COMPUTER GRAPHICS

PROCEEDINGS

Annual Conference Series   1998

SIGGRAPH 98
Conference Proceedings
July 19–24, 1998
Papers Chair: Michael Cohen

A Publication of ACM SIGGRAPH

Sponsored by the ACM's Special
Interest Group on Computer
Graphics

SIGGRAPH 98

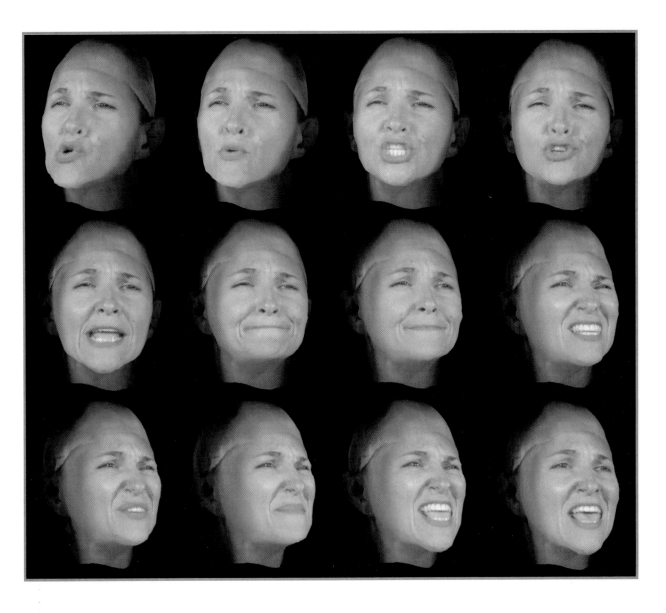

The Association for Computing Machinery, Inc.
1515 Broadway
New York, NY 10036

Sample Citation Information:
...Proceedings of SIGGRAPH 98 (Orlando, Florida, July 19–24, 1998). In *Computer Graphics* Proceedings, Annual Conference Series, 1998, ACM SIGGRAPH, pp. xx – yy.

Orders from members of ACM:

U.S.A. and Canada:
ACM Order Department
P.O. Box 12114
Church Street Station
New York, NY 10257
    Telephone: +1-800-342-6626
    Telephone: +1-212-626-0500
    Fax: +1-212-944-1318
    E-mail: `orders@acm.org`
    URL: `http://www.acm.org/`

All other countries:
ACM European Service Center
108 Cowley Road
Oxford OX4 1JF
United Kingdom
    Telephone: +44-1-865-382338
    Fax: +44-1-865-381338
    E-mail: `acm_europe@acm.org`

ACM Order Number: 428980
ACM ISBN: 0-89791-999-8
ACM ISSN: 1069-529X

Orders from nonmembers of ACM:

Addison-Wesley will pay postage and handling on orders accompanied by check. Credit card orders may be placed by mail or by calling the Addison-Wesley Order Department at the number above. Followup inquiries should be directed at the same number. Please include the Addison-Wesley ISBN with your order:
    A-W Softcover Proceedings and
    CD-ROM Package ISBN:
    0-201-30988-2

United States:
Addison-Wesley Publishing Company
Order Department
Jacob Way
Reading, MA 01867
    Telephone: +1-800-447-2226

Europe/Middle East:
Addison-Wesley Publishing Group
Concertgebouwplein 25
1071 LM Amsterdam
The Netherlands
    Telephone: +31-20-6717296
    Fax: +31-20-6645334

Germany/Austria/Switzerland:
Addison-Wesley Verlag Deutschland GmbH
Hildachstraße 15d
Wachsbleiche 7-12
53111 Bonn
Germany
    Telephone: +49-228-98-515-0
    Fax: +49-228-98-515-99

United Kingdom/Africa:
Addison-Wesley Publishers Ltd.
Finchampstead Road
Wokingham, Berkshire RG11 2NZ
United Kingdom
    Telephone: +44-734-794000
    Fax: +44-734-794035

Asia:
Addison-Wesley Singapore Pte. Ltd.
15 Beach Road
#05-02/09/10 Beach Centre
Singapore 0718
    Telephone: +65-339-7503
    Fax: +65-339-9709

Japan:
Addison-Wesley Publishers Japan Ltd.
Nichibo Building
1-2-2 Sarugakucho
Chiyoda-ku, Tokyo 101
Japan
    Telephone: +81-33-2914581
    Fax: +81-33-2914592

Australia/New Zealand:
Addison-Wesley Publishers Pty. Ltd.
6 Byfield Street
North Ryde, N.S.W. 2113
Australia
    Telephone: +61-2-878-5411
    Fax: +61-2-878-5830

Latin America:
Addison-Wesley Iberoamericana S.A.
Boulevard de las Cataratas #3
Colonia Jardines del Pedregal
Delegacion Alvaro Obregon
01900 Mexico D.F.
    Telephone: +52-5-660-2695
    Fax: +52-5-660-4930

Canada:
Addison-Wesley Publishing (Canada) Ltd.
26 Prince Andrew Place
Don Mills, Ontario M3C 2T8 Canada
    Telephone: +1-416-447-5101
    Fax: +1-416-443-0948

Contents

Papers Sessions, Wednesday, 22 July

Papers Sessions, Thursday, 23 July

Papers Sessions, Friday, 24 July

Papers Preface

In the 25 years that the SIGGRAPH conference has taken place, our world has changed in many ways. We now almost take for granted that medical devices can peer inside of us and reconstruct 3D images of our organs. We are barely surprised when dinosaurs of incredible realism walk across our movie screens. We are perhaps even bored now when shiny 3D logos fly across our TV screens. Some of this is due, in no small part, to the work reported in the past two and a half decades in the predecessors to these proceedings. It is almost a certainty that the information contained in this book will have a profound impact on how we will be educated, cared for by medical professionals, and entertained in the years to come.

For the 25th anniversary of SIGGRAPH, 303 papers were submitted by January 16, 1998 to be considered for inclusion in the SIGGRAPH 98 technical program. Never before had close to this many papers been received. Each submission contained six copies of the paper along with videotapes and other supporting materials. Dealing with such a huge mound of express packages was an interesting and challenging task. Microsoft Research generously set aside an office to process the submissions and the entire graphics research staff was temporarily enlisted as mail handlers. Two administrative aides assisted with opening and logging each entry and with getting the submissions to the papers committee. Alyn Rockwood, who will serve as next year's chair, and John Snyder helped sort the papers into 29 piles for the committee members.

Each submission was forwarded to two senior reviewers (members of the Papers Committee). The primary senior reviewer solicited reviews from at least three other experts in the field and was responsible for collecting and summarizing their feedback. The secondary senior reviewer reviewed the submissions assigned to them. Each member of the Papers Committee took on the role of primary reviewer for 10-12 papers and the role of secondary reviewer for another 10-12 papers.

The 29 members of the 1998 Papers Committee met in Seattle the weekend of March 7–8, to confer, occasionally argue, and to ultimately select 45 outstanding papers from among the 303 submissions. One cannot overstate the thanks due to the members of the committee for their dedication and hard work. The amount of effort and time each member of the committee provided is way beyond the call of duty. In addition, the hundreds of reviewers enlisted by the senior reviewers deserve our gratitude.

Accepted papers were forwarded to Stephen Spencer, SIGGRAPH Director for Publications. Videotapes accompanying papers were forwarded to Jim Rose. Both have done an outstanding job of assembling the printed, CD, and video versions of the Conference Proceedings and deserve sincere thanks.

Over the last 25 years, SIGGRAPH conferences have been a wonderful venue to bring together scientists, artists and members of the business community to share ideas about computer graphics. I'm looking forward to the next 25 years of exciting developments in the field, some of which are contained in these proceedings.

Michael F. Cohen
SIGGRAPH 98 Papers Chair

1998 ACM SIGGRAPH Awards

Computer Graphics Achievement Award Michael F. Cohen

ACM SIGGRAPH is pleased to present the 1998 Computer Graphics Achievement Award to Michael F. Cohen for the development of practical radiosity methods for realistic image synthesis. His research is the key to making radiosity usable with complex scenes. The beautiful images created by Michael and his colleagues still remain among the state of the art – both technically and artistically.

Michael's first major achievement was the development of the hemi-cube algorithm for computing form factors in the presence of occlusion. Soon afterward he developed the progressive refinement radiosity algorithm. By reordering light bounces to match their relative contribution to the final radiosity solution, images could be generated relatively quickly and gracefully refined. Michael also developed other major radiosity extensions: adaptive meshing, an extension to dynamic environments; and wavelet radiosity. He also extended the radiosity algorithm to include specular in addition to diffuse reflection, and was involved in one of the few studies to quantitatively compare real and synthetic imagery. He also showed how inverse methods could be used to control light sources to achieve the desired effect in the final image. His work in radiosity culminated in the publication of a book, with John Wallace, titled "Radiosity and Realistic Image Synthesis."

He also contributed to many other areas of computer graphics, most notably animation, technical illustration, and image-based rendering. For computer animation, he has developed dynamic and kinematic specifications of motion, interactive and hierarchical space-time control algorithms, and the automatic and efficient generation of motion and camera parameters. For the technical illustration speciality, he developed an early system to create informative illustrations of mechanical parts. His recent contribution on the lumigraph and layered depth images is seminal in the relatively new specialty of computer graphics – image-based rendering.

His work has unusual breadth and creativity attributable to his multi-disciplinary background and approach to problems. He holds two undergraduate degrees, one in Art, from Beloit, and another in Civil Engineering from Rutgers, a MS degree in Computer Graphics from Cornell, and a Ph.D. degree in Computer Science from Utah. Michael taught at Cornell, Utah and Princeton before accepting his current position at Microsoft, where he is a senior researcher and manager of the computer graphics group. He is an admired teacher and is sought out by his colleagues in the computer graphics community. An active participant in many SIGGRAPH activities, he is the SIGGRAPH 98 Papers Chair.

Michael Cohen exemplifies the tradition of outstanding individuals in computer graphics. SIGGRAPH is happy to recognize his many achievements by awarding him the Computer Graphics Achievement Award.

References

1. Michael F. Cohen and Donald P. Greenberg. "The Hemi-Cube: A Radiosity Solution for Complex Environments," SIGGRAPH 85 Proceedings, pp 31-40.

2. Gary W. Meyer, Holly E. Rushmeier, Michael F. Cohen, Donald P. Greenberg, and Kenneth E. Torrance. "An Experimental Evaluation of Computer Graphics Imagery," ACM Transactions on Graphics, Vol. 5, No. 1, 1986, pp 30-50.

3. Michael Cohen, Donald P. Greenberg, Dave S. Immel, and Philip J. Brock. "An Efficient Radiosity Approach for Realistic Image Synthesis," IEEE Computer Graphics and Applications (6),3, pp 26-35, 1986.

4. Daniel R. Baum, John R. Wallace, Michael F. Cohen, and Donald P. Greenberg. "The Back Buffer Algorithm: An Extension of the Radiosity Method to Dynamic Environments," The Visual Computer, Vol. 2, 1986.

5. David S. Immel, Michael F. Cohen, and Donald P. Greenberg. "A Radiosity Method for Non Diffuse Environments," SIGGRAPH 86 Proceedings, pp 133-142.

6. Paul M. Isaacs and Michael F. Cohen. "Controlling Dynamic Simulation with Kinematic Constraints, Behavior Functions and Inverse Dynamics", SIGGRAPH '87 Proceedings, pp 215-224.

7. John R. Wallace, Michael F. Cohen, and Donald P. Greenberg. "A Two-Pass Solution to the Rendering Equation: A Synthesis of Ray Tracing and Radiosity Methods", SIGGRAPH 87 Proceedings, pp 311-320.

8. Michael F. Cohen, Shenchang Eric Chen, John R. Wallace, and Donald P. Greenberg. "A Progressive Refinement Approach to Fast Radiosity Image Generation," SIGGRAPH 88 Proceedings, pp 45-84.

9. Michael F. Cohen. "Interactive spacetime control for animation," SIGGRAPH 92 Proceedings, pp 293-302.

10. Michael F. Cohen and John R. Wallace. Radiosity and Realistic Image Synthesis. Cambridge, MA: Academic Press, 1993.

11. John K. Kawai, James S. Painter, and Michael F. Cohen. "Radioptimization - Goal Based Rendering," SIGGRAPH 93 Proceedings, pp 147-154.

12. Steven J. Gortler, Peter Schroder, Michael F. Cohen, Pat Hanrahan. "Wavelet Radiosity," SIGGRAPH 93 Proceedings, pp 221-230.

13. Zicheng Liu, Steven J. Gortler, and Michael F. Cohen. "Hierarchical Spacetime Control," SIGGRAPH 93 Proceedings, pp 35-42.

14. Steven J. Gortler, Michael F. Cohen, and Phillip Slusallek. "Radiosity and Relaxation Methods," IEEE Computer Graphics and Applications (14), 6, pp 28-58, 1994.

15. Brian Guenter, Charles F. Rose, Bobby Bodenheimer, and Michael F. Cohen. "Efficient Generation of Motion Transitions using Spacetime Constraints," SIGGRAPH 96 Proceedings, pp 147-154.

16. Li-wei He, Michael F. Cohen, and David H. Salesin. "The Virtual Cinematographer: A Paradigm for Automatic Real-Time Camera Control and Directing," SIGGRAPH 96 Proceedings, pp 217-224.

17. Steven J. Gortler, Radek Grzeszczuk, Richard Szeliski, and Michael F. Cohen. "The Lumigraph," SIGGRAPH 96 Proceedings, pp 43-54.

Previous Award Recipients

1997	Przemyslaw Prusinkiewicz
1996	Marc Levoy
1995	Kurt Akeley
1994	Kenneth E. Torrance
1993	Pat Hanrahan
1992	Henry Fuchs
1991	James T. Kajiya
1990	Richard Shoup and Alvy Ray Smith
1989	John Warnock
1988	Alan H. Barr
1987	Robert Cook
1986	Turner Whitted
1985	Loren Carpenter
1984	James H. Clark
1983	James F. Blinn

NeuroAnimator:
Fast Neural Network Emulation and Control of Physics-Based Models

Radek Grzeszczuk [1]   Demetri Terzopoulos [2,1]   Geoffrey Hinton [2]

[1] Intel Corporation   [2] University of Toronto

Abstract: Animation through the numerical simulation of physics-based graphics models offers unsurpassed realism, but it can be computationally demanding. Likewise, the search for controllers that enable physics-based models to produce desired animations usually entails formidable computational cost. This paper demonstrates the possibility of replacing the numerical simulation and control of dynamic models with a dramatically more efficient alternative. In particular, we propose the NeuroAnimator, a novel approach to creating physically realistic animation that exploits neural networks. NeuroAnimators are automatically trained off-line to emulate physical dynamics through the observation of physics-based models in action. Depending on the model, its neural network emulator can yield physically realistic animation one or two orders of magnitude faster than conventional numerical simulation. Furthermore, by exploiting the network structure of the NeuroAnimator, we introduce a fast algorithm for learning controllers that enables either physics-based models or their neural network emulators to synthesize motions satisfying prescribed animation goals. We demonstrate NeuroAnimators for a variety of physics-based models.

CR Categories: I.3.7 [Computer Graphics]: Three-Dimensional Graphics and Realism—Animation; I.6.8 [Simulation and Modeling]: Types of Simulation—Animation

Keywords: physics-based animation, neural networks, learning, motion control, backpropagation, dynamical systems, simulation.

1 Introduction

Animation based on physical principles has been an influential trend in computer graphics. This is not only due to the unsurpassed realism that physics-based techniques offer. In conjunction with suitable control and constraint mechanisms, physical models also facilitate the production of copious quantities of realistic animation in a highly automated fashion. Physics-based animation techniques are beginning to find their way into high-end commercial systems. However, a well-known drawback has retarded their broader penetration—compared to geometric models, physical models typically entail formidable numerical simulation costs.

This paper proposes a new approach to creating physically realistic animation that differs radically from the conventional approach of numerically simulating the equations of motion of physics-based models. We replace physics-based models by fast *emulators* which automatically learn to produce similar motions by observing the models in action. Our emulators have a neural network structure, hence we dub them *NeuroAnimators*. The network structure of NeuroAnimators furthermore enables a new solution to the control problem associated with physics-based models, leading to a remarkably fast algorithm for synthesizing motions that satisfy prescribed animation goals.

1.1 Overview of the NeuroAnimator Approach

Our approach is motivated by the following considerations: Whether we are dealing with rigid [6, 1], articulated [7, 19], or non-rigid [17, 10] dynamic animation models, the numerical simulation of the associated equations of motion leads to the computation of a discrete-time dynamical system of the form

$$\mathbf{s}_{t+\delta t} = \Phi[\mathbf{s}_t, \mathbf{u}_t, \mathbf{f}_t]. \qquad (1)$$

These (generally nonlinear) equations express the vector $\mathbf{s}_{t+\delta t}$ of state variables of the system (values of the system's degrees of freedom and their velocities) at time $t + \delta t$ in the future as a function Φ of the state vector $\mathbf{s}_t$, the vector $\mathbf{u}_t$ of control inputs, and the vector $\mathbf{f}_t$ of external forces acting on the system at time t.

Physics-based animation through the numerical simulation of a dynamical system (1) requires the evaluation of the map Φ at every timestep, which usually involves a non-trivial computation. Evaluating Φ using explicit time integration methods incurs a computational cost of $O(N)$ operations, where N is proportional to the dimensionality of the state space. Unfortunately, for many dynamic models of interest, explicit methods are plagued by instability, necessitating numerous tiny timesteps δt per unit simulation time. Alternatively, implicit time-integration methods usually permit larger timesteps, but they compute Φ by solving a system of N algebraic equations, generally incurring a cost of $O(N^3)$ operations per timestep.

We pose an intriguing question: Is it possible to replace the conventional numerical simulator, which must repeatedly compute Φ, by a significantly cheaper alternative? A crucial realization is that the substitute, or emulator, need not compute the map Φ exactly, but merely approximate it to a degree of precision that preserves the perceived faithfulness of the resulting animation to the simulated dynamics of the physical model.

Neural networks [2] offer a general mechanism for approximating complex maps in higher dimensional spaces.[2] Our premise is that, to a sufficient degree of accuracy and at significant computational savings, trained neural networks can approximate maps Φ

[1] 2200 Mission College Blvd., Santa Clara, CA 95052, RN6-35
E-mail: radek.grzeszczuk@intel.com
[2] 10 King's College Road, Toronto, Ontario, Canada, M5S 3G4
E-mail: {dt|hinton}@cs.toronto.edu

---

[2]Note that Φ in (1) is in general a high-dimensional map from $\Re^{s+u+f} \mapsto \Re^s$, where s, u, and f denote the dimensionalities of the state, control, and external force vectors.

not just for simple dynamical systems, but also for those associated with dynamic models that are among the most complex reported in the graphics literature to date.

The NeuroAnimator, which uses neural networks to emulate physics-based animation, learns an approximation to the dynamic model by observing instances of state transitions, as well as control inputs and/or external forces that cause these transitions. Training a NeuroAnimator is quite unlike recording motion capture data, since the network observes isolated examples of state transitions rather than complete motion trajectories. By generalizing from the sparse examples presented to it, a trained NeuroAnimator can emulate an infinite variety of continuous animations that it has never actually seen. Each emulation step costs only $O(N^2)$ operations, but it is possible to gain additional efficiency relative to a numerical simulator by training neural networks to approximate a lengthy chain of evaluations of (1). Thus, the emulator network can perform "super timesteps" $\Delta t = n\delta t$, typically one or two orders of magnitude larger than δt for the competing implicit time-integration scheme, thereby achieving outstanding efficiency without serious loss of accuracy.

The NeuroAnimator offers an additional bonus which has crucial consequences for animation control: Unlike the map Φ in the original dynamical system (1), its neural network approximation is analytically differentiable. In fact, the derivative of NeuroAnimator state outputs with respect to control and external force inputs is efficiently computable by applying the chain rule of differentiation. Easy differentiability enables us to arrive at a remarkably fast gradient descent optimization algorithm to compute optimal or near-optimal controllers. These controllers produce a series of control inputs $\mathbf{u}_t$ that enable NeuroAnimators to synthesize motions satisfying prescribed constraints on the desired animation. NeuroAnimator controllers are equally applicable to controlling the original physics-based models.

1.2 Related Work

To date, network architectures have found only a few applications in computer graphics. One application has been the control of animated characters. Ridsdale [14] reports a method for skill acquisition using a connectionist model of skill memory. The sensor-actuator networks of van de Panne and Fiume [19] are recurrent networks of units that take sensory information as input and produce actuator controls as output. Sims [16] employed a network architecture to structure simple "brains" that control evolved creatures. Our work differs fundamentally from these efforts.

The basis of our approach is related to work presented in the mainstream neural network literature on connectionist control of complex systems. Nguyen and Widrow demonstrated the neural network based approximation and control of a nonlinear kinematic system in their "truck backer-upper" [12]. More recently, Jordan and Rumelhart [9] proposed a two step approach to learning controllers for physical robots. In step one, a neural net learns a predictive internal model of the robot, which maps from actions to state transitions. In step two this forward model is used to learn an inverse model that maps from intentions to actions, by training the inverse model so that it produces an identity transformation in cascade with the established forward model.

Inspired by these results, we exploit neural networks to produce controlled, physically realistic animation satisfying user-specified constraints at a fraction of the computational cost of conventional numerical simulation.

2 Artificial Neural Networks

In this section we define a common type of artificial neural network and describe the backpropagation training algorithm. Neu-

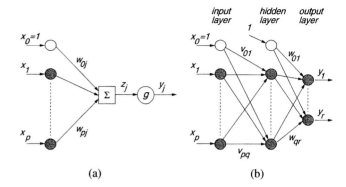

(a)   (b)

Figure 1: (a) Mathematical model of a neuron j. (b) Three-layer feedforward neural network $\mathbf{N}$. Bias units are not shaded.

roAnimator makes use of a neural network simulator called *Xerion* which was developed at the University of Toronto and is available publicly.[3] The public availability of software such as Xerion contributes to making our NeuroAnimator approach easily accessible to the graphics community.

2.1 Neurons and Neural Networks

In mathematical terms, a *neuron* is an operator that maps $\Re^p \mapsto \Re$. Referring to Fig. 1(a), neuron j receives a signal z_j that is the sum of p inputs x_i scaled by associated connection weights w_{ij}:

$$z_j = w_{0j} + \sum_{i=1}^{p} x_i w_{ij} = \sum_{i=0}^{p} x_i w_{ij} = \mathbf{x}^T \mathbf{w}_j, \qquad (2)$$

where $\mathbf{x} = [x_0, x_1, \ldots, x_p]^T$ is the input vector (the superscript T denotes transposition), $\mathbf{w}_j = [w_{0j}, w_{1j}, \ldots, w_{pj}]^T$ is the weight vector of neuron j, and w_{0j} is the bias parameter, which can be treated as an extra connection with constant unit input, $x_0 = 1$, as shown in the figure. The neuron outputs a signal $y_j = g(z_j)$, where g is a continuous, monotonic, and often nonlinear activation function, commonly the logistic sigmoid $g(z) = \sigma(z) = 1/(1 + e^{-z})$.

A *neural network* is a set of interconnected neurons. In a simple *feedforward neural network*, the neurons are organized in layers so that a neuron in layer l receives inputs only from the neurons in layer $l - 1$. The first layer is commonly referred to as the input layer and the last layer as the output layer. The intermediate layers are called hidden layers.

Fig. 1(b) shows a fully connected network with only a single hidden layer. We use this popular type of network in our algorithms. The hidden and output layers include bias units that group together the bias parameters of all the neurons in those layers. The input and output layers use linear activation functions, while the hidden layer uses the logistic sigmoid activation function. The output of the jth hidden unit is therefore given by $h_j = \sigma\left(\sum_{i=0}^{p} x_i v_{ij}\right)$.

2.2 Approximation by Learning

We denote a 3-layer feedforward network with p input units, q hidden units, r output units, and weight vector $\mathbf{w}$ as $\mathbf{N}(\mathbf{x}, \mathbf{w})$. It defines a continuous map $\mathbf{N} : \Re^p \mapsto \Re^r$. With sufficiently large q, a feedforward neural network with this architecture can approximate as accurately as necessary any continuous map $\Phi : \Re^p \mapsto \Re^r$ over

---

[3]Available from `ftp://ftp.cs.toronto.edu/pub/xerion`

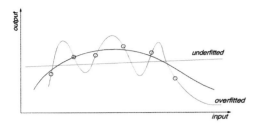

Figure 2: Depicted in a low-dimensional setting, a neural network with too few neurons underfits the training data. One with too many neurons overfits the data. The solid curve represents a properly chosen network which provides a good compromise between approximation (fits the training data) and generalization (generates reasonable output values away from the training examples).

a compact domain $\mathbf{x} \in \mathcal{X}$ [3, 8]; i.e., for an arbitrarily small $\epsilon > 0$ there exists a network $\mathbf{N}$ such that

$$\forall \mathbf{x} \in \mathcal{X}, \quad e(\mathbf{x}, \mathbf{w}) = \|\Phi(\mathbf{x}) - \mathbf{N}(\mathbf{x}, \mathbf{w})\|^2 < \epsilon, \qquad (3)$$

where e is the approximation error.

A neural network can *learn* an approximation to a map Φ by observing training data consisting of input-output pairs that sample Φ. The training sequence is a set of *examples*, such that the τth example comprises the pair

$$\begin{cases} \mathbf{x}^\tau = [x_1^\tau, x_2^\tau, \dots, x_p^\tau]^T; \\ \mathbf{y}^\tau = \Phi(\mathbf{x}^\tau) = [y_1^\tau, y_2^\tau, \dots, y_r^\tau]^T, \end{cases} \qquad (4)$$

where $\mathbf{x}^\tau$ is the input vector and $\mathbf{y}^\tau$ is the associated desired output vector. The goal of training is to utilize the examples to find a set of weights $\mathbf{w}$ for the network $\mathbf{N}(\mathbf{x}, \mathbf{w})$ such that, for all inputs of interest, the difference between the network output and the true output is sufficiently small, as measured by the approximation error (3).

Training a neural network to approximate a map is analogous to fitting a polynomial to data and it suffers from the same problems. Mainly, a network with two few free parameters (weights) will underfit the data, while a network with too many free parameters will overfit the data. Fig. 2 depicts these problems in a low-dimensional setting. To avoid underfitting, we use networks with a sufficient number of weights. To avoid overfitting, we make sure that we use sufficient training data. We use 8-10 times as many examples as there are weights in the network, which seems sufficient to avoid serious overfitting or underfitting.

2.3 Backpropagation Learning Algorithm

Rumelhart, Hinton and Williams [15] proposed an efficient algorithm for training multi-layer feedforward networks, called the *backpropagation algorithm*. The backpropagation algorithm seeks to minimize the objective function

$$E(\mathbf{w}) = \sum_{\tau=1}^{n} e(\mathbf{x}^\tau, \mathbf{w}) = \sum_{\tau=1}^{n} E^\tau(\mathbf{w}) \qquad (5)$$

which sums the approximation errors e from (3) over the n training examples. The off-line training version of the algorithm adjusts the weights of the network using the gradient descent formula

$$\mathbf{w}^{l+1} = \mathbf{w}^l + \eta \nabla_\mathbf{w} E(\mathbf{w}^l), \qquad (6)$$

where $\nabla_\mathbf{w} E$ denotes the gradient of the objective function with respect to the weights and $\eta < 1$ is referred to as the *learning rate*.

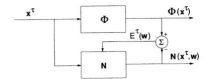

Figure 3: The backpropagation algorithm learns a map Φ by adjusting the weights $\mathbf{w}$ of the network $\mathbf{N}$ in order to reduce the difference between in the network output $\mathbf{N}(\mathbf{x}^\tau, \mathbf{w})$ and the desired output $\Phi(\mathbf{x}^\tau)$. Depicted here is the on-line version of the algorithm that adjusts the weights of the network after observing each training example.

An on-line training version of the backpropagation algorithm that adjusts the weights of the network after each training example is presented in [15]. Fig. 3 illustrates this process.

Backpropagation refers to the practical, recursive method to calculate the component error derivatives of the gradient term in (6). Applying the chain rule of differentiation, the backpropagation algorithm first computes the derivatives with respect to weights in the output layer and chains its way back to the input layer, computing the derivatives with respect to weights in each hidden layer as it proceeds.

To improve the learning rate, the gradient descent rule of the basic backpropagation algorithm (6), which takes a fixed step in the direction of the gradient, can be replaced by more sophisticated nonlinear optimization techniques. Line search offers one way to accelerate the training by searching for the optimal size step in the gradient direction. Additional performance improvement can be achieved by taking at each optimization step a direction orthogonal to previous directions. This is known as the conjugate gradient method [13]. A simple but effective method for increasing the learning rate augments the gradient descent update rule with a *momentum term*. The momentum method updates the weights as follows:

$$\begin{aligned} \delta \mathbf{w}^{l+1} &= -\eta_w \nabla_\mathbf{w} E(\mathbf{w}^l) + \alpha_w \delta \mathbf{w}^l, & (7) \\ \mathbf{w}^{l+1} &= \mathbf{w}^l + \delta \mathbf{w}^{l+1}, & (8) \end{aligned}$$

where the momentum parameter α_w must be between 0 and 1. The neural network simulator Xerion includes the above optimization techniques and several others. Later in the paper we discuss the types of optimization methods that we used to train NeuroAnimators and to synthesize controllers.

3 From Physics-Based Models to NeuroAnimators

In this section we explain the practical application of neural network concepts to the construction and training of different classes of NeuroAnimators. Among other subjects, this includes network input/output structure, the use of hierarchical networks to tackle physics-based models with large state spaces, and strategies for generating good training datasets. We also discuss the practical issue of applying the Xerion neural network simulator to train NeuroAnimators. Finally, we show sample results demonstrating the accurate emulation of various dynamic models.

Our task is to construct neural networks that approximate Φ in the dynamical system (1). We propose to employ backpropagation to train feedforward networks $\mathbf{N}_\Phi$ to predict future states using super timesteps $\Delta t = n \delta t$ while containing the approximation error so as not to appreciably degrade the physical realism of the resulting animation. Analogous to (1), the basic emulation step is

$$\mathbf{s}_{t+\Delta t} = \mathbf{N}_\Phi[\mathbf{s}_t, \mathbf{u}_t, \mathbf{f}_t]. \qquad (9)$$

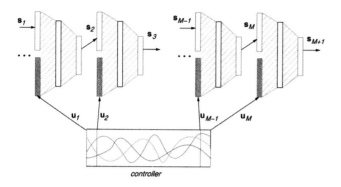

Figure 4: Forward emulation using a neural network. At each iteration, the network output becomes the state input at the next iteration of the algorithm. Note that the same emulator network is used recursively.

The trained emulator network N_Φ takes as input the state of the model, its control inputs, and the external forces acting on it at time t, and produces as output the state of the model at time $t + \Delta t$ by evaluating the network. The emulation process is a sequence of these evaluations. After each evaluation, the network control and force inputs receive new values, and the network state inputs receive the emulator outputs from the previous evaluation. Fig. 4 illustrates the emulation process. The figure represents each emulation step by a separate network whose outputs become the inputs to the next network. In reality, the emulation process employs a recurrent network whose outputs become inputs for the subsequent evaluation step.

Since the emulation step is large compared with the physical simulation step, we often find the sampling rate of the motion trajectory produced by the emulator too coarse for animation. To avoid motion artifacts, we resample the motion trajectory at the animation frame rate, computing intermediate states through linear interpolation of states obtained from the emulation. Linear interpolation produces satisfactory motion, although a more sophisticated scheme could improve the result.

3.1 Network Input/Output Structure

The emulator network has a single set of output variables specifying $s_{t+\Delta t}$. The number of input variable sets depends on whether the physical model is active or passive and the type of forces involved. A dynamical system of the form (1), such as the multi-link pendulum illustrated in Fig. 5(a), with control inputs u comprising joint motor torques is known as active, otherwise, it is passive.

Fig. 5(b) illustrates different emulator input/output structures. If we wish, in the fully general case, to emulate an active model under the influence of unpredictable applied forces, we employ a full network with three sets of input variables: s_t, u_t, and f_t, as shown in the figure. For passive models, the control $u_t = 0$ and the network simplifies to one with two sets of inputs, s_t and f_t.

In the special case when the forces f_t are completely determined by the state of the system s_t, we can suppress the f_t inputs, allowing the network to learn the effects of these forces from the state transition training data. For example, the active multi-link pendulum illustrated in Fig. 5(a) is under the influence of gravity g and joint friction forces τ. However, since both g and τ are completely determined by s_t, they need not be provided as emulator inputs. A simple emulator with two input sets s_t and u_t can learn the response of the multi-link pendulum to those external forces.

The simplest type of emulator has only a single set of inputs s_t. This emulator can approximate passive models acted upon by deterministic external forces.

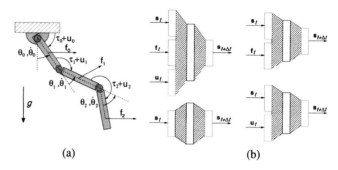

(a)　　　　　(b)

Figure 5: Three-link physical pendulum and network emulators. (a) An active pendulum with joint friction τ_i, motor torques u_i, applied forces f_i, and gravity g. Without motor torques, the pendulum is passive. (b) Different types of emulators.

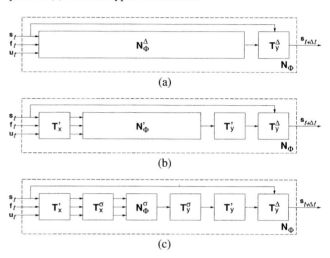

Figure 6: Transforming a simple feedforward neural network N_Φ into a practical emulator network N_Φ^σ that is easily trained to emulate physics-based models. The following operators perform the appropriate pre- and post-processing: T_x' transforms inputs to local coordinates, T_x^σ normalizes inputs, T_y^σ unnormalizes outputs, T_y' transforms outputs to global coordinates, T_y^Δ converts from a state change to the next state (see text).

3.2 Input and Output Transformations

The accurate approximation of complex functional mappings using neural networks can be challenging. We have observed that a simple feedforward neural network with a single layer of sigmoid units has difficulty producing an accurate approximation to the dynamics of physical models. In practice, we often must transform the emulator to ensure a good approximation of the map Φ, as we explain next.

A fundamental problem is that the state variables of a dynamical system can have a large dynamic range (e.g., the position and velocity of an unconstrained particle can take values from $-\infty$ to $+\infty$). A single sigmoid unit is nonlinear only over a small region of its input space and approximately constant elsewhere. To approximate a nonlinear map Φ accurately over a large domain, we would need to use a neural network with many sigmoid units, each shifted and scaled so that their nonlinear segments cover different parts of the domain. The direct approximation of Φ is therefore impractical.

A successful strategy is to train networks to emulate *changes* in state variables rather than their actual values, since state changes over small timesteps will have a significantly smaller dynamic range. Hence, in Fig. 6(a) we restructure our simple network N_Φ as a network N_Φ^Δ which is trained to emulate the change in the state vector $\Delta\mathbf{s}_t$ for given state, external force, and control inputs, followed by an operator $\mathbf{T}_y^\Delta$ that computes $\mathbf{s}_{t+\Delta t} = \mathbf{s}_t + \Delta\mathbf{s}_t$ to recover the next state.

We can further improve the approximation power of the emulator network by exploiting natural invariances. In particular, note that the map Φ is invariant under rotation and translation; i.e., the state changes are independent of the absolute position and orientation of the physical model relative to the world coordinate system. Hence, in Fig. 6(b) we replace $\mathbf{N}_\Phi^\Delta$ with an operator $\mathbf{T}_x'$ that converts the inputs from the world coordinate system to the local coordinate system of the model, a network $\mathbf{N}_\Phi'$ that is trained to emulate state changes represented in the local coordinate system, and an operator $\mathbf{T}_y'$ that converts the output of $\mathbf{N}_\Phi'$ back to world coordinates.

A final improvement in the ability of the NeuroAnimator to approximate the map Φ accrues from the normalization of groups of input and output variables. Since the values of state, force, and control variables can deviate significantly, their effect on the network outputs is uneven, causing problems when large inputs must have a small influence on outputs. To make inputs contribute more evenly to the network outputs, we normalize groups of variables so that they have zero means and unit variances. Appendix A provides the mathematical details. With normalization, we can furthermore expect the weights of the trained network to be of order unity and they can be given a simple random initialization prior to training. Hence, in Fig. 6(c) we replace $\mathbf{N}_\Phi'$ with an operator $\mathbf{T}_x^\sigma$ that normalizes its inputs, a network $\mathbf{N}_\Phi^\sigma$ that assumes zero mean, unit variance inputs and outputs, and an operator $\mathbf{T}_y^\sigma$ that unnormalizes the outputs to recover their original distributions.

Although the final emulator in Fig. 6(c) is structurally more complex than the standard feedforward neural network $\mathbf{N}_\Phi$ that it replaces, the operators denoted by the letter $\mathbf{T}$ are completely determined by the state of the model and the distribution of the training data, and the emulator network $\mathbf{N}_\Phi^\sigma$ is much easier to train. A more detailed presentation of the restructured emulator can be found in [4].

3.3 Hierarchical Networks

As a universal function approximator, a neural network should in principle be able to approximate the map Φ in (1) for any dynamical system given enough sigmoid hidden units and training data. In practice, however, significant performance improvements accrue from tailoring the neural network to the physics-based model.

In particular, neural networks are susceptible to the "curse of dimensionality". The number of neurons needed in hidden layers and the training data requirements grow quickly with the size of the network, often making the training of large networks impractical. We have found it prudent to structure NeuroAnimators for all but the simplest physics-based models as hierarchies of smaller networks rather than as large, monolithic networks. The strategy behind a hierarchical representation is to group state variables according to their dependencies and approximate each tightly coupled group with a subnet that takes part of its input from a parent network.

A natural example of hierarchical networks arises when approximating complex articulated models, such as Hodgins' mechanical human runner model [7] which has a tree structure with a torso and limbs. Rather than collect all of its 30 controlled degrees of freedom into a single large network, it is natural to emulate the model using 5 smaller networks: a torso network plus left and right arm and leg networks.

Hierarchical representations are also useful when dealing with deformable models with large state spaces, such as the biomechanical model of a dolphin described in [5] which we use in our experiments. The mass-spring-damper dolphin model (Fig. 7) consists of

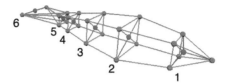

Figure 7: Hierarchical state representation for the dolphin mechanical model. Red nodes mark point masses and green nodes mark numbered local centers of mass. Green lines associate groups of point masses to their local center.

23 point masses, yielding a state space with $23 \times 3 = 69$ positions and 69 velocities, plus 6 controlled degrees of freedom—one for each independent actuator. Rather than constructing a monolithic neural network with $69 + 69 = 138$ state inputs $\mathbf{s}_t$ and outputs $\mathbf{s}_{t+\Delta t}$, we subdivide hierarchically. A natural subdivision is to represent each of the 6 body segments as a separate sub-network in the local center of mass coordinates of the segment, as shown in the figure.

3.4 Training NeuroAnimators

To arrive at a NeuroAnimator for a given physics-based model, we train the constituent neural network(s) by invoking the back-propagation algorithm on training examples generated by simulating the model. Training requires the generation and processing of many examples, hence it is typically slow, often requiring several CPU hours. However, it is important to realize that training takes place off-line, in advance. Once a NeuroAnimator is trained, it can be reused readily to produce an infinite variety of fast animations. Training a NeuroAnimator is quite unlike recording motion capture data. In fact, the network never observes complete motion trajectories, only sparse examples of individual state transitions. The important point is that by generalizing from the sparse examples that it has learned, a trained NeuroAnimator will produce an infinite variety of extended, continuous animations that it has never seen.

More specifically, each training example consists of an input vector $\mathbf{x}$ and an output vector $\mathbf{y}$. In the general case, the input vector $\mathbf{x} = [\mathbf{s}_0^T, \mathbf{f}_0^T, \mathbf{u}_0^T]^T$ comprises the state of the model, the external forces, and the control inputs at time $t = 0$. The output vector $\mathbf{y} = \mathbf{s}_{\Delta t}$ is the state of the model at time $t = \Delta t$, where Δt is the duration of the super timestep. To generate each training example, we would start the numerical simulator of the physics-based model with the initial conditions $\mathbf{s}_0$, $\mathbf{f}_0$, and $\mathbf{u}_0$, and run the dynamic simulation for n numerical time steps δt such that $\Delta t = n\delta t$. In principle, we could generate an arbitrarily large set of training examples $\{\mathbf{x}^\tau; \mathbf{y}^\tau\}$, $\tau = 1, 2, \ldots$, by repeating this process with different initial conditions.

The initial conditions can be sampled at random among all valid state, external force, and control combinations. To learn a good neural network approximation $\mathbf{N}_\Phi$ of the map Φ in (1), we would like ideally to sample Φ as uniformly as possible over its domain. Unfortunately, for most physics-based models of interest, the domain has high dimensionality, often making a uniform sampling impractical. However, we can make the best use of computational resources by concentrating them on sampling those state, force, and control inputs that typically occur as a physics-based model is used in practice.

Fig. 8 illustrates an effective sampling strategy using the dynamic dolphin model as an example. We simulate the model over an extended period of time with a fixed timestep δt. During the simulation, we apply typical control inputs to the model. For the dolphin, the control inputs are coordinated muscle actions that produce locomotion. At well-separated times $t = t_k$ during the simulation, we

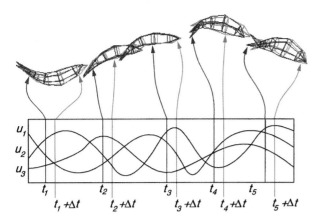

Figure 8: An effective state transition sampling strategy illustrated using the dynamic dolphin model. The dynamic model is simulated numerically with typical control input functions $\mathbf{u}$. For each training example generated, the blue model represents the input state (and/or control and external forces) at time t_k, while the red model represents the output state at time $t_k + \Delta t$. The long time lag enforced between samples reduces the correlation of the training examples that are produced.

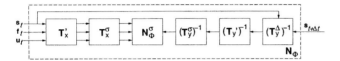

Figure 9: Transforming the training data for consumption by the network $\mathbf{N}_\Phi^\sigma$ in Fig. 6(c). The inputs of the training set are transformed through the operators on the input side of the network in Fig. 6(c). The outputs of the training set are transformed through the inverses of the operators at the output side of the network in Fig. 6(c).

record a set of training examples $\{[\mathbf{s}_{t_k}^T, \mathbf{f}_{t_k}^T, \mathbf{u}_{t_k}^T]^T; \mathbf{s}_{t_k+\Delta t}\}$, $k = 1, 2, \ldots$ The lag between successive samples is drawn randomly from a uniform distribution over the interval $\Delta t \leq (t_{k+1} - t_k) \leq 5\Delta t$. The considerable separation of successive samples in time helps reduce the correlation of the training data, improving learning. Furthermore, we randomize the order of the training samples before starting the backpropagation training algorithm. Clearly, the network observes many independent examples of typical state transitions, rather than any continuous motion.

3.5 Network Training in Xerion

As mentioned earlier, to train the emulator shown in Fig. 6(c) we need only train the network $\mathbf{N}_\Phi^\sigma$ because the operators denoted by the letter $\mathbf{T}$ are predetermined. As shown in Fig. 9 before presenting the training data to the network $\mathbf{N}_\Phi^\sigma$, we transform the inputs of the training set through the operators $\mathbf{T}_x'$ and $\mathbf{T}_x^\sigma$ and transform the associated outputs through the operators $(\mathbf{T}_y^\Delta)^{-1}$, $(\mathbf{T}_y')^{-1}$, and $(\mathbf{T}_y^\sigma)^{-1}$ which are the inverses of the corresponding operators used during the forward emulation step shown in Fig. 6(c).

We begin the off-line training process by initializing the weights of $\mathbf{N}_\Phi^\sigma$ to random values from a uniform distribution in the range $[0, 1]$ (due to the normalization of inputs and outputs). Xerion automatically terminates the backpropagation learning algorithm when it can no longer reduce the network approximation error (3) significantly.

We use the conjugate gradient method to train networks of small and moderate size. This method converges faster than gradient

Model Description	State Inputs	Force Inputs	Control Inputs	Hidden Units	State Outputs	Training Examples
Pendulum						
passive	6	—	—	20	6	2,400
active	6	—	3	20	6	3,000
ext. force	6	3	3	20	6	3,000
Lander	13	—	4	50	13	13,500
Truck	6	—	2	40	6	5,200
Dolphin						
global net	78	—	6	50	78	64,000
local net	72	—	6	40	36	32,000

Table 1: Structure of the NeuroAnimators used in our experiments. Columns 2, 3, and 4 indicate the input groups of the emulator, column 4 indicates the number of hidden units, and column 5 indicates the number of outputs. The final column shows the size of the data set used to train the model. The dolphin NeuroAnimator includes six local nets, one for each body segment.

descent, but the efficiency becomes less significant when training large networks. Since this technique works in batch mode, as the number of training examples grows, the weight updates become too time consuming. For this reason, we use gradient descent with the momentum term (7–8) when training large networks. We divide the training examples into small sets, called *mini-batches*, each consisting of approximately 30 uncorrelated examples, and update the network weights after processing each mini-batch.

Appendix B contains an example Xerion script which specifies and trains a NeuroAnimator.

3.6 Example NeuroAnimators

We have successfully constructed and trained several NeuroAnimators to emulate a variety of physics-based models, including the 3-link pendulum from Fig. 5(a), a lunar lander spacecraft, a truck, and the dolphin model from Fig. 7. We used SD/FAST[4] to simulate the dynamics of the rigid body and articulated models, and we employ the simulator developed in [18] to simulate the deformable-body dynamics of the dolphin. Fig. 10 shows rendered stills from animations created using NeuroAnimators trained with these models.

Table 1 summarizes the structures of the NeuroAnimators developed to emulate these models (note that for the hierarchical dolphin NeuroAnimator, the table indicates the dimensions for only one of its six sub-networks; the other five are similar). In our experiments we have not attempted to minimize the number of network weights required for successful training. We have also not tried to minimize the number of hidden units, but rather used enough units to obtain networks that generalize well while not overfitting the training data. We can always expect to be able to satisfy these guidelines in view of our ability to generate sufficient training data. Section 5 will present a detailed analysis of our results, including performance benchmarks indicating that the neural network emulators can yield physically realistic animation one or two orders of magnitude faster than conventional numerical simulation of the associated physics-based models.

4 NeuroAnimator Controller Synthesis

We have demonstrated that it is possible to emulate a dynamical system using a trained neural network. We turn next to the problem of control; i.e., producing physically realistic animation that satisfies goals specified by the animator.

---

[4]SD/FAST is a commercial system for simulating rigid body dynamics, available from Symbolic Dynamics, Inc.

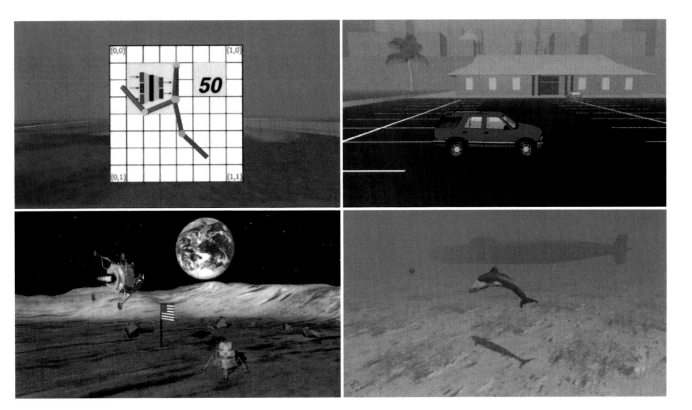

Figure 10: NeuroAnimators used in our experiments. The image at the upper left shows the emulator of a physics-based model of a planar multi-link pendulum suspended in gravity, subject to joint friction forces, external forces applied on the links, and controlled by independent motor torques at each of the three joints. The image at the upper right shows the emulator of a physics-based model of a truck implemented as a rigid body, subject to friction forces where the tires contact the ground, controlled by rear-wheel drive (forward and reverse) and steerable front wheels. The image at the lower left shows the emulator of a physics-based model of a lunar lander, implemented as a rigid body subject to gravitational forces and controlled by a main rocket thruster and three independent attitude jets. The image at the lower right shows the emulator of a physics-based deformable (mass-spring-damper) model of a dolphin capable of locomoting via the coordinated contraction of 6 independently controlled muscle actuators which deform its body, producing hydrodynamic propulsion forces.

4.1 Motivation

A popular approach to the animation control problem is *controller synthesis* [11, 19, 5]. Controller synthesis is a generate-and-test strategy. Through repeated forward simulation of the physics-based model, controller synthesis optimizes a control objective function that measures the degree to which the animation generated by the controlled physical model achieves the desired goals. Each simulation is followed by an evaluation of the motion through the function, thus guiding the search.

While the controller synthesis technique readily handles the complex optimal control problems characteristic of physics-based animation, it is computationally very costly. Evaluation of the objective function requires a forward simulation of the dynamic model, often subject to complex applied forces and constraints. Hence the function is almost never analytically differentiable, prompting the application of non-gradient optimization methods such as simulated annealing [19, 5] and genetic algorithms [11]. In general, since gradient-free optimization methods perform essentially a random walk through the huge search space of possible controllers, computing many dynamic simulations before finding a good solution, they generally converge slowly compared to optimization methods guided by gradient directions.

The NeuroAnimator enables a novel, highly efficient approach to controller synthesis. Outstanding efficiency results not only because of fast controller evaluation through NeuroAnimator emulation of the dynamics of the physical model. To a large degree it also

stems from the fact that we can exploit the neural network approximation in the trained NeuroAnimator to compute partial derivatives of output states with respect to control inputs. This enables the computation of a gradient, hence the use of fast gradient-based optimization for controller synthesis.

In the remainder of this section, we first describe the objective function and its discrete approximation. We then propose an efficient gradient based optimization procedure that computes derivatives of the objective function with respect to the control inputs through a backpropagation algorithm.

4.2 Objective Function and Optimization

Using (9) we write a sequence of emulation steps

$$\mathbf{s}_{i+1} = \mathbf{N}_\Phi[\mathbf{s}_i, \mathbf{u}_i, \mathbf{f}_i]; \qquad 1 \le i \le M, \qquad (10)$$

where i indexes the emulation step, and $\mathbf{s}_i$, $\mathbf{u}_i$ and $\mathbf{f}_i$ denote, respectively, the state, control inputs and external forces in the ith step. Figure 4 illustrates forward emulation by the NeuroAnimator according to this index notation.

Following the control learning formulation in [5], we define a discrete objective function

$$J(\mathbf{u}) = \mu_u J_u(\mathbf{u}) + \mu_s J_s(\mathbf{s}), \qquad (11)$$

a weighted sum (with scalar weights μ_u and μ_s) of a term J_u that evaluates the controller $\mathbf{u} = [\mathbf{u}_1, \mathbf{u}_2, \ldots, \mathbf{u}_M]$ and a term J_s that evaluates the motion $\mathbf{s} = [\mathbf{s}_1, \mathbf{s}_2, \ldots, \mathbf{s}_{M+1}]$ produced by the NeuroAnimator using $\mathbf{u}$, according to (10). Via the controller evaluation term J_u, we may wish to promote a preference for controllers with certain desirable qualities, such as smooth lower amplitude controllers. The distinction between good and bad control functions also depends on the goals that the animation must satisfy. In our applications, we used trajectory criteria J_s such as the final distance to the goal, the deviation from a desired speed, etc. The objective function provides a quantitative measure of the progress of the controller learning process, with larger values of J indicating better controllers.

A typical objective function used in our experiments seeks an efficient controller that leaves the model in some desired state $\mathbf{s}_d$ at the end of simulation. Mathematically, this is expressed as

$$J(\mathbf{u}) = \frac{\mu_u}{2} \sum_{i=1}^{M} \mathbf{u}_i^2 + \frac{\mu_s}{2} (\mathbf{s}_{M+1} - \mathbf{s}_d)^2, \qquad (12)$$

where the first term maximizes the efficiency of the controller and the second term constrains the final state of the model at the end of the animation.

4.3 Backpropagation Through Time

Assuming a trained NeuroAnimator with a set of fixed weights, the essence of our control learning algorithm is to iteratively update the control parameters $\mathbf{u}$ so as to maximize the objective function J in (11). As mentioned earlier, we exploit the NeuroAnimator structure to arrive at an efficient gradient descent optimizer:

$$\mathbf{u}^{l+1} = \mathbf{u}^l + \eta_x \nabla_{\mathbf{u}} J(\mathbf{u}^l), \qquad (13)$$

where l denotes the iteration of the minimization step, and the constant η_x is the learning rate parameter.

At each iteration l, the algorithm first emulates the forward dynamics according to (10) using the control inputs $\mathbf{u}^l = [\mathbf{u}_1^l, \mathbf{u}_2^l, \ldots, \mathbf{u}_M^l]$ to yield the motion sequence $\mathbf{s}^l = [\mathbf{s}_1^l, \mathbf{s}_2^l, \ldots, \mathbf{s}_{M+1}^l]$, as is illustrated in Fig. 4. Next, it computes the components of $\nabla_{\mathbf{u}} J$ in (13) in an efficient manner. The cascade network structure enables us to apply the chain rule of differentiation within each network, chaining backwards across networks, yielding a variant of the backpropagation algorithm called *backpropagation through time* [15]. Instead of adjusting weights as in normal backpropagation, however, the algorithm adjusts neuronal inputs, specifically, the control inputs. It thus proceeds in reverse through the network cascade computing components of the gradient. Fig. 11 illustrates the backpropagation through time process, showing the sequentially computed controller updates $\delta \mathbf{u}_M$ to $\delta \mathbf{u}_0$.

The forward emulation and control adjustment steps are repeated for each iteration of (13), quickly yielding a good controller. The efficiency stems from two factors. First, each NeuroAnimator emulation of the physics-based model consumes only a fraction of the time it would take to numerically simulate the model. Second, quick gradient descent towards an optimum is possible because the trained NeuroAnimator provides a gradient direction.

The control algorithm based on the differentiation of the emulator of the forward model has important advantages. First, the backpropagation through time can solve fairly complex sequential decision problems where early decisions can have substantial effects on the final results. Second, the algorithm can be applied to dynamic environments with changing control objectives since it relearns very quickly.

More efficient optimization techniques can be applied to improve a slow convergence rate of the gradient descent algorithm (13). Adding momentum (7–8) to the gradient descent rule improves the

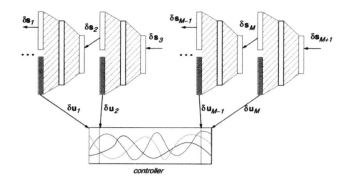

Figure 11: The backpropagation through time algorithm. At each iteration the algorithm computes the derivatives of the objective function with respect to the inputs of the emulator using the chain rule and it adjusts the control inputs to decrease the value of the objective function.

effective learning:

$$
\begin{aligned}
\delta \mathbf{u}^{l+1} &= \eta_x \nabla_{\mathbf{u}} J(\mathbf{u}^l) + \alpha_x \delta \mathbf{u}^l, \qquad &(14)\\
\mathbf{u}^{l+1} &= \mathbf{u}^l + \delta \mathbf{u}^{l+1}, \qquad &(15)
\end{aligned}
$$

where α_x is the momentum parameter used to update the inputs, and l is the iteration of the minimization step. Learning with the momentum term is very fast. Section 6 includes a performance comparison of the different optimization techniques.

Up to now we have assumed that the objective is a known analytic function of the states and the controls of the model, as in (11). Although this definition covers a wide range of practical problems, our approach to control learning can handle objective functions whose analytic form is unknown in advance. See [4] for further discussion.

An additional advantage of our approach is that once an optimal controller has been computed, it can be applied to control either the NeuroAnimator emulator or to the original physical model, yielding animations that in most cases differ only minimally.

5 NeuroAnimator Synthesis Results

As we discussed earlier, we have successfully constructed and trained several NeuroAnimators to emulate a variety of physics-based models pictured in Fig. 10. The ensuing discussion presents performance benchmarks and an error analysis.

5.1 Performance Benchmarks

An important advantage of using neural networks to emulate dynamical systems is the speed at which they can be iterated to produce animation. Since the emulator for a dynamical system with the state vector of size N never uses more than $O(N)$ hidden units, it can be evaluated using only $O(N^2)$ operations. Appendix C contains the computer code for the forward step. By comparison, a single simulation timestep using an implicit time integration scheme requires $O(N^3)$ operations. Moreover, a forward pass through the neural network is often equivalent to as many as 50 physical simulation steps, so the efficiency is even more dramatic, yielding performance improvements up to two orders of magnitude faster than the physical simulator.

In the remainder of this section we use $\mathbf{N}_\Phi^n$ to denote a neural network model that was trained with super timestep $\Delta t = n \delta t$. Table 2 compares the physical simulation times obtained using the

Model Description	Physical Simulation	N_Φ^{25}	N_Φ^{50}	N_Φ^{100}	N_Φ^{50} with Regularization
Passive Pendulum	4.70	0.10	0.05	0.02	—
Active Pendulum	4.52	0.12	0.06	0.03	—
Truck	4.88	—	0.07	—	—
Lunar Lander	6.44	—	0.12	—	—
Dolphin	63.00	—	0.95	—	2.48

Table 2: Comparison of simulation time between the physical simulator and different neural network emulators. The duration of each test was 20,000 physical simulation timesteps.

SD/FAST physical simulator and 3 different neural network models: N_Φ^{25}, N_Φ^{50}, and N_Φ^{100}. For the truck model and the lunar lander model, we have trained only N_Φ^{50} emulators. The neural network model that predicts over 100 physical simulation steps offers a speedup of anywhere between 50 and 100 times depending on the type of physical model.

5.2 Approximation Error

As Fig. 12 shows, an interesting property of the neural network emulation is that the error does not increase appreciably for emulators with increasingly larger super timesteps; i.e., in the graphs, the error over time for N_Φ^{25}, N_Φ^{50}, and N_Φ^{100} is nearly constant. This is attributable to the fact that an emulator that can predict further into the future must be iterated fewer steps per given interval of animation than an emulator that cannot predict so far ahead. Thus, although the error per iteration may be higher for the longer-range emulator, the growth of the error over time can remain nearly the same for both the longer and shorter range predictors. This means that the only penalty for using emulators that predict far ahead might be a loss of detail (high frequency components in the motion) due to coarse sampling. However, we did not observe this effect for the physical models with which we experimented, suggesting that the physical systems are locally smooth. Of course, it is not possible to increase the neural network prediction time indefinitely, because eventually the network will no longer be able to approximate the physical system at all adequately.

Although it is hard to totally eliminate error, we noticed that the approximation error remained within reasonable bounds for the purposes of computer animation. The neural network emulation appears comparable to the physical simulation, and although the emulated trajectory differs slightly from the trajectory produced by the physical simulator, the emulator reproduces all of the visually salient properties of the physical motion.

5.3 Regularization of Deformable Models

When emulating spring-mass systems in which the degrees of freedom are subject to soft constraints, we discovered that the modest approximation error of even a well-trained emulator network can accumulate as the network is applied repeatedly to generate a lengthy animation. Unlike an articulated system whose state is represented by joint angles and hence is kinematically constrained to maintain its connectivity, the emulation of mass-spring systems can result in some unnatural deformations after many (hundreds or thousands) emulation steps. Accumulated error can be annihilated by periodically performing regularization steps through the application of the true dynamical system (1) using an inexpensive, explicit Euler time-integration step

$$\mathbf{v}_{t+\delta t} = \mathbf{v}_t + \delta t \mathbf{d}(\mathbf{s}_t),$$
$$\mathbf{x}_{t+\delta t} = \mathbf{x}_t + \delta t \mathbf{v}_{t+\delta t},$$

where the state is $\mathbf{s}_t = [\mathbf{v}_t^T, \mathbf{x}_t^T]^T$ and $\mathbf{d}(\mathbf{s}_t)$ are the deformation forces generated by the springs at time t. It is important to note that

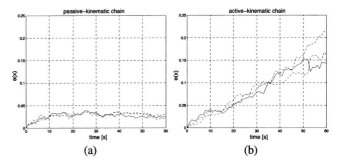

(a) (b)

Figure 12: The error $e(\mathbf{x})$ in the state estimation incurred by different neural network emulators, measured as the absolute difference between the state variables of the emulator and the associated physical model. Plot (a) compares the approximation error for the passive pendulum for 3 different emulator networks: N_Φ^{25} (solid), N_Φ^{50} (dashed), N_Φ^{100} (dot-dashed). Plot (b) shows the same comparison for the active pendulum. All experiments show the averaged error over 30 simulation trials and over all state variables. The duration of each trial was 6000 physical simulation timesteps.

this inexpensive, explicit Euler step is adequate as a regularizer, but it is impractical for long-term physical simulation because of its inherent instability. To improve the stability when applying the explicit Euler step, we used a smaller spring stiffness and larger damping factor when compared to the semi-implicit Euler step used during the numerical simulation [18]. Otherwise the system would oscillate too much or would simply become unstable.

We achieve the best results when performing a few regularization steps after each emulation step. This produces much smoother motion than performing more regularization step but less frequently. Referring to Table 2 for the case of the deformable dolphin model, the second column indicates the simulation time using the physical simulator described in [18], the fourth column shows the simulation time using the N_Φ^{50} emulator, and the last column reveals the impact of regularization on the emulation time. In this case, each emulation step includes 5 iterations of the above explicit Euler regularizer.

6 Control Learning Results

We have successfully applied our backpropagation through time controller learning algorithm to the NeuroAnimators presented in Section 5. We find the technique very effective—it routinely computes solutions to non-trivial control problems in just a few iterations. The efficiency of the fast convergence rate is further amplified by the replacement of costly physical simulation with much faster NeuroAnimator emulation. These two factors yield outstanding speedups, as we report below.

Fig. 13(a) shows the progress of the control learning algorithm for the 3-link pendulum. The purple pendulum, animated by a NeuroAnimator, is given the goal to end the animation with zero velocity in the position indicated in green. We make the learning problem very challenging by setting a low upper limit on the internal motor torques of the pendulum, so that it cannot reach its target in one shot, but must swing back and forth to gain the momentum necessary to reach the goal state. Our algorithm takes 20 backpropagation through time iterations to learn a successful controller.

Fig. 13(b) shows the truck NeuroAnimator learning to park. The translucent truck in the background indicates the desired position and orientation of the model at the end of the simulation. The NeuroAnimator produces a parking controller in 15 learning iterations.

Fig. 13(c) shows the lunar lander NeuroAnimator learning a soft landing maneuver. The translucent lander resting on the surface indicates the desired position and orientation of the model at the end of the animation. An additional constraint is that the descent velocity prior to landing should be small in order to land softly. A successful landing controller was computed in 15 learning iterations.

Fig. 13(d) shows the dolphin NeuroAnimator learning to swim forward. The simple objective of moving as far forward as possible produces a natural, sinusoidal swimming pattern.

All trained controllers have a duration of 20 seconds of animation time; i.e., they take the equivalent of 2,000 physical simulation timesteps, or 40 emulator super-timesteps using $\mathbf{N}_\Phi^{50}$ emulator. The number of control variables (M in $\mathbf{u} = [\mathbf{u}_1, \mathbf{u}_2, \ldots, \mathbf{u}_M]$) optimized varies: the pendulum optimizes 60 variables, 20 for each actuator; the lunar lander optimizes 80 variables, 20 for the main thruster, and 20 for each of the 3 attitude thrusters; the truck optimizes 40 variables—20 for acceleration/deceleration, and 20 for the rate of turning; finally, the dolphin optimizes 60 variables—one variable for every 2 emulator steps for each of the 6 muscle actuators.

Referring to the locomotion learning problem studied in [5], we next compare the efficiency of our new backpropagation through time control learning algorithm using NeuroAnimators and the undirected search techniques—simulated annealing and simplex—reported in [5]. The locomotion learning problem requires the dolphin to learn how to actuate its 6 independent muscles over time in order to swim forward as efficiently as possible, as defined by an objective function that includes actuator work and distance traveled. Our earlier techniques take from 500 to 3500 learning iterations to converge because they need to perform extensive sampling of the control space in the absence of gradient information. By contrast, the gradient directed algorithm converges to a similar solution in as little as 20 learning iterations. Thus, the use of the neural network emulator offers a two orders of magnitude reduction in the number of iterations and a two orders of magnitude reduction in the execution time of each learning iteration. In terms of actual running times, the synthesis of the swimming controller which took more than 1 hour using the technique in [5] now takes less than 10 seconds on the same computer.

Hierarchically structured emulators, in which a global network represents the global aspects of motion and a set of sub-networks refine the motion produced by the global network, enable us to enhance the performance of our controller learning algorithm. For example, when applying the dolphin NeuroAnimator to learn locomotion controllers, we improve efficiency by employing only the global deformation network which accounts for the deformation of the entire body and suppressing the sub-networks that account for the local deformation of each body segment relative to its own center-of-mass coordinate system, since these small deformations do not significantly impact the locomotion. Similarly for a hierarchical human NeuroAnimator, when learning a controller that uses a subset of joints, we need only activate the sub-networks that represent the active joints.

We next compare the convergence of simple gradient descent and gradient descent with the momentum term on the control synthesis problem. Fig. 14 illustrates the progress of learning for the lunar lander problem. The results obtained using the momentum term are shown in the plot on the left and were generated using the parameters $\eta_x = 1.5$, $\alpha_x = 0.5$ in (14). The results obtained using the simple gradient descent are shown in the plot on the right and were generated using $\eta_x = 1.0$ in (13)—the largest learning rate that would converge. Clearly, the momentum term decreases the error much more rapidly, yielding an improved learning rate.

7 Conclusion

We have introduced the NeuroAnimator, an efficient alternative to the conventional approach of producing physically realistic anima-

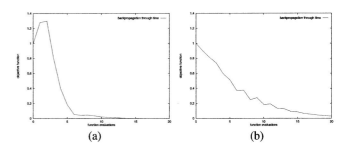

(a)   (b)

Figure 14: The plots show the value of the objective as a function of the iteration of the control learning algorithm. The plot on the left was produced using the momentum term. It converges faster than simple gradient descent plotted on the right.

tion through numerical simulation. NeuroAnimator involves the learning of neural network emulators of physics-based models by observing the dynamic state transitions produced by such models in action. The training takes place off-line and in advance. Animations subsequently produced by a trained NeuroAnimator approximate physical dynamics with dramatic efficiency, yet without serious loss of apparent fidelity. We have demonstrated the practicality of our technique by constructing NeuroAnimators for a variety of nontrivial physics-based models. Our unusual approach to physics-based animation furthermore led us to a novel controller synthesis method which exploits fast emulation and the differentiability of the NeuroAnimator approximation. We presented a "backpropagation through time" learning algorithm which computes controllers that satisfy nontrivial animation goals. Our new control learning algorithm is orders of magnitude faster than prior algorithms.

Acknowledgments

We thank Zoubin Ghahramani for valuable discussions that led to the idea of the rotation and translation invariant emulator, which was crucial to the success of this work. We are indebted to Steve Hunt for procuring the equipment that we needed to carry out our research at Intel. We thank Sonja Jeter for her assistance with the Viewpoint models and Mike Gendimenico for setting up the video editing suite and helping us to use it. We thank John Funge and Michiel van de Panne for their assistance in producing animations, Mike Revow and Drew van Camp for assistance with Xerion, and Alexander Reshetov for his valuable suggestions about building physical models.

A Normalizing Network Inputs & Outputs

In Section 3.2 we recommended the normalization of emulator inputs and outputs. Variables in different groups (state, force, or control) require independent normalization. We normalize each variable so that it has zero mean and unit variance as follows:

$$\tilde{x}_k^n = \frac{x_k^n - \mu_i^x}{\sigma_i^x}, \tag{16}$$

where the mean of the ith group of inputs is

$$\mu_i^x = \frac{1}{NK} \sum_{n=1}^{N} \sum_{k=k_i}^{k_i+K_i} x_k^n, \tag{17}$$

and its variance is

$$\sigma_i^x = \frac{1}{(N-1)(K-1)} \sum_{n=1}^{N} \sum_{k=k_i}^{k_i+K_i} (x_k^n - \mu_i)^2. \tag{18}$$

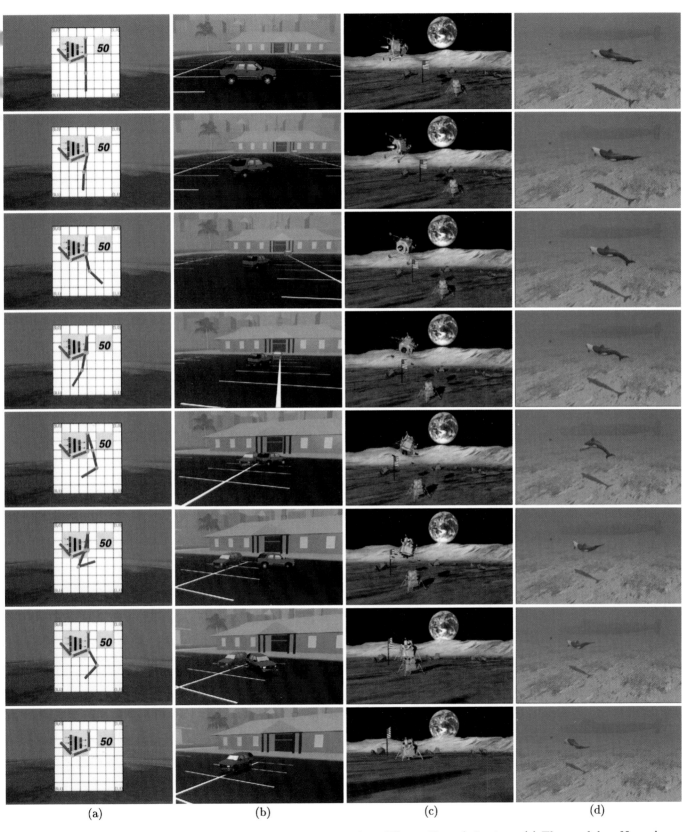

Figure 13: Results of applying the control learning algorithm to four different NeuroAnimators. (a) The pendulum NeuroAnimator shown in purple needs to reach the state indicated by the green pendulum, with zero final velocity. (b) The truck NeuroAnimator learning to park in the position and orientation indicated by the translucent vehicle in the background. (c) The lunar lander NeuroAnimator learning to land in the position and orientation of the translucent vehicle sitting on the ground, with minimal descent velocity. (d) The dolphin NeuroAnimator learning to swim. The objective of locomoting as far forward as possible produces a natural, periodic swimming pattern.

Here $n = 1, \ldots, N$ indexes the training example, $k = k_i, \ldots, k_i + K_i$ indexes the variables in group i, K_i represents the size of group i, and x_k^n denotes the kth input variable for the nth training example. A similar set of equations computes the means μ_j^y and the variances σ_j^y for the output layer of the network:

$$\tilde{y}_k^n = \frac{y_k^n - \mu_j^y}{\sigma_j^y}. \tag{19}$$

B   Example Xerion Script

The following is a Xerion script that specifies and trains the network $\mathbf{N}_\Phi^\sigma$ used to build the NeuroAnimator for the lunar lander model.

```
#! /u/xerion/uts/bin/bp_sh

# The network has 13 inputs, 50 hidden units, and
# 13 outputs. The hidden layer uses the logistic
# sigmoid as the activation function (default).
uts_simpleNet landerNet 13 50 13
bp_groupType landerNet.Hidden {HIDDEN DPROD LOGISTIC}

# Initialize the example set. Read
# the training data from a file.
set trainSet "landerNet.data"
uts_exampleSet   $trainSet
uts_loadExamples $trainSet landerNet.data

# Randomize the weights in the network.
random seed 3
uts_randomizeNet landerNet

# Initialize the minimizer and tell it to use
# the network and the training set defined above.
bp_netMinimizer mz
mz configure -net landerNet -exampleSet trainSet

# Start the training and save the weights
# of the network after the training is finished.
mz run
uts_saveWeights landerNet landerNet.weights
```

C   Forward Pass Through the Network

The following is a C++ function for calculating the outputs of a neural network from the inputs. It implements the core loop that takes a single super timestep in an animation sequence with a trained NeuroAnimator.

```
BasicNet::forwardStep(void)
{
  int i,j,k;

  double *input = inputLayer.units;
  double *hidden = hiddenLayer.units;
  double *output = outputLayer.units;
  double **ww = inputHiddenWeights;
  double **vv = hiddenOutputWeights;

  // compute the activity of the hidden layer
  for (j=0;j<hiddenSize;j++) {
    hidden[j] = biasHiddenWeights[j];
    for (k=0;k<inputSize;k++)
      hidden[j] += input[k]*ww[k][j];
    hidden[j]=hiddenLayer.transFunc(hidden[j]);
  }

  // compute the activity of the output layer
  for (i=0;i<outputSize;i++) {
    output[i] = biasOutputWeights[i];
    for (j=0;j<hiddenSize;j++)
      output[i] += hidden[j]*vv[j][i];
    output[i]=outputLayer.transFunc(output[i]);
  }
}
```

References

[1] David Baraff. Analytical methods for dynamic simulation of non-penetrating rigid bodies. In Jeffrey Lane, editor, *Computer Graphics (SIGGRAPH '89 Proceedings)*, volume 23, pages 223–232, July 1989.

[2] C. M. Bishop. *Neural Networks for Pattern Recognition*. Clarendon Press, 1995.

[3] G. Cybenko. Approximation by superposition of sigmoidal function. *Mathematics of Control Signals and Systems*, 2(4):303–314, 1989.

[4] R. Grzeszczuk. *NeuroAnimator: Fast Neural Network Emulation and Control of Physics-Based Models*. PhD thesis, Department of Computer Science, University of Toronto, May 1998.

[5] Radek Grzeszczuk and Demetri Terzopoulos. Automated learning of Muscle-Actuated locomotion through control abstraction. In Robert Cook, editor, *SIGGRAPH 95 Conference Proceedings*, Annual Conference Series, pages 63–70. ACM SIGGRAPH, Addison Wesley, August 1995. held in Los Angeles, California, 06-11 August 1995.

[6] James K. Hahn. Realistic animation of rigid bodies. In John Dill, editor, *Computer Graphics (SIGGRAPH '88 Proceedings)*, volume 22, pages 299–308, August 1988.

[7] Jessica K. Hodgins, Wayne L. Wooten, David C. Brogan, and James F. O'Brien. Animating human athletics. In Robert Cook, editor, *SIGGRAPH 95 Conference Proceedings*, Annual Conference Series, pages 71–78. ACM SIGGRAPH, Addison Wesley, August 1995. held in Los Angeles, California, 06-11 August 1995.

[8] K. Hornik, M. Stinchcomb, and H. White. Multilayer feedforward networks are universal approximators. *Neural Networks*, 2:359–366, 1989.

[9] M. I. Jordan and D. E. Rumelhart. Supervised learning with a distal teacher. *Cognitive Science*, 16:307–354, 1992.

[10] Gavin S. P. Miller. The motion dynamics of snakes and worms. In John Dill, editor, *Computer Graphics (SIGGRAPH '88 Proceedings)*, volume 22, pages 169–178, August 1988.

[11] J. Thomas Ngo and Joe Marks. Spacetime constraints revisited. In James T. Kajiya, editor, *Computer Graphics (SIGGRAPH '93 Proceedings)*, volume 27, pages 343–350, August 1993.

[12] D. Nguyen and B. Widrow. The truck backer-upper: An example of self-learning in neural networks. In *Proceedings of the International Joint Conference on Neural Networks*, volume 2, pages 357–363. IEEE Press, 1989.

[13] W. H. Press, S. A. Teukolsky, W. T. Vetterling, and B. P. Flannery. *Numerical Recipes: The Art of Scientific Computing, Second Edition*. Cambridge University Press, 1992.

[14] G. Ridsdale. Connectionist modeling of skill dynamics. *Journal of Visualization and Computer Animation*, 1(2):66–72, 1990.

[15] D. E. Rumelhart, G. E. Hinton, and R. J. Williams. Learning internal representations by error backpropagation. In D. E. Rumelhart, J. L. McCleland, and the PDP Research Group, editors, *Parallel Distributed Processing: Explorations in the Microstructure of Cognition*, volume 1, pages 318–362. MIT Press, 1986.

[16] Karl Sims. Evolving virtual creatures. In Andrew Glassner, editor, *Proceedings of SIGGRAPH '94 (Orlando, Florida, July 24–29, 1994)*, Computer Graphics Proceedings, Annual Conference Series, pages 15–22. ACM SIGGRAPH, ACM Press, July 1994. ISBN 0-89791-667-0.

[17] Demetri Terzopoulos, John Platt, Alan Barr, and Kurt Fleischer. Elastically deformable models. In Maureen C. Stone, editor, *Computer Graphics (SIGGRAPH '87 Proceedings)*, volume 21, pages 205–214, July 1987.

[18] Xiaoyuan Tu and Demetri Terzopoulos. Artificial fishes: Physics, locomotion, perception, behavior. In Andrew Glassner, editor, *Proceedings of SIGGRAPH '94 (Orlando, Florida, July 24–29, 1994)*, Computer Graphics Proceedings, Annual Conference Series, pages 43–50. ACM SIGGRAPH, ACM Press, July 1994. ISBN 0-89791-667-0.

[19] Michiel van de Panne and Eugene Fiume. Sensor-actuator networks. In James T. Kajiya, editor, *Computer Graphics (SIGGRAPH '93 Proceedings)*, volume 27, pages 335–342, August 1993.

A Beam Tracing Approach to Acoustic Modeling for Interactive Virtual Environments

Thomas Funkhouser,* Ingrid Carlbom, Gary Elko,
Gopal Pingali, Mohan Sondhi, and Jim West
Bell Laboratories

Abstract

Virtual environment research has focused on interactive image generation and has largely ignored acoustic modeling for spatialization of sound. Yet, realistic auditory cues can complement and enhance visual cues to aid navigation, comprehension, and sense of presence in virtual environments. A primary challenge in acoustic modeling is computation of reverberation paths from sound sources fast enough for real-time auralization. We have developed a system that uses precomputed spatial subdivision and "beam tree" data structures to enable real-time acoustic modeling and auralization in interactive virtual environments. The spatial subdivision is a partition of 3D space into convex polyhedral regions (cells) represented as a cell adjacency graph. A beam tracing algorithm recursively traces pyramidal beams through the spatial subdivision to construct a beam tree data structure representing the regions of space reachable by each potential sequence of transmission and specular reflection events at cell boundaries. From these precomputed data structures, we can generate high-order specular reflection and transmission paths at interactive rates to spatialize fixed sound sources in real-time as the user moves through a virtual environment. Unlike previous acoustic modeling work, our beam tracing method: 1) supports evaluation of reverberation paths at interactive rates, 2) scales to compute high-order reflections and large environments, and 3) extends naturally to compute paths of diffraction and diffuse reflection efficiently. We are using this system to develop interactive applications in which a user experiences a virtual environment immersively via simultaneous auralization and visualization.

Key Words: Beam tracing, acoustic modeling, auralization, spatialized sound, virtual environment systems, virtual reality.

1 Introduction

Interactive virtual environment systems combine graphics, acoustics, and haptics to simulate the experience of immersive exploration of a three-dimensional virtual world by rendering the environment as perceived from the viewpoint of an observer moving under real-time control by the user. Most prior research in virtual environment systems has focused on visualization (i.e., methods for rendering more realistic images or for increasing image refresh rates), while relatively little attention has been paid to auralization (i.e., rendering spatialized sound based on acoustical modeling). Yet, it is clear that

we must pay more attention to producing realistic sound in order to create a complete immersive experience in which aural cues combine with visual cues to support more natural interaction within a virtual environment. First, qualitative changes in sound reverberation, such as more absorption in a room with more lush carpets, can enhance and reinforce visual comprehension of the environment. Second, spatialized sound can be useful for providing audio cues to aid navigation, communication, and sense of presence [14]. For example, the sounds of objects requiring user attention can be spatialized according to their positions in order to aid object location and binaural selectivity of desired signals (e.g., "cocktail party" effect). The goal of this work is to augment a previous interactive image generation system to support real-time auralization of sound based on realistic acoustic modeling in large virtual environments. We hope to use this system to support virtual environment applications such as distributed training, simulation, education, home shopping, virtual meetings, and multiplayer games.

A primary challenge in acoustic modeling is computation of reverberation paths from a sound source to a listener (receiver) [30]. As sound may travel from source to receiver via a multitude of reflection, transmission, and diffraction paths, accurate simulation is extremely compute intensive. For instance, consider the simple example shown in Figure 1. In order to present an accurate model of a sound source (labeled 'S') at a receiver location (labeled 'R'), we must account for an infinite number of possible reverberation paths (some of which are shown). If we are able to model the reverberation paths from a sound source to a receiver, we can render a spatialized representation of the sound according to their delays, attenuations, and source and receiver directivities.

Figure 1: Example reverberation paths.

Since sound and light are both wave phenomena, acoustic modeling is similar to global illumination in computer graphics. However, there are several significant differences. First, the wavelengths of audible sound fall between 0.02 and 17 meters (20kHz to 20Hz), more than five orders of magnitude longer than visible light. As a result, though reflection of sound waves off large walls tends to be primarily specular, significant diffraction does occur around edges of objects like walls and tables. Small objects (like coffee mugs) have significant effect on the sound field only at frequencies beyond 4 kHz, and can usually be excluded from models of acoustic environments, especially in the presence of other significant sources of reflection and diffraction. Second, sound travels through air 10^6 times slower than light, causing significantly different arrival times for sound propagating along different paths, and the resulting acoustic signal is perceived as a combination of direct and reflected sound

---

*Princeton University

(reverberation). The time distribution of the reverberation paths of the sound in a typical room is much longer than the integration period of the perception of sound by a human. Thus, it is important to accurately compute the exact time/frequency distribution of the reverberation. In contrast, the speed of light and the perception of light is such that the eye integrates out the transient response of a light source and only the energy steady-state response needs to be calculated. Third, since sound is a coherent wave phenomenon, the calculation of the reflected and scattered sound waves must incorporate the phase (complex amplitude) of the incident and reflected wave(s), while for incoherent light, only the power must be summed.

Although acoustic modeling has been well-studied in the context of non-interactive applications [34], such as concert hall design, there has been relatively little prior research in real-time acoustic modeling for virtual environment systems [15]. Currently available auralization systems generally model only early specular reflections, while late reverberations and diffractions are modeled with statistical approximations [1, 25, 40, 53]. Also, due to the computational complexity of current systems, they generally consider only simple geometric arrangements and low-order specular reflections. For instance, the Acoustetron [17] computes only first- and second-order specular reflections for box-shaped virtual environments. Video games provide spatialized sound with ad hoc localization methods (e.g., pan effects) rather than with realistic geometrical acoustic modeling methods. The 1995 National Research Council Report on Virtual Reality Scientific and Technological Challenges [15] states that "current technology is still unable to provide interactive systems with real-time rendering of acoustic environments with complex, realistic room reflections."

In this paper, we describe a beam tracing method that computes high-order specular reflection and transmission paths from fixed sources in large polygonal models fast enough to be used for auralization in interactive virtual environment systems. The key idea behind our method is to precompute and store spatial data structures that encode all possible transmission and specular reflection paths from each audio source and then use these data structures to compute reverberation paths to an arbitrarily moving observer viewpoint for real-time auralization during an interactive user session. Our algorithms for construction and query of these data structures have the unique features that they scale well with increasing numbers of reflections and global geometric complexity, and they extend naturally to model paths of diffraction and diffuse reflection. We have incorporated these algorithms and data structures into a system that supports real-time auralization and visualization of large virtual environments.

2 Previous Work

There has been a large amount of work in acoustic modeling. Prior methods can be classified into four types: 1) image source methods, 2) radiant exchange methods 3) path tracing, and 4) beam tracing.

2.1 Image Source Methods

Image source methods [2, 6] compute specular reflection paths by considering *virtual sources* generated by mirroring the location of the audio source, S, over each polygonal surface of the environment (see Figure 2). For each virtual source, S_i, a specular reflection path can be constructed by iterative intersection of a line segment from the source position to the receiver position, R, with the reflecting surface planes (such a path is shown for virtual source S_c in Figure 2). Specular reflection paths can be computed up to any order by recursive generation of virtual sources.

The primary advantage of image source methods is their robustness. They can guarantee that all specular paths up to a given order or reverberation time will be found. The disadvantages of image source methods are that they model only specular reflections, and

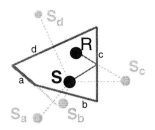

Figure 2: Image source method.

their expected computational complexity has exponential growth. In general, $O(n^r)$ virtual sources must be generated for r reflections in environments with n surface planes. Moreover, in all but the simplest environments (e.g., a box), complex validity/visibility checks must be performed for each of the $O(n^r)$ virtual sources since not all of the virtual sources represent physically realizable specular reflection paths [6]. For instance, a virtual source generated by reflection over the non-reflective side of a surface is "invalid." Likewise, a virtual source whose reflection is blocked by another surface in the environment or intersects a point on a surface's plane which is outside the surface's boundary (e.g., S_a in Figure 2) is "invisible." During recursive generation of virtual sources, descendents of invalid virtual sources can be ignored. However, descendents of invisible virtual sources must still be considered, as higher-order reflections may generate visible virtual sources (consider mirroring S_a over surface d). Due to the computational demands of $O(n^r)$ visibility checks, image source methods are practical only for acoustic modeling of few reflections in simple environments [32].

2.2 Radiant Exchange Methods

Radiant exchange methods have been used extensively in computer graphics to model diffuse reflection of radiosity between patches [21]. Briefly, radiosity methods consider every patch a potential emitter and reflector of radiosity. Conceptually, for every pair of patches, A and B, a form factor is computed which measures the fraction of the radiosity leaving patch A that arrives at patch B. This approach yields a set of simultaneous equations which are solved to obtain the radiosity for each patch.

Although this approach has been used with good results for modeling diffuse indirect illumination in computer graphics, it is not easily extensible to acoustics. In acoustics modeling, transport equations must account for phase, specular reflection tends to dominate diffuse reflection, and "extended form factor" computations must consider paths of diffraction as well as specular reflection. Furthermore, to meet error tolerances suitable for acoustic modeling, patches must be substructured to a very fine element mesh (typically much less than the acoustic wavelength), the solution must be computed for many frequencies, and the representation of the sound leaving an element must be very data intensive, a complex function of phase, direction, and frequency usually requiring thousands of bytes. As a result, direct extensions to prior radiosity methods [36, 39, 52] do not seem practical for large environments.

2.3 Path Tracing Methods

Ray tracing methods [33, 61] find reverberation paths between a source and receiver by generating rays emanating from the source position and following them through the environment until an appropriate set of rays has been found that reach a representation of the receiver position (see Figure 3).

Monte Carlo path tracing methods consider randomly generated paths from the source to the receiver [28]. For instance, the Metropolis Light Transport algorithm [54] generates a sequence of light transport paths by randomly mutating a single current path by

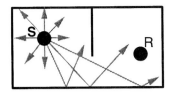

Figure 3: Ray tracing method.

adding, deleting, or replacing vertices. Mutated paths are accepted according to probabilities based on the estimated contribution they make to the solution. As contributing paths are found, they are logged and then mutated further to generate new paths in a Markov chain. Mutation strategies and acceptance probabilities are chosen to insure that the method is unbiased, stratified, and ergodic.

A primary advantage of these methods is their simplicity. They depend only on ray-surface intersection calculations, which are relatively easy to implement and have computational complexity that grows sublinearly with the number of surfaces in the model. Another advantage is generality. As each ray-surface intersection is found, paths of specular reflection, diffuse reflection, diffraction, and refraction can be sampled [10], thereby modeling arbitrary types of indirect reverberation, even for models with curved surfaces.

The primary disadvantages of path tracing methods stem from the fact that the continuous 5D space of rays is sampled by a discrete set of paths, leading to aliasing and errors in predicted room responses [35]. For instance, in ray tracing, the receiver position and diffracting edges are often approximated by volumes of space (in order to admit intersections with infinitely thin rays), which can lead to false hits and paths counted multiple times [35]. Moreover, important reverberation paths may be missed by all samples. In order to minimize the likelihood of large errors, path tracing systems often generate a large number of samples, which requires a large amount of computation. Another disadvantage of path tracing is that the results are dependent on a particular receiver position, and thus these methods are not directly applicable in virtual environment applications where either the source or receiver is moving continuously.

2.4 Beam Tracing Methods

Beam tracing methods [23] classify reflection paths from a source by recursively tracing pyramidal beams (i.e., sets of rays) through the environment. Briefly, a set of pyramidal beams are constructed that completely cover the 2D space of directions from the source. For each beam, polygons are considered for intersection in order from front to back. As intersecting polygons are detected, the original beam is clipped to remove the shadow region, a transmission beam is constructed matching the shadow region, and a reflection beam is constructed by mirroring the transmission beam over the polygon's plane (see Figure 4).

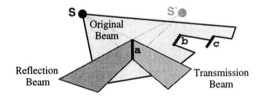

Figure 4: Beam tracing method.

As compared to image source methods, the primary advantage of beam tracing is that fewer virtual sources must be considered for environments with arbitrary geometry. Since each beam represents the region of space for which a corresponding virtual source (at the apex of the beam) is visible, higher-order virtual sources must be considered only for reflections of polygons intersecting the beam. For instance, in Figure 5, consider the virtual source S_a, which results from reflection of S over polygon a. The corresponding reflection beam, R_a, contains exactly the set of receiver points for which S_a is valid and visible. Similarly, R_a intersects exactly the set of polygons (c and d) for which second-order reflections are possible after specular reflection off polygon a. Other polygons (b, e, f, and g) need not be considered for second order specular reflections after a. Beam tracing allows the recursion tree of virtual sources to be pruned significantly. On the other hand, the image source method is more efficient for a box-shaped environment for which a regular lattice of virtual sources can be constructed that are guaranteed to be visible for all receiver locations [2].

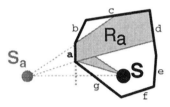

Figure 5: Beam tracing culls invisible virtual sources.

As compared to path tracing methods, the primary advantage of beam tracing is that it takes advantage of spatial coherence, as each beam-surface intersection represents an infinite number of ray-surface intersections. Also, pyramidal beam tracing does not suffer from sampling artifacts of ray tracing [35] or the overlap problems of cone tracing [3, 55], since the entire 2D space of directions leaving the source can be covered by beams exactly.

The primary disadvantage of beam tracing is that the geometric operations required to trace a beam through a 3D model (i.e., intersection and clipping) are relatively complex, as each beam may be reflected and/or obstructed by several surfaces. Another limitation is that reflections off curved surfaces and refractions are difficult to model.

Geometric beam tracing has been used in a variety of applications, including acoustic modeling [13, 38, 46, 57], illumination [9, 19, 20, 22, 23, 59], and radio propagation [16]. The challenge is to perform geometric operations (i.e., intersection, clipping, and mirroring) on beams efficiently as they are traced recursively through a complex environment.

Some systems avoid the geometric complexity of beam tracing by approximating each beam by its medial axis ray for intersection and mirror operations [36], possibly splitting rays as they diverge with distance [31, 42]. In this case, the beam representation is only useful for modeling the distribution of rays/energy with distance and for avoiding large tolerances in ray-receiver intersection calculations. If beams are not clipped or split when they intersect more than one surface, significant reverberation paths can be missed.

Heckbert and Hanrahan [23] described an algorithm for illumination in which pyramidal beams represented by their 2D polygonal cross-sections are traced recursively either forward from a viewpoint or backward from a point light source. For each beam, all polygons are processed in front to back order. For each polygon intersecting the beam, the shadow region is "cut out" of the original beam using a polygon clipping algorithm capable of handling concavities and holes. The authors describe construction of an intermediate "light beam tree" data structure that encodes the beam tracing recursion and is used for later evaluation of light paths. Their implementation does not scale well to large environments since its computational complexity grows with $O(n^2)$ for n polygons.

Dadoun et al. [12, 13] described a beam tracing algorithm for acoustic modeling in which a hierarchical scene representation (HSR) is used to accelerate polygon sorting and intersection testing. During a preprocessing phase, a binary space partition (BSP) tree structure is constructed and augmented with storage for the convex hull for each subtree. Then, during beam tracing, the HSR is used to accelerate queries to find an ordered set of polygons potentially intersecting each beam. As in [23], beams are represented by their 2D polygonal cross-sections and are updated using the Weiler-Atherton clipping algorithm [60] at polygon intersections.

Fortune [16] described a beam tracing algorithm for indoor radio propagation prediction in which a spatial data structure comprising "layers" of 2D triangulations is used to accelerate polygon intersection testing. A method is proposed in which beams are partitioned into convex regions by planes supporting the edges of occluding polygons. However, Fortune expects that method to be too expensive for use in indoor radio propagation (where attenuation due to transmission is small) due to the exponential growth in the number of beams. Instead, he has implemented a system in which beams are traced directly from the source and along paths of reflection, but are not clipped by occluding polygons. Instead, attenuation due to occlusion is computed for each path, taking into account the attenuation of each occluding polygon along the path. This implementation trades-off more expensive computation during path generation for less expensive computation during beam tracing.

Jones [27] and Teller [51] have described beam tracing algorithms to compute a "potentially visible set" of polygons to render from a particular viewpoint in a computer graphics scene. These algorithms preprocess the scene into a spatial subdivision of cells (convex polyhedra) and portals (transparent, boundaries between cells). Polyhedral beams are traced through portals to determine the region of space potentially visible from a view frustum in order to produce a conservative and approximate solution to the hidden surface problem.

In this paper, we describe beam tracing data structures and algorithms for real-time acoustic modeling in interactive virtual environment applications. Our method is most closely related to work in [23] and [51]. As compared to previous acoustic modeling methods, the unique features of our method are the ability to: 1) generate specular reflection and transmission paths at interactive rates, 2) scale to support large virtual environments, 3) scale to compute high-order reflection and transmission paths, and 4) extend to support efficient computation of diffraction and diffuse reflection paths. We have included these algorithms and data structures in an interactive virtual environment system that supports immersive auralization and visualization in complex polygonal environments.

3   System Organization

Our virtual environment system takes as input: 1) a description of the geometry and visual/acoustic surface properties of the environment (i.e., sets of polygons), and 2) a set of anechoic audio source signals at fixed locations. As a user moves through the virtual environment interactively, the system generates images as seen from a simulated observer viewpoint, along with a stereo audio signal spatialized according to the computed reverberation paths from each audio source to the observer location.

In order to support real-time auralization, we partition our system into four distinct phases (see Figure 6), two of which are preprocessing steps that execute off-line, while the last two execute in real-time as a user interactively controls an observer viewpoint moving through a virtual environment. First, during the *spatial subdivision phase*, we precompute spatial relationships inherent in the set of polygons describing the environment and represent them in a cell adjacency graph data structure that supports efficient traversals of space. Second, during the *beam tracing phase*, we recursively follow beams of transmission and specular reflection through space for each audio source. The output of the beam tracing phase is a beam tree data structure that explicitly encodes the region of space reachable by each sequence of reflection and transmission paths from each source point. Third, during the *path generation* phase,

we compute reverberation paths from each source to the receiver via lookup into the precomputed beam tree data structure as the receiver (i.e., the observer viewpoint) is moved under interactive user control. Finally, during the *auralization phase*, we spatialize each source audio signal (in stereo) according to the lengths, attenuations, and directions of the computed reverberation paths. The spatialized audio output is synchronized with real-time graphics output to provide an immersive virtual environment experience.

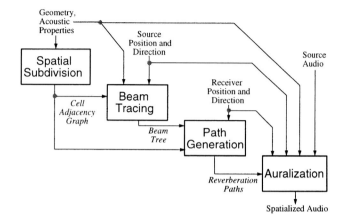

Figure 6: System organization.

3.1   Spatial Subdivision

Our system preprocesses the geometric properties of the environment and builds a spatial subdivision to accelerate beam tracing. The goal of this phase is to precompute spatial relationships inherent in the set of polygons describing the environment and to represent them in a data structure that supports efficient traversals of space. The spatial subdivision is constructed by partitioning 3D space into a set of convex polyhedral regions and building a graph that explicitly represents the adjacencies between the regions of the subdivision.

We build the spatial subdivision using a Binary Space Partition (BSP) [18], a recursive binary split of 3D space into convex polyhedral regions (*cells*) separated by planes. To construct the BSP, we recursively split cells by candidate planes selected by the method described in [41]. The binary splitting process continues until no input polygon intersects the interior of any BSP cell. The result of the BSP is a set of convex polyhedral cells whose convex, planar boundaries contain all the input polygons.

An adjacency graph is constructed that explicitly represents the neighbor relationships between cells of the spatial subdivision. Each cell of the BSP is represented by a node in the graph, and two nodes have a *link* between them for each planar, polygonal boundary shared by the corresponding adjacent cells in the spatial subdivision. Construction of the cell adjacency graph is integrated with the binary space partitioning algorithm. If a leaf in the BSP is split into two by a plane, we create new nodes in the graph corresponding to the new cells in the BSP, and we update the links of the split leaf's neighbors to reflect the new adjacencies. We create a separate link between two cells for each convex polygonal region that is entirely either transparent or opaque along the cells' shared boundary.

A simple 2D example model (on left) and its cell adjacency graph (on right) are shown in Figure 7. Input "polygons" appear as solid line segments labeled with lower-case letters ($a - q$); transparent cell boundaries introduced by the BSP are shown as dashed line segments labeled with lower-case letters ($r - u$); constructed cell regions are labeled with upper-case letters ($A - E$); and, links are drawn between adjacent cells sharing a convex "polygonal" boundary.

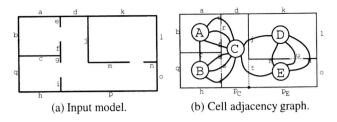

(a) Input model.	(b) Cell adjacency graph.

Figure 7: Example spatial subdivision.

3.2 Beam Tracing

After the spatial subdivision has been constructed, we use it to accelerate traversals of space in our beam tracing algorithm. Beams are traced through the cell adjacency graph via a recursive depth-first traversal starting in the cell containing the source point. Adjacent cells are visited recursively while a beam representing the region of space reachable from the source by a sequence of cell boundary reflection and transmission events is incrementally updated. As the algorithm traverses a cell boundary into a new cell, the current convex pyramidal beam is "clipped" to include only the region of space passing through the convex polygonal boundary polygon. At reflecting cell boundaries, the beam is mirrored across the plane supporting the cell boundary in order to model specular reflections. As an example, Figure 8 shows a sequence of beams (green polyhedra) traced up to one reflection from a source (white point) through the spatial subdivision (blue 'X's are cell boundaries) for a simple set of input polygons (red surfaces).

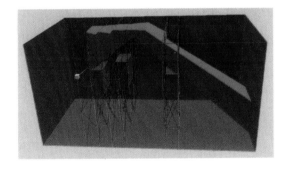

Figure 8: A beam clipped and reflected at cell boundaries.

Throughout the traversal, the algorithm maintains a *current cell* (a reference to a cell in the spatial subdivision) and a *current beam* (an infinite convex pyramidal beam whose apex is the source point). Initially, the *current cell* is set to be the cell containing the source point and the *current beam* is set to cover all of space. During each step of the depth-first traversal, the algorithm continues recursively for each boundary polygon, P, of the *current cell*, C, that intersects the *current beam*, B. If P does not coincide with an opaque input surface, the algorithm follows a transmission path, recursing to the cell adjacent to C across P with a *transmission beam*, B_t, constructed as the intersection of B with a pyramidal beam whose apex is the source point and whose sides pass through the edges of P. Likewise, if P coincides with a reflecting input surface, the algorithm follows a specular reflection path, recursing in cell C with a *specular reflection beam*, B_r, constructed by mirroring the *transmission beam* over the plane supporting P. The depth-first traversal along any path terminates when the length of a path exceeds a user-specified threshold or when the cumulative absorption due to transmission and reflection exceeds a preset threshold. The traversal may also be terminated when the total number of reflections or transmissions exceeds a third threshold.

Figure 9 contains an illustration of the beam tracing algorithm execution for specular reflections through the simple 2D example

model shown in Figure 7. The depth-first traversal starts in the cell (labeled 'D') containing the source point (labeled 'S') with a beam containing the entire cell (shown as dark green). Beams are created and traced for each of the six boundary polygons of cell 'D' (j, k, l, m, n, and u). For example, transmission through the cell boundary labeled 'u' results in a beam (labeled T_u) that is trimmed as it enters cell 'E.' T_u intersects only the polygon labeled 'o,' which spawns a reflection beam (labeled $T_u R_o$). That beam intersects only the polygon labeled 'p,' which spawns a reflection beam (labeled $T_u R_o R_p$). Execution continues recursively for each beam until the length of every path exceeds a user-specified threshold or when the absorption along every path becomes too large.

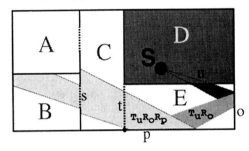

Figure 9: Beam tracing through cell adjacency graph.

While tracing beams through the spatial subdivision, our algorithm constructs a *beam tree* data structure [23] to be used for rapid determination of reverberation paths from the source point later during the path generation phase. The beam tree corresponds directly to the recursion tree generated during the depth-first traversal through the cell adjacency graph. It is similar to the "stab tree" data structure used by Teller to encode visibility relationships for occlusion culling [51]. Each node of the beam tree stores: 1) a reference to the cell being traversed, 2) the cell boundary most recently traversed (if there is one), and 3) the convex beam representing the region of space reachable by the sequence of reflection and transmission events along the current path of the depth-first traversal. To further accelerate reverberation path generation, each node of the beam tree also stores the cumulative attenuation due to reflective and transmissive absorption, and each cell of the spatial subdivision stores a list of "back-pointers" to its beam tree nodes. Figure 10 shows a partial beam tree corresponding to the traversal shown in Figure 9.

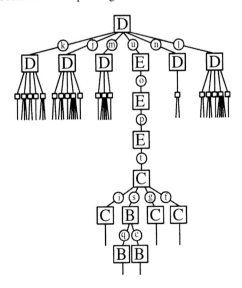

Figure 10: Beam tree.

3.3 Path Generation

During an interactive session in which the user navigates a simulated observer (receiver) through the virtual environment, reverberation paths from a particular source point, S, to the moving receiver point, R, can be generated quickly via lookup in the beam tree data structure. First, the cell containing the receiver point is found by logarithmic-time search of the BSP. Then, each beam tree node, T, associated with that cell is checked to see whether the beam stored with T contains the receiver point. If it does, a viable ray path from the source point to the receiver point has been found, and the ancestors of T in the beam tree explicitly encode the set of reflections and transmissions through the boundaries of the spatial subdivision that a ray must traverse from the source to the receiver along this path (more generally, to any point inside the beam stored with T).

The attenuation, length, and directional vectors for the corresponding reverberation path can be derived quickly from the data stored with the beam tree node, T. Specifically, the attenuation due to reflection and transmission can be retrieved from T directly. The length of the reverberation path and the directional vectors at the source and receiver points can be easily computed as the source's reflected image for this path is stored explicitly in T as the apex of its pyramidal beam. The actual ray path from the source point to the receiver point can be generated by iterative intersection with the reflecting cell boundaries stored with the ancestors of T. For example, Figure 11 shows the specular reflection path to a particular receiver point (labeled 'R') for the example shown in Figure 9.

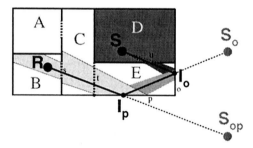

Figure 11: Reverberation path to receiver point ('R') computed via lookup in beam tree for source point ('S').

3.4 Auralization

Once a set of reverberation paths from a source to the receiver has been computed, the source-receiver impulse response is generated by adding one pulse corresponding to each distinct path from the source to the receiver. The delay associated with each pulse is given by L/C, where L is the length of the corresponding reverberation path, and C is the speed of sound. Since the pulse is attenuated by every reflection and dispersion, the amplitude of each pulse is given by A/L, where A is the product of all the frequency-independent reflectivity and transmission coefficients for each of the reflecting and transmitting surfaces along the corresponding reverberation path.

At the receiver, the binaural impulse responses (response of the left and right ears) are different due to the directivity of each ear. These binaural impulse responses are generated by multiplying each pulse of the impulse response by the cardioid directivity function $(1/2(1 + \cos(\theta)))$, where θ is the angle of arrival of the pulse with respect to the normal vector pointing out of the ear) corresponding to each ear. This rough approximation to actual head scattering and diffraction is similar to the standard two-point stereo microphone technique used in high fidelity audio recording. Finally, the (anechoic) input audio signal is auralized by convolving it

with the binaural impulse responses to produce a stereo spatialized audio signal. In the future, we intend to incorporate source directivity, frequency-dependent absorption [34], and angle-dependent absorption [11, 43] into our acoustic models.

A separate, concurrently executing process is spawned to perform convolution of the computed binaural impulse responses with the input audio signal. In order to support real-time auralization, transfer of the impulse responses from the path generation process to the convolution process utilizes double buffers synchronized by a semaphore. Each new pair of impulse responses is loaded by the path generation process into a "back buffer" as the convolution process continues to access the current impulse responses stored in the "front buffer." A semaphore is used to synchronize the processes as the front and back buffer are switched.

4 Results

The 3D data structures and algorithms described in the preceding sections have been implemented in C++ and run on Silicon Graphics and PC/Windows computers.

To test whether the algorithms scale well as the complexity of the 3D environment and the number of specular reflections increase, we executed a series of experiments with our system computing spatial subdivisions, beam trees, and specular reflection paths for various architectural models of different complexities. Our test models ranged from a simple box to a complex building, Soda Hall, the computer science building at UC Berkeley (an image and description of each test model appears in Figure 12). The experiments were run on a Silicon Graphics Octane workstation with 640MB of memory and used one 195MHz R10000 processor.

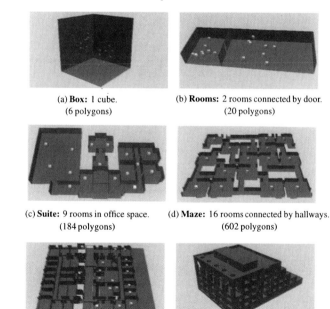

(a) **Box:** 1 cube.
(6 polygons)

(b) **Rooms:** 2 rooms connected by door.
(20 polygons)

(c) **Suite:** 9 rooms in office space.
(184 polygons)

(d) **Maze:** 16 rooms connected by hallways.
(602 polygons)

(e) **Floor:** ~50 rooms of Soda Hall.
(1,772 polygons)

(f) **Building:** ~250 rooms of Soda Hall.
(10,057 polygons)

Figure 12: Test models (source locations are gray dots).

4.1 Spatial Subdivision Results

We first constructed the spatial subdivision data structure (cell adjacency graph) for each test model. Statistics from this phase of the experiment are shown in Table 1. Column 2 lists the number of input polygons in each model, while Columns 3 and 4 contain the numbers of cells and links, respectively, generated by the spatial subdivision algorithm. Column 5 contains the wall-clock time (in seconds) for the algorithm to execute, while Column 6 shows the storage requirements (in MBs) for the resulting spatial subdivision.

Model Name	# Polys	# Cells	# Links	Time (sec)	Storage (MB)
Box	6	7	18	0.0	0.004
Rooms	20	12	43	0.1	0.029
Suite	184	98	581	3.0	0.352
Maze	602	172	1,187	4.9	0.803
Floor	1,772	814	5,533	22.7	3.310
Bldg	10,057	4,512	31,681	186.3	18.694

Table 1: Spatial subdivision statistics.

Empirically, we find that the numbers of cells and links created by our spatial subdivision algorithm grow linearly with the number of input polygons for typical architectural models (see Figure 13), rather than quadratically as is possible for worst case geometric arrangements. The reason for linear growth can be seen intuitively in the two images inlaid in Figure 13, which compare spatial subdivisions for the Maze test model (on the left) and a 2x2 grid of Maze test models (on the right). The 2x2 grid of Mazes has exactly four times as many polygons and approximately four times as many cells. The storage requirements of the spatial subdivision data structure also grow linearly as they are dominated by the vertices of link polygons.

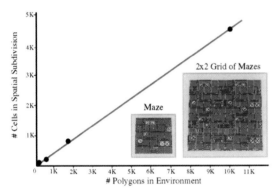

Figure 13: Plot of subdivision size vs. polygonal complexity.

The time required to construct the spatial subdivisions grows super-linearly, dominated by the code that selects and orders splitting planes during BSP construction (see [41]). It is important to note that the spatial subdivision phase must be executed only once off-line for each geometric model, as its results are stored in a file, allowing rapid reconstruction in subsequent beam tracing executions.

4.2 Beam Tracing Results

We experimented with our beam tracing algorithm for sixteen source locations in each test model. The source locations were chosen to represent typical audio source positions (e.g., in offices, in common areas, etc.) – they are shown as gray dots in Figure 12 (experiments with the Building test used the same source locations as are shown in the Floor model). For each source location, we traced beams (i.e., constructed a beam tree) five times, each time with a different limit on the maximum number of specular reflections (e.g., up to 0, 1, 2, 4, or 8 reflections). Other termination criteria based on attenuation or path length were disabled, and transmission was ignored, in order

to isolate the impact of input model size and maximum number of specular reflections on computational complexity.

Table 2 contains statistics gathered during the beam tracing experiment – each row represents an execution with a particular test model and maximum number of reflections, averaged over all 16 source locations. Columns 2 and 3 show the number of polygons describing each test model and the maximum number of specular reflections allowed in each test, respectively. Column 4 contains the average number of beams traced by our algorithm (i.e., the average number of nodes in the resulting beam trees), and Column 5 shows the average wall-clock time (in milliseconds) for the beam tracing algorithm to execute.

Model Name	# Polys	# Rfl	Beam Tracing # Beams	Beam Tracing Time (ms)	Path Generation # Paths	Path Generation Time (ms)
Box	6	0	1	0	1.0	0.0
		1	7	1	7.0	0.1
		2	37	3	25.0	0.3
		4	473	42	129.0	6.0
		8	10,036	825	833.0	228.2
Rooms	20	0	3	0	1.0	0.0
		1	31	3	7.0	0.1
		2	177	16	25.1	0.3
		4	1,939	178	127.9	5.2
		8	33,877	3,024	794.4	180.3
Suite	184	0	7	1	1.0	0.0
		1	90	9	6.8	0.1
		2	576	59	25.3	0.4
		4	7,217	722	120.2	6.5
		8	132,920	13,070	672.5	188.9
Maze	602	0	11	1	0.4	0.0
		1	167	16	2.3	0.0
		2	1,162	107	8.6	0.1
		4	13,874	1,272	36.2	2.0
		8	236,891	21,519	183.1	46.7
Floor	1,772	0	23	4	1.0	0.0
		1	289	39	6.1	0.1
		2	1,713	213	21.5	0.4
		4	18,239	2,097	93.7	5.3
		8	294,635	32,061	467.0	124.5
Bldg	10,057	0	28	5	1.0	0.0
		1	347	49	6.3	0.1
		2	2,135	293	22.7	0.4
		4	23,264	2,830	101.8	6.8
		8	411,640	48,650	529.8	169.5

Table 2: Beam tracing and path generation statistics.

Scale with Increasing Polygonal Complexity

We readily see from the results in Column 4 that the number of beams traced by our algorithm (i.e., the number of nodes in the beam tree) does *not* grow at an exponential rate with the number of polygons in these environments (as it does using the image source method). Each beam traced by our algorithm pre-classifies the regions of space according to whether the corresponding virtual source (i.e., the apex of the beam) is visible to a receiver. Rather than generating $O(n)$ virtual sources (beams) at each step of the recursion as in the image source method, we directly find only the potentially visible virtual sources via beam-polygon intersection and cell adjacency graph traversal. We use the current beam and the current cell of the spatial subdivision to find the small set of polygon reflections that admit visible higher-order virtual sources.

The benefit of this approach is particularly important for large environments in which the boundary of each convex cell is simple, and yet the entire environment is very complex. As an example, consider computation of up to 8 specular reflections in the Building test model (the last row of Table 2). The image source method must consider approximately 1,851,082,741 virtual sources ($\sum_{r=0}^{8}(10,057/2)^r$), assuming half of the 10,057 polygons are front-facing to each virtual source. Our beam tracing method considers only 411,640 virtual sources, a difference of four orders of magnitude. In most cases, it would be impractical to build and store the recursion tree without such effective pruning.

In "densely-occluded" environments, in which all but a little part of the environment is occluded from any source point (e.g., most buildings, cities, etc.), the number of beams traced by our algorithm does not even grow linearly with the total number of polygons in the environment (see Figure 14). In these environments, the number of boundaries on each cell is nearly constant, and a nearly constant number of cells are reached by each beam, leading to near-constant expected-case complexity of our beam tracing algorithm with increasing global environment complexity. As an example, the two images inlaid in Figure 14 show that the number of beams (green) traced in the Maze test model (left) does not increase significantly if the model is increased to be a 2x2 grid of Maze models (right). *The beam tracing algorithm is impacted only by local complexity, and not by global complexity.*

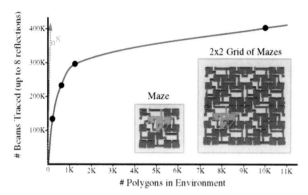

Figure 14: Plot of beam tree size vs. polygonal complexity.

Scale with Increasing Reflections

We see that the number of beams traced by our algorithm grows exponentially, but far slower than $O(n^r)$, as we increase the maximum number of reflections. Figure 15 shows a logscale plot of the average number of beams traced in the Building model with increasing numbers of specular reflections. The beam tree growth is less than $O(n^r)$ because each beam narrows as it is clipped by the cell boundaries it has traversed, and thus it tends to intersect fewer cell boundaries (see the example beam inlaid in Figure 15). In the limit, each beam becomes so narrow that it intersects only one or two cell boundaries, on average, leading to a beam tree with a small branching factor (rather than a branching factor of $O(n)$, as in the image source method).

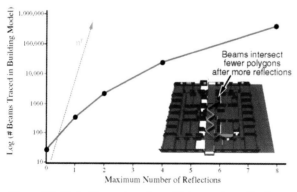

Figure 15: Plot of beam tree size with increasing reflections.

Tree Depth	Total Nodes	Interior Nodes	Leaf Nodes	Branching Factor
0	1	1	0	16.0000
1	16	16	0	6.5000
2	104	104	0	4.2981
3	447	446	1	2.9193
4	1,302	1,296	6	2.3920
5	3,100	3,092	8	2.0715
6-10	84,788	72,469	12,319	1.2920
11-15	154,790	114,664	40,126	1.2685
>15	96,434	61,079	35,355	1.1789

Table 3: Example beam tree branching statistics.

As an example, consider Table 3 which shows the average branching factor for nodes at each depth of the beam tree constructed for up to 8 specular reflections in the Building model from one source location. The average branching factor (Column 5) generally decreases with tree depth and is generally bounded by a small constant in lower levels of the tree.

On the other hand, if a beam is trimmed by many cell boundaries and becomes too narrow, the advantages of beam tracing over ray tracing are diminished. This observation suggests a possible future hybrid approach in which medial rays are used to approximate intersections for beams whose cross-sectional area falls below a threshold.

4.3 Path Generation Results

In order to verify that specular reflection paths can be computed from fixed sources at interactive rates as the receiver moves, we conducted experiments to quantify the complexity of generating specular reflection paths to different receiver locations from precomputed beam trees. For each beam tree constructed in the previous experiment, we logged statistics during generation of specular reverberation paths to 16 different receiver locations. Receivers were chosen randomly within a two foot sphere around the source to represent a typical audio scenario in which the source and receiver are in close proximity within the same "room." We believe this represents a worst-case scenario as fewer paths would likely be found to more remote and more occluded receiver locations.

Columns 6 and 7 of Table 2 contain statistics gathered during path generation for each combination of model and termination criterion averaged over all 256 source-receiver pairs (i.e., 16 receivers for each of the 16 sources). Column 6 contains the average number of reverberation paths generated, while Column 7 shows the average wall-clock time (in milliseconds) for execution of the path generation algorithm. Figure 16 shows a plot of the wall-clock time required to generate up to eighth-order specular reflection paths for each test model.

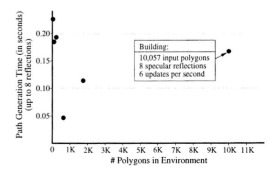

Figure 16: Path compute time vs. polygonal complexity.

We find that the number of specular reflection paths between a source and receiver in close proximity of one another is nearly constant across all of our test models. Also, the time required by our path generation algorithm is generally *not* dependent on the number of polygons in the environment (see Figure 16), nor is it dependent on the total number of nodes in the precomputed beam tree. This result is due to the fact that our path generation algorithm considers only nodes of the beam tree with beams residing inside the cell containing the receiver location. Therefore, the computation time required by the algorithm is *not* dependent on the complexity of the whole environment, but instead on the number of beams that traverse the receiver's cell.

Overall, we find that our algorithm supports generation of specular reflection paths between a fixed source and any (arbitrarily moving) receiver at interactive rates in complex environments. For instance, we are able to compute up to 8th order specular reflection paths in the Building environment with more than 10,000 polygons at a rate of approximately 6 times per second (i.e., the rightmost point in the plot of Figure 16).

4.4 Auralization Results

We have integrated the acoustic modeling method described in this paper into an interactive system for audio/visual exploration of virtual environments (e.g., using VRML). The system allows a user to move through a virtual environment while images and spatialized audio are rendered in real-time according to the user's simulated viewpoint. Figure 17 shows one application we have developed, called VirtualWorks, in which a user may interact with objects (e.g., click on them with the mouse) in the virtual environment to invoke behaviors that present information in various media, including text, image, video, and spatialized audio. For instance, if the user clicks on the workstation sitting on the desk, the application invokes a video which is displayed on the screen of that workstation. We are using this system to experiment with 3D user interfaces for presentation of multimedia data and multi-user interaction.

We ran experiments with this application using a Silicon Graphics Octane workstation with 640MB of memory and two 195MHz R10000 processors. One processor was used for image generation and acoustic modeling (i.e., reverberation path generation), while the second processor was dedicated solely to auralization (i.e., convolution of the computed stereo impulse responses with audio signals).

Due to the differences between graphics and acoustics described in Section 1, the geometry and surface characteristics of the virtual environment were input and represented in two separate forms, one for graphics and another for acoustics. The graphical model (shown in Figure 17) was represented as a scene graph containing 80,372 polygons, most of which describe the furniture and other small, detailed, visually-important objects in the environment. The acoustical model contained only 184 polygons, which described the ceilings, walls, cubicles, floors, and other large, acoustically-important features of the environment (it was identical to the Suite test model shown in Figure 12c).

We gathered statistics during sample executions of this application. Figures 17b-c show an observer viewpoint path (red) along which the application was able to render between eight and twelve images per second, while simultaneously auralizing four audio sources (labeled 1-4) in stereo according to fourth-order specular reflection paths updated during each frame. While walking along this path, it was possible to notice subtle acoustic effects due to reflections and occlusions. In particular, near the viewpoint labeled 'A' in Figure 17b, audio source '2' became very reverberant due to reflections (cyan lines) in the long room. Likewise, audio source '3' suddenly became much louder and then softer as the observer passed by an open doorway near the viewpoint labeled 'B' in Figure 17c.

Throughout our experiments, the auralization process was the bottleneck. Our C++ convolution code running on a R10000 pro-cessor could execute fast enough to output 8 KHz stereo audio for a set of impulse responses cumulatively containing around 500 non-zero elements. We are planning to integrate DSP-based hardware [37] with our system to implement real-time convolution in the near future.

5 Discussion

5.1 Geometric Limitations

Our method is not practical for all virtual environments. First, the geometric input must comprise only planar polygons. Each acoustic reflector is assumed to be locally reacting and to have dimensions far exceeding the wavelength of audible sound (since initially we are assuming that specular reflections are the dominant components of reverberation).

Second, the efficiency of our method is greatly impacted by the complexity and quality of the constructed spatial subdivision. For best results, the polygons should be connected (e.g., without small cracks between them) and arranged such that a large part of the model is occluded from any position in space (e.g., like most buildings or cities). Specifically, our method would not perform well for geometric models with high local geometric complexity (e.g., a forest of trees). In these cases, beams traced through boundaries of cells enclosing free space would quickly become fragmented into many smaller beams, leading to disadvantageous growth of the beam tree. For this reason, our method is not as well suited for global illumination as it is for acoustic modeling, in which small objects can be ignored and large surfaces can be modeled with little geometric surface detail due to the longer wavelengths of audible sound.

Third, the major occluding and reflecting surfaces of the virtual environment must be static during interactive path generation and auralization. If any acoustically significant polygon moves, the spatial subdivision and every beam tree must be recomputed.

The class of geometric models for which our method does work well includes most architectural and urban environments. In these models, acoustically significant surfaces are generally planar, large, and stationary, and the acoustical effects of any sound source are limited to a local region of the environment.

5.2 Diffraction and Diffuse Reflection

Our current 3D implementation traces beams only along paths of specular reflection and transmission, and it does not model other scattering effects. Of course, paths of diffraction and diffuse reflection are also important for accurate acoustic modeling [34, 26]. Fortunately, our beam tracing algorithm and beam tree representation can be generalized to model these effects. For instance, new beams can be traced that enclose the region of space reached by diffracting and diffuse reflection paths, and new nodes can be added to the beam tree representing diffractions and diffuse reflection events at cell boundaries. For these more complex scattering phenomena, the geometry of the beams is most useful for computing candidate reverberation paths, while the amplitude of the signal along any of the these paths can be evaluated for a known receiver during path generation. We have already included these extensions in a 2D beam tracing implementation, and we are currently working on a similar 3D implementation.

First, consider diffraction. According to the Geometrical Theory of Diffraction [29], an acoustic field that is incident on a discontinuity along an edge has a diffracted wave that propagates into the shadow region. The diffracted wave can be modeled in geometric terms by considering the edge to be a source of new waves emanating from the edge. Higher order reflections and diffractions occur as diffracted waves impinge upon other surfaces and edge discontinuities. By using edge-based adjacency information in our

(a)

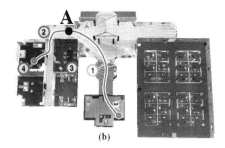
(b)

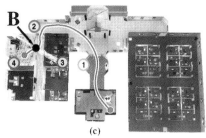
(c)

Figure 17: VirtualWorks application. User's view is shown in (a), while a bird's eye view of fourth-order reverberation paths (color coded lines) from four sources (numbered circles) to Viewpoints 'A' and 'B' (black circles) are shown in (b) and (c), respectively.

spatial subdivision data structure, we can quickly perform the geometric operations required to construct and trace beams along paths of diffraction. For a given beam, we can find edges causing diffraction, as they are the ones: 1) intersected by the beam, and 2) shared by cell boundaries with different acoustic properties (e.g., one is transparent and another is opaque). For each such edge, we can determine the region of space reached by diffraction at that edge by tracing a beam whose "source" coincides with the portion of the edge intersected by the impinging beam, and whose extent is bounded by the solid wedge of opaque surfaces sharing the edge. For densely-occluded environments, each such diffraction beam can be computed and traced in expected-case constant time.

Second, consider diffuse reflection. We may model complex reflections and diffractions from some highly faceted surfaces as diffuse reflections from planar surfaces emanating equally in all directions. To compute the region of space reached by such a reflection using our approach, we can construct a beam whose "source" is the convex polygonal region of the surface intersected by an impinging beam and whose initial extent encloses the entire halfspace in front of the surface. We can trace the beam through the cell adjacency graph to find the region of space reached from any point on the reflecting part of the surface (i.e., the anti-penumbra [50]).

We have implemented these methods so far in 2D using a planar winged-edge representation [5] for the spatial subdivision and a bow-tie representation [49] for the beams. Unfortunately, tracing 3D "beams" of diffraction and diffuse reflection is more complicated. First, the source of each diffraction beam is no longer a point, but a finite edge, and the source of each diffuse reflection beam is generally a convex polygon. Second, as we trace such beams through the spatial subdivision, splitting and trimming them as they passes through multiple convex polygonal cell boundaries, their bounding surfaces can become quadric surfaces (i.e., reguli) [50]. Finally, evaluation of the amplitude of the signal along a "path" of diffraction or diffuse reflection requires integration over (possibly multiple) edges and polygons. We are currently extending our 3D data structures and algorithms to model these effects. Initially, we are planning to trace polyhedral beams that conservatively over-estimate the region covered by an exact, more complex, representation of the scattering patterns. Then, as each reverberation path to a particular receiver is considered, we will check whether it lies within the exact scattering region, or whether it should be discarded because it lies in the over-estimating region of the polyhedral beam.

5.3 Visualization

In order to aid understanding and debugging of our acoustic modeling method, we have found it extremely valuable to use interactive visualization. So far, we have concentrated on visualization of our data structures and algorithms. Our system provides menu and keyboard commands that may be used to toggle display of the: 1) input polygons (red), 2) source point (white), 3) receiver point (purple), 4) boundaries of the spatial subdivision (gray), 5) pyramidal beams

(green), 6) image sources (cyan), and 7) reverberation paths (yellow). The system also supports visualization of acoustic metrics (e.g., power, clarity, etc.) computed for a set of receiver locations on a regular planar grid displayed with a textured polygon. Example visualizations are shown in Figures 18-20.

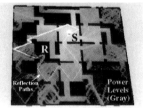

Figure 18: Eighth-order specular reflection beams (left) and predicted power levels (right) in Maze model.

Of course, many commercial [7, 8, 40] and research systems [38, 47] provide elaborate tools for visualizing computed acoustic metrics. The critical difference in our system is that it supports continuous interactive updates of reverberation paths and debugging information as a user moves the receiver point with the mouse. For instance, Figures 18 and 20 show eighth-order specular reflection paths (yellow lines) from a single audio source (white points) to a receiver location (purple points) which can be updated more than six times per second as the receiver location is moved arbitrarily. The user may select any reverberation path for further inspection by clicking on it and then independently toggle display of reflecting cell boundaries, transmitting cell boundaries, and the associated set of pyramidal beams for the selected path.

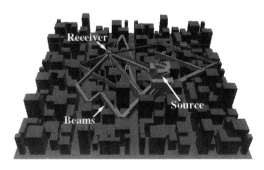

Figure 19: Beams (green) containing all eighth-order specular reflection paths from a source to a receiver in City model.

Separate pop-up windows provide real-time display of other useful visual debugging and acoustic modeling information. For instance, one popup window shows a diagram of the beam tree data structure. Each beam tree node is dynamically colored in the diagram according to whether the receiver point is inside its associated beam (white) or cell (green). Another popup window shows a plot of the impulse response representing the reverberation paths from source to receiver (see Figure 20). A third popup window shows values of various acoustic metrics, including power, clarity, reverberation time, and frequency response. All of the information displayed is updated in real-time as the user moves the receiver interactively with the mouse.

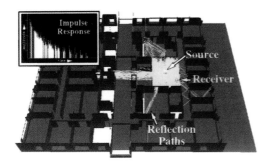

Figure 20: Impulse response (inset) derived from eighth-order specular reflection paths (yellow) in Floor model.

6 Future Work

6.1 System Extensions

Our system could be extended in many ways. For instance, the beam tracing algorithm is well-suited for parallelization, with much of the previous work in parallel ray tracing directly applicable [4]. Also, the geometric regions covered by each node of the beam tree could be stored in a single hierarchical spatial structure (e.g., a BSP), allowing logarithmic search during path generation, rather than linear search of the beams inside a single cell. HRFT (Head-Related Transfer Functions) directional filtering, angle-dependent and frequency-dependent acoustic properties of absorption, and source directivity should be included in our acoustical models. Of course, we could also use beam trees to allow a user to manipulate the acoustic properties of individual surfaces of the environment interactively with real-time feedback, like parameterized ray tracing [44].

6.2 Moving Sources

In order to support acoustic modeling in real-time, our current approach is to fix the position of each sound source and to precompute and store potential reverberation paths from that position to all points in space (i.e., the beam tree) so that reverberation paths to a specific receiver can be generated quickly. This method achieves interactive performance by trading real-time processing for storage and precomputation time. Yet, it requires that each sound source be stationary, which is not adequate to support all virtual environment applications (e.g., multi-user chat). In order to extend our method to support real-time acoustic modeling for virtual environments with moving sound sources, one approach is to precompute and store beam trees for a finite number of source locations (e.g., on a grid), and then derive the impulse response for any arbitrary source location via interpolation.

A second approach is to rework our beam tracing algorithm (i.e., the second phase, which currently executes as a preprocessing step) to execute in real-time at interactive rates. Although real-time beam tracing requires improvement of one or two orders of magnitude (beam tracing times for our test models ranged from 0.8 to 49 seconds for eigth-order specular reflections), we are optimistic that

this is possible. In contrast to our current beam tracing precomputation, which must consider potential receivers at any point in space, *a real-time beam tracing algorithm must compute reverberation paths only to a specific set of known receiver positions* (e.g., the locations of other avatars in a multi-user chat). Therefore, we can implement a far more efficient beam tracing algorithm by employing aggressive path pruning methods and importance heuristics [45] to trace only beams that represent (psychoacoustically) significant reverberation paths between some source-receiver pair. Bi-directional beam tracing (computing kth-order reflections by combining beams traced up to $k/2$ reflections from both the source and the receiver positions [23, 24]) should also improve performance. We plan to experiment with these techniques and to incorporate moving sound sources into our system in the near future.

6.3 Simulation Verification

Verification of our simulation results by comparison to measured data is an important topic for further discussion. Unlike sound rendering systems for animation in virtual environments [48, 53], we aim to simulate room impulse responses accurately enough to be used also for architectural and concert hall design applications.

Although we do not present verification results in this paper due to space limitations, it is useful to note that our current system computes (more efficiently) the same specular reflection paths as the source image method, for which verification results have been published [56]. We are currently making impulse response measurements for verification of our simulations in the Varechoic Chamber, a specially constructed acoustics facility that allows one to vary the reverberation time by more than a factor of 10 by adjusting the acoustic reflection coefficient of 384 individually computer controllable acoustic panels [58].

6.4 Psychoacoustics Experiments

Perhaps the most interesting direction of future work is to investigate the possible applications of *interactive* acoustic modeling. What can we do with interactive manipulation of acoustic model parameters that would be difficult to do otherwise?

As a first application, we hope to build a system that uses our interactive acoustic simulations to investigate the psychoacoustic effects of varying different acoustic modeling parameters. Our system will allow a user to interactively change various acoustics parameters with real-time auralization and visualization feedback. With this interactive simulation system, it may be possible to address psychoacoustic questions, such as "how many reflections are psychoacoustically important to model?," or "which surface reflection model provides a psychoacoustically better approximation?" Moreover, we hope to investigate the interaction of visual and aural cues on spatial perception. We believe that the answers to such questions are of critical importance to future designers of 3D virtual environment systems.

7 Conclusion

We have described a system that uses beam tracing data structures and algorithms to compute high-order specular reflection and transmission paths from static sources to a moving receiver at interactive rates for real-time auralization in large virtual environments.

As compared to previous acoustic modeling approaches, our beam tracing method takes unique advantage of *precomputation* and *convexity*. Precomputation is used twice, once to encode in the spatial subdivision data structure a depth-ordered sequence of (cell boundary) polygons to be considered during any traversal of space, and once to encode in the beam tree data structure the region of space reachable from a static source by sequences of specular reflections and transmissions at cell boundaries. We use the convexity of the beams, cell regions, and cell boundary polygons to enable efficient and robust computation of beam-polygon and beam-receiver intersections. As a result, our method is uniquely able to: 1) support evaluation of reverberation paths at interactive rates, 2) scale to compute high-order reflections in large environments, and 3) extend to compute paths of diffraction and diffuse reflection.

Our virtual environment system integrates real-time auralization with visualization of large virtual environments. Based on our initial experiences with this system, we believe that accurately spatialized audio is a very important cue for experiencing and navigating virtual environments. We are continuing this research in order to further investigate the perceptual interaction of visual and acoustics effects and to better realize the opportunities possible with interactive acoustic modeling.

Acknowledgements

The authors thank Arun C. Surendran and Michael Gatlin for their valuable discussions and contributions to the project. We are also grateful to Bob Kubli who helped record audio for the accompanying video tape.

References

[1] Ahnert, Wolfgang. EARS Auralization Software. *J. Audio Eng. Soc.*, 41, 11, November, 1993, 894-904.

[2] Allen, J.B., Berkley, D.A. *Image Method for Efficiently Simulating Small-Room Acoustics*, J. Acoust. Soc. Am., 65, 4, April, 1979, 943–951.

[3] Amanatides, J. Ray Tracing with Cones. *Computer Graphics* (SIGGRAPH 84). 18, 3, 129-135.

[4] Arvo, J. and D. Kirk. A Survey of Ray Tracing Acceleration Techniques. in *An Introduction to Ray Tracing*, Andrew Glassner editor, Academic Press, San Diego, CA, 1989.

[5] Baumgart, Bruce G. *Winged Edge Polyhedron Representation*. Ph.D. Thesis, Computer Science Department, Stanford University, 1972.

[6] Borish, Jeffrey. Extension of the Image Model to Arbitrary Polyhedra. *J. Acoust. Soc. Am.*, 75, 6, June, 1984, 1827-1836.

[7] *Bose Modeler*, Bose Corporation, Framingham, MA. http://www.bose.com.

[8] *CATT-Acoustic*, CATT, Gothenburg, Sweden, http://www.netg.se/ catt.

[9] Chuang, J.H. and S.A. Cheng. Computing caustic effects by backward beam tracing. *The Visual Computer*, 11, 3, 1995, 156–166.

[10] Cook, Robert, L., Thomas Porter, and Loren Carpenter. Distributed Ray Tracing. *Computer Graphics* (SIGGRAPH 84). 18, 3, 137-146.

[11] D'Antonio, Peter, and John Konnert. The Directional Scattering Coefficient: Experimental Determination. *J, Audio Eng. Soc.*, 40, 12, December, 1992, 997-1017.

[12] Dadoun, N., D.G. Kirkpatrick, and J.P. Walsh. Hierarchical Approaches to Hidden Surface Intersection Testing. *Graphics Interface '82*, Toronto, Canada, May, 1982, 49-56.

[13] Dadoun, N., D.G. Kirkpatrick, and J.P. Walsh. The Geometry of Beam Tracing. *Proceedings of the Symposium on Computational Geometry*, Baltimore, June, 1985, 55-71.

[14] Durlach, N.I., R.W. Pew, W.A. Aviles, P.A. DiZio, and D.L. Zeltzer. *Virtual Environment Technology for Training (VETT)*. Report No. 7661, Bolt, Beranek, and Newmann, Cambridge, MA, 1992.

[15] Durlach, N.I, and A.S. Mavor, editors, *Virtual Reality Scientific and Technological Challenges*, National Research Council Report, National Academy Press, Washington, D.C., 1995.

[16] Fortune, Steve. Algorithms for Prediction of Indoor Radio Propagation. *Technical Memorandum*, Document #11274-960117-03TM, Bell Laboratories, 1996. A partial version of this paper appears in *Applied Computational Geometry, Towards Geometric Engineering*, proceedings of the *FCRC '96 Workshop* in conjunction with *WACG '96*, Philadelphia, PA, May, 1996, 157-166.

[17] Foster, S.H., E.M. Wenzel, and R.M. Taylor. Real-time Synthesis of Complex Acoustic Environments. *Proceedings of the IEEE Workshop on Applications of Signal Processing to Audio and Acoustics*, New Paltz, NY, 1991.

[18] Fuchs, H. Kedem, Z., and Naylor, B. On Visible Surface Generation by a Priori Tree Structures. *Computer Graphics* (Proc. SIGGRAPH '80), 124-133.

[19] Fujomoto, Akira. Turbo Beam Tracing - A Physically Accurate Lighting Simulation Environment. *Knowledge Based Image Computing Systems*, May, 1988, 1-5.

[20] Ghazanfarpour, G. and J. Marc Hasenfratz. A Beam Tracing with Precise Antialiasing for Polyhedral Scenes. *Computer & Graphics*, 22, 1, 1998.

[21] Goral, Cindy M., Kenneth E. Torrance, Donald P. Greenberg, and Bennett Battaile. Modeling the Interaction of Light Between Diffuse Surfaces. *Computer Graphics* (Proc. SIGGRAPH '84), 18, 3, July, 1984, 213-222.

[22] Haines, Eric A. Beams O' Light: Confessions of a Hacker. *Frontiers in Rendering Course Notes, SIGGRAPH '91*, 1991.

[23] Heckbert, Paul, and Pat Hanrahan. Beam Tracing Polygonal Objects. *Computer Graphics* (SIGGRAPH 84), 18, 3, 119-127.

[24] Heckbert, Paul. Adaptive Radiosity Textures for Bidirectional Ray Tracing. *Computer Graphics* (SIGGRAPH 90), 24, 4, 145-154.

[25] Heinz, R. Binaural Room Simulation Based on an Image Source Model with Addition of Statistical Methods to Include the Diffuse Sound Scattering of Walls and to Predict the Reverberant Tail *J. Applied Acoustics*, 38, 2-4, 1993, 145-160.

[26] Hodgson, M. Evidence of Diffuse Surface Reflections in Rooms. *J. Acoust. Soc. Am.*, 89, 1991, 765-771.

[27] Jones, C.B. A New Approach to the 'Hidden Line' Problem. *The Computer Journal*, 14, 3 (August 1971), 232-237.

[28] Kajiya, James T. The Rendering Equation. *Computer Graphics* (SIGGRAPH 86), 143-150.

[29] Keller, Joseph B. Geometrical Theory of Diffraction. *Journal of the Optical Society of America*, 52, 2, February, 1962, 116-130.

[30] Kleiner, Mendel, Bengt-Inge Dalenback, and Peter Svensson. Auralization – An Overview. *J. Audio Eng. Soc.*, 41, 11, November, 1993, 861-875.

[31] Kreuzgruber, P., P. Unterberger, and R. Gahleitner. A Ray Splitting Model for Indoor Radio Propagation Associated with Complex Geometries. *Proceedings of the 1993 43rd IEEE Vehicular Technology Conference*, 1993, 227-230.

[32] Kristiansen, U.R., A. Krokstad, and T. Follestad. Extending the Image Method to Higher-Order Reflections. *J. Applied Acoustics*, 38, 2-4, 1993, 195-206.

[33] Krockstadt, U.R. *Calculating the Acoustical Room Response by the Use of a Ray Tracing Technique*, J. Sound and Vibrations, 8, 18, 1968.

[34] Kuttruff, Heinrich *Room Acoustics*, 3rd Edition, Elsevier Science, London, England, 1991.

[35] Lehnert, Hilmar. Systematic Errors of the Ray-Tracing Algorithm. *J. Applied Acoustics*, 38, 2-4, 1993, 207-221.

[36] Lewers, T. A Combined Beam Tracing and Radiant Exchange Computer Model of Room Acoustics. *J. Applied Acoustics*, 38, 2-4, 1993, 161-178.

[37] McGrath, David, and Andrew Reilly. Convolution Processing for Realistic Reverberation. *The 98th Convention of the Audio Engineering Society*, February, 1995.

[38] Monks, Michael, Byong Mok Oh, and Julie Dorsey. Acoustic Simulation and Visualization using a New Unified Beam Tracing and Image Source Approach. *Meeting of the Audio Engineering Society*, November, 1996.

[39] Moore, G.R. *An Approach to the Analysis of Sound in Auditoria*. Ph.D. Thesis, Cambridge, UK, 1984.

[40] Naylor, G.M. ODEON - Another Hybrid Room Acoustical Model. *J. Applied Acoustics*, 38, 2-4, 1993, 131-144.

[41] Naylor, B.F. Constructing Good Partitioning Trees. *Graphics Interface '93*, Toronto, CA, May, 1993.

[42] Rajkumar, A., B.F. Naylor, and L. Rogers. Predicting RF Coverage in Large Environments using Ray-Beam Tracing and Partitioning Tree Represented Geometry. *Wireless Networks*, 1995.

[43] Rindel, J.H. Modelling the Angle-Dependent Pressure Reflection Factor. *J. Applied Acoustics*, 38, 2-4, 1993, 223-234.

[44] Sequin, Carlo, and Eliot Smyrl. Parameterized Ray Tracing. *Computer Graphics* (SIGGRAPH 89), 23, 3, 307-314.

[45] Smits, Brian, James R. Arvo, and David H. Salesin. An Importance-Driven Radiosity Algorithm. *Computer Graphics* (SIGGRAPH 92), 26, 2, 273-282.

[46] Stephenson, U., and U. Kristiansen. Pyramidal Beam Tracing and Time Dependent Radiosity. *Fifteenth International Congress on Acoustics*, Tapir, June, 1995, 657-660.

[47] Stettner, Adam, and Donald P. Greenberg. Computer Graphics Visualization for Acoustic Simulation. *Computer Graphics* (SIGGRAPH 89), 23, 3, 195-206.

[48] Takala, Tapio, and James Hahn. Sound Rendering. *Computer Graphics* (SIGGRAPH 92), 26, 2, 211-220.

[49] Teller, Seth J., and Carlo H. Séquin, Visibility Preprocessing for Interactive Walkthroughs. *Computer Graphics* (SIGGRAPH 91), 25, 4, 61-69.

[50] Teller, Seth J. Computing the Antiumbra Cast by an Area Light Source. *Computer Graphics (Proc. SIGGRAPH '92)*, 26, 2 (August 1992), 139-148.

[51] Teller, Seth J. *Visibility Computations in Densely Occluded Polyhedral Environments*. Ph.D. thesis, Computer Science Division (EECS), University of California, Berkeley, 1992. Also available as UC Berkeley technical report UCB/CSD-92-708.

[52] Tsingos, Nicolas, and Jean-Dominique Gascuel. A General Model for Simulation of Room Acoustics Based On Hierarchical Radiosity. Technical Sketches, *SIGGRAPH 97 Visual Proceedings*, 1997.

[53] Tsingos, Nicolas, and Jean-Dominique Gascuel. Soundtracks for Computer Animation: Sound Rendering in Dynamic Environments with Occlusions. *Graphics Interface '97*, Kelowna, May 21-23, 1997, 9-16.

[54] Veach, Eric, and Leonidas J. Guibas. Metropolis Light Transport. *Computer Graphics* (SIGGRAPH 97), 65-76.

[55] Vian, J.P. and D. van Maercke. Calculation of the Room Response Using a Ray Tracing Method. *Proceedings of the ICA Symposium on Acoustics and Theater Planning for the Performing Arts*, Vancouver, CA, 1986, 74-78.

[56] Vorlander, M. International Round Robin on Room Acoustical Computer Simulations. *Proceedings of the 15th International Congress of Acoustics*, Trondheim, Norway, June, 1995.

[57] Walsh, John P., and Norm Dadoun. What Are We Waiting for? The Development of Godot, II. *presented at the 103rd Meeting of the Acoustical Society of America*, Chicago, April, 1982.

[58] Ward, William C., Gary, W. Elko, Robert A. Kubli, and W. Craig McDougald. The New Varechoic chamber at AT&T Bell Labs. *Proceeding of Wallace Clement Sabine Centennial Symposium*, Acoustical Society of America, New York, June, 1994, 343-346.

[59] Watt, Mark. Light-Water Interaction Using Backward Beam Tracing. *Computer Graphics* (SIGGRAPH 90), 24, 377-385.

[60] Weiler, K. and P. Atherton. Hidden Surface Removal Using Polygon Area Sorting. *Computer Graphics* (SIGGRAPH 77), 11, 2, 214-222.

[61] Whitted, Turner. An Improved Illumination Model for Shaded Display. *Communications of the ACM*, 23, 6, June, 1980, 343-349.

Retargetting Motion to New Characters

Michael Gleicher *

Autodesk Vision Technology Center

Abstract

In this paper, we present a technique for *retargetting* motion: the problem of adapting an animated motion from one character to another. Our focus is on adapting the motion of one articulated figure to another figure with identical structure but different segment lengths, although we use this as a step when considering less similar characters. Our method creates adaptations that preserve desirable qualities of the original motion. We identify specific features of the motion as constraints that must be maintained. A spacetime constraints solver computes an adapted motion that re-establishes these constraints while preserving the frequency characteristics of the original signal. We demonstrate our approach on motion capture data.

CR Categories and Subject Descriptors: I.3.7 [Computer Graphics]: Three Dimensional Graphics and Realism - Animation

Additional Keywords: motion editing, motion signal-processing, spacetime constraints, motion capture.

1 Introduction

In this paper, we present techniques for *retargetting* motion: the problem of adapting an animated motion from one character to another. Our goal is to re-use motions created for one character on other characters, independently of how that motion was created. We aim to preserve as many of the desirable properties of the original motion as possible. That is, if we begin with the motion of a tall adult person, we expect to end up with a motion of a small child walking like an adult, or a crocodile swing dancing as if it were an adult human. Admittedly, this faithfulness to the original motion is not always artistically desirable. However, we prefer to relegate the difficult creative decisions (How do crocodiles dance?) to the user's selection of an initial motion.

Our focus is on applying motion created for one articulated figure to another figure with identical structure (connectivity of limbs, types of joints, number of degrees of freedom) but different segment lengths. Even when two articulated figures share structure, the motion of one may not trivially apply to the other and therefore require adaptation. Good adaptations preserve important aspects of the motion by altering less important ones: in a walking motion, it is important that the feet touch the floor, not that the pelvis is 32 inches above the floor as in the original. The important properties of

a given motion may not always be simple; realism, grace, like–in–Singing–in–the–Rain–ness, or other high-level properties may be desirable to preserve during adaptation. In practice, we are limited by our ability to define high-level qualities of the motion mathematically, by our ability to compute adaptations efficiently when the metrics become complex, and by the amount of effort we wish to expend in identifying (or having the user identify) these properties. These issues motivate a more pragmatic approach to retargetting.

This paper presents a method for finding the adaptations needed to retarget motions from one articulated figure to another. We accomplish this by requiring the basic features of the motion – for example that the feet touch the floor when walking – to be identified as constraints. If the constraints are violated when the motion is applied to a different figure, we find an adaptation to the motion that re-establishes the constraints in a manner that fits with the motion. Our premise is that by maintaining the basic features and avoiding uncharacteristic (in a basic signal-processing sense) changes, we find adaptations that generally preserve the desirable characteristics of a motion, without explicitly modeling them.

The core of our retargetting method is a numerical solver that computes an adaptation to the original motion. The adaptation re-establishes the constraints while attempting to avoid adding any undesirable artifacts. Our solver is a spacetime constraints method that considers the entire motion simultaneously, computing whole motions, not just individual frames. To preserve the qualities of the original motion, we minimize the magnitude of the changes and restrict their frequency content.

After a review of previous work, we introduce our method in Section 3, and summarize the technique in Section 4. Section 5 describes how the method can be applied to creating motions when the character is changing (morphing). In section 6, we discuss issues in solving the non-linear constraint problems. We provide a gallery of examples in Section 7 and consider the problem of retargetting a motion to a character with different structure in Section 8.

1.1 An Example

We motivate our approach with an example: retargetting motion capture data of an actress walking up to, picking up, and carrying away a box. During pre-processing, we augment the motion data by specifying constraints that are essential to the action: the hands must grab the box in the middle frame, the hands must remain the correct distance apart while carrying the box, and the feet must be planted and not skid when they are on the ground.

Without adaptation, our motion capture data does not apply to figures of different sizes or proportions than our actress: the resulting motions have the feet skating and the hands failing to reach the object. Our method enables us to re-use this data on figures of varying proportions, as shown in Figure 1. The method computes an adapted motion for each new character using the approach detailed in Section 3. Because the technique looks at the entire motion, it can make adjustments based on all the requirements. For example, it adjusts the footplant positions so that the characters reach the box using natural footstep sizes.

Our approach makes many sacrifices to achieve practicality. We tell our solver little about the original motion or general motion properties, and our choice of the mathematical problem is heavily

---
*Autodesk VTC, 2465 Latham St, Mountain View, CA 94040.
gleicher@cs.cmu.edu, http://www.gleicher.com/mike

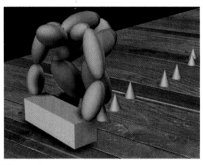  

Figure 1: Differently sized characters pick up an object. Their positions are determined by the position of the object. The left shows the original actress. The center shows a figure 60% as large. The right shows a figure with extremely short legs and arms and an extremely long body. The yellow cones represent footplant positions.

influenced by what can be solved efficiently. We sometimes pay for these sacrifices in the quality of the resulting motions. For example, because our system did not consider gravity or posture we get an unrealistically unbalanced result in the right frame of Figure 1. The payoff is that our approach provides a practical solution to the retargetting problem and a framework in which to employ more sophisticated constraints, like balance, in the future.

2 Previous Work

Few techniques specifically address the retargetting problem. Generally, users are forced to adapt motions using the same tools that are used for motion creation: each frame or key must be manually tweaked. Some commercial systems, such as Kinetix's Character Studio [11], are beginning to support retargetting. For example, Character Studio can adjust keyframes to maintain footplants and balance when a motion is re-applied to a new character.

Hodgins and Pollard [9] address a variant of the motion re-use problem, adjusting parameters of a physical simulation to adapt a controller for use with a new character or a character that is changing. In general, procedural- and simulation- based approaches to animation offer representations independent of the character and therefore may be used generate new motions for new characters. Many of the procedural and simulation controllers are able to adjust to different characters easily. Such methods do not address the retargetting problem: they can generate new motions for new characters but not reuse existing motions. Re-generation of motion risks losing qualities in the original. Our goal is to create methods that adapt existing motions obtained from a variety of sources, including motion capture and keyframing as well as simulation and procedural generation.

Recently, there is an interest in tools that allow motion to be altered in ways that are independent of how it was created. At their core, these tools treat animated motions as time-varying signals and apply signal processing techniques to these signals. Litwinowicz's Inkwell system [12] first demonstrated the utility of applying signal processing methods to animation data. Perlin [17] showed how existing motions could be blended together, and how the addition of noise to a motion could be used to transform it. Bruderlin and Williams [2] showed that many signal processing techniques could be applied to motion. Simultaneously, other authors showed some of these methods in greater detail. Unuma et al. [21] showed how band-pass filtering methods could adjust emotional content, and Witkin and Popović [23] introduced motion-warping, a variant of Bruderlin and Williams' motion displacement mapping.

2.1 Spacetime Constraints

The spacetime constraint approach, introduced by Witkin and Kass [22], poses the motion synthesis problem as a constrained optimiza-

tion: what is the best motion that meets a specified set of constraints? Cohen [3] extended this with a more complete system that allowed the user to focus the solution process. Recently, Rose et al. [19] applied the approach to the problem of generating transitions between motion segments, and Gleicher and Litwinowicz [7] showed how the methods can be used for adjusting motions so that the characters have new goals. Gleicher [6] extends this work by simplifying the spacetime problem to achieve interactive performance for interactive editing.

What differentiates spacetime from other constraint methods is that it poses a single large problem over a duration of motion, rather than on an individual frame. The original spacetime work, as well as most that followed, used spacetime to derive physically valid motions: constraints enforced Newton's laws, and the objective function minimized energy consumption. Previously, we [6] have suggested removing the physical constraints to achieve better performance and to apply the techniques to non-physical motions.

Although Ngo and Marks[15] re-used the term spacetime constraints to describe their work, their method belongs to a different family of approaches that generates control systems that create motions, rather than generating the motions themselves. We prefer to reserve the term *spacetime constraints* for methods that compute specific motions.

3 An Approach to Retargetting

In this section, we motivate and describe our approach to retargetting the motion between articulated figures with identical structure but different segment lengths. We assume that the configuration of an articulated figure is specified by a position for the root of the hierarchy and the angles of its joints. We will denote these configurations as a vector that concatenates all of these parameters, often denoted by $\mathbf{q}$, or by $\mathbf{q}^t$ to refer to its value at time t. A motion is a vector-valued function that provides a configuration given a time. While we often represent the initial motion as a dense array of samples or as a set of key values that are interpolated, our methods are independent of how this motion is obtained. We refer to the retargetted motion as $\mathbf{m}(t)$, and often use the concept of a motion displacement which represents the difference between two motions, e.g. $\mathbf{m}(t) = \mathbf{m_0}(t) + \mathbf{d}(t)$.

Because the target character has the same parameters as the original, reusing the original motion data will cause the new character to move its limbs as the original, but not necessarily lead to a desirable result as shown in the example of Figure 2. Because the length of the limbs are different, the parts of the new character do not end up in the same place as in the original. Therefore, they may fail to interact correctly with other objects in the world or may move differently. In the example these problems appear as the feet not touching the floor and "skating" horizontally when planted, as

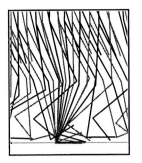 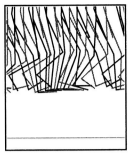

Figure 2: Left: Frames from a rotoscoped walking motion are shown. Right: Applying this motion to a character that is 60% of the size of the original yields a motion that skates along horizontally above the floor.

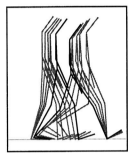 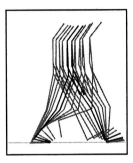

Figure 3: Adaptations are applied to the motion of Figure 2 to re-establish the constraints. The figure shows five frames before and after a heel strike, with the frame immediately before and after the heel strike darkened. A constraint on the heel's position applies on the frames after the strike. Left: inverse kinematics is applied to individual frames, causing a noticeable discontinuity. Right: our approach re-establishes the constraints while maintaining the frequency characteristics of the original motion.

seen in Figure 2. The naive retargetting fails to preserve important properties of the initial motion.

3.1 Inverse Kinematics

The principal problem with the naively retargetted motion is that it violates some of the constraints that we expect in a satisfactory walking motion. For example, a walking motion requires character's feet to touch the floor and to not skid during footplants. Retargetting must re-establish these constraints.

Inverse kinematics (IK) is a common technique for positioning end effectors of articulated figures in individual frames of an animation. An IK solver could be used to adjust the configuration of the character to meet the constraints in each frame. Figure 3 shows the result of such a retargetting approach, re-establishing the planted foot positions. Because the IK solver considers each frame independently, it makes different alterations to each frame. This lack of consistency adds many undesirable artifacts to the motion. For example, because frame i does not know that a foot will be planted in frame $i + 1$, it cannot move towards this constraint, so that in frame $i + 1$, the foot will snap to its new location. Even within a footplant, there is a lack of consistency: on each frame the solver will use a different combination of straightening the leg and lowering the pelvis. These artifacts appear as high frequency "jerkiness," shown for the example in Figure 3.

3.2 Motion Frequency Response

The problem with the IK solution is that we have added high frequencies to a primarily smooth motion. Extending the leg from bent to straight in $1/15th$ of a second might be acceptable if this were a karate master's kick, but, this discontinuity is inappropriate in our walking motion. Generally, the high frequencies of a motion (or the lack thereof) are important, and therefore must not be disturbed. An adaptation that removed the snap from a karate kick might be just as inappropriate as adding the snap to our slow walking motion.

The importance of preserving the high-frequency content of a motion (or the lack thereof) is an explanation for the success of motion-displacement mapping [2, 23] (also called motion-warping) techniques.[1] The key spacing of the displacement curves restricts their frequency content such that the high frequencies of the motion are not disturbed.

Changes should not necessarily be made at the lowest possible frequency. Consider retargetting a motion where a smaller character must grab an object in the middle frame, but there are no other constraints on the arm. To meet the constraint, the character must extend his arm in this one frame. This alteration can be made at any frequency: the single frame can be adjusted (e.g. the arm shoots out for the $1/30th$ of a second), or the adjustment can be applied to the whole motion (e.g. the arm is extended while the character walks up to the object to pick it up). While the extreme high-frequencies of the former are undesirable, so are the extreme low frequencies of the latter (the added signal has only a DC component).

A simple approach to avoiding the addition of high frequencies is to low-pass filter the displacement signal generated by the inverse kinematics process. Unfortunately this change does not necessarily maintain the constraints that IK was used to achieve as shown in Figure 4.

3.3 Motivating Spacetime

The failure of the per-frame approach to meet the needs of automatic retargetting suggests that we require a constraint-based method that can take into consideration a span of the motion, e.g. spacetime constraints. The more global view of such a method allows it to consider relationships among multiple frames. Spacetime constraint's use of constrained optimization allows us to address both parts of the retargetting problem: establishing the constraints on the motion, while minimizing the changes our original motion.

The spacetime constraints approach poses the retargetting problem mathematically. We seek a motion $\mathbf{m}(t)$ that, subject to satisfying a set of constraints on the motion $\mathbf{f}(\mathbf{m}(t)) = 0$ and $\mathbf{f}_i(\mathbf{m}(t)) \geq 0$ (we divide the constraints as equality and inequality constraints for notational convenience), minimizes an objective function $g(\mathbf{m})$. For retargetting, the objective compares the motion with the original motion, $\mathbf{m_0}(t)$. By encoding the retargetting problem in this form, we can use numerical methods to solve the constrained optimization problem for our desired result.

Because the spacetime approach looks at the entire motion, it can make choices based on other parts of the motion. For example, it can move footplants based on where the character needs to end up. Such look-ahead and -behind is not possible in approaches that consider each frame independently.

3.4 Spacetime in Practice

Ideally, the constrained optimization problem would fully encode our desires mathematically: there would be a single solution that was the desired motion. Realizing this ideal requires a rich set of constraints and objectives. For example, we could find constraints that enforce the laws of physics, biomechanical limitations due to strength, and proper ballet form. We could define objective functions that measure visual properties such as "grace," "Charlie–Chaplin–ness," and "like–Joe–did–it–yesterday–ness." We would

---

[1]Albeit, one that is not emphasized in [2] but is a motivation for [23].

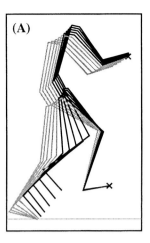   

Figure 4: Ten frames of a ladder-climbing motion are shown. In the last 5 frames (shown darker), the hand is constrained to be attached to the handhold. (A) shows the original motion capture data. (B) shows the motion adapted to a smaller character by applying Inverse kinematics (IK) to each frame, causing a noticeable snap. (C) shows low-pass filtering of the results of the IK process. This removes the snaps at the expense of violating the constraints. (D) shows our approach applied to the example.

aim to maintain the constraints that were satisfied in the original motion while minimizing the amount of change in the important properties.

There are central difficulties in realizing the spacetime ideal for retargetting: first, some properties are difficult to encode mathematically as constraints or objectives either because the forms of the equations are complex or because they elude a mathematical encoding; second, we may not know all the properties required, such as the mass distribution of an imaginary character or the physical laws of an imaginary world; third, we must decide which properties are important in a given setting; fourth, many of the properties and constraints may be specific to a small set of examples, and therefore not worth the effort to define.

Even if we encoded the desired animation completely in a constrained optimization, we still need to find the solution to these problems. Generally, richer sets of constraints and objective functions are likely to lead to more difficult problems to solve. The challenges of solution lead us to take a pragmatic view in defining spacetime problems. An extreme case of this pragmatism is our work on spacetime editing [6] where many sacrifices were made in order to achieve interactive performance.

Our approach to spacetime for retargetting is motivated by the pragmatic issues of defining, specifying, and solving constraints and objectives. We use constraints to define specific features of the motion that must be maintained and use the objective function to limit certain generally unacceptable types of changes. Besides the constraints and objectives, we have two more pragmatic tools that we can use to help define a spacetime problem with the desired solution: the representation used for the motion and the starting point for the constrained optimization. We will discuss these four in more detail in the following sections.

3.5 Sources of Constraints

Constraints are the primary tool used to identify features of the original motion that must be present in the retargetted result. In general, our constraints will either come from restrictions on the character (e.g. the elbows do not bend backwards), the environment (nothing should be below the floor), or the motion (the character must pick up the box in frame 50). Specification of these constraints typically involves only a small amount of work in comparison with the tasks of creating the characters and motions, especially with semi-automatic detection (for example finding footplants), graphical specification, and generic constraints (e.g. we use the same joint

limits for most humanoid characters). Constraints are generally defined once for each motion, and this one set of constraints is used for any retargettings (or editing, using the techniques of [6]) done with the motion. Even with these tools, augmenting our characters and motions with constraints does require some additional work. However, we feel this incremental effort is worthwhile because of the potential for reuse afforded by augmentation.

Mathematically, constraints are differentiable functions of the parameters of the character. Although it is not required by the methods, our implementation always places constraints on configurations at particular instants of time. Variational constraints, that is constraints that are to hold over a range of the motion curves, are approximated by sampling. Therefore, constraints are generally written as $f(\mathbf{q}^{t_i}) \diamond c$, where $\diamond$ is $\{\leq, \geq, =\}$ and c is a constant. Some constraints consider two instants in time, and therefore have the form $f(\mathbf{q}^{t_i}, \mathbf{q}^{t_j}) \diamond c$.

In our system, the user never needs to see an equation: the system includes a variety of pre-defined constraints that can be applied to a motion through a graphical user interface or via a scripting language. We have emphasized finding (and using) constraints that we believe are applicable over a wide range of motions. Some of these include:

1. a parameter's value is in a range (useful for joint limits);

2. a point on the character (such as an end-effector) is in a specific location (useful for footplants or grabbing an object);

3. a point on the character is in a certain region (for example, above the floor);

4. a point on the character is in the same place at two different times (useful to prevent skidding), although this position is unspecified so that it can be adjusted;

5. a point on the character is following the path of another point;

6. two points are a specified distance apart (useful for when a character is carrying an object of a fixed size);

7. the vector between two points has a specified orientation.

The architecture of our system is designed to minimize the effort required to add new types of constraints, although this does require programming and must be done at compile-time.

In developing a new type of constraint, it is important to make restrictions in ways that are invariant of other aspects of the motion. For example, if one defines a footplant by the positions of the heel and toe strikes, the constraint cannot be satisfied if the foot size is changed. Similarly, we often do not care where a footplant is, providing that is is on the floor and that the foot does not skate while planted. For the examples in this paper, we will distinguish between footplant constraints that maintain the position on the floor and those that only restrict height and skating. When the solver is permitted to move footplants, the resulting motion may cover a different distance, e.g. if the footsteps of a walk are made smaller, the character will travel a shorter distance since the system does not generate new footsteps.

3.6 Objective Functions

Since there are typically many possible motions that satisfy the constraints, we use an objective function to select the best choice. For retargetting, a simple objective is "minimize the amount of noticeable change." This does not necessarily lead to a simple, generic manifestation: consider a ballet motion where a very slight bend of the knee might be a very noticeable deviation from the otherwise perfect form of the original with its straight leg. However, our strategy is to use constraints to prevent specific changes that are unwanted, and use the objective function to avoid undesirable frequency content and unnecessary large alterations, as discussed in Section 3.2. We avoid designing objective functions tuned to specific high-level goals.

The most basic comparative objective function would be to compare the values of the parameters, matching pose in parameter space. For example,

$$g(\mathbf{m}) = \int_t (\mathbf{m}(t) - \mathbf{m}_0(t))^2 = \int_t \mathbf{d}(t)^2, \qquad (1)$$

minimizes the magnitude of signal differences in the motions over time. This objective is similar to performing per-frame inverse kinematics as it provides no coupling between constraints at different times. The minimum magnitude solution effectively maximizes high frequency content. Intuitively, it prefers not to "waste" change preparing to meet goals at other times. Other frequency criteria can be implemented with an objective function that minimizes the output of a filter that selects undesirable frequencies.

In practice, we find that pragmatic concerns outweigh most other choices in the design of an objective function. For the experiments described in this paper, we use the objective function to minimize the magnitude of the changes, approximating Equation 1. Methods described in the next section restrict high frequency content of the changes. This tactic affords the use of more efficient solving techniques (as we will describe in Section 6).

3.7 Representation

Another issue in a spacetime approach is how to represent the motions so that the optimization problems can be solved effectively. Liu et al. [13] first made use of a carefully selected representation by using wavelets to speed computations. Gleicher and Litwinowicz [7] introduced the use of motion-displacement maps as a representation for spacetime problems where the objective function related two motions. This approach defines

$$\mathbf{m}(t) = \mathbf{m}_0(t) + \mathbf{d}(t)$$

and uses the solver to find $\mathbf{d}(t)$. The approach has a number of advantages. First, it decouples the solution from the form of the initial motion, providing generality. Secondly, it simplifies placing constraints and objectives on the changes. Third, it allows a representation for $\mathbf{d}(t)$ to be chosen that includes constraints on the changes so they do not need to be expressed as explicit functions.

To constrain the displacement signal not to include high frequencies, we use a representation for it that cannot represent the high frequencies: specifically, cubic B-splines [14] with control point spacing determined by the desired frequency limits. The control points of the displacement curve need not be uniformly spaced: we can place controls closer together for portions of the motion where higher frequencies are acceptable. Similarly, we do not need to use the same key spacing for all parameters, for example, if a chef is chopping, we might allow high frequencies in the motion of his arm (to accommodate the abrupt motions of the knife), and only permit smoother changes to the rest of his body.

The spacing of B-spline control points allows us to determine the frequency response of our adaptations, although we do not have the fine control afforded by carefully crafted filters placed in an objective function. We must determine how to place the control points to achieve the desired effect. For our experiments, we have limited our choices to using the uniformly spaced control points on all parameters of a motion.[2] For the examples in this paper, we further restrict ourselves to control points spaced every 2, 4 or 8 frames. We have developed a simple heuristic method for determining which of these to apply: we compute a bandpass decomposition of the original motion (as described in [2]) and choose the key spacing that coincides with the lowest, that is highest-frequency, level of the pyramid whose energy contribution exceeds a threshold. While this simple heuristic has resulted in the correct recommendation for almost all of our examples, the speed of our solver makes it practical to produce all three adaptations and to select the one that gives the most appealing result.

With the constraints imposed by the restricted representation, there may not be a solution to the constraints. In such cases, there is a fitting problem: find the frequency-limited signal that comes closest to satisfying the constraints (where the constraints are the explicit equations from Section 3.5). In such a scheme, the nature of the mathematical problem is flipped: our constraint is the frequency response, and our optimization objective attempts to minimize the residual of the constraints. We use a least-squares metric for the residual which enables simpler solution methods, as we will discuss in Section 6.

3.8 Starting Points

Cohen [3] pointed out the importance of having good starting points for spacetime problems. Seitz and Dyer [20] observed the utility of a previously captured motion as a starting point for speeding their numerical solutions. With our retargetting approach, the initial estimate of the solution is even more critical because our simple objective function explicitly defines the result in terms of the initial estimate. To improve the quality of our results, we must apply some simple transformations to the original motion so it better estimates the desired result. The process described in this section is summarized in Figure 5.

Simply re-using the initial motion is possible because our figures share the same parameters. For articulated figures, most of the parameters are angles and are independent of the scaling of the limbs: the angular value for a straight leg is the same, no matter how long the thigh and calf are. However, the positional offset of the root of the hierarchy is not scale-independent. The translation is a distance (from the origin), and therefore should be scaled as the limbs were. Such scalings are difficult to create with the additive displacement maps, so we perform the scaling as a separate step. If the character

---

[2]This was problematic only for the example of Figure 1 where the footsteps have different frequency content than the grabbing motion. The artifacts of this problem are subtle.

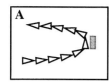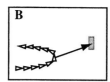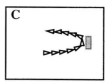

Figure 5: A: An abstracted aerial view of a character walking up to, picking up, and carrying away an object. B: When the motion is scaled about the origin (the lower left corner of the frame), the character does not come close to the object. C: Because the position of the object is the only constraint that specifies a position for the character, the entire motion can be translated.

is scaled uniformly and does not interact with the world (or if the world is scaled similarly), the scaling is sufficient for retargetting. In cases where the character is scaled non-uniformly, we make an estimate of the overall scaling to apply to the positions.

Multiplying the positional parameters scales the motion around an arbitrary point, the center of the coordinate system. Typically, there is a better center for the scaling. For example, we might scale the heights around the floor, which may not be zero. We recenter the scaling of the positional parameters by adding a translational component to them.

To find the translation, we note that a constant positional shift of a motion is not noticeable, except in conjunction with constraints that relate the character to the world. Therefore, if we could re-establish the constraints by a simple shift of the motion, this would be ideal. We find the shift of the motion that comes closest to re-establishing the constraints by computing the average of the displacements. By displacement, we refer to the vector between the point on the character and a position that it is attached to. Constraints only have displacements for axes that they restrict with a fixed position, for example, a footplant constraint may only specify the vertical direction if it only places non-skid restrictions on the other axes.

Since the center of scaling might not be constant over the whole motion, we compute a translational signal to add to the positions. We perform the displacement averaging process on each frame individually. Adding the per-frame constraint displacements to the motion may add undesirable high frequencies. Therefore, we interpolate the offsets to frames that do not have any displacements and apply low-pass filtering to remove high frequencies.

The utility of interpolation can be seen in the example of Section 1.1 where a figure walks up to, picks up, and carries away an object. In this example, the only constraint on the figure's position on the floor is provided by the constraint that the hands touch the object on the middle frame of the motion. When the motion is scaled, the entire motion is moved far away from the goal point. Interpolating the displacement of this one constraint shifts the entire motion back to the object, as shown in Figure 5. The desirability of constant shifts is unique to position; for angles it can have the undesirable behavior described in Section 3.2.

4 The Motion Retargetting Method

To summarize, our approach to retargetting motion to another articulated figure with different limb lengths consists of the following steps:

1. Begin with an initial motion with identified constraints.

2. Find an initial estimate $\mathbf{m_1}(t)$ of the solution by scaling the translational parameters of the motion, and then adding a translation to define the center of scaling. This translation is computed by finding the constraint displacements of the scaled motion for the target character, interpolating these values, and smoothing.

3. Choose a representation for the motion-displacement curve based on the frequency decomposition of the original motion.

4. Solve the non-linear constraint problem for a displacement that when added to the result of step 2 provides a motion that satisfies the constraints.

5. (optional) If the result of step 4 does not satisfy the constraints sufficiently, solve using the result of the step $(\mathbf{m_1}(t) + \mathbf{d}(t))$ as the initial motion, and a denser set of control points for the new displacement.

5 Motion for Morphing

The same methods that are used to adapt a character to new segment lengths can be used when the target lengths are not constant, i.e. when the target character is morphing. A simple example of a motion generated for morphing is shown in Figure 6. A more complex example is shown in Figure 10.

The difference between motion for morphing and standard retargetting is that the segment lengths of the target character is not constant over the motion. Therefore, it is better to use a different scaling amount on each frame in Step 2. As with the constant case, we estimate the scale in the event that the limb scalings are non-uniform. To apply this time-varying scale to the character's position, we scale the changes in translation between frames by the scale of the character in the frame, and add these changes together to find the characters positions.

6 Solving the Non-Linear Optimization

The key computation of the retargetting approach is the solution of the spacetime constraint problem. In this section, we briefly discuss our solver implementation. We emphasize that our approach casts retargetting as a standard mathematical problem, constrained optimization, for which there is a rich literature of solution methods. For a more detailed discussion of solution methods, we suggest a text on the subject such as Fletcher [4] or Gill et al. [5].

For simplicity of our discussion, we consider only equality constraints as we implement inequality constraints using an active set method [4] that creates inequality constraints by switching sets of equality constraints on and off. The constrained optimization problem we solve is generically:

$$\text{minimize } g(\mathbf{x}) \text{ subject to } \mathbf{f}(\mathbf{x}) = \mathbf{c}. \tag{2}$$

The unknown in our spacetime problem is the motion-displacement curve, or more precisely, the values for the B-Spline control points of the displacement curve. The vector of parameters $\mathbf{x}$ is the concatenation of these points. We must express all of the constraints and objectives in terms of these variables, and solution methods require us to compute the values and derivatives of

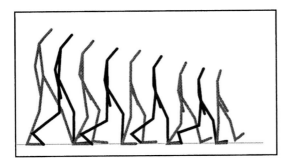 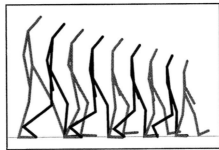

Figure 6: The retargetting process is used to adapt the motion of Figure 2 as the character morphs to 60% of its original size. Left: the footplant positions are fixed to be the same as the original motion. Right: the solver repositions the footplants.

these functions. We approximate the objective of Equation 1 as a weighted sum of squares of the controls

$$g(\mathbf{x}) = \frac{1}{2}\mathbf{x}\mathbf{M}\mathbf{x} \qquad (3)$$

where $\mathbf{M}$ is a diagonal matrix. We usually compute the entries in $\mathbf{M}$ to account for differing sensitivities in the variables as described in [6] and [7]. The importance of the choice of $\mathbf{M}$ is reduced by the large number of constraints, both explicit in equations and implicit in the representation, in the retargetting problems.

Since our constraints are always defined on instants of time, the sampling of the continuous variational problem is implicit in their definition. While the expressions for individual constraints may grow complicated, we note that they are composed of smaller pieces that are more manageable. For example, a constraint specifying the height of a characters foot would combine the kinematic function that takes the character's parameters and returns the foot height $f_k(\mathbf{q})$ composed with the function that computed the value of the parameters at the instant of time in question $\mathbf{q}^{t_i} = \mathbf{m_0}(t_i) + \mathbf{d}(t_i)$, which in turn must sample the B-splines $\mathbf{d}(t_i) = \mathbf{b}(t, \mathbf{x})$. Through the use of automatic differentiation [8, 10], we can construct these pieces independently.

Most previous spacetime work has used constrained optimization solvers that are variants of sequential quadratic programming (SQP). This standard method is described in texts such as [4], as well as spacetime papers such as [22] and [3]. In [6], we provided a variant of SQP that is more efficient for cases where the objective function has the special form of Equation 3. Our system includes solvers that operate both ways.

An alternative solution approach focuses on minimizing the constraint residual $r = 1/2(\mathbf{f}(\mathbf{x}) - \mathbf{c}) \cdot (\mathbf{f}(\mathbf{x}) - \mathbf{c})$ (because of the implicit constraints of the representation, it is unreasonable to expect that there will be an exact solution to the explicit, equational constraints). Because the constraints may not fully determine the solution, for example on a walking motion the legs may be over-determined while there are no constraints on the arms, we add additional constraints that specify that each variable should have a zero value. These constraints receive a smaller weighting. Such problems are called damped least-squares problems [5, 16], and can be solved by performing an unconstrained minimization on the residual

$$r = \frac{1}{2}(\mathbf{f}(\mathbf{x}) - \mathbf{c}) \cdot (\mathbf{f}(\mathbf{x}) - \mathbf{c}) + \epsilon\frac{1}{2}\mathbf{x} \cdot \mathbf{x}, \qquad (4)$$

where ϵ is a small constant, or a diagonal matrix of weights.

Our non-linear least-squares solver iteratively improves on an estimate of the solution. At each step, we construct a linear approximation of the constraint problem using Taylor expansion around the current estimate for $\mathbf{x}$,

$$\mathbf{f}(\mathbf{x} + \mathbf{\Delta}) \approx \mathbf{f}(\mathbf{x_i}) + \frac{\partial\mathbf{f}}{\partial\mathbf{x}}\mathbf{\Delta},$$

which gives us a linearized version of the constraint equations,

$$\mathbf{J}\mathbf{\Delta} = \mathbf{f}(\mathbf{x}) - \mathbf{c}.$$

This linear least-squares problem can be solved in a variety of ways. We solve for $\mathbf{\Delta}$ using a damped pseudo-inverse

$$(\mathbf{J}^\mathbf{T}\mathbf{J} + \epsilon\mathbf{I})\mathbf{\Delta} = \mathbf{J}^\mathbf{T}(\mathbf{f}(\mathbf{x}) - \mathbf{c}). \qquad (5)$$

Because Equation 5 is a positive definite linear system, we can solve it efficiently using either a Cholesky decomposition [18] or conjugate gradient solver[1]. We use the latter exclusively as it allows us to exploit the sparsity in the matrix to achieve good performance.

In both our constrained-optimization and least-squares solvers we use a line search [18] to determine how to use best the results of the linear subproblem. That is, once we compute $\mathbf{\Delta}$, we determine a value of k such that $\mathbf{x} + k\mathbf{\Delta}$ best satisfies the non-linear constraints.

In most cases, we find the least-squares solver to be faster than either of the SQP style solvers while providing equivalent results. For the rest of the paper, we will refer to the solvers as SQP (for the solver similar to that described in [3]), LMULT (for our implementation of the method in [6]), and least squares (for the pseudo-inverse based solver). The running times of the iterative methods used in our solvers depend on many factors, including number of variables, number of constraints, sparsity, and desired stopping tolerance. Small changes, especially in tolerance, can cause dramatic changes in solver times.

7 Examples

We have used the retargetting approach of this paper on a number of examples. While there is nothing specific to motion capture data in our approach, our examples are exclusively done on performance data because of its availability. Other than the rotoscoped 2D walking motion of Figure 2, the motions in this paper were captured with an optical motion capture system at a commercial studio. In all examples, the 120 Hz motion capture data was downsampled to 30Hz. Marker positions were converted to articulated figure parameters using our experimental automated software.

Because of the differences in processing technologies, we have some diversity in the parameters for the figures in different motions. In all cases, we use Euler angle representations for the joints. We do not have positional information for the hands. Therefore, we treat the end of the forearm as the "hand." Similarly, some motion data is missing information for the feet, in which case the ankles are used as the end effectors. For many of the motions, we did not compute the head and neck parameters as they do not affect the computations. Joints generally have three degrees of freedom, except for the elbows, knees, and ankles which have one or two parameters.

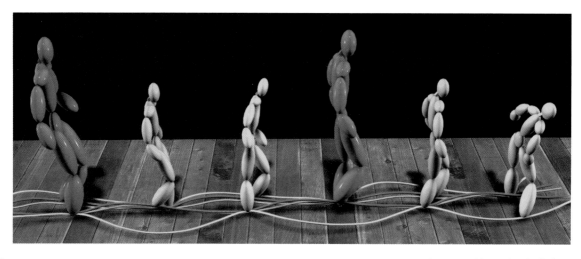

Figure 7: A walk adapted to a figure 60% of the size of the original actor. The smaller character is forced to use the original footplant positions. When the displacement keys are too distant, overfitting causes the wide swings shown in the alternate (yellow) foot traces. Proper key spacing (blue) results in a motion similar to the original (purple).

When given, timing information refers to our prototype system running on an Apple Power Macintosh 8500/180 computer with a 180Mhz PowerPC 604e processor and enough physical memory to complete the retargetting without paging. Timings are reported for the task of solving the non-linear optimization as the other parts of our retargetting approach take negligible amounts of computation.

7.1 Walking

The initial 2D walking motion of Figure 2 was created by rotoscoping marker points and using a capture process like that described in Section 8 to compute the parameters of the articulated figure. Our character has 14 degrees of freedom (2 for position and 12 joint angles), and the motion is 15Hz. On the 82 frame motion, footplant constraints on the heels and toes give 146 scalar constraints, to which we add 328 inequality constraints to keep the feet above the floor in each frame, and 1968 joint limit constraints.

Our 3D walking example is similar. The character has 34 degrees of freedom, and does not have hands or feet. Because the "feet" in the motion are actually ankles, they were not planted in the original motion and skated. We therefore used our solver to establish these constraints initially. Including joint limits and feet-above-floor constraints there are a total of 4193 scalar equations on the 112 frame motion, although during solving there are generally only 354 active constraints.

We have adapted the walking motion to a number of differently proportioned figures. An example is shown in Figure 7. With fixed footplant positions to match the tall figure, the shorter legged figures must take unnaturally long strides, seen in Figure 8. As predicted by the pyramid level heuristic of Section 3.7, a key spacing of 4 provides a better result to spacings of 8 or 2. With a key spacing of 8 there is considerable over-fitting that can be clearly seen in the yellow foot path traces of Figure 7. A key spacing of 2 provides a motion that is reasonable, however, the character seems to slow down with each step. While this is different from the original motion, the character is taking very large steps, so it seems natural for it to regain its balance each time. Our system was able to generate all 3 motions in under 10 seconds of solution time, so it is practical to create all 3 motions and choose the one we find visually most desirable.

Figure 8: Forcing a character with short legs to walk in the footsteps of a longer-legged character leads to an unnatural motion.

7.2 Climbing a Ladder

The ladder example, shown in Figure 4, gives constraints on both hands and feet. The figure has 35 degrees of freedom, no hands, and no neck or head. We use fixed position constraints for the footplants and handplants on the ladder. The least-squares solver takes approximately 9 seconds for keys spaced every other frame, and 7 seconds every fourth frame. The LMULT solver takes 6 and 4 seconds, although its answers do not satisfy the constraints as accurately. With the key spacing of 4, the LMULT solution has some constraints being violated by over half an inch, while the least-squares solution satisfies all constraints to within a quarter of an inch.

The fixed position of the hand and footplants on the ladder lead to slightly unnatural motions: the small figure must reach over its head to grasp the handholds and sometimes stands on its tip-toes to reach. We have implemented some less restrictive constraints: footplants that the solver can move along the ladder step (so the width of the steps is not an issue) and hand-holds that can be positioned along the rail. These constraints are relatively special purpose: they probably will be useful for ladder climbing motions. The motion obtained from using these constraints more closely resembles the original motion, although it is still unnatural as the ladder is very large in comparison to the resized character.

Figure 11: A walking motion is adapted from a human to a soda can by first adapting it to a human with the proportions of a can, then using this motion to drive the motion of the can (shown transparently surrounding the humanoid).

Figure 9: Two frames are shown of a swing dance motion adapted to a smaller female character. Left: original motion. Center: only female motion adapted. Right: both characters adapted.

7.3 Swing Dancing

When there are two characters in a scene, we may wish to adapt both together, even if only one changes size. For example, consider the swing dance motion in Figure 9. In this motion, the hands of the two characters must remain connected, in addition to the footplant constraints. If we change the size of the female figure without changing the motion of the male figure, the smaller figure gets lifted by the hand-hold when spinning. If we adjust both motions simultaneously, the male's part is adapted, and the female's spin is less noticeably forced. In Figure 10, the female shrinks in size while spinning and the male part responds accordingly.

On the 276 frame motion, we use 1200 equality constraints for the female character's footplants (which are free to be repositioned by the solver) and the connection between the characters hands. We only allow the upper body of the male character to be altered. If we adapt just the female motion, there are 33 parameters. Adapting both motions gives 44 parameters per key. The least-squares solver took approximately 14 seconds, while the LMULT solver ran for slightly over a minute, but with a solution that better satisfies the constraints (all to within an eighth of an inch).

8 Differing Characters

When the characters share structure there is a direct mapping between the parameters of one to the other. The more general retargetting problem is harder. When we apply a human motion to a figure with a different structure, there are creative choices in how the motion applies. What will the character use for knees? How do we choose a motion for the parts of the character that the human does not have? These creative choices correspond to mathematical problems: there may be different types of degrees of freedom, and there may be different numbers of degrees of freedom.

Our initial attempts at "automatic anthropomorphism" allow the user to make the creative choices, while having the system do the more tedious aspects. The user identifies correspondences between externally visible features of the characters, not the degrees of freedom that determine their positions. For example, we identify points on the new character that will serve as its feet when it walks, even if the foot is not at the end of a two-segment leg like the human. These correspondences pose a constraint problem, almost identical to the problem of motion capture processing: we must compute a motion that puts the character's features in the right location in each frame.

We can use the same spacetime constraints techniques that we have used for retargetting for the anthropomorphic case. Our constraints connect each feature on the new character to its corresponding feature on the original in each frame. If there are fewer degrees of freedom on the character, the motions will not be able to match exactly, and we find the "best matching motion" in a least squares sense. We have not yet developed a method for handling extra degrees of freedom.

For the spatial correspondences to apply, the characters must be approximately the same size. We use the retargetting methods of this paper to adapt the initial human motion to a new figure that has proportions more similar to the target character. We then use this motion as the source of constraints to compute the target motion. Figure 11 shows an example in which we adapt a human motion to a rigid can (a cylinder with the same proportions as a soda can). We correspond three points on the can to the human: the ends of the legs are connected to points on the bottom of the can, and the center of the hips is attached to the center of the can. Even with the can's extremely limited degrees of freedom (it is a rigid body), it can convey a sense of the original human motion. In our tests, we have made the can walk, skip, and run.

9 Discussion

In this paper we presented an approach to retargetting motions from one character to another by posing the problem of computing an adaptation as a constrained optimization. To realize the approach in a practical manner, we used geometric constraints and a simple objective function. This pragmatic strategy dodges difficulties in using spacetime constraints. We compute retargettings of complex motions despite: not having developed mathematical encodings of

Figure 10: The female character morphs into a smaller character during her spin.

concepts such as "grace" and "Charlie–Chaplin–ness" in motion; not having presented too many choices of constraints and objectives to users; and not having solved optimization problems for which we do not have efficient solution methods.

While our pragmatism pays off in the practicality of the method, we sometimes pay a cost in the quality of the resulting motions. Some of the problems we see are artifacts of the specific simple objective we have chosen and our reliance on simple frequency limits on the adaptations. For instance, in the example of Figure 1 the balance between reaching, bending, and positioning is chosen by artifacts of the representation of the character's configuration and different spatial frequencies in reaching and walking make selection of a single frequency limit for the adaptation problematic. Other problems occur because we have no guarantees on the many properties we do not explicitly model in our constraints and objective. For instance, our lack of physics constraints can lead to unrealistic situations like Figure 8 and the right image of Figure 1. Richer sets of constraints and objective functions, combined with improved solvers for the resulting numerical problems and techniques to avoid the burden of specification, would cause our approach to provide better results for a wider range of motions.

Acknowledgments

Jim Spohrer was instrumental in getting Apple Computer to give me access to the Timelines source code and sample data. Peter Litwinowicz suggested the retargetting problem to me, and suffered through my early attempts to solve it. My colleagues at the Autodesk Vision Technology Center provided critical reads of this paper. Jane Wilhelms, Sebastian Grassia, Zoran Popović and Jessica Hodgins gave much needed writing advice. Lori Gleicher was my dance critic.

References

[1] Richard Barrett, Michael Berry, Tony Chan, James Demmel, June Donato, Jack Dongarra, Victor Eikhout, Roldan Pozo, Charles Romine, and Henk van der Vorst. *Templates for the solution of linear systems: Building Blocks for Iterative Methods*. SIAM, 1994.

[2] Armin Bruderlin and Lance Williams. Motion signal processing. In Robert Cook, editor, *SIGGRAPH 95 Conference Proceedings*, Annual Conference Series, pages 97–104, August 1995.

[3] Michael F. Cohen. Interactive spacetime control for animation. In Edwin E. Catmull, editor, *Computer Graphics (SIGGRAPH '92 Proceedings)*, volume 26, pages 293–302, July 1992.

[4] Roger Fletcher. *Practical Methods of Optimization*. John Wiley and Sons, 1987.

[5] Phillip Gill, Walter Murray, and Margaret Wright. *Practical Optimization*. Academic Press, New York, NY, 1981.

[6] Michael Gleicher. Motion editing with spacetime constraints. In Michael Cohen and David Zeltzer, editors, *Proceedings 1997 Symposium on Interactive 3D Graphics*, pages 139–148, apr 1997.

[7] Michael Gleicher and Peter Litwinowicz. Constraint-based motion adaptation. *Journal of Visualization and Computer Animation*, to appear.

[8] Michael Gleicher and Andrew Witkin. Supporting numerical computations in interactive contexts. In Tom Calvert, editor, *Proceedings of Graphics Interface '93*, pages 138–145, May 1993.

[9] Jessica Hodgins and Nancy Pollard. Adapting simulated behaviors for new characters. In Turner Whitted, editor, *SIGGRAPH 97 Conference Proceedings*, pages 153–162, August 1997.

[10] Masao Iri. History of automatic differentiation and rounding error estimation. In Andreas Griewank and George Corliss, editors, *Automatic Differentiation of Algorithms: Theory, Implementation and Application*, pages 3–16. SIAM, January 1991.

[11] Kinetix Division of Autodesk Inc. Character studio. Computer Program, 1997.

[12] Peter C. Litwinowicz. Inkwell: A $2\frac{1}{2}$-D animation system. In Thomas W. Sederberg, editor, *Computer Graphics (SIGGRAPH '91 Proceedings)*, volume 25, pages 113–122, July 1991.

[13] Zicheng Liu, Steven J. Gortler, and Michael F. Cohen. Hierarchical spacetime control. In Andrew Glassner, editor, *SIGGRAPH 94 Conference Proceedings*, Annual Conference Series, pages 35–42, July 1994.

[14] Michael Mortenson. *Geometric Modelling*. John Wiley & Sons, second edition, 1997.

[15] J. Thomas Ngo and Joe Marks. Spacetime constraints revisited. In James Kajiya, editor, *Computer Graphics (SIGGRAPH '93 Proceedings)*, volume 27, pages 343–350, August 1993.

[16] Christopher Paige and Michael Saunders. LSQR: an algorithm for sparse linear equations and sparse least squares. *ACM Transactions on Mathematical Software*, 8(1):43–71, March 1982.

[17] Ken Perlin. Real time responsive animation with personality. *IEEE Transactions on Visualization and Computer Graphics*, 1(1):5–15, March 1995. ISSN 1077-2626.

[18] William Press, Brian Flannery, Saul Teukolsky, and William Vetterling. *Numerical Recipes in C*. Cambridge University Press, Cambridge, England, 1986.

[19] Charles F. Rose, Brian Guenter, Bobby Bodenheimer, and Michael F. Cohen. Efficient generation of motion transitions using spacetime constraints. In Holly Rushmeier, editor, *SIGGRAPH 96 Conference Proceedings*, Annual Conference Series, pages 147–154, August 1996.

[20] Steven Seitz and Chuck Dyer. Analogically-guided animation. Masters Project Report, Department of Computer Science, University of Wisconsin, May 1993. unpublished.

[21] Munetoshi Unuma, Ken Anjyo, and Ryozo Takeuchi. Fourier principles for emotion-based human figure animation. In Robert Cook, editor, *SIGGRAPH 95 Conference Proceedings*, Annual Conference Series, pages 91–96. ACM SIGGRAPH, Addison Wesley, August 1995.

[22] Andrew Witkin and Michael Kass. Spacetime constraints. In John Dill, editor, *Computer Graphics (SIGGRAPH '88 Proceedings)*, volume 22, pages 159–168, August 1988.

[23] Andrew Witkin and Zoran Popović. Motion warping. In Robert Cook, editor, *SIGGRAPH 95 Conference Proceedings*, Annual Conference Series, pages 105–108, August 1995.

Large Steps in Cloth Simulation

David Baraff   Andrew Witkin

Robotics Institute
Carnegie Mellon University

Abstract

The bottle-neck in most cloth simulation systems is that time steps must be small to avoid numerical instability. This paper describes a cloth simulation system that can stably take large time steps. The simulation system couples a new technique for enforcing constraints on individual cloth particles with an implicit integration method. The simulator models cloth as a triangular mesh, with internal cloth forces derived using a simple continuum formulation that supports modeling operations such as local anisotropic stretch or compression; a unified treatment of damping forces is included as well. The implicit integration method generates a large, unbanded sparse linear system at each time step which is solved using a modified conjugate gradient method that simultaneously enforces particles' constraints. The constraints are always maintained exactly, independent of the number of conjugate gradient iterations, which is typically small. The resulting simulation system is significantly faster than previous accounts of cloth simulation systems in the literature.

Keywords—Cloth, simulation, constraints, implicit integration, physically-based modeling.

1 Introduction

Physically-based cloth animation has been a problem of interest to the graphics community for more than a decade. Early work by Terzopoulos et al. [17] and Terzopoulos and Fleischer [15, 16] on deformable models correctly characterized cloth simulation as a problem in deformable surfaces, and applied techniques from the mechanical engineering and finite element communities to the problem. Since then, other research groups (notably Carignan et al. [4] and Volino et al. [20, 21]; Breen et al. [3]; and Eberhardt et al. [5]) have taken up the challenge of cloth.

Although specific details vary (underlying representations, numerical solution methods, collision detection and constraint methods, etc.), there is a deep commonality amongst all the approaches: physically-based cloth simulation is formulated as a time-varying partial differential equation which, after discretization, is numerically solved as an ordinary differential equation

$$\ddot{\mathbf{x}} = \mathbf{M}^{-1} \left(-\frac{\partial E}{\partial \mathbf{x}} + \mathbf{F} \right). \tag{1}$$

In this equation the vector $\mathbf{x}$ and diagonal matrix $\mathbf{M}$ represent the geometric state and mass distribution of the cloth, E—a scalar func-

tion of $\mathbf{x}$—yields the cloth's internal energy, and $\mathbf{F}$ (a function of $\mathbf{x}$ and $\dot{\mathbf{x}}$) describes other forces (air-drag, contact and constraint forces, internal damping, etc.) acting on the cloth.

In this paper, we describe a cloth simulation system that is much faster than previously reported simulation systems. Our system's faster performance begins with the choice of an *implicit* numerical integration method to solve equation (1). The reader should note that the use of implicit integration methods in cloth simulation is far from novel: initial work by Terzopoulos et al. [15, 16, 17] applied such methods to the problem.[1] Since this time though, research on cloth simulation has generally relied on *explicit* numerical integration (such as Euler's method or Runge-Kutta methods) to advance the simulation, or, in the case of energy minimization, analogous methods such as steepest-descent [3, 10].

This is unfortunate. Cloth strongly resists stretching motions while being comparatively permissive in allowing bending or shearing motions. This results in a "stiff" underlying differential equation of motion [12]. Explicit methods are ill-suited to solving stiff equations because they require many small steps to stably advance the simulation forward in time.[2] In practice, the computational cost of an explicit method greatly limits the realizable resolution of the cloth. For some applications, the required spatial resolution—that is, the dimension n of the state vector $\mathbf{x}$—can be quite low: a resolution of only a few hundred particles (or nodal points, depending on your formulation/terminology) can be sufficient when it comes to modeling flags or tablecloths. To animate clothing, which is our main concern, requires much higher spatial resolution to adequately represent realistic (or even semi-realistic) wrinkling and folding configurations.

In this paper, we demonstrate that implicit methods for cloth overcome the performance limits inherent in explicit simulation methods. We describe a simulation system that uses a triangular mesh for cloth surfaces, eliminating topological restrictions of rectangular meshes, and a simple but versatile formulation of the internal cloth energy forces. (Unlike previous metric-tensor-based formulations [15, 16, 17, 4] which model deformation energies as quartic functions of positions, we model deformation energies only as quadratic functions with suitably large scaling. Quadratic energy models mesh well with implicit integration's numerical properties.) We also introduce a simple, unified treatment of damping forces, a subject which has been largely ignored thus far. A key step in our simulation process is the solution of an $O(n) \times O(n)$ sparse linear system, which arises from the implicit integration method. In this respect, our implementation differs greatly from the implementation by Terzopoulos et al. [15, 17], which for large simulations

---

[1] Additional use of implicit methods in animation and dynamics work includes Kass and Miller [8], Terzopoulos and Qin [18], and Tu [19].

[2] Even worse, the number of time steps per frame tends to increase along with the problem size, for an explicit method. Cloth simulations of size n—meaning $\mathbf{x} \in \mathbf{R}^{O(n)}$—generally require $O(n)$ explicit steps per unit simulated time. Because the cost of an explicit step is also $O(n)$ (setting aside complications such as collision detection for now) explicit methods for cloth require time $O(n^2)$—or worse.

used an "alternating-direction" implicit (ADI) method [12]. An ADI method generates a series of tightly banded (and thus quickly solved) linear systems rather than one large sparse system. (The price, however, is that some of the forces in the system—notably between diagonally-adjacent and non-adjacent nodes involved in self-collisions—are treated explicitly, not implicitly.) The speed (and ease) with which our sparse linear systems can be robustly solved—even for systems involving 25,000 variables or more—has convinced us that there is no benefit to be gained from using an ADI method instead (even if ADI methods could be applied to irregular triangular meshes). Thus, regardless of simulation size, we treat *all* forces as part of the implicit formulation. Even for extremely stiff systems, numerical stability has not been an issue for our simulator.

1.1 Specific Contributions

Much of the performance of our system stems from the development of an implicit integration formulation that handles contact and geometric constraints in a direct fashion. Specifically, our simulator enforces constraints without introducing additional penalty terms in the energy function E or adding Lagrange-multiplier forces into the force $\mathbf{F}$. (This sort of direct constraint treatment is trivial if equation (1) is integrated using explicit techniques, but is problematic for implicit methods.) Our formulation for directly imposing and maintaining constraints is harmonious with the use of an extremely fast iterative solution algorithm—a modified version of the conjugate gradient (CG) method—to solve the $O(n) \times O(n)$ linear system generated by the implicit integrator. Iterative methods do not in general solve linear systems exactly—they are run until the solution error drops below some tolerance threshold. A property of our approach, however, is that the constraints are maintained exactly, regardless of the number of iterations taken by the linear solver. Additionally, we introduce a simple method, tailored to cloth simulation, for dynamically adapting the size of time steps over the course of a simulation.

The combination of implicit integration and direct constraint satisfaction is very powerful, because this approach almost always allows us to take large steps forward. In general, most of our simulations require on average from two to three time steps per frame of 30 Hz animation, even for (relatively) fast moving cloth. The large step sizes complement the fact that the CG solver requires relatively few iterations to converge. For example, in simulating a 6,000 node system, the solver takes only 50–100 iterations to solve the $18,000 \times 18,000$ linear system formed at each step. Additionally, the running time of our simulator is remarkably insensitive to the cloth's material properties (quite the opposite behavior of explicit methods). All of the above advantages translate directly into a fast running time. For example, we demonstrate results similar to those in Breen *et al.* [3] and Eberhardt *et al.* [5] (draping of a 2,600 node cloth) with a running time just over 2 seconds per frame on an SGI Octane R10000 195 Mhz processor. Similarly, we show garments (shirts, pants, skirts) exhibiting complex wrinkling and folding behavior on both key-framed and motion-captured characters. Representative running times include a long skirt with 4,530 nodes (8,844 triangles) on a dancing character at a cost of 10 seconds per frame, and a shirt with 6,450 nodes (12,654 triangles) with a cost varying between 8 to 14 seconds per frame, depending on the underlying character's motion.

1.2 Previous Work

Terzopoulos *et al.* [15, 17] discretized cloth as a rectangular mesh. Energy functions were derived using a continuum formulation. This work recognized the need for damping forces; however, only a simple viscous drag force $-k\dot{x}$ was used. The linear systems result-

ing from the use of implicit integration techniques were solved, for small systems, by direct methods such as Choleski factorization, or using iterative techniques such as Gauss-Seidel relaxation or conjugate gradients. (For a square system of n nodes, the resulting linear system has bandwidth $\sqrt{n}$. In this case, banded Choleski factorization [6] requires time $O(n^2)$.) As previously discussed, Terzopoulos *et al.* made use of an ADI method for larger cloth simulations.

Following Terzopoulos *et al.*'s treatment of deformable surfaces, work by Carignan *et al.* [4] described a cloth simulation system using rectangular discretization and the same formulation as Terzopoulos *et al.* Explicit integration was used. Carignan *et al.* recognized the need for damping functions which do not penalize rigid-body motions of the cloth (as simple viscous damping does) and they added a force which damps cloth stretch and shear (but not bend). Later work by the same group includes Volino *et al.* [20], which focuses mainly on collision detection/response and uses a triangular mesh; no mention is made of damping forces. The system uses the midpoint method (an explicit method) to advance the simulation. Thus far, the accumulated work by this group (see Volino *et al.* [21] for an overview) gives the only published results we know of for simulated garments on moving characters. Reported resolutions of the garments are approximately two thousand triangles per garment (roughly 1,000 nodal points) [21] with running times of several minutes per frame for each garment on an SGI R4400 150 Mhz processor.

Breen *et al.* [3] depart completely from continuum formulations of the energy function, and describe what they call a "particle-based" approach to the problem. By making use of real-world cloth material properties (the Kawabata measuring system) they produced highly realistic static images of draped rectangular cloth meshes with reported resolutions of up to 51×51 nodes. The focus of this work is on static poses for cloth, as opposed to animation: thus, their simulation process is best described as energy minimization, although methods analogous to explicit methods are used. Speed was of secondary concern in this work. Refinements by Eberhardt *et al.* [5]—notably, the use of higher-order explicit integration methods and Maple-optimized code, as well as a dynamic, not static treatment of the problem—obtain similarly realistic results, while dropping the computational cost to approximately 20–30 minutes per frame on an SGI R8000 processor. No mention is made of damping terms. Provot [13] focuses on improving the performance of explicit methods by a post-step modification of nodal positions. He iteratively adjusts nodal positions to eliminate unwanted stretch; the convergence properties of this method are unclear. A more comprehensive discussion on cloth research can be found in the survey paper by Ng and Grimsdale [9].

2 Simulation Overview

In this section, we give a brief overview of our simulator's architecture and introduce some notation. The next section derives the linear system used to step the simulator forward implicitly while section 4 describes the specifics of the internal forces and their derivatives that form the linear system. Section 5 describes how constraints are maintained (once established), with a discussion in section 6 on collision detection and constraint initialization. Section 7 describes our adaptive step-size control, and we conclude in section 8 with some simulation results.

2.1 Notation and Geometry

Our simulator models cloth as a triangular mesh of particles. Given a mesh of n particles, the position in world-space of the ith particle is $\mathbf{x}_i \in \mathbf{R}^3$. The geometric state of all the particles is simply $\mathbf{x} \in \mathbf{R}^{3n}$.

The same component notation applies to forces: a force $\mathbf{f} \in \mathbf{R}^{3n}$ acting on the cloth exerts a force $\mathbf{f}_i$ on the ith particle. Real-world cloth is cut from flat sheets of material and tends to resist deformations away from this initial flat state (creases and pleats not withstanding). We capture the rest state of cloth by assigning each particle an unchanging coordinate (u_i, v_i) in the plane.[3] Section 4 makes use of these planar coordinates.

Collisions between cloth and solid objects are handled by preventing cloth particles from interpenetrating solid objects. Our current implementation models solid objects as triangularly faced polyhedra. Each face has an associated thickness and an orientation; particles found to be sufficiently near a face, and on the wrong side, are deemed to have collided with that face, and become subject to a contact constraint. (If relative velocities are extremely high, this simple test may miss some collisions. In this case, analytically checking for intersection between previous and current positions can guarantee that no collisions are missed.) For cloth/cloth collisions, we detect both face-vertex collisions between cloth particles and triangles, as well as edge/edge collisions between portions of the cloth. As in the case of solids, close proximity or actual intersection of cloth with itself initiates contact handling.

2.2 Energy and Forces

The most critical forces in the system are the internal cloth forces which impart much of the cloth's characteristic behavior. Breen *et al.* [3] describes the use of the Kawabata system of measurement for realistic determination of the in-plane shearing and out-of-plane bending forces in cloth. We call these two forces the shear and bend forces. We formulate the shear force on a per triangle basis, while the bend force is formulated on a per edge basis—between pairs of adjacent triangles.

The strongest internal force—which we call the stretch force—resists in-plane stretching or compression, and is also formulated per triangle. Under normal conditions, cloth does not stretch appreciably under its own weight. This requires the stretch force to have a high coefficient of stiffness, and in fact, it is the stretch force that is most responsible for the stiffness of equation (1). A common practice in explicitly integrated cloth systems is to improve running time by decreasing the strength of the stretch force; however, this leads to "rubbery" or "bouncy" cloth. Our system uses a very stiff stretch force to combat this problem, without any detrimental effects on the run-time performance. While the shear and bend force stiffness coefficients depend on the material being simulated, the stretch coefficient is essentially the same (large) value for all simulations. (Of course, if stretchy cloth is specifically called for, the stretch coefficient can be made smaller.)

Complementing the above three internal forces are three damping forces. In section 5, we formulate damping forces that subdue any oscillations having to do with, respectively, stretching, shearing, and bending motions of the cloth. The damping forces do not dissipate energy due to other modes of motion. Additional forces include air-drag, gravity, and user-generated generated mouse-forces (for interactive simulations). Cloth/cloth contacts generate strong repulsive linear-spring forces between cloth particles.

Combining all forces into a net force vector $\mathbf{f}$, the acceleration $\ddot{\mathbf{x}}_i$ of the ith particle is simply $\ddot{\mathbf{x}}_i = \mathbf{f}_i / m_i$, where m_i is the ith particle's mass. The mass m_i is determined by summing one third the mass

of all triangles containing the ith particle. (A triangle's mass is the product of the cloth's density and the triangle's fixed area in the uv coordinate system.) Defining the diagonal mass matrix $\mathbf{M} \in \mathbf{R}^{3n \times 3n}$ by $\mathrm{diag}(\mathbf{M}) = (m_1, m_1, m_1, m_2, m_2, m_2, \ldots, m_n, m_n, m_n)$, we can write simply that

$$\ddot{\mathbf{x}} = \mathbf{M}^{-1} \mathbf{f}(\mathbf{x}, \dot{\mathbf{x}}). \tag{2}$$

2.3 Sparse Matrices

The use of an implicit integration method, described in the next section, generates large unbanded sparse linear systems. We solve these systems through a modified conjugate gradient (CG) iterative method, described in section 5. CG methods exploit sparsity quite easily, since they are based solely on matrix-vector multiplies, and require only rudimentary sparse storage techniques. The sparsity of the matrix generated by the implicit integrator is best represented in block-fashion: for a system with n particles, we deal with an $n \times n$ matrix, whose non-zero entries are represented as dense 3×3 matrices of scalars. The matrix is represented as an array of n rows; each row is a linked list of the non-zero elements of that row, to accommodate possible run-time changes in the sparsity pattern, due to cloth/cloth contact. The (dense) vectors that are multiplied against this matrix are stored simply as n element arrays of three-component vectors. The overall implementation of sparsity is completely straightforward.

2.4 Constraints

An individual particle's position and velocity can be completely controlled in either one, two, or three dimensions. Particles can thus be attached to a fixed or moving point in space, or constrained to a fixed or moving surface or curve. Constraints are either user-defined (the time period that a constraint is active is user-controlled) or automatically generated, in the case of contact constraints between cloth and solids. During cloth/solid contacts, the particle may be attached to the surface, depending on the magnitudes of the frictional forces required; otherwise, the particle is constrained to remain on the surface, with sliding allowed. The mechanism for releasing a contact constraint, or switching between sliding or not sliding, is described in section 5.

The constraint techniques we use on individual particles work just as well for collections of particles; thus, we could handle cloth/cloth intersections using the technique described in section 5, but the cost is potentially large. For that reason, we have chosen to deal with cloth/cloth contacts using penalty forces: whenever a particle is near a cloth triangle or is detected to have passed through a cloth triangle, we add a stiff spring with damping to pull the particle back to the correct side of the triangle. The implicit solver easily tolerates these stiff forces.

3 Implicit Integration

Given the known position $\mathbf{x}(t_0)$ and velocity $\dot{\mathbf{x}}(t_0)$ of the system at time t_0, our goal is to determine a new position $\mathbf{x}(t_0 + h)$ and velocity $\dot{\mathbf{x}}(t_0 + h)$ at time $t_0 + h$. To compute the new state and velocity using an implicit technique, we must first transform equation (2) into a first-order differential equation. This is accomplished simply by defining the system's velocity $\mathbf{v}$ as $\mathbf{v} = \dot{\mathbf{x}}$ and then writing

$$\frac{d}{dt} \begin{pmatrix} \mathbf{x} \\ \dot{\mathbf{x}} \end{pmatrix} = \frac{d}{dt} \begin{pmatrix} \mathbf{x} \\ \mathbf{v} \end{pmatrix} = \begin{pmatrix} \mathbf{v} \\ \mathbf{M}^{-1} \mathbf{f}(\mathbf{x}, \mathbf{v}) \end{pmatrix}. \tag{3}$$

To simplify notation, we will define $\mathbf{x_0} = \mathbf{x}(t_0)$ and $\mathbf{v_0} = \mathbf{v}(t_0)$. We also define $\Delta \mathbf{x} = \mathbf{x}(t_0 + h) - \mathbf{x}(t_0)$ and $\Delta \mathbf{v} = \mathbf{v}(t_0 + h) - \mathbf{v}(t_0)$.

---

[3]In general, each particle has a unique (u, v) coordinate; however, to accommodate pieces of cloth that have been topologically seamed together (such as a sleeve), particles lying on the seam must have multiple (u, v) coordinates. For these particles, we let the (u, v) coordinate depend on which triangle we are currently examining. The (u, v) coordinates are useful for texturing.

The explicit *forward* Euler method applied to equation (3) approximates $\Delta\mathbf{x}$ and $\Delta\mathbf{v}$ as

$$\left(\begin{array}{c} \Delta\mathbf{x} \\ \Delta\mathbf{v} \end{array}\right) = h\left(\begin{array}{c} \mathbf{v_0} \\ \mathbf{M}^{-1}\mathbf{f_0} \end{array}\right)$$

where the force $\mathbf{f_0}$ is defined by $\mathbf{f_0} = \mathbf{f}(\mathbf{x_0}, \mathbf{v_0})$. As previously discussed, the step size h must be quite small to ensure stability when using this method. The implicit *backward* Euler method appears similar at first: $\Delta\mathbf{x}$ and $\Delta\mathbf{v}$ are approximated by

$$\left(\begin{array}{c} \Delta\mathbf{x} \\ \Delta\mathbf{v} \end{array}\right) = h\left(\begin{array}{c} \mathbf{v_0} + \Delta\mathbf{v} \\ \mathbf{M}^{-1}\mathbf{f}(\mathbf{x_0} + \Delta\mathbf{x}, \mathbf{v_0} + \Delta\mathbf{v}) \end{array}\right). \qquad (4)$$

The difference in the two methods is that the forward method's step is based solely on conditions at time t_0 while the backward method's step is written in terms of conditions at the terminus of the step itself.[4]

The forward method requires only an evaluation of the function $\mathbf{f}$ but the backward method requires that we *solve* for values of $\Delta\mathbf{x}$ and $\Delta\mathbf{v}$ that satisfy equation (4). Equation (4) is a nonlinear equation: rather than solve this equation exactly (which would require iteration) we apply a Taylor series expansion to $\mathbf{f}$ and make the first-order approximation

$$\mathbf{f}(\mathbf{x_0} + \Delta\mathbf{x}, \mathbf{v_0} + \Delta\mathbf{v}) = \mathbf{f_0} + \frac{\partial\mathbf{f}}{\partial\mathbf{x}}\Delta\mathbf{x} + \frac{\partial\mathbf{f}}{\partial\mathbf{v}}\Delta\mathbf{v}.$$

In this equation, the derivative $\partial\mathbf{f}/\partial\mathbf{x}$ is evaluated for the state $(\mathbf{x_0}, \mathbf{v_0})$ and similarly for $\partial\mathbf{f}/\partial\mathbf{v}$. Substituting this approximation into equation (4) yields the linear system

$$\left(\begin{array}{c} \Delta\mathbf{x} \\ \Delta\mathbf{v} \end{array}\right) = h\left(\begin{array}{c} \mathbf{v_0} + \Delta\mathbf{v} \\ \mathbf{M}^{-1}(\mathbf{f_0} + \frac{\partial\mathbf{f}}{\partial\mathbf{x}}\Delta\mathbf{x} + \frac{\partial\mathbf{f}}{\partial\mathbf{v}}\Delta\mathbf{v}) \end{array}\right). \qquad (5)$$

Taking the bottom row of equation (5) and substituting $\Delta\mathbf{x} = h(\mathbf{v_0} + \Delta\mathbf{v})$ yields

$$\Delta\mathbf{v} = h\mathbf{M}^{-1}\left(\mathbf{f_0} + \frac{\partial\mathbf{f}}{\partial\mathbf{x}}h(\mathbf{v_0} + \Delta\mathbf{v}) + \frac{\partial\mathbf{f}}{\partial\mathbf{v}}\Delta\mathbf{v}\right).$$

Letting $\mathbf{I}$ denote the identity matrix, and regrouping, we obtain

$$\left(\mathbf{I} - h\mathbf{M}^{-1}\frac{\partial\mathbf{f}}{\partial\mathbf{v}} - h^2\mathbf{M}^{-1}\frac{\partial\mathbf{f}}{\partial\mathbf{x}}\right)\Delta\mathbf{v} = h\mathbf{M}^{-1}\left(\mathbf{f_0} + h\frac{\partial\mathbf{f}}{\partial\mathbf{x}}\mathbf{v_0}\right) \qquad (6)$$

which we then solve for $\Delta\mathbf{v}$. Given $\Delta\mathbf{v}$, we trivially compute $\Delta\mathbf{x} = h(\mathbf{v_0} + \Delta\mathbf{v})$.

Thus, the backward Euler step consists of evaluating $\mathbf{f_0}$, $\partial\mathbf{f}/\partial\mathbf{x}$ and $\partial\mathbf{f}/\partial\mathbf{v}$; forming the system in equation (6); solving the system for $\Delta\mathbf{v}$; and then updating $\mathbf{x}$ and $\mathbf{v}$. We use the sparse data structures described in section 2.3 to store the linear system. The sparsity pattern of equation (6) is described in the next section, while solution techniques are deferred to section 5.

---

[4]The method is called "backward" Euler because starting from the output state $(\mathbf{x_0} + \Delta\mathbf{x}, \mathbf{v_0} + \Delta\mathbf{v})$ and using a forward Euler step to run the system *backward* in time (i.e. taking the step $-h(\mathbf{v}(t_0 + h), \mathbf{f}(\mathbf{x}(t_0 + h), \mathbf{v}(t_0 + h)))$ brings you back to $(\mathbf{x_0}, \mathbf{v_0})$. What is the value in this? Forward Euler takes no notice of wildly changing derivatives, and proceeds forward quite blindly. Backward Euler, however, forces one to find an output state whose derivative at least points back to where you came from, imparting, essentially, an additional layer of consistency (or sanity-checking, if you will).

4 Forces

Cloth's material behavior is customarily described in terms of a scalar potential energy function $E(\mathbf{x})$; the force $\mathbf{f}$ arising from this energy is $\mathbf{f} = -\partial E/\partial\mathbf{x}$. Equation (6) requires both the vector $\mathbf{f}$ and the matrix $\partial\mathbf{f}/\partial\mathbf{x}$. Expressing the energy E as a single monolithic function—encompassing all aspects of the cloth's internal behavior—and then taking derivatives is impractical, from a bookkeeping point of view. A better approach is decompose E into a sum of sparse energy functions; that is, to write $E(\mathbf{x}) = \sum_\alpha E_\alpha(\mathbf{x})$ where each E_α depends on as few elements of $\mathbf{x}$—as few particles—as possible.

However, even decomposing E into sparse energy functions is not enough. Energy functions are an undesirable starting point because sensible damping functions cannot be derived from energy functions. Instead, we define internal behavior by formulating a vector condition $\mathbf{C}(\mathbf{x})$ which we want to be zero, and then defining the associated energy as $\frac{k}{2}\mathbf{C}(\mathbf{x})^T\mathbf{C}(\mathbf{x})$ where k is a stiffness constant. In section 4.5, we show how sensible damping functions can be constructed based on this formulation. An added bonus is that starting from this vector-based energy description tends to result in a simpler, more compact, and more easily coded formulation for $\partial\mathbf{f}/\partial\mathbf{x}$ than proceeding from an energy function in which the structure of $\mathbf{C}$ has been lost.

4.1 Forces and Force Derivatives

Given a condition $\mathbf{C}(\mathbf{x})$ which we want to be zero, we associate an energy function $E_\mathbf{C}$ with $\mathbf{C}$ by writing $E_\mathbf{C}(\mathbf{x}) = \frac{k}{2}\mathbf{C}(\mathbf{x})^T\mathbf{C}(\mathbf{x})$ where k is a stiffness constant of our choice. Assuming that $\mathbf{C}$ depends on only a few particle, $\mathbf{C}$ gives rise to a sparse force vector $\mathbf{f}$. Recall from section 2.1 that we view the vector $\mathbf{f}$ in block form; each element $\mathbf{f}_i$ is a vector in $\mathbf{R}^3$. For each particle i that $\mathbf{C}$ depends on,

$$\mathbf{f}_i = -\frac{\partial E_\mathbf{C}}{\partial\mathbf{x}_i} = -k\frac{\partial\mathbf{C}(\mathbf{x})}{\partial\mathbf{x}_i}\mathbf{C}(\mathbf{x}); \qquad (7)$$

all the other elements of $\mathbf{f}$ are zero.

Similarly, the derivative of $\mathbf{f}$ is also sparse. Defining the derivative matrix $\mathbf{K} = \partial\mathbf{f}/\partial\mathbf{x}$, the nonzero entries of $\mathbf{K}$ are $\mathbf{K}_{ij}$ for all *pairs* of particles i and j that $\mathbf{C}$ depends on. Again, we treat $\mathbf{K}$ in block fashion: $\mathbf{K} \in \mathbf{R}^{3n\times 3n}$, so an element $\mathbf{K}_{ij}$ is a 3×3 matrix. From equation (7), we have

$$\mathbf{K}_{ij} = \frac{\partial\mathbf{f}_i}{\partial\mathbf{x}_j} = -k\left(\frac{\partial\mathbf{C}(\mathbf{x})}{\partial\mathbf{x}_i}\frac{\partial\mathbf{C}(\mathbf{x})}{\partial\mathbf{x}_j}^T + \frac{\partial^2\mathbf{C}(\mathbf{x})}{\partial\mathbf{x}_i\partial\mathbf{x}_j}\mathbf{C}(\mathbf{x})\right). \qquad (8)$$

Additionally, since $\mathbf{K}_{ij}$ is a second derivative—that is, $\mathbf{K}_{ij} = \partial\mathbf{f}_i/\partial\mathbf{x}_j = \partial^2 E/\partial\mathbf{x}_i\partial\mathbf{x}_j$—we have $\mathbf{K}_{ij} = \mathbf{K}_{ji}^T$ so $\mathbf{K}$ is symmetric. Note that since $\mathbf{C}$ does not depend on $\mathbf{v}$, the matrix $\partial\mathbf{f}/\partial\mathbf{v}$ is zero.

We can now easily describe the internal forces acting on the cloth, by just writing condition functions. Forces and their derivatives are easily derived using equations (7) and (8).

4.2 Stretch Forces

Recall that every cloth particle has a changing position $\mathbf{x}_i$ in world space, and a fixed plane coordinate (u_i, v_i). Even though our cloth is modeled as a discrete set of points, grouped into triangles, it will be convenient to pretend momentarily that we have a single continuous function $\mathbf{w}(u, v)$ that maps from plane coordinates to world space. Stretch can be measured at any point in the cloth surface by examining the derivatives $\mathbf{w}_u = \partial\mathbf{w}/\partial u$ and $\mathbf{w}_v = \partial\mathbf{w}/\partial v$ at that point. The magnitude of $\mathbf{w}_u$ describes the stretch or compression in the u direction; the material is unstretched wherever $\|\mathbf{w}_u\| = 1$. Stretch in the

v direction is measured by $\|\mathbf{w}_v\|$. (Some previous continuum formulations have modeled stretch energy along an axis as essentially $(\mathbf{w}_u^T\mathbf{w}_u - 1)^2$, which is a quartic function of position [15, 16, 17, 4]. We find this to be needlessly stiff; worse, near the rest state, the force gradient—a quadratic function of position—is quite small, which partially negates the advantage implicit integration has in exploiting knowledge of the force gradient. A quadratic model for energy is, numerically, a better choice.)

We apply this stretch/compression measure to a triangle as follows. Let us consider a triangle whose vertices are particles i, j and k. Define $\Delta\mathbf{x}_1 = \mathbf{x}_j - \mathbf{x}_i$ and $\Delta\mathbf{x}_2 = \mathbf{x}_k - \mathbf{x}_i$. Also, let $\Delta u_1 = u_j - u_i$, while $\Delta u_2 = u_k - u_i$ and similarly for Δv_1 and Δv_2. We approximate $\mathbf{w}(u, v)$ as a linear function over each triangle; this is equivalent to saying that $\mathbf{w}_u$ and $\mathbf{w}_v$ are constant over each triangle. This lets us write $\Delta\mathbf{x}_1 = \mathbf{w}_u\Delta u_1 + \mathbf{w}_v\Delta v_1$ and $\Delta\mathbf{x}_2 = \mathbf{w}_u\Delta u_2 + \mathbf{w}_v\Delta v_2$. Solving for $\mathbf{w}_u$ and $\mathbf{w}_v$ yields

$$(\mathbf{w}_u \quad \mathbf{w}_v) = (\Delta\mathbf{x}_1 \quad \Delta\mathbf{x}_2) \begin{pmatrix} \Delta u_1 & \Delta u_2 \\ \Delta v_1 & \Delta v_2 \end{pmatrix}^{-1}. \qquad (9)$$

Note that $\mathbf{x}_1$ and $\mathbf{x}_2$ vary during the simulation but the matrix in the above equation does not.

We can treat $\mathbf{w}_u$ and $\mathbf{w}_v$ as functions of $\mathbf{x}$, realizing that they depend only on $\mathbf{x}_i$, $\mathbf{x}_j$ and $\mathbf{x}_k$ and using equation (9) to obtain derivatives. The condition we use for the stretch energy is

$$\mathbf{C}(\mathbf{x}) = a \begin{pmatrix} \|\mathbf{w}_u(\mathbf{x})\| - b_u \\ \|\mathbf{w}_v(\mathbf{x})\| - b_v \end{pmatrix} \qquad (10)$$

where a is the triangle's area in uv coordinates. Usually, we set $b_u = b_v = 1$, though we need not always do so. In particular, if we want to slightly lengthen a garment (for example, a sleeve) in the u direction, we can increase b_u, which causes $\mathbf{w}_u$ to seek a larger value, and tends to induce wrinkles across the u direction. Likewise, we might decrease b_v near the end of a sleeve, inducing a tight cuff, as on a sweatshirt. We have found the ability to control shrink/stretch anisotropically to be an indispensable modeling tool.

4.3 Shear and Bend Forces

Cloth likewise resists shearing in the plane. We can measure the extent to which cloth has sheared in a triangle by considering the inner product $\mathbf{w}_u^T\mathbf{w}_v$. In its rest state, this product is zero. Since the stretch term prevents the magnitudes of $\mathbf{w}_u$ and $\mathbf{w}_v$ from changing overly much, we need not normalize. By the small angle approximation, the product $\mathbf{w}_u^T\mathbf{w}_v$ is a reasonable approximation to the shear angle. The condition for shearing is simply

$$C(\mathbf{x}) = a\mathbf{w}_u(\mathbf{x})^T\mathbf{w}_v(\mathbf{x})$$

with a the triangle's area in the uv plane.

We measure bend between pairs of adjacent triangles. The condition we write for the bend energy depends upon the four particles defining the two adjoining triangles. If we let $\mathbf{n}_1$ and $\mathbf{n}_2$ denote the unit normals of the two triangles and let $\mathbf{e}$ be a unit vector parallel to the common edge, the angle θ between the two faces is defined by the relations $\sin\theta = (\mathbf{n}_1 \times \mathbf{n}_2) \cdot \mathbf{e}$ and $\cos\theta = \mathbf{n}_1 \cdot \mathbf{n}_2$. We define a condition for bending by writing simply $C(\mathbf{x}) = \theta$ which results in a force that counters bending.[5] The assumption that the stretch energy will keep the cloth from stretching much allows us to treat $\mathbf{n}_1$,

---

[5]For reasonably equilateral triangles, as edge lengths decrease, the curvature represented by a particular angle θ between triangles increases. Since the square of the curvature—a a good measure of the bend energy in cloth—increases at the same rate that the triangle's area decreases, the condition C should *not* be scaled by the triangles' areas. See Breen *et al.* [3] for a further discussion of relating curvature to bend angle.

$\mathbf{n}_2$ and $\mathbf{e}$ as having a constant length at each step of the simulation. This makes differentiating θ with respect to $\mathbf{x}$ a manageable task.

Rectangular meshes make it simple to treat bending anisotropically. The uv coordinates associated with particles make this possible for triangular meshes as well. Given material for which bending in the u and v directions are weighted by stiffnesses k_u and k_v, we can emulate this anisotropy as follows. Let the edge between the triangles be between particles i and j, and define $\Delta u = u_i - u_j$ and $\Delta v = v_i - v_j$. The stiffness weighting for this edge should simply be

$$\frac{k_u(\Delta u)^2 + k_v(\Delta v)^2}{(\Delta u)^2 + (\Delta v)^2}.$$

4.4 Additional Forces

To the above forces we also add easily implemented forces such as gravity and air-drag (which is formulated on a per-triangle basis, and opposes velocities along the triangle's normal direction). When the simulation is fast enough to interact with, we add user-controlled "mouse" forces. These forces and their gradients are easily derived.

4.5 Damping

The energies we have just described are functions of position only. Robust dynamic cloth simulation, however, is critically dependent on well-chosen damping forces that are a function of both position *and* velocity. For example, the strong stretch force must be accompanied by a suitably strong damping force if we are to prevent anomalous in-plane oscillations from arising between connected particles. However, this strong damping force must confine itself solely to damping in-plane stretching/compressing motions: stretch damping should not arise due to motions that are not causing stretch or compression. Terzopoulos *et al.*'s [16, 17] treatment of cloth used a simple viscous damping function which dissipated kinetic energy, independent of the type of motion. Carignan *et al.* [4] improved upon this somewhat, borrowing a formulation due to Platt and Barr [11]; however, their damping function—a linear function of velocity—does not match the quartic energy functions of their continuum formulation. In this section we describe a general treatment for damping that is independent of the specific energy function being damped.

It is tempting to formulate a damping function for an energy function $E(\mathbf{x})$ by measuring the velocity of the energy, $\dot{E} = \frac{d}{dt}E(\mathbf{x})$. This is an easy trap to fall into, but it gives nonsensical results. At an equilibrium point of E, the gradient $\partial E/\partial\mathbf{x}$ vanishes. Since $\dot{E} = (\partial E/\partial\mathbf{x})^T\dot{\mathbf{x}}$, we find that $\dot{E}$ is zero when E is at its minimum, *regardless* of the system's velocity $\dot{\mathbf{x}} = \mathbf{v}$. In general, $\dot{E}$ is always too small near the system's rest state. Clearly, basing the damping force on $\dot{E}$ is not what we want to do.

We believe that the damping function should be defined not in terms of the energy E, but in terms of the condition $\mathbf{C}(\mathbf{x})$ we have been using to define energies. The force $\mathbf{f}$ arising from the energy acts only in the direction $\partial\mathbf{C}(\mathbf{x})/\partial\mathbf{x}$, and so should the damping force. Additionally, the damping force should depend on the component of the system's velocity in the $\partial\mathbf{C}(\mathbf{x})/\partial\mathbf{x}$ direction; in other words, the damping strength should depend on $(\partial\mathbf{C}(\mathbf{x})/\partial\mathbf{x})^T\dot{\mathbf{x}} = \dot{\mathbf{C}}(\mathbf{x})$. Putting this together, we propose that the damping force $\mathbf{d}$ associated with a condition $\mathbf{C}$ have the form

$$\mathbf{d} = -k_d\frac{\partial\mathbf{C}(\mathbf{x})}{\partial\mathbf{x}}\dot{\mathbf{C}}(\mathbf{x}). \qquad (11)$$

This neatly parallels the fact that $\mathbf{f} = -k_s\frac{\partial\mathbf{C}(\mathbf{x})}{\partial\mathbf{x}}\mathbf{C}(\mathbf{x})$.

Given the condition functions $\mathbf{C}$ we have defined in this section for stretch, bend and shear forces, we can now add accompanying damping forces by applying equation (11). As before, $\mathbf{d}_i$ is nonzero only for those particles that $\mathbf{C}$ depends on, and $\partial \mathbf{d}/\partial \mathbf{x}$ has the same sparsity pattern as $\partial \mathbf{f}/\partial \mathbf{x}$. Differentiating equation (11), we obtain

$$\frac{\partial \mathbf{d}_i}{\partial \mathbf{x}_j} = -k_d \left(\frac{\partial \mathbf{C}(\mathbf{x})}{\partial \mathbf{x}_i} \frac{\partial \dot{\mathbf{C}}(\mathbf{x})}{\partial \mathbf{x}_j}^T + \frac{\partial^2 \mathbf{C}(\mathbf{x})}{\partial \mathbf{x}_i \partial \mathbf{x}_j} \dot{\mathbf{C}}(\mathbf{x}) \right). \quad (12)$$

Note that $\partial \mathbf{d}/\partial \mathbf{x}$ is *not* a second derivative of some function as was the case in equation (8) so we cannot expect $\partial \mathbf{d}/\partial \mathbf{x}$ to be symmetrical. In equation (12), it is the term $(\partial \mathbf{C}(\mathbf{x})/\partial \mathbf{x}_i)(\partial \dot{\mathbf{C}}(\mathbf{x})/\partial \mathbf{x}_j)^T$ which breaks the symmetry. Anticipating section 5.2, we find it expedient simply to leave this term out, thereby restoring symmetry. This simplification is clearly not physically justifiable, but we have not observed any ill effects from this omission. (Omitting *all* of equation (12), however, causes serious problems.)

Finally, equation (6) requires the derivative $\partial \mathbf{d}/\partial \mathbf{v}$. Since $\dot{\mathbf{C}}(\mathbf{x}) = (\partial \mathbf{C}(\mathbf{x})/\partial \mathbf{x})^T \mathbf{v}$, we have

$$\frac{\partial \dot{\mathbf{C}}(\mathbf{x})}{\partial \mathbf{v}} = \frac{\partial}{\partial \mathbf{v}} \left(\frac{\partial \mathbf{C}(\mathbf{x})}{\partial \mathbf{x}}^T \mathbf{v} \right) = \frac{\partial \mathbf{C}(\mathbf{x})}{\partial \mathbf{x}}.$$

Using this fact, we can write

$$\frac{\partial \mathbf{d}_i}{\partial \mathbf{v}_j} = -k_d \frac{\partial \mathbf{C}(\mathbf{x})}{\partial \mathbf{x}_i} \frac{\partial \dot{\mathbf{C}}(\mathbf{x})}{\partial \mathbf{v}_j}^T = -k_d \frac{\partial \mathbf{C}(\mathbf{x})}{\partial \mathbf{x}_i} \frac{\partial \mathbf{C}(\mathbf{x})}{\partial \mathbf{x}_j}^T.$$

In this case, the result is symmetrical without dropping any terms.

5 Constraints

In this section, we describe how constraints are imposed on individual cloth particles. The constraints we discuss in this section are either automatically determined by the user (such as geometric attachment constraints on a particle) or are contact constraints (generated by the system) between a solid object and a particle. The techniques we describe in this section could be used for multi-particle constraints; however, constraints that share particle would need to be merged. Thus, a set of four-particle constraints (such as vertex/triangle or edge/edge contacts in the cloth) might merge to form a single constraint on arbitrarily many particles, which would be expensive to maintain. Because of this, we handle cloth/cloth contacts with strong springs (easily dealt with, given the simulator's underlying implicit integration base) and "position alteration," a technique described in section 6.

At any given step of the simulation, a cloth particle is either completely unconstrained (though subject to forces), or the particle may be constrained in either one, two or three dimensions. Given the differential nature of our formulation, it is the particle's acceleration, or equivalently, the change in the particle's velocity, that is constrained. If the particle is constrained in all three dimensions, then we are explicitly setting the particle's velocity (at the next step). If the constraint is in two or one dimensions, we are constraining the particle's velocity along either two or one mutually orthogonal axes. Before describing our constraint method, we discuss several other possible enforcement mechanisms and explain why we chose not to use them.

Reduced Coordinates

An obvious and quite exact method for constraining a particle is to reduce the number of coordinates describing the particle's position and velocity. A completely constrained particle would have no coordinates, while a particle with one dimension of constraint would have two coordinates. This is possible—but it complicates the system immensely. If we change the number of coordinates per particle, we alter the size of the derivative matrices in equation (6), as well as the sparsity pattern (this happens when a particle changes from having no coordinates to some coordinates, or vice versa). Given the transient nature of contact constraints between cloth and solids, this is most unappealing. The computation of the derivative matrices' entries is also greatly complicated, because we must now introduce extra Jacobian matrices that relate a particle's reduced coordinates to its motion in world-space. Finally, correct constraint-release behavior between cloth and solid objects is difficult to achieve using a reduced coordinate formulation. Considering all of this, we immediately rejected this method of constraints.

Penalty Methods

We could constrain particles through the use of strong energy functions—essentially, stiff springs that attempt to prevent illegal particle motions. Since our entire formulation is geared to handle stiffness, the usual objections to enforcing constraints with springs—very stiff equations—do not carry as much weight. We tried this for a time, and found it to be a not unreasonable constraint enforcement mechanism. However, penalty methods do not enforce constraints exactly, and they do add some additional stiffness to the system. Since the mechanism we describe enforces constraints exactly, and adds no extra stiffness, we turned away from penalty methods except in the case of cloth/cloth interactions.

Lagrange Multipliers

We could introduce additional constraint forces—that is, Lagrange multipliers—into our system to satisfy the constraints. This involves augmenting the linear system of equation (6) with extra variables (the multipliers) and extra equations (the constraint conditions). Unfortunately, this turns a positive definite system into an indefinite system, which means that iterative methods such as CG will need to square the system first, thereby doubling the running time and degrading the numerical conditioning of the linear system. Additionally, an iterative method will generally not enforce the constraints exactly without a large number of iterations. (A direct method for solving the augmented system would, however, avoid this problem.) Again, the constraint method we describe steps past these difficulties, so we turned away from using Lagrange multipliers.

5.1 Mass Modification

The idea behind our constraint enforcement mechanism is described quite simply, although the actual implementation is somewhat more complicated, to maximize performance. A dynamic simulation usually requires knowledge of the *inverse* mass of objects; for example, note the appearance of $\mathbf{M}^{-1}$, and not $\mathbf{M}$ in equation (6). In the case of a single particle, we write $\ddot{\mathbf{x}}_i = \frac{1}{m_i} \mathbf{f}_i$ to describe a particle's acceleration. When inverse mass is used, it becomes trivial to enforce constraints by altering the mass.

Suppose for example that we want to keep particle i's velocity from changing. If we take $1/m_i$ to be zero, we give the particle an infinite mass, making it ignore all forces exerted on it. Complete control over a particle's acceleration is thus taken care of by storing a value of zero for the particle's inverse mass. What if we wish to constrain the particle's acceleration in only one or two dimensions? Although we normally think of a particle's mass as a scalar, we need not always do so. Suppose we write $\ddot{\mathbf{x}}_i = \begin{pmatrix} 1/m_i & 0 & 0 \\ 0 & 1/m_i & 0 \\ 0 & 0 & 0 \end{pmatrix} \mathbf{f}_i$. Now $\ddot{\mathbf{x}}_i$

must lie in the xy plane; no acceleration in the z direction is possible. Note than an unconstrained particle can be considered to have the 3×3 inverse mass matrix $\frac{1}{m_i}\mathbf{I}$, with $\mathbf{I}$ the identity matrix.

Of course, we are not restricted to coordinate-aligned constraints. More generally, given a unit vector $\mathbf{p} \in \mathbf{R}^3$, a particle is prevented from accelerating along $\mathbf{p}$ by using an inverse mass matrix $\frac{1}{m_i}(\mathbf{I} - \mathbf{pp}^T)$; this follows from the fact that $(\mathbf{I} - \mathbf{pp}^T)\mathbf{p} = \mathbf{0}$. Similarly, given two mutually orthogonal unit vectors $\mathbf{p}$ and $\mathbf{q}$, we prevent a particle from accelerating in either the $\mathbf{p}$ or $\mathbf{q}$ direction by using the inverse mass matrix $\frac{1}{m_i}(\mathbf{I} - \mathbf{pp}^T - \mathbf{qq}^T)$.

By allowing constrained particles to have these sorts of inverse masses, we can build constraints directly into equation (6). We will create a modified version $\mathbf{W}$ of $\mathbf{M}^{-1}$; $\mathbf{W}$ will be a block-diagonal matrix, with off-diagonal blocks being zero, and diagonal blocks defined as follows: let ndof(i) indicate the number of degrees of freedom particle i has, and let particle i's prohibited directions be $\mathbf{p}_i$ (if ndof(i) = 2) or $\mathbf{p}_i$ and $\mathbf{q}_i$ (if ndof(i) = 1) with $\mathbf{p}_i$ and $\mathbf{q}_i$ mutually orthogonal unit vectors. $\mathbf{W}$'s diagonal blocks are $\mathbf{W}_{ii} = \frac{1}{m_i}\mathbf{S}_i$ where

$$
\mathbf{S}_i = \begin{cases} \mathbf{I} & \text{if ndof}(i) = 3 \\ (\mathbf{I} - \mathbf{p}_i\mathbf{p}_i^T) & \text{if ndof}(i) = 2 \\ (\mathbf{I} - \mathbf{p}_i\mathbf{p}_i^T - \mathbf{q}_i\mathbf{q}_i^T) & \text{if ndof}(i) = 1 \\ \mathbf{0} & \text{if ndof}(i) = 0. \end{cases} \tag{13}
$$

We are not limited to constraining particles to have zero accelerations in certain directions; rather, we control exactly *what* the change in velocity is along the constrained directions. For every particle i, let $\mathbf{z}_i$ be the change in velocity we wish to enforce in the particle's constrained direction(s). (This implies we can choose any value of $\mathbf{z}_i$ for a completely constrained particle, since all directions are constrained; an unconstrained particle must have $\mathbf{z}_i = \mathbf{0}$ since it has *no* constrained directions.) Using $\mathbf{W}$ and $\mathbf{z}$, we rewrite equation (6) to directly enforce constraints. If we solve

$$
\left(\mathbf{I} - h\mathbf{W}\frac{\partial \mathbf{f}}{\partial \mathbf{v}} - h^2\mathbf{W}\frac{\partial \mathbf{f}}{\partial \mathbf{x}}\right)\Delta\mathbf{v} = h\mathbf{W}\left(\mathbf{f}_0 + h\frac{\partial \mathbf{f}}{\partial \mathbf{x}}\mathbf{v}_0\right) + \mathbf{z} \tag{14}
$$

for $\Delta\mathbf{v}$, we will obtain a $\Delta\mathbf{v}$ which is consistent with our constraints. Completely constrained particles will have $\Delta\mathbf{v}_i = \mathbf{z}_i$, while partially constrained particles will have a $\Delta\mathbf{v}_i$ whose component in the constrained direction(s) is equal to $\mathbf{z}_i$.

5.2 Implementation

We initially implemented constraints using equation (14) and found that it worked exactly as advertised. For very small test systems, we solved equation (14) using a direct method (Gaussian elimination) without any problems. For larger systems, we planned to use the iterative, sparsity-exploiting CG method, which immediately presents us with a problem: equation (14) is not a symmetric linear system. (For that matter, neither is equation (6) unless all particles have the same mass.) CG methods, however, require symmetric matrices.[6] We *could* apply a CG method to the unsymmetric matrix of equation (14) by use of the "normal equations"; but this involves multiplying the matrix of equation (14) with its transpose which doubles the cost of each iteration while squaring the condition number of the system [14]—a less than desirable plan. We decided that using a CG method to solve the unsymmetric problem was not acceptable.

Note that without constraints, applying a CG method to equation (6) is not difficult, because we can transform this equation to

---

[6] In fact, they work best on positive definite symmetric matrices. The matrices we ultimately hand to our CG method are positive definite.

a symmetric (and positive definite) system by left-multiplying the entire equation by $\mathbf{M}$: the system

$$
\left(\mathbf{M} - h\frac{\partial \mathbf{f}}{\partial \mathbf{v}} - h^2\frac{\partial \mathbf{f}}{\partial \mathbf{x}}\right)\Delta\mathbf{v} = h\left(\mathbf{f}_0 + h\frac{\partial \mathbf{f}}{\partial \mathbf{x}}\mathbf{v}_0\right) \tag{15}
$$

is symmetric and has the same solution $\Delta\mathbf{v}$ as equation (6). Unfortunately, we cannot apply the same transformation to equation (14), because $\mathbf{W}$ is singular—the filtering blocks in equation (13) are rank deficient—so we cannot multiply through by $\mathbf{W}^{-1}$.

The solution to the problem of asymmetry is to modify the CG method so that it can operate on equation (15), while procedurally applying the constraints inherent in the matrix $\mathbf{W}$ at each iteration. The modified method will need to know about the particles' constraints and the vector $\mathbf{z}$. Let us define the symmetric positive definite matrix $\mathbf{A}$ by

$$
\mathbf{A} = \left(\mathbf{M} - h\frac{\partial \mathbf{f}}{\partial \mathbf{v}} - h^2\frac{\partial \mathbf{f}}{\partial \mathbf{x}}\right) \tag{16}
$$

and the vector $\mathbf{b}$ and residual vector $\mathbf{r}$ as

$$
\mathbf{b} = h\left(\mathbf{f}_0 + h\frac{\partial \mathbf{f}}{\partial \mathbf{x}}\mathbf{v}_0\right) \qquad \text{and} \qquad \mathbf{r} = \mathbf{A}\Delta\mathbf{v} - \mathbf{b}.
$$

Given $\mathbf{A}$, $\mathbf{b}$, constraints on the particles, and $\mathbf{z}$, our modified CG method will try to find $\Delta\mathbf{v}$ that satisfies two conditions:

- For each particle i, the component of $\mathbf{r}_i$ in the particle's *unconstrained* direction(s) will be made equal to zero (assuming the method is run for sufficiently many iterations).

- For each particle i, the component of $\Delta\mathbf{v}_i$ in the particle's *constrained* direction(s) will be exactly $\mathbf{z}_i$ (no matter how many iterations are taken).

Note that these two conditions imply that unconstrained particles have $\mathbf{r}_i$ close to zero, while completely constrained particles have $\Delta\mathbf{v}_i = \mathbf{z}_i$. Thus in the case when no particles are constrained, our modified CG method should produce the same result as the regular CG method.

5.3 The Modified Conjugate Gradient Method

The CG method (technically, the preconditioned CG method) takes a symmetric positive semi-definite matrix $\mathbf{A}$, a symmetric positive definite preconditioning matrix $\mathbf{P}$ of the same dimension as $\mathbf{A}$, a vector $\mathbf{b}$ and iteratively solves $\mathbf{A}\Delta\mathbf{v} = \mathbf{b}$. The iteration stops when $\|\mathbf{b} - \mathbf{A}\Delta\mathbf{v}\|$ is less than $\epsilon\|\mathbf{b}\|$ where ϵ is a user-defined tolerance value. The preconditioning matrix $\mathbf{P}$, which must be easily invertible, speeds convergence to the extent that $\mathbf{P}^{-1}$ approximates $\mathbf{A}$. We wholeheartedly refer the reader to Shewchuk [14] for information on the CG method.

We derive our modified conjugate gradient method by observing that the effect of the matrix $\mathbf{W}$ in equation (14) is to filter out velocity changes in the constrained directions. Our idea then is to define an invariant— for all i, the component of $\Delta\mathbf{v}_i$ in the constrained direction(s) of particle i is equal to $\mathbf{z}_i$—and then establish and maintain the invariant at each iteration, by defining a filtering procedure **filter**. The role of **filter** is to take a vector $\mathbf{a}$ and perform the same filtering operation (see equation (13)) as multiplying by $\mathbf{W}$, but leaving out the scaling by $1/m_i$:

```
procedure filter(a)
for i = 1 to n
    âᵢ = Sᵢaᵢ
return â
```

Using **filter**, we define the modified CG method **modified-pcg** as follows:

```
1      procedure modified-pcg
2      Δv = z
3      δ₀ = filter(b)ᵀP filter(b)
4      r = filter(b − AΔv)
5      c = filter(P⁻¹r)
6      δnew = rᵀc
7      while δnew > ε²δ₀
8          q = filter(Ac)
9          α = δnew/(cᵀq)
10         Δv = Δv + αc
11         r = r − αq
12         s = P⁻¹r
13         δold = δnew
14         δnew = rᵀs
15         c = filter(s + (δnew/δold)c)
```

Line 2 of the procedure establishes our invariant. Lines 5 and 15 maintain the invariant by filtering $\mathbf{c}$ before adding it to $\Delta\mathbf{v}$. The unmodified conjugate gradient method establishes a stopping criterion based on $\mathbf{b}^T\mathbf{Pb}$. Since our constrained formulation ignores certain components of $\mathbf{b}$, our stopping criterion should as well, so we add filtering to line 3. The vector $\mathbf{r}$ measures the solution error $\mathbf{b} - \mathbf{A}\Delta\mathbf{v}$, and should not include error due to the constraints; hence we add filtering at lines 4 and 8. (Note that removing the calls to **filter** and changing line 2 to $\Delta\mathbf{v} = \mathbf{0}$ yields the standard preconditioned conjugate gradient method.)

We use a simple preconditioner $\mathbf{P}$ by making $\mathbf{P}$ be a diagonal matrix with $\mathbf{P}_{ii} = 1/\mathbf{A}_{ii}$ so products involving $\mathbf{P}^{-1}$ are trivially computed. More elaborate preconditioners could be used, though we doubt there is a large speedup to be gained. Matrix-vector products with $\mathbf{A}$ are of course implemented in sparse matrix-vector fashion, using the data structures defined in section 2.3.

Given **modified-pcg**, obvious questions are "does it work?" followed by "how does it compare with the unmodified CG method?" Proofs about CG methods are difficult in general; in practice, our method always converges, which answers the first question. Prior to implementing **modified-pcg**, we used a penalty method and applied the standard CG method to equation (15). When we began using procedure **modified-pcg**, we did not notice any substantial change in the number of iterations required by the method. Empirically, we conclude that the two methods have similar convergence behavior. Result in section 8 indicate that the running time is close to $O(n^{1.5})$, which is what unmodified CG would be expected to deliver on this sort of problem [14].

5.4 Determining the Constraint Forces

For contact constraints (between cloth and solid objects) we need to know what the actual force of constraint is, in order to determine when to terminate a constraint. Additionally, we need to know the constraint force actually exerted in order to model frictional forces properly. Fortunately, it is easy to add one more step to **modified-pcg** to determine the constraint force. When **modified-pcg** terminates, the residual error $\mathbf{e} = \mathbf{A}\Delta\mathbf{v} - \mathbf{b}$ has the property that $\mathbf{e}_i$ need not be close to zero if particle i is constrained. In fact, $\mathbf{e}_i$ is exactly the extra constraint force that must have been supplied to enforce the constraint. Thus, we can compute constraint forces at the end of **modified-pcg** by performing one last matrix-vector product to compute $\mathbf{A}\Delta\mathbf{v} - \mathbf{b}$. (The vector $\mathbf{r}$ in **modified-pcg** is equal to **filter**$(\mathbf{A}\Delta\mathbf{v} - \mathbf{b})$, so the extra matrix-vector product to compute $\mathbf{e}$ really is necessary.)

The particles' accelerations are inherently dependent on one another through the matrix $\mathbf{A}$ of equation (16). This means that the correct approach to determing constraint release is combinatoric, as in Baraff [2]. We reject this approach as impractical given the dimension of $\mathbf{A}$. Instead, we allow contacts to release when the constraint force between a particle and a solid switches from a repulsive force to an attractive one. In practice, this has proven to work well.

Friction presents a similar problem. When cloth contacts a solid, we lock the particle onto the surface, if the relative tangential velocity is low. We monitor the constraint force, and if the tangential force exceeds some fraction of the normal force, we allow the particle to slide on the surface. For high sliding velocities, we apply a dissipative tangential force, opposite the relative sliding direction, proportional to the normal force.

6 Collisions

Much has been written about collision detection for cloth; we have nothing substantial to add to the subject of collision detection *per se*. Cloth/cloth collisions are detected by checking pairs (p, t) and (e_1, e_2) for intersections, where p and t are a cloth particle and a cloth triangle respectively, and e_1 and e_2 are edges of cloth triangles. Given a previous known legal state of the cloth, we postulate a linear motion for the cloth particles to the current (possibly illegal) state and check for either particle/triangle or edge/edge crossings. To avoid $O(n^2)$ comparisons, we use a coherency-based bounding-box approach [1] to cull out the majority of pairs.

When collisions between a cloth vertex and triangle, or two cloth edges are detected, we insert a strong damped spring force to push the cloth apart. A dissipative force tangent to the contact is also applied, countering any sliding motion. The force is not, strictly speaking, a frictional force: rather it is proportional to the slip velocity, so it is in actuality a damping force, although it reasonably emulates dynamic friction. Applying static friction forces to cloth contacts is far more difficult, and is a problem we have not solved yet. The forces, and their derivatives with respect to position and velocity, are of course included in equation (15).

Our system detects collisions between cloth particles and solid objects by testing each individual cloth particle against the faces of each solid object. A solid object's faces are grouped in a hierarchical bounding box tree, with the leaves of the tree being individual faces of the solid. The tree is created by a simple recursive splitting along coordinate axes. The maintenance of contacts and the application of friction forces was described in the previous section.

6.1 Constraint Initiation

Both cloth/cloth and cloth/solid collisions give rise to the same problem whenever two contacts form. For both types of collisions, our detection algorithm reports an intersection, and then takes action to remedy the situation: either by enforcing a constraint (cloth/solid collisions) or by adding a penalty force (cloth/cloth) collisions. However, since our simulator proceeds in discrete steps, collisions resulting in a reasonably substantial interpenetration depth can occur between one step and the next. Clearly, this situation needs to be remedied.

For cloth/cloth collisions, this would not appear to be a problem: the spring forces that are added work to counter the colliding velocities and then push the cloth apart. For cloth/solid collisions, however, the situation is more complicated. If we simply enforce a constraint which causes the colliding cloth particle to have a velocity consistent with the solid object's velocity, and continue to enforce that constraint, the cloth particle will continue to remain embedded somewhere below the solid object's surface. This is unacceptable.

One solution is to use Baumgarte stabilization [18], which schedules the particle's acceleration so that the position and velocity error of the particle with respect to the surface decay asymptotically to zero. We experimented with this technique, but found it lacking. In particular, a fast rise to the surface was prone to noise and "jumpiness"; this could be eliminated, but at the cost of decreasing the step size. A slower rise to the surface caused visual artifacts.

We tried a simpler solution: when intersections occurred, rather than wait for a scheduled constraint or a penalty force to eliminate the intersection, we simply altered the positions of the cloth particles, effecting an instantaneous (and discontinuous) change in position. While this would be problematic when using a multi-step differential equation solver which expects continuity (such as a Runge-Kutta method), it should not interfere with a one-step solver such as the backward Euler method. Unfortunately, simply changing particle positions produced disastrous results. The stretch energy term in a cloth system is extremely strong, and altering particle positions arbitrarily introduced excessively large deformation energies in an altered particle's neighborhood. This resulted in visibly "jumpy" behavior of the cloth in localized regions.

6.2 Position Alteration

Despite its initial failure, the ability to make arbitrary small changes in a particle's position continued to attract our attention. The entire process of implicit integration can be considered to be a filtering process [7], and we postulated that a mechanism for filtering energy changes caused by displacing particles might make position alteration a viable technique. We considered that perhaps some sort of extra implicit step could be used as a filter, but forming and solving an additional linear system at each step seemed too expensive. Happily, we can make use of the filtering effect of implicit integration without any extra work.

Consider a particle that has collided with a solid object. The particle's change in velocity at each step is under our control, using the constraint techniques described in section 5. Meanwhile, the particle's *position* at the next step follows from equation (4):

$$\Delta \mathbf{x}_i = h(\mathbf{v}_{0_i} + \Delta \mathbf{v}_i)$$

(recall that $\mathbf{v}_{0_i}$ is the particle's current velocity). The reason that changing positions *after* a step has been taken doesn't work is because the particle's neighbors receive no advance notification of the change in position: they are confronted with the alteration at the beginning of the next step. This presents an obvious solution: we simply modify the top row of equation (4) to

$$\Delta \mathbf{x}_i = h(\mathbf{v}_{0_i} + \Delta \mathbf{v}_i) + \mathbf{y}_i \qquad (17)$$

where $\mathbf{y}_i$ is an arbitrary correction term of our choice, introduced solely to move a particle to a desired location during the backward Euler step. Having modified the top row of equation (4), we must follow this change through: using equation (17) and repeating the derivation of section 3 and the symmetric transform from section 5 yields the modified symmetric system

$$\left(\mathbf{M} - h\frac{\partial \mathbf{f}}{\partial \mathbf{v}} - h^2 \frac{\partial \mathbf{f}}{\partial \mathbf{x}} \right) \Delta \mathbf{v} = h \left(\mathbf{f}_0 + h\frac{\partial \mathbf{f}}{\partial \mathbf{x}}\mathbf{v}_0 + \frac{\partial \mathbf{f}}{\partial \mathbf{x}}\mathbf{y} \right). \qquad (18)$$

This modification gives us complete control over both the position and velocity of a constrained particle in just one step, without any extra computational cost. We use this technique to bring particles quickly and stably to the surface of solid objects without creating visual artifacts or limiting the allowable step size. We can also add correction terms to particles involved in cloth/cloth collisions. Without a constraint on those particles' velocities there is no guarantee that they will go exactly where we want in one step, but the ability to induce sizeable jumps in position without excessively stiff spring forces adds greatly to the stability of the simulation.

7 Adaptive Time Stepping

The methods introduced in all of the previous sections usually allow us to take sizeable steps forward, without loss of stability. Even so, there are still times when the step size must be reduced to avoid divergence. There are a large number of methods for altering the size of a time step, for both explicit and implicit integrators, but these methods tend to concentrate on the accuracy of the simulation, and not the stability. Our goal is animation, not engineering; thus visually pleasing results, meaning a numerically stable solution, rather than overall accuracy, is the deciding voice. The trick is to recognize instability before you see it on your screen—by then it's too late.

Stiffness, and thus any potential instability, arises almost completely from the strong stretch forces in the cloth. After each implicit step, we treat the resulting $\Delta \mathbf{x}$ as a proposed change in the cloth's state, and examine the stretch terms (section 4.2) for each triangle in the newly proposed state. If any triangle undergoes a drastic change in its stretch (in either the u or v direction) we discard the proposed state, reduce the step size, and try again. Subtlety is not required: we find that an unstable step invariably results in stretch changes that are quite large, and are thus easily detected.

Our simulation is run with a parameter that indicates the maximum allowable step size: this parameter is set by the user, and is always less than or equal to one frame. (Most of our simulations involving human motions use a step size of 0.02 seconds.) Whenever the simulator reduces the step size, after two successes with the reduced step size the simulator tries to increase the step size. If the simulator fails at the larger step size, it reduces the size again, and waits for a longer period of time before retrying to increase the step size. At its limit, the simulator will try increasing the step size every 40 steps; thus, if the user chooses too large a step, the simulator settles down to wasting only one out of every 40 steps in attempting too large a step. This method, though simple, has served us well.

8 Results

Table 1 gives a performance summary of assorted animations, shown in figures 1–6. Unaccounted overhead of the simulation (typically about 5%) includes tasks such as geometry transformations, memory allocation, etc. The clothes in figures 3–6 were modeled as discrete planar panels, and then topologically seamed. The simulator was used to relax the clothing from an initial deformed state, that got the clothes around the characters, to a well-fitting state on the characters. The b_u and b_v parameters (see equation (10)) were then made smaller in certain regions to produce cuffs and waistbands, or strategically increased to induce wrinkling behavior in other regions.

We also ran the simulation in figure 1 with a range of stiffnesses for the bend term. Using the stiffness parameters in figure 1 as a reference, we ran the simulation with those bend stiffnesses multiplied by 0.1, 1.0, 10, 100 and 1,000 (for a total range of 10,000 in the stiffness). The variance in the running times was under 5%. We doubt that simulators based on explicit integration methods could make a similar claim.

Finally, we tried to estimate our simulator's performance as a function of n, the number of cloth particles. We ran the simulation in figure 1 with cloth resolutions of 500, 899, 2,602 (shown in figure 1) and 7,359 particles. The running times were, respectively, 0.23 seconds/frame, 0.46 seconds/frame, 2.23 seconds/frame, and 10.3 seconds/frame. This is slightly better than $O(n^{1.5})$ performance, which is in line with the convergence rates of the conjugate gradient method [14] for systems such as equation (18).

figure		no. vertices/no. triangles		time/frame	step size	total frames/	task breakdown percentage			
		cloth	solid	(CPU sec.)	min/max (ms)	total steps	EVAL	CG	C/C	C/S
1		2,602/4,9442	322/640	2.23	16.5/33	75/80	25.7	50.4	18.3	1.4
2		2,602/4,9442	322/640	3.06	16.5/33	75/80	17.9	63.6	15.3	0.2
3		6,450/12,654	9,941/18,110	7.32	16.5/33	50/52	18.9	37.9	30.9	2.6
4	(shirt)	6,450/12,654	9,941/18,110	14.5	2.5/20	430/748	16.7	29.9	46.1	2.2
	(pants)	8,757/17,352	9,941/18,110	38.5	0.625/20	430/1214	16.4	35.7	42.5	1.7
5	(skirt)	2,153/4,020	7,630/14,008	3.68	5/20	393/715	18.1	30.0	44.5	1.5
	(blouse)	5,108/10,016	7,630/14,008	16.7	5/20	393/701	11.2	26.0	57.7	1.3
6	(skirt)	4,530/8,844	7,630/14,008	10.2	10/20	393/670	20.1	36.8	29.7	2.6
	(blouse)	5,188/10,194	7,630/14,008	16.6	1.25/20	393/753	13.2	30.9	50.2	1.4

Table 1: System performance for simulations in figures 1–6. Minimum and maximum time steps are in milliseconds of simulation time. Time/frame indicates actual CPU time for each frame, averaged over the simulation. Percentages of total running time are given for four tasks: EVAL— forming the linear system of equation (18); CG—solving equation (18); C/C—cloth/cloth collision detection; and C/S—cloth/solid collision detection.

9 Acknowledgments

This research was supported in part by an ONR Young Investigator award, an NSF CAREER award, and grants from the Intel Corporation. We thank Alias|Wavefront for supplying the models and motion capture data used in figures 5 and 6.

References

[1] D. Baraff. *Dynamic Simulation of Non-penetrating Rigid Bodies*. PhD thesis, Cornell University, May 1992.

[2] D. Baraff. Fast contact force computation for nonpenetrating rigid bodies. *Computer Graphics (Proc. SIGGRAPH)*, 28:23–34, 1994.

[3] D.E. Breen, D.H. House, and M.J. Wozny. Predicting the drape of woven cloth using interacting particles. *Computer Graphics (Proc. SIGGRAPH)*, pages 365–372, 1994.

[4] M. Carignan, Y. Yang, N. Magenenat-Thalmann, and D. Thalmann. Dressing animated synthetic actors with complex deformable clothes. *Computer Graphics (Proc. SIGGRAPH)*, pages 99–104, 1992.

[5] B. Eberhardt, A. Weber, and W. Strasser. A fast, flexible, particle-system model for cloth draping. *IEEE Computer Graphics and Applications*, 16:52–59, 1996.

[6] G. Golub and C. Van Loan. *Matrix Computations*. John Hopkins University Press, 1983.

[7] M. Kass. *An Introduction To Physically Based Modeling*, chapter Introduction to Continuum Dynamics for Computer Graphics. SIGGRAPH Course Notes, ACM SIGGRAPH, 1995.

[8] M. Kass and G. Miller. Rapid, stable fluid dynamics for computer graphics. *Computer Graphics (Proc. SIGGRAPH)*, pages 49–58, 1990.

[9] H.N. Ng and R.L. Grimsdale. Computer graphics techniques for modeling cloth. *IEEE Computer Graphics and Applications*, 16:28–41, 1996.

[10] H. Okabe, H. Imaoka, T. Tomiha, and H. Niwaya. Three dimensional apparel cad system. *Computer Graphics (Proc. SIGGRAPH)*, pages 105–110, 1992.

[11] J.C. Platt and A.H. Barr. Constraint methods for flexible models. In *Computer Graphics (Proc. SIGGRAPH)*, volume 22, pages 279–288. ACM, July 1988.

[12] W.H. Press, B.P. Flannery, S.A. Teukolsky, and W.T. Vetterling. *Numerical Recipes*. Cambridge University Press, 1986.

[13] X. Provot. Deformation constraints in a mass-spring model to describe rigid cloth behavior. In *Graphics Interface*, pages 147–155, 1995.

[14] J. Shewchuk. An introduction to the conjugate gradient method without the agonizing pain. Technical Report CMU-CS-TR-94-125, Carnegie Mellon University, 1994. (See also http://www.cs.cmu.edu/~quake-papers/ painless-conjugate-gradient.ps.).

[15] D. Terzopoulos and K. Fleischer. Deformable models. *Visual Computer*, 4:306–331, 1988.

[16] D. Terzopoulos and K. Fleischer. Modeling inelastic deformation: Viscoelasticity, plasticity, fracture. In *Computer Graphics (Proc. SIGGRAPH)*, volume 22, pages 269–278. ACM, August 1988.

[17] D. Terzopoulos, J.C. Platt, and A.H. Barr. Elastically deformable models. *Computer Graphics (Proc. SIGGRAPH)*, 21:205–214, 1987.

[18] D. Terzopoulos and H. Qin. Dynamics nurbs with geometric constraints for interactive sculpting. *ACM Transactions on Graphics*, 13:103–136, 1994.

[19] X. Tu. *Artificial Animals for Computer Animation: Biomechanics, Locomotion, Perception and Behavior*. PhD thesis, University of Toronto, May 1996.

[20] P. Volino, M. Courchesne, and N. Magnenat Thalmann. Versatile and efficient techniques for simulating cloth and other deformable objects. *Computer Graphics (Proc. SIGGRAPH)*, pages 137–144, 1995.

[21] P. Volino, N. Magnenat Thalmann, S. Jianhua, and D. Thalmann. An evolving system for simulating clothes on virtual actors. *IEEE Computer Graphics and Applications*, 16:42–51, 1996.

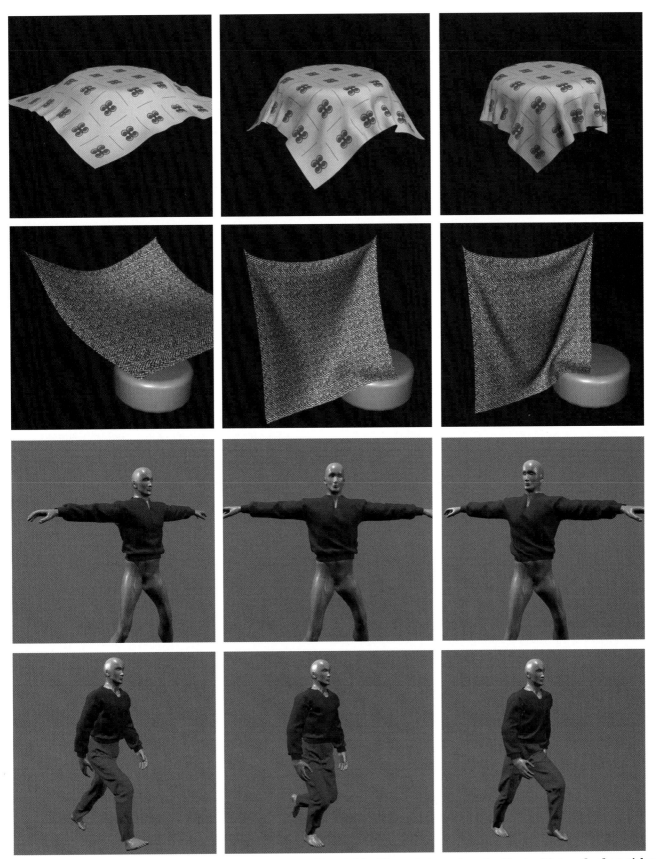

Figure 1 (top row): Cloth draping on cylinder; frames 8, 13 and 35. **Figure 2 (second row):** Sheet with two fixed particles; frames 10, 29 and 67. **Figure 3 (third row):** Shirt on twisting figure; frames 1, 24 and 46. **Figure 4 (bottom row):** Walking man; frames 30, 45 and 58.

Figure 5 (top row): Dancer with short skirt; frames 110, 136 and 155. Figure 6 (middle row): Dancer with long skirt; frames 185, 215 and 236. Figure 7 (bottom row): Closeups from figures 4 and 6.

Making Faces

Brian Guenter[†]   Cindy Grimm[†]   Daniel Wood[‡]
Henrique Malvar[†]   Fredrick Pighin[‡]
[†]**Microsoft Corporation**   [‡]**University of Washington**

ABSTRACT

We have created a system for capturing both the three-dimensional geometry and color and shading information for human facial expressions. We use this data to reconstruct photorealistic, 3D animations of the captured expressions. The system uses a large set of sampling points on the face to accurately track the three dimensional deformations of the face. Simultaneously with the tracking of the geometric data, we capture multiple high resolution, registered video images of the face. These images are used to create a texture map sequence for a three dimensional polygonal face model which can then be rendered on standard 3D graphics hardware. The resulting facial animation is surprisingly life-like and looks very much like the original live performance. Separating the capture of the geometry from the texture images eliminates much of the variance in the image data due to motion, which increases compression ratios. Although the primary emphasis of our work is not compression we have investigated the use of a novel method to compress the geometric data based on principal components analysis. The texture sequence is compressed using an MPEG4 video codec. Animations reconstructed from 512x512 pixel textures look good at data rates as low as 240 Kbits per second.

CR Categories: I.3.7 [Computer Graphics]: Three Dimensional Graphics and Realism: Animation; I.3.5 [Computer Graphics]: Computational Geometry and Object Modeling

1   Introduction

One of the most elusive goals in computer animation has been the realistic animation of the human face. Possessed of many degrees of freedom and capable of deforming in many ways the face has been difficult to simulate accurately enough to convince the average person that a piece of computer animation is actually an image of a real person.

We have created a system for capturing human facial expression and replaying it as a highly realistic 3D "talking head" consisting of a deformable 3D polygonal face model with a changing texture map. The process begins with video of a live actor's face, recorded from multiple camera positions simultaneously. Fluorescent colored 1/8" circular paper fiducials are glued on the actor's face and their 3D position reconstructed over time as the actor talks and emotes. The 3D fiducial positions are used to distort a 3D polygonal face model in mimicry of the distortions of the real face. The fiducials are removed using image processing techniques and the video streams from the multiple cameras are merged into a single texture map. When the resulting fiducial-free texture map is applied to the 3D reconstructed face mesh the result is a remarkably life-like 3D animation of facial expression. Both the time varying texture created from the video streams and the accurate reproduction of the 3D face structure contribute to the believability of the resulting animation.

Our system differs from much previous work in facial animation, such as that of Lee [10], Waters [14], and Cassel [3], in that we are not synthesizing animations using a physical or procedural model of the face. Instead, we capture facial movements in three dimensions and then replay them. The systems of [10], [14] are designed to make it relatively easy to animate facial expression manually. The system of [3] is designed to automatically create a dialog rather than faithfully reconstruct a particular person's facial expression. The work of Williams [15] is most similar to ours except that he used a single static texture image of a real person's face and tracked points only in 2D. The work of Bregler et al [2] is somewhat less related. They use speech recognition to locate visemes[1] in a video of a person talking and then synthesize new video, based on the original video sequence, for the mouth and jaw region of the face to correspond with synthetic utterances. They do not create a three dimensional face model nor do they vary the expression on the remainder of the face. Since we are only concerned with capturing and reconstructing facial performances out work is unlike that of [5] which attempts to recognize expressions or that of [4] which can track only a limited set of facial expressions.

An obvious application of this new method is the creation of believable virtual characters for movies and television. Another application is the construction of a flexible type of video compression. Facial expression can be captured in a studio, delivered via CDROM or the internet to a user, and then reconstructed in real time on a user's computer in a virtual 3D environment. The user can select any

---

[1]Visemes are the visual analog of phonemes.

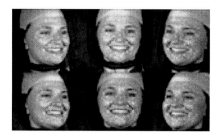

Figure 1: The six camera views of our actress' face.

arbitrary position for the face, any virtual camera viewpoint, and render the result at any size.

One might think the second application would be difficult to achieve because of the huge amount of video data required for the time varying texture map. However, since our system generates accurate 3D deformation information, the texture image data is precisely registered from frame to frame. This reduces most of the variation in image intensity due to geometric motion, leaving primarily shading and self shadowing effects. These effects tend to be of low spatial frequency and can be compressed very efficiently. The compressed animation looks good at data rates of 240 kbits per second for texture image sizes of 512x512 pixels, updating at 30 frames per second.

The main contributions of the paper are a method for robustly capturing both a 3D deformation model and a registered texture image sequence from video data. The resulting geometric and texture data can be compressed, with little loss of fidelity, so that storage requirements are reasonable for many applications.

Section 2 of the paper explains the data capture stage of the process. Section 3 describes the fiducial correspondence algorithm. In Section 4 we discuss capturing and moving the mesh. Sections 5 and 6 describe the process for making the texture maps. Section 7 of the paper describes the algorithm for compressing the geometric data.

2 Data Capture

We used six studio quality video cameras arranged in the pattern shown in Plate 1 to capture the video data. The cameras were synchronized and the data saved digitally. Each of the six cameras was individually calibrated to determine its intrinsic and extrinsic parameters and to correct for lens distortion. The details of the calibration process are not germane to this paper but the interested reader can find a good overview of the topic in [6] as well as an extensive bibliography.

We glued 182 dots of six different colors onto the actress' face. The dots were arranged so that dots of the same color were as far apart as possible from each other and followed the contours of the face. This made the task of determining frame to frame dot correspondence (described in Section 3.3) much easier. The dot pattern was chosen to follow the contours of the face (i.e., outlining the eyes, lips, and nasio-labial furrows), although the manual application of the dots made it difficult to follow the pattern exactly.

The actress' head was kept relatively immobile using a padded foam box; this reduced rigid body motions and ensured that the actress' face stayed centered in the video images. Note that rigid body motions can be captured later using a 3D motion tracker, if desired.

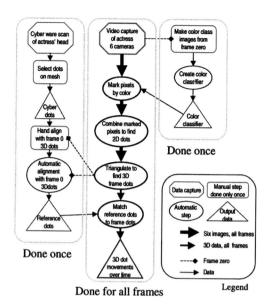

Figure 2: The sequence of operations needed to produce the labeled 3D dot movements over time.

The actress was illuminated with a combination of visible and near UV light. Because the dots were painted with fluorescent pigments the UV illumination increased the brightness of the dots significantly and moved them further away in color space from the colors of the face than they would ordinarily be. This made them easier to track reliably. Before the video shoot the actress' face was digitized using a cyberware scanner. This scan was used to create the base 3D face mesh which was then distorted using the positions of the tracked dots.

3 Dot Labeling

The fiducials are used to generate a set of 3D points which act as control points to warp the cyberware scan mesh of the actress' head. They are also used to establish a stable mapping for the textures generated from each of the six camera views. This requires that each dot have a unique and consistent label over time so that it is associated with a consistent set of mesh vertices.

The dot labeling begins by first locating (for each camera view) connected components of pixels which correspond to the fiducials. The 2D location for each dot is computed by finding the two dimensional centroid of each connected component. Correspondence between 2D dots in different camera views is established and potential 3D locations of dots reconstructed by triangulation. We construct a reference set of dots and pair up this reference set with the 3D locations in each frame. This gives a unique labeling for the dots that is maintained throughout the video sequence.

A flowchart of the dot labeling process is shown in Figure 2. The left side of the flowchart is described in Section 3.3.1, the middle in Sections 3.1, 3.2, and 3.3.2, and the right side in Section 3.1.1.

3.1 Two-dimensional dot location

For each camera view the 2D coordinates of the centroid of each colored fiducial must be computed. There are three

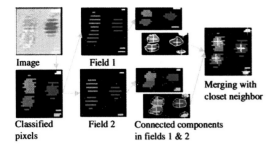

Figure 3: Finding the 2D dots in the images.

steps to this process: color classification, connected color component generation, and centroid computation.

First, each pixel is classified as belonging to one of the six dot colors or to the background. Then depth first search is used to locate connected blobs of similarly colored pixels. Each connected colored blob is grown by one pixel to create a mask used to mark those pixels to be included in the centroid computation. This process is illustrated in Figure 3.

The classifier requires the manual marking of the fiducials for one frame for each of the six cameras. From this data a robust color classifier is created (exact details are discussed in Section 3.1.1). Although the training set was created using a single frame of a 3330 frame sequence, the fiducial colors are reliably labeled throughout the sequence. False positives are quite rare, with one major exception, and are almost always isolated pixels or two pixel clusters. The majority of exceptions arise because the highlights on the teeth and mouth match the color of the white fiducial training set. Fortunately, the incorrect white fiducial labelings occur at consistent 3D locations and are easily eliminated in the 3D dot processing stage.

The classifier generalizes well so that even fairly dramatic changes in fiducial color over time do not result in incorrect classification. For example, Figure 5(b) shows the same green fiducial in two different frames. This fiducial is correctly classified as green in both frames.

The next step, finding connected color components, is complicated by the fact that the video is interlaced. There is significant field to field movement, especially around the lips and jaw, sometimes great enough so that there is no spatial overlap at all between the pixels of a fiducial in one field and the pixels of the same fiducial in the next field. If the two fields are treated as a single frame then a single fiducial can be fragmented, sometimes into many pieces.

One could just find connected color components in each field and use these to compute the 2D dot locations. Unfortunately, this does not work well because the fiducials often deform and are sometimes partially occluded. Therefore, the threshold for the number of pixels needed to classify a group of pixels as a fiducial has to be set very low. In our implementation any connected component which has more than three pixels is classified as a fiducial rather than noise. If just the connected pixels in a single field are counted then the threshold would have to be reduced to one pixel. This would cause many false fiducial classifications because there are typically a few 1 pixel false color classifications per frame and 2 or 3 pixel false clusters occur occasionally. Instead, we find connected components and generate lists of potential 2D dots in each field. Each potential 2D dot in field one is then paired with the closest 2D potential dot in field two. Because fiducials of the same color are spaced far apart, and because the field to field movement is not very large,

the closest potential 2D dot is virtually guaranteed to be the correct match. If the sum of the pixels in the two potential 2D dots is greater than three pixels then the connected components of the two 2D potential dots are merged, and the resulting connected component is marked as a 2D dot.

The next step is to find the centroid of the connected components marked as 2D dots in the previous step. A two dimensional gradient magnitude image is computed by passing a one dimensional first derivative of Gaussian along the x and y directions and then taking the magnitude of these two values at each pixel. The centroid of the colored blob is computed by taking a weighted sum of positions of the pixel (x, y) coordinates which lie inside the gradient mask, where the weights are equal to the gradient magnitude.

3.1.1 Training the color classifier

We create one color classifier for each of the camera views, since the lighting can vary greatly between cameras. In the following discussion we build the classifier for a single camera.

The data for the color classifier is created by manually marking the pixels of frame zero that belong to a particular fiducial color. This is repeated for each of the six colors. The marked data is stored as 6 *color class images*, each of which is created from the original camera image by setting all of the pixels *not* marked as the given color to black (we use black as an out-of-class label because pure black never occurred in any of our images). A typical color class image for the yellow dots is shown in Figure 4. We generated the color class images using the "magic wand" tool available in many image editing programs.

A seventh color class image is automatically created for the background color (e.g., skin and hair) by labeling as out-of-class any pixel in the image which was previously marked as a fiducial in any of the fiducial color class images. This produces an image of the face with black holes where the fiducials were.

The color classifier is a discrete approximation to a nearest neighbor classifier [12]. In a nearest neighbor classifier the item to be classified is given the label of the closest item in the training set, which in our case is the color data contained in the color class images. Because we have 3 dimensional data we can approximate the nearest neighbor classifier by subdividing the RGB cube uniformly into voxels, and assigning class labels to each RGB voxel. To classify a new color you quantize its RGB values and then index into the cube to extract the label.

To create the color classifier we use the color class images to assign color classes to each voxel. Assume that the color class image for color class C_i has n distinct colors, $c_1...c_n$. Each of the voxels corresponding to the color c_j is labeled with the color class C_i. Once the voxels for all of the known colors are labeled, the remaining unlabeled voxels are assigned labels by searching through all of the colors in each color class C_i and finding the color closest to p in RGB space. The color p is given the label of the color class containing the nearest color. Nearness in our case is the Euclidean distance between the two points in RGB space.

If colors from different color classes map to the same sub-cube, we label that sub-cube with the background label since it is more important to avoid incorrect dot labeling than it is to try to label every dot pixel. For the results shown in this paper we quantized the RGB color cube into a 32x32x32 lattice.

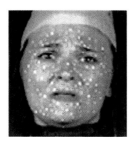

Figure 4: An image of the actress's face. A typical training set for the yellow dots, selected from the image on the left.

3.2 Camera to camera dot correspondence and 3D reconstruction

In order to capture good images of both the front and the sides of the face the cameras were spaced far apart. Because there are such extreme changes in perspective between the different camera views, the projected images of the colored fiducials are very different. Figure 5 shows some examples of the changes in fiducial shape and color between camera views. Establishing fiducial correspondence between camera views by using image matching techniques such as optical flow or template matching would be difficult and likely to generate incorrect matches. In addition, most of the camera views will only see a fraction of the fiducials so the correspondence has to be robust enough to cope with occlusion of fiducials in some of the camera views. With the large number of fiducials we have placed on the face false matches are also quite likely and these must be detected and removed. We used ray tracing in combination with a RANSAC [7] like algorithm to establish fiducial correspondence and to compute accurate 3D dot positions. This algorithm is robust to occlusion and to false matches as well.

First, all potential point correspondences between cameras are generated. If there are k cameras, and n 2D dots in each camera view then $\binom{k}{2} n^2$ point correspondences will be tested. Each correspondence gives rise to a 3D candidate point defined as the closest point of intersection of rays cast from the 2D dots in the two camera views. The 3D candidate point is projected into each of the two camera views used to generate it. If the projection is further than a user-defined epsilon, in our case two pixels, from the centroid of either 2D point then the point is discarded as a potential 3D point candidate. All the 3D candidate points which remain are added to the 3D point list.

Each of the points in the 3D point list is projected into a reference camera view which is the camera with the best view of all the fiducials on the face. If the projected point lies within two pixels of the centroid of a 2D dot visible in the reference camera view then it is added to the list of potential 3D candidate positions for that 2D dot. This is the list of potential 3D matches for a given 2D dot.

For each 3D point in the potential 3D match list, $\binom{n}{3}$ possible combinations of three points in the 3D point list are computed and the combination with the smallest variance is chosen as the true 3D position. Then all 3D points which lie within a user defined distance, in our case the sphere subtended by a cone two pixels in radius at the distance of the 3D point, are averaged to generate the final 3D dot position. This 3D dot position is assigned to the corresponding 2D dot in the reference camera view.

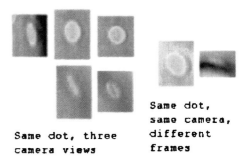

Same dot, three camera views

Same dot, same camera, different frames

Figure 5: Dot variation. Left: Two dots seen from three different cameras (the purple dot is occluded in one camera's view). Right: A single dot seen from a single camera but in two different frames.

This algorithm could clearly be made more efficient because many more 3D candidate points are generated then necessary. One could search for potential camera to camera correspondences only along the epipolar lines and use a variety of space subdivision techniques to find 3D candidate points to test for a given 2D point. However, because the number of fiducials in each color set is small (never more than 40) both steps of this simple and robust algorithm are reasonably fast, taking less than a second to generate the 2D dot correspondences and 3D dot positions for six camera views. The 2D dot correspondence calculation is dominated by the time taken to read in the images of the six camera views and to locate the 2D dots in each view. Consequently, the extra complexity of more efficient stereo matching algorithms does not appear to be justified.

3.3 Frame to frame dot correspondence and labeling

We now have a set of unlabeled 3D dot locations for each frame. We need to assign, across the entire sequence, consistent labels to the 3D dot locations. We do this by defining a reference set of dots D and matching this set to the 3D dot locations given for each frame. We can then describe how the reference dots move over time as follows: Let $d_j \in D$ be the neutral location for the reference dot j. We define the position of d_j at frame i by an offset, i.e.,

$$d_j^i = d_j + \vec{v}_j^i \qquad (1)$$

Because there are thousands of frames and 182 dots in our data set we would like the correspondence computation to be automatic and quite efficient. To simplify the matching we used a fiducial pattern that separates fiducials of a given color as much as possible so that only a small subset of the unlabeled 3D dots need be checked for a best match. Unfortunately, simple nearest neighbor matching fails for several reasons: some fiducials occasionally disappear, some 3D dots may move more than the average distance between 3D dots of the same color, and occasionally extraneous 3D dots appear, caused by highlights in the eyes or teeth. Fortunately, neighboring fiducials move similarly and we can exploit this fact, modifying the nearest neighbor matching algorithm so that it is still efficient but also robust.

For each frame i we first move the reference dots to the locations found in the previous frame. Next, we find a (possibly incomplete) match between the reference dots and the

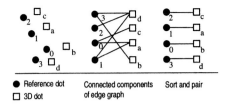

Figure 6: Matching dots.

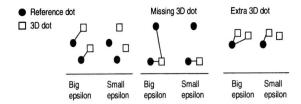

Figure 7: Examples of extra and missing dots and the effect of different values for ϵ.

3D dot locations for frame i. We then move each matched reference dot to the location of its corresponding 3D dot. If a reference dot does not have a match we "guess" a new location for it by moving it in the same direction as its neighbors. We then perform a final matching step.

3.3.1 Acquiring the reference set of dots

The cyberware scan was taken with the dots glued onto the face. Since the dots are visible in both the geometric and color information of the scan, we can place the reference dots on the cyberware model by manually clicking on the model. We next need to align the reference dots and the model with the 3D dot locations found in frame zero. The coordinate system for the cyberware scan differs from the one used for the 3D dot locations, but only by a rigid body motion plus a uniform scale. We find this transform as follows: we first hand-align the 3D dots from frame zero with the reference dots acquired from the scan, then call the matching routine described in Section 3.3.2 below to find the correspondence between the 3D dot locations, f_i, and the reference dots, d_i. We use the method described in [9] to find the exact transform, T, between the two sets of dots. Finally, we replace the temporary locations of the reference dots with

$$d_i = f_i.$$

and use T^{-1} to transform the cyberware model into the coordinate system of the video 3D dot locations.

3.3.2 The matching routine

The matching routine is run twice per frame. We first perform a conservative match, move the reference dots (as described below in Section 3.3.3), then perform a second, less conservative, match. By moving the reference dots between matches we reduce the problem of large 3D dot position displacements.

The matching routine can be thought of as a graph problem where an edge between a reference dot and a frame dot indicates that the dots are potentially paired (see Figure 6). The matching routine proceeds in several steps; first, for each reference dot we add an edge for every 3D dot of the same color that is within a given distance ϵ. We then search for connected components in the graph that have an equal number of 3D and reference dots (most connected components will have exactly two dots, one of each type). We sort the dots in the vertical dimension of the plane of the face and use the resulting ordering to pair up the reference dots with the 3D dot locations (see Figure 6).

In the video sequences we captured, the difference in the 3D dot positions from frame to frame varied from zero to about 1.5 times the average distance separating closest dots. To adjust for this, we run the matching routine with several values of ϵ and pick the run that generates the most matches. Different choices of ϵ produce different results (see Figure 7): if ϵ is too small we may not find matches for 3D dots that

have moved a lot. If ϵ is too large then the connected components in the graph will expand to include too many 3D dots. We try approximately five distances ranging from 0.5 to 1.5 of the average distance between closest reference dots.

If we are doing the second match for the frame we add an additional step to locate matches where a dot may be missing (or extra). We take those dots which have not been matched and run the matching routine on them with smaller and smaller ϵ values. This resolves situations such as the one shown on the right of Figure 7.

3.3.3 Moving the dots

We move all of the matched reference dots to their new locations then interpolate the locations for the remaining, unmatched reference dots by using their nearest, matched neighbors. For each reference dot we define a valid set of neighbors using the routine in Section 4.2.1, ignoring the blending values returned by the routine.

To move an unmatched dot d_k we use a combination of the offsets of all of its valid neighbors (refer to Equation 1). Let $n_k \subset D$ be the set of neighbor dots for dot d_k. Let $\hat{n}_k$ be the set of neighbors that have a match for the current frame i. Provided $\hat{n}_k \neq \emptyset$, the offset vector for dot d_k^i is calculated as follows: let $\vec{v}_j^i = d_j^i - d_j$ be the offset of dot j (recall that d_j is the initial position for the reference dot j).

$$\vec{v}_k^i = \frac{1}{||\hat{n}_k||} \sum_{d_j^i \in \hat{n}_k} \vec{v}_j^i$$

If the dot has no matched neighbors we repeat as necessary, treating the moved, unmatched reference dots as matched dots. Eventually, the movements will propagate through all of the reference dots.

4 Mesh construction and deformation

4.1 Constructing the mesh

To construct a mesh we begin with a cyberware scan of the head. Because we later need to align the scan with the 3D video dot data, we scanned the head with the fiducials glued on. The resulting scan suffers from four problems:

- The fluorescent fiducials caused "bumps" on the mesh.

- Several parts of the mesh were not adequately scanned, namely, the ears, one side of the nose, the eyes, and under the chin. These were manually corrected.

- The mesh does not have an opening for the mouth.

- The scan has too many polygons.

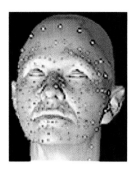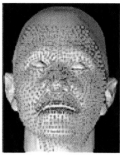

Figure 8: Left: The original dots plus the extra dots (in white). The labeling curves are shown in light green. Right: The grid of dots. Outline dots are green or blue.

The bumps caused by the fluorescent fiducials were removed by selecting the vertices which were out of place (approximately 10-30 surrounding each dot) and automatically finding new locations for them by blending between four correct neighbors. Since the scan produces a rectangular grid of vertices we can pick the neighbors to blend between in (u, v) space, i.e., the nearest valid neighbors in the positive and negative u and v direction.

The polygons at the mouth were split and then filled with six rows of polygons located slightly behind the lips. We map the teeth and tongue onto these polygons when the mouth is open.

We reduced the number of polygons in the mesh from approximately $460,000$ to 4800 using Hoppe's simplification method [8].

4.2   Moving the mesh

The vertices are moved by a linear combination of the offsets of the nearest dots (refer to Equation 1). The linear combination for each vertex v_j is expressed as a set of blend coefficients, α_k^j, one for each dot, such that $\sum_{d_k \in D} \alpha_k^j = 1$ (most of the α_k^js will be zero). The new location p_j^i of the vertex v_j at frame i is then

$$p_j^i = p_j + \sum_k \alpha_k^j ||d_k^i - d_k||$$

where p_j is the initial location of the vertex v_j.

For most of the vertices the α_k^js are a weighted average of the closest dots. The vertices in the eyes, mouth, behind the mouth, and outside of the facial area are treated slightly differently since, for example, we do not want the dots on the lower lip influencing vertices on the upper part of the lip. Also, although we tried to keep the head as still as possible, there is still some residual rigid body motion. We need to compensate for this for those vertices that are not directly influenced by a dot (e.g., the back of the head).

We use a two-step process to assign the blend coefficients to the vertices. We first find blend coefficients for a grid of points evenly distributed across the face, then use this grid of points to assign blend coefficients to the vertices. This two-step process is helpful because both the fluorescent fiducials and the mesh vertices are unevenly distributed across the face, making it difficult to get smoothly changing blend coefficients.

The grid consists of roughly 1400 points, evenly distributed and placed by hand to follow the contours of the face (see Figure 8). The points along the nasolabial furrows,

nostrils, eyes, and lips are treated slightly differently than the other points to avoid blending across features such as the lips.

Because we want the mesh movement to go to zero outside of the face, we add another set of unmoving dots to the reference set. These new dots form a ring around the face (see Figure 8) enclosing all of the reference dots. For each frame we determine the rigid body motion of the head (if any) using a subset of those reference dots which are relatively stable. This rigid body transformation is then applied to the new dots.

We label the dots, grid points, and vertices as being *above*, *below*, or *neither* with respect to each of the eyes and the mouth. Dots which are *above* a given feature can not be combined with dots which are *below* that same feature (or vice-versa). Labeling is accomplished using three curves, one for each of the eyes and one for the mouth. Dots directly above (or below) a curve are labeled as *above* (or *below*) that curve. Otherwise, they are labeled *neither*.

4.2.1   Assigning blends to the grid points

The algorithm for assigning blends to the grid points first finds the closest dots, assigns blends, then filters to more evenly distribute the blends.

Finding the ideal set of reference dots to influence a grid point is complicated because the reference dots are not evenly distributed across the face. The algorithm attempts to find two or more dots distributed in a rough circle around the given grid point. To do this we both compensate for the dot density, by setting the search distance using the two closest dots, and by checking for dots which will both "pull" in the same direction.

To find the closest dots to the grid point p we first find δ_1 and δ_2, the distance to the closest and second closest dot, respectively. Let $D_n \subset D$ be the set of dots within $1.8\frac{\delta_1 + \delta_2}{2}$ distance of p whose labels do not conflict with p's label. Next, we check for pairs of dots that are more or less in the same direction from p and remove the furthest one. More precisely, let $\hat{v}_i$ be the normalized vector from p to the dot $d_i \in D_n$ and let $\hat{v}_j$ be the normalized vector from p to the dot $d_j \in D_n$. If $\hat{v}_1 \cdot \hat{v}_2 > 0.8$ then remove the furthest of d_i and d_j from the set D_n.

We assign blend values based on the distance of the dots from p. If the dot is not in D_n then its corresponding α value is 0. For the dots in D_n let $l_i = \frac{1.0}{||d_i - p||}$. Then the corresponding α's are

$$\alpha_i = \frac{l_i}{(\sum_{d_i \in D_n} l_i)}$$

We next filter the blend coefficients for the grid points. For each grid point we find the closest grid points – since the grid points are distributed in a rough grid there will usually be 4 neighboring points – using the above routine (replacing the dots with the grid points). We special case the outlining grid points; they are only blended with other outlining grid points. The new blend coefficients are found by taking 0.75 of the grid point's blend coefficients and 0.25 of the average of the neighboring grid point's coefficients. More formally, let $g_i = [\alpha_0, \ldots, \alpha_n]$ be the vector of blend coefficients for the grid point i. Then the new vector g_i' is found as follows, where N_i is the set of neighboring grid points for the grid point i:

$$g_i' = 0.75 g_i + \frac{0.25}{||N_i||} \sum_{j \in N_i} g_j$$

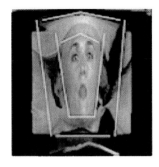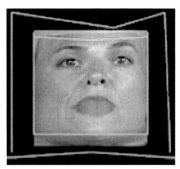

Figure 9: Masks surrounding important facial features. The gradient of a blurred version of this mask is used to orient the low-pass filters used in the dot removal process.

Figure 10: Standard cylindrical texture map. Warped texture map that focuses on the face, and particularly on the eyes and mouth. The warp is defined by the line pairs shown in white.

We apply this filter twice to simulate a wide low pass filter.

To find the blend coefficients for the vertices of the mesh we find the closest grid point with the same label as the vertex and copy the blend coefficients. The only exception to this is the vertices for the polygons inside of the mouth. For these vertices we take β of the closest grid point on the top lip and $1.0 - \beta$ of the closest grid point on the bottom lip. The β values are 0.8, 0.6, 0.4, 0.25, and 0.1 from top to bottom of the mouth polygons.

5 Dot removal

Before we create the textures, the dots and their associated illumination effects have to be removed from the camera images. Interreflection effects are surprisingly noticeable because some parts of the face fold dramatically, bringing the reflective surface of some dots into close proximity with the skin. This is a big problem along the naso-labial furrow where diffuse interreflection from the colored dots onto the face significantly alters the skin color.

First, the dot colors are removed from each of the six camera image sequences by substituting skin texture for pixels which are covered by colored dots. Next, diffuse interreflection effects and any remaining color casts from stray pixels that have not been properly substituted are removed.

The skin texture substitution begins by finding the pixels which correspond to colored dots. The nearest neighbor color classifier described in Section 3.1.1 is used to mark all pixels which have any of the dot colors. A special training set is used since in this case false positives are much less detrimental than they are for the dot tracking case. Also, there is no need to distinguish between dot colors, only between dot colors and the background colors. The training set is created to capture as much of the dot color and the boundary region between dots and the background colors as possible.

A dot mask is generated by applying the classifier to each pixel in the image. The mask is grown by a few pixels to account for any remaining pixels which might be contaminated by the dot color. The dot mask marks all pixels which must have skin texture substituted.

The skin texture is broken into low spatial frequency and high frequency components. The low frequency components of the skin texture are interpolated by using a directional low pass filter oriented parallel to features that might introduce intensity discontinuities. This prevents bleeding of colors across sharp intensity boundaries such as the boundary between the lips and the lighter colored regions around

the mouth. The directionality of the filter is controlled by a two dimensional mask which is the projection into the image plane of a three dimensional polygon mask lying on the 3D face model. Because the polygon mask is fixed on the 3D mesh, the 2D projection of the polygon mask stays in registration with the texture map as the face deforms.

All of the important intensity gradients have their own polygon mask: the eyes, the eyebrows, the lips, and the naso-labial furrows (see 9). The 2D polygon masks are filled with white and the region of the image outside the masks is filled with black to create an image. This image is low-pass filtered. The intensity of the resulting image is used to control how directional the filter is. The filter is circularly symmetric where the image is black, i.e., far from intensity discontinuities, and it is very directional where the image is white. The directional filter is oriented so that its long axis is orthogonal to the gradient of this image.

The high frequency skin texture is created from a rectangular sample of skin texture taken from a part of the face that is free of dots. The skin sample is highpass filtered to eliminate low frequency components. At each dot mask pixel location the highpass filtered skin texture is first registered to the center of the 2D bounding box of the connected dot region and then added to the low frequency interpolated skin texture.

The remaining diffuse interreflection effects are removed by clamping the hue of the skin color to a narrow range determined from the actual skin colors. First the pixel values are converted from RGB to HSV space and then any hue outside the legal range is clamped to the extremes of the range. Pixels in the eyes and mouth, found using the eye and lip masks shown in Figure 9, are left unchanged.

Some temporal variation remains in the substituted skin texture due to imperfect registration of the high frequency texture from frame to frame. A low pass temporal filter is applied to the dot mask regions in the texture images, because in the texture map space the dots are relatively motionless. This temporal filter effectively eliminates the temporal texture substitution artifacts.

6 Creating the texture maps

Figure 11 is a flowchart of the texture creation process. We create texture maps for every frame of our animation in a four-step process. The first two steps are performed only once per mesh. First we define a parameterization of the mesh. Second, using this parameterization, we create a

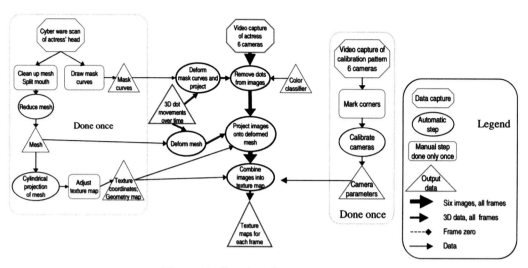

Figure 11: Creating the texture maps.

geometry map containing a location on the mesh for each texel. Third, for every frame, we create six preliminary texture maps, one from each camera image, along with weight maps. The weight maps indicate the relative quality of the data from the different cameras. Fourth, we take a weighted average of these texture maps to make our final texture map.

We create an initial set of texture coordinates for the head by tilting the mesh back 10 degrees to expose the nostrils and projecting the mesh vertices onto a cylinder. A texture map generated using this parametrization is shown on the left of Figure 10. We specify a set of line pairs and warp the texture coordinates using the technique described by Beier and Neely[1]. This parametrization results in the texture map shown on the right of Figure 10. Only the front of the head is textured with data from the six video streams.

Next we create the geometry map containing a mesh location for each texel. A mesh location is a triple (k, β_1, β_2) specifying a triangle k and barycentric coordinates in the triangle $(\beta_1, \beta_2, 1 - \beta_1 - \beta_2)$. To find the triangle identifier k for texel (u, v) we exhaustively search through the mesh's triangles to find the one that contains the texture coordinates (u, v). We then set the β_is to be the barycentric coordinates of the point (u, v) in the texture coordinates of the triangle k. When finding the mesh location for a pixel we already know in which triangles its neighbors above and to the left lie. Therefore, we speed our search by first searching through these triangles and their neighbors. However, the time required for this task is not critical as the geometry map need only be created once.

Next we create preliminary texture maps for frame f one for each camera. This is a modified version of the technique described in [11]. To create the texture map for camera c, we begin by deforming the mesh into its frame f position. Then, for each texel, we get its mesh location, (k, β_1, β_2), from the geometry map. With the 3D coordinates of triangle k's vertices and the barycentric coordinates β_i, we compute the texel's 3D location t. We transform t by camera c's projection matrix to obtain a location, (x, y), on camera c's image plane. We then color the texel with the color from camera c's image at (x, y). We set the texel's weight to the dot product of the mesh normal at t, $\hat{n}$, with the direction back to the camera, $\hat{d}$ (see Figure 12). Negative values are clamped to zero. Hence, weights are low where the camera's view is glancing. However, this weight map is not smooth at triangle boundaries, so we smooth it by convolving it with a Gaussian kernel.

Last, we merge the six preliminary texture maps. As they do not align perfectly, averaging them blurs the texture and loses detail. Therefore, we use only the texture map of our bottom, center camera for the center 46 % of the final texture map. We smoothly transition (over 23 pixels) to using a weighted average of each preliminary texture map at the sides.

We texture the parts of the head not covered by the aforementioned texture maps with the captured reflectance data from our Cyberware scan, modified in two ways. First, because we replaced the mesh's ears with ears from a stock mesh (Section 4.1), we moved the ears in the texture to achieve better registration. Second, we set the alpha channel to zero (with a soft edge) in the region of the texture for the front of the head. Then we render in two passes to create an image of the head with both texture maps applied.

7 Compression

7.1 Principal Components Analysis

The geometric and texture map data have different statistical characteristics and are best compressed in different ways. There is significant long-term temporal correlation in the geometric data since similar facial expressions occur throughout the sequence. The short term correlation of the texture data is significantly increased over that of the raw video footage because in the texture image space the fiducials are essentially motionless. This eliminates most of the intensity changes associated with movement and leaves primarily shading changes. Shading changes tend to have low spatial frequencies and are highly compressible. Compression schemes such as MPEG, which can take advantage of short term temporal correlation, can exploit this increase in short term correlation.

For the geometric data, one way to exploit the long term correlation is to use principal component analysis. If we represent our data set as a matrix A, where frame i of the data maps column i of A, then the first principal component of A is

$$\max_u (A^T u)^T (A^T u) \qquad (2)$$

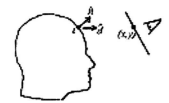

Figure 12: Creating the preliminary texture map.

The u which maximizes Equation 2 is the eigenvector associated with the largest eigenvalue of AA^T, which is also the value of the maximum. Succeeding principal components are defined similarly, except that they are required to be orthogonal to all preceding principal components, i.e., $u_i^T u_j = 0$ for $j \neq i$. The principal components form an orthonormal basis set represented by the matrix U where the columns of U are the principal components of A ordered by eigenvalue size with the most significant principal component in the first column of U.

The data in the A matrix can be projected onto the principal component basis as follows:

$$W = U^T A$$

Row i of W is the projection of column A_i onto the basis vector u_i. More precisely, the jth element in row i of W corresponds to the projection of frame j of the original data onto the ith basis vector. We will call the elements of the W matrix projection *coefficients*.

Similarly, A can be reconstructed exactly from W by multiplication by the basis set, i.e., $A = UW$.
The most important property of the principal components for our purposes is that they are the best linear basis set for reconstruction in the l_2 norm sense. For any given matrix U_k, where k is the number of columns of the matrix and $k < rank(A)$, the reconstruction error

$$e = ||A - U_k U_k^T A||_F^2 \qquad (3)$$

where $||B||_F^2$ is the Frobenius norm defined to be

$$||B||_F^2 = \sum_{i=1}^{m} \sum_{j=1}^{n} b_{ij}^2 \qquad (4)$$

will be minimized if U_k is the matrix containing the k most significant principal components of A.

We can compress a data set A by quantizing the elements of its corresponding W and U matrices and entropy coding them. Since the compressed data cannot be reconstructed without the principal component basis vectors both the W and U matrices have to be compressed. The basis vectors add overhead that is not present with basis sets that can be computed independent of the original data set, such as the DCT basis.

For data sequences that have no particular structure the extra overhead of the basis vectors would probably outweigh any gain in compression efficiency. However, for data sets with regular frame to frame structure the residual error for reconstruction with the principal component basis vectors can be much smaller than for other bases. This reduction in residual error can be great enough to compensate for the overhead bits of the basis vectors.

The principal components can be computed using the singular value decomposition (SVD) [13]. Efficient implementations of this algorithm are widely available. The SVD of a matrix A is

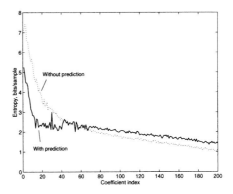

Figure 13: Reduction in entropy after temporal prediction.

$$A = U\Sigma V^T \qquad (5)$$

where the columns of U are the eigenvectors of AA^T, the singular values, σ_i, along the diagonal matrix Σ are the square roots of the eigenvalues of AA^T, and the columns of V are the eigenvectors of $A^T A$. The ith column of U is the ith principal component of A. Computing the first k left singular vectors of A is equivalent to computing the first k principal components.

7.2 Geometric Data

The geometric data has the long term temporal coherence properties mentioned above since the motion of the face is highly structured. The overhead of the basis vectors for the geometric data is fixed because there are only 182 fiducials on the face. The maximum number of basis vectors is $182 * 3$ since there are three numbers, x, y, and z, associated with each fiducial. Consequently, the basis vector overhead steadily diminishes as the length of the animation sequence increases.

The geometric data is mapped to matrix form by taking the 3D offset data for the ith frame and mapping it the ith column of the data matrix A_g. The first k principal components, U_g, of A_g are computed and A_g is projected into the U_g basis to give the projection coefficients W_g.

There is significant correlation between the columns of projection coefficients because the motion of the dots is relatively smooth over time. We can reduce the entropy of the quantized projection coefficients by temporally predicting the projection coefficients in column i from column $i-1$, i.e., $c_i = c_{i-1} + \Delta_i$ where we encode Δ_i.

For our data set, only the projection coefficients associated with the first 45 principal components, corresponding to the first 45 rows of W_g, have significant temporal correlation so only the first 45 rows are temporally predicted. The remaining rows are entropy coded directly. After the temporal prediction the entropy is reduced by about 20 percent (Figure 13).

The basis vectors are compressed by choosing a peak error rate and then varying the number of quantization levels allocated to each vector based on the standard deviation of the projection coefficients for each vector.

We visually examined animation sequences with W_g and U_g compressed at a variety of peak error rates and chose a level which resulted in undetectable geometric jitter in reconstructed animation. The entropy of W_g for this error level is 26 Kbits per second and the entropy of U_g is 13 kbits per second for a total of 40 kbits per second for all the geometric data. These values were computed for our 3330 frame animation sequence.

8 Results

Figure 16 shows some typical frames from a reconstructed sequence of 3D facial expressions. These frames are taken from a 3330 frame animation in which the actress makes random expressions while reading from a script[2].

The facial expressions look remarkably life-like. The animation sequence is similarly striking. Virtually all evidence of the colored fiducials and diffuse interreflection artifacts is gone, which is surprising considering that in some regions of the face, especially around the lips, there is very little of the actress' skin visible – most of the area is covered by colored fiducials.

Both the accurate 3D geometry and the accurate face texture contribute to the believability of the reconstructed expressions. Occlusion contours look correct and the subtle details of face geometry that are very difficult to capture as geometric data show up well in the texture images. Important examples of this occur at the nasolabial furrow which runs from just above the nares down to slightly below the lips, eyebrows, and eyes. Forehead furrows and wrinkles also are captured. To recreate these features using geometric data rather than texture data would require an extremely detailed 3D capture of the face geometry and a resulting high polygon count in the 3D model. In addition, shading these details properly if they were represented as geometry would be difficult since it would require computing shadows and possibly even diffuse interreflection effects in order to look correct. Subtle shading changes on the smooth parts of the skin, most prominent at the cheekbones, are also captured well in the texture images.

There are still visible artifacts in the animation, some of which are polygonization or shading artifacts, others of which arise because of limitations in our current implementation.

Some polygonization of the face surface is visible, especially along the chin contour, because the front surface of the head contains only 4500 polygons. This is not a limitation of the algorithm – we chose this number of polygons because we wanted to verify that believable facial animation could be done at polygon resolutions low enough to potentially be displayed in real time on inexpensive ($200) 3D graphics cards[3]. For film or television work, where real time rendering is not an issue, the polygon count can be made much higher and the polygonization artifacts will disappear. As graphics hardware becomes faster the differential in quality between offline and online rendered face images will diminish.

Several artifacts are simply the result of our current implementation. For example, occasionally the edge of the face, the tips of the nares, and the eyebrows appear to jitter. This usually occurs when dots are lost, either by falling below the minimum size threshold or by not being visible to three or more cameras. When a dot is lost the algorithm synthesizes dot position data which is usually incorrect enough that it is visible as jitter. More cameras, or

better placement of the cameras, would eliminate this problem. However, overall the image is extremely stable.

In retrospect, a mesh constructed by hand with the correct geometry and then fit to the cyberware data [10] would be much simpler and possibly reduce some of the polygonization artifacts.

Another implementation artifact that becomes most visible when the head is viewed near profile is that the teeth and tongue appear slightly distorted. This is because we do not use correct 3D models to represent them. Instead, the texture map of the teeth and tongue is projected onto a sheet of polygons stretching between the lips. It is possible that the teeth and tongue could be tracked using more sophisticated computer vision techniques and then more correct geometric models could be used.

Shading artifacts represent an intrinsic limitation of the algorithm. The highlights on the eyes and skin remain in fixed positions regardless of point of view, and shadowing is fixed at the time the video is captured. However, for many applications this should not be a limitation because these artifacts are surprisingly subtle. Most people do not notice that the shading is incorrect until it is pointed out to them, and even then frequently do not find it particularly objectionable. The highlights on the eyes can probably be corrected by building a 3D eye model and creating synthetic highlights appropriate for the viewing situation. Correcting the skin shading and self shadowing artifacts is more difficult. The former will require very realistic and efficient skin reflectance models while the latter will require significant improvements in rendering performance, especially if the shadowing effect of area light sources is to be adequately modeled. When both these problems are solved then it will no longer be necessary to capture the live video sequence – only the 3D geometric data and skin reflectance properties will be needed.

The compression numbers are quite good. Figure 14 shows a single frame from the original sequence, the same frame compressed by the MPEG4 codec at 460 Kbps and at 260 KBps. All of the images look quite good. The animated sequences also look good, with the 260 KBps sequence just beginning to show noticeable compression artifacts. The 260 KBps video is well within the bandwidth of single speed CDROM drives. This data rate is probably low enough that decompression could be performed in real time in software on the fastest personal computers so there is the potential for real time display of the resulting animations. We intend to investigate this possibility in future work.

There is still room for significant improvement in our compression. A better mesh parameterization would significantly reduce the number of bits needed to encode the eyes, which distort significantly over time in the texture map space. Also the teeth, inner edges of the lips, and the tongue could potentially be tracked over time and at least partially stabilized, resulting in a significant reduction in bit rate for the mouth region. Since these two regions account for the majority of the bit budget, the potential for further reduction in bit rate is large.

9 Conclusion

The system produces remarkably lifelike reconstructions of facial expressions recorded from live actors' performances. The accurate 3D tracking of a large number of points on the face results in an accurate 3D model of facial expression. The texture map sequence captured simultaneously with the 3D deformation data captures details of expres-

---

[2]The rubber cap on the actress' head was used to keep her hair out of her face.

[3]In this paper we have not addressed the issue of real time texture decompression and rendering of the face model, but we plan to do so in future work

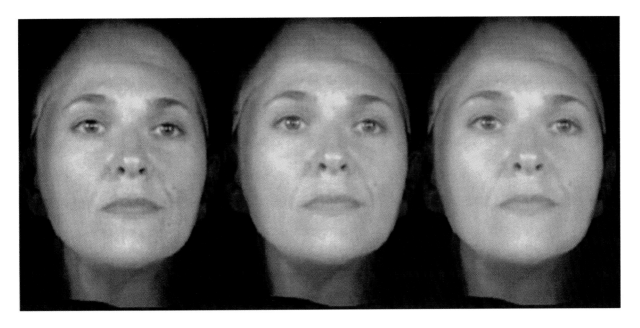

Figure 14: Left to Right: Mesh with uncompressed textures, compressed to 400 kbits/sec, and compressed to 200 kbits/sec

sion that would be difficult to capture any other way. By using the 3D deformation information to register the texture maps from frame to frame the variance of the texture map sequence is significantly reduced which increases its compressibility. Image quality of 30 frame per second animations, reconstructed at approximately 300 by 400 pixels, is still good at data rates as low as 240 Kbits per second, and there is significant potential for lowering this bit rate even further. Because the bit overhead for the geometric data is low in comparison to the texture data one can get a 3D talking head, with all the attendant flexibility, for little more than the cost of a conventional video sequence. With the true 3D model of facial expression, the animation can be viewed from any angle and placed in a 3D virtual environment, making it much more flexible than conventional video.

REFERENCES

[1] BEIER, T., AND NEELY, S. Feature-based image metamorphosis. In *Computer Graphics (SIGGRAPH '92 Proceedings)* (July 1992), E. E. Catmull, Ed., vol. 26, pp. 35–42.

[2] BREGLER, C., COVELL, M., AND SLANEY, M. Video rewrite: Driving visual speech with audio. *Computer Graphics 31*, 2 (Aug. 1997), 353–361.

[3] CASSELL, J., PELACHAUD, C., BADLER, N., STEEDMAN, M., ACHORN, B., BECKET, T., DOUVILLE, B., PREVOST, S., AND STONE, M. Animated conversation: Rule-based generation of facial expression, gesture and spoken intonation for multiple conversational agents. *Computer Graphics 28*, 2 (Aug. 1994), 413–420.

[4] DECARLO, D., AND METAXAS, D. The integration of optical flow and deformable models with applications to human face shape and motion estimation. *Proceedings CVPR* (1996), 231–238.

[5] ESSA, I., AND PENTLAND, A. Coding, analysis, interpretation and recognition of facial expressions. *IEEE Transactions on Pattern Analysis and Machine Intelligence 19*, 7 (1997), 757–763.

[6] FAUGERAS, O. *Three-dimensional computer vision.* MIT Press, Cambridge, MA, 1993.

[7] FISCHLER, M. A., AND BOOLES, R. C. Random sample consensus: A paradigm for model fitting with applications to image analysis and automated cartography. *Communications of the ACM 24*, 6 (Aug. 1981), 381–395.

[8] HOPPE, H. Progressive meshes. In *SIGGRAPH 96 Conference Proceedings* (Aug. 1996), H. Rushmeier, Ed., Annual Conference Series, ACM SIGGRAPH, Addison Wesley, pp. 99–108. held in New Orleans, Louisiana, 04-09 August 1996.

[9] HORN, B. K. P. Closed-form solution of absolute orientation using unit quaternions. *Journal of the Optical Society of America 4*, 4 (Apr. 1987).

[10] LEE, Y., TERZOPOULOS, D., AND WATERS, K. Realistic modeling for facial animation. *Computer Graphics 29*, 2 (July 1995), 55–62.

[11] PIGHIN, F., AUSLANDER, J., LISHINSKI, D., SZELISKI, R., AND SALESIN, D. Realistic facial animation using image based 3d morphing. Tech. Report TR-97-01-03, Department of Computer Science and Engineering, University of Washington, Seattle, Wa, 1997.

[12] SCHÜRMANN, J. *Pattern Classification: A Unified View of Statistical and Neural Approaches.* John Wiley and Sons, Inc., New York, 1996.

[13] STRANG. *Linear Algebra and its Application.* HBJ, 1988.

[14] WATERS, K. A muscle model for animating three-dimensional facial expression. In *Computer Graphics (SIGGRAPH '87 Proceedings)* (July 1987), M. C. Stone, Ed., vol. 21, pp. 17–24.

[15] WILLIAMS, L. Performance-driven facial animation. *Computer Graphics 24*, 2 (Aug. 1990), 235–242.

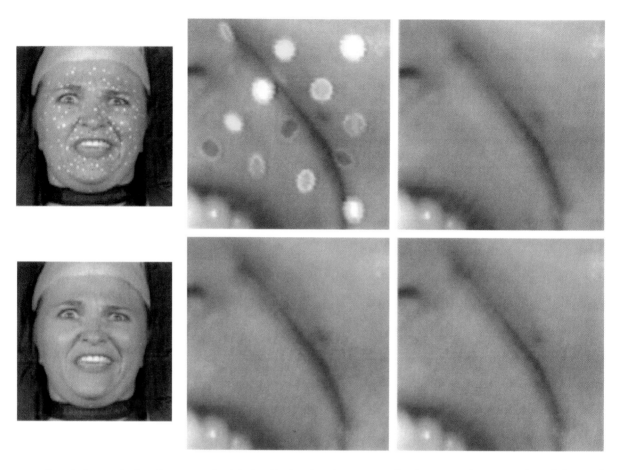

Figure 14: Face before and after dot removal, with details showing the steps in the dot removal process. From left to right, top to bottom: Face with dots, dots replaced with low frequency skin texture, high frequency skin texture added, hue clamped.

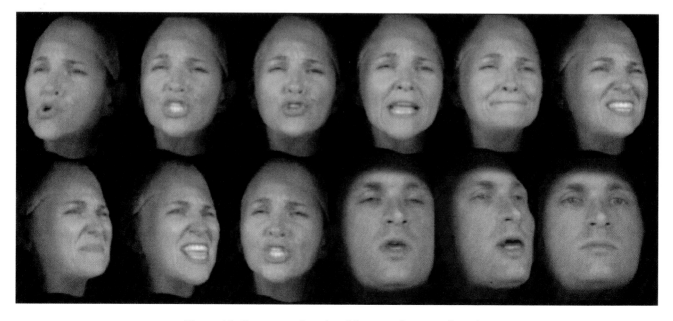

Figure 15: Sequence of rendered images of textured mesh.

An Anthropometric Face Model using Variational Techniques

Douglas DeCarlo, Dimitris Metaxas and Matthew Stone

Department of Computer and Information Science, University of Pennsylvania

{dmd@gradient | dnm@central | matthew@linc}.cis.upenn.edu

Abstract

We describe a system that automatically generates varied geometric models of human faces. A collection of random measurements of the face is generated according to anthropometric statistics for likely face measurements in a population. These measurements are then treated as constraints on a parameterized surface. Variational modeling is used to find a smooth surface that satisfies these constraints while using a prototype shape as a reference.

Keywords: face modeling, anthropometry, variational modeling, crowd generation

1 Introduction

A hallmark of the diversity and individuality of the people we encounter in daily life is the range of variation in the shape of their faces. A simulation or animation that fails to reproduce this diversity—whether by design or circumstance—deprives its characters of independent identities. To animate a bustling scene realistically or to play out an extended virtual interaction believably requires hundreds of different facial geometries, maybe even a distinct one for each person, as in real life.

It is a monumental challenge to achieve such breadth with existing modeling techniques. One possibility might be to use range scanning technology. This involves all the complexities of casting extras for a film: with scanning, each new face must be found on a living subject. And although scanning permits detailed geometries to be extracted quickly, scanned data frequently includes artifacts that must be touched up by hand. Another alternative is manual construction of face models, by deforming an existing model or having an artist design one from scratch; this tends to be slow and expensive.

This paper describes a new alternative: a system capable of automatically generating distinct, plausible face geometries. This system constructs a face in two steps. The first step is the generation of a random set of *measurements* that characterize the face. The form and values of these measurements are computed according to *face anthropometry*, the science dedicated to the measurement of the human face. Anthropometric studies like [11, 12] report statistics on reliable differences in shape across faces within and across populations. Random measurements generated according to the

anthropometric profile of a population characterize the distinctive features of a likely face in that population.

In the second step, our system constructs the best surface that satisfies the geometric constraints that a set of measurements imposes, using *variational modeling* [16, 31, 33]. Variational modeling is a framework for building surfaces by constrained optimization; the output surface minimizes a measure of *fairness*, which in our case formalizes how much the surface bends and stretches away from the kind of shape that faces normally have. Having a fairness measure is necessary, since the anthropometric measurements leave the resulting surface underdetermined. Bookstein [4] uses this same fairness measure as a method of data interpolation for sparse biometric data, supporting its utility for determining the geometry of an underdetermined biological shape. Variational modeling provides a powerful and elegant tool for capturing the commonalities in shape among faces along with the differences. Its use reduces the problem of generating face geometries into the problem of generating sets of anthropometric measurements.

The remainder of the paper describes our techniques in more detail. We begin in Section 1.1 by introducing the problem of representing and specifying face geometry. In Section 2, we summarize the research from face anthropometry that we draw on; Section 3 describes how random measurements are generated from these results. In Section 4, we describe our use of variational techniques to derive natural face geometries that satisfy anthropometric measurements. We finish in Section 5 with illustrations of the output of our system.

1.1 Background and related work

Human face animation is a complex task requiring modeling and rendering not only of face geometry, but also of distinctive facial features (such as skin, hair, and tongue) and their motions. Most research in face modeling in computer graphics has addressed these latter problems [21, 23, 25, 26].

Research on human geometry itself falls into two camps, both crucially dependent (in different ways) on human participation. The first approach is to extract geometry automatically from the measurement of a live subject. Lee, et al. [21] use a range scan of a subject, and produce a physics-based model capable of animation. Akimoto, et al. [1] use front and profile images of a subject to produce a model.

The second approach is to facilitate manual specification of new face geometry by a user. A certain facility is offered already by commercial modelers (though of course their use demands considerable artistic skill); several researchers have sought to provide higher levels of control. Parke [25] provides parameters which can control the face shape; and Magnenat-Thalmann, et al. [23] describe a more comprehensive set of localized deformation parameters. Patel [27] offers an alternative set of parameters similar in scope to [23] but more closely tied to the structure of the head. DiPaola [8] uses a set of localized volumetric deformations, with a similar feel to [23] in their effects. Lewis [22] discusses the use of stochastic noise functions as a means of deforming natural objects (including faces). In this case, the control maintained by the user is limited to noise generation parameters.

In contrast, we adopt a different approach: generating new face geometries automatically. More so than interactive methods, this approach depends on a precise mathematical description of possible face geometries. Many conventional representations of face shape seem inadequate for this purpose.

For example, the simple scaling parameters used by manual modeling techniques can perform useful effects like changing the width of the mouth or the height of the head; but they are unlikely to provide sufficient generality to describe a wide sampling of face geometries.

Meanwhile, for models based on principal components analysis (PCA)—an alternative representation derived from work in face recognition [32]—the opposite problem is likely. PCA describes a face shape as a weighted sum of an orthogonal basis of 3D shapes (called principal components). This basis is constructed from a large bank of examples that have been placed in mutual correspondence. (This correspondence is very much like that required for image morphing [3]; establishing it is a considerable task, but not one that has evaded automation [32].)

PCA typically allows faces nearly identical to those in the bank to be accurately represented by weighting a truncated basis that only includes a few hundred of the most significant components. However, because components are individually complex and combined simply by addition, alternative weightings could easily encode implausible face shapes. Identifying which basis weights are reasonable is just the original problem (of characterizing possible faces) in a different guise. Bookstein [5] describes this problem in terms of "latent variables," and notes that principal components often bear little resemblance to the underlying interdependent structure of biological forms. (In other words, it is quite difficult to extract non-linear dependencies between different shape aspects using a linear model like PCA.) At the same time, there is no guarantee that faces considerably outside the example set will be approximated well at all.

We therefore adopt a representation of face shape based on constrained optimization. The constraints—generated as described in Section 3—are based on the anthropometric studies of the face of [11, 12, 20] described in the next section; we avoid the difficulty of learning possible geometries since these studies identify the range of variation in real faces. The constraint optimization, as described in Section 4, is accomplished by variational surface modeling.

2 Face Anthropometry

Anthropometry is the biological science of human body measurement. Anthropometric data informs a range of enterprises that depend on knowledge of the distribution of measurements across human populations. For example, in human-factors analysis, a known range for human measurements can help guide the design of products to fit most people [9]; in medicine, quantitative comparison of anthropometric data with patients' measurements before and after surgery furthers planning and assessment of plastic and reconstructive surgery [12]; in forensic anthropology, conjectures about likely measurements, derived from anthropometry, figure in the determination of individuals' appearance from their remains [12, 30]; and in the recovery of missing children, by aging their appearance taken from photographs [12]. This paper describes a similar use of anthropometry in the construction of face models for computer graphics applications.[1]

---

[1] An alternative source of such information might come from morphometrics [5], the study of the overall shape of biological forms, their development, and the interrelations of different aspects of their geometry. Morphometric analyses also provide detailed characterizations of the variability in the shape of faces.

In order to develop useful statistics from anthropometric measurements, the measurements are made in a strictly defined way [19]. The rest of this section outlines one popular regime of such measurements and the information available from analyses of the resulting data. This provides an overview first of the anthropometric structure that our model embodies and then of the statistical results our model exploits.

Anthropometric evaluation begins with the identification of particular locations on a subject, called *landmark* points, defined in terms of visible or palpable features (skin or bone) on the subject. A series of measurements between these landmarks is then taken using carefully specified procedures and measuring instruments (such as calipers, levels and measuring tape). As a result, repeated measurements of the same individual (taken a few days apart) are very reliable, and measurements of different individuals can be successfully compared.

Farkas [12] describes a widely used set of measurements for describing the human face. A large amount of anthropometric data using this system is available [11, 12]. The system uses a total of 47 landmark points to describe the face; Figure 1 illustrates many of them. The landmarks are typically identified by abbreviations of corresponding anatomical terms. For example, the inner corner of the eye is *en* for *endocanthion*, while the top of the flap of cartilage (the tragus) in front of the ear is *t* for *tragion*.

Two of the landmarks determine a canonical horizontal orientation for the head. The horizontal plane is determined by the two lines (on either side of the head) connecting the landmark *t* to the landmark *or* (for *orbitale*), the lowest point of the eye socket on the skull. In measurement, anthropometrists actually align the head to this horizontal, in what is known as Frankfurt horizontal (FH) position [12, 20], so that measurements can be made easily and accurately with respect to this coordinate system. In addition to this, a vertical mid-line axis is defined by the landmarks *n* (for *nasion*), a skull feature roughly between the eyebrows; *sn* (for *subnasale*) the center point where the nose meets the upper lip; and *gn* (for *gnathion*), the lowest point on the chin.

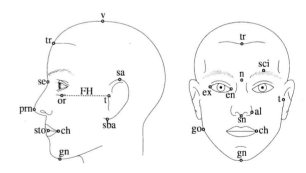

Figure 1: Anthropometric landmarks on the face [12]

Farkas's inventory includes the five types of facial measurements described below and illustrated in Figure 2:

- the *shortest distance* between two landmarks. An example is *en-ex*, the distance between the landmarks at the corners of the eye
- the *axial distance* between two landmarks—the distance measured along one of the axes of the canonical coordinate system, with the head in FH position. An example is *v-tr*, the vertical distance (height difference) between the top of the head (*v* for *vertex*) and hairline (*tr* for *trichion*).
- the *tangential distance* between two landmarks—the distance measured along a prescribed path on the surface of the face. An example is *ch-t*, the surface distance from the corner of the mouth (*ch* for *cheilion*) to the tragus.

- the *angle of inclination* between two landmarks with respect to one of the canonical axes. An example is the inclination of the ear axis with respect to the vertical.
- the *angle between locations*, such as the mentocervical angle (the angle at the chin).

We must represent measurements of each of these types to apply Farkas's anthropometry in creating models for graphics.

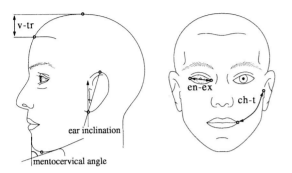

Figure 2: Example anthropometric measurements [12]

Farkas describes a total of 132 measurements on the face and head. Some of the measurements are *paired*, when there is a corresponding measurement on the left and right side of the face. Until recently, the measurement process could only be carried out by experienced anthropometrists by hand. However, recent work has investigated 3-D range scanners as an alternative to manual measurement [6, 12, 20].

Systematic collection of anthropometric measurements has made possible a variety of statistical investigations of groups of subjects. Subjects have been grouped on the basis of gender, race, age, "attractiveness" or the presence of a physical syndrome. Means and variances for the measurements within a group, tabulated in [12, 15], effectively provide a set of measurements which captures virtually all of the variation that can occur in the group.

In addition to statistics on measurements, statistics on the *proportions* between measurements have also been derived. The description of the human form by proportions goes back to Dürer and da Vinci; anthropometrists have found that proportions give useful information about the correlations between features, and can serve as more reliable indicators of group membership than can simple measurements [11]. Many facial proportions have been found to show statistically significant differences across population groups [19]. These proportions are averaged over a particular population group, and means and variances are provided in [11].

3   Generating measurements

The rich descriptions of human geometry developed in anthropometry provide an invaluable resource for human modeling in computer graphics. This goes for artists as well as automatic systems: Parke and Waters [26] describe the importance of having a set of "conformation guidelines" for facial shape, which draw from artistic rules of face design. These guidelines provide qualitative information about the shape and proportion of faces, respecting the quantitative information found in anthropometric measurements.

In using such descriptions, automatic systems immediately confront the problem of bringing a model into correspondence with a desired set of measurements. A widely-used approach is to design a model whose degrees of freedom can be directly specified by anthropometric measurements. For example, in the early visualization frameworks for human factors engineering surveyed in [9]—where anthropometric data first figured in graphics—articulated

humans were made to exhibit specified body measurements by rigidly scaling each component of the articulation. Grosso, et al. [17] describe a similar model, but scale physical characteristics (such as mass) as well, to produce a model suitable for dynamic simulation and animation. Azuola [2] builds on Grosso's work, and generates random sets of (axis-aligned distance) measurements using covariance information (but not proportions). The purpose of this generation is to produce a fairly small sampling of differently sized people for human factors analysis.

Our work represents a departure in that we use anthropometric data to constrain the degrees of freedom of the model indirectly (as described in Section 4). This is a must for the diverse, abstract and interrelated measurements of face anthropometry. The flexibility of generating measurements as constraints offers additional benefits. In particular, it allows statistics about proportions to be taken into account as precisely as possible.

This section describes how our system uses published facial measurement and proportion statistics [11, 12] to generate random sets of measurements. The generated measurements both respect a given population distribution, and—thanks to the use of proportions—produce a believable face.

3.1   The need for proportions

Start with a given population, whose anthropometric measurements are tabulated for mean and standard deviation (we later use the measurements from [12]). We can assume that the measurements are given by a Gaussian normal distribution, as corroborated by statistical tests on the raw data [12]. This gives a naive algorithm for deriving a set of measurements—generate each measurement independently as if sampled from the normal distribution with its (estimated) mean and variance. Such random values are easily computed [29]; then, given the constraint-based framework we use, a shape can be generated to fit the resulting suite of measurements as long as the measurements are geometrically consistent.

Mere geometric consistency of measurements is no guarantee of the reasonable appearance of the resulting face shape, however. Anthropometric measurements are not independent. On the face, one striking illustration comes from the inclinations of the profile, which are highly intercorrelated. In the population described in [11], the inclinations to the front of the chin from under the nose (*sn-pg*) and from the lower lip (*li-pg*) take a wide range of values, but, despite the many curves in this part of the face, tend to agree very closely.

Published proportions provide the best available resource to model correlations between measurements such as these. For example, [11] tabulates the mean and variance for statistically significant ratios between anthropometric measurements for a population of young North American Caucasian men and women. Given a calculated value for one measurement, the proportion allows the other measurement to be determined using a random value from the estimated distribution of the proportion. Since the proportion reflects a correlation between these values, the resulting pair of measurements is more representative of the population than the two measurements would be if generated independently.

With many measurements come many useful proportions, but each value will be calculated only once. We must find the proportions that provide the most evidence about the distribution. The next section describes the algorithm we use to do that. It assumes that proportions can be applied in either direction (by approximating the distribution for the inverse proportion) and that we are generating a set of measurements all of which are related by proportions. (We can split the measurements into groups before applying this algorithm.) The algorithm also assumes that we are given a fixed initial measurement (or measurements) in this set from which other measurements could be generated. If we are generating a random face, the choice of which initial measurement to use is up in the air. We therefore find the best calculation scheme for each possible initial measurement, and then use the best of those. Random values for this initial measurement are generated by sampling its distribution. Thereafter, randomly generated proportions are used to generate the remaining dependent measurements.

The same algorithm could also be used to fill in measurements specified by a user (as a rough guide of the kind of face needed) or selected to be representative of an extreme in the population (for use in human-factors analysis). In this case, the algorithm gives a way of generating a plausible, random variation on this given information.

3.2 An algorithm for proportions

Given base measurements, our goal is to find the best way to use an inventory of proportions to calculate dependent measurements. We can describe this problem more precisely by viewing measurements as vertices and proportions as edges in a graph. Figure 3(a) shows a portion of this graph, given the measurements and proportions from [11, 12] (some edge labels are omitted for the sake of readability). The presence of cycles in this graph exhibits the need to select proportions. A particular method for calculating measurements using proportions can be represented as a *branching* in this graph—an acyclic directed graph in which each vertex has at most one incident edge. The edge e from s to d in this branching indicates that d is calculated by proportion e from s. By assumption, we will require this branching to span the graph (this means adding dummy edges connecting multiple base measurements). An example branching is illustrated in Figure 3(b), and contains a single base measurement (the vertex marked with a double circle).

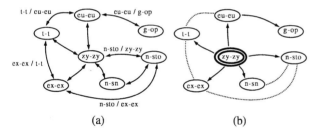

(a)   (b)

Figure 3: Interpreting measurements and proportions as a graph (a); Example branching used to compute measurements (b)

The algorithm associates each vertex v in the branching with a mean μ_v and variance σ_v^2. The variance is an indication of the precision of the statistical information applied in generating the measurement at v from given information. The smaller σ_v/μ_v, the more constrained the measurement. We take σ_v/μ_v as the weight of d.

For base measurements, σ_v is simply the standard deviation of the measurement. Thereafter, if an edge connects s to d with a proportion with mean μ_e and standard deviation σ_e, and s has mean μ_s and standard deviation σ_s, then the induced distribution at d is characterized by:

$$\mu_d = \mu_s \mu_e$$
$$\sigma_d^2 = \mu_s^2 \sigma_e^2 + \mu_e^2 \sigma_s^2 + \sigma_e^2 \sigma_s^2$$

(This assumes proportions and measurements are independent and Gaussian.) Note that the weight of d is always larger than the weight of s—this means the precision of the information concerning the distribution decreases as we go deeper into the branching.

Our goal in selecting proportions is to derive a branching T_M which assigns a minimum total weight to its vertices. This allows

the most constrained features to determine the remaining features via proportionality relationships. We can modify Prim's algorithm for minimum spanning tree to solve this problem. Our algorithm maintains a subtree T of some optimal branching. Initially, the subtree contains just the root for the initial measurement. At subsequent stages, each vertex is associated with the least weight induced by any edge running from the branching to it. The algorithm incorporates the vertex v whose weight is the least into the tree, by the appropriate new edge e.

As with Prim's algorithm (c.f. [13]), the argument that this algorithm works ensures inductively that if T is a subtree of some optimal branching T_M, then so is $T + e$. If e is not an edge in T_M, then T_M contains some other directed path to v, ending with a different edge e'. This path starts at the root of T, so it must at some point leave T. Because e was chosen with minimum weight and weights increase along paths, in fact the path must leave T at e'; since the algorithm chose e, e and e' induce the same weight for v. The inductive property is now established, since $(T_M - e') + e$ is an optimal branching of which T is a subtree.

4 Variational Modeling

Using the method outlined in Section 3, we generate complete sets of anthropometric measurements in Farkas's system. These constraints describe the geometry of the face in great detail, but they by no means specify a unique geometry for the face surface. For example, Farkas's measurements are relatively silent about the distribution of curvature over the face—the particular measurement that specifies the angle formed at the tip of the chin (the mentocervical angle; as in Figure 2), does not actually specify how sharply curved the chin is. What is needed then, intuitively, is a mechanism for generating a shape that shares the important properties of a typical face, as far as possible, but still respects a given set of anthropometric measurements. This intuition allows the problem of building an anthropometric face model to be cast as a constrained optimization problem—anthropometric measurements are treated as constraints, and the remainder of the face is determined by optimizing a surface objective function. This characterization allows us to apply variational modeling techniques [7, 16, 18, 24, 31, 33, 34].

This section briefly introduces variational modeling, and describes how we adapt existing variational modeling techniques to develop the anthropometric face model. Our approach to variational modeling greatly resembles the framework in [33]; a key difference is that we perform most of the variational computation in advance and share results across different face generation runs. This amortization of computational cost makes it feasible to construct larger models subject to many constraints. However, it requires careful formulation of constraints and algorithms to exploit the constancy of the face model and its inventory of constraints.

As described in Section 4.1, we begin by specifying a space of possible face geometries using a parametric surface $s(u, v)$, and locating the landmark points on the surface. We use a B-spline surface [10] to represent s. This surface is specified by a control mesh, where the mesh degrees of freedom are collected into a vector p. A particular instantiation p' of p provides a *prototype shape*, a reference geometry that epitomizes the kind of shape faces have. Both $s(u, v)$ and p' are designed by hand, but the same parameterized surface and prototype shape are used to model any set of anthropometric measurements.

Given this shape representation, the task of the face modeling system is to allow a given set of anthropometric measurements m to be used as degrees of freedom for s, *in place of* p. It does so in two logical steps: (1), expressing m as constraints on p in terms of the landmark points as described in Section 4.2; and (2), using variational techniques as described in Section 4.3 through Section 4.5

to find a surface that satisfies the constraints and which minimizes bending and stretching away from the prototype face shape.

4.1 Surface representation

We choose a B-spline surface as a shape representation because of the demands both of anthropometric modeling and variational techniques. Our shape must be smooth, must permit evaluation of our constraints, and must have surface points and tangent vectors that are defined as linear combinations of its control mesh points. This scheme meets all of these requirements.

The specification of $\mathbf{s}(u,v)$ involved the manual construction of a B-spline control mesh for the face, shown in Figure 4. The mesh is a tube with openings at the mouth and neck; the geometry follows an available polygonal face model and (as required for accurate variational modeling) is parameterized to avoid excessive distortion of (u,v) patches.

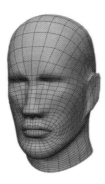

Figure 4: The prototype face model

Anthropometric landmarks are assigned fixed locations on the surface in (u,v) parameter space; some are also associated with constraints that enforce their fixed geometric interpretations. For example, in the case of the v landmark, which represents the top of the head, we ensure that the tangent to the surface at the point representing the landmark is in fact horizontal. We likewise add constraints to keep the model in FH position, so that the horizontal axis of the model is consistent with the axis by which landmarks are identified (and measurements taken). These constraints together constitute a set of *base* constraints which must be satisfied to apply any anthropometric measurement. Further constraints are then added to the model—one for each measurement.

4.2 Surface constraints

Our framework derives a shape by applying both linear and nonlinear constraints. The linear constraints are derived from axial distance anthropometric measurements and the base constraints on the model; both can be represented as a linear function of the degrees of freedom of the model, $\mathbf{p}$. A matrix $\mathbf{A}$ describes how the values of all linear constraints are calculated, while a vector $\mathbf{b}$ encodes the intended values for those measurements. Thus solutions to these constraints satisfy:

$$\mathbf{Ap} = \mathbf{b} \qquad (1)$$

Because $\mathbf{A}$ depends only on the *types* of constraint measurements, $\mathbf{A}$ can be solved in advance; then values of $\mathbf{p}$ can be computed directly from $\mathbf{b}$ given particular measurements $\mathbf{m}$.

Many of the constraints are non-linear, however. Each non-linear constraint is associated with a positive function measuring how far the surface is from the correct measurement. These functions are summed to give an overall penalty function $\mathcal{P}$ so that non-linear constraints impose the equation:

$$\mathcal{P}(\mathbf{p}) = 0 \qquad (2)$$

($\mathcal{P}(\mathbf{p}) \geq 0$ for all $\mathbf{p}$). The remainder of this section describes the penalty functions associated with each type of measurement constraint.

The shortest distance measurement constrains the points $\mathbf{x}_i$ and $\mathbf{x}_j$ at a distance r apart using the penalty:

$$\mathcal{P}_{\text{dist}}(\mathbf{x}_i, \mathbf{x}_j) = \left(\|\mathbf{x}_i - \mathbf{x}_j\| - r \right)^2 \qquad (3)$$

The tangential distance constraint, which specifies the length of a surface curve to be r, is approximated using the chord-length approximation of a curve [10] using the points $\mathbf{x}_1 \ldots \mathbf{x}_n$:

$$\mathcal{P}_{\text{arc-len}}(\mathbf{x}_1, \ldots, \mathbf{x}_n) = \left(\sum_{i=1}^{n-1} \|\mathbf{x}_i - \mathbf{x}_{i+1}\| - r \right)^2 \qquad (4)$$

The points $\mathbf{x}_i$ all lie on a predetermined curve specified in (u,v)-space (using a B-spline), and are adaptively sampled as to achieve a good estimate of the arc length using the chord-length approximation.

The inclination measurement constraint fixes a vector $\mathbf{v}$ at an angle θ to a fixed axis $\mathbf{a}$:

$$\mathcal{P}_{\text{incl}}(\mathbf{v}) = (\hat{\mathbf{v}} - Rot(\mathbf{a}, \theta))^2 \qquad (5)$$

Using the rotation Rot, the axis $\mathbf{a}$ is aligned with the "goal" direction. $\mathbf{v}$ can be the direction between two points on the surface, as well as a surface tangent vector.

The angle measurement constraint positions the vectors $\mathbf{v}_1$ and $\mathbf{v}_2$ to be separated by the angle θ. It is treated as two independent inclination constraints:

$$\begin{aligned} \mathcal{P}_{\text{angle}_1}(\mathbf{v}_1) &= (\hat{\mathbf{v}}_1 - Rot(\hat{\mathbf{v}}_2, \theta))^2 \\ \mathcal{P}_{\text{angle}_2}(\mathbf{v}_2) &= (\hat{\mathbf{v}}_2 - Rot(\hat{\mathbf{v}}_1, -\theta))^2 \end{aligned} \qquad (6)$$

4.3 Fairing

A fair surface can be constructed by minimizing an objective function $E(\mathbf{s})$. We will be using the *thin-plate* functional [7, 18, 33] which measures the bending of the surface $\mathbf{s}$. It includes the thin-plate term E_p to measure bending, and a membrane term E_m which ensures the approximation does not become inaccurate:

$$\begin{aligned} E_p(\mathbf{s}) &= \int (\mathbf{s}_{uu} \cdot \mathbf{s}_{uu} + 2\mathbf{s}_{uv} \cdot \mathbf{s}_{uv} + \mathbf{s}_{vv} \cdot \mathbf{s}_{vv}) du\, dv, \\ E_m(\mathbf{s}) &= \int (\mathbf{s}_u \cdot \mathbf{s}_u + 2\mathbf{s}_u \cdot \mathbf{s}_v + \mathbf{s}_v \cdot \mathbf{s}_v) du\, dv \end{aligned} \qquad (7)$$

where the subscripts on $\mathbf{s}$ denote parametric differentiation. The overall fairness of the surface is determined by combining these terms together using weights α and β (where typically α is just large enough to prevent approximation error):

$$E(\mathbf{s}) = \alpha E_m(\mathbf{s}) + \beta E_p(\mathbf{s}) \qquad (8)$$

For linear surface representation schemes (including B-splines), the objective function in (8) can be evaluated exactly as a quadratic form $\frac{1}{2}\mathbf{p}^\top \mathbf{H} \mathbf{p}$ [18, 33], where $\mathbf{H}$ is determined based on the surface representation scheme; the construction for B-splines is given in [33]. Due to the local refinement property of B-splines, $\mathbf{H}$ is sparse.

The objective function can also be measured with respect to the prototype shape $\mathbf{p}'$ [33], so that the minimization is performed with respect to $(\mathbf{p} - \mathbf{p}')$, resulting in $\frac{1}{2}(\mathbf{p} - \mathbf{p}')^\top \mathbf{H}(\mathbf{p} - \mathbf{p}')$. The use of a prototype shape instructs the fairing process to ignore expected regions of sharp curvature, such as the ears and nose on the face.

Given $\mathbf{H}$, the problem of fairing given purely linear constraints as in (1) is reduced to the following linearly constrained quadratic optimization problem [18, 33]:

$$\min_{\mathbf{p}} \left\| \frac{1}{2}(\mathbf{p} - \mathbf{p}')^\top \mathbf{H}(\mathbf{p} - \mathbf{p}') \right\| \quad \text{subject to } \mathbf{Ap} = \mathbf{b} \qquad (9)$$

4.4 Fairing with constraints

There are a number of approaches for solving the constrained minimization problem in (9) including Lagrange multipliers and penalty methods [33] and null-space projection [18], each of which transform the problem to a unconstrained problem.

The Lagrange multiplier $\mathbf{y}$ yields the unconstrained minimization:

$$\min_{\mathbf{p}, \mathbf{y}} \left\| \frac{1}{2}(\mathbf{p} - \mathbf{p}')^\top \mathbf{H}(\mathbf{p} - \mathbf{p}') + (\mathbf{Ap} - \mathbf{b})^\top \mathbf{y} \right\| \qquad (10)$$

At the minimum, the partial derivatives of the bracketed terms vanish. Differentiation leads to the linear system:

$$\left| \begin{array}{cc} \mathbf{H} & \mathbf{A}^\top \\ \mathbf{A} & 0 \end{array} \right| \left| \begin{array}{c} \mathbf{p} \\ \mathbf{y} \end{array} \right| = \left| \begin{array}{c} \mathbf{Hp}' \\ \mathbf{b} \end{array} \right| \qquad (11)$$

Solving such a system requires selecting a technique that is mathematically sound and computationally feasible. For example, interactive modeling, with varying constraints and response time demands, requires the use of iterative solution methods, such as the conjugate gradient technique [16, 34]. However, we can solve this system without iteration, using a sparse LU decomposition technique [14]; producing the decomposition takes $O(n^2)$ time given a $O(n)$ sparse $n \times n$ system. This technique is applicable because the set of constraints is hand-constructed, so we can guarantee that the constraint matrix $\mathbf{A}$ contains no dependent rows, and hence that the LU decomposition is well defined. It is feasible because the control mesh topology and the constraint matrix are unchanging, so that only one decomposition ever needs to be generated. Finding solutions is then quite efficient. In general, solving a system given an LU decomposition takes $O(n^2)$ time. However, we have found that the LU decomposition is roughly $O(n)$ sparse given our constraints. (This is not too surprising given that the each constraint involves only a few points on the surface; note that an LU decomposition can be sparse even if the actual inverse is dense.) This means that, in practice, solution steps require roughly linear time.

4.5 Non-linear constraints

As described in Section 4.2, the non-linear constraints are specified using the penalty function $\mathcal{P}(\mathbf{p})$. Since this function is positive, it is simply added into the minimization (10) [28, 33]. The extended linear system (11) has $\mathbf{Hp}' - \partial\mathcal{P}(\mathbf{p})/\partial\mathbf{p}$ in place of $\mathbf{Hp}'$. Due to the non-linearity of $\mathcal{P}$, this system must be solved iteratively. (By contrast, Section 4.2 described a non-iterative method for solving the linear constraints.)

At iteration i, we determine C_i to be used in place of $-\partial\mathcal{P}(\mathbf{p})/\partial\mathbf{p}$ as:

$$C_i = C_{i-1} - \mu_i \frac{\partial\mathcal{P}(\mathbf{p}_{i-1})}{\partial\mathbf{p}} \qquad (12)$$

with $C_0 = \mathbf{0}$. The scalar value μ is a positive weight (analogous to a time-step in ODE integration), determined using an adaptive method such as step-doubling (for ODE solution) [29]. This results in the iterative linear system:

$$\left| \begin{array}{cc} \mathbf{H} & \mathbf{A}^\top \\ \mathbf{A} & 0 \end{array} \right| \left| \begin{array}{c} \mathbf{p}_i \\ \mathbf{y} \end{array} \right| = \left| \begin{array}{c} \mathbf{Hp}' + C_i \\ \mathbf{b} \end{array} \right| \qquad (13)$$

where $\mathbf{p}_0$ is the solution corresponding to (11). Note that we still exploit the LU decomposition to allow steps to be solved quickly and exactly; this technique is stabler and faster to converge than the combination of a conjugate gradient technique with the penalty method. We experimented with linearizations of some of the non-linear constraints (and added them into $\mathbf{A}$), but found little gain in efficiency, and decreased stability in solving.

In practice, the simultaneous use of all anthropometric constraints will lead to conflict. For example, some measurements lead to linearly dependent constraints; they are easily identified by inspection, and culled to keep $\mathbf{A}$ invertible. Similarly, when multiple measurements place non-linear constraints on similar features of nearby points on the model (without providing additional variation in shape), including all can introduce a source of geometric inconsistency and prevent the convergence of C. Our constraint set was selected by following a strategy of including only those constraints with the most locally confining definitions (i.e. constraints which affected fewer facial locations or more proximate facial locations were favored).

5 Results and discussion

Sample face models derived using this technique are shown in Figure 5. To produce the measurements for these models, we ran the generation algorithm described in Section 3 on the measurements from [12] and the proportions from [11] for North American Caucasian young adult men and women. Faces for the random measurements were realized by applying the variational framework to a B-spline mesh (a grid 32 by 32) so as to satisfy the base constraints (a total of 15) and 65 measurements that give good coverage both of the shape of the face and of the kinds of measurements used in Farkas's system. There were a total of 120 proportions used as input to the algorithm in Section 3.2.

Producing the LU decomposition used for all these examples involved a one-time cost of roughly 3 minutes on an SGI 175 MHz R10000. Faces typically found their rough shape within 50 iterations; our illustrations were allowed to run for up to 200 iterations to ensure convergence to millimeter accuracy, resulting in runs that took about 1 minute for each face. Models were rendered using RenderMan.

Individual variation across the example males and females in Figure 5 encompass a range of features; for example, clear differences are found in the length and width of the nose and mouth, the inclinations of forehead and nose, as well as the overall shape of the face. At the same time, traits that distinguish men and women—such as the angle at the chin, the slope of the eyes and the height of the lower face (particularly at the jaw)—vary systematically and correctly (based on qualitative comparisons with the anthropometric data). Examining the variation within a population group, the thirty generated males in Figure 6 exhibit the expected range of geometric variation.

In order to quantify this comparison, the proportion-based measurement generation algorithm from Section 3.2 was validated by generating a large number of measurement sets, and comparing the resulting measurement distributions to the published figures from the corresponding population groups. On average, the means differed by about 1% (with a maximum deviation of 4.5%)—well below the differences in means between population groups. The standard deviations agreed comparably, where the generated measurements had standard deviations that range from being 5% lower to 20% higher than the published values. While this validation guarantees the plausibility of measurements on the generated face models, data is unfortunately not available for comparing the entire geometry (this would require having, for example, a set of measurements of an individual along with a corresponding range scan). One would not expect such a comparison to precisely agree anyway, as the prototype shape has a measurable effect on the resulting geometry. However, this effect decreases with the use of additional measurements, which suggests the need to search out additional data on face geometry (morphometrics [5] seems to be a good starting point).

Despite the many changes, a single prototype shape was used for all examples. This gives the models commonalities in shape where anthropometric data is silent. Further, all the faces use the same texture so as not to exaggerate their differences (having a variety of textures would of course produce nicer results, but would be overlooking the main point of this work). The ears remain coarsely modeled (partly as a result of scarcity of measurements within the ear).

6   Conclusions

This paper has described a two step procedure for generating novel face geometries. The first step produces a plausible set of constraints on the geometry using anthropometric statistics; the second derives a surface that satisfies the constraints using variational modeling. This fruitful combination of techniques offers broader lessons for modeling: in particular, ways to scale up variational modeling—a technique previously restricted to modeling frameworks that have seen limited use to surface fitting tasks—for constrained classes of shapes, and ways to apply anthropometric proportions—long valued by artists and scientists alike—in graphics model generation.

Of course, our models must ultimately be more richly represented. Possible extensions might apply variational techniques to construct the face surface and the interior skull simultaneously; this would form the basis of a face animation model as in [21]. Similarly, landmarks on the face could be used to drive texture synthesis, deriving distinct but plausible patterns of skin and hair.

In the meantime, our work already suggests new computational approaches for tasks that rely on anthropometric results, like forensic anthropology, plastic surgery planning, and child aging. It could also figure in a user interface for editing face models, by allowing features to be edited while related features systematically changed—preserving natural proportions or ensuring that faces respect anthropometric properties common to their population group. Both tasks underscore the importance of continuing to gather and analyze anthropometric data of diverse human populations.

Acknowledgements

We would like to thank Will Welch, Nick Foster, Michael Collins, Max Mintz, Michael Gleicher, Scott King, Nathan Loofbourrow and Charles Loop for their helpful comments and discussion. This research is partially supported by ONR-YIP grant K-5-55043/3916-1552793; ONR DURIP N0001497-1-0396 and N00014-97-1-0385; NSF IRI 95-04372; NSF Career Award grant 9624604; NASA-96-OLMSA-01-147; NIST grant 60NANB7D0058; and ARO grant DAAH-04-96-1-007.

References

[1]   T. Akimoto, Y. Suenaga, and R.Wallace. Automatic creation of 3D facial models. *IEEE Computer Graphics and Applications*, 13(5):16–22, September 1993.

[2]   F. Azuola. *Error in representation of standard anthropometric data by human figure models*. PhD thesis, University of Pennsylvania, 1996.

[3]   T. Beier and S. Neely. Feature-based image metamorphosis. In *Proceedings SIGGRAPH '92*, volume 26, pages 35–42, July 1992.

[4]   F. Bookstein. Principal warps: Thin-plate splines and the decomposition of deformations. *IEEE Pattern Analysis and Machine Intelligence*, 11(6):567–585, 1989.

[5]   F. Bookstein. *Morphometric Tools for Landmark Data: Geometry and Biloogy*. Cambridge University Press, 1991.

[6]   K. Bush and O. Antonyshyn. 3-dimensional facial anthropometry using a laser-surface scanner–validation of the technique. *Plastic and reconstructive surgery*, 98(2):226–235, August 1996.

[7]   G. Celniker and D. Gossard. Deformable curve and surface finite elements for free-form shape design. In *Proceedings SIGGRAPH '91*, volume 25, pages 257–266, 1991.

[8]   S. DiPaola. Extending the range of facial types. *Journal of Visualization and Computer Animation*, 2(4):129–131, 1991.

[9]   M. Dooley. Anthropometric modeling programs – a survey. *IEEE Computer Graphics and Applications*, 2:17–25, November 1982.

[10]   G. Farin. *Curves and Surfaces for Computer Aided Geometric Design*. Academic Press, 1993.

[11]   L. Farkas. *Anthropometric Facial Proportions in Medicine*. Thomas Books, 1987.

[12]   L. Farkas. *Anthropometry of the Head and Face*. Raven Press, 1994.

[13]   A. Gibbons. *Algorithmic Graph Theory*. Cambridge University Press, 1985.

[14]   G. Golub and C. Van Loan. *Matrix Computations*. Johns Hopkins University Press, 1989.

[15]   C. Gordon. *1988 anthropometric survey of U.S. Army personnel: methods and summary statistics*. United States Army Natick Research, Development and Engineering Center, 1989.

[16]   S. Gortler and M. Cohen. Hierarchical and variational geometric modeling with wavelets. In *1995 Symposium on Interactive 3D Graphics*, pages 35–42, April 1995.

[17]   M. Grosso, R. Quach, and N. Badler. Anthropometry for computer animated human figures. In N. Magnenat-Thalmann and D. Thalmann, editors, *State-of-the-art in Computer Animation: Proceedings of Computer Animation '89*, New York, 1989. Springer-Verlag.

[18]   M. Halstead, M. Kass, and T. DeRose. Efficient, fair interpolation using Catmull-Clark surfaces. In *Proceedings SIGGRAPH '93*, volume 27, pages 35–44, August 1993.

[19]   A. Hrdlicka. *Practical anthropometry*. AMS Press, 1972.

[20]   J. Kolar and E. Salter. *Craniofacial Anthropometry: Practical Measurement of the Head and Face for Clinical, Surgical and Research Use*. Charles C. Thomas Publisher, LTD, 1996.

[21]   Y. Lee, D. Terzopoulos, and K.Waters. Realistic face modeling for animation. In *Proceedings SIGGRAPH '95*, pages 55–62, 1995.

[22]   J. P. Lewis. Algorithms for solid noise synthesis. *Proceedings SIGGRAPH '89*, 23(3):263–270, 1989.

[23]   N. Magnenat-Thalmann, H. Minh, M. de Angelis, and D. Thalmann. Design, transformation and animation of human faces. *The Visual Computer*, 5(1/2):32–39, March 1989.

[24]   H. Moreton and C. Séquin. Functional optimization for fair surface design. In *Proceedings SIGGRAPH '92*, volume 26, pages 167–176, 1992.

[25]   F. Parke. Parameterized models for facial animation. *IEEE Computer Graphics and Applications*, 2(9):61–68, 1982.

[26]   F. Parke and K. Waters. *Computer Facial Animation*. A K Peters, 1996.

[27]   M. Patel and P. Willis. FACES: The facial animation construction and editing system. In *Eurographics '91*, 1991.

[28]   J. Platt and A. Barr. Constraint methods for flexible models. In *Proceedings SIGGRAPH '88*, volume 22, pages 279–288, 1988.

[29]   W. Press, S. Teukolsky, W. Vetterling, and B. Flannery. *Numerical Recipes in C: The Art of Scientific Computing*. Cambridge University Press, 1992.

[30]   S. Rogers. *Personal Identification from Human Remains*. Charles C. Thomas Publisher, LTD, 1984.

[31]   D. Terzopoulos and H. Qin. Dynamic nurbs with geometric constrains for interactive sculpting. *ACM Transactions on Graphics*, 13(2):103–136, 1994.

[32]   T. Vetter and T. Poggio. Linear object classes and image synthesis from a single example image. *IEEE Pattern Analysis and Machine Intelligence*, 19(7):733–742, 1997.

[33]   W. Welch and A. Witkin. Variational surface modeling. In *Proceedings SIGGRAPH '92*, volume 26, pages 157–166, 1992.

[34]   W. Welch and A. Witkin. Free–Form shape design using triangulated surfaces. In *Proceedings SIGGRAPH '94*, volume 28, pages 247–256, July 1994.

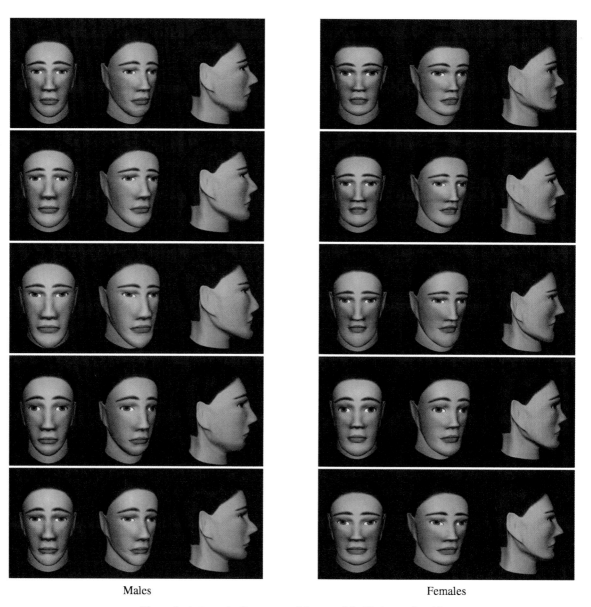

Males   Females

Figure 5: Automatically generated face models (3 views of each)

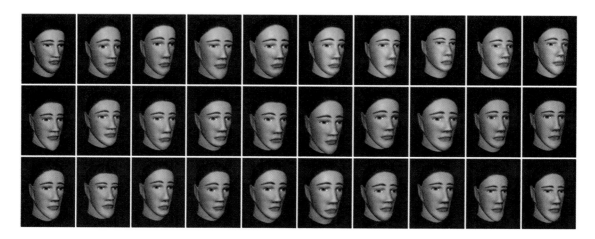

Figure 6: A male a minute

Synthesizing Realistic Facial Expressions from Photographs

Frédéric Pighin   *Jamie Hecker*   *Dani Lischinski*[†]   *Richard Szeliski*[‡]   *David H. Salesin*

University of Washington   [†]The Hebrew University   [‡]Microsoft Research

Abstract

We present new techniques for creating photorealistic textured 3D facial models from photographs of a human subject, and for creating smooth transitions between different facial expressions by morphing between these different models. Starting from several uncalibrated views of a human subject, we employ a user-assisted technique to recover the camera poses corresponding to the views as well as the 3D coordinates of a sparse set of chosen locations on the subject's face. A scattered data interpolation technique is then used to deform a generic face mesh to fit the particular geometry of the subject's face. Having recovered the camera poses and the facial geometry, we extract from the input images one or more texture maps for the model. This process is repeated for several facial expressions of a particular subject. To generate transitions between these facial expressions we use 3D shape morphing between the corresponding face models, while at the same time blending the corresponding textures. Using our technique, we have been able to generate highly realistic face models and natural looking animations.

CR Categories: I.2.10 [Artificial Intelligence]: Vision and Scene Understanding — Modeling and recovery of physical attributes; I.3.7 [Computer Graphics]: Three-Dimensional Graphics — Animation; I.3.7 [Computer Graphics]: Three-Dimensional Graphics — Color, shading, shadowing and texture.

Additional Keywords: facial modeling, facial expression generation, facial animation, photogrammetry, morphing, view-dependent texture-mapping

1 Introduction

> *There is no landscape that we know as well as the human face. The twenty-five-odd square inches containing the features is the most intimately scrutinized piece of territory in existence, examined constantly, and carefully, with far more than an intellectual interest. Every detail of the nose, eyes, and mouth, every regularity in proportion, every variation from one individual to the next, are matters about which we are all authorities.*
>
> — Gary Faigin [14],
> from *The Artist's Complete Guide to Facial Expression*

Realistic facial synthesis is one of the most fundamental problems in computer graphics — and one of the most difficult. Indeed, attempts to model and animate realistic human faces date back to the early 70's [34], with many dozens of research papers published since.

The applications of facial animation include such diverse fields as character animation for films and advertising, computer games [19], video teleconferencing [7], user-interface agents and avatars [44], and facial surgery planning [23, 45]. Yet no perfectly realistic facial animation has ever been generated by computer: no "facial animation Turing test" has ever been passed.

There are several factors that make realistic facial animation so elusive. First, the human face is an extremely complex geometric form. For example, the human face models used in Pixar's *Toy Story* had several thousand control points each [10]. Moreover, the face exhibits countless tiny creases and wrinkles, as well as subtle variations in color and texture — all of which are crucial for our comprehension and appreciation of facial expressions. As difficult as the face is to model, it is even more problematic to animate, since facial movement is a product of the underlying skeletal and muscular forms, as well as the mechanical properties of the skin and subcutaneous layers (which vary in thickness and composition in different parts of the face). All of these problems are enormously magnified by the fact that we as humans have an uncanny ability to read expressions — an ability that is not merely a learned skill, but part of our deep-rooted instincts. For facial expressions, the slightest deviation from truth is something any person will immediately detect.

A number of approaches have been developed to model and animate realistic facial expressions in three dimensions. (The reader is referred to the recent book by Parke and Waters [36] for an excellent survey of this entire field.) Parke's pioneering work introduced simple geometric interpolation between face models that were digitized by hand [34]. A radically different approach is performance-based animation, in which measurements from real actors are used to drive synthetic characters [4, 13, 47]. Today, face models can also be obtained using laser-based cylindrical scanners, such as those produced by Cyberware [8]. The resulting range and color data can be fitted with a structured face mesh, augmented with a physically-based model of skin and muscles [29, 30, 43, 46]. The animations produced using these face models represent the state-of-the-art in automatic physically-based facial animation.

For sheer photorealism, one of the most effective approaches to date has been the use of 2D morphing between photographic images [3]. Indeed, some remarkable results have been achieved in this way — most notably, perhaps, the Michael Jackson video produced by PDI, in which very different-looking actors are seemingly transformed into one another as they dance. The production of this video, however, required animators to painstakingly specify a few dozen carefully chosen correspondences between physical features of the actors in almost every frame. Another problem with 2D image morphing is that it does not correctly account for changes in viewpoint or object pose. Although this shortcoming has been recently addressed by a technique called "view morphing" [39], 2D morphing still lacks some of the advantages of a 3D model, such as the complete freedom of viewpoint and the ability to composite the image with other 3D graphics. Morphing has also been applied in 3D: Chen *et al.* [6] applied Beier and Neely's 2D morphing technique [3] to morph between cylindrical laser scans of human heads. Still, even in this case the animator must specify correspondences for every pair of expressions in order to produce a transition between them. More recently,

Bregler *et al.* [5] used morphing of mouth regions to lip-synch existing video to a novel sound-track.

In this paper, we show how 2D morphing techniques can be combined with 3D transformations of a geometric model to automatically produce 3D facial expressions with a high degree of realism. Our process consists of several basic steps. First, we capture multiple views of a human subject (with a given facial expression) using cameras at arbitrary locations. Next, we digitize these photographs and manually mark a small set of initial corresponding points on the face in the different views (typically, corners of the eyes and mouth, tip of the nose, etc.). These points are then used to automatically recover the camera parameters (position, focal length, etc.) corresponding to each photograph, as well as the 3D positions of the marked points in space. The 3D positions are then used to deform a generic 3D face mesh to fit the face of the particular human subject. At this stage, additional corresponding points may be marked to refine the fit. Finally, we extract one or more texture maps for the 3D model from the photos. Either a single view-independent texture map can be extracted, or the original images can be used to perform view-dependent texture mapping. This whole process is repeated for the same human subject, with several different facial expressions. To produce facial animations, we interpolate between two or more different 3D models constructed in this way, while at the same time blending the textures. Since all the 3D models are constructed from the same generic mesh, there is a natural correspondence between all geometric points for performing the morph. Thus, transitions between expressions can be produced entirely automatically once the different face models have been constructed, without having to specify pairwise correspondences between any of the expressions.

Our modeling approach is based on photogrammetric techniques in which images are used to create precise geometry [31, 40]. The earliest such techniques applied to facial modeling and animation employed grids that were drawn directly on the human subject's face [34, 35]. One consequence of these grids, however, is that the images used to construct geometry can no longer be used as valid texture maps for the subject. More recently, several methods have been proposed for modeling the face photogrammetrically without the use of grids [20, 24]. These modeling methods are similar in concept to the modeling technique described in this paper. However, these previous techniques use a small predetermined set of features to deform the generic face mesh to the particular face being modeled, and offer no mechanism to further improve the fit. Such an approach may perform poorly on faces with unusual features or other significant deviations from the normal. Our system, by contrast, gives the user complete freedom in specifying the correspondences, and enables the user to refine the initial fit as needed. Another advantage of our technique is its ability to handle fairly arbitrary camera positions and lenses, rather than using a fixed pair that are precisely oriented. Our method is similar, in concept, to the work done in architectural modeling by Debevec *et al.* [9], where a set of annotated photographs are used to model buildings starting from a rough description of their shape. Compared to facial modeling methods that utilize a laser scanner, our technique uses simpler acquisition equipment (regular cameras), and it is capable of extracting texture maps of higher resolution. (Cyberware scans typically produce a cylindrical grid of 512 by 256 samples). The price we pay for these advantages is the need for user intervention in the modeling process.

We employ our system not only for creating realistic face models, but also for performing realistic transitions between different expressions. One advantage of our technique, compared to more traditional animatable models with a single texture map, is that we can capture the subtle changes in illumination and appearance (e.g., facial creases) that occur as the face is deformed. This degree of realism is difficult to achieve even with physically-based models, because of the complexity of skin folding and the difficulty of simulating interreflections and self-shadowing [18, 21, 32].

This paper also presents several new expression synthesis techniques based on extensions to the idea of morphing. We develop a morphing technique that allows for different regions of the face to have different "percentages" or "mixing proportions" of facial expressions. We also introduce a painting interface, which allows users to locally add in a little bit of an expression to an existing composite expression. We believe that these novel methods for expression generation and animation may be more natural for the average user than more traditional animation systems, which rely on the manual adjustments of dozens or hundreds of control parameters.

The rest of this paper is organized as follows. Section 2 describes our method for fitting a generic face mesh to a collection of simultaneous photographs of an individual's head. Section 3 describes our technique for extracting both view-dependent and view-independent texture maps for photorealistic rendering of the face. Section 4 presents the face morphing algorithm that is used to animate the face model. Section 5 describes the key aspects of our system's user interface. Section 6 presents the results of our experiments with the proposed techniques, and Section 7 offers directions for future research.

2 Model fitting

The task of the model-fitting process is to adapt a generic face model to fit an individual's face and facial expression. As input to this process, we take several images of the face from different viewpoints (Figure 1a) and a generic face model (we use the generic face model created with Alias|Wavefront [2] shown in Figure 1c). A few features points are chosen (13 in this case, shown in the frames of Figure 1a) to recover the camera pose. These same points are also used to refine the generic face model (Figure 1d). The model can be further refined by drawing corresponding curves in the different views (Figure 1b). The output of the process is a face model that has been adapted to fit the face in the input images (Figure 1e), along with a precise estimate of the camera pose corresponding to each input image.

The model-fitting process consists of three stages. In the *pose recovery* stage, we apply computer vision techniques to estimate the viewing parameters (position, orientation, and focal length) for each of the input cameras. We simultaneously recover the 3D coordinates of a set of *feature points* on the face. These feature points are selected interactively from among the face mesh vertices, and their positions in each image (where visible) are specified by hand. The *scattered data interpolation* stage uses the estimated 3D coordinates of the feature points to compute the positions of the remaining face mesh vertices. In the *shape refinement* stage, we specify additional correspondences between facial vertices and image coordinates to improve the estimated shape of the face (while keeping the camera pose fixed).

2.1 Pose recovery

Starting with a rough knowledge of the camera positions (e.g., frontal view, side view, etc.) and of the 3D shape (given by the generic head model), we iteratively improve the pose and the 3D shape estimates in order to minimize the difference between the predicted and observed feature point positions. Our formulation is based on the non-linear least squares structure-from-motion algorithm introduced by Szeliski and Kang [41]. However, unlike the method they describe, which uses the Levenberg-Marquardt algorithm to perform a complete iterative minimization over all of the unknowns simultaneously, we break the problem down into a series of linear least squares problems that can be solved using very simple

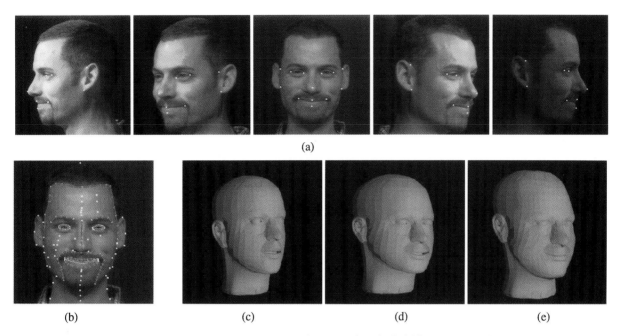

Figure 1 Model-fitting process: (a) a set of input images with marked feature points, (b) facial features annotated using a set of curves, (c) generic face geometry (shaded surface rendering), (d) face adapted to initial 13 feature points (after pose estimation) (e) face after 99 additional correspondences have been given.

and numerically stable techniques [16, 37].

To formulate the pose recovery problem, we associate a rotation matrix $\boldsymbol{R}^k$ and a translation vector $\boldsymbol{t}^k$ with each camera pose k. (The three rows of $\boldsymbol{R}^k$ are $\boldsymbol{r}_x^k$, $\boldsymbol{r}_y^k$, and $\boldsymbol{r}_z^k$, and the three entries in $\boldsymbol{t}^k$ are t_x^k, t_y^k, t_z^k.) We write each 3D feature point as $\boldsymbol{p}_i$, and its 2D screen coordinates in the k-th image as (x_i^k, y_i^k).

Assuming that the origin of the (x, y) image coordinate system lies at the optical center of each image (i.e., where the optical axis intersects the image plane), the traditional 3D projection equation for a camera with a focal length f^k (expressed in pixels) can be written as

$$x_i^k = f^k \frac{\boldsymbol{r}_x^k \cdot \boldsymbol{p}_i + t_x^k}{\boldsymbol{r}_z^k \cdot \boldsymbol{p}_i + t_z^k} \qquad y_i^k = f^k \frac{\boldsymbol{r}_y^k \cdot \boldsymbol{p}_i + t_y^k}{\boldsymbol{r}_z^k \cdot \boldsymbol{p}_i + t_z^k} \qquad (1)$$

(This is just an explicit rewriting of the traditional projection equation $\boldsymbol{x}_i^k \propto \boldsymbol{R}^k \boldsymbol{p}_i + \boldsymbol{t}^k$ where $\boldsymbol{x}_i^k = (x_i^k, y_i^k, f^k)$.)

Instead of using (1) directly, we reformulate the problem to estimate inverse distances to the object [41]. Let $\eta^k = 1/t_z^k$ be this inverse distance and $s^k = f^k \eta^k$ be a world-to-image scale factor. The advantage of this formulation is that the scale factor s^k can be reliably estimated even when the focal length is long, whereas the original formulation has a strong coupling between the f^k and t_z^k parameters.

Performing these substitution, we obtain

$$x_i^k = s^k \frac{\boldsymbol{r}_x^k \cdot \boldsymbol{p}_i + t_x^k}{1 + \eta^k \boldsymbol{r}_z^k \cdot \boldsymbol{p}_i}$$
$$y_i^k = s^k \frac{\boldsymbol{r}_y^k \cdot \boldsymbol{p}_i + t_y^k}{1 + \eta^k \boldsymbol{r}_z^k \cdot \boldsymbol{p}_i}.$$

If we let $w_i^k = (1 + \eta^k (\boldsymbol{r}_z^k \cdot \boldsymbol{p}_i))^{-1}$ be the inverse denominator, and collect terms on the left-hand side, we get

$$w_i^k \left(x_i^k + x_i^k \eta^k (\boldsymbol{r}_z^k \cdot \boldsymbol{p}_i) - s^k (\boldsymbol{r}_x^k \cdot \boldsymbol{p}_i + t_x^k) \right) = 0 \qquad (2)$$
$$w_i^k \left(y_i^k + y_i^k \eta^k (\boldsymbol{r}_z^k \cdot \boldsymbol{p}_i) - s^k (\boldsymbol{r}_y^k \cdot \boldsymbol{p}_i + t_y^k) \right) = 0$$

Note that these equations are linear in each of the unknowns that we wish to recover, i.e., $\boldsymbol{p}_i$, t_x^k, t_y^k, η^k, s^k, and $\boldsymbol{R}^k$, if we ignore the variation of w_i^k with respect to these parameters. (The reason we keep the w_i^k term, rather than just dropping it from these equations, is so that the linear equations being solved in the least squares step have the same magnitude as the original measurements (x_i^k, y_i^k). Hence, least-squares will produce a *maximum likelihood* estimate for the unknown parameters [26].)

Given estimates for initial values, we can solve for different subsets of the unknowns. In our current algorithm, we solve for the unknowns in five steps: first s^k, then $\boldsymbol{p}_i$, $\boldsymbol{R}^k$, t_x^k and t_y^k, and finally η^k. This order is chosen to provide maximum numerical stability given the crude initial pose and shape estimates. For each parameter or set of parameters chosen, we solve for the unknowns using linear least squares (Appendix A). The simplicity of this approach is a result of solving for the unknowns in five separate stages, so that the parameters for a given camera or 3D point can be recovered independently of the other parameters.

2.2 Scattered data interpolation

Once we have computed an initial set of coordinates for the feature points $\boldsymbol{p}_i$, we use these values to deform the remaining vertices on the face mesh. We construct a smooth interpolation function that gives the 3D displacements between the original point positions and the new adapted positions for every vertex in the original generic face mesh. Constructing such an interpolation function is a standard problem in scattered data interpolation. Given a set of known displacements $\boldsymbol{u}_i = \boldsymbol{p}_i - \boldsymbol{p}_i^{(0)}$ away from the original positions $\boldsymbol{p}_i^{(0)}$ at every constrained vertex i, construct a function that gives the displacement $\boldsymbol{u}_j$ for every unconstrained vertex j.

There are several considerations in choosing the particular data interpolant [33]. The first consideration is the embedding space, that is, the domain of the function being computed. In our case, we use the original 3D coordinates of the points as the domain. (An alternative would be to use some 2D parameterization of the surface mesh, for instance, the cylindrical coordinates described in Section 3.) We therefore attempt to find a smooth vector-valued function $\boldsymbol{f}(\boldsymbol{p})$ fitted to the known data $u_i = f(p_i)$, from which we can compute $u_j = f(p_j)$.

There are also several choices for how to construct the interpolating function [33]. We use a method based on *radial basis functions*, that is, functions of the form

$$f(p) = \sum_i c_i \phi(\|p - p_i\|),$$

where $\phi(r)$ are radially symmetric basis functions. A more general form of this interpolant also adds some low-order polynomial terms to model global, e.g., affine, deformations [27, 28, 33]. In our system, we use an affine basis as part of our interpolation algorithm, so that our interpolant has the form:

$$f(p) = \sum_i c_i \phi(\|p - p_i\|) + Mp + t, \qquad (3)$$

To determine the coefficients c_i and the affine components M and t, we solve a set of linear equations that includes the interpolation constraints $u_i = f(p_i)$, as well as the constraints $\sum_i c_i = 0$ and $\sum_i c_i p_i^{\mathrm{T}} = 0$, which remove affine contributions from the radial basis functions.

Many different functions for $\phi(r)$ have been proposed [33]. After experimenting with a number of functions, we have chosen to use $\phi(r) = e^{-r/64}$, with units measured in inches.

Figure 1d shows the shape of the face model after having interpolated the set of computed 3D displacements at 13 feature points shown in Figure 1 and applied them to the entire face.

2.3 Correspondence-based shape refinement

After warping the generic face model into its new shape, we can further improve the shape by specifying additional correspondences. Since these correspondences may not be as easy to locate correctly, we do not use them to update the camera pose estimates. Instead, we simply solve for the values of the new feature points p_i using a simple least-squares fit, which corresponds to finding the point nearest the intersection of the viewing rays in 3D. We can then re-run the scattered data interpolation algorithm to update the vertices for which no correspondences are given. This process can be repeated until we are satisfied with the shape.

Figure 1e shows the shape of the face model after 99 additional correspondences have been specified. To facilitate the annotation process, we grouped vertices into polylines. Each polyline corresponds to an easily identifiable facial feature such as the eyebrow, eyelid, lips, chin, or hairline. The features can be annotated by outlining them with hand-drawn curves on each photograph where they are visible. The curves are automatically converted into a set of feature points by stepping along them using an arc-length parametrization. Figure 1b shows annotated facial features using a set of curves on the front view.

3 Texture extraction

In this section we describe the process of extracting the texture maps necessary for rendering photorealistic images of a reconstructed face model from various viewpoints.

The texture extraction problem can be defined as follows. Given a collection of photographs, the recovered viewing parameters, and the fitted face model, compute for each point p on the face model its texture color $T(p)$.

Each point p may be visible in one or more photographs; therefore, we must identify the corresponding point in each photograph and decide how these potentially different values should be combined

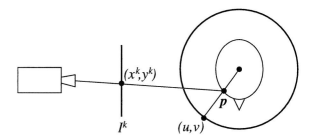

Figure 2 Geometry for texture extraction

(blended) together. There are two principal ways to blend values from different photographs: *view-independent blending*, resulting in a texture map that can be used to render the face from any viewpoint; and *view-dependent blending*, which adjusts the blending weights at each point based on the direction of the current viewpoint [9, 38]. Rendering takes longer with view-dependent blending, but the resulting image is of slightly higher quality (see Figure 3).

3.1 Weight maps

As outlined above, the texture value $T(p)$ at each point on the face model can be expressed as a convex combination of the corresponding colors in the photographs:

$$T(p) = \frac{\sum_k m^k(p) I^k(x^k, y^k)}{\sum_k m^k(p)}.$$

Here, I^k is the image function (color at each pixel of the k-th photograph,) and (x^k, y^k) are the image coordinates of the projection of p onto the k-th image plane. The *weight map $m^k(p)$* is a function that specifies the contribution of the k-th photograph to the texture at each facial surface point.

The construction of these weight maps is probably the trickiest and the most interesting component of our texture extraction technique. There are several important considerations that must be taken into account when defining a weight map:

1. *Self-occlusion:* $m^k(p)$ should be zero unless p is front-facing with respect to the k-th image and visible in it.

2. *Smoothness:* the weight map should vary smoothly, in order to ensure a seamless blend between different input images.

3. *Positional certainty:* $m^k(p)$ should depend on the "positional certainty" [24] of p with respect to the k-th image. The positional certainty is defined as the dot product between the surface normal at p and the k-th direction of projection.

4. *View similarity:* for view-dependent texture mapping, the weight $m^k(p)$ should also depend on the angle between the direction of projection of p onto the j-th image and its direction of projection in the new view.

Previous authors have taken only a subset of these considerations into account when designing their weighting functions. For example, Kurihara and Arai [24] use positional certainty as their weighting function, but they do not account for self-occlusion. Akimoto *et al.* [1] and Ip and Yin [20] blend the images smoothly, but address neither self-occlusion nor positional certainty. Debevec *et al.* [9], who describe a view-dependent texture mapping technique for modeling and rendering buildings from photographs, do address occlusion but do not account for positional certainty. (It should be noted, however, that positional certainty is less critical in photographs of buildings, since most buildings do not tend to curve away from the camera.)

To facilitate fast visibility testing of points on the surface of the face from a particular camera pose, we first render the face model using the recovered viewing parameters and save the resulting depth map from the Z-buffer. Then, with the aid of this depth map, we can quickly classify the visibility of each facial point by applying the viewing transformation and comparing the resulting depth to the corresponding value in the depth map.

3.2 View-independent texture mapping

In order to support rapid display of the textured face model from any viewpoint, it is desirable to blend the individual photographs together into a single texture map. This texture map is constructed on a virtual cylinder enclosing the face model. The mapping between the 3D coordinates on the face mesh and the 2D texture space is defined using a cylindrical projection, as in several previous papers [6, 24, 29].

For view-independent texture mapping, we will index the weight map m^k by the (u, v) coordinates of the texture being created. Each weight $m^k(u, v)$ is determined by the following steps:

1. Construct a feathered visibility map F^k for each image k. These maps are defined in the same cylindrical coordinates as the texture map. We initially set $F^k(u, v)$ to 1 if the corresponding facial point p is visible in the k-th image, and to 0 otherwise. The result is a binary visibility map, which is then smoothly ramped (feathered) from 1 to 0 in the vicinity of the boundaries [42]. A cubic polynomial is used as the ramping function.

2. Compute the 3D point p on the surface of the face mesh whose cylindrical projection is (u, v) (see Figure 2). This computation is performed by casting a ray from (u, v) on the cylinder towards the cylinder's axis. The first intersection between this ray and the face mesh is the point p. (Note that there can be more than one intersection for certain regions of the face, most notably the ears. These special cases are discussed in Section 3.4.) Let $P^k(p)$ be the positional certainty of p with respect to the k-th image.

3. Set weight $m^k(u, v)$ to the product $F^k(u, v) P^k(p)$.

For view-independent texture mapping, we will compute each pixel of the resulting texture $T(u, v)$ as a weighted sum of the original image functions, indexed by (u, v).

3.3 View-dependent texture mapping

The main disadvantage of the view-independent cylindrical texture map described above is that its construction involves blending together resampled versions of the original images of the face. Because of this resampling, and also because of slight registration errors, the resulting texture is slightly blurry. This problem can be alleviated to a large degree by using a view-dependent texture map [9] in which the blending weights are adjusted dynamically, according to the current view.

For view-dependent texture mapping, we render the model several times, each time using a different input photograph as a texture map, and blend the results. More specifically, for each input photograph, we associate texture coordinates and a blending weight with each vertex in the face mesh. (The rendering hardware performs perspective-correct texture mapping along with linear interpolation of the blending weights.)

Given a viewing direction d, we first select the subset of photographs used for the rendering and then assign blending weights to each of these photographs. Pulli et al. [38] select three photographs based on a Delaunay triangulation of a sphere surrounding the object. Since our cameras were positioned roughly in the same plane,

Figure 3 Comparison between view-independent (left) and view-dependent (right) texture mapping. Higher frequency details are visible in the view-dependent rendering.

we select just the two photographs whose view directions d^ℓ and $d^{\ell+1}$ are the closest to d and blend between the two.

In choosing the view-dependent term $V^k(d)$ of the blending weights, we wish to use just a single photo if that photo's view direction matches the current view direction precisely, and to blend smoothly between the nearest two photos otherwise. We used the simplest possible blending function having this effect:

$$V^k(d) = \begin{cases} d \cdot d^k - d^\ell \cdot d^{\ell+1} & \text{if } \ell \leq k \leq \ell+1 \\ 0 & \text{otherwise} \end{cases}$$

For the final blending weights $m^k(p, d)$, we then use the product of all three terms $F^k(x^k, y^k) P^k(p) V^k(d)$.

View-dependent texture maps have several advantages over cylindrical texture maps. First, they can make up for some lack of detail in the model. Second, whenever the model projects onto a cylinder with overlap, a cylindrical texture map will not contain data for some parts of the model. This problem does not arise with view-dependent texture maps if the geometry of the mesh matches the photograph properly. One disadvantage of the view-dependent approach is its higher memory requirements and slower speed due to the multi-pass rendering. Another drawback is that the resulting images are much more sensitive to any variations in exposure or lighting conditions in the original photographs.

3.4 Eyes, teeth, ears, and hair

The parts of the mesh that correspond to the eyes, teeth, ears, and hair are textured in a separate process. The eyes and teeth are usually partially occluded by the face; hence it is difficult to extract a texture map for these parts in every facial expression. The ears have an intricate geometry with many folds and usually fail to project without overlap on a cylinder. The hair has fine-detailed texture that is difficult to register properly across facial expressions. For these reasons, each of these facial elements is assigned an individual texture map. The texture maps for the eyes, teeth, and ears are computed by projecting the corresponding mesh part onto a selected input image where that part is clearly visible (the front view for eyes and teeth, side views for ears).

The eyes and the teeth are usually partially shadowed by the eyelids and the mouth respectively. We approximate this shadowing by modulating the brightness of the eye and teeth texture maps according to the size of the eyelid and mouth openings.

Figure 4 A global blend between "surprised" (left) and "sad" (center) produces a "worried" expression (right).

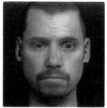  

Figure 5 Combining the upper part of a "neutral" expression (left) with the lower part of a "happy" expression (center) produces a "fake smile" (right).

4 Expression morphing

A major goal of this work is the generation of continuous and realistic transitions between different facial expressions. We achieve these effects by morphing between corresponding face models.

In general the problem of morphing between arbitrary polygonal meshes is a difficult one [22], since it requires a set of correspondences between meshes with potentially different topology that can produce a reasonable set of intermediate shapes. In our case, however, the topology of all the face meshes is identical. Thus, there is already a natural correspondence between vertices. Furthermore, in creating the models we attempt to mark facial features consistently across different facial expressions, so that the major facial features correspond to the same vertices in all expressions. In this case, a satisfactory 3D morphing sequence can be obtained using simple linear interpolation between the geometric coordinates of corresponding vertices in each of the two face meshes.

Together with the geometric interpolation, we need to blend the associated textures. Again, in general, morphing between two images requires pairwise correspondences between images features [3]. In our case, however, correspondences between the two textures are implicit in the texture coordinates of the two associated face meshes. Rather than warping the two textures to form an intermediate one, the intermediate face model (obtained by geometric interpolation) is rendered once with the first texture, and again with the second. The two resulting images are then blended together. This approach is faster than warping the textures (which typically have high resolution), and it avoids the resampling that is typically performed during warping.

4.1 Multiway blend and localized blend

Given a set of facial expression meshes, we have explored ways to enlarge this set by combining expressions. The simplest approach is to use the morphing technique described above to create new facial expressions, which can be added to the set. This idea can be generalized to an arbitrary number of starting expressions by taking convex combinations of them all, using weights that apply both to the coordinates of the mesh vertices and to the values in the texture map. (Extrapolation of expressions should also be possible by allowing weights to have values outside of the interval [0, 1]; note, however, that such weights might result in colors outside of the allowable gamut.)

We can generate an even wider range of expressions using a localized blend of the facial expressions. Such a blend is specified by a set of blend functions, one for each expression, defined over the vertices of the mesh. These blend functions describe the contribution of a given expression at a particular vertex.

Although it would be possible to compute a texture map for each new expression, doing so would result in a loss of texture quality. Instead, the weights for each new blended expression are always factored into weights over the vertices of the original set of expressions. Thus, each blended expression is rendered using the texture map of an original expression, along with weights at each vertex, which control the opacity of that texture. The opacities are linearly interpolated over the face mesh using Gouraud shading.

4.2 Blend specification

In order to design new facial expressions easily, the user must be provided with useful tools for specifying the blending functions. These tools should satisfy several requirements. First, it should be possible to edit the blend at different resolutions. Moreover, we would like the specification process to be continuous so that small changes in the blend parameters do not trigger radical changes in the resulting expression. Finally, the tools should be intuitive to the user; it should be easy to produce a particular target facial expression from an existing set.

We explored several different ways of specifying the blending weights:

- *Global blend.* The blending weights are constant over all vertices. A set of sliders controls the mixing proportions of the contributing expressions. Figure 4 shows two facial expressions blended in equal proportions to produce a halfway blend.

- *Regional blend.* According to studies in psychology, the face can be split into several regions that behave as coherent units [11]. Usually, three regions are considered: one for the forehead (including the eyebrows), another for the eyes, and another for the lower part of the face. Further splitting the face vertically down the center results in six regions and allows for asymmetric expressions. We similarly partition the face mesh into several (softly feathered) regions and assign weights so that vertices belonging to the same region have the same weights. The mixing proportions describing a selected region can be adjusted by manipulating a set of sliders. Figure 5 illustrates the blend of two facial expressions with two regions: the upper part of the face (including eyes and forehead) and the lower part (including nose, mouth, and chin.)

- *Painterly interface.* The blending weights can be assigned to the vertices using a 3D painting tool. This tool uses a palette in which the "colors" are facial expressions (both geometry and color), and the "opacity" of the brush controls how much the expression contributes to the result. Once an expression is selected, a 3D brush can be used to modify the blending weights in selected areas of the mesh. The fraction painted has a gradual drop-off and is controlled by the opacity of the brush. The strokes are applied directly on the rendering of the current facial blend, which is updated in real-time. To improve the rendering speed, only the portion of the mesh that is being painted is re-rendered. Figure 7 illustrates the design of a debauched smile: starting with a neutral expression, the face is locally modified using three other expressions. Note that in the last step, the use of a partially transparent brush with the "sleepy" expression results in the actual geometry of the eyelids becoming partially lowered.

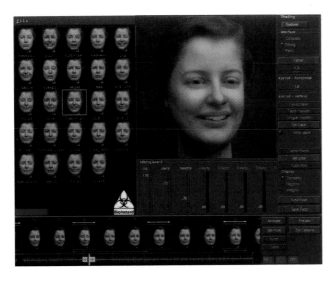

Figure 6 Animation interface. On the left is the "expression gallery"; on the right an expression is being designed. At the bottom expressions and poses are scheduled on the timeline.

Combining different original expressions enlarges the repertoire of expressions obtained from a set of photographs. The expressions in this repertoire can themselves be blended to create even more expressions, with the resulting expression still being representable as a (locally varying) linear combination of the original expressions.

5 User interface

We designed an interactive tool to fit a 3D face mesh to a set of images. This tool allows a user to select vertices on the mesh and mark where these curves or vertices should project on the images. After a first expression has been modeled, the set of annotations can be used as an initial guess for subsequent expressions. These guesses are automatically refined using standard correlation-based search. Any resulting errors can be fixed up by hand. The extraction of the texture map does not require user intervention, but is included in the interface to provide feedback during the modeling phase.

We also designed a keyframe animation system to generate facial animations. Our animation system permits a user to blend facial expressions and to control the transitions between these different expressions (Figure 6). The expression gallery is a key component of our system; it is used to select and display (as thumbnails) the set of facial expressions currently available. The thumbnails can be dragged and dropped onto the timeline (to set keyframes) or onto the facial design interface (to select or add facial expressions). The timeline is used to schedule the different expression blends and the changes in viewing parameters (pose) during the animation. The blends and poses have two distinct types of keyframes. Both types of keyframes are linearly interpolated with user-controlled cubic Bézier curves. The timeline can also be used to display intermediate frames at low resolution to provide a quick feedback to the animator. A second timeline can be displayed next to the composition timeline. This feature is helpful for correctly synchronizing an animation with live video or a soundtrack. The eyes are animated separately from the rest of the face, with the gaze direction parameterized by two Euler angles.

6 Results

In order to test our technique, we photographed both a man (J. R.) and a woman (Karla) in a variety of facial expressions. The photog-

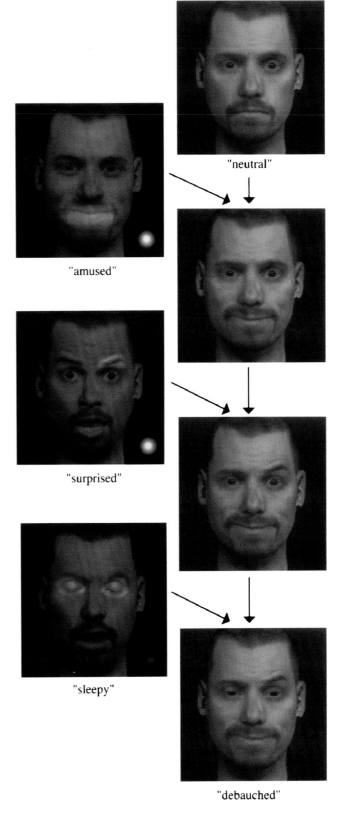

Figure 7 Painterly interface: design of a debauched smile. The right column shows the different stages of the design; the left column shows the portions of the original expressions used in creating the final expression. The "soft brush" used is shown at the bottom-right corner of each contributing expression.

raphy was performed using five cameras simultaneously. The cameras were not calibrated in any particular way, and the lenses had different focal lengths. Since no special attempt was made to illuminate the subject uniformly, the resulting photographs exhibited considerable variation in both hue and brightness. The photographs were digitized using the Kodak PhotoCD process. Five typical images (cropped to the size of the subject's head) are shown in Figure 1a.

We used the interactive modeling system described in Sections 2 and 3 to create the same set of eight face models for each subject: "happy," "amused," "angry," "surprised," "sad," "sleepy," "pained," and "neutral."

Following the modeling stage, we generated a facial animation for each of the individuals starting from the eight original expressions. We first created an animation for J. R. We then applied the very same morphs specified by this animation to the models created for Karla. For most frames of the animation, the resulting expressions were quite realistic. Figure 8 shows five frames from the animation sequence for J. R. and the purely automatically generated frames in the corresponding animation for Karla. With just a small amount of additional retouching (using the blending tools described in Section 4.2), this derivative animation can be made to look as good as the original animation for J. R.

7 Future work

The work described in this paper is just the first step towards building a complete image-based facial modeling and animation system. There are many ways to further enhance and extend the techniques that we have described:

Color correction. For better color consistency in facial textures extracted from photographs, color correction should be applied to simultaneous photographs of each expression.

Improved registration. Some residual ghosting or blurring artifacts may occasionally be visible in the cylindrical texture map due to small misregistrations between the images, which can occur if geometry is imperfectly modeled or not detailed enough. To improve the quality of the composite textures, we could locally warp each component texture (and weight) map before blending [42].

Texture relighting. Currently, extracted textures reflect the lighting conditions under which the photographs were taken. Relighting techniques should be developed for seamless integration of our face models with other elements.

Automatic modeling. Our ultimate goal, as far as the facial modeling part is concerned, is to construct a fully automated modeling system, which would automatically find features and correspondences with minimal user intervention. This is a challenging problem indeed, but recent results on 2D face modeling in computer vision [25] give us cause for hope.

Modeling from video. We would like to be able to create face models from video or old movie footage. For this purpose, we would have to improve the robustness of our techniques in order to synthesize face meshes and texture maps from images that do not correspond to different views of the same expression. Adding anthropomorphic constraints to our face model might make up for the lack of coherence in the data [48].

Complex animations. In order to create complex animations, we must extend our vocabulary for describing facial movements beyond blending between different expressions. There are several potential ways to attack this problem. One would be to adopt an action-unit-based system such as the Facial Action Coding System

(a)   (b)

Figure 8 On the left are frames from an original animation, which we created for J. R. The morphs specified in these frames were then directly used to create a derivative animation for Karla, shown on the right.

(FACS) [12]. Another possibility would be to apply modal analysis (principal component analysis) techniques to describe facial expression changes using a small number of motions [25]. Finding natural control parameters to facilitate animation and developing realistic-looking temporal profiles for such movements are also challenging research problems.

Lip-synching. Generating speech animation with our keyframe animation system would require a large number of keyframes. However, we could use a technique similar to that of Bregler *et al.* [5] to automatically lip-synch an animation to a sound-track. This would require the synthesis of face models for a wide range of visemes. For example, such database of models could be constructed using video footage to reconstruct face models automatically [17].

Performance-driven animation. Ultimately, we would also like to support performance-driven animation, i.e., the ability to automatically track facial movements in a video sequence, and to automatically translate these into animation control parameters. Our current techniques for registering images and converting them into 3D movements should provide a good start, although they will probably need to be enhanced with feature-tracking techniques and some rudimentary expression-recognition capabilities. Such a system would enable not only very realistic facial animation, but also a new level of video coding and compression techniques (since only the expression parameters would need to be encoded), as well as real-time control of avatars in 3D chat systems.

8 Acknowledgments

We would like to thank Katrin Petersen and Andrew Petty for modeling the generic face model, Cassidy Curtis for his invaluable advice on animating faces, and Joel Auslander and Jason Griffith for early contributions to this project. This work was supported by an NSF Presidential Faculty Fellow award (CCR-9553199), an ONR Young Investigator award (N00014-95-1-0728), and industrial gifts from Microsoft and Pixar.

References

[1] Takaaki Akimoto, Yasuhito Suenaga, and Richard S. Wallace. Automatic Creation of 3D Facial Models. *IEEE Computer Graphics and Applications*, 13(5):16–22, September 1993.

[2] Alias | Wavefront, Toronto, Ontario. *Alias V7.0*, 1995.

[3] Thaddeus Beier and Shawn Neely. Feature-based Image Metamorphosis. In *SIGGRAPH 92 Conference Proceedings*, pages 35–42. ACM SIGGRAPH, July 1992.

[4] Philippe Bergeron and Pierre Lachapelle. Controlling Facial Expressions and Body Movements in the Computer-Generated Animated Short "Tony De Peltrie". In *SIGGRAPH 85 Advanced Computer Animation seminar notes*. July 1985.

[5] Christoph Bregler, Michele Covell, and Malcolm Slaney. Video Rewrite: Driving Visual Speech with Audio. In *SIGGRAPH 97 Conference Proceedings*, pages 353–360. ACM SIGGRAPH, August 1997.

[6] David T. Chen, Andrei State, and David Banks. Interactive Shape Metamorphosis. In *1995 Symposium on Interactive 3D Graphics*, pages 43–44. ACM SIGGRAPH, April 1995.

[7] Chang S. Choi, Kiyoharu, Hiroshi Harashima, and Tsuyoshi Takebe. Analysis and Synthesis of Facial Image Sequences in Model-Based Image Coding. In *IEEE Transactions on Circuits and Systems for Video Technology*, volume 4, pages 257 – 275. June 1994.

[8] Cyberware Laboratory, Inc, Monterey, California. *4020/RGB 3D Scanner with Color Digitizer*, 1990.

[9] Paul E. Debevec, Camillo J. Taylor, and Jitendra Malik. Modeling and Rendering Architecture from Photographs: A Hybrid Geometry- and Image-Based Approach. In *SIGGRAPH 96 Conference Proceedings*, pages 11–20. ACM SIGGRAPH, August 1996.

[10] Eben Ostby, Pixar Animation Studios. Personal communication, January 1997.

[11] Paul Ekman and Wallace V. Friesen. *Unmasking the Face. A guide to recognizing emotions fron facial clues*. Prentice-Hall, Inc., Englewood Cliffs, New Jersey, 1975.

[12] Paul Ekman and Wallace V. Friesen. *Manual for the Facial Action Coding System*. Consulting Psychologists Press, Inc., Palo Alto, California, 1978.

[13] Irfan Essa, Sumit Basu, Trevor Darrell, and Alex Pentland. Modeling, Tracking and Interactive Animation of Faces and Heads Using Input from Video. In *Computer Animation Conference*, pages 68–79. June 1996.

[14] Gary Faigin. *The Artist's Complete Guide to Facial Expression*. Watson-Guptill Publications, New York, 1990.

[15] Olivier Faugeras. *Three-Dimensional Computer Vision: A Geometric Viewpoint*. MIT Press, Cambridge, Massachusetts, 1993.

[16] G. Golub and C. F. Van Loan. *Matrix Computation, third edition*. The John Hopkins University Press, Baltimore and London, 1996.

[17] Brian Guenter, Cindy Grimm, Daniel Wood, Henrique Malvar, and Frédéric Pighin. Making Faces. In *SIGGRAPH 98 Conference Proceedings*. ACM SIGGRAPH, July 1998.

[18] Pat Hanrahan and Wolfgang Krueger. Reflection from Layered Surfaces Due to Subsurface Scattering. In *SIGGRAPH 93 Conference Proceedings*, volume 27, pages 165–174. ACM SIGGRAPH, August 1993.

[19] Bright Star Technologies Inc. *Beginning Reading Software*. Sierra On-Line, Inc., 1993.

[20] Horace H. S. Ip and Lijun Yin. Constructing a 3D Individualized Head Model from Two Orthogonal Views. *The Visual Computer*, 12:254–266, 1996.

[21] Gregory Ward J., Francis M. Rubinstein, and Robert D. Clear. A Ray Tracing Solution for Diffuse Interreflection. In *SIGGRAPH 88 Conference Proceedings*, volume 22, pages 85–92. August 1988.

[22] James R. Kent, Wayne E. Carlson, and Richard E. Parent. Shape Transformation for Polyhedral Objects. In *SIGGRAPH 92 Proceedings Conference*, volume 26, pages 47–54. ACM SIGGRAPH, July 1992.

[23] Rolf M. Koch, Markus H. Gross, Friedrich R. Carls, Daniel F. von Büren, George Fankhauser, and Yoav I. H. Parish. Simulating Facial Surgery Using Finite Element Methods. In *SIGGRAPH 96 Conference Proceedings*, pages 421–428. ACM SIGGRAPH, August 1996.

[24] Tsuneya Kurihara and Kiyoshi Arai. A Transformation Method for Modeling and Animation of the Human Face from Photographs. In Nadia Magnenat Thalmann and Daniel Thalmann, editors, *Computer Animation 91*, pages 45–58. Springer-Verlag, Tokyo, 1991.

[25] A. Lanitis, C. J. Taylor, and T. F. Cootes. A Unified Approach for Coding and Interpreting Face Images. In *Fifth International Conference on Computer Vision (ICCV 95)*, pages 368–373. Cambridge, Massachusetts, June 1995.

[26] C. L. Lawson and R. J. Hansen. *Solving Least Squares Problems*. Prentice-Hall, Englewood Cliffs, 1974.

[27] Seung-Yong Lee, Kyung-Yong Chwa, Sung Yong Shin, and George Wolberg. Image Metamorphosis Using Snakes and Free-Form Deformations. In *SIGGRAPH 95 Conference Proceedings*, pages 439–448. ACM SIGGRAPH, August 1995.

[28] Seung-Yong Lee, George Wolberg, Kyung-Yong Chwa, and Sung Yong Shin. Image Metamorphosis with Scattered Feature Constraints. *IEEE Transactions on Visualization and Computer Graphics*, 2(4), December 1996.

[29] Yuencheng Lee, Demetri Terzopoulos, and Keith Waters. Realistic Modeling for Facial Animation. In *SIGGRAPH 95 Conference Proceedings*, pages 55–62. ACM SIGGRAPH, August 1995.

[30] Yuencheng C. Lee, Demetri Terzopoulos, and Keith Waters. Constructing Physics-Based Facial Models of Individuals. In *Proceedings of Graphics Interface 93*, pages 1–8. May 1993.

[31] Francis H. Moffitt and Edward M. Mikhail. *Photogrammetry*. Harper & Row, New York, 3 edition, 1980.

[32] Shree K. Nayar, Katsushi Ikeuchi, and Takeo Kanade. Shape from Interreflections. *International Journal of Computer Vision*, 6:173–195, 1991.

[33] Gregory M. Nielson. Scattered Data Modeling. *IEEE Computer Graphics and Applications*, 13(1):60–70, January 1993.

[34] Frederic I. Parke. Computer Generated Animation of Faces. *Proceedings ACM annual conference.*, August 1972.

[35] Frederic I. Parke. A Parametric Model for Human Faces. PhD thesis, University of Utah, Salt Lake City, Utah, December 1974. UTEC-CSc-75-047.

[36] Frederic I. Parke and Keith Waters. *Computer Facial Animation*. A K Peters, Wellesley, Massachusetts, 1996.

[37] W. H. Press, B. P. Flannery, S. A. Teukolsky, and W. T. Vetterling. *Numerical Recipes in C: The Art of Scientific Computing*. Cambridge University Press, Cambridge, England, second edition, 1992.

[38] Kari Pulli, Michael Cohen, Tom Duchamp, Hugues Hoppe, Linda Shapiro, and Werner Stuetzle. View-based rendering: Visualizing real objects from scanned range and color data. In *Proc. 8th Eurographics Workshop on Rendering*. June 1997.

[39] Steven M. Seitz and Charles R. Dyer. View Morphing. In *SIGGRAPH 96 Conference Proceedings*, Annual Conference Series, pages 21–30. ACM SIGGRAPH, August 1996.

[40] Chester C. Slama, editor. *Manual of Photogrammetry*. American Society of Photogrammetry, Falls Church, Virginia, fourth edition, 1980.

[41] Richard Szeliski and Sing Bing Kang. Recovering 3D Shape and Motion from Image Streams using Nonlinear Least Squares. *Journal of Visual Communication and Image Representation*, 5(1):10–28, March 1994.

[42] Richard Szeliski and Heung-Yeung Shum. Creating Full View Panoramic Image Mosaics and Texture-Mapped Models. In *SIGGRAPH 97 Conference Proceedings*, pages 251–258. ACM SIGGRAPH, August 1997.

[43] Demetri Terzopoulos and Keith Waters. Physically-based Facial Modeling, Analysis, and Animation. *Journal of Visualization and Computer Animation*, 1(4):73–80, March 1990.

[44] Kristinn R. Thórisson. Gandalf: An Embodied Humanoid Capable of Real-Time Multimodal Dialogue with People. In *First ACM International Conference on Autonomous Agents*. 1997.

[45] Michael W. Vannier, Jeffrey F. Marsh, and James O. Warren. Three-dimensional Computer Graphics for Craniofacial Surgical Planning and Evaluation. In *SIGGRAPH 83 Conference Proceedings*, volume 17, pages 263–273. ACM SIGGRAPH, August 1983.

[46] Keith Waters. A Muscle Model for Animating Three-Dimensional Facial Expression. In *SIGGRAPH 87 Conference Proceedings)*, volume 21, pages 17–24. ACM SIGGRAPH, July 1987.

[47] Lance Williams. Performance-Driven Facial Animation. In *SIGGRAPH 90 Conference Proceedings*, volume 24, pages 235–242. August 1990.

[48] Z. Zhang, K. Isono, and S. Akamatsu. Euclidean Structure from Uncalibrated Images Using Fuzzy Domain Knowledge: Application to Facial Images Synthesis. In *Proc. International Conference on Computer Vision (ICCV'98)*. January 1998.

A   Least squares for pose recovery

To solve for a subset of the parameters given in Equation (2), we use linear least squares. In general, given a set of linear equations of the form

$$a_j \cdot x - b_j = 0, \tag{4}$$

we solve for the vector x by minimizing

$$\sum_j (a_j \cdot x - b_j)^2. \tag{5}$$

Setting the partial derivative of this sum with respect to x to zero, we obtain

$$\sum_j (a_j a_j^T) x - b_j a_j = 0, \tag{6}$$

i.e., we solve the set of *normal equations* [16]

$$\left(\sum_j a_j a_j^T \right) x = \sum_j b_j a_j. \tag{7}$$

More numerically stable methods such as QR decomposition or Singular Value Decomposition [16] can also be used to solve the least squares problem, but we have not found them to be necessary for our application.

To update one of the parameters, we simply pull out the relevant linear coefficient a_j and scalar value b_j from Equation (2). For example, to solve for p_i, we set

$$a_{2k+0} = w_i^k(x_i^k \eta^k r_z^k - s^k r_x^k), \qquad b_{2k+0} = w_i^k(s^k t_x^k - x_i^k)$$
$$a_{2k+1} = w_i^k(y_i^k \eta^k r_z^k - s^k r_y^k), \qquad b_{2k+1} = w_i^k(s^k t_y^k - y_i^k).$$

For a scalar variable like s^k, we obtain scalar equations

$$a_{2k+0} = w_i^k(r_x^k \cdot p_i + t_x^k), \qquad b_{2k+0} = w_i^k \left(x_i^k + x_i^k \eta^k (r_z^k \cdot p_i) \right)$$
$$a_{2k+1} = w_i^k(r_y^k \cdot p_i + t_y^k), \qquad b_{2k+1} = w_i^k \left(y_i^k + y_i^k \eta^k (r_z^k \cdot p_i) \right).$$

Similar equations for a_j and b_j can be derived for the other parameters t_x^k, t_y^k, and η^k. Note that the parameters for a given camera k or 3D point i can be recovered independently of the other parameters.

Solving for rotation is a little trickier than for the other parameters, since R must be a valid rotation matrix. Instead of updating the elements in R_k directly, we replace the rotation matrix R^k with $\tilde{R}R^k$ [42], where $\tilde{R}$ is given by Rodriguez's formula [15]:

$$\tilde{R}(\hat{n}, \theta) = I + \sin\theta X(\hat{n}) + (1 - \cos\theta)X^2(\hat{n}), \tag{8}$$

where θ is an incremental rotation angle, $\hat{n}$ is a rotation axis, and $X(v)$ is the cross product operator

$$X(v) = \begin{bmatrix} 0 & -v_z & v_y \\ v_z & 0 & -v_x \\ -v_y & v_x & 0 \end{bmatrix} \tag{9}$$

A first order expansion of $\tilde{R}$ in terms of the entries in $v = \theta\hat{n} = (v_x, v_y, v_z)$ is given by $I + X(v)$.

Substituting into Equation (2) and letting $q_i = R^k p_i$, we obtain

$$w_i^k \left(x_i^k + x_i^k \eta^k (\tilde{r}_z^k \cdot q_i) - s^k(\tilde{r}_x^k \cdot q_i + t_x^k) \right) = 0 \tag{10}$$
$$w_i^k \left(y_i^k + y_i^k \eta^k (\tilde{r}_z^k \cdot q_i) - s^k(\tilde{r}_y^k \cdot q_i + t_y^k) \right) = 0,$$

where $\tilde{r}_x^k = (1, -v_z, v_y)$, $\tilde{r}_y^k = (v_z, 1, -v_x)$, $\tilde{r}_z^k = (-v_y, v_x, 1)$, are the rows of $[I + X(v)]$. This expression is linear in (v_x, v_y, v_z), and hence leads to a 3×3 set of normal equations in (v_x, v_y, v_z). Once the elements of v have been estimated, we can compute θ and $\hat{n}$, and update the rotation matrix using

$$R^k \leftarrow \tilde{R}(\hat{n}^k, \theta^k)R^k.$$

Subdivision Surfaces in Character Animation

Tony DeRose   Michael Kass   Tien Truong

Pixar Animation Studios

Figure 1: Geri.

Abstract

The creation of believable and endearing characters in computer graphics presents a number of technical challenges, including the modeling, animation and rendering of complex shapes such as heads, hands, and clothing. Traditionally, these shapes have been modeled with NURBS surfaces despite the severe topological restrictions that NURBS impose. In order to move beyond these restrictions, we have recently introduced subdivision surfaces into our production environment. Subdivision surfaces are not new, but their use in high-end CG production has been limited.

Here we describe a series of developments that were required in order for subdivision surfaces to meet the demands of high-end production. First, we devised a practical technique for construct-

ing provably smooth variable-radius fillets and blends. Second, we developed methods for using subdivision surfaces in clothing simulation including a new algorithm for efficient collision detection. Third, we developed a method for constructing smooth scalar fields on subdivision surfaces, thereby enabling the use of a wider class of programmable shaders. These developments, which were used extensively in our recently completed short film *Geri's game*, have become a highly valued feature of our production environment.

CR Categories: I.3.5 [Computer Graphics]: Computational Geometry and Object Modeling; I.3.3 [Computer Graphics]: Picture/Image Generation.

1   Motivation

The most common way to model complex smooth surfaces such as those encountered in human character animation is by using a patchwork of trimmed NURBS. Trimmed NURBS are used primarily because they are readily available in existing commercial systems such as Alias-Wavefront and SoftImage. They do, however, suffer from at least two difficulties:

1. Trimming is expensive and prone to numerical error.

2. It is difficult to maintain smoothness, or even approximate smoothness, at the seams of the patchwork as the model is

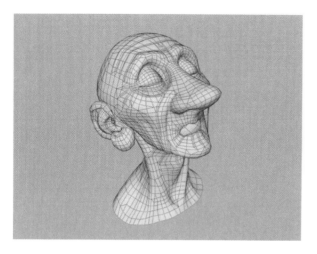

Figure 2: The control mesh for Geri's head, created by digitizing a full-scale model sculpted out of clay.

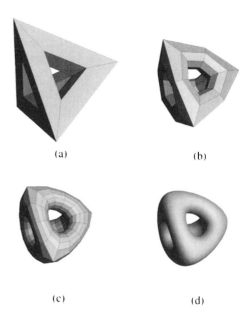

Figure 3: Recursive subdivision of a topologically complicated mesh: (a) the control mesh; (b) after one subdivision step; (c) after two subdivision steps; (d) the limit surface.

animated. As a case in point, considerable manual effort was required to hide the seams in the face of Woody, a principal character in *Toy Story*.

Subdivision surfaces have the potential to overcome both of these problems: they do not require trimming, and smoothness of the model is automatically guaranteed, even as the model animates.

The use of subdivision in animation systems is not new, but for a variety of reasons (several of which we address in this paper), their use has not been widespread. In the mid 1980s for instance, Symbolics was possibly the first to use subdivision in their animation system as a means of creating detailed polyhedra. The LightWave 3D modeling and animation system from NewTek also uses subdivision in a similar fashion.

This paper describes a number of issues that arose when we added a variant of Catmull-Clark [2] subdivision surfaces to our animation and rendering systems, Marionette and RenderMan [17], respectively. The resulting extensions were used heavily in the creation of Geri (Figure 1), a human character in our recently completed short film *Geri's game*. Specifically, subdivision surfaces were used to model the skin of Geri's head (see Figure 2), his hands, and his clothing, including his jacket, pants, shirt, tie, and shoes.

In contrast to previous systems such as those mentioned above, that use subdivision as a means to embellish polygonal models, our system uses subdivision as a means to define piecewise smooth surfaces. Since our system reasons about the limit surface itself, polygonal artifacts are never present, no matter how the surface animates or how closely it is viewed.

The use of subdivision surfaces posed new challenges throughout the production process, from modeling and animation to rendering. In modeling, subdivision surfaces free the designer from worrying about the topological restrictions that haunt NURBS modelers, but they simultaneously prevent the use of special tools that have been developed over the years to add features such as variable radius fillets to NURBS models. In Section 3, we describe an approach for introducing similar capabilities into subdivision surface models. The basic idea is to generalize the infinitely sharp creases of Hoppe *et. al.* [10] to obtain semi-sharp creases – that is, creases whose sharpness can vary from zero (meaning smooth) to infinite.

Once models have been constructed with subdivision surfaces, the problems of animation are generally easier than with corresponding NURBS surfaces because subdivision surface models are seamless, so the surface is guaranteed to remain smooth as the model is animated. Using subdivision surfaces for physically-based animation of clothing, however, poses its own difficulties which we address in Section 4. First, it is necessary to express the energy function of the clothing on subdivision meshes in such a way that the resulting motion does not inappropriately reveal the structure of the subdivision control mesh. Second, in order for a physical simulator to make use of subdivision surfaces it must compute collisions very efficiently. While collisions of NURBS surfaces have been studied in great detail, little work has been done previously with subdivision surfaces.

Having modeled and animated subdivision surfaces, some formidable challenges remain before they can be rendered. The topological freedom that makes subdivision surfaces so attractive for modeling and animation means that they generally do not admit parametrizations suitable for texture mapping. Solid textures [12, 13] and projection textures [9] can address some production needs, but Section 5.1 shows that it is possible to go a good deal further by using programmable shaders in combination with smooth scalar fields defined over the surface.

The combination of semi-sharp creases for modeling, an appropriate and efficient interface to physical simulation for animation, and the availability of scalar fields for shading and rendering have made subdivision surfaces an extremely effective tool in our production environment.

2 Background

A single NURBS surface, like any other parametric surface, is limited to representing surfaces which are topologically equivalent to a sheet, a cylinder or a torus. This is a fundamental limitation for any surface that imposes a global planar parameterization. A single subdivision surface, by contrast, can represent surfaces of arbitrary topology. The basic idea is to construct a surface from an arbitrary polyhedron by repeatedly subdividing each of the faces, as illustrated in Figure 3. If the subdivision is done appropriately, the limit of this subdivision process will be a smooth surface.

Catmull and Clark [2] introduced one of the first subdivision schemes. Their method begins with an arbitrary polyhedron called the control mesh. The control mesh, denoted M^0 (see Figure 3(a)), is subdivided to produce the mesh M^1 (shown in Figure 3(b)) by splitting each face into a collection of quadrilateral subfaces. A face having n edges is split into n quadrilaterals. The vertices of M^1 are computed using certain weighted averages as detailed below. The same subdivision procedure is used again on M^1 to produce the mesh M^2 shown in Figure 3(c). The subdivision surface is defined to be the limit of the sequence of meshes $M^0, M^1, \ldots$ created by repeated application of the subdivision procedure.

To describe the weighted averages used by Catmull and Clark it is convenient to observe that each vertex of M^{i+1} can be associated with either a face, an edge, or a vertex of M^i; these are called face, edge, and vertex points, respectively. This association is indicated in Figure 4 for the situation around a vertex v^0 of M^0. As indicated in the figure, we use f's to denote face points, e's to denote edge points, and v's to denote vertex points. Face points are positioned at the centroid of the vertices of the corresponding face. An edge point e_j^{i+1}, as indicated in Figure 4 is computed as

$$e_j^{i+1} = \frac{v^i + e_j^i + f_{j-1}^{i+1} + f_j^{i+1}}{4}, \qquad (1)$$

where subscripts are taken modulo the valence of the central vertex v^0. (The valence of a vertex is the number of edges incident to it.) Finally, a vertex point v^i is computed as

$$v^{i+1} = \frac{n-2}{n} v^i + \frac{1}{n^2} \sum_j e_j^i + \frac{1}{n^2} \sum_j f_j^{i+1} \qquad (2)$$

Vertices of valence 4 are called ordinary; others are called extraordinary.

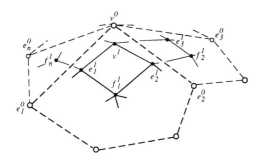

Figure 4: The situation around a vertex v^0 of valence n.

These averaging rules — also called subdivision rules, masks, or stencils — are such that the limit surface can be shown to be tangent plane smooth no matter where the control vertices are placed [14, 19].[1]

Whereas Catmull-Clark subdivision is based on quadrilaterals, Loop's surfaces [11] and the Butterfly scheme [6] are based on triangles. We chose to base our work on Catmull-Clark surfaces for two reasons:

1. They strictly generalize uniform tensor product cubic B-splines, making them easier to use in conjunction with existing in-house and commercial software systems such as Alias-Wavefront and SoftImage.

2. Quadrilaterals are often better than triangles at capturing the symmetries of natural and man-made objects. Tube-like surfaces — such as arms, legs, and fingers — for example, can be modeled much more naturally with quadrilaterals.

---

[1] Technical caveat for the purist: The surface is guaranteed to be smooth except for control vertex positions in a set of measure zero.

Figure 5: Geri's hand as a piecewise smooth Catmull-Clark surface. Infinitely sharp creases are used between the skin and the finger nails.

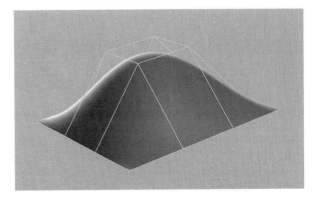

Figure 6: A surface where boundary edges are tagged as sharp and boundary vertices of valence two are tagged as corners. The control mesh is yellow and the limit surface is cyan.

Following Hoppe *et. al.* [10] it is possible to modify the subdivision rules to create piecewise smooth surfaces containing infinitely sharp features such as creases and corners. This is illustrated in Figure 5 which shows a close-up shot of Geri's hand. Infinitely sharp creases were used to separate the skin of the hand from the finger nails. Sharp creases can be modeled by marking a subset of the edges of the control mesh as sharp and then using specially designed rules in the neighborhood of sharp edges. Appendix A describes the necessary special rules and when to use them.

Again following Hoppe *et. al.*, we deal with boundaries of the control mesh by tagging the boundary edges as sharp. We have also found it convenient to tag boundary vertices of valence 2 as corners, even though they would normally be treated as crease vertices since they are incident to two sharp edges. We do this to mimic the behavior of endpoint interpolating tensor product uniform cubic B-spline surfaces, as illustrated in Figure 6.

3 Modeling fillets and blends

As mentioned in Section 1 and shown in Figure 5, infinitely sharp creases are very convenient for representing piecewise-smooth surfaces. However, real-world surfaces are never infinitely sharp. The corner of a tabletop, for instance, is smooth when viewed sufficiently closely. For animation purposes it is often desirable to capture such tightly curved shapes.

To this end we have developed a generalization of the Catmull-

Clark scheme to admit semi-sharp creases – that is, creases of controllable sharpness, a simple example of which is shown in Figure 7.

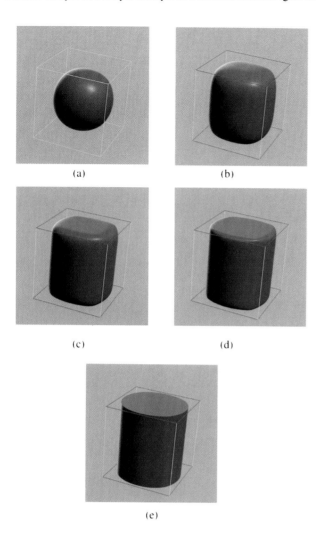

(a)

(b)

(c)

(d)

(e)

Figure 7: An example of a semi-sharp crease. The control mesh for each of these surfaces is the unit cube, drawn in wireframe, where crease edges are red and smooth edges are yellow. In (a) the crease sharpness is 0, meaning that all edges are smooth. The sharpnesses for (b), (c), (d), and (e) are 1, 2, 3, and infinite, respectively.

One approach to achieve semi-sharp creases is to develop subdivision rules whose weights are parametrized by the sharpness s of the crease. This approach is difficult because it can be quite hard to discover rules that lead to the desired smoothness properties of the limit surfaces. One of the roadblocks is that subdivision rules around a crease break a symmetry possessed by the smooth rules: typical smooth rules (such as the Catmull-Clark rules) are invariant under cyclic reindexing, meaning that discrete Fourier transforms can be used to prove properties for vertices of arbitrary valence (cf. Zorin [19]). In the absence of this invariance, each valence must currently be considered separately, as was done by Schweitzer [15]. Another difficulty is that such an approach is likely to lead to a zoo of rules depending on the number and configuration of creases through a vertex. For instance, a vertex with two semi-sharp creases passing through it would use a different set of rules than a vertex with just one crease through it.

Our approach is to use a very simple process we call hybrid subdivision. The general idea is to use one set of rules for a finite but

arbitrary number of subdivision steps, followed by another set of rules that are applied to the limit. Smoothness therefore depends only on the second set of rules. Hybrid subdivision can be used to obtain semi-sharp creases by using infinitely sharp rules during the first few subdivision steps, followed by use of the smooth rules for subsequent subdivision steps. Intuitively this leads to surfaces that are sharp at coarse scales, but smooth at finer scales.

Now the details. To set the stage for the general situation where the sharpness can vary along a crease, we consider two illustrative special cases.

Case 1: A constant integer sharpness s crease: We subdivide s times using the infinitely sharp rules, then switch to the smooth rules. In other words, an edge of sharpness $s > 0$ is subdivided using the sharp edge rule. The two subedges created each have sharpness $s - 1$. A sharpness $s = 0$ edge is considered smooth, and it stays smooth for remaining subdivisions. In the limit where $s \to \infty$ the sharp rules are used for all steps, leading to an infinitely sharp crease. An example of integer sharpness creases is shown in Figure 7. A more complicated example where two creases of different sharpnesses intersect is shown in Figure 8.

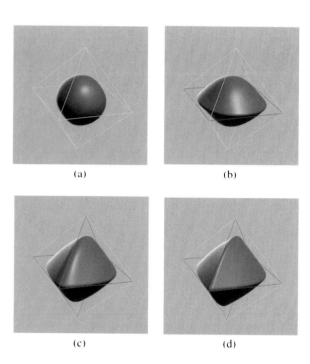

(a)

(b)

(c)

(d)

Figure 8: A pair of crossing semi-sharp creases. The control mesh for all surfaces is the octahedron drawn in wire frame. Yellow denotes smooth edges, red denotes the edges of the first crease, and magenta denotes the edges of the second crease. In (a) the crease sharpnesses are both zero; in (b), (c), and (d) the sharpness of the red crease is 4. The sharpness of the magenta crease in (b), (c), and (d) is 0, 2, and 4, respectively.

Case 2: A constant, but not necessarily integer sharpness s: the main idea here is to interpolate between adjacent integer sharpnesses. Let $s{\downarrow}$ and $s{\uparrow}$ denote the floor and ceiling of s, respectively. Imagine creating two versions of the crease: the first obtained by subdividing $s{\downarrow}$ times using the sharp rules, then subdividing one additional time using the smooth rules. Call the vertices of this first version $v{\downarrow}_0, v{\downarrow}_1, \ldots$. The second version, the vertices of which we denote by $v{\uparrow}_0, v{\uparrow}_1, \ldots$, is created by subdividing $s{\uparrow}$ times using the sharp rules. We take the $s{\uparrow}$-times subdivided semi-sharp crease to

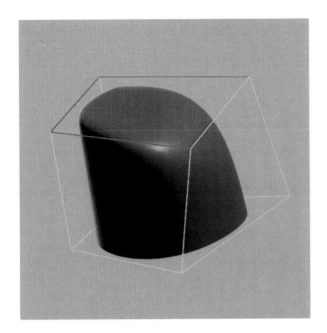

Figure 9: A simple example of a variable sharpness crease. The edges of the bottom face of the cubical control mesh are infinitely sharp. Three edges of the top face form a single variable sharpness crease with edge sharpnesses set to 2 (the two magenta edges), and 4 (the red edge).

Figure 10: A more complex example of variable sharpness creases. This model, inspired by an Edouard Lanteri sculpture, contains numerous variable sharpness creases to reduce the size of the control mesh. The control mesh for the model made without variable sharpness creases required 840 faces; with variable sharpness creases the face count dropped to 627. Model courtesy of Jason Bickerstaff.

have vertex positions $v_i^{s\uparrow}$ computed via simple linear interpolation:

$$v_i^{s\uparrow} = (1-\sigma)v\!\downarrow_i + \sigma v\!\uparrow_i \qquad (3)$$

where $\sigma = (s - s\!\downarrow)/(s\!\uparrow - s\!\downarrow)$. Subsequent subdivisions are done using the smooth rules. In the case where all creases have the same non-integer sharpness s, the surface produced by the above process is identical to the one obtained by linearly interpolating between the integer sharpness limit surfaces corresponding to $s\!\downarrow$ and $s\!\uparrow$. Typically, however, crease sharpnesses will not all be equal, meaning that the limit surface is not a simple blend of integer sharpness surfaces.

The more general situation where crease sharpness is non-integer and varies along a crease is presented in Appendix B. Figure 9 depicts a simple example. A more complex use of variable sharpness is shown in Figure 10.

4 Supporting cloth dynamics

The use of simulated physics to animate clothing has been widely discussed in the literature (cf. [1, 5, 16]). Here, we address the issues that arise when interfacing a physical simulator to a set of geometric models constructed out of subdivision surfaces. It is not our intent in this section to detail our cloth simulation system fully – that would require an entire paper of its own. Our goal is rather to highlight issues related to the use of subdivision surfaces to model both kinematic and dynamic objects.

In Section 4.1 we define the behavior of the cloth material by constructing an energy functional on the subdivision control mesh. If the material properties such as the stiffness of the cloth vary over the surface, one or more scalar fields (see Section 5.1) must be defined to modulate the local energy contributions. In Section 4.2 we describe an algorithm for rapidly identifying potential collisions involving the cloth and/or kinematic obstacles. Rapid collision detection is crucial to achieving acceptable performance.

4.1 Energy functional

For physical simulation, the basic properties of a material are generally specified by defining an energy functional to represent the attraction or resistance of the material to various possible deformations. Typically, the energy is either specified as a surface integral or as a discrete sum of terms which are functions of the positions of surface samples or control vertices. The first type of specification typically gives rise to a finite-element approach, while the second is associated more with finite-difference methods.

Finite-element approaches are possible with subdivision surfaces, and in fact some relevant surface integrals can be computed analytically [8]. In general, however, finite-element surface integrals must be estimated through numerical quadrature, and this gives rise to a collection of special cases around extraordinary points. We chose to avoid these special cases by adopting a finite-difference approach, approximating the clothing with a mass-spring model [18] in which all the mass is concentrated at the control points.

Away from extraordinary points, Catmull-Clark meshes under subdivision become regular quadrilateral grids. This makes them ideally suited for representing woven fabrics which are also generally described locally by a gridded structure. In constructing the energy functions for clothing simulation, we use the edges of the subdivision mesh to correspond with the warp and weft directions of the simulated woven fabrics.

Since most popular fabrics stretch very little along the warp or weft directions, we introduce relatively strong fixed rest-length springs along each edge of the mesh. More precisely, for each edge from p_1 to p_2, we add an energy term $k_s E_s(p_1, p_2)$ where

$$E_s(p_1, p_2) = \frac{1}{2}\left(\frac{|p_1 - p_2|}{|p_1^* - p_2^*|} - 1\right)^2. \qquad (4)$$

Here, p_1^* and p_2^* are the rest positions of the two vertices, and k_s is the corresponding spring constant.

With only fixed-length springs along the mesh edges, the simulated clothing can undergo arbitrary skew without penalty. One way to prevent the skew is to introduce fixed-length springs along the diagonals. The problem with this approach is that strong diagonal springs make the mesh too stiff, and weak diagonal springs allow the mesh to skew excessively. We chose to address this problem by introducing an energy term which is proportional to the product of the energies of two diagonal fixed-length springs. If p_1 and p_2 are vertices along one diagonal of a quadrilateral mesh face and p_3 and p_4 are vertices along the other diagonal, the energy is given by $k_d E_d(p_1, p_2, p_3, p_4)$ where k_d is a scalar parameter that functions analagously to a spring constant, and where

$$E_d(p_1, p_2, p_3, p_4) = E_s(p_1, p_2) E_s(p_3, p_4). \qquad (5)$$

The energy $E_d(p_1, p_2, p_3, p_4)$ reaches its minimum at zero when either of the diagonals of the quadrilateral face are of the original rest length. Thus the material can fold freely along either diagonal, while resisting skew to a degree determined by k_d. We sometimes use weak springs along the diagonals to keep the material from wrinkling too much.

With the fixed-length springs along the edges and the diagonal contributions to the energy, the simulated material, unlike real cloth, can bend without penalty. To add greater realism to the simulated cloth, we introduce an energy term that establishes a resistance to bending along virtual threads. Virtual threads are defined as a sequence of vertices. They follow grid lines in regular regions of the mesh, and when a thread passes through an extraordinary vertex of valence n, it continues by exiting along the edge $\lfloor n/2 \rfloor$-edges away in the clockwise direction. If p_1, p_2, and p_3 are three points along a virtual thread, the anti-bending component of the energy is given by $k_p E_p(p_1, p_2, p_3)$ where

$$E_p(p_1, p_2, p_3) = \frac{1}{2} * [C(p_1, p_2, p_3) - C(p_1^*, p_2^*, p_3^*)]^2 \qquad (6)$$

$$C(p_1, p_2, p_3) = \left| \frac{p_3 - p_2}{|p_3^* - p_2^*|} - \frac{p_2 - p_1}{|p_2^* - p_1^*|} \right| \qquad (7)$$

and p_1^*, p_2^*, and p_3^* are the rest positions of the three points.

By adjusting k_s, k_d and k_p both globally and locally, we have been able to simulate a reasonably wide variety of cloth behavior. In the production of *Geri's game*, we found that Geri's jacket looked a great deal more realistic when we modulated k_p over the surface of the jacket in order to provide more stiffness on the shoulder pads, on the lapels, and in an area under the armpits which is often reinforced in real jackets. Methods for specifying scalar fields like k_p over a subdivision surface are discussed in more detail in section 5.1.

4.2 Collisions

The simplest approach to detecting collisions in a physical simulation is to test each geometric element (i.e. point, edge, face) against each other geometric element for a possible collision. With N geometric elements, this would take N^2 time, which is prohibitive for large N. To achieve practical running times for large simulations, the number of possible collisions must be culled as rapidly as possible using some type of spatial data structure. While this can be done in a variety of different ways, there are two basic strategies: we can distribute the elements into a two-dimensional surface-based data structure, or we can distribute them into a three-dimensional volume-based data structure. Using a two-dimensional structure has several advantages if the surface connectivity does not change. First, the hierarchy can be fixed, and need not be regenerated each time the geometry is moved. Second, the storage can all be statically allocated. Third, there is never any need to rebalance the tree.

Finally, very short edges in the surface need not give rise to deep branches in the tree, as they would using a volume-based method.

It is a simple matter to construct a suitable surface-based data structure for a NURBS surface. One method is to subdivide the (s, t) parameter plane recursively into an quadtree. Since each node in the quadtree represents a subsquare of the parameter plane, a bounding box for the surface restricted to the subsquare can be constructed. An efficient method for constructing the hierarchy of boxes is to compute bounding boxes for the children using the convex hull property; parent bounding boxes can then be computed in a bottom up fashion by unioning child boxes. Having constructed the quadtree, we can find all patches within ε of a point p as follows. We start at the root of the quadtree and compare the bounding box of the root node with a box of size 2ε centered on p. If there is no intersection, then there are no patches within ε of p. If there is an intersection, then we repeat the test on each of the children and recurse. The recursion terminates at the leaf nodes of the quadtree, where bounding boxes of individual subpatches are tested against the box around p.

Subdivision meshes have a natural hierarchy for levels finer than the original unsubdivided mesh, but this hierarchy is insufficient because even the unsubdivided mesh may have too many faces to test exhaustively. Since there is there is no global (s, t) plane from which to derive a hierarchy, we instead construct a hierarchy by "unsubdividing" or "coarsening" the mesh: We begin by forming leaf nodes of the hierarchy, each of which corresponds to a face of the subdivision surface control mesh. We then hierarchically merge faces level by level until we finish with a single merged face corresponding to the entire subdivision surface.

The process of merging faces proceeds as follows. In order to create the ℓth level in the hierarchy, we first mark all non-boundary edges in the $\ell - 1$st level as candidates for merging. Then until all candidates at the ℓth level have been exhausted, we pick a candidate edge e, and remove it from the mesh, thereby creating a "superface" f^* by merging the two faces f_1 and f_2 that shared e. The hierarchy is extended by creating a new node to represent f^* and making its children be the nodes corresponding to f_1 and f_2. If f^* were to participate immediately in another merge, the hierarchy could become poorly balanced. To ensure against that possibility, we next remove all edges of f^* from the candidate list. When all the candidate edges at one level have been exhausted, we begin the next level by marking non-boundary edges as candidates once again. Hierarchy construction halts when only a single superface remains in the mesh.

The coarsening hierarchy is constructed once in a preprocessing phase. During each iteration of the simulation, control vertex positions change, so the bounding boxes stored in the hierarchy must be updated. Updating the boxes is again a bottom up process: the current control vertex positions are used to update the bounding boxes at the leaves of the hierarchy. We do this efficiently by storing with each leaf in the hierarchy a set of pointers to the vertices used to construct its bounding box. Bounding boxes are then unioned up the hierarchy. A point can be "tested against" a hierarchy to find all faces within ε of the point by starting at the root of the hierarchy and recursively testing bounding boxes, just as is done with the NURBS quadtree.

We build a coarsening hierarchy for each of the cloth meshes, as well as for each of the kinematic obstacles. To determine collisions between a cloth mesh and a kinematic obstacle, we test each vertex of the cloth mesh against the hierarchy for the obstacle. To determine collisions between a cloth mesh and itself, we test each vertex of the mesh against the hierarchy for the same mesh.

5 Rendering subdivision surfaces

In this section, we introduce the idea of smoothly varying scalar fields defined over subdivision surfaces and show how they can be used to apply parametric textures to subdivision surfaces. We then describe a collection of implementation issues that arose when subdivision surfaces and scalar fields were added to RenderMan.

5.1 Texturing using scalar fields

NURBS surfaces are textured using four principal methods: parametric texture mapping, procedural texture, 3D paint [9], and solid texture [12, 13]. It is straightforward to apply 3D paint and solid texturing to virtually any type of primitive, so these techniques can readily be applied to texture subdivision surfaces. It is less clear, however, how to apply parametric texture mapping, and more generally, procedural texturing to subdivision surfaces since, unlike NURBS, they are not defined parametrically.

With regard to texture mapping, subdivision surfaces are more akin to polygonal models since neither possesses a global (s, t) parameter plane. The now-standard method of texture mapping a polygonal model is to assign texture coordinates to each of the vertices. If the faces of the polygon consist only of triangles and quadrilaterals, the texture coordinates can be interpolated across the face of the polygon during scan conversion using linear or bilinear interpolation. Faces with more than four sides pose a greater challenge. One approach is to pre-process the model by splitting such faces into a collection of triangles and/or quadrilaterals, using some averaging scheme to invent texture coordinates at newly introduced vertices. One difficulty with this approach is that the texture coordinates are not differentiable across edges of the original or pre-processed mesh. As illustrated in Figures 11(a) and (b), these discontinuities can appear as visual artifacts in the texture, especially as the model is animated.

Fortunately, the situation for subdivision surfaces is profoundly better than for polygonal models. As we prove in Appendix C, smoothly varying texture coordinates result if the texture coordinates (s, t) assigned to the control vertices are subdivided using the same subdivision rules as used for the geometric coordinates (x, y, z). (In other words, control point positions and subdivision can be thought of as taking place in a 5-space consisting of (x, y, z, s, t) coordinates.) This is illustrated in Figure 11(c), where the surface is treated as a Catmull-Clark surface with infinitely sharp boundary edges. A more complicated example of parametric texture on a subdivision surface is shown in Figure 12.

As is generally the case in real productions, we used a combination of texturing methods to create Geri: the flesh tones on his head and hands were 3D-painted, solid textures were used to add fine detail to his skin and jacket, and we used procedural texturing (described more fully below) for the seams of his jacket.

The texture coordinates s and t mentioned above are each instances of a scalar field; that is, a scalar-valued function that varies over the surface. A scalar field f is defined on the surface by assigning a value f_v to each of the control vertices v. The proof sketch in Appendix C shows that the function $f(p)$ created through subdivision (where p is a point on the limit surface) varies smoothly wherever the subdivision surface itself is smooth.

Scalar fields can be used for more than just parametric texture mapping — they can be used more generally as arbitrary parameters to procedural shaders. An example of this occurs on Geri's jacket. A scalar field is defined on the jacket that takes on large values for points on the surface near a seam, and small values elsewhere. The procedural jacket shader uses the value of the this field to add the apparent seams to the jacket. We use other scalar fields to darken Geri's nostril and ear cavities, and to modulate various physical parameters of the cloth in the cloth simulator.

We assign scalar field values to the vertices of the control mesh in a variety of ways, including direct manual assignment. In some cases, we find it convenient to specify the value of the field directly at a small number of control points, and then determine the rest by interpolation using Laplacian smoothing. In other cases, we specify the scalar field values by painting an intensity map on one or more rendered images of the surface. We then use a least squares solver to determine the field values that best reproduce the painted intensities.

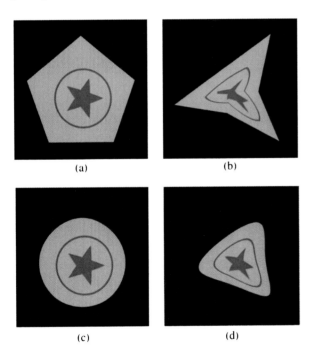

(a)

(b)

(c)

(d)

Figure 11: (a) A texture mapped regular pentagon comprised of 5 triangles; (b) the pentagonal model with its vertices moved; (c) A subdivision surface whose control mesh is the same 5 triangles in (a), and where boundary edges are marked as creases; (d) the subdivision surface with its vertices positioned as in (b).

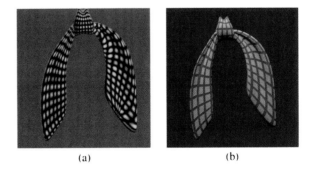

(a)

(b)

Figure 12: Gridded textures mapped onto a bandanna modeled using two subdivision surfaces. One surface is used for the knot, the other for the two flaps. In (a) texture coordinates are assigned uniformly on the right flap and nonuniformly using smoothing on the left to reduce distortion. In (b) smoothing is used on both sides and a more realistic texture is applied.

5.2 Implementation issues

We have implemented subdivision surfaces, specifically semi-sharp Catmull-Clark surfaces, as a new geometric primitive in Render-Man.

Our renderer, built upon the REYES architecture [4], demands that all primitives be convertible into grids of micropolygons (i.e. half-pixel wide quadrilaterals). Consequently, each type of primitive must be capable of splitting itself into a collection of subpatches, bounding itself (for culling and bucketing purposes), and dicing itself into a grid of micropolygons.

Each face of a Catmull-Clark control mesh can be associated with a patch on the surface, so the first step in rendering a Catmull-Clark surface is to split it in into a collection of individual patches. The control mesh for each patch consists of a face of the control mesh together with neighboring faces and their vertices. To bound each patch, we use the knowledge that a Catmull-Clark surface lies within the convex hull of its control mesh. We therefore take the bounding box of the mesh points to be the bounding box for the patch. Once bounded, the primitive is tested to determine if it is diceable; it is not diceable if dicing would produce a grid with too many micropolygons or a wide range of micropolygon sizes. If the patch is not diceable, then we split each patch by performing a subdivision step to create four new subpatch primitives. If the patch is diceable, it is repeatedly subdivided until it generates a grid with the required number of micropolygons. Finally, we move each of the grid points to its limit position using the method described in Halstead *et. al.* [8].

An important property of Catmull-Clark surfaces is that they give rise to bicubic B-splines patches for all faces except those in the neighborhood of extraordinary points or sharp features. Therefore, at each level of splitting, it is often possible to identify one or more subpatches as B-spline patches. As splitting proceeds, more of the surface can be covered with B-spline patches. Exploiting this fact has three advantages. First, the fixed 4×4 size of a B-spline patch allows for efficiency in memory usage because there is no need to store information about vertex connectivity. Second, the fact that a B-spline patch, unlike a Catmull-Clark patch, can be split independently in either parametric direction makes it possible to reduce the total amount of splitting. Third, efficient and well understood forward differencing algorithms are available to dice B-spline patches [7].

We quickly learned that an advantage of semi-sharp creases over infinitely sharp creases is that the former gives smoothly varying normals across the crease, while the latter does not. This implies that if the surface is displaced in the normal direction in a creased area, it will tear at an infinitely sharp crease but not at a semi-sharp one.

6 Conclusion

Our experience using subdivision surfaces in production has been extremely positive. The use of subdivision surfaces allows our model builders to arrange control points in a way that is natural to capture geometric features of the model (see Figure 2), without concern for maintaining a regular gridded structure as required by NURBS models. This freedom has two principal consequences. First, it dramatically reduces the time needed to plan and build an initial model. Second, and perhaps more importantly, it allows the initial model to be refined locally. Local refinement is not possible with a NURBS surface, since an entire control point row, or column, or both must be added to preserve the gridded structure. Additionally, extreme care must be taken either to hide the seams between NURBS patches, or to constrain control points near the seam to create at least the illusion of smoothness.

By developing semi-sharp creases and scalar fields for shading,

we have removed two of the important obstacles to the use of subdivision surfaces in production. By developing an efficient data structure for culling collisions with subdivisions, we have made subdivision surfaces well suited to physical simulation. By developing a cloth energy function that takes advantage of Catmull-Clark mesh structure, we have made subdivision surfaces the surfaces of choice for our clothing simulations. Finally, by introducing Catmull-Clark subdivision surfaces into our RenderMan implementation, we have shown that subdivision surfaces are capable of meeting the demands of high-end rendering.

A Infinitely Sharp Creases

Hoppe *et. al.* [10] introduced infinitely sharp features such as creases and corners into Loop's surfaces by modifying the subdivision rules in the neighborhood of a sharp feature. The same can be done for Catmull-Clark surfaces, as we now describe.

Face points are always positioned at face centroids, independent of which edges are tagged as sharp. Referring to Figure 4, suppose the edge $v^i e^i_j$ has been tagged as sharp. The corresponding edge point is placed at the edge midpoint:

$$e^{i+1}_j = \frac{v^i + e^i_j}{2}. \tag{8}$$

The rule to use when placing vertex points depends on the number of sharp edges incident at the vertex. A vertex with one sharp edge is called a dart and is placed using the smooth vertex rule from Equation 2. A vertex v^i with two incident sharp edges is called a crease vertex. If these sharp edges are $e^i_j v^i$ and $v^i e^i_k$, the vertex point v^{i+1} is positioned using the crease vertex rule:

$$v^{i+1} = \frac{e^i_j + 6v^i + e^i_k}{8}. \tag{9}$$

The sharp edge and crease vertex rules are such that an isolated crease converges to a uniform cubic B-spline curve lying on the limit surface. A vertex v^i with three or more incident sharp edges is called a corner; the corresonding vertex point is positioned using the corner rule

$$v^{i+1} = v^i \tag{10}$$

meaning that corners do not move during subdivision. See Hoppe *et. al.* [10] and Schweitzer [15] for a more complete discussion and rationale for these choices.

Hoppe *et. al.* found it necessary in proving smoothness properties of the limit surfaces in their Loop-based scheme to make further distinctions between so-called regular and irregular vertices, and they introduced additional rules to subdivide them. It may be necessary to do something similar to prove smoothness of our Catmull-Clark based method, but empirically we have noticed no anamolies using the simple strategy above.

B General semi-sharp creases

Here we consider the general case where a crease sharpness is allowed to be non-integer, and to vary along the crease. The following procedure is relatively simple and strictly generalizes the two special cases discussed in Section 3.

We specify a crease by a sequence of edges $e_1, e_2, \ldots$ in the control mesh, where each edge e_i has an associated sharpness $e_i.s$. We associate a sharpness per edge rather than one per vertex since there is no single sharpness that can be assigned to a vertex where two or more creases cross.[2]

---

[2]In our implementation we do not allow two creases to share an edge.

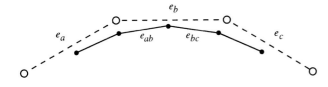

Figure 13: Subedge labeling.

During subdivision, face points are always placed at face centroids. The rules used when placing edge and vertex points are determined by examining edge sharpnesses as follows:

- An edge point corresponding to a smooth edge (i.e, $e.s = 0$) is computed using the smooth edge rule (Equation 1).

- An edge point corresponding to an edge of sharpness $e.s >= 1$ is computed using the sharp edge rule (Equation 8).

- An edge point corresponding to an edge of sharpness $e.s < 1$ is computed using a blend between smooth and sharp edge rules: specifically, let v_{smooth} and v_{sharp} be the edge points computed using the smooth and sharp edge rules, respectively. The edge point is placed at

$$(1 - e.s)v_{smooth} + e.sv_{sharp}. \qquad (11)$$

- A vertex point corresponding to a vertex adjacent to zero or one sharp edges is computed using the smooth vertex rule (Equation 2).

- A vertex point corresponding to a vertex v adjacent to three or more sharp edge is computed using the corner rule (Equation 10).

- A vertex point corresponding to a vertex v adjacent to two sharp edges is computed using the crease vertex rule (Equation 9) if $v.s \geq 1$, or a linear blend between the crease vertex and corner masks if $v.s < 1$, where $v.s$ is the average of the incidence edge sharpnesses.

When a crease edge is subdivided, the sharpnesses of the resulting subedges is determined using Chaikin's curve subdivision algorithm [3]. Specifically, if e_a, e_b, e_c denote three adjacent edges of a crease, then the subedges e_{ab} and e_{bc} as shown in Figure 13 have sharpnesses

$$e_{ab}.s = \max(\frac{e_a.s + 3e_b.s}{4} - 1, 0)$$

$$e_{bc}.s = \max(\frac{3e_b.s + e_c.s}{4} - 1, 0)$$

A 1 is subtracted after performing Chaikin's averaging to account for the fact that the subedges (e_{ab}, e_{bc}) are at a finer level than their parent edges (e_a, e_b, e_c). A maximum with zero is taken to keep the sharpnesses non-negative. If either e_a or e_b is infinitely sharp, then e_{ab} is; if either e_b or e_c is infinitely sharp, then e_{bc} is. This relatively simple procedure generalizes cases 1 and 2 described in Section 3. Examples are shown in Figures 9 and 10.

C   Smoothness of scalar fields

In this appendix we wish to sketch a proof that a scalar field f is smooth as a function on a subdivision surface wherever the surface itself is smooth. To say that a function on a smooth surface S is smooth to first order at a point p on the surface is to say that there

exists a parametrization $S(s,t)$ for the surface in the neighborhood of p such that $S(0,0) = p$, and such that the function $f(s,t)$ is differentiable and the derivative varies continuously in the neighborhood of $(0,0)$.

The characteristic map, introduced by Reif [14] and extended by Zorin [19], provides such a parametrization: the characteristic map allows a subdivision surface S in three space in the neighborhood of a point p on the surface to be written as

$$S(s,t) = (x(s,t), y(s,t), z(s,t)) \qquad (12)$$

where $S(0,0) = p$ and where each of $x(s,t)$, $y(s,t)$, and $z(s,t)$ is once differentiable if the surface is smooth at p. Since scalar fields are subdivided according to the same rules as the x, y, and z coordinates of the control points, the function $f(s,t)$ must also be smooth.

Acknowledgments

The authors would like to thank Ed Catmull for creating the *Geri's game* project, Jan Pinkava for creating Geri and for writing and directing the film, Karen Dufilho for producing it, Dave Haumann and Leo Hourvitz for leading the technical crew, Paul Aichele for building Geri's head, Jason Bickerstaff for modeling most of the rest of Geri and for Figure 10, and Guido Quaroni for Figure 12. Finally, we'd like to thank the entire crew of *Geri's game* for making our work look so good.

References

[1] David E. Breen, Donald H. House, and Michael J. Wozny. Predicting the drape of woven cloth using interacting particles. In Andrew Glassner, editor, *Proceedings of SIGGRAPH '94 (Orlando, Florida, July 24–29, 1994)*, Computer Graphics Proceedings, Annual Conference Series, pages 365–372. ACM SIGGRAPH, ACM Press, July 1994. ISBN 0-89791-667-0.

[2] E. Catmull and J. Clark. Recursively generated B-spline surfaces on arbitrary topological meshes. *Computer Aided Design*, 10(6):350–355, 1978.

[3] G. Chaikin. An algorithm for high speed curve generation. *Computer Graphics and Image Processing*, 3:346–349, 1974.

[4] Robert L. Cook, Loren Carpenter, and Edwin Catmull. The Reyes image rendering architecture. In Maureen C. Stone, editor, *Computer Graphics (SIGGRAPH '87 Proceedings)*, pages 95–102, July 1987.

[5] Martin Courshesnes, Pascal Volino, and Nadia Magnenat Thalmann. Versatile and efficient techniques for simulating cloth and other deformable objects. In Robert Cook, editor, *SIGGRAPH 95 Conference Proceedings*, Annual Conference Series, pages 137–144. ACM SIGGRAPH, Addison Wesley, August 1995. held in Los Angeles, California, 06-11 August 1995.

[6] Nira Dyn, David Leven, and John Gregory. A butterfly subdivision scheme for surface interpolation with tension control. *ACM Transactions on Graphics*, 9(2):160–169, April 1990.

[7] James D. Foley, Andries van Dam, Steven K. Feiner, and John F. Hughes. *Computer Graphics: Principles and Practice*. Prentice-Hall, 1990.

[8] Mark Halstead, Michael Kass, and Tony DeRose. Efficient, fair interpolation using Catmull-Clark surfaces. *Computer Graphics*, 27(3):35–44, August 1993.

[9] Pat Hanrahan and Paul E. Haeberli. Direct WYSIWYG painting and texturing on 3D shapes. In Forest Baskett, editor, *Computer Graphics (SIGGRAPH '90 Proceedings)*, volume 24, pages 215–223, August 1990.

[10] H. Hoppe, T. DeRose, T. Duchamp, M. Halstead, H. Jin, J. McDonald, J. Schweitzer, and W. Stuetzle. Piecewise smooth surface reconstruction. *Computer Graphics*, 28(3):295–302, July 1994.

[11] Charles T. Loop. Smooth subdivision surfaces based on triangles. Master's thesis, Department of Mathematics, University of Utah, August 1987.

[12] Darwyn R. Peachey. Solid texturing of complex surfaces. In B. A. Barsky, editor, *Computer Graphics (SIGGRAPH '85 Proceedings)*, volume 19, pages 279–286, July 1985.

[13] Ken Perlin. An image synthesizer. In B. A. Barsky, editor, *Computer Graphics (SIGGRAPH '85 Proceedings)*, volume 19, pages 287–296, July 1985.

[14] Ulrich Reif. A unified approach to subdivision algorithms. Mathematisches Institute A 92-16, Universitaet Stuttgart, 1992.

[15] Jean E. Schweitzer. *Analysis and Application of Subdivision Surfaces*. PhD thesis, Department of Computer Science and Engineering, University of Washington, 1996.

[16] Demetri Terzopoulos, John Platt, Alan Barr, and Kurt Fleischer. Elastically deformable models. In Maureen C. Stone, editor, *Computer Graphics (SIGGRAPH '87 Proceedings)*, volume 21, pages 205–214, July 1987.

[17] Steve Upstill. *The RenderMan Companion*. Addison-Wesley, 1990.

[18] Andrew Witkin, David Baraff, and Michael Kass. An introduction to physically based modeling. SIGGRAPH Course Notes, Course No. 32, 1994.

[19] Denis Zorin. *Stationary Subdivision and Multiresolution Surface Representations*. PhD thesis, Caltech, Pasadena, 1997.

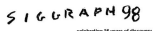

MAPS: Multiresolution Adaptive Parameterization of Surfaces

Aaron W. F. Lee*
Princeton University

Wim Sweldens[†]
Bell Laboratories

Peter Schröder[‡]
Caltech

Lawrence Cowsar[§]
Bell Laboratories

David Dobkin[¶]
Princeton University

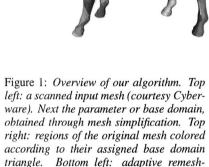

Figure 1: *Overview of our algorithm. Top left: a scanned input mesh (courtesy Cyberware). Next the parameter or base domain, obtained through mesh simplification. Top right: regions of the original mesh colored according to their assigned base domain triangle. Bottom left: adaptive remeshing with subdivision connectivity ($\varepsilon = 1\%$). Bottom middle: multiresolution edit.*

Abstract

We construct smooth parameterizations of irregular connectivity triangulations of arbitrary genus 2-manifolds. Our algorithm uses hierarchical simplification to efficiently induce a parameterization of the original mesh over a base domain consisting of a small number of triangles. This initial parameterization is further improved through a hierarchical smoothing procedure based on Loop subdivision applied in the parameter domain. Our method supports both fully automatic and user constrained operations. In the latter, we accommodate point and edge constraints to force the alignment of iso-parameter lines with desired features. We show how to use the parameterization for fast, hierarchical subdivision connectivity remeshing with guaranteed error bounds. The remeshing algorithm constructs an adaptively subdivided mesh directly without first resorting to uniform subdivision followed by subsequent sparsification. It thus avoids the exponential cost of the latter. Our parameterizations are also useful for texture mapping and morphing applications, among others.

CR Categories and Subject Descriptors: I.3.3 [Computer Graphics]: *Picture/Image Generation – Display Algorithms, Viewing Algorithms*; I.3.5 [Computer Graphics]: *Computational Geometry and Object Modeling - Curve, Surface, Solid and Object Representations, Hierarchy and Geometric Transformations, Object Hierarchies.*

Additional Key Words and Phrases: Meshes, surface parameterization, mesh simplification, remeshing, texture mapping, multiresolution, subdivision surfaces, Loop scheme.

*wailee@cs.princeton.edu
[†]wim@bell-labs.com
[‡]ps@cs.caltech.edu
[§]cowsar@bell-labs.com
[¶]dpd@cs.princeton.edu

1 Introduction

Dense triangular meshes routinely result from a number of 3D acquisition techniques, e.g., laser range scanning and MRI volumetric imaging followed by iso-surface extraction (see Figure 1 top left). The triangulations form a surface of arbitrary topology—genus, boundaries, connected components—and have irregular connectivity. Because of their complex structure and tremendous size, these meshes are awkward to handle in such common tasks as storage, display, editing, and transmission.

Multiresolution representations are now established as a fundamental component in addressing these issues. Two schools exist. One approach extends classical multiresolution analysis and subdivision techniques to arbitrary topology surfaces [19, 20, 7, 3]. The alternative is more general and is based on sequential mesh simplification, e.g., progressive meshes (PM) [12]; see [11] for a review. In either case, the objective is to represent triangulated 2-manifolds in an efficient and flexible way, and to use this description in fast algorithms addressing the challenges mentioned above. Our approach fits in the first group, but draws on ideas from the second group.

An important element in the design of algorithms which manipulate mesh approximations of 2-manifolds is the construction of "nice" parameterizations when none are given. Ideally, the manifold is parameterized over a base domain consisting of a small number of triangles. Once a surface is understood as a function from the base domain into $\mathbf{R}^3$ (or higher-D when surface attributes are considered), many tools from areas such as approximation theory, signal processing, and numerical analysis are at our disposal. In particular, classical multiresolution analysis can be used in the design and analysis of algorithms. For example, error controlled, adaptive remeshing can be performed easily and efficiently. Figure 1 shows the outline of our procedure: beginning with an irregular input mesh (top left), we find a base domain through mesh simplification (top middle). Concurrent with simplification, a mapping is constructed which assigns every vertex from the original mesh to a base triangle (top right). Using this mapping an adaptive remesh with subdivision connectivity can be built (bottom left) which is now suitable for such applications as multiresolution editing (bottom middle). Additionally, there are other practical payoffs to good parameterizations, for example in texture mapping and morphing.

In this paper we present an algorithm for the fast computation of smooth parameterizations of dense 2-manifold meshes with arbitrary topology. Specifically, we make the following contributions

- We describe an $O(N \log N)$ time and storage algorithm to construct a logarithmic level hierarchy of arbitrary topology, irregular connectivity meshes based on the Dobkin-Kirkpatrick (DK) algorithm. Our algorithm accommodates geometric criteria such as area and curvature as well as vertex and edge constraints.

- We construct a smooth parameterization of the original mesh over the base domain. This parameterization is derived through repeated conformal remapping during graph simplification followed by a parameter space smoothing procedure based on the Loop scheme. The resulting parameterizations are of high visual and numerical quality.

- Using the smooth parameterization, we describe an algorithm for adaptive, hierarchical remeshing of arbitrary meshes into subdivision connectivity meshes. The procedure is fully automatic, but also allows for user intervention in the form of fixing point or path features in the original mesh. The remeshed manifold meets conservative approximation bounds.

Even though the ingredients of our construction are reminiscent of mesh simplification algorithms, we emphasize that our goal is not the construction of another mesh simplification procedure, but rather the construction of smooth parameterizations. We are particularly interested in using these parameterizations for remeshing, although they are useful for a variety of applications.

1.1 Related Work

A number of researchers have considered—either explicitly or implicitly—the problem of building parameterizations for arbitrary topology, triangulated surfaces. This work falls into two main categories: (1) algorithms which build a smoothly parameterized approximation of a set of samples (e.g. [14, 1, 17]), and (2) algorithms which remesh an existing mesh with the goal of applying classical multiresolution approaches [7, 8].

A related, though quite different problem, is the maintenance of a *given* parameterization during mesh simplification [4]. We emphasize that our goal is the *construction* of mappings when none are given.

In the following two sections, we discuss related work and contrast it to our approach.

1.1.1 Approximation of a Given Set of Samples

Hoppe and co-workers [14] describe a fully automatic algorithm to approximate a given polyhedral mesh with Loop subdivision patches [18] respecting features such as edges and corners. Their algorithm uses a non-linear optimization procedure taking into account approximation error and the number of triangles of the base domain. The result is a smooth parameterization of the original polyhedral mesh over the base domain. Since the approach only uses subdivision, small features in the original mesh can only be resolved accurately by increasing the number of triangles in the base domain accordingly. A similar approach, albeit using A-patches, was described by Bajaj and co-workers [1]. From the point of view of constructing parameterizations, the main drawback of algorithms in this class is that the number of triangles in the base domain depends heavily on the geometric complexity of the goal surface.

This problem was addressed in work of Krishnamurthy and Levoy [17]. They approximate densely sampled geometry with bicubic spline patches and displacement maps. Arguing that a fully automatic system cannot put iso-parameter lines where a skilled animator would want them, they require the user to lay out the entire network of top level spline patch boundaries. A coarse to fine matching procedure with relaxation is used to arrive at a high quality patch mesh whose base domain need not mimic small scale geometric features.

The principal drawback of their procedure is that the user is required to define the *entire* base domain rather then only selected features. Additionally, given that the procedure works from coarse to fine, it is possible for the procedure to "latch" onto the wrong surface in regions of high curvature [17, Figure 7].

1.1.2 Remeshing

Lounsbery and co-workers [19, 20] were the first to propose algorithms to extend classical multiresolution analysis to arbitrary topology surfaces. Because of its connection to the mathematical foundations of wavelets, this approach has proven very attractive (e.g. [22, 7, 27, 8, 3, 28]). The central requirement of these methods is that the input mesh have subdivision connectivity. This is generally not true for meshes derived from 3D scanning sources.

To overcome this problem, Eck and co-workers [7] developed an algorithm to compute smooth parameterizations of high resolution polyhedral meshes over a low face count base domain. Using such a mapping, the original surface can be remeshed using subdivision connectivity. After this conversion step, adaptive simplification, compression, progressive transmission, rendering, and editing become simple and efficient operations [3, 8, 28].

Eck et al. arrive at the base domain through a Voronoi tiling of the original mesh. Using a sequence of local harmonic maps, a parameterization which is smooth over each triangle in the base domain and which meets with C^0 continuity at base domain edges [7, Plate 1(f)] is constructed. Runtimes for the algorithm can be long because of the many harmonic map computations. This problem was recently addressed by Duchamp and co-workers [6], who reduced the harmonic map computations from their initial $O(N^2)$ complexity to $O(N \log N)$ through hierarchical preconditioning. The hierarchy construction they employed for use in a multigrid solver is related to our hierarchy construction.

The initial Voronoi tile construction relies on a number of heuristics which render the overall algorithm fragile (for an improved version see [16]). Moreover, there is no explicit control over the number of triangles in the base domain or the placement of patch boundaries.

The algorithm generates only uniformly subdivided meshes which later can be decimated through classical wavelet methods. Many extra globally subdivided levels may be needed to resolve one small local feature; moreover, each additional level quadruples the amount of work and storage. This can lead to the intermediate construction of many more triangles than were contained in the input mesh.

1.2 Features of MAPS

Our algorithm was designed to overcome the drawbacks of previous work as well as to introduce new features. We use a fast coarsification strategy to define the base domain, avoiding the potential difficulties of finding Voronoi tiles [7, 16]. Since our algorithm proceeds from fine to coarse, correspondence problems found in coarse to fine strategies [17] are avoided, and all features are correctly resolved. We use conformal maps for continued remapping during coarsification to immediately produce a global parameterization of the original mesh. This map is further improved through the use of a hierarchical Loop smoothing procedure obviating the need for iterative numerical solvers [7]. Since the procedure is performed globally, derivative discontinuities at the edges of the base domain are avoided [7]. In contrast to fully automatic methods [7], the algorithm supports vertex and edge tags [14] to constrain the parameterization to align with selected features; however, the user is not required to specify the entire patch network [17]. During remeshing we take advantage of the original fine to coarse hierarchy to output a sparse, adaptive, subdivision connectivity mesh directly without resorting to a depth first oracle [22] or the need to produce a uniform subdivision connectivity mesh at exponential cost followed by wavelet thresholding [3].

2 Hierarchical Surface Representation

In this section we describe the main components of our algorithm, coarsification and map construction. We begin by fixing our notation.

2.1 Notation

When describing surfaces mathematically, it is useful to separate the topological and geometric information. To this end we introduce some notation adapted from [24]. We denote a triangular mesh as a pair $(\mathcal{P}, \mathcal{K})$, where $\mathcal{P}$ is a set of N point positions $p_i = (x_i, y_i, z_i) \in \mathbf{R}^3$ with $1 \leq i \leq N$, and $\mathcal{K}$ is an *abstract simplicial complex* which contains all the topological, i.e., adjacency information. The complex $\mathcal{K}$ is a set of subsets of $\{1, \ldots, N\}$. These subsets are called simplices and come in 3 types: vertices $v = \{i\} \in \mathcal{K}$, edges $e = \{i, j\} \in \mathcal{K}$, and faces $f = \{i, j, k\} \in \mathcal{K}$, so that any nonempty subset of a simplex of $\mathcal{K}$ is again a simplex of $\mathcal{K}$, e.g., if a face is present so are its edges and vertices.

Let e_i denote the standard i-th basis vector in $\mathbf{R}^N$. For each simplex s, its *topological realization* $|s|$ is the strictly convex hull of $\{e_i \mid i \in s\}$. Thus $|\{i\}| = e_i$, $|\{i, j\}|$ is the open line segment between e_i and e_j, and $|\{i, j, k\}|$ is an open equilateral triangle. The topological realization $|\mathcal{K}|$ is defined as $\cup_{s \in \mathcal{K}} |s|$. The *geometric realization* $\varphi(|\mathcal{K}|)$ relies on a linear map $\varphi : \mathbf{R}^N \to \mathbf{R}^3$ defined by

$\varphi(e_i) = p_i$. The resulting polyhedron consists of points, segments, and triangles in $\mathbf{R}^3$.

Two vertices $\{i\}$ and $\{j\}$ are *neighbors* if $\{i, j\} \in \mathcal{K}$. A set of vertices is *independent* if no two vertices are neighbors. A set of vertices is *maximally independent* if no larger independent set contains it (see Figure 3, left side). The 1-ring neighborhood of a vertex $\{i\}$ is the set

$$\mathcal{N}(i) = \{j \mid \{i, j\} \in \mathcal{K}\}.$$

The *outdegree* K_i of a vertex is its number of neighbors. The *star* of a vertex $\{i\}$ is the set of simplices

$$\text{star}(i) = \bigcup_{i \in s, s \in \mathcal{K}} s.$$

We say that $|K|$ is a two dimensional manifold (or 2-manifold) with boundaries if for each i, $|\text{star}(i)|$ is homeomorphic to a disk (interior vertex) or half-disk (boundary vertex) in $\mathbf{R}^2$. An edge $e = \{i, j\}$ is called a *boundary edge* if there is only one face f with $e \subset f$.

We define a conservative curvature estimate, $\kappa(i) = |\kappa_1| + |\kappa_2|$ at p_i, using the principal curvatures κ_1 and κ_2. These are estimated by the standard procedure of first establishing a tangent plane at p_i and then using a second degree polynomial to approximate $\varphi(|\text{star}(i)|)$.

2.2 Mesh Hierarchies

An important part of our algorithm is the construction of a mesh hierarchy. The original mesh $(\mathcal{P}, \mathcal{K}) = (\mathcal{P}^L, \mathcal{K}^L)$ is successively simplified into a series of homeomorphic meshes $(\mathcal{P}^l, \mathcal{K}^l)$ with $0 \leq l < L$, where $(\mathcal{P}^0, \mathcal{K}^0)$ is the coarsest or base mesh (see Figure 4).

Several approaches for such mesh simplification have been proposed, most notably progressive meshes (PM) [12]. In PM the basic operation is the "edge collapse." A sequence of such atomic operations is prioritized based on approximation error. The linear sequence of edge collapses can be partially ordered based on topological dependence [25, 13], which defines levels in a hierarchy. The depth of these hierarchies appears "reasonable" in practice, though can vary considerably for the same dataset [13].

Our approach is similar in spirit, but inspired by the hierarchy proposed by Dobkin and Kirkpatrick (DK) [5], which guarantees that the number of levels L is $O(\log N)$. While the original DK hierarchy is built for convex polyhedra, we show how the idea behind DK can be used for general polyhedra. The DK atomic simplification step is a *vertex remove*, followed by a retriangulation of the hole.

The two basic operations "vertex remove" and "edge collapse" are related since an edge collapse into one of its endpoints corresponds to a vertex remove with a particular retriangulation of the resulting hole (see Figure 2). The main reason we chose an algorithm based on the ideas of the DK hierarchy is that it guarantees a logarithmic bound on the number of levels. However, we emphasize that the ideas behind our map constructions apply equally well to PM type algorithms.

2.3 Vertex Removal

One DK simplification step $\mathcal{K}^l \to \mathcal{K}^{l-1}$ consists of removing a maximally independent set of vertices with low outdegree (see Figure 3). To find such a set, the original DK algorithm used a greedy approach based only on *topological* information. Instead, we use a priority queue based on both *geometric and topological* information.

At the start of each level of the original DK algorithm, none of the vertices are marked and the set to be removed is empty. The algorithm randomly selects a non-marked vertex of outdegree less than 12, removes it and its star from $\mathcal{K}^l$, marks its neighbors as

Vertex removal followed by retriangulation

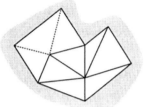 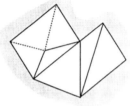

Half edge collapse as vertex removal with special retriangulation

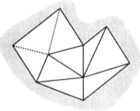 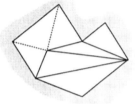

General Edge collapse operation

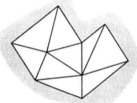 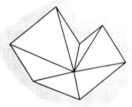

Figure 2: *Examples of different atomic mesh simplification steps. At the top vertex removal, in the middle half-edge collapse, and edge collapse at the bottom.*

unremovable and iterates this until no further vertices can be removed. In a triangulated surface the average outdegree of a vertex is 6. Consequently, no more than half of the vertices can be of outdegree 12 or more. Thus it is guaranteed that at least $1/24$ of the vertices will be removed at each level [5]. In practice, it turns out one can remove roughly $1/4$ of the vertices reflecting the fact that the graph is four-colorable. Given that a constant fraction can be removed on each level, the number of levels behaves as $O(\log N)$. The entire hierarchy can thus be constructed in linear time.

In our approach, we stay in the DK framework, but replace the random selection of vertices by a priority queue based on geometric information. Roughly speaking, vertices with small and flat 1-ring neighborhoods will be chosen first. At level l, for a vertex $p_i \in \mathcal{P}^l$, we consider its 1-ring neighborhood $\varphi(|\text{star}(i)|)$ and compute its area $a(i)$ and estimate its curvature $\kappa(i)$. These quantities are computed relative to $\mathcal{K}^l$, the current level. We assign a priority to $\{i\}$ inversely proportional to a convex combination of relative area and curvature

$$w(\lambda, i) = \lambda \frac{a(i)}{\max_{p_i \in \mathcal{P}^l} a(i)} + (1-\lambda) \frac{\kappa(i)}{\max_{p_i \in \mathcal{P}^l} \kappa(i)}.$$

(We found $\lambda = 1/2$ to work well in our experiments.) Omitting all vertices of outdegree greater than 12 from the queue, removal of a constant fraction of vertices is still guaranteed. Because of the sort implied by the priority queue, the complexity of building the entire hierarchy grows to $O(N \log N)$.

Figure 4 shows three stages (original, intermediary, coarsest) of the DK hierarchy. Given that the coarsest mesh is homeomorphic to the original mesh, it can be used as the domain of a parameterization.

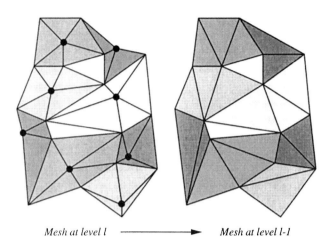

Mesh at level l ⟶ *Mesh at level $l-1$*

Figure 3: *On the left a mesh with a maximally independent set of vertices marked by heavy dots. Each vertex in the independent set has its respective star highlighted. Note that the star's of the independent set do not tile the mesh (two triangles are left white). The right side gives the retriangulation after vertex removal.*

2.4 Flattening and Retriangulation

To find $\mathcal{K}^{l-1}$, we need to retriangulate the holes left by removing the independent set. One possibility is to find a plane into which to project the 1-ring neighborhood $\varphi(|\text{star}(i)|)$ of a removed vertex $\varphi(|i|)$ without overlapping triangles and then retriangulate the hole in that plane. However, finding such a plane, which may not even exist, can be expensive and involves linear programming [4].

Instead, we use the conformal map z^a [6] which minimizes metric distortion to map the neighborhood of a removed vertex into the plane. Let $\{i\}$ be a vertex to be removed. Enumerate cyclically the K_i vertices in the 1-ring $\mathcal{N}(i) = \{j_k \mid 1 \leq k \leq K_i\}$ such that $\{j_{k-1}, i, j_k\} \in \mathcal{K}^l$ with $j_0 = j_{K_i}$. A piecewise linear approximation of z^a, which we denote by μ_i, is defined by its values for the center point and 1-ring neighbors; namely, $\mu_i(p_i) = 0$ and $\mu_i(p_{j_k}) = r_k^a \exp(i\theta_k a)$, where $r_k = \|p_i - p_{j_k}\|$,

$$\theta_k = \sum_{l=1}^{k} \angle(p_{j_{l-1}}, p_i, p_{j_l}),$$

and $a = 2\pi/\theta_{K_i}$. The advantages of the conformal map are numerous: it always exists, it is easy to compute, it minimizes metric distortion, and it is a bijection and thus never maps two triangles on top of each other. Once the 1-ring is flattened, we can retriangulate the hole using, for example, a constrained Delaunay triangulation (CDT) (see Figure 5). This tells us how to build $\mathcal{K}^{l-1}$.

When the vertex to be removed is a boundary vertex, we map to a half disk by setting $a = \pi/\theta_{K_i}$ (assuming j_1 and j_{K_i} are boundary vertices and setting $\theta_1 = 0$). Retriangulation is again performed with a CDT.

3   Initial Parameterization

To find a parameterization, we begin by constructing a bijection Π from $\varphi(|\mathcal{K}^L|)$ to $\varphi(|\mathcal{K}^0|)$. The parameterization of the original mesh over the base domain follows from $\Pi^{-1}(\varphi(|\mathcal{K}^0|))$. In other words, the mapping of a point $p \in \varphi(|\mathcal{K}^L|)$ through Π is a point $p^0 = \Pi(v) \in \varphi(|\mathcal{K}^0|)$, which can be written as

$$p^0 = \alpha p_i + \beta p_j + \gamma p_k,$$

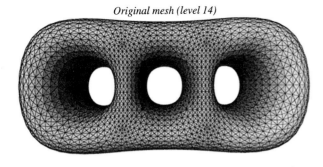

Original mesh (level 14)

Intermediate mesh (level 6)

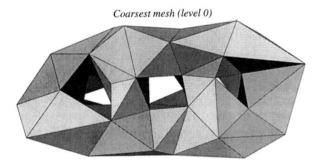

Coarsest mesh (level 0)

Figure 4: *Example of a modified DK mesh hierarchy. At the top the finest (original) mesh* $\varphi(|\mathcal{K}^L|)$ *followed by an intermediate mesh, and the coarsest (base) mesh* $\varphi(|\mathcal{K}^0|)$ *at the bottom (original dataset courtesy University of Washington).*

where $\{i,j,k\} \in \mathcal{K}^0$ is a face of the base domain and α, β and γ are barycentric coordinates, i.e., $\alpha + \beta + \gamma = 1$.

The mapping can be computed concurrently with the hierarchy construction. The basic idea is to successively compute piecewise linear bijections Π^l between $\varphi(|\mathcal{K}^L|)$ and $\varphi(|\mathcal{K}^l|)$ starting with Π^L, which is the identity, and ending with $\Pi^0 = \Pi$.

Notice that we only need to compute the value of Π^l at the vertices of $\mathcal{K}^L$. At any other point it follows from piecewise linearity.[1] Assume we are given Π^l and want to compute Π^{l-1}. Each vertex $\{i\} \in \mathcal{K}^L$ falls into one of the following categories:

1. $\{i\} \in \mathcal{K}^{l-1}$: The vertex is not removed on level l and survives on level $l-1$. In this case nothing needs to be done. $\Pi^{l-1}(p_i) = \Pi^l(p_i) = p_i$.

2. $\{i\} \in \mathcal{K}^l \setminus \mathcal{K}^{l-1}$: The vertex gets removed when going from l to $l-1$. Consider the flattening of the 1-ring around p_i (see Figure 5). After retriangulation, the origin lies in a triangle which corresponds to some face $t = \{j,k,m\} \in \mathcal{K}^{l-1}$ and has barycentric coordinates (α, β, γ) with respect to the vertices of

<hr>

[1] In the vicinity of vertices in $\mathcal{K}^l$ a triangle $\{i,j,k\} \in \mathcal{K}^L$ can straddle multiple triangles in $\mathcal{K}^l$. In this case the map depends on the flattening strategy used (see Section 2.4).

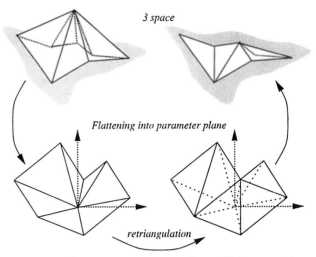

3 space

Flattening into parameter plane

retriangulation

Figure 5: *In order to remove a vertex* p_i, *its star* (i) *is mapped fr 3-space to a plane using the map* z^a. *In the plane the central ver is removed and the resulting hole retriangulated (bottom right).*

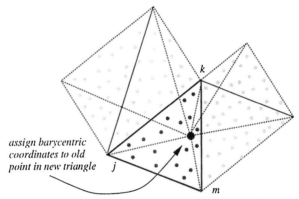

assign barycentric coordinates to old point in new triangle

Figure 6: *After retriangulation of a hole in the plane (see Figure the just removed vertex gets assigned barycentric coordinates w respect to the containing triangle on the coarser level. Similarly, the finest level vertices that were mapped to a triangle of the h now need to be reassigned to a triangle of the coarser level.*

that face, i.e., $\alpha \mu_i(p_j) + \beta \mu_i(p_k) + \gamma \mu_i(p_m)$ (see Figure 6). that case, let $\Pi^{l-1}(p_i) = \alpha p_j + \beta p_k + \gamma p_m$.

3. $\{i\} \in \mathcal{K}^L \setminus \mathcal{K}^l$: The vertex was removed earlier, th $\Pi^l(p_i) = \alpha' p_{j'} + \beta' p_{k'} + \gamma' p_{m'}$ for some triangle t' $\{j',k',m'\} \in \mathcal{K}^l$. If $t' \in \mathcal{K}^{l-1}$, nothing needs to be done; o erwise, the independent set guarantees that exactly one v tex of t' is removed, say $\{j'\}$. Consider the conformal m $\mu_{j'}$ (Figure 6). After retriangulation, the $\mu_{j'}(p_i)$ lies in a angle which corresponds to some face $t = \{j,k,m\} \in \mathcal{K}^l$ with barycentric coordinates (α, β, γ) (black dots within hi¦ lighted face in Figure 6). In that case, let $\Pi^{l-1}(p_i) = \alpha p$, $\beta p_k + \gamma p_m$ (i.e., all vertices in Figure 6 are reparameteriz in this way).

Note that on every level, the algorithm requires a sweep through the vertices of the finest level resulting in an overall complexity $O(N \log N)$.

Figure 7 visualizes the mapping we just computed. For e¦ point p_i from the original mesh, its mapping $\Pi(p_i)$ is shown wit dot on the base domain.

Caution: Given that every association between a 1-ring and retriangulated hole is a bijection, so is the mapping Π. Howe\

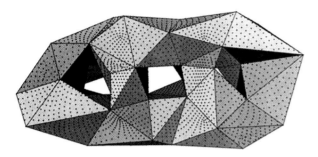

Figure 7: *Base domain* $\varphi(|\mathcal{K}^0|)$. *For each point p_i from the original mesh, its mapping $\Pi(p_i)$ is shown with a dot on the base domain.*

Π does not necessarily map a finest level triangle to a triangular region in the base domain. Instead the image of a triangle may be a non-convex region. In that case connecting the mapped vertices with straight lines can cause flipping, i.e., triangles may end up on top of each other (see Figure 8 for an example). Two methods exist for dealing with this problem. First one could further subdivide the original mesh in the problem regions. Given that the underlying continuous map is a bijection, this is guaranteed to fix the problem. The alternative is to use some brute force triangle unflipping mechanism. We have found the following scheme to work well: adjust the parameter values of every vertex whose 2-neighborhood contains a flipped triangle, by replacing them with the averaged parameter values of its 1-ring neighbors [7].

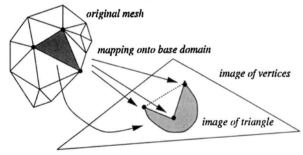

Figure 8: *Although the mapping Π from the original mesh to a base domain triangle is a bijection, triangles do not in general get mapped to triangles. Three vertices of the original mesh get mapped to a concave configuration on the base domain, causing the piecewise linear approximation of the map to flip the triangle.*

3.1 Tagging and Feature Lines

In the algorithm described so far, there is no *a priori* control over which vertices end up in the base domain or how they will be connected. However, often there are features which one wants to preserve in the base domain. These features can either be detected automatically or specified by the user.

We consider two types of features on the finest mesh: vertices and paths of edges. Guaranteeing that a certain vertex of the original mesh ends up in the base domain is straightforward. Simply mark that vertex as unremovable throughout the DK hierarchy.

We now describe an algorithm to guarantee that a certain path of edges on the finest mesh gets mapped to an edge of the base domain. Let $\{v_i \mid 1 \leq i \leq I\} \subset \mathcal{K}^L$ be a set of vertices on the finest level which form a path, i.e., $\{v_i, v_{i+1}\}$ is an edge. Tag all the edges in the path as feature edges. First tag v_1 and v_I, so called *dart points* [14], as unremovable so they are guaranteed to end up in the base domain. Let v_i be the first vertex on the interior of the path which gets marked for removal in the DK hierarchy, say, when going from

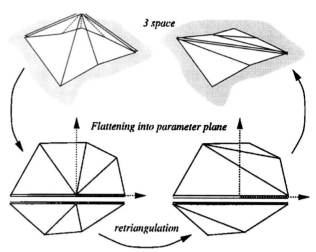

Figure 9: *When a vertex with two incident feature edges is removed, we want to ensure that the subsequent retriangulation adds a new feature edge to replace the two old ones.*

level l to $l - 1$. Because of the independent set property, v_{i-1} and v_{i+1} cannot be removed and therefore must belong to $\mathcal{K}^{l-1}$. When flattening the hole around v_i, tagged edges are treated like a boundary. We first straighten out the edges $\{v_{i-1}, v_i\}$ and $\{v_i, v_{i+1}\}$ along the x-axis, and use two boundary type conformal maps to the half disk above and below (cf. the last paragraph of Section 2.4). When retriangulating the hole around v_i, we put the edge $\{v_{i-1}, v_{i+1}\}$ in $\mathcal{K}^{l-1}$, tag it as a feature edge, and compute a CDT on the upper and lower parts (see Figure 9). If we apply similar procedures on coarser levels, we ensure that v_1 and v_I remain connected by a path (potentially a single edge) on the base domain. This guarantees that Π maps the curved feature path onto the coarsest level edge(s) between v_1 and v_I.

In general, there will be multiple feature paths which may be closed or cross each other. As usual, a vertex with more than 2 incident feature edges is considered a corner, and marked as unremovable.

The feature vertices and paths can be provided by the user or detected automatically. As an example of the latter case, we consider every edge whose dihedral angle is below a certain threshold to be a feature edge, and every vertex whose curvature is above a certain threshold to be a feature vertex. An example of this strategy is illustrated in Figure 13.

3.2 A Quick Review

Before we consider the problem of remeshing, it may be helpful to review what we have at this point. We have established an initial bijection Π of the original surface $\varphi(|\mathcal{K}^L|)$ onto a base domain $\varphi(|\mathcal{K}^0|)$ consisting of a small number of triangles (e.g. Figure 7). We use a simplification hierarchy (Figure 4) in which the holes after vertex removal are flattened and retriangulated (Figures 5 and 9). Original mesh points get successively reparametrized over coarser triangulations (Figure 6). The resulting mapping is always a bijection; triangle flipping (Figure 8) is possible but can be corrected.

4 Remeshing

In this section, we consider remeshing using subdivision connectivity triangulations since it is both a convenient way to illustrate the properties of a parameterization and is an important subject in its own right. In the process, we compute a smoothed version of our initial parameterization. We also show how to efficiently construct an adaptive remeshing with guaranteed error bounds.

4.1 Uniform Remeshing

Since Π is a bijection, we can use Π^{-1} to map the base domain to the original mesh. We follow the strategy used in [7]: regularly (1:4) subdivide the base domain and use the inverse map to obtain a regular connectivity remeshing. This introduces a hierarchy of regular meshes $(Q^m, \mathcal{R}^m)$ (Q is the point set and $\mathcal{R}$ is the complex) obtained from m-fold midpoint subdivision of the base domain $(\mathcal{P}^0, \mathcal{K}^0) = (Q^0, \mathcal{R}^0)$. Midpoint subdivision implies that all new domain points lie *in* the base domain, $Q^m \subset \varphi(|\mathcal{R}^0|)$ and $|\mathcal{R}^m| = |\mathcal{R}^0|$. All vertices of $\mathcal{R}^m \setminus \mathcal{R}^0$ have outdegree 6. The uniform remeshing of the original mesh on level m is given by $(\Pi^{-1}(Q^m), \mathcal{R}^m)$.

We thus need to compute $\Pi^{-1}(q)$ where q is a point in the base domain with dyadic barycentric coordinates. In particular, we need to compute which triangle of $\varphi(|\mathcal{K}^L|)$ contains $\Pi^{-1}(q)$, or, equivalently, which triangle of $\Pi(\varphi(|\mathcal{K}^L|))$ contains q. This is a standard *point location* problem in an irregular triangulation. We use the point location algorithm of Brown and Faigle [2] which avoids looping that can occur with non-Delaunay meshes [10, 9]. Once we have found the triangle $\{i, j, k\}$ which contains q, we can write q as

$$q = \alpha\Pi(p_i) + \beta\Pi(p_j) + \gamma\Pi(p_k),$$

and thus

$$\Pi^{-1}(q) = \alpha p_i + \beta p_j + \gamma p_k \in \varphi(|\mathcal{K}^L|).$$

Figure 10 shows the result of this procedure: a level 3 uniform remeshing of a 3-holed torus using the Π^{-1} map.

A note on complexity: The point location algorithm is essentially a walk on the finest level mesh with complexity $O(\sqrt{N})$. Hierarchical point location algorithms, which have asymptotic complexity $O(\log N)$, exist [15] but have a much larger constant. Given that we schedule the queries in a systematic order, we almost always have an excellent starting guess and observe a constant number of steps. In practice, the finest level "walking" algorithm beats the hierarchical point location algorithms for all meshes we encountered (up to $100K$ faces).

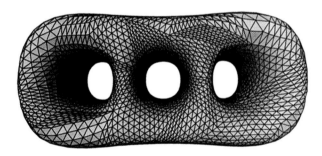

Figure 10: *Remeshing of 3 holed torus using midpoint subdivision. The parameterization is smooth within each base domain triangle, but clearly not across base domain triangles.*

4.2 Smoothing the Parameterization

It is clear from Figure 10 that the mapping we used is not smooth across global edges. One way to obtain global smoothness is to consider a map that minimizes a global smoothness functional and goes from $\varphi(|\mathcal{K}^L|)$ to $|\mathcal{K}^0|$ rather than to $\varphi(|\mathcal{K}^0|)$. This would require an iterative PDE solver. We have found computation of mappings to topological realizations that live in a high dimensional space to be needlessly cumbersome.

Instead, we use a much simpler and cheaper smoothing technique based on Loop subdivision. The main idea is to compute Π^{-1} at a smoothed version of the dyadic points, rather then at the dyadic points themselves (which can equivalently be viewed as changing the parameterization). To that end, we define a map $\mathcal{L}$ from the base domain to itself by the following modification of Loop:

- If all the points of the stencil needed for computing either a new point or smoothing an old point are inside the same triangle of the base domain, we can simply apply the Loop weights and the new points will be in that same face.

- If the stencil stretches across two faces of the base domain, we flatten them out using a "hinge" map at their common edge. We then compute the point's position in this flattened domain and extract the triangle in which the point lies together with its barycentric coordinates.

- If the stencil stretches across multiple faces, we use the conformal flattening strategy discussed earlier.

Note that the modifications to Loop force $\mathcal{L}$ to map the base domain onto the base domain. We emphasize that we do *not* apply the classic Loop scheme (which would produce a "blobby" version of the base domain). Nor are the surface approximations that we later produce Loop surfaces.

The composite map $\Pi^{-1} \circ \mathcal{L}$ is our *smoothed parameterization* that maps the base domain onto the original surface. The m-th level of uniform remeshing with the smoothed parameterization is $(\Pi^{-1} \circ \mathcal{L}(Q^m), \mathcal{R}^m)$, where Q^m, as before, are the dyadic points on the base domain. Figure 11 shows the result of this procedure: a level 3 uniform remeshing of a 3-holed torus using the smoothed parameterization.

When the mesh is tagged, we cannot apply smoothing across the tagged edges since this would break the alignment with the features. Therefore, we use modified versions of Loop which can deal with corners, dart points and feature edges [14, 23, 26] (see Figure 13).

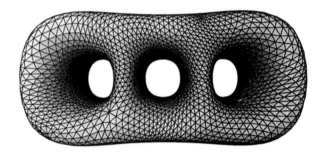

Figure 11: *The same remeshing of the 3-holed torus as in Figure 10, but this time with respect to a Loop smoothed parameterization.* **Note:** *Because the Loop scheme only enters in smoothing the parameterization the surface shown is still a sampling of the original mesh, not a Loop surface approximation of the original.*

4.3 Adaptive Remeshing

One of the advantages of meshes with subdivision connectivity is that classical multiresolution and wavelet algorithms can be employed. The standard wavelet algorithms used, e.g., in image compression, start from the finest level, compute the wavelet transform, and then obtain an efficient representation by discarding small wavelet coefficients. Eck et al. [7, 8] as well as Certain et al. [3] follow a similar approach: remesh using a uniformly subdivided grid followed by decimation through wavelet thresholding. This has the drawback that in order to resolve a small local feature on the original mesh, one may need to subdivide to a very fine level. Each extra

Dataset	Input size (triangles)	Hierarchy creation	Levels	$\mathcal{P}^0$ size (triangles)	Remeshing tolerance	Remesh creation	Output size (triangles)
3-hole	11776	18 (s)	14	120	(NA)	8 (s)	30720
fandisk	12946	23 (s)	15	168	1%	10 (s)	3430
fandisk	12946	23 (s)	15	168	5%	5 (s)	1130
head	100000	160 (s)	22	180	0.5%	440 (s)	74698
horse	96966	163 (s)	21	254	1%	60 (s)	15684
horse	96966	163 (s)	21	254	0.5%	314 (s)	63060

Table 1: *Selected statistics for the examples discussed in the text. All times are in seconds on a 200 MHz PentiumPro.*

duce. The resulting meshes may also find application in numerical analysis algorithms, such as fast multigrid solvers. Clearly there are many other applications which benefit from smooth parameterizations, e.g., texture mapping and morphing, which would be interesting to pursue in future work. Because of its independent set selection the standard DK hierarchy creates topologically uniform simplifications. We have begun to explore how the selection can be controlled using geometric properties. Alternatively, one could use a PM framework to control geometric criteria of simplification. Perhaps the most interesting question for future research is how to incorporate topology changes into the MAPS construction.

Acknowledgments

Aaron Lee and David Dobkin were partially supported by NSF Grant CCR-9643913 and the US Army Research Office Grant DAAH04-96-1-0181. Aaron Lee was also partially supported by a Wu Graduate Fellowship and a Summer Internship at Bell Laboratories, Lucent Technologies. Peter Schröder was partially supported by grants from the Intel Corporation, the Sloan Foundation, an NSF CAREER award (ASC-9624957), a MURI (AFOSR F49620-96-1-0471), and Bell Laboratories, Lucent Technologies. Special thanks to Timothy Baker, Ken Clarkson, Tom Duchamp, Tom Funkhouser, Amanda Galtman, and Ralph Howard for many interesting and stimulation discussions. Special thanks also to Andrei Khodakovsky, Louis Thomas, and Gary Wu for invaluable help in the production of the paper. Our implementation uses the triangle facet data structure and code of Ernst Mücke.

References

[1] BAJAJ, C. L., BERNADINI, F., CHEN, J., AND SCHIKORE, D. R. Automatic Reconstruction of 3D CAD Models. Tech. Rep. 96-015, Purdue University, February 1996.

[2] BROWN, P. J. C., AND FAIGLE, C. T. A Robust Efficient Algorithm for Point Location in Triangulations. Tech. rep., Cambridge University, February 1997.

[3] CERTAIN, A., POPOVIĆ, J., DEROSE, T., DUCHAMP, T., SALESIN, D., AND STUETZLE, W. Interactive Multiresolution Surface Viewing. In *Computer Graphics (SIGGRAPH 96 Proceedings)*, 91–98, 1996.

[4] COHEN, J., MANOCHA, D., AND OLANO, M. Simplifying Polygonal Models Using Successive Mappings. In *Proceedings IEEE Visualization 97*, 395–402, October 1997.

[5] DOBKIN, D., AND KIRKPATRICK, D. A Linear Algorithm for Determining the Separation of Convex Polyhedra. *Journal of Algorithms 6* (1985), 381–392.

[6] DUCHAMP, T., CERTAIN, A., DEROSE, T., AND STUETZLE, W. Hierarchical Computation of PL harmonic Embeddings. Tech. rep., University of Washington, July 1997.

[7] ECK, M., DEROSE, T., DUCHAMP, T., HOPPE, H., LOUNSBERY, M., AND STUETZLE, W. Multiresolution Analysis of Arbitrary Meshes. In *Computer Graphics (SIGGRAPH 95 Proceedings)*, 173–182, 1995.

[8] ECK, M., AND HOPPE, H. Automatic Reconstruction of B-Spline Surfaces of Arbitrary Topological Type. In *Computer Graphics (SIGGRAPH 96 Proceedings)*, 325–334, 1996.

[9] GARLAND, M., AND HECKBERT, P. S. Fast Polygonal Approximation of Terrains and Height Fields. Tech. Rep. CMU-CS-95-181, CS Dept., Carnegie Mellon U., September 1995.

[10] GUIBAS, L., AND STOLFI, J. Primitives for the Manipulation of General Subdivisions and the Computation of Voronoi Diagrams. *ACM Transactions on Graphics 4*, 2 (April 1985), 74–123.

[11] HECKBERT, P. S., AND GARLAND, M. Survey of Polygonal Surface Simplification Algorithms. Tech. rep., Carnegie Mellon University, 1997.

[12] HOPPE, H. Progressive Meshes. In *Computer Graphics (SIGGRAPH 96 Proceedings)*, 99–108, 1996.

[13] HOPPE, H. View-Dependent Refinement of Progressive Meshes. In *Computer Graphics (SIGGRAPH 97 Proceedings)*, 189–198, 1997.

[14] HOPPE, H., DEROSE, T., DUCHAMP, T., HALSTEAD, M., JIN, H., MCDONALD, J., SCHWEITZER, J., AND STUETZLE, W. Piecewise Smooth Surface Reconstruction. In *Computer Graphics (SIGGRAPH 94 Proceedings)*, 295–302, 1994.

[15] KIRKPATRICK, D. Optimal Search in Planar Subdivisions. *SIAM J. Comput. 12* (1983), 28–35.

[16] KLEIN, A., CERTAIN, A., DEROSE, T., DUCHAMP, T., AND STUETZLE, W. Vertex-based Delaunay Triangulation of Meshes of Arbitrary Topological Type. Tech. rep., University of Washington, July 1997.

[17] KRISHNAMURTHY, V., AND LEVOY, M. Fitting Smooth Surfaces to Dense Polygon Meshes. In *Computer Graphics (SIGGRAPH 96 Proceedings)*, 313–324, 1996.

[18] LOOP, C. Smooth Subdivision Surfaces Based on Triangles. Master's thesis, University of Utah, Department of Mathematics, 1987.

[19] LOUNSBERY, M. *Multiresolution Analysis for Surfaces of Arbitrary Topological Type*. PhD thesis, Department of Computer Science, University of Washington, 1994.

[20] LOUNSBERY, M., DEROSE, T., AND WARREN, J. Multiresolution Analysis for Surfaces of Arbitrary Topological Type. *Transactions on Graphics 16*, 1 (January 1997), 34–73.

[21] MÜCKE, E. P. Shapes and Implementations in Three-Dimensional Geometry. Technical Report UIUCDCS-R-93-1836, University of Illinois at Urbana-Champaign, 1993.

[22] SCHRÖDER, P., AND SWELDENS, W. Spherical Wavelets: Efficiently Representing Functions on the Sphere. In *Computer Graphics (SIGGRAPH 95 Proceedings)*, Annual Conference Series, 1995.

[23] SCHWEITZER, J. E. *Analysis and Application of Subdivision Surfaces*. PhD thesis, University of Washington, 1996.

[24] SPANIER, E. H. *Algebraic Topology*. McGraw-Hill, New York, 1966.

[25] XIA, J. C., AND VARSHNEY, A. Dynamic View-Dependent Simplification for Polygonal Models. In *Proceedings Visualization 96*, 327–334, October 1996.

[26] ZORIN, D. *Subdivision and Multiresolution Surface Representations*. PhD thesis, California Institute of Technology, 1997.

[27] ZORIN, D., SCHRÖDER, P., AND SWELDENS, W. Interpolating Subdivision for Meshes with Arbitrary Topology. In *Computer Graphics (SIGGRAPH 96 Proceedings)*, 189–192, 1996.

[28] ZORIN, D., SCHRÖDER, P., AND SWELDENS, W. Interactive Multiresolution Mesh Editing. In *Computer Graphics (SIGGRAPH 97 Proceedings)*, 259–268, 1997.

4.1 Uniform Remeshing

Since Π is a bijection, we can use Π^{-1} to map the base domain to the original mesh. We follow the strategy used in [7]: regularly (1:4) subdivide the base domain and use the inverse map to obtain a regular connectivity remeshing. This introduces a hierarchy of regular meshes $(Q^m, \mathcal{R}^m)$ (Q is the point set and $\mathcal{R}$ is the complex) obtained from m-fold midpoint subdivision of the base domain $(\mathcal{P}^0, \mathcal{K}^0) = (Q^0, \mathcal{R}^0)$. Midpoint subdivision implies that all new domain points lie *in* the base domain, $Q^m \subset \varphi(|\mathcal{R}^0|)$ and $|\mathcal{R}^m| = |\mathcal{R}^0|$. All vertices of $\mathcal{R}^m \setminus \mathcal{R}^0$ have outdegree 6. The uniform remeshing of the original mesh on level m is given by $(\Pi^{-1}(Q^m), \mathcal{R}^m)$.

We thus need to compute $\Pi^{-1}(q)$ where q is a point in the base domain with dyadic barycentric coordinates. In particular, we need to compute which triangle of $\varphi(|\mathcal{K}^L|)$ contains $\Pi^{-1}(q)$, or, equivalently, which triangle of $\Pi(\varphi(|\mathcal{K}^L|))$ contains q. This is a standard *point location* problem in an irregular triangulation. We use the point location algorithm of Brown and Faigle [2] which avoids looping that can occur with non-Delaunay meshes [10, 9]. Once we have found the triangle $\{i, j, k\}$ which contains q, we can write q as

$$q = \alpha \Pi(p_i) + \beta \Pi(p_j) + \gamma \Pi(p_k),$$

and thus

$$\Pi^{-1}(q) = \alpha p_i + \beta p_j + \gamma p_k \in \varphi(|\mathcal{K}^L|).$$

Figure 10 shows the result of this procedure: a level 3 uniform remeshing of a 3-holed torus using the Π^{-1} map.

A note on complexity: The point location algorithm is essentially a walk on the finest level mesh with complexity $O(\sqrt{N})$. Hierarchical point location algorithms, which have asymptotic complexity $O(\log N)$, exist [15] but have a much larger constant. Given that we schedule the queries in a systematic order, we almost always have an excellent starting guess and observe a constant number of steps. In practice, the finest level "walking" algorithm beats the hierarchical point location algorithms for all meshes we encountered (up to $100K$ faces).

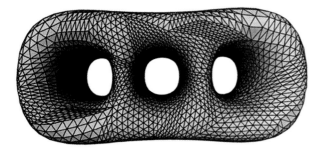

Figure 10: *Remeshing of 3 holed torus using midpoint subdivision. The parameterization is smooth within each base domain triangle, but clearly not across base domain triangles.*

4.2 Smoothing the Parameterization

It is clear from Figure 10 that the mapping we used is not smooth across global edges. One way to obtain global smoothness is to consider a map that minimizes a global smoothness functional and goes from $\varphi(|\mathcal{K}^L|)$ to $|\mathcal{K}^0|$ rather than to $\varphi(|\mathcal{K}^0|)$. This would require an iterative PDE solver. We have found computation of mappings to topological realizations that live in a high dimensional space to be needlessly cumbersome.

Instead, we use a much simpler and cheaper smoothing technique based on Loop subdivision. The main idea is to compute Π^{-1} at a smoothed version of the dyadic points, rather then at the dyadic points themselves (which can equivalently be viewed as changing the parameterization). To that end, we define a map $\mathcal{L}$ from the base domain to itself by the following modification of Loop:

- If all the points of the stencil needed for computing either a new point or smoothing an old point are inside the same triangle of the base domain, we can simply apply the Loop weights and the new points will be in that same face.

- If the stencil stretches across two faces of the base domain, we flatten them out using a "hinge" map at their common edge. We then compute the point's position in this flattened domain and extract the triangle in which the point lies together with its barycentric coordinates.

- If the stencil stretches across multiple faces, we use the conformal flattening strategy discussed earlier.

Note that the modifications to Loop force $\mathcal{L}$ to map the base domain onto the base domain. We emphasize that we do *not* apply the classic Loop scheme (which would produce a "blobby" version of the base domain). Nor are the surface approximations that we later produce Loop surfaces.

The composite map $\Pi^{-1} \circ \mathcal{L}$ is our *smoothed parameterization* that maps the base domain onto the original surface. The m-th level of uniform remeshing with the smoothed parameterization is $(\Pi^{-1} \circ \mathcal{L}(Q^m), \mathcal{R}^m)$, where Q^m, as before, are the dyadic points on the base domain. Figure 11 shows the result of this procedure: a level 3 uniform remeshing of a 3-holed torus using the smoothed parameterization.

When the mesh is tagged, we cannot apply smoothing across the tagged edges since this would break the alignment with the features. Therefore, we use modified versions of Loop which can deal with corners, dart points and feature edges [14, 23, 26] (see Figure 13).

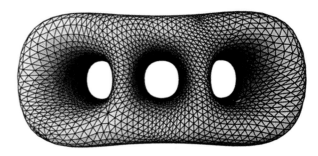

Figure 11: *The same remeshing of the 3-holed torus as in Figure 10, but this time with respect to a Loop smoothed parameterization.* **Note:** *Because the Loop scheme only enters in smoothing the parameterization the surface shown is still a sampling of the original mesh, not a Loop surface approximation of the original.*

4.3 Adaptive Remeshing

One of the advantages of meshes with subdivision connectivity is that classical multiresolution and wavelet algorithms can be employed. The standard wavelet algorithms used, e.g., in image compression, start from the finest level, compute the wavelet transform, and then obtain an efficient representation by discarding small wavelet coefficients. Eck et al. [7, 8] as well as Certain et al. [3] follow a similar approach: remesh using a uniformly subdivided grid followed by decimation through wavelet thresholding. This has the drawback that in order to resolve a small local feature on the original mesh, one may need to subdivide to a very fine level. Each extra level quadruples the number of triangles, most of which will later be decimated using the wavelet procedure. Imagine, e.g., a plane which is coarsely triangulated except for a narrow spike. Making the spike width sufficiently small, the number of levels needed to resolve it can be made arbitrarily high.

In this section we present an algorithm which avoids first building a full tree and later pruning it. Instead, we immediately build the adaptive mesh with a guaranteed conservative error bound. This is possible because the DK hierarchy contains the information on how much subdivision is needed in any given area. Essentially, we let the irregular DK hierarchy "drive" the adaptive construction of the regular pyramid.

We first compute for each triangle $t \in \mathcal{K}^0$ the following error quantity:

$$E(t) = \max_{p_i \in \mathcal{P}^L \text{and } \Pi(p_i) \in \varphi(|t|)} \text{dist}(p_i, \varphi(|t|)).$$

This measures the distance between one triangle in the base domain and the vertices of the finest level mapped to that triangle.

The adaptive algorithm is now straightforward. Set a certain relative error threshold ε. Compute $E(t)$ for all triangles of the base domain. If $E(t)/B$, where B is the largest side of the bounding box, is larger than ε, subdivide the domain triangle using the Loop procedure above. Next, we need to reassign vertices to the triangles of level $m = 1$. This is done as follows: For each point $p_i \in \mathcal{P}^L$ consider the triangle t of $\mathcal{K}^0$ to which it is currently assigned. Next consider the 4 children of t on level 1, t_j with $j = 0, 1, 2, 3$ and compute the distance between p_i and each of the $\varphi(|t_j|)$. Assign p_i to the closest child. Once the finest level vertices have been reassigned to level 1 triangles, the errors for those triangles can be computed. Now iterate this procedure until all triangles have an error below the threshold. Because all errors are computed from the finest level, we are guaranteed to resolve all features within the error bound. Note that we are not computing the true distance between the original vertices and a given approximation, but rather an easy to compute upper bound for it.

In order to be able to compute the Loop smoothing map $\mathcal{L}$ on an adaptively subdivided grid, the grid needs to satisfy a *vertex restriction criterion*, i.e., if a vertex has a triangle incident to it with depth i, then it must have a complete 1-ring at level $i - 1$ [28]. This restriction may necessitate subdividing some triangles even if they are below the error threshold. Examples of adaptive remeshing can be seen in Figure 1 (lower left), Figure 12, and Figure 13.

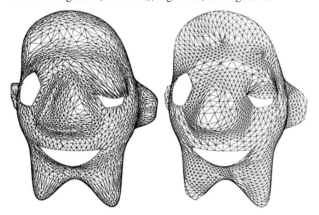

Figure 12: *Example remesh of a surface with boundaries.*

5 Results

We have implemented MAPS as described above and applied it to a number of well known example datasets, as well as some new

ones. The application was written in C++ using standard computational geometry data structures, see e.g. [21], and all timings reported in this section were measured on a 200 MHz PentiumPro personal computer.

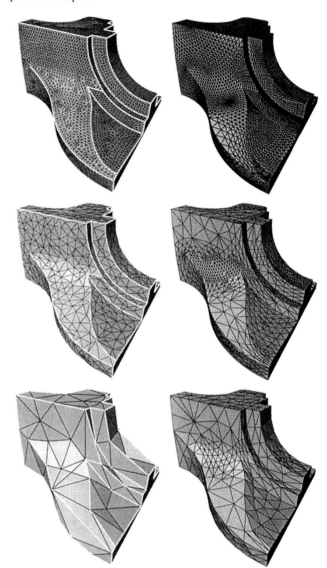

Figure 13: *Left (top to bottom): three levels in the DK pyramid, finest ($L = 15$) with 12946, intermediate ($l = 8$) with 1530, and coarsest ($l = 0$) with 168 triangles. Feature edges, dart and corner vertices survive on the base domain. Right (bottom to top): adaptive mesh with $\varepsilon = 5\%$ and 1120 triangles (bottom), $\varepsilon = 1\%$ and 3430 triangles (middle), and uniform level 3 (top). (Original dataset courtesy University of Washington.)*

The first example used throughout the text is the 3-holed torus. The original mesh contained 11776 faces. These were reduced in the DK hierarchy to 120 faces over 14 levels implying an average removal of 30% of the faces on a given level. The remesh of Figure 11 used 4 levels of uniform subdivision for a total of 30720 triangles.

The original sampled geometry of the 3-holed torus is smooth and did not involve any feature constraints. A more challenging case is presented by the fandisk shown in Figure 13. The original mesh (top left) contains 12946 triangles which were reduced to 168

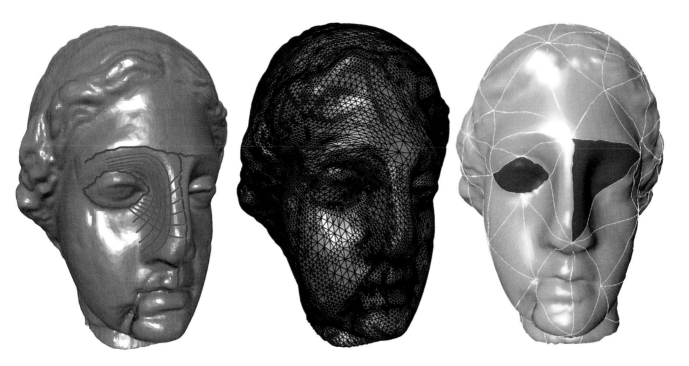

Figure 14: *Example of a constrained parameterization based on user input. Top: original input mesh (100000 triangles) with edge tags superimposed in red, green lines show some smooth iso-parameter lines of our parameterization. The middle shows an adaptive subdivision connectivity remesh. The bottom one patches corresponding to the eye regions (right eye was constrained, left eye was not) are highlighted to indicate the resulting alignment of top level patches with the feature lines. (Dataset courtesy Cyberware.)*

faces in the base domain over 15 levels (25% average face removal per level). The initial mesh had all edges with dihedral angles below 75° tagged (1487 edges), resulting in 141 tagged edges at the coarsest level. Adaptive remeshing to within $\varepsilon = 5\%$ and $\varepsilon = 1\%$ (fraction of longest bounding box side) error results in the meshes shown in the right column. The top right image shows a uniform resampling to level 3, in effect showing iso-parameter lines of the parameterization used for remeshing. Note how the iso-parameter lines conform perfectly to the initially tagged features.

This dataset demonstrates one of the advantages of our method—inclusion of feature constraints—over the earlier work of Eck et al. [7]. In the original PM paper [12, Figure 12], Hoppe shows the simplification of the fandisk based on Eck's algorithm which does not use tagging. He points out that the multiresolution approximation is quite poor at low triangle counts and consequently requires many triangles to achieve high accuracy. The comparison between our Figure 13 and Figure 12 in [12] demonstrates that our multiresolution algorithm which incorporates feature tagging solves these problems.

Another example of constrained parameterization and subsequent adaptive remeshing is shown in Figure 14. The original dataset (100000 triangles) is shown on the left. The red lines indicate user supplied feature constraints which may facilitate subsequent animation. The green lines show some representative iso-parameter lines of our parameterization subject to the red feature constraints. Those can be used for computing texture coordinates. The middle image shows an adaptive subdivision connectivity remesh with 74698 triangles ($\varepsilon = 0.5\%$). On the right we have highlighted a group of patches, 2 over the right (constrained) eye and 1 over the left (unconstrained) eye. This indicates how user supplied constraints force domain patches to align with desired features. Other enforced patch boundaries are the eyebrows, center of the nose, and middle of lips (see red lines in left image). This

example illustrates how one places constraints like Krishnamurthy and Levoy [17]. We remove the need in their algorithms to specify the entire base domain. A user may want to control patch outlines for editing in one region (e.g., on the face), but may not care about what happens in other regions (e.g., on the back of the head).

We present a final example in Figure 1. The original mesh (96966 triangles) is shown on the top left, with the adaptive, subdivision connectivity remesh on the bottom left. This remesh was subsequently edited in a interactive multiresolution editing system [28] and the result is shown on the bottom middle.

6 Conclusions and Future Research

We have described an algorithm which establishes smooth parameterizations for irregular connectivity, 2-manifold triangular meshes of arbitrary topology. Using a variant of the DK hierarchy construction, we simplify the original mesh and use piecewise linear approximations of conformal mappings to incrementally build a parameterization of the original mesh over a low face count base domain. This parameterization is further improved through a hierarchical smoothing procedure which is based on Loop smoothing in parameter space. The resulting parameterizations are of high quality, and we demonstrated their utility in an adaptive, subdivision connectivity remeshing algorithm that has guaranteed error bounds. The new meshes satisfy the requirements of multiresolution representations which generalize classical wavelet representations and are thus of immediate use in applications such as multiresolution editing and compression. Using edge and vertex constraints, the parameterizations can be forced to respect feature lines of interest without requiring specification of the entire patch network.

In this paper we have chosen remeshing as the primary application to demonstrate the usefulness of the parameterizations we pro-

Dataset	Input size (triangles)	Hierarchy creation	Levels	$\mathcal{P}^0$ size (triangles)	Remeshing tolerance	Remesh creation	Output size (triangles)
3-hole	11776	18 (s)	14	120	(NA)	8 (s)	30720
fandisk	12946	23 (s)	15	168	1%	10 (s)	3430
fandisk	12946	23 (s)	15	168	5%	5 (s)	1130
head	100000	160 (s)	22	180	0.5%	440 (s)	74698
horse	96966	163 (s)	21	254	1%	60 (s)	15684
horse	96966	163 (s)	21	254	0.5%	314 (s)	63060

Table 1: *Selected statistics for the examples discussed in the text. All times are in seconds on a 200 MHz PentiumPro.*

duce. The resulting meshes may also find application in numerical analysis algorithms, such as fast multigrid solvers. Clearly there are many other applications which benefit from smooth parameterizations, e.g., texture mapping and morphing, which would be interesting to pursue in future work. Because of its independent set selection the standard DK hierarchy creates topologically uniform simplifications. We have begun to explore how the selection can be controlled using geometric properties. Alternatively, one could use a PM framework to control geometric criteria of simplification. Perhaps the most interesting question for future research is how to incorporate topology changes into the MAPS construction.

Acknowledgments

Aaron Lee and David Dobkin were partially supported by NSF Grant CCR-9643913 and the US Army Research Office Grant DAAH04-96-1-0181. Aaron Lee was also partially supported by a Wu Graduate Fellowship and a Summer Internship at Bell Laboratories, Lucent Technologies. Peter Schröder was partially supported by grants from the Intel Corporation, the Sloan Foundation, an NSF CAREER award (ASC-9624957), a MURI (AFOSR F49620-96-1-0471), and Bell Laboratories, Lucent Technologies. Special thanks to Timothy Baker, Ken Clarkson, Tom Duchamp, Tom Funkhouser, Amanda Galtman, and Ralph Howard for many interesting and stimulation discussions. Special thanks also to Andrei Khodakovsky, Louis Thomas, and Gary Wu for invaluable help in the production of the paper. Our implementation uses the triangle facet data structure and code of Ernst Mücke.

References

[1] BAJAJ, C. L., BERNADINI, F., CHEN, J., AND SCHIKORE, D. R. Automatic Reconstruction of 3D CAD Models. Tech. Rep. 96-015, Purdue University, February 1996.

[2] BROWN, P. J. C., AND FAIGLE, C. T. A Robust Efficient Algorithm for Point Location in Triangulations. Tech. rep., Cambridge University, February 1997.

[3] CERTAIN, A., POPOVIĆ, J., DEROSE, T., DUCHAMP, T., SALESIN, D., AND STUETZLE, W. Interactive Multiresolution Surface Viewing. In *Computer Graphics (SIGGRAPH 96 Proceedings)*, 91–98, 1996.

[4] COHEN, J., MANOCHA, D., AND OLANO, M. Simplifying Polygonal Models Using Successive Mappings. In *Proceedings IEEE Visualization 97*, 395–402, October 1997.

[5] DOBKIN, D., AND KIRKPATRICK, D. A Linear Algorithm for Determining the Separation of Convex Polyhedra. *Journal of Algorithms 6* (1985), 381–392.

[6] DUCHAMP, T., CERTAIN, A., DEROSE, T., AND STUETZLE, W. Hierarchical Computation of PL harmonic Embeddings. Tech. rep., University of Washington, July 1997.

[7] ECK, M., DEROSE, T., DUCHAMP, T., HOPPE, H., LOUNSBERY, M., AND STUETZLE, W. Multiresolution Analysis of Arbitrary Meshes. In *Computer Graphics (SIGGRAPH 95 Proceedings)*, 173–182, 1995.

[8] ECK, M., AND HOPPE, H. Automatic Reconstruction of B-Spline Surfaces of Arbitrary Topological Type. In *Computer Graphics (SIGGRAPH 96 Proceedings)*, 325–334, 1996.

[9] GARLAND, M., AND HECKBERT, P. S. Fast Polygonal Approximation of Terrains and Height Fields. Tech. Rep. CMU-CS-95-181, CS Dept., Carnegie Mellon U., September 1995.

[10] GUIBAS, L., AND STOLFI, J. Primitives for the Manipulation of General Subdivisions and the Computation of Voronoi Diagrams. *ACM Transactions on Graphics 4*, 2 (April 1985), 74–123.

[11] HECKBERT, P. S., AND GARLAND, M. Survey of Polygonal Surface Simplification Algorithms. Tech. rep., Carnegie Mellon University, 1997.

[12] HOPPE, H. Progressive Meshes. In *Computer Graphics (SIGGRAPH 96 Proceedings)*, 99–108, 1996.

[13] HOPPE, H. View-Dependent Refinement of Progressive Meshes. In *Computer Graphics (SIGGRAPH 97 Proceedings)*, 189–198, 1997.

[14] HOPPE, H., DEROSE, T., DUCHAMP, T., HALSTEAD, M., JIN, H., MCDONALD, J., SCHWEITZER, J., AND STUETZLE, W. Piecewise Smooth Surface Reconstruction. In *Computer Graphics (SIGGRAPH 94 Proceedings)*, 295–302, 1994.

[15] KIRKPATRICK, D. Optimal Search in Planar Subdivisions. *SIAM J. Comput. 12* (1983), 28–35.

[16] KLEIN, A., CERTAIN, A., DEROSE, T., DUCHAMP, T., AND STUETZLE, W. Vertex-based Delaunay Triangulation of Meshes of Arbitrary Topological Type. Tech. rep., University of Washington, July 1997.

[17] KRISHNAMURTHY, V., AND LEVOY, M. Fitting Smooth Surfaces to Dense Polygon Meshes. In *Computer Graphics (SIGGRAPH 96 Proceedings)*, 313–324, 1996.

[18] LOOP, C. Smooth Subdivision Surfaces Based on Triangles. Master's thesis, University of Utah, Department of Mathematics, 1987.

[19] LOUNSBERY, M. *Multiresolution Analysis for Surfaces of Arbitrary Topological Type*. PhD thesis, Department of Computer Science, University of Washington, 1994.

[20] LOUNSBERY, M., DEROSE, T., AND WARREN, J. Multiresolution Analysis for Surfaces of Arbitrary Topological Type. *Transactions on Graphics 16*, 1 (January 1997), 34–73.

[21] MÜCKE, E. P. Shapes and Implementations in Three-Dimensional Geometry. Technical Report UIUCDCS-R-93-1836, University of Illinois at Urbana-Champaign, 1993.

[22] SCHRÖDER, P., AND SWELDENS, W. Spherical Wavelets: Efficiently Representing Functions on the Sphere. In *Computer Graphics (SIGGRAPH 95 Proceedings)*, Annual Conference Series, 1995.

[23] SCHWEITZER, J. E. *Analysis and Application of Subdivision Surfaces*. PhD thesis, University of Washington, 1996.

[24] SPANIER, E. H. *Algebraic Topology*. McGraw-Hill, New York, 1966.

[25] XIA, J. C., AND VARSHNEY, A. Dynamic View-Dependent Simplification for Polygonal Models. In *Proceedings Visualization 96*, 327–334, October 1996.

[26] ZORIN, D. *Subdivision and Multiresolution Surface Representations*. PhD thesis, California Institute of Technology, 1997.

[27] ZORIN, D., SCHRÖDER, P., AND SWELDENS, W. Interpolating Subdivision for Meshes with Arbitrary Topology. In *Computer Graphics (SIGGRAPH 96 Proceedings)*, 189–192, 1996.

[28] ZORIN, D., SCHRÖDER, P., AND SWELDENS, W. Interactive Multiresolution Mesh Editing. In *Computer Graphics (SIGGRAPH 97 Proceedings)*, 259–268, 1997.

Interactive Multi-Resolution Modeling on Arbitrary Meshes

Leif Kobbelt[*]   Swen Campagna   Jens Vorsatz   Hans-Peter Seidel

University of Erlangen–Nürnberg

Abstract

During the last years the concept of multi-resolution modeling has gained special attention in many fields of computer graphics and geometric modeling. In this paper we generalize powerful multi-resolution techniques to arbitrary triangle meshes without requiring subdivision connectivity. Our major observation is that the hierarchy of nested spaces which is the structural core element of most multi-resolution algorithms can be replaced by the sequence of intermediate meshes emerging from the application of incremental mesh decimation. Performing such schemes with local frame coding of the detail coefficients already provides effective and efficient algorithms to extract multi-resolution information from unstructured meshes. In combination with discrete fairing techniques, i.e., the constrained minimization of discrete energy functionals, we obtain very fast mesh smoothing algorithms which are able to reduce noise from a geometrically specified frequency band in a multi-resolution decomposition. Putting mesh hierarchies, local frame coding and multi-level smoothing together allows us to propose a flexible and intuitive paradigm for interactive detail-preserving mesh modification. We show examples generated by our mesh modeling tool implementation to demonstrate its functionality.

1 Introduction

Traditionally, geometric modeling is based on piecewise polynomial surface representations [8, 16]. However, while special polynomial basis functions are well suited for describing and modifying smooth triangular or quadrilateral *patches*, it turns out to be rather difficult to smoothly join several pieces of a composite surface along common (possibly trimmed) boundary curves. As flexible patch layout is crucial for the construction of non-trivial geometric shapes, spline-based modeling tools do spend much effort to maintain the global smoothness of a surface.

Subdivision schemes can be considered as an algorithmic generalization of classical spline techniques enabling control meshes with arbitrary topology [2, 5, 6, 18, 22, 39]. They provide easy access to globally smooth surfaces of arbitrary shape by iteratively applying simple refinement rules to the given control mesh. A sequence of meshes generated by this process quickly converges to a smooth limit surface. For most practical applications, the refined

meshes are already sufficiently close to the smooth limit after only a few refinement steps.

Within a multi-resolution framework, subdivision schemes provide a set of basis functions $\phi_{i,j} = \phi(2^i \cdot -j)$ which are suitable to build a cascade of nested spaces $V_i = \mathrm{span}([\phi_{i,j}]_j)$ [4, 33]. Since the functions $\phi_{i,j}$ are defined by uniform refinement of a given control mesh $\mathcal{M}_0 \cong V_0$, the spaces V_i have to be isomorphic to meshes $\mathcal{M}_i$ with *subdivision connectivity*.

While being much more flexible than classical (tensor-product) spline techniques, the multi-resolution representation based on the uniform refinement of a polygonal base mesh is still rather rigid. When analyzing a given mesh $\mathcal{M}_k$, i.e., when decomposing the mesh into disjoint frequency bands $W_i = V_{i+1} \setminus V_i$, we have to *invert* the uniform refinement operation $V_i \to V_{i+1}$. Hence, the input mesh always has to be topologically isomorphic to an iteratively refined base grid. In general this requires a global remeshing/resampling of the input data prior to the multi-resolution analysis [7]. Moreover, if we want to fuse several separately generated subdivision meshes (e.g. laser range scans) into one model, restrictive compatibility conditions have to be satisfied. Hence, subdivision schemes are able to deal with arbitrary *topology* but not with arbitrary *connectivity*!

The *scales* of subdivision based multi-resolution mesh representations are defined in terms of topological distances. Since every vertex $\mathbf{p}_{i,j}$ on each level of subdivision $\mathcal{M}_i$ represents the weight coefficient of a particular basis function $\phi_{i,j}$ with fixed support, its region of influence is determined by topological neighborhood in the mesh instead of geometric proximity. Being derived from the regular functional setting, the refinement rules of stationary subdivision schemes only depend on the valences of the vertices but not on the length of the adjacent edges. Hence, surface artifacts can occur when the given base mesh is locally strongly distorted.

Assume we have a subdivision connectivity mesh and want to apply modifications on a specific scale V_i. The usual way to implement this operation is to run a decomposition scheme several steps until the desired resolution level is reached. On this level the mesh $\mathcal{M}_i$ is modified and the reconstruction starting with $\mathcal{M}_i'$ yields the final result. The major draw-back of this procedure is the fact that coarse basis functions exist for the coarse-mesh vertices only and hence all low-frequency modifications have to be *aligned* to the grid imposed by the subdivision connectivity. Shifted low-frequency modifications can be faked by moving a *group* of vertices from a finer scale simultaneously but this annihilates the mathematical elegance of multi-resolution representations.

A standard demo example for multi-resolution modeling is pulling the nose tip of a human head model. Depending on the chosen scale either the whole face is affected or just the nose is elongated. On uniformly refined meshes this operation only works if a coarse-scale control vertex happens to be located right at the nose tip. However, for an *automatic* remeshing algorithm it is very difficult, if not impossible, to place the coarse-scale vertices at the semantically relevant features of an object.

In this paper we present an alternative approach to multi-resolution modeling which avoids these three major difficulties, i.e. the restriction to subdivision connectivity meshes, the restriction to basis functions with fixed support and the alignment of potential coarser-scale modifications.

[*]Computer Sciences Department (IMMD9), University of Erlangen-Nürnberg, Am Weichselgarten 9, 91058 Erlangen, Germany, Leif.Kobbelt@informatik.uni-erlangen.de

The first problem is solved by using mesh hierarchies which emerge from the application of a mesh decimation scheme. In Section 2 we derive the necessary equipment to extract multi-resolution information from arbitrary meshes and geometrically encode detail information with respect to local frames which adapt to the local geometry of the coarser approximation of the object.

To overcome the problems arising from the fixed support and aligned distribution of subdivision basis functions, we drop the structural concept of considering a surface in space to be a linear combination of scalar-valued basis functions. On each level of detail, the lower-frequency components of the geometric shape are simply characterized by energy minimization (*fairing*). In Section 3 we overview the discrete fairing technique [19, 38] and show how a combination with the non-uniform mesh hierarchy leads to highly efficient mesh optimization algorithms. Due to the local smoothing properties of the fairing operators, we are able to define a *geometric* threshold for the wavelength up to which a low-pass filter should remove noise.

With an efficient hierarchical mesh smoothing scheme available, we propose a flexible mesh modification paradigm in Section 4. The basic idea is to let the designer freely define the region of influence and the characteristics of the modification which both can be adapted to the surface geometry instead of being determined by the connectivity. The selected region defines the "frequency" of the modification since it provides the boundary conditions for a constrained energy minimization. Nevertheless the detail information within the selected region is preserved and does change according to the global modification. Exploiting the efficient schemes from Section 3 leads to interactive response times for moderately complex models.

Throughout the paper, we consider a modeling scenario where a triangle mesh $\mathcal{M}$ with arbitrary connectivity is *given* (no from-scratch design). All modifications just alter the position of the vertices but not their adjacency. In particular, we do not consider ad infinitum subdivision to establish infinitesimal smoothness. The given mesh $\mathcal{M} = \mathcal{M}_k$ represents per definition the finest level of detail.

2 Multi-resolution representations

Most schemes for the multi-resolution representation and modification of triangle meshes emerge from generalizing harmonic analysis techniques like the wavelet transform [1, 23, 30, 33]. Since the fundamentals have been derived in the scalar-valued functional setting $\mathbf{R}^d \to \mathbf{R}$, difficulties emerge from the fact that manifolds in space are in general not topologically equivalent to simply connected regions in $\mathbf{R}^d$.

The philosophy behind multi-resolution modeling on surfaces is hence to mimic the algorithmic structure of the related functional transforms and preserve some of the important properties like locality, smoothness, stability or polynomial precision which have related meaning in both settings [9, 12, 40]. Accordingly, the nested sequence of spaces underlying the decomposition into disjoint frequency bands is thought of being generated bottom-up from a coarse base mesh up to finer and finer resolutions. This implies that subdivision connectivity is mandatory on higher levels of detail. Not only the mesh has to consist of large regular regions with isolated extra-ordinary vertices in between. Additionally, we have to make sure that the topological distance between the singularities is the same for every pair of neighboring singularities and this topological distance has to be a power of 2.

Such special topological requirements prevent the schemes from being applicable to arbitrary input meshes. Global remeshing and resampling is necessary to obtain a proper hierarchy which gives rise to alias-errors and requires involved computations [7].

Luckily, the restricted topology is not necessary to define different levels of resolution or approximation for a triangle mesh.

In the literature on mesh decimation we find many examples for hierarchies built on arbitrary meshes [11, 15, 20, 24, 27, 31, 35]. The key is always to build the hierarchy top-down by eliminating vertices from the current mesh (*incremental reduction, progressive meshes*). Running a mesh decimation algorithm, we can stop, e.g., every time a certain percentage of the vertices is removed. The intermediate meshes can be used as a level-of-detail representation [15, 23].

In both cases, i.e., the bottom-up or the top-down generation of nested (vertex-) grids, the multi-resolution concept is rigidly attached to topological entities. This makes sense if hierarchies are merely used to reduce the complexity of the representation. In the context of multi-resolution modeling, however, we want the hierarchy not necessarily to rate meshes according to their *coarseness* but rather according to their *smoothness* (cf. Fig 1).

We will use multi-resolution hierarchies for two purposes. First we want to derive highly efficient algorithms for mesh optimization. In Section 3 we will see that topologically reduced meshes are the key to significantly increase the performance (levels of coarseness). On the other hand, we want to avoid any restrictions that are imposed by topological peculiarities. In particular, when interactively modifying a triangle mesh, we do not want any alignment. The *support* of a modification should have no influence on *where* this modification can be applied (levels of smoothness).

To describe the different set-ups for multi-resolution representation uniformly, we define a generic decomposition scheme $\mathbf{A} = (\mathbf{A}_\Phi | \mathbf{A}_\Psi)^T$ (*analysis*) as a general procedure that transforms a given mesh $\mathcal{M}_i$ into a coarser/smoother one $\mathcal{M}_{i-1} = \mathbf{A}_\Phi \mathcal{M}_i$ plus detail coefficients $\mathcal{D}_{i-1} = \mathbf{A}_\Psi \mathcal{M}_i$. In the standard wavelet setting the cardinalities satisfy $\#\mathcal{D}_{i-1} + \#\mathcal{M}_{i-1} = \#\mathcal{M}_i$ since decomposition is a proper basis transform.

If a (bi-orthogonal) wavelet basis is not known, we have to store more detail information ($\#\mathcal{D}_{i-1} + \#\mathcal{M}_{i-1} > \#\mathcal{M}_i$) since the reconstruction operator $\mathbf{A}^{-1}$ might be computationally expensive or not even uniquely defined. Well-known examples for this kind of decomposition with extra detail coefficients are the Laplacian-pyramid type of representation in [40] and the progressive mesh representation [15].

When $\mathbf{A}_\Phi$ is merely a smoothing operator which does not change the topological mesh structure of $\mathcal{M}_i$ we have $\mathbf{A}_\Psi = \mathbf{I}d - \mathbf{A}_\Phi$ and $\#\mathcal{D}_{i-1} = \#\mathcal{M}_{i-1} = \#\mathcal{M}_i$.

2.1 Local Frames

In a multi-resolution representation of a geometric object $\mathcal{M} = \mathcal{M}_k$, the detail coefficients $\mathcal{D}_{i-1}$ describe the difference between two approximations $\mathcal{M}_{i-1}$ and $\mathcal{M}_i$ having different levels of detail. For parametric surfaces, the detail coefficients, i.e., the spatial location of the vertices in $\mathcal{M}_i$ have to be encoded relative to the local geometry of the coarser approximation $\mathcal{M}_{i-1}$. This is necessary since modifications on the coarser level should have an intuitive effect on the geometric features from finer scales.

First proposed by [10] it has become standard to derive local coordinate frames from the partial derivative information of the coarse representation $\mathcal{M}_{i-1}$. Since we do not assume the existence of any global structure or auxiliary information in the sequence of meshes $\mathcal{M}_i$, we have to rely on intrinsic geometric properties of the triangles themselves. Depending on the intended application we assign the local frames to the triangles or the vertices of $\mathcal{M}_{i-1}$. A detail vector is then defined by three coordinate values $[u, v, n]$ plus an index i identifying the affine frame $F_i = [\mathbf{p}_i, U_i, V_i, N_i]$ with respect to which the coordinates are given.

2.1.1 Vertex-based frames

We can use any heuristic to estimate the normal vector N_i at a vertex $\mathbf{p}_i$ in a polygonal mesh, e.g., taking the average of the adjacent triangle normals. The vector $U_i = E - (E^T N_i) N_i$ is ob-

Figure 1: The well-known Stanford-Bunny. Although the original mesh does not have subdivision connectivity, mesh decimation algorithms easily generate a hierarchy of topologically simplified meshes. On the other hand, multi-resolution modeling also requires hierarchies of differently *smooth* approximations. Notice that the meshes in the lower row have identical connectivity.

tained by projecting any adjacent edge E into the tangent plane and $V_i := N_i \times U_i$. The data structure for storing the mesh $\mathcal{M}_{i-1}$ has to make sure that E is uniquely defined, e.g. as the first member in a list of neighbors.

2.1.2 Face-based frames

It is tempting to simply use the local frame which is given by two triangle edges and their cross product. However, this will not lead to convincing detail reconstruction after modifying the coarser level. The reason for this is that the local frames would be rigidly attached to one coarse triangle. In fact, tracing the dependency over several levels of detail shows that the original mesh is implicitly partitioned into sub-meshes being assigned to the same coarse triangle T. Applying a transformation to T implies the same transformation for all vertices being defined relative to T. This obviously leads to artifacts between neighboring sub-meshes in the fine mesh.

A better choice is to use local low order polynomial interpolants or approximants that depend on more than one single triangle. Let $\mathbf{p}_0$, $\mathbf{p}_1$, and $\mathbf{p}_2$ be the vertices of a triangle $T \in \mathcal{M}_{i-1}$ and $\mathbf{p}_3$, $\mathbf{p}_4$, and $\mathbf{p}_5$ be the opposite vertices of the triangles adjacent to T (cf. Fig. 2). To construct a quadratic polynomial

$$\mathbf{F}(u, v) = \mathbf{f} + u\,\mathbf{f}_u + v\,\mathbf{f}_v + \frac{u^2}{2}\,\mathbf{f}_{uu} + u\,v\,\mathbf{f}_{uv} + \frac{v^2}{2}\,\mathbf{f}_{vv}$$

approximating the $\mathbf{p}_i$ we have to define a parameterization first. Note that the particular choice of this parameterization controls the quality of the approximant. Since we want to take the geometric constellation of the $\mathbf{p}_i$ into account, we define a parameterization by projecting the vertices into the supporting plane of T.

Exploiting the invariance of the polynomial interpolant with respect to affine re-parameterizations, we can require $\mathbf{F}(0, 0) := \mathbf{p}_0$, $\mathbf{F}(1, 0) := \mathbf{p}_1$, and $\mathbf{F}(0, 1) := \mathbf{p}_2$ which implies

$$\begin{aligned} \mathbf{f} &= \mathbf{p}_0 \\ \mathbf{f}_u &= \mathbf{p}_1 - \mathbf{p}_0 - \tfrac{1}{2}\mathbf{f}_{uu} \\ \mathbf{f}_v &= \mathbf{p}_2 - \mathbf{p}_0 - \tfrac{1}{2}\mathbf{f}_{vv}. \end{aligned} \quad (1)$$

Let the vertices $\mathbf{p}_3$, $\mathbf{p}_4$, and $\mathbf{p}_5$ be projected to (u_3, v_3), (u_4, v_4), and (u_5, v_5) according to the frame $[\mathbf{p}_0, \mathbf{p}_1, \mathbf{p}_2]$. To additionally stabilize the interpolation scheme, we introduce a tension parameter $\tau \in [0, 1]$ which trades approximation error at $\mathbf{p}_3$, $\mathbf{p}_4$, and $\mathbf{p}_5$ for minimizing the bending energy $\mathbf{f}_{uu}^2 + 2\,\mathbf{f}_{uv}^2 + \mathbf{f}_{vv}^2$. Using (1) we obtain

$$\begin{pmatrix} \tfrac{1}{2} u_3 (u_3 - 1) & u_3 v_3 & \tfrac{1}{2} v_3 (v_3 - 1) \\ \tfrac{1}{2} u_4 (u_4 - 1) & u_4 v_4 & \tfrac{1}{2} v_4 (v_4 - 1) \\ \tfrac{1}{2} u_5 (u_5 - 1) & u_5 v_5 & \tfrac{1}{2} v_5 (v_5 - 1) \\ \tau & 0 & 0 \\ 0 & 2\tau & 0 \\ 0 & 0 & \tau \end{pmatrix} \begin{pmatrix} \mathbf{f}_{uu} \\ \mathbf{f}_{uv} \\ \mathbf{f}_{vv} \end{pmatrix} =$$

$$\begin{pmatrix} (\mathbf{p}_3 - \mathbf{p}_0) + u_3 (\mathbf{p}_0 - \mathbf{p}_1) + v_3 (\mathbf{p}_0 - \mathbf{p}_2) \\ (\mathbf{p}_4 - \mathbf{p}_0) + u_4 (\mathbf{p}_0 - \mathbf{p}_1) + v_4 (\mathbf{p}_0 - \mathbf{p}_2) \\ (\mathbf{p}_5 - \mathbf{p}_0) + u_5 (\mathbf{p}_0 - \mathbf{p}_1) + v_5 (\mathbf{p}_0 - \mathbf{p}_2) \\ 0 \\ 0 \\ 0 \end{pmatrix}$$

which has to be solved in a least squares sense.

To compute the detail coefficients $[\hat{u}, \hat{v}, h]$ for a point $\mathbf{q}$ with respect to T, we start from the center $(u, v) = (\tfrac{1}{3}, \tfrac{1}{3})$ and simple Newton iteration steps $(u, v) \leftarrow (u, v) + (\triangle u, \triangle v)$ with $\mathbf{d} = \mathbf{q} - \mathbf{F}(u, v)$ and

$$\begin{pmatrix} \mathbf{F}_u^T \mathbf{F}_u & \mathbf{F}_u^T \mathbf{F}_v \\ \mathbf{F}_u^T \mathbf{F}_v & \mathbf{F}_v^T \mathbf{F}_v \end{pmatrix} \begin{pmatrix} \triangle u \\ \triangle v \end{pmatrix} = \begin{pmatrix} \mathbf{F}_u^T \mathbf{d} \\ \mathbf{F}_u^T \mathbf{d} \end{pmatrix}$$

quickly converge to the point $\mathbf{F}(\hat{u}, \hat{v})$ with the detail vector $\mathbf{d}$ perpendicular to the surface $\mathbf{F}(u, v)$. The third coefficient is then $h = \text{sign}(\mathbf{d}^T (\mathbf{F}_u \times \mathbf{F}_v)) \, \|\mathbf{d}\|$.

Although the parameter values $(\hat{u}, \hat{v})$ can lie outside the unit triangle (which occasionally occurs for extremely distorted configurations) the detail coefficient $[\hat{u}, \hat{v}, h]$ is still well-defined and reconstruction works. Notice that the scheme might produce counterintuitive results if the maximum dihedral angle between T and one of its neighbors becomes larger than $\frac{\pi}{2}$. In this case the parameterization for $\mathbf{p}_3$, $\mathbf{p}_4$, and $\mathbf{p}_5$ could be derived by rotation about T's edges instead of projection.

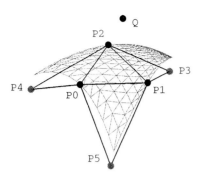

Figure 2: Vertex labeling for the construction of a local frame.

Obviously, the detail coefficient $[\hat{u}, \hat{v}, h]$ is not coded with respect to a local frame in the narrow sense. However, it has a similar semantics. Recovering the vertex position $\mathbf{q}'$ requires to construct the approximating polynomial $\mathbf{F}'(u, v)$ for the possibly modified vertices $\mathbf{p}'_i$, evaluate at $(\hat{u}, \hat{v})$ and move in normal direction by h. The distance h is a measure for the "size" of the detail.

In our current implementation on a SGI R10000/195 MHz workstation the analysis $\mathbf{q} \rightarrow [\hat{u}, \hat{v}, h]$ takes about $20\mu S$ while the reconstruction $[\hat{u}, \hat{v}, h] \rightarrow \mathbf{q}$ takes approximately $8\mu S$. Since a progressive mesh representation introduces two triangles per vertex split, this means that for the reconstruction of a mesh with 10^5 triangles, the computational overhead due to the local frame representation is less than half a second.

2.2 Decomposition and reconstruction

To complete our equipment for the multi-resolution set-up we have to define the decomposition and reconstruction operations which separate the high-frequency detail from the low-frequency shape and eventually recombine the two to recover the original mesh. We apply different strategies depending on whether decomposition generates a coarser approximation of the original geometry or a smoother approximation.

In either case the decomposition operator $\mathbf{A}$ is applied to the original mesh $\mathcal{M}_i$ and the details $\mathcal{D}_{i-1}$ are coded in local frame coordinates with respect to $\mathcal{M}_{i-1}$. Since the reconstruction is an extrapolation process, it is numerically unstable. To stabilize the operation we have to make the details as small as possible, i.e., when encoding the spatial position of a point $\mathbf{q} \in \mathbf{R}^3$ we pick that local frame on $\mathcal{M}_{i-1}$ which is closest to $\mathbf{q}$.

Usually the computational complexity of generating the detail coefficients is higher than the complexity of the evaluation during reconstruction. This is an important feature since for interactive modeling the (dynamic) reconstruction has to be done in real-time while the requirements for the (static) decomposition are not as demanding.

2.2.1 Mesh decimation based decomposition

When performing an incremental mesh decimation algorithm, each reduction step removes one vertex and retriangulates the remaining hole [15, 31]. We use a simplified version of the algorithm described in [20] that controls the reduction process in order to optimize the fairness of the coarse mesh while keeping the global approximation error below a prescribed tolerance.

The basic topological operation is the *half edge collapse* which shifts one vertex $\mathbf{p}$ into an adjacent vertex $\mathbf{q}$ and removes the two

degenerate triangles. In [20] a fast algorithm is presented to determine that triangle T in the neighborhood of the collapse which lies closest to the removed vertex $\mathbf{p}$. The position of $\mathbf{p}$ is then coded with respect to the local frame associated with this triangle.

The inverse operation of an edge collapse is the *vertex split* [15]. Since during reconstruction the vertices are inserted in the reverse order of their removal, it is guaranteed that, when $\mathbf{p}$ is inserted, the topological neighborhood looks the same as when it was deleted and hence the local frame to transform the detail coefficient for $\mathbf{p}$ back into world coordinates is well-defined.

During the iterative decimation, each intermediate mesh could be considered as one individual level of detail approximation. However, if we want to define disjoint frequency bands, it is reasonable to consider a whole sub-sequence of edge collapses as one atomic transformation from one level $\mathcal{M}_i$ to $\mathcal{M}_{i-1}$.

There are several criteria to determine which levels mark the boundaries between successive frequency bands. One possibility is to simply define $\mathcal{M}_i$ to be the coarsest mesh that still keeps a maximum tolerance of less than some ε_i to the original data. Alternatively we can require the number of vertices in $\mathcal{M}_{i-1}$ to be a fixed percentage of the number of vertices in $\mathcal{M}_i$. This simulates the geometric decrease of complexity known from classical multi-resolution schemes. We can also let the human user decide when a significant level of detail is reached by allowing her to browse through the sequence of incrementally reduced meshes.

In order to achieve optimal performance with the multi-level smoothing algorithm described in the next section, we decided in our implementation to distribute the collapses evenly over the mesh: When a collapse $\mathbf{p} \rightarrow \mathbf{q}$ is performed, all vertices adjacent to $\mathbf{q}$ are locked for further collapsing (independent set of collapses). If no more collapses are possible, the current mesh defines the next level of detail and all vertices are un-locked. One pass of this reduction scheme removes about 25% of the vertices in average.

2.2.2 Mesh smoothing based decomposition

For multi-resolution *modeling* we have to separate high frequency features from the global shape in order to modify both individually. Reducing the mesh complexity cannot help in this case since coarser meshes do no longer have enough degrees of freedom to be smooth, i.e., to have small angles between adjacent triangles. Hence, the decomposition operator $\mathbf{A}_\Phi$ becomes a mere smoothing operator that reduces the discrete bending energy in the mesh without changing the topology (cf. Section 3).

A natural way to define the detail coefficients would be to store the difference vectors between the original vertex position $\mathbf{q}$ and the shifted position $\mathbf{q}'$ with respect to the local frame defined at $\mathbf{q}'$. However, in view of numerical stability this choice is not optimal. Depending on the special type of smoothing operator $\mathbf{A}_\Phi$ the vertices can move "within" the surface such that another vertex $\mathbf{p}' \in \mathcal{M}_{i-1} = \mathbf{A}_\Phi \mathcal{M}_i$ could lie closer to $\mathbf{q}$ than $\mathbf{q}'$ (cf. Fig. 3).

 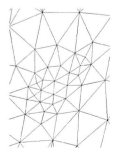

Figure 3: Although the bending energy minimizing smoothing operator $\mathbf{A}_\Phi$ is applied to a *plane* triangulation, the vertices are moved within the plane since linear operators always do the fairing with respect to a specific parameterization (cf. Section 3).

To stabilize the reconstruction, i.e., to minimize the length of the detail vectors, we apply a simple local search procedure to find the nearest vertex $\mathbf{p}' \in \mathcal{M}_{i-1}$ to $\mathbf{q}$ and express the detail vector with respect to the local frame at $\mathbf{p}'$ or one of its adjacent triangles. This searching step does not noticeably increase the computation time (which is usually dominated by the smoothing operation $\mathbf{A}_\Phi$) but leads to much shorter detail vectors (cf. Fig 4).

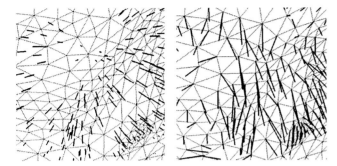

Figure 4: The shortest detail vectors are obtained by representing the detail coefficients with respect to the nearest local frame (left) instead of attaching the detail vectors to the topologically corresponding original vertices.

3 Discrete fairing

From CAGD it is well-known that constrained energy minimization is a very powerful technique to generate high quality surfaces [3, 13, 25, 28, 37]. For efficiency, one usually defines a simple quadratic energy functional $\mathcal{E}(f)$ and searches among the set of functions satisfying prescribed interpolation constraints for that function f which minimizes $\mathcal{E}$.

Transferring the continuous concept of energy minimization to the discrete setting of triangle mesh optimization leads to the discrete fairing approach [19, 38]. Local polynomial interpolants are used to estimate derivative information at each vertex by divided difference operators. Hence, the differential equation characterizing the functions with minimum energy is discretized into a linear system for the vertex positions.

Since this system is global and sparse, we apply iterative solving algorithms like the Gauß-Seidel-scheme. For such algorithms one iteration step merely consists in the application of a simple local averaging operator. This makes discrete fairing an easy accessible technique for mesh optimization.

3.1 The umbrella-algorithm

The most prominent energy functionals that are used in the theory and practice of surface design are the membrane energy

$$\mathcal{E}_M(f) := \int f_u^2 + f_v^2 \qquad (2)$$

which prefers functions with smaller surface area and the thin plate energy

$$\mathcal{E}_{TP}(f) := \int f_{uu}^2 + 2 f_{uv}^2 + f_{vv}^2 \qquad (3)$$

which punishes strong bending. The variational calculus leads to simple characterizations of the corresponding minimum energy surfaces

$$\triangle f = f_{uu} + f_{vv} = 0 \qquad (4)$$

or

$$\triangle^2 f = f_{uuuu} + 2 f_{uuvv} + f_{vvvv} = 0 \qquad (5)$$

respectively. Obviously, low degree polynomials satisfy both differential equations and hence appropriate (Dirichlet-) boundary conditions have to be imposed which make the semi-definite functionals $\mathcal{E}_M$ and $\mathcal{E}_{TP}$ positive-definite.

The discrete fairing approach discretizes either the energy functionals (2–3) [19, 38] or the corresponding Euler-Lagrange equations (4–5) [17, 36] by replacing the differential operators with divided difference operators. To construct these operators, we have to choose an appropriate parameterization in the vicinity of each vertex. In [38] for example a discrete analogon to the exponential map is chosen. In [17] the *umbrella-algorithm* is derived by choosing a symmetric parameterization

$$(u_i, v_i) := \left(\cos(2\pi \frac{i}{n}), \sin(2\pi \frac{i}{n}) \right), \quad i = 0, \ldots, n-1 \quad (6)$$

with n being the valence of the center vertex $\mathbf{p}$ (cf. Fig 5). This parameterization does not adapt to the local geometric constellation but it simplifies the construction of the corresponding difference operators which are otherwise obtained by solving a Vandermonde system for local polynomial interpolation. With the special parameterization (6) the discrete analogon of the Laplacian $\triangle f$ turns out to be the umbrella-operator

$$\mathcal{U}(\mathbf{p}) = \frac{1}{n} \sum_{i=0}^{n-1} \mathbf{p}_i - \mathbf{p}$$

with $\mathbf{p}_i$ being the direct neighbors of $\mathbf{p}$ (cf. Fig. 5). The umbrella-operator can be applied recursively leading to

$$\mathcal{U}^2(\mathbf{p}) = \frac{1}{n} \sum_{i=0}^{n-1} \mathcal{U}(\mathbf{p}_i) - \mathcal{U}(\mathbf{p})$$

as a discretization of $\triangle^2 f$.

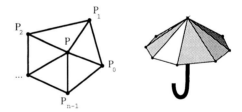

Figure 5: To compute the discrete Laplacian, we need the 1-neighborhood of a vertex $\mathbf{p}$ ($\rightarrow$ umbrella-operator).

The boundary conditions are imposed to the discrete problem by freezing certain vertices. When minimizing the discrete version of $\mathcal{E}_M$ we hold a closed boundary polygon fixed and compute the membrane that is spanned in between. For the minimization of $\mathcal{E}_{TP}$ we need two rings of boundary vertices, i.e., we keep a closed strip of triangles fixed. This imposes a (discrete) C^1 boundary condition to the optimization problem (cf. Fig 6). All internal vertices can be moved freely to minimize the global energy. The properly chosen boundary conditions imply positive-definiteness of the energy functional and guarantee the convergence of the iterative solving algorithm [29].

The characteristic (linear) system for the corresponding unconstrained minimization problem has rows $\mathcal{U}(\mathbf{p}_i) = 0$ or $\mathcal{U}^2(\mathbf{p}_i) = 0$ respectively for the free vertices $\mathbf{p}_i$. An iterative solving scheme approaches the optimal solution by solving each row of the system separately and cycling through the list of free vertices until a stable solution is reached. In case of the membrane energy $\mathcal{E}_M$ this leads to the local update rule

$$\mathbf{p}_i \leftarrow \mathbf{p}_i + \mathcal{U}(\mathbf{p}_i) \qquad (7)$$

and for the thin plate energy $\mathcal{E}_{TP}$, we obtain

$$\mathbf{p}_i \;\leftarrow\; \mathbf{p}_i - \frac{1}{\nu}\,\mathcal{U}^2(\mathbf{p}_i) \tag{8}$$

with the "diagonal element"

$$\nu \;=\; 1 + \frac{1}{n_i}\sum_j \frac{1}{n_{i,j}}$$

where n_i and $n_{i,j}$ are the valences of the center vertex $\mathbf{p}_i$ and its jth neighbor respectively.

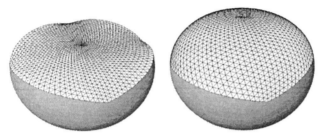

Figure 6: A closed polygon or a closed triangle strip provide C^0 or C^1 boundary conditions for the discrete fairing. On the left the triangle mesh minimizes $\mathcal{E}_M$ on the right it minimizes $\mathcal{E}_{TP}$.

Although the rule (8) can be implemented recursively, the performance is optimized if we use a two step process where all umbrella vectors $\mathcal{U}(\mathbf{p}_i)$ are computed in a first pass and $\mathcal{U}^2(\mathbf{p}_i)$ in the second. This avoids double computation but it also forces us to use in fact a plain Jacobi-solver since no intermediate updates from neighboring vertices can be used. However the $(n+2):2$ speed-up for a vertex with valence n amortizes the slower convergence of Jacobi compared to Gauß-Seidel.

3.2 Connection to Taubin's signal processing approach

The local update operator (7) in the iterative solving scheme for constrained energy minimization is exactly the Laplace smoothing operator proposed by Taubin in [34] where he derived it (also in the context of mesh smoothing) from a filter formalism based on generalized Fourier analysis for arbitrary polygonal meshes. In his paper, Taubin starts with a matrix version of the scaled update rule (7)

$$[\mathbf{p}_i'] \;:=\; (I + \lambda\,\mathcal{U})\,[\mathbf{p}_i]$$

where λ is a damping factor and formally rewrites it by using a transfer function notation

$$f(k) \;:=\; 1 - \lambda\,k$$

with respect to the eigenbasis of the (negative) Laplace operator. Since no proper boundary conditions are imposed, the continued filtering by $f(k)$ leads to severe shrinking and hence he proposes combined filters

$$f(k) \;:=\; (1 - \lambda\,k)(1 - \mu\,k) \tag{9}$$

where λ and μ are set in order to minimize the shrinking. A feasible heuristic is to choose a *pass-band frequency*

$$k_{PB} \;=\; \frac{1}{\lambda} + \frac{1}{\mu} \;\in\; [0.01 \ldots 0.1]$$

and set λ and μ while observing the stability of the filter.

Obviously, the update rule for the difference equation $\mathcal{U}(\mathbf{p}_i) = 0$ which characterizes meshes with minimum membrane energy corresponds to a special low-pass filter with transfer function $f_{\mathcal{U}}(k) = (1 - k)$. For the minimization of the total curvature, characterized by $\mathcal{U}^2(\mathbf{p}_i) = 0$, the iteration rule (8) can be re-written in transfer function notation as

$$f_{\mathcal{U}^2}(k) \;=\; \left(1 - \frac{1}{\nu}\,k^2\right) \;=\; \left(1 + \frac{1}{\sqrt{\nu}}\,k\right)\left(1 - \frac{1}{\sqrt{\nu}}\,k\right)$$

which corresponds to a combined Laplace filter of the form (9) with pass-band frequency $k_{PB} = 0$. Although this is not optimal for reducing the shrinking effect, we observe that the transfer function happens to have a vanishing derivative at $k = 0$. From signal processing theory it is known that this characterizes maximal smoothness [26], i.e., among the two step Laplace filters, the $\mathcal{U}^2$-filter achieves optimal smoothing properties. To stabilize the filter we might want to introduce a damping factor $0 < \sigma < \frac{1}{2}\nu$ into the update-rule

$$\mathbf{p}_i \;\leftarrow\; \mathbf{p}_i - \frac{\sigma}{\nu}\,\mathcal{U}^2(\mathbf{p}_i)$$

3.3 Multi-level smoothing

A well-known negative result from numerical analysis is that straight forward iterative solvers like the Gauß-Seidel scheme are not appropriate for large sparse problems [32]. More sophisticated solvers exploit knowledge about the *structure* of the problem. The important class of multi-grid solvers achieve linear running times in the number of degrees of freedom by solving the same problem on grids with different step sizes and combining the approximate solutions [14].

For difference (= discrete differential) equations of elliptic type the Gauß-Seidel iteration matrices have a special eigenstructure that causes high frequencies in the error to be attenuated very quickly while for lower frequencies no practically useful rate of convergence can be observed. Multi-level schemes hence solve a given problem on a very coarse scale first. This solution is used to predict initial values for a solution of the same problem on the next refinement level. If these predicted values have only small deviations from the true solution in low-frequency sub-spaces, then Gauß-Seidel performs well in reducing the high-frequency error. The alternating refinement and smoothing leads to highly efficient variational subdivision schemes [19] which generate fair high-resolution meshes with a rate of several thousand triangles per second (linear complexity!).

As we saw in Section 2, the bottom-up way to build multi-resolution hierarchies is just one of two possibilities. To get rid of the restriction that the uniform multi-level approach to fairing cannot be applied to arbitrary meshes, we generate the hierarchy top-down by incremental mesh decimation.

A complete V-cycle multi-grid solver recursively applies operators $\Phi_i = \Psi\,P\,\Phi_{i-1}\,R\,\Psi$ where the first (right) Ψ is a generic (pre-)smoothing operator — a Gauß-Seidel scheme in our case. R is a restriction operator to go one level coarser. This is where the mesh decimation comes in. On the coarser level, the same scheme is applied recursively, Φ_{i-1}, until on the coarsest level the number of degrees of freedom is small enough to solve the system directly (or any other stopping criterion is met). On the way back-up, the prolongation operator P inserts the previously removed vertices to go one level finer again. P can be considered as a non-regular subdivision operator which has to predict the positions of the vertices in the next level's solution. The re-subdivided mesh is an approximative solution with mostly high frequency error. (Post-)smoothing by some more iterations Ψ removes the noise and yields the final solution.

Fig 7 shows the effect of multi-level smoothing. On the left you see the original bunny with about 70K triangles. In the center left, we applied the Laplace-filter proposed in [34] with $\lambda = 0.6307$

Figure 7: Four versions of the Stanford bunny. On the left the original data set. In the center left the same object after 200 iterations of the non-shrinking Laplace-filter. On the center right and far right the original data set after applying the multi-level umbrella filter with three or six levels respectively.

and $\mu = -0.6732$. The iterative application of the local smoothing operator

$$\mathbf{p}_i \;\leftarrow\; \mathbf{p}_i + [\lambda|\mu]\,\mathcal{U}(\mathbf{p}_i) \qquad (10)$$

removes the highest frequency noise after a few iterations but does not have enough impact to flatten out the fur even after several hundred iterations. On the right you see the meshes after applying a multi-level smoothing with the following schedule: Hierarchy levels are generated by incremental mesh decimation where each level has about 50% of the next finer level's vertices. The pre-smoothing rule (8) is applied twice on every level before going downwards and five times after coming back up. On the center right model we computed a three level V-cycle and on the far right model a six level V-cycle. Notice that the computation time of the multi-level filters (excluding restriction and prolongation) corresponds to about $(2+5)(1+0.5+0.5^2+\ldots) < 14$ double-steps of the one-level Laplace-Filter (10).

3.4 Geometric filtering

The bunny example in Fig. 7 is well suited for demonstrating the effect of multi-level smoothing but we did not impose any boundary conditions and thus we applied the smoothing as a mere filter and not as a solving scheme for a well-posed optimization problem. This is the reason why we could use the number of levels to control the impact of the smoothing scheme on the final result. For constrained optimization, it does not make any sense to stop the recursion after a fixed number of decimation levels: we always reduce the mesh down to a small fixed number of triangles. Properly chosen boundary condition will ensure the convergence to the true solution and prevent the mesh from shrinking.

Nevertheless, we can exploit the effect observed in Fig. 7 to define more sophisticated geometric low-pass filters. Since the support of the Laplace-filters is controlled by the neighborhood relation in the underlying mesh, the smoothing characteristics are defined relative to a "topological wavelength". Noise which affects every other vertex is removed very quickly independent from the length of the edges while global distortions affecting a larger sub-mesh are hardly reduced. For *geometric* filters however we would like to set the pass-band frequency in terms of Euclidian distances by postulating that all geometric features being smaller than some threshold ε are considered as noise and should be removed.

Such filters can be implemented by using an appropriate mesh reduction scheme that tends to generate intermediate meshes with strong coherence in the length of the edges. In [20] we propose a mesh decimation scheme that rates the possible edge collapses according to some generic fairness functional. A suitable objective function for our application is to maximize the *roundness* of triangles, i.e., the ratio of its inner circle radius to its longest edge. If the mesh decimation scheme prefers those collapses that improve the global roundness, the resulting meshes tend to have only little variance in the lengths of the edges. For the bunny example, we can

keep the standard deviation from the average edge length below one percent for incremental decimation down to about 5K triangles.

By selecting the lowest level $\mathcal{M}_0$ down to which the V-cycle multi-level filtering iterates, we set the threshold $\varepsilon = \varepsilon(\mathcal{M}_0)$ for detail being removed by the multi-level smoothing scheme. The thresholding works very well due to the strong local and poor global convergence of the iterative update rule (8). Fig. 8 shows the base meshes for the multi-level smoothing during the computation of the two right bunnies of Fig. 7.

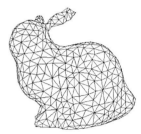

Figure 8: Base meshes where the V-cycle recursion stopped when generating the right models in Fig. 7. The final meshes do not loose significant detail (watch the silhouette). Notice how in the left example the fur is removed but the bunny's body preserved while in the right example the leg and the neck start to disappear.

4 Multi-resolution modeling on triangle meshes

In this section we describe a flexible and intuitive multi-resolution mesh modeling metaphor which exploits the techniques presented in the last two sections. As we discussed in the introduction, our goal is to get rid of topological restrictions for the mesh but also to get rid of difficulties emerging from the alignment of the basis functions in a hierarchical representation and the rigid shape of the basis function's support.

From a designer's point of view, we have to distinguish three *semantic* levels of detail. These levels are defined relative to a specific modeling operation since, of course, in a multi-resolution environment the features that are detail in a (global) modification become the global shape for a minute adjustment.

- The *global shape* is that part of the geometry that is the subject of the current modification. Intuitively, the designer selects a piece of the global shape and applies a transformation to it.

- The *structural detail* are features that are too small to be modified by hand but still represent actual geometry. This detail should follow the modification applied to the global shape in a geometrically intuitive manner. The preservation of structural

Figure 9: The wooden cat model $\mathcal{M}_k$ (178K triangles, left) is in progressive mesh representation. The high resolution is necessary to avoid alias errors in the displacement texture. The center left model $\mathcal{M}_i$ (23K triangles) is extracted by stopping the mesh reduction when a prescribed complexity is reached. On this level interactive mesh modification is done which yields the model $\mathcal{M}_i'$ (center right). The final result $\mathcal{M}_k'$ (right) is obtained by running the reconstruction on the modified mesh.

detail during interactive modeling is crucial for plausible visual feed-back (cf. the eyes and ears of the wooden cat model in Fig. 9).

- The *textural detail* does not really describe geometric shape. It is necessary to let the surface appear more realistic and is often represented by displacement maps [21]. In high quality mesh models it is the source for the explosive increase in complexity (cf. the wood texture in Fig. 9).

Having identified these three semantic levels of detail, we suggest a mesh modeling environment which provides flexible mesh modification functionality and allows the user to adapt the mesh complexity to the available hardware resources.

In an off-line preprocessing step, an incremental mesh decimation algorithm is applied and the detail coefficients are stored with respect to local frames as explained in Section 2.2.1. This transforms the highly complex input model into a progressive-mesh type multi-resolution representation without any remeshing or resampling. The representation allows the user to choose an appropriate number of triangles for generating a mesh model that is fine enough to contain at least all the structural detail but which is also coarse enough to be modified in realtime. This pre-process removes the textural detail prior to the actual interactive mesh modification.

Suppose the original mesh model $\mathcal{M}_k$ is transformed into the progressive mesh sequence $[\mathcal{M}_k, \ldots, \mathcal{M}_0]$ with $\mathcal{M}_0$ being the coarsest base mesh. If the user picks the mesh $\mathcal{M}_i$ and applies modifications then this invalidates the subsequence $[\mathcal{M}_{i-1}, \ldots, \mathcal{M}_0]$. If the working resolution is to be reduced afterwards to $\mathcal{M}_j$ $(j < i)$ then the intermediate meshes have to be recomputed by online mesh decimation. The textural detail encoded in the subsequence $[\mathcal{M}_k, \ldots, \mathcal{M}_{i+1}]$ however remains unchanged since it is stored with respect to local frames such that reconstruction starting from a modified mesh $\mathcal{M}_i'$ leads to the intended result $\mathcal{M}_k'$. Fig. 9 shows an example of this procedure.

4.1 Interactive mesh modeling by discrete fairing

The most important feature in the proposed multi-resolution mesh modeling environment is the modification functionality itself (*modeling metaphor*) which hides the mesh connectivity to the designer.

The designer starts by marking an arbitrary region on the mesh $\mathcal{M}_i$. In fact, she picks a sequence of surface points (not necessarily vertices) on the triangle mesh and these points are connected either by geodesics or by projected lines. The strip of triangles $\mathcal{S}$ which are intersected by the geodesic (projected) boundary polygon separates an interior region $\mathcal{M}_*$ and an exterior region $\mathcal{M}_i \setminus (\mathcal{M}_* \cup \mathcal{S})$. The interior region $\mathcal{M}_*$ is to be affected by the following modification.

A second polygon (not necessarily closed) is marked within the first one to define the *handle*. The semantics of this arbitrarily shaped handle is quite similar to the handle metaphor in [37]: when the designer moves or scales the virtual tool, the same geometric transformation is applied to the rigid handle and the surrounding mesh $\mathcal{M}_*$ follows according to a constrained energy minimization principle.

The freedom to define the boundary strip $\mathcal{S}$ and the handle geometry allows the designer to build "custom tailored" basis functions for the intended modification. Particularly interesting is the definition of a *closed* handle polygon which allows to control the characteristics of a bell-shaped dent: For the same region $\mathcal{M}_*$, a tiny ring-shaped handle in the middle causes a rather sharp peak while a bigger ring causes a wider bubble (cf. Fig 10). Notice that the mesh vertices in the interior of the handle polygon move according to the energy minimization.

Figure 10: Controlling the characteristics of the modification by the size of a closed handle polygon.

Since we are working on triangle meshes, the energy minimization on $\mathcal{M}_*$ is done by discrete fairing techniques (cf. Section 3). The boundary triangles $\mathcal{S}$ provide the correct C^1 boundary conditions for minimizing the thin plate energy functional (3).

The handle imposes additional interpolatory constraints on the location only — derivatives should not be affect by the handle. Hence, we cannot have triangles being part of the handle geometry. We implemented the handle constraint in the following way: like the boundary polygon, the handle polygon defines a strip of triangles being intersected by it. Whether the handle polygon is open or closed, we find two polygons of mesh edges on either side of that strip. We take any one of the two polygons and collect every other mesh vertex in a set of *handle vertices*. Keeping these handle vertices fixed during the mesh optimization is the additional interpolatory constraint.

The reason for freezing only every other handle vertex is that three fixed vertices directly connected by two edges build a rigid constellation leaving no freedom to adjust the *angle* between them. During discrete optimization this would be the source of undesired artifacts in the smooth mesh.

With the boundary conditions properly set we perform the thin plate energy minimization by using the umbrella algorithm described in Section 3.1. To obtain interactive response times, we exploit the multi-level technique: a mesh decimation algorithm is applied to the mesh $\mathcal{M}_* \cup \mathcal{S}$ to build up a hierarchy. Then starting from the coarsest level, we apply the $\mathcal{U}^2$ smoothing filter alternating with mesh refinement. This process is fast enough to obtain several frames per second when modeling with meshes of $\#\mathcal{M}_* \approx 5K$ triangles (SGI R10000/195MHz). Typically, we set the ratio of the complexities between successive meshes in the hierarchy to $1 : 2$ or $1 : 4$ and iterate the smoothing filter 3 to 5 times on each level.

During the interactive mesh smoothing we do not compute the full V-cycle algorithm of Sect. 3.3. In fact, we omit the pre-smoothing and always start from the coarsest level. When a vertex is inserted during a mesh refinement step we place it initially at its neighbor's center of gravity unless the vertex is a handle vertex. Handle vertices are placed at the location prescribed by the designer's interaction (*handle interpolation constraint*). Hence the mesh is computed from scratch in every iteration instead of just updating the last position. This is very important for the modeling dialog since only the current position, orientation and scale of the handle determines the smoothed mesh and not the whole history of movements.

For the fast convergence of the optimization procedure it turns out to be important that the interpolation constraints imposed by the handle vertices show up already on rather coarse levels in the mesh hierarchy. Otherwise their impact cannot propagate far enough through the mesh such that cusps remain in the smoothed mesh which can only be removed by an excessive number of smoothing iterations. This additional requirement can easily be included into the mesh reduction scheme by lowering the priority ranking of collapses involving handle vertices.

4.2 Detail preservation

If the modified mesh $\mathcal{M}'_*$ is merely defined by constrained energy minimization, we obviously loose all the detail of the originally selected submesh $\mathcal{M}_*$. Since only the boundary and the handle vertices put constraints on the mesh, all other geometric features are smoothed out.

To preserve the detail, we use the multi-resolution representation explained in Section 2.2.2. After the boundary $\mathcal{S}$ and the handle polygon are defined but before the handle is moved by the designer, we apply the multi-level smoothing scheme once. Although the original mesh $\mathcal{M}_*$ and the smoothed mesh $\widetilde{\mathcal{M}}_*$ are topologically equivalent, they do have different levels of (geometric) resolution and hence constitute a two-scale decomposition based on varying levels of smoothness. We encode the difference $\mathcal{D}_*$ between the two meshes, i.e., the detail coefficients for the vertices $\mathbf{p}_i \in \mathcal{M}_*$ by storing the displacement vectors with respect to the local frame associated with the nearest triangle in $\widetilde{\mathcal{M}}_*$.

When the designer moves the handle, the bottom-up mesh smoothing is performed to re-adjust the mesh to the new interpolation conditions. On the resulting smooth mesh $\widetilde{\mathcal{M}}'_*$, the detail $\mathcal{D}_*$ is added and the final mesh $\mathcal{M}'_*$ is rendered on the screen. Due to the geometric coding of the detail information, this leads to intuitive changes in the surface shape (cf. Figs. 11, 12). The "frequency" of the modification is determined by the size of the area, i.e., by the boundary conditions and the fact that the *supporting mesh* is optimal with respect to the thin-plate functional.

5 Conclusions and future work

We presented a new approach to multi-resolution mesh representation and modeling which does not require the underlying triangle mesh to have subdivision connectivity. By adapting multi-level techniques known from numerical analysis to the non-regular setting of arbitrary mesh hierarchies, we are able to approximately solve constrained mesh optimization in realtime. Combining the two results allows us to present a flexible metaphor for interactive mesh modeling where the shape of the modification is controlled by energy minimization while the geometric detail is preserved and updated according to the change of the global shape.

Our current implementation of an experimental mesh modeling tool already provides sufficient functionality to apply sophisticated realtime modifications to arbitrary input meshes with up to 100K triangles. However, all changes do affect the *geometry* of the meshes only. So far we did not consider *topological* modifications of triangle meshes. In the future, when modifying a given mesh, we would like new vertices to be inserted where the mesh is locally stretched too much and, on the other hand, we would like vertices to be removed when strong global modification causes local self-intersection of the reconstructed detail.

References

[1] BONNEAU, G., HAHMANN, S., AND NIELSON, G. Blac-wavelets: a multiresolution analysis with non-nested spaces. In *Visualization Proceedings* (1996), pp. 43–48.

[2] CATMULL, E., AND CLARK, J. Recursively Generated B-Spline Surfaces on Arbitrary Topological Meshes. *Computer Aided Design 10*, 6 (Nov. 1978), 239–248.

[3] CELNIKER, G., AND GOSSARD, D. Deformable curve and surface finite elements for free-form shape design. In *Computer Graphics (SIGGRAPH 91 Proceedings)* (July 1991), pp. 257–265.

[4] DAUBECHIES, I. *Ten Lectures on Wavelets.* CBMS-NSF Regional Conf. Series in Appl. Math., Vol. 61. SIAM, Philadelphia, PA, 1992.

[5] DOO, D., AND SABIN, M. Behaviour of recursive division surfaces near extraordinary points. *CAD* (1978).

[6] DYN, N., LEVIN, D., AND GREGORY, J. A. A butterfly subdivision scheme for surface interpolation with tension control. *ACM Transactions on Graphics 9*, 2 (April 1990), 160–169.

[7] ECK, M., DEROSE, T., DUCHAMP, T., HOPPE, H., LOUNSBERY, M., AND STUETZLE, W. Multiresolution Analysis of Arbitrary Meshes. In *Computer Graphics (SIGGRAPH 95 Proceedings)* (1995), pp. 173–182.

[8] FARIN, G. *Curves and Surfaces for CAGD*, 3rd ed. Academic Press, 1993.

[9] FINKELSTEIN, A., AND SALESIN, D. H. Multiresolution Curves. In *Computer Graphics (SIGGRAPH 94 Proceedings)* (July 1994), pp. 261–268.

[10] FORSEY, D. R., AND BARTELS, R. H. Hierarchical B-spline refinement. In *Computer Graphics (SIGGRAPH 88 Proceedings)* (1988), pp. 205–212.

[11] GARLAND, M., AND HECKBERT, P. S. Surface Simplification Using Quadric Error Metrics. In *Computer Graphics (SIGGRAPH 97 Proceedings)* (1997), pp. 209–218.

[12] GORTLER, S. J., AND COHEN, M. F. Hierarchical and Variational Geometric Modeling with Wavelets. In *Proceedings Symposium on Interactive 3D Graphics* (May 1995).

[13] GREINER, G. Variational design and fairing of spline surfaces. *Computer Graphics Forum 13* (1994), 143–154.

[14] HACKBUSCH, W. *Multi-Grid Methods and Applications.* Springer Verlag, Berlin, 1985.

[15] HOPPE, H. Progressive Meshes. In *Computer Graphics (SIGGRAPH 96 Proceedings)* (1996), pp. 99–108.

[16] HOSCHEK, J., AND LASSER, D. *Fundamentals of Computer Aided Geometric Design.* AK Peters, 1993.

[17] KOBBELT, L. *Iterative Erzeugung glatter Interpolanten.* Shaker Verlag, ISBN 3-8265-0540-9, 1995.

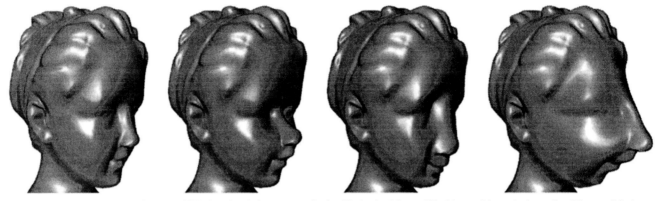

Figure 11: The mesh model of a bust (62K triangles, left, courtesy Stefan Karbacher) is modified by multi-resolution edits. The modified area $\mathcal{M}_*$ is the bust's face while the handle polygon lies around the nose. From left to right, we apply rotation, scaling and translation.

Figure 12: Some more modifications on the bust model. The support of the modification and the handle geometry adapt to the intended design operation. The detail is preserved while the global modification is controlled by discrete fairing.

[18] KOBBELT, L. Interpolatory Subdivision on Open Quadrilateral Nets with Arbitrary Topology. In *Computer Graphics Forum, Proceedings of Eurographics '96* (1996), pp. C407–C420.

[19] KOBBELT, L. Discrete fairing. In *Proceedings of the Seventh IMA Conference on the Mathematics of Surfaces* (1997), pp. 101–131.

[20] KOBBELT, L., CAMPAGNA, S., AND SEIDEL, H.-P. A general framework for mesh decimation. In *Proceedings of the Graphics Interface conference '98* (1998).

[21] KRISHNAMURTHY, V., AND LEVOY, M. Fitting smooth surfaces to dense polygon meshes. In *Computer Graphics (SIGGRAPH 96 Proceedings)* (1996), pp. 313–324.

[22] LOOP, C. Smooth spline surfaces over irregular meshes. In *Computer Graphics Proceedings* (1994), Annual Conference Series, ACM Siggraph, pp. 303–310.

[23] LOUNSBERY, M., DEROSE, T., AND WARREN, J. Multiresolution Analysis for Surfaces of Arbitrary Topological Type. *ACM Transactions on Graphics 16, 1* (January 1997), 34–73.

[24] LUEBKE, D., AND ERIKSON, C. View-Dependent Simplification of Arbitrary Polygonal Environments. In *Computer Graphics (SIGGRAPH 97 Proceedings)* (1997), pp. 199–208.

[25] MORETON, H., AND SÉQUIN, C. Functional optimization for fair surface design. In *Computer Graphics (SIGGRAPH 92 Proceedings)* (1992), pp. 167–176.

[26] OPPENHEIM, A., AND SCHAFER, R. *Discrete-Time Signal Processing.* Prentice Hall, 1989.

[27] ROSSIGNAC, J. Simplification and Compression of 3D Scenes, 1997. Tutorial Eurographics '97.

[28] SAPIDIS, N. E. *Designing Fair Curves and Surfaces.* SIAM, 1994.

[29] SCHABAK, R., AND WERNER, H. *Numerische Mathematik.* Springer Verlag, 1993.

[30] SCHRÖDER, P., AND SWELDENS, W. Spherical wavelets: Efficiently representing functions on the sphere. In *Computer Graphics (SIGGRAPH 95 Proceedings)* (1995), pp. 161–172.

[31] SCHROEDER, W. J., ZARGE, J. A., AND LORENSEN, W. E. Decimation of Triangle Meshes. In *Computer Graphics (SIGGRAPH 92 Proceedings)* (1992), pp. 65–70.

[32] STOER, J. *Einführung in die Numerische Mathematik I.* Springer Verlag, 1983.

[33] STOLLNITZ, E., DEROSE, T., AND SALESIN, D. *Wavelets for Computer Graphics.* Morgan Kaufmann Publishers, 1996.

[34] TAUBIN, G. A signal processing approach to fair surface design. In *Computer Graphics (SIGGRAPH 95 Proceedings)* (1995), pp. 351–358.

[35] TURK, G. Re-Tiling Polygonal Surfaces. In *Computer Graphics (SIGGRAPH 92 Proceedings)* (1992), pp. 55–64.

[36] WARREN, J. Subdivision schemes for variational splines, 1997. Preprint.

[37] WELCH, W., AND WITKIN, A. Variational surface modeling. In *Computer Graphics (SIGGRAPH 92 Proceedings)* (1992), pp. 157–166.

[38] WELCH, W., AND WITKIN, A. Free–Form shape design using triangulated surfaces. In *Computer Graphics (SIGGRAPH 94 Proceedings)* (1994), A. Glassner, Ed., pp. 247–256.

[39] ZORIN, D., SCHRÖDER, P., AND SWELDENS, W. Interpolating subdivision for meshes with arbitrary topology. In *Computer Graphics (SIGGRAPH 96 Proceedings)* (1996), pp. 189–192.

[40] ZORIN, D., SCHRÖDER, P., AND SWELDENS, W. Interactive multiresolution mesh editing. In *Computer Graphics (SIGGRAPH 97 Proceedings)* (1997), pp. 259–268.

Appearance-Preserving Simplification

Jonathan Cohen   Marc Olano   Dinesh Manocha

University of North Carolina at Chapel Hill

Abstract

We present a new algorithm for appearance-preserving simplification. Not only does it generate a low-polygon-count approximation of a model, but it also preserves the appearance. This is accomplished for a particular display resolution in the sense that we properly sample the surface position, curvature, and color attributes of the input surface. We convert the input surface to a representation that decouples the sampling of these three attributes, storing the colors and normals in texture and normal maps, respectively. Our simplification algorithm employs a new *texture deviation metric*, which guarantees that these maps shift by no more than a user-specified number of pixels on the screen. The simplification process filters the surface position, while the run-time system filters the colors and normals on a per-pixel basis. We have applied our simplification technique to several large models achieving significant amounts of simplification with little or no loss in rendering quality.

CR Categories: I.3.5: Object hierarchies, I.3.7: Color, shading, shadowing, and texture

Additional Keywords: simplification, attributes, parameterization, color, normal, texture, maps

1 INTRODUCTION

Simplification of polygonal surfaces has been an active area of research in computer graphics. The main goal of simplification is to generate a low-polygon-count approximation that maintains the high fidelity of the original model. This involves preserving the model's main features and overall appearance. Typically, there are three *appearance attributes* that contribute to the overall appearance of a polygonal surface:

1. **Surface position**, represented by the coordinates of the polygon vertices.

2. **Surface curvature**, represented by a field of normal vectors across the polygons.

3. **Surface color**, also represented as a field across the polygons.

The number of samples necessary to represent a surface accurately depends on the nature of the model and its area in screen pixels (which is related to its distance from the viewpoint). For a simplification algorithm to preserve the appearance of the input surface, it must guarantee adequate sampling of these three attributes. If it does, we say that it has preserved the appearance with respect to the display resolution.

e-mail: {cohenj,dm}@cs.unc.edu, olano@engr.sgi.com
WWW: http://www.cs.unc.edu/~geom/APS

The majority of work in the field of simplification has focused on *surface approximation* algorithms. These algorithms bound the error in surface position only. Such bounds can be used to guarantee a maximum deviation of the object's silhouette in units of pixels on the screen. While this guarantees that the object will cover the correct pixels on the screen, it says nothing about the final colors of these pixels.

Of the few simplification algorithms that deal with the remaining two attributes, most provide some threshold on a maximum or average deviation of these attribute values across the model. While such measures do guarantee adequate sampling of all three attributes, they do *not* generally allow increased simplification as the object becomes smaller on the screen. These threshold metrics do not incorporate information about the object's distance from the viewpoint or its area on the screen. As a result of these metrics and of the way we typically represent these appearance attributes, simplification algorithms have been quite restricted in their ability to simplify a surface while preserving its appearance.

1.1 Main Contribution

We present a new algorithm for appearance-preserving simplification. We convert our input surface to a *decoupled representation*. Surface position is represented in the typical way, by a set of triangles with 3D coordinates stored at the vertices. Surface colors and normals are stored in texture and normal maps, respectively. These colors and normals are mapped to the surface with the aid of a surface parameterization, represented as 2D texture coordinates at the triangle vertices.

The surface position is filtered using a standard surface approximation algorithm that makes local, complexity-reducing simplification operations (e.g. edge collapse, vertex removal, etc.). The color and normal attributes are filtered by the run-time system at the pixel level, using standard mip-mapping techniques [1].

Because the colors and normals are now decoupled from the surface position, we employ a new *texture deviation metric,* which effectively bounds the deviation of a mapped attribute value's position from its correct position on the original surface. We thus guarantee that each attribute is appropriately sampled and mapped to screen-space. The deviation metric necessarily constrains the simplification algorithm somewhat, but it is much less restrictive than retaining sufficient tessellation to accurately represent colors and normals in a standard, per-vertex representation. The preservation of colors using texture maps is possible on all current graphics systems that supports real-time texture maps. The preservation of normals using normal maps is possible on prototype machines today, and there are indications that hardware

Figure 1: Bumpy Torus Model. *Left*: 44,252 triangles full resolution mesh. *Middle and Right*: 5,531 triangles, 0.25 mm maximum image deviation. *Middle*: per-vertex normals. *Right*: normal maps

support for real-time normal maps will become more widespread in the next several years.

One of the nice properties of this approach is that the user-specified error tolerance, ε, is both simple and intuitive; it is a screen-space deviation in pixel units. A particular point on the surface, with some color and some normal, may appear to shift by at most ε pixels on the screen.

We have applied our algorithm to several large models. Figure 1 clearly shows the improved quality of our appearance-preserving simplification technique over a standard surface approximation algorithm with per-vertex normals. By merely controlling the switching distances properly, we can discretely switch between a few statically-generated levels of detail (sampled from a progressive mesh representation) with no perceptible artifacts. Overall, we are able to achieve a significant speedup in rendering large models with little or no loss in rendering quality.

1.2 Paper Organization

In Section 2, we review the related work from several areas. Section 3 presents an overview of our appearance-preserving simplification algorithm. Sections 4 through 6 describe the components of this algorithm, followed by a discussion of our particular implementation and results in Section 7. Finally, we mention our ongoing work and conclude in Section 8.

2 RELATED WORK

Research areas related to this paper include geometric levels-of-detail, preservation of appearance attributes, and map-based representations. We now briefly survey these.

2.1 Geometric Levels-Of-Detail

Given a polygonal model, a number of algorithms have been proposed for generating levels-of-detail. These methods differ according to the local or global error metrics used for simplification and the underlying data structures or representations. Some approaches based on vertex clustering [2, 3] are applicable to all polygonal models and do not preserve the topology of the original models. Other algorithms assume that the input model is a valid mesh. Algorithms based on vertex removal [4, 5] and local error metrics have been proposed by [6-10]. Cohen et al. [11] and Eck et al. [12] have presented algorithms that preserve topology and use a global error bound. Our appearance-preserving simplification algorithm can be combined with many of these.

Other simplification algorithms include decimation techniques based on vertex removal [4], topology modification [13], and controlled simplification of genus [14]. All of these algorithms compute static levels-of-detail. Hoppe [15] has introduced an incremental representation, called the *progressive mesh*, and based on that representation view-dependent algorithms have been proposed by [16, 17]. These algorithms use different view-dependent criteria like local illumination, screen-space surface approximation error, and silhouette edges to adaptively refine the meshes. Our appearance preserving simplification algorithm generates a progressive mesh, which can be used by these view-dependent algorithms.

2.2 Preserving Appearance Attributes

Bajaj and Schikore [18] have presented an algorithm to simplify meshes with associated scalar fields to within a given tolerance. Hughes et al. [19] have presented an algorithm to simplify radiositized meshes. Erikson and Manocha[20] grow error volumes for appearance attributes as well as geometry. Many algorithms based on multi-resolution analysis have been proposed as well. Schroeder and Sweldens [21] have presented algorithms for simplifying functions defined over a sphere. Eck et al. [12]

apply multi-resolution analysis to simplify arbitrary meshes, and Certain et al. [22] extend this to colored meshes by separately analyzing surface geometry and color. They make use of texture mapping hardware to render the color at full resolution. It may be possible to extend this approach to handle other functions on the mesh. However, algorithms based on vertex removal and edge collapses [11, 15] have been able to obtain more drastic simplification (in terms of reducing the polygon count) and produce better looking simplifications [15].

Hoppe [15] has used an optimization framework to preserve discrete and scalar surface appearance attributes. Currently, this algorithm measures a maximum or average deviation of the scalar attributes across the model. Our approach can be incorporated into this comprehensive optimization framework to preserve the appearance of colors and normals, while allowing continued simplification as an object's screen size is reduced.

2.3 Map-based Representations

Texture mapping is a common technique for defining color on a surface. It is just one instance of mapping, a general technique for defining attributes on a surface. Other forms of mapping use the same texture coordinate parameterization, but with maps that contain something other than surface color. *Displacement maps* [23] contain perturbations of the surface position. They are typically used to add surface detail to a simple model. *Bump maps* [24] are similar, but instead give perturbations of the surface normal. They can make a smooth surface appear bumpy, but will not change the surface's silhouette. *Normal maps* [25] can also make a smooth surface appear bumpy, but contain the actual normal instead of just a perturbation of the normal.

Texture mapping is available in most current graphics systems, including workstations and PCs. We expect to see bump mapping and similar surface shading techniques on graphics systems in the near future [26]. In fact, many of these mapping techniques are already possible using the procedural shading capabilities of PixelFlow[27].

Several researchers have explored the possibility of replacing geometric information with texture. Kajiya first introduced the "hierarchy of scale" of geometric models, mapping, and lighting[28]. Cabral et. al. [29] addressed the transition between bump mapping and lighting effects. Westin et. al. [30] generated BRDFs from a Monte-Carlo ray tracing of an idealized piece of surface. Becker and Max [31] handle transitions from geometric detail in the form of displacement maps to shading in the form of bump maps. Fournier [25] generates maps with normal and shading information directly from surface geometry. Krishnamurthy and Levoy [32] fit complex, scanned surfaces with a set of smooth B-spline patches, then store some of the lost geometric information in a displacement map or bump map. Many algorithms first capture the geometric complexity of a scene in an image-based representation by rendering several different views and then render the scene using texture maps [33-36].

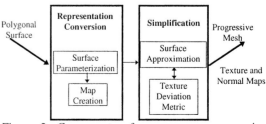

Figure 2: Components of an appearance-preserving simplification system.

3 OVERVIEW

We now present an overview of our appearance-preserving simplification algorithm. Figure 2 presents a breakdown of the algorithm into its components. The input to the algorithm is the polygonal surface, M_0, to be simplified. The surface may come from one of a wide variety of sources, and thus may have a variety of characteristics. The types of possible input models include:

- **CAD models**, with per-vertex normals and a single color
- **Radiositized models**, with per-vertex colors and no normals
- **Scientific visualization models**, with per-vertex normals and per-vertex colors
- **Textured models**, with texture-mapped colors, with or without per-vertex normals

To store the colors and normals in maps, we need a parameterization of the surface, $F_0(X): M_0 \rightarrow P$, where P is a 2D texture domain (*texture plane*), as shown in Figure 3. If the input model is already textured, such a parameterization comes with the model. Otherwise, we create one and store it in the form of per-vertex texture coordinates. Using this parameterization, per-vertex colors and normals are then stored in texture and normal maps.

The original surface and its texture coordinates are then fed to the surface simplification algorithm. This algorithm is responsible for choosing which simplification operations to perform and in what order. It calls our texture deviation component to measure the deviation of the texture coordinates caused by each proposed operation. It uses the resulting error bound to help make its choices of operations, and stores the bound with each operation in its progressive mesh output.

We can use the resulting progressive mesh with error bounds to create a static set of levels of detail with error bounds, or we can use the progressive mesh directly with a view-dependent simplification system at run-time. Either way, the error bound allows the run-time system to choose or adjust the tessellation of the models to meet a user-specified tolerance. It is also possible for the user to choose a desired polygon count and have the run-time system increase or decrease the error bound to meet that target.

4 REPRESENTATION CONVERSION

Before we apply the actual simplification component of our algorithm, we perform a representation conversion (as shown in Figure 2). The representation we choose for our surface has a significant impact on the amount of simplification we can perform for a given level of visual fidelity. To convert to a form which decouples the sampling rates of the colors and normals from the sampling rate of the surface, we first parameterize the surface, then store the color and normal information in separate maps.

4.1 Surface Parameterization

To store a surface's color or normal attributes in a map, the surface must first have a 2D parameterization. This function, $F_0(X): M_0 \rightarrow P$, maps points, X, on the input surface, M_0, to points, x,[*] on the texture plane, P (see Figure 3). The surface is typically decomposed into several *polygonal patches*, each with its own parameterization. The creation of such parameterizations has been an active area of research and is fundamental for shape transformation, multi-resolution analysis, approximation of meshes by NURBS, and texture mapping. Though we do not present a new algorithm for such parameterization here, it is useful to consider

---

[*] Capital letters (e.g. X) refer to points in 3D, while lowercase letters (e.g. x) refer to points in 2D.

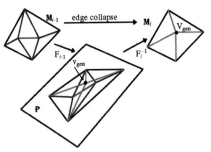

Figure 3: A look at the ith edge collapse. Computing V_{gen} determines the shape of the new mesh, M_i. Computing v_{gen} determines the new mapping F_i, to the texture plane, P.

the desirable properties of such a parameterization for our algorithm. They are:

1. **Number of patches**: The parameterization should use as few patches as possible. The triangles of the simplified surface must each lie in a single patch, so the number of patches places a bound on the minimum mesh complexity.

2. **Vertex distribution**: The vertices should be as evenly distributed in the texture plane as possible. If the parameterization causes too much area compression, we will require a greater map resolution to capture all of our original per-vertex data.

3. **One-to-one mapping**: The mapping from the surface to the texture plane should be one-to-one. If the surface has folds in the texture plane, parts of the texture will be incorrectly stored and mapped back to the surface

Our particular application of the parameterization makes us somewhat less concerned with preserving aspect ratios than some other applications are. For instance, many applications apply $F^{-1}(x)$ to map a pre-synthesized texture map to an arbitrary surface. In that case, distortions in the parameterization cause the texture to look distorted when applied to the surface. However, in our application, the color or normal data originates on the surface itself. Any distortion created by applying $F(X)$ to map this data onto P is reversed when we apply $F^{-1}(x)$ to map it back to M.

Algorithms for computing such parameterizations have been studied in the computer graphics and graph drawing literature.

Computer Graphics: In the recent computer graphics literature, [12, 37, 38] use a spring system with various energy terms to distribute the vertices of a polygonal patch in the plane. [12, 32, 38, 39] provide methods for subdividing surfaces into separate patches based on automatic criteria or user-guidance. This body of research addresses the above properties one and two, but unfortunately, parameterizations based on spring-system algorithms do not generally guarantee a one-to-one mapping.

Graph Drawing: The field of graph drawing addresses the issue of one-to-one mappings more rigorously. Relevant topics include straight-line drawings on a grid [40] and convex straight-line drawings [41]. Battista et al. [42] present a survey of the field. These techniques produce guaranteed one-to-one mappings, but the necessary grids for a graph with V vertices are worst case (and typically) O(V) width and height, and the vertices are generally unevenly spaced.

To break a surface into polygonal patches, we currently apply an automatic subdivision algorithm like that presented in [12]. Their application requires a patch network with more constraints than ours. We can generally subdivide the surface into fewer patches. During this process, which grows Voronoi-like patches, we simply require that each patch not expand far enough to touch itself. To produce the parameterization for each patch, we employ

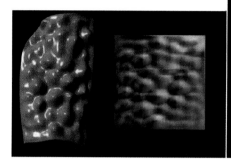

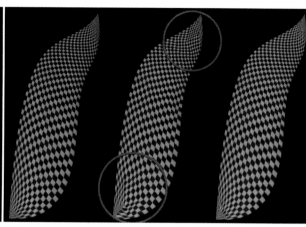

Figure 4: A patch from the leg of an armadillo model and its associated normal map.

Figure 5: Lion model.

Figure 6: Texture coordinate deviation and correction on the lion's tail. *Left*: 1,740 triangles full resolution. *Middle and Right*: 0.25 mm maximum image deviation. *Middle*: 108 triangles, no texture deviation metric. *Right*: 434 triangles with texture metric.

a spring system with uniform weights. A side-by-side comparison of various choices of weights in [12] shows that uniform weights produce more evenly-distributed vertices than some other choices. For parameterizations used only with one particular map, it is also possible to allow more area compression where data values are similar. While this technique will generally create reasonable parameterizations, it would be better if there were a way to *also* guarantee that $\mathbf{F}(\mathbf{X})$ is one-to-one, as in the graph drawing literature.

4.2 Creating Texture and Normal Maps

Given a polygonal surface patch, $\mathbf{M}_0$, and its 2D parameterization, $\mathbf{F}$, it is straightforward to store per-vertex colors and normals into the appropriate maps using standard rendering software. To create a map, scan convert each triangle of $\mathbf{M}_0$, replacing each of its vertex coordinates, $\mathbf{V}_j$, with $\mathbf{F}(\mathbf{V}_j)$, the texture coordinates of the vertex. For a texture map, apply the Gouraud method for linearly interpolating the colors across the triangles. For a normal map, interpolate the per-vertex normals across the triangles instead (Figure 4).

The most important question in creating these maps is what the maximum resolution of the map images should be. To capture all the information from the original mesh, each vertex's data should be stored in a unique texel. We can guarantee this conservatively by choosing $1/d$ x $1/d$ for our map resolution, where d is the minimum distance between vertex texture coordinates:

$$d = \min_{\mathbf{V}_i, \mathbf{V}_j \in \mathbf{M}_0, i \neq j} \left\| \mathbf{F}(\mathbf{V}_i) - \mathbf{F}(\mathbf{V}_j) \right\| \qquad (1)$$

If the vertices of the polygonal surface patch happen to be a uniform sampling of the texture space (e.g. if the polygonal surface patch was generated from a parametric curved surface patch), then the issues of scan conversion and resolution are simplified considerably. Each vertex color (or normal) is simply stored in an element of a 2D array of the appropriate dimensions, and the array itself is the map image.

It is possible to trade off accuracy of the map data for run-time texturing resources by scaling down the initial maps to a lower resolution.

5 SIMPLIFICATION ALGORITHM

Once we have decomposed the surface into one or more parameterized polygonal patches with associated maps, we begin the actual simplification process. Many simplification algorithms perform a series of edge collapses or other local simplification operations to gradually reduce the complexity of the input surface.

The order in which these operations are performed has a large impact on the quality of the resulting surface, so simplification algorithms typically choose the operations in order of increasing error according to some metric. This metric may be local or global in nature, and for surface approximation algorithms, it provides some bound or estimate on the error in surface position. The operations to be performed are typically maintained in a priority queue, which is continually updated as the simplification progresses. This basic design is applied by many of the current simplification algorithms, including [6-8, 15].

To incorporate our appearance-preservation approach into such an algorithm, the original algorithm is modified to use our texture deviation metric in addition to its usual error metric. When an edge is collapsed, the error metric of the particular surface approximation algorithm is used to compute a value for $\mathbf{V}_{gen}$, the surface position of the new vertex (see Figure 3). Our texture deviation metric is then applied to compute a value for $\mathbf{v}_{gen}$, the texture coordinates of the new vertex.

For the purpose of computing an edge's priority, there are several ways to combine the error metrics of surface approximation along with the texture deviation metric, and the appropriate choice depends on the algorithm in question. Several possibilities for such a *total error metric* include a weighted combination of the two error metrics, the maximum or minimum of the error metrics, or one of the two error metrics taken alone. For instance, when integrating with Garland and Heckbert's algorithm [6], it would be desirable to take a weighted combination in order to retain the precedence their system accords the topology-preserving collapses over the topology-modifying collapses. Similarly, a weighted combination may be desirable for an integration with Hoppe's system [15], which already optimizes error terms corresponding to various mesh attributes.

The interactive display system later uses the error metrics to determine appropriate distances from the viewpoint either for switching between static levels of detail or for collapsing/splitting the edges dynamically to produce adaptive, view-dependent tessellations. If the system intends to guarantee that certain tolerances are met, the maximum of the error metrics is often an appropriate choice.

6 TEXTURE DEVIATION METRIC

A key element of our approach to appearance-preservation is the measurement of the *texture coordinate deviation* caused by the simplification process. We provide a bound on this deviation, to

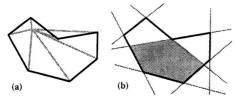

Figure 7: (a) An invalid choice for $\mathbf{v}_{gen}$ in $\mathbf{P}$, causing the new triangles extend outside the polygon. (b) Valid choices must lie in the shaded *kernel*.

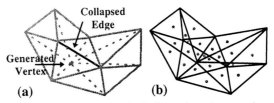

Figure 8: (a) An overlay in $\mathbf{P}$ determines the mapping between M_{i-1} and M_i. (b) A set of polygonal *mapping cells*, each containing a dot.

be used by the simplification algorithm to prioritize the potential edge collapses and by the run-time visualization system to choose appropriate levels of detail based on the current viewpoint. The lion's tail in Figure 6 demonstrates the need to measure texture coordinate deviation. The center figure is simplified by a surface approximation algorithm without using a texture deviation metric. The distortions are visible in the areas marked by red circles. The right tail is simplified using our texture deviation metric and does not have visible distortions. The image-space deviation bound now applies to the texture as well as to the surface.

For a given point, $\mathbf{X}$, on simplified mesh M_i, this deviation is the distance in 3D from $\mathbf{X}$ to the point on the input surface with the same texture coordinates:

$$T_i(\mathbf{X}) = \left\| \mathbf{X} - \mathbf{F}_0^{-1}(\mathbf{F}_i(\mathbf{X})) \right\| \qquad (2)$$

We define the texture coordinate deviation of a whole triangle to be the maximum deviation of all the points in the triangle, and similarly for the whole surface:

$$T_i(\Delta) = \max_{\mathbf{X} \in \Delta} T_i(\mathbf{X}); \quad T_i(M_i) = \max_{\mathbf{X} \in M_i} T_i(\mathbf{X}) \qquad (3)$$

To compute the texture coordinate deviation incurred by an edge collapse operation, our algorithm takes as input the set of triangles before the edge collapse and $\mathbf{V}_{gen}$, the 3D coordinates of the new vertex generated by the collapse operation. The algorithm outputs $\mathbf{v}_{gen}$, the 2D texture coordinates for this generated vertex, and a bound on $T_i(\Delta)$ for each of the triangles after the collapse.

6.1 Computing New Texture Coordinates

We visualize the neighborhood of an edge to be collapsed in the texture plane, $\mathbf{P}$, as shown in Figure 3. The boundary of the edge neighborhood is a polygon in $\mathbf{P}$. The edge collapse causes us to replace the two vertices of the edge with a single vertex. The 3D coordinates, $\mathbf{V}_{gen}$ of this generated vertex are provided to us by the surface approximation algorithm. The first task of the texture deviation algorithm is to compute $\mathbf{v}_{gen}$, the 2D texture coordinates of this generated vertex.

For $\mathbf{v}_{gen}$ to be valid, it must lie in the convex *kernel* of our polygon in the texture plane [43] (see Figure 7). Meeting this criterion ensures that the set of triangles after the edge collapse covers exactly the same portion of the texture plane as the set of triangles before the collapse.

Given a candidate point in the texture plane, we efficiently test the kernel criterion with a series of dot products to see if it lies on the inward side of each polygon edge. We first test some heuristic choices for the texture coordinates – the midpoint of the original edge in the texture plane or one of the edge vertices. If the heuristic choices fail we compute a point inside the kernel by averaging three corners, found using linear programming techniques [43].

6.2 Patch Borders & Continuity

Unlike an interior edge collapse, an edge collapse on a patch border can change the coverage in the texture plane, either by cutting off some of texture space or by extending into a portion of texture space for which we have no map data. Since neither of these is acceptable, we add additional constraints on the choice of $\mathbf{v}_{gen}$ at patch borders.

We assume that the area of texture space for which we have map data is rectangular (though the method works for any map that covers a polygonal area in texture space), and that the edges of the patch are also the edges of the map. If the entire edge to be collapsed lies on a border of the map, we restrict $\mathbf{v}_{gen}$ to lie on the edge. If one of the vertices of the edge lies on a corner of the map, we further restrict $\mathbf{v}_{gen}$ to lie at that vertex. If only one vertex is on the border, we restrict $\mathbf{v}_{gen}$ to lie at that vertex. If one vertex of the edge lies on one border of the map and the other vertex lies on a different border, we do not allow the edge collapse.

The surface parameterization component typically breaks the input model into several connected patches. To preserve geometric and texture continuity across the boundary between them, we add further restrictions on the simplifications that are performed along the border. The shared border edges must be simplified on both patches, with matching choices of $\mathbf{V}_{gen}$ and $\mathbf{v}_{gen}$.

6.3 Measuring Texture Deviation

Texture deviation is a measure of the parametric distortion caused by the simplification process. We measure this deviation using a method similar to the one presented to measure surface deviation in [8]. The main difference is that we now measure the deviation using our mapping in the texture plane, rather than in the plane of some planar projection. While [8] presents an overview of this technique, we present it more formally.

Given the overlay (see Figure 8(a)) in the texture plane, $\mathbf{P}$, of two simplified versions of the surface, M_i and M_j, we define the *incremental texture deviation* between them:

$$\mathbf{E}_{i,j}(\mathbf{x}) = \left\| \mathbf{F}_i^{-1}(\mathbf{x}) - \mathbf{F}_j^{-1}(\mathbf{x}) \right\| \qquad (4)$$

This is the deviation between corresponding 3D points on the surfaces, both with texture coordinates, $\mathbf{x}$. Between any two sequential surfaces, M_i and M_{i-1}, differing only by an edge collapse, the incremental deviation, $\mathbf{E}_{i,i-1}(\mathbf{x})$, is only non-zero in the neighborhood of the collapsed edge (i.e. only in the triangles that actually move).

The edges on the overlay in $\mathbf{P}$ partition the region into a set of convex, polygonal *mapping cells* (each identified by a dot in Figure 8(b)). Within each mapping cell, the incremental deviation function is linear, so the maximum incremental deviation for each cell occurs at one of its boundary points. Thus, we bound the incremental deviation using only the deviation at the cell vertices, $\mathbf{v}_k$:

$$\mathbf{E}_{i,i-1}(\mathbf{P}) = \max_{\mathbf{x} \in \mathbf{P}} \mathbf{E}_{i,i-1}(\mathbf{x}) = \max_{\mathbf{v}_k} \mathbf{E}_{i,i-1}(\mathbf{v}_k) \qquad (5)$$

In terms of the incremental deviation, the *total texture deviation*, defined in (2) (the distance from points on M_i to corresponding points on the original surface, M_0) is

$$T_i(\mathbf{X}) = \mathbf{E}_{i,0}(\mathbf{F}_i(\mathbf{X})) \qquad (6)$$

We approximate $\mathbf{E}_{i,0}(\mathbf{x})$ using a set of axis-aligned boxes. This provides a convenient representation of a bound on $T_i(\mathbf{X})$, which we can update from one simplified mesh to the next without having to refer to the original mesh. Each triangle, Δ_k in $\mathbf{M}_i$, has its own axis-aligned box, $\boldsymbol{b}_{i,k}$ such that at every point on the triangle, the Minkowski sum of the 3D point with the box gives a region that contains the point on the original surface with the same texture coordinates.

$$\forall \mathbf{X} \in \Delta_k, \, \mathbf{F}_0^{-1}\big(\mathbf{F}_i(\mathbf{X})\big) \in \mathbf{X} \oplus \boldsymbol{b}_{i,k} \qquad (7)$$

Figure 9(a) shows an original surface (curve) in black and a simplification of it, consisting of the thick blue and green lines. The box associated with the blue line, $\boldsymbol{b}_{i,0}$, is shown in blue, while the box for the green line, $\boldsymbol{b}_{i,1}$, is shown in green. The blue box slides along the blue line; at every point of application, the point on the base mesh with the same texture coordinate is contained within the translated box. For example, one set of corresponding points is shown in red, with its box also in red.

From (2) and (7), we produce $\widetilde{T}_i(\mathbf{X})$, a bound on the total texture deviation, $T_i(\mathbf{X})$. This our texture deviation output.

$$T_i(\mathbf{X}) \le \widetilde{T}_i(\mathbf{X}) = \max_{\mathbf{X}' \in \mathbf{X} \oplus b_{i,j}} \|\mathbf{X} - \mathbf{X}'\| \qquad (8)$$

$\widetilde{T}_i(\mathbf{X})$ is the distance from $\mathbf{X}$ to the farthest corner of the box at $\mathbf{X}$. This will always bound the distance from $\mathbf{X}$ to $\mathbf{F}_0^{-1}(\mathbf{F}_i(\mathbf{X}))$. The maximum deviation over an edge collapse neighborhood is the maximum $\widetilde{T}_i(\mathbf{X})$ for any cell vertex.

The boxes, $\boldsymbol{b}_{i,k}$, are the only information we keep about the position of the original mesh as we simplify. We create a new set of boxes, $\boldsymbol{b}_{i+1,k}$, for mesh $\mathbf{M}_{i+1}$ using an incremental computation (described in Figure 10). Figure 9(b) shows the propagation from $\mathbf{M}_i$ to $\mathbf{M}_{i+1}$. The blue and green lines are simplified to the pink line. The new box, $\boldsymbol{b}_{i+1,0}$ is constant as it slides across the pink line. The size and offset is chosen so that, at every point of application, the pink box, $\boldsymbol{b}_{i+1,0}$, contains the corresponding blue or green boxes, $\boldsymbol{b}_{i,0}$ or $\boldsymbol{b}_{i,1}$.

If $\mathbf{X}$ is a point on $\mathbf{M}_i$ in triangle k, and $\mathbf{Y}$ is the point with the same texture coordinate on $\mathbf{M}_{i+1}$, the containment property of (7) holds:

$$\mathbf{F}_0^{-1}\big(\mathbf{F}_{i+1}(\mathbf{Y})\big) \in \mathbf{X} \oplus \boldsymbol{b}_{i,k} \subseteq \mathbf{Y} \oplus \boldsymbol{b}_{i+1,k'} \qquad (9)$$

For example, all three red dots Figure 9(b) have the same texture coordinates. The red point on $\mathbf{M}_0$ is contained in the smaller red box, $\mathbf{X} \oplus \boldsymbol{b}_{i,0}$, which is contained in the larger red box, $\mathbf{Y} \oplus \boldsymbol{b}_{i+1,0}$.

Because each mapping cell in the overlay between $\mathbf{M}_i$ and $\mathbf{M}_{i+1}$ is linear, we compute the sizes of the boxes, $\boldsymbol{b}_{i+1,k'}$, by considering

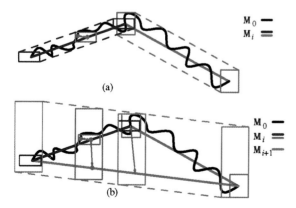

(a)

(b)

Figure 9: 2D illustration of the box approximation to total deviation error. a) A curve has been simplified to two segment, each with an associated box to bound the deviation. b) As we simplify one more step, the approximation is propagated to the newly created segment.

```
PropagateError():
foreach cell vertex, v
    foreach triangle, T_old, in M_{i-1} touching v
        foreach triangle, T_new, in M_i touching v
            PropagateBox(v, T_old, T_new)
PropagateBox(v, T_old, T_new):
P_old = F_{i-1}^{-1}(v), P_new = F_i^{-1}(v)
Enlarge T_old.box so that T_old.box applied at
    P_old contains T_new.box applied at P_new
```

Figure 10: Pseudo-code for the propagation of deviation error from mesh $\mathbf{M}_{i-1}$ to mesh $\mathbf{M}_i$.

only the box correspondences at cell vertices. In Figure 9(b), there are three places we must consider. If the magenta box contains the blue and green boxes in all three places, it will contain them everywhere.

Together, the propagation rules, which are simple to implement, and the box-based approximation to the texture deviation, provide the tools we need to efficiently provide a texture deviation for the simplification process.

7 IMPLEMENTATION AND RESULTS

In this section we present some details of our implementation of the various components of our appearance-preserving simplification algorithm. These include methods for representation conversion, simplification and, finally, interactive display.

7.1 Representation Conversion

We have applied our technique to several large models, including those listed in Table 1. The bumpy torus model (Figure 1) was created from a parametric equation to demonstrate the need for greater sampling of the normals than of the surface position. The lion model (Figure 5) was designed from NURBS patches as part of a much larger garden environment, and we chose to decorate it with a marble texture (and a checkerboard texture to make texture deviation more apparent in static images). Neither of these models required the computation of a parameterization. The armadillo (Figure 12) was constructed by merging several laser-scanned meshes into a single, dense polygon mesh. It was decomposed into polygonal patches and parameterized using the algorithm presented in [32], which eventually converts the patches into a NURBS representation with associated displacement maps.

Because all these models were not only parameterized, but available in piecewise-rational parametric representations, we generated polygonal patches by uniformly sampling these representations in the parameter space. We chose the original tessellation of the models to be high enough to capture all the detail available in their smooth representations. Due to the uniform sampling, we were able to use the simpler method of map creation (described in Section 4.2), avoiding the need for a scan-conversion process.

7.2 Simplification

We integrated our texture deviation metric with the successive mapping algorithm for surface approximation [8]. The error metric for the successive mapping algorithm is simply a 3D surface deviation. We used this deviation only in the computation of $\mathbf{V}_{gen}$. Our total error metric for prioritizing edges and choosing switching distances is just the texture deviation. This is sensible because the texture deviation metric is also a measure of surface deviation, whose particular mapping is the parameterization. Thus, if the successive mapping metric is less than the texture deviation metric, we must apply the texture deviation metric, because it is the minimum bound we know that guarantees the bound on our texture deviation. On the other hand, if the successive mapping metric is greater than the texture deviation metric, the texture deviation bound is still sufficient to guarantee a bound on both the surface deviation and the texture.

To achieve a simple and efficient run-time system, we apply a post-process to convert the progressive mesh output to a static set of levels of detail, reducing the mesh complexity by a factor of two at each level.

Our implementation can either treat each patch as an independent object or treat a connected set of patches as one object. If we simplify the patches independently, we have the freedom to switch their levels of detail independently, but we will see cracks between the patches when they are rendered at a sufficiently large error tolerance. Simplifying the patches together allows us to prevent cracks by switching the levels of detail simultaneously.

Table 1 gives the computation time to simplify several models,

Model	Patches	Input Tris	Time	Map Res.
Torus	1	44,252	4.4	512x128
Lion	49	86,844	7.4	N.A.
Armadillo	102	2,040,000	190	128x128

Table 1: Several models used to test appearance-preserving simplification. Simplification time is in minutes on a MIPS R10000 processor.

as well as the resolution of each map image. Figure 11 and Figure 12 show results on the armadillo model. It should be noted that the latter figure is not intended to imply equal computational costs for rendering models with per-vertex normals and normal maps. Simplification using the normal map representation provides measurable quality and reduced triangle overhead, with an additional overhead dependent on the screen resolution.

7.3 Interactive Display System

We have implemented two interactive display systems: one on top of SGI's IRIS Performer library, and one on top of a custom library running on a PixelFlow system. The SGI system supports color preservation using texture maps, and the PixelFlow system supports color and normal preservation using texture and normal maps, respectively. Both systems apply a bound on the distance from the viewpoint to the object to convert the texture deviation error in 3D to a number of pixels on the screen, and allow the user to specify a tolerance for the number of pixels of deviation. The tolerance is ultimately used to choose the primitives to render from among the statically generated set of levels of detail.

Our custom shading function on the PixelFlow implementation performs a mip-mapped look-up of the normal and applies a

Figure 11: Levels of detail of the armadillo model shown with 1.0 mm maximum image deviation. Triangle counts are: 7,809, 3,905, 1,951, 975, 488

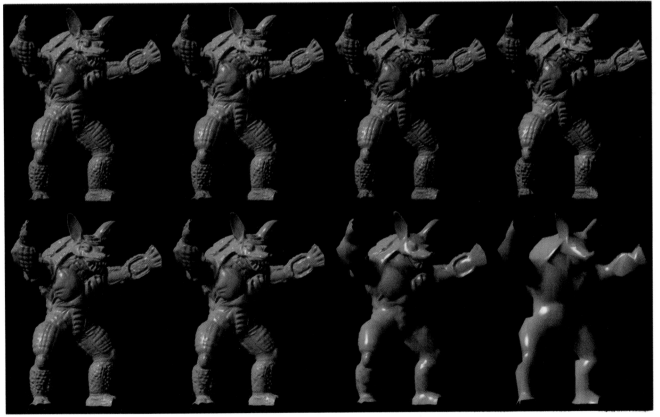

249,924 triangles	62,480 triangles	7,809 triangles	975 triangles
0.05 mm max image deviation	0.25 mm max image deviation	1.3 mm max image deviation	6.6 mm max image deviation

Figure 12: Close-up of several levels of detail of the armadillo model. *Top*: normal maps *Bottom*: per-vertex normals

Phong lighting model to compute the output color of each pixel. The current implementation looks up normals with 8 bits per component, which seems sufficient in practice (using [44])

8 ONGOING WORK AND CONCLUSIONS

There are several directions to pursue to improve our system for appearance-preserving simplification. We would like to experiment more with techniques to generate parameterizations that allow efficient representations of the mapped attributes as well as guarantee a one-to-one mapping to the texture plane.

It would be nice for the simplification component to do a better job of optimizing the 3D and texture coordinates of the generated vertex for each edge collapse, both in 3D and the texture plane. Also, it may be interesting to allow the attribute data of a map to influence the error metric. We would also like to integrate our technique with a simplification algorithm like [6] that deals well with imperfect input meshes and allows some topological changes. Finally, we want to display our resulting progressive meshes in a system that performs dynamic, view-dependent management of LODs.

Our current system demonstrates the feasibility and desirability of our approach to appearance-preserving simplification. It produces high-fidelity images using a small number of high-quality triangles. This approach should complement future graphics systems well as we strive for increasingly realistic real-time computer graphics.

ACKNOWLEDGMENTS

We would like to thank Venkat Krishnamurthy and Marc Levoy at the Stanford Computer Graphics Laboratory and Peter Schröder for the armadillo model, and Lifeng Wang and Xing Xing Computer for the lion model. Our visualization system implementation was made possible by the UNC PixelFlow Project and the Hewlett Packard Visualize PxFl team. We also appreciate the assistance of the UNC Walkthrough Project. This work was supported in part by an Alfred P. Sloan Foundation Fellowship, ARO Contract DAAH04-96-1-0257, NSF Grant CCR-9625217, ONR Young Investigator Award, Honda, Intel, NSF/ARPA Center for Computer Graphics and Scientific Visualization, and NIH/National Center for Research Resources Award 2P41RR02170-13 on Interactive Graphics for Molecular Studies and Microscopy.

REFERENCES

[1] L. Williams, "Pyramidal Parametrics," *SIGGRAPH 83 Conference Proceedings*, pp. 1--11, 1983.

[2] J. Rossignac and P. Borrel, "Multi-Resolution 3D Approximations for Rendering," in *Modeling in Computer Graphics*: Springer-Verlag, 1993, pp. 455--465.

[3] G. Schaufler and W. Sturzlinger, "Generating Multiple Levels of Detail from Polygonal Geometry Models," *Virtual Environments'95 (Eurographics Workshop)*, pp. 33-41, 1995.

[4] W. J. Schroeder, J. A. Zarge, and W. E. Lorensen, "Decimation of Triangle Meshes," in *Proc. of ACM Siggraph*, 1992, pp. 65--70.

[5] G. Turk, "Re-tiling polygonal surfaces," *Comput. Graphics*, vol. 26, pp. 55--64, 1992.

[6] M. Garland and P. Heckbert, "Surface Simplification using Quadric Error Bounds," *SIGGRAPH'97 Conference Proceedings*, pp. 209-216, 1997.

[7] A. Gueziec, "Surface Simplification with Variable Tolerance," in *Second Annual Intl. Symp. on Medical Robotics and Computer Assisted Surgery (MRCAS '95)*, November 1995, pp. 132--139.

[8] J. Cohen, D. Manocha, and M. Olano, "Simplifying Polygonal Models Using Successive Mappings," *Proc. of IEEE Visualization'97*, pp. 395-402, 1997.

[9] R. Ronfard and J. Rossignac, "Full-range approximation of triangulated polyhedra," *Computer Graphics Forum*, vol. 15, pp. 67--76 and 462, August 1996.

[10] R. Klein, G. Liebich, and W. Straßer, "Mesh Reduction with Error Control," in *IEEE Visualization '96*: IEEE, October 1996.

[11] J. Cohen, A. Varshney, D. Manocha, G. Turk, H. Weber, P. Agarwal, F. Brooks, and W. Wright, "Simplification Envelopes," in *SIGGRAPH'96 Conference Proceedings*, 1996, pp. 119--128.

[12] M. Eck, T. DeRose, T. Duchamp, H. Hoppe, M. Lounsbery, and W. Stuetzle, "Multiresolution Analysis of Arbitrary Meshes," in *SIGGRAPH'95 Conference Proceedings*, 1995, pp. 173--182.

[13] W. Schroeder, "A Topology Modifying Progressive Decimation Algorithm," *Proc. of IEEE Visualization'97*, pp. 205-212, 1997.

[14] J. El-Sana and A. Varshney, "Controlled Simplification of Genus for Polygonal Models," *Proc. of IEEE Visualization'97*, pp. 403-410, 1997.

[15] H. Hoppe, "Progressive Meshes," in *SIGGRAPH 96 Conference Proceedings*: ACM SIGGRAPH, 1996, pp. 99--108.

[16] H. Hoppe, "View-Dependent Refinement of Progressive Meshes," *SIGGRAPH'97 Conference Proceedings*, pp. 189-198, 1997.

[17] J. Xia, J. El-Sana, and A. Varshney, "Adaptive Real-Time Level-of-detail-based Rendering for Polygonal Models," *IEEE Transactions on Visualization and Computer Graphics*, vol. 3, pp. 171--183, 1997.

[18] C. Bajaj and D. Schikore, "Error-bounded reduction of triangle meshes with multivariate data," *SPIE*, vol. 2656, pp. 34--45, 1996.

[19] M. Hughes, A. Lastra, and E. Saxe , "Simplification of Global-Illumination Meshes," *Proceedings of Eurographics '96, Computer Graphics Forum*, vol. 15, pp. 339-345, 1996.

[20] C. Erikson and D. Manocha, "Simplification Culling of Static and Dynamic Scene Graphs," UNC-Chapel Hill Computer Science TR98-009, 1998.

[21] P. Schroder and W. Sweldens, "Spherical Wavelets: Efficiently Representing Functions on the Sphere," *SIGGRAPH 95 Conference Proceedings*, pp. 161--172, August 1995.

[22] A. Certain, J. Popovic, T. Derose, T. Duchamp, D. Salesin, and W. Stuetzle, "Interactive Multiresolution Surface Viewing," in *Proc. of ACM Siggraph*, 1996, pp. 91--98.

[23] R. L. Cook, "Shade trees," in *Computer Graphics (SIGGRAPH '84 Proceedings)*, vol. 18, H. Christiansen, Ed., July 1984, pp. 223--231.

[24] J. Blinn, "Simulation of Wrinkled Surfaces," *SIGGRAPH '78 Conference Proceedings*, vol. 12, pp. 286--292, 1978.

[25] A. Fournier, "Normal distribution functions and multiple surfaces," *Graphics Interface '92 Workshop on Local Illumination*, pp. 45--52, 1992.

[26] M. Peercy, J. Airey, and B. Cabral, "Efficient Bump Mapping Hardware," *SIGGRAPH'97 Conference Proceedings*, pp. 303-306, 1997.

[27] M. Olano and A. Lastra, "A Shading Language on Graphics Hardware: The PixelFlow Shading System," *SIGGRAPH 98 Conference Proceedings*, 1998.

[28] J. Kajiya, "Anisotropic Reflection Models," *SIGGRAPH '85 Conference Proceedings*, pp. 15--21, 1985.

[29] B. Cabral, N. Max, and R. Springmeyer, "Bidirectional Reflection Functions From Surface Bump Maps," *SIGGRAPH '87 Conference Proceedings*, pp. 273--281, 1987.

[30] S. Westin, J. Arvo, and K. Torrance, "Predicting Reflectance Functions From Complex Surfaces," *SIGGRAPH '92 Conference Proceedings*, pp. 255--264, 1992.

[31] B. G. Becker and N. L. Max, "Smooth Transitions between Bump Rendering Algorithms," in *Computer Graphics (SIGGRAPH '93 Proceedings)*, vol. 27, J. T. Kajiya, Ed., August 1993, pp. 183--190.

[32] V. Krishnamurthy and M. Levoy, "Fitting Smooth Surfaces to Dense Polygon Meshes," *SIGGRAPH 96 Conference Proceedings*, pp. 313--324, 1996.

[33] D. G. Aliaga, "Visualization of Complex Models using Dynamic Texture-based Simplification," *Proc. of IEEE Visualization'96*, pp. 101--106, 1996.

[34] L. Darsa, B. Costa, and A. Varshney, "Navigating Static Environments using Image-space simplification and morphing," *Proc. of 1997 Symposium on Interactive 3D Graphics*, pp. 25-34, 1997.

[35] P. W. C. Maciel and P. Shirley, "Visual Navigation of Large Environments Using Textured Clusters," *Proc. of 1995 Symposium on Interactive 3D Graphics*, pp. 95--102, 1995.

[36] J. Shade, D. Lischinski, D. Salesin, T. DeRose, and J. Snyder, "Hierarchical Image Caching for Accelerated Walkthroughs of Complex Environments," *SIGGRAPH 96 Conference Proceedings*, pp. 75--82, August 1996.

[37] J. Kent, W. Carlson, and R. Parent, "Shape transformation for polyhedral objects," *SIGGRAPH '92 Conference Proceedings*, pp. 47--54, 1992.

[38] J. Maillot, H. Yahia, and A. Veroust, "Interactive Texture Mapping," *SIGGRAPH'93 Conference Proceedings*, pp. 27--34, 1993.

[39] H. Pedersen, "A Framework for Interactive Texturing Operations on Curved Surfaces," in *SIGGRAPH 96 Conference Proceedings, Annual Conference Series*, H. Rushmeier, Ed., August 1996, pp. 295--302.

[40] H. d. Fraysseix, J. Pach, and R. Pollack, "How to Draw a Planar Graph on a Grid," *Combinatorica*, vol. 10, pp. 41--51, 1990.

[41] N. Chiba, T. Nishizeki, S. Abe, and T. Ozawa, "A Linear Algorithm for Embedding Planar Graphs Using PQ-Trees," *J. Comput. Syst. Sci.*, vol. 30, pp. 54--76, 1985.

[42] G. D. Battista, P. Eades, R. Tamassia, and I. G. Tollis, "Algorithms for drawing graphs: an annotated bibliography," *Comput. Geom. Theory Appl.*, vol. 4, pp. 235--282, 1994.

[43] M. d. Berg, M. v. Kreveld, M. Overmars, and O. Schwarzkopf, *Computational Geometry: Algorithms and Applications*: Springer-Verlag, 1997.

[44] R. F. Lyon, "Phong Shading Reformulation for Hardware Renderer Simplification," Apple Computer #43, 1993.

Progressive Forest Split Compression

Gabriel Taubin [1]   André Guéziec [1]   William Horn [1]   Francis Lazarus [2]

IBM T. J. Watson Research Center

ABSTRACT

In this paper we introduce the Progressive Forest Split (PFS) representation, a new adaptive refinement scheme for storing and transmitting manifold triangular meshes in progressive and highly compressed form. As in the Progressive Mesh (PM) method of Hoppe, a triangular mesh is represented as a low resolution polygonal model followed by a sequence of refinement operations, each one specifying how to add triangles and vertices to the previous level of detail to obtain a new level. The PFS format shares with PM and other refinement schemes the ability to smoothly interpolate between consecutive levels of detail. However, it achieves much higher compression ratios than PM by using a more complex refinement operation which can, at the expense of reduced granularity, be encoded more efficiently. A *forest split* operation doubling the number n of triangles of a mesh requires a maximum of approximately $3.5n$ bits to represent the connectivity changes, as opposed to approximately $(5 + \log_2(n))n$ bits in PM.

We describe algorithms to efficiently encode and decode the PFS format. We also show how any surface simplification algorithm based on edge collapses can be modified to convert single resolution triangular meshes to the PFS format. The modifications are simple and only require two additional topological tests on each candidate edge collapse. We show results obtained by applying these modifications to the Variable Tolerance method of Guéziec.

CR Categories and Subject Descriptors:

I.3.5 [**Computer Graphics**]: Computational Geometry and Object Modeling - surface, solid, and object representations.

General Terms: Geometric Compression, Algorithms, Graphics.

1 INTRODUCTION

Although modeling systems in Mechanical Computer Aided Design and in animation are expanding their geometric domain to free form surfaces, polygonal models remain the primary 3D representation used in the manufacturing, architectural, and entertainment industries. Polygonal models are particularly effective for hardware assisted rendering, which is important for video-games, virtual reality, fly-through, and digital prototyping.

A polygonal model is defined by the position of its vertices (geometry); by the association between each face and its sustaining vertices (connectivity); and optional colors, normals and texture coordinates (properties). In this paper we concentrate on manifold polygonal models described by *triangular meshes* without attached properties. However, we address issues of non-triangular polygons, properties, and non-manifolds in Section 7. A method to triangulate arbitrary polygonal faces is described by Ronfard and Rossignac [16]. A method to convert non-manifold polygonal models to manifold polygonal models is described by Guéziec *et al.* [7].

[1] IBM T.J.Watson Research Center, P.O.Box 704, Yorktown Heights, NY 10598, {taubin,gueziec,hornwp}@watson.ibm.com

[2] IRCOM-SIC (UMR CNRS 6615), SP2MI, Bvd. 3, Teleport 2, B.P. 179, 86960 Futuroscope Cedex, France, lazarus@sic.univ-poitiers.fr

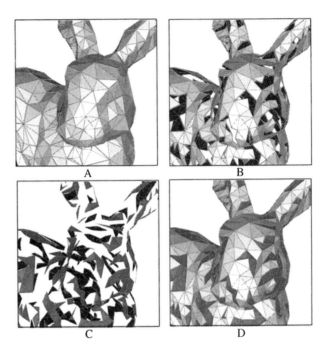

Figure 1: The forest split operation. A: A triangular mesh with a forest of edges marked in red. B: Resulting mesh after cutting through the forest edges and splitting vertices in the resulting tree boundary loops. C: Simple polygons to be stitched to the boundary loops. The correspondence between polygon boundaries and tree boundary loops is implicit. D: The refined mesh. Normally, to produce a smooth transition, the vertices are displaced only after the boundary loops are triangulated. In the figure they have been displaced immediately after the cutting to illustrate the connectivity refinement process.

Polygonal models are typically stored in file servers and exchanged over computer networks. It is frequently desirable to compress models to reduce storage and transmission time requirements. Effective single-resolution-compression schemes have been recently introduced by Deering [3] and Taubin and Rossignac [20].

While single resolution schemes can be used to reduce transmission bandwidth, it is frequently desirable to send the model in a progressive fashion. For example a progressive scheme may start by sending a compressed version of the lowest resolution level of a level-of-detail (LOD) hierarchy. After the lowest level has been sent, a sequence of additional refinement operations may be sent in parallel to the rendering operation. In this manner, successively finer levels of detail may be displayed while even more detailed levels are still arriving.

To prevent visual artifacts, sometimes referred to as "popping", it is also desirable to be able to transition smoothly, or *geomorph*, from one level of the LOD hierarchy to the next by interpolating the positions of corresponding vertices in consecutive levels of detail as a function of time.

The Progressive Forest Split (PFS) scheme is introduced in this paper and features a new adaptive refinement scheme for storing and transmitting triangle meshes in progressive and highly compressed form. In this scheme a manifold triangular mesh is represented as a low resolution polygonal model followed by a sequence of refinement operations. The scheme permits the smooth transition between successive levels of refinement. High compression ratios are achieved by using a new refinement operation which can produce more changes per bit than existing schemes. The scheme requires only $O(n)$ bits to double the size of a mesh with n vertices.

The *forest split* operation, the refinement operation of the PFS scheme, is illustrated in Figure 1. It is specified by a forest in the graph of vertices and edges of the mesh, a sequence of simple polygons (triangulated with no internal vertices), and a sequence of vertex displacements. The mesh is refined by cutting the mesh through the forest, splitting the resulting boundaries apart, filling each of the resulting *tree boundary loops* with one of the simple polygons, and finally displacing the new vertices.

In Section 3 we describe the algorithms for efficiently encoding and decoding PFS meshes. We show how any surface simplification algorithm based on edge collapses can be modified to convert single resolution triangular meshes to PFS format. The modifications require performing two simple additional topological tests on each candidate edge collapse.

In Section 6 we show results obtained by applying these modifications to the Variable Tolerance surface simplification method of Guéziec [6]. Using this method we guarantee simplification error bounds on all levels of details as a measure of the approximation quality. We finish the paper with a short discussion on extensions and future work.

2 PREVIOUS WORK

Single-resolution mesh compression schemes

Deering's method [3] is designed to compress the data for transmission from the CPU to the graphics adapter. The method uses a stack-buffer to store 16 of the previously used vertices instead of having random access to all the vertices of the model. The triangles of the mesh are partitioned into *generalized triangle meshes*, and the connectivity of the triangular mesh is lost. The vertex positions are quantized and the differences between consecutive values are entropy encoded.

The Topological Surgery (TS) method of Taubin and Rossignac [20] was designed for fast network transmission and compact storage. In this method the connectivity of a manifold triangular mesh is encoded without loss of information, with storage rates approaching one bit per triangle for large models. In this scheme the vertices are organized as a spanning tree, and the triangles as a simple polygon. The vertex positions and properties are quantized, predicted as a linear combination of ancestors along the vertex tree, and the corrections are entropy encoded. A more detailed description is presented in Section 3.1. The method has been extended to handle all the polygonal models which can be represented in the Virtual Reality Modeling Language (VRML) [19], including all properties and property bindings permitted by the language. Compression ratios of up to 50:1 or more can be achieved for large VRML models.

Recursive subdivision and refinement

Recursive subdivision schemes [2, 4, 13] provide a truly progressive representation for a limited family of meshes. Most have the ability to transition smoothly between consecutive levels of detail. In a recursive subdivision scheme a polygonal mesh is defined as a low resolution base mesh followed by a sequence of subdivision steps. Each subdivision step can be further decomposed into a connectivity refinement step, and a smoothing or geometry update step. In the connectivity refinement step more vertices and faces are added to the mesh. These additions usually do not change the topological

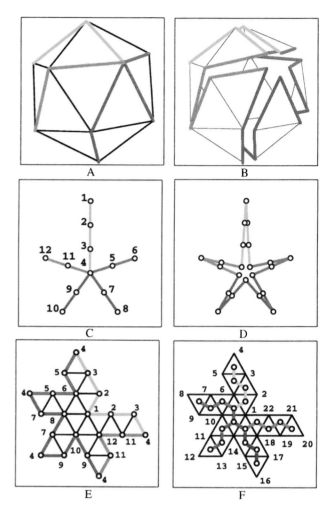

Figure 2: The topological surgery method of Taubin and Rossignac [20]. A: The vertex tree on the surface. Each run is painted with a different color. B: The result of cutting through the edges of the vertex tree (the vertex positions have been modified here to artificially enlarge the gap created by the topological cut) is the simple polygon. C: The structure of the vertex tree with the vertex tree traversal indices. D: The vertex tree becomes the boundary loop after cutting through its edges. E: The simple polygon (artificially flattened) has no internal vertices. Simple polygon vertices are labeled here with their corresponding vertex tree traversal indices. F: The dual graph of the simple polygon is the triangle tree. One marching bit per regular node is also required to describe the triangulation of its runs. The order for the vertex indices is derived from the vertex tree traversal order. Simple polygon vertices are labeled here with their boundary loop indices. The correspondence between boundary loop indices and vertex tree indices is stored in a lookup table constructed by traversing the vertex tree.

type and new vertices are positioned such that the overall geometry does not change. In the smoothing step, depending on whether the method is approximating or interpolating, some or all of the vertices of the mesh with refined connectivity are displaced. Usually the goal is to show that after an infinite number of subdivision steps, the sequence of polygonal meshes converges to a smooth continuous surface, but in practice only a few subdivision steps are applied.

Uniform subdivision schemes can be regarded as the optimal compression schemes. Both the connectivity refinement and the smoothing steps are defined globally by a few parameters per subdivision step [18] and the schemes are optimal in the sense that the number of parameters is independent of the number of vertices and faces created at each subdivision step. However, these high compression ratios are obtained only for meshes with recursive subdivision connectivity. Eck *et al.* [5] describe a method to approximate a triangular mesh by a new mesh with recursive subdivision connectivity and approximately the same geometry, but very often the option of changing the connectivity of the mesh in this way is not possible.

Adaptive subdivision schemes [9, 21] must specify how and where the mesh connectivity is to be refined. This may require as little as only one bit per vertex, edge, or face to specify each connectivity refinement step. These schemes may also require vertex displacements for the newly created vertices, instead of, or in addition to, the global parameters defining the smoothing step.

As noted above, the main problem with existing uniform and adaptive subdivision schemes is that a general triangular mesh usually does not satisfy subdivision requirements and cannot be compressed with these methods. The Progressive Mesh (PM) scheme introduced by Hoppe [11] solves this problem. The scheme is not a subdivision scheme but an *adaptive refinement* scheme where new faces are not created by subdividing existing faces, but by inserting them in between existing faces. Every triangular mesh can be represented as a base mesh followed by a sequence of refinements referred to as *vertex splits*. Each vertex split is specified for the current level of detail by identifying two edges and a shared vertex. The mesh is refined by cutting it through the pair of edges, splitting the common vertex into two vertices and creating a quadrilateral hole, which is filled with two triangles sharing the edge connecting the two new vertices. The PM scheme is not an efficient compression scheme. Since the refinement operations perform very small and localized changes the scheme requires $O(n\log_2(n))$ bits to double the size of a mesh with n vertices.

The refinement operation of the PFS scheme introduced in this paper, the forest split, can be seen as a grouping of several consecutive edge split operations into a set, instead of a sequence. In the PFS scheme there is a tradeoff between compression ratios and granularity. The highest compression ratios are achieved by minimizing the number of levels of detail. Most often the high number of levels of detail produced by the PM scheme are not required. Hoppe typically defines the levels of the LOD hierarchy of his PM representation using exponential steps.

3 THE PFS REPRESENTATION

A multi-resolution mesh represented in the PFS format is composed of an initial low resolution level of detail followed by a sequence of forest split operations. Although any method could be used to represent the lowest resolution level of detail, we use the TS method because the PFS representation is a natural extension of the representation used in this scheme. For both the lowest resolution base mesh and the forest split operations we make a distinction between the representation and the encoding of the representation.

3.1 Topological Surgery

In this section we give a brief description of the TS representation for a *simple mesh*, that is, a triangle mesh with sphere topology. With a few minor additions, manifolds of arbitrary genus, with or without boundaries, and orientable or non-orientable can also be represented. Since these additional concepts are not needed to describe the PFS format, we refer the interested reader to the original reference for the details.

Representation Figure 2 illustrates the main concepts of the TS representation. In this method the vertices of a triangular mesh are organized as a rooted spanning tree in the graph of the mesh, called the *vertex tree* (Figure 2-A). As shown in Figure 2-B,E, when a simple mesh is cut through the vertex tree edges, the connectivity

of the resulting mesh is a simple polygon. The edges of the simple polygon form a *boundary loop*.

The order of traversal of the vertex tree (Figure 2-C) defines a one-to-two correspondence between the edges of the vertex tree and the edges of the *boundary loop* (Figure 2-D). This correspondence defines which pairs of boundary loop edges should be stitched together to reconstruct the connectivity of the original mesh.

Encoding The encoding of this representation in the compressed data stream is composed of, in order: the encoding of the vertex tree, the compressed coordinate information, and the encoding of the simple polygon.

The vertex tree is run-length encoded. The tree is decomposed into *runs* (shown in different colors in Figure 2-A,C). A run connects a leaf or branching node to another leaf or branching node through a path of zero or more regular nodes. The order of traversal of the tree defines an order of traversals of the runs, and a first and last node for each run. Each run is encoded as a record composed of three fields *(is-last-run,length-of-run,ends-in-leaf)*. The *is-last-run* field is a bit that determines if the runs shares the first node with the next run or not. It determines the pushing of branching node indices onto a *traversal stack*. The *length-of-run* field is a variable length integer (same number of bits for all the runs in the tree) with a value equal to the number of edges in the run. The *ends-in-leaf* field is a bit which determines if the run ends in a leaf or branching node, and the popping of branching node indices from the traversal stack.

The coordinate information is placed in the compressed stream in the order of traversal of the vertex tree. The coordinate data is compressed by storing errors instead of absolute coordinates. The errors are calculated with respect to a predictor. The predictor is computed as a linear combination of several ancestors in the tree and is quantized to a certain number of bits per coordinate with respect to a bounding box. The errors are then Huffman-encoded. Once the coordinate information is received, the geometry of the mesh can be reconstructed as an array of vertex coordinates.

The dual graph of the simple polygon is also a tree (Figure 2-F). The structure of this *triangle tree* is run-length encoded in the same way as the vertex tree, except that the *is-last-run* field is not necessary, because the triangle tree is a binary tree. The structure of the triangle tree does not completely describe the triangulation of the polygon. To complete the description, an extra bit per triangle associated with each regular node of the triangle tree must be included. These *marching bits* determine how to triangulate the runs of the tree by advancing either on the left or on the right on the boundary of the polygon. This encoding scheme produces very good results for polygons with very few and long runs. Another encoding scheme for simple polygons is described in the next section.

3.2 The forest split operation

Representation A forest split operation, illustrated in Figure 1, is represented by: a forest in the graph of vertices and edges of a mesh; a sequence of simple polygons; and a sequence of vertex displacements. The mesh is refined by cutting the mesh through the forest, splitting the resulting boundaries apart, filling each of the resulting tree boundary loops with one of the simple polygons, and finally, displacing the new vertices.

Applying a forest split operation involves: 1) cutting the mesh through the forest edges; 2) triangulating each tree loop according to the corresponding simple polygon; and 3) displacing the new vertices to their new positions. As will be explained in the next section, some of the information required to perform these steps, such as the correspondence between trees of the forest and simple polygons, and between tree boundary loop edges and polygon boundary loop edges of each corresponding tree-polygon pair, is not given

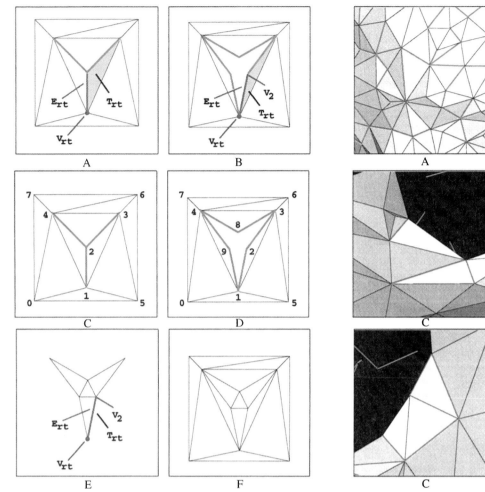

Figure 3: When a mesh is cut through a tree of edges (red and green edges in A), a tree boundary loop (red and green edges in B) is created with each edge of the tree corresponding to two edges of the boundary loop. Some vertex indices are assigned before cutting (C) to new tree boundary loop vertices, others are assigned subsequent indices (D). The hole created by the cutting operation is filled by triangulating the boundary loop using a simple polygon (E) resulting in a refined mesh (F) with the same topological type as the initial mesh.

Figure 4: Construction and triangulation of tree boundary loops. A,B: No tree vertices in the mesh boundary. C,D: A tree vertex isolated in the mesh boundary requires an extra tree loop edge. E,F: A tree edge on the mesh boundary edges does not require an extra tree loop edge, but some of the new vertex indices may only be used by new triangles. Note that the tree may have several contacts with the mesh boundary.

explicitly, but is based on an implicit convention for enumerating mesh elements.

Enumeration of mesh elements

Given a triangular mesh with V vertices and T triangles, we assume that the vertices have consecutive *vertex indices* in the range $0, \ldots, V-1$, and the triangles have consecutive *triangle indices* in the range $0, \ldots, T-1$. The edges of the mesh, which are represented by pairs of vertex indices (i, j) with $i < j$, are ordered lexicographically and assigned consecutive *edge indices* in the range $0, \ldots, E-1$. The trees in the forest are ordered according to the minimum vertex index of each tree. The *root vertex* v_{rt} of each tree in the forest is the leaf of the tree with the minimum index. Starting at the root, the boundary loop created by cutting along the tree can be traversed in cyclic fashion in one of the two directions. The *root edge* e_{rt} of the tree is the only edge of the tree which has the root vertex as an endpoint. Of the two triangles incident to the root edge of the tree, the *root triangle* t_{rt} of the tree is the one with the minimum triangle index. The root triangle of the tree determines the direction of traversal of the tree boundary loop. Of the two edges of the tree boundary loop

corresponding to the root edge of the tree, the *root edge* e_{rt} of the tree boundary loop is the one incident to the root triangle. Figures 3-A,B illustrate these concepts.

Each simple polygon has a boundary edge identified as the *root edge* e_{rt}, with one of the two endpoints labeled as the *root vertex* v_{rt}, and the other endpoint labeled as the *second vertex* v_2. Figure 3-E illustrates these concepts. The cyclical direction of traversal of the polygon boundary loop is determined by visiting the root vertex first, followed by the second vertex. The correspondence between vertices and edges in a tree boundary loop and the polygon boundary loop is defined by their directions of cyclical traversal and by the matching of their root vertices.

Cutting through forest edges

Cutting through a forest of edges can be performed sequentially, cutting through one tree at time. Each cut is typically a local operation, affecting only the triangles incident to vertices and edges of the tree. However, as in the TS method, a single cut could involve all the triangles of the mesh. Cutting requires duplicating some tree vertices, assigning additional indices to the new vertices and fixing the specification of the affected triangles.

As illustrated in Figure 4-A,B, if no tree vertex is a boundary vertex of the mesh, then the tree is completely surrounded by triangles. Starting at the root triangle, all the corners of affected triangles can be visited in the order of traversal of the tree boundary loop, by jumping from triangle to neighboring triangle, while always keeping contact with the tree. This process produces a list of triangle corners, called the *corner loop*, whose values need to be updated with the new vertex indices. While traversing this list, we encounter runs of corners corresponding to the same vertex index before the cut. A new vertex index must be assigned to each one of these runs. To prevent gaps in the list of vertex indices we first need to reuse the vertex indices of the tree vertices, which otherwise would not be corner values of any triangles. The first visited run corresponding to one of these vertices is assigned that vertex index. The next visited run corresponding to the same vertex index is assigned the first vertex index not yet assigned above the number of vertices of the mesh before the cut. This procedure performs the topological cut. For example, in Figure 3-C, the vertex index values of the corners in the corner loop list are:

$$[1233333244444421111] \; .$$

The list can be decomposed into 6 runs [11111], [2], [33333], [2], [444444], and [2]. As shown in Figure 3-D, the vertex indices assigned to these runs are 1, 2, 3, 8, 4, 9.

A tree with m edges containing no mesh boundary vertices creates a tree boundary loop of $2m$ edges. This may not be the case when one or more tree vertices are also part of the mesh boundary. As illustrated in Figures 4-C,D,E,F, several special cases, must be considered. These special cases treat collapsed edges incident to or on the mesh boundary produced by the PFS generation algorithms as described in Section 5.

Triangulating tree boundary loops By replacing each run of corners in the corner loop with the assigned vertex index, we construct a new list representing the tree boundary loop, If the tree boundary loop has m vertices, so does the corresponding polygon boundary loop. Each triangle $t = \{i, j, k\}$ of the simple polygon defines a new triangle of the refined mesh by replacing the polygon boundary loop indices i, j, k with their corresponding tree boundary loop indices. This is done using the list representing the tree boundary loop as a lookup table. The triangles of the simple polygon are visited in the order of a depth first traversal of its dual tree. The traversal starts with the triangle opposite to the root triangle and always traverses the left branch of a branching triangle first.

Displacing vertices To satisfy the smooth transition property, vertex coordinates corresponding to new vertices are first assigned the same coordinates as the corresponding tree vertices before the cut. To prevent the appearance of holes, these vertices are displaced after the boundary loops are triangulated. Optionally, all affected vertices may be repositioned.

4 COMPRESSION AND ENCODING

In this section we describe how a model represented in PFS format is encoded/compressed for efficient transmission and storage. Compression and encoding of the first (lowest) resolution level of detail was discussed in Section 3.1. This block of data is followed by the compressed/encoded forest split operations in the order they are applied. The encoding of each forest split operation is composed of, in order: 1) the encoding of the forest of edges, 2) the encoding of the sequence of simple polygons, and 3) the compression/encoding of the vertex displacements.

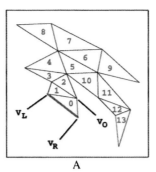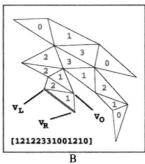

Figure 5: Constant-length encoding of a simple polygon. A: Triangles labels according to their order of traversal. B: Triangles labels according to their two bit code. The encoding of the polygon is the sequence between the brackets.

Encoding the forest A simple encoding of the forest requires one bit per edge, for example a value 1 for the edges which belong to the forest and 0 for the rest. These bits are placed in the compressed data stream in the edge index order defined above. However, since any subset of edges of a forest form a forest, the edges with bit value 1 read up to a certain point may determine that certain edges with higher edge index should have bit value 0, otherwise they would create loops in the forest defined so far by the bits with bit value 1. These edges can be skipped in the compressed data stream. When very few edges belong to the forest, run-length encoding this bit-stream may result in fewer bits. In the experiments that we have performed so far, where the number of triangles increase by 50-70% with each forest split operation, the skipping of predictable bits described above trims the length of the forest bit-stream by only about 1-8% and the simple encoding of the resulting bit-stream is usually shorter that the run-length encoded stream.

Encoding a simple polygon The variable length encoding scheme described in section 3.1 uses one record per triangle tree run and one marching bit per regular node of the triangle tree to encode a simple polygon. This encoding is not very efficient when the simple polygon is composed of a few triangles or short runs. A constant length encoding scheme, requiring exactly 2 bits per triangle, has been proposed by Frank Bossen as an alternative for the MPEG4 standard [1]. This scheme produces better results for polygons with few triangles or short runs.

In the current implementation we compute both encodings for all simple polygons and put the shortest one in the compressed data stream, preceded by one bit to indicate which encoding is used. That is, the simple polygons are either all constant length encoded or all run-length encoded.

The constant-length encoding scheme, illustrated in Figure 5, is performed by traversing the triangle tree. The traversal starts by entering the first triangle through the root edge, with the root vertex assigned to *left vertex* v_L, and the second vertex assigned to *right vertex* v_R. The third vertex of the triangle is assigned to the *opposite vertex* $v_O = (v_L, v_O)$ is the *left edge*, and the edge $e_R = (v_R, v_O)$ is the *right edge*. One bit is used to indicate whether each edge (left and right) is a boundary edge or an internal edge of the polygon. If only the left edge is internal, we set $v_R = v_O$ and we continue with the other triangle incident to e_L. If only the right edge is internal, we set $v_L = v_O$ and we continue with the other triangle incident to e_R. If both edges are internal, we push v_O and v_R onto a traversal stack, we set $v_R = v_O$ and we continue with the other triangle incident to e_L. If both edges are boundary and the traversal stack is not empty, we pop v_R and v_L from the traversal stack, and we continue with the other triangle incident to the edge (v_L, v_R). If both edges are boundary, and the traversal stack is empty, we have finished visiting all the triangles of the simple polygon. For example, in Figure 5-A, the triangles are labeled with their order of traversal, and in Figure 5-B, with their corresponding two-bit code, as a number in the range $0, \ldots, 3$. Here, for each digit the first bit equals 0 if the left edge is boundary, 1 if the left edge is interior. The second bit represents the right side and uses the same convention. The encoding of this polygon is [12122331001210]. Note that there is a very simple transformation from the constant-length encoding to the variable-length encoding. The 3s and 0s in the constant-length encoded sequence mark the end of the triangle runs. In this example, the triangle-runs are defined by the sub sequences [121223], [3], [10], [0], and [1210], which are in the same order defined by the variable-length scheme. The length-of-run field value is the number of two-bit codes in the corresponding sub sequence $(6,1,2,1,$ and 4 in this case). The ends-in-leaf bit value is determined by the last code in the sub sequence ($3 \rightarrow 0, 0 \rightarrow 1$), and the marching bits by the other codes in the sequence, skipping the 3s and 0s (($1 \rightarrow 0, 2 \rightarrow 1$). In this example the marching pattern is the following sequence of bits [010110010]. The transformation from the variable-length encoding to the constant-length encoding is also straightforward.

Decoding a simple polygon As described in Section 3.2, applying the forest split operation requires the triangles of each simple polygon to be represented by triplets $t = \{i, j, k\}$ of polygon boundary loop indices. These indices are subsequently replaced with the vertex indices assigned to the corresponding tree boundary loop indices.

Since the order in which the polygon vertices are visited during tree traversal is usually not the sequential order of the boundary loop, the following recursive procedure is used to reconstruct the triangles of each simple polygon. As described above the traversal of a simple polygon starts by entering the first triangle crossing the root edge, with the left boundary loop index $i_L = 0$ corresponding to the root vertex, and the right boundary loop index $i_R = 1$ corresponding to the second vertex. In general, when we enter a triangle, we know the values of i_L and i_R, and only the opposite boundary loop index i_O must be determined.

If the two-bit code is 1 (leaf node with next triangle on the left), we set $i_O = i_R + 1$ (addition and subtraction is modulo the length of the polygon boundary loop) and reconstruct the triangle $\{i_L, i_O, i_R\}$, we set $i_R = i_O$, and continue. If the two-bit code is 2 (leaf node with next triangle on the right), we set $i_O = i_L - 1$, reconstruct the triangle $\{i_L, i_O, i_R\}$, we set $i_L = i_O$, and continue. To determine the value of i_O for a branching triangle, if we know the distance d along the boundary loop from the left vertex to the right vertex for the run attached to the left edge, we set $i_O = i_L + d$, reconstruct the triangle $\{i_L, i_O, i_R\}$, push i_R and i_O onto the traversal stack, set $i_R = i_O$, and continue. As explained by Taubin and Rossignac [20], these lengths can be recursively computed for all the runs from the encoding of the polygon based on the formula $d = l - 1 + d_L + d_R$, there d is the distance of one run, l is the length of the run. If the run ends in a branching node, d_L is the distance of the run attached to the left edge of the last triangle of the run, and d_R is the distance of the run attached to the right edge of the last triangle of the run. If the run ends in a leaf node, $d_L = d_R = 1$. If the two-bit code of the triangle has the value 0 (leaf node of the triangle tree), we set $i_O = i_L - 1$ or $i_O = i_R + 1$, and reconstruct the triangle $\{i_L, i_O, i_R\}$. If the stack is empty we have finished reconstructing the polygons. Otherwise we pop i_L and i_R values from the stack, and continue.

Encoding the sequence of simple polygons We encode a sequence of constant-length encoded simple polygons by specifying the total number of triangles in the complete sequence of simple polygons followed by a concatenation of the two-bit encoding sequences. It is not necessary to include special markers

in the compressed data stream to indicate the beginning and end of each polygon. The following procedure, which uses a single integer variable called *depth*, determines the limits of the polygons. The depth variable is initialized to 1 before starting traversing a polygon. Each time a two-bit code with the value 3 is found (branching triangle), depth is incremented by one. Each time a two-bit code with the value 0 is found (leaf triangle), depth is decremented by one. The variable depth is always positive while inside the polygon. The end of the polygon is reached after the depth becomes equal to zero. If the polygons are run-length encoded, instead of the total number of runs, the *(length-of-run,ends-in-leaf)* records are put into the data stream in the order of traversal of the trees, preceded by the total number of runs in the sequence, and the number of bits per length-of-run. The same procedure described above (using a depth variable) can be used to determine the limits of the simple polygon.

Encoding the vertex displacements Rather than encoding the new absolute positions of the marked vertices, their positions after and before the forest split operation are first quantized to a certain number of bits per coordinate with respect to a global bounding box enclosing all the levels of detail. The differences between these values are then Huffman encoded. The Huffman encoding table, the specification of the bounding box, and the number of bits per coordinate error, are included at the beginning of the compressed stream. The same bounding box and number of bits per coordinate is used by the TS scheme, described in Section 3.1, to encode the coordinates of the lowest resolution level of detail, but because the errors are computed in a different way, different Huffman tables are used. Also, since the errors keep growing smaller as more forest split operations are applied, we use a different Huffman table for each forest split operation.

Pre and post smoothing The differences between vertex positions before and after each forest split operation can be made smaller by representing these errors as the sum of a global predictor plus a correction. We use the smoothing method of Taubin [18] as a global predictor. The method requires only three global parameters which are included in the compressed data stream. After the connectivity refinement step of a forest split operation is applied, the new vertices are positioned where their corresponding vertices in the previous level of detail were positioned and the mesh has many edges of zero length (all the new triangles have zero surface area). The smoothing method of Taubin, which tends to equalize the size of neighboring triangles, brings the endpoints of most such edges apart, most often reducing the distance to the desired vertex positions. The corrections, the differences between the vertex positions after the split operation and the result of smoothing the positions before the split operation, are then quantized according to the global quantization grid and entropy encoded. To make sure that the resulting vertex positions have values on the quantization grid, the smoothed coordinates must be quantized before computing the corrections. In our experiments, this procedure reduces the total length of the entropy encoded corrections by up to 20-25%.

If the polygonal model approximates a smooth shape, a post-smoothing step can be applied to reduced the visual artifacts produced by the quantization process. In many cases, even fewer bits per coordinate can be used in the quantization process without a significant perceptual difference, also reducing the total length of the encoded vertex displacements. Figure 6 illustrates the effect of post-smoothing.

Compression ratios The simple encoding of the forest with one bit per edge and the constant-length encoding of the simple polygons provide an upper bound to the number of bits required to encode a forest split operation. Since the number of edges in the mesh is independent of the number of triangles added, the minimum

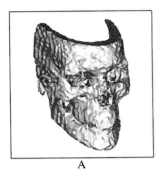 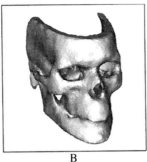

A	B

Figure 6: Effect of post-smoothing. A: Coordinates quantized to 6 bits per coordinate. B: Result of applying the smoothing algorithm of Taubin [18] with parameters $n = 16$ $\lambda = 0.60$ $\mu = -0.64$. Compare with the original in Figure 8-D.

number of bits per triangle are obtained when the most triangles are added with one forest split operation.

The most triangles we can add with one forest split operation is approximately equal to the current number of triangles. As the number of edges in the forest increases, so does the number of triangles added. The forest with the largest number of edges for a triangle mesh with V vertices has $V - 1$ edges and corresponds to a forest composed of a single spanning tree. Ignoring the case of meshes with boundaries, this single tree creates a tree boundary loop with $2V - 2$ edges, and a simple polygon with that many boundary edges is composed of $2V - 4$ triangles. Since typical meshes have about twice as many triangles as vertices, the number of triangles in this simple polygon is approximately equal to T, the number of triangles in the mesh. If we also assume that the mesh has low Euler number ($V - E + T \approx 0$), then $E \approx 1.5T$. If $\Delta T = \alpha T$ is the number of triangles added by the forest split operation ($0 < \alpha < 1$), the total number of bits required to encode the connectivity information of this forest split operation is approximately equal to $(1.5/\alpha + 2)\Delta T$. This is 3.5 bits per triangle for $\alpha = 1$, 4 bits per triangle for $\alpha = 0.75$, and 5 bits per triangle for $\alpha = 0.5$.

In the PM scheme each vertex split operation requires an average of $5 + \log_2(n)$ bits to specify the refinement in the connectivity of the mesh ($\log_2(n)$ bits to specify the index of the common vertex, and an average of 5 bits to specify the two incident edges), to a total storage of about $n(5 + \log_2(n))$ bits to double the number of vertices of the mesh. For example, let us consider a relatively small mesh with 1,000 triangles, and a forest split operation which increases the number of triangles by 75%. The PFS scheme needs about 4 bits per new triangles to represent the connectivity changes while the PM scheme needs about $5 + 10 = 15$ bits per triangle or almost four times the number of bits required by the PFS scheme. For larger meshes the differences become more pronounced.

If no pre or post smoothing is used, the number of bits used to encode each vertex displacement is about the same as in PM. As discussed above, pre and post smoothing can be used to decrease the total size of the encoded vertex displacements by up to 20-25%. Because of the small granularity, it is not practical to apply pre smoothing before each vertex split operation in PM.

Complexity of encoding and decoding
Since the two triangles incident to an edge defined by a pair of vertex indices can be accessed in constant time, the forest split operation is linear in the number of triangles added. We represent the edges as quadruplets, with two vertex indices and two face indices, and keep them in a hash table or array of linked lists. For typical surfaces this provides constant or almost constant access time.

5 CONVERSION TO PFS FORMAT

In this section we discuss simplification algorithms to convert a single-resolution triangular mesh to PFS format. We show that most edge-collapse based simplification algorithms can be modified to represent a simplification LOD hierarchy as a sequence of *forest collapse* operations.

Clustered multi-resolution models Several existing methods to generate multi-resolution polygonal models are based on *vertex clustering algorithms* [17]. In the multi-resolution polygonal model produced by these algorithms, the vertices of each level of detail are partitioned into disjoint subsets of vertices called *clusters*. All the vertices in each cluster are collapsed into a single vertex of the next (lower resolution) level of detail. Other examples of clustering algorithms for automatic surface simplification are based on triangle collapsing [10], and edge collapsing [12, 15, 6, 11].

For a clustering algorithm producing an LOD hierarchy with L levels, the vertices of consecutive levels are related by *clustering functions* $c_l : \{1, \ldots, V_l\} \to \{1, \ldots, V_{l+1}\}$ which map vertex indices of level l onto vertex indices of level $l+1$. Here, V_l denotes the number of vertices of the l-th. level. Triangles at each level of detail are completely specified by the triangles of the first (highest resolution) level of detail and the clustering functions. If $t_l = \{i, j, k\}$ is a triangle of the l-th. level, then $t_{l+1} = \{c_l(i), c_l(j), c_l(k)\}$ is a triangle of the next level if it is composed of three different indices; otherwise we say that t_l was *collapsed* at the next level.

Clustered multi-resolution polygonal models have the smooth transition property. Vertex i of the l-th. level is linearly interpolated with vertex $c_l(i)$ of the level as a function of time. A closely related, but more compact data structure, optimized for fast switching between levels of detail was recently introduced by Guéziec *et al.* [8] to represent clustered multi-resolution polygonal models.

The forest collapse operation The set of triangles of each level of detail that collapses in the next level can be partitioned into connected components, where two triangles are considered connected if they share an edge. A clustering function defines a forest collapse operation if the following two conditions are satisfied: 1) each connected component is a simple polygon (triangulated with no internal vertices); and 2) no vertex is shared by two or more connected components. If these two conditions are satisfied, the boundary edges of each connected component form a disconnected tree in the next level of detail. If the edges formed a graph with loops instead of a tree then the connected component would not be simply connected. Also, connected components with no common vertices always produce disconnected trees.

To test whether or not a clustering function defines a forest collapse operation, it is sufficient to: 1) check that the Euler numbers of the connected components are all equal to one ($V - E - T = 1$), where the edges which separate the triangles of each component from other triangles are consdiered boundary edges; and 2) count the number of times that each vertex of the mesh belongs to the boundary of a connected component and then check that all these numbers are equal to 0 or 1.

Permutations of vertex and triangle indices If all the clustering functions of a clustered multi-resolution model define forest collapse operations, the transition from the lowest to the highest resolution level of detail can be represented as a sequence of forest split operations. The order of vertices and triangles in the highest resolution level of detail and those induced by the clustering functions in the lower resolution levels will, in general, not be the same as those produced by decompressing the low resolution mesh and applying the forest split operations. Special care must be taken to determine the permutations which put the vertices and faces of

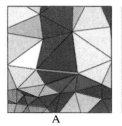  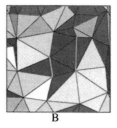

A   C   B

Figure 7: Collapsibility tests. A: Acceptable edge of multiplicity 1. B: Rejected edge of multiplicity 1. C: Rejected edge of multiplicity > 1.

different levels in the order that the decoder expects as described in Section 3.2.

Edge-collapse simplification algorithms In several simplification algorithms based on edge collapsing, the edges of the mesh are ordered in a priority queue according to certain criteria, usually based on the geometry of a neighborhood, and on the changes that the edge would produce if collapsed. The first edge is removed from the queue and certain connectivity and geometry tests are applied to it. If it passes the tests it is classified as *collapsible*, and the edge is collapsed. Otherwise, it is discarded. The collapsing of an edge may require changing the order of some of the neighboring edges in the queue. The process continues removing edges from the queue until the queue is exhausted, or until a termination condition, such as maximum number of collapsed triangles, is reached. To prevent visual artifacts the collapsibility test should take into account the values of properties bound to vertices, triangles, or corners, and the discontinuity curves that such property fields define, as in the PM simplification algorithm [11].

The initial mesh, before the simplification algorithm starts collapsing edges, defines one level of detail, and the resulting mesh, after the collapsing stops, defines the next level of detail. An extended collapsibility test must be performed to ensure that the clustering function defined by a proposed edge collapse also defines a valid forest collapse operation. This extended test requires two additional, simple tests to be performed on each candidate edge collapse. Figure 7 illustrates these tests. Both tests are straightforward.

The first test determines whether or not the connected components of the set of collapsed triangles are simple polygons after the edge is collapsed. The test can be implemented using an auxiliary data structure to maintain a forest in the dual graph of the mesh, with each tree of this forest corresponding to one connected component (simple polygon) constructed so far. When an edge collapse is accepted by the simplification algorithm, it not only identifies the two endpoints of the edge, but also the two remaining edges of each of the two (one for the case involving mesh boundary) collapsed triangles. This defines a *multiplicity* for each edge of the simplified mesh. Initially all edges in the current level of detail are assigned a multiplicity of one. When two edges are identified as the result of an edge collapse, they are removed from the priority queue, and a new edge with the sum of the two multiplicities is reinserted in the queue. Of the four (two for the case involving mesh boundary) boundary edges of the quadrilateral defined by the two (one) collapsed triangles, between 0 and 4 (2) edges are boundary edges of neighboring connected components. The test is passed if all of these neighboring connected components are different, in which case, adding the collapsed edge and the edges shared with the connected components to the dual forest would not destroy the forest structure. Otherwise, one or more loops would be created. Two triangles incident to an edge with multiplicity higher than one correspond to two mesh triangles which each share an edge with a boundary edge of the same connected component but are not neigh-

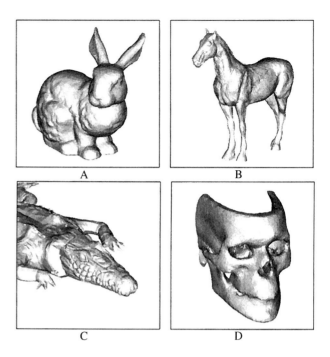

A   B

C   D

Figure 8: Highest resolution models used to converted to PFS format in Section 6. A: bunny. B: horse. C: crocodile. D: skull. All the models are flat-shaded. Properties are ignored.

bors in the original mesh. Either one or two of the edges of each one of these triangles in the original mesh are boundary edges of the neighboring connected component, otherwise the previous test would have been violated. The test is passed if only one edge is shared with the neighboring connected component.

The second test is applied only if the edge passes the first test. This test prevents vertices from being shared by two or more connected components and can be implemented using an auxiliary data structure to keep track of the vertices of the mesh which are boundary vertices of simple polygons constructed so far. An array of boolean variables, initialized to false, is sufficient for this purpose. We call a vertex of the quadrilateral defined by the collapse of an edge with multiplicity 1 *isolated*, if neither one of the two boundary edges of the quadrilateral shared by the vertex are shared by neighboring connected components. The same name is given to the two vertices of the two triangles incident to an edge with multiplicity higher than 1, which are not endpoints of the collapsed edge. The second test is passed if neither one of the isolated vertices are boundary vertices of any connected component. If an edge passes both tests then the edge is collapsed, the priority queue and the data structures needed to perform the two new tests are updated, and the process repeats until the queue is exhausted.

As explained in Section 4, the most triangles a forest split operation can add to a mesh with T triangles is approximately T. Therefore, when the simplification algorithm (with the two additional tests) stops because the queue has been exhausted, the resulting mesh cannot have less than half the triangles of the original mesh. In our experiments, a forest split operation adds between 45-90% T to a mesh of T triangles.

6   IMPLEMENTATION AND RESULTS

Our prototype implementation is composed of three programs: 1) a simplification program, 2) an encoding program, and 3) a decoding program. The current implementation handles manifold triangular meshes without properties.

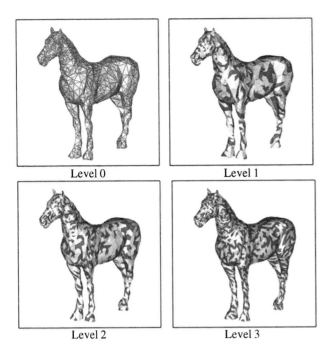

Figure 9: LOD hierarchy generated automatically from the horse of figure 8-B (Level 4). Red triangles collapse in the next level

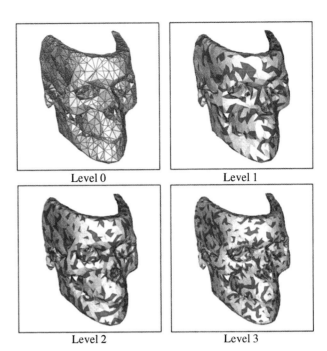

Figure 10: LOD hierarchy generated automatically from the skull of figure 8-D (Level 4). Red triangles collapse in the next level

For the simplification progam we implemented the variable tolerance simplification method of Guéziec [6] with the modifications described in Section 5. The combined procedure takes a single-resolution triangular mesh as input, and produces as output a file in *clustered multi-resolution* format. This is an ASCII file containing the connectivity of the original mesh, the vertices coordinates of all the levels produced, and the clustering functions represented as arrays of vertex indices. The encoder program takes this file format as input, checks whether the data is PFS compressible or not, and if so, produces a compressed data stream as described in Section 4. The decoder program takes this compressed data stream as input and produces a file in clustered multi-resolution format.

We report results for four models, each displayed in full resolution in figures 8-A,B,C,D. The models all have roughly the same number of vertices and triangles (except the bunny) and represent different topological types. The bunny has the topology of a sphere with four holes (in the bottom). The horse is composed of three connected components each with the topology of a sphere without boundary (body and eyes). The crocodile is composed of 65 connected components each with the topology of a sphere (body, mandibles, eyes and teeth) and with large variations in the number of vertices and triangles in each component. The skull is connected, has no boundary and a very high genus.

The simplification program produced four levels of detail for the bunny, and five levels of detail for each one of the other models. Figure 9 shows the LOD hierarchy generated from the horse. Figure 10 shows the LOD hierarchy generated from the skull. The number of vertices and triangles for each level, as well as the number of bytes needed to encode the base meshes and forest split operations are shown in the Figure 11. Overall, the single resolution scheme used to encode and compress the lowest resolution level of detail has better compression rates (bits per triangle) than the forest split operations. However, the forest split operation compression rates approach the single resolution compression rates as the size of the forests grow and the vertex displacements decrease in magnitude.

7 EXTENSIONS

To simplify the description of the representation, algorithms and data structures, and to reflect the limitations of the current implementation, we have limited the scope of this paper to manifold triangular meshes without properties. Some of these extensions are straightforward, others will require further work.

Polygonal faces Just as the TS method was extended to handle the simply connected polygonal faces found in VRML models [19], the PFS method can be extended to handle manifold polygonal models with simply connected polygonal faces. The representation and encoding of the forest of edges do not require any modification. Tree boundary loops would be polygonized instead of triangulated. Tree boundary loops can be polygonized by sending one extra bit per marching edge to indicate which of the internal edges of the triangulated simple polygon are actually face edges.

Properties The current implementation supports topology and vector coordinates. The TS method has been extended to handle properties (colors, normals and texture coordinates) and property bindings for faces and corners [19]. The same techniques can be used to extend the PFS method to handle additional properties and property bindings. Normals can be quantized in a special way, taking into account the unit length nature of normals vectors [19]. When properties are bound to corners, they define *discontinuity curves* [11, 19]. Encoding these discontinuity curves by simply requiring an extra bit per edge may be too expensive. A scheme to progressively update the discontinuity curves may be necessary. We intend to work on this issue in the near future.

Non-manifolds and topology changing refinement
The topological type of the lowest resolution level of detail stays constant during the refinement process for bothe the PFS and PM methods. The Progressive Simplicial Complexes (PSC) scheme was introduced by Popovic and Hoppe [14], to allow changes in topological type (genus) to occur during the refinement process.

CROCODILE					(1.89)
Level	0	1	2	3	4
T	3,506	5,128	7,680	12,408	21,628
ΔT	3,506	1,622	2,552	4,728	9,220
ΔT (%)	∞	46	50	62	74
C/ΔT	3.42	5.29	5.04	4.45	4.02
(C+G)/ΔT	13.29	26.71	24.20	20.82	17.27
HORSE					(2.76)
T	2,894	4,306	6,774	11,754	22,258
ΔT	2,894	1,412	2,468	4,980	10,504
ΔT (%)	∞	49	57	74	90
C/ΔT	3.44	5.12	4.64	4.05	3.68
(C+G)/ΔT	13.74	25.04	25.04	19.16	17.91
SKULL					(1.48)
T	4,464	6,612	9,966	14,896	22,104
ΔT	4,464	2,148	3,354	4,930	7,208
ΔT (%)	∞	48	51	50	48
C/ΔT	4.51	5.15	4.97	5.04	5.10
(C+G)/ΔT	14.86	29.85	28.15	26.71	24.58
BUNNY					(1.73)
T	2,008	3,169	5,072	7,698	
ΔT	2,008	1,161	1,903	2,626	
ΔT (%)	∞	58	60	44	
C/ΔT	3.27	4.69	4.56	4.95	
(C+G)/ΔT	14.37	27.97	25.68	26.38	

Figure 11: Numerical results. T: number of triangles. ΔT: increment with respect to previous level. C/ΔT: bits per triangle for connectivity. (C+G)/ΔT: total number of bits per triangle. The number in parentheses is the relative cost of progressive vs. single resolution transmission of connectivity (ratio of connectivity bits per triangle in Progressive Forest Split / Topological Surgery).

The PSC representation retains most of the advantages of the PM representation, including smooth transitions between consecutive levels of detail and progressive transmission. However, the increased generality of the method requires a higher number of bits to specify each refinement operation.

We believe that a recursive subdivision approach related to the one taken in this paper, but with a more complex refinement operation, can solve the problem of dealing with non-manifolds and changes of topological type. We intend to work on this issue in the near future as well.

8 CONCLUSIONS

In this paper we introduced the PFS representation as a new adaptive refinement scheme for storing and transmitting triangular meshes in a progressive and highly compressed form. We started the paper by putting this new method and the PM method of Hoppe in the general context of recursive subdivision/refinement schemes. We showed that PFS allows the user to tradeoff granularity in refinement levels for complexity in the data stream. For a fine granularity (PM) $O(n \log_2(n))$ bits are required to double the connectivity size of a mesh with $O(n)$ levels of detail. For a coarse granularity (PFS) $O(n)$ bits are required to perform the same doubling for $O(1)$ levels of detail.

We have described algorithms for efficiently encoding to and decoding from a data stream containing the PFS format. We also showed how to reduce the number of bits required to encode the geometry the mesh by using pre and post global smoothing steps.

We showed how, with the addition of two simple tests, to modify any simplification algorithm based on edge collapses to convert single resolution triangular meshes to PFS format. We presented results obtained by applying these modifications to the Variable

Tolerance method of Guéziec. Finally, we discussed how to extend the scheme to handle polygonal faces and various property bindings.

Acknowledgments

Our thanks to Rhythm & Hues Studios, Inc. and Greg Turk for the Horse model. Thanks to Marc Levoy for the Bunny model.

REFERENCES

[1] MPEG4/SNHC verification model 5.0, July 1997. ISO/IEC JTC1/-SC29/WG11 Document N1820, Caspar Horne (ed.).

[2] E. Catmull and J. Clark. Recursively generated B-spline surfaces on arbitrary topological meshes. *Computer Aided Design*, 10:350–355, 1978.

[3] M. Deering. Geometric compression. In *Siggraph'95 Conference Proceedings*, pages 13–20, August 1995.

[4] D. Doo and M. Sabin. Behaviour of recursive division surfaces near extraordinary points. *Computer Aided Design*, 10:356–360, 1978.

[5] M. Eck, T. DeRose, T. Duchamp, H. Hoppe, M. Lounsbery, and W. Stuetzle. Multiresolution analysis of arbitrary meshes. In *Siggraph'95 Conference Proceedings*, pages 173–182, August 1995.

[6] A. Guéziec. Surface simplification with variable tolerance. In *Second Annual International Symposium on Medical Robotics and Computer Assisted Surgery*, pages 132–139, Baltimore, MD, November 1995.

[7] A. Guéziec, G. Taubin, F. Lazarus, and W. Horn. Cutting and Stitching: Efficient Conversion of a Non-Manifold Polygonal Surface to a Manifold. Technical Report RC-20935, IBM Research, July 1997.

[8] A. Guéziec, G. Taubin, F. Lazarus, and W. Horn. Simplicial maps for progressive transmission of polygonal surfaces. In *VRML 98*. ACM, February 1998.

[9] M. Hall and J. Warren. Adaptive polygonalization of implicitly defined surfaces. *IEEE Computer Graphics and Applications*, pages 33–42, November 1990.

[10] B. Hamann. A data reduction scheme for triangulated surfaces. *Computer Aided Geometric Design*, 11(2):197–214, 1994.

[11] H. Hoppe. Progressive meshes. In *Siggraph'96 Conference Proceedings*, pages 99–108, August 1996.

[12] H. Hoppe, T. DeRose, T. Duchamp, J. McDonald, and W. Stuetzle. Mesh optimization. In *Siggraph'93 Conference Proceedings*, pages 19–25, July 1993.

[13] C. Loop. Smooth subdivision surfaces based on triangles. Master's thesis, Dept. of Mathematics, University of Utah, August 1987.

[14] J. Popović and H. Hoppe. Progressive simplicial complexes. In *Siggraph'97 Conference Proceedings*, pages 217–224, August 1997.

[15] R. Ronfard and J. Rossignac. Simplifying a triangular mesh with multiple planar constraints. Technical report, IBM Research, 1994.

[16] R. Ronfard and J. Rossignac. Triangulating multiply-connected polygons: A simple, yet efficient algorithm. *Computer Graphics Forum*, 13(3):C281–C292, 1994. Proc. Eurographics'94, Oslo, Norway.

[17] J. Rossignac and P. Borrel. *Geometric Modeling in Computer Graphics*, chapter Multi-resolution 3D approximations for rendering complex scenes, pages 455–465. Springer Verlag, 1993.

[18] G. Taubin. A signal processing approach to fair surface design. In *Siggraph'95 Conference Proceedings*, pages 351–358, August 1995.

[19] G. Taubin, W.P. Horn, F. Lazarus, and J. Rossignac. Geometric Coding and VRML. *Proceedings of the IEEE*, July 1998. (to appear) Also IBM Research TR RC-20925, July 1997.

[20] G. Taubin and J. Rossignac. Geometry Compression through Topological Surgery. *ACM Transactions on Graphics*, April 1998. (to appear).

[21] D. Zorin, P. Schröder, and W. Sweldens. Interactive multiresolution mesh editing. In *Siggraph'97 Conference Proceedings*, pages 259–268, August 1997.

Real Time Compression of Triangle Mesh Connectivity

Stefan Gumhold, Wolfgang Straßer[*]

WSI/GRIS University of Tübingen

Abstract

In this paper we introduce a new compressed representation for the
connectivity of a triangle mesh. We present local compression and
decompression algorithms which are fast enough for real time applications. The achieved space compression rates keep pace with
the best rates reported for any known global compression algorithm.
These nice properties have great benefits for several important applications. Naturally, the technique can be used to compress triangle meshes without significant delay before they are stored on external devices or transmitted over a network. The presented decompression algorithm is very simple allowing a possible hardware realization of the decompression algorithm which could significantly
increase the rendering speed of pipelined graphics hardware.

CR Categories: I.3.1 [Computer Graphics]: Hardware Architecture; I.3.3 [Computer Graphics]: Picture/Image Generation—
Display algorithms

Keywords: Mesh Compression, Algorithms, 3D Graphics Hardware, Graphics

1 Introduction and Related Work

The ability to handle very large geometric data sets becomes more
and more important. Powerful compression techniques are mandatory to solve this task. The compression approach presented in this
paper has several advantages. The compression and decompression
algorithms are fast and simple. The achieved space compression ratios are among the best known results and the algorithms act locally
such that only a fraction of the vertices must be accessible. None
of the available techniques combines these properties. All lack a
very fast compression algorithm and therefore the compressed representation must be pre-computed before rendering. No speed up
through compression could be achieved so far in the visualization of
meshes with changing connectivity. The related work concentrates
either on fast rendering or on maximum compression and therefore
the following discussion is divided into two sections.

1.1 Compression for Fast Rendering

In this section we discuss representations of triangle meshes that
are used for transmission to graphics hardware. 3D-hardware support is primarily based on the rendering of triangles. Each triangle

---

[*]Email: {sgumhold/strasser}@gris.uni-tuebingen.de

is specified by its three vertices, where each vertex contains three
coordinates, possibly the surface normal, material attributes and/or
texture coordinates. The coordinates and normals are specified with
floating point values, such that a vertex may contain data of up to
36 bytes[1]. Thus the transmission of a vertex is expensive and the
simple approach of specifying each triangle by the data of its three
vertices is wasteful as for an average triangle mesh each vertex must
be transmitted six times.

The introduction of triangle strips helped to save unnecessary
transmission of vertices. Two successive triangles in a triangle strip
join an edge. Therefore, from the second triangle on, the vertices
of the previous triangle can be combined with only one new vertex
to form the next triangle. As with each triangle at least one vertex
is transmitted and as an average triangle mesh has twice as many
triangles as vertices, the maximal gain is that each vertex has to
be transmitted only about two times. Two kinds of triangle strips
are commonly used – the *sequential* and the *generalized triangle
strips*. In generalized triangle strips an additional bit is sent with
each vertex to specify to which of the free edges of the previous
triangle the new vertex is attached. *Sequential strips* even drop this
bit and impose that the triangles are attached alternating. OpenGL
[7] which evolved to the commonly used standard for graphics libraries allowed [5] generalized triangle strips in earlier versions, but
the current version is restricted to sequential strips. Therefore, the
demands on the stripping algorithms increased. None of the existing algorithms reaches the optimum that each vertex is transmitted
only twice. The algorithm of Evans et al. [4] produces strips such
that each vertex is transmitted about 2.5 times and this is currently
the best algorithm.

Arkin et al. [1] examined the problem of testing whether a triangulation can be covered with one triangle strip. For generalized
triangle strips this problem is NP-complete, but for sequential strips
there exists a simple linear time algorithm. But no results or algorithms were given to cover a mesh with several strips.

To break the limit of sending each vertex at least twice Deering [3] suggests the use of an on-board vertex buffer of sixteen
vertices. With this approach, which he calls *generalized mesh*
theoretically only six percent of the vertices have to be transmitted twice. But up to now no corresponding algorithms have been
presented. Bar-Yehuda et al. [2] examined different sized vertex
buffers. They prove that a triangle mesh with n vertices can be
optimally rendered, i.e. each vertex is transmitted only once, if
a buffer for $12.72\sqrt{n}$ vertices is provided. They also show that
this upper bound is tight and no algorithm can work with less than
$1.649\sqrt{n}$ buffered vertices. In their estimation they neglect the time
consumed by the referencing of buffered vertices, which makes it
impossible to determine the suitability of the approach for connectivity compression. Again the algorithms to compute the rendering
sequences are not fast enough for on-line generation.

Our connectivity compression technique also utilizes a vertex
buffer where each vertex has to be transmitted only once. As our
technique is hard to analyze theoretically, we can only give experimental results of the size. These are all less than $12.72\sqrt{n}$. By
defining a fixed traverse order our approach minimizes the number

---

[1]where we assumed four bytes per floating point value and one byte per
color component

of indices needed to reference vertices in the buffer, which results in an additional speed up for rendering. If these indices are Huffman-encoded, in the average only two bits per triangle are needed for references.

1.2 Maximum Mesh Compression

The work on fast rendering explained in section 1.1 can also be used for the compression of triangle mesh connectivity. Instead of retransmitting a vertex, a reference is inserted into a compressed representation. If a vertex from the buffer is referenced its index within the buffer enters the compressed representation. In the triangle strips of Evans et al. [4] each vertex appears about 2.5 times. The vertices can be rearranged into the order they appear the first time and only the indices of $1.5n$ vertices need to be inserted in the compressed representation. One additional bit per triangle is needed to specify whether the next vertex is used the first time or the index of an already used vertex follows. This sums up to about $1 + 0.75 \cdot \lceil \log_2 n \rceil$ bits per triangle. The disadvantage of this approach is that the storage needs grow with the size of the triangle mesh. The measurements of Deering in [3] show that the generalized mesh approach theoretically consumes between eight and eleven bits per triangle if an optimal stripper is available.

The work of Bar-Yehuda et al. [2] cannot be compared to our work as no appropriate measurements are available.

Taubin et al. [8] propose a very advanced global compression technique for the connectivity of triangle meshes. The method is based on a similar optimization problem as for sequential triangle strips and the authors guess that it is NP-complete. Their approximation allows compression to only two bits per triangle and there exist triangle meshes which consume only one bit per triangle. The decompression splits into several processing steps over the complete mesh, which makes the approach unsuitable to speed up hardware driven rendering. Their compression and decompression algorithms are more complex than ours and although the asymptotic running time should be the same we strongly believe that a comparable optimized implementation of our algorithms is several times faster than the algorithms proposed by Taubin. Our compression technique yields nearly equivalent compression of the mesh connectivity.

So far we described only lossless compression techniques. For applications which allow lossy compression also the vertex data can be compressed and the connectivity can be simplified. Deering [3] uses the proximity of the vertices independently of the connectivity. Taubin et al. [8] propose to predict the coordinates v_n of the vertex, which is to be compressed next, from the preceding K vertices $v_{n-1}, \ldots, v_{n-K}$ and only encode the difference $\epsilon(v_n)$ to the predicted position

$$\epsilon(v_n) = v_n - P(\lambda, v_{n-1}, \ldots, v_{n-K}),$$

where λ specifies the parameters for the predictor function P, which was implemented as the linear filter $\sum_{i=1}^{K} \lambda_i v_i$ and the parameters where chosen to minimize the square sum of all $\epsilon(v_n)$. In both approaches of vertex data compression the positions are additionally entropy encoded after the delta compression. Similar techniques are used to compress the normals and the material data. Our approach of connectivity compression can be used with both of these geometry compression techniques. The result is a significant speed up in both cases and the improvement of the compression ratios of Deering's approach[2].

---

[2] The compression ratios for the models (triceratops, galleon, viper, 57chevy, insect) measured in Deering's paper would increase from (5.8X, 8.2X, 9.2X, 9.2X, 7.2X) to (7.4X, 11.2X, 11.6X, 12.0X, 11.4X)

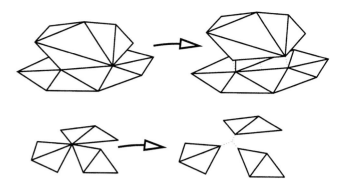

Figure 1: Non manifold vertices must be duplicated in order to make their neighborhood 2-manifold with border.

2 Compression and Decompression

Let us introduce the ideas of compression and decompression by comparison with generalized triangle strips. This approach utilizes a vertex buffer of only three vertices but in turn has to transmit each vertex twice. Thus the first idea is to simply increase the size of the vertex buffer, such that all the undecided vertices can be stored. The undecided vertices are those, which have not finally been incorporated into the so far decompressed triangle mesh, i.e. for these vertices exist adjacent triangles which will be transmitted later.

The increased vertex buffer is not very useful, if still indices of the vertices must be transmitted to localize them within the buffer. The transmission of most indices can be avoided by fixing the order in which the edges formed by the vertices in the vertex buffer are traversed. Therefore, the traverse order need not be encoded. The rules to fix the traverse order must be chosen carefully as they constitute most degrees of freedom for optimization. In turn the compression algorithm becomes nearly as fast as the decompressed algorithm. In the case of generalized triangle strips the traverse order is not fixed. Each of the additional bits encodes which of the two free edges of the previous triangle the next triangle is attached to.

To allow the encoding of an arbitrarily connected and oriented triangle mesh in one run, several basic building operations must be encodable. In the case of triangle strips there is only one operation – the attachment of a new triangle to an existing edge. This has the advantage that the type of operation need not be encoded. In our approach all of the building operations also introduce one new triangle, but the new triangle can additionally be formed exclusively by buffered vertices.

Section 2.1 introduces the rules which fix the order in which the triangle mesh is traversed. Then the different building operations are discussed in section 2.2. The building operations are Huffman encoded in a variable length bit stream to achieve the best compression of the connectivity. Section 2.3 explains how to combine the bit stream with the vertex data and additional data.

In what follows we assume that the triangle meshes consist of several connected components, all orientable and locally 2-manifold with borders. Thus the neighborhood of each vertex can be continuously mapped to a plane or to a half-plane if the vertex belongs to the border of a component. Our approach is extended to non orientable 2-manifold triangle meshes in section 5.1. Non manifold models must be cut into manifold models by duplication of non manifold vertices as indicated in figure 1.

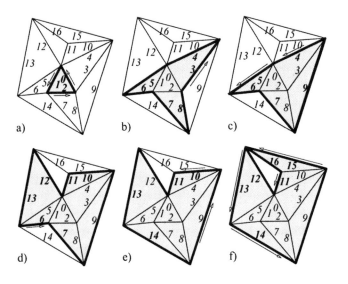

Figure 2: The shown sample triangle mesh is traversed in a breadth-first order.

2.1 Traverse Order

Figure 2 illustrates a breadth-first traverse order of a sample triangle mesh. The buffered vertices are connected with bold lines. The collection of these lines is called the *cut-border*. The cut-border divides the triangle mesh into two parts, the so far decompressed part – the *inner part* (shaded) – and the rest – the *outer part*. The edges on the cut-border are enumerated in the order they are processed. Each time a cut-border edge is processed, a new triangle is added to this edge with a basic building operation imposed by the connectivity of the triangle mesh. The new triangle introduces new cut-border edges and the processed edge is removed from the cut-border.

These are the basic rules which define the traverse order. The degrees of freedom lay in the choice of the initial triangle, which constitutes the initial cut-border, and in the way the new edges are enumerated. It will turn out in section 4.2, that the choice of the initial triangle doesn't influence the compression significantly. In the breadth-first strategy the new cut-border edges obtain increasing numbers, such that the cut-border is grown in a cyclic way. A depth-first order is achieved by enumerating the new cut-border edges in a decreasing order, such that the last introduced cut-border edges are processed first. The complete information in the vertex buffer can be used to determine the position of the new cut-border edges. As we concentrate on real time compression, only the strategies which consume no additional computation time are analyzed in section 4.2.

2.2 Building Operations

Let us take a closer look at figure 2 as nearly all basic building operations arise in this small example. The triangle mesh is always built from an initial triangle consisting of the first three vertices. The initial building operation is not encoded but will be denoted with the symbol "Δ". Between figure 2a and 2b to each of the three initial cut-border edges a triangle is attached in the same way as to a triangle strip. Each operation introduces a new vertex and two new edges to the cut-border. Let us call this building operation *"new vertex"* and abbreviate it with the symbol "$*$". The new cut-border edges are enumerated in the order they are added to the cut-border in order to bring about a breadth-first traverse order.

Between figure 2b and 2c the triangle of the outer part, which is

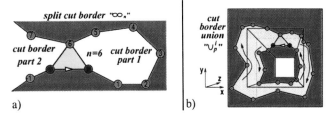

Figure 3: The *"split cut-border"*-/*"cut-border union"*-operation needs one/two indices to specify the third vertex with which the current cut-border edge forms the next triangle. The vertices of the current edge are shaded dark and the newly attached triangle light.

adjacent to edge **3**, is added to the so far (de)compressed triangle mesh. This time no new vertex is inserted, but edge **3** forms a triangle with the preceding cut-border edge. This operation will be called *"connect backward"* and is represented by the symbol "$\leftarrow$".

Moving on to figure 2d, two *"new vertex"*-operations arise at the cut-border edges **4** and **5**. At the cut-border edge **6** the mirror image of the *"connect backward"*-operation is applied to connect this edge to the subsequent edge. Naturally, this operation is called *"connect forward"* and is abbreviated with "$\rightarrow$". No triangle is added to cut-border edge **9** as it is part of the mesh border. This fact has to be encoded, too, and is called *"border"*("$_-$")-operation.

A more complex operation appears at cut-border edge **10** in figure 2e. The adjacent triangle in the outer part is neither formed with the preceding nor with the subsequent cut-border vertex, but with a vertex further apart. The result is that the cut-border splits into two parts. In figure 2f the first part is formed by the edges **11**, **12** and **16** and the second part by **13**, **14** and **15**. This operation will be called *"split cut-border"* ("∞_i"), which takes the index i to specify the third vertex relative to the current cut-border edge. Figure 3a shows another *"split cut-border"*-operation. The relative indices are written into the cut-border vertices. The *"split cut-border"*-operation has two consequences. Firstly, the cut-border cannot be represented anymore by a simple linked list, but by a list of linked lists. And secondly, the choice of the next cut-border part to be processed after a *"split cut-border"*-operation yields a new degree of freedom for the traverse order. To minimize the number of cut-border parts the cut-border part with fewer vertices is chosen.

Another operation arises in figure 2f at cut-border edge **11**. The adjacent triangle closes the triangle mesh and the current cut-border part is removed. This operation is called *"close cut-border"* and is denoted by "∇". As the size of the current cut-border part is known during compression and decompression, the *"close cut-border"*-operation can also be encoded with *"connect forward"* or *"connect backward"* and the different symbol is only introduced for didactic reasons. On the other hand if there really is a hole in the form of a triangle, three *"border"*-operations are encoded.

Finally, there exists a somewhat inverse operation to the *"split cut-border"*-operation – the *"cut-border union"*-operation. An example is visualized in figure 3b. The figure shows in perspective a cube with a quadratic hole. The so far compressed inner part consists of the two green shaded regions. There are two cut-border parts which are connected by the new yellow triangle, which is attached to the current edge (dark blue vertices). Therefore, this operation is called *"cut-border union"* or for short "$\bigcup_p^i$". Two indices are needed to specify the second cut-border part p and the index i of the vertex within the second cut-border part. The vertices in a cut-border part are enumerated according to the cut-border edges. Therefore, the vertex at the beginning of the cut-border edge with the smallest index in the cut-border part p is numbered zero, the vertex at the second smallest cut-border edge is numbered one and so forth.

op.:	vertex	inner edge	border edge	triangle
$\triangle$	3	0	0	1
$\star$	1	1	0	1
$\rightarrow/\leftarrow$	0	2	0	1
$-$	0	0	1	0
∞_i	0	1	0	1
∇	0	3	0	1
$\bigcup_p^i$	0	1	0	1

Table 1: The table shows for each basic building operation which mesh elements are finally placed into the inner part.

It can be shown that the number of *"cut-border union"*-operations is exactly the genus of the compressed triangle mesh. Seen from a different angle, the operations $"\nabla"$, $"\rightarrow/\leftarrow"$, $"\infty_i"$ and $"\bigcup_p^i"$ provide the possibility to connect the current cut-border edge to any possible vertex in the cut-border, whereas the operations $"\triangle"$ and $"\star"$ utilize new vertices.

2.3 Compressed Representation

The encoding of the sequence of atomic building operations uniquely defines the connectivity of a triangle mesh. The connectivity of the sample mesh in figure 2 can be encoded by the following sequence of operations:

$$\star\star\star\leftarrow\star\star\rightarrow_-\infty_2\rightarrow_{-\,-\,-}$$

The symbols for the different operations can be encoded with Huffman Codes to achieve good compression rates. Therefore, the mesh connectivity is sequentially stored in a *bit stream*.

The geometry and material data must be supplied additionally. For each vertex this data can include the vertex position, the surface normal at the vertex and the texture coordinates or some material information. We will refer to all this data with the term *vertex data*. The material of the mesh can also be given for each triangle. Similarly, data can be supplied for the inner edges and the border edges of the mesh. We will collect the different kinds of data in the terms *triangle data*, the *inner edge data* and the *border edge data*. Thus for each type of mesh element, data can be supplied with the connectivity of the mesh. We refer to the collection of all additional data with the term *mesh data*.

Depending on the application there exist two approaches to combine the connectivity and the mesh data of a compressed triangle mesh.

If an application is supplied with enough storage for the complete mesh data, the bit stream for the connectivity can be stored separately. For each type of mesh element the specific data is stored in an array. While the triangle mesh is traversed a vertex, triangle, inner edge and border edge index is incremented after each operation, such that the current mesh elements can be found in the corresponding arrays with the suitable indices. Table 1 shows the increments for each index after the different operations. For example after a *"connect forward"*-operation the inner edge index is incremented by two and the triangle index by one. The advantage of this representation is that the mesh data can be processed without traversing the mesh, for example to apply transformations to the coordinates and normals.

If the compressed triangle mesh is passed to the graphics board or if the mesh data is encoded with variable length values, no random access to the vertex data is possible. Then the mesh data is inserted into the bit stream for the mesh connectivity. After each operation symbol in the stream, the corresponding mesh data is sent

to the stream appropriately. For example after a *"split cut border"*-symbol the mesh data for one inner edge and one triangle is transmitted (see table 1). If we only assume vertex and triangle data and denote the vertex data for the ith vertex with v_i and the triangle data for triangle j with t_j, the extended bit stream representation of the mesh in figure 2 would be:

$$v_0v_1v_2t_0\star v_3t_1\star v_4t_2\star v_5t_3\leftarrow t_4\star v_6t_5\star v_7t_6\rightarrow t_7-\infty_2t_8\rightarrow t_9{-\,-\,-}$$

Remember that the initial triangle is implicitly stored without symbol and introduces the vertices v_0, v_1, v_2 and the triangle t_0.

If the triangle mesh consists of several unconnected components, the compressed bit stream representation consists of the concatenation of the bit streams of the different components.

3 Implementation

All algorithms which process the compressed representation are based on the implementation of the data structure for the cut-border as introduced in section 3.1. This data structure implements the rules which define the traverse order. All other algorithms such as the compression and decompression algorithms presented in the sections 3.2 and 3.3 use this implementation. Further algorithms such as homogeneous transformations of the mesh geometry would also use the cut-border data structure to iterate through the compressed representation

The data structures and algorithms in this section are given in a C++-like syntax. For readability and brevity parentheses were replaced by indentation and additional key-words.

3.1 Cut-Border Data Structure

Data Structure 1	cut border

```
struct Part
    int          rootElement, nrEdges, nrVertices;
struct Element
    int          prev, next;
    Data         data;
    bool         isEdgeBegin;
struct CutBorder
    Part         *parts, *part;
    Element      *elements, *element;
    Element      *emptyElements;

                 CutBorder (int maxParts, int maxElems);
    bool         atEnd();
    void         traverseStep (Data &v₀, Data &v₁);

    void         initial (Data v₀, Data v₁, Data v₂);
    void         newVertex (Data v);
    Data         connectForward/Backward();
    void         border();
    Data         splitCutBorder (int i);
    Data         cutBorderUnion (int i, int p);

    bool         findAndUpdate (Data v, int i, int p);
```

The data structure for the cut-border is a list of doubly linked lists storing the vertex data of the buffered vertices. All elements in the doubly linked lists of the different parts are stored within one homogeneous buffer named *elements*. The maximum number of vertices in the buffer during the compression or decompression defines its size. The maximum buffer size is known once the triangle mesh is compressed and can be transmitted in front of the compressed representation. For the first compression of the mesh the maximum number of vertices can be estimated by $10\sqrt{n}$ (see section 4.2), where n is the number of vertices in the triangle mesh. With this approach a simple and efficient memory management as described in [6] is feasible. Only the pointer *emptyElements* is needed, which points to the first of the empty elements in the buffer. Any time a new element is needed, it is taken from the empty elements and the deleted elements are put back to the empty elements. On the one hand the memory management avoids dynamic storage allocation which is not available on graphics boards and on the other hand it speeds up the algorithms by a factor of two if no memory caches influence the performance.

The different parts can be managed with an array *parts* with enough space for the maximum number of parts which are created while the mesh is traversed. Again this number must be estimated for the first compression and can be transmitted in front of the compressed representation. Thus the constructor for the cut-border data structure takes the maximum number of parts and the maximum number of cut-border elements.

part and *element* point to the current part and the current element within the current part respectively. Each part stores the index of its root element, the number of edges and the number of vertices. These numbers may differ as each part is not simply a closed polygon. Any time a *"border"*-operation arises one cut-border edge is eliminated but the adjacent cut-border vertices can only be removed if they are adjacent to two removed edges. Therefore, each cut-border element stores in addition to the indices of the previous and next element and the vertex data, a flag which denotes whether the edge beginning at this cut-border element belongs to the cut-border or not.

The cut-border data structure provides methods to steer the traversal via a bit stream or with the help of a triangle mesh. The methods $atEnd()$ and $traverseStep(\&v_0, \&v_1)$ are used to form the main loop. The method $traverseStep(\&v_0, \&v_1)$ steps to the next edge in the cut-border data structure and returns the vertex data of the two vertices forming this edge. If no more edges are available, $atEnd()$ becomes true.

During decompression the operations are read from the bit stream and the cut-border data structure is updated with the corresponding methods *initial*, *newVertex*, *connectForward/Backward*, *border*, *splitCutBorder* and *cutBorderUnion*. For compression additionally the method *findAndUpdate* is needed to localize a vertex within the cut-border data structure. The part index and vertex index are returned and can be used to deduce the current building operation. If the vertex has been found by the *findAndUpdate*-method, it is connected with the current cut-border edge.

3.2 Compression Algorithm

Besides the cut-border we need two further data structures for the compression algorithm — a triangle mesh, with random access to the third vertex of a triangle given a half edge, and a permutation. The random access representation of the triangle mesh provides two methods – the $chooseTriangle(v_0, v_1, v_2)$ -method, which returns the vertex data v_0, v_1, v_2 of the three vertices in an initial triangle, and the method $getVertexData(i_0, i_1)$, which takes the vertex indices i_0 and i_1 of a half edge v_0v_1 and returns the vertex data of the third vertex of the triangle containing v_0v_1. The permutation is used to build a bijection between the vertex indices in the random access representation and the vertex indices in the compressed representation. It allows to map an index of the first kind to an index of the second kind and to determine whether a certain vertex index in the random access representation has been mapped.

Given a random access triangle mesh, the compression algorithm computes the mentioned permutation and the compressed represen-

---

Algorithm 1		compression	
Input:	*RAM*	...	random access representation
Output:	*bitStream*	...	compressed representation
	perm	...	permutation of the vertices

```
vertexIdx  = 3;
RAM.chooseTriangle (v₀, v₁, v₂) ;
perm.map ( (v₀.idx, 0) ,  (v₁.idx, 1) ,  (v₂.idx, 2) ) ;
bitStream << v₀ << v₁ << v₂ ;
cutBorder.initial (v₀, v₁, v₂) ;
while not  cutBorder.atEnd () do
    cutBorder.traversalStep (v₀, v₁) ;
    v₂  = RAM.getVertexData (v₁.idx, v₀.idx) ;
    if v₂.isUndefined () then
        bitStream << "_";
        cutBorder.border () ;
    else
        if not  perm.isMapped (v₂.idx) then
            bitStream << "*" << v₂ ;
            cutBorder.newVertex (v₂) ;
            perm.map ( (v₂.idx, vertexIdx++) ) ;
        else
            cutBorder.findAndUpdate (v₂, i, p) ;
            if p > 0 then bitStream << "∪ᵢₚ" ;
            else if i == ±1 then bitStream << "→/←";
            else bitStream << "∞ᵢ";
```

---

tation of the mesh, which is sent to a bit stream. The current vertex index of the compressed representation is counted in the index *vertexIdx*. After the initial triangle is processed, the cut-border data structure is used to iterate through the triangle mesh. In each step the vertex data v_0 and v_1 of the current cut-border edge is determined. From the vertex indices the vertex data of the third vertex in the triangle adjacent to the current edge is looked up in the random access triangle mesh. If no triangle is found, a *"border"*-operation is sent to the bit stream. Otherwise it is checked whether the new vertex has already been mapped, i.e. sent to the cut-border. If not, a *"new vertex"*-operation is sent to the bit stream and the vertex index is mapped to the current index in the compressed representation. If the third vertex of the new triangle is contained in the cut-border, the *findAndUpdate*-method is used to determine the part index and the vertex index within that cut-border part. If the part index is greater than zero, a *"cut-border union"*-operation is written. Otherwise a *"connect forward/backward"*-operation or a *"split cut-border"*-operation is written dependent on the vertex index.

3.3 Decompression Algorithm

The decompression algorithm reads the compressed representation from an input bit stream and enumerates all triangles. The triangles are processed with the subroutine $handle(v_0, v_1, v_2)$, which for example renders the triangles. As in the compression algorithm, firstly, the initial triangle is processed and then the mesh is re-built with the help of the cut-border methods *atEnd* and *traversalStep*. In each step the next operation is read from the bit stream and the corresponding method of the cut-border data structure is called such that the third vertex of the new triangle is determined in order to send it to the subroutine *handle*.

4 Measurements and Optimizations

In this section we analyze our software implementation of the compression and decompression algorithm. Firstly, we introduce the

Algorithm 2   decompression

Input:	*bitStream*	... compressed representation
Output:	*handle*	... processes triangles

```
bitStream >> v₀ >> v₁ >> v₂ ;
handle (v₀, v₁, v₂) ;
cutBorder.initial (v₀, v₁, v₂) ;
while not cutBorder.atEnd () do
    cutBorder.traversalStep (v₀, v₁) ;
    bitStream >> operation ;
    switch (operation)
        case "→/←":
            handle (v₁, v₀,
                cutBorder.connectForward/Backward ()) ;
        case "∞ᵢ":
            handle (v₁, v₀, cutBorder.splitCutBorder (i)) ;
        case "⋃ᵢₚ":
            handle (v₁, v₀, cutBorder.cutBorderUnion (i,p)) ;
        case "⋆":
            bitStream >> v₂ ;
            cutBorder.newVertex (v₂) ;
            handle (v₁, v₀, v₂) ;
        case "_":
            cutBorder.border () ;
```

triangle mesh				compr	decom	storage
name	**t**	**n**	**|bd|**	$k\Delta/s$	$k\Delta/s$	*bits/t*
genus5	144	64	0	386	782	4.23±5.7%
vase	180	97	12	511	796	2.15±6.0%
club	515	262	6	541	857	2.09±3.5%
surface	2449	1340	213	490	790	1.87±0.8%
spock	3525	1779	30	496	820	1.97±0.7%
face	24118	12530	940	430	791	1.81±0.3%
jaw	77692	38918	148	332	809	1.62±0.5%
head	391098	196386	1865	321	796	1.71±0.1%

Table 2: The basic characteristics of the models, the compression and decompression speed and the storage needs per triangle.

test set of models in section 4.1. Then we examine the influence of the traverse order on the compression ratio and the size of the cut-border (section 4.2). And finally we gather the important results on the performance of the presented algorithms in section 4.3.

4.1 The Models

The measurements were performed on the models shown in figure 4. All models are simple connected 2-manifolds and differ in their size. From top left: genus5, vase, club, surface, spock, jaw, face, head. The detail of the head model is hidden in the small interior structures. Therefore, we present in figure 4 a view into the inside of the head.

The basic characteristics of the models are shown in the left half of table 2. Here the number of triangles **t**, the number of vertices **n** and the number of border edges |**bd**| are tabulated for each model.

4.2 Traverse Order and Cut-Border Size

In section 2.1 we defined the traverse order up to the choice of the initial triangle and the enumeration of newly introduced cut-border edges. To study the influence of the initial triangle we measured the storage needs for the compressed connectivity of each model

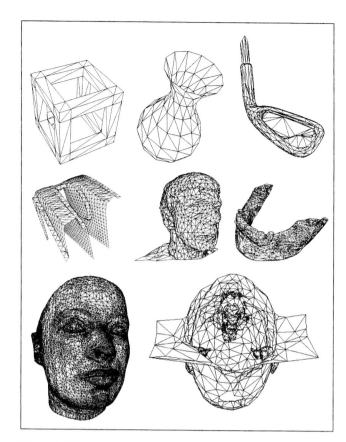

Figure 4: The models used to analyze the compression and decompression algorithms.

several times with randomly chosen initial triangles. Then we computed for each model the average value and the standard deviation as tabulated on the very right of table 2. The influence of the initial triangle vanishes with increasing size of the model and is still less than ten percent for the smallest models. With the same measurements the fluctuation of the cut-border size was determined as shown in table 3. Here the fluctuation is higher and reaches up to twenty percent for the jaw and the club models.

There are a large number of enumeration strategies for the newly introduced cut-border edges. For performance reasons and the simplicity of the implementation, we favored the enumeration strategies which can be implicitly handled with the cut-border data structure introduced in section 3.1. Therefore a newly introduced cut-border edge may either be delayed until all present edges are processed or the new edge is processed next. These two strategies apply to the *"connect forward/backward"*-operations and correspond to attaching the next highest and the next smallest edge index respectively to the new edge. In the case of a *"new vertex"*-operation two new edges are introduced to the cut-border. In this case three possible strategies are feasible. Either the first/second new edge is processed next or both edges are delayed. The *"split cut-border"*- and the *"cut-border union"*-operations arise much more rarely and therefore were excluded from the analysis of the traversal strategy. Thus we were left with twelve strategies, three choices for the *"new vertex"*-operation and for each *"connect"*-operation two choices. Luckily, it turned out that the strategy, where the new edge is processed next after both *"connect"*-operations and where the second edge is processed next after a *"new vertex"*-operation, is superior over all others. This strategy achieved best compression and kept the cut-border smallest for all models.

Table 3 shows for each model the maximum number of parts and the maximum number of buffered vertices needed for mesh traver-

name	$part_{max}$	$vert_{max}$	$prop$
genus5	3.21±12.7%	32.75±15.4%	5.35
vase	2.30±24.2%	22.56±10.2%	2.99
club	3.11±11.9%	44.24±21.0%	4.45
surface	3.10± 9.7%	83.16±12.1%	3.10
spock	3.24±13.2%	120.10± 4.5%	3.23
face	3.40±15.6%	329.08±14.5%	4.22
jaw	4.76±10.7%	564.42±19.7%	4.55
head	9.00±11.1%	1255.20± 8.6%	3.56

Table 3: The maximum number of parts and the maximum number of buffered vertices needed for mesh traversal. The last column gives the quantity $prop = (vert_{max} + 6 \cdot s_{vert})/\sqrt{n}$.

sal. The values are averaged over several random choices of the initial triangle. As the values fluctuate significantly we add three standard deviations to the values such that 99.73% of the values are smaller than our estimation if we suppose a normal distribution. The maximum number of cut-border parts is comparably small and can safely be estimated by 100 for the first compression of a triangle mesh. To show that the maximum number of buffered vertices increases with $\sqrt{n}$ we divide the measured values plus three standard deviations by $\sqrt{n}$ and get values between three and six independent of the size of the model. Thus a save estimation for the size of the vertex buffer in a first compression of a triangle mesh is $10\sqrt{n}$.

4.3 Performance

The last column of table 2 shows that our approach allows compression of the connectivity of a triangle mesh to two bits per triangle[3] and less. The theoretical lower limit is 1.5 bits per triangle which is achieved with uniform triangle meshes. To understand this fact let us neglect the *"split cut-border"*- and *"cut-border union"*-operations. Each *"new vertex"*-operation introduces one vertex and one triangle, whereas each *"connect"*-operation only introduces a triangle to the mesh. To arrive at a mesh with twice as many triangles as vertices, equally many *"new vertex"*- and *"connect"*-operations must appear. The Huffman code for the *"new vertex"*-operation consumes one bit and the *"connect"*-operations are encoded with two and three bits as still other operations must be encoded. If both *"connect"*-operations are equally likely, we get a compression to 1.75 bits per triangle. If on the other hand one *"connect"*-operation is completely negligible a compression to 1.5 bits is feasible. The optimal traversal strategy found in the previous section avoids *"connect backward"*-operation and therefore allows for better Huffman-encoding than the other strategies.

Table 2 also shows the compression and decompression speed in thousands of triangles per second measured on a 175MHz SGI/O2 R10000. The decompression algorithm clearly performs in linear time in the number of triangles with about 800,000 triangles per second. But the performance of the compression algorithm seems to decrease with increasing n. Actually, this impression is caused by the 1 MB data cache of the O2 which cannot keep the complete random access representation of the larger models, whereas the small cut-border data structure nicely fits into the cache during decompression. On machines without data cache the performance of the compression algorithm is also independent of n. The compression algorithm is approximately half as fast as the decompression algorithm. About 40% of the compression time is consumed by the random access representation of the triangle mesh in order to find the third vertex of the current vertex. The other ten percent are used to determine the part and vertex index within the cut-border.

If our compression scheme is used to increase the bandwidth of transmission, storage or rendering, we can easily compute the break-even point of the bandwidth. The total time consumed by our compression scheme is the sum of the times spent for compression, transmission and decompression. The total time must be compared to the transmission time of the uncompressed mesh. Let us assume for the uncompressed representation an index size of 2 bytes, such that each triangle is encoded in 6 bytes. If we further use the estimation that the triangle mesh contains twice as many triangles as vertices, the break-even point computes[4] to a bandwidth of 12MBit/sec. Thus the compression scheme can be used to improve transmission of triangle meshes over standard 10MBit Ethernet lines. As our approach allows us to compress and decompress the triangle mesh incrementally, the triangle mesh can also be compressed and decompressed in parallel to the transmission process. Then even the transmission over a 100MBit Ethernet line could be improved.

5 Extensions

In this section we describe how to extend our method on non orientable triangle meshes. Additionally, we show how to encode attributes which are attached to vertex-triangle pairs.

5.1 Non Orientable Triangle Meshes

As we restricted ourselves to 2-manifold triangle meshes, the neighborhood of each vertex must still be orientable even for non orientable meshes. From this follows that each cut-border part must be orientable at any time: a cut-border part is a closed loop of adjacent edges. The orientation of one edge is passed on to an adjacent edge through the consistent orientation of the neighborhood of their common vertex. Therefore, only the *"split cut-border"*- and *"cut-border union"*-operations need to be extended as they introduce or eliminate cut-border parts. Both operations connect the current cut-border edge to a third vertex in the cut-border, which is either in the same or in another cut-border part. The only thing which can be different in a non orientable triangle mesh is that the orientation of the cut-border around this third vertex is in the opposite direction as in the orientable case. Therefore, only one additional bit is needed for each *"∞_i"*- and *"$\bigcup_p^i$"*-operation, which encodes whether the orientation around the third vertex is different. During compression the value of the additional bit can be checked from the neighborhood of the third vertex. Previously a *"split cut-border"*-operation produced a new cut-border part. In the new case with different orientations around the third vertex, the orientation of one of the new parts must be reversed and the parts are concatenated again as illustrated in figure 5. In a *"cut-border union"*-operation the cut-border part containing the third vertex is concatenated to the current cut-border part and in the new case the orientation of the cut-border part with the third vertex is reversed before concatenation.

5.2 Attributes For Vertex-Triangle Pairs

A lot of triangle meshes contain discontinuities that force attachment of certain vertex attributes to vertex-triangle pairs. See for example the genus5 model in figure 4, which contains a lot of creases. For each vertex on a crease exist two or more different normals which must be attached to the same vertex which is contained in different triangles. Thus for models with creases it must be possible to store several different vertex normals for different vertex-triangle pairs. Similarly, discontinuities in the color attribute force storage

---

[3] The genus5 model consumes more storage as its genus forces five *"cut-border union"*-operations and the model is relatively small.

[4] with a compression rate of 400,000 triangles per second and a decompression rate of 800,000 triangles per second

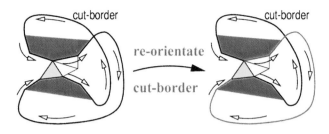

Figure 5: After some *"split cut-border"*-operations of a non orientable manifold half of the cut-border (drawn in red) must be re-oriented and no new part is generated.

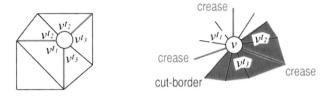

Figure 6: Creases divide the neighborhood of a vertex into regions. Each region contains the triangles with one vertex-triangle attribute.

of several RGBA values within the vertex-triangle pairs. A simple solution to support vertex-triangle attributes is to encode these attributes with every appearance of a vertex-triangle pair. This implies that the same vertex-triangle attributes for one vertex may be replicated several times. On the other hand if we duplicated these vertices, which lay on creases, the vertex coordinates would be replicated.

With a small amount of overhead we can do better and encode each vertex location and each vertex-triangle attribute exactly once. Let us denote the collection of all vertex specific data as for example its coordinates with v and the different collections of the vertex-triangle data with $v^{t1}, v^{t2}, \ldots$. As an example let us describe the encoding of v^t in the case of creases as illustrated in figure 6. The neighborhood of each vertex is split by the creases into several regions. Within each region there is exactly one vertex-triangle attribute valid for the vertex and all triangles in this region. On the right side of figure 6 a cut-border vertex is shown during compression or decompression. We see that at any time it is sufficient to store besides the vertex data v two vertex-triangle attributes $v^{t\text{left}}$ and $v^{t\text{right}}$ for each vertex within the cut-border. When a new triangle is added to the cut-border, the vertex-triangle attributes of a vertex can only change, if the vertex is part of the current cut-border edge and if this edge is a crease. If one of the vertex-triangle attributes for example $v^{t\text{left}}$ changes after an operation which adds a triangle, there are two possible cases. Either a new vertex-triangle attribute is transmitted over the bit stream or the new attribute is copied from $v^{t\text{right}}$.

To encode when a new vertex-triangle attribute has to be transmitted we transmit one or two control bits after each operation, which adds a triangle to the current cut-border edge. Two control bits are needed only for the *"connect"*-operations as the new triangle contains two cut-border edges. The control bits encode whether the affected cut-border edges are creases. Afterwards, for each cut-border vertex on a cut-border edge, which is a crease, we transmit one further bit which encodes whether a new vertex-triangle attribute is transmitted or the attribute should be copied from the other vertex-triangle attribute stored in the cut-border. If we denote the total number of inner edges with e and the total number of crease edges with e_c this approach results in an overhead of less

than $e + 2e_c$ bits.

6 Conclusion

The presented compression technique provides not only a fast decompression algorithm but also a compression algorithm which performs in only double the amount of time of the decompression algorithm. The slow down of the compression algorithm is primarily caused by the uncompressed random access mesh representation. Faster mesh data structures must be investigated as well as the usage of hash tables to speed up the search for vertices within the cut-border.

The simplicity of the algorithms allow for hardware implementation and suitable hardware will be designed in future work. But also software implementations perform extremely well as shown in the previous section. Beside the good performance and the simplicity of the approach the connectivity of a triangle mesh is compressed similarly well as by the best known compression methods. Therefore even globally optimizing compression algorithms can be replaced by the faster and simpler approach.

Acknowledgments

Many thanks to Reinhard Klein and Andreas Schilling for inspiring discussions and to Michael Doggett for reviewing the paper.

References

[1] E. M. Arkin, M. Held, J. S. B. Mitchell, and S. S. Skiena. Hamiltonian triangulations for fast rendering. *Lecture Notes in Computer Science*, 855:36–57, 1994.

[2] Rueven Bar-Yehuda and Craig Gotsman. Time/space tradeoffs for polygon mesh rendering. *ACM Transactions on Graphics*, 15(2):141–152, April 1996.

[3] M. Deering. Geometry compression. In *Computer Graphics (SIGGRAPH '95 Proceedings)*, pages 13–20, 1995.

[4] Francine Evans, Steven S. Skiena, and Amitabh Varshney. Optimizing triangle strips for fast rendering. In *IEEE Visualization '96*. IEEE, October 1996. ISBN 0-89791-864-9.

[5] Silicon Graphics Inc. GL programming guide. 1991.

[6] Scott Meyers. *Effective C++: 50 specific ways to improve your programs and designs. – 2. ed.* Addison-Wesley, Reading, MA, USA, 1997.

[7] Jackie Neider, Tom Davis, and Mason Woo. *OpenGL Programming Guide — The Official Guide to Learning OpenGL, Version 1.1*. Addison-Wesley, Reading, MA, USA, 1997.

[8] Gabriel Taubin and Jarek Rossignac. Geometric compression through topological surgery. Technical report, Yorktown Heights, NY 10598, January 1996. IBM Research Report RC 20340.

The Design of a Parallel Graphics Interface

Homan Igehy   Gordon Stoll   Pat Hanrahan

Computer Science Department

Stanford University

Abstract

It has become increasingly difficult to drive a modern high-performance graphics accelerator at full speed with a serial immediate-mode graphics interface. To resolve this problem, retained-mode constructs have been integrated into graphics interfaces. While retained-mode constructs provide a good solution in many cases, at times they provide an undesirable interface model for the application programmer, and in some cases they do not solve the performance problem. In order to resolve some of these cases, we present a parallel graphics interface that may be used in conjunction with the existing API as a new paradigm for high-performance graphics applications.

The parallel API extends existing ideas found in OpenGL and X11 that allow multiple graphics contexts to simultaneously draw into the same image. Through the introduction of synchronization primitives, the parallel API allows parallel traversal of an explicitly ordered scene. We give code examples which demonstrate how the API can be used to expose parallelism while retaining many of the desirable features of serial immediate-mode programming. The viability of the API is demonstrated by the performance of our implementation which achieves scalable performance on a 24 processor system.

CR Categories and Subject Descriptors: C.0 [Computer Systems Organization]: Hardware/Software Interfaces; D.1.3 [Programming Techniques]: Concurrent Programming; I.3.1 [Computer Graphics]: Hardware Architecture.

1 INTRODUCTION

Computer graphics hardware has been rapidly increasing in performance. This has motivated immediate-mode graphics interfaces like OpenGL [20] to adopt constructs such as display lists and packed vertex arrays in order to alleviate system bottlenecks. However, these constructs may impose an undesired paradigm shift for the application programmer, and they may not be useful in resolving the particular performance bottleneck. Furthermore, with the increasing use of multiprocessor systems for graphics applications, a serial interface to the graphics system can be inele-

gant. A parallel graphics interface seeks to resolve these issues. To provide a common framework, we first review three key issues in graphics interfaces.

The first issue in designing a graphics interface is state. In a stateless interface, the behavior of every command is independent of every other command; thus, every command must include all the information required to execute that command. Conversely, in an interface with state, a command's behavior can be affected by previous commands. Some of the information required for the execution of commands may reside within the state maintained by the interface, and some commands modify that state. While stateless interfaces simplify many issues (especially with regard to parallelism), they are not well-suited to full-featured rendering systems. The problem is that a large amount of data is needed for each drawing command, and much of it is changed infrequently. Respecifying this data with each primitive is tedious and inefficient, so most graphics interfaces contain state.

The second key issue is whether the graphics interface is immediate-mode or retained-mode. In an immediate-mode API, the application sends commands to the graphics system one at a time, and the graphics system executes them more or less immediately. In a retained-mode API, the application first specifies an entire scene that is built on the graphics system and subsequently requests the scene to be rendered with certain viewing parameters. Though retained-mode interfaces can sometimes provide performance benefits, programmers prefer immediate-mode interfaces due to their flexibility and ease of use. Many well-designed interfaces use the best of both worlds: they are based on immediate-mode semantics, and some retained-mode constructs are included to allow performance benefits.

The third major issue that arises in graphics interface design is ordering. Ordering semantics are the set of rules that constrain the order in which API commands may be executed. In a strictly ordered interface, primitives must be drawn in the order in which they are specified. This behavior is essential for many algorithms such as the placement of ground-plane shadows [3] and transparency through alpha-compositing [21]. Sometimes, however, a programmer may not care whether or not primitives are drawn in the order specified. For example, depth buffering alleviates the need for drawing a scene of opaque 3D primitives in any particular order. In these cases, the programmer would gladly use less constrained ordering semantics if it meant increased performance.

In the rest of the paper, we present the motivations and issues involved in designing a parallel extension to a serial immediate-mode graphics interface with strict ordering and state. By adding synchronization commands (such as barriers and semaphores) into multiple graphics command streams, application threads can issue explicitly ordered primitives in parallel without blocking. We also introduce the notion of a wait context command for synchronizing contexts at the level of application

---

{homan,gws,hanrahan}@graphics.stanford.edu

threads. Given the resulting API, we explore how an application programmer would attain parallel issue of graphics commands. These ideas are demonstrated by an implementation which achieves scalable performance on a 24 processor system. We also discuss the issues surrounding the various ways of implementing the parallel API. Very little research has been done in the area of parallel graphics interfaces. This paper provides a common framework on which a new class of research and commercial systems can be built as well as a common framework on which a new class of parallel algorithms can be designed.

2 MOTIVATION

Graphics interfaces have been around for many years, so why investigate a parallel API now? While it is true that some applications are most naturally expressed through a parallel graphics API, the main motivation is performance: it is becoming more and more difficult to drive a graphics system at full speed using a single CPU. First we look into the reasons behind this, and then we examine possible solutions.

2.1 Performance Limitations

Although graphics systems are on the same technology curve as microprocessors, graphics systems have reached a level of performance at which they can process graphics commands faster than microprocessors can produce them: a single CPU running an immediate-mode interface cannot keep up with modern graphics hardware. This is primarily due to an increasing use of parallelism within graphics hardware. Within a computer, there are three sources of bottlenecks in a graphics application. First, performance may be limited by the speed of the graphics system. In this case, the only solution is to use a faster graphics system. Second, performance may be limited by the rate of data generation. In this case, the programmer can use either a faster data generation algorithm or else, if the algorithm is parallelizable, multiple processors. Third, performance may be limited by the interface between the host system and the graphics system. Possible sources of this limitation are:

1) Overhead for encoding API commands.
2) Data bandwidth from the API host.
3) Data bandwidth into the graphics system.
4) Overhead for decoding API commands.

2.2 Performance Solutions

There are several possible ways to extend a serial immediate-mode API in order to address the interface bottlenecks. First, we describe two techniques that are currently in widespread use, packed primitive arrays and display lists. Then we describe a proposed technique, compression. Finally, we describe our proposal, a parallel graphics interface. It is important to note that many of these techniques can complement each other in resolving performance bottlenecks.

2.2.1 Packed Primitive Arrays

A packed primitive array is an array of primitives that reside in system memory. By using a single API call to issue the entire array of primitives instead of one API call per primitive, the cost of encoding API commands is amortized. Furthermore, because the arrays may be transferred by direct memory access (DMA), bandwidth limitations from the API processor may be bypassed.

Nothing is done, however, about the bandwidth limitations into the graphics system. Furthermore, although the decoding may be somewhat simplified, all the primitives in the array still have to be decoded on the graphics system. While packed primitive arrays are useful in a wide variety of applications, they may introduce an awkward programming model.

2.2.2 Display Lists

A display list is a compiled set of graphics commands that resides on the graphics system. In a fashion similar to retained-mode interfaces, the user first specifies the list of commands to be stored in the display list and later invokes the commands within the display list. Because they are essentially command macros, display lists work well semantically with immediate-mode interfaces. In cases where the scene is small enough to fit in the graphics system and the frame-to-frame scene changes are modest, display lists trivially resolve the first three bottlenecks. If the scene is too large and therefore must reside in system memory, display lists are similar to packed primitive arrays and only the first two bottlenecks are resolved. Display lists provide an excellent solution for performance bottlenecks if the same objects are drawn from frame to frame. But on applications that recompute the graphics data on every frame (e.g., [11, 24]), display lists are not useful. Furthermore, the use of display lists burdens the programmer with the task of managing handles to the display lists.

2.2.3 Compression

Whereas the idea of quantizing the data sent through the API has been used for quite some time, the idea of compressing the data has only recently been proposed. One system compresses the geometric data sent through the API [6]; other systems compress the texture data [2, 25]. All compression schemes increase the decoding costs, and systems which compress the data interactively increase the encoding costs. Systems which compress the data off-line, on the other hand, are useful only when the graphics data does not change.

2.2.4 Parallel Interface

The motivation behind a parallel graphics interface is scalability: bottlenecks are overcome with increased parallelism. If the graphics system is too slow, it can be scaled by adding more graphics nodes. If the data generation is too slow, more processors can be used to generate the data in parallel. Similarly, if the serial interface is too slow, then it should be parallelized. In a system with a single graphics port, a parallel API can be used to overcome the first two interface limitations. However, by building a scalable system with multiple graphics ports, all interface limitations can be overcome.

There are many challenges to designing a good parallel graphics interface; in formulating our design, we had several goals in mind. First and foremost were the ability to issue graphics primitives in parallel and the ability to explicitly constrain the ordering of these primitives. Ideally, the API should allow parallel issue of a set of primitives that need to be drawn in an exact order. The parallel API should be a minimal set of extensions to an immediate-mode interface such as OpenGL, and it should be compatible with existing features such as display lists. The design is constrained by the presence of state; this is required for a large feature set. A well designed parallel interface should be intuitive and useful in a wide variety of applications. And finally, the new API should extend the current framework of graphics architectures to provide a rich set of implementation choices.

3 RELATED WORK

In the field of parallel graphics interfaces, Crockett introduced the Parallel Graphics Library (PGL) for use in visualizing 3D graphics data produced by message-passing supercomputers [5]. Due to the characteristics of its target architecture and target applications, PGL was designed as a retained-mode interface. In parallel, each processor adds objects to a scene by passing pointers to graphics data residing in system memory. A separate command is used to render the objects into a framebuffer, and no ordering constraints are imposed by the interface. PixelFlow [8, 18] is another system designed to support multiple simultaneous inputs from a parallel host machine, and PixelFlow OpenGL includes extensions for this purpose. However, due to the underlying image composition architecture, PixelFlow OpenGL also imposes frame semantics and does not support ordering. Because of these constraints, PGL and PixelFlow OpenGL do not meet the requirements of many graphics applications.

The X11 window system provides a parallel 2D graphics interface [9, 23]. A client with the proper permissions may open a connection to an X server and ask for X resources to be allocated. Among these resources are drawables (which are on- or off-screen framebuffers) and X contexts (which hold graphics state). Since resources are globally visible, any client may subsequently use the resource within X commands. Since X drawing calls always include references to a drawable and an X context, client requests are simply inserted into a global queue and processed one at a time by the X server. Though it is not explicitly encouraged, multiple clients may draw into the same drawable or even use the same graphics context.

While a 3D graphics interface was beyond the scope of the original design of X, OpenGL is a 3D interface that has been coupled with X. For explicitness, OpenGL within X will serve as our example API due to its popularity and elegant design [20]. OpenGL is an immediate-mode interface whose state is kept within an X resource called the GLX context. In the interest of efficiency, both display lists and packed primitive arrays are supported. Furthermore, both texture data and display lists may be shared between contexts in order to allow the efficient sharing of hardware resources amongst related contexts [12].

Strict ordering semantics are enforced in X and OpenGL: from the point of view of the API, every command appears to be executed once the API call returns. However, in the interest of efficiency, both interfaces allow implementations to indefinitely buffer commands. This introduces the need for two types of API calls. Upon return from the *flush* call (XFlush, glFlush), the system guarantees that all previous commands will execute in a finite amount of time from the point of view of the drawable. Upon return from a *finish* call (XSync, glFinish), the system guarantees that all previous commands have been executed from the point of view of the drawable.

Since OpenGL and X solve different problems, programs often use both. Because of buffering, however, a program must synchronize the operations of the two streams. Imagine a program that wants to draw a 3D scene with OpenGL and then place text on top of it with X. It is insufficient to simply make the drawing calls in the right order because commands do not execute immediately. Furthermore, a flush is insufficient because it only guarantees eventual execution. A finish, on the other hand, guarantees the right order by forcing the application to wait for the OpenGL commands to execute before issuing X commands. In a sense, however, the finish is too much: the application need not wait for

the actual execution of the OpenGL commands; it only needs a guarantee that all prior OpenGL commands execute before any subsequent X commands. The call glXWaitGL provides this guarantee, and glXWaitX provides the complement.

Hardware implementations of OpenGL typically provide support for a single context, and sharing of the hardware is done through a context switch. Though context switches are typically inexpensive enough to allow multiple windows, they are expensive enough to discourage fine-grained sharing of the graphics hardware between application threads. A few architectures actually provide hardware support for multiple simultaneous contexts drawing into the same framebuffer [13, 26], but all commands must go through a single graphics port. Furthermore, these architectures do not have a mechanism for maintaining the parallel issue of graphics commands when an exact ordering of primitives is desired.

4 THE PARALLEL API EXTENSIONS

While OpenGL is not intended for multithreaded use in most implementations, the interface provides mechanisms for having multiple application threads work simultaneously on the same image. In this section, we first demonstrate how such an interface may be used to attain parallel issue of graphics commands. Then, we show how additional extensions can be used to increase the performance of parallel issue. The specification of the API extensions is given in Figure 1, and the reader is encouraged to look back to it as necessary.

The API extensions are most easily motivated through the use of an example. Suppose that we want to draw a 3D scene composed of opaque and transparent objects. Though depth buffering alleviates the need to draw the opaque primitives in any particular order, blending arithmetic requires that the transparent objects be drawn in back-to-front order after all the opaque objects have been drawn. By utilizing the strict ordering semantics of the serial graphics API, a serial program simply issues the primitives in the desired order. With a parallel API, order must be explicitly constrained. We assume the existence of two arrays: one holds opaque primitives, and the other holds transparent primitives in

```
glpNewBarrier(GLuint barrier, GLuint numCtxs)
    barrier->numCtxs = numCtxs;
    barrier->count = numCtxs;

glpBarrier(GLuint barrier)
    barrier->count--;
    if (barrier->count == 0)
        barrier->count = barrier->numCtxs;
        signal(all waiting contexts);
    else
        wait();

glpDeleteBarrier(GLuint barrier)
```

```
glpNewSema(GLuint sema, GLuint count)
    sema->count = count;

glpPSema(GLuint sema)
    if (sema->count == 0)
        wait();
    sema->count--;

glpVSema(GLuint sema)
    sema->count++;
    signal(one waiting context, if any);

glpDeleteSema(GLuint sema)
```

```
glpWaitContext(GLXContext ctx)
    Upon return, all subsequent commands from the issuing
    context are guaranteed to execute after all prior commands
    from ctx have finished execution.
```

Figure 1: The Parallel Graphics Interface Extensions.

back-to-front order. We also assume the existence of the following function:

```
DrawPrimitives(prims[first..last])
  glBegin(GL_TRIANGLE_STRIP)
  for p = first..last
    glColor(prims[p].color)
    glVertex(prims[p].coord)
  glEnd()
```

4.1 Existing Constructs

As a first attempt at parallel issue, imagine two application threads using the same context to draw into the same framebuffer. In such a situation, a "set current color" command intended for a primitive from one application thread could be used for a primitive from the other application thread. In general, the sharing of contexts between application threads provides unusable semantics because of the extensive use of state. By using separate contexts, dependencies between the state-modifying graphics commands of the two streams are trivially resolved. Given two application threads using separate contexts on the same framebuffer, the following code could be used to attain parallel issue of the opaque primitives:

```
Thread1                        Thread2
DrawPrimitives(opaq[1..256])   DrawPrimitives(opaq[257..512])
                               glFinish()
appBarrier(appBarrierVar)      appBarrier(appBarrierVar)
DrawPrimitives(tran[1..256])
glFinish()
appBarrier(appBarrierVar)      appBarrier(appBarrierVar)
                               DrawPrimitives(tran[257..512])
```

Both application threads first issue their share of opaque primitives without regard for order. After synchronizing in lock-step at the application barrier, *Thread1* issues its half of the transparent primitives. These transparent primitives are guaranteed to be drawn in back-to-front order after *Thread1*'s share of opaque primitives through the strict ordering semantics of the serial API. They are also guaranteed to be drawn after *Thread2*'s share of opaque primitives through the combination of the barrier and the finish: the finish guarantees the drawing of all previously issued commands from *Thread2*. By using this same synchronization mechanism again, *Thread2*'s share of transparent primitives are then drawn in back-to-front order after *Thread1*'s share of transparent primitives.

4.2 The Wait Construct

One inefficiency in the above code is the use of the finish command; in a sense, it is too much. Synchronization between the threads does not require the actual execution of the graphics commands; it only requires a guarantee on the order of execution between the two graphics streams. In a fashion similar to what is used for synchronizing X and OpenGL, we introduce the *wait context* call in order to make guarantees about the execution of commands between contexts. We refer the reader to Figure 1 for an exact specification. In synchronization situations, the wait call is more efficient than the finish call because it does not require any application thread to wait for the completion of graphics commands. The following code demonstrates how the example scene may be drawn using the wait command:

```
Thread1                        Thread2
DrawPrimitives(opaq[1..256])   DrawPrimitives(opaq[257..512])
appBarrier(appBarrierVar)      appBarrier(appBarrierVar)
glpWaitContext(Thread2Ctx)
DrawPrimitives(tran[1..256])
appBarrier(appBarrierVar)      appBarrier(appBarrierVar)
                               glpWaitContext(Thread1Ctx)
                               DrawPrimitives(tran[257..512])
```

Intergraph uses a different mechanism to provide the same effect as the wait call [13]. Due to the underlying implementation of the single graphics port, returning from a flush call guarantees that all of a context's primitives will be drawn before any subsequent primitives from any other context. While similar in spirit to the wait call, this mechanism does not scale very well to systems with multiple ports because of its underlying broadcast requirement. The wait construct uses point-to-point communication.

4.3 Synchronization Constructs

While the wait command provides an improvement over the finish command, a large problem remains: the synchronization of the graphics streams is done by the application threads. Consequently, application threads are forced to wait. But why should an application thread wait when it could be doing something more useful? For example, in the code of Section 4.2, the first thread must issue its entire half of the transparent primitives before the second thread can begin issuing its half; thus, the second thread is forced to wait. Every time an explicit ordering is needed between primitives from different threads, the interface essentially degrades to a serial solution.

The answer to this problem is the key idea of our parallel API: synchronization that is intended to synchronize graphics streams should be done between graphics streams—not between application threads. To this end, we introduce a graphics barrier command into the API. As with other API calls, the application thread merely issues the barrier command, and the command is later executed within the graphics system. Thus, the blocking associated with the barrier is done on graphics contexts, not on the application threads. The code below achieves our primary objective—the parallel issue of explicitly ordered primitives: both application threads may execute this code without ever blocking if the graphics system provides sufficient buffering.

```
Thread1                        Thread2
DrawPrimitives(opaq[1..256])   DrawPrimitives(opaq[257..512])
glpBarrier(glpBarrierVar)      glpBarrier(glpBarrierVar)
DrawPrimitives(tran[1..256])
glpBarrier(glpBarrierVar)      glpBarrier(glpBarrierVar)
                               DrawPrimitives(tran[257..512])
```

We see the utility of the barrier primitive in the above code example, but what other synchronization primitives provide useful semantics within the realm of a parallel graphics interface? Whereas the barrier is an excellent mechanism for synchronizing a set of streams in lock-step, it is not the best mechanism for doing point-to-point synchronization. Borrowing from the field of concurrent programming, we find that semaphores provide an elegant solution for many problems [7]. Among them is a mechanism for signal-and-wait semantics between multiple streams. The specification of the barrier and semaphore commands can be found in Figure 1. As with texture data and display lists, the data associated with barriers and semaphores should be sharable between contexts.

Barriers and semaphores have been found to be good synchronization primitives in the applications we have considered. If found to be useful, other synchronization primitives can also be added to the API. It is important to note that the requirements for synchronization primitives within a graphics API are somewhat constrained. Because the expression of arbitrary computation through a graphics API is not feasible, a synchronization primitive's utility cannot rely on computation outside of its own set of predefined operations. For example, condition variables are not a suitable choice.

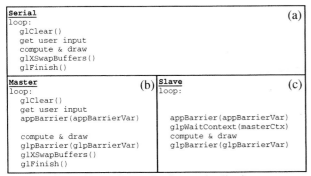

Figure 2: A Simple Interactive Loop. Application computation and rendering are parallelized across slave threads, and a master thread coordinates per-frame operations.

5 USING THE PARALLEL GRAPHICS API

In order to illustrate how the parallel graphics interface may be used to provide scalable command issue, we present two examples. The first example is a generic interactive loop, and the second example is the marching cubes algorithm.

5.1 Simple Interactive Loop

Figure 2a shows a simple interactive loop expressed in a strictly ordered serial interface. The goal in this example is to parallelize the compute and draw stage. This can yield improved performance in the host computation, the issue of the graphics commands, and the execution of graphics commands.

For parallel issue, a master thread (Figure 2b) creates a number of slave threads (Figure 2c) to help with the compute and draw stage. The master first issues a clear command and gets the user input. The application barrier ensures that the worker threads use the correct user input data for the rendering of each frame. This synchronizes the application threads, but not the graphics command streams. The slaves issue wait commands to ensure that the clear command issued by the master is executed first. The master is assured that the clear occurs first due to the strict ordering semantics of a single stream. After each thread issues its graphics commands, a graphics barrier is issued to restrict the swap operation to occur only after all the graphics streams have finished drawing their share of the frame. Finally, a finish operation is needed to ensure that the image is completed and displayed before getting user input for the next frame. The finish itself is a context-local operation which only guarantees that all previous commands issued by the master are completed. However, in conjunction with the graphics barrier, the finish guarantees that the commands of the slaves are also completed.

5.2 Marching Cubes

As a more demanding example, we consider the marching cubes algorithm [16]. Marching cubes is used to extract the polygonal approximation of an isosurface of a function which is sampled on a 3D grid. The grid is divided into a set of cells, and each cell is composed of one or more voxels. In Figure 3a, we present a simplification of marching cubes to 2D. The mechanics of surface extraction and rendering are abstracted as *ExtractAndRender*. *ExtractAndRender* operates on a single cell of the grid independently. If any portion of the desired isosurface lies within the cell, polygons approximating it are calculated and issued to the graph-

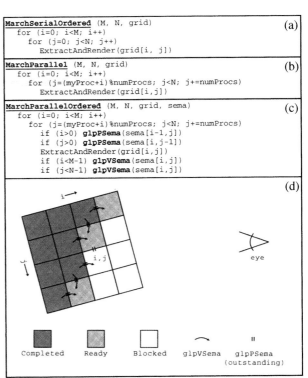

Figure 3: Parallel Marching Cubes. As the rendering of a cell completes, glpVSema operations are performed by the graphics context to release dependent neighboring cells closer to the eye. The rendering commands of the white cells are blocked on glpPSema operations which are waiting for the rendering of adjacent or more distant cells.

ics system immediately. Due to the grid structure, it is fairly simple to perform the traversal in back-to-front order based on the current viewpoint, thus eliminating the need for depth buffering and allowing for alpha-based translucency. In our example, this corresponds to traversing the grid in raster order.

Due to the independence of the processing of different cells, marching cubes is easily parallelized. In Figure 3b, traversal is parallelized by interleaving the cells across processing elements. Unfortunately, this simple approach sacrifices back-to-front ordering. Figure 3d illustrates the dependence relationships between cells and their neighbors which must be obeyed in the ordered drawing of primitives. These dependencies can be expressed directly using semaphores injected into the graphics command streams. Such an implementation is shown in Figure 3c. Before processing a cell, a thread issues two *P* operations to constrain the rendering of a cell to occur after rendering of its two rear neighbor cells. After processing the cell, it issues two *V* operations to signal the rendering of its other neighbors. Note that the dependencies and traversal order given here are non-ideal; more efficient (and more complicated) approaches are possible.

6 IMPLEMENTATION

In order to test the viability of the parallel API extensions, we have implemented a software graphics library which is capable of handling multiple simultaneous graphics contexts. The name of this implementation is Argus, and the performance achieved with the parallel API using this system demonstrates the utility and feasibility of the ideas presented in this paper.

The Argus Pipeline

The diagram on the right shows the flow of data through the Argus pipeline. The pipeline contains several threads, shown as gray boxes, which communicate through a variety of queues. In this example, two application threads are drawing into the same framebuffer through two different contexts. The graphics data from the two contexts is shown in red and blue.

One key design issue that comes up in implementing the parallel API is the handling of the graphics state since most commands affect rendering through state changes. API commands are issued by the 'App' threads shown at the top of the diagram. Commands that modify state which is not necessary for the rendering of the current GL primitive (e.g., the bottom entries of the matrix stack) are tracked in the context state (e.g., CS). Commands that modify state which is necessary for rendering the current GL primitive (e.g., the top entry of the matrix stack) are tracked in the current geometry state (e.g., GS_2), but old versions of the geometry state (e.g., GS_1) are kept until they are no longer needed by the rest of the pipeline. Commands which specify the current primitive (i.e., commands which are allowed within glBegin and glEnd, such as glNormal and glVertex) are grouped into fixed-size primitive blocks (denoted by P_i). A primitive block and its related geometry state contain all the information necessary for the rendering of the primitives, and multiple primitive blocks can share the same geometry state. For example, primitive blocks P_2 and P_3 both use the same geometry state GS_2. Every time a primitive block fills up or the geometry state changes, a pair of pointers (which are represented in the diagram by parentheses) is added to the local command queue (LCQ) by the 'App' thread; synchronization commands (Sema) are inserted into this queue directly.

Another key implementation design issue that comes up in any parallel API implementation is the merging of graphics streams and the resolution of synchronization commands. In Argus, each context has a 'Sync' thread which is responsible for moving data from its LCQ onto a global command queue (GCQ). 'Sync' threads execute the synchronization commands found in the LCQ (as illustrated by the dotted green line). When 'Sync' threads are not blocked due to synchronization, they copy the pointers from their LCQ onto the GCQ. This creates a sequence in the GCQ which is strictly ordered with respect to any one context and consistent with the constraints imposed by the synchronization commands. For example, the sequence found in the GCQ of the diagram keeps the order { P_1, P_2, P_3 } and { P_1, P_2, P_3 }. The sequence is also consistent with the semaphore pair (which requires an ordering that puts { P_1, P_2 } in front of { P_3, P_3 }).

Beyond the GCQ, the Argus pipeline is very similar to a graphics pipeline which implements a serial API. The 'Geom' threads drain the GCQ and fill the triangle queue by converting the geometry state (GS_i) and the 3D data from primitive blocks (P_i) into rasterization state (RS_i) and 2D triangle blocks (T_i). Each 'Rast' thread is responsible for drawing into one tile of the framebuffer, and the 'Geom' threads insert pointers into the appropriate rasterization buffers based on the tiles which are overlapped by the triangles in the triangle block. These reorder buffers are used as a mechanism for maintaining the ordering found in the GCQ across the rasterizers.

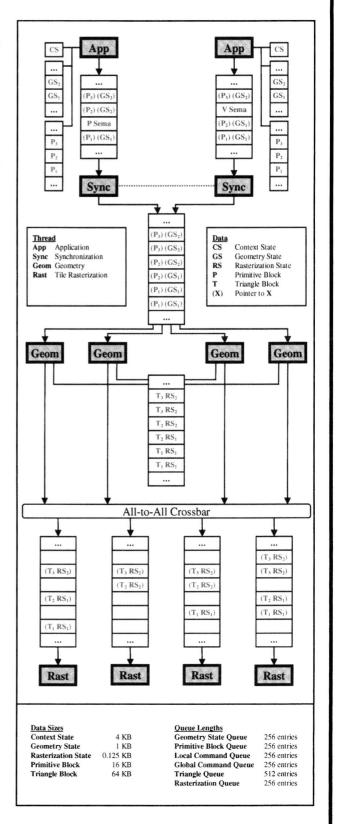

Thread	
App	Application
Sync	Synchronization
Geom	Geometry
Rast	Tile Rasterization

Data	
CS	Context State
GS	Geometry State
RS	Rasterization State
P	Primitive Block
T	Triangle Block
(X)	Pointer to **X**

Data Sizes			Queue Lengths	
Context State	4 KB		**Geometry State Queue**	256 entries
Geometry State	1 KB		**Primitive Block Queue**	256 entries
Rasterization State	0.125 KB		**Local Command Queue**	256 entries
Primitive Block	16 KB		**Global Command Queue**	256 entries
Triangle Block	64 KB		**Triangle Queue**	512 entries
			Rasterization Queue	256 entries

6.1 Argus

Argus is a shared memory multiprocessor graphics library which was designed to serve as a test-bed for various studies in graphics architecture. Argus implements a subset of OpenGL as well as the parallel API extensions. At the heart of Argus is a lightweight multiprocessor threads package. We implement a graphics architecture by allocating a thread for each processing node in the architectural design. A custom scheduler is used to schedule these threads onto system processors appropriately. Furthermore, if a system processor running application code is blocked for some reason due to the graphics (e.g., a buffer fills up or a glFinish is pending), the threads package will run graphics threads on the otherwise idle application processor.

There are three basic types of threads in the serial API version of Argus. An application thread runs application code and manages the graphics context. A geometry thread transforms and shades the primitives encoded in the graphics instruction stream. A rasterization thread is responsible for drawing these transformed primitives into the framebuffer. The version of Argus that implements the serial API is a sort-middle tiled parallel graphics system [17]. Graphics commands from a single application thread fill a global command queue which is drained by many geometry threads. The number of geometry threads is scalable since the data in this global command queue can be read in parallel. Of course, the geometry threads must synchronize at a single point of contention in order to distribute the work in the queue amongst themselves, but because the contention is amortized over a large number of primitives, this cost is insignificant in our implementation. After the appropriate computation, the geometry threads distribute the transformed primitives among the appropriate tile rasterizers. Though the details are beyond the scope of this paper, reorder buffers in front of each rasterizer are used to maintain the ordering found in the global command queue across the rasterizers. Since each tile rasterizer is responsible for a contiguous portion of the screen, no one rasterizer needs to see all of the primitives; thus, the rasterization architecture is scalable. Argus supports a variety of schemes for load balancing tile rasterization. For the results presented here, we used distributed task queues with stealing.

The version of Argus that implements the parallel API extends the serial API architecture to allow multiple simultaneous graphics streams. Each application thread is augmented by a local command queue and a synchronization thread. Instead of entering graphics commands onto the global command queue, each application thread fills its local command queue. The synchronization thread is then responsible for transferring commands from this local command queue onto the global command queue. Since the global command queue may be written in parallel, the architecture is scalable. The box on the adjacent page describes the pipeline in greater detail and explains how state management and synchronization commands are implemented within Argus.

6.2 Performance

Because poor performance often hides architectural bottlenecks, Argus was designed with performance as one of its main criteria. Although Argus can run on many architectures, particular care was taken to optimize the library for the Silicon Graphics Origin system [15]. The Origin is composed of 195 MHz R10000 processors interconnected in a scalable NUMA architecture. Depending on the rendering parameters, the single processor version of Argus is able to render up to 200K triangles per second; this

rendering rate scales up to 24 processors. In its original incarnation, Argus was designed for a serial interface and many serial applications were not able to keep up with the scalable performance of the graphics system. Remedying this situation led us to the development of the parallel API.

To study the performance of our parallel API implementation, we ran two applications: *Nurbs* and *March*. *Nurbs* is an immediate-mode patch tessellator parallelized by distributing the individual patches of a scene across processors in a round-robin manner. By tessellating patches on every frame, the application may vary the resolution of the patches interactively, and because depth buffering is enabled, no ordering constraints are imposed in the drawing of the patches—synchronization commands are utilized only on frame boundaries. Our second application, *March*, is a parallel implementation of the marching cubes algorithm [16]. By extracting the isosurface on every frame, the application may choose the desired isosurfaces interactively. Rendering is performed in back-to-front order to allow transparency effects by issuing graphics semaphores which enforce the dependencies described in Section 5.2. One noteworthy difference between our implementation and the one outlined in Section 5.2 is that cells are distributed from a centralized task queue rather than in round-robin order because the amount of work in each cell can be highly unbalanced. The input characteristics and parameter settings used with each of these applications are shown below:

Nurbs	March
armadillo dataset	skull dataset
102 patches	256K voxels (64x64x64)
196 control points per patch	cell size at 16x16x16
117504 stripped triangles	53346 independent triangles
1200x1000 pixels	1200x1000 pixels

Figure 4a and Figure 4b show the processor speedup curves for *Nurbs* and *March*, respectively. The various lines in the graph represent different numbers of application threads. The serial application bottleneck can be seen in each case by the flattening of the "1 Context" curve: as more processors are utilized, no more performance is gained. Whereas the uniprocessor version of *Nurbs* attains 1.65 Hz, and the serial API version is limited to 8.8 Hz, the parallel API version is able to achieve 32.2 Hz by using four contexts. Similarly, the uniprocessor version of *March* gets 0.90 Hz, and the serial API version of *March* is limited to 6.3 Hz, but the parallel API version is able to attain 17.8 Hz by utilizing three contexts. These speedups show high processor utilization and highlight the implementation's ability to handle extra contexts gracefully.

One extension to Argus that we have been considering is the use of commodity hardware for tile rasterization. Although this introduces many difficulties, it also increases rasterization rate significantly. In order to simulate the effects of faster rasterization on the viability of the parallel API, we stress the system by running Argus in a simulation mode which imitates infinite pixel fill rate. In this mode, the slope calculations for triangle setup do occur, as does the movement of the triangle data between the geometry processors and the tile rasterizers. Only the rasterization itself is skipped. The resulting system increases the throughput of Argus and stresses the parallel API: Figure 4c and Figure 4d show how a greater number of contexts are required to keep up with the faster rendering rate. The parallel API allows Argus to achieve peak frame rates of 50.5 Hz in *Nurbs* and 40.9 Hz in *March*. This corresponds to 5.9 million stripped triangles per second in *Nurbs* and 2.2 million independent triangles per second in *March*. These rates are approximately double the rate at which a single application thread can issue primitives into Argus even

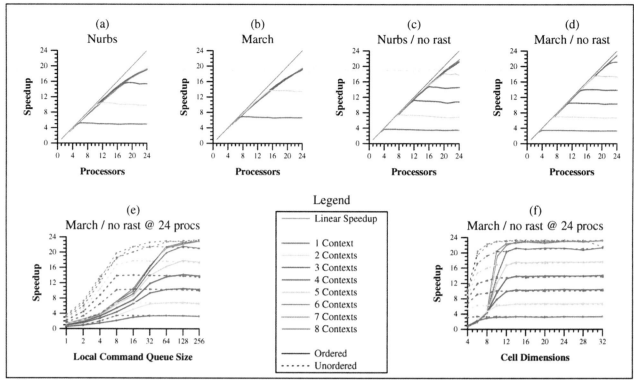

Figure 4: Performance Graphs. The speedup curves for two applications, *Nurbs* and *March*, are drawn in (a) and (b) for a varying numbers of contexts using the Argus graphics library. These same graphs are plotted for a version of Argus which assumes infinite fill rate in (c) and (d). The effects of buffering are illustrated in (e), and the effects of synchronization granularity are demonstrated in (f).

when *no* application computation is involved, thus demonstrating the importance of multiple input ports. Again, the graphs illustrate Argus's capability of handling extra contexts without performance penalties.

One important aspect of any implementation of the parallel API is the amount of buffering required to make the API work. Without enough buffering, the parallel API serializes: in Argus, if a local command queue fills up before its synchronization commands are resolved, the application thread is forced to wait. Intuitively, we expect the amount of buffering required to be sensitive to the amount of synchronization between different threads. This is quantified in the speedup curves of Figure 4e for 24 processors. The number of entries in the local command queue (which can each point to a 16 KB block of primitive commands or hold a single synchronization command) was varied from 1 to 256. The runs were performed on the *March* application with the semaphores both enabled (the solid "Ordered" lines) and disabled (the dotted "Unordered" lines). As one would expect, the ordered version requires significantly larger buffers.

Another key aspect of any parallel API implementation is its ability to minimize the cost of synchronization. If the granularity of the application is too fine, synchronization costs can dominate, and the application is forced to use a coarser subdivision of work. If the work is subdivided too coarsely, load imbalance can occur within the application. The effects of granularity on Argus were tested by varying the dimensions of the cells on both the ordered and unordered versions of *March*. The number of processors was held at 24 and timings were taken with varying numbers of contexts, as illustrated in Figure 4f. A granularity which is too fine deteriorates performance in both the application (as demonstrated

by the unordered runs) as well as in the graphics system (as demonstrated by the extra performance hit taken by the ordered runs). For the *March* application, there is a wide range of granularities (well over an order of magnitude in the number of voxels) that work well since Argus was designed to keep the cost of synchronization low. When *March* is run without isosurface extraction and rendering (i.e., nothing but the synchronization primitives are issued), several hundred thousand semaphore operations are resolved per second.

7 DISCUSSION

Argus is one implementation of the parallel API which performs well. Obviously, the architecture embodied by Argus is not the only possible choice, and it is instructive to examine the design considerations of alternative implementations due to the special architectural requirements imposed by the extensions.

7.1 Consistency and Synchronization

Until now, we have not said much about how the operations of the parallel API can be interleaved. Supporting multiple contexts that share a framebuffer means that the system must provide a consistency model. We borrow the notion of sequential consistency from the field of computer architecture [14]. Imagine a system consisting of multiple processes simultaneously performing atomic operations. A sequentially consistent system computes a result that is realizable by some serial interleaving of these atomic operations. By making a single API command be the level of apparent atomicity, we define the notion of *command-sequential consistency*, the strongest form of consistency possible within the parallel API. At the other end of the spectrum is framebuffer-sequential consistency—only framebuffer accesses are atomic. A whole spectrum of consistency models can be enumerated in such a fashion. The OpenGL specification does not require an implementation to support any consistency model. In order to support the parallel API, however, a graphics system should provide at least *fragment-sequential consistency* in order to support features which depend on an atomic read-modify-write operation on the framebuffer (such as depth buffering).

The consistency model which an architecture supports is related to the location in the pipeline where synchronization constraints between graphics streams are resolved. The Argus pipeline described in Section 6.1 synchronizes and merges multiple graphics streams early in the pipeline, thus supporting command-sequential consistency. One problem with such an architecture is that geometry processing cannot occur on primitives which are blocked due to synchronization constraints. Another problem is that ordering dependencies not required by the synchronization commands are introduced early in the pipeline at the global command queue.

An alternate architecture addresses these problems by merging graphics streams at the rasterizers, thus supporting fragment-sequential consistency. We implemented such an alternate version of Argus in which the entire pipeline up to and including the tile rasterization threads is replicated for each context. Every tile thread executes every synchronization command, and threads which share the same tile merge their streams by obtaining exclusive access to the tile. One disadvantage of this approach is the extra buffering requirements due to the fact that the size of the graphics data expands as it gets farther down the pipeline. Another problem with this alternate approach is the high cost of synchronization since synchronization commands must be executed by every tile rasterizer—this proved prohibitively expensive in the framework of Argus. Of course, many architectures other than the two we tried are possible, and an architect should evaluate the effects of a proposed architecture on these same issues.

7.2 Architectural Requirements

While a graphics system which implements the parallel API is in many respects similar to one which implements a serial API, an architecture should take special care in addressing three particular areas. First, the architecture must have a mechanism that efficiently handles multiple simultaneous input streams. Second, the state management capabilities of the architecture must be able to handle multiple simultaneous graphics states. And third, the rasterization system must be able to handle texture data for multiple streams efficiently.

In designing current systems, graphics architects have gone to great lengths to allow the seamless sharing of the graphics hardware between multiple windows by significantly reducing the context switch time. Although this same mechanism can be used for the parallel API, the context switch time must be reduced even further in order to handle multiple input streams at a much finer granularity. Argus does this by making use of a thread library which can switch threads in less than a microsecond as well as allowing multiple input ports. A hardware system could allow multiple input ports by replicating command processors. Ideally, each of the command processors could handle either a single graphics stream at a high rate or multiple graphics streams at lower rates. This would result in peak performance on serial applications and good performance on highly parallel applications.

The parallel API imposes special requirements on the handling of state. In past architectures, state changes have been expensive due to pipeline flushing. Recent graphics architectures, however, have taken measures to allow large numbers of state changes [19]. To a first order, the number of state changes for a given scene as issued by one application thread is the same as the number of state changes for the same scene as issued by multiple application threads since the number of inherent state changes in a scene is constant. However, the parallel API increases the amount of state that has to be accessible to the different portions of the graphics system: the various graphics processors must be able to switch between the states of different graphics streams without dramatically affecting performance. Hardware implementations which allow for multiple simultaneous contexts have already been demonstrated [13, 26]. In Argus, multiple simultaneous contexts are handled efficiently by taking advantage of state coherence in the state management algorithm through the use of shared memory and processor caching.

One type of state which requires special attention is texture. Unlike the rest of the state associated with a context (with the exception of display lists), texture state can be shared amongst multiple contexts, thus exposing the need for efficient download of and access to shared texture data. The semantics of texture download are the same as all other graphics commands: it is susceptible to buffering, and synchronization must occur to guarantee its effects from the point of view of other contexts. Efficient implementations of synchronized texture download can be realized by extending the idea of the "texture download barrier" found in the SGI InfiniteReality [19]. The access of texture memory may also require special care. Since hardware systems have a limited amount of local texture memory, applications issue primitives in an order which exploits texture locality. The parallel API can reduce this locality since the rasterizers can interleave the rendering of several command streams. In architectures which use implicit caching [4, 10], the effectiveness of the cache can possibly be reduced. In architectures which utilize local texture memory as an explicit cache, texture management is complicated. In Argus, shared texture download is facilitated by shared memory, and locality of texture access is provided by the caching hardware.

8 FUTURE WORK

The parallel API provides a new paradigm for writing parallel graphics applications. Many graphics algorithms exist that need an immediate-mode interface but are limited by application computation speed (e.g., [11, 24]), and parallelizing them can help greatly. There are two other uses of the parallel API which are of special interest. Scene graph libraries such as Performer [22] are parallel applications which traverse, cull, and issue scenes on multiple processors. Pipeline parallelism is used to distribute different tasks among different processors, but Performer is limited on most applications by the single processor responsible for the issuing of the graphics commands. The parallel API can be used to write such libraries in a homogeneous, scalable fashion. A second novel use of the parallel API is to write a "compiler" that can automatically parallelize the graphics calls of a serial graphics application. Recent advances in compiler technology allow automatic parallelization of regular serial applications [1], and extending this work to encompass graphics applications would be an interesting research direction.

Another significant step in validating the parallel API is implementing an architecture with hardware acceleration. While

Argus is an excellent software system for studying the issues in the design of the parallel API, its performance is limited by poor rasterization speed, especially when texturing is enabled. One possible architecture consists of implementing the parallel API on a cluster of interconnected PCs with rasterization hardware. Another possibility is to extend the basic sort-middle interleaved architecture [17] of a high-end system such as the SGI InfiniteReality [19]. Though this task is by no means easy, we believe that such a system is feasible with the techniques described in Section 7.2. The parallel API can also be implemented by a variety of other, more exotic architectures.

Image composition architectures such as PixelFlow [8, 18] are one class of rendering architectures that have not been addressed by the parallel API. Because these machines are not designed to do ordered drawing of primitives, the parallel API needs to be extended to allow a relaxed ordering model in which the requirement of drawing in strict order can be enabled and disabled.

9 CONCLUSION

We have designed a parallel immediate-mode graphics interface. By introducing synchronization commands into the API, ordering between multiple graphics streams can be explicitly constrained. Since synchronization is done between graphics streams, an application thread is able to continue issuing graphics commands even when its graphics stream is blocked. The API provides a natural paradigm for parallel graphics applications that can be used in conjunction with the existing retained-mode constructs of an immediate-mode interface. The feasibility of this API has been demonstrated by a sample implementation which provides scalable performance on a 24 processor system.

Acknowledgements

We would like to thank Matthew Eldridge, Kekoa Proudfoot, Milton Chen, John Owens, and the rest of the Stanford Graphics Lab for their insights about this work. We thank Kurt Akeley and the anonymous reviewers for their helpful comments in revising the paper. We thank Dale Kirkland for describing the parallel interface used by Intergraph. For support, we thank Silicon Graphics, Intel, and DARPA contract DABT63-95-C-0085-P00006. For machine time, we thank Chris Johnson and the University of Utah. And finally, we thank our loved ones.

References

[1] S. Amarasinghe, J. Anderson, C. Wilson, S. Liao, B. Murphy, R. French, M. Lam, and M. Hall. Multiprocessors from a Software Perspective. *IEEE Micro*, 16:3, pages 52-61, 1996.

[2] A. Beers, M. Agrawala, and N. Chaddha. Rendering from Compressed Textures. *Computer Graphics* (SIGGRAPH 96 Proceedings), volume 30, pages 373-378, 1996.

[3] J. Blinn. Me and My (Fake) Shadow. *IEEE Computer Graphics and Applications*, 8:1, pages 82-86, 1988.

[4] M. Cox, N. Bhandari, and M. Shantz. Multi-Level Texture Caching for 3D Graphics Hardware. *Proceedings of the 25th International Symposium on Computer Architecture*, 1998.

[5] T. Crockett. Design Considerations for Parallel Graphics Libraries. *Proceedings of the Intel Supercomputer Users Group 1994*, 1994.

[6] M. Deering. Geometry Compression. *Computer Graphics* (SIGGRAPH 95 Proceedings), volume 29, pages 13-20, 1995.

[7] E. Dijkstra. Cooperating Sequential Processes. *Programming Languages*, pages 43-112, 1968.

[8] J. Eyles, S. Molnar, J. Poulton, T. Greer, A. Lastra, N. England, and L. Westover. PixelFlow: The Realization. *Proceedings of the 1997 SIGGRAPH/Eurographics Workshop on Graphics Hardware*, pages 57-68, 1997.

[9] J. Gettys and P. Karlton. The X Window System, Version 11. *Software—Practice and Experience*, 20:S2, pages 35-67, 1990.

[10] Z. Hakura and A. Gupta. The Design and Analysis of a Cache Architecture for Texture Mapping. *Proceedings of the 24th International Symposium on Computer Architecture*, 1997.

[11] H. Hoppe. View-Dependent Refinement of Progressive Meshes. *Computer Graphics* (SIGGRAPH 97 Proceedings), volume 31, pages 189-198, 1997.

[12] M. Kilgard. *OpenGL Programming for the X Window System,* Addison-Wesley, 1996.

[13] D. Kirkland. Personal Communication. Intergraph Corp., 1998.

[14] L. Lamport. How to Make a Multiprocessor Computer that Correctly Executes Multiprocess Programs. *IEEE Transactions on Computers*, 28:9, pages 241-248, 1979.

[15] J. Laudon and D. Lenoski. The SGI Origin: A ccNUMA Highly Scalable Server. *Proceedings of the 24th Annual Symposium on Computer Architecture*, 1997.

[16] W. Lorensen and H. Cline. Marching Cubes: A High-Resolution 3D Surface Reconstruction Algorithm. *Computer Graphics* (SIGGRAPH 87 Proceedings), volume 21, pages 163-169, 1987.

[17] S. Molnar, M. Cox, D. Ellsworth, and H. Fuchs. A Sorting Classification of Parallel Rendering. *IEEE Computer Graphics and Applications*, 14:4, pages 23-32, 1994.

[18] S. Molnar, J. Eyles, and J. Poulton. PixelFlow: High-Speed Rendering Using Image Composition. *Computer Graphics* (SIGGRAPH 92 Proceedings), volume 26, pages 231-240, 1992.

[19] J. Montrym, D. Baum, D. Dignam, and C. Migdal. InfiniteReality: A Real-Time Graphics System. *Computer Graphics* (SIGGRAPH 97 Proceedings), volume 31, pages 293-302, 1997.

[20] J. Neider, T. Davis, and M. Woo. *OpenGL Programming Guide.* Addison-Wesley, 1993.

[21] T. Porter and T. Duff. Compositing Digital Images. *Computer Graphics* (SIGGRAPH 84 Proceedings), volume 18, pages 253-259, 1984.

[22] J. Rohlf and J. Helman. IRIS Performer: A High Performance Multiprocessing Toolkit for Real-Time 3D Graphics. *Computer Graphics* (SIGGRAPH 94 Proceedings), volume 28, pages 381-395, 1994.

[23] R. Scheifler and J. Gettys. The X Window System. *ACM Transactions on Graphics*, 5:2, pages 79-109, 1986.

[24] T. Sederberg and S. Parry. Free-Form Deformation of Solid Geometric Models. *Computer Graphics* (SIGGRAPH 86 Proceedings), volume 20, pages 151-160, 1986.

[25] J. Torborg and J. Kajiya. Talisman: Commodity Real-Time 3D Graphics for the PC. *Computer Graphics* (SIGGRAPH 96 Proceedings), volume 30, pages 57-68, 1996.

[26] D. Voorhies, D. Kirk, and O. Lathrop. Virtual Graphics. *Computer Graphics* (SIGGRAPH 88 Proceedings), volume 22, pages 247-253, 1988.

The Clipmap: A Virtual Mipmap

Christopher C. Tanner, Christopher J. Migdal, and Michael T. Jones
Silicon Graphics Computer Systems

ABSTRACT

We describe the *clipmap*, a dynamic texture representation that efficiently caches textures of arbitrarily large size in a finite amount of physical memory for rendering at real-time rates. Further, we describe a software system for managing clipmaps that supports integration into demanding real-time applications. We show the scale and robustness of this integrated hardware/software architecture by reviewing an application virtualizing a 170 gigabyte texture at 60 Hertz. Finally, we suggest ways that other rendering systems may exploit the concepts underlying clipmaps to solve related problems.

CR Categories and Subject Descriptors: I.3.1 [Computer Graphics]: Hardware Architecture—Graphics Processors; I.3.3 [Computer Graphics]: Picture/Image Generation—Display Algorithms; I.3.4 [Computer Graphics]: Graphics Utilities—Graphics Packages; I.3.7 [Computer Graphics]: Three-Dimensional Graphics and Realism—Color, shading, shadowing, and texture.

Additional Keywords: clipmap, mipmap, texture, image exploitation, terrain visualization, load management, visual simulation.

1 INTRODUCTION

Textures add important visual information to graphical applications. Their scope, fidelity, and presentation directly affects the level of realism and immersion achievable for a given object or environment. From being able to discern each brush stroke in every mural in a virtual Vatican to counting tire tracks in the sand halfway around a simulated globe, the amount of visual information applications require is growing without bound. It is this enormous visual dynamic range that illuminates the limitations of current texture representations and defines our problem space.

Specifically, our representation addresses all of the issues relevant to the real-time rendering of the earth's surface as a single high resolution texture. Representing the earth with one meter texels requires a 40 million by 20 million texel texture and an overall square, power of two mipmap size of approximately 11 petabytes.

We identified six goals for an effective solution to this problem. First, the new texture system must support full speed rendering using a small subset of an arbitrarily large texture. Second, it must be possible to rapidly update this subset simultaneously with real-time rendering. Third, the texture technique must not force subdivision or other constraints onto geometric scene components. Fourth, load control must be robust and automatic to avoid distracting visual discontinuities under overload. Fifth, it must be possible for the representation to be seamlessly integrated into existing applications. Finally, the incremental implementation cost should be small relative to existing hardware.

Author Contacts: {cct|migdal|mtj}@sgi.com

Our initial clipmap implementation addresses these goals through a combination of low-level hardware and higher-level system level software. The hardware provides real-time rendering capabilities based on the clipmap representation, while the software manages the representation and interfaces with applications. This paper describes our clipmap implementation and reviews how well it meets the goals and challenges already outlined: §2 presents past approaches to managing large texture images, §3 describes exactly what a clipmap is and what it achieves, §4 explains how the clipmap is updated and addresses memory bandwidth issues, §5 shows how the clipmap representation is a modification of mipmap rendering, §6 describes how clipmaps are generalized to overcome hardware resource and precision limits, §7 discusses the higher-level software used to update clipmaps, manage system load, and deal with data on disk, §8 examines several applications of the system, and finally, §9 considers the success of our first implementation and suggests directions for further research.

2 PREVIOUS APPROACHES

The common method for dealing with large textures requires subdividing a huge texture image into small tiles of sizes directly supportable by typical graphics hardware. This approach provides good paging granularity for the system both from disk to main memory and from main memory to texture memory. In practice, however, this approach has several drawbacks. First, geometric primitives must not straddle texture-tile boundaries, forcing unwanted geometric subdivision. Second, texture border support is required for each level of each tile if correct sampling is to be performed at tile boundaries. Lastly, the level of detail mechanisms take place at the granularity of the tiles themselves—producing disconcerting visual pops of whole texture/geometry tiles. These limitations limit visual effectiveness and add an extra level of complexity to geometric modeling, morphing, and LOD definition—all of which must take the texture tile boundaries into account.

The higher-quality system of Sanz-Pastor and Barcena [4] blends multiple active textures of differing resolutions. Each of these levels roams based on its dynamic relationship to the eyepoint; polygons slide from one texture to another with textures closer to the eyepoint at higher-resolution. The drawback of such a system is that geometry is still tied directly to one of these textures so texture LOD decisions are made at the per-polygon rather than per-pixel level. Developers must also obey a complex algorithm to subdivide geometry based on the boundaries between the different textures of different resolutions. Further, texture LOD choices made by the algorithm are based on coarse eyepoint range rather than the fine display space projection of texel area.

An advanced solution outlined by Cosman [1] offers per-pixel LOD selection in a static multiresolution environment. Although similar to our clipmap approach in some ways, Cosman does not address look-ahead caching, load control, or the virtualization of the algorithm beyond hardware limits.

Although these approaches have solved large scale problems, they do not appear generalizable to fully address all six goals of §1.

3 THE CLIPMAP REPRESENTATION

3.1 Observations about Mipmaps

The following review summarizes the key mipmap concepts on

which clipmaps are based. A *mipmap* as defined by Williams [6] is a collection of correlated images of increasingly reduced resolution arranged, in spirit, as a resolution pyramid. Starting with level 0, the largest and finest level, each lower level represents the image using half as many texels in each dimension: 1D = 1/2, 2D = 1/4, and 3D = 1/8 the texels. The 2D case is illustrated in Figure 1.

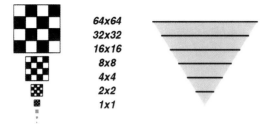

Figure 1: Mipmap Image Pyramid and Side-View Diagram

When rendering with a mipmap, pixels are projected into mipmap space using texture coordinates, underlying geometric positions, geometric transformations, and texture transformations to define the projection. Each rendered pixel is derived from one or more texel samples taken from one or more levels of the mipmap hierarchy. In particular, the samples chosen are taken from the immediate neighborhood of the mipmap level where the display's pixel-to-texel mapping is closest to a 1:1 mapping, a level dictated in part by display resolution. The texels are then filtered to produce a single value for further processing.

Given this simple overview of mipmap processing, we now ask which texels within a mipmap might be accessed during the rendering of an image. Clearly there can be many variations in the factors that control pixel to display projection, such as differing triangle locations within a large database, so it may seem that all of the texels are potentially used if the universe of possible geometry is taken into consideration. Refer to Figure 2 for an illustration of the relationship between eyepoint position and texel access.

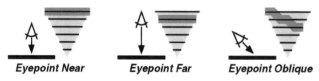

Figure 2: Texel Access within a Mipmap

Mipmaps are potentially fully accessed during rendering when their size in texels is less than twice the size of the maximum display extent in pixels. This observation derives from interactions between mipmap sample selection logic and finite display resolution. For example, when rendering a 32768^2 texel mipmap to a 1024^2 pixel display, the mipmap sample-selection logic will choose the texels that are closest to having a 1:1 mapping to pixel area. Thus it will use at most 1024^2 texels from a level before accessing an adjacent level. Implementations that blend samples from adjacent levels (as in *trilinear filtering*) potentially access twice as many texels in each dimension. For an example of this refer to the center diagram in Figure 2, where texels from level 1 are being fully used. If the eyepoint were just slightly closer, then samples would be blended from both level 0 and level 1, but 1024^2 texels from level 1 would still be accessible. The corresponding texels from level 0 needed to blend with these 1024^2 level 1 texels are distributed over a 2048^2 texel extent in level 0.

When the indexing arithmetic for very large mimpaps is analyzed, it becomes clear that the majority of the mipmap pyramid will not be used in the rendering of a single image no matter what geometry is rendered. The basis of our system is this realization that eyepoint and display resolution control access into the mip-

map and that in the case of the very large textures we are concerned with, only a minute fraction of the texels in the mipmap are accessible. We can build hardware to exploit this fact by rendering from the minimal subset of the mipmap needed for each frame—a structure we term a clipmap.

3.2 The Anatomy of a Clipmap

A *clipmap* is an updatable representation of a partial mipmap, in which each level has been clipped to a specified maximum size. This parameterization results in an obelisk shape for clipmaps as opposed to the pyramid of mipmaps. It also defines the size of the texture memory cache needed to fully represent the texture hierarchy.

3.2.1 Defining Clipmap Region with ClipSize

ClipSize represents the limit, specified in texels, of texture cache extent for any single level of a clipmap texture. Each level of a normal mipmap is clipped to ClipSize if it would have been larger than ClipSize, as shown in Figure 3. All levels retain the logical size and render-time accessing arithmetic of the corresponding level of a full mipmap.

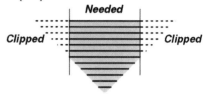

Figure 3: Clipmap Region within a Mipmap

Based on this mipmap subset representation, we further define the *Clipmap Stack* to be the set of levels that have been clipped from full mipmap-size by the limit imposed by ClipSize. These levels are not fully resident within the clipmap; only a ClipSize^2 subset is cached. These levels are the topmost levels in Figure 4. Below the Clipmap Stack is the *Clipmap Pyramid,* defined as the set of levels of sizes not greater than the ClipSize limit. These levels are completely contained in texture memory and are identical to the corresponding portions of a full mipmap.

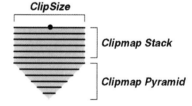

Figure 4: Clipmap Stack and Pyramid Levels

3.2.2 Defining Clipmap Contents with ClipCenter

Given the notion of clipping a mipmap to fit in a subset clipmap cache, we specify the data present in this cache by specifying a ClipCenter for each stack level. A *ClipCenter* is an arbitrary texture space coordinate that defines the center of a cached layer. By defining ClipSize and ClipCenter for each level, we precisely select the texture region being cached by the ClipStack levels of our representation.

One implementation is to specify the ClipCenter for stack level 0 and derive the ClipCenter of lower levels by shifting the center based on depth. This forces each level to be centered along a line from the level 0 center to the clipmap apex. This center is the dot indicated at the top of Figure 4. This type of centering yields concentric rings of resolution surrounding the level 0 ClipCenter. The center location may be placed anywhere in full mipmap space. The image in Figure 5 shows an orthogonal view of a polygon (viewed from the "Eyepoint Near" position of Figure 2) that has been textured with a clipmap having a very small ClipSize in order to demonstrate the concentric rings of texture resolution.

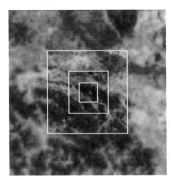

Figure 5: Rings of Texture Resolution

When the cache is insufficient, due either to an overly small ClipSize or a poor choice of ClipCenter, the best available lower resolution data from lower in the clipmap stack or pyramid is used. This "clip texture accesses to best available data" nature is a second reason why we chose the name clipmap for this approach.

In normal use, however, the ClipSize is set to equal or exceed the display size, in which case the rings of resolution shown in Figure 5 are large enough that, with a properly chosen ClipCenter, these rings form a superset of the needed precision. Thus, the subset nature of clipmaps does not limit the texture sample logic—every texel addressed is present in the clipped mipmap and the resulting image will be pixel-exact with one drawn using the full mipmap, meeting the first of the goals outlined for this texture system.

3.2.3 Invalid Border for Parallel Update

The previous subsection presents rendering from a Clipmap Stack level as a static subset of the complete mipmap level; it does not address the need to pre-page data needed for future frames concurrently with rendering. In order to provide storage for paged data and for load control, we introduce another parameter, the *Invalid-Border*, defined as a border of texels existing within each stack level that is InvalidBorder texels wide. Texels within the Invalid-Border are inactive and are not accessed by the texel-sample indexing logic. They provide a destination region into which higher-level software prefetches data. The size of the active portion of a clip map is simply ClipSize minus twice the InvalidBorder, known as the *EffectiveSize* of each stack level. The relationship and position of the InvalidBorder and EffectiveSize are illustrated in Figure 6.

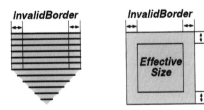

Figure 6: Clipmap with InvalidBorder and EffectiveSize

3.2.4 TextureOffset for Efficient Update

The final fundamental parameter of our low-level clipmap representation is the *TextureOffset*, the starting address used by the texture address generator to locate the logical center of a clipmap's EffectiveSize within the ClipSize^2 memory region allocated for each Clipmap Stack level. The addressing logic uses the Texture-Offset and modular addressing to roam efficiently through the level's ClipSize^2 memory region as discussed in detail in §4, where

the process of clipmap updating and rendering is presented. This offset is specified per level and affects addressing for the level exactly as a texture matrix translation with a wrap-style texture clamp mode.

3.3 Clipmap Storage Efficiency

Consider a 16 level 32768^2 clipmap to be rendered on a 1024^2 display. We begin our analysis with pixel-exact rendering. Given the display size, we know that the upper bound on texture usage from a single level is 2048^2, so we set the ClipSize to 2048. There will be four clipped levels forming our Clipmap Stack and 12 levels in the Clipmap Pyramid. The storage required for this is 2048^2 texels * 4 levels + 4/3 * 2048^2 texels for the pyramid = 42.7 MB at 2 bytes per texel. This perfect clipmap configuration requires only 42.7 MB of the full 2.8 GB present in the complete mipmap. A more typical configuration using a 1024 ClipSize will achieve attractive results using 1024^2*5 stack texels + 1024^2*4/3 pyramid texels = 12.7 MB. Finally, a 512 texel ClipSize yields reasonable results with 512^2*6 stack texels + 512^2*4/3 pyramid texels = 3.7 MB of storage.

In general, a 2^nx2^n clipmap with a ClipSize of 2^m requires only $4^m(n - m + 4/3) - 1/3$ texels of texture storage. For full mipmaps, the storage needed is $(4^{n+1} - 1)/3$ texels. Both of the equations must be scaled by the number of bytes per texel to compute physical memory use. Note that total mipmap storage is exponential in n where clipmap storage is linear, underscoring the practical ability of clipmaps to handle much larger textures than mipmaps.

Comparative storage use is tabulated in Table 1, where KB = 1024 Bytes, and 16-bit texels are used. The final column shows memory use for a 2^{26}x2^{26} image large enough to represent the earth at 1 meter per texel; the 34.7 MB clipmap requirement fits nicely into the texture memory of a modern high-performance graphics workstation, confirming the ability of clipmaps to address the problem identified in §1.

Type and Size	512^2	1024^2	4096^2	32768^2	67108864^2
Full Mipmap	682KB	2.7MB	42.7MB	2.7GB	10923TB
512^2 **Clipmap**	682KB	1.1MB	2.2MB	3.7MB	9.1MB
1024^2 **Clipmap**	682KB	2.7MB	6.7MB	12.7MB	34.7MB
2048^2 **Clipmap**	682KB	2.7MB	18.7MB	42.7MB	131.7MB

Table 1: Clipmap Storage Requirements

4 UPDATING CLIPMAPS

Clipmap caches are by intent just large enough to effectively cache the texels needed to render one view. It is therefore important to update the cache as the viewpoint changes, typically before each frame is rendered. This update is performed by considering the texture regions needed for each level as described in §3 and loading them into texture memory. Moreover, to take advantage of the significant frame-to-frame coherence in cache contents, we can reuse cached texels in subsequent frames. We define each level as an independently roaming 2D image cache that moves through the entire region of that level within the complete mipmap using toroidal addressing, a commonly used approach in image processing applications [5]. We then update each level incrementally by downloading the new data into the cache and letting this addressing scheme define the destination. The same logic is used when reading memory to render the texture. The four steps of this loading/addressing scheme are presented in Figure 7. The process begins with a 2D image centered in the cache as shown on the left. We then specify a new ClipCenter, in this case d texels above and to the right of the old center. Comparing the old and new image regions, note that the central texels are unchanged *(SAME)* in each, so only the top *(T)*, corner *(C)*, and right *(R)* border areas are updated, as indicated in the third diagram.

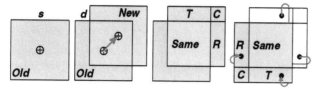

Figure 7: 2D Image Roam using Toroidal Addressing

Using toroidal addressing, new data at the top of the image is loaded at the bottom, data on the right is loaded at the left, and the upper right corner is loaded at the lower left. Implementation is easy: compute the virtual texel address by adding the ClipCenter to the texel address and then use the remainder modulo ClipSize as the physical address. The cache start address moves from $(s/2, s/2)$ to $(s/2+d, s/2+d)$, so the TextureOffset for this level is set to this new origin address, identifying the starting address of the cached image to the addressing unit.

Given that each stack level roams independently based on its center and assuming that we are centering all the levels based on the same ClipCenter, we can visualize the complete multi-level update process as shown in Figure 8.

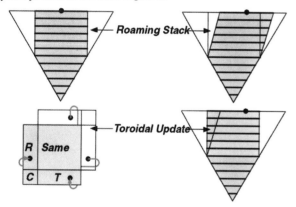

Figure 8: 2D Image Roam of Complete Stack

This side view of the toroidal indexing scheme shows how the entire set of stack levels appears to have moved when in fact all updates are performed in place as described previously. The overlap areas are unchanged and require no update. In practice, this area is relatively large so only minor paging at the edges is required to update a clipmap stack. Since lower levels are coarser resolutions as in normal mipmapping, the same movement of center point will result in only half as much movement of a lower level than the level above it, and less movement means less paging.

When movement of the TextureCenter is smaller than the InvalidBorder for a given level, then the update regions can be loaded while texture is being drawn with the previous center. This is true because the InvalidBorder guarantees those texels will not be used. This also allows large updates to be performed in an incremental manner across multiple frames before the ClipCenter is moved.

4.1 Update Bandwidth Considerations

In addition to rendering, implementations must also offer enough texture download bandwidth to meet the demands implied by Clipmap Stack depth, ClipSize, and the speed of eyepoint travel through texture space as defined by ClipCenter. An upper limit to cache update time is that time needed to replace all clipmap stack

levels. In the case of the 32768^2 clipmap with a 1024 StackSize that our implementation is designed to handle, reloading the cache levels requires 10MBytes of texture paging. Given memory-to-graphics rates of 270MBytes per second, a flush requires $1/27^{th}$ second. Fortunately, the cache need not be completely flushed due to the texel reuse and incremental update allowed by toroidal addressing. With this efficiency, the ClipCenter can be moved 1000 texels on the highest level map in this configuration in less than $1/60^{th}$ of a second. This corresponds to an eyepoint speed of 134,160 miles per hour when 1 meter texels are used, a rate that easily exceeds our update goals.

5 RENDERING WITH CLIPMAPS

Rendering with a clipmap is much the same as rendering with a mipmap. The only modifications to the normal mipmap rendering are slight changes to the level-of-detail selection algorithm and to the texture memory addressing system. However, it is important to note that building clipmapping support into low level hardware is crucial. With this in mind, here are the steps to sample texture for a given pixel using a clipmap representation:

1. Determine the S, T coordinates for the current pixel. This is done exactly as addressing an equivalent mipmap.

2. Calculate the level of detail based on normal mipmapping criteria. This calculation yields a floating-point LOD where the fractional part of the number represents blending between two LODs. If this LOD resides completely in the pyramidal portion of the clipmap then we simply proceed with addressing the appropriate LODs as a normal mipmap. If the finer LOD being blended resides in the Clipmap Stack and the coarser LOD resides in the pyramid, then we address the coarser LOD as a mipmap but continue on the clipmap path for the finer LOD addressing.

3. Calculate the finest LOD available given the texture coordinates established in Step 1. This calculation is done by comparing the texture coordinate to all of the texture regions described in §3. This calculation has to be done in case the texels are not present at the LOD requested. There are several hardware optimizations that can be performed to make this Finest LOD for a texture coordinate calculation tenable and efficient in hardware. For cost sensitive solutions, a restriction can be made where all levels must be centered concentrically, such that calculating a simple maximum distance from the TextureCenter to the texture coordinate generated can yield the finest available LOD based on the following:

   Sdist = roundUp(abs(Scenter – s))
   Tdist = roundUp(abs(Tcenter – t))
   MaxDist = max(Sdist, Tdist)
   FinestLODAvailable = roundUp(log2(MaxDist) – log2(ClipSize))

   The equation for FinestLODAvailable is adjusted to consider the InvalidBorder designed to prevent accessing texels that are in the process of being asynchronously updated. Having calculated the LODmip and LODAvailable, we simply use the coarser of the two. We emphasize that it is possible to configure a system and application where the LODAvailable never limits the LOD calculation. This is done by selecting a sufficiently large ClipSize and placing the ClipCenter appropriately.

4. Convert the s and t coordinates into level-specific and cache-specific coordinates. First, we split the calculation into two to account for the blending between two active LODs (fine and coarse).

   Sf = (s >> LODclip) – 0.5
   Tf = (t >> LODclip) – 0.5
   Sc = (s >> (LODclip + 1)) – 0.5
   Tc = (t >> (LODclip + 1)) – 0.5

Then, determine the offsets necessary to address the fine and coarse LOD given the data currently cached inside each level.

Sfoff = ClipCenter[LODclip].S – TextureSize[LODclip]/2
Tfoff = ClipCenter[LODclip].T – TextureSize[LODclip]/2
Scoff = ClipCenter[LODclip+1].S – TextureSize[LODclip]/2
Tcoff = ClipCenter[LODclip+1].T – TextureSize[LODclip]/2

Finally, determine the actual S, T address within the clipmap level cache for both the fine and coarse LODs by using the actual texture coordinate, the recently computed center offset, and the user specified TextureOffset. These addresses are interpreted using modular addressing consistent with the way that §4 describes cache updates based on TextureOffset.

Sclipfine = (Sf – Sfoff – TextureOffset[LODclip].S)% ClipSize
Tclipfine = (Tf – Tfoff – TextureOffset[LODclip].T)% ClipSize
Sclipcoarse = (Sc – Scoff – TextureOffset[LODclip+1].S)% ClipSize
Tclipcoarse = (Tc – Tcoff – TextureOffset[LODclip+1].T)% ClipSize

5. Use the two sets of texture coordinates (fine and coarse) to generate a filtered texture value for the pixel exactly as for a mipmap texture.

6 VIRTUAL CLIPMAPS

Having defined the low-level architecture of the clipmap representation, we consider a key implementation issue—the numerical range and precision required throughout the texture system. This issue is central because it controls cost and complexity in an implementation, factors that we seek to minimize as goals of our development. Previous mipmap implementations have supported texture sizes as large as 2^8 to 2^{12} in each dimension, far less than the 2^{26} needed by a 1 meter per texel whole earth texture. Thus, having first solved the storage problem for huge texture images, we must now find an affordable way to address their compact representation.

The hardware environment of our first implementation [3] dictated that directly enlarging the numerical range and precision throughout the system to match the needs of 27-level and larger clipmaps was not practical. The impact would have included bus widths, gate counts, circuit complexity, logic delays, and packaging considerations; full-performance rendering would have been impossible. These issues, along with the practical matter of schedule, encouraged us to solve the 2^{26} clipmap problem within the 2^{15} precision supported in hardware.

Our approach to virtualizing clipmaps is based on the observation that while the polygons comprising a scene extend from the eyepoint to the horizon, each individual polygon only subtends a portion of this range. Thus, while a scene may need the full 27-level clipmap for proper texturing, individual polygons can be properly rendered with the 16-level hardware support so long as two conditions are met: the texture extent across each polygon fits within the hardware limit, and an appropriate adjustment is made as polygons are rendered to select the proper 16 levels from the full 27 level virtual clipmap.

We implement virtual clipmaps by adding two extensions to the clipmap system. First, we provide a fixed offset that is added to all texture addresses. This value is used to virtually locate a physical clipmap stack within a taller virtual clipmap stack, in essence making one of the virtual stack levels appear to be the top level to the hardware. Second, we add a scale and bias step to texture coordinate processing. This operation is equivalent to the memory address offset but modifies texture coordinates rather than texel memory addresses. In concert, these extensions provide address precision accurate to the limit of either user specification or coordinate transformation. With a 32-bit internal implementation, this is sufficient to represent the entire earth at 1 centimeter per texel resolution, which exceeds our stated goal.

This virtualization requires that the low-level clipmap algorithm be extended to address a sub-clipmap out of an arbitrary clipmap

when the depth exceeds the directly supported precision. Given the stack and pyramid structure defined in a clipmap, we observe three possible types of addressing that must be supported as illustrated in Figure 9.

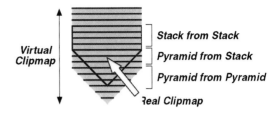

Figure 9: Virtual Addressing in Stack and Pyramid Levels

1. Address a stack level as a stack level. No address modifications necessary other than the upstream scale and bias.

2. Address a stack level as a pyramid level. Need to provide an offset into the level to get to the correct data. This can be done by starting from the center texel, and offsetting backwards to find the origin texel of the sub-level based on desired level size.

3. Address a pyramid level as a pyramid level. This can be implemented by knowing the actual level size, finding the center texel, and offsetting backwards to find the origin texel of the sub-level based on desired level size.

These three cases define the additional addressing hardware used to switch between the normal stack address processing (as described in §5), sub-addressing as defined above for cases 2 and 3, and normal mipmap addressing. With these addressing extensions, software can select sub-clipmaps and implement texture coordinate scale and bias.

Why add this additional complexity to an otherwise simple low-level implementation? Because there is seemingly no limit to desired texture size. While the size of directly supported clipmaps will likely grow in future implementations, so will the demand for larger textures. Since each extra level directly supported by hardware forces expensive precision-related system costs onto implementations, we believe that virtual clipmap support will always be useful.

7 DYNAMIC CLIPMAP MANAGEMENT

Having described the clipmap representation, the architecture, and the refinements needed to virtualize a clipmap beyond implementation limits, we now consider the remaining issue—keeping the clipmap updated as the eyepoint moves through texture space. This is a significant part of any implementation, since the tremendous efficiency of the clipmap representation reduces only the number of texels resident in texture memory at any one time, not the total number of texels in the mipmap. A series of images rendered interactively may visit the entire extent of the texture image over the course of time; an image which for a one meter per texel earth is an intimidating 10,923 TBytes of data.

Our goals for dynamic clipmap management are these: effective use of system memory as a second-level cache to buffer disk reads, efficient management of multiple disk drives of differing speeds and latencies as the primary source for texture images, automated load management of the clipmap update process to avoid distracting visual artifacts in cases of system bandwidth overload, support for high resolution inset areas (which implies a sparse tile cache on disk), and finally, complete integration of this higher-level clipmap support into software tools in order to provide developers the sense that clipmaps are as complete, automatic, and easy to use as standard mipmaps.

7.1 Main Memory as Second-Level Cache

To use main memory as a second level cache we must optimize throughput on two different paths: we need to optimize throughput from disk devices to memory and we need to optimize throughput from memory to the underlying hardware clipmap cache. In order to optimize utilization of system resources we use separate threads to manage all aspects of data flow. We need at least one process scheduling data flow, one process moving data from disk to memory, and one process incrementally feeding clipmap updates to the graphics subsystem. In the context of our high-level graphics software toolkit, IRIS Performer [2], this means that scheduling is done by the software rendering pipeline in the Cull process, downloading of data to the graphics pipeline is done in the Draw process, and a new lightweight asynchronous disk reading process is created to manage file system activities.

The second level cache represents each level of the mipmap using an array of tiles. These tiles must be large enough to enable maximum throughput from disk, but small enough to keep overall paging latency low. We use sizes between 128^2 and 1024^2 depending on disk configurations. For this second level cache to operate as a real-time look-ahead cache, we load into parts of the cache that are not currently needed by the underlying hardware. Thus each cache level contains at least enough tiles to completely hold the underlying clipmap level that is currently resident while prefetching border tiles. With a ClipSize of 1024 and a tile size of 256^2, the cache must be configured to be at least 6 by 6 tiles or 1536 by 1536 texels, as shown in Figure 10.

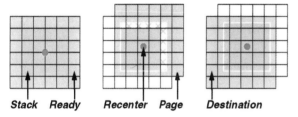

Stack   Ready   Recenter   Page   Destination

Figure 10: Tiled Main-Memory Image Cache

Due to memory alignment issues, low-level texture updates must be implemented as individual downloads based on tile boundaries. In Figure 10, the left drawing shows a minimal cache for one stack level. This cache has already copied the texels in the ClipSize^2 central area down to the clipmap in texture memory. The cache has also pre-fetched the minimal single-tile border of image tiles, the "ready" area. The center illustration indicates that the ClipCenter (the dot) has been moved up and to the right by half of a tile (128 texels in this case). What actions are implied by this recentering action? First, the clipmap must be updated. This is done by accessing the border tiles above and to the right of the existing stack data. The white square indicates the new clipmap area, and the nine crosshatched rectangles are the texture downloads required to update the hardware clipmap stack for this level. Multiple downloads are performed because it is infeasible to perform real-time memory to memory copies to realign memory when overall texture load rates are 270 MB per second. Once the clipmap layer is updated, the main memory tile-cache must be roamed up and to the right, by scheduling disk reads to retrieve the newly uncovered tiles, indicated as the "page" area in the diagram. While the new tiles are logically up and to the right, we store them at the bottom and the left, using the same toroidal addressing used in the clipmap itself—as in that case, unchanged data is never updated.

This main memory clipmap cache is very much a larger tiled version of the underlying hardware representation. It has a section of static pyramid levels and a section of cached roaming stack levels. The biggest difference being that an external tile border is used for paging in main memory and an internal InvalidBorder-sized region

serves the same purpose within the clipmap. Each cache roams through its level of the full mipmap texture independently based on the level's ClipCenter. Each cache level performs look-ahead paging, requesting disk reads for image tiles that are likely to be loaded into the clipmap in the near future. Each level is responsible for managing the corresponding level of the underlying hardware clipmap implementation: recentering the underlying hardware level and incrementally downloading the relevant texture data from its tiled cache.

To configure the main memory cache system, developers specify information for each clipmap level. For stack levels, they provide image cache configurations that describe how to load tiles (such as an *sprintf* format-string to convert tile row and column indices into a full filesystem path name for each level), how big the cache should be, how big the underlying hardware clipmap level is, and other basic information. For pyramid levels, they simply provide the static image. Global clipmap data is also provided, such as the ClipSize for the clipmap, the storage format of the texels, and parameterization for load control.

7.2 Cache Centering Algorithms

In addition to the low and high level representations we have defined so far, there is still an important issue we have not yet discussed: how to decide which part of the image should be cached. We encourage developers to set the center directly in both the lower and higher-level software since the optimal place to center the cache is inherently application dependent. Some applications use narrow fields of view and thus look at data in the distance, which is where the ClipCenter should be located. Other applications, such as head-tracked ground-based virtual reality applications, want to ensure that quick panning will not cause the clipmap cache to be exceeded, arguing for placing the ClipCenter at the viewer's virtual foot position. Our higher-level software provides utilities to automatically set the clipmap ClipCenter based on a variety of simple viewpoint projections and viewing frustum related intersection calculations as a convenience in those cases where default processing is appropriate.

7.3 Managing Filesystem Paging

The low-level clipmap representation provides fully deterministic performance because it is updated with whatever texels are required before rendering begins. Unfortunately, this is not true of the second-level cache in main memory due to the vagaries of filesystem access in terms of both bandwidth and latency. Compared to memory-to-graphics throughput of 200-450 MBytes/second, individual disk bandwidths of 3-15 MBytes per second are very slow. This could lead to a situation where speedy eyepoint motion exceeds the pace of second-level tile paging, causing the Effective-Size cache region to "stall" at the edge of a cache level awaiting data from disk before being recentered. We must anticipate this problem since we do not limit eyepoint speed, but we can avoid visual distraction should it occur.

The important realization is that the requested data is always present in the clipmap, albeit at a coarser resolution than desired, since the top-most of the pyramid levels in the clipmap caches the entire image. We use the MaxTextureLOD feature already present in the hardware to disable render access to a hardware stack level whenever updating a level requires unavailable data. The clipmap software system attempts to catch up to outstanding paging requests, and will re-enable a level by changing the MaxTexture-LOD as soon as the main memory texture tile cache is up to date. Thus MaxTextureLOD converts the stack levels into a resolution bellows, causing the clipmap to always use the best available data without ever waiting for tardy data. This makes it possible for clipmaps to allow arbitrary rates of eyepoint motion no matter what filesystem configuration is used. In underpowered systems it is perfectly acceptable if the texture becomes slightly blurry when the ClipCenter is moved through the data faster than the tiles can be read. Recovery from this overload condition is automatic once the data is available; the system downloads the level and tells the hardware to incrementally fade that level back in by slowly changing the MaxTextureLOD over an interval of several frames.

To control latency in paging-limited cases, we provide a lightweight process to optimize the contents of the disk read queues. Without this the read queue could grow without bound when cache levels make requests that the filesystem cannot service, causing the system to get ever further behind. The queue manager process orders tile read requests by priorities which are determined based on the stack level issuing the request (with higher priorities for coarser data) and on the estimated time until a tile will be needed. The priorities of outstanding requests are asynchronously updated by the cache software managing each level every frame and the read manager thread sorts the disk read queue based on these changing priorities, removing entries that are no longer relevant. This priority sort limits the read queue size and minimizes latency of read requests for more important tiles, thus ensuring that tiles needed to update coarser levels are loaded and used sooner.

7.4 Managing Stack Level Updates

We now address load management issues in paging data from main memory to texture hardware. Since memory-to-graphics bandwidth is at a premium in immediate-mode graphics systems, it is important to understand and control its expenditure. A typical application might devote 75% of the throughput for sending geometric information to the graphics subsystem, leaving 25% of the 16.67ms (60 Hz) frame time for incremental texture paging, including both mipmaps and clipmaps. The time allocated for clipmap updates may be less than the time needed to fully update a clipmap because the center is moved a great distance requiring many texels to be updated or because the time allowed for updates is so little that even the smallest update may not be performed. Since unwavering 60 Hz update rates are a fundamental goal of our system, we must plan for and avoid these situations.

To control clipmap update duration we precisely estimate the time required to perform the downloads for a given frame. A table of the measured time for texture downloads of each size that could potentially be performed based on clipmap and system configuration is generated at system start-up. Then, as we schedule downloads, we start at the lowest (coarsest) cache level and work our way up the cache levels one by one. The total projected time is accumulated and updates are terminated when insufficient time remains to load a complete level. Coarse LODs are updated first, since they are both the most important and require the least bandwidth. Finer levels are disabled using MaxTextureLOD if there is insufficient time for the required updates.

We also expose the MaxTextureLOD parameter for explicit coarse-grain adjustments to required download bandwidth. Since each higher stack level requires four times the paging of the next lower one, adjustment of maximum LOD has a powerful ability to reduce overall paging time. The visual effect of coarsening the MaxTextureLOD by one level is to remove the innermost of the concentric rings of texture precision. Since this has a visually discernible effect, it must be gradually done over a few tens of frames by fractionally changing the MaxTextureLOD until an entire stack level is no longer in use, after which rendering and paging are disabled for that level. This method is illustrated in the right-most column of Figure 11, where the inner resolution ring has been removed by decreasing the MaxTextureLOD.

For fine-grain control of paging bandwidth, we use the Invalid-Border control as described in §3.2.3 to reduce the area of texels

that must be updated in each stack level. Our implementation allows the InvalidBorder to be adjusted on a per-frame basis with little overhead. Increasing the InvalidBorder reduces the EffectiveArea, reducing the radius of each concentric band of precision. This is illustrated at the bottom row of Figure 11, where rendering with a larger InvalidBorder is seen to scale the Stack Levels closer to the ClipCenter. Only the stack levels are modified by the InvalidBorder, as indicated by the outer region in the left diagram.

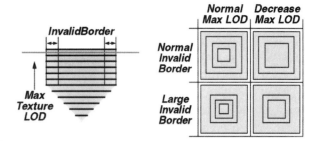

Figure 11: Visual Effect of Load Control

The load control mechanisms presented here have proven to be effective, allowing existing applications to integrate clipmaps virtualizing terabytes of filesystem backing store, maintaining constant 60 Hz real-time rendering rates irrespective of disk speeds and latencies.

7.5 High-Resolution Insets

High-resolution insets are regions of extra-high texture resolution embedded into a larger, lower-resolution texture image. They are important since applications often have areas within their database where higher-fidelity is needed. An example occurs in commercial flight simulators, where texture resolution at airports must be very high to support taxi, approach, and departure training, while the terrain areas traversed in flight between airports require more moderate texture resolution.

Our implementation supports insets as a side effect of the integrated filesystem paging load control that constantly sorts tile read requests. To implement insets, developers specify sparse tile arrays in the filesystem for each clip level. Sparse tile arrays are those where some or nearly all tiles are undefined, resulting in "islands" of resolution in various portions of an otherwise empty tile array (near airports, for the example above). In this situation the higher-level software uses the inset data when it can—skipping the empty regions automatically using the TextureMaxLOD load-control mechanism as it discovers that nonexistent tiles are perpetually late in arriving from the filesystem. The load control algorithm naturally falls back on coarser LODs when inset level data is not available.

To allow insets to blend in smoothly, tiles containing the inset texels must be surrounded by a border at least ClipSize texels wide using data magnified from the next lower level in a recursive manner, a requirement easily met by automatic database construction tools. This restriction exists because the decision to enable or disable a clipmap level is made for the level in its entirety using TextureMaxLOD, and therefore partially valid cache levels—partly in the inset region and partly outside of it—would normally be disabled. Providing this border ensures that the load-management algorithm will enable the entire level when any pixel of the inset is addressed.

8 IMPLEMENTATION RESULTS

We have implemented the clipmap rendering system described here. The implementation consists of low-level support for real and virtual clipmaps within the InfiniteReality [3] graphics subsystem;

special OpenGL clipmap control and virtualization extensions; and support within the IRIS Performer [2] real-time graphics software toolkit for clipmap virtualization, second-level tile caches, tile paging from the filesystem, and for automatic load-management controls as described above.

In working with the system, developers find the results of using the clipmap approach to be excellent. Real-time graphics applications can now use textures of any desired precision at full speed—examples include planet-wide textures from satellite data, country and continent scale visual simulation applications with centimeter scale insets, architectural walkthrough applications showing murals with minute brush strokes visible at close inspection, and numerous advanced uses in government.

The image in Figure 12 shows an overhead view of a 8192^2 texture image of the Moffet Field Naval Air Station in Mountain View, California rendered onto a single polygon. The colored markers are diagnostic annotations indicating the extent of each clipmap level. The EffectiveArea has been significantly reduced by enlarging the InvalidBorder to make these concentric bands of precision easily visible.

Figure 12: Concentric Resolution Bands

The image in Figure 13 shows a very small portion of a 25m per texel clipmap of the entire United States—the area shown here is the southern half of the Yosemite National Park. That our approach makes this single 170 GByte texture displayable at 60 Hertz with an approximately 16 MByte clipmap cache is impressive; equally so is the fact that the application being used need not know about clipmaps—all clipmap definition, updating, load-management and default ClipCenter selection happens automatically within IRIS Performer.

9 CONCLUSIONS

We have developed a new texture representation—the *clipmap*—a look-ahead cache configured to exploit insights about mipmap rendering, spatial coherence, and object to texture space coordinate mappings. This representation is simply parameterized and can be implemented in hardware via small modifications to existing mipmap rendering designs. It has been implemented in a system featuring a fast system-to-graphics interface allowing real-time update of clipmap caches. This system renders high quality images in real-time from very large textures using relatively little texture memory. The hardware supports virtualization for textures larger than it can address directly. This approach is not only important for representing textures of arbitrary scale. Equally important is that it also liberates geometric modeling and level of detail decisions from texture management concerns.

The guiding insights about mipmap utilization that made the

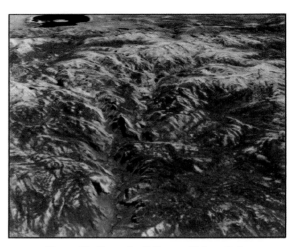

Figure 13: Yosemite Valley and Mono Lake

clipmap solution possible can be applied to related problems in computer graphics. Display resolution provides an upper bound to the amount of data needed in any rendering. It seems possible to develop a system that stages geometric level-of-detail information for large databases similarly to the way clipmaps stage image data. If an adaptive rendering algorithm were defined to create continuous tessellations from partially specified geometric levels of detail, then the same look ahead cache notions could be used to stage geometry. At a system level, this approach has predetermined throughputs and bandwidths that can be established to ensure both high fidelity and robust real-time behavior. In this way, the overall data flow of large systems can be easily sized and tuned for a wide range of applications.

Since the original development of clipmaps and their hardware and software implementations, we have explored several extensions including 3D clipmaps, texture download optimizations, and new inter-level texture blend modes. This work leads us to believe that there is considerably more to be discovered. We have seen realism in real-time visual simulation revolutionized in the wake of the introduction of clipmaps and we eagerly anticipate new ways in which clipmaps can have this effect in other application areas.

Acknowledgments

We would like to recognize Jim Foran for his original idea, Don Hatch and Tom McReynolds of IRIS Performer, Mark Peercy of OpenGL and the technical marketing team for their contribution.

References

[1] Cosman, Michael. Global Terrain Texture: Lowering the Cost. In Eric G. Monroe, editor, *Proceedings of 1994 IMAGE VII Conference*, pages 53-64. The IMAGE Society, 1994.

[2] Rohlf, John and James Helman. IRIS Performer: A High Performance Multiprocessing Toolkit for Real-Time 3D Graphics. In Andrew Glassner, editor, *SIGGRAPH 94 Conference Proceedings*. Annual Conference Series, pages 381-394. ACM SIGGRAPH, Addison Wesley, July 1994. ISBN 0-89791-667-0.

[3] Montrym, John S, Daniel R Baum, David L Dignam and Christopher J Migdal. InfiniteReality: A Real-Time Graphics System. In Turner Whitted, editor, *SIGGRAPH 97 Conference Proceedings*. Annual Conference Series, pages 293-301. ACM SIGGRAPH, Addison Wesley, August 1997. ISBN 0-89791-896-7.

[4] Sanz-Pastor, Nacho and Luis Barcena. Computer Arts & Development, Madrid, Spain. Private communication.

[5] Walker, Chris, Nancy Cam, Jon Brandt and Phil Keslin. Image Vision Library 3.0 Programming Guide. Silicon Graphics Computer Systems, 1996.

[6] Williams, Lance. Pyramidal Parametrics. In Peter Tanner, editor, *Computer Graphics (SIGGRAPH 83 Conference Proceedings)*, volume 17, pages 1-11. ACM SIGGRAPH, July 1983. ISBN 0-89791-109-1.

A Shading Language on Graphics Hardware:
The PixelFlow Shading System

Marc Olano[†]   Anselmo Lastra[‡]

University of North Carolina at Chapel Hill

Abstract

Over the years, there have been two main branches of computer graphics image-synthesis research; one focused on interactivity, the other on image quality. Procedural shading is a powerful tool, commonly used for creating high-quality images and production animation. A key aspect of most procedural shading is the use of a shading language, which allows a high-level description of the color and shading of each surface. However, shading languages have been beyond the capabilities of the interactive graphics hardware community. We have created a parallel graphics multi-computer, PixelFlow, that can render images at 30 frames per second using a shading language. This is the first system to be able to support a shading language in real-time. In this paper, we describe some of the techniques that make this possible.

CR Categories and Subject Descriptors: D.3.2 [Language Classifications] Specialized Application Languages; I.3.1 [Computer Graphics] Hardware Architecture; I.3.3 [Computer Graphics] Picture/Image Generation; I.3.6 [Computer Graphics] Methodologies and Techniques; I.3.7 [Computer Graphics] Three-dimensional Graphics and Realism.

Additional Keywords: real-time image generation, procedural shading, shading language.

1 INTRODUCTION

We have created a SIMD graphics multicomputer, PixelFlow, which supports *procedural shading* using a shading language. Even a small (single chassis) PixelFlow system is capable of rendering scenes with procedural shading at 30 frames per second or more. Figure 1 shows several examples of shaders that were written in our shading language and rendered on PixelFlow.

In procedural shading, a user (someone other than a system designer) creates a short procedure, called a *shader*, to determine the final color for each point on a surface. The shader is responsible

[†] Now at Silicon Graphics, Inc., 2011 N. Shoreline Blvd., M/S #590, Mountain View, CA 94043 (email: olano@engr.sgi.com)

[‡] UNC Department of Computer Science, Sitterson Hall, CB #3175, Chapel Hill, NC 27599 (email: lastra@cs.unc.edu)

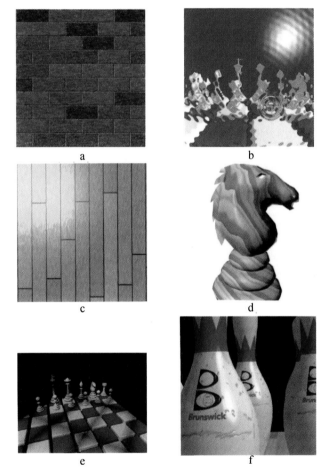

Figure 1: Some PixelFlow surface shaders. a) brick. b) mirror with animated ripple. c) wood planks. d) a volume-based wood. e) light shining through a paned window. f) view of a bowling scene.

for color variations across the surface and the interaction of light with the surface. Shaders can use an assortment of input *appearance parameters*, usually including the surface normal, texture coordinates, texture maps, light direction and colors.

Procedural shading is quite popular in the production industry where it is commonly used for rendering in feature films and commercials. The best known examples of this have been rendered using Pixar's PhotoRealistic RenderMan software [Upstill90]. A key aspect of RenderMan is its shading language. The shading language provides a high-level description of each procedural shader. Shaders written in the RenderMan shading language can be used by any compliant renderer, no matter what rendering method it uses.

There are several reasons to provide procedural shading instead of just image texturing on a real-time graphics system:

- It is easy to add noise and random variability to make a surface look more realistic.
- It can be easier to create a procedural shader for a complicated surface than to try to eliminate the distortions caused by wrapping a flat, scanned texture over the surface.
- It is easier to "tweak" a procedural shader than to rescan or repaint an image texture.
- It is often easier to create detail on an object using a procedural shader instead of modifying the object geometry.
- A procedurally shaded surface can change with time, distance, or viewing angle.

Usually procedural shading is associated with images that take a while to generate – from a few minutes to a day or so. Recently, graphics hardware reached the point where image texture mapping was not just possible, but common; now hardware is reaching the point where shading languages for interactive graphics are possible.

We have produced a shading language and shading language compiler for our high-end graphics machine, PixelFlow. This language is called *pfman* (*pf* for PixelFlow, *man* because it is similar to Pixar's RenderMan shading language). One of the great advantages of a shading language for procedural shading, particularly on a complex graphics engine, is that it effectively hides the implementation details from the shader-writer. The specifics of the graphics architecture are hidden in the shading language compiler, as are all of the tricks, optimizations, and special adaptations required by the machine. In this paper, we describe shading on PixelFlow, the pfman language, and the optimizations that were necessary to make it run in real-time.

Section 2 is a review of the relevant prior work. Section 3 covers features of the pfman shading language, paying particular attention to the ways that it differs from the RenderMan shading language. Section 4 describes our extensions to the OpenGL API [Neider93] to support procedural shading. Section 5 gives a brief overview of the PixelFlow hardware. Section 6 covers our implementation and the optimizations that are done by PixelFlow and the pfman compiler. Finally, Section 7 has some conclusions.

2 RELATED WORK

Early forms of programmable shading were accomplished by re-writing the shading code for the renderer (see, for example, [Max81]). Whitted and Weimer specifically allowed this in their testbed system [Whitted81]. Their *span buffers* are an implementation of a technique now called *deferred shading*, which we use on PixelFlow. In this technique, the parameters for shading are scan converted for a later shading pass. This allowed them to run multiple shaders on the same scene without having to re-render. Previous uses of deferred shading for interactive graphics systems include [Deering88] and [Ellsworth91].

More recently, easier access to procedural shading capabilities has been provided to the graphics programmer. Cook's *shade trees* [Cook84] were the base of most later shading works. He turned simple expressions, describing the shading at a point on the surface, into a parse tree form, which was interpreted. He introduced the name *appearance parameters* for the parameters that affect the shading calculations. He also proposed an orthogonal subdivision of types of programmable functions into displacement, surface shading, light, and atmosphere trees.

Perlin's image synthesizer extends the simple expressions in Cook's shade trees to a full language with control structures [Perlin85]. He also introduced the powerful Perlin noise function, which produces random numbers with a band-limited frequency

spectrum. This style of noise plays a major role in many procedural shaders.

The RenderMan shading language [Hanrahan90][Upstill90] further extends the work of Cook and Perlin. It suggests new procedures for transformations, image operations, and volume effects. The shading language is presented as a standard, making shaders portable to any conforming implementation.

In addition to the shading language, RenderMan also provides a geometry description library (the RenderMan API) and a geometric file format (called RIB). The reference implementation is Pixar's PhotoRealistic RenderMan based on the *REYES* rendering algorithm [Cook87], but other implementations now exist [Slusallek94][Gritz96].

The same application will run on all of these without change. RenderMan effectively hides the details of the implementation. Not only does this allow multiple implementations using completely different rendering algorithms, but it means the user writing the application and shaders doesn't need to know anything about the rendering algorithm being used. Knowledge of basic graphics concepts suffices.

Previous efforts to support user-written procedural shading on a real-time graphics system are much more limited. The evolution of graphics hardware is only just reaching the point where procedural shading is practical. The only implementation to date was Pixel-Planes 5, which supported a simple form of procedural shading [Rhoades92]. The language used by this system was quite low level. It used an assembly-like interpreted language with simple operations like copy, add, and multiply and a few more complex operations like a Perlin noise function. The hardware limitations of Pixel-Planes 5 limited the complexity of the shaders, and the low-level nature of the language limited its use.

Lastra et. al. [Lastra95] presents previous work on the PixelFlow shading implementation. It analyzes results from a PixelFlow simulator for hand-coded shaders and draws a number of conclusions about the hardware requirements for procedural shading. At the time of that paper, the shading language compiler was in its infancy, and we had not addressed many of the issues that make a real-time shading language possible. [Lastra95] is the foundation on which we built our shading language.

3 SHADING LANGUAGE

A surface shader produces a color for each point on a surface, taking into account the color variations of the surface itself and the lighting effects. As an example, we will show a shader for a brick wall. The wall is rendered as a single polygon with texture coordinates to parameterize the position on the surface.

The shader requires several additional parameters to describe the size, shape, and color of the brick. These are the width and height of the brick, the width of the mortar, and the colors of the mortar and brick (Figure 2). These parameters are used to wrap the texture coordinates into *brick coordinates* for each brick. These are (0,0) at the lower left corner of each brick, and are used

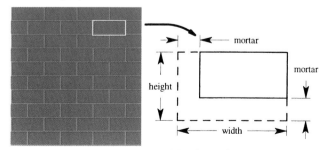

Figure 2: Example bricks and the size and shape parameters for the brick shader.

```
      // figure out which row of bricks this is (row is 8-bit integer)
fixed<8,0> row = tt / height;
      // offset even rows by half a row
if (row % 2 == 0) ss += width/2;
      // wrap texture coordinates to get "brick coordinates"
ss = ss % width;
tt = tt % height;
      // pick a color for the brick surface
float surface_color[3] = brick_color;
if (ss < mortar || tt < mortar)
    surface_color = mortar_color;
```

Figure 3: Code from a simple brick shader

to choose either the brick or mortar color. A portion of the brick shader is shown in Figure 3. The brick image in Figure 2 was generated with this shader.

One advantage of procedural shading is the ease with which shaders can be modified to produce the desired results. Figure 1a shows a more realistic brick that resulted from small modifications to the simple brick shader. It includes a simple procedurally-defined bump map to indent the mortar, high-frequency band-limited noise to simulate grains in the mortar and brick, patches of color variation within each brick to simulate swirls of color in the clay, and variations in color from brick to brick.

The remainder of this section covers some of the details of the pfman shading language and some of the differences between it and the RenderMan shading language. These differences are

1. the introduction of a fixed-point data type,
2. the use of arrays for points and vectors,
3. the introduction of transformation attributes,
4. the explicit listing of all shader parameters, and
5. the ability to link with external functions.

Of these changes, 1 and 2 allow us to use the faster and more efficient fixed-point math on our SIMD processing elements. The third covers a hole in the RenderMan standard that has since been fixed. The fourth was not necessary, but simplified the implementation of our compiler. Finally, item 5 is a result of our language being compiled instead of interpreted (in contrast to most off-line renderer implementations of RenderMan).

3.1 Types

As with the RenderMan shading language, variables may be declared to be either `uniform` or `varying`. A `varying` variable is one that might vary from pixel to pixel – texture coordinates for example. A `uniform` variable is one that will never vary from pixel to pixel. For the brick shader presented above, the width, height and color of the bricks and the thickness and color of the mortar are all uniform parameters. These control the appearance of the brick, and allow us to use the same shader for a variety of different styles of brick.

RenderMan has one representation for all numbers: floating-point. We also support floating-point (32-bit IEEE single precision format) because it is such a forgiving representation. This format has about 10^{-7} relative error for the entire range of numbers from 10^{-38} to 10^{38}. However, for some quantities used in shading this range is overkill (for colors, an 8 to 16 bit fixed-point representation can be sufficient [Hill97]). Worse, there are cases where floating-point has too much range but not enough precision. For example, a Mandelbrot fractal shader has an insatiable appetite for precision, but only over the range [−2,2] (Figure 4). In this case, it makes much more sense to use a fixed-point format instead of a 32 bit floating-point format: the floating-point format wastes one of the four bytes for an exponent that is hardly used. In general, it is easiest to prototype a shader using floating-point,

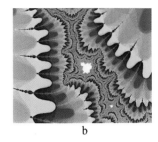

a   b

Figure 4: Fixed-point vs. floating-point comparison.
a) Mandelbrot set computed using floating-point.
b) Mandelbrot set computed using fixed-point

then change to fixed-point as necessary for memory usage, precision, and speed. Our fixed-point types may be signed or unsigned and have two parameters: the size in bits and an exponent, written `fixed<size,exponent>`. Fixed-point behaves like floating-point where the exponent is a compile-time constant. Small exponents can be interpreted as the number of fractional bits: a two byte integer is `fixed<16,0>`, while a two byte pure fraction is `fixed<16,16>`.

Like recent versions of the RenderMan shading language [Pixar97], pfman supports arrays of its basic types. However, where RenderMan uses separate types for points, vectors, normals, and colors, pfman uses arrays with *transformation attributes*. By making each point be an array of floating-point or fixed-point numbers, we can choose the appropriate representation independently for every point. A transformation attribute indicates how the point or vector should be transformed. For example, points use the regular transformation matrix, vectors use the same transformation but without translation, and normals use the adjoint or inverse without translation. We also include a transformation attribute for texture coordinates, which are transformed by the OpenGL texture transformation matrix.

3.2 Explicit Shader Parameters

RenderMan defines a set of *standard parameters* that are implicitly available for use by every surface shader. The surface shader does not need to declare these parameters and can use them as if they were global variables. In pfman, these parameters must be explicitly declared. This allows us to construct a transfer map (discussed later in Section 6) that contains only those parameters that are actually needed by the shader.

In retrospect, we should have done a static analysis of the shader function to decide which built-in parameters are used. This would have made pfman that much more like RenderMan, and consequently that much easier for new users already familiar with RenderMan.

3.3 External Linking

Compiling a pfman shader is a two-stage process. The pfman compiler produces C++ source code. This C++ code is then compiled by a C++ compiler to produce an object file for the shader. The function definitions and calls in pfman correspond directly to C++ function definitions and calls. Thus, unlike most RenderMan implementations, we support calling C++ functions from the shading language and vice versa. This facility is limited to functions using types that the shading language supports.

Compiling to C++ also provides other advantages. We ignore certain optimizations in the pfman compiler since the C++ compiler does them. One could also use the generated C++ code as a starting point for a hand-optimized shader. Such a hand-optimized shader would no longer be portable, and performing the optimization would require considerable understanding of the PixelFlow

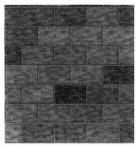 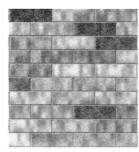

Figure 5: Instances of a brick surface shader.

internals normally hidden by the shading language. Not surprisingly, no one has done this yet.

4 API

The RenderMan standard [Upstill90] defines not only the shading language, but also a graphics application program interface (API). This is a library of graphics functions that the graphics application can call to describe the scene to the renderer. We elected to base our API on OpenGL [Neider93] instead of RenderMan. OpenGL is a popular API for interactive graphics applications, supported on a number of graphics hardware platforms. It provides about the same capabilities as the RenderMan API, with a similar collection of functions, but with more focus on interactive graphics. By using OpenGL as our base we can easily port applications written for other hardware.

We extended OpenGL to support procedural shading [Leech98]. We required that the procedural shading extensions have no impact on applications that do not use procedural shading. We also endeavored to make them fit the framework and philosophy of OpenGL. Our efforts to extend OpenGL should be readily usable by future real-time shading language systems.

Following the OpenGL standard, all of our extensions have the suffix EXT. We will follow that convention here to help clarify what is already part of OpenGL and what we added. OpenGL functions also include suffix letters (f, i, s, etc.) indicating the operand type. For brevity, we omit these in the text.

4.1 Loading Functions

Procedural surface shaders and lights are written as pfman functions. The new API call, glLoadExtensionCodeEXT, loads a shader. Currently, we do not support dynamic linking of surface or light functions, so this call just declares which shaders will be used. In the future, we do plan to dynamically load shaders.

4.2 Shading Parameters

On PixelFlow, the default shader implements the OpenGL shading model. Applications that do not "use" procedural shading use this default *OpenGL shader* without having to know any of the shading extensions to OpenGL.

We set the values for shading parameters using the glMaterial call, already used by OpenGL to set parameters for the built-in shading model. Parameters set in this fashion go into the OpenGL global state, where they may be used by any shader. Any shader can use the same parameters as the OpenGL shader simply by sharing the same parameter names, or it can define its own new parameter names.

OpenGL also has a handful of other, parameter-specific, calls. glColor can be set to change any of several possible color parameters, each of which can also be changed with glMaterial. We created similar parameter name equivalents for glNormal and glTexCoord. Other shaders may use these names to access

the normals set with glNormal and texture coordinates from glTexcoord.

4.3 Shader Instances

The RenderMan API allows some parameter values to be set when a shader function is chosen. Our equivalent is to allow certain *bound* parameter values. A shading function and its bound parameters together make a *shader instance* (or sometimes just *shader*) that describes a particular type of surface. Because the character of a shader is as much a product of its parameter settings as its code, we may create and use several instances of each shading function. For example, given the brick shading function of Figure 3, we can define instances for fat red bricks and thin yellow bricks by using different bound values for the width, height, and color of the bricks (Figure 5).

To set the bound parameter values for an instance, we use a glBoundMaterialEXT function. This is equivalent to glMaterial, but operates only on bound parameters.

We create a new instance with a glNewShaderEXT, glEndShaderEXT pair. This is similar to the way OpenGL defines other objects, for example display list definitions are bracketed by calls to glNewList and glEndList. glNewShaderEXT takes the shading function to use and returns a *shader ID* that can be used to identify the instance later. Between the glNewShaderEXT and glEndShaderEXT we use glShaderParameterBindingEXT, which takes a parameter ID and one of GL_MATERIAL_EXT or GL_BOUND_MATERIAL_EXT. This indicates whether the parameter should be set by calls to glMaterial (for ordinary parameters) or glBoundMaterialEXT (for bound parameters).

To choose a shader instance, we call glShaderEXT with a shader ID. Primitives drawn after the glShaderEXT call will use the specified shader instance.

4.4 Lights

OpenGL normally supports up to eight lights, GL_LIGHT0 through GL_LIGHT7. New light IDs beyond these eight are created with glNewLightEXT. Lights are turned on and off through calls to glEnable and glDisable. Parameters for the lights are set with glLight, which takes the light ID, the parameter name, and the new value. As with surface shaders, we have a built-in OpenGL light that implements the OpenGL lighting model. The eight standard lights are pre-loaded to use this function.

The OpenGL lighting model uses multiple colors for each light, with a different color for each of the ambient, diffuse and specular shading computations. In contrast, the RenderMan lighting model has only one color for each light. We allow a mix of these two styles. The only constraint is that surface shaders that use three different light colors can only be used with lights that provide three light colors. Surface shaders that follow the RenderMan model will use only the diffuse light color from lights that follow the OpenGL model.

5 PIXELFLOW

We implemented the pfman shading language on PixelFlow, a high-performance graphics machine. The following sections give a brief overview of PixelFlow. For more details, refer to [Molnar92] or [Eyles97]

5.1 Low-level View

A typical PixelFlow system consists of a host, a number of rendering nodes, a number of shading nodes, and a frame buffer node

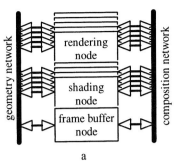
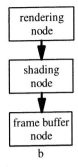

Figure 6: PixelFlow: a) machine organization.
b) simplified view of the system.

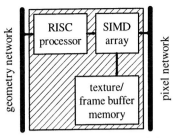

Figure 7: Simple block diagram of a PixelFlow node.

(Figure 6a). The rendering nodes and shading nodes are identical, so the balance between rendering performance and shading performance can be decided for each application. The frame buffer node is also the same, though it includes an additional *daughter card* to produce video output. The host is connected through a daughter card on one of the rendering nodes.

The pipelined design of PixelFlow allows the rendering performance to scale linearly with the number of rendering nodes and the shading performance to scale linearly with the number of shading nodes.

Each rendering node is responsible for an effectively random subset of the primitives in the scene. The rendering nodes handle one 128x64 pixel *region* at a time. More precisely, the region is 128x64 image samples. When antialiasing, the image samples are blended into a smaller block of pixels after shading. For brevity, we will continue to use the word "pixel", with the understanding that sometimes they may be image samples instead of actual pixels.

Since each rendering node has only a subset of the primitives, a region rendered by one node will have holes and missing polygons. The different versions of the region are merged using a technique called *image composition*. PixelFlow includes a special high-bandwidth *composition network* that allows image composition to proceed at the same time as pixel data communication. As all of the rendering nodes simultaneously transmit their data for a region, the hardware on each node compares, pixel-by-pixel, the data it is transmitting with the data from the upstream nodes. It sends the closer of each pair of pixels downstream. By the time all of the pixels reach their destination, one of the system's shading nodes, the composition is complete.

Once the shading node has received the data, it does the surface shading for the entire region. In a PixelFlow system with n shading nodes, each shades every n^{th} region. Once each region has been shaded, it is sent over the composition network (without compositing) to the frame buffer node, where the regions are collected and displayed.

Each node has two RISC processors (HP PA-8000's), a custom SIMD array of pixel processors, and a texture memory store. Each processing element of the SIMD array has 256 bytes of memory, an 8-bit ALU with support for integer multiplication, and an enable flag indicating the active processors. All enabled processors in the 128x64 array simultaneously compute, on their own data, the result of any operation. This provides a speedup of up to 8192 times the rate of a single processing element.

5.2 High-level View

The hardware and basic system software handle the details of scheduling primitives for the rendering nodes, compositing pixel samples from these nodes, assigning them to shading nodes, and moving the shaded pixel information to the frame buffer. Consequently, it is possible to take the simplified view of PixelFlow as a simple pipeline (Figure 6b). This view is based on the passage of a single displayed pixel through the system. Each displayed pixel arrives at the frame buffer, having been shaded by a single shading node. We can ignore the fact that displayed pixels in other regions were shaded by different physical shading nodes. Before arriving at the shading node, the pixel was part of a primitive on just one of the rendering nodes. We can ignore the fact that other pixels may display different primitives from different rendering nodes.

Only the rendering nodes make use of the second RISC processor. The primitives assigned to the node are split between the processors. We can take the simplified view that there is only one processor on the node, and let the lower level software handle the scheduling between the physical processors. Figure 7 is simple block diagram of a PixelFlow node with these simplifications. Each node is connected to two communication networks. The geometry network (800 MB/s in each direction), handles information about the scene geometry, bound parameter values, and other data bound for the RISC processors. It is 32 bits wide, operating at 200 MHz. The composition network (6.4 GB/s in each direction) handles transfers of pixel data from node to node. It is 256 bits wide, also operating at 200 MHz. Since our simplified view of the PixelFlow system hides the image composition, it is reasonable to simply refer to the composition network as a pixel network.

6 IMPLEMENTATION

Implementation of a shading language on PixelFlow requires optimizations. Some are necessary to achieve the targeted interactive rates of 20-30 frames per second, whereas others are necessary just to enable shaders to run on PixelFlow. The three scarce resources impact our PixelFlow implementation: time, communication bandwidth, and memory. In this section, we present optimizations to address each.

6.1 Execution Optimizations

Our target frame rate of 30 frames per second translates to 33 ms per frame. The system pipelining means that most of this time is actually available for shading. Each shading node can handle one 128x64 region at a time and a 1280x1024 screen (or 640x512 screen with 4-sample antialiasing) contains 160 such regions. On a system with four shading nodes, each is responsible for 40 regions and can take an average of 825 µs shading each region. On a larger system with 16 shading nodes, each is responsible for 10 regions and can spend an average of 3.3 ms shading a region. Table 1 shows per-region execution times fore some sample shaders. The first four shaders appear in Figure 1. The other shaders were written by the UNC nanoManipulator project for surface data visualization.

shader	bytes free	execution time
brick	46	613.15 µs
ripple reflection	59	1058.07 µs
planks	105	532.30 µs
bowling pin	86	401.96 µs
nanoManipulator 1	75	567.95 µs
nanoManipulator 2	1	2041.44 µs
nanoManipulator 3	51	1638.67 µs

Table 1: Memory and performance summary.

6.1.1 Deferred Shading

Deferred shading is the technique of performing shading computations on pixels only after the visible pixels have been determined [Whitted81][Deering88][Ellsworth91]. It provides several advantages for the execution of surface shading functions. First, no time is wasted on shading computations for pixels that will not be visible. Second, our SIMD array can simultaneously evaluate a single surface shader instance on every primitive that uses it in a 128x64 region. Finally, it decouples the rendering performance and shading performance of the system. To handle more complex shading, add more shading hardware. To handle more complex geometry, add more rendering hardware.

6.1.2 Uniform and Varying

RenderMan has *uniform* and *varying* types (Section 3.1), in part for the efficiency of their software renderer. A *uniform expression* uses only uniform operands and has a uniform result; a *varying expression* may have both uniform and varying operands but has a varying result. As Pixar's prman renderer evaluates the shading on a surface, it computes uniform expressions only once, sharing the results with all of the surface samples, but loops over the surface samples to compute the varying expressions.

We can use a similar division of labor. The microprocessor on each PixelFlow node can compute the result of a single operation much faster than the SIMD array; but the microprocessor produces one result, while the SIMD array can produce a different result on each of the 8K pixel processing elements. If the value is the same everywhere, it is faster for the microprocessor to compute and broadcast the result to the pixel processors. If the value is different at different pixel processors, it is much faster to allow the SIMD array to compute all of the results in parallel.

Since uniform expressions do not vary across the pixels, it is much more efficient to compute them using the microprocessor and store them in microprocessor memory. In contrast, varying expressions are the domain of the pixel processors. They can potentially have different values at every pixel, so must exist in pixel memory. They are fast and efficient because their storage and operations are replicated across the SIMD array. This same distinction between shared (*uniform*) and SIMD array (*varying*) memory was made by Thinking Machines for the Connection Machine [ThinkingMachines89], though they called them *mono* and *poly*, and by MasPar for the MP-1 [MasPar90], though their terms were *singular* and *plural*.

Operation	16-bit fixed	32-bit fixed	32-bit float
+	0.07 µs	0.13 µs	3.08 µs
*	0.50 µs	2.00 µs	2.04 µs
/	1.60 µs	6.40 µs	7.07 µs
sqrt	1.22 µs	3.33 µs	6.99 µs
noise	5.71 µs	—	21.64 µs

Table 2: Fixed-point and floating-point execution times for 128x64 SIMD array.

6.1.3 Fixed-point

We can achieve significant speed improvements by using fixed-point operations for varying computations instead of floating-point. Our pixel processors do not support floating-point in hardware: every floating-point operation is built from basic integer math operations. These operations consist of the equivalent integer operation with bitwise shifts to align the operands and result. Fixed-point numbers may also require shifting to align the decimal points, but the shifts are known at compile-time. The timings of some fixed-point and floating-point operations are shown in Table 2. These operations may be done by as many as 8K pixel processors at once, yet we would still like them to be as fast as possible.

6.1.4 Math Functions

We provide floating-point versions of the standard math library functions. An efficient SIMD implementation of these functions has slightly different constraints than a serial implementation. Piece-wise polynomial approximation is the typical method to evaluate transcendental math functions.

This approach presents a problem on PixelFlow due to the handling of conditionals on a SIMD array. On a SIMD array, the condition determines which processing elements are enabled. The true part of an if/else is executed with some processing elements enabled, the set of enabled processors is flipped and the false part is executed. Thus the SIMD array spends the time to execute both branches of the if.

This means that using a table of 32 polynomials takes as much time as a single polynomial with 32 times as many terms covering the entire domain. Even so, a polynomial with, say, 160 terms is not practical. For each PixelFlow math function, we reduce the function domain using identities, but do not reduce it further. For example, the log of a floating-point number, $m*2^e$, is $e*\log(2)+\log(m)$. We fit $\log(m)$ with a single polynomial. Each polynomial is chosen to use as few terms as possible while remaining accurate to within the floating-point precision. Thus, we still do a piece-wise fit, but fit a single large piece with a polynomial of relatively high degree.

While we provide accurate versions of the math functions, often shaders do not really need the "true" function. With the ripple reflection shader in Figure 1b, it is not important that the ripples **be** sine waves. They just need to **look like** sine waves. For that reason, we also provide faster, visually accurate but numerically poor, versions of the math functions. The fast versions use simpler polynomials, just matching value and first derivative at each endpoint of the range fit by the more exact approximations. This provides a function that appears visually correct but executes in about half the time.

function	exact	fast
sin	81.36 µs	45.64 µs
cos	81.36 µs	48.77 µs
tan	93.25 µs	52.65 µs
asin, acos	78.52 µs	47.50 µs
atan	66.41 µs	35.34 µs
atan2	66.17 µs	35.15 µs
exp	53.37 µs	37.86 µs
exp2	51.09 µs	35.58 µs
log	57.76 µs	21.57 µs
log2	57.68 µs	21.49 µs

Table 3: Execution times for floating-point math functions on 128x64 SIMD array.

```
// setup, compute base surface color
illuminance() {
    // add in  the contribution of one light
}
// wrap-up
```

Figure 8: Outline of a typical surface shader.

6.1.5 Combined Execution

Many shading functions have similar organizations. Combining the execution of the common sections of code in multiple shaders can lead to large gains in performance. In the next few sections, we will discuss some of these methods. The easiest and most automatic of this class of optimizations is combined execution of lights for all surface shaders. For some of the more traditional surface shaders, involving image texture lookups and Phong shading, we can do further overlapped computation.

6.1.5.1 Lights

One of the jobs of a surface shader is to incorporate the effects of each light in the scene. As in the RenderMan shading language, this is accomplished through the `illuminance` construct, which behaves like a loop over the active lights (Figure 8). This means that each surface shader effectively includes a loop over every light. For m shaders and n lights, this results in m*n light executions. This can be quite expensive since the lights themselves are procedural, and could be arbitrarily complex. Since the lights are the same for each of the m shaders, we compute each light just once and share its results among all of the shaders, resulting in only n light executions. We do this by interleaving the execution of all of the lights and shaders.

We accomplish this interleaving by having each surface shader generate three instruction streams for the SIMD array. The first stream, which we call *pre-illum*, contains only the setup code (until the `illuminance` in Figure 8). The second stream contains the body of the `illuminance` construct. We call this the *illum* stream. Finally, the *post-illum* stream contains everything after the `illuminance`. The lights themselves create their own stream of SIMD commands. The interleaving pattern of these streams is shown in Figure 9.

The SIMD memory usage of the surfaces and lights must be chosen in such a way that each has room to operate, but none conflict. The surface shaders will not interfere with each other since any one pixel can only use one surface shader. Different surface shaders already use different pixel memory maps. Lights, however, must operate in an environment that does not disturb any surface shader, but provides results in a form that all surface shaders can use. The results of the lighting computation, the color and direction of the light hitting each pixel, are stored in a special

shader	stage	setup	add light 1	add light 2	wrap-up
		— time (not to scale) →			
Surface 1	pre-illum	▓			
	illum		▓	▓	
	post-illum				▓
Surface 2	pre-illum	▓			
	illum		▓	▓	
	post-illum				▓
Surface 3	pre-illum	▓			
	illum		▓	▓	
	post-illum				▓
Light 1			▓		
Light 2				▓	

Figure 9: Interleaving of surface shaders and lights.

communications area to be shared by all surface shaders. The light functions themselves operate in the SIMD memory left over by the retained result of the greediest of the surface shader pre-illum stages. Above this *high water mark*, the light can freely allocate whatever memory it needs. The illum, and post-illum streams of all shaders can use all available memory without interfering with either the other surfaces or the lights.

6.1.5.2 Surface Position

For image composition, every pixel must contain the Z-buffer depth of the closest surface visible at that pixel. This Z value, along with the position of the pixel on the screen, is sufficient to compute where the surface sample is in 3D. Since the surface position can be reconstructed from these pieces of information, we do not store the surface position in pixel memory during rendering or waste composition bandwidth sending it from the rendering nodes to the shading nodes. Instead, we compute it on the shading nodes in a phase we call pre-shade, which occurs before any shading begins. Thus, we share the execution time necessary to reconstruct the surface position. We also save memory and bandwidth early in the graphics pipeline, helping with the other two forms of optimization, to be mentioned later.

6.1.5.3 Support for Traditional Shaders

Some optimizations have been added to assist in cases that are common for forms of the OpenGL shading model. Unlike the earlier execution optimizations, these special-purpose optimizations are only enabled by setting flags in the shader.

Surface shaders that use only the typical Phong shading model can use a shared illum stream. This allows shaders to set up different parameters to the Phong shader, but the code for the Phong shading model runs only once.

Surface shaders that use a certain class of texture lookups can share the lookup computations. These shaders know what texture they want to look up in the pre-illum phase, but don't require the results until the post-illum phase. The PixelFlow hardware does not provide any significant improvement in actual lookup time for shared lookups, but this optimization allows the SIMD processors to perform other operations while the lookup is in progress. To share the lookup processing, they place their *texture ID* and *texture coordinates* in special shared "magic" parameters. The results of the lookup are placed in another shared magic parameter by the start of the post-illum stage.

6.1.6 Cached Instruction Streams

On PixelFlow, the microprocessor code computes the uniform expressions and all of the uniform control flow (if's with uniform conditions, while's, for's, etc.), generating a stream of SIMD processor instructions. This SIMD instruction stream is buffered for later execution. The set of SIMD instructions for a shader only changes when some uniform parameter of the shader changes, so we cache the instruction stream and re-use it. Any parameter change sets a flag that indicates that the stream must be regenerated. For most non-animated shaders, this means that the uniform code executes only once, when the application starts.

6.2 Bandwidth Optimizations

Communication bandwidth is another scarce resource on PixelFlow. As mentioned in Section 5, there are two communication paths between nodes in the PixelFlow system, the geometry net and composition net. We are primarily concerned with the composition net bandwidth. While its total bandwidth is 6.4 GB/s, four bytes of every transfer are reserved for the pixel depth, giving an effective bandwidth of 5.6 GB/s.

Since PixelFlow uses deferred shading, the complete set of varying shading parameters and the shader ID must be transferred across the composition network. The final color must also be transferred from the shader node to the frame buffer. However, the design of the composition network allows these two transfers to be overlapped, so we really only pay for the bandwidth to send data for each visible pixel from the rendering nodes to shading nodes. At 30 frames per second on a 1280x1024 screen, the maximum communication budget is 142 bytes per pixel. To deal with this limited communication budget, we must perform some optimizations to reduce the number of parameters that need to be sent from renderer node to shader node.

6.2.1 Shader-Specific Maps

Even though each 128x64 pixel region is sent as a single transfer, every pixel could potentially be part of a different surface. Rather than use a transfer that is the union of all the parameters needed by all of those surface shaders, we allow each to have its own tailored transfer map. The first two bytes in every map contain the *shader ID*, which indicates what transfer map was used and which surface shader to run.

6.2.2 Bound Parameters

The bound parameters of any shader instance cannot change from pixel to pixel (Section 4.3), so they are sent over the geometry network directly to the shading nodes. Since the shader nodes deal with visible pixels without any indication of when during the frame they were rendered, we must restrict bound parameters to only change between frames. Bound uniform parameters are used directly by the shading function running on the microprocessor. Any bound varying parameters must be loaded into pixel memory. Based on the shader ID stored in each pixel, we identify which pixels use each shader instance and load their bound varying parameters into pixel memory before the shader executes.

Any parameter that is bound in every instance of a shader should probably be uniform, since this gives other memory and execution time gains. However, it is occasionally helpful to have bound values for varying shading parameters. For example, our brick shader may include a `dirtiness` parameter. Some brick walls will be equally dirty everywhere. Others will be dirtiest near the ground and clean near the top. The instance used in one wall may have `dirtiness` as a bound parameter, while the instance used in a second wall allows `dirtiness` to be set using `glMaterial` with a different value at each vertex.

However, the set of parameters that should logically be bound in some instances and not in others is small. Allowing bound values for varying parameters would be only a minor bandwidth savings, were it not for another implication of deferred shading. Since bound parameters can only change once per frame, we find parameters that would otherwise be uniform are being declared as varying solely to allow them to be changed with `glMaterial` from primitive to primitive (instead of requiring hundreds of instances). This means that someone writing a PixelFlow shader may make a parameter varying for flexibility even though it will never actually vary across any primitives. Allowing instances to have bound values for all parameters helps counter the resulting explosion of pseudo-varying parameters.

6.3 Memory Optimizations

The most limited resource when writing shaders on PixelFlow is pixel memory. The texture memory size (64 megabytes) affects the size of image textures a shader can use in its computations, but does not affect the shader complexity. The microprocessor memory (128 megabytes), is designed to be sufficient to hold large geometric databases. For shading purposes it is effectively unlimited. However, the pixel memory, at only 256 bytes, is quite limited. From those 256 bytes, we further subtract the shader input parameters and an area used for communication between the light shaders and surface shaders. What is left is barely enough to support a full-fledged shading language. The memory limitations of Pixel-Planes 5 were one of the reasons that, while it supported a form of procedural shading, it could not handle a true shading language. In this section we highlight some of the pfman features and optimizations made by the pfman compiler to make this limited memory work for real shaders.

6.3.1 Uniform vs. Varying

We previously mentioned uniform and varying parameters in the context of execution optimizations. Bigger gains come from the storage savings: uniform values are stored in the large main memory instead of the much more limited pixel memory.

6.3.2 Fixed-point

PixelFlow can only allocate and operate on multiples of single bytes, yet we specify the size of our fixed-point numbers in bits. This is because we can do a much better job of limiting the sizes of intermediate results in expressions with a more accurate idea of the true range of the values involved. For example, if we add two two-byte integers, we need three bytes for the result. However, if we know the integers really only use 14 bits, the result is only 15 bits, which still fits into two bytes.

A two-pass analysis determines the sizes of intermediate fixed-point results. A *bottom-up* pass determines the sizes necessary to keep all available precision. It starts with the sizes it knows (e.g. from a variable reference) and combines them according to simple rules. A *top-down* pass limits the fixed-point sizes of the intermediate results to only what is necessary.

6.3.3 Memory Allocation

The primary feature that allows shaders to have any hope of working on PixelFlow is the memory allocation done by the compiler. Since every surface shader is running different code, we use a different memory map for each. We spend considerable compile-time effort creating these memory maps.

Whereas even the simplest of shaders may define more than 256 bytes of varying variables, most shaders do not use that many variables at once. We effectively treat pixel memory as one giant register pool, and perform register allocation on it during compilation. This is one of the most compelling reasons to use a compiler when writing surface shaders to run on graphics hardware. It is possible to manually analyze which variables can coexist in the same place in memory, but it is not easy. One of the authors did just such an analysis for the Pixel-Planes 5 shading code. It took about a month. With automatic allocation, it suddenly becomes possible to prototype and change shaders in minutes instead of months.

The pfman memory allocator performs variable lifetime analysis by converting the code to a static single assignment (SSA) form [Muchnick97][Briggs92] (Figure 10). First, we go through the shader, creating a new temporary variable for the result of every assignment. This is where the method gets its name: we do a static analysis, resulting in one and only one assignment for every variable. In some places, a variable reference will be ambiguous, potentially referring to one of several of these new temporaries. During the analysis, we perform these references using a ϕ-*function*. The ϕ-function is a pseudo-function-call indicating that, depending on the control flow, one of several variables could be referenced. For example, the value of i in the last line of Figure 10b, could have come from either `i2` or `i3`. In these cases, we

```
i = 1;              i1 = 1;              i1 = 1;
i = i + 1;          i2 = i1 + 1;         i2_3 = i1 + 1;
if (i > j)          if (i2 > j1)         if (i2_3 > j1)
    i = 5;              i3 = 5;              i2_3 = 5;
j = i;              j2 = φ(i2,i3);       j2 = i2_3;
        a                   b                   c
```

Figure 10: Example of lifetime analysis using SSA. a) original code fragment. b) code fragment in SSA form. Note the new variables used for every assignment and the use of the φ-function for the ambiguous assignment. c) final code fragment with φ-functions merged.

merge the separate temporaries back together into a single variable. What results is a program with many more variables, but each having as short a lifetime as possible.

Following the SSA lifetime analysis, we make a linear pass through the code, mapping these new variables to free memory as soon as they become live, and unmapping them when they are no longer live. Variables can only become live at assignments and can only die at their last reference. As a result of these two passes, variables with the same name in the user's code may shift from memory location to memory location. We only allow these shifts when the SSA name for the variable changes. One of the most noticeable effects of the this analysis is that a variable that is used independently in two sections of code does not take space between execution of the sections.

Table 4 shows the performance of the memory allocation on an assortment of shaders. Table 1 shows the amount of memory left after the shading parameters, shader, light, and all overhead have been factored out.

7 CONCLUSIONS

We have demonstrated an interactive graphics platform that supports procedural shading through a shading language. With our system, we can write shaders in a high-level shading language, compile them, and generate images at 30 frames per second or more. To accomplish this, we modified a real-time API to support procedural shading and an existing shading language to include features beneficial for a real-time implementation.

Our API is based on OpenGL, with extensions to support the added flexibility of procedural shading. We believe the decision to extend OpenGL instead of using the existing RenderMan API was a good one. Many existing interactive graphics applications are already written in OpenGL, and can be ported to PixelFlow with relative ease. Whereas the RenderMan API has better support of curved surface primitives important for its user community, OpenGL has better support for polygons, triangle strips and display lists, important for interactive graphics hardware.

Our shading language is based on the RenderMan shading language. Of the differences we introduced, only the fixed-point data type was really necessary. We expect that future hardware-assisted shading language implementations may also want similar fixed-point extensions. The other changes were either done for implementation convenience or to fill holes in the RenderMan shading language definition that have since been addressed by more recent versions of RenderMan. If we were starting the project over again today, we would just add fixed-point to the current version of the RenderMan shading language.

We have only addressed surface shading and procedural lights. RenderMan also allows other types of procedures, all of which could be implemented on PixelFlow, but have not been. We also do not have derivative functions, an important part of the RenderMan shading language. Details on how these features could be implemented on PixelFlow can be found in [Olano98]

shader	total (uniform + varying)	varying only	varying with allocation
simple brick	171	97	16
fancy brick	239	175	101
ripple reflection	341	193	137
wood planks	216	152	97

Table 4: Shader memory usage in bytes.

We created a shading language compiler, which hides the details of our hardware architecture. The compiler also allows us to invisibly do the optimizations necessary to run on our hardware. We found the most useful optimizations to be those that happen automatically. This is consistent with the shading language philosophy of hiding system details from the shader writer.

Using a compiler and shading language to mask details of the hardware architecture has been largely successful, but the hardware limitations do peek through as shaders become short on memory. Several of our users have been forced to manually convert portions of their large shaders to fixed-point to allow them to run. Even after such conversion, one of the shaders in Table 1 has only a single byte free. If a shader exceeds the memory resources after it is converted to fixed-point, it cannot run on PixelFlow. If this becomes a problem, we can add the capability to spill pixel memory into texture memory, at a cost in execution speed.

Any graphics engine capable of real-time procedural shading will require significant pixel-level parallelism, though this parallelism may be achieved through MIMD processors instead of SIMD as we used. For the near future, this level of parallelism will imply a limited per-pixel memory pool. Consequently, we expect our memory optimization techniques to be directly useful for at least the next several real-time procedural-shading machines. Our bandwidth optimization techniques are somewhat specific to the PixelFlow architecture, though should apply to other deferred shading systems since they need to either transmit or store the per-pixel appearance parameters between rendering and shading. Deferred shading and our experience with function approximation will be of interest for future SIMD machines. The other execution optimizations, dealing with tasks that can be done once instead of multiple times, will be of lasting applicability to anyone attempting a procedural shading machine.

There is future work to be done extending some of our optimization techniques. In particular, we have barely scratched the surface of automatic combined execution of portions of different shaders. We do only the most basic of these optimizations automatically. Some others we do with hints from the shader-writer, whereas other possible optimizations are not done at all. For example, we currently run every shader instance independently. It would be relatively easy to identify and merge instances of the same shader function that did not differ in any uniform parameters. For a SIMD machine like ours, this would give linear speed improvement with the number of instances we can execute together. Even more interesting would be to use the techniques of [Dietz92] and [Guenter95] to combine code within a shader and between shader instances with differing uniform parameter values.

Creating a system that renders in real-time using a shading language has been richly rewarding. We hope the experiences we have outlined here will benefit others who attempt real-time procedural shading.

8 ACKNOWLEDGMENTS

PixelFlow was a joint project of the University of North Carolina and Hewlett-Packard and was supported in part by DARPA order numbers A410 and E278, and NSF grant numbers MIP-9306208 and MIP-9612643.

The entire project team deserves recognition and thanks; this work exists by virtue of their labors. We would like to single out Voicu Popescu for his work on pfman memory allocation as well as the other project members who worked on the pfman compiler, Peter McMurry and Rob Wheeler. Thanks to Steve Molnar and Yulan Wang for their early work on programmable shading on PixelFlow. Thanks to Jon Leech for his work on the OpenGL extensions. We would also like to express special thanks to the other people who worked on the PixelFlow shading system and the API extensions: Dan Aliaga, Greg Allen, Jon Cohen, Rich Holloway, Roman Kuchkuda, Paul Layne, Carl Mueller, Greg Pruett, Brad Ritter, and Lee Westover.

Finally, we would like to gratefully acknowledge the help and patience of those who have used pfman, and provided several of the shaders used in this paper. They are Arthur Gregory, Chris Wynn, and members of the UNC nanoManipulator project, under the direction of Russ Taylor (Alexandra Bokinsky, Chun-Fa Chang, Aron Helser, Sang-Uok Kum, and Renee Maheshwari).

References

[Briggs92] Preston Briggs, *Register Allocation via Graph Coloring*, PhD Dissertation, Department of Computer Science, Rice University, Houston, Texas, 1992.

[Cook84] Robert L. Cook, "Shade Trees", Proceedings of SIGGRAPH 84 (Minneapolis, Minnesota, July 23–27, 1984). In *Computer Graphics*, v18n3. ACM SIGGRAPH, July 1984. pp. 223–231.

[Cook87] Robert L. Cook, "The Reyes Image Rendering Architecture", Proceedings of SIGGRAPH 87 (Anaheim, California, July 27–31, 1987). In *Computer Graphics*, v21n4. ACM SIGGRAPH, July 1987. pp. 95–102.

[Deering88] Michael Deering, Stephanie Winner, Bic Schediwy, Chris Duffy and Neil Hunt, "The Triangle Processor and Normal Vector Shader: A VLSI System for High Performance Graphics", Proceedings of SIGGRAPH 88 (Atlanta, Georgia, August 1–5, 1988). In *Computer Graphics*, v22n4, ACM SIGGRAPH, August 1988. pp. 21–30.

[Dietz92] Henry G. Dietz, "Common Subexpression Induction", Proceedings of the 1992 International Conference on Parallel Processing (Saint Charles, Illinois, August 1992). pp. 174–182.

[Ellsworth91] David Ellsworth, "Parallel Architectures and Algorithms for Real-time Synthesis of High-quality Images using Deferred Shading". Workshop on Algorithms and Parallel VLSI Architectures (Pont-á-Mousson, France, June 12, 1990).

[Eyles97] John Eyles, Steven Molnar, John Poulton, Trey Greer, Anselmo Lastra, Nick England and Lee Westover, "PixelFlow: The Realization", Proceedings of the 1997 SIGGRAPH/Eurographics Workshop on Graphics Hardware (Los Angeles, California, August 3–4, 1992). ACM SIGGRAPH, August 1997. pp. 57–68.

[Gritz96] Larry Gritz and James K. Hahn, "BMRT: A Global Illumination Implementation of the RenderMan Standard", *Journal of Graphics Tools*, v1n3, 1996. pp. 29–47.

[Guenter95] Brian Guenter, Todd B. Knoblock and Erik Ruf, "Specializing Shaders", Proceedings of SIGGRAPH 95 (Los Angeles, California, August 6–11, 1995). In *Computer Graphics* Proceedings, Annual Conference Series, ACM SIGGRAPH, 1995. pp. 343–348.

[Hanrahan90] Pat Hanrahan and Jim Lawson, "A Language for Shading and Lighting Calculations", Proceedings of SIGGRAPH 90 (Dallas, Texas, August 6–10, 1990). In *Computer Graphics*, v24n4. ACM SIGGRAPH, August 1990. pp. 289–298.

[Hill97] B. Hill, Th. Roger and F. W. Vorhagen, "Comparative Analysis of the Quantization of Color Spaces on the Basis of the CIELAB Color-Difference Formula", *ACM Transactions on Graphics*, v16n2. ACM, April 1997. pp. 109–154.

[Lastra95] Anselmo Lastra, Steven Molnar, Marc Olano and Yulan Wang, "Real-time Programmable Shading", Proceedings of the 1995 Symposium on Interactive 3D Graphics (Monterey, California, April 9–12, 1995). ACM SIGGRAPH, 1995. pp. 59–66.

[Leech98] Jon Leech, "OpenGL Extensions and Restrictions for PixelFlow", Technical Report TR98-019, Department of Computer Science, University of North Carolina at Chapel Hill.

[MasPar90] MasPar Computer Corporation, MasPar Parallel Application Language (MPL) User Guide, 1990.

[Max81] Nelson L. Max, "Vectorized Procedural Models for Natural Terrain: Waves and Islands in the Sunset", Proceedings of SIGGRAPH 81 (Dallas, Texas, July 1981). In *Computer Graphics*, v15n3. ACM SIGGRAPH, August 1981. pp. 317–324.

[Molnar92] Steven Molnar, John Eyles and John Poulton, "PixelFlow: High-speed Rendering Using Image Composition", Proceedings of SIGGRAPH 92 (Chicago, Illinois, July 26–31, 1992). In *Computer Graphics*, v26n2. ACM SIGGRAPH, July 1992. pp. 231–240.

[Muchnick97] Steven Muchnick, *Compiler Design and Implementation*. Morgan Kaufmann, San Francisco, CA, 1997.

[Neider93] Jackie Neider, Tom Davis and Mason Woo, *OpenGL Programming Guide: the official guide to learning OpenGL release 1.*, Addison-Wesley, 1993.

[Olano98] Marc Olano, *A Programmable Pipeline for Graphics Hardware*, PhD Dissertation, Department of Computer Science, University of North Carolina at Chapel Hill, 1998.

[Perlin85] Ken Perlin, "An Image Synthesizer", Proceedings of SIGGRAPH 85 (San Francisco, California, July 22–26, 1985). In *Computer Graphics*, v19n3. ACM SIGGRAPH, July 1985. pp. 287–296.

[Pixar97] Pixar Animation Studios, *PhotoRealistic RenderMan 3.7 Shading Language Extensions*. Pixar animation studios, March 1997.

[Rhoades92] John Rhoades, Greg Turk, Andrew Bell, Andrei State, Ulrich Neumann and Amitabh Varshney, "Real-time procedural textures", Proceedings of the 1992 Symposium on Interactive 3D Graphics (Cambridge, Massachusetts, March 29–April 1, 1992). In *Computer Graphics* special issue. ACM SIGGRAPH, March 1992. pp. 95–100.

[Slusallek94] Philipp Slusallek, Thomas Pflaum and Hans-Peter Seidel, "Implementing RenderMan–Practice, Problems and Enhancements", Proceedings of Eurographics '94. In *Computer Graphics Forum*, v13n3, 1994. pp. 443–454.

[ThinkingMachines89] Thinking Machines Corporation, *Connection Machine Model CM-2 Technical Summary*. Thinking Machines Corporation, Version 5.1, May 1989.

[Upstill90] Steve Upstill, *The RenderMan Companion*, Addison-Wesley, 1990.

[Whitted81] T. Whitted and D. M. Weimer, "A software test-bed for the development of 3-D raster graphics systems", Proceedings of SIGGRAPH 81 (Dallas, Texas, July 1981). In *Computer Graphics*, v15n3. ACM SIGGRAPH, August 1981. pp. 271–277.

Efficiently Using Graphics Hardware
in Volume Rendering Applications

Rüdiger Westermann, Thomas Ertl

Computer Graphics Group
Universität Erlangen-Nürnberg, Germany*

Abstract

OpenGL and its extensions provide access to advanced per-pixel operations available in the rasterization stage and in the frame buffer hardware of modern graphics workstations. With these mechanisms, completely new rendering algorithms can be designed and implemented in a very particular way. In this paper we extend the idea of extensively using graphics hardware for the rendering of volumetric data sets in various ways. First, we introduce the concept of clipping geometries by means of stencil buffer operations, and we exploit pixel textures for the mapping of volume data to spherical domains. We show ways to use 3D textures for the rendering of lighted and shaded iso-surfaces in real-time without extracting any polygonal representation. Second, we demonstrate that even for volume data on unstructured grids, where only software solutions exist up to now, both methods, iso-surface extraction and direct volume rendering, can be accelerated to new rates of interactivity by simple polygon drawing and frame buffer operations.

CR Categories: I.3.7 [Computer Graphics]: Three-Dimensional Graphics and Realism—*Graphics Hardware, 3D Textures, Volume Rendering, Unstructured Grids*

1 Introduction

Over the past few years workstations with hardware support for the interactive rendering of complex 3D polygonal scenes consisting of directly lit and shaded triangles have become widely available. The last two generations of high-end graphics workstations [1, 17], however, besides providing impressive rates of geometry processing, also introduced new functionality in the rasterization and frame buffer hardware, like texture and environment mapping, fragment tests and manipulation as well as auxiliary buffers. The ability to exploit these features through OpenGL and its extensions allows completely new classes of rendering algorithms to be developed. Anticipating similar trends for the more advanced imaging functionality of todays high-end machines we are actively investigating possibilities to accelerate expensive visualization algorithms by using these extensions.

---

*Lehrstuhl für Graphische Datenverarbeitung (IMMD9), Universität Erlangen-Nürnberg, Am Weichselgarten 9, 91054 Erlangen, Germany, Email: wester@informatik.uni-erlangen.de

In this paper we are dealing with the efficient generation of a visual representation of the information present in volumetric data sets. For scalar-valued volume data two standard techniques, the rendering of iso-surfaces, and the direct volume rendering, have been developed to a high degree of sophistication. However, due to the huge number of volume cells which have to be processed and to the variety of different cell types only a few approaches allow parameter modifications and navigation at interactive rates for realistically sized data sets. To overcome these limitations we provide a basis for hardware accelerated interactive visualization of both iso-surfaces and direct volume rendering on arbitrary topologies.

Direct volume rendering tries to convey a visual impression of the complete 3D data set by taking into account the emission and absorption effects as seen by an outside viewer. The underlying theory of the physics of light transport is simplified to the well known volume rendering integral when scattering and frequency effects are neglected [9, 10, 15, 29]. A few standard algorithms exist for computing the intensity contribution along a ray of sight, enhanced by a wide variety of optimization strategies [13, 15, 12, 4, 11]. But only recently, since hardware supported 3D texture mapping is available, has direct volume rendering become interactively feasible on graphics workstations [2, 3, 30]. We extend this approach with respect to flexible editing options and advanced mapping and rendering techniques.

Our goal is the visualization and manipulation of volumetric data sets of arbitrary data type and grid topology at interactive rates within one application on standard graphics workstations. In this paper we focus on scalar-valued volumes and show how to accelerate the rendering process by exploiting features of advanced graphics hardware implementations through standard APIs like OpenGL. Our approach is pixel oriented, taking advantage of rasterization functionality such as color interpolation, texture mapping, color manipulation in the pixel transfer path, various fragment and stencil tests, and blending operations. In this way we

- **extend volume rendering via 3D textures** with respect to arbitrary clipping geometries and exploit pixel textures for volume rendering in spherical domains

- **render shaded iso-surfaces** at interactive rates combining 3D textures and fragment operations thus avoiding any polygonal representation

- **accelerate volume visualization of tetrahedral grids** employing polygon rendering of cell faces and fragment operations for both shaded iso-surfaces and direct volume rendering.

In the remainder of this paper we first introduce the basic concept of direct volume rendering via 3D textures. We then describe our extension for arbitrary clipping geometries, and we introduce the pixel texture mechanism for spherical domains be reused later on. Basic algorithms for rendering shaded iso-surfaces from regular voxel grids will be described. Finally, we propose a general framework for the visualization of unstructured grids. Some of the earlier ideas can be used here again, but 3D textures have to be abandoned in favor of polygon rendering of the cell faces. We conclude our paper with detailed results and additional ideas for future work.

2 Volume rendering via 3D textures

When 3D textures became available on graphics workstations their potential benefit in volume rendering applications was soon recognized [3, 2]. The basic idea is to interpret the voxel array as a 3D texture defined over $[0,1]^3$ and to understand 3D texture mapping as the trilinear interpolation of the volume data set at an arbitrary point within this domain. At the core of the algorithm multiple planes parallel to the image plane are clipped against the parametric texture domain (see Figure 1) and sent to the geometry processing unit. The hardware is then exploited for interpolating 3D texture coordinates issued at the polygon vertices and for reconstructing the texture samples by trilinearly interpolating within the volume. Finally, pixel values are blended appropriately into the frame buffer in order to approximate the continuous volume rendering integral.

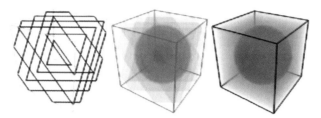

Figure 1: Volume rendering by 3D texture slicing.

Nevertheless, besides interactive frame rates, in many practical applications editing the data in a free and easy way is of particular interest. Although texture lookup tables might be modified in order to enhance or suppress portions of the data, the relevant structures can often be separated in a much more convenient and intuitive way by using additional clipping geometries. Planar clipping planes available as core OpenGL mechanisms may be utilized, but from the user's point of view more complex geometries are necessary.

2.1 Arbitrary clipping geometries

A straightforward approach which is implemented quite often is the use of multiple clipping planes to construct more complex geometries. However, notice that the simple task of clipping an arbitrarily scaled box cannot be realized in this way.

Even more flexibility and ease of manipulation can be achieved by taking advantage of the per-pixel operations provided in the rasterization stage. As we will outline, as long as the object against which the volume is to be clipped is a closed surface represented by a list of triangles it can be efficiently used as the clipping geometry.

The basic idea is to determine all pixels which are covered by the cross-section between the object and the actual slicing plane (see Figure 2). These pixels, then, are locked, thus preventing the textured polygon from getting drawn to these locations.

The locking mechanism is implemented exploiting the OpenGL stencil buffer test. It allows pixel updates to be accepted or rejected based on the outcome of a comparison between a user defined reference value and the value of the corresponding entry in the stencil buffer. Before the textured polygon gets rendered the stencil buffer has to be initialized in such a way that all color values written to pixels inside the cross-section will be rejected.

In order to determine for a certain plane whether a pixel is covered by a cross-section or not we render the clipping object in polygon mode. However, since we are only interested in setting the stencil buffer we do not alter any of the frame buffer values. At first, an additional clipping plane is enabled which has the same orientation and position as the slicing plane. All back faces with respect to the actual viewing direction are drawn, and everything in front of

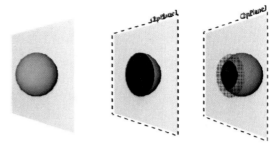

Figure 2: The use of arbitrary clipping geometries is demonstrated for the case of a sphere. In regions where the object intersects the actual slice the stencil buffer is locked. The intuitive approach of rendering only the back faces might result in the patterned erroneous region.

the plane is clipped. Wherever a pixel would have been drawn the stencil buffer is set. Finally, by changing the stencil test appropriately, rendering the textured polygon, now, only affects those pixels where the stencil buffer is unchanged.

In general, however, depending on the clipping geometry this procedure fails in determining the cross-section exactly (see rightmost image in Figure 2). Therefore, before the textured polygon is rendered all stencil buffer entries which are set improperly have to be updated. Notice that in front of a back face which was written erroneously there is always a front face due to the topology of the clipping object. The front faces are thus rendered into those pixels where the stencil buffer is set and the stencil buffer is cleared where a pixel also passes the depth test. Now the stencil buffer is correctly initialized and all further drawing operations are restricted to those pixels where it is set or vice versa. Of course, the stencil buffer has to be cleared in order to process the next slice.

Since this approach is independent of the used geometry it allows arbitrary shapes to be specified. In particular, it turns out that adaptive manipulations of individual vertices can be handled quite easily thus providing a flexible tool for carving portions out of the data in an intuitive way.

2.2 Spherical domains

Traditionally, 3D texture space is parameterized over a Cartesian domain. Because the texture is mapped to a cube, all cross-sections between a slice parallel to the image plane and the volume still remain planar in parametric texture space. As a consequence it suffices to assign texture coordinates on a per-vertex basis and to bilinearly interpolate between them during rasterization.

However, in many applications the texture has to be mapped to domains which are not Cartesian. For instance, observe that in geoscience atmospheric data is often parameterized in spherical coordinates and mapped to the corresponding domain.

Now 3D texture mapping becomes difficult because planar slicing planes are mapped to non-planar surfaces in texture space. No longer can bilinear interpolation on a per-vertex basis be used. One way to deal with this limitation is to assign texture coordinates for each pixel separately rather than to interpolate the values across polygons. With the **pixel texgen** OpenGL extension available on SGI Impact architectures this becomes possible in a quite efficient way by giving the user direct control of texture coordinates on a per-pixel basis.

Pixel textures are specified in the same way as standard 3D textures. Once a pixel texture has been activated all pixel values which are drawn from main memory into the frame buffer are interpreted as texture coordinates into this texture. At first, each RGB color triple is mapped to the texture. Then, instead of the color values the interpolated texture values are drawn.

Let us consider a simple example to demonstrate the relevance of pixel textures in volume rendering. A spherical object is rendered having smooth color interpolation across polygons. Red and green color components are set according to the normalized spherical coordinates. The blue component is initialized by a constant value (see left of Figure 3). By reading the frame buffer and drawing it back with enabled pixel texture each of the RGB values is treated as a texture coordinate into the 3D map.

Figure 3: Using pixel textures to perform texture mapping and distortion on spherical domains. The right image was created by using constant color across faces.

Since texture coordinates can be modified in main memory on the per-pixel basis it is easy to apply arbitrary transformations without manipulating and re-loading the texture. For example, in Figure 3 the original texture was just a simple striped pattern, but texture coordinates were distorted with respect to a vector field before they got mapped (see middle of Figure 3).

Arbitrary homogeneous transformations can be applied using the OpenGL pixel transfer operations. Before pixel data gets written to the frame buffer it is multiplied with the **color matrix** and finally scaled and biased by vector-valued factors. More precisely, if **CM** is the 4x4 color matrix and **b** and **s** are the four component bias and scale vectors providing separate factors for each color channel, then each RGBα quadruple, **p**, becomes $\mathbf{b} + \mathbf{s} \cdot \mathbf{CM} \cdot \mathbf{p}$.

Even more efficiently pixel textures can be exploited in volume rendering applications. For example, image c) in Figure 10 was produced by rendering the spherical object multiple times, each time which a slightly increased radius coded into the blue color channel. The pixel data was then re-used to map to the 3D texture before it was blended into the frame buffer thus simulating volumetric effects.

3 Rendering shaded iso-surfaces via 3D textures

So far, with our extensions to texture mapped volume rendering we introduced concepts for adaptive exploration of volumetric data sets as well as for the application to rather unusual domains.

In practice, however, the display of shaded iso-surfaces has been shown as one of the most dominant visualization options, which is particularly useful to enhance the spatial relationship between structures. Moreover, this kind of representation often meets the physical characteristics of the real object in a more natural way.

Different algorithms have been proposed for efficiently reconstructing polygonal representations of iso-surfaces from scalar volume data [14, 16, 19, 26], but unfortunately none of these approaches can effectively be used in interactive applications. This is due to the effort that has to be spent to fit the surface and also to the enormous amount of triangles produced.

For example, the iso-surface shown in Figure 4 was reconstructed from a 512^2x128 abdomen data set. It took about half a minute to generate 1.4 million triangles. Rendering the triangle list on a high-end graphics workstation takes several seconds. Thus, interactively manipulating the iso-value is quite impossible,

Figure 4: Iso-surface reconstructed with the MC algorithm.

and also rendering the surface at acceptable frame rates can hardly be achieved. In contrast, with the method we propose the surface can be rendered in approximately one second, including arbitrary updates of the iso-value.

In order to design an algorithm that completely avoids any polygonal representation we combine 3D texture mapping and advanced pixel transfer operations in a way that allows the iso-surface to be rendered on a per-pixel basis. Since the maximum possible feature size is a single pixel we expect our method to be able to capture even the smallest features in the data.

Recently, first approaches for combining hardware accelerated volume rendering via 3D texture maps with lighting and shading were presented. In [24] the sum of pre-computed ambient and reflected light components is stored in the texture volume and standard 3D texture composition is performed. On the contrary, in [8] the orientation of voxel gradients is stored together with the volume density as the 3D texture map. Lighting is achieved by indexing into an appropriately replicated color table. The inherent drawbacks to these techniques is the need for reloading the texture memory each time any of the lighting parameters change (including changes in the orientation of the object) [24], and the difficulty to achieve smoothly shaded surfaces due to the limited quantization of the normal orientation and the intrinsic hardware interpolation problems [8].

Basically, our approach is similar to the one used in traditional volume ray-casting for the display of shaded iso-surfaces. Let us consider that the surface is hit if the material values along the ray do exceed the iso-value for the first time. At this location the material gradient is computed which is then used in the lighting calculations.

By recognizing that we do already exploit texture interpolation to re-sample the data, all that needs to be evaluated is how to capture those texture samples above the iso-value which are nearest to the image plane. Therefore we have employed the OpenGL **alpha test**, which is used to reject pixels based on the outcome of a comparison between their alpha component and a reference value.

Each element of the 3D texture gets assigned the material value as it's alpha component. Then, texture mapped volume rendering is performed as usual, but pixel values are only drawn if they pass the z-buffer test and if the alpha value is larger than or equal to the selected iso-value. In any of the affected pixels in the frame buffer, now, the color present at the first surface point is being displayed.

In order to obtain the shaded iso-surface from the pixel values already drawn into the frame buffer we propose two different approaches:

- **Gradient shading**: A four component 3D texture is stored which holds in each element the material gradient as well as the material value. Shading is performed in image space by means of matrix multiplication using an appropriately initialized color matrix.

- **Gradientless shading**: Shading is simulated by simple frame buffer arithmetic computing forward differences with respect to the light source direction. Pixel texturing is exploited to encompass multiple rendering passes.

Both approaches account for diffuse shading with respect to a parallel light source positioned at infinity. Then the diffuse term reduces to the scalar product between the surface normal, **N**, and the direction of the light source, **L**, scaled by the material diffuse reflectivity, k_d.

The texture elements in gradient shading each consist of an RGBα quadruple which holds the gradient components in the color channels and the material value in the alpha channel. Before the texture is stored and internally clamped to the range [0,1] the gradient components are being scaled and translated by a factor of 0.5.

By slicing the texture thereby exploiting the alpha test as described the transformed gradients at the surface points are finally displayed in the RGB frame buffer components (see left image in Figure 5). For the surface shading to proceed properly, pixel values have to be scaled and translated back to the range [-1,1]. We also have to account for changes in the orientation of the object. Thus, the normal vectors have to be transformed by the model rotation matrix. Finally, the diffuse shading term is calculated by computing the scalar product between the light source direction and the transformed normals.

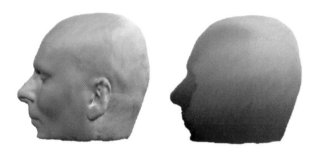

Figure 5: On the left, for an iso-surface the gradient components are displayed in the RGB pixel values. On the right, for the same iso-surface the coordinates in texture space are displayed in the RGB components.

All three transformations can be applied simultaneously using one 4x4 matrix. It is stored in the currently selected color matrix which post-multiplies each of the four-component pixel values if pixel data is copied within the active frame buffer.

For the color matrix to accomplish the transformations it has to be initialized as follows:

$$CM = \begin{pmatrix} L_x & L_y & L_z & 0 \\ L_x & L_y & L_z & 0 \\ L_x & L_y & L_z & 0 \\ 0 & 0 & 0 & 1 \end{pmatrix} \mathbf{M}_{rot} \begin{pmatrix} 2 & 0 & 0 & -1 \\ 0 & 2 & 0 & -1 \\ 0 & 0 & 2 & -1 \\ 0 & 0 & 0 & 1 \end{pmatrix}$$

By just copying the frame buffer contents onto itself each pixel gets multiplied by the color matrix. In addition, it is scaled and biased in order to account for the material diffuse reflectivity and the ambient term. The resulting pixel values are

$$\begin{bmatrix} I_a \\ I_a \\ I_a \\ 0 \end{bmatrix} + \begin{bmatrix} k_d \\ k_d \\ k_d \\ 1 \end{bmatrix} \mathbf{CM} \begin{bmatrix} R \\ G \\ B \\ \alpha \end{bmatrix} = \begin{bmatrix} k_d \langle L, N_{rot} \rangle + I_a \\ k_d \langle L, N_{rot} \rangle + I_a \\ k_d \langle L, N_{rot} \rangle + I_a \\ \alpha \end{bmatrix}$$

where obviously different ambient terms and reflectivities can be specified for each color component.

To circumvent the additional amount of memory that is needed to store the gradient texture we propose a second technique which

applies concepts borrowed from [18] but in an essentially different scenario. The diffuse shading term can be simulated by simple frame buffer arithmetic if the surface is locally orthogonal to the surface normal and the normal as well as the light source direction are orthonormal vectors.

Notice that the diffuse shading term is then proportional to the directional derivative towards the light source. Thus, it can be simulated by taking forward differences toward the light source with respect to the material values:

$$\frac{\partial \mathbf{X}}{\partial L} \approx \mathbf{X}(\vec{p}_0) - \mathbf{X}(\vec{p}_0 + \triangle \cdot \vec{L})$$

By rendering the material values twice, once at the original surface points and then shifted towards the light source, OpenGL blending operations can be exploited to compute the differences.

In order to obtain the coordinates of the surface points we take advantage of the alpha test as proposed and we also apply pixel textures to re-sample the material values. Therefore it is important to know that each vertex comes with a texture coordinate as well as a color value. Usually the color values provide a base color and opacity in order to modulate the interpolated texture samples.

Let us consider that to each vertex the computed texture coordinate (u, v, w) is assigned as RGB color value. Since texture coordinates are computed in parametric texture space they are within the range [0,1]. Moreover, the color values interpolated during rasterization correspond to the texture space coordinates of points on the slicing plane. As a consequence we now have the position of surface points available in the frame buffer rather than the material gradients.

In order to display the correct color values they must not be modulated by the texture samples. However, remember that in gradientless shading we use the same texture format as in traditional texture slicing. Each element comprises a single-valued color entry which is mapped via a RGBα lookup table. This allows us to temporarily set all RGB values in the lookup table to one thus avoiding any modulation of color values.

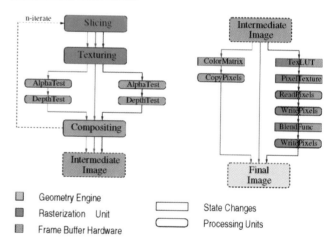

Figure 6: Process flow for texture based volume rendering techniques. Green: Standard; Red: Gradient Shading; Blue: Gradientless Shading

At this point, the real strength of pixel textures can be exploited. The RGB entries of the texture lookup table are reset in order to produce the original scalar values. Then, the pixel data is read into main memory and it is drawn twice into the frame buffer with enabled pixel texture. In the second pass pixel values are shifted towards the light source by means of the OpenGL pixel bias. Changing the blending equation appropriately let values get subtracted from those already in the frame buffer. Figure 6 summarizes the basic stages and instructions involved in the outlined methods.

So far, we have accepted that only the first material value exceeding the iso-value will be captured. In practice, however, it is often useful to visualize the exterior and the interior of an iso-surface, the latter one often characterized by material values falling below the iso-value. For example, the left image in Figure 7 was generated using our approach. Since close to the volume boundaries data larger than the iso-value is present the first pixel drawn locks the frame buffer.

This problem is solved by a multi-pass rendering approach. At first, the depth buffer is initialized with a value right behind the first intersection with the texture bounding box. All structures close to the boundary which are drawn, therefore, fail the depth test. At these locations the stencil buffer is set. Now the volume is rendered with the alpha test performed as usual into pixels where the stencil buffer is unchanged. Then, the alpha test is reversed and the volume is rendered into pixels where the stencil buffer has already been set. The result is shown in Figure 7.

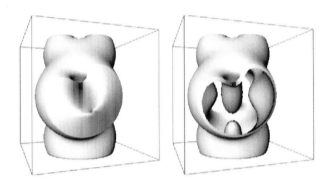

Figure 7: Multi-pass rendering to determine the exterior and the interior of iso-surfaces.

3.1 Bricking

All presented approaches work equally well if the volume data has to be split into smaller blocks which are small enough to fit into texture memory. Each brick is rendered separately from front to back starting with the one nearest to the image plane. Since the stencil buffer is immediately locked whenever a hit with the surface occurs, once a value has been set correctly it will never be changed.

Even when pixel textures are used the same algorithm proceeds without essential modifications. Since the rendered color values are always specified with respect to the parametric domain of the actual block the pixel texture will always be accessed correctly.

4 Volume rendering of unstructured grids

Now we turn our attention to tetrahedral grids most familiar in CFD simulation, which have also recently shown their importance in adaptive refinement strategies. Since most grid types which provide the data at unevenly spaced sample points can be quite easily converted into this representation, our technique, in general, is potentially attractive to a wide area of different applications.

Caused by the irregular topology of the grids to be processed the intrinsic problem showing up in direct volume rendering is to find the correct visibility ordering of the involved primitives. Different ways have been proposed to attack this problem, e.g. by improving sorting algorithms [23, 28, 5], by using space partitioning strategies [27], by taking advantage of hardware assisted polygon rendering [20, 23, 31, 25] and by exploiting the coherence within

cutting planes in object space [6, 21]. Similar to the marching cubes algorithm, the marching tetrahedra approach suffers from the same limitations, i.e., the large amount of generated triangles.

In each tetrahedron (hereafter termed the volume primitive or cell) we have a linear range in the material distribution and therefore a constant gradient. The affine interpolation function $f(x,y,z) = a + bx + cy + dz$ which defines the material distribution within one cell is computed by solving the system of equations

$$\begin{pmatrix} 1 & x_0 & y_0 & z_0 \\ 1 & x_1 & y_1 & z_1 \\ 1 & x_2 & y_2 & z_2 \\ 1 & x_3 & y_3 & z_3 \end{pmatrix} \begin{bmatrix} a \\ b \\ c \\ d \end{bmatrix} = \begin{bmatrix} f_0 \\ f_1 \\ f_2 \\ f_3 \end{bmatrix}$$

for the unknowns a, b, c and d. f_i are the function values given at locations (x_i, y_i, z_i).

Now the partial derivatives, b, c and d, provide the gradient components of each cell. Gradients at the vertices are computed by simply averaging all contributions from different cells. These are stored in addition to the vertex coordinates and the scalar material values, the latter ones given as one-component color indices into a RGBα lookup table.

4.1 Shaded iso-surfaces

In contrast to regular volume data we are no longer able to perform the rendering process by means of 3D textures. However, geometry processing and advanced per-pixel operations will be exploited in a highly effective way which again allows us to avoid any polygonal representation.

At first, let us consider a ray of sight passing through one tetrahedron in order to re-sample the material values. Since along the ray the material distribution is linear it suffices to evaluate the data within the appropriate front and back face and to linearly interpolate in between. This, again, can be solved quite efficiently using the graphics hardware. Therefore the material values are issued as the color of each vertex before the smoothly shaded cell faces are rendered. The correctly interpolated samples are then being displayed and can be grabbed from the frame buffer.

Obviously, the same procedure can be applied by choosing an appropriate shading model and by issuing the material gradient as the vertex normal. Then the rendered triangles will be illuminated with respect to the gradients of the volume material.

Nevertheless, since we are interested in rendering a specific iso-surface we have to find those elements the surface is passing through. But even more difficult, the exact location of the surface within these cells has to be determined in order to compute appropriate interpolation weights (see Figure 8).

The key idea lies in a multi-pass approach:

a: **Faces are rendered having smooth color interpolation in order to compute the interpolation weights.**

b: **Faces are rendered having smooth shading in order to compute illuminated pixels.**

c: **The interpolation weights are used to modulate the results properly.**

In order to compute the interpolation weights we duplicate the material values given at the vertices into RGBα-quadruples. These are used as the current color values. Next, all the back faces are rendered, but only those pixels nearest to the image plane with an alpha value larger than the threshold are maintained by exploiting the alpha test and the z-buffer test. The stencil buffer is set whenever a pixel passes both tests.

We proceed by inverting the alpha test and by drawing the front faces. Although z-buffer comparison is in effect, z-values are never going to be changed since they are needed later. Pixel values may

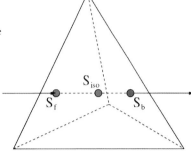

Hit with front face

Hit with iso-surface

Hit with back face

Figure 8: Interpolation weights are computed as $q = \frac{(S_b - S_f)}{S_{iso} - S_f}$ and $1 - q$ in order to obtain the iso-surface.

be affected where the stencil buffer is set, but, in fact, not all components will be altered in order to retain the previously written results.

Instead of processing all front faces at once we alternatively render each element's back faces again. By setting their alpha values to zero it is guaranteed that they always pass the alpha test. Notice that if pixels were accepted in the first pass the corresponding z-values are still present since we did not alter the z-buffer. Choosing an appropriate stencil function allows the stencil buffer to be locked whenever a pixel is written with a z-value equal to the stored one. At these locations the frame buffer is locked in order to prevent the correctly drawn pixels from being destroyed. Finally, the pixel data is read into main memory and the interpolation weights are computed and stored into two distinct pixel images I_f and I_b, respectively.

Once again, the entire procedure is repeated, but now the hardware is exploited to render illuminated faces instead of colored ones. The results of the first rendering pass are blended with the pixel image I_f and the modulated pixel data is transfered to the accumulation buffer [7]. Pixel data produced in the second pass is blended with the pixel image I_b and added to the data already stored in the accumulation buffer. During both passes blending ensures that the shaded faces are interpolated correctly in order to produce the surface shading. Finally, entire image is drawn back into the frame buffer.

However, even without computing the interpolation weights, just by equally blending the lighted front and back faces, this method produces sufficient results (see Figure 9). It is quite evident that sometimes the geometric structure of the cells shows up, but this seems to be tolerable during interactive sessions.

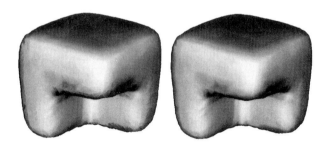

Figure 9: Iso-surface reconstructed from a tetrahedral grid. Color values of the image were equalized to enhance the effects. The left image was generated without using the interpolation weights necessary to achieve smooth results.

4.2 Directly slicing unstructured grids

It is now easy to derive an algorithm which allows us to reconstruct arbitrary slices out of the data. For each vertex we also store it's distance to the image plane and use it temporarily as the scalar material value. But then, a slice just corresponds to a planar iso-surface defined by an iso-value that is equal to the distance of that slice to the image plane. As a consequence our method for reconstructing shaded iso-surfaces can be applied directly. Even more efficiently, since we are only interested in the scalar material values faces are always rendered having smooth color interpolation.

For the method to proceed properly, we store the scalar values in the RG color components and the distance values in the Bα components issued at each vertex. Again we start rendering the back faces. For a slice at the distance d from the image plane only pixel values with an alpha value larger than or equal to d are accepted. We only allow RB pixel values to be written to the frame buffer. As usual, the stencil buffer is set where a pixel passes the depth test and the alpha test. Now the front faces are rendered but only the Gα components are going to be altered. Locking the stencil buffer is done in the same way as described.

Finally, all values necessary to correctly interpolate the scalar values within the actual slice are available in the pixel data. We read the data and calculate

$$S = \frac{R - d}{R - B} \cdot G + \frac{d - B}{R - B} \cdot \alpha,$$

for each RGBα pixel value. Before the resulting scalar value are written back into the frame buffer they get mapped via a lookup table provided by the graphics hardware. In order to approximate the volume rendering integral the grid is sliced multiple times and the generated images are blended properly.

The remarkable fact is that we never need to explicitly use the geometric description of primitives or the topology of the underlying grid. Sorting is implicitly done on the per-pixel basis in the rasterization unit. Polygon drawing is exploited for reconstructing scalar values on the cell faces. All values necessary to interpolate within one slice are accessed from the frame buffer. Moreover, adaptive slicing can easily be performed. For example, to preview the result at a very coarse level only a few slices have to be rendered.

4.3 Data Structures

In this section we briefly discuss the basic data structures used in the presented approaches. In particular the following two issues will be addressed:

- **Find all elements a particular iso-surface passes through**

- **Which elements contribute to a particular slice**

It is important that the decision whether a cell has to be rendered or not can be done in a predictive way. The naive approach to render every cell in each pass of the algorithm would cause the graphics hardware to collapse for sufficiently large data sets.

In iso-surface rendering we prefer a simple byte stream data structure which is easy to access and efficient to store. All scalar material values are scaled to the range [0,1] which is partitioned into an arbitrary number of equally spaced intervals.

Let us consider that we have N cells to process. For each interval a stream of $\lceil N/8 \rceil$ bytes is stored. A bit is set if not all of the values given at the vertices of the corresponding cell are completely less or larger than the bounds of the interval. For a surface to be rendered with respect to a particular iso-value it now suffices to find those entries in the relevant stream which are set. Since in general many adjacent entries within the same interval will be empty this kind of representation provides an effective data structure to be runlength encoded. In addition, this encoding scheme allows empty intervals to be skipped quite efficiently.

In our slicing approach to simulate direct volume rendering we mainly borrowed ideas from [31]. Each cell occurs twice in a set of lists, each of which is stored for exactly one slice. Since each element, in general, contribute to multiple slices, it is included into those lists which are stored for the first and the last slice that is covered by the element. In addition, an active cell list is utilized which captures all cells contributing to the slice that is actually being rendered. Obviously, other data structures [27] might be well suited for this kind of application, but we found the present one to be optimal in our test cases. Tree-like data structures, of course, avoid the incremental update from slice to slice and from viewpoint to viewpoint, but in order to keep the memory overhead moderate much more cells have to be rendered in general. In all our experiments the time necessary to update the cell lists was negligible compared to the final rendering times. We believe that the additional amount of memory introduced by this approach is fairly acceptable compared to the gains it offers.

5 Results

Compared to pure software solutions the accuracy of the results produced by our approaches strongly depends on the available frame buffer hardware. Whenever pixel values are read and processed further on the number of bits per color channel determines the precision that can be achieved. This turns out to be most critical in rendering shaded iso-surfaces with the pixel texture where we may access wrong locations in the texture domain. For example, let us consider a 1024^3 texture which should be processed using a 8 Bit frame buffer. Since pixel values are only precise within $\frac{1}{256}$ we may access voxel values which are about 4 cells aside.

Limited precision is also a problem in direct rendering of unstructured grids where the frame buffer is accessed multiple times to retrieve the scalar material values and the values necessary to perform the interpolation. By repeatedly blending the quantized data samples the final image might get degraded.

Throughout our experiments we used the 8 bit frame buffer on a SGI Maximum Impact where pixel textures have been exploited and in all other cases the 12 bit frame buffer of the RealityEngineII. The **SGIX_pbuffer**, an additional frame buffer invisible to the user, was used throughout the implementations since it can be locked exclusively in order to prevent other applications from drawing into pixel data to be read.

All the results were run on different data sets carefully chosen to outline the basic features of our approaches. The first row of Figure 10 shows a selection of images demonstrating the extensions to the traditional texture based volume rendering we developed. In the images a) and b) a simple box was used to clip the interior and the exterior of a MRI-scan. Image c) shows the benefits of pixel textures for the visualization of atmospheric data. The multi-pass algorithm as described was employed.

In the second row we compare results of the proposed rendering techniques for shaded iso-surfaces. The surface on the leftmost image was rendered in roughly 15 seconds using a software based ray-caster. 3D texture based gradient shading was run with 6 frames per second on the next image. The distance between successive slices was equal to the sampling intervals used in the software approach. The surface on the right appears somewhat brighter with a little less contrast, but basically there can hardly be seen any differences.

The next two images show the comparison between gradient shading and gradientless shading. Obviously, surfaces rendered by the latter one exhibit low contrast and even incorrect results are produced especially in regions where the variation of the gradient magnitude across the surface is high. Although the material distribution in the example data is almost iso-metric, at some points the differences can be easily recognized. At these surface points the step size

used to compute the forward difference has to be increased, which, of course, can not be realized by our approach.

However, only one fourth of the memory needed in gradient shading is used in gradientless shading, and also the rendering times differ insignificantly. The only difference lies in the way the shading is finally computed. In gradient shading we copy the whole frame buffer once. In gradientless shading we have to read the pixel data and we have to write it twice with enabled pixel texturing. For a 512x512 viewport the difference was 0.08 seconds. Compared to the traditional rendering via 3D textures gradient shading ran about 0.04 seconds slower. On the other hand, since the overhead does not depend on the data resolution but on the size of the viewport we expect it's relative contribution to decrease rapidly with increasing data size.

Our final results illustrate the rendering of scalar volume data defined on tetrahedral grids (see last row in Figure 10). The first image shows an iso-surface from the NASA bluntfin which was converted into 225000 tetrahedra. To generate the 512x512 pixel image it took 0.2 seconds on a RE2 with one R10000 195 Mhz cpu.

Direct volume rendering of a finite-element data set is demonstrated by the second example. Notice the adaptive manipulation of the transfer function in order to indicate increasing temperature from blue to yellow. The glowing inner kernel can be clearly distinguished. In Table 1 we compare timings for various parts of the algorithm. These are mainly the elapsed times needed to read and write the frame buffer (**FbOps**) and to render the element's faces (**GrOps**), and the cpu time required to calculate the interpolation weights for all slices (**Cmp**).

Table 1: Processed primitives and timings (seconds) for the finite-element data set. (400 slices, 400x400 viewport)

	#Tetra	FbOps	GrOps	Cmp	Total
fedata0	60000	5.0	9.2	6.4	20.6
fedata1	110000	5.0	11.5	6.4	22.9
fedata2	150000	5.0	15.3	6.4	25.7
fedata3	200000	5.0	18.0	6.4	29.4

Observe that the time needed to compute the interpolation weights does not change since the number of pixels which have to be processed remains constant.

The experimental times are significantly faster than the times proposed in [31, 25, 22] without noticeable losses in the image quality. Compared to the lazy sweep algorithm [21], however, our method is slightly slower. The significant improvement is that the expected times do not depend on the grid topology. As a consequence we end up with constant frame rates for arbitrary topologies but equal number of primitives. This is a major difference to a variety of existing approaches which exploit the connectivity between cells. Once the first intersection with the boundaries has been computed the grid can be traversed very efficiently taking benefit of the pre-computed neighborhood information.

Our final image shows a particular state of a binary cellular automaton. A test case for which we expect other techniques taking advantage of the coherence between primitives to be significantly slower. Each primitive represents a living cell in the automaton. Originally, 8000 cells were generated. Each cell has been converted to 12 tetrahedra which have the center point of the original cell in common. In order to show a potential surface around the centers of the cells, there, the material values were set to one. At all other vertices they were set to zero. No connectivity information was used. The time needed to render the shown iso-surface was 1.8 seconds. Direct volume rendering with the same settings as described took 14.1 seconds.

Obviously, since the performance of our algorithms strongly depends on the throughput of the geometry engine as well as the rasterization unit, we expect them to be accelerated considerably if run on the currently available high-end systems like the InfiniteReality or future architectures.

6   Conclusion

In this paper we have presented many different ideas to exploit advanced features offered by modern high-end graphics workstations through standard APIs like OpenGL in volume rendering applications. In particular, real-time rendering of shaded iso-surfaces has been made possible for Cartesian and tetrahedral grids avoiding any polygonal representation. Furthermore, we have presented a direct volume rendering algorithm for unstructured grids with arbitrary topology by means of hardware supported geometry processing and color interpolation. Since any connectivity information has been abandoned we expect the frame rates to be independent of the grid topology.

Our results have shown that the presented methods are significantly faster than other methods previously proposed while only introducing slight image degradations. Since we take advantage of graphics hardware whenever possible, the number of operations to be performed in software is minimized making the algorithms relatively simple and easy to implement. However, there are still several areas to be explored in this research:

- **Hardware supported specular lighting effects and shadows** will help to improve the spatial perception of volumetric objects and may also be integrated in global illumination algorithms.

- **Image based pixel manipulations** are useful in a variety of applications, e.g. image based rendering, volume morphing or vector field visualization. In this context, the benefits of pixel textures have to be explored more carefully.

- **Multi-block data sets and arbitrary cell primitives** are a major challenge in scientific visualization. Efficient rendering algorithms for these kinds of representation still need to be developed.

7   Acknowledgments

Special thanks to Wolgang Heidrich for valuable suggestions and advice concerning the OpenGL implementation, and Ove Sommer who did integrate some of the ideas into our OpenInventor based visualization tool.

References

[1] K. Akeley. Reality Engine Graphics. *ACM Computer Graphics, Proc. SIGGRAPH '93*, pages 109–116, July 1993.

[2] B. Cabral, N. Cam, and J. Foran. Accelerated Volume Rendering and Tomographic Reconstruction Using Texture Mapping Hardware. In *ACM Symposium on Volume Visualization '94*, pages 91–98, 1994.

[3] T.J. Cullip and U. Neumann. Accelerating Volume Reconstruction with 3D Texture Hardware. Technical Report TR93-027, University of North Carolina, Chapel Hill N.C., 1993.

[4] J. Danskin and P. Hanrahan. Fast Algorithms for Volume Ray Tracing. In *ACM Workshop on Volume Visualization '92*, pages 91–98, 1992.

[5] M. Garrity. Ray Tracing Irregular Volume Data. In *ACM Workshop on Volume Visualization '90*, pages 35–40, 1990.

[6] C. Giertsen. Volume Visualization of Sparse Irregular Meshes. *Computer Graphics and Applications*, 12(2):40–48, 1992.

[7] P. Haeberli and K. Akeley. The Accumulation Buffer: Hardware Support for High-Quality Rendering. *ACM Computer Graphics, Proc. SIGGRAPH '90*, pages 309–318, July 1990.

[8] M. Haubner, Ch. Krapichler, A. Lösch, K.-H. Englmeier, and van Eimeren W. Virtual Reality in Medicine - Computer Graphics and Interaction Techiques. *IEEE Transactions on Information Technology in Biomedicine*, 1996.

[9] J. T. Kajiya and B. P. Von Herzen. Ray Tracing Volume Densities. *ACM Computer Graphics, Proc. SIGGRAPH '84*, 18(3):165–174, July 1984.

[10] W. Krüger. The Application of Transport Theory to the Visualization of 3-D Scalar Data Fields. In *IEEE Visualization '90*, pages 273–280, 1990.

[11] P. Lacroute and M Levoy. Fast Volume Rendering Using a Shear-Warp Factorization of the Viewing Transform. *Computer Graphics, Proc. SIGGRAPH '94*, 28(4):451–458, 1994.

[12] D. Laur and P. Hanrahan. Hierarchical Splatting: A Progressive Refinement Algorithm for Volume Rendering. *ACM Computer Graphics, Proc. SIGGRAPH '93*, 25(4):285–288, July 1991.

[13] M. Levoy. Efficient Ray Tracing of Volume Data. *ACM Transactions on Graphics*, 9(3):245–261, July 1990.

[14] W.E. Lorensen and H.E. Cline. Marching Cubes: A High Resolution 3D Surface Construction Algorithm. *ACM Computer Graphics, Proc. SIGGRAPH '87*, 21(4):163–169, 1987.

[15] N. Max, P. Hanrahan, and R. Crawfis. Area and Volume Coherence for Efficient Visualization of 3D Scalar Functions. In *ACM Workshop on Volume Visualization '91*, pages 27–33, 1991.

[16] C. Montani, R. Scateni, and R. Scopigno. Discretized Marching Cubes. In *IEEE Visualization'94*, pages 281–287, 1994.

[17] J. Montrym, D. Baum, D. Dignam, and C. Migdal. Infinite Reality: A Real-Time Graphics System. *Computer Graphics, Proc. SIGGRAPH '97*, pages 293–303, July 1997.

[18] M. Peercy, J. Airy, and B. Cabral. Efficient Bump Mapping Hardware. *Computer Graphics, Proc. SIGGRAPH '97*, pages 303–307, July 1997.

[19] H. Shen and C. Johnson. Sweeping Simplices: A Fast Iso-Surface Axtraction Algorithm for Unstructured Grids. In *IEEE Visualization '95*, pages 143–150, 1995.

[20] P. Shirley and A. Tuchman. A Polygonal Approximation to Direct Scalar Volume Rendering. *ACM Computer Graphics, Proc. SIGGRAPH '90*, 24(5):63–70, 1990.

[21] C. Silva and J. Mitchell. The Lazy Sweep Ray Casting Algorithm for Rendering Irregular Grids. *Transactions on Visualization and Computer Graphics*, 4(2), June 1997.

[22] C. Silva, J. Mitchell, and A. Kaufman. Fast Rendering of Irregular Grids. In *ACM Symposium on Volume Visualization '96*, pages 15–23, 1996.

[23] C. Stein, B. Becker, and N. Max. Sorting and hardware assisted rendering for volume visualization. In *ACM Symposium on Volume Visualization '94*, pages 83–90, 1994.

[24] A. Van Gelder and K. Kwansik. Direct Volume Rendering with Shading via Three-Dimensional Textures. In R. Crawfis and Ch. Hansen, editors, *ACM Symposium on Volume Visualization '96*, pages 23–30, 1996.

[25] R. Westermann and T. Ertl. The VSBUFFER: Visibility Ordering unstructured Volume Primitives by Polygon Drawing. In *IEEE Visualization '97*, pages 35–43, 1997.

[26] J. Wilhelms and A. Van Gelder. Octrees for faster Iso-Surface Generation. *ACM Transactions on Graphics*, 11(3):201–297, July 1992.

[27] J. Wilhelms, A. van Gelder, P. Tarantino, and J. Gibbs. Hierarchical and Parallelizable Direct Volume Rendering for Irregular and Multiple Grids. In *IEEE Visualization 1996*, pages 57–65, 1996.

[28] P. Williams. Visibility Ordering Meshed Polyhedra. *ACM Transactions on Graphics*, 11(2):102–126, 1992.

[29] P. Williams and N. Max. A Volume Density Optical Model. In *ACM Workshop on Volume Visualization '92*, pages 61–69, 1992.

[30] O. Wilson, A. Van Gelder, and J. Wilhelms. Direct Volume Rendering via 3D Textures. Technical Report UCSC-CRL-94-19, University of California, Santa Cruz, 1994.

[31] R. Yagel, D. Reed, A. Law, P. Shih, and N. Shareef. Hardware Assisted Volume Rendering of Unstructured Grids by Incremental Slicing. In *ACM Symposium on Volume Visualization '96*, pages 55–63, 1996.

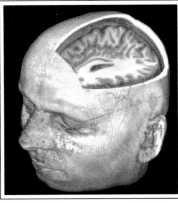

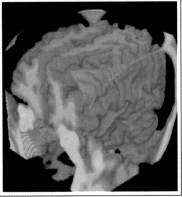

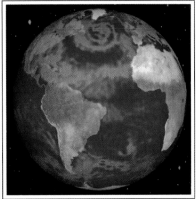

(a) Box clipping performed with the stencil buffer.

(b) Inverse box clipping of the brain.

(c) Visualizing atmospheric volume data with the pixel texture.

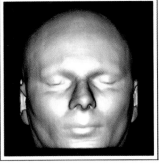

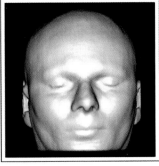

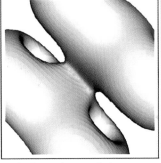

(d) Iso-surface rendering by software ray-casting.

(e) Iso-surface rendering performed with a 3D gradient texture.

(f) Iso-surface rendering performed with a 3D gradient texture.

(g) Iso-surface rendering by frame buffer arithmetic.

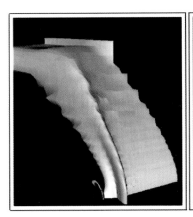

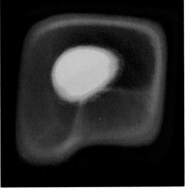

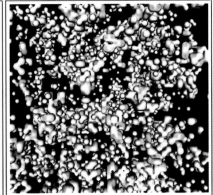

(h) Shaded iso-surface extracted from the NASA bluntfin data set.

(i) Direct volume rendering of a finite-element data set.

(j) Iso-surface displayed from a highly irregular topology.

Figure 10: Image plate showing the results of hardware supported volume visualization.

The Office of the Future: A Unified Approach to Image-Based Modeling and Spatially Immersive Displays

Ramesh Raskar, Greg Welch, Matt Cutts, Adam Lake, Lev Stesin,

and

Henry Fuchs

University of North Carolina at Chapel Hill and
the NSF Science and Technology Center for Computer Graphics and Scientific Visualization[†]

Abstract

We introduce ideas, proposed technologies, and initial results for an *office of the future* that is based on a unified application of computer vision and computer graphics in a system that combines and builds upon the notions of the CAVE™, tiled display systems, and image-based modeling. The basic idea is to use real-time computer vision techniques to dynamically extract per-pixel depth and reflectance information for the visible surfaces in the office including walls, furniture, objects, and people, and then to either project images *on* the surfaces, render images *of* the surfaces, or interpret changes *in* the surfaces. In the first case, one could designate every-day (potentially irregular) real surfaces in the office to be used as *spatially immersive display* surfaces, and then project high-resolution graphics and text onto those surfaces. In the second case, one could transmit the dynamic image-based models over a network for display at a remote site. Finally, one could interpret dynamic changes in the surfaces for the purposes of tracking, interaction, or augmented reality applications.

To accomplish the simultaneous capture and display we envision an office of the future where the ceiling lights are replaced by computer controlled cameras and "smart" projectors that are used to capture dynamic image-based models with *imperceptible structured light* techniques, and to display high-resolution images on designated display surfaces. By doing both simultaneously on the designated display surfaces, one can dynamically adjust or autocalibrate for geometric, intensity, and resolution variations resulting from irregular or changing display surfaces, or overlapped projector images.

Our current approach to dynamic image-based modeling is to use an optimized structured light scheme that can capture per-pixel depth and reflectance at interactive rates. Our system implementation is not yet imperceptible, but we can demonstrate the approach in the laboratory. Our approach to rendering on the designated (potentially irregular) display surfaces is to employ a two-pass projective texture scheme to generate images that when projected onto the surfaces appear correct to a moving head-tracked observer. We present here an initial implementation of the overall vision, in an office-like setting, and preliminary demonstrations of our dynamic modeling and display techniques.

† CB 3175, Sitterson Hall, Chapel Hill, NC, 27599-3175
{raskar, welch, cutts, lake, stesin, fuchs}@cs.unc.edu
http://www.cs.unc.edu/~{raskar, welch, cutts, lake, stesin, fuchs}
http://www.cs.brown.edu/stc/

CR Categories and Subject Descriptors: I.3.3 [Computer Graphics]: Picture/Image Generation—Digitizing and scanning; Display algorithms; Viewing algorithms; I.3.7 [Computer Graphics]: Three-Dimensional Graphics and Realism—Virtual reality; I.4.1 [Image Processing and Computer Vision]: Digitization and Image Capture—Imaging geometry; Reflectance; Sampling; Scanning; I.4.8 [Image Processing and Computer Vision]: Scene Analysis—Color; Range data; Shading; Shape; Surface fitting; Time-varying imagery; Tracking; I.4.9 [Image Processing and Computer Vision]: Applications; B.4.2 [Input/Output and Data Communications] Input/Output Devices—Image display

Additional Key Words and Phrases: display, spatially immersive display, intensity blending, image-based modeling, image-based rendering, range, depth, reflectance, projection, virtual environments, calibration, autocalibration.

Figure 1: A conceptual sketch of the *office of the future*. By replacing the normal office lights with projectors, one could obtain precise control over all of the light in the office. With the help of synchronized cameras, the geometry and reflectance information can be captured for all of the visible surfaces in the office so that one can project images *on* the surfaces, render images *of* the surfaces, or interpret changes *in* the surfaces. The inset image is intended to help differentiate between the projected images and the real objects in the sketch.

1 INTRODUCTION

The impetus for this work is Henry Fuchs's long-time desire to build more compelling and useful systems for shared telepresence and telecollaboration between distant individuals. It was Fuchs who first inspired us with ideas for using a "sea of cameras" [39]

and imperceptible lights to extract a 3D scene and to reconstruct it at a remote location. These ideas have been refined over several years of collaboration with Ruzena Bajcsy of the University of Pennsylvania's GRASP Laboratory [18], and with our colleagues in the NSF Science and Technology Center for Computer Graphics and Scientific Visualization.

While we are making progress toward our vision for the *office of the future*, we do not yet have a complete working system—the ideas are by definition futuristic. As such, throughout the paper we present a mix of demonstrated results from new methods, and plausible ideas for future systems. We do our best to distinguish between the two lest the reader be led to believe that we have implemented something that we have not.

In the remainder of this section we present motivation for the idea in the form of a story that outlines the developments that led to the vision as presented in this paper. In section 2 we discuss the principal components of the envisioned system, without necessarily discussing a specific implementation. In section 3 we present our approach to actually implementing such an office of the future. In section 4 we discuss our current implementation, and in section 5 we discuss work to be done and future research topics. Note that rather than including a specific "previous work" section we have chosen to discuss related work throughout the paper.

Telecollaboration Interfaces

While telecollaboration systems using 2D "talking heads" and shared white boards have improved significantly over the years, we believe that the through-the-window paradigm itself often inhibits much of the interaction that would otherwise take place if the collaborators were actually together in the same room. In [5] Buxton identifies several tasks for which commercial televideo systems provide only limited support. Aside from limited resolution, part of the problem is that users are forced to maintain two separate *egocenters* (notions of where they are and who they are with): one in their local environment, and another egocenter with the remote collaborators. The participants must then consider and adjust normal behavior to "fit through the window."

One alternative is to implement a shared immersive virtual environment where a user dons a head-mounted display (HMD), disappears from the real world, and enters a shared virtual environment "inside the display" where for example they might see virtual objects along with 2D video avatars of their collaborators. Indeed, we have experimented with such paradigms, as have others. However this interface has several disadvantages. Most obvious are the typical ergonomic problems, for example size, weight, mobility, limited resolution, and limited field of view. Furthermore, for immersive HMD's, the resulting disassociation from a person's comfortable surroundings can be disconcerting and can limit their ability to interact with other people and real objects in the environment.

A more attractive alternative is to get the display off of the user's head, and to instead use a *spatially immersive display* (SID). A SID is a display that physically surrounds the viewer with a panorama of imagery [4]. SID's are typically room-sized, thus accommodating multiple viewers, and are usually implemented with multiple fixed front or rear-projection display units. Probably the most well-known examples of general-purpose SID's are the Cave Automated Virtual Environment (CAVE™) [12], the related tiled-display PowerWall and Infinity Wall™ systems, and Alternate Realities' VisionDome [2]. There are several good examples of telecollaboration applications where the users see and interact with their remote collaborators using a CAVE™ or CAVE™-like system, for example [34]. Such large systems typically require significant physical floor space, for example in a laboratory where there is room for both the screens and the projection units. But we would like to *avoid* going "down the hall"

to use the system, instead we would like something as convenient as the telephone—a SID built into an office.

While such an endeavor would probably not be cost-effective solely for the purpose of telecollaboration, if it were of high enough quality one could use it for every-day 2D computer work, video, and 3D immersive visualization. However not only does the construction of such SID's require very careful engineering and assembly, but certain characteristics vary with time and environmental factors such as temperature or vibration. Such time-varying characteristics include the intrinsic and extrinsic projector parameters, intensity balance, color balance, edge alignment, and blending. These problems are most often addressed by periodic mechanical projector calibration, however this approach becomes increasingly difficult and less reliable as the number of projectors increases. Flight simulator developers have faced such problems for some time, and while they have developed digital calibration systems, the systems tend to be highly specialized, thus increasing development cost and overall complexity. A more general-purpose autocalibration scheme would be preferable so that one could modify the display surface or projector configuration as needed. If one could modify the display surface, one could spontaneously add a "drawing board" onto their desktop and the system would account for it. If one had some flexibility over projector placement, one could for example add projectors in an overlapping manner to increase the display resolution (a high-resolution region), or image intensity, or side-by-side to increase the display surface area.

Telecollaboration Infrastructure and Applications

There exists a relatively large body of work in telecollaboration infrastructures and applications, not to mention a large body of work in the area of Computer-Supported Cooperative Work (CSCW). Some representative examples are [34, 37, 6, 15, 28, 19, 27, 36, 3, 41, 10, 33, 37]. Our vision for the office of the future is one in which all of this and similar work can be applied, we hope in new and exciting ways. We envision our office as a particularly compelling interface to be used in support of these efforts, and every-day applications. We are aware of no other one system that attempts to achieve what we do in a similar unified approach.

Of the existing telecollaboration efforts that we know about, the only one that attempts to provide an office-like interface is TelePort [20]. The TelePort system uses wall-sized displays that each show a synthetic scene that is blended with video images of remote participants. As participants move, their locations are tracked so that the images are rendered from the proper perspective. The TelePort display is built into a room that is carefully designed to match the rendered room. The goal is for the virtual room to seem as an extension of the real room. They use carefully constructed geometric models for the office environment, and video-based human avatars obtained by separating the remote participants from the original background (via delta-keying). Rather than building a specialized telecollaboration system that resembles an office, we want to build capability for a life-like shared-room experience *into* existing offices.

"Every Millimeter at Every Millisecond"

One question in our minds was how should remote collaborators and their environment appear remotely? While acceptable for some tasks, we believe that 2D video-based avatars do not effectively engender the sense of being with another person that is necessary for effective interpersonal communication. We want to see and interact with collaborators in 3D, as naturally as we do when we are in the same physical room: gesturing, pointing, walking, waving, using all of the subtle nuances of both verbal and nonverbal communication. A visually attractive possibility would be to use a high-quality 3D image-based rendering or modeling system for each participant (see for example [30, 38, 40, 43]). However we dream of a room-sized working volume, not only because we want mobility, but also because we want to be able to see multiple participants, and to see everyone in their natural surroundings, i.e. their offices. In short, we envision a system similar to [20] where the local and remote offices appear to be physically joined together along some common junction such as a designated wall that is actually a SID. But unlike [20] which overlays 2D video of the remote participants onto a virtual adjoining office, we want to see an image-based 3D reconstruction of the remote office and all of its real contents including people and every-day clutter. That is, we have the ability to capture and remotely display a dynamic image-based model of an entire office.

At some point when considering all of these factors, we came to the realization that if we had access to a dynamic image-based model of the entire office, *including* the designated SID surfaces, we could automatically correct for changes in the time-varying geometric characteristics of the SID. Furthermore, if several cameras could see the display surfaces from a variety of angles, we should be able to observe view-dependent intensity and color variations in the designated display surfaces, thus inferring the surface reflectance properties. In other words, while obtaining an image-based model for the office we could autocalibrate all of the designated display surfaces. Thus the realization that *the SID could in effect be almost anything or anywhere in the office*! It wouldn't matter if the surfaces were irregularly shaped, or if the geometry was changing over time, the image-based model would indicate the variations. And if one was willing to sacrifice some dynamic range in the projected images, one might even be able to use the surface reflectance information to account for slight variations in view-dependent intensity. Note that a crucial advantage of this unified approach is that because the autocalibration and the projection are done by the same device, one eliminates the problems of calibration and drift of the calibration system itself.

Finally, we also note that if one has access to a dynamic image-based model of the entire office, including the occupants, one could potentially extract higher-level representations of the data, assign semantics to those higher-level objects, and then in real-time interpret and respond to object motion or collisions for the purpose of tracking, interaction, or augmented reality (AR). With such capability one could implement untethered interaction as in the Luminous Room, where cameras and projectors serve as "I/O Bulbs" [46, 47]. In this way for example one might be able to track a person's hands so that they could reach out and manipulate a floating 3D model, or perhaps one could detect collisions between real and virtual objects so that virtual objects could be placed on the desk.

Figure 1 depicts a conceptual sketch of our *office of the future,* replicated and in use at three different sites. Note the ceiling-mounted projectors and cameras, the use of lightly-colored material on the designated SID wall and desk area, and the mixed use of that SID for simultaneous image-based and geometric model visualization.

To achieve the above capabilities of acquisition, calibration, and display in a continuously changing office scene with both local and remote participants, we dream of being able to control light in the office over "every millimeter at every millisecond."

2 FUNDAMENTAL COMPONENTS

Our idea for the *office of the future* brings together several fundamental areas of computer science, components that can be enumerated independently from descriptions of their actual implementations. While one goal of this paper is to present the specific implementation of such a system, this does not preclude the use of any of the techniques others have developed in each of these areas. Quite to the contrary, we believe there are trade-offs with all of these techniques which warrant further investigation.

2.1 Dynamic Image-Based Modeling

One of the major components of the system is the module that will capture, continually and in real time, image-based models of the office environment including all of the designated display surfaces. A large body of literature exists from computer vision regarding the determination of depth from a scene. Some of the more common approaches include depth from motion, stereo, focus, and defocus. For our system we are interested not only in dynamic image-based modeling, but over a large volume also. With real-time in mind, many of the techniques traditionally used are difficult because of computational and bandwidth requirements. At CMU, a specialized hardware real-time depth from stereo architecture system has been developed [31]. It can take input from six cameras and produce, at 30 frames/second, a 256×240 depth map aligned with an intensity image. They also have the ability to produce an uncertainty estimation for each pixel. One advantage of this technique is the instantaneous sample-and-hold nature of depth from stereo. In contrast, using a laser scanner that cannot complete a scan of the image in a single frame may result in distorted shapes as objects in the scene move. Any technique which depends on computations made with several frames sampled at different times, including the structured light method described in section 3.1, will have this problem.

Another real-time depth system has been developed by the Columbia University Automated Visual Environment Group [38]. They have demonstrated the ability to produce 512×480 depth estimates at 30 Hz with an accuracy of 0.3%. Their technique relies on a precise physical model of all the optical sensing and computational elements in the system: the optical transfer function, defocus, image sensing and sampling, and focus measure operators. They project a high frequency texture onto the scene and, via the same optical path, image the scene. An advantage of this system over the depth from stereo is that they do not have to worry about the correspondence problem faced by depth from stereo. One concern is the distracting high frequency textures which much be projected onto the scene. These patterns could prove unacceptable if the user wants to be in the environment while the scene is being captured.

2.2 Rendering

Our vision for the *office of the future* requires the ability to generate images that when projected onto the display surfaces appear correct to a moving head-tracked observer. This is true also for systems such as the CAVE™, but our situation is somewhat unusual in that we want to be able to project onto general surfaces whereas the CAVE™ system is tailored to planar surfaces. Future capabilities in image generation will allow the increased burden of display on arbitrary surfaces to be realized.

An interesting technique is presented in [16] for the use of computer graphics systems in theater design, where she models the appearance of backdrops from the audience's perspective. If left uncorrected, the backdrops would appear distorted. Essentially, we are faced with the same problem in our system, except with multiple projectors. We need to determine how to predistort the images such that, when projected from the projector's viewpoint, it will look correct from the user's viewpoint. Dorsey *et al.* also extend this technique to model the projector optics and demonstrates an extended radiosity method to simulate directional lighting characteristics.

2.3 Spatially Immersive Displays

The most well known spatially immersive display in the graphics community is probably the CAVE™ [12]. The CAVE™ exists in many forms, typically it is configured as a left, right, and rear wall rear projection system. In some implementations they use a mirror above the CAVE™ that projects an image onto the floor. While the

CAVE™ does provide head-tracked stereo views surrounding the user of the system, current implementations are limited to 1 projector displayed on each wall. The CAVE™ does not deal with intensity blending and has no method of capturing the geometry of the environment, which is reasonable since this was not an intended goal of their system.

The military simulation/flight simulator industry is full of numerous examples of spatially immersive displays [9, 23, 29, 32, 35]. These systems typical use CRT projectors which need frequent calibration. Also, they usually (but not always) restrict themselves to matching the seams of the display instead of considering the whole display area as something that needs to be blended seamlessly. Another technique of the flight simulator industry is to place a high resolution display in the center of view of the user and project a low resolution image on the surrounding screen, or to only project an image in the view frustum of the user. While this is effective, it cannot easily be repositioned and may show a seam where the high resolution image meets the low resolution image. The seam is a problem because it is disconcerting and severely disrupts the goal of achieving a feeling of being somewhere else—the user is always reminded they are looking at an imperfect display surface. The attempts at creating a seamless display are discussed in the previously cited flight simulator papers.

Domed displays are another example [2]. Such systems are often limited to only one high resolution projector and have rarely employed a mechanism to capture depth or projection surface information from the scene. A method is presented in [29] that corrects the warping of the dome by modeling a dome with a 5-degree polygon mesh and a GUI for manipulating the coordinates of this mesh, but this is not done in real-time or automatically: direct user intervention is required. This method is meant to only be used when the system is moved or for some infrequent reason falls out of alignment, it is not meant to be a method that can update the projection in real-time as the display surface changes shape or occlusion properties.

A final important point about all of these systems is that they rely on special geometric configurations and they present no general solution, which is a completely reasonable design decision on their part: typically they had an unchanging environment with uniform, ideal display surfaces. Also, they had control of every issue of the display system, from the lighting to the precise calibration of the projectors. Instead, we propose a general solution to the problem of projecting onto arbitrary display surfaces with real-time, automatic calibration procedures. Understand that we do not necessarily believe people will want to project on every type of surface or object, but we feel that thinking about the problem in this way is useful.

3 METHODS

In this section we describe the idea of using cameras and projectors that can be operated in either a capture or display mode. (See Figure 2 and Figure 8.) When in capture mode, the projectors and cameras can be used together to obtain per-pixel depth and reflectance information from the designated display surfaces. When in display mode, the image-based models may be used to render and then project geometrically and photometrically correct images onto the (potentially irregular) display surfaces.

3.1 Dynamic Image-Based Modeling

Image-based modeling is a difficult problem, one that has occupied the computer vision community for many years.

Depth Extraction

The depth extraction method for office scenes should work in large working volumes populated with areas with high frequency texture as well as surfaces that lack texture. To model display surfaces, we

Figure 2: Our current implementation of the *office of the future.* (a) The cameras and digital light projectors are mounted near the ceiling using Unistrut material. (b) The walls consist of white foam-core board mounted on vertical posts. As shown in (b), they are used as display surfaces for a spatially-immersive display (SID).

typically need high accuracy so that the projections are correct. To model dynamically changing scenes we need higher update rates to represent motion with potentially decreased resolution or accuracy. The method should be non-intrusive so that people can work in the environment. This prevents the use of lasers or other invasive methods.

Our system currently uses one video camera and one projector in a pair, although multiple cameras could work with one projector [43]. The correspondence problem is solved by projecting binary coded vertical bars [14]. The camera looks at a set of n successive images, creates binary images using adaptive thresholding on a per-pixel basis, and generates an n-bit code for every pixel corresponding to the code for the vertical bar that was imaged at this pixel. This allows us to distinguish between 2^n projected vertical bars. A pre-computed sparse triangulation lookup table based on calibration data allows trilinear interpolation to compute intersection of pseudo-camera rays and projected vertical planes. The 3D coordinates of the surface points imaged at every pixel are later used with color information to complete the image-based model. The vertical bars can be projected repeatedly to compute depth for dynamic scenes. The same method can be used for scanning walls, people or moving objects with different levels of sophistication for sub-pixel image thresholding. See Figure 3 for some still-frame sample results.

A choice of a camera and projector to actively scan 3D environments is necessitated by the fact that display surfaces may lack texture to provide enough correspondence cues. Use of the same projector for scanning and display allows unification of the two tasks and the only additional component is a camera. Speed versus accuracy trade-offs led us to two types of camera-projector pairs. Relatively static display surfaces such as walls and furniture in office scenes are modeled more accurately and slowly by the outward looking pairs of camera-projector than people and moving objects, which are scanned by inward looking pairs of camera-projectors.

The difficult part of using two separate devices for depth extraction is calibration. We use [45] first to find intrinsic and extrinsic parameters of the camera using a checkerboard pattern on

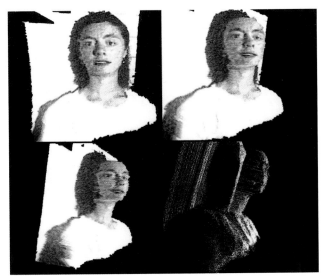

Figure 3: Some example results (still frames from live updates) of depth extraction using binary coded structured light.

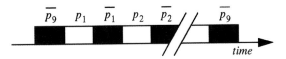

Sequence of patterns and their complements.

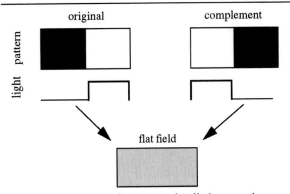

Figure 4: Pattern and complement are visually integrated over time, the result is the appearance of a flat field, or "white" light.

a flat surface. Then the same method is used to calibrate the projector with respect to the same flat surface. Combining the two gives the relationship between the camera and the projector. To find the relationship between two camera-projector pairs, the transformation between the two cameras is first determined by viewing a common checkerboard pattern on a flat surface. Then, using the method described above, the two pairs are calibrated with respect to the working volume. The procedure is easier if the frustums of the two cameras overlap considerably.

Detection of changes in scene geometry by camera image differencing is not robust when display surfaces lack texture. However, changes in a projected random texture can be imaged The random texture itself will be imperceptible to the human eye as described in section 3.2. Detected changes in scene geometry over a period of time could be the result of either actual changes in the surfaces or drift in the calibrated system.

The use of cameras allow the possibility to self-calibrate the system periodically to compensate for errors due to environmental factors such as temperature or vibrations in the setup.

Color and Reflectance

The projector is used in two modes, scene extraction and display. To get color information about the surfaces the projector is used as a bright light source along with a synchronized camera. However, the modes can be interleaved by inserting completely white frames in between the display frames. In the binary pulse-coded modulation (PCM) coded light projectors, only a few bits are used to project white frames while other bits can be used to project the display frames at reduced color resolution.

Currently we illuminate the scene with a black followed by white pattern and observe the resultant dark image and bright image from one view point to estimate the per-pixel reflectance function. The reflectance function is primarily used to threshold images of projected binary coded structured light patterns assuming the camera response is linear to intensity. Camera response curves can be estimated by illuminating the scene with different levels of intensity. To complete the image based model, surfaces in the scene can be sampled from multiple view points to estimate a bidirectional reflectance distribution (BRDF) function.

The camera is used for per-pixel depth extraction as well as color extraction. Since the two procedures share the same optical axis, there is no drift. Similarly, the same projector is used for projecting structured light patterns, for depth extraction, and for

display on the depth extracted surface. This eliminating problems due to drift or misalignment.

3.2 Imperceptible Structured Light

With respect to the structured light described in section 3.1, our goal is to make it appear to the casual observer as nothing more than incandescent white light, not a succession of flashing binary patterns. Our method for doing this is to use *imperceptible structured light.* The approach is a combination of time-division multiplexing and light cancellation techniques to hide the patterns in a rapid series of white-light projections. Figure 4 depicts a sequence of patterns projected in time. A binary structured light approach such as ours uses n patterns to resolve 2^n projected vertical bars. The period of pattern repetition would be, for example, $1/60$ second for a 60 Hz depth extraction rate. Figure 4 depicts how a given pattern p_i and complement $\bar{p}_i$ are integrated by the visual system in such a way that the sequence appears to be the projection of a flat field or white light. The same approach can be applied to project imperceptible structured light along with video or graphics images, facilitating imperceptible autocalibration of designated display surfaces. We use a digital light projector [25, 26] which uses PCM to project the pattern and its complement. A synchronized camera can measure the structured light by integrating light during the pattern projection.

While limited access to digital light projector specifications currently limits our ability to implement completely imperceptible image-based modeling, we are able to separately demonstrate real-time capture and imperceptible structured light. Figure 5 shows the effect in a laboratory experiment. Figure 6 shows the use of a similar approach to embed imperceptible structured light in a still image as opposed to white light. We are working together with the developers of the projector technology to obtain lower-level access to the technology, which will introduce a whole new realm of possibilities for dynamic structured light and display.

3.3 Geometric Registration

The depth data acquired from different cameras needs to be zipped together to complete the display surface geometry. This is required for generating correct images from a single projector for multisurfaces [42] and also for intensity blending if the projections from multiple projectors overlap. The depth images are taken from distinct cameras and are in different coordinate systems. Thus in order to tile the extracted surfaces together corresponding points

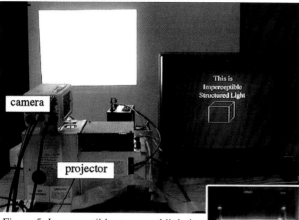

Figure 5: Imperceptible structured light is demonstrated in the laboratory. The digital projector on the left is projecting the text shown in the monitor and its complement , however the text can only be seen with a synchronized camera such as that sitting on the projector above. The inset snapshot of an oscilloscope shows the pulses that correspond to the brief time when the pattern (text in this case) is being projected.

Figure 6: Imperceptible structured light embedded in images. (a) An initial image (Tokaj, Hungary). (b) The binary image that is to be imperceptible. (c) The two images combined and mapped to the proper time-division bit sequence. (d) The final result, showing the initial image (with reduced dynamic range) being projected on the wall, while the embedded imperceptible image is captured and displayed on the monitor (lower left).

from overlap regions are used. The corresponding points are generated using the binary coded structured light approach for rows and columns of projector pixels. The binary code of an imaged point uniquely identifies the corresponding projector pixel. Pairs of pixels in two cameras that share the binary code are used to compute transformation between depth data sets. Note that this transformation between two cameras can also be pre-computed during calibration stage but is usually not sufficiently accurate to register two depth data sets. Otherwise, for blending purposes, the geometric correspondence between pixels of two different projectors is established by observing the projection overlap region from a single camera. We assume that every pair of images has a substantial overlap (about one-third of its total area).

3.4 Rendering and Display

Our goal is to generate images that appear correct to an observer when projected onto (potentially irregular) display surfaces. Since the observer can move around in the office, we currently use magnetic head-tracking to determine the viewer's location. The inputs to the algorithm are a model of the surface, the projector's intrinsic and extrinsic parameters, the viewer's location, and a "desired image," the image which we want the viewer to see. The desired image will typically be the result of conventional 3-D rendering.

Our algorithm can work with any general type of surface representation (e.g. NURBs), as long as the model of the real-world display surface is accurate. Likewise, rendering could be done with many different methods (e.g. ray-tracing); our current implementation uses projective textures with OpenGL primitives to achieve hardware acceleration. The underlying projective textures [44] technique is an extension of perspectively-correct texture mapping that can be used to do arbitrary projection of two dimensional images onto geometry in real-time.

We describe a two pass approach for rendering and displaying images of 3D scenes on potentially irregular surfaces. In the first pass, we compute the "desired image" for the viewer by rendering the 3D scene from the observer's viewpoint. This desired image is stored as a texture map. In the second pass the texture is effectively projected from the user's viewpoint onto the polygonal model of the display surface. The display surface (with the desired image texture mapped onto it) is then rendered from the projector's viewpoint. The resulting image, when displayed by the projector, will produce the desired image for the viewer. As the user moves, the desired image changes and it is also projected from the user's new location.

Multiple projectors can be used to increase the display surface area. To ensure complete coverage of the display surface, every part of the display surface must be visible to at least one projector. To ensure complete coverage from a given viewpoint, at least one projector must be able to image on every surface visible from that viewpoint. The projectors' viewpoints in the second pass typically remains fixed. Neither projector overlap nor self-occlusions of display surfaces from observer's viewpoint need hinder the effective image from the user's viewpoint. See Figure 7.

To specify the viewing direction for projecting textures with monocular viewing, we only need the position of the user and not orientation. A field of view that contains all the polygons of the synthetic object is sufficient for the frustum of texture projection. This frustum may be trimmed if it exceeds the frustum of the display surface model. The frustum is oriented from the viewer's location toward the polygonal model of display surfaces. The user's frustum parameters during the first pass and texture projection in the second pass are identical.

We assume that the projectors have no radial distortion and hence the projectors can be modeled with a pinhole camera. For the optics of digital micromirror device (DMD) projectors, this assumption is valid. However, if the projector has radial distortion, we must pre-distort the rendered image before it is sent to the projector framebuffer. This pre-distortion can be done using non-linear 3D warp of display surface geometry or using screen space 2D warp with texture mapping.

Challenges
Speed.
The two pass rendering method consists of normal 3D rendering in the first pass, followed by a second pass that maps the desired image to a display surface model. The additional cost of the algorithm comes from transferring the framebuffer from the first pass into texture memory and rendering the display surface model with texture mapping applied in the second pass. Thus it is crucial to simplify the display surface geometries.

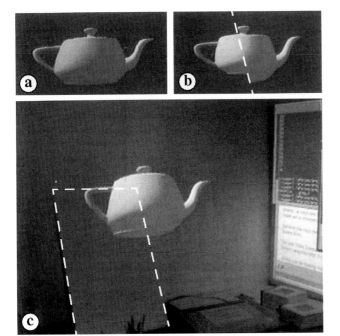

Figure 7: Multisurface rendering. (a) A teapot projected onto a single planar surface. (b) A distorted projection resulting from the introduction of a second planar display surface. (c) The final corrected projection obtained by extracting the display surface geometry and then employing our two-pass rendering scheme. The edges of the second planar surface—shown leaning against the wall on the desk in (c)—are highlighted with a dashed line.

Parallelization

If more than one projector is used, each projector can have a separate display engine. Rendering can be done in parallel, and each display engine need only load those parts of the display surface model that are visible from the corresponding projector. We have some initial evidence [42] that our method is faster versus conventional rendering techniques with multiple projectors, complex displays, or complex graphics models. The reason is that the first pass of the algorithm (conventional rendering) only needs to be done once, and then the second pass can be performed for each projector. Conventional techniques require the graphics model to be re-rendered for each projector or even for each polygon in the display surface.

If the first pass is also parallelized, all the corresponding graphics pipelines need to access the synthetic model being displayed simultaneously. This could be a problem if the model is dynamically changing and the graphics pipeline must read the model during every display iteration. Other parallelization issues include if the display surface model is dynamic, as well as network issues if the display engines are on different machines.

Latency

There is inherent latency in the system in addition to traditional tracking and rendering latency due to two pass method for drawing models. For large models, rendering times could be different for different projectors so that there is inter-projector delay during rendering. If all the projectors are driven from a single machine, then setting up viewports within a single rendering program for each projector and synchronously updating the framebuffers will eliminate this problem.

3.5 Generating Blending Functions

We use the traditional computer graphics phrase "alpha values" to describe the blending functions. When building some sort of a tiled multi-projector SID, one is faced with two approaches for handling

the transitions between the projected images: one can either design the system such that the images do not overlap but can be adjusted so that they are barely touching and thus "seamless," or one can allow projected images to overlap and employ some means of blending. The second approach typically uses a roll-off function such as a linear ramp or a cosine curve to smooth the transition between projectors.

Designers of the CAVE™ exercise the first option by limiting the system to a well-defined, relatively simple screen arrangement whereby no projectors overlap. However we want to be able to project images onto arbitrary potentially irregular display surfaces in the office, which means that we cannot use the first approach as we assume no control over the surfaces. Furthermore, we envision a more flexible setup whereby multiple projectors can be used to project into the same space in order to achieve higher resolution (e.g., via a "high-resolution insert") or increased light.

We implemented a weighting function by assigning alpha values between 0 and 1 to every pixel in every projector, and as described in section 3.3 ensure that every illuminated world point corresponding to a single camera pixel has an alpha sum equal to one. This assumes that the projectors have similar intensity response. There are two cases: a point resulting from a projection of only one projector and a point resulting from a number of projectors. In the first case the solution is trivial. However, in the second case, the case where overlap occurs, we make alpha values a function of the distance to the beginning/end of overlapping region, with the constraint that alpha values of points from different projectors, corresponding to the same point in space, must sum up to one. To assign different weights to projector pixels, we actually create an alpha image for each projector. This image contains (1 - *desired_alpha*) at each pixel. This alpha image is rendered last. In our OpenGL implementation this is achieved using transparent textures. A camera in the closed loop system allows one to photometrically correct images even when the projectors have different brightness or when the display surface has non-uniform reflectance properties. Although the digital light projectors have linear intensity response, they use a de-gamma correction [25]. Use of alpha image allows us to compensate the de-gamma correction.

3.6 Simplification of Depth Data

Dynamic image-based modeling of an entire office will result in tremendously large data sets, given that the data would be per-pixel for multiple cameras, occurring at video rates. However it is reasonable to expect that the majority of the data is highly correlated both temporally and spatially. In fact most of the office is unlikely to change dramatically over short periods of time, in particular this is likely to be true for the office walls and most designated display surfaces. It makes sense to attempt to simplify the data so that the system does not have to deal with such a horrendous volume of data. For example, Radim Sara and Ruzena Bajcsy at the University of Pennsylvania have created a depth data set of an office that has approximately half a million vertices. The simplification method must be careful not to simplify in regions of rapid change or high curvature where information might be lost. The automatic reconstruction of surfaces from range data is explored in [13, 1, 8, 11, 17, 22].

Unfortunately, the dynamic nature and the presence of noise in our system, disallow the use of well-established simplification algorithms. The method we currently employ is not a well-defined mathematical approach, but rather a heuristic-based method that produced qualitatively pleasing results based on the characteristics of our data sets. We first apply a curvature approach to the data set using a tangent method similar to [24], and we then use a Euclidean distance approach on the remaining points. We chose this particular sequence of steps because the curvature method is usually much more successful in eliminating points than the second one. This approach produces elimination rates of 80% to 90% without any visible loss of information. This is because most of the objects in the office environment are locally planar.

3.7 Tracking

While our office of the future could certainly and possibly very effectively be used in a 2D-only mode, we believe that it is more compelling to consider its additional use as a 3D visualization environment. We need the ability to track viewers' heads in order to render perspectively correct images. Interestingly enough, for monoscopic viewing one does not need the orientation of the eye because the display image is uniquely determined by the eye position. For stereoscopic viewing one needs to be able to either track one eye and the user's head orientation, or two eyes, each with position only. The system involves projecting synthetic

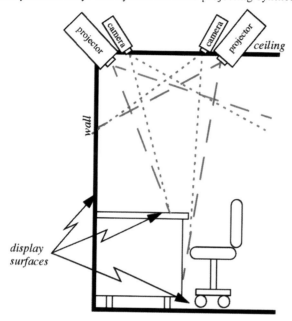

Figure 8: Digital projectors and cameras work together to capture depth, color, and surface reflectance information for objects and participants in the scene. A subset of the projectors is also used for display purposes; captured display surface depth, color, and reflectance information can be used to autocalibrate the display surfaces so that projected images are geometrically and photometrically correct from the viewer's viewpoint, and so overlapping projections are properly blended

images onto real surfaces for which the extracted surface model is assumed to be correct in world space. Any small error in tracker reading (after transformation) in world space will result in visibly incorrect registration between projected images and the display surfaces. This situation is similar to augmented reality systems where traditionally a vision based registration system is used to correct the tracker readings. A similar closed loop system may be necessary for accurate rendering for our system.

4 CURRENT IMPLEMENTATION

While a complete realization of such an office of the future is, by definition, years away, we are making steady progress and present here some promising results and demonstrations. We have implemented a working system using projective textures. We have also independently demonstrated 1) a depth extraction system running at 3 Hz, 2) imperceptible structured light, and 3) initial experiments in intensity blending.

The office size is $10 \times 10 \times 10$ feet, and is populated with five 800×600 resolution *digital light projectors* and two

640×480 resolution video cameras (Figure 2). The outward looking five projectors are driven simultaneously from an SGI Infinite Reality. Four of these project on relatively vertical surfaces and one projects down on the table and the floor. The binary PCM coded light projectors project 24 bit color at a 60Hz update rate. The projectors allow off-axis projection with a small offset without significant focus problems. The camera framegrabbers are SGI O2s and currently we use a video switcher to switch between the video cameras while capturing images of the environment. We expect that in the very near future the rendering will be done in different viewports of a single window and hence can be used to maintain synchronous updates of all projector framebuffers. The system also includes an Ascension magnetic tracker for tracking user position.

The walls of the office are made up of relatively inexpensive foam-core board, and does not need solid support because the system supports non-planar surfaces and off-axis projection. A separate projector-camera pair setup is used to create dynamic image based model in a small working volume of $3 \times 3 \times 2$ feet, and can be used for dynamic image-based modeling of human faces (see Figure 3) [43]. The system creates a 640×240 depth map at three updates per second, which is texture mapped with live video. Using a direct digital interface to the digital light projectors from a PC, we have been able to project patterns that are imperceptible to human eye but visible from a synchronized camera (see Figure 5). We have capability to change the binary PCM coding of light for the projectors allowing us to use different bits for different purposes; in particular we have the ability to burn an equal-bit-time PROM for the projectors which allows us to demonstrate compelling imperceptible structured light (see Figure 5). With the equal-bit-time PROM, a binary pattern can be displayed 24 times per 60 Hz frame, i.e. every 694 microseconds. Thus a pattern and its complement can be displayed sequentially in approximately 1.4 milliseconds. The synchronized camera with exposure time less than 700 microsecond was used in Figure 5. Using this PROM we could in theory project and capture $60 \times 24 = 1440$ binary patterns per second. Our current framegrabbers, however, can process only 60 images per second. A better digital interface to DLP's will also allow us to render stereo images at 60 Hz.

Although we expect the participants to be seating in a chair most of the time (Figure 2), the current setup allows participants of average height (under 6 feet) to stand and move around without blocking the projection on the walls if they are at least 4 feet away from the walls.

The office of the future setup allows scalability in terms of more pairs of camera and projector to either increase resolution of extracted surfaces, or resolution of display on surfaces. The system other than computer hardware costs approximately $35,000. We expect minimal maintenance of projector, cameras or display surfaces because the system employs self-calibration methods.

5 FUTURE WORK

Much work remains to be done, some of which we have concrete plans to attack, some we are attacking with collaborations, and some we hope others will pursue.

We plan to integrate scene acquisition and display in such a way that the acquisition is imperceptible, or at least unobtrusive. This will involve some combination of light control and cameras, possibly wide-field-of-view high-resolution clusters as described in [7]. Together with our collaborators in the GRASP Laboratory at the University of Pennsylvania, we are exploring the continuum of options between strict control of all of the lights in the environment (as outlined herein) and little or no control of the lights but using multiple cameras and passive correlation-based techniques. We expect to have within the coming year a new multibaseline correlation system on hand for experiments with our structured light acquisition and display environment.

As part of scene acquisition, one can detect display surface changes and adapt the rendering accordingly. Currently it can be done at non-interactive rates. Eventually we also want to explore methods as in [21] to detect surface changes for purposes such as tracking and gestural input.

We also want to improve image generation with better blending, by exploiting image-based rendering methods to construct a target image from multiple reference images. There is a good possibility that a distributed rendering scheme employing the multiprojector and multisurface display algorithms that we present and analyze in [42] will prove to be effective. In addition, we want to correct for surface reflectance discontinuities *dynamically*, and to make use of the information during run-time to adjust the rendered images.

We are planning to use our system in an on-going telecollaboration involving multi-disciplinary mechanical design and manufacturing with our collaborators in the NSF Science and Technology Center for Graphics and Visualization. In addition as part of The Tele-Immersion Initiative we are planning to make use of the CAVE™ library or similar framework to connect several laboratories over high speed networks with novel immersive display environments.

6 SUMMARY AND CONCLUSIONS

We have shown initial results for a novel semi-immersive display in an office-like environment, one that combines acquisition and display. We have developed techniques to acquire the geometry of an irregular surface and then modify rendering to allow projection onto that irregular surface so that it looks correct to an observer at a known location. We have described a method of injecting structured light into a scene that is imperceptible to the participants but measurable to synchronized cameras. These techniques can be applied to other display environments which use multiple projectors or that involve complex display geometries.

In conclusion, we note that a major trend in computer science over the past few decades has been from one to many, from being restricted by resources' proximity to employing resources irrespective of their locations. One field unaffected by this global development has been the computer display or the area where the results of our work are being presented. Our system pushes this envelope, thus enabling any object, or a collection of such, located anywhere to be used as a display surface. From now on, one does not have to cramp the information into a relatively small monitor, but to have as much space as possible and to be limited only by the amount of space around. Anything can be a display surface - a wall or a table, and anywhere - be it an office or a conference hall. Of course, the system faces many challenges, but they can be overcome by the increasing power of graphics hardware and general purpose computing.

7 ACKNOWLEDGMENTS

This work was supported by (1) the National Science Foundation Cooperative Agreement no. ASC-8920219: "Science and Technology Center for Computer Graphics and Scientific Visualization", Center Director Andy van Dam (Brown University). Principal Investigators Andy van Dam, Al Barr (California Institute of Technology), Don Greenberg (Cornell University), Henry Fuchs (University of North Carolina at Chapel Hill), Rich Riesenfeld (University of Utah); (2) the "National Tele-Immersion Initiative" which is sponsored by Advanced Networks and Services, President and Chief Executive Officer Al Weis, Chief Scientist Jaron Lanier; and (3) DARPA grant no. N66001-97-1-8919: "Three Applications of Digital Light Projection for Tiled Display and 3-D Scene Capture."

We thank Nick England for sharing his significant knowledge about wide-area tiled display systems, both in terms of past work and fundamental issues; Mary Whitton, David Harrison, John Thomas, Kurtis Keller, and Jim Mahaney for their help in designing, arranging, and constructing the prototype office of the future; Todd Gaul for help with our video taping; Jean-Yves Bouguet of Caltech for the camera calibration code and useful discussions; Nick Vallidis for his work on creating new DLP binary PCM coding; Andy Ade and Jai Glasgow for their administrative help; our department's Computer Services staff members for keeping our networks and machines humming in spite of our experimental modifications; and Hans Weber and Rui Bastos for help photographing the imperceptible structured light demonstrations. Finally, we gratefully acknowledge Andrei State for his illustrations of the office of the future (Figure 1).

References

[1] Bajaj, C.L., F. Bernardini, and G. Xu. "Automatic reconstruction of surfaces and scalar fields from 3D scans," SIGGRAPH 95 Conference Proceedings, Annual Conference Series, ACM SIGGRAPH, Addison-Wesley, pp. 109-118, August 1995.

[2] Bennett, David T. Chairman and Co-Founder of Alternate Realities Corporation. Internet: http://www.virtual-reality.com. 215 Southport Drive Suite 1300 Morrisville, NC 27560.

[3] Bowen, Loftin, R. "Hands Across the Atlantic," IEEE Computer Graphics and Applications, Vol. 17, No. 2, pp. 78-79, March-April 1997.

[4] Bryson, Steve, David Zeltzer, Mark T. Bolas, Bertrand de La Chapelle, and David Bennett. "The Future of Virtual Reality: Head Mounted Displays Versus Spatially Immersive Displays," SIGGRAPH 97 Conference Proceedings, Annual Conference Series, ACM SIGGRAPH, Addison-Wesley, pp. 485-486, August 1997.

[5] Buxton, W., Sellen, A. & Sheasby, M. "Interfaces for multiparty videoconferencing," In K. Finn, A. Sellen & S. Wilber (Eds.). Video Mediated Communication. Hillsdale, N.J.: Erlbaum, pp. 385-400, 1997.

[6] Capin, Tolga K., Hansrudi Noser, Daniel Thalmann, Igor Sunday Pandzic and Nadia Magnenat Thalman. "Virtual Human Representation and Communication in VLNet," IEEE Computer Graphics and Applications, Vol. 17, No. 2, pp. 42-53, March-April 1997.

[7] Chi, Vern, Matt Cutts, Henry Fuchs, Kurtis Keller, Greg Welch, Mark Bloomenthal, Elaine Cohen, Sam Drake, Russ Fish, Rich Riesenfeld. 1998. "A Wide Field-of-View Camera Cluster", University of North Carolina at Chapel Hill, Dept of Computer Science, Technical Report TR98-018.

[8] Chien, C.H., Y.B. Sim, and J.K. Aggarwal. "Generation of volume/surface octree from range data," In The Computer Graphics Society Conference on Computer Vision and Pattern Recognition, pp. 254-260, June 1988.

[9] Clodfelter, Robert M. "Predicting Display System Performance," Presented at the 1996 IMAGE Conference, Scottsdale, AZ, pp. 1-5, June 23-28, 1996.

[10] Conner, D.B, Cutts, M., Fish, R., Fuchs, H., Holden, L., Jacobs, M., Loss, B., Markosian, L., Riesenfeld, R., and Turk, G. "An Immersive Tool for Wide-Area Collaborative Design," TeamCAD, the First Graphics Visualization, and Usability (GVU) Workshop on Collaborative Design. Atlanta, Georgia, May 12-13, 1997.

[11] Connolly, C.I. "Cumulative generation of octree models from range data," Proceedings, Int'l. Conference Robotics, pp. 25-32, March 1984.

[12] Cruz-Neira, Carolina, Daniel J. Sandin, and Thomas A. DeFanti. "Surround-Screen Projection-Based Virtual Reality: The Design and Implementation of the CAVE," Computer Graphics, SIGGRAPH Annual Conference Proceedings, 1993.

[13] Curless, Brian, and Marc Levoy. "A Volumetric Method for Building Complex Models from Range Images," SIGGRAPH 96 Conference Proceedings, Annual Conference Series, ACM SIGGRAPH, Addison-Wesley. pp. 303-312, 1996.

[14] DePiero, F.W., and Trivedi, M.M., "3-D Computer Vision using Structured Light: Design, Calibration, and Implementation Issues," Advances in Computers(43), 1996, Academic Press, pp.243-278

[15] Dias, José Miguel Salles, Ricardo Galli, António Carlos Almeida, Carlos A. C. Belo, and José Manuel Rebordã. "mWorld: A Multiuser 3D Virtual Environment," IEEE Computer Graphics and Applications, Vol. 17, No. 2., pp. 55-64, March-April 1997.

[16] Dorsey, Julie O'B., Fransco X. Sillion, Donald Greenberg. "Design and Simulation of Opera Lighting and Projection Effects," SIGGRAPH 91 Conference Proceedings, Annual Conference Series, ACM SIGGRAPH, Addison-Wesley, pp. 41-50, 1991.

[17] Edelsbrunner, H. and E.P. Mucke. "Three-dimensional alpha shapes," In Workshop on Volume Visualization, pp. 75-105, October 1992.

[18] Fuchs, Henry, Gary Bishop, Kevin Arthur, Leonard McMillan, Ruzena Bajcsy, Sang Lee, Hany Farid, and Takeo Kanade. "Virtual Space Teleconferencing Using a Sea of Cameras," Proceedings of the First International Symposium on Medical Robotics and Computer Assisted Surgery, (Pittsburgh, PA.) Sept 22-24, 1994.

[19] Gajewska , Hania , Jay Kistler, Mark S. Manasse, and David D. Redell. "Argo: A System for Distributed Collaboration," (DEC, Multimedia '94)

[20] Gibbs, Simon, Constantin Arapis and Christian J. Breiteneder. "TELEPORT-Towards Immersive Copresence," accepted for publication in ACM Multimedia Systems Journal, 1998.

[21] Goncalves, Luis , Enrico Di Bernardo, Enrico Ursella, Pietro Perona. "Monocular Tracking of the Human Arm in 3D," Proc. of the 5th Inter. Conf. on Computer Vision, ICCV 95.

[22] Hilton, A., A.J. Toddart, J. Illingworth, and T. Windeatt. "Reliable surface reconstruction from multiple range images," In Fouth European Conference on Computer Vision, Volume 1, pp. 117-126. April 1996.

[23] Holmes, Richard E. "Common Projector and Display Modules for Aircraft Simulator Visual Systems," Presented at the IMAGE V Conference, Phoenix, AZ, June 19-22, pp. 81-88, 1990.

[24] Hoppe, Hugues, Tony DeRose, Tom Duchamp, John McDonald, Werner Stuetzle. "Surface Reconstruction from Unorganized Points," SIGGRAPH 92 Conference Proceedings, Annual Conference Series, ACM SIGGRAPH, Addison-Wesley, pp. 71-76, 1992.

[25] Hornbeck, Larry J., "Deformable-Mirror Spatial Light Modulators,"Proceedings SPIE, Vol. 1150, Aug 1989.

[26] Hornbeck, Larry J., "Digital Light Processing for High-Brightness High-Resolution Applications," [cited 21 April 1998]. Available from http://www.ti.com/dlp/docs/business/resources/white/hornbeck.pdf, 1995.

[27] Ichikawa, Y., Okada, K., Jeong, G., Tanaka, S. and Matsushita, Y.: "MAJIC Videoconferencing System: Experiments, Evaluation and Improvement'," In Proceedings of ECSCW'95, pp. 279-292, Sept. 1995.

[28] Ishii, Hiroshi, Minoru Kobayashi, Kazuho Arita. "Iterative Design of Seamless Collaboration Media," CACM, Volume 37, Number 8, pp. 83-97, August 1994.

[29] Jarvis, Kevin. "Real-time 60Hz Distortion Correction on a Silicon Graphics IG," Real-time Graphics, Vol. 5, No. 7, pp. 6-7. February 1997.

[30] Kanade, Takeo and Haruhiko Asada. "Noncontact Visual Three-Dimensional Ranging Devices," Proceedings of SPIE: 3D Machine Perception. Volume 283, Pages 48-54. April 23-24, 1981.

[31] Kanade, Takeo, Hiroshi Kano, Shigeru Kimura, Atsushi Yoshida, Kazuo Oda. "Development of a Video-Rate Stereo Machine," Proceedings of International Robotics and Systems Conference (IROS '95). pp. 95-100, Pittsburgh, PA., August 5-9, 1995.

[32] Lacroix, Michel. "A HDTV Projector For Wide Field of View Flight Simulators," pp. 493-500. Presented at the IMAGE VI Conference, Scottsdale, AZ, July 14-17, 1992.

[33] Lamotte, Wim, Eddy Flerackers, Frank Van Reeth, Rae Earnshaw, Joao Mena De Matos. Visinet: Collaborative 3D Visualization and VR over ATM Networks. IEEE Computer Graphics and Applications, Vol. 17, No. 2, pp. 66-75, March-April 1997.

[34] Lehner, Valerie D., and Thomas A. DeFanti. "Distributed Virtual Reality: Supporting Remote Collaboration in Vehicle Design," IEEE Computer Graphics and Applications, Vol. 17, No. 2, pp. 13-17, March-April 1997.

[35] Lyon, Paul. "Edge-blending Multiple Projection Displays On A Dome Surface To Form Continuous Wide Angle Fields-of-View," pp. 203-209. Proceedings of 7th I/ITEC, 1985.

[36] Macedonia, Michale R. and Stefan Noll. "A Transatlantic Research and Development Environment," IEEE Computer Graphics and Applications, Vol. 17, No. 2, pp. 76-82, March-April 1997.

[37] Mandeville, J., T. Furness, M. Kawahata, D. Campbell, P. Danset, A. Dahl, J. Dauner, J. Davidson, K. Kandie, and P. Schwartz. "GreenSpace: Creating a Distributed Virtual Environment for Global Applications," Proceedings of IEEE Networked Virtual Reality Workshop, 1995.

[38] Nayar, Shree, Masahiro Watanabe, Minori Noguchi. "Real-time Focus Range Sensor," Columbia University, CUCS-028-94.

[39] Neumann, Ulrich and Henry Fuchs, "A Vision of Telepresence for Medical Consultation and Other Applications," Proceedings of the Sixth International Symposium on Robotics Research, Hidden Valley, PA, Oct. 1-5, 1993, pp. 565-571.

[40] Ohya, Jun, Kitamura, Yasuichi, Takemura, Haruo, et al. "Real-time Reproduction of 3D Human Images in Virtual Space Teleconferencing," IEEE Virtual Reality International Symposium. Sep 1993.

[41] Panorama Project, WWW description. [cited 13 January 1998]. Available from http://www.tnt.uni-hannover.de/project/eu/panorama/overview.html

[42] Raskar, Ramesh, Matt Cutts, Greg Welch, Wolfgang Stüerzlinger. "Efficient Image Generation for Multiprojector and Multisurface Displays," University of North Carolina at Chapel Hill, Dept of Computer Science, Technical Report TR98-016, 1998.

[43] Raskar, Ramesh, Henry Fuchs, Greg Welch, Adam Lake, Matt Cutts. "3D Talking Heads : Image Based Modeling at Interactive rate using Structured Light Projection,"University of North Carolina at Chapel Hill, Dept of Computer Science, Technical Report TR98-017, 1998

[44] Segal, Mark, Carl Korobkin, Rolf van Widenfelt, Jim Foran and Paul Haeberli, "Fast Shadows and Lighting Effects using Texture Mapping," Computer Graphics (SIGGRAPH 92 Proceedings), pp. 249-252, July, 1992.

[45] Tsai , Roger Y. "An Efficient and Accurate Camera Calibration Technique for 3D Machine Vision," Proceedings of IEEE Conference on Computer Vision and Pattern Recognition, Miami Beach, FL, pp. 364-374, 1986.

[46] Underkoffler, J. "A View From the Luminous Room," Personal Technologies, Vol. 1, No. 2, pp. 49-59, June 1997.

[47] Underkoffler, J., and Hiroshi Ishii. "Illuminating Light: An Optical Design Tool with a Luminous-Tangible Interface," Proceedings of CHI '98, ACM, April 1998.

Rendering Synthetic Objects into Real Scenes:
Bridging Traditional and Image-based Graphics with Global Illumination and High Dynamic Range Photography

Paul Debevec

University of California at Berkeley[1]

ABSTRACT

We present a method that uses measured scene radiance and global illumination in order to add new objects to light-based models with correct lighting. The method uses a high dynamic range image-based model of the scene, rather than synthetic light sources, to illuminate the new objects. To compute the illumination, the scene is considered as three components: the distant scene, the local scene, and the synthetic objects. The distant scene is assumed to be photometrically unaffected by the objects, obviating the need for reflectance model information. The local scene is endowed with estimated reflectance model information so that it can catch shadows and receive reflected light from the new objects. Renderings are created with a standard global illumination method by simulating the interaction of light amongst the three components. A differential rendering technique allows for good results to be obtained when only an estimate of the local scene reflectance properties is known.

We apply the general method to the problem of rendering synthetic objects into real scenes. The light-based model is constructed from an approximate geometric model of the scene and by using a light probe to measure the incident illumination at the location of the synthetic objects. The global illumination solution is then composited into a photograph of the scene using the differential rendering technique. We conclude by discussing the relevance of the technique to recovering surface reflectance properties in uncontrolled lighting situations. Applications of the method include visual effects, interior design, and architectural visualization.

CR Descriptors: I.2.10 [**Artificial Intelligence**]: Vision and Scene Understanding - *Intensity, color, photometry and thresholding*; I.3.7 [**Computer Graphics**]: Three-Dimensional Graphics and Realism - *Color, shading, shadowing, and texture*; I.3.7 [**Computer Graphics**]: Three-Dimensional Graphics and Realism - *Radiosity*; I.4.1 [**Image Processing**]: Digitization - *Scanning*; I.4.8 [**Image Processing**]: Scene Analysis - *Photometry, Sensor Fusion*.

[1]Computer Science Division, University of California at Berkeley, Berkeley, CA 94720-1776. Email: debevec@cs.berkeley.edu. More information and additional results may be found at: http://www.cs.berkeley.edu/~debevec/Research

1 Introduction

Rendering synthetic objects into real-world scenes is an important application of computer graphics, particularly in architectural and visual effects domains. Oftentimes, a piece of furniture, a prop, or a digital creature or actor needs to be rendered seamlessly into a real scene. This difficult task requires that the objects be lit consistently with the surfaces in their vicinity, and that the interplay of light between the objects and their surroundings be properly simulated. Specifically, the objects should cast shadows, appear in reflections, and refract, focus, and emit light just as real objects would.

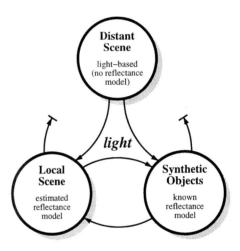

Figure 1: **The General Method** *In our method for adding synthetic objects into light-based scenes, the scene is partitioned into three components: the distant scene, the local scene, and the synthetic objects. Global illumination is used to simulate the interplay of light amongst all three components, except that light reflected back at the distant scene is ignored. As a result, BRDF information for the distant scene is unnecessary. Estimates of the geometry and material properties of the local scene are used to simulate the interaction of light between it and the synthetic objects.*

Currently available techniques for realistically rendering synthetic objects into scenes are labor intensive and not always successful. A common technique is to manually survey the positions of the light sources, and to instantiate a virtual light of equal color and intensity for each real light to illuminate the synthetic objects. Another technique is to photograph a reference object (such as a gray sphere) in the scene where the new object is to be rendered, and use its appearance as a qualitative guide in manually configuring the lighting environment. Lastly, the technique of reflection mapping is useful for mirror-like reflections. These methods typically require considerable hand-refinement and none of them easily simulates the effects of indirect illumination from the environment.

Accurately simulating the effects of both direct and indirect lighting has been the subject of research in global illumination. With a global illumination algorithm, if the entire scene were modeled with its full geometric and reflectance (BRDF) characteristics, one could correctly render a synthetic object into the scene simply by adding it to the model and recomputing the global illumination solution. Unfortunately, obtaining a full geometric and reflectance model of a large environment is extremeley difficult. Furthermore, global illumination solutions for large complex environments are extremely computationally intensive.

Moreover, it seems that having a full reflectance model of the large-scale scene should be unnecessary: under most circumstances, a new object will have no significant effect on the appearance of most of the of the distant scene. Thus, for such distant areas, knowing just its radiance (under the desired lighting conditions) should suffice.

Recently, [9] introduced a high dynamic range photographic technique that allows accurate measurements of scene radiance to be derived from a set of differently exposed photographs. This technique allows both low levels of indirect radiance from surfaces and high levels of direct radiance from light sources to be accurately recorded. When combined with image-based modeling techniques (e.g. [22, 24, 4, 10, 23, 17, 29]), and possibly active techniques for measuring geometry (e.g. [35, 30, 7, 27]) these derived radiance maps can be used to construct spatial representations of scene radiance.

We will use the term **light-based model** to refer to a representation of a scene that consists of radiance information, possibly with specific reference to light leaving surfaces, but not necessarily containing material property (BRDF) information. A light-based model can be used to evaluate the 5D plenoptic function [1] $P(\theta, \phi, V_x, V_y, V_z)$ for a given virtual or real subset of space[1]. A material-based model is converted to a light-based model by computing an illumination solution for it. A light-based model is differentiated from an image-based model in that its light values are actual measures of radiance[2], whereas image-based models may contain pixel values already transformed and truncated by the response function of an image acquisition or synthesis process.

In this paper, we present a general method for using accurate measurements of scene radiance in conjunction with global illumination to realistically add new objects to light-based models. The synthetic objects may have arbitrary material properties and can be rendered with appropriate illumination in arbitrary lighting environments. Furthermore, the objects can correctly interact with the environment around them: they cast the appropriate shadows, they are properly reflected, they can reflect and focus light, and they exhibit appropriate diffuse interreflection. The method can be carried out with commonly available equipment and software.

In this method (see Fig. 1), the scene is partitioned into three components. The first is the distant scene, which is the visible part of the environment too remote to be perceptibly affected by the synthetic object. The second is the local scene, which is the part of the environment which will be significantly affected by the presence of the objects. The third component is the synthetic objects. Our approach uses global illumination to correctly simulate the interaction of light amongst these three elements, with the exception that light radiated toward the distant environment will not be considered in the calculation. As a result, the BRDF of the distant environment need not be known — the technique uses BRDF information only for the local scene and the synthetic objects. We discuss the challenges in estimating the BRDF of the local scene, and methods for obtaining usable approximations. We also present a differential rendering

technique that produces perceptually accurate results even when the estimated BRDF is somewhat inaccurate.

We demonstrate the general method for the specific case of rendering synthetic objects into particular views of a scene (such as background plates) rather than into a general image-based model. In this method, a light probe is used to acquire a high dynamic range panoramic radiance map near the location where the object will be rendered. A simple example of a light probe is a camera aimed at a mirrored sphere, a configuration commonly used for acquiring environment maps. An approximate geometric model of the scene is created (via surveying, photogrammetry, or 3D scanning) and mapped with radiance values measured with the light probe. The distant scene, local scene, and synthetic objects are rendered with global illumination from the same point of view as the background plate, and the results are composited into the background plate with a differential rendering technique.

1.1 Overview

The rest of this paper is organized as follows. In the next section we discuss work related to this paper. Section 3 introduces the basic technique of using acquired maps of scene radiance to illuminate synthetic objects. Section 4 presents the general method we will use to render synthetic objects into real scenes. Section 5 describes a practical technique based on this method using a *light probe* to measure incident illumination. Section 6 presents a differential rendering technique for rendering the local environment with only an approximate description of its reflectance. Section 7 presents a simple method to approximately recover the diffuse reflectance characteristics of the local environment. Section 8 presents results obtained with the technique. Section 9 discusses future directions for this work, and we conclude in Section 10.

2 Background and Related Work

The practice of adding new objects to photographs dates to the early days of photography in the simple form of pasting a cut-out from one picture onto another. While the technique conveys the idea of the new object being in the scene, it usually fails to produce an image that as a whole is a believable photograph. Attaining such realism requires a number of aspects of the two images to match. First, the camera projections should be consistent, otherwise the object may seem too foreshortened or skewed relative to the rest of the picture. Second, the patterns of film grain and film response should match. Third, the lighting on the object needs to be consistent with other objects in the environment. Lastly, the object needs to cast realistic shadows and reflections on the scene. Skilled artists found that by giving these considerations due attention, synthetic objects could be painted into still photographs convincingly.

In optical film compositing, the use of object mattes to prevent particular sections of film from being exposed made the same sort of cut-and-paste compositing possible for moving images. However, the increased demands of realism imposed by the dynamic nature of film made matching camera positions and lighting even more critical. As a result, care was taken to light the objects appropriately for the scene into which they were to be composited. This would still not account for the objects casting shadows onto the scene, so often these were painted in by an artist frame by frame [13, 2, 28]. Digital film scanning and compositing [26] helped make this process far more efficient.

Work in global illumination [16, 19] has recently produced algorithms (e.g. [31]) and software (e.g. [33]) to realistically simulate lighting in synthetic scenes, including indirect lighting with both specular and diffuse reflections. We leverage this work in order to create realistic renderings.

Some work has been done on the specific problem of compositing objects into photography. [25] presented a procedure for ren-

---

[1] Time and wavelength dependence can be included to represent the general 7D plenoptic function as appropriate.

[2] In practice, the measures of radiance are with respect to a discrete set of spectral distributions such as the standard tristimulus model.

dering architecture into background photographs using knowledge of the sun position and measurements or approximations of the local ambient light. For diffuse buildings in diffuse scenes, the technique is effective. The technique of *reflection mapping* (also called *environment mapping*) [3, 18] produces realistic results for mirror-like objects. In reflection mapping, a panoramic image is rendered or photographed from the location of the object. Then, the surface normals of the object are used to index into the panoramic image by reflecting rays from the desired viewpoint. As a result, the shiny object appears to properly reflect the desired environment[3]. However, the technique is limited to mirror-like reflection and does not account for objects casting light or shadows on the environment.

A common visual effects technique for having synthetic objects cast shadows on an existing environment is to create an approximate geometric model of the environment local to the object, and then compute the shadows from the various light sources. The shadows can then be subtracted from the background image. In the hands of professional artists this technique can produce excellent results, but it requires knowing the position, size, shape, color, and intensity of each of the scene's light sources. Furthermore, it does not account for diffuse reflection from the scene, and light reflected by the objects onto the scene must be handled specially.

To properly model the interaction of light between the objects and the local scene, we pose the compositing problem as a global illumination computation as in [14] and [12]. As in this work, we apply the effect of the synthetic objects in the lighting solution as a differential update to the original appearance of the scene. In the previous work an approximate model of the entire scene and its original light sources is constructed; the positions and sizes of the light sources are measured manually. Rough methods are used to estimate diffuse-only reflectance characteristics of the scene, which are then used to estimate the intensities of the light sources. [12] additionally presents a method for performing fast updates of the illumination solution in the case of moving objects. As in the previous work, we leverage the basic result from incremental radiosity [6, 5] that making a small change to a scene does not require recomputing the entire solution.

3 Illuminating synthetic objects with real light

In this section we propose that computer-generated objects be lit by actual recordings of light from the scene, using global illumination. Performing the lighting in this manner provides a unified and physically accurate alternative to manually attempting to replicate incident illumination conditions.

Accurately recording light in a scene is difficult because of the high dynamic range that scenes typically exhibit; this wide range of brightness is the result of light sources being relatively concentrated. As a result, the intensity of a source is often two to six orders of magnitude larger than the intensity of the non-emissive parts of an environment. However, it is necessary to accurately record both the large areas of indirect light from the environment and the concentrated areas of direct light from the sources since both are significant parts of the illumination solution.

Using the technique introduced in [9], we can acquire correct measures of scene radiance using conventional imaging equipment. The images, called *radiance maps*, are derived from a series of images with different sensor integration times and a technique for computing and accounting for the imaging system response function f. We can use these measures to illuminate synthetic objects exhibiting arbitrary material properties.

Fig. 2 shows a high-dynamic range lighting environment with electric, natural, and indirect lighting. This environment was

recorded by taking a full dynamic range photograph of a mirrored ball on a table (see Section 5). A digital camera was used to acquire a series images in one-stop exposure increments from $\frac{1}{4}$ to $\frac{1}{10000}$ second. The images were fused using the technique in [9].

The environment is displayed at three exposure levels (-0, -3.5, and -7.0 stops) to show its full dynamic range. Recovered RGB radiance values for several points in the scene and on the two major light sources are indicated; the color difference between the tungsten lamp and the sky is evident. A single low-dynamic range photograph would be unable to record the correct colors and intensities over the entire scene.

Fig. 3(a-e) shows the results of using this panoramic radiance map to synthetically light a variety of materials using the RADIANCE global illumination algorithm [33]. The materials are: (a) perfectly reflective, (b) rough gold, (c) perfectly diffuse gray material, (d) shiny green plastic, and (e) dull orange plastic. Since we are computing a full illumination solution, the objects exhibit self-reflection and shadows from the light sources as appropriate. Note that in (c) the protrusions produce two noticeable shadows of slightly different colors, one corresponding to the ceiling light and a softer shadow corresponding to the window.

The shiny plastic object in (d) has a 4 percent specular component with a Gaussian roughness of 0.04 [32]. Since the object's surface both blurs and attenuates the light with its rough specular component, the reflections fall within the dynamic range of our display device and the different colors of the light sources can be seen. In (e) the rough plastic diffuses the incident light over a much larger area.

To illustrate the importance of using high dynamic range radiance maps, the same renderings were produced using just one of the original photographs as the lighting environment. In this single image, similar in appearance to Fig. 2(a), the brightest regions had been truncated to approximately 2 percent of their true values. The rendering of the mirrored surface (f) appears similar to (a) since it is displayed in low-dynamic range printed form. Significant errors are noticeable in (g-j) since these materials blur the incident light. In (g), the blurring of the rough material darkens the light sources, whereas in (b) they remain saturated. Renderings (h-j) are very dark due to the missed light; thus we have brightened by a factor of eight on the right in order to make qualitative comparisons to (c-e) possible. In each it can be seen that the low-dynamic range image of the lighting environment fails to capture the information necessary to simulate correct color balance, shadows, and highlights.

Fig. 4 shows a collection of objects with different material properties illuminated by two different environments. A wide variety of light interaction between the objects and the environment can be seen. The (synthetic) mirrored ball reflects both the synthetic objects as well as the environment. The floating diffuse ball shows a subtle color shift along its right edge as it shadows itself from the windows and is lit primarily by the incandescent lamp in Fig. 4(a). The reflection of the environment in the black ball (which has a specular intensity of 0.04) shows the colors of the light sources, which are too bright to be seen in the mirrored ball. A variety of shadows, reflections, and focused light can be observed on the resting surface.

The next section describes how the technique of using radiance maps to illuminate synthetic objects can be extended to compute the proper photometric interaction of the objects with the scene. It also describes how high dynamic range photography and image-based modeling combine in a natural manner to allow the simulation of arbitrary (non-infinite) lighting environments.

4 The General Method

This section explains our method for adding new objects to light-based scene representations. As in Fig. 1, we partition our scene into three parts: the distant scene, the local scene, and the synthetic

---

[3]Using the surface normal indexing method, the object will not reflect itself. Correct self-reflection can be obtained through ray tracing.

Figure 2: **An omnidirectional radiance map** This full dynamic range lighting environment was acquired by photographing a mirrored ball balanced on the cap of a pen sitting on a table. The environment contains natural, electric, and indirect light. The three views of this image adjusted to (a) +0 stops, (b) -3.5 stops, and (c) -7.0 stops show that the full dynamic range of the scene has been captured without saturation. As a result, the image usefully records the direction, color, and intensity of all forms of incident light.

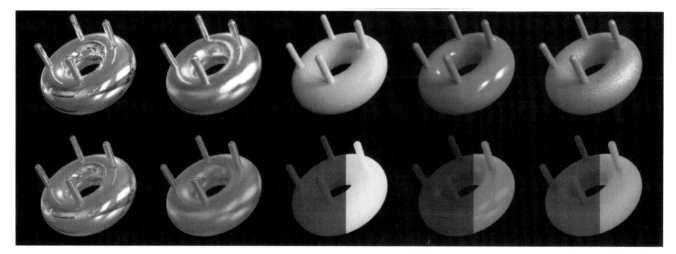

Figure 3: **Illuminating synthetic objects with real light (Top row: a,b,c,d,e)** *With full dynamic range measurements of scene radiance from Fig. 2.* **(Bottom row: f,g,h,i,j)** *With low dynamic range information from a single photograph of the ball. The right sides of images (h,i,j) have been brightened by a factor of six to allow qualitative comparison to (c,d,e). The high dynamic range measurements of scene radiance are necessary to produce proper lighting on the objects.*

Figure 4: **Synthetic objects lit by two different environments (a)** *A collection of objects is illuminated by the radiance information in 2. The objects exhibit appropriate interreflection.* **(b)** *The same objects are illuminated by different radiance information obtained in an outdoor urban environment on an overcast day. The radiance map used for the illumination is shown in the upper left of each image. Candle holder model courtesy of Gregory Ward Larson.*

objects. We describe the geometric and photometric requirements for each of these components.

1. **A light-based model of the distant scene**
   The distant scene is constructed as a light-based model. The synthetic objects will receive light from this model, so it is necessary that the model store true measures of radiance rather than low dynamic range pixel values from conventional images. The light-based model can take on any form, using very little explicit geometry [23, 17], some geometry [24], moderate geometry [10], or be a full 3D scan of an environment with view-dependent texture-mapped [11] radiance. What is important is for the model to provide accurate measures of incident illumination in the vicinity of the objects, as well as from the desired viewpoint. In the next section we will present a convenient procedure for constructing a minimal model that meets these requirements.

   In the global illumination computation, the distant scene radiates light toward the local scene and the synthetic objects, but ignores light reflected back to it. We assume that no area of the distant scene will be significantly affected by light reflecting from the synthetic objects; if that were the case, the area should instead belong to the local scene, which contains the BRDF information necessary to interact with light. In the RADIANCE [33] system, this exclusively emissive behavior can be specified with the "glow" material property.

2. **An approximate material-based model of the local scene**
   The local scene consists of the surfaces that will photometrically interact with the synthetic objects. It is this geometry onto which the objects will cast shadows and reflect light. Since the local scene needs to fully participate in the illumination solution, both its geometry and reflectance characteristics should be known, at least approximately. If the geometry of the local scene is not readily available with sufficient accuracy from the light-based model of the distant scene, there are various techniques available for determining its geometry through active or passive methods. In the common case where the local scene is a flat surface that supports the synthetic objects, its geometry is determined easily from the camera pose. Methods for estimating the BRDF of the local scene are discussed in Section 7.

   Usually, the local scene will be the part of the scene that is geometrically close to the synthetic objects. When the local scene is mostly diffuse, the rendering equation shows that the visible effect of the objects on the local scene decreases as the inverse square of the distance between the two. Nonetheless, there is a variety of circumstances in which synthetic objects can significantly affect areas of the scene not in the immediate vicinity. Some common circumstances are:

   - If there are concentrated light sources illuminating the object, then the object can cast a significant shadow on a distant surface collinear with it and the light source.

   - If there are concentrated light sources and the object is flat and specular, it can focus a significant amount of light onto a distant part of the scene.

   - If a part of the distant scene is flat and specular (e.g. a mirror on a wall), its appearance can be significantly affected by a synthetic object.

   - If the synthetic object emits light (e.g. a synthetic laser), it can affect the appearance of the distant scene significantly.

   These situations should be considered in choosing which parts of the scene should be considered local and which parts distant. Any part of the scene that will be significantly affected in

its appearance from the desired viewpoint should be included as part of the local scene.

Since the local scene is a full BRDF model, it can be added to the global illumination problem as would any other object. The local scene may consist of any number of surfaces and objects with different material properties. For example, the local scene could consist of a patch of floor beneath the synthetic object to catch shadows as well as a mirror surface hanging on the opposite wall to catch a reflection. The local scene replaces the corresponding part of the light-based model of the distant scene.

Since it can be difficult to determine the precise BRDF characteristics of the local scene, it is often desirable to have only the *change* in the local scene's appearance be computed with the BRDF estimate; its appearance due to illumination from the distant scene is taken from the original light-based model. This differential rendering method is presented in Section 6.

3. **Complete material-based models of the objects**
   The synthetic objects themselves may consist of any variety of shapes and materials supported by the global illumination software, including plastics, metals, emitters, and dielectrics such as glass and water. They should be placed in their desired geometric correspondence to the local scene.

Once the distant scene, local scene, and synthetic objects are properly modeled and positioned, the global illumination software can be used in the normal fashion to produce renderings from the desired viewpoints.

5 Compositing using a light probe

This section presents a particular technique for constructing a light-based model of a real scene suitable for adding synthetic objects at a particular location. This technique is useful for compositing objects into actual photography of a scene.

In Section 4, we mentioned that the light-based model of the distant scene needs to appear correctly in the vicinity of the synthetic objects as well as from the desired viewpoints. This latter requirement can be satisfied if it is possible to directly acquire radiance maps of the scene from the desired viewpoints. The former requirement, that the appear photometrically correct in all directions in the vicinity of the synthetic objects, arises because this information comprises the incident light which will illuminate the objects.

To obtain this part of the light-based model, we acquire a full dynamic range omnidirectional radiance map near the location of the synthetic object or objects. One technique for acquiring this radiance map is to photograph a spherical first-surface mirror, such as a polished steel ball, placed at or near the desired location of the synthetic object[4]. This procedure is illustrated in Fig. 7(a). An actual radiance map obtained using this method is shown in Fig. 2.

The radiance measurements observed in the ball are mapped onto the geometry of the distant scene. In many circumstances this model can be very simple. In particular, if the objects are small and resting on a flat surface, one can model the scene as a horizontal plane for the resting surface and a large dome for the rest of the environment. Fig. 7(c) illustrates the ball image being mapped onto a table surface and the walls and ceiling of a finite room; 5 shows the resulting light-based model.

5.1 Mapping from the probe to the scene model

To precisely determine the mapping between coordinates on the ball and rays in the world, one needs to record the position of the ball

---

[4]Parabolic mirrors combined with telecentric lenses [34] can be used to obtain hemispherical fields of view with a consistent principal point, if so desired.

relative to the camera, the size of the ball, and the camera parameters such as its location in the scene and focal length. With this information, it is straightforward to trace rays from the camera center through the pixels of the image, and reflect rays off the ball into the environment. Often a good approximation results from assuming the ball is small relative to the environment and that the camera's view is orthographic.

The data acquired from a single ball image will exhibit a number of artifacts. First, the camera (and possibly the photographer) will be visible. The ball, in observing the scene, interacts with it: the ball (and its support) can appear in reflections, cast shadows, and can reflect light back onto surfaces. Lastly, the ball will not reflect the scene directly behind it, and will poorly sample the area nearby. If care is taken in positioning the ball and camera, these effects can be minimized and will have a negligible effect on the final renderings. If the artifacts are significant, the images can be fixed manually in image editing program or by selectively combining images of the ball taken from different directions; Fig. 6 shows a relatively artifact-free enviroment constructed using the latter method. We have found that combining two images of the ball taken ninety degrees apart from each other allows us to eliminate the camera's appearance and to avoid poor sampling.

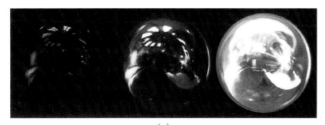

(a)

(b)

Figure 6: **Rendering with a Combined Probe Image** *The full dynamic range environment map shown at the top was assembled from two light probe images taken ninety degrees apart from each other. As a result, the only visible artifact is small amount of the probe support visible on the floor. The map is shown at -4.5, 0, and +4.5 stops. The bottom rendering was produced using this lighting information, and exhibits diffuse and specular reflections, shadows from different sources of light, reflections, and caustics.*

5.2 Creating renderings

To render the objects into the scene, a synthetic local scene model is created as described in Section 4. Images of the scene from the desired viewpoint(s) are taken (Fig. 7(a)), and their position relative to the scene is recorded through pose-instrumented cameras or (as in our work) photogrammetry. The location of the ball in the scene is also recorded at this time. The global illumination software is then run to render the objects, local scene, and distant scene from the desired viewpoint (Fig. 7(d)).

The objects and local scene are then composited onto the background image. To perform this compositing, a mask is created by rendering the objects and local scene in white and the distant scene in black. If objects in the distant scene (which may appear in front of the objects or local scene from certain viewpoints) are geometrically modeled, they will properly obscure the local scene and the objects as necessary. This compositing can be considered as a subset of the general method (Section 4) wherein the light-based model of the distant scene acts as follows: if (V_x, V_y, V_z) corresponds to an actual view of the scene, return the radiance value looking in direction (θ, ϕ). Otherwise, return the radiance value obtained by casting the ray $(\theta, \phi, V_x, V_y, V_z)$ onto the radiance-mapped distant scene model.

In the next section we describe a more robust method of compositing the local scene into the background image.

6 Improving quality with differential rendering

The method we have presented so far requires that the local scene be modeled accurately in both its geometry and its spatially varying material properties. If the model is inaccurate, the appearance of the local scene will not be consistent with the appearance of adjacent distant scene. Such a border is readily apparent in Fig. 8(c), since the local scene was modeled with a homogeneous BRDF when in reality it exhibits a patterned albedo (see [21]). In this section we describe a method for greatly reducing such effects.

Suppose that we compute a global illumination solution for the local and distant scene models without including the synthetic objects. If the BRDF and geometry of the local scene model were perfectly accurate, then one would expect the appearance of the rendered local scene to be consistent with its appearance in the light-based model of the entire scene. Let us call the appearance of the local scene from the desired viewpoint in the light-based model LS_b. In the context of the method described in Section 5, LS_b is simply the background image. We will let LS_{noobj} denote the appearance of the local scene, without the synthetic objects, as calculated by the global illumination solution. The error in the rendered local scene (without the objects) is thus: $Err_{ls} = LS_{noobj} - LS_b$. This error results from the difference between the BRDF characteristics of the actual local scene as compared to the modeled local scene.

Let LS_{obj} denote the appearance of the local environment as calculated by the global illumination solution with the synthetic objects in place. We can compensate for the error if we compute our final rendering LS_{final} as:

$$LS_{final} = LS_{obj} - Err_{ls}$$

Equivalently, we can write:

$$LS_{final} = LS_b + (LS_{obj} - LS_{noobj})$$

In this form, we see that whenever LS_{obj} and LS_{noobj} are the same (i.e. the addition of the objects to the scene had no effect on the local scene) the final rendering of the local scene is equivalent to LS_b (e.g. the background plate). When LS_{obj} is darker than LS_{noobj}, light is subtracted from the background to form shadows,

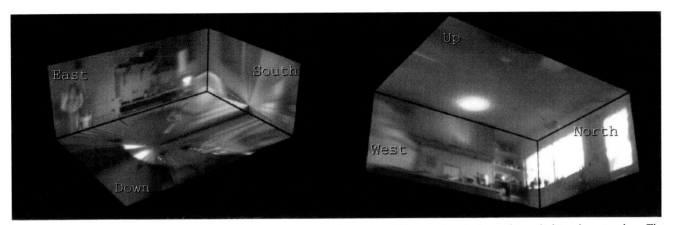

Figure 5: **A Light-Based Model** *A simple light-based model of a room is constructed by mapping the image from a light probe onto a box. The box corresponds to the upper half of the room, with the bottom face of the box being coincident with the top of the table. The model contains the full dynamic range of the original scene, which is not reproduced in its entirety in this figure.*

and when LS_{obj} is lighter than LS_{noobj} light is added to the background to produce reflections and caustics.

Stated more generally, the appearance of the local scene without the objects is computed with the correct reflectance characteristics lit by the correct environment, and the change in appearance due to the presence of the synthetic objects is computed with the modeled reflectance characteristics as lit by the modeled environment. While the realism of LS_{final} still benefits from having a good model of the reflectance characteristics of the local scene, the perceptual effect of small errors in albedo or specular properties is considerably reduced. Fig. 8(g) shows a final rendering in which the local environment is computed using this differential rendering technique. The objects are composited into the image directly from the LS_{obj} solution shown in Fig. 8(c).

It is important to stress that this technique can still produce abitrarily wrong results depending on the amount of error in the estimated local scene BRDF and the inaccuracies in the light-based model of the distance scene. In fact, Err_{ls} may be larger than LS_{obj}, causing LS_{final} to be negative. An alternate approach is to compensate for the *relative* error in the appearance of the local scene: $LS_{final} = LS_b(LS_{obj}/LS_{noobj})$. Inaccuracies in the local scene BDRF will also be reflected in the objects.

In the next section we discuss techniques for estimating the BRDF of the local scene.

7   Estimating the local scene BRDF

Simulating the interaction of light between the local scene and the synthetic objects requires a model of the reflectance characteristics of the local scene. Considerable recent work [32, 20, 8, 27] has presented methods for measuring the reflectance properties of materials through observation under controlled lighting configurations. Furthermore, reflectance characteristics can also be measured with commercial radiometric devices.

It would be more convenient if the local scene reflectance could be estimated directly from observation. Since the light-based model contains information about the radiance of the local scene as well as its irradiance, it actually contains information about the local scene reflectance. If we hypothesize reflectance characteristics for the local scene, we can illuminate the local scene with its known irradiance from the light-based model. If our hypothesis is correct, then the appearance should be consistent with the measured appearance. This suggests the following iterative method for recovering the reflectance properties of the local scene:

1. Assume a reflectance model for the local scene (e.g. diffuse only, diffuse + specular, metallic, or arbitrary BRDF, including

spatial variation)

2. Choose approximate initial values for the parameters of the reflectance model

3. Compute a global illumination solution for the local scene with the current parameters using the observed lighting configuration or configurations.

4. Compare the appearance of the rendered local scene to its actual appearance in one or more views.

5. If the renderings are not consistent, adjust the parameters of the reflectance model and return to step 3.

Efficient methods of performing the adjustment in step 5 that exploit the properties of particular reflectance models are left as future work. However, assuming a diffuse-only model of the local scene in step 1 makes the adjustment in step 5 straightforward. We have:

$$L_{r1}(\theta_r, \phi_r) = \int_0^{2\pi} \int_0^{\pi/2} \rho_d L_i(\theta_i, \phi_i) \cos \theta_i \sin \theta_i \, d\theta_i \, d\phi_i =$$

$$\rho_d \int_0^{2\pi} \int_0^{\pi/2} L_i(\theta_i, \phi_i) \cos \theta_i \sin \theta_i \, d\theta_i \, d\phi_i$$

If we initialize the local scene to be perfectly diffuse ($\rho_d = 1$) everywhere, we have:

$$L_{r2}(\theta_r, \phi_r) = \int_0^{2\pi} \int_0^{\pi/2} L_i(\theta_i, \phi_i) \cos \theta_i \sin \theta_i \, d\theta_i \, d\phi_i$$

The updated diffuse reflectance coefficient for each part of the local scene can be computed as:

$$\rho_d' = \frac{L_{r1}(\theta_r, \phi_r)}{L_{r2}(\theta_r, \phi_r)}$$

In this manner, we use the global illumination calculation to render each patch as a perfectly diffuse reflector, and compare the resulting radiance to the observed value. Dividing the two quantities yields the next estimate of the diffuse reflection coefficient ρ_d'. If there is no interreflection within the local scene, then the ρ_d' estimates will make the renderings consistent. If there is interreflection, then the algorithm should be iterated until there is convergence.

For a trichromatic image, the red, green, and blue diffuse reflectance values are computed independently. The diffuse characteristics of the background material used to produce Fig. 8(c) were

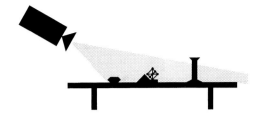

(a) Acquiring the background photograph

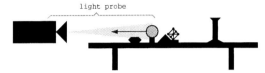

(b) Using the light probe

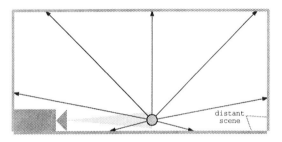

(c) Constructing the light-based model

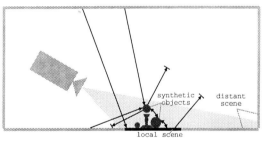

(d) Computing the global illumination solution

Figure 7: **Using a light probe (a)** *The background plate of the scene (some objects on a table) is taken.* **(b)** *A light probe (in this case, the camera photographing a steel ball) records the incident radiance near the location of where the synthetic objects are to be placed.* **(c)** *A simplified light-based model of the distant scene is created as a planar surface for the table and a finite box to represent the rest of the room. The scene is texture-mapped in high dynamic range with the radiance map from the light probe. The objects on the table, which were not explicitly modeled, become projected onto the table.* **(d)** *Synthetic objects and a BRDF model of the local scene are added to the light-based model of the distant scene. A global illumination solution of this configuration is computed with light coming from the distant scene and interacting with the local scene and synthetic objects. Light reflected back to the distant scene is ignored. The results of this rendering are composited (possibly with differential rendering) into the background plate from (a) to achieve the final result.*

computed using this method, although it was assumed that the entire local scene had the same diffuse reflectance.

In the standard "plastic" illumination model, just two more coefficients – those for specular intensity and roughness – need to be specified. In Fig. 8, the specular coefficients for the local scene were estimated manually based on the specular reflection of the window in the table in Fig. 2.

8 Compositing Results

Fig. 5 shows a simple light-based model of a room constructed using the panoramic radiance map from Fig. 2. The room model begins at the height of the table and continues to the ceiling; its measurements and the position of the ball within it were measured manually. The table surface is visible on the bottom face. Since the room model is finite in size, the light sources are effectively local rather than infinite. The stretching on the south wall is due to the poor sampling toward the silhouette edge of the ball.

Figs. 4 and 6 show complex arrangements of synthetic objects lit entirely by a variety of light-based models. The selection and composition of the objects in the scene was chosen to exhibit a wide variety of light interactions, including diffuse and specular reflectance, multiple soft shadows, and reflected and focused light. Each rendering was produced using the RADIANCE system with two diffuse light bounces and a relatively high density of ambient sample points.

Fig. 8(a) is a background plate image into which the synthetic objects will be rendered. In 8(b) a calibration grid was placed on the table in order to determine the camera pose relative to the scene and to the mirrored ball, which can also be seen. The poses were determined using the photogrammetric method in [10]. In 8(c), a model of the local scene as well as the synthetic objects is geometrically matched and composited onto the background image. Note that the local scene, while the same average color as the table, is readily distinguishable at its edges and because it lacks the correct variations in albedo.

Fig. 8(d) shows the results of lighting the local scene model with the light-based model of the room, without the objects. This image will be compared to 8(c) in order to determine the effect the synthetic objects have on the local scene. Fig. 8(e) is a mask image in which the white areas indicate the location of the synthetic objects. If the distant or local scene were to occlude the objects, such regions would be dark in this image.

Fig. 8(f) shows the difference between the appearance of the local scene rendered with (8(c)) and without (8(d)) the objects. For illustration purposes, the difference in radiance values have been offset so that zero difference is shown in gray. The objects have been masked out using image 8(e). This difference image encodes both the shadowing (dark areas) and reflected and focussed light (light areas) imposed on the local scene by the addition of the synthetic objects.

Fig. 8(g) shows the final result using the differential rendering method described in Section 6. The synthetic objects are copied directly from the global illumination solution 8(c) using the object mask 8(e). The effects the objects have on the local scene are included by adding the difference image 8(f) (without offset) to the background image. The remainder of the scene is copied directly from the background image 8(a). Note that in the mirror ball's reflection, the modeled local scene can be observed without the effects of differential rendering — a limitation of the compositing technique.

In this final rendering, the synthetic objects exhibit a consistent appearance with the real objects present in the background image 8(a) in both their diffuse and specular shading, as well as the direction and coloration of their shadows. The somewhat speckled nature of the object reflections seen in the table surface is due to

(a) Background photograph

(b) Camera calibration grid and light probe

(c) Objects and local scene matched to background

(d) Local scene, without objects, lit by the model

(e) Object matte

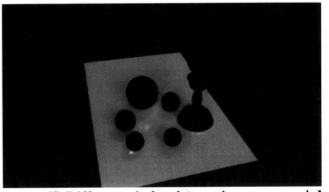

(f) Difference in local scene between **c** and **d**

(g) Final result with differential rendering

the stochastic nature of the particular global illumination algorithm used.

The differential rendering technique successfully eliminates the border between the local scene and the background image seen in 8(c). Note that the albedo texture of the table in the local scene area is preserved, and that a specular reflection of a background object on the table (appearing just to the left of the floating sphere) is correctly preserved in the final rendering. The local scene also exhibits reflections from the synthetic objects. A caustic from the glass ball focusing the light of the ceiling lamp onto the table is evident.

9 Future work

The method proposed here suggests a number of areas for future work. One area is to investigate methods of automatically recovering more general reflectance models for the local scene geometry, as proposed in Section 7. With such information available, the program might also also be able to suggest which areas of the scene should be considered as part of the local scene and which can safely be considered distant, given the position and reflectance characteristics of the desired synthetic objects.

Some additional work could be done to allow the global illumination algorithm to compute the ilumination solution more efficiently. One technique would be to have an algorithm automatically locate and identify concentrated light sources in the light-based model of the scene. With such knowledge, the algorithm could compute most of the direct illumination in a forward manner, which could dramatically increase the efficiency with which an accurate solution could be calculated. To the same end, use of the method presented in [15] to expedite the solution could be investigated. For the case of compositing moving objects into scenes, greatly increased efficiency could be obtained by adapting incremental radiosity methods to the current framework.

10 Conclusion

We have presented a general framework for adding new objects to light-based models with correct illumination. The method leverages a technique of using high dynamic range images of real scene radiance to synthetically illuminate new objects with arbitrary reflectance characteristics. We leverage this technique in a general method to simulate interplay of light between synthetic objects and the light-based environment, including shadows, reflections, and caustics. The method can be implemented with standard global illumination techniques.

For the particular case of rendering synthetic objects into real scenes (rather than general light-based models), we have presented a practical instance of the method that uses a light probe to record incident illumination in the vicinity of the synthetic objects. In addition, we have described a differential rendering technique that can convincingly render the interplay of light between objects and the local scene when only approximate reflectance information for the local scene is available. Lastly, we presented an iterative approach for determining reflectance characteristics of the local scene based on measured geometry and observed radiance in uncontrolled lighting conditions. It is our hope that the techniques presented here will be useful in practice as well as comprise a useful framework for combining material-based and light-based graphics.

Acknowledgments

The author wishes to thank Chris Bregler, David Forsyth, Jianbo Shi, Charles Ying, Steve Chenney, and Andrean Kalemis for the various forms of help and advice they provided. Special gratitude is also due to Jitendra Malik for helping make this work possible. Discussions with Michael Naimark and Steve Saunders helped motivate this work. Tim Hawkins provided extensive assistance on improving and revising this paper and provided invaluable assistance with image acquisition. Gregory Ward Larson deserves great thanks for the RADIANCE lighting simulation system and his invaluable assistance and advice in using RADIANCE in this research, for assisting with reflectance measurements, and for very helpful comments and suggestions on the paper. This research was supported by a Multidisciplinary University Research Initiative on three dimensional direct visualization from ONR and BMDO, grant FDN00014-96-1-1200.

References

[1] ADELSON, E. H., AND BERGEN, J. R. *Computational Models of Visual Processing*. MIT Press, Cambridge, Mass., 1991, ch. 1. The Plenoptic Function and the Elements of Early Vision.

[2] AZARMI, M. *Optical Effects Cinematography: Its Development, Methods, and Techniques*. University Microfilms International, Ann Arbor, Michigan, 1973.

[3] BLINN, J. F. Texture and reflection in computer generated images. *Communications of the ACM 19*, 10 (October 1976), 542–547.

[4] CHEN, E. QuickTime VR - an image-based approach to virtual environment navigation. In *SIGGRAPH '95* (1995).

[5] CHEN, S. E. Incremental radiosity: An extension of progressive radiosity to an interactive synthesis system. In *SIGGRAPH '90* (1990), pp. 135–144.

[6] COHEN, M. F., CHEN, S. E., WALLACE, J. R., AND GREENBERG, D. P. A progressive refinement approach to fast radiosity image generation. In *SIGGRAPH '88* (1988), pp. 75–84.

[7] CURLESS, B., AND LEVOY, M. A volumetric method for building complex models from range images. In *SIGGRAPH '96* (1996), pp. 303–312.

[8] DANA, K. J., GINNEKEN, B., NAYAR, S. K., AND KOENDERINK, J. J. Reflectance and texture of real-world surfaces. In *Proc. IEEE Conf. on Comp. Vision and Patt. Recog.* (1997), pp. 151–157.

[9] DEBEVEC, P. E., AND MALIK, J. Recovering high dynamic range radiance maps from photographs. In *SIGGRAPH '97* (August 1997), pp. 369–378.

[10] DEBEVEC, P. E., TAYLOR, C. J., AND MALIK, J. Modeling and rendering architecture from photographs: A hybrid geometry- and image-based approach. In *SIGGRAPH '96* (August 1996), pp. 11–20.

[11] DEBEVEC, P. E., YU, Y., AND BORSHUKOV, G. D. Efficient view-dependent image-based rendering with projective texture-mapping. Tech. Rep. UCB//CSD-98-1003, University of California at Berkeley, 1998.

[12] DRETTAKIS, G., ROBERT, L., AND BOUGNOUX, S. Interactive common illumination for computer augmented reality. In *8th Eurographics workshop on Rendering, St. Etienne, France* (May 1997), J. Dorsey and P. Slusallek, Eds., pp. 45–57.

[13] FIELDING, R. *The Technique of Special Effects Cinematography*. Hastings House, New York, 1968.

[14] FOURNIER, A., GUNAWAN, A., AND ROMANZIN, C. Common illumination between real and computer generated scenes. In *Graphics Interface* (May 1993), pp. 254–262.

[15] GERSHBEIN, R., SCHRODER, P., AND HANRAHAN, P. Textures and radiosity: Controlling emission and reflection with texture maps. In *SIGGRAPH '94* (1994).

[16] GORAL, C. M., TORRANCE, K. E., GREENBERG, D. P., AND BATTAILE, B. Modeling the interaction of light between diffuse surfaces. In *SIGGRAPH '84* (1984), pp. 213–222.

[17] GORTLER, S. J., GRZESZCZUK, R., SZELISKI, R., AND COHEN, M. F. The Lumigraph. In *SIGGRAPH '96* (1996), pp. 43–54.

[18] HECKBERT, P. S. Survey of texture mapping. *IEEE Computer Graphics and Applications 6*, 11 (November 1986), 56–67.

[19] KAJIYA, J. The rendering equation. In *SIGGRAPH '86* (1986), pp. 143–150.

[20] KARNER, K. F., MAYER, H., AND GERVAUTZ, M. An image based measurement system for anisotropic reflection. In *EUROGRAPHICS Annual Conference Proceedings* (1996).

[21] KOENDERINK, J. J., AND VAN DOORN, A. J. Illuminance texture due to surface mesostructure. *J. Opt. Soc. Am. 13*, 3 (1996).

[22] LAVEAU, S., AND FAUGERAS, O. 3-D scene representation as a collection of images. In *Proceedings of 12th International Conference on Pattern Recognition* (1994), vol. 1, pp. 689–691.

[23] LEVOY, M., AND HANRAHAN, P. Light field rendering. In *SIGGRAPH '96* (1996), pp. 31–42.

[24] MCMILLAN, L., AND BISHOP, G. Plenoptic Modeling: An image-based rendering system. In *SIGGRAPH '95* (1995).

[25] NAKAMAE, E., HARADA, K., AND ISHIZAKI, T. A montage method: The overlaying of the computer generated images onto a background photograph. In *SIGGRAPH '86* (1986), pp. 207–214.

[26] PORTER, T., AND DUFF, T. Compositing digital images. In *SIGGRAPH 84* (July 1984), pp. 253–259.

[27] SATO, Y., WHEELER, M. D., AND IKEUCHI, K. Object shape and reflectance modeling from observation. In *SIGGRAPH '97* (1997), pp. 379–387.

[28] SMITH, T. G. *Industrial Light and Magic: The Art of Special Effects*. Ballantine Books, New York, 1986.

[29] SZELISKI, R. Image mosaicing for tele-reality applications. In *IEEE Computer Graphics and Applications* (1996).

[30] TURK, G., AND LEVOY, M. Zippered polygon meshes from range images. In *SIGGRAPH '94* (1994), pp. 311–318.

[31] VEACH, E., AND GUIBAS, L. J. Metropolis light transport. In *SIGGRAPH '97* (August 1997), pp. 65–76.

[32] WARD, G. J. Measuring and modeling anisotropic reflection. In *SIGGRAPH '92* (July 1992), pp. 265–272.

[33] WARD, G. J. The radiance lighting simulation and rendering system. In *SIGGRAPH '94* (July 1994), pp. 459–472.

[34] WATANABE, M., AND NAYAR, S. K. Telecentric optics for computational vision. In *Proceedings of Image Understanding Workshop (IUW 96)* (February 1996).

[35] Y.CHEN, AND MEDIONI, G. Object modeling from multiple range images. *Image and Vision Computing 10*, 3 (April 1992), 145–155.

Multiple-Center-of-Projection Images

Paul Rademacher   Gary Bishop

University of North Carolina at Chapel Hill

ABSTRACT

In image-based rendering, images acquired from a scene are used to represent the scene itself. A number of reference images are required to fully represent even the simplest scene. This leads to a number of problems during image acquisition and subsequent reconstruction. We present the *multiple-center-of-projection image*, a single image acquired from multiple locations, which solves many of the problems of working with multiple range images.

This work develops and discusses multiple-center-of-projection images, and explains their advantages over conventional range images for image-based rendering. The contributions include greater flexibility during image acquisition and improved image reconstruction due to greater connectivity information. We discuss the acquisition and rendering of multiple-center-of-projection datasets, and the associated sampling issues. We also discuss the unique epipolar and correspondence properties of this class of image.

CR Categories: I.3.3 [Computer Graphics]: Picture/Image Generation – *Digitizing and scanning, Viewing algorithms*; I.3.7 [Computer Graphics]: Three-Dimensional Graphics and Realism; I.4.10 [Image Processing]: Scene Analysis

Keywords: image-based rendering, multiple-center-of-projection images

1   INTRODUCTION

In recent years, image-based rendering (IBR) has emerged as a powerful alternative to geometry-based representations of 3-D scenes. Instead of geometric primitives, the dataset in IBR is a collection of samples along viewing rays from discrete locations. Image-based methods have several advantages. They provide an alternative to laborious, error-prone geometric modeling. They can produce very realistic images when acquired from the real world, and can improve image quality when combined with geometry (e.g., texture mapping). Furthermore, the rendering time for an image-based dataset is dependent on the image sampling density, rather than the underlying spatial complexity of the scene. This can yield significant rendering speedups by replacing or augmenting traditional geometric methods [7][23][26][4].

The number and quality of viewing samples limits the quality of images reconstructed from an image-based dataset.

CB #3175 Sitterson Hall, Chapel Hill, NC, 27599-3175

rademach@cs.unc.edu, bishop@cs.unc.edu   http://www.cs.unc.edu/~ibr

Clearly, if we sample from every possible viewing position and along every possible viewing direction (thus sampling the entire *plenoptic function* [19][1]), then any view of the scene can be reconstructed perfectly. In practice, however, it is impossible to store or even acquire the complete plenoptic function, and so one must sample from a finite number of discrete viewing locations, thereby building a set of *reference images*. To synthesize an image from a new viewpoint, one must use data from *multiple* reference images. However, combining information from different images poses a number of difficulties that may decrease both image quality and representation efficiency. The *multiple-center-of-projection (MCOP) image* approaches these problems by combining samples from multiple viewpoints into a *single image*, which becomes the complete dataset. Figure 1 is an example MCOP image.

Figure 1 Example MCOP image of an elephant

The formal definition of multiple-center-of-projection images encompasses a wide range of camera configurations. This paper mainly focuses on one particular instance, based on the photographic *strip camera* [9]. This is a camera with a vertical slit directly in front of a moving strip of film (shown in Figure 2 without the lens system). As the film slides past the slit a continuous image-slice of the scene is acquired. If the camera is moved through space while the film rolls by, then different columns along the film are acquired from different vantage points. This allows the single image to capture continuous information from multiple viewpoints. The strip camera has been used extensively, e.g., in aerial photography. In this work's notion of a digital strip camera, each pixel-wide column of the image is acquired from a different center-of-projection. This single image becomes the complete dataset for IBR.

Features of multiple-center-of-projection images include:

- greater connectivity information compared with collections of standard range images, resulting in improved rendering quality,
- greater flexibility in the acquisition of image-based datasets, for example by sampling different portions of the scene at different resolutions, and
- a unique *internal* epipolar geometry which characterizes optical flow within a single image.

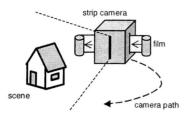

Figure 2 A *strip camera* consists of a moving strip of film behind a vertical slit.

Furthermore, MCOP images retain the desirable properties of conventional range images, such as fast incremental projection and moderate storage requirements.

In this paper we formally develop the concept of multiple-center-of-projection images, and discuss their acquisition and reprojection for image-based rendering. We describe different data structures to maintain these images, and discuss the implications of sampling during their acquisition. We also show how to perform point correspondence using a single MCOP image. We conclude by presenting several examples of MCOP images, and demonstrate their advantage over conventional range images.

2 PREVIOUS WORK

Early work in image-based rendering includes the rangeless panoramas of Chen and Williams [3][4] and Regan and Pose[22], which allow view reconstruction from a set of fixed eye locations. Plenoptic modeling [19] adds range to panoramic images, thereby allowing reprojection from arbitrary viewpoints. The concept of the plenoptic function is further explored by light slab methods [10][16], which attempt to fully sample the function within a subset of space.

Several methods exist for handling IBR range images from multiple viewpoints. *Layered depth images* [23] store multiple hits of a viewing ray in different layers of a single image, allowing, e.g., the front and back of a surface to be kept in a single data structure. The *delta tree* [6] acquires a hierarchical set of reference images on a sampling sphere around a target object, discarding redundant information when possible.

The work most closely related to this paper is the *multiperspective panorama for cel animation* [30]. This method constructs an image from multiple viewpoints for use as a backdrop in traditional cel animation. A continuous set of views along a pre-specified path can be extracted from this single backdrop. The construction of multiperspective panoramas is similar to the use of *manifold projections* in computer vision [20].

Another related work is the *extended camera for ray tracing* [11]. This method allows a ray-tracing camera to undergo arbitrary transformations as it traverses each pixel of the output image, thereby achieving a number of artistic effects.

Imaging devices similar to strip cameras have recently been explored in computer vision by Zheng and Tsuji [31] and by Hartley [13]. The former discusses their use in robot navigation, while the latter discusses the *pushbroom camera*, used in satellite imagery. One-dimensional cameras are also the basis of Cyberware scanners, which sweep a linear or circular path around an object, and systems by 3D Scanners, Ltd., which attach a 1-D scanning head to a Faro Technologies arm.

3 MULTIPLE-CENTER-OF-PROJECTION IMAGES

3.1 Definition

A multiple-center-of-projection image is an extension of a conventional image, characterized by having a *set* of cameras contributing to it, rather than only a single camera. Individual pixels or sets of pixels are acquired by different cameras, subject to certain constraints.

A *multiple-center-of-projection image* consists of a two dimensional image and a parameterized set of cameras, meeting the following conditions:
1) the cameras must lie on either a continuous curve or a continuous surface
2) each pixel is acquired by a single camera
3) viewing rays vary continuously across neighboring pixels
4) two neighboring pixels must either correspond to the same camera or to neighboring cameras.

This definition states that the camera locations are not an unorganized set of points, but rather define a continuous curve or surface (condition 1). Condition 2 states each pixel is from a single camera, rather than a blend of samples from multiple cameras. Condition 3 imposes smoothness on the viewing rays, thereby ensuring they do not vary discontinuously. The last condition imposes an organization on the mapping of camera samples to the resulting image; it ensures we move smoothly from camera to camera as we traverse from pixel to pixel in an image.

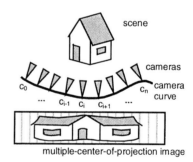

Figure 3 A multiple-center-of-projection image acquired by capturing a discrete number of image-slices along a curve. This single image (bottom) sees three sides of the house simultaneously. A similar configuration was used to create Figure 1.

Note that while the definition contains several parts, a continuous strip camera – along any continuous path – automatically satisfies the four criteria (section 4.4 discusses the sampling implications for discrete images). The remainder of this paper thus deals exclusively with the strip camera instance, unless otherwise noted.

3.2 Distinctions From Other Methods

Before delving into the details of MCOP images, we should clarify what these images *are not*. For example, what is the difference between an MCOP image and an arbitrary collection of conventional images? As will be shown in sections 4 and 5, the four constraints on an MCOP image yield advantages not found with conventional range images. These include improved image reconstruction quality, greater flexibility during image acquisition, and unique epipolar and correspondence properties. MCOP images are *not* a data structure for maintaining collections of images.

What is the difference between an MCOP image and the multiperspective panorama [30]? Multiperspective panoramas may be considered subsets of MCOP images, since they meet the definition of section 3.1. However, a multiperspective panorama is not intended as a dataset for arbitrary view construction; it does not permit 3D reprojection, and thus can only provide views along a single predetermined path. Also, a primary goal in multiperspective panoramas is to minimize the local distortion in the bitmap – otherwise, output images will suffer from perspective errors. This will not occur with MCOP images.

What is the difference between an MCOP dataset and a polygonal mesh? MCOP images retain the same desirable characteristics that separate all image-based range datasets from polygonal datasets. Because of strong spatial coherence across neighboring pixels, the projection of image points can be computed incrementally using McMillan and Bishop's 3D warping equations [19]. Also, since the image dataset is a regular grid, the 2D pixel coordinates are implicit for all points – each pixel only needs to contain intensity and range, in contrast with intensity, x, y, and z. Finally, an MCOP image has projective and epipolar properties not found in polygonal meshes.

We must also distinguish between MCOP images and images with arbitrary-manifold projection surfaces. That is, we can construct a single-COP image in which the projection surface is not a plane, cylinder, or sphere, but rather an arbitrary manifold surface. Each pixel in this image is then given by an intersection of a ray from the COP through the surface. While MCOP images *do* have curved image surfaces, the two are not equivalent, since the arbitrary-manifold image can still only capture scene points visible to the single center of projection, whereas MCOP images can view from more than one location.

4 ACQUIRING MCOP IMAGES

Multiple-center-of-projection images are well-suited to applications where a useful path can be defined through or around a scene; by not tying every pixel in a reference image to the same viewpoint, they allow greater flexibility during acquisition than conventional images. For example, sampling a nearly-convex object (such as in Figure 4) results in several poorly-sampled areas, as the cameras' viewing rays approach grazing angle with the object. The MCOP image on the right, however, samples every point at a near-normal angle, thus acquiring good samples everywhere. This occurs for both quantities being measured – color and range. Other relevant sampling issues are discussed in section 4.4.

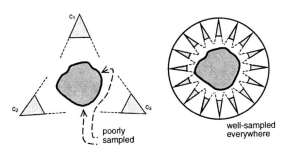

Figure 4 The three regular cameras on the left have difficulty sampling the object well. The MCOP image on the right can easily sample well the complete object.

4.1 Data Structures for MCOP Images

Although each pixel in an MCOP image may conceptually belong to a different camera, in practice we minimize storage requirements by describing the cameras parametrically in a variety of ways. At the highest level, for example, we can divide the camera curve into equally-spaced segments, then use the column index of each pixel as an implicit curve coordinate to compute the camera location. At the next level, each column of the image may explicitly store the parametric coordinate of the camera, thus allowing irregular camera spacing along the curve. Each column may instead *explicitly* contain the complete camera model, thus requiring n camera descriptions for an $n{\times}n$-sized image. Or, at the extreme level, each *pixel* can explicitly store a camera model. Clearly, the most compact method should be selected given a particular application.

4.2 Synthesizing From a 3D Model

To synthesize an MCOP image from a 3D model, we first define a path through the 3D scene. This path need not be closed, nor do the viewing rays need to be normal to the curve. We then smoothly animate a camera along this curve, extracting a single-pixel-wide color image and depth map at each frame of the animation. As each slice is captured, we concatenate the color image and range map into a rectangular buffer, and store the camera information for that column (four vectors, described in 5.1) in an array. Since there is much coherence from one camera position to the next along the path, a method such as *multiple viewpoint rendering* [12] may be used to accelerate the rendering.

Figures 5 through 8 show a rendered 1000×500 MCOP image of a castle model. Details of the rendering process are given in section 8. Note that the single image captures the complete exterior of the model, which is then rendered as a single mesh. This demonstrates the increased acquisition flexibility and improved connectivity properties of the MCOP technique.

4.3 Acquiring From Real-World Scenes

We can acquire an MCOP image of the real world by constructing the digital equivalent of a strip camera. For example, we can use a 1-D CCD camera, translated along a path. One-dimensional image-strips are captured at discrete points on the path and concatenated into the image buffer. The CCD camera must be accurately tracked to prevent errors during reprojection, using for example the techniques in [28].

This method has the disadvantage of introducing a temporal element into the image, since every 1-D strip is captured at a different time. This may lead to mismatched data unless the scene is static (static scenes are a common assumption in IBR [4][19][16][10]).

Active range-finding techniques, such as laser range-finders, can be applied to MCOP images almost exactly as with regular images: simply register the laser scanner with the color camera. A Cyberware scanner, for example, is a 1-D laser range-finder registered with a 1-D linear camera. Section 6 discusses how the epipolar constraint - critical to passive range-finding methods - can be extended to MCOP images.

Figure 5 Castle model. The red curve is the path the camera was swept on, and the arrows indicate the direction of motion. The blue triangles are the thin frusta of each camera. Every 64th camera is shown.

Figure 6 The resulting 1000×500 MCOP image. The first fourth of the image, on the left side, is from the camera sweeping over the roof. Note how the courtyard was sampled more finely, for added resolution.

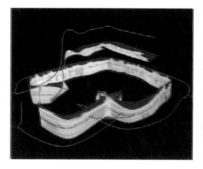 

Figure 7 The projection surface (image plane) of the camera curve.

Figure 8 Three views of the castle, reconstructed solely from the single MCOP image above. This dataset captures the complete exterior of the castle.

4.4   Sampling Issues

The construction of an MCOP image is inherently a sampling process; there are two primary questions that must be asked. First, *how much* of the plenoptic function does an MCOP image capture? The light field and Lumigraph methods approach this by attempting to fully sample the function, but only over a subset of space. The MCOP method is better suited to the opposite approach - sampling the plenoptic function only partially (specifically, not capturing view-dependent lighting), but over large regions. Furthermore, MCOP range images are not bound by the *free space assumption* of light slab methods, since the range at each pixel is used to resolve visibility. Thus, MCOP images can contain both foreground and background objects (by sweeping the camera over both areas), and the reprojection viewpoint is not limited to lying between the camera path and the projection surface.

Second, *how well* does an MCOP image sample the plenoptic function? Since the functions being sampled (color and range) are not bandlimited, aliasing is inevitable. To minimize it, we must prefilter the signals (that is, perform area sampling rather than point sampling) as we must with light field rendering [16]. In that work the camera spacing is constant, and thus also the filtering kernel. However, in MCOP images the camera spacing and orientation may vary across the image. Therefore, a larger filtering kernel is required in regions of greater camera translation or rotation. However, as the filtering kernel is increased, the resolution of each sample is effectively reduced, since a greater portion of the scene is blurred into each sample. To avoid excessively-large kernels (that is, excessive blurring), the sampling rate should be increased in regions of fast camera motion.

5   REPROJECTING MCOP IMAGES

This section describes how to render a new viewpoint using an MCOP reference image. This consists of two steps: computing each pixel's reprojected location in world-space, and rendering the reprojected points using an appropriate reconstruction method. Alternatively, we may skip the reprojection into world-space, instead projecting from the 2D reference image directly into the 2D output image, as described in [18].

5.1   Reprojection Formula

Since an MCOP image conceptually contains a full camera description plus range for each pixel, the reprojection step is straightforward (in the strip camera case, we need only one camera model per column). Our implementation stores the camera information for each column i as four vectors: a center of projection C_i, a vector O_i from C_i to the image plane origin, a U_i vector defining the horizontal axis of the projection plane, and a V_i vector defining the vertical axis. Each pixel (i,j) contains *disparity* rather then depth, defined here as the distance from C_i to the image plane at a given pixel, divided by the distance from C_i to the pixel's corresponding world-space point. Thus disparity is inversely proportional to range.

Given this camera model and the disparity $\delta_{i,j}$ for a pixel (i, j), the 3-space reprojection (x, y, z) is:

$$\begin{pmatrix} x \\ y \\ z \end{pmatrix} = \frac{1}{\delta_{i,j}} \begin{bmatrix} U_{i_x} & V_{i_x} & O_{i_x} \\ U_{i_y} & V_{i_y} & O_{i_y} \\ U_{i_z} & V_{i_z} & O_{i_z} \end{bmatrix} \begin{pmatrix} i \\ j \\ 1 \end{pmatrix} + \begin{pmatrix} C_{i_x} \\ C_{i_y} \\ C_{i_z} \end{pmatrix}$$

If the dataset is rendered in column-major order, we can reproject the pixels incrementally, since C_i, O_i, U_i, and V_i are constant for each column. Also note the (i, j) coordinates of a pixel are *implicit* (since the image is a regular grid) and do not have to be explicitly maintained.

5.2 Image Reconstruction

After calculating the reprojected coordinates of each pixel in the reference image, there are two common methods for reconstructing a *conventional* range image from a new viewpoint: splatting and meshing. Splatting consists of directly rendering each point using a variable-size reconstruction kernel (e.g., a Gaussian blob), with size dependent on distance from the eye to the point [25][29]. Meshing consists of connecting adjacent pixels with triangles, quadrilaterals, or some higher-order surface. Visibility can be determined for both methods by z-buffering.

Splatting with MCOP images is exactly as with conventional images, since each point is rendered independently: we compute each pixel's 3-space location, then render that point with an appropriate reconstruction kernel. Meshing can also be employed as with conventional images; although neighboring pixels may come from different cameras, the constraints of the MCOP definition ensure that neighboring pixels in the image represent neighboring points in space.

For proper meshing of conventional or MCOP images, discontinuities in the range image must first be detected. For example, three adjacent pixels with one belonging to a foreground object and the others belonging to the background should not be connected in the rendered image. Methods for detecting these *silhouette edges* are discussed in [17][7][27]. Such algorithms can be easily extended to the MCOP domain. For example, our silhouette-detection implementation for a *single*-COP image will not connect adjacent pixels if the surface they define is sampled by a nearly parallel ray (see Figure 9). It assumes these points probably span empty space, rather than a real surface. This method is directly extended to MCOP images by testing each triangle (from three adjacent pixels) against the rays of the two or three cameras that contribute to it: if the triangle is nearly parallel to them all, it is not rendered; otherwise, it *is* rendered. This comparison is only performed once, as a preprocess.

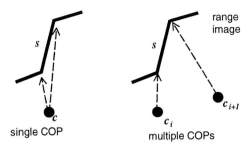

Figure 9 In the single-COP case the surface s is nearly parallel to the rays of camera c, and so is not rendered. In the MCOP case, s is not parallel to the ray from the second camera, and therefore *is* rendered.

MCOP images have an advantage over conventional images when rendering with meshes. In the conventional case a large number of separate images may be required to fully sample an object. One can only easily connect adjacent pixels *within each image*, but points from different images cannot be connected with a mesh unless a "zippering" preprocess [5] is performed. The amount of zippering required increases with the number of images, since each image's boundaries will tend to produce additional seams. With the MCOP method, this problem is minimized, since there is only one image in the dataset. By reducing the number of boundaries to consider, MCOP images can greatly reduce the amount of zippering necessary to fully connect a scene.

5.3 Multiple Sampling of Scene Points

An MCOP image may contain multiple samplings of the same scene point. Since these samples map to the same area in the new, reconstructed image, simple meshing or splatting methods leave only the last-rendered of the frontmost samples in the image. This, however, may not be the best sample. A better method is to blend successive samples as they are written to the image buffer, as described in [7] and [21].

6 EPIPOLAR GEOMETRY

A fundamental relationship between a pair of conventional images is the epipolar geometry they define: a pixel with unknown range in one image will map to a line in the other (planar) image [8][2]. This property characterizes the *optical flow* between the two images, and aids in solving the *correspondence problem* - if one image's pixel views a feature **x**, then to find that feature in the other image, we need only search the corresponding line that the pixel maps to. This property has led to the

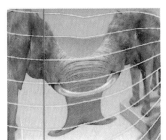

Figure 10 Internal epipolar geometry for an MCOP image. a) Elephant model. The camera first sweeps the head in one direction, then in the other direction b) the MCOP image c) rays cast by a camera, and acquired by every other camera. Positive rays are yellow, negative rays green. d) the epipolar curves induced by the rays of the leftmost eye's camera, marked in red. Note how the curve that crosses the first viewing of the eye also crosses the second viewing of the eye. Given these two corresponding points, we can find the range of the eye by triangulation.

development of occlusion-compatible rendering order for range images and layered depth images [19][23], and greatly simplifies passive range-finding methods based on correspondence.

We can similarly define an epipolar geometry between an MCOP image and a conventional image, or between two MCOP images, by merely projecting the rays of one image's pixels into the other image. However, these will usually map to curves in an MCOP image, rather than to lines.

We can also define an *internal* epipolar geometry using only a *single* MCOP image. Pick some camera c_i of the MCOP image, and project its rays into every other camera of the image (Figure 10). The result will be a family of curves, which characterizes the optical flow between c_i and the other cameras. If some feature **x** is seen multiple times in the image (e.g., the elephant's eye in the image, which is seen twice), then all sightings must lie along an epipolar curve. Thus the *epipolar constraint* holds for MCOP images, although it remains as future work whether the internal epipolar geometry will lead to useful correspondence algorithms.

7 CAMERAS ALONG A SURFACE

This paper has dealt exclusively with MCOP images constructed by placing cameras along a curve. However, the definition of multiple-center-of-projection images also allows the cameras to define a surface. This approach allows more independence among viewing locations and rays by providing an additional dimension of parameterization. We can, for example, parameterize a 3D surface by s and t, then define a camera for m and n discrete points along s and t, respectively. The viewing rays need not be normal to the surface, but must vary smoothly across neighboring pixels.

A useful case where the cameras define a surface can be constructed as follows: consider a static rig in the shape of an arc, lined with a curved one-dimensional CCD array on the inside (Figure 12). This rig is then rotated around a target object (the CCDs need not point directly at the center of rotation). Since each CCD is considered a camera, this case constructs an MCOP image where the camera forms a surface, rather than a curve. Note that although the camera locations and orientations now differ *for every pixel* in the resulting image, they can be efficiently described by a parametric surface, and thus do not significantly increase the dataset size.

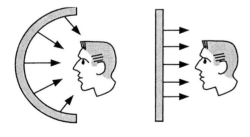

Figure 12 Cameras along an arc (left) define a surface of revolution when rotated, and may be used to capture a greater solid angle compared to conventional cylindrical scanners (right)

This configuration is very similar to Cyberware scanners, except their rig is not curved, so all of their viewing rays are parallel. A limitation of non-curved scanners is that they cannot appropriately sample the tops or bottom of many commonly scanned objects, such as the human head. The curved camera surface, however, will adequately handle this.

8 RESULTS

Figures 5 through 8 and 13 through 17 show the multiple-center-of-projection method applied to two synthetic scenes. Each MCOP image was rendered in 3D Studio MAX as described in section 4.2: we defined one curve around the model for the camera location, another curve for the camera's *lookat* point, and then rendered a single-pixel-wide image at each step along these curves. We used a custom plug-in to extract the Z-buffer and camera information (C, O, U, and V vectors) for each pixel-wide image. The color, range, and camera information were then concatenated into a rectangular color image, a rectangular disparity map, and an array of camera descriptors.

The castle model demonstrates the MCOP method's improved connectivity by rendering the entire image with a single mesh. The Titanic model demonstrates the method's flexible image acquisition, by sampling the flag at a higher resolution than the rest of the ship.

Figure 11 shows the results of an early experiment to acquire real-world data. A UNC HiBall optoelectronic tracker was rigidly attached to an Acuity Research AccuRange4000 laser range finder, which reflected from a rotating mirror. This rig was moved along the path shown in Figure 11b, sweeping out columns of range and reflectance at discrete points on the path. The camera swept over the scene a total of six times (note that the scene photographed is a recreation of that which the laser actually

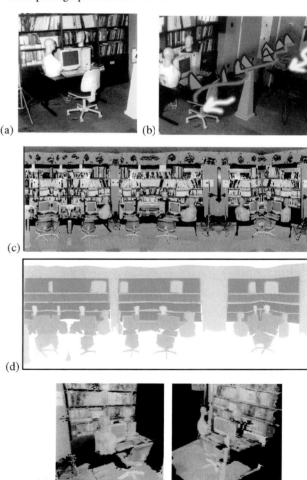

Figure 11 Results of early experiment (see section 8 for details). (a) Scene. (b) Camera path used to acquire it. (c) The grayscale acquired image. (d) Color mask applied to it. (e) Reprojected views.

scanned, since equipment was moved between the day of the experiment and the day of the photographs). The MCOP image shown in (c) is the grayscale reflectance reported by the laser. The color mask was hand-created to better distinguish the separate objects. Two reprojections of the entire dataset. The results from this early experiment were reasonable, and proved the feasibility of the MCOP method for real-world usage. The main problems encountered were static misregistration between the tracker and laser, and poor range data resulting from specular surfaces.

9 LIMITATIONS AND FUTURE WORK

The tradeoffs and limitations of MCOP images are similar to those of conventional images. In order to capture view-dependent lighting in an MCOP image, we must acquire a feature multiple times; this is analogous to sampling a point from different locations with conventional images. As with all image-based methods, the rendering quality is limited by the original image sampling; this is in contrast with geometric methods, which can represent objects as continuous entities. Also, since the number of viewpoints in an MCOP image tends to be larger than in a set of conventional images, there are more opportunities for error to be introduced by the camera tracking. Finally, while MCOP images allow greater acquisition flexibility, they do not solve the problem of finding a set of viewpoints that fully cover a scene, or sample it at some optimal quality.

Conventional range images can be rendered in occlusion-compatible order [19], a scene-independent list-priority technique that eliminates the need for z-buffering with a single reference image. This cannot be applied directly to multiple-center-of-projection images, however, due to their complex epipolar geometries. It remains as future work to classify what subsets of all possible MCOP configurations *can* be rendered in occlusion compatible order.

Another area of future work concerns the construction of complete polygonal meshes for CAD or geometric rendering [5][27], given an MCOP range image. The problem is simplified somewhat in the MCOP domain since we have connectivity information across *all* neighboring pixels, as opposed to dealing with an unorganized set of points, or multiple reference images which only contain connectivity information within themselves. Nonetheless, while MCOP images may reduce the number of seams that must be stitched, they are not altogether eliminated. Whenever a surface is viewed multiple times, the spatial connectivity across the different viewings must still be determined.

10 CONCLUSION

In this paper we have developed and discussed the multiple-center-of-projection image for image-based rendering. MCOP images alleviate many problems of image-based rendering by maintaining a *single* image, containing information from multiple viewpoints. They allow for better image reconstruction than conventional range images. They are capable of sampling different portions of a scene at different resolutions. They provide greater control over the sampling process, allowing the directions of viewing rays to vary over the image, thereby acquiring better samples than if all were bound to the same COP. They also posses a unique internal epipolar geometry that defines how multiple viewings of scene points relate to each other.

Multiple-center-of-projection images have already proven their usefulness in real-world domains, though under different names. The strip camera, for example, has existed for almost a hundred years, and has been used for such important tasks as aerial photography for the last fifty. The Cyberware scanner, another MCOP device, has proven invaluable to a wide range of computer graphics applications. This paper presents a framework by which these existing methods can be exploited further. More importantly, it extends the notion of what it means to be an "image" in image-based rendering.

ACKNOLEDGEMENTS

We would like to thank Mary Whitton, Nick England, Russ Taylor, Anselmo Lastra, Henry Fuchs, and the UNC IBR group for their assistance and insight at various stages of this work. Special thanks to Fred Brooks for his thorough critique of an early draft, and to Lars Nyland for his collaboration on the laser experiment. Thanks also to the SIGGRAPH reviewers. Photographs are by Todd Gaul. The models were provided by REM Infografica. This work is supported by DARPA ITO contract number E278, NSF MIP-9612643, DARPA ETO contract number N00019-97-C-2013, and an NSF Graduate Fellowship. Thanks also to Intel for their generous donation of equipment.

REFERENCES

[1] E. H. Adelson and J. R. Bergen. The Plenoptic Function And The Elements Of Early Vision. In *Computational Models of Visual Processing*, pp. 3-20, Edited by Michael Landy and J. Anthony Movshon, The MIT Press, Cambridge, 1991.

[2] Robert C. Bolles, H. Harlyn Baker, and David H. Marimont. Epipolar-Plane Image Analysis: An Approach To Determining Structure From Motion. In *International Journal of Computer Vision*, volume 1, page 7-55. Boston, 1987.

[3] Shenchang Eric Chen and Lance Williams. View Interpolation For Image Synthesis. In *Proceedings of SIGGRAPH 93*, pp. 279-288, New York, 1993. ACM.

[4] Shenchang Eric Chen. Quicktime VR: An Image-Based Approach To Virtual Environment Navigation. In *Proceedings of SIGGRAPH 95*, pp. 29-38, New York, 1995. ACM.

[5] Brian Curless and Marc Levoy. A Volumetric Method For Building Complex Models From Range Images. In *Proceedings of SIGGRAPH 96*, pp. 303-312. New York, 1996. ACM.

[6] William J. Dally, Leonard McMillan, Gary Bishop, and Henry Fuchs. The Delta Tree: An Object-Centered Approach To Image-Based Rendering. MIT AI Lab Technical Memo 1604, May 1996.

[7] Lucia Darsa, Bruno Costa Silva, and Amitabh Varshney. Navigating Static Environments Using Image-Space Simplification And Morphing. In *Proceedings of 1997 Symposium on Interactive 3D Graphics*, pp. 25-34. April 1997.

[8] Olivier Faugeras. *Three-Dimensional Computer Vision: A Geometric Approach*. MIT Press, Cambridge, Massachusetts, 1993.

[9] Sanjib K. Ghosh. *Analytical Photogrammetry*, second edition. Pergamon, 1988.

[10] Steven J. Gortler, Radek Grzeszczuk, Richard Szeliski, and Michael F. Cohen. The Lumigraph. In *Proceedings of SIGGRAPH 96*, pp. 43-54, New York, 1996. ACM.

[11] Eduard Gröller and Helwig Löffelmann. Extended Camera Specifications for Image Synthesis. In *Machine Graphics and Vision*, 3 (3), pp. 513-530. 1994.

[12] Michael Halle. Multiple Viewpoint Rendering. To appear in *Proceedings of SIGGRAPH 98*. New York, 1998. ACM

[13] Richard Hartley and Rajiv Gupta. Linear Pushbroom Cameras. In *Proceedings of Third European Conference on Computer Vision*, pp. 555-566. New York, 1994.

[14] Hugues Hoppe, Tony DeRose, Tom Duchamp, John McDonald, and Werner Stuetzle. Surface Reconstruction From Unorganized Points. In *Computer Graphics (SIGGRAPH 92 Conference Proceedings)*, volume 26, pp. 71-78. New York, July 1992. ACM.

[15] Stephane Lavaeu and Olivier Faugeras. 3-D Scene Representation As A Collection Of Images. INRIA Technical Report RR-2205. February 1994, INRIA.

[16] Marc Levoy and Pat Hanrahan. Light Field Rendering. In *Proceedings of SIGGRAPH 96*, pp. 31-42, New York, 1996. ACM.

[17] William R. Mark, Leonard McMillan and Gary Bishop. Post-Rendering 3D Warping. In *Proceedings of the 1997 Symposium on Interactive 3D Graphics*, page 7-16, Providence, Rhode Island, April 1997.

[18] Leonard McMillan and Gary Bishop. Shape As A Perturbation To Projective Mapping, UNC Computer Science Technical Report TR95-046, University of North Carolina, April 1995.

[19] Leonard McMillan and Gary Bishop. Plenoptic Modeling: An Image-Based Rendering System. In *Proceedings of SIGGRAPH 95*, pp. 39-46, New York, 1995. ACM.

[20] Shmuel Peleg and Joshua Herman. Panoramic Mosaics by Manifold Projection. In *Proceedings of Computer Vision and Pattern Recognition*, pp. 338-343, Washington, June 1997. IEEE.

[21] Kari Pulli, Michael Cohen, Tom Duchamp, Hugues Hoppe, Linda Shapiro, Werner Stuetzle. View-Based Rendering: Visualizing Real Objects from Scanned Range and Color Data. In *Proceedings of Eighth Eurographics Workshop on Rendering*, pp. 23-34. Eurographics, June 1997.

[22] Matthew Regan and Ronald Pose. Priority Rendering with a Virtual Reality Address Recalculation Pipeline. In *Proceedings of SIGGRAPH 94*, pp. 155-162, New York, 1994. ACM.

[23] Jonathan Shade, Steven Gortler, Li-wei He, and Richard Szeliski. Layered Depth Images. To appear in *Proceedings of SIGGRAPH 98*. New York, 1998. ACM

[24] François X. Sillion, George Drettakis and Benoit Bodelet. Efficient Impostor Manipulation For Real-Time Visualization Of Urban Scenery. In *Proceedings of Eurographics 97*, pp. 207-218. Budapest, Hungary, September 1997.

[25] Edward Swan, Klaus Mueller, Torsten Moller, Naeem Shareef, Roger Crawfis, and Roni Yagel. An Anti-Aliasing Technique For Splatting. In *Proceedings of IEEE Visualization 97*, pp. 197-204, 1997

[26] Jay Torborg, James T. Kajiya. Talisman: Commodity Real-Time Graphics For The PC. In *Proceedings of SIGGRAPH 96*, pp. 353-363. New York, August 1996. ACM.

[27] Greg Turk and Marc Levoy. Zippered Polygon Meshes From Range Images. In *Proceedings of SIGGRAPH 94*, pp. 311-318. New York, July 1994. ACM.

[28] Gregory Welch and Gary Bishop. SCAAT: Incremental Tracking With Incomplete Information. In *Proceedings of SIGGRAPH 97*, pp. 333-344. Los Angeles , August 1997. ACM.

[29] Lee Westover. Footprint Evaluation For Volume Rendering. In *Computer Graphics (SIGGRAPH 90 Conference Proceedings)*, volume 24, pp. 367-376. New York, August 1990. ACM.

[30] Daniel N. Wood, Adam Finkelstein, John F. Hughes, Craig E. Thayer, and David H. Salesin. Multiperspective Panoramas For Cel Animation. In *Proceedings of SIGGRAPH 97*, pp. 243-250. New York, 1997. ACM.

[31] Jiang Yu Zheng and Saburo Tsuji. Panoramic Representation for Route Recognition by a Mobile Robot. In *International Journal of Computer Vision* 9 (1): 55-76. Netherlands, 1992. Kluwer.

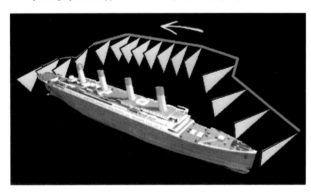

Figure 13 Titanic. We sample the fore and aft more closely than the midsection, for better reconstruction at those areas. The camera moves very close at the end of the path, to capture a small flag at the rear of the ship.

Figure 14 The resulting 1000×500 MCOP image. Because the fore and aft of the ship were sampled at a higher resolution, they occupy a larger portion of the image. The right side of the image shows the finely-sampled flag.

Figure 15 The image on the left is constructed by splatting every fourth column in the MCOP dataset. This shows the image-slices acquired by each camera on the curve. On the right is the dataset rendered by connecting adjacent points with triangles.

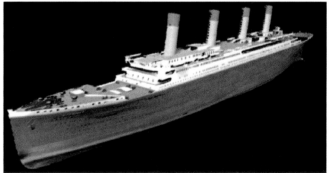

Figure 16 A full view of the reprojected dataset. The back sides of the funnels are not seen, because they were not sampled by the cameras (see Figure 13).

Recovering Photometric Properties Of Architectural Scenes From Photographs

Yizhou Yu   Jitendra Malik

Computer Science Division
University Of California At Berkeley *

Abstract

In this paper, we present a new approach to producing photorealistic computer renderings of real architectural scenes under novel lighting conditions, such as at different times of day, starting from a small set of photographs of the real scene. Traditional texture mapping approaches to image-based modeling and rendering are unable to do this because texture maps are the product of the interaction between lighting and surface reflectance and one cannot deal with novel lighting without dissecting their respective contributions. To obtain this decomposition into lighting and reflectance, our basic approach is to solve a series of optimization problems to find the parameters of appropriate lighting and reflectance models that best explain the measured values in the various photographs of the scene. The lighting models include the radiance distributions from the sun and the sky, as well as the landscape to consider the effect of secondary illumination from the environment. The reflectance models are for the surfaces of the architecture. Photographs are taken for the sun, the sky, the landscape, as well as the architecture at a few different times of day to collect enough data for recovering the various lighting and reflectance models. We can predict novel illumination conditions with the recovered lighting models and use these together with the recovered reflectance values to produce renderings of the scene. Our results show that our goal of generating photorealistic renderings of real architectural scenes under novel lighting conditions has been achieved.

CR Categories: I.2.10 [**Artificial Intelligence**]: Vision and Scene Understanding—modeling and recovery of physical attributes I.3.7 [**Computer Graphics**]: Three-dimensional Graphics and Realism—color, shading, shadowing, and texture , visible line/surface algorithms I.4.8 [**Image Processing**]: Scene Analysis—color, photometry, shading

Keywords: Photometric Properties, Image-based Rendering, Illumination, Sky Model, Reflectance, BRDF, Photometric Stereo

1 INTRODUCTION

It is light that reveals the form and material of architecture. In keeping with its rhythms of light and dark, clear and cloudy, the architec-

---

*Berkeley, CA 94720, e-mail: {yyz,malik}@cs.Berkeley.edu, website: http://http.cs.berkeley.edu/~{yyz,malik}

ture evokes distinct visual moods and impressions, something that many photographers and painters have sought to capture. Perhaps the most noteworthy of these attempts is the famous series of studies of the Cathedral at Rouen by Claude Monet–he painted the same facade at many different times of day and in different seasons of the year, seeking to capture the different 'impressions' of the scene.

Our goal in this paper is to develop this theme in the context of computer graphics. We will develop and demonstrate techniques to produce photorealistic computer renderings of real architectural scenes under different lighting conditions, such as at different times of day, starting from a small set of photographs of the real scene. Previous work on the FACADE system[4] has shown that it is possible to use a combination of geometric models recovered from photographs, and projective texture mapping with textures derived from the same photographs, to generate extremely photorealistic renderings of the scene from novel viewpoints. However while we have the ability to vary viewpoint, we are unable to produce renderings under new lighting conditions–the texture maps are the product of the interaction between the lighting and surface reflectance and one cannot deal with novel lighting without dissecting their respective contributions. Other approaches to image-based rendering [14, 12, 6, 21] share the same general difficulty.

To obtain this decomposition into lighting and reflectance, our basic approach is to solve a series of optimization problems to find the parameters of appropriate lighting and reflectance models that best explain the measured values in the various photographs of the scene. The lighting models include those for the radiance distribution from the sun and the sky, as well as a landscape radiance model to consider the effect of illumination from the secondary sources in the environment. Note that illumination from these secondary sources, such as the ground near the floor of a building can be very important and is often the dominant term in shadowed areas. To have sufficient data for parameter recovery, we take several photographs–of the sun, the sky, the architecture, and the environment surrounding the architecture. This enables us to recover radiance models for the sun, sky and environment for that time of day. The process is repeated for a few different times of the day; collectively all these data are used to estimate the reflectance properties of the architecture. It is assumed that a geometric model of the architecture had previously been created using a modeling system such as FACADE, so at this stage enough information is available to rerender the building under novel lighting conditions. The data-flow diagram of the system is given in Figure 1.

There are several technical challenges that must be overcome. We highlight a few of them here:

1. The photographs do not directly give us radiance measurements–there is a nonlinear mapping which relates the digital values from the photograph to the radiance in the direction of that image pixel. This can be estimated using the technique from [3], and subsequent processing performed using radiance images.

2. Any measurements that we make from photographs cannot be used to recover the full spectral BRDF. We need to define a

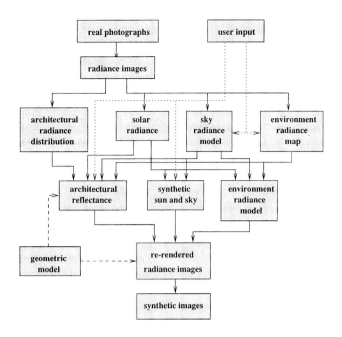

Figure 1: Data-flow diagram of the re-rendering system.

new concept, the pseudo-BRDF associated with a particular spectral distribution of the illuminant. This is done in Section 2. Our system is based on recovering pseudo-BRDFs for the architecture, and then subsequently using them for re-rendering. We recover two pseudo-BRDFs, one corresponding to the spectral distribution of the sun and one corresponding to the integrated light from the sky and landscape.

3. Producing renderings of the scene at novel times of day requires being able to predict lighting from the sun, sky and environment at such times. For the sun and sky, we rely on interpolated/extrapolated radiance models of the sun and sky (Section 5). Prediction of radiance from the environment at a novel time requires use of the computer vision technique of photometric stereo to recover a low resolution surface normal map of the environment, which can then be used in conjunction with the new sun position to yield the new environment radiance map.

This paper is organized as follows. In Section 2, we will discuss the pseudo-BRDF. In Section 3, we will introduce the methods for measuring the illumination. In Section 4, we will introduce the methods for recovering reflectance. In Section 5, we will propose approaches for simulating novel lighting conditions. In Section 6, we will give re-rendering results. Conclusions and future work will be given in the last section. In the appendices, we will give an algorithm for irradiance calculation and an algorithm for visibility processing.

2 THE PSEUDO-BRDF CONCEPT

The traditional way to formally define reflectance is using the concept of the bidirectional reflectance distribution function (BRDF) defined as follows:

$$\rho(\theta_i, \phi_i, \theta_r, \phi_r, \lambda) = \frac{dI(\theta_r, \phi_r, \lambda)}{I(\theta_i, \phi_i, \lambda)cos\theta_i d\omega_i} \quad (1)$$

where $I(\theta_i, \phi_i, \lambda)$ is the incident radiance and $dI(\theta_r, \phi_r, \lambda)$ is the reflected differential radiance.

Note the dependence on wavelength λ. There has been some some previous work using a spectrophotometer to carefully measure spectral BRDFs [2]. However, we concluded that it is impractical to use such a technique to measure the BRDFs of complex, outdoor scenes. Our philosophy is to work with whatever information can be extracted from photographs, and we will use just an ordinary hand-held digital video camcorder to acquire these photographs. Assume that the camera is geometrically calibrated, permitting us to identify ray directions from pixel locations.

In such a photograph, the value V obtained at a particular pixel in a particular channel (R, G, B) is the result of integration with the spectral response function $R(\lambda)$

$$V = \int R(\lambda)E(\lambda)d\lambda . \quad (2)$$

where $E(\lambda)$ is the incident radiance.

Suppose we take photographs of an area light source and of an object illuminated by this light source. Let us check the impact of this spectral integration over the traditional BRDF reflection model. What we can get from the photograph of the area light source is

$$I_{image}(\theta_i, \phi_i) = \int I(\theta_i, \phi_i, \lambda)R(\lambda)d\lambda \quad (3)$$

and what we can get from the photograph of the object is

$$I_{image}(\theta_r, \phi_r) = \int I(\theta_r, \phi_r, \lambda)R(\lambda)d\lambda$$

$$= \int \int I(\theta_i, \phi_i, \lambda)\rho(\theta_i, \phi_i, \theta_r, \phi_r, \lambda)R(\lambda)d\lambda \, cos\theta_i d\omega_i. \quad (4)$$

If we follow the definition of BRDF, but use $I_{image}(\theta_i, \phi_i)$ and $I_{image}(\theta_r, \phi_r)$ instead, we can define the following quantity which we will call the *pseudo-BRDF*

$$\rho_{pseudo}(\theta_i, \phi_i, \theta_r, \phi_r) = \frac{dI_{image}(\theta_r, \phi_r)}{I_{image}(\theta_i, \phi_i)cos\theta_i d\omega_i} \quad (5)$$

$$= \frac{\int I(\theta_i, \phi_i, \lambda)\rho(\theta_i, \phi_i, \theta_r, \phi_r, \lambda)R(\lambda) \, d\lambda}{\int I(\theta_i, \phi_i, \lambda)R(\lambda) \, d\lambda} \quad (6)$$

We note some properties of the pseudo-BRDF here:

- The pseudo-BRDF is equal to the real BRDF when the real BRDF does not vary with the wavelength. So they usually are not the same.

- In general, the pseudo-BRDF varies as the spectral distribution of the light source varies.

- If the spectral response function $R(\lambda) = \delta(\lambda - \lambda_0)$, then $\rho_{pseudo}(\theta_i, \phi_i, \theta_r, \phi_r) = \rho(\theta_i, \phi_i, \theta_r, \phi_r, \lambda_0)$.

Suppose we have a geometric model of some building. For the purpose of re-rendering under different lighting conditions, we need to recover the reflectance of the faces in the model. Since only pseudo-BRDFs can be recovered directly from photographs for each color channel and pseudo-BRDFs are sensitive to the spectral distribution of the light source, theoretically, we should divide the sky and the environment into small regions which have almost uniform spectral distributions spatially and recover distinct pseudo-BRDFs for each region. This is impractical because all these regions have their lighting effects on the considered architecture altogether and it is impossible to turn on only one of them and shut down the rest to recover individual pseudo-BRDFs. What we want to do is to recover as few pseudo-BRDFs as possible, but still get good approximations in rendering. It is possible to separate the sun from the sky since the solar position changes a lot during a day and a face of a building can be lit or unlit at different times. This has the same effect as turning the sun on or off for that face. It is also necessary to do this separation because the sun is the most important light source and its spectral distribution is so different from the blue sky. As to the rest of the sky and the environment, we find from experiments that recovering only one set of pseudo-BRDFs for them works very well. From now on, we will always recover two sets of pseudo-BRDFs, one of which corresponds to the spectral distribution of the sun, and the other to the integrated effect of the sky and environment. They will be used for re-rendering under novel lighting conditions under the assumption that the spectral distribution of daylight does not change much. Under extreme conditions, sunrise and sunset, we may expect these pseudo-BRDF's to cease being accurate.

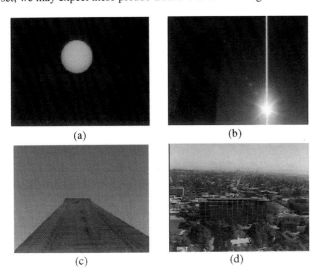

Figure 2: (a)Solar image obtained using a couple of neutral density filters, (b) Solar aureole obtained using fast shutter speed, (c) a photograph for the zenith, (d) a photograph for the landscape and the sky near the horizon.

3 MEASURING AND MODELING ILLUMINATION

We consider three sources of illumination. Light can be from the sun, the sky and the surrounding environment which serves as a secondary light source. Of course, in some fundamental sense, the sun is the only true light source. Both skylight and the light from the environment are ultimately derived from the sun. However, with an image-based approach, we need to measure and model these three sources separately. We shall not be constructing a physically correct global illumination model of the atmosphere and environment taking into account all the scattering and reflection effects!

To model these illumination sources, we take photographs of the sun, the sky and environment using a handheld CCD camera. To accurately measure the radiance, we need to convert the photographs into radiance images by inverting the nonlinear mapping between the incident radiance of the camera and its digital output. To recover this nonlinear mapping, we use the technique described in [3].

3.1 The Sun

We can measure the radiance of the sun with a camera and a couple of neutral density filters(Figure 2(a)) to make it unsaturated so that we can recover its dynamic radiance using the nonlinear mapping introduced before. The solid angle subtended by the sun can

be obtained from the diameter of the sun and the distance between the sun and the earth. The solar position(altitude and azimuth) can be obtained from formula given in the appendix of [18], provided that the latitude and longitude of the site on the earth's surface, and the time and date are known. We model the sun as a parallel light source.

3.2 The Sky

We can take photographs of the sky in order to measure its radiance distribution. But there exist a couple of problems. First, it is hard to know the camera pose because there is no feature in the sky to calibrate camera orientation if the sky is clear; second, it is hard to get a picture of the whole sky even with a fish-eye lens because there might be some objects occluding part of the sky, such as trees, buildings, and mountains; third, the intensity of circumsolar region or solar aureole can be very high, and can easily get saturated at a normal shutter speed. To solve the first problem, we decided to include some buildings as landmarks in each photograph so that we can use them to recover the camera pose later. But this means we are going to have more occlusions. While we will take multiple photographs(Figure 2(c)(d)) and hope the invisible part of the sky in one photograph will become visible in some other photograph, there is no way to guarantee that every part of the sky will be seen. Our approach to this difficulty is to have a sky model which we can fit to the visible parts of the sky and extrapolate into the invisible parts. To solve the last problem, we use a set of different shutter speeds for the solar aureole with each speed capturing the radiance inside a circular band centered at the solar position(Figure 2(b)).

Several papers present physical models of sky radiance [22, 9, 23]. However, we do not know how closely they approximate the real sky. Furthermore, physical models often give the spectral distribution of any point in the sky. It is very hard to fit these models to RGB data taken from photographs.

On the other hand, there are also many empirical models for sky luminance or radiance distribution [16, 1, 13, 8]. All CIE standard sky formulae are fixed sky luminance distributions. They can not be used for the purpose of data-fitting. The all-weather sky luminance model proposed in [16] is a generalization of the CIE standard clear sky formula. It is given by

$$Ls(\xi,\gamma) = Lvz \, f(\xi,\gamma)/f(0,Z) \qquad (7)$$

where ξ is the zenith angle of the considered sky element and γ is the angle between this sky element and the position of the sun, Lvz is zenith luminance, Z is the zenith angle of the sun, and

$$f(\xi,\gamma) = [1 + a \exp(b/\cos\xi)][1 + c \exp(d\gamma) + e \cos^2\gamma] \quad (8)$$

where $a, b, c, d,$ and e are adjustable coefficients. These variable coefficients make this empirical model more flexible than others, which means we might have a better fit by using this model. Since both Lvz and $f(0, Z)$ in the above model are unknown constants, we replace them with one new variable coefficient which can be optimized during data fitting. Empirically, we also find it is better to have one more variable coefficient as the exponent of γ in the term with c and d. Thus, we obtain the following revised seven-parameter sky model

$$Ls(\xi,\gamma) = Lz[1 + a \exp(b/\cos\xi)][1 + c \exp(d\gamma^h) + e \cos^2\gamma]$$
$$(9)$$

where $a, b, c, d, e, h,$ and Lz are variable coefficients.

Up to now, we still only have a sky luminance model which does not have colors. We have not seen in the literature any approach converting sky luminance models to RGB color distributions. The

   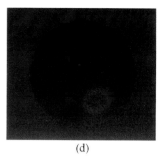

<table>
<tr><td>(a)</td><td>(b)</td><td>(c)</td><td>(d)</td></tr>
</table>

Figure 3: (a) A sky radiance model obtained by data-fitting,(b)-(d) the R,G,B channels of the sky model in (a). All color channels are generated using the same sky luminance model, but each color channel has its own distinct parameters.

method proposed in [23] converts luminance data to color temperatures and then to spectral distributions. The relationship they use between luminance and color temperatures is not necessarily accurate for different weather conditions. Based on the fact that the sky radiance distribution at each color channel has a similar shape, we decided to use the same model but a distinct set of coefficients for each color channel by fitting the above revised model to the data from each channel. In practice, the error of data-fitting remains very small for each channel, which means our method is appropriate. Skies thus obtained have convincing colors.

Since there might be trees, buildings or mountains in photographs, we interactively pick some sky regions from each photograph and fit the revised sky model to the chosen sky radiance data by using Levenberg-Marquardt method [17] to minimize the weighted least-square

$$\sum_{i=1}^{N}[\frac{y_i - Ls(\xi_i, \gamma_i)}{\sigma_i}]^2 \qquad (10)$$

where y_i's are the chosen sky radiance data from photographs and σ_i's are weights. We tried different weighting schemes, such as $\sigma_i = 1$, $y_i/\log(y_i)$, $y_i/\text{sqrt}(y_i)$, or y_i, and found the best result was obtained when $\sigma_i = y_i/\log(y_i)$. With this weighting scheme, the fitting error at most places is within 5%. A recovered sky radiance model is given in Figure 3.

 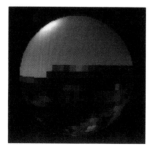

Figure 4: Two views of a spherical environment map. The upper hemisphere corresponds to the sky and the lower hemisphere has the radiance values from the surrounding landscape.

3.3 The Environment

By our definition, the environment of an outdoor object is its surrounding landscape. It can be a more significant light source than the dark side of a clear sky. There are mutual interreflections between an object and its environment. For reflectance recovery, we need to measure the radiance distribution of the whole environment which includes radiance from all visible objects and is the equilibrium state of mutual interreflections. It is assumed that we do not interfere with this equilibrium state when we take photographs of the environment.

For our purpose, we only need a coarse-grain environment radiance map to do irradiance calculation because irradiance results from an integrated effect of the incident radiance distribution. High-frequency components can therefore be ignored. We subdivide the environment sphere along latitudinal and longitudinal directions and get a set of rectangular spherical regions. Once we have those environment photographs(Figure 2(d)) and their camera orientations, we project every pixel into one of the spherical regions. Finally, we average the color of the pixels projected into each region and give the result as the average radiance from that region. If the architecture has large size, we may need to capture more than one environment map at different locations because the surrounding light field is a four dimensional distribution. However, since the integrated irradiance over the surfaces changes smoothly and slowly, we do not need to capture more than a small number of coarse-grain environment maps.

Two images of a spherical environment map including radiance distribution from both the sky and the landscape are shown in Figure 4.

Figure 5: Some photographs of a bell tower for reflectance recovery.

4 RECOVERING REFLECTANCE

We need to recover the reflectance of the faces in the geometric model for the purpose of re-rendering under different lighting conditions. There has been a lot of previous work [24, 19, 20, 11, 2] trying

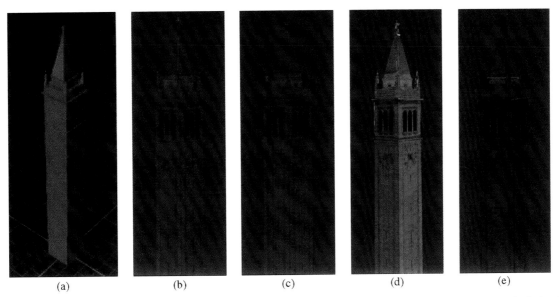

Figure 6: (a) A simple geometric model of a bell tower, (b)-(c) Diffuse pseudo-albedo recovered by using irradiance from both the sky and the landscape, (d) diffuse pseudo-albedo recovered incorrectly by only using irradiance from the sky, (e) diffuse pseudo-albedo corresponding to the spectral distribution of the sun.

to fit empirical or physics-based models to measured data and then using the obtained model into illumination calculation. The experiments were done for small objects or material samples in laboratory settings where only one single point light source was used and global illumination effects could be ignored. Usually only one set of pseudo-BRDF's were recovered if the data were obtained from images, which, as we know, is not adequate in our outdoor natural lighting context.

Recall from Section 2, that we decided to recover two sets of pseudo-BRDFs: one corresponding to the spectral distribution of the sun, and the other corresponding to the spectral distribution of the irradiance from both the sky and environment.

4.1 Recovering Diffuse Pseudo-Albedos

We use Lambertian model for diffuse component. So the recovery of diffuse pseudo-albedos at each surface point needs the incident irradiance and the outgoing diffuse radiance. The incident irradiance is obtained by gathering light from the sun, the sky, the environment, and possibly other polygonal faces occluding part of the previous three sources. We can get the irradiance from the sun by using the surface normal, the color and solid angle of the sun which we got from Section 3.1. We will discuss gathering light from the sky and environment in Appendix A. Gathering light from occluding faces can be done using the method in [15]. We use one-bounce reflection to approximate the interreflection among different faces.

Multiple photographs are taken for the considered building at different viewing directions and times(Figure 5). Since most architectural materials are only weakly specular except for windows, if our viewing direction is far away from the mirror angle of the current solar position, we can assume only diffuse radiance is captured in the photograph. Since each photograph can only cover some part of the architecture and there are occlusions among different faces, we need to decide which face is visible to which photographs. Visibility testing and polygon clipping will be discussed in Appendix B.

Since every surface of the building has its own surface texture, we need to incorporate these spatial variations into its pseudo-albedos. Each polygon in the geometric model is first triangulated and a dense grid is set up on each triangle in order to capture the variations. This step is similar to that introduced in [20]. Each grid point

is projected onto the photographs to which it is visible and a radiance value is taken from each photograph. The diffuse pseudo-albedo at the grid point is obtained by dividing the average radiance by the irradiance.

We need at least two photographs for each face of the building to recover both sets of pseudo-BRDF's. And it should not be lit by the sun in one photograph and should be lit in the other. Thus we have two equations for each surface point, one from each photograph.

$$\pi I^{(1)} = \rho^{se} E_{se}^{(1)} \tag{11}$$

$$\pi I^{(2)} = \rho^{se} E_{se}^{(2)} + \rho^{sun} E_{sun} \tag{12}$$

where $I^{(1)}$ and $I^{(2)}$ are radiance values obtained from the two photographs, $E_{se}^{(1)}$ and $E_{se}^{(2)}$ are the irradiance from the sky and environment, E_{sun} is the irradiance from the sun, ρ^{se} is the pseudo-albedo corresponding to the spectral distribution of the sky and environment, and ρ^{sun} is the pseudo-albedo corresponding to the spectral distribution of the sun.

From (11), we can solve ρ^{se}. By substituting it into (12), we can solve ρ^{sun} too. Of course, if we have more than two photographs, these estimations can be made more robust. Figure 6 displays the recovered diffuse pseudo-albedo. Figure 6(b)&(c) shows the diffuse pseudo-albedos of four different sides of a bell tower. These recovered pseudo-albedos are quite consistent with each other, providing an independent verification of our procedure since we recovered them from different photographs shot at different times.

We can choose solar positions to avoid large shadows cast on the architecture. When large shadows are inavoidable, we can interactively label the shadow boundaries to separate sunlit regions from shadowed ones. If there are several buildings located close to each other such that some sides of the buildings can not be lit by the sun or we can not simply take photographs for them, our method can not be used. A solution to this difficulty might be to fill in reflectance values from adjacent faces.

4.2 Recovering The Specular Lobes Of The Pseudo-BRDFs

We adopt the empirical model in [11] to recover specular lobes because this model can effectively simulate effects such as specular-

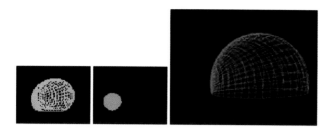

Figure 7: RGB specular lobes, recovered for the sun, of the associated pseudo-BRDF of the lower block of the geometric model in Fig. 6(a) at incident direction $(0.5, 0.0, 0.86)$.

ity at grazing angles, off-specular reflections and etc. Putting diffuse and specular lobes together, for each color channel, we have the following reflection model expressed in a local coordinate system of each triangular patch

$$\rho(u,v) = \rho_d + \rho_s [C_x u_x v_x + C_y u_y v_y + C_z u_z v_z]^n. \quad (13)$$

where $u = (u_x, u_y, u_z)$ is the incident direction, $v = (v_x, v_y, v_z)$ is the viewing direction and $\rho_d, \rho_s, C_x, C_y, C_z, n$ are adjustable coefficients.

We take multiple photographs at diferent times and viewing directions(Figure 5), such as grazing angles, directions close to mirror angles of the solar positions and other directions, to sample the radiance distribution from the architecture.

4.2.1 Specular Lobe For The Sky And Environment Pseudo-BRDF

Since the sky and the environment are extended light sources, to recover specular lobe of the associated pseudo-BRDF, we need to divide them into small pieces and plug the vector flux from each piece into the specular model. Let the set of incident irradiance from these pieces are $\{e_1, e_2, \cdots, e_n\}$, the set of corresponding incident directions are $\{u_1, u_2, \cdots, u_n\}$, the set of viewing directions are $\{v_1, v_2, \cdots, v_m\}$ and the corresponding radiance values are $\{I_1, I_2, \cdots, I_m\}$, this problem can be considered as minimizing the following least-square objective

$$\sum_{i=1}^{m} \left(\frac{\sum_{j=1}^{n} e_j \rho(u_j, v_i) - I_i}{\sigma_i} \right)^2. \quad (14)$$

This double summation needs to be evaluated at each iteration of the optimization. The number of patches in the sky and environment might be quite large, so it is time-consuming to run the optimization. This prevents us from using optimization at each grid point in the model. On the other hand, the parameter estimation can become unreliable at places where there are not enough data available for the specular component. Therefore, we assume each block in the model has the same specular lobe except for windows which are left for further investigation.

For each block, we interactively pick some regions on the surface that are visible to multiple photographs. Thus each grid point in the regions has multiple radiance values corresponding to different viewing directions. Subtracting the estimated diffuse component from these radiance values and then running the optimization for each block with Levenberg-Marquardt method, we can get the coefficients related to the specular lobe.

4.2.2 Specular Lobe For The Sun Pseudo-BRDF

Recovering specular lobe corresponding to the spectral distribution of the sun is less time-consuming because the sun is considered as a

directional(parallel) light source, we do not need to evaluate the inner summation in (14) any more. This means it is possible to apply better but more expensive global optimization techniques. We use the downhill simplex method with simulated annealing [17], which allows us to apply some techniques [17, 7] for robust parameter estimation. Robust estimation tries to minimize

$$\sum_{i=1}^{N} \varrho \left(\frac{y_i - y(x_i; \theta)}{\sigma_i} \right) \quad (15)$$

where $\varrho(z)$ is a nonlinear function of a single variable $z \equiv [y_i - y(x_i)]/\sigma_i$, in order to estimate θ, the vector of parameters. Classic least squares corresponds to using $\varrho(z) = z^2$, and is very sensitive to outliers. By a suitable choice of $\varrho(z)$, in our experiments $\varrho(z) = \frac{1 - \exp(-|z|/2)}{1 + \exp(-|z|/2)}$, one can suppress the influence of outliers in the data. We refer the reader to [7] for extensive discussion on this topic, as well as a technique for estimating σ_i. The recovered RGB specular lobes of a block of the bell tower is given in Figure 7.

5 MODELING ILLUMINATION AT NOVEL TIMES OF DAY

To generate renderings of the scene at a novel time of day, we need to predict what the illumination will be at that time. This requires us to construct sun, sky and environment illumination models appropriate to that time. We have available as a starting point, the illumination models for a few times of day where we took the initial photographs, recovered using the techniques introduced in Section 3.

5.1 The Sun And Sky

Given the local time of day, the solar position(altitude and azimuth) can be obtained directly from formula given in the appendix of [18], provided that the latitude and longitude of the site on the earth's surface and the day number in a year are all known.

Finding the appropriate sky model requires more work. First we consider sky interpolation during the main part of the day, ignoring sunrise and sunset. Note that the sky radiance distribution changes with the solar position, and naive pointwise radiance interpolation at each point in the sky would not work as shown in Figure 8.

(a)	(b)

Figure 8: 1D Schematic of sky interpolation where peaks represent sky radiance at solar aureole. (a) A new sky(solid) obtained by pointwise interpolating two sky models(dot). It is not correct because it has two peaks. (b) A new sky(solid) obtained with our interpolating scheme.

Instead, let's examine the sky model in (9). It has three parts. The first part is the scaling factor Lz which controls the overall brightness of the sky. If not during sunrise or sunset, it should be almost a constant. The second part is the sky background. We denote it by $Bg(\xi)$. The third part is the solar aureole. We denote it by $Sa(\gamma)$. The shapes of $Bg(\xi)$ and $Sa(\gamma)$ remain unchanged during most times of a day. What changes is their relative position. $Sa(\gamma)$ rotates relative to $Bg(\xi)$ as the sun moves across the sky. Based on this observation, we derive a sky interpolation scheme. Suppose we

Figure 9: (a)-(d) Environment maps for four different times, obtained from multiple photographs, (e)-(h) corresponding environment maps generated with the recovered environment radiance models which were obtained by data-fitting. There is one recovered radiance model for each environment region.

have recovered k sky models. If we need a new sky model at a different time, a grid is first set up on the sky hemisphere. At each grid point with parameters (ξ_i, γ_i) corresponding to the new solar position, we can get three data sets $\{Lz^j, Bg^j(\xi_i), Sa^j(\gamma_i); j = 1, \cdots, k\}$ from the existing models. Set the sky radiance at the grid point to be the product of three weighted averages of the three data sets. The weight for each existing sky model is proportional to the reciprocal of the angular distance between the new solar position and the solar position of that sky model. Finally, with the radiance values at the grid points, we can run an optimization to fit a new sky model.

During sunrise or sunset, there is less light from short wavelengths. So the sun and solar aureole appear more red. The whole sky is darker. But the color of the rest of the sky only changes a little. It is well known, e.g. [9], that the color of the sky and sun is caused by scattering in the atmosphere. If a light beam travels a distance d in a medium with scattering particles, its intensity will be decreased by a factor of $\exp(-\beta d)$ where β is a constant coefficient. With different β's for different wavelengths, the color of the beam will also change. The distance d that the sunlight travels through the atmosphere is the smallest when solar direction is perpendicular to the ground and it increases when the sun moves closer to the horizon. The optical depth of the atmosphere at the horizon is about 38 times that at the zenith. A formula to compute d for any solar position can be found in [9] which tries to get the color of the sun and sky from physics-based models. However, we want to fit the above scattering model to real measurements. We measured solar radiance during the day and sunset and fit a distinct β for each color channel. We use the same coefficients to get the color of solar aureole. For the sky background, we use an average β for all three color channels to decrease the brightness but keep the color unchanged.

5.2 Environment Radiance Model

Predicting radiance models for the sun and sky is not enough, because the building also receives light reflected from other surfaces in the environment. Predicting the environment radiance map at a novel time is a challenging problem, and it may appear that the only solution would be to completely geometrically model the rest of the environment and then solve a global illumination problem to render the entire scene. However we have found an acceptable approximation for our purposes by a much simpler technique.

The idea is to recover not the detailed geometric structure of the environment, but rather a very crude, low frequency model adequate enough for our purpose – obtaining an approximation to the illumination resulting from it on the primary architectural piece of interest.

We use the technique of photometric stereo for shape-from-shading in computer vision [25] to recover the average reflectance, assumed lambertian, and surface normal for each region of the environment. One can solve for the albedo and normal orientation at each pixel location in an overdetermined system by taking multiple images of the same object with the same camera position but differ-

ent positions of the single light source. In our context, the different positions of the light source are generated by the movement of the sun during the day. Interreflections within the environment are neglected. The Lambertian model appears reasonable because most surfaces in an outdoor scene are pretty diffuse. The big change is that we do not have a single light source, but must consider both the sky and the sun as light sources. Considering the sky as an ambient light source and the sun as a directional light source, we have the following formulation

$$I_{env} = \begin{cases} \rho^{sky} E_{sky} + \rho^{sun} E_{sun}(n_{env} \cdot l_{sun}) \\ \qquad\qquad , \text{if } n_{env} \cdot l_{sun} \geq 0, \\ \rho^{sky} E_{sky} \qquad\qquad , \text{otherwise.} \end{cases} \quad (16)$$

where ρ^{sky} is the pseudo-albedo corresponding to the spectral distribution of the sky, E_{sky} is the magnitude of the total flux from the sky because we consider the sky as an ambient source, ρ^{sun} is the pseudo-albedo corresponding to the spectral distribution of the sun, E_{sun} is the irradiance from the sun, n_{env} is the normal of the considered region and l_{sun} is the solar position. The reason why we allow ρ^{sky} and ρ^{sun} to be independent because they are related to pseudo-BRDF's corresponding to the spectral distributions of the sky and the sun and we expect them to be very different.

Since we have three color channels, both ρ^{sky} and ρ^{sun} have three components, and n_{env} has two degrees of freedom because it has unit length. There are eight unknowns for each environment region. If we photograph the environment for at least three solar positions and get the corresponding sky flux values, we would have at least nine equations at each environment region and the unknowns can be estimated by weighted least-square method. Note that the trajectory of the sun seen from the surface of the earth is not a planar curve, otherwise the three solar positions would not give us independent information. The estimated pseudo-albedos and normal can then be used to predict radiance under new lighting conditions.

How can we impose the constraint that n_{env} has unit length ? We could just add a penalty term in (16) to do this. However we find, among the six variables in ρ^{sun} and n_{env}, there are only five degrees of freedom. We can just set one of them to be a constant to impose the constraint more strictly. Any component of n_{env} can be either zero or nonzero. It is more appropriate to set one component of ρ^{sun} to be a positive constant, say 0.1. Now n_{env} does not necessarily have unit length. (16) should be rewritten in the following way

$$I_{env} = \begin{cases} \rho^{sky} E_{sky} + (\rho^{sun} \|n_{env}\|) E_{sun}\left(\frac{n_{env}}{\|n_{env}\|} \cdot l_{sun}\right) \\ \qquad\qquad , \text{if } n_{env} \cdot l_{sun} \geq 0, \\ \rho^{sky} E_{sky} \qquad\qquad , \text{otherwise.} \end{cases}$$
$$(17)$$

We use the Levenberg-Marquardt method to solve this nonlinear least-squares problem. However this technique requires the objective function to have a derivative everywhere while our formulation above does not have one when $n_{env} \cdot l_{sun} = 0$. One way to get around this is to reformulate (17) as follows

$$I_{env} = \begin{cases} \rho^{sky}E_{sky} + (\rho^{sun}\|n_{env}\|)E_{sun}(\frac{n_{env}}{\|n_{env}\|} \cdot l_{sun}) \\ \qquad\qquad\qquad\qquad , \text{if } n_{env} \cdot l_{sun} \geq 0, \\ \rho^{sky}E_{sky} + (\rho^{sun}\|n_{env}\|)E_{sun}\cdot \\ \{\frac{1}{\alpha}[\exp(\frac{\alpha}{\|n_{env}\|}n_{env} \cdot l_{sun}) - 1]\} \qquad , \text{otherwise.} \end{cases}$$
(18)

where α can be any large positive constant, say 1000.

We can check that (18) has derivative everywhere and its second term keeps very close to zero when $n_{env} \cdot l_{sun} < 0$, which is a good approximation to (17). Levenberg-Marquardt method can be easily used to minimize the least-square error criterion for (18). The start point of ρ^{sky} is set to the ratio between the average radiance and the average magnitude of incident flux from the sky, and the start point of ρ^{sun} is set to the ratio between the average radiance and the average irradiance from the sun. We may obtain meaningless values for the normal if some region is never lit by the sun. To alleviate this problem, during the optimization, if the data fitting error at some region is larger than a threshold and the obtained normal is pointing away from the building, we remove the solar term in the above model and only try to get an estimation for ρ^{sky}. Adding a smoothing term between adjacent regions may also help. Some recovered environment radiance maps with the above modeling method are given in Figure 9(e)-(h). For every region of the environment, we have eight unknowns in the model and twelve equations obtained from four different times of day. Since the system is overdetermined, the good fit in Figure 9 provides justification for our simplifying assumptions that the environment is Lambertian and that interreflections within the environment can be neglected.

6 RESULTS

We chose the Berkeley bell tower(Campanile) as our target architecture and took a total of about 100 photographs for the tower, the sky and the landscape at four different times. These photographs are used as source in data-fitting. They can be considered as training data. From the various measurements and recovered models, we found the relative importance of each illumination component and reflectance component in our example. On shaded sides of the tower, the irradiance from both the sky and landscape has the same order of magnitude, but the irradiance from the landscape is larger. On sunlit sides, the sun dominates the illumination if its incident angle is not too large. The percentage varies with different color channels. If the incident angle is less than 60 degrees, the light from the sun may exceed 90% in the red channel, and 60% in the blue channel. As to reflectance models, the ratio between the maximum specular reflectance and the diffuse reflectance is about 1 : 18. So we only kept the specular reflection from the sun and ignored the rest of the light sources to speed up re-rendering.

We also took photographs at a fifth time. Those photographs are used for comparison with re-rendered images. They can be considered as testing data.

Relative positions and orientations of the cameras are currently calibrated by using the FACADE system in [4]. Alternatively, we could use any standard mosaicing technique for the environment photographs. Exterior orientation is calibrated with a compass map or the solar position.

Photometric calibration of the camera is done using the technique in [3]. Once we have recovered the nonlinear mapping between incident radiance and camera output, we can use it to further recover the radiance at each pixel. To extend the dynamic range, it is necessary to take photographs at different shutter speeds. The technique from [3] enables the combined use of these to recover a high dynamic range radiance image. All subsequent processing in the system uses radiance values. At the end, re-rendered radiance images

are converted back to normal images using the nonlinear response curve of the sensor.

6.1 Comparison With Ground Truth

Our approach makes a number of simplifying assumptions and approximations. It is therefore necessary to check the accuracy of our re-rendering by rendering the bell tower at the fifth time and comparing the synthetic images with real photographs shot at the same time. Three pairs of images from three different viewpoints are shown in Figure 10. The sky in the synthetic images are obtained by clear sky interpolation introduced in Section 5.1.

6.2 Sunrise To Sunset Simulation

A sequence of images are shown in Figure 11. It includes images at sunrise and sunset simulated with the technique in Section 5.1. Images rendered for sunrise and sunset can only be considered as approximations to real photographs because the solar spectrum changes at these periods, but we still use previously recovered pseudo-BRDF's. However, these approximations look realistic.

6.3 Intermediate And Overcast Sky Simulation

By intermediate and overcast skies, we mean there is a uniform layer of clouds covering the sky which blocks some or all of the sunlight. To simulate this kind of sky, we can either get a overcast sky model by data fitting or use CIE standard overcast sky luminance model along with a user-specified color for the clouds which is usually close to gray. A coefficient specifying the percentage of the sunlight blocked by the clouds should also be given. Then the color at a point in the sky is simply a linear interpolation between the color of a clear sky and the color of the overcast sky. Actually some sky luminance models reviewed in [13] really use this kind of interpolation between two extreme sky models.

A sequence of images are shown in Figure 12. It gives rerendering results with various sky interpolation coefficients.

The above simulation sequences may be found in the SIGGRAPH video tape.

6.4 High Resolution Re-Rendering

Since we used a fixed size grid on each triangular patch to capture the spatial variation of surface reflectance, as the viewpoint moves sufficiently close to the surface of the object, each grid cell will correspond to multiple image pixels. The resulting rendering then takes on a somewhat blurred appearance, as variation in surface texture at a resolution finer than the grid size is lost. In this section we show results from a simple technique by which the resolution can be boosted to the pixel resolution. The basic idea is to use a high resolution zoom photograph of the architecture available as a texture map in the "right" way. Since the lighting conditions can be different, we need pixel wise reflectance values. Let $I(x, y)$ be the radiance measured from the high-resolution photograph at pixel (x, y) and $\rho(x, y)$, and $E(x, y)$ be the corresponding high-resolution pseudo-albedo and irradiance at the surface point corresponding to pixel (x, y). $\tilde{I}(x, y)$, $\tilde{\rho}(x, y)$ and $\tilde{E}(x, y)$ are the corresponding low-resolution versions. Both $\rho(x, y)$ and $E(x, y)$ are unknown, but we can exploit the fact that the spatial variation in lighting $E(x, y)$ has only low frequency components, and therefore is quite well approximated by $\tilde{E}(x, y)$. We can obtain $\tilde{\rho}(x, y)$ from previously recovered pseudo-albedo at surface grid points, and $\tilde{I}(x, y)$ by smoothing $I(x, y)$; then $\tilde{E}(x, y) = \frac{\tilde{I}(x,y)}{\tilde{\rho}(x,y)}$ and the high resolution pseudo-albedo $\rho(x, y)$ can be estimated by

$$\rho(x, y) = \frac{I(x, y)}{E(x, y)} \approx \frac{I(x, y)}{\tilde{E}(x, y)}$$
(19)

Figure 10: (a)-(c) Three real photographs of a bell tower taken with shutter duration 1/1500 a second, (d)-(f) three corresponding synthetic images for the same time and shutter speed. They look similar although the real photographs in (a)-(c) are not used for training and generating the synthetic images.

Figure 11: Five synthetic images of a bell tower under a clear sky with shutter duration 1/1500 a second. They represent the appearances of the bell tower at different times(solar positions) on a sunny day close to the end of August at a location with latitude 37.8 and longitude -122.3. (a) 7am, (b) 1pm, (c) 4pm, (d) 6pm, (e) 6:30pm.

The recovered high-resolution pseudo-albedo $\rho(x, y)$ can be used for re-rendering under novel lighting conditions. In Figure 13, we give a resulting image from this kind of re-rendering. A low-resolution image from previously recovered reflectance is also given for comparison. By taking zoom-in photographs at various camera positions, we can combine this technique with view-dependent texture mapping [4].

7 CONCLUSIONS AND FUTURE WORK

In this paper, we proposed a method to extend image-based modeling and rendering techniques to deal with producing renderings under novel lighting conditions. The input to the process is a small number of photographs of the architectural scene, at a few different times of day, taken using a handheld camera. These photographs are used to recover underlying radiance and reflectance models, which are subsequently used for producing re-renderings of the scene under novel illumination conditions.

As part of this process, we introduced the pseudo-BRDF concept. We recovered two sets of pseudo-BRDF's for re-rendering under

daylight. This approach is reasonable so long as the spectral distribution of the sunlight and skylight doesn't change too significantly. Extending the approach to work under more extreme conditions is left for further investigation.

For more complex situations, such as a cluster of buildings, our approach can still work if we have the geometric models of these buildings and recover the reflectance of the buildings one by one in a sequential mode. We need some new techniques if we want to recover their reflectance simultaneously.

Acknowledgments

This research was supported by a Multidisciplinary University Research Initiative on three dimensional direct visualization from ONR and BMDO, grant FDN00014-96-1-1200, the California MICRO program and Philips Corporation. The authors wish to thank Paul E. Debevec and George Borshukov for providing the bell tower models, Charles Ying for helping make the video sequences, David Forsyth, Gregory Ward Larson, Carlo Sequin, Charles Benton and our reviewers for their valuable comments during the preparation of this paper.

| (a) | (b) | (c) | (d) |

Figure 12: Four synthetic images of a bell tower with shutter duration 1/1500 a second under an overcast sky with different percentages of blocked sunlight(PBS). (a) PBS=0.0, (b) PBS=0.5, (c) PBS=0.9, (d) PBS=0.95.

References

[1] BRUNGER, A., AND HOOPER, F. Anisotropic sky radiance model based on narrow field of view measurements of short-wave radiance. *Solar Energy 51*, 1 (1993), 53–64.

[2] DANA, K., VAN GINNEKEN, B., NAYAR, S., AND KOENDERINK, J. Reflectance and texture of real-world surfaces. In *proceedings of CVPR* (1997), pp. 151–157.

[3] DEBEVEC, P., AND MALIK, J. Recovering high dynamic range radiance maps from photographs. In *Computer Graphics Proceedings, Annual Conference Series* (1997), pp. 369–378.

[4] DEBEVEC, P., TAYLOR, C., AND MALIK, J. Modeling and rendering architecture from photographs: A hybrid geometry-and image-based approach. In *Computer Graphics Proceedings, Annual Conference Series* (1996), pp. 11–20.

[5] DEBEVEC, P., YU, Y., AND BORSHUKOV, G. Efficient view-dependent image-based rendering with projective texture-mapping. UC Berkeley technical report #UCB//CSD-98-1003.

[6] GORTLER, S., GRZESZCZUK, R., SZELISKI, R., AND COHEN, M. The lumigraph. In *Computer Graphics Proceedings, Annual Conference Series* (1996), pp. 43–54.

[7] HAMPEL, F., ROUSSEEUW, P., RONCHETTI, E., AND STAHEL, W. *Robust Statistics*. John Wiley & Sons, New York, 1986.

[8] INEICHEN, P., MOLINEAUX, B., AND PEREZ, R. Sky luminance data validation: Comparison of seven models with four data banks. *Solar Energy 52*, 4 (1994), 337–346.

[9] KLASSEN, R. Modeling the effect of the atmosphere on light. *ACM Transactions on Graphics 6*, 3 (1987), 215–237.

[10] KOENDERINK, J., AND VAN DOORN, A. Illuminance texture due to surface mesostructure. *J. Opt. Soc. Am.A 13*, 3 (1996), 452–463.

[11] LAFORTUNE, E., FOO, S., TORRANCE, K., AND GREENBERG, D. Non-linear approximation of reflectance functions. In *Computer Graphics Proceedings, Annual Conference Series* (1997), pp. 117–126.

[12] LEVOY, M., AND HANRAHAN, P. Light field rendering. In *Computer Graphics Proceedings, Annual Conference Series* (1996), pp. 31–42.

[13] LITTLEFAIR, P. A comparison of sky luminance models with measured data from garston, united kingdom. *Solar Energy 53*, 4 (1994), 315–322.

[14] MCMILLAN, L., AND BISHOP, G. Plenoptic modeling: An image-based rendering system. In *Computer Graphics Proceedings, Annual Conference Series* (1995), pp. 39–46.

[15] NISHITA, T., AND NAKAMAE, E. Continuous tone representation of three-dimensional objects illuminated by sky light. *Computer Graphics 20*, 4 (1986), 125–132.

[16] PEREZ, R., SEALS, R., AND MICHALSKY, J. All-weather model for sky luminance distribution–preliminary configuration and validation. *Solar Energy 50*, 3 (1993), 235–245.

[17] PRESS, W., FLANNERY, B., TEUKOLSKY, S., AND VETTERLING, W. *Numerical Recipes in C*. Cambridge Univ. Press, New York, 1988.

[18] REES, W. *Physical Principles of Remote Sensing*. Cambridge Univ. Press, 1990.

[19] SATO, Y., AND IKEUCHI, K. Reflectance analysis for 3d computer graphics model generation. *Graphical Models and Image Processing 58*, 5 (1996), 437–451.

[20] SATO, Y., WHEELER, M., AND IKEUCHI, K. Object shape and reflectance modeling from observation. In *Computer Graphics Proceedings, Annual Conference Series* (1997), pp. 379–388.

[21] SZELISKI, R., AND SHUM, H. Creating full view panoramic mosaics and environment maps. In *Computer Graphics Proceedings, Annual Conference Series* (1997), pp. 251–258.

[22] TADAMURA, K., NAKAMAE, E., KANEDA, K., BABA, M., YAMASHITA, H., AND NISHITA, T. Modeling of skylight and rendering of outdoor scenes. *Proceedings of EUROGRAPHICS'93, Computer Graphics Forum 12*, 3 (1993), 189–200.

[23] TAKAGI, A., TAKAOKA, H., OSHIMA, T., AND OGATA, Y. Accurate rendering technique based on colorimetric conception. *Computer Graphics 24*, 4 (1990), 1990.

[24] WARD, G. Measuring and modeling anisotropic reflection. *Computer Graphics 26*, 2 (1992), 265–272.

[25] WOODHAM, R. Photometric method for determining surface orientation from multiple images. In *Shape from Shading*, B. Horn and M. Brooks, Eds. MIT Press, 1989, pp. 513–532.

A IRRADIANCE CALCULATION

We designed an efficient algorithm for gathering light from the sky based on adaptive subdivision. Since irradiance is an integration of the incident radiance, it varies slowly over the surface of the architecture. Thus we assume the irradiance over a triangular patch is a constant. For each triangle, we only gather the light at its centroid, and the centroid can always be handled as the effective center of the sky dome hemisphere because of the dome's very large radius. Each triangle defines a plane and only the part of the sky which is on the correct side of this plane, can be seen by the triangle. Further, there might be other faces in front of the triangle occluding part of the sky. So clipping the sky is necessary. The algorithm is summarized as follows

- Give each original polygon in the architecture model an id number; for each triangle, set its centroid as the viewpoint, Z-buffer the polygons with their id numbers as their color, scan the color buffer to retrieve the polygons in front of the current triangle.

- Discretize the sky hemisphere into a small set of large rectangular spherical polygons. For each triangle, use its tangent plane and those occluding polygons to clip these spherical polygons. As a result, we get back a list of visible spherical polygons. Subdivide these spherical polygons until the sky radiance over each of them is almost uniform. The sky vector flux is the summation of the flux vectors of these subdivided sky patches. Finally, the irradiance from the sky is the inner product between the sky vector flux and the local surface normal.

The vector flux of a sky patch gives the direction and magnitude of the flux of that sky patch [10]. This algorithm is efficient because we only do visibility clipping on the initial small set of spherical polygons. This does not affect the accuracy because we do adaptive subdivision after the clipping.

The vector flux of a spherical triangle with uniform unit radiance can be obtained using a formula from [10]. We can assume the sky hemisphere has unit radius and its center is O because the irradiance from the sky is determined by its solid angle which is fixed no matter how large the radius is. Let A, B, C be three vertices on the sphere, L_{AB} be the length of the arc on the great circle passing through A and B, Π_{AB} be normalized $-(\vec{OA} \times \vec{OB})$. Then the vector flux of the spherical triangle ABC is

$$F(\triangle ABC) = \frac{L_{AB}}{2}\Pi_{AB} + \frac{L_{BC}}{2}\Pi_{BC} + \frac{L_{CA}}{2}\Pi_{CA}. \quad (20)$$

This formula can be easily generalized to compute the vector flux of any kind of spherical polygons.

Clipping a spherical polygon with a planar polygon can be done by connecting its vertices with straight line segments and treating it as a planar polygon. The only thing we need to remedy after clipping is pushing back onto the sphere every new vertex generated by clipping.

We calculate the irradiance from the environment in the same way except that we do not subdivide each environment region adaptively. We only have a constant radiance value over each region and adaptive subdivision will not help improve the accuracy here.

B   VISIBILITY PREPROCESSING

We need to decide in which photographs a particular triangular patch from the model is visible. If a triangle is partially visible in a photograph, we should clip it so that each resulting triangle is either totally visible or totally invisible. The reason to do this is to correctly and efficiently assign radiance values from the photographs to the visible triangles.

This preprocessing operates in both image space and object space. It is outlined as follows.

- Clip the triangles against all image boundaries so that any resulting triangle is either totally inside an image or totally outside the image.
- Set each camera position as the viewpoint in turn, Z-buffer the original large polygons from the geometric model using their id numbers as their colors.
- At each camera position, scan-convert each triangle so we can know which pixels are covered by it. If at some covered pixel location, the retrieved polygon id from the color buffer is different from the current polygon id, we find an occluding polygon.
- Clip each triangle with its list of occluders in the object space.

- Associate with each triangle a list of photographs to which it is totally visible.

Clipping in object-space takes very little time and the performance of this algorithm is almost determined by the scan-conversion part because we use the original large polygons in Z-buffering, which results in a very small set of occluding polygons for each triangle. So this algorithm has nearly the speed of image-space algorithms and the accuracy of object-space algorithms as long as the original polygons in the model are all larger than a pixel.

This is a modified version of the visibility algorithm presented in [5].

(a)   (b)

(c)

Figure 13: (a) A re-rendered zoom-in image with shutter duration 1/500 a second with the sun behind the bell tower using the previously recovered surface pseudo-BRDF's, (b) a reference photograph at the same viewpoint, but with a different solar position, (c) a synthetic image with the same illumination and shutter speed as in (a), but with higher resolution, rendered using the view-dependent re-rendering technique. It uses both the reference photograph and the previously recovered low-resolution surface pseudo-BRDF's.

Visibility Sorting and Compositing without Splitting
for Image Layer Decompositions

John Snyder and Jed Lengyel
Microsoft Research

Abstract

We present an efficient algorithm for visibility sorting a set of moving geometric objects into a sequence of image layers which are composited to produce the final image. Instead of splitting the geometry as in previous visibility approaches, we detect mutual occluders and resolve them using an appropriate image compositing expression or merge them into a single layer. Such an algorithm has many applications in computer graphics; we demonstrate two: rendering acceleration using image interpolation and visibility-correct depth of field using image blurring.

We propose a new, incremental method for identifying mutually occluding sets of objects and computing a visibility sort among these sets. Occlusion queries are accelerated by testing on convex bounding hulls; less conservative tests are also discussed. Kd-trees formed by combinations of directions in object or image space provide an initial cull on potential occluders, and incremental collision detection algorithms are adapted to resolve pairwise occlusions, when necessary. Mutual occluders are further analyzed to generate an image compositing expression; in the case of nonbinary occlusion cycles, an expression can always be generated without merging the objects into a single layer. Results demonstrate that the algorithm is practical for real-time animation of scenes involving hundreds of objects each comprising hundreds or thousands of polygons.

CR Categories: I.3.3 [Computer Graphics]: Picture/Image Generation - Display algorithms.

Additional Keywords: visibility sorting, compositing, nonsplitting layered decomposition, occlusion cycle, occlusion graph, sprite, kd-tree.

1 Introduction

This paper addresses the problem of how to efficiently sort dynamic geometry into image layers. Applications include:

1. image-based rendering acceleration – by using image warping techniques rather than re-rendering to approximate appearance, rendering resources can be conserved [Shade96,Schaufler96,Torborg96, Lengyel97].

2. image stream compression – segmenting a synthetic image stream into visibility-sorted layers yields greater compression by exploiting the greater coherence present in the segmented layers [Wang94,Ming97].

3. fast special effects generation – effects such as motion blur and depth-of-field can be efficiently computed via image post-processing techniques [Potmesil81,Potmesil83,Max85,Rokita93]. Visibility sorting corrects errors due to the lack of information on occluded surfaces in [Potmesil81,Potmesil83,Rokita93] (see [Cook84] for a discussion of these errors), and uses a correct visibility sort instead of the simple depth sort proposed in [Max85].

Address: 1 Microsoft Way, Redmond WA 98052.
Email: johnsny@microsoft.com, jedl@microsoft.com

4. animation playback with selective display/modification – by storing the image layers associated with each object and the image compositing expression for these layers, layers may be selectively added, removed, or modified for fast preview or interactive playback. Unchanged layers require no re-rendering.

5. incorporation of external image streams – hand-drawn character animation, recorded video, or off-line rendered images can be inserted into a 3D animation using a geometric proxy which is ordered along with the 3D synthetic elements, but drawn using the 2D image stream.

6. rendering with transparency – while standard z-buffers fail to properly render arbitrarily-ordered transparent objects, visibility sorting solves this problem provided the (possibly grouped) objects themselves can be properly rendered.

7. fast hidden-line rendering – by factoring the geometry into sorted layers, we reduce the hidden line problem [Appel67,Markosian97] into a set of much simpler problems. Rasterized hidden line renderings of occluding layers simply overwrite occluded layers beneath.

8. rendering without or with reduced z-buffer use – the software visibility sort allows elimination or reduced use of hardware z-buffers. Z-buffer resolution can also be targeted to the extent of small groups of mutually occluding objects, rather than the whole scene's.

To understand the usefulness of visibility sorting, we briefly focus on rendering acceleration. The goal is to render each coherent object at the appropriate spatial and temporal resolution and interpolate with image warps between renderings. Several approaches have been used to compose the set of object images. We use pure image sprites without z information, requiring software visibility sorting [Lengyel97]. Another approach caches images with sampled (per-pixel) z information [Molnar92,Regan94,Mark97, Schaufler97], but incurs problems with antialiasing and depth uncovering (disocclusion). A third approach is to use texture-mapped geometric impostors like single quadrilaterals [Shade96,Schaufler96] or polygonal meshes [Maciel95,Sillion97]. Such approaches use complex 3D rendering rather than simple 2D image transformations and require geometric impostors suitable for visibility determination, especially demanding for dynamic scenes. By separating visibility determination from appearance approximation, we exploit the simplest appearance representation (a 2D image without z) and warp (affine transformation), without sacrificing correct visibility results.

In our approach, the content author identifies geometry that forms the lowest level layers, called *parts*. Parts (*e.g.*, a tree, car, space vehicle, or joint in an articulated figure) contain many polygons and form a perceptual object or object component that is expected to have coherent motion. Very large continuous objects, like terrain, are *a priori* split into component objects. At runtime, for every frame, the visibility relations between parts are incrementally analyzed to generate a sorted list of layers, each containing one or more parts, and an image compositing expression ([Porter84]) on these layers that produces the final image. We assume the renderer can correctly produce hidden-surface-eliminated images for each layer when necessary, regardless of whether the layer contains one or more parts.

Once defined, our approach never splits parts at run-time as in BSP-tree or octree visibility algorithms; the parts are rendered alone or in groups. There are two reasons for this. First, real-time software visibility sorting is practical for hundreds of parts but not for the millions of polygons they

Figure 1: Sorting without splitting: This configuration can be visibility sorted for any viewpoint even though no non-splitting partitioning plane exists.

contain. Second, splitting is undesirable and often unnecessary. In dynamic situations, the number of splits and their location in image space varies as the corresponding split object or other objects in its environment move. Not only is this a major computational burden, but it also destroys coherence, thereby reducing the reuse rate in image-based rendering acceleration or the compression ratio in a layered image stream.

BSP and octree decompositions require global separating planes which induce unnecessary splitting, even though a global separating plane is not required for a valid visibility ordering (Figure 1). We use pairwise occlusion tests between convex hulls or unions of convex hulls around each part. Such visibility testing is conservative, since it fills holes in objects and counts intersections as occlusions even when the intersection occurs only in the invisible (back-facing) part of one object. This compromise permits fast sorting and, in practice, does not cause undue occlusion cycle growth. Less conservative special cases can also be developed, such as between a sphere/cylinder joint (see Appendix B). Our algorithm always finds a correct visibility sort if it exists, with respect to a pairwise occlusion test, or aggregates mutual occluders and sorts among the resulting groups. Moreover, we show that splitting is unnecessary even in the presence of occlusion cycles having no mutually occluding pairs (*i.e.*, no binary occlusion cycles).

The main contribution of this work is the identification of a new and useful problem in computer graphics, that of visibility sorting and occlusion cycle detection on dynamic, multi-polygon objects without splitting, and the description of a fast algorithm for its solution. We introduce the notion of an occlusion graph, which defines the "layerability" criterion using pairwise occlusion relations without introducing unnecessary global partitioning planes. We present a fast method for occlusion culling, and a hybrid incremental algorithm for performing occlusion testing on convex bounding polyhedra. We show how non-binary occlusion cycles can be dynamically handled without grouping the participating objects, by compiling and evaluating an appropriate image compositing expression. We also show how binary occlusion cycles can be eliminated by pre-splitting geometry. Finally, we demonstrate the practicality of these ideas in several situations and applications. Visibility sorting of collections of several hundred parts can be computed at more than 60Hz on a PC.

2 Previous Work

The problem of visibility has many guises. Recent work has considered invisibility culling [Greene93,Zhang97], analytic hidden surface removal [McKenna87,Mulmuley89,Naylor92], and global visibility [Teller93,Durand97]. The problem we solve, production of a layered decomposition that yields the hidden-surface eliminated result, is an old problem in computer graphics of particular importance before hardware z-buffers became widely available [Schumacker69,Newell72,Sutherland74, Fuchs80]. In our approach, we do not wish to eliminate occluded surfaces, but to find the correct layering order, since occluded surfaces in the current frame might be revealed in the next. Unlike the early work, we handle dynamic, multi-polygon objects without splitting; we call this variant of the visibility problem *non-splitting layered decomposition*.

Much previous work in visibility focuses on walkthroughs of static scenes, but a few do consider dynamic situations. [Sudarsky96] uses octrees for the invisibility culling problem, while [Torres90] uses dynamic BSP trees to compute a visibility ordering on all polygons in the scene. Neither technique treats the non-splitting layered decomposition problem, and the algorithms of [Torres90] remain impractical for real-time animations. Visibility algorithms can not simply segregate the dynamic and static elements of the scene and process them independently. A dynamic object can form an occlusion cycle with static objects that were formerly orderable. Our algorithms detect such situations without expending much

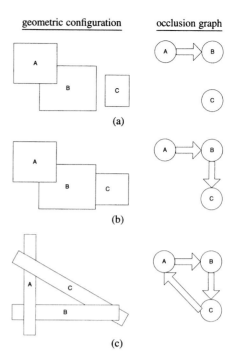

Figure 2: Occlusion graphs: The figure illustrates the occlusion graphs for some simple configurations. (a) and (b) are acyclic, while (c) contains a cycle.

computation on static components.

To accelerate occlusion testing, we use a spatial hierarchy (kd-tree) to organize parts. Such structures (octrees, bintrees, kd-trees, and BSP trees) are a staple of computer graphics algorithms [Fuchs80,Teller91,Funkhouser92, Naylor92,Greene93,Sudarsky96,Shade96]. Our approach generalizes octrees [Greene93,Sudarsky96] and 3D kd-trees [Teller91,Funkhouser92, Shade96] in that it allows a fixed but arbitrarily chosen number of directions in both object and image space. This allows maximum flexibility to tightly bound scenes with a few directions. Our hierarchy is also dynamic, allowing fast rebalancing, insertion, and deletion of objects.

Collision and occlusion detection are similar. We use convex bounding volumes to accelerate occlusion testing, as in [Baraff90,Cohen95, Ponamgi97], and track extents with vertex descent on the convex polyhedra, as in [Cohen95] (although this technique is generalized to angular, or image space, extent tracking as well as spatial). Still, occlusion detection has several peculiarities, among them that an object A can occlude B even if they are nonintersecting, or in fact, very far apart. For this reason, the sweep and prune technique of [Cohen95,Ponamgi97] is inapplicable to occlusion detection. We instead use kd-trees that allow dynamic deactivation of objects as the visibility sort proceeds. Pairwise collision of convex bodies can be applied to occlusion detection; we hybridize techniques from [Chung96a,Chung96b,Gilbert88].

The work of [Max85] deserves special mention as an early example of applying visibility sorting and image compositing to special effects generation. Our work develops the required sorting theory and algorithms.

3 Occlusion Graphs

The central notion for our visibility sorting algorithms is the pairwise occlusion relation. We use the notation $A \rightarrow_E B$ meaning object A occludes object B with respect to eye point E. Mathematically, this relation signifies that there exists a ray emanating from E such that the ray intersects A and then B.[1] It is useful notationally to make the dependence on the eye point implicit so that $A \rightarrow B$ means that A occludes B with respect to an implicit eye point. The arrow "points" to the object that is occluded.

The set of occlusion relations between pairs of the n parts comprising the entire scene forms a directed graph, called the occlusion graph. This notion of occlusion graph is very similar to the priority graph of

---

[1] A definition for $A \rightarrow_E B$ more suitable for closed objects but harder to compute is that a ray emanating from E hits a front face of A followed by a front face of B.

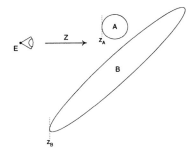

Figure 3: Depth ordering does not indicate visibility ordering: While the minimum depth of object B is smaller than A's ($z_B < z_A$), A occludes B as seen from eye point E. Similarly, by placing E on the right side of the diagram, it can be seen that maximum depth ordering also fails to correspond to visibility ordering.

[Schumacker69] but uses actual occlusion of the objects rather than the results of plane equation tests for pairwise separating planes chosen *a priori* (view independently). Figure 2 illustrates some example occlusion graphs. When the directed occlusion graph is acyclic, visibility sorting is equivalent to topological sorting of the occlusion graph, and produces a (front-to-back) ordering of the objects $\langle O_1, O_2, \ldots, O_n \rangle$ such that $i < j$ implies $O_j \not\to O_i$. Objects so ordered can thus be rendered with correct hidden surface elimination simply by using "Painter's algorithm"; *i.e.*, by rendering O_n, followed by O_{n-1}, and so on until O_1. Thus the final image, I, can be constructed by a sequence of "over" operations on the image layers of each of the objects:

$$I \equiv I_1 \text{ over } I_2 \text{ over } \ldots \text{ over } I_n \qquad (1)$$

where I_i is the *shaped image* of O_i, containing both color and coverage/transparency information [Porter84].

Cycles in the occlusion graph mean that no visibility ordering exists (see Figure 2c). In this case, parts in the cycle are grouped together and analyzed further to generate an image compositing expression (Section 5). The resulting image for the cycle can then be composited in the chain of over operators as above.

This notion of occlusion ignores the viewing direction; only the eye point matters. By taking account of visibility relationships all around the eye, the algorithm described here can respond to rapid shifts in view direction common in interactive settings and critical in VR applications [Regan94].

4 Incremental Visibility Sorting

Our algorithm for incremental visibility sorting and occlusion cycle detection (IVS) is related to the Newell, Newell, and Sancha (NNS) algorithm for visibility ordering a set of polygons [Newell72,Sutherland74]. In brief, NNS sorts a set of polygons by furthest depth and tests whether the resulting order is actually a visibility ordering. NNS traverses the depth-sorted list of polygons; if the next polygon does not overlap in depth with the remaining polygons in the list, the polygon can be removed and placed in the ordered output. Otherwise, NNS examines the collection of polygons that overlap in depth using a series of occlusion tests of increasing complexity. If the polygon is not occluded by any of these overlapping polygons, it can be sent to the output; otherwise, it is marked and reinserted behind the overlapping polygons. When NNS encounters a marked polygon, a cyclic occlusion is indicated and NNS splits the polygon to remove the cycle.

IVS differs from NNS in that it orders aggregate geometry composed of many polygons rather than individual polygons, and identifies and groups occlusion cycles rather than splitting to remove them. Most important, IVS orders incrementally, based on the visibility ordering computed previously, rather than starting from an ordering based on depth.

This fundamental change has both advantages and disadvantages. It is advantageous because depth sorting is an unreliable indicator of visibility order as shown in Figure 3. Applying the NNS algorithm to a coherently changing scene repeatedly computes the same object reorderings (with their attendant costly occlusion tests) to convert the initial depth sort to a visibility sort. The disadvantage is that the sort from the last invocation provides no restriction on the set of objects that can occlude a given object for the current invocation. The NNS depth sort, in contrast, has the useful

---

<u>IVS</u>(L,G)　　*[computes visibility sort]*

Input: ordering of non-grouped objects from previous invocation (L)
Output: front-to-back ordering with cyclic elements grouped together (G)
Algorithm:

```
G ← ∅
unmark all elements of L
while L is nonempty
    pop off top(L): A
    if A is unmarked
        if nothing else in L occludes A
            insert A onto G
            unmark everything in L
        else
            [reinsert A onto L]
            mark A
            find element in L occluding A furthest from top(L): F_A
            reinsert A into L after F_A
        endif
    else    [A is marked]
        form list S ≡ ⟨A, L_1, L_2, ..., L_n⟩ where L_1, ..., L_n
            are the largest consecutive sequence of marked elements,
            starting from top(L)
        if detect_cycle(S) then
            [insert cycle as grouped object onto L]
            group cycle-forming elements of S into grouped object C
            delete all members of C from L
            insert C (unmarked) as top(L)
        else
            [reinsert A onto L]
            find element in L occluding A furthest from top(L): F_A
            reinsert A into L after F_A
        endif
    endif
endwhile
```

Figure 4: IVS algorithm. The top object, A, in the current ordering (list L) is examined for occluders. If nothing occludes A, it is inserted in the output list G. Otherwise, A is marked and reinserted behind the furthest object in the list that occludes it, F_A. When a marked object is encountered, the sequence of consecutively marked objects starting at the top of the list is checked for an occlusion cycle using detect_cycle. If an occlusion cycle is found, the participating objects are grouped and reinserted on top of L. This loop is repeated until L is empty; G then contains the sorted list of parts with mutual occluders grouped together.

---

detect_cycle(S)　　*[finds a cycle]*

Input: list of objects $S \equiv \langle S_1, S_2, \ldots, S_n \rangle$
Output: determination of existence of a cycle and a list of
　　　　　cycle-forming objects, if a cycle is found.
Algorithm:

```
if n ≤ 1 return NO_CYCLE
i_1 ← 1
for j = 2 to n + 1
    if S_{i_k} occludes S_{i_{j-1}} for k < j − 1 then
        cycle is ⟨S_{i_k}, S_{i_{k+1}}, ..., S_{i_{j-1}}⟩
        return CYCLE
    else if no occluder of S_{i_{j-1}} exists in S then
        return NO_CYCLE
    else
        let S_k be an occluder of S_{i_{j-1}}
        i_j ← k
    endif
endfor
```

Figure 5: Cycle detection algorithm used in IVS. This algorithm will find a cycle if any initial contiguous subsequence of $1 < m \le n$ vertices $\langle S_1, S_2, \ldots, S_m \rangle$ forms a *cyclically-connected subgraph*; *i.e.*, a subgraph in which every part is occluded by at least one other member of the subgraph. For subgraphs which are not cyclically connected, the algorithm can fail to find existing cycles, but this is not necessary for the correctness of IVS (for example, consider the occlusion graph with three nodes A, B, and C where $A \to B \to A$ and initial list $\langle C, A, B \rangle$).

L	G	comment
ABC	∅	initial state
BC	A	insert A onto G
C	AB	insert B onto G
∅	ABC	insert C onto G

Figure 6: IVS Example 1: Each line shows the state of L and G after the next while loop iteration, using the graph of Figure 2(b) and initial ordering ABC.

L	G	comment
CBA	∅	initial state
BC^*A	∅	mark C and reinsert after B
C^*AB^*	∅	mark B and reinsert after A
AB^*C^*	∅	A unmarked, so reinsert C
BC	A	insert A onto G, unmark everything
C	AB	insert B onto G
∅	ABC	insert C onto G

Figure 7: IVS Example 2: Using the graph of Figure 2(b), this time with initial ordering CBA. The notation P^* is used to signify marking. The step from 3 to 4 reinserts C into L because there is an unmarked element, A, between C and the furthest element occluding it, B.

L	G	comment
ABC	∅	initial state
BCA^*	∅	mark A and reinsert
CA^*B^*	∅	mark B and reinsert
$A^*B^*C^*$	∅	mark C and reinsert
(ABC)	∅	group cycle
∅	(ABC)	insert (ABC) onto G

Figure 8: IVS Example 3: Using the graph of Figure 2(c) with initial ordering ABC. The notation $(P_1, P_2, \ldots, P_r)$ denotes grouping.

property that an object Q further in the list from a given object P, and all objects after Q, can not occlude P if Q's min depth exceeds the max depth of P. Naively, IVS requires testing potentially all n objects to see if any occlude a given one, resulting in an $O(n^2)$ algorithm. Fortunately, we will see in the next section how the occlusion culling may be sped up using simple hierarchical techniques, actually improving upon NNS occlusion culling (see Section 8).

The IVS algorithm is presented in Figures 4 and 5. Mathematically, the IVS algorithm computes an incremental topological sort on the strongly connected components of the directed occlusion graph (see [Sedgewick83] for background on directed graphs, strongly connected components, and topological sort). A strongly connected component (SCC) in the occlusion graph is a set of mutually occluding objects, in that for any object pair A and B in the SCC, either $A \rightarrow B$ or there exist objects, $X_1, X_2, ..., X_s$ also in the SCC such that

$$A \rightarrow X_1 \rightarrow X_2 \rightarrow ... \rightarrow X_s \rightarrow B.$$

The IVS algorithm finds the parts comprising each SCC, and optionally computes the occlusion subgraph of the members of each SCC to resolve nonbinary cycles without aggregating layers (Section 5).

A series of example invocations of the IVS algorithm for some of the occlusion graphs in Figure 2 are presented in Figures 6, 7, and 8. A proof of correctness is contained in [Snyder97].

The IVS algorithm takes advantage of coherence in the visibility ordering from the previous frame. When a given object A is popped off the list, it is likely that few objects further in the list will occlude it. Typically, no objects will be found to occlude A and it will be immediately inserted onto G. If we can quickly determine that no objects occlude A, and the new ordering requires no rearrangements, the algorithm verifies that the new order is identical to the old with computation $O(n \log n)$ in the total number of objects. In essence, the algorithm's incrementality allows it to examine only a small subset of the potentially $O(n^2)$ arcs in the occlusion graph.

We assume that occlusion cycles (SCCs) will be small and of limited duration in typical scenes. This assumption is important since the cycle detection algorithm has quadratic complexity in the number of cycle elements. The visibility sorting algorithm does not attempt to exploit coherence in persistent occlusion cycles.

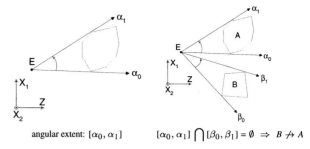

angular extent: $[\alpha_0, \alpha_1]$ $[\alpha_0, \alpha_1] \bigcap [\beta_0, \beta_1] = \emptyset \Rightarrow B \not\rightarrow A$

Figure 9: Angular extent occlusion culling: Angular extents are defined with respect to an eye point E and a orthogonal coordinate frame (X_1, X_2, Z) where X_2 (out of the page) is perpendicular to the plane in which angles are measured, Z defines the zero angle, and X_1 defines an angle of $+\pi/2$ radians. The resulting extent is simply an interval: $[\alpha_0, \alpha_1]$. To determine that $B \not\rightarrow A$ (right side of figure), we test for empty interval intersection.

As the number of re-arrangements required in the new order increases (*i.e.*, as the coherence of the ordering decreases) the IVS algorithm slows down, until a worst case scenario of starting from what is now a completely reversed ordering requires $O(n^2)$ outer while loop iterations. This is analogous to using insertion sort for repeatedly sorting a coherently changing list: typically, the sort is $O(n)$, but can be $O(n^2)$ in pathologically incoherent situations.

The algorithm's complexity is bounded by $(n + r)(s + co + c^2)$ where r is the number of reinsertions required, c is the maximum number of objects involved in an occlusion cycle, o is the maximum number of primitive occluders of a (possibly grouped) object, and s is the complexity of the search for occluders of a given object. The first factor represents the number of outer while-loop iterations of IVS. In the second factor, the three terms represent time to find potential occluders, to reduce this set to actual occluders (see Section 4.1.3), and to detect occlusion cycles. Typically, $r \sim O(n)$, $c \sim O(1)$, $o \sim O(1)$, and $s \sim O(\log n)$ resulting in an $O(n \log n)$ algorithm. In the worst case, many reinsertions are required, many objects are involved in occlusion cycles, and many objects occlude any given object so that $r \sim O(n^2)$, $c \sim O(n)$, $o \sim O(n)$, and $s \sim O(n)$ resulting in an $O(n^4)$ algorithm. This analysis assumes that occlusion detection between a pair of parts requires constant time.

When the animation is started and at major changes of scene, there is no previous visibility sort to be exploited. In this case, we use an initial sort by distance from the eye point to the centroid of each part's bounding hull. Using a sort by z is less effective because it sorts objects behind the eye in reverse order; sorting by distance is effective even if the view direction swings around rapidly.

4.1 Occlusion Culling

The fundamental query of the IVS algorithm determines which current objects occlude a given (possibly grouped) object. To quickly cull the list of candidate occluders to as small a set as possible, we bound each part with a convex polyhedron and determine the spatial extent of this convex bound with respect to a predetermined set of directions, as in [Kay86]. These directions are of two types. *Spatial extents* are projections along a given 3D vector. *Angular extents* are projected angles with respect to a given eye point and axis. Spatial extents are defined by extremizing (maximizing and minimizing) $\mathcal{S}(P) \equiv D \cdot P$ over all points P in the convex hull. Angular extents are defined similarly by extremizing[2]

$$\mathcal{A}(P) \equiv \tan^{-1} \left(\frac{(P - E) \cdot Z}{(P - E) \cdot X_1} \right) \quad (2)$$

where E is the "eye" point, Z defines the zero angle direction, and X_1 defines the positive angles.

Given two objects, A and B, with interval bounds for each of their extents, occlusion relationships can be tested with simple interval intersection tests performed independently for each extent, as shown in Figures 9 and 10. The content author chooses the number of spatial (k_s) and angular (k_a) extents and their directions; let $k \equiv k_s + k_a$ be the total number. If any of

---

[2] Care must be taken when the denominator is close to 0. This is easily accomplished in the C math library by using the function atan2.

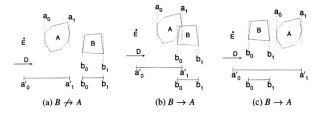

Figure 10: Spatial extent occlusion culling: Spatial extents are defined with respect to a direction D. To test whether $B \to A$, A's spatial extent $[a_0, a_1]$ is expanded by $E \cdot D$ to yield $[a'_0, a'_1]$. Three cases can occur. In (a), $[a'_0, a'_1]$ is disjoint from B's extent $[b_0, b_1]$, so $B \not\to A$. In (b), $[a'_0, a'_1]$ overlaps with $[b_0, b_1]$, so $B \to A$ is possible. In (c), $[a'_0, a'_1]$ overlaps with $[b_0, b_1]$ even though A's extent $[a_0, a_1]$ is disjoint from B. Again, $B \to A$ is possible. Note that in case (b) and (c), the occlusion cull tests must determine $B \to A$ for all k extents before concluding B is a possible occluder of A.

the k tests finds that $B \not\to A$ then the test can be concluded and B rejected as an occluder without testing more extents.

Note that the algorithm computes all intersecting pairs, which is a useful computational by-product for simulation. View frustum culling is made trivial by computing the angular extents of the visible region once at the start of each frame and determining whether each objects' angular extents intersect it.

4.1.1 Tracking Extents on Convex Hulls

Spatial extent directions can be fixed in space (*e.g.*, the coordinate axes, but note that arbitrary directions are allowed) or tied to the camera. Camera-independent spatial extents only need to be updated when the object moves; camera-dependent spatial extents must be updated when the object or the camera moves. Angular extents must also be updated whenever the object or camera moves. For the results in Section 8, in one case (Tumbling Toothpicks) we used two orthogonal angular extents (screen x and y directions) and the orthogonal camera-dependent spatial extent (Z). In another case with many unmoving objects (Canyon Flyby), we used 3 mutually orthogonal camera-independent spatial extents.

For convex bounding polyhedra, spatial and angular extents can be updated simply by "sliding downhill" (*i.e.*, gradient descent) from vertex to neighboring vertex, evaluating the objective function (S or $\mathcal{A}$) at each vertex. At each iteration, the neighboring vertex having the minimum value is accepted as the starting point for the next iteration. If no neighbors have a smaller objective function, then the computation is halted with the current vertex returned as the minimizer. Small motions of the convex hull or the spatial/angular reference frame move the new extremal vertex at most a few neighbors away from the last one. By starting with the extremal vertex from the last query, coherence in object and camera motions is thus exploited.

4.1.2 Accelerating Occlusion Queries with Kd-Trees

We have reduced the problem of finding all potential occluders of an object A to

1. forming a query extent for A, in which an k-dimensional interval is created by taking the angular extents without change and the spatial extents after enlarging by $E \cdot D$, and

2. finding all objects that overlap this query.

We hierarchically organize part extents using a kd-tree to accelerate finding the set of overlapping extents for a given query.

A kd-tree [Bentley75] is a binary tree which subdivides along k fixed dimensions. Each node T in the tree stores both the dimension subdivided ($T.i$) and the location of the partitioning point ($T.v$). Object extents whose $T.i$-th dimension interval lower bound is less than $T.v$ are placed in the left child of node T; those whose upper bound is greater than $T.v$ are placed in the right child. Objects which straddle kd-planes are simply inserted into both subtrees. Note that the planes are not used directly to determine the visibility order; the structure simply accelerates occlusion queries.

A simple minimum cost metric is used to determine a subdivision point for a list of intervals, representing the 1D extents of the set of objects with respect to one of the k_a angular or k_s spatial directions. Our cost metric sums the length of the longer of the left and right sublists and the number of

intervals shared between left and right. Avoiding lopsided trees and trees in which many objects are repeated in both subtrees is desirable since such trees tend to degrade query performance in the average case. The cost can be computed with a simple traversal of a sorted list containing both upper and lower bounds; details can be found in [Snyder97].

To build the kd-tree, we begin by sorting each of the k interval sets to produce k *1D sorted bound lists*, containing both upper and lower bounds. The kd-tree is then built recursively in a top-down fashion. To subdivide a node, the partitioning cost is computed for each of the k bound lists, and the dimension of lowest cost actually used to partition. Bound lists for the partitioned children are built in sorted order by traversing the sorted parent's list, inserting to either or both child lists according to the computed partitioning. We then recurse to the left and right sides of the kd-tree. The algorithm is terminated when the longer child list is insufficiently smaller than its parent (we use a threshold of 10). A node T in the final kd-tree stores the 1D sorted bound list only for dimension $T.i$, which is used to update the subdivision value $T.v$ in future queries, and to shift objects between left and right subtrees as they move. The other lists are deleted.

Since rebuilding is relatively expensive, the algorithm also incorporates a quick kd-tree rebalancing pass. To rebalance the kd-tree as object extents change, we visit all its nodes depth-first. At each node T, the 1D sorted bound list is re-sorted using insertion sort and the cost algorithm is invoked to find a new optimal subdivision point, $T.v$. Extents are then repartitioned with respect to the new $T.v$, shifting extents between left and right subtrees. Extent addition is done lazily (*i.e.*, only to the immediate child), with further insertion occurring when the child nodes are visited. Extent deletion is done immediately for all subtrees in which the extent appears, an operation that can be done efficiently by recording a (possibly null) left and right child pointer for each extent stored in T. Note that coherent changes to the object extents yield an essentially linear re-sort of bound lists, and few objects that must be shifted between subtrees.

It is important to realize that the coherence of kd-tree rebalancing depends on fixing the subdivision dimension $T.i$ at each node. If changes in the subdivided dimension were allowed, large numbers of extents could be shifted between left and right subtrees, eliminating coherence in all descendants. Fixing $T.i$ but not $T.v$ restores coherence, but since $T.i$ is computed only once, the tree can gradually become less efficient for query acceleration as object extents change. This problem can be dealt with by rebuilding the tree after a specified number of frames or after measures of tree effectiveness (*e.g.*, tree balance) so indicate. A new kd-tree can then be rebuilt as a background process over many frames while simultaneously rebalancing and querying an older version.

Querying the kd-tree involves simple descent guided by the query. At a given node T, if the query's $T.i$-th interval lower bound is less than $T.v$, then the left subtree is recursively visited. Similarly, if the query's $T.i$-th interval upper bound is greater than $T.v$ then the right subtree is recursively visited. When a terminal node is reached, extents stored there are tested for overlap with respect to all k dimensions. Overlapping extents are accumulated into an occluder list. An extent is inserted only once in the occluder list, though it may occur in multiple leaf nodes.

An additional concern is that the occlusion query should return occluders of an object A *that have not already been inserted into the output list*. Restricting the set of occluders to the set remaining in L can be accomplished by activating/deactivating extents in the kd-tree. When A is popped off the list L in the IVS algorithm, all objects grouped within it are deactivated. Deactivated objects are handled by attaching a flag to each object in the list stored at each terminal node of the kd-tree. Deactivating an object involves following its left and right subtree pointers, beginning at the kd root, to arrive at terminal lists containing the object to be deactivated. Activation is done similarly, with the flag set oppositely. Counts of active objects within each kd-tree node are kept so that nodes in which all objects have been deactivated can be ignored during queries.

4.1.3 Avoiding Occlusion Cycle Growth

The occlusion testing described so far is conservative, in the sense that possible occluders of an object can be returned which do not in fact occlude it. There are two sources of this conservativeness. First, occlusion is tested with respect to a fixed set of spatial and/or angular extents, which essentially creates an object larger than the original convex hull and thus more likely to be occluded. Second, extents for grouped objects are computed by simple

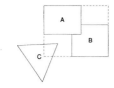

Figure 11: Occlusion cycle growth with grouped objects: In this example, A and B have been grouped because they are mutually occluding. A simple bound around their union, shown by the dashed lines, is occluded by object C, even though the objects themselves are not. We therefore use the bounded extents around grouped objects for a quick cull of nonoccluders, but further test objects which are not so culled to make sure they occlude at least one primitive element of the grouped object.

unioning of the extents of the members, even though the unioned bound may contain much empty space, as shown in Figure 11. The next section will show how to compute an exact occlusion test between a pair of convex objects, thus handling the first problem. This section describes a more stringent test for grouped objects which removes the second problem.

Occlusion testing that is too conservative can lead very large groupings of objects in occlusion cycles. In the extreme case every object is inserted into a single SCC. This is especially problematic because of the second source of conservatism – that bounds essentially grow to encompass all members of the current SCC, which in turn occlude further objects, and so on, until the SCC becomes very large.

To handle this problem, we perform additional tests when a grouped object A is tested for occlusion. A's unioned extents are used to return a candidate list of possible occluders, as usual. Then the list of occluders is scanned to make sure each occludes at least one of the primitive members of A, using a simple k-dimensional interval intersection test. Any elements of the list that do not occlude at least one member of A are rejected, thus ensuring that "holes" within the grouped object can be seen through without causing occlusions. Finally, remaining objects can be tested against primitive members of A using the exact occlusion test.

4.2 Occlusion Testing

The algorithms in Section 4.1 provide a fast but conservative pruning of the set of objects that can possibly occlude a given object A. To produce the set of objects that actually occlude A with respect to the convex hull bounds, we apply an exact test of occlusion for primitive object pairs (A, B), which determines whether $B \rightarrow A$. The test is used in the IVS algorithm by scanning the list of primitive elements of the possibly grouped object A and ensuring that at least one occluder in the returned list occludes it, with respect to the exact test. The exact test is thus used as a last resort when the faster methods fail to reject occluders.

The exact occlusion test algorithm is as follows:

ExactConvexOcclusion(A,B,E)   *[returns whether $B \rightarrow_E A$]*

  if all (non eye-expanded) spatial extents of A and B intersect
     initiate 3D collision tracking for $\langle A, B \rangle$, if not already
     if A and B collide, return $B \rightarrow A$
        if E on same side of separating plane as A, return $B \not\rightarrow A$
  endif

  if B contains eye point E, return $B \rightarrow A$ *[B occludes everything]*
  initiate occlusion tracking for $\langle B, A \rangle$, if not already
  return result of occlusion test

Both the collision and occlusion query used in the above algorithm can be computed using the algorithm in Appendix A. While the collision query is not strictly necessary, it is more efficient in the case of a pair of colliding objects to track the colliding pair once rather than tracking two queries which bundle the eye point with each of the respective objects. For scenes in which collisions are rare, the direct occlusion test should be used.

The IVS algorithm is extended to make use of a hash table of object pairs for which 3D collision or occlusion tracking have been initialized, allowing fast access to the information. Tracking is discontinued for a pair if the information is not accessed after more than one frame.

Note that further occlusion resolution is also possible with respect to the actual objects rather than convex bounds around them. It is also possible to inject special knowledge in the occlusion resolution process, such as the fact that a given separating plane is known to exist between certain pairs of objects, like joints in an articulated character or adjacent cells in a

pre-partitioned terrain. Special purpose pairwise visibility codes can also be developed; Appendix B provides an example for a cylinder with endcap tangent to a sphere that provides a visibility heuristic for articulated joints in animal-like creatures.

4.3 Conditioning Sort

After each IVS invocation, we have found it useful to perform a conditioning sort on the output that "bubbles up" SCCs based on their midpoint with respect to a given extent. More precisely, we reorder according to the absolute value of the difference of the midpoint and the projection of the eye point along the spatial extents. The camera-dependent Z direction is typically used as the ordering extent, but other choices also provide benefit. An SCC is only moved up in the order if doing so does not violate the visibility ordering; *i.e.*, the object does not occlude the object before which it is inserted. This conditioning sort smooths out computation over many queries. Without it, unoccluding objects near the eye can remain well back in the ordering until they finally occlude something, when they must be moved in front of many objects in the order, reducing coherence. The conditioning sort also sorts parts within SCCs according to extent midpoint, but ignoring occlusion relationships (since the SCC is not visibility sortable).

5 Resolving Non-Binary Cycles

Following [Porter84], we represent a shaped image as a 2D array of 4-tuples, written

$$A \equiv [A_r, A_g, A_b, A_\alpha]$$

where A_r, A_g, A_b are the color components of the image and A_α is the transparency, in the range [0, 1].

Consider the cyclic occlusion graph and geometric situation shown in Figure 2c. Clearly,

$$A \text{ over } B \text{ over } C$$

produces an incorrect image because $C \rightarrow A$ but no part of C comes before A in the ordering. A simple modification though produces the correct answer:

$$A \text{ out } C + B \text{ out } A + C \text{ out } B.$$

where "out" is defined as

$$A \text{ out } B \equiv A(1 - B_\alpha).$$

This expression follows from the idea that objects should be attenuated by the images of all occluding objects. Another correct expression is

$$(C \text{ atop } A) \text{ over } B \text{ over } C$$

where "atop" is defined as

$$A \text{ atop } B \equiv A B_\alpha + (1 - A_\alpha) B.$$

In either case, the expression correctly overlays the relevant parts of occluding objects over the occluded objects, using only shaped images for the individual objects (refer to Figure 12). Technically, the result is not correct at any pixels partially covered by all three objects, since the matte channel encodes coverage as well as transparency. Such pixels tend to be isolated, if they exist, and the resulting errors of little significance.[3]

The above example can be generalized to any collection of objects with a known occlusion graph having no *binary cycles*: cycles of the form $A \rightarrow B, B \rightarrow A$. The reason binary cycles can not be handled is that in the region of intersection of the bounding hulls of A and B, we simply have no information about which object occludes which. Note also that the compositing expression in this case reduces to $A \text{ out } B + B \text{ out } A$ which incorrectly eliminates the part of the image where $A \bigcap B$ projects.

A correct compositing expression for n shaped images I_i is given by

$$\sum_{i=1}^{n} I_i \operatorname*{OUT}_{\{j \,|\, O_j \rightarrow O_i\}} I_j \qquad (3)$$

The notation OUT with a set subscript is analogous to the multiplication accumulator operator Π, creating a chain of "out" operations, as in

$$D \operatorname*{OUT}_{\{A,B,C\}} = D \text{ out } A \text{ out } B \text{ out } C.$$

---

[3] Recall too that overlaying shaped images where the matte channel encodes coverage is itself an approximation since it assumes uncorrelated silhouette edges.

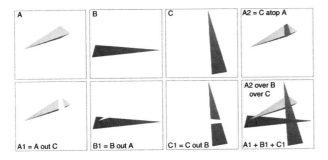

Figure 12: Compositing expressions for cycle breaking: The original sprite images are shown as A, B, C. Using "over-atop", the final image is formed by (C atop A) over B over C. Using "sum-of-outs", the final image is formed by (A out C) + (B out A) + (C out B).

In words, (3) sums the image for each object O_i, attenuated by the "out" chain of products for each object O_j that occludes O_i (Figure 12, bottom row).

An alternate recursive formulation using atop is harder to compile but generates simpler expressions. As before, we have a set of objects $O = \{O_i\}$ together with an occlusion graph G for O containing no binary cycles. The subgraph of G induced by an object subset $X \subset O$ is written G_X. Then for any $O_* \in O$

$$I(G_O) = \left(I(G_{\{O_i | O_i \to O_*\}}) \text{ atop } I(O_*)\right) \text{ over } I(G_{O-\{O_*\}}) \quad (4)$$

where $I(G)$ represents the shaped image of the collection of objects using the occlusion graph G. In other words, to render the scene, we can pick any isolated object O_*, find the expression for the subgraph induced by those objects occluding O_*, and compute that expression "atop" O_* (Figure 12, top right). That result is then placed "over" the expression for the subgraph induced by removing O_* from the set of objects O. Note also that the above expression assumes $I(G_\emptyset) = 0$.

Proofs of correctness of the two expressions is available in a technical report [Snyder98].

Compositing Expression Compilation

An efficient approach to generating an image compositing expression for the scene uses the IVS algorithm to produce a visibility sorted list of SCCs. Thus the images for each SCC can be combined using a simple sequence of "over" operations as in Expression (1). Most SCCs are *singletons* (containing a single object). Non-singleton SCCs are further processed to merge binary cycles, using the occlusion subgraph of the parts comprising the SCC. Merging must take place iteratively in case binary cycles are present between objects that were merged in a previous step, until there are no binary cycles between merged objects. We call such merged groups BMCs, for *binary merged components*. Expression (3) or (4) is then evaluated using the resulting merged occlusion graph to produce an expression for the SCC. Each BMC must be grouped into a single layer, but not the entire SCC. For example, Figure 2(c) involves one SCC but three BMCs, since there are no binary cycles.

It is clear that Expression (3) can be evaluated using two image registers: one for accumulating a series of "out" operations for all image occluders of a given object, and another for summing the results. Expression (4) can be similarly compiled into an expression using two image resisters: one for "in" or "out" operations and one for sum accumulation [Snyder98]. Two image registers thus suffice to produce the image result for any SCC. An efficient evaluation for the scene's image requires a third register to accumulate the results of the "over" operator on the sorted sequence of SCCs. This third register allows segregation of the SCCs into separately compilable units.

Given such a three-register implementation, it can be seen why Expression (4) is more efficient. For example, for a simple ring cycle of n objects; *i.e.*, a graph

$$O_1 \to O_2 \to \cdots \to O_n \to O_1$$

the "sum-of-outs" formulation (Expression 3) produces

$$I(O_1)\text{out}I(O_n) + I(O_2)\text{out}I(O_1) + I(O_3)\text{out}I(O_2) + \cdots + I(O_n)\text{out}I(O_{n-1})$$

with n "out" and $n - 1$ addition operations, while the "over-atop" formulation (Expression 4) produces

$$\left(I(O_n) \text{ in } I(O_1) + I(O_1) \text{ out } I(O_n)\right) \text{ over } I(O_2) \text{ over } \cdots \text{ over } I(O_n)$$

with $n - 1$ "over", 1 "in", 1 "out", and 1 addition operators. Assuming "over" is an indispensable operator for hardware implementations and is thus atomic, the second formulation takes advantage of "over" to reduce the expression complexity.

6 Pre-Splitting to Remove Binary Cycles

The use of convex bounding hulls in occlusion testing is sometimes overly conservative. For example, consider a pencil in a cup or an aircraft flying within a narrow valley. If the cup or valley form a single part, our visibility sorting algorithm will always group the pencil and cup, and the aircraft and valley, in a single layer (BMC) because their convex hulls intersect. In fact, in the case of the valley it is likely that nearly all of the scene's geometry will be contained inside the convex hull of the valley, yielding a single layer for the entire scene.

To solve this problem, we pre-split objects that are likely to cause unwanted aggregation of parts. Objects that are very large, like terrain, are obvious candidates. Foreground objects that require large rendering resources and are known to be "containers", like the cup, may also be pre-split. Pre-splitting means replacing an object with a set of parts, called *split parts*, whose convex hull is less likely to intersect other moving parts. With enough splitting, the layer aggregation problem can be sufficiently reduced or eliminated.

Simple methods for splitting usually suffice. Terrain height fields can be split using a 2D grid of splitting planes, while rotationally symmetric containers, like a cup, can be split using a cylindrical grid. A 3D grid of splitting planes can be used for objects without obvious projection planes or symmetry (*e.g.*, trees). On the other hand, less naive methods that split more in less convex regions can reduce the number of split parts, improving performance. Such methods remain to be investigated in future work.

Pre-splitting produces a problem however. At the seam between split neighbors the compositor produces a pixel-wide gap, because its assumption of uncorrelated edges is incorrect. The split geometry exactly tessellates any split surfaces; thus alpha (coverage) values should be added at the seam, not over'ed. The result is that seams become visible.

To solve this problem, we extend the region which is included in each split object to produce overlapping split parts, a technique also used in [Shade96]. While this eliminates the visible seam artifact, it causes split parts to intersect, and the layer aggregation problem recurs. Fortunately, adjacent split parts contain the same geometry in their region of overlap. We therefore add pairwise separating planes between neighbors, because both agree on the appearance within the region of overlap so either may be drawn. This breaks the mutual occlusion relationship between neighbors and avoids catastrophic layer growth. But we use the convex hulls around the "inflated" split parts for testing with all other objects, so that the correct occlusion relationship is still computed.

Note that the occlusion sort does not preclude splitting arrangements like hexagonal terrain cells that permit no global partitioning planes. All that is required is pairwise separation.

7 Visibility Correct Depth of Field

2D image blurring is a fast method for simulating depth of field effects amenable to hardware implementation [Rokita93]. Unfortunately, as observed in [Cook84], any approximation that uses a single hidden-surface-eliminated image, including [Potmesil81,Rokita93], causes artifacts because no information is available for occluded surfaces made visible by depth of field. The worst case is when a blurry foreground object occludes a background object in focus (Figure 13). As shown in the figure, the approximation of [Potmesil81] sharpens the edge between the foreground and background objects, greatly reducing the illusion. Following [Max85], but using correct visibility sorting, we take advantage of the information in layer images that would ordinarily be eliminated to correct these problems.

The individual image layers are still approximated by spatially invariant blurring in the case of objects having small depth extent, or by the spatially varying convolution from [Potmesil81]. Image compositing is used between layers. Since a substantial portion of depth of field cues come from

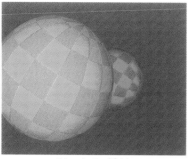
(a) no depth of field

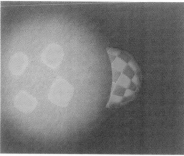
(b) single layer depth of field approx.

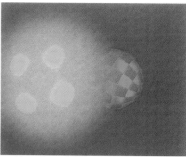
(c) two layer visibility compositing approx.

Figure 13: Simulating depth of field with image blurring.

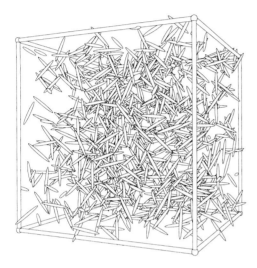

Figure 14: Toothpick example (nobjs=800, uniform scale): This image shows a frame from the first experiment, drawn with hidden line elimination by using Painter's algorithm with the computed visibility order. For the hidden line processing, singleton SCCs are simply drawn by finding the part's silhouette, filling its interior in white and then its boundary as a black polyline. Nonsingleton SCCs are further processed to find visible intersection and silhouette edges dynamically, but only the few objects comprising the SCC need be considered, not the entire scene.

edge relations between foreground and background objects, we consider this a good approximation, although blurring without correctly integrating over the lens only approximates the appearance of individual parts.

Grouping parts in a BMC because of occlusion undecomposability exacts a penalty. Such grouping increases the depth extent of the members of the group so that the constant blur approximation or even the more expensive depth-based convolution incur substantial error. For groupings of large extent, the renderer could resort to rendering integration using the accumulation buffer [Haeberli90]. Such integration requires many rendering passes (23 were used in images from [Haeberli90]), representing a large allocation of system resources to be avoided when simple blurring suffices.

8 Results

All timings are reported for *one processor* of a Gateway E5000-2300MMX PC with dual Pentium II 300MHz processors and 128MB of memory. Measured computation includes visibility sorting and kd-tree building and rebalancing. The kd-tree was built only once at the start of each animation; the amortized cost to build it is included in the "average" cpu times reported.

Tumbling Toothpicks

The first results involve a simulation of tumbling "toothpicks", eccentric ellipsoids, moving in a cubical volume (Figure 14). The toothpicks bounce off the cube sides, but are allowed to pass through each other. Each toothpick contains 328 polygons and forms one part. There are 250 frames in the animation.

In the first series of experiments, we measured cpu time per frame, as a function of number of toothpicks (Figure 15). Time per frame averaged over the entire animation and maximum time for any frame are both reported. One experiment, labeled "us" for *uniform scale* in the figure, adds more toothpicks of the same size to the volume. This biases the occlusion complexity superlinearly with number of objects, since there are many more collisions and the size of the average occlusion cycle increases. With enough toothpicks, the volume becomes filled with a solid mass of moving geometry, forming a single SCC. As previously discussed, the algorithm is designed for situations in which occlusion cycles are relatively small.

A more suitable measure of the algorithm's complexity preserves the average complexity per unit volume and simply increases the visible volume. This effect can be achieved by scaling the toothpicks by the cube root of their number ratio, so as to preserve average distance between toothpicks as a fraction of their length. The second experiment, labeled "ud" for *uniform density* presents these results. The results demonstrate the expected $O(n \log n)$ rate of growth. The two experiments are normalized so that the simulations are identical within timing noise for nobjs=200: the uniform density experiment applies the scale $(200/\text{nobjs})^{\frac{1}{3}}$ to the toothpicks of the other trials. In particular, note that a simulation with 200 toothpicks (220 total objects including cube parts), can be computed at over 100Hz, making it practical for real-time applications. To verify the above scaling assumptions, the following table summarizes some visibility statistics (averaged over all frames of the animation) for the baseline scene with 200 toothpicks and the two scenes with 1600 toothpicks (uniform density, uniform scale):

measurement	nobjs=200	nobjs=1600 (uniform density)	nobjs=1600 (uniform scale)
fraction of SCCs that are nonsingleton	.0454	.04633	.2542
fraction of parts in non-singleton SCCs	.0907	0.0929	.5642
average size of nonsingleton SCCs	2.097	2.107	3.798
max size of SCCs	2.64	3.672	45.588

With the exception of the "max size of nonsingleton SCC" which we would expect to increase given that the 1600 object simulation produces greater probability that bigger SCCs will develop, the first two columns in the table are comparable, indicating a reasonable scaling, while the third indicates much greater complexity. Note also that the large maximum cpu time for the 1400 and 1600 uniform scale trials is due to the brief existence of much larger than average sized occlusion cycles.

The second experiment measures cpu time with varying coherence. We globally scale the rate of camera movement and the linear and angular velocities of the toothpicks (Figure 16). The number of toothpicks was fixed at 200; the trial with velocity scale of 1 is thus identical to the trial with nobjs=200 in Figure 15. The algorithm is clearly sensitive to changing coherence, but exhibits only slow growth as the velocities become very large. Not surprisingly, the difference between average and worst case query times increases as coherence decreases, but the percentage difference remains fairly constant, between 17% and 30%.

To calibrate the results of the second experiment, let S be the length of the image window and W the length of the cube side containing the

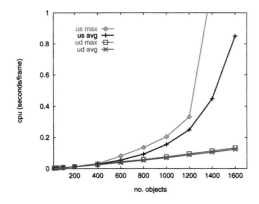

no. objs	25	50	100	200	400	800	1600
avg. cpu (ms) [ud]	1.51	2.51	4.81	9.97	23.1	51.7	122
max cpu (ms) [ud]	2.40	3.55	6.28	11.8	26.3	56.9	131
avg. cpu (ms) [us]	1.32	2.17	4.21	10.1	27.0	92.5	849
max cpu (ms) [us]	2.28	3.11	5.57	11.9	30.5	134	3090

Figure 15: Performance with increasing number of objects.

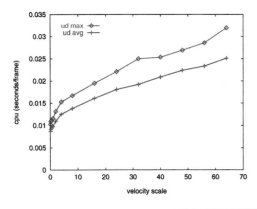

vel. scl.	.25	.5	1	2	4	8	16	32	64
avg cpu (ms)	9.15	9.52	9.78	11.0	12.6	13.8	16.1	19.3	25.2
max cpu (ms)	10.9	11.2	11.6	13.2	15.3	16.7	19.5	25.0	32.0

Figure 16: Performance with increasing velocity (decreasing coherence).

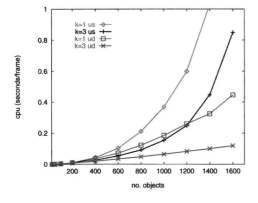

no. objs	50	100	200	400	800	1600
$k = 3$ cpu (ms) [ud]	2.51	4.81	9.97	23.1	51.7	122
$k = 1$ cpu (ms) [ud]	2.65	5.48	12.7	38.0	124	447
% diff. [ud]	5.55%	14.0%	27.7%	64.6%	140%	267%
$k = 3$ cpu (ms) [us]	2.17	4.21	10.1	27.0	92.5	849
$k = 1$ cpu (ms) [us]	2.28	4.79	12.9	47.2	215	1780
% diff. [us]	5.05%	13.6%	28.7%	74.4%	132%	109%

Figure 17: Comparison of kd-tree culling with different numbers of extents. Cpu times are for the average case.

toothpicks. For the unit scale trial the velocity measured at one toothpick end and averaged over all frames and toothpicks was 0.117% S per frame (image space) and 0.269% W per frame (world space). This amounts to an average of 14.2 and 6.2 seconds to traverse the image or cube side respectively at a 60Hz frame rate.[4]

In a third experiment (Figure 17), we compared performance of the algorithm using kd-trees that sort by different numbers of extents. The same simulations were run as in the first experiment, either exactly as before ($k = 3$, using two angular extents and the perpendicular camera-dependent spatial extent Z), or using kd-tree partitioning only in a single dimension ($k = 1$, using only Z). In the second case, the two angular extents were still used for occlusion culling, but not for kd-tree partitioning. This roughly simulates the operation of the NNS algorithm, which first examines objects that overlap in depth before applying further culls using screen bounding boxes. It can be seen that simultaneously searching all dimensions is much preferable, especially as the number of objects increases. For example, in the uniform density case, using a single direction rather than three degrades performance by 14% for 100 objects, 28% for 200, 65% for 400, up to 267% for 1600. The differences in the uniform scale case are still significant but less dramatic, since occlusion culling forms a less important role than layer reordering and occlusion cycle detection.

We used the visibility sorting results to create a depth of field blurred result using compositing operations as described in Section 7, and compared it to a version created with 21 accumulation buffer passes. The results are shown in Figure 18. For the visibility compositing result, a constant blur factor was determined from the circle of confusion at the centroid of the object or object group, for all objects except the cube sides. Because of the large depth extent of the cube sides, these few parts were generated using the accumulation buffer technique on the individual layer parts and composited into the result with the rest.

Canyon Flyby

The second results involve a set of aircraft flying in formation inside a winding valley (Figure 19). We pre-split the valley terrain (see Section 6) into split parts using 2D grids of separating planes and an inflation factor of 20%. The animation involves six aircraft each divided into six parts (body, wing, rudder, engine, hinge, and tail); polygon counts are given in the table below:

object	polygons	hull polygons
body	1558	192
engine	1255	230
wing	1421	80
tail	22	22
rudder	48	28
hinge	64	46
sky (sphere)	480	-
terrain (unsplit)	2473	-

Using terrain splitting grids of various resolutions, we investigated rendering acceleration using image-based interpolation of part images. The following table shows average polygon counts per split part for terrain splits using 2D grids of 20×20, 14×14, 10×10, 7×7, and 5×5:

grid	split objects	polygons/object	hull polygons/object
20 × 20	390	31.98	29.01
14 × 14	191	48.91	37.78
10 × 10	100	76.48	42.42
7 × 7	49	130.45	57.51
5 × 5	25	225.32	72.72

Note that the "polygons" and "polygons/object" column in the above tables are a measure of the average rendering cost of each part, while the "hull polygons" and "hull polygons/object" column is an indirect measure of computational cost for the visibility sorting algorithm, since it deals with hulls rather than actual geometry.

Following results from [Lengyel97], we assumed the 6 parts of each aircraft required a 20% update rate (*i.e.*, could be rendered every fifth frame and interpolated the rest), the terrain a 70% update rate, and the sky a 40% update rate. These choices produce a result in which the interpolation artifacts are almost imperceptible. To account for the loss

---

[4]While this baseline may seem somewhat slow-moving, it should be noted that small movements of the parts in this simulation can cause large changes in their occlusion graph with attendant computational cost. We believe this situation to be more difficult than typical computer graphics animations. Stated another way, most computer graphics animations will produce similar occlusion topology changes only at much higher velocities.

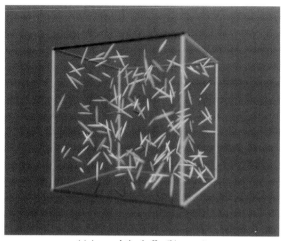

(a) Accumulation buffer (21 passes)

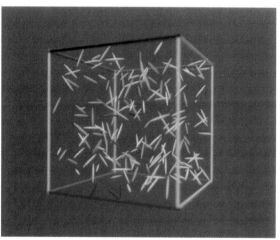

(b) Visibility compositing

Figure 18: Comparison of depth of field generation methods: The images show two different depth of field renderings from the tumbling toothpicks experiment. Toothpicks comprising a multi-object layer share a common color; singleton layers are drawn in white. Note the occlusion relationships between the sphere/cylinder joints at the cube sides, computed using the algorithm in Appendix B. While pairs of spheres and cylinders are sometimes mutually occluding, the algorithm is able to prevent any further occlusion cycle growth.

Figure 19: Scene from canyon flyby: computed using image compositing of sorted layers with 14 × 14 terrain split. The highlighted terrain portion is one involved in a detected occlusion cycle with the ship above it, with respect to the bounding convex hulls.

of coherence which occurs when parts are aggregated into a single layer, we conservatively assumed that all parts so aggregated must be rendered every frame (100% update rate), which we call the *aggregation penalty*. The results are summarized in Figure 20.

The column "cpu" shows average and maximum cpu time per frame in milliseconds. The next column ("terrain expansion factor") is the factor increase in number of polygons due to splitting and overlap; this is equal to the total number of polygons in the split terrain divided by the original number, 2473. The next columns show the fraction of visible layers that include more than one part ("aggregate layers fraction"), followed by the fraction of visible parts that are aggregated ("aggregated parts fraction"). Visible in this context means not outside the viewable volume. Average re-rendering (update) rates under various weightings and assumptions follow: unit weighting per part with and without the aggregation penalty ("update rate, unit weighting, (agg)" and ". . . (no agg)"), followed by the analogs for polygon number weighting. Smaller rates are better in that they indicate greater reuse of image layers through interpolation and less actual rendering. The factors without aggregation are included to show how much the rendering rate is affected by the presence of undecomposable multi-object layers. The polygon-weighted rates account for the fact that the terrain has been decomposed into an increased number of polygons. This is done by scaling the rates of all terrain objects by the terrain expansion factor.

In summary, the best polygon-weighted reuse rate in this experiment, 38%, is achieved by the 14 × 14 split. Finer splitting incurs a penalty for increasing the number of polygons in the terrain, without enough payoff in terms of reducing aggregation. Coarser splitting decreases the splitting penalty but also increases the number of layer aggregations, in turn reducing the reuse rate via the aggregation penalty. Note the dramatic increase from 7 × 7 to 5 × 5 in poly-weighted update rate with aggregation penalty (second rightmost column) – splits below this level fill up concavities in the valley too much, greatly increasing the portion of aggregated objects.

It should be noted that the reuse numbers in this experiment become higher if the fraction of polygons in objects with more coherence (in this case, the aircraft) are increased or more such objects are added. Allowing independent update of the terrain's layers would also improve reuse, although as pointed out in [Lengyel97] this results in artificial apparent motion between terrain parts.

9 Conclusion

Many applications exist for an algorithm that performs visibility sorting without splitting, including rendering acceleration, fast special effects generation, animation design, and incorporation of external image streams into a synthetic animation. These techniques all derive from the observation that 2D image processing is cheaper than 3D rendering and often suffices. By avoiding unnecessary splitting, these techniques better exploit the temporal coherence present in most animations, and allow sorting at the level of objects rather than polygons. We have shown that the non-splitting visibility sorting required in these applications can be computed in real-time on PCs, for scenes of high geometric and occlusion complexity, and demonstrated a few of the many applications.

Much future work remains. Using more adaptive ways of splitting container objects is a straightforward extension. Incorporation of space-time volumes would allow visibility-correct motion blur using 2D image processing techniques. Further work is needed to incorporate visibility sorting in animation design systems allowing preview of modifications in their complete context without re-rendering unmodified elements. Opportunities also exist to invent faster and less conservative occlusion tests for special geometric cases. Finally, further development is needed for fast hardware which exploits software visibility sorting and performs 3D rendering and 2D real-time image operations, such as compositing with multiple image registers, blurring, warping, and interpolation.

Acknowledgments

We thank the Siggraph reviewers for their careful reading and many helpful suggestions. Jim Blinn suggested the "sum of outs" resolution for nonbinary cycles. Brian Guenter provided a most helpful critical reading. Susan Temple has been an early adopter of a system based on these ideas and has contributed many helpful suggestions. Jim Kajiya and Conal Elliot were involved in many discussions during the formative phase of this work.

split	cpu (ms)		terrain expan. fac.	layers agg. fraction	parts agg. fraction	update rate			
	avg	max				unit weighting		poly weighting	
						(agg)	(no agg)	(agg)	(no agg)
20×20	17.33	29.82	5.04	0.1%	0.2%	58.3%	58.1%	41.8%	40.7%
14×14	8.08	14.59	3.78	0.4%	1.0%	51.3%	50.2%	38.0%	36.0%
10×10	5.17	9.88	3.09	1.9%	6.4%	48.7%	40.9%	40.4%	30.7%
7×7	4.51	9.68	2.58	5.2%	22.5%	51.9%	37.8%	42.4%	27.8%
5×5	5.37	11.01	2.28	13.0%	53.1%	71.5%	32.3%	72.0%	26.1%

Figure 20: Canyon flyby results.

References

[Appel67] Appel A., "The Notion of Quantitative Invisibility and the Machine Rendering of Solids," In *Proceedings of the ACM National Conference*, pp. 387-393, 1967.

[Baraff90] Baraff, David, "Curved Surfaces and Coherence for Non-Penetrating Rigid Body Simulation," *Siggraph '90*, August 1990, pp. 19-28.

[Bentley75] Bentley, J.L., "Multidimensional Binary Search Trees Used for Associative Searching," *Communications of the ACM*, 18(1975), pp. 509-517.

[Chen96] Chen, Han-Ming, and Wen-Teng Wang, "The Feudal Priority Algorithm on Hidden-Surface Removal," *Siggraph '96*, August 1996, pp. 55-64.

[Chung96a] Chung, Kelvin, and Wenping Wang, "Quick Collision Detection of Polytopes in Virtual Environments," *ACM Symposium on Virtual Reality Software and Technology 1996*, July 1996, pp. 1-4.

[Chung96b] Chung, Tat Leung (Kelvin), "An Efficient Collision Detection Algorithm for Polytopes in Virtual Environments," M. Phil Thesis at the University of Hong Kong, 1996 [www.cs.hku.hk/ tlchung/collision_library.html].

[Cohen95] Cohen, D.J., M.C. Lin, D. Manocha, and M. Ponamgi, "I-Collide: An Interactive and Exact Collision Detection System for Large-Scale Environments," *Proceedings of the Symposium on Interactive 3D Graphics,*, 1995, pp. 189-196.

[Cook84] Cook, Robert, "Distributed Ray Tracing," *Siggraph '84*, July 1984, pp. 137-145.

[Durand97] Durand, Fredo, George Drettakis, and Claude Puech, "The Visibility Skeleton: A Powerful and Efficient Multi-Purpose Global Visibility Tool," *Siggraph '97*, August 1997, pp. 89-100.

[Fuchs80] Fuchs, H., Z.M. Kedem, and B.F. Naylor, "On Visible Surface Generation by A Priori Tree Structures," *Siggraph '80*, July 1980, pp. 124-133.

[Funkhouser92] Funkhouser, T.A., C.H. Sequin, and S.J. Teller, "Management of Large Amounts of Data in Interactive Building Walkthroughs," *Proceedings of 1992 Symposium on Interactive 3D Graphics,* July 1991, pp. 11-20.

[Gilbert88] Gilbert, Elmer G., Daniel W. Johnson, and S. Sathiya A. Keerthi, "A Fast Procedure for Computing the Distance Between Complex Objects in Three-Dimensional Space," IEEE Journal of Robotics and Automation, 4(2), April 1988, pp. 193-203.

[Greene93] Greene, N., M. Kass, and G. Miller, "Hierarchical Z-buffer Visibility," *Siggraph '93*, August 1993, pp. 231-238.

[Haeberli90] Haeberli, Paul, and Kurt Akeley, "The Accumulation Buffer: Hardware Support for High-Quality Rendering," *Siggraph '90*, August 1990, pp. 309-318.

[Kay86] Kay, Tim, and J. Kajiya, "Ray Tracing Complex Scenes," *Siggraph '86*, August 1986, pp. 269-278.

[Lengyel97] Lengyel, Jed, and John Snyder, "Rendering with Coherent Layers," *Siggraph '97*, August 1997, pp. 233-242.

[Maciel95] Maciel, Paolo W.C. and Peter Shirley, "Visual Navigation of Large Environments Using Textured Clusters," *Proceedings 1995 Symposium on Interactive 3D Graphics,* April 1995, pp. 95-102.

[Mark97] Mark, William R., Leonard McMillan, and Gary Bishop, "Post-Rendering 3D Warping," *Proceedings 1997 Symposium on Interactive 3D Graphics,* April 1997, pp. 7-16.

[Markosian97] Markosian, Lee, M.A. Kowalski, S.J. Trychin, L.D. Bourdev, D. Goodstein, and J.F. Hughes, "Real-Time Nonphotorealistic Rendering," *Siggraph '97*, August 1997, pp. 415-420.

[Max85] Max, Nelson, and Douglas Lerner, "A Two-and-a-Half-D Motion-Blur Algorithm," *Siggraph '85*, July 1985, pp. 85-93.

[McKenna87] McKenna, M., "Worst-Case Optimal Hidden Surface Removal," *ACM Transactions on Graphics*, 1987, 6, pp. 19-28.

[Ming97] Ming-Chieh Lee, Wei-ge Chen, Chih-lung Bruce Lin, Chunag Gu, Tomislav Markoc, Steven I. Zabinsky, and Richard Szeliski, "A Layered Video Object Coding System Using Sprite and Affine Motion Model," *IEEE Transactions on Circuits and Systems for Video Technology,* 7(1), February 1997, pp. 130-145.

[Molnar92] Molnar, Steve, John Eyles, and John Poulton, "PixelFlow: High-Speed Rendering Using Image Compositing," *Siggraph '92*, August 1992, pp. 231-140.

[Mulmuley89] Mulmuley, K., "An Efficient Algorithm for Hidden Surface Removal," *Siggraph '89*, July 1989, pp. 379-388.

[Naylor92] Naylor, B.F., "Partitioning Tree Image Representation and Generation from 3D Geometric Models," *Proceedings of Graphics Interface '92*, May 1992, pp. 201-212.

[Newell72] Newell, M. E., R. G. Newell, and T. L. Sancha, "A Solution to the Hidden Surface Problem," *Proc. ACM National Conf.*, 1972.

[Ponamgi97] Ponamgi, Madhav K., Dinesh Manocha, and Ming C. Lin, "Incremental Algorithms for Collision Detection between Polygonal Models," IEEE Transactions on Visualization and Computer Graphics, 3(1), March 1997, pp 51-64.

[Porter84] Porter, Thomas, and Tom Duff, "Compositing Digital Images," Siggraph '84, July 1984, pp. 253-258.

[Potmesil81] Potmesil, Michael, and Indranil Chakravarty, "A Lens and Aperture Camera Model for Synthetic Image Generation," *Siggraph '81*, August 1981, pp. 389-399.

[Potmesil83] Potmesil, Michael, and Indranil Chakravarty, "Modeling Motion Blur in Computer-Generated Images," *Siggraph '83*, July 1983, pp. 389-399.

[Regan94] Regan, Matthew, and Ronald Pose, "Priority Rendering with a Virtual Address Recalculation Pipeline," *Siggraph '94*, August 1994, pp. 155-162.

[Rokita93] Rokita, Przemyslaw, "Fast Generation of Depth of Field Effects in Computer Graphics," *Computers and Graphics*, 17(5), 1993, pp. 593-595.

[Schaufler96] Schaufler, Gernot, and Wolfgang Stürzlinger, "A Three Dimensional Image Cache for Virtual Reality," *Proceedings of Eurographics '96*, August 1996, pp. 227-235.

[Schaufler97] Schaufler, Gernot, "Nailboards: A Rendering Primitive for Image Caching in Dynamic Scenes," in *Proceedings of the 8th Eurographics Workshop on Rendering '97*, St. Etienne, France, June 16-18, 1997, pp. 151-162.

[Schumacker69] Schumacker, R.A., B. Brand, M. Gilliland, and W. Sharp, "Study for Applying Computer-Generated Images to Visual Simulation," AFHRL-TR-69-14, U.S. Air Force Human Resources Laboratory, Sept. 1969.

[Sedgewick83] Sedgewick, Robert, *Algorithms*, Addison-Wesley, Reading, MA, 1983.

[Shade96] Shade, Jonathan, Dani Lischinski, David H. Salesin, Tony DeRose, and John Snyder, "Hierarchical Image Caching for Accelerated Walkthroughs of Complex Environments," *Siggraph '96*, August 1996, pp. 75-82.

[Sillion97] Sillion, François, George Drettakis, and Benoit Bodelet, "Efficient Impostor Manipulation for Real-Time Visualization of Urban Scenery," *Proceedings of Eurographics '97*, Sept 1997, pp. 207-218.

[Snyder97] Snyder, John, and Jed Lengyel, "Visibility Sorting and Compositing for Image-Based Rendering," Microsoft Technical Report, MSR-TR-97-11, April 1997.

[Snyder98] Snyder, John, Jed Lengyel, and Jim Blinn, "Resolving Non-Binary Cyclic Occlusions with Image Compositing," Microsoft Technical Report, MSR-TR-98-05, March 1998.

[Sudarsky96] Sudarsky, Oded, and Craig Gotsman, "Output-Sensitive Visibility Algorithms for Dynamic Scenes with Applications to Virtual Reality," Computer Graphics Forum, 15(3), *Proceedings of Eurographics '96*, pp. 249-258.

[Sutherland74] Sutherland, Ivan E., Robert F. Sproull, and Robert A. Schumacker, "A Characterization of Ten Hidden-Surface Algorithms," *Computing Surveys*, 6(1), March 1974, pp. 293-347.

[Teller91] Teller, Seth, and C.H. Sequin, "Visibility Preprocessing for Interactive Walkthroughs," *Siggraph '91*, July 1991, pp. 61-19.

[Teller93] Teller, Seth, and P. Hanrahan, "Global Visibility Algorithms for Illumination Computations," *Siggraph '93*, August 1993, pp. 239-246.

[Torborg96]   Torborg, Jay, and James T. Kajiya, "Talisman: Commodity Realtime 3D Graphics for the PC," *Siggraph '96*, August 1996, pp. 353-364.

[Torres90]   Torres, E., "Optimization of the Binary Space Partition Algorithm (BSP) for the Visualization of Dynamic Scenes," *Proceedings of Eurographics '90*, Sept. 1990, pp. 507-518.

[Wang94]   Wang, J.Y.A., and E.H. Adelson, "Representing Moving Images with Layers," *IEEE Trans. Image Processing*, vol. 3, September 1994, pp. 625-638.

[Zhang97]   Zhang, Hansong, Dinesh Manocha, Thomas Hudson, and Kenneth Hoff III, "Visibility Culling Using Hierarchical Occlusion Maps," Siggraph '97, August 1997, pp. 77-88.

A   Convex Collision/Occlusion Detection

To incrementally detect collisions and occlusions between moving 3D convex polyhedra, we use a modification of Chung's algorithm [Chung96a, Chung96b]. The main idea is to iterate over a potential separating plane direction between the two objects. Given a direction, it is easy to find the extremal vertices with respect to that direction as already discussed in Section 4.1.1. If the current direction D points outward from the first object A, and the respective extremal vertices with respect to D are v_A on object A and v_B on object B,[5] then D is a separating direction if

$$D \cdot v_A < D \cdot v_B.$$

If D fails to separate the objects, then it is updated by reflecting with respect to the line joining the two extremal points. Mathematically,

$$D' \equiv D - 2(R \cdot D) R$$

where R is the unit vector in the direction $v_B - v_A$. [Chung96b] proves that if the objects are indeed disjoint, then this algorithm converges to a separating direction for the objects A and B. Coherence is achieved for disjoint objects because the separating direction from the previous invocation often suffices as a witness to their disjointness in the current invocation, or suffices after a few of the above iterations.

While it is well known that collisions between linearly transforming and translating convex polyhedra can be detected with efficient, coherent algorithms, Chung's algorithm has several advantages over previous methods, notably Voronoi feature tracking algorithm ([Ponamgi97]) and Gilbert's algorithm ([Gilbert88]). The inner loop of Chung's algorithm finds the extremal vertex with respect to a current direction, a very fast algorithm for convex polyhedra. Also, the direction can be transformed to the local space of each convex hull once and then used in the vertex gradient descent algorithm. Chung found a substantial speedup factor in experiments comparing his algorithm with its fastest competitors. Furthermore, Chung found that most queries were resolved with only a few iterations (< 4) of the separating direction.

To detect the case of object collision, Chung's algorithm keeps track of the directions from v_A to v_B generated at each iteration and detects when these vectors span greater than a hemispherical set of directions in S^2. This approach works well in the 3D simulation domain where collision responses are generated that tend to keep objects from interpenetrating, making collisions relatively evanescent. In the visibility sorting domain however, there is no guarantee that a collision between the convex hulls of some object pairs will not persist in time. For example, a terrain cell's convex hull may encompasses several objects for many frames. In this case, Chung's algorithm is quite inefficient.

To achieve coherence for colliding objects, we use a variant of Gilbert's algorithm [Gilbert88]. In brief, Gilbert's algorithm iterates over vertices on the Minkowski difference of the two objects, by finding extremal vertices on the two objects with respect to computed directions. A set of up to four vertex pairs are stored, and the closest point to the origin on the convex hull of these points computed at each iteration, using Johnson's algorithm for computing the closest point on a simplex to the origin. If the convex hull contains the origin, then the two objects intersect. Otherwise, the direction to this point becomes the direction to locate extremal vertices for the next iteration. In the case of collision, a tetrahedron on the Minkowski difference serves as a coherent witness to the objects' collision. We also note that the extremal vertex searching employed in Gilbert's algorithm can be made more spatially coherent by caching the vertex from the previous

---

[5]Here, v_A maximizes the dot product with respect to D over object A and v_B minimizes the dot product over object B, in a common coordinate system.

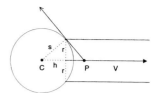

Figure 21: Sphere/cylinder joint occlusion: A cylinder of radius r in direction V is tangent to the sphere of radius s with center C. An occlusion relationship can be derived using the plane through the intersection, at distance h from C along V, and the cone with apex at P such that lines tangent to the sphere through P pass through the circle of intersection.

search on each of the two objects and always starting from that vertex in a search query.

The final, hybrid algorithm uses up to 4 Chung iterations if in the previous invocation the objects were disjoint. If the algorithm finds a separating plane, it is halted. Otherwise, Gilbert's iteration is used to find a witness to collision or find a separating plane. In the case in which Chung iteration fails, Gilbert's algorithm is initialized with the 4 pairs of vertices found in the Chung iterations. The result is an algorithm which functions incrementally for both colliding and disjoint objects and requires only a single query on geometry that returns the extremal vertex on the object given a direction.

The algorithm can be used to detect collisions between two convex polyhedra, or for point inclusion queries (*i.e.*, single point vs. convex polyhedron). It can also be used for occlusion detection between convex polyhedra given an eye point E. To detect whether $A \rightarrow B$, we can test whether $B' \equiv \text{convex\_hull}(B \bigcup E)$ intersects with A. Fortunately, there is no need to actually compute the polytope B'. Instead, the extremal direction search of B' is computed by first searching B as before. We then simply compare that result with the dot product of the direction with E to see if is more extreme and, if so, return E.

B   Occlusion Testing for Sphere/Cylinder Joint

This section presents an method for testing occlusion between a sphere and a cylinder tangent to it with respect to its end cap. Let the sphere have center at C and radius s. The cylinder has unit-length central axis in direction V away from the sphere, and radius r, $r \leq s$. Note that the convex hulls of such a configuration intersect (one cylindrical endcap is entirely inside the sphere), and thus the methods of Section 4.2 always indicate mutual occlusion. However, two exact tests can be used to "split" the cycle, indicating a single occlusion arc between the sphere and cylinder. We assume the eye point E is not inside either object.

The cylinder occludes the sphere (and not vice versa) if the eye is on cylinder side of endcap plane; *i.e.*

$$V \cdot (E - C) - h \geq 0$$

where E is the eye point, and where $h \equiv \sqrt{s^2 - r^2}$ is the distance from C to the plane of intersection.

The sphere occludes the cylinder (and not vice versa) if the circle where the sphere and cylinder intersect is invisible. This can be tested using the cone formed by the apex P along the cylinder's central axis for which emanating rays are tangent to the sphere at the circle of intersection. If the eye point is inside this cone, then the circle of intersection is entirely occluded by the sphere. We define $l \equiv \frac{sr}{h} + h$ representing the distance from P to C; P is thus given by $C + lV$. Then the sphere completely occludes the circle of intersection if

$$(E - P) \cdot (C - P) \geq 0$$

and

$$[(E - P) \cdot (C - P)]^2 \geq (l^2 - s^2)(E - P) \cdot (E - P)$$

where the first test indicates whether E is in front of the cone apex, and the second efficiently tests the square of the cosine of the angle, without using square roots. Note that h and l can be computed once as a preprocess, even if C and v vary as the joint moves.

If both these tests fails, then the sphere and cylinder are mutually occluding.

Layered Depth Images

Jonathan Shade   Steven Gortler*   Li-wei He[†]   Richard Szeliski[‡]

University of Washington   **Harvard University*   *†Stanford University*   *‡Microsoft Research*

Abstract

In this paper we present a set of efficient image based rendering methods capable of rendering multiple frames per second on a PC. The first method warps Sprites with Depth representing smooth surfaces without the gaps found in other techniques. A second method for more general scenes performs warping from an intermediate representation called a Layered Depth Image (LDI). An LDI is a view of the scene from a single input camera view, but with multiple pixels along each line of sight. The size of the representation grows only linearly with the observed depth complexity in the scene. Moreover, because the LDI data are represented in a single image coordinate system, McMillan's warp ordering algorithm can be successfully adapted. As a result, pixels are drawn in the output image in back-to-front order. No z-buffer is required, so alpha-compositing can be done efficiently without depth sorting. This makes splatting an efficient solution to the resampling problem.

1 Introduction

Image based rendering (IBR) techniques have been proposed as an efficient way of generating novel views of real and synthetic objects. With traditional rendering techniques, the time required to render an image increases with the geometric complexity of the scene. The rendering time also grows as the requested shading computations (such as those requiring global illumination solutions) become more ambitious.

The most familiar IBR method is texture mapping. An image is remapped onto a surface residing in a three-dimensional scene. Traditional texture mapping exhibits two serious limitations. First, the pixelization of the texture map and that of the final image may be vastly different. The aliasing of the classic infinite checkerboard floor is a clear illustration of the problems this mismatch can create. Secondly, texture mapping speed is still limited by the surface the texture is applied to. Thus it would be very difficult to create a texture mapped tree containing thousands of leaves that exhibits appropriate parallax as the viewpoint changes.

Two extensions of the texture mapping model have recently been presented in the computer graphics literature that address these two difficulties. The first is a generalization of *sprites*. Once a complex scene is rendered from a particular point of view, the image that would be created from a nearby point of view will likely be similar. In this case, the original 2D image, or *sprite*, can be slightly altered by a 2D affine or projective transformation to approximate the view from the new camera position [30, 26, 14].

The sprite approximation's fidelity to the correct new view is highly dependent on the geometry being represented. In particular, the

errors increase with the amount of depth variation in the real part of the scene captured by the sprite. The amount of virtual camera motion away from the point of view of sprite creation also increases the error. Errors decrease with the distance of the geometry from the virtual camera.

The second recent extension is to add depth information to an image to produce a *depth image* and to then use the optical flow that would be induced by a camera shift to warp the scene into an approximation of the new view [2, 21].

Each of these methods has its limitations. Simple sprite warping cannot produce the *parallax* induced when parts of the scenes have sizable differences in distance from the camera. Flowing a depth image pixel by pixel, on the other hand, can provide proper parallax but will result in gaps in the image either due to visibility changes when some portion of the scene become unoccluded, or when a surface is magnified in the new view.

Some solutions have been proposed to the latter problem. Laveau and Faugeras suggest performing a backwards mapping from the output sample location to the input image [13]. This is an expensive operation that requires some amount of searching in the input image. Another possible solution is to think of the input image as a mesh of micro-polygons, and to scan-convert these polygons in the output image. This is an expensive operation, as it requires a polygon scan-convert setup for each input pixel [17], an operation we would prefer to avoid especially in the absence of specialized rendering hardware. Alternatively one could use multiple input images from different viewpoints. However, if one uses n input images, one effectively multiplies the size of the scene description by n, and the rendering cost increases accordingly.

This paper introduces two new extensions to overcome both of these limitations. The first extension is primarily applicable to smoothly varying surfaces, while the second is useful primarily for very complex geometries. Each method provides efficient image based rendering capable of producing multiple frames per second on a PC.

In the case of sprites representing smoothly varying surfaces, we introduce an algorithm for rendering *Sprites with Depth*. The algorithm first forward maps (i.e., warps) the depth values themselves and then uses this information to add parallax corrections to a standard sprite renderer.

For more complex geometries, we introduce the *Layered Depth Image*, or LDI, that contains potentially multiple depth pixels at each discrete location in the image. Instead of a 2D array of depth pixels (a pixel with associated depth information), we store a 2D array of layered depth pixels. A layered depth pixel stores a set of depth pixels along one line of sight sorted in front to back order. The front element in the layered depth pixel samples the first surface seen along that line of sight; the next pixel in the layered depth pixel samples the next surface seen along that line of sight, etc. When rendering from an LDI, the requested view can move away from the original LDI view and expose surfaces that were not visible in the first layer. The previously occluded regions may still be rendered from data stored in some later layer of a layered depth pixel.

There are many advantages to this representation. The size of the

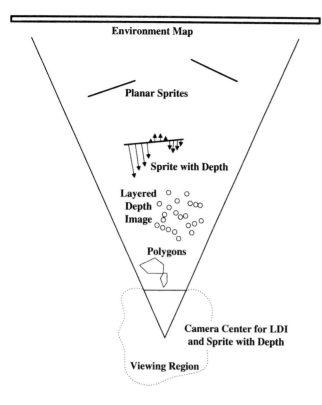

Figure 1 Different image based primitives can serve well depending on distance from the camera

representation grows linearly only with the depth complexity of the image. Moreover, because the LDI data are represented in a single image coordinate system, McMillan's ordering algorithm [20] can be successfully applied. As a result, pixels are drawn in the output image in back to front order allowing proper alpha blending without depth sorting. No z-buffer is required, so alpha-compositing can be done efficiently without explicit depth sorting. This makes splatting an efficient solution to the reconstruction problem.

Sprites with Depth and Layered Depth Images provide us with two new image based primitives that can be used in combination with traditional ones. Figure 1 depicts five types of primitives we may wish to use. The camera at the center of the frustum indicates where the image based primitives were generated from. The viewing volume indicates the range one wishes to allow the camera to move while still re-using these image based primitives.

The choice of which type of image-based or geometric primitive to use for each scene element is a function of its distance, its internal depth variation relative to the camera, as well as its internal geometric complexity. For scene elements at a great distance from the camera one might simply generate an environment map. The environment map is invariant to translation and simply translates as a whole on the screen based on the rotation of the camera. At a somewhat closer range, and for geometrically planar elements, traditional planar sprites (or *image caches*) may be used [30, 26]. The assumption here is that although the part of the scene depicted in the sprite may display some parallax relative to the background environment map and other sprites, it will not need to depict any parallax within the sprite itself. Yet closer to the camera, for elements with smoothly varying depth, Sprites with Depth are capable of displaying internal parallax but cannot deal with disocclusions

due to image flow that may arise in more complex geometric scene elements. Layered Depth Images deal with both parallax and disocclusions and are thus useful for objects near the camera that also contain complex geometries that will exhibit considerable-like parallax. Finally, traditional polygon rendering may need to be used for immediate foreground objects.

In the sections that follow, we will concentrate on describing the data structures and algorithms for representing and rapidly rendering Sprites with Depth and Layered Depth Images.

2 Previous Work

Over the past few years, there have been many papers on image based rendering. In [16], Levoy and Whitted discuss rendering point data. Chen and Williams presented the idea of rendering from images [2]. Laveau and Faugeras discuss IBR using a backwards map [13]. McMillan and Bishop discuss IBR using cylindrical views [21]. Seitz and Dyer describe a system that allows a user to correctly model view transforms in a user controlled image morphing system [28]. In a slightly different direction, Levoy and Hanrahan [15] and Gortler *et al.* [7] describe IBR methods using a large number of input images to sample the high dimensional radiance function.

Max uses a representation similar to an LDI [18], but for a purpose quite different than ours; his purpose is high quality anti-aliasing, while our goal is efficiency. Max reports his rendering time as 5 minutes per frame while our goal is multiple frames per second. Max warps from *n* input LDIs with different camera information; the multiple depth layers serve to represent the high depth complexity of trees. We warp from a single LDI, so that the warping can be done most efficiently. For output, Max warps to an LDI. This is done so that, in conjunction with an A-buffer, high quality, but somewhat expensive, anti-aliasing of the output picture can be performed.

Mark *et al.*[17] and Darsa *et al.*[4] create triangulated depth maps from input images with per-pixel depth. Darsa concentrates on limiting the number of triangles by looking for depth coherence across regions of pixels. This triangle mesh is then rendered traditionally taking advantage of graphics hardware pipelines. Mark *et al.*describe the use of multiple input images as well. In this aspect of their work, specific triangles are given lowered priority if there is a large discontinuity in depth across neighboring pixels. In this case, if another image fills in the same area with a triangle of higher priority, it is used instead. This helps deal with disocclusions.

Shade *et al.*[30] and Shaufler *et al.*[26] render complex portions of a scene such as a tree onto alpha matted billboard-like sprites

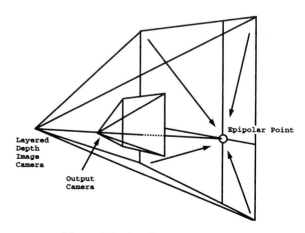

Figure 2 Back to front output ordering

and then reuse them as textures in subsequent frames. Lengyel and Snyder [14] extend this work by warping sprites by a best fit affine transformation based on a set of sample points in the underlying 3D model. These affine transforms are allowed to vary in time as the position and/or color of the sample points change. Hardware considerations for such system are discussed in [31].

Horry *et al.* [10] describe a very simple sprite-like system in which a user interactively indicates planes in an image that represent areas in a given image. Thus, from a single input image and some user supplied information, they can warp an image and provide approximate three dimensional cues about the scene.

The system presented here relies heavily on McMillan's ordering algorithm [20, 19, 21]. Using input and output camera information, a warping order is computed such that pixels that map to the same location in the output image are guaranteed to arrive in back to front order.

In McMillan's work, the depth order is computed by first finding the projection of the output camera's location in the input camera's image plane, that is, the intersection of the line joining the two camera locations with the input camera's image plane. The line joining the two camera locations is called the epipolar line, and the intersection with the image plane is called an epipolar point [6] (see Figure 1). The input image is then split horizontally and vertically at the epipolar point, generally creating 4 image quadrants. (If the epipolar point lies off the image plane, we may have only 2 or 1 regions.) The pixels in each of the quadrants are processed in a different order. Depending on whether the output camera is in front of or behind the input camera, the pixels in each quadrant are processed either towards the epipolar point or outwards away from it. In other words, one of the quadrants is processed left to right, top to bottom, another is processed left to right, bottom to top, etc. McMillan discusses in detail the various special cases that arise and proves that this ordering is guaranteed to produce depth ordered output [19].

When warping from an LDI, there is effectively only one input camera view. Therefore one can use the ordering algorithm to order the layered depth pixels visited. Within each layered depth pixel, the layers are processed in back to front order. The formal proof of [19] applies, and the ordering algorithm is guaranteed to work.

3 Rendering Sprites

Sprites are texture maps or images with alphas (transparent pixels) rendered onto planar surfaces. They can be used either for locally caching the results of slower rendering and then generating new views by warping [30, 26, 31, 14], or they can be used directly as drawing primitives (as in video games).

The texture map associated with a sprite can be computed by simply choosing a 3D viewing matrix and projecting some portion of the scene onto the image plane. In practice, a view associated with the current or expected viewpoint is a good choice. A 3D plane equation can also be computed for the sprite, e.g., by fitting a 3D plane to the z-buffer values associated with the sprite pixels. Below, we derive the equations for the 2D perspective mapping between a sprite and its novel view. This is useful both for implementing a backward mapping algorithm, and lays the foundation for our Sprites with Depth rendering algorithm.

A sprite consists of an alpha-matted image $I_1(x_1, y_1)$, a 4×4 camera matrix C_1 which maps from 3D world coordinates $(X, Y, Z, 1)$ into

the sprite's coordinates $(x_1, y_1, z_1, 1)$,

$$
\begin{bmatrix} w_1 x_1 \\ w_1 y_1 \\ w_1 z_1 \\ w_1 \end{bmatrix} = C_1 \begin{bmatrix} X \\ Y \\ Z \\ 1 \end{bmatrix}, \tag{1}
$$

(z_1 is the z-buffer value), and a plane equation. This plane equation can either be specified in world coordinates, $AX + BY + CZ + D = 0$, or it can be specified in the sprite's coordinate system, $ax_1 + by_1 + cz_1 + d = 0$. In the former case, we can form a new camera matrix $\hat{C}_1$ by replacing the third row of C_1 with the row $[A\ B\ C\ D]$, while in the latter, we can compute $\hat{C}_1 = PC_1$, where

$$
P = \begin{bmatrix} 1 & 0 & 0 & 0 \\ 0 & 1 & 0 & 0 \\ a & b & c & d \\ 0 & 0 & 1 & 0 \end{bmatrix}
$$

(note that $[A\ B\ C\ D] = [a\ b\ c\ d]C_1$).

In either case, we can write the modified projection equation as

$$
\begin{bmatrix} w_1 x_1 \\ w_1 y_1 \\ w_1 d_1 \\ w_1 \end{bmatrix} = \hat{C}_1 \begin{bmatrix} X \\ Y \\ Z \\ 1 \end{bmatrix}, \tag{2}
$$

where $d_1 = 0$ for pixels on the plane. For pixels off the plane, d_1 is the scaled perpendicular distance to the plane (the scale factor is 1 if $A^2 + B^2 + C^2 = 1$) divided by the pixel to camera distance w_1.

Given such a sprite, how do we compute the 2D transformation associated with a novel view $\hat{C}_2$? The mapping between pixels $(x_1, y_1, d_1, 1)$ in the sprite and pixels $(w_2 x_2, w_2 y_2, w_2 d_2, w_2)$ in the output camera's image is given by the transfer matrix $T_{1,2} = \hat{C}_2 \cdot \hat{C}_1^{-1}$.

For a flat sprite ($d_1 = 0$), the transfer equation can be written as

$$
\begin{bmatrix} w_2 x_2 \\ w_2 y_2 \\ w_2 \end{bmatrix} = H_{1,2} \begin{bmatrix} x_1 \\ y_1 \\ 1 \end{bmatrix} \tag{3}
$$

where $H_{1,2}$ is the 2D planar perspective transformation (*homography*) obtained by dropping the third row and column of $T_{1,2}$. The coordinates (x_2, y_2) obtained after dividing out w_2 index a pixel address in the output camera's image. Efficient backward mapping techniques exist for performing the 2D perspective warp [8, 34], or texture mapping hardware can be used.

3.1 Sprites with Depth

The descriptive power (realism) of sprites can be greatly enhanced by adding an out-of-plane displacement component d_1 at each pixel in the sprite.[1] Unfortunately, such a representation can no longer be rendered directly using a backward mapping algorithm.

Using the same notation as before, we see that the transfer equation is now

$$
\begin{bmatrix} w_2 x_2 \\ w_2 y_2 \\ w_2 \end{bmatrix} = H_{1,2} \begin{bmatrix} x_1 \\ y_1 \\ 1 \end{bmatrix} + d_1 e_{1,2}, \tag{4}
$$

[1]The d_1 values can be stored as a separate image, say as 8-bit signed depths. The full precision of a traditional z-buffer is not required, since these depths are used only to compute local parallax, and not to perform z-buffer merging of primitives. Furthermore, the d_1 image could be stored at a lower resolution than the color image, if desired.

where $e_{1,2}$ is called *epipole* [6, 25, 11], and is obtained from the third column of $T_{1,2}$.

Equation (4) can be used to *forward map* pixels from a sprite to a new view. Unfortunately, this entails the usual problems associated with forward mapping, e.g., the necessity to fill gaps or to use larger splatting kernels, and the difficulty in achieving proper resampling. Notice, however, that Equation (4) could be used to perform a backward mapping step by interchanging the 1 and 2 indices, if only we knew the displacements d_2 in the output camera's coordinate frame.

A solution to this problem is to first *forward map* the displacements d_1, and to then use Equation (4) to perform a backward mapping step with the new (view-based) displacements. While this may at first appear to be no faster or more accurate than simply forward warping the color values, it does have some significant advantages.

First, small errors in displacement map warping will not be as evident as errors in the sprite image warping, at least if the displacement map is smoothly varying (in practice, the shape of a simple surface often varies more smoothly than its photometry). If bilinear or higher order filtering is used in the final color (backward) resampling, this two-stage warping will have much lower errors than forward mapping the colors directly with an inaccurate forward map. We can therefore use a quick single-pixel splat algorithm followed by a quick hole filling, or alternatively, use a simple 2×2 splat.

The second main advantage is that we can design the forward warping step to have a simpler form by factoring out the planar perspective warp. Notice that we can rewrite Equation (4) as

$$\begin{bmatrix} w_2 x_2 \\ w_2 y_2 \\ w_2 \end{bmatrix} = H_{1,2} \begin{bmatrix} x_3 \\ y_3 \\ 1 \end{bmatrix}, \tag{5}$$

with

$$\begin{bmatrix} w_3 x_3 \\ w_3 y_3 \\ w_3 \end{bmatrix} = \begin{bmatrix} x_1 \\ y_1 \\ 1 \end{bmatrix} + d_1 e_{1,2}^*, \tag{6}$$

where $e_{1,2}^* = H_{1,2}^{-1} e_{1,2}$. This suggests that Sprite with Depth rendering can be implemented by first shifting pixels by their local parallax, filling any resulting gaps, and then applying a global homography (planar perspective warp). This has the advantage that it can handle large changes in view (e.g., large zooms) with only a small amount of gap filling (since gaps arise only in the first step, and are due to variations in displacement).

Our novel two-step rendering algorithm thus proceeds in two stages:

1. forward map the displacement map $d_1(x_1, y_1)$, using only the parallax component given in Equation (6) to obtain $d_3(x_3, y_3)$;

2a. backward map the resulting warped displacements $d_3(x_3, y_3)$ using Equation (5) to obtain $d_2(x_2, y_2)$ (the displacements in the new camera view);

2b. backward map the original sprite colors, using both the homography $H_{2,1}$ and the new parallax d_2 as in Equation (4) (with the 1 and 2 indices interchanged), to obtain the image corresponding to camera C_2.

The last two operations can be combined into a single raster scan over the output image, avoiding the need to perspective warp d_3 into d_2. More precisely, for each output pixel (x_2, y_2), we compute (x_3, y_3) such that

$$\begin{bmatrix} w_3 x_3 \\ w_3 y_3 \\ w_3 \end{bmatrix} = H_{2,1} \begin{bmatrix} x_2 \\ y_2 \\ 1 \end{bmatrix} \tag{7}$$

to compute where to look up the displacement $d_3(x_3, y_3)$, and form the final address of the source sprite pixel using

$$\begin{bmatrix} w_1 x_1 \\ w_1 y_1 \\ w_1 \end{bmatrix} = \begin{bmatrix} w_3 x_3 \\ w_3 y_3 \\ w_3 \end{bmatrix} + d_3(x_3, y_3) e_{2,1}. \tag{8}$$

We can obtain a quicker, but less accurate, algorithm by omitting the first step, i.e., the pure parallax warp from d_1 to d_3. If we assume the depth at a pixel before and after the warp will not change significantly, we can use d_1 instead of d_3 in Equation (8). This still gives a useful illusion of 3-D parallax, but is only valid for a much smaller range of viewing motions (see Figure 3).

Another variant on this algorithm, which uses somewhat more storage but fewer computations, is to compute a 2-D displacement field in the first pass, $u_3(x_3, y_3) = x_1 - x_3$, $v_3(x_3, y_3) = y_1 - y_3$, where (x_3, y_3) is computed using the pure parallax transform in Equation (6). In the second pass, the final pixel address in the sprite is computed using

$$\begin{bmatrix} x_1 \\ y_1 \end{bmatrix} = \begin{bmatrix} x_3 \\ y_3 \end{bmatrix} + \begin{bmatrix} u_3(x_3, y_3) \\ v_3(x_3, y_3) \end{bmatrix}, \tag{9}$$

where this time (x_3, y_3) is computed using the transform given in Equation (7).

We can make the pure parallax transformation (6) faster by avoiding the per-pixel division required after adding homogeneous coordinates. One way to do this is to approximate the parallax transformation by first moving the epipole to infinity (setting its third component to 0). This is equivalent to having an *affine* parallax component (all points move in the same direction, instead of towards a common vanishing point). In practice, we find that this still provides a very compelling illusion of 3D shape.

Figure 3 shows some of the steps in our two-pass warping algorithm. Figures 3a and 3f show the original sprite (color) image and the depth map. Figure 3b shows the sprite warped with no parallax. Figures 3g, 3h, and 3i shows the depth map forward warped with only pure parallax, only the perspective projection, and both. Figure 3c shows the backward warp using the incorrect depth map d_1 (note how dark "background" colors are mapped onto the "bump"), whereas Figure 3d shows the backward warp using the correct depth map d_3. The white pixels near the right hand edge are a result of using only a single step of gap filling. Using three steps results in the better quality image shown in Figure 3e. Gaps also do not appear for a less quickly slanting d maps, such as the pyramid shown in Figure 3j.

The rendering times for the 256×256 image shown in Figure 3 on a 300 MHz Pentium II are as follows. Using bilinear pixel sampling, the frame rates are 30 Hz for no z-parallax, 21 Hz for "crude" one-pass warping (no forward warping of d_1 values), and 16 Hz for two-pass warping. Using nearest-neighbor resampling, the frame rates go up to 47 Hz, 24 Hz, and 20 Hz, respectively.

3.2 Recovering sprites from image sequences

While sprites and sprites with depth can be generated using computer graphics techniques, they can also be extracted from image sequences using computer vision techniques. To do this, we use a layered motion estimation algorithm [32, 1], which simultaneously segments the sequence into coherently moving regions, and computes a parametric motion estimate (planar perspective transformation) for each layer. To convert the recovered layers into sprites, we need to determine the plane equation associated with each region. We do this by tracking features from frame to frame and applying

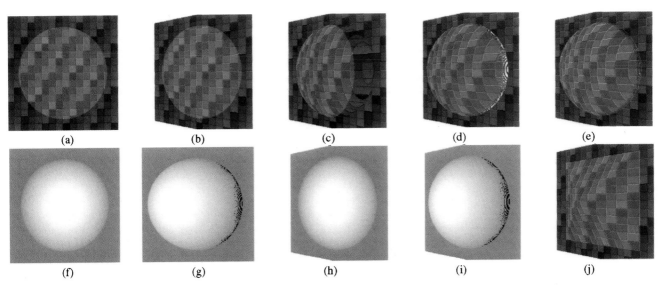

Figure 3 Plane with bump rendering example: (a) input color (sprite) image $I_1(x_1, y_1)$; (b) sprite warped by homography only (no parallax); (c) sprite warped by homography and crude parallax (d_1); (d) sprite warped by homography and true parallax (d_2); (e) with gap fill width set to 3; (f) input depth map $d_1(x_1, y_1)$; (g) pure parallax warped depth map $d_3(x_3, y_3)$; (h) forward warped depth map without parallax correction; (i) forward warped depth map $d_2(x_2, y_2)$; (j) sprite with "pyramid" depth map.

Figure 4 Results of sprite extraction from image sequence: (a) third of five images; (b) initial segmentation into six layers; (c) recovered depth map; (d) the five layer sprites; (e) residual depth image for fifth layer; (f) re-synthesized third image (note extended field of view); (g) novel view without residual depth; (h) novel view with residual depth (note the "rounding" of the people).

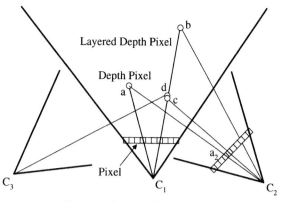

Figure 5 Layered Depth Image

a standard structure from motion algorithm to recover the camera parameters (viewing matrices) for each frame [6]. Tracking several points on each sprite enables us to reconstruct their 3D positions, and hence to estimate their 3D plane equations [1]. Once the sprite pixel assignment have been recovered, we run a traditional stereo algorithm to recover the out-of-plane displacements.

The results of applying the layered motion estimation algorithm to the first five images from a 40-image stereo dataset[2] are shown in Figure 4. Figure 4(a) shows the middle input image, Figure 4(b) shows the initial pixel assignment to layers, Figure 4(c) shows the recovered depth map, and Figure 4(e) shows the residual depth map for layer 5. Figure 4(d) shows the recovered sprites. Figure 4(f) shows the middle image re-synthesized from these sprites, while Figures 4(g–h) show the same sprite collection seen from a novel viewpoint (well outside the range of the original views), both with and without residual depth-based correction (parallax). The gaps visible in Figures 4(c) and 4(f) lie *outside* the area corresponding to the middle image, where the appropriate parts of the background sprites could not be seen.

4 Layered Depth Images

While the use of sprites and Sprites with Depth provides a fast means to warp planar or smoothly varying surfaces, more general scenes require the ability to handle more general disocclusions and large amounts of parallax as the viewpoint moves. These needs have led to the development of Layered Depth Images (LDI).

Like a sprite with depth, pixels contain depth values along with their colors (i.e., a *depth pixel*). In addition, a Layered Depth Image (Figure 5) contains potentially multiple depth pixels per pixel location. The farther depth pixels, which are occluded from the LDI center, will act to fill in the disocclusions that occur as the viewpoint moves away from the center.

The structure of an LDI is summarized by the following conceptual representation:

```
DepthPixel =
    ColorRGBA: 32 bit integer
    Z: 20 bit integer
    SplatIndex: 11 bit integer

LayeredDepthPixel =
    NumLayers: integer
    Layers[0..numlayers-1]: array of DepthPixel
```

[2]Courtesy of Dayton Taylor.

```
LayeredDepthImage =
    Camera: camera
    Pixels[0..xres-1,0..yres-1]: array of LayeredDepthPixel
```

The layered depth image contains camera information plus an array of size *xres* by *yres* layered depth pixels. In addition to image data, each layered depth pixel has an integer indicating how many valid depth pixels are contained in that pixel. The data contained in the depth pixel includes the color, the depth of the object seen at that pixel, plus an index into a table that will be used to calculate a splat size for reconstruction. This index is composed from a combination of the normal of the object seen and the distance from the LDI camera.

In practice, we implement Layered Depth Images in two ways. When creating layered depth images, it is important to be able to efficiently insert and delete layered depth pixels, so the *Layers* array in the *LayeredDepthPixel* structure is implemented as a linked list. When rendering, it is important to maintain spatial locality of depth pixels in order to most effectively take advantage of the cache in the CPU [12]. In Section 5.1 we discuss the compact render-time version of layered depth images.

There are a variety of ways to generate an LDI. Given a synthetic scene, we could use multiple images from nearby points of view for which depth information is available at each pixel. This information can be gathered from a standard ray tracer that returns depth per pixel or from a scan conversion and z-buffer algorithm where the z-buffer is also returned. Alternatively, we could use a ray tracer to sample an environment in a less regular way and then store computed ray intersections in the LDI structure. Given multiple real images, we can turn to computer vision techniques that can infer pixel correspondence and thus deduce depth values per pixel. We will demonstrate results from each of these three methods.

4.1 LDIs from Multiple Depth Images

We can construct an LDI by warping n depth images into a common camera view. For example the depth images C_2 and C_3 in Figure 5 can be warped to the camera frame defined by the LDI (C_1 in figure 5). [3] If, during the warp from the input camera to the LDI camera, two or more pixels map to the same layered depth pixel, their Z values are compared. If the Z values differ by more than a preset epsilon, a new layer is added to that layered depth pixel for each distinct Z value (i.e., *NumLayers* is incremented and a new depth pixel is added), otherwise (e.g., depth pixels c and d in figure 5), the values are averaged resulting in a single depth pixel. This preprocessing is similar to the rendering described by Max [18]. This construction of the layered depth image is effectively decoupled from the final rendering of images from desired viewpoints. Thus, the LDI construction does not need to run at multiple frames per second to allow interactive camera motion.

4.2 LDIs from a Modified Ray Tracer

By construction, a Layered Depth Image reconstructs images of a scene well from the center of projection of the LDI (we simply display the nearest depth pixels). The quality of the reconstruction from another viewpoint will depend on how closely the distribution of depth pixels in the LDI, when warped to the new viewpoint, corresponds to the pixel density in the new image. Two common events that occur are: (1) disocclusions as the viewpoint changes,

[3]Any arbitrary single coordinate system can be specified here. However, we have found it best to use one of the original camera coordinate systems. This results in fewer pixels needing to be resampled twice; once in the LDI construction, and once in the rendering process.

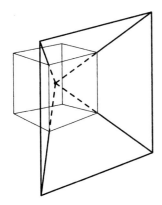

Figure 6 An LDI consists of the 90 degree frustum exiting one side of a cube. The cube represents the region of interest in which the viewer will be able to move.

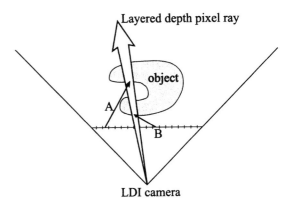

Figure 7 Intersections from sampling rays A and B are added to the same layered depth pixel.

and (2) surfaces that grow in terms of screen space. For example, when a surface is edge on to the LDI, it covers no area. Later, it may face the new viewpoint and thus cover some screen space.

When using a ray tracer, we have the freedom to sample the scene with any distribution of rays we desire. We could simply allow the rays emanating from the center of the LDI to pierce surfaces, recording each hit along the way (up to some maximum). This would solve the disocclusion problem but would not effectively sample surfaces edge on to the LDI.

What set of rays should we trace to sample the scene, to best approximate the distribution of rays from all possible viewpoints we are interested in? For simplicity, we have chosen to use a cubical region of empty space surrounding the LDI center to represent the region that the viewer is able to move in. Each face of the viewing cube defines a 90 degree frustum which we will use to define a single LDI (Figure 6). The six faces of the viewing cube thus cover all of space. For the following discussion we will refer to a single LDI.

Each ray in free space has four coordinates, two for position and two for direction. Since all rays of interest intersect the cube faces, we will choose the outward intersection to parameterize the position of the ray. Direction is parameterized by two angles.

Given no *a priori* knowledge of the geometry in the scene, we assume that every ray intersection the cube is equally important. To achieve a uniform density of rays we sample the positional coordinates uniformly. A uniform distribution over the hemisphere of directions requires that the probability of choosing a direction is proportional to the *projected* area in that direction. Thus, the direction is weighted by the cosine of the angle off the normal to the cube face.

Choosing a cosine weighted direction over a hemisphere can be accomplished by uniformly sampling the unit disk formed by the base of the hemisphere to get two coordinates of the ray direction, say x and y if the z-axis is normal to the disk. The third coordinate is chosen to give a unit length ($z = \sqrt{1 - x^2 - y^2}$). We make the selection within the disk by first selecting a point in the unit square, then applying a measure preserving mapping [23] that maps the unit square to the unit disk.

Given this desired distribution of rays, there are a variety of ways to perform the sampling:

Uniform. A straightforward stochastic method would take as input the number of rays to cast. Then, for each ray it would choose an origin on the cube face and a direction from the cosine distribution

and cast the ray into the scene. There are two problems with this simple scheme. First, such *white noise* distributions tend to form unwanted clumps. Second, since there is no coherence between rays, complex scenes require considerable memory thrashing since rays will access the database in a random way [24]. The model of the chestnut tree seen in the color images was too complex to sample with a pure stochastic method on a machine with 320MB of memory.

Stratified Stochastic. To improve the coherence and distribution of rays, we employ a stratified scheme. In this method, we divide the 4D space of rays uniformly into a grid of $N \times N \times N \times N$ strata. For each stratum, we cast M rays. Enough coherence exists within a stratum that swapping of the data set is alleviated. Typical values for N and M are 32 and 16, generating approximately 16 million rays per cube face.

Once a ray is chosen, we cast it into the scene. If it hits an object, and that object lies in the LDI's frustum, we reproject the intersection into the LDI, as depicted in Figure 7, to determine which layered depth pixel should receive the sample. If the new sample is within an epsilon tolerance in depth of an existing depth pixel, the color of the new sample is averaged with the existing depth pixel. Otherwise, the color, normal, and distance to the sample create a new depth pixel that is inserted into the Layered Depth Pixel.

4.3 LDIs from Real Images

The dinosaur model in Figure 13 is constructed from 21 photographs of the object undergoing a 360 degree rotation on a computer-controlled calibrated turntable. An adaptation of Seitz and Dyer's voxel coloring algorithm [29] is used to obtain the LDI representation directly from the input images. The regular voxelization of Seitz and Dyer is replaced by a view-centered voxelization similar to the LDI structure. The procedure entails moving outward on rays from the LDI camera center and projecting candidate voxels back into the input images. If all input images agree on a color, this voxel is filled as a depth pixel in the LDI structure. This approach enables straightforward construction of LDI's from images that do not contain depth per pixel.

5 Rendering Layered Depth Images

Our fast warping-based renderer takes as input an LDI along with its associated camera information. Given a new desired camera position, the warper uses an incremental warping algorithm to efficiently create an output image. Pixels from the LDI are splatted into the output image using the *over* compositing operation. The size and footprint of the splat is based on an estimated size of the reprojected pixel.

5.1 Space Efficient Representation

When rendering, it is important to maintain the spatial locality of depth pixels to exploit the second level cache in the CPU [12]. To this end, we reorganize the depth pixels into a linear array ordered from bottom to top and left to right in screen space, and back to front along a ray. We also separate out the number of layers in each layered depth pixel from the depth pixels themselves. The layered depth pixel structure does not exist explicitly in this implementation. Instead, a double array of offsets is used to locate each depth pixel. The number of depth pixels in each scanline is accumulated into a vector of offsets to the beginning of each scanline. Within each scanline, for each pixel location, a total count of the depth pixels from the beginning of the scanline to that location is maintained. Thus to find any layered depth pixel, one simply offsets to the beginning of the scanline and then further to the first depth pixel at that location. This supports scanning in right-to-left order as well as the clipping operation discussed later.

5.2 Incremental Warping Computation

The incremental warping computation is similar to the one used for certain texture mapping operations [9, 27]. The geometry of this computation has been analyzed by McMillan [22], and efficient computation for the special case of orthographic input images is given in [3].

Let C_1 be the 4×4 matrix for the LDI camera. It is composed of an affine transformation matrix, a projection matrix, and a viewport matrix, $C_1 = V_1 \cdot P_1 \cdot A_1$. This camera matrix transforms a point from the global coordinate system into the camera's projected image coordinate system. The projected image coordinates (x_1, y_1), obtained after multiplying the point's global coordinates by C_1 and dividing out w_1, index a screen pixel address. The z_1 coordinate can be used for depth comparisons in a z buffer.

Let C_2 be the output camera's matrix. Define the transfer matrix as $T_{1,2} = C_2 \cdot C_1^{-1}$. Given the projected image coordinates of some point seen in the LDI camera (e.g., the coordinates of a in Figure 5), this matrix computes the image coordinates as seen in the output camera (e.g., the image coordinates of a_2 in camera C_2 in Figure 5).

$$T_{1,2} \cdot \begin{bmatrix} x_1 \\ y_1 \\ z_1 \\ 1 \end{bmatrix} = \begin{bmatrix} x_2 \cdot w_2 \\ y_2 \cdot w_2 \\ z_2 \cdot w_2 \\ w_2 \end{bmatrix} = \textbf{result}$$

The coordinates (x_2, y_2) obtained after dividing by w_2, index a pixel address in the output camera's image.

Using the linearity of matrix operations, this matrix multiply can be factored to reuse much of the computation from each iteration through the layers of a layered depth pixel; **result** can be computed as

$$T_{1,2} \cdot \begin{bmatrix} x_1 \\ y_1 \\ z_1 \\ 1 \end{bmatrix} = T_{1,2} \cdot \begin{bmatrix} x_1 \\ y_1 \\ 0 \\ 1 \end{bmatrix} + z_1 \cdot T_{1,2} \cdot \begin{bmatrix} 0 \\ 0 \\ 1 \\ 0 \end{bmatrix} = \textbf{start} + z_1 \cdot \textbf{depth}$$

To compute the warped position of the next layered depth pixel along a scanline, the new **start** is simply incremented.

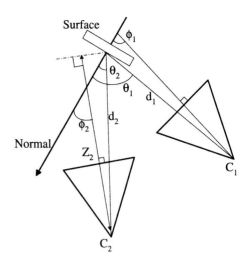

Figure 8 Values for size computation of a projected pixel.

$$T_{1,2} \cdot \begin{bmatrix} x_1 + 1 \\ y_1 \\ 0 \\ 1 \end{bmatrix} = T_{1,2} \cdot \begin{bmatrix} x_1 \\ y_1 \\ 0 \\ 1 \end{bmatrix} + T_{1,2} \cdot \begin{bmatrix} 1 \\ 0 \\ 0 \\ 0 \end{bmatrix} = \textbf{start} + \textbf{xincr}$$

The warping algorithm proceeds using McMillan's ordering algorithm [20]. The LDI is broken up into four regions above and below and to the left and right of the epipolar point. For each quadrant, the LDI is traversed in (possibly reverse) scan line order. At the beginning of each scan line, **start** is computed. The sign of **xincr** is determined by the direction of processing in this quadrant. Each layered depth pixel in the scan line is then warped to the output image by calling *Warp*. This procedure visits each of the layers in back to front order and computes **result** to determine its location in the output image. As in perspective texture mapping, a divide is required per pixel. Finally, the depth pixel's color is splatted at this location in the output image.

The following pseudo code summarizes the warping algorithm applied to each layered depth pixel.

```
procedure Warp(ldpix, start, depth, xincr)
    for k ←0 to dpix.NumLayers-1
        z1 ←ldpix.Layers[k].Z
        result ←start + z1 * depth
        //cull if the depth pixel goes behind the output camera
        //or if the depth pixel goes out of the output cam's frustum
        if result.w > 0 and IsInViewport(result) then
            result ←result / result.w
            // see next section
            sqrtSize ←z2 * lookupTable[ldpix.Layers[k].SplatIndex]
            splat(ldpix.Layers[k].ColorRGBA, x2, y2, sqrtSize)
        end if
        // increment for next layered pixel on this scan line
        start ←start + xincr
    end for
end procedure
```

5.3 Splat Size Computation

To splat the LDI into the output image, we estimate the projected area of the warped pixel. This is a rough approximation to the footprint evaluation [33] optimized for speed. The proper size can be computed (differentially) as

$$size = \frac{(d_1)^2 \, cos(\theta_2) \, res_2 \, tan(fov_1/2)}{(d_2)^2 \, cos(\theta_1) \, res_1 \, tan(fov_2/2)}$$

where d_1 is the distance from the sampled surface point to the LDI camera, fov_1 is the field of view of the LDI camera, $res_1 = (w_1 h_1)^{-1}$ where w_1 and h_1 are the width and height of the LDI, and θ_1 is the angle between the surface normal and the line of sight to the LDI camera (see Figure 8). The same terms with subscript 2 refer to the output camera.

It will be more efficient to compute an approximation of the square root of size,

$$\sqrt{size} = \frac{1}{d_2} \cdot \frac{d_1\sqrt{cos(\theta_2)res_2 tan(fov_1/2)}}{\sqrt{cos(\theta_1)res_1 tan(fov_2/2)}}$$

$$\approx \frac{1}{Z_2} \cdot \frac{d_1\sqrt{cos(\phi_2)res_2 tan(fov_1/2)}}{\sqrt{cos(\phi_1)res_1 tan(fov_2/2)}}$$

$$\approx z_2 \cdot \frac{d_1\sqrt{cos(\phi_2)res_2 tan(fov_1/2)}}{\sqrt{cos(\phi_1)res_1 tan(fov_2/2)}}$$

We approximate the θs as the angles ϕ between the surface normal vector and the z axes of the camera's coordinate systems. We also approximate d_2 by Z_2, the z coordinate of the sampled point in the output camera's unprojected eye coordinate system. During rendering, we set the projection matrix such that $z_2 = 1/Z_2$.

The current implementation supports 4 different splat sizes, so a very crude approximation of the size computation is implemented using a lookup table. For each pixel in the LDI, we store d_1 using 5 bits. We use 6 bits to encode the normal, 3 for n_x, and 3 for n_y. This gives us an eleven-bit lookup table index. Before rendering each new image, we use the new output camera information to precompute values for the 2048 possible lookup table indexes. At each pixel we obtain $\sqrt{size}$ by multiplying the computed z_2 by the value found in the lookup table.

$$\sqrt{size} \approx z_2 \cdot \text{lookup[nx,ny,d1]}$$

To maintain the accuracy of the approximation for d_1, we discretize d_1 nonlinearly using a simple exponential function that allocates more bits to the nearby d_1 values, and fewer bits to the distant d_1 values.

The four splat sizes we currently use have 1 by 1, 3 by 3, 5 by 5, and 7 by 7 pixel footprints. Each pixel in a footprint has an alpha value to approximate a Gaussian splat kernel. However, the alpha values are rounded to 1, 1/2, or 1/4, so the alpha blending can be done with integer shifts and adds.

5.4 Depth Pixel Representation

The size of a cache line on current Intel processors (Pentium Pro and Pentium II) is 32 bytes. To fit four depth pixels into a single cache line we convert the floating point Z value to a 20 bit integer. This is then packed into a single word along with the 11 bit splat table index. These 32 bits along with the R, G, B, and alpha values fill out the 8 bytes. This seemingly small optimization yielded a 25 percent improvement in rendering speed.

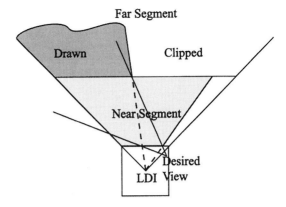

Figure 9 LDI with two segments

5.5 Clipping

The LDI of the chestnut tree scene in Figure 11 is a large data set containing over 1.1 million depth pixels. If we naively render this LDI by reprojecting every depth pixel, we would only be able to render at one or two frames per second. When the viewer is close to the tree, there is no need to flow those pixels that will fall outside of the new view. Unseen pixels can be culled by intersecting the view frustum with the frustum of the LDI. This is implemented by intersecting the view frustum with the near and far plane of the LDI frustum, and taking the bounding box of the intersection. This region defines the rays of depth pixels that could be seen in the new view. This computation is conservative, and gives suboptimal results when the viewer is looking at the LDI from the side (see Figure 9). The view frustum intersects almost the entire cross section of the LDI frustum, but only those depth pixels in the desired view need be warped. Our simple clipping test indicates that most of the LDI needs to be warped. To alleviate this, we split the LDI into two segments, a near and a far segment (see Figure 9). These are simply two frustra stacked one on top of the other. The near frustum is kept smaller than the back segment. We clip each segment individually, and render the back segment first and the front segment second. Clipping can speed rendering times by a factor of 2 to 4.

6 Results

Sprites with Depth and Layered Depth Images have been implemented in C++. The color figures show two examples of rendering sprites and three examples of rendering LDIs. Figures 3a through 3j show the results of rendering a sprite with depth. The hemisphere in the middle of the sprite pops out of the plane of the sprite, and the illusion of depth is quite good. Figure 4 shows the process of extracting sprites from multiple images using the vision techniques discussed in Section 3. There is a great deal of parallax between the layers of sprites, resulting in a convincing and inexpensive image-based-rendering method.

Figure 10 shows two views of a barnyard scene modeled in Softimage. A set of 20 images was pre-rendered from cameras that encircle the chicken using the Mental Ray renderer. The renderer returns colors, depths, and normals at each pixel. The images were rendered at 320 by 320 pixel resolution, taking approximately one minute each to generate. In the interactive system, the 3 images out of the 17 that have the closest direction to the current camera are chosen. The preprocessor (running in a low-priority thread) uses these images to create an LDI in about 1 second. While the LDIs are allocated with a maximum of 10 layers per pixel, the average depth complexity for these LDIs is only 1.24. Thus the use of three input images only increases the rendering cost by 24 percent. The fast

Figure 10 Barnyard scene

Figure 11 Near segment of chestnut tree

Figure 12 Chestnut tree in front of environment map

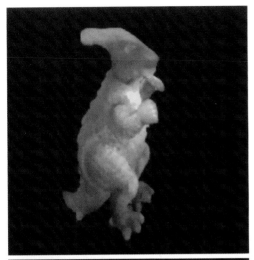

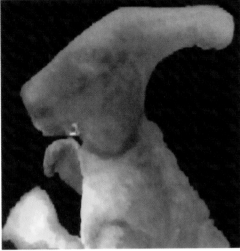

Figure 13 Dinosaur model reconstructed from 21 photographs

renderer (running concurrently in a high-priority thread) generates images at 300 by 300 resolution. On a Pentium II PC running at 300MHz, we achieved frame rate of 8 to 10 frames per second.

Figures 11 and 12 show two cross-eye stereo pairs of a chestnut tree. In Figure 11 only the near segment is displayed. Figure 12 shows both segments in front of an environment map. The LDIs were created using a modified version of the Rayshade raytracer. The tree model is very large; Rayshade allocates over 340 MB of memory to render a single image of the tree. The stochastic method discussed in Section 4.2 took 7 hours to trace 16 million rays through this scene using an SGI Indigo2 with a 250 MHz processor and 320MB of memory. The resulting LDI has over 1.1 million depth pixels, 70,000 of which were placed in the near segment with the rest in the far segment. When rendering this interactively we attain frame rates between 4 and 10 frames per second on a Pentium II PC running at 300MHz.

7 Discussion

In this paper, we have described two novel techniques for image based rendering. The first technique renders Sprites with Depth without visible gaps, and with a smoother rendering than traditional forward mapping (splatting) techniques. It is based on the observation that a forward mapped displacement map does not have to be as

accurate as a forward mapped color image. If the displacement map is smooth, the inaccuracies in the warped displacement map result in only sub-pixel errors in the final color pixel sample positions.

Our second novel approach to image based rendering is a Layered Depth Image representation. The LDI representation provides the means to display the parallax induced by camera motion as well as reveal disoccluded regions. The average depth complexity in our LDI's is much lower that one would achieve using multiple input images (e.g., only 1.24 in the Chicken LDI). The LDI representation takes advantage of McMillan's ordering algorithm allowing pixels to be splatted back to Front with an *over* compositing operation.

Traditional graphics elements and planar sprites can be combined with Sprites with Depth and LDIs in the same scene if a back-to-front ordering is maintained. In this case they are simply composited onto one another. Without such an ordering a z-buffer approach will still work at the extra cost of maintaining depth information per frame.

Choosing a single camera view to organize the data has the advantage of having sampled the geometry with a preference for views very near the center of the LDI. This also has its disadvantages. First, pixels undergo two resampling steps in their journey from input image to output. This can potentially degrade image quality. Secondly, if some surface is seen at a glancing angle in the LDIs view the depth complexity for that LDI increases, while the spatial sampling resolution over that surface degrades. The sampling and aliasing issues involved in our layered depth image approach are still not fully understood; a formal analysis of these issues would be helpful.

With the introduction of our two new representations and rendering techniques, there now exists a wide range of different image based rendering methods available. At one end of the spectrum are traditional texture-mapped models. When the scene does not have too much geometric detail, and when texture-mapping hardware is available, this may be the method of choice. If the scene can easily be partitioned into non-overlapping sprites (with depth), then triangle-based texture-mapped rendering can be used without requiring a z buffer [17, 4].

All of these representations, however, do not explicitly account for certain variation of scene appearance with viewpoint, e.g., specularities, transparency, etc. View-dependent texture maps [5], and 4D representations such as lightfields or Lumigraphs [15, 7], have been designed to model such effects. These techniques can lead to greater realism than static texture maps, sprites, or Layered Depth Images, but usually require more effort (and time) to render.

In future work, we hope to explore representations and rendering algorithms which combine several image based rendering techniques. Automatic techniques for taking a 3D scene (either synthesized or real) and re-representing it in the most appropriate fashion for image based rendering would be very useful. These would allow us to apply image based rendering to truly complex, visually rich scenes, and thereby extend their range of applicability.

Acknowledgments

The authors would first of all like to thank Michael F. Cohen. Many of the original ideas contained in this paper as well as much of the discussion in the paper itself can be directly attributable to him. The authors would also like to thank Craig Kolb for his help in obtaining and modifying Rayshade. Steve Seitz is responsible for creating the LDI of the dinosaur from a modified version of his earlier code. Andrew Glassner was a great help with some of the illustrations in the paper. Finally, we would like to thank Microsoft Research for helping to bring together the authors to work on this project.

References

[1] S. Baker, R. Szeliski, and P. Anandan. A Layered Approach to Stereo Reconstruction. In *IEEE Computer Society Conference on Computer Vision and Pattern Recognition (CVPR'98)*. Santa Barbara, June 1998.

[2] Shenchang Eric Chen and Lance Williams. View Interpolation for Image Synthesis. In James T. Kajiya, editor, *Computer Graphics (SIGGRAPH '93 Proceedings)*, volume 27, pages 279–288. August 1993.

[3] William Dally, Leonard McMillan, Gary Bishop, and Henry Fuchs. The Delta Tree: An Object Centered Approach to Image Based Rendering. AI technical Memo 1604, MIT, 1996.

[4] Lucia Darsa, Bruno Costa Silva, and Amitabh Varshney. Navigating Static Environments Using Image-Space Simplification and Morphing. In *Proc. 1997 Symposium on Interactive 3D Graphics*, pages 25–34. 1997.

[5] Paul E. Debevec, Camillo J. Taylor, and Jitendra Malik. Modeling and Rendering Architecture from Photographs: A Hybrid Geometry- and Image-Based Approach. In Holly Rushmeier, editor, *SIGGRAPH 96 Conference Proceedings*, Annual Conference Series, pages 11–20. ACM SIGGRAPH, Addison Wesley, August 1996.

[6] O. Faugeras. *Three-dimensional computer vision: A geometric viewpoint*. MIT Press, Cambridge, Massachusetts, 1993.

[7] Steven J. Gortler, Radek Grzeszczuk, Richard Szeliski, and Michael F. Cohen. The Lumigraph. In Holly Rushmeier, editor, *SIGGRAPH 96 Conference Proceedings*, Annual Conference Series, pages 43–54. ACM SIGGRAPH, Addison Wesley, August 1996.

[8] Paul S. Heckbert. Survey of Texture Mapping. *IEEE Computer Graphics and Applications*, 6(11):56–67, November 1986.

[9] Paul S. Heckbert and Henry P. Moreton. Interpolation for Polygon Texture Mapping and Shading. In David Rogers and Rae Earnshaw, editors, *State of the Art in Computer Graphics: Visualization and Modeling*, pages 101–111. Springer-Verlag, 1991.

[10] Youichi Horry, Ken ichi Anjyo, and Kiyoshi Arai. Tour Into the Picture: Using a Spidery Mesh Interface to Make Animation from a Single Image. In Turner Whitted, editor, *SIGGRAPH 97 Conference Proceedings*, Annual Conference Series, pages 225–232. ACM SIGGRAPH, Addison Wesley, August 1997.

[11] R. Kumar, P. Anandan, and K. Hanna. Direct recovery of shape from multiple views: A parallax based approach. In *Twelfth International Conference on Pattern Recognition (ICPR'94)*, volume A, pages 685–688. IEEE Computer Society Press, Jerusalem, Israel, October 1994.

[12] Anthony G. LaMarca. Caches and Algorithms. Ph.D. thesis, University of Washington, 1996.

[13] S. Laveau and O. D. Faugeras. 3-D Scene Representation as a Collection of Images. In *Twelfth International Conference on Pattern Recognition (ICPR'94)*, volume A, pages 689–691. IEEE Computer Society Press, Jerusalem, Israel, October 1994.

[14] Jed Lengyel and John Snyder. Rendering with Coherent Layers. In Turner Whitted, editor, *SIGGRAPH 97 Conference Proceedings*, Annual Conference Series, pages 233–242. ACM SIGGRAPH, Addison Wesley, August 1997.

[15] Marc Levoy and Pat Hanrahan. Light Field Rendering. In Holly Rushmeier, editor, *SIGGRAPH 96 Conference Proceedings*, Annual Conference Series, pages 31–42. ACM SIGGRAPH, Addison Wesley, August 1996.

[16] Mark Levoy and Turner Whitted. The Use of Points as a Display Primitive. Technical Report 85-022, University of North Carolina, 1985.

[17] William R. Mark, Leonard McMilland, and Gary Bishop. Post-Rendering 3D Warping. In *Proc. 1997 Symposium on Interactive 3D Graphics*, pages 7–16. 1997.

[18] Nelson Max. Hierarchical Rendering of Trees from Precomputed Multi-Layer Z-Buffers. In Xavier Pueyo and Peter Schröder, editors, *Eurographics Rendering Workshop 1996*, pages 165–174. Eurographics, Springer Wein, New York City, NY, June 1996.

[19] Leonard McMillan. Computing Visibility Without Depth. Technical Report 95-047, University of North Carolina, 1995.

[20] Leonard McMillan. A List-Priority Rendering Algorithm for Redisplaying Projected Surfaces. Technical Report 95-005, University of North Carolina, 1995.

[21] Leonard McMillan and Gary Bishop. Plenoptic Modeling: An Image-Based Rendering System. In Robert Cook, editor, *SIGGRAPH 95 Conference Proceedings*, Annual Conference Series, pages 39–46. ACM SIGGRAPH, Addison Wesley, August 1995.

[22] Leonard McMillan and Gary Bishop. Shape as a Pertebation to Projective Mapping. Technical Report 95-046, University of North Carolina, 1995.

[23] Don P. Mitchell. *personal communication*. 1997.

[24] Matt Pharr, Craig Kolb, Reid Gershbein, and Pat Hanrahan. Rendering Complex Scenes with Memory-Coherent Ray Tracing. In Turner Whitted, editor, *SIGGRAPH 97 Conference Proceedings*, Annual Conference Series, pages 101–108. ACM SIGGRAPH, Addison Wesley, August 1997.

[25] H. S. Sawhney. 3D Geometry from Planar Parallax. In *IEEE Computer Society Conference on Computer Vision and Pattern Recognition (CVPR'94)*, pages 929–934. IEEE Computer Society, Seattle, Washington, June 1994.

[26] Gernot Schaufler and Wolfgang Stürzlinger. A Three-Dimensional Image Cache for Virtual Reality. In *Proceedings of Eurographics '96*, pages 227–236. August 1996.

[27] Mark Segal, Carl Korobkin, Rolf van Widenfelt, Jim Foran, and Paul E. Haeberli. Fast shadows and lighting effects using texture mapping. In Edwin E. Catmull, editor, *Computer Graphics (SIGGRAPH '92 Proceedings)*, volume 26, pages 249–252. July 1992.

[28] Steven M. Seitz and Charles R. Dyer. View Morphing: Synthesizing 3D Metamorphoses Using Image Transforms. In Holly Rushmeier, editor, *SIGGRAPH 96 Conference Proceedings*, Annual Conference Series, pages 21–30. ACM SIGGRAPH, Addison Wesley, August 1996.

[29] Steven M. seitz and Charles R. Dyer. Photorealistic Scene Reconstruction by Voxel Coloring. In *Proc. Computer Vision and Pattern Recognition Conf.*, pages 1067–1073. 1997.

[30] Jonathan Shade, Dani Lischinski, David Salesin, Tony DeRose, and John Snyder. Hierarchical Image Caching for Accelerated Walkthroughs of Complex Environments. In Holly Rushmeier, editor, *SIGGRAPH 96 Conference Proceedings*, Annual Conference Series, pages 75–82. ACM SIGGRAPH, Addison Wesley, August 1996.

[31] Jay Torborg and Jim Kajiya. Talisman: Commodity Real-time 3D Graphics for the PC. In Holly Rushmeier, editor, *SIGGRAPH 96 Conference Proceedings*, Annual Conference Series, pages 353–364. ACM SIGGRAPH, Addison Wesley, August 1996.

[32] J. Y. A. Wang and E. H. Adelson. Layered Representation for Motion Analysis. In *IEEE Computer Society Conference on Computer Vision and Pattern Recognition (CVPR'93)*, pages 361–366. New York, New York, June 1993.

[33] Lee Westover. Footprint Evaluation for Volume Rendering. In Forest Baskett, editor, *Computer Graphics (SIGGRAPH '90 Proceedings)*, volume 24, pages 367–376. August 1990.

[34] G. Wolberg. *Digital Image Warping*. IEEE Computer Society Press, Los Alamitos, California, 1990.

Multiple Viewpoint Rendering

Michael Halle

Brigham and Women's Hospital

Abstract

This paper presents an algorithm for rendering a static scene from multiple perspectives. While most current computer graphics algorithms render scenes as they appear from a single viewpoint (the location of the camera) multiple viewpoint rendering (MVR) renders a scene from a range of spatially-varying viewpoints. By exploiting perspective coherence, MVR can produce a set of images orders of magnitude faster than conventional rendering methods. Images produced by MVR can be used as input to multiple-perspective displays such as holographic stereograms, lenticular sheet displays, and holographic video. MVR can also be used as a geometry-to-image prefilter for image-based rendering algorithms. MVR techniques are adapted from single viewpoint computer graphics algorithms and can be accelerated using existing hardware graphics subsystems. This paper describes the characteristics of MVR algorithms in general, along with the design, implementation, and applications of a particular MVR rendering system.

1 Introduction

Many of the important techniques and algorithms of computer graphics are specifically focused on accelerating the conversion of geometric primitives to images by using coherence of some kind. Published taxonomies of coherence [17] have presented the spectrum of possible coherence types, but common practice has put greater emphasis on some areas and left others generally untouched. In particular, most computer graphics algorithms heavily emphasize the use of image and geometric coherence to accelerate the rendering of a single image. These techniques include some of the most important in computer graphics: polygon scan conversion and incremental shading.

Less common rendering techniques have been used to exploit coherence over multiple views of an object. For example, temporal coherence can be used to speed the rendition of the frames of a computer animation. Coherence across several images, referred to under the blanket name *frame-to-frame coherence*, is very general and scene dependent because of the sheer variety of changes that an object in a scene can experience from one frame to the next. Fully general temporal coherence algorithms must deal with potentially complex camera motion as well as arbitrary object transfor-

mation and other changes to the scene. In part because of this generality, the observation made by Sutherland *et. al.* from 1974 is still mostly true today: "It is really hard to make much use of object and frame coherence, so perhaps it is not surprising that not much [use of it] has been made." Recent developments such as the Talisman graphics architecture [19] demonstrate both the promise and the complexities of using temporal coherence.

2 Perspective coherence

While temporal coherence of time-varying image sequences is an important subclass of frame-to-frame coherence, it is not the only subclass. Another coherence type, *perspective coherence*, is the similarity between images of a static scene as viewed from different locations. Simple observation demonstrates the prevalence of perspective coherence in common "real world" scenes: viewing typical objects by alternating between your left and right eyes produces little apparent change in appearance. Small shifts of your head side to side or up and down usually yields similarly small changes.

Because perspective coherence results from the apparent change of a scene's appearance due solely to a change in camera perspective, it is much more restricted and less general than temporal coherence. Geometric and shading changes to the scene's appearance are usually related to the change in the camera position in a simple way. With the appropriate rendering constructs, perspective coherence is easier to find and to exploit than more general frame-to-frame coherence. This paper describes a method of rendering whereby perspective coherence can be harnessed to efficiently render sets of perspective images.

3 Multiple viewpoint rendering

This text refers to rendering methods that generate perspective image sets as *multiple viewpoint rendering*, or *MVR*, and those algorithms that create single images as *single viewpoint rendering (SVR)*. MVR algorithms treat the process of rendering a set of perspective images as a unit, and use the structured coherence of spatio-perspective space to accelerate the process of image data generation. For instance, using a relatively small number of transformation and shading calculations, MVR can interpolate location and appearance of an object through an entire range of views.

4 Applications

Perspective image sets such as those generated by MVR are used less frequently than are animations or other temporally varying image sequences. But perspective image sets have their own important class of emerging uses in computer graphics. This class of applications approximate optical capture, distortion, or display of a field of light emitted by a scene. Two diverse examples of potential applications for MVR-generated image sets include synthetic three-dimensional display and image-based rendering.

4.1 Three-dimensional displays

Multi-perspective 3D or parallax displays, a classification which include lenticular sheet displays, parallax panoramagrams, holographic stereograms, and holographic video displays, mimic the

75 Francis Street, Boston, MA 02115, USA. Email: mhalle@bwh.harvard.edu.
This work was performed while the author was at the MIT Media Laboratory.

appearance of three-dimensional scenes by displaying different perspectives of the scene in different directions [10][15]. Most multi-perspective displays are horizontal parallax only: they use a range of perspectives that vary only horizontally in order to provide stereopsis to a viewer. Depending on the exact technology used in the display, the number of perspectives required as input to the display device may range from two to tens of thousands. For three-dimensional images of synthetic scenes, these perspectives must be rendered. The high cost of computing this large amount of image information is currently a major impediment for the development of three-dimensional displays; MVR can be used to produce 3D images of virtual scenes much faster than existing rendering methods.

4.2 Image-based rendering

Another use for perspective image sets is as input to image-based rendering algorithms. Image-based rendering densely samples light traveling through a space as a set of images and transforms this data to produce new images seen from viewpoints spatially disparate from any of the originals. Image algorithms such as those developed by Gortler *et. al.* [8] and Levoy and Hanrahan [14] produce a single output image from a perspective image set, while similar algorithms developed for optical predistortion in synthetic holography derive not just one but an entirely new set of images [10]. Either of these types of image-based rendering algorithms requires a set of rendered perspectives in order to image a synthetic scene. MVR serves as a prefilter for the image-based rendering pipeline, transforming scene geometry into a basis set of the light field from which new images are derived. Perspective coherence, in turn, provides the means to efficiently compute this perspective image set.

5 Camera geometries

The exact relationship between a change in camera viewpoint and the resulting change in the appearance of a scene depends on

the capture camera geometry. Choice of camera geometry depends on how the output data will be used and how well a particular geometry lends itself to efficient use of perspective coherence. Image-based rendering algorithms have shown that a sufficiently dense sampling perspectives in a single plane provides enough information to synthesize arbitrary perspectives within a volume free of occluders; this property permits the set of perspective images from one camera geometry to be converted to that of another, different camera geometry. The ability to convert sets of perspective images between different camera geometries allows the choice of a convenient geometry to maximize the use of perspective coherence to accelerate rendering. This paper will focus on a planar camera geometry specifically designed to simplify interpolation between different views.

6 PRS camera geometry

One of the simplest multi-perspective camera geometries consists of an planar array of cameras arranged in a regular grid, with all of the cameras' optical axes mutually parallel. The film plane of each camera in the grid is sheared in a plane orthogonal to the camera's view vector in order to recenter the image of points on an image plane located a constant distance from the camera plane. This camera geometry has been used in computer vision and synthetic holography since the late 1970's; it is identical to the one described by Levoy and Hanrahan [14].

We will refer to this geometry as a *planar regular shearing* camera geometry, or *PRS* camera. The one-dimensional analog of the PRS camera consists of a regularly spaced line of cameras; this geometry is called a *linear regular shearing* geometry, or *LRS*. The PRS camera can be decomposed into a set of simpler LRS cameras arranged in a regular array. Collectively, the PRS and LRS geometries are called *regular shearing* (*RS*) cameras. PRS and LRS camera geometries are shown in Figure 1.

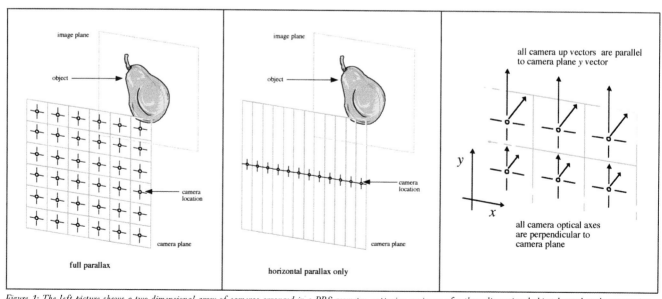

Figure 1: The left picture shows a two-dimensional array of cameras arranged in a PRS geometry, capturing an image of a three-dimensional object located at the recentering plane. The PRS camera geometry captures both vertical and horizontal parallax (full parallax information) of the object. The middle picture depicts a one-dimensional LRS camera geometry, which captures only horizontal parallax. A PRS camera can be created from a set of LRS camera positioned in a regular grid. The right picture shows a detail of the individual camera orientation for RS camera geometries: the cameras are positioned at regular grid locations, with their optical axes (view vectors) all parallel, and their film planes shifted so as to recenter the image plane in each view.

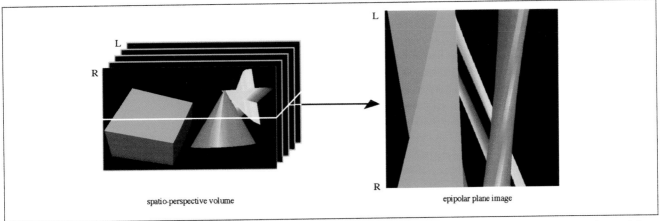

Figure 2: This spatio-perspective volume of a simple polygonal scene is formed by the frames captured by an LRS camera. An epipolar plane image (EPI) is a horizontal slice through this volume. In the scene, the cube and star are diffuse surfaces while the cone is shiny with a specular highlight.

The use of an RS camera introduces several simplifying constraints to the geometry and the mathematics of rendering multiple images. Assuming that a pinhole camera imaging model is used, an unoccluded point in the scene will translate in position from one camera image to the next at a velocity constant for all views and linearly proportional to the point's distance from the recentering plane and the spacing between the cameras in the grid. The relationship between camera position and the point's location in the corresponding image is separable. In other words, a point translating horizontally from one camera's image to another can only be due to a change in horizontal camera position (and similarly true in any other axis of lateral camera displacement). The separable linearity between camera location and image position is the key to maximizing perspective coherence.

7 Spatio-perspective image volume

Considered as a single unit, the set of perspective images from an RS camera form an image volume that spans a region of spatio-perspective space. The three-dimensional perspective image volume from an LRS camera is formed by stacking the individual camera images on top of each other like playing cards. A PRS camera forms an analogous four-dimensional volume. For the purposes of illustration, we will for the moment restrict our explanation to a LRS camera geometry where the camera is moving strictly horizontally.

The original perspectives of the RS camera are slices through the perspective image space. The volume can also be sliced in other ways. The computer vision community has used a construct known as an *epipolar plane image*, or *EPI*, to analyze the output of cameras arranged in (or moved through) a set of spatially disparate locations [4]. EPIs are slices of spatio-perspective space cut parallel to the direction of camera motion. The scanlines that make up EPI *n* are the *n*th scanline from each of the original camera views. Figure 2 shows the frames of a polygonal scene stacked up to form a spatio-perspective image volume. A horizontal slice through the volume at the location shown forms the EPI at right.

EPIs are useful because they expose the perspective coherence of the RS camera geometry. The linear relationship between camera position and the location of image detail manifests itself as linear features called tracks in the EPI. A point in the scene, for instance, sweeps out a linear *point track* in the EPI. Tracks are visible in the EPI as long as objects are visible and in frame as seen from a particular camera location. If an object is occluded by

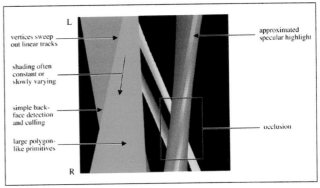

Figure 3: This figure shows some of the graphical properties of an LRS EPI. The large size of the track primitives, the regularity of the linear features, and the assimilation of shading make EPIs appealing to render. Note that specular highlights are not attached to the surface upon which they appear, but instead have their own slope. Since the renderer that produced this image implements Phong lighting but not Phong shading, the specular highlight on the cone is approximate.

another object in one viewpoint, its track will be correspondingly occluded by the other point's track in the EPI. Since points in a scene tend to remain visible over a range of viewing locations, tracks tend to be fairly long in EPI space.

Surfaces in the spatio-perspective volume swept out by lines in the scene are called *line tracks*. Line tracks are twisted quadrilaterals that interpolate between the point tracks of the line segment's two endpoints. A line in the scene that lies in an *epipolar plane* (a plane that includes the line of the camera track and a horizontal scanline) has a line track restricted to a single EPI. The EPI of the line track is formed by projecting its twisted 3D shape into 2D. A line track can occlude or intersect the tracks of other objects in the scene, or even twist itself into a bowtie shape as seen in 2D projection. The occlusion relationship between two different line tracks can be determined by interpolating the depth coordinate of the two endpoint tracks for each line track and occluding the more distant of the two line tracks at every point. These occlusion calculations are very similar to those performed in conventional single viewpoint rendering.

8 Properties of EPIs

The simple EPI shown in Figure 2 demonstrates some of the reasons why EPIs are useful for rendering. Linear track features are compatible with interpolation algorithms implemented in conventional rendering software and hardware. The shape of line tracks are similar to, but even more regular than, the shape of the polygons that are frequently used to describe the geometry of scenes. Tracks are usually very long, spanning many pixels, so that the ratio of pixels spanned by a track versus the vertices needed to describe it is high. Occlusion relationships are essentially the same as in ordinary scenes. The color of objects tends to change slowly with varying viewpoint. Figure 3 shows examples of these and other graphical properties of objects in the EPI from Figure 2.

9 MVR rendering algorithm

The length of the tracks of geometric primitives in spatio-perspective space hints that EPIs of a scene contain more coherence than conventional perspective views of the same scene. This observation, combined with the other graphical properties of LRS EPIs, leads to the basic idea of the MVR algorithm: decompose a geometric scene into primitives that are rendered efficiently into EPIs, then render the spatio-perspective volume, EPI by EPI, until the entire volume is computed. To render a four-dimensional PRS spatio-perspective volume, decompose it into simpler three-dimensional LRS subvolumes that can be rendered individually. (A more sophisticated algorithm could render the 4D spatio-perspective volume as a single unit.) In many ways, MVR can be thought of as a higher-dimensional version of established scan conversion algorithms.

The basic steps of the MVR pipeline are as follows:

Preprocessing and transformation:

- Perform initial scene transformation and view independent lighting calculations for each vertex in the scene,

- Decompose the two-dimensional PRS camera geometry into a set of simpler horizontal LRS cameras,

- For each LRS camera, transform the vertices of the original scene geometry to find its position as seen from the two most extreme camera viewpoints,

Geometric slicing:

- Decompose the scene polygons into horizontal slices that lie along the scanlines of the final image,

- Sort these polygon slices by scanline into a scanline slice table,

Rasterization and hidden surface removal:

- For each scanline entry in the slice table, scan convert the slices for that scanline into tracks in EPI space, performing view-dependent shading calculations and hidden surface removal in the process,

- Combine all EPIs from all LRS cameras into a complete spatio-perspective volume.

The rest of this section describes more specific details of the different stages of the MVR rendering pipeline.

9.1 Preprocessing and transformation

Several of the computational steps used to calculate the appearance of a single image in conventional rendering can be performed once for the entire set of perspective images in multiple viewpoint rendering. For a Gouraud-shaded object, for instance, view independent lighting calculations such as Lambertian reflection can be performed once at each vertex of the scene. The cost of these lighting calculations is independent of the number of views to be rendered; their computational expense is amortized over the entire set of images.

Per-sequence MVR calculations proceed as follows. The geometry of the scene is either read from disk or accessed from memory. For each LRS image set to be rendered, the model is transformed into homogeneous screen space as seen from the two extreme camera viewpoints. (This paper uses a right-handed coordinate system where the x coordinate increases to the right of the screen, y increases up, and z increases out of the screen.) These two camera views differ only in the horizontal direction; because of the RS camera geometry, a vertex seen from these two viewpoints differs strictly in its x coordinate. The redundancy of the calculation means that the cost of performing both endpoint camera transformations is only 1.25 times the cost of performing a single transformation. Following this step, each vertex will have screen space coordinates (x_L, x_R, y, z, w), where x_L and x_R are the x coordinates of the vertex as seen from the extreme left and right camera views.

Next, clipping is performed on the transformed vertex coordinates. Polygons lying completely above or below the view window can be culled, as can those outside the near and far clipping planes. Clipping polygons that partially fall within the view window of at least one view is straightforward but somewhat more complicated than for SVR. In our prototype implementation, we chose to perform no polygon clipping at this stage for simplicity, while risking some performance penalty.

As another result of the RS camera geometry, both the z and w screen-space coordinates of each vertex remain constant over the entire range of viewpoints. Because w is fixed, the homogeneous divide required for perspective transformation are performed as a preprocessing step, reducing the computational cost of transformation. The w coordinate should be maintained, however, to permit perspective-correct shading and texture interpolation during scan conversion [3].

9.2 Geometric slicing

Polygon tracks, or *PT*s, are three-dimensional volume primitives in the spatio-perspective space of an LRS camera geometry. Two-dimensional scan conversion of a PT requires the original polygon be decomposed, or sliced, into a set of line segments that lie along the scanlines of the image set's final perspective images. These line segments are called *polygon slices*.

Slicing a polygon along scanlines is very similar to conventional scan conversion, except that the slices retain their continuous three-dimensionality. As each horizontal slice is generated, a data structure describing it is added to a scanline slice table. This table has one entry per scanline: each entry is a list of polygon slices that the scanline intersects. Thus, each scanline table entry contains all the information needed to render the scanline's EPI, which is in turn the scanline's appearance from all viewpoints.

9.3 Rasterization

When it is rendered, each polygon slice is converted into a special kind of line track called a *polygon slice track* (*PST*) and rendered into the appropriate EPI. The PST is the key rendering primitive of MVR. Figure 4 shows some of the PST shapes from which different slice orientations can result. PSTs have two types of edges. *P-edges* (projection edges) are the projections of the polygon slice as seen from two most extreme camera views. *I-edges* (interpolating edges) interpolate the position of a slice endpoint through the range of views. The geometry of PSTs is very regular; without clipping or culling and disregarding degenerate cases, p-edges are always horizontal and lie at the top and bottom scanline of the EPI, while i-edges cross all EPI scanlines.

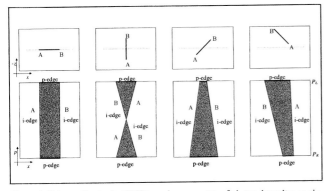

Figure 4: Polygon slice tracks (PSTs) can have a variety of shapes depending on the orientation of the corresponding polygon with respect to the image plane. P-edges are the edges of the PST that are projected onto the camera plane; i-edges interpolate the endpoints of the p-edges through a range of viewpoints. This figure shows several polygon slice orientations (top) and the corresponding PST shape (bottom). The dotted line represents the image or recentering plane of the capture camera.

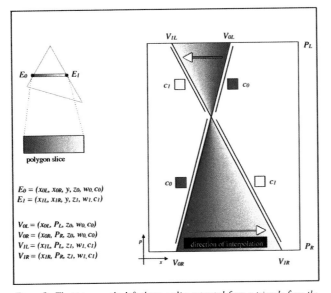

Figure 5: The picture on the left shows a slice extracted from a triangle from the original scene geometry. The coordinates E_0 and E_1 have been interpolated from the triangle's vertices and represent the homogeneous location of the vertex (x_L, x_R, y, z, w) and the view independent per-vertex color (c) calculated there. From these endpoint coordinates, the vertices of the PST V_{0L}, V_{0R}, V_{1L}, and V_{1R} are found. PST rasterization requires linear interpolation of geometric and Gouraud shading parameters in the horizontal direction.

Figure 5 shows how the coordinates of the PST vertices in spatio-perspective space are derived from the endpoints of the polygon slice in screen space. Rasterization of a PST of a diffuse Gouraud-shaded polygon proceeds by interpolating the perspective coordinate in the vertical (p) direction, and all other parameters in the horizontal (x) direction. Every horizontal scanline of the PST crosses through the same range of values for each parameter, but at a different rate of sampling depending on the width of the PST at that scanline. If the i-edges of a PST cross at a point, the direction of interpolation will be opposite from one side of the crossing point to the other, as the figure demonstrates.

Geometric slicing and PST rasterization most distinguish the MVR rendering process from that of a more conventional renderer. By way of example, Figure 6 shows how a single triangle is rendered using MVR and an LRS camera geometry.

9.4 Hidden surface removal

Hidden surface removal (HSR) is performed in spatio-perspective space in the same way it would be performed in image space, and many of the algorithms for HSR can be adapted to work on PSTs instead of polygons. The widely-used Z-buffer algorithm for HSR can be easily implemented by storing a depth value for each pixel in an EPI, and comparing the interpolated depth value for each pixel of the PST being rasterized to see if it is in front of all previous surfaces.

Some aspects of HSR can be simplified in MVR by using the inherent perspective coherence of the scene. Backface culling, for instance, can be performed once per PST instead of once per polygon per viewpoint by observing that the orientation of a polygon slice with respect to the camera changes slowly and predictably. If the i-edges of a PST do not intersect, a backfacing test is required only once for the entire PST, accepting or rejecting it as a whole. If a PST does cross itself, one of the triangles of the PST is back facing and the other is front facing. The back facing piece of the PST need not be rendered.

9.5 Texture mapping

Texture mapping is a type of shading that applies image detail to the surfaces of geometric objects. The appearance of texture maps is view independent: while the geometry onto which the texture is mapped may change depending on the location of the viewer, the appearance of the texture itself does not. Other types of image-level mapping algorithms such as reflection or environment mapping are not view independent; a reflection on a surface can change in appearance as the viewer moves around it. Figure 7 shows a simple polygonal scene with both texture and reflection maps applied to different objects. The corresponding EPI shows how the texture mapped onto the cube and star changes gradually over the entire range of views, in contrast to the less predictable reflection mapped cone. The view independence of texture mapping lends itself to an efficient MVR implementation.

In its simplest form, MVR texture mapping is similar to the analogous algorithms in SVR. Texture coordinates are assigned to each vertex of the original scene geometry, hyperbolic texture coordinates[3] are interpolated to find the texture of each slice endpoint, and textures are further interpolated across the surface of the PST. This simple texturing technique can be used when adapting existing rendering algorithms to render PSTs.

When rendering a large number of views, a more efficient MVR texture map algorithm can be implemented using the fact that each horizontal line of a PST is a resampling of the same texture at a different rate. Figure 8 outlines the steps of this algorithm. The texture for each polygon slice is extracted from two-dimensional texture memory using MIP [21] or area sampling techniques and stored in a one-dimensional texture map at a sampling rate appropriate for the slice's greatest width under transformation. Non-linear sampling of the two-dimensional texture takes care of distortions due to perspective: further resampling of the one-dimensional texture can be performed linearly without need for complex and expensive hyperbolic interpolation when rendering every pixel.

This 1D map is the basis for a new MIP map that is applied to different regions of the PST. Using the 1D map has several advantages over existing texturing algorithms. The width of a PST changes slowly and regularly, so the appropriate level of the MIP map needed to avoid sampling artifacts can readily be chosen. 2D texture memory is probed in a more predictable way, improving

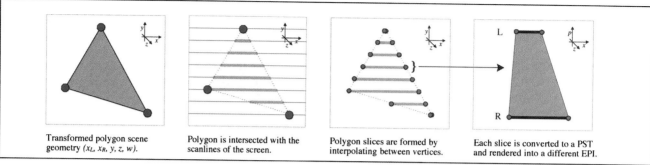

Figure 6: The basic MVR rendering pipeline for the LRS camera geometry, applied to rendering a single triangle.

| Transformed polygon scene geometry (x_L, x_R, y, z, w). | Polygon is intersected with the scanlines of the screen. | Polygon slices are formed by interpolating between vertices. | Each slice is converted to a PST and rendered into a different EPI. |

texture prefetching strategies. The size of the 1D map is small enough to allow efficient caching in fast memory, where the texture of a PST pixel can be computed using linear indexing and simple interpolation. These simple operations suggest the possible use of specialized hardware including image warping subsystems to perform MVR texturing.

9.6 View-dependent shading

View dependent shading of surfaces in MVR can, like texture mapping, be implemented using modified SVR algorithms. Reflection and environment mapping are the most common view dependent shading algorithms in current use. Reflection algorithms calculate reflection vectors at each polygon vertex based on eye, light, and surface orientation vectors, interpolating the reflection vectors across the polygon, and perform a lookup into a reflection map using the interpolated vector. MVR reflection mapping works the same way, except that the eye vector can potentially vary over a large angle through the range of camera positions. Figure 9 describes the relationship between camera geometry and the assignment of reflection vectors to a PST.

When implementing reflection mapping in MVR, care must be taken to assure that reflection calculations are accurate over a large angular change in eye vectors. For example, spherical reflection mapping [16] substitutes complex spherical interpolation with simpler linear interpolation across the extent of polygons. Over large angles, this approximation becomes invalid and results in noticeably incorrect shading of PSTs. One recourse to solve this problem with spherical maps is to uniformly subdivide PSTs in the perspective dimension at the cost of performance. Cubic reflection maps, on the other hand, correctly interpolate reflection vectors and can be used without subdivision.

Although view dependent shading does not attain the level of efficiency in MVR as does view independent shading, it can still be more efficient than a comparable SVR algorithm. Computational savings result from the precalculation and incremental interpolation of reflection vectors over PSTs and the regularity of the reflection vector's mapping into the reflection map memory.

10 Implementation

The MVR algorithm described in this paper generates a set of perspective images from cameras arranged in a PRS camera geometry, using computer graphics hardware to accelerate the rendering process. The prototype implementation described here is designed to fairly compare the relative efficiency of MVR and conventional SVR algorithms. The implementation consists of shared modules for file input and output, scene transformation, and texturing and reflection mapping, as well as MVR or SVR-specific modules for primitive generation, rendering and image

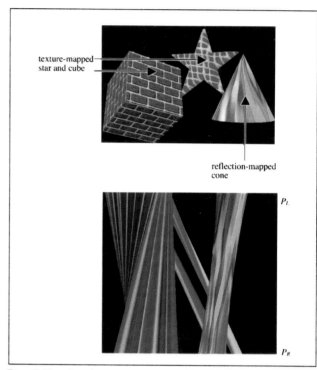

Figure 7: The cube and star in this polygonal scene are texture mapped, while the cone is reflection mapped. The EPI of a scanline of the scene is extracted and shown in the lower picture.

assembly. The code for the implementation is written in ANSI C and uses the OpenGL™ graphics library to provide device-independent graphics acceleration. The algorithm has been tested on a range of workstations from Silicon Graphics Inc., including an Indigo^2 workstation with Maximum Impact graphics and a 150 MHz R4400 CPU, and an Onyx with RealityEngine^2 graphics and two 150 MHz R4400 CPUs. Further tests were done using a Sun Microsystems Ultra 1 workstation with Creator3D graphics.

Input data for the tests consisted of two polygonal models: one of a teacup, the other of a Ferio automobile body shell provided by the Honda R&D Company (Figure 10). These scenes were created using Alias/Wavefront Corporation's Alias Studio modeling program. From original surface models, Alias Studio calculates per-vertex view independent lighting and texture coordinate values, and outputs a collection of independent triangles to a file. This triangle data eliminates the need for view independent lighting to be implemented in the rendering testbed itself. In

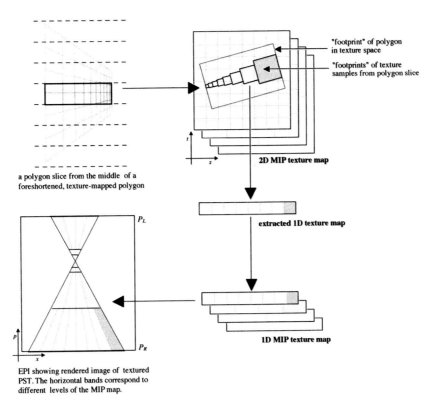

a polygon slice from the middle of a
foreshortened, texture-mapped polygon

"footprint" of polygon
in texture space

"footprints" of texture
samples from polygon slice

2D MIP texture map

extracted 1D texture map

1D MIP texture map

P_L

P_R

EPI showing rendered image of textured
PST. The horizontal bands correspond to
different levels of the MIP map.

Figure 8: An MVR-specific algorithm for texture mapping extracts the texture for a polygon slice from two-dimensional memory, builds a 1D MIP map, and repeatedly resamples it to apply the texture to scanlines of the PST. This process eliminates the need for a per-pixel homogeneous divide.

addition the teacup was tessellated to produce 4K, 16K, 63K, 99K, and 143K triangle count models in order to compare the efficiency of MVR when rendering polygons of different average sizes.

10.1 MVR renderer

The MVR module consists of a polygon slicer, a scanline slice table, a slice-to-PST converter, and an EPI rasterizer. PSTs are rendered in hardware by approximating them as polygons. Although PST shading and interpolation is actually easier than shading triangles because of their regular geometry, current rendering hardware designed for optimized triangle rendering produces shading artifacts across the PST (and many other quadrilaterals [22]). Such errors can be reduced by minimizing the size of polygons, reducing the range of viewpoints, or decomposing the PST into smaller primitives. During testing, a minimal decomposition of PSTs into no more than four triangles was used for both timing and rendering accuracy tests. A hardware rendering system specifically designed for MVR could provide higher quality rendering at rates faster than the fastest rates described here.

Texturing and reflection mapping were implemented in the MVR module without using MVR-specific algorithms in order to use existing graphics hardware to accelerate these operations. Reflection mapping uses spherical environment maps to simulate surrounding objects and Phong-like specular highlights. Figure 11 shows a two-dimensional array of images rendered using MVR with both texture and reflection mapping. Figure 12 is an EPI from the teacup, from a scanline near the cup's lip.

10.2 SVR renderer

The SVR module was designed to minimize redundant operations consistent with rendering a set of images. For instance, the initial transformation of the scene triangles, performed on the CPU and not in the graphics engine, is done only once for all views. The graphics hardware's transformation matrices were not updated from view to view for the SVR speed tests: only the image of the central view was used as an approximation of the per-frame rendering speed. If anything, this approximation should underestimate the rendering time for the SVR algorithm. For both the SVR and MVR modules, speed tests do not include the time required to read back data from framebuffer memory. Applications that use a set of perspective images are almost certain to need the rendered images as data in main memory, not just on the screen, but reading framebuffer memory requires approximately the same time in either SVR or MVR.

The next section presents the results of speed and rendering accuracy tests performed using the prototype rendering implementation.

11 Performance

11.1 Timing tests

The graph in Figure 13 shows the performance of the different stages of the MVR pipeline when rendering the Ferio database at a resolution of 640 by 480 pixels per view over a varying number of views of an LRS camera. Only view independent shading was performed for this test. Timings were performed on the SGI Indigo². The cost of reading triangles, transforming them (includ-

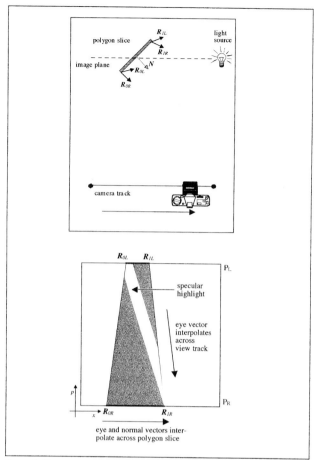

Figure 9: The top figure shows an LRS camera viewing a polygon slice with a surface normal **N** across its surface. The slice endpoints each have two reflection vectors **R** that result from view vectors from the two camera track endpoints. These four reflection vectors are assigned to the PST shown in the EPI in the bottom figure.

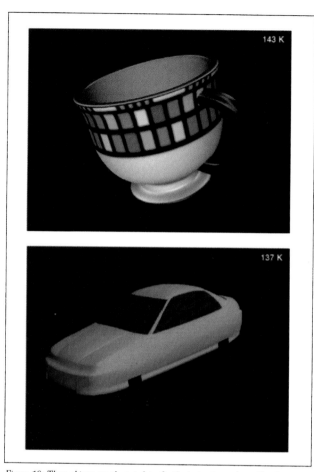

Figure 10: These objects are the test data for the prototype renderer. Numbers indicate the triangle count of the two models shown here. These images are extracted from a set of MVR-rendered perspective images.

ing conventional transformation and the additional cost of calculating horizontally and vertically varying parallax information), and slicing the polygons is constant. The cost of rendering less than about 400 primitives is also constant: the hardware setup time for the PSTs is greater than the cost of concurrently painting the pixels of the PSTs onto the screen. The line on the far left side of the graph shows the relative cost of rendering using the SVR module. In this test, MVR is more efficient than SVR for images sets larger than about 10 views.

Figure 14 directly compares the time required to render scenes of different tessellation using both MVR and SVR. The teacup models of different tessellation densities were rendered using both algorithms using the SGI Onyx. The graph shows that the smaller the polygons, the better MVR performed relative to SVR. This behavior is due to the increased spatial coherence in the smaller polygon scenes: SVR better amortizes per-polygon setup costs over a larger number of pixels drawn to the screen. At best case for this resolution, MVR is about 26 times faster than SVR.

Figure 15 shows a comparison between SVR and MVR using a polygon database of fixed size, but with a varying pixel resolution of the output images. The Indigo[2] system was used to render the Ferio database for this test. In the SVR timing results, the hardware is not pixel fill rate limited at any of the resolutions. Thus, rendering times are independent of the pixel size of the

image. MVR performance is, on the other hand, dependent on image resolution. Smaller images result in fewer PSTs to render. At the lowest image resolution, for example, MVR is more than 200 times faster than SVR. These low-resolution images have application in three-dimensional display devices, where light modulators may have a low pixel count.

The shape of the MVR timing curves reflects the different types of cost savings when rendering different numbers of views. For a small view count, geometry costs dominate pixel fill and adding more views are essentially free. The knee of the curve represents the point where the cost of the concurrently-performed geometry and fill operations are equal. The slope to the right of the knee of the curve levels off as the costs of sequential preprocessing operations are amortized over increasingly many views.

11.2 Rendering accuracy

Ideally in the most common case, there should be no difference between the image sets rendered using MVR and those rendered conventionally with MVR. However, some errors in shading may occur because of algorithm-dependent differences in rasterization or shading. To test the accuracy of MVR, the 143K teacup was used as a model for both MVR and SVR to render sixteen views at 640 by 480 pixels. From these two collections of

Figure 11: A set of texture mapped and reflection mapped images computed using MVR.

Figure 12: An EPI of the teacup.

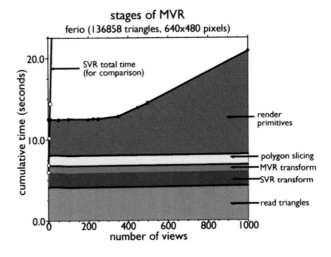

Figure 13: Relative costs of the different stages of MVR, using an LRS camera, when rendering different numbers of views. Total rendering time of SVR is included for reference.

views, four pairs were extracted, and the absolute values of their pixel-by-pixel differences computed. Rendering was done using the Sun Ultra 1. No PST subdivision was used when rendering using MVR.

The result of this difference is shown in Figure 16. An enlarged piece of the error image is shown in Figure 17. The largest errors located along the edge of the cup are most likely due to small differences in transformation between the two rendering modules; these differences are never more than one pixel wide in any view. Errors on the interior of the teacup result from differences in

shading between the two algorithms. Neither error is generally noticeable in practice.

When rendering small numbers of widely disparate views, however, shading differences between MVR and SVR can be significant. The reason for this difference is SVR makes no guarantees that the track of a object in spatio-perspective space is continuous, while MVR does; the track of any MVR-rendered feature is bandlimited so that the images of the feature abut from view to view. The MVR behavior, while different than that of SVR, provides sufficient sampling to avoid aliasing artifacts in image-based rendering and synthetic holographic displays [12].

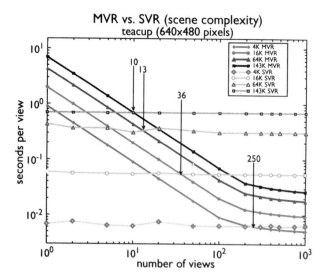

Figure 14: This graph compares the performance of SVR and MVR algorithms while rendering the same scene at different tessellation densities. The arrows in the graph show the "break even" points where SVR and MVR take the same amount of time to render the image volume.

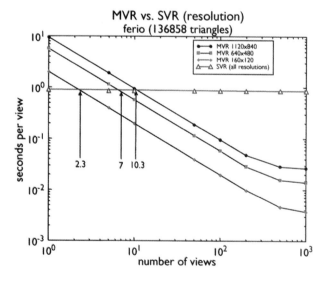

Figure 15: The graph compares SVR and MVR performance at different image resolutions.

11.3 Interpreting the results

These results for scenes with view independent shading demonstrate that MVR is capable of exceeding the performance of SVR algorithms by one to two orders of magnitude. Further testing confirms that these savings are also true for texture- and reflection-mapped scenes, and for PRS cameras constructed from multiple LRS cameras. MVR is faster than SVR for rendering large sets of perspective images for several reasons. First, a significant number of transformation and shading operations are performed as preprocessing steps, incurring a constant cost that is amortized over the entire set of images. In the RS camera geometry, this preprocess-

ing can include the otherwise-costly homogeneous divide required during perspective transformations.

Second, the ratio of the pixel size of rendered primitives to the number of vertices that describe those primitives' geometry is much higher for PSTs in MVR than for ordinary polygons when rendering many viewpoints. Since rendering hardware often uses more expensive floating point representations to describe and transform vertices, and fixed-point or integer calculations to deal with pixels, improving the pixel-to-vertex ratio of geometric primitives can often lead to dramatic improvements in performance. Many other techniques exist for changing the pixel-to-vertex ratio, including building geometry strips and compressing the scene's geometric description [7]. The use of these techniques and the tuning of software and hardware that makes up a specific rendering pipeline can control whether rendering of a given scene is geometry or pixel fill limited. MVR is an additional technique that shifts the balance towards high pixel-to-vertex ratios; it can also be combined with other techniques such as geometry strips or compression to achieve still more pixels per vertex.

Third, shading and texturing PSTs is less complex than the equivalent operations on polygons. PSTs have a more regular shape and size than do polygons from the same scene. PSTs can be shaded and textured using only horizontal interpolation between i-edges for each scanline of a PST. Perspective-correct texture mapping can be performed using only linear resampling of a perspective-predistorted subtexture, eliminating a per-pixel divide, improving memory access and cache performance, and simplifying possible hardware implementation. Backface culling and hidden surface removal can both be implemented to take advantage of perspective coherence.

The exact impact of these cost-saving properties on the time required to render a perspective image set depends on the architecture of the computer rendering subsystem (including the relative costs of vertex operations, pixel fills, memory access and communication), the resolution and count of the output images, and the properties of the particular scene being rendered. A graphics system with a very limited pixel fill rate, for example, may experience little or no savings from MVR. The following rule can be used to determine the general applicability of MVR to a particular application: if the height in pixels of an average polygon in a scene is smaller than the number of viewpoints to be rendered, MVR will likely be as fast or faster than an SVR algorithm. For this number of views, the pixel-to-vertex ratio for SVR and MVR is approximately equal.

12 Comparison to other work

Several other researchers have developed computer graphics algorithms that use some form of frame-to-frame coherence. Badt [2], Chapman *et. al.* [5], and Groeller and Purgathofer [9] have produced ray-tracing algorithms that use temporal coherence to improve multi-frame rendering performance. Each of these algorithms produce modest computational savings over conventional ray-tracing techniques. Tost and Brunet characterized a variety of frame coherent algorithms in a 1990 taxonomy[20]. Adelson *et. al.* [1] used perspective coherence to compute pairs of images for stereoscopic displays. Because their algorithm only computes pairs of images, only limited acceleration due to perspective coherence is possible.

The computer vision and image processing fields have used epipolar plane image analysis as a way to interpolate intermediate viewpoints from a set of photographically acquired images. Takahashi *et. al.* [18] have used these methods to generate images

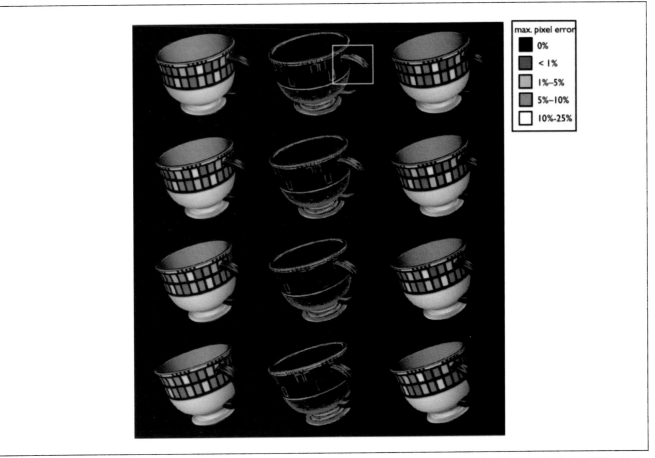

Figure 16: *The four images on the left side of the figure were calculated using conventional SVR rendering techniques. The set on the right was rendered using MVR, with the four images extracted from a set of sixteen. In the middle is the per-pixel absolute value of the difference between the two sets (as a percentage of the maximum possible difference), colorized to more clearly show error regions. The rectangular area is enlarged in Figure 17.*

Figure 17: *An enlargement of the difference image from Figure 16. The blue and green interior areas are the result of shading differences, while the broken red and white lines are probably the result of slight misregistration of geometry.*

for holographic stereograms. Image interpolation of this kind requires finding corresponding points in different images (the underconstrained "correspondence problem" of computer vision).

Hybrid computer graphics and image processing algorithms reduce the need to solve the correspondence problem by augmenting image information with more data from the original scene. Zeghers *et. al.* [23] use motion-compensated interpolation to produce a series of intermediate frames in an image sequence of fully computed frames. The disadvantages of this algorithm are the need to compute a motion field, and the loss of fine detail in the scene because of image space interpolation.

Chen and Williams [6] also use geometry information to guide viewpoint interpolation. Using known camera geometries, their algorithm builds an image space morph map from two images and depth buffers. This technique can be used to reduce the cost of shadow and motion blur generation, since intermediate images can be computed in time independent of the geometric complexity of the scene. They propose methods for reducing the "overlaps" and "holes" in the data between two images. These problems can only be minimized, not eliminated, however. The image space interpolation cannot correctly deal with anti-aliased input images, specular highlights, and other view dependent scene changes.

Instead of using a limited amount of scene information from an image space buffer, MVR interpolates intermediate views using the object precision of the original scene geometry. It incorporates image interpolation as part of the rendering process without any need to deal with the difficult computer vision problems of correspondence. The cost of rendering intermediate views is dependent on the complexity of the scene geometry. However, MVR is more compatible with the interpolation hardware found in hardware graphics systems.

13 Conclusions and future work

New applications in computer graphics such as three-dimensional display and image-based rendering need large sets of perspective images as input. MVR extends conventional scanline rendering algorithms to provide these sets of images at rates one to two orders of magnitude faster than existing methods. MVR can generate high quality images using texture and reflection maps, and can be accelerated using both existing and future graphics hardware. Many rendering techniques not described here can be adapted for use with MVR. MVR techniques can also be extended to alternate camera geometries, geometry compression, and transmission of three-dimensional geometry information.

Acknowledgments

The work described in this paper was done as part of my doctoral dissertation at the Spatial Imaging Group of the MIT Media Laboratory. Thanks to everyone in the group who helped me think through these ideas and reviewed drafts of this paper, including Wendy Plesniak, Ravikanth Pappu, and John Underkoffler. Wendy Plesniak also modeled the teacup used in the figures. My advisor Stephen Benton and my thesis committee members V. Michael Bove and Seth Teller provided great comments and support. Ron Kikinis and Ferenc Jolesz at BWH supported me during the last year of this work, in part through funding from Robert Sproull at Sun Microsystems. Both Silicon Graphics and Sun Microsystems provided equipment used in this research. Also, thanks to the SIGGRAPH reviewers for their thoughtful comments and suggestions.

This work was funded in part by the Design Staff of the General Motors Corporation, the Honda R&D Company, IBM, NEC, and the Office of Naval Research (Grant N0014-96-11200).

References

[1] Stephen J. Adelson, Jeffrey B. Bentley, In Seok Chung, Larry F. Hodges, and Joseph Winograd. Simultaneous Generation of Stereoscopic Views. *Computer Graphics Forum*, 10(1):3-10, March 1991.

[2] Sig Badt, Jr. Two Algorithms for Taking Advantage of Temporal Coherence in Ray Tracing. *The Visual Computer*, 4(3):123-132, September 1988.

[3] James F. Blinn. Jim Blinn's corner: Hyperbolic Interpolation. *IEEE Computer Graphics and Applications*, 12(4):89-94, July 1992.

[4] R. C. Bolles, H. H. Baker, and D. H. Marimont. Epipolar-Plane Image Analysis: An Approach to Determining Structure from Motion. *Inter. J. Computer Vision*, 1:7-55, 1987.

[5] J. Chapman, T. W. Calvert, and J. Dill. Exploiting Temporal Coherence in Ray Tracing. In *Proceedings of Graphics Interface '90*, pages 196-204, May 1990.

[6] Shenchang Eric Chen and Lance Williams. View Interpolation for Image Synthesis. In James T. Kajiya, editor, *Computer Graphics* (SIGGRAPH 93 Proceedings), volume 27, pages 279-288, August 1993.

[7] Michael Deering. Geometry Compression. In Robert Cook, editor, *SIGGRAPH 95 Conference Proceedings*, Annual Conference Series, pages 13–20, August 1995.

[8] Steven J. Gortler, Radek Grzeszczuk, Richard Szeliski, and Michael F. Cohen. The Lumigraph. In Holly Rushmeier, editor, *SIGGRAPH 96 Conference Proceedings*, Annual Conference Series, pages 43-54, August 1996.

[9] E. Groeller and W. Purgathofer. Using Temporal and Spatial Coherence for Accelerating the Calculation of Animation Sequences. In Werner Purgathofer, editor, *Eurographics '91*, pages 103-113. North-Holland, September 1991.

[10] Michael W. Halle. Autostereoscopic Displays and Computer Graphics. In *Computer Graphics*, ACM SIGGRAPH. 31(2), pages 58-62.

[11] Michael W. Halle. The Generalized Holographic Stereogram. Master's thesis, Department of Architecture and Planning, Massachusetts Institute of Technology, February 1991.

[12] Michael W. Halle. Holographic Stereograms as Discrete Imaging Systems. In *Practical Holography VIII*, vol. 2176, pages 73–84, SPIE, May 1994.

[13] Michael W. Halle. Multiple Viewpoint Rendering for Autostereoscopic Displays. Ph.D. thesis, Media Arts and Sciences Section, Massachusetts Institute of Technology, May 1997.

[14] Marc Levoy and Pat Hanrahan. Light Field Rendering. In Holly Rushmeier, editor, *SIGGRAPH 96 Conference Proceedings*, Annual Conference Series, pages 31-42, August 1996.

[15] T. Okoshi. *Three-Dimensional Imaging Techniques*. Academic Press, New York, 1976.

[16] Mark Segal, Carl Korobkin, Rolf van Widenfelt, Jim Foran, and Paul E. Haeberli. Fast Shadows and Lighting Effects using Texture Mapping. In Edwin E. Catmull, editor, *Computer Graphics* (SIGGRAPH 92 Proceedings), volume 26, pages 249-252, July 1992.

[17] Ivan E. Sutherland, Robert F. Sproull, and Robert A. Schumacker. A Characterization of Ten Hidden-Surface Algorithms. *Computing Surveys*, 6(1), March 1974.

[18] S. Takahashi, T. Honda, M. Yamaguchi, N. Ohyama, and F. Iwata. Generation of Intermediate Parallax-images for Holographic stereograms. In *Practical Holography VII: Imaging and Materials*, pages 2+, SPIE, 1993.

[19] Jay Torborg and Jim Kajiya. Talisman: Commodity Real-time 3D Graphics for the PC. In Holly Rushmeier, editor, *SIGGRAPH 96 Conference Proceedings*, Annual Conference Series, pages 353-364, August 1996.

[20] Daniele Tost and Pere Brunet. A Definition of Frame-To-Frame Coherence. In N. Magnenat-Thalmann and D. Thalmann, editors, *Computer Animation '90*, pages 207-225, April 1990.

[21] Lance Williams. Pyramidal Parametrics. In *Computer Graphics* (SIGGRAPH '83 Proceedings), volume 17, pages 1-11, July 1983.

[22] Andrew Woo, Andrew Pearce, and Marc Ouellette. It's Really Not a Rendering Bug, You See.... *IEEE Computer Graphics and Applications*, 16(5):21-25, September 1996.

[23] Eric Zeghers, Kadi Bouatouch, Eric Maisel, and Christian Bouville. Faster Image Rendering in Animation Through Motion Compensated Interpolation. In *Graphics, Design and Visualization*, pages 49+. International Federation for Information Processing Transactions, 1993.

Progressive Radiance Evaluation Using Directional Coherence Maps

Baining Guo
Intel Corporation*

Abstract

We develop a progressive refinement algorithm that generates an approximate image quickly, then gradually refines it towards the final result. Our algorithm can reconstruct a high-quality image after evaluating only a small percentage of the pixels. For a typical scene, evaluating only 6% of the pixels yields an approximate image that is visually hard to distinguish from an image with all the pixels evaluated. At this low sampling rate, previous techniques such as adaptive stochastic sampling suffer from artifacts including heavily jagged edges, missing object parts, and missing high-frequency details.

A key ingredient of our algorithm is the directional coherence map (DCM), a new technique for handling general radiance discontinuities in a progressive ray tracing framework. Essentially an encoding of the directional coherence in image space, the DCM performs well on discontinuities that are usually considered extremely difficult, e.g. those involving non-polygonal geometry or caused by secondary light sources. Incorporating the DCM into a ray tracing system incurs only a negligible amount of additional computation. More importantly, the DCM uses little memory and thus it preserves the strengths of ray tracing systems in dealing with complex scenes.

We have implemented our algorithm on top of RADIANCE. Our enhanced system can produce high-quality images significantly faster than RADIANCE – sometimes by orders of magnitude. Moreover, when the baseline system becomes less effective as its Monte Carlo components are challenged by difficult lighting configurations, our system will still produce high quality images by redistributing computation to the small percentage of pixels as dictated by the DCM.

CR Categories: I.3.7 [Computer Graphics]: Three-Dimensional Graphics and Realism; I.3.3 [Computer Graphics]: Picture/Image Generation.

Keywords: Progressive refinement, image-space discontinuities, directional coherence, radiance evaluation, rendering

1 Introduction

Despite the rapidly increasing power of computers, global illumination is far from being a real-time process. Accurate radiance evaluations often require hours of computation for complex scenes. To balance rendering speed and visual realism, global illumination algorithms often take a "progressive refinement" approach. In the radiosity framework, Cohen [8] extended earlier work by Bergman [2] and developed a progressive refinement algorithm that produces successive approximations, refining continuously towards the final radiosity solution.

As an acceleration strategy, the idea of progressive refinement is readily applicable to radiance evaluation, which must account for all major modes of light transport. One approach to progressive radiance evaluation is to combine progressive radiosity with ray tracing in a multi-pass system (e.g. [6, 27]). Alternatively, we can use a progressive ray tracing algorithm based on Monte Carlo light transport [16]. Compared to the multi-pass approach, progressive ray tracing has several important advantages in real-world applications. In particular, ray tracing uses much less memory than radiosity, while placing fewer restrictions on surface geometry and reflectance models.

This paper develops a radiance evaluation algorithm using progressive ray tracing. Based on the hierarchical integration technique by Kajiya [16], Painter has proposed an adaptive sampling method for progressively refining a ray traced image [23] (see also [37]). One of his important contributions was to recognize that in a progressive ray tracing system, different sampling strategies apply to the task of locating image features and the task of increasing pixel confidence [23].[1] Our main goal is to capture image features early and generate high-quality images as quickly as possible. A fundamental obstacle facing adaptive sampling techniques (including the edge following methods for anti-aliasing [3, 12, 38]) is that these techniques cannot produce high-quality images before densely sampling all the high-frequency details. We overcome this obstacle with knowledge about discontinuities.

Researchers have been aware of the importance of discontinuities for decades, and investigations in this area have led to algorithms for shadows (e.g. [10, 7, 5, 30, 32, 28, 11]) and discontinuity meshing (e.g. [14, 20]). The discontinuities computed by these object-space algorithms may be projected and inserted into an image-plane discontinuity mesh (IPDM), as was proposed by Pighin [24]. The IPDM produces dramatically better shadows from early on, but there are problems, including difficulties in handling non-polygonal geometry and discontinuities caused by secondary sources, as well as the substantial space requirements for discontinuity computations with a complex scene. A big source of inefficiency in the existing discontinuity algorithms is that they try to locate *potential* discontinuities instead of the actual discontinuities. In addition, these object-space algorithms cannot deal with the view-dependent specular components of radiance discontinuities.

A key ingredient of our algorithm is the *directional coherence map* (DCM), a new technique for handling general radiance discontinuities in a progressive ray tracing framework. The DCM includes

---

*Microcomputer Research Labs, RN6-35, 2200 Mission College Blvd, Santa Clara, CA 95052, email: baining_guo@ccm.sc.intel.com

---

[1]The task of increasing pixel confidence has attracted extensive research in the context of anti-aliasing [13]. We do not develop new anti-aliasing techniques; instead we construct our progressive renderer on top of a baseline ray tracer such that the pixel confidences of our system depend on the sampling strategy of the baseline system. By building our progressive renderer this way, we know in advance that we will capture the same set of features as the baseline system does.

two main components: an adaptive partition of the image plane into square blocks, such that each block is simple enough to have at most one discontinuity edge, and an estimation of the orientation of the discontinuity edge in each block. The DCM helps us to capture radiance discontinuities through a finite element approximation to the radiance function, with the finite elements on each block oriented in accordance with the orientation of the discontinuity within that block.

In facing the challenge of treating general radiance discontinuities, our overall strategy is to combine object-space and image-space data. Specifically, we efficiently obtain object boundaries in the image using the Z-buffer hardware [36]. By doing so we benefit from the *a priori* knowledge of the scene. We extract other discontinuities from densely evaluated pixels on the block boundaries in the DCM. Extracting discontinuity information from radiance samples is a unique feature of our algorithm. This feature not only allows us to treat several types of discontinuities ignored by previous algorithms, but also saves us time by focusing on the *actual* discontinuities.

We have implemented our progressive rendering algorithm using RADIANCE [33] as the baseline system. To render images of comparable quality, our system typically takes $1/4$ to $1/15$ of the time needed by RADIANCE. When their Monte Carlo components are challenged by difficult lighting configurations, RADIANCE and other ray tracing systems for global illumination [27] will become less effective. In this situation, our system can still produce high quality images by reallocating computational resources to increase the accuracy of the small percentage of pixels needed by the DCM. Fig. 12 demonstrates this capability. The DCM performs well on a variety of discontinuities, including those that can be handled by existing discontinuity algorithms (see, e.g., Fig. 10 with fine shadows cast by polygonal occluders) and those that cannot (see, e.g., Fig. 13 with closely packed surfaces which are both curved and specular). Finally, compared to Painter's successful system based on progressive adaptive sampling [23], our system generates far better images for the same amount of computation time, as Fig. 2 (c) and Fig. 4 show.

The remainder of the paper is organized as follows. In Section 2, we give a high level overview of the progressive rendering pipeline in our system. Section 3 describes the treatment of a block with simple discontinuities, which serves as the foundation of the DCM and is based on the least discrepancy direction and oriented finite elements. Section 4 discusses the initialization and refinements of the DCM, detailing steps for partitioning the image plane into blocks and tests for determining if a block has only simple discontinuities. Section 5 provides the details of our implementation. Results are presented in Section 6, followed in Section 7 by conclusions and suggestions for future work.

2 System Overview

Our progressive rendering system relies on a baseline ray tracing system for pixel radiance evaluations. This type of ray tracing system was first proposed by Kajiya [16], building on earlier work by Cook [9] and Whitted [35]. For simplicity, we assume the baseline system generates an anti-aliased image by filtering an enlarged *work image* of super-sample resolution (this assumption can be relaxed to allow baseline ray tracers that collect super-samples for individual pixels of the output image). Our progressive rendering system augments the baseline system with a component responsible for deciding where to sample and how to reconstruct an approximate image on user demand.

The rendering pipeline of our system, shown in Fig. 1, has two main stages. The first is the regular subdivision stage, in which we use a quadtree to partition the image plane into small blocks. We refer to these blocks as elementary blocks. To perform the regular

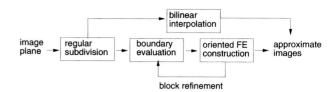

Figure 1: The rendering pipeline of our system. The approximate image is available any time, on demand. When all blocks are of the pixel size, the iterative block refinement terminates with the approximate image output as the final image.

subdivision, we start with the entire image plane as the root block and recursively subdivide each block in four until the current block has become an elementary one. During the regular subdivision, the four corners of each block are sampled, and an approximate image may be created for display at any time by interpolating the corner values. Fig. 2 (a) shows an example image at the end of the regular subdivision stage.

The second stage is an iterative process in which we begin constructing and refining the DCM. In each iteration, we select a subset of blocks as edge blocks and analyze them for discontinuities; blocks not selected simply go through another step of regular subdivision. On each edge block, we densely sample the block boundary (not just the four corners) and subdivide the block into four quads for the next iteration. From the evaluated boundary pixels and some additional object-space data, we infer the discontinuities on each edge block and record the information into the DCM. With this information, an oriented finite element approximation is constructed on the block. The oriented finite elements on edge blocks and the bilinear interpolants on the other blocks may be resampled into an approximate image at the user's request. Figs. 2 (b) and (c) are images from the second stage. Fig. 2 (d) is the final image.

3 Blocks with Simple Discontinuities

Taking a divide-and-conquer approach, the DCM treats discontinuities by partitioning the image plane into small blocks so that most blocks are crossed by no more than one discontinuity edge. Moreover, the edge is expected to have small curvature like the example in Fig. 3 (a) as opposed to the corner in Fig. 3 (b). Since the effectiveness of the DCM depends on its performance on blocks with simple discontinuities, we wish to capture such discontinuities using a small number of samples. Traditionally, adaptive sampling techniques [22, 23, 13] are used to reduce the amount of sampling needed to capture features or discontinuities. Adaptive sampling is effective in that it significantly reduces sampling in areas away from discontinuities. However, adaptive sampling is not completely satisfactory for us because it does not produce good images unless the discontinuity areas have been densely sampled. In this section, we explore an alternative based on least discrepancy directions and oriented finite elements.

3.1 Discontinuity Characteristics

A simple way to capture a discontinuity edge within a block is to build a mathematical model for the edge. Since the block is small, the edge can be regarded as straight, and we can model its behavior by locating the endpoints on the block boundary. This is essentially the approach we take, even though the basic idea is modified in several ways to accommodate the special properties of image data.

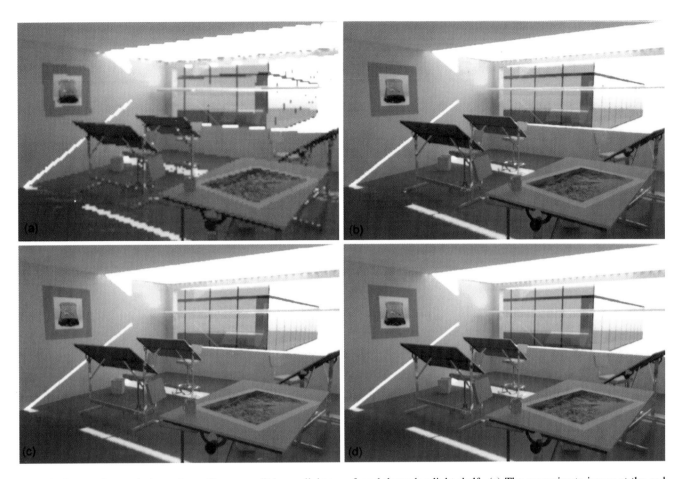

Figure 2: Progressive renderings of an office scene lit by sunlight transferred through a light shelf. (a) The approximate image at the end of the regular subdivision, with 1.6% evaluated pixels located at the corners of the 8×8 blocks in the work image. (b) The approximate image after boundary evaluations for all 8×8 edge blocks in the work image, with 5% of pixels evaluated. (c) The approximate image after evaluating about 6% of the pixels, whose locations are shown in Fig. 5 (bottom left). (d) The final image as rendered by the baseline RADIANCE system. The scene model was supplied courtesy of Greg W. Larson.

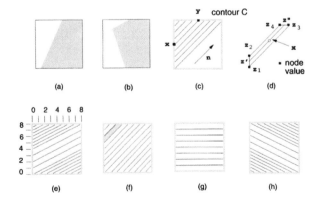

Figure 3: Discontinuity analysis on a block. The discontinuity in (a) is considered simple whereas that in (b) is not, because of the corner. The geometry for the least-discrepancy direction is given in (c). In (d) we show the construction of a typical bilinear element $f_e(\mathbf{x})$ on a quadrilateral $Q = [\mathbf{z}_1\mathbf{z}_2\mathbf{z}_3\mathbf{z}_4]$ with known node values $f_n(\mathbf{z}_i)$, $i = 1 : 4$. Essentially this construction is a Gouraud interpolation with the scanline rotated to be parallel with the least-discrepancy direction. Note that (d) is a zoomed version of the shaded element in (f). Finally, oriented finite elements are shown in (e) through (h) for four different orientations.

Working with image data differs fundamentally from working with geometric data. The discontinuity edges computed by discontinuity meshing algorithms have two properties. First, the discontinuities are abstract mathematical lines with no shape or width. Second, discontinuities are either present or absent at a given location. In contrast, image edges have spatial scales (e.g. sharp or fuzzy) and their existence at a given location is modulated by their strength [21] (a weak edge may be just a faint wisp). These properties of image edges create challenges. For example, it is no longer trivial to define the location of the edge. In addition, the fact that image edges have characteristics such as shape and strength requires more information to be estimated with the small amount of sampling at our disposal.

The least discrepancy direction and oriented finite element discussed below form an integrated approach to extracting discontinuity information from image data and modeling the discontinuities in a finite element approximation to the block radiance function. This approach does not explicitly refer to discontinuity locations, and it models edge shape as well as strength. Our discussions on the least-discrepancy direction and oriented finite elements can be easily extended to any convex image blocks, including the non-square blocks often encountered in a quadtree subdivision of the image plane.

3.2 The Least Discrepancy Direction

The least discrepancy direction $\mathbf{m}(B_k)$ of a $k \times k$ block B_k is defined to be the unit vector that minimizes the contour integral

$$d(\mathbf{n}) = \frac{1}{s} \int_C \left(f(\mathbf{x} + t(\mathbf{x})\,\mathbf{n}) - f(\mathbf{x}) \right)^2 ds,$$

where C is the boundary contour of B_k and s is arc length (the reader may observe that the integration actually only needs to extend over half the contour). For a fixed direction $\mathbf{n}$ and a point $\mathbf{x}$ on C, the scalar $t(\mathbf{x})$ is chosen such that the parametric line $\mathbf{y}(t) = \mathbf{x} + t\,\mathbf{n}$ intersects the contour C at $\mathbf{x}$ and $\mathbf{y} = \mathbf{x} + t(\mathbf{x})\,\mathbf{n}$, as is shown Fig. 3 (c). Once the radiance function $f(\mathbf{x})$ is known on the contour C through boundary evaluation, the *directional discrepancy* $d(\mathbf{n})$ is a well-defined function of the direction $\mathbf{n}$.

For implementation, we let $\mathbf{n} = [\cos\theta, \sin\theta]$ and discretize the angular range $0 \le \theta < \pi$ into h different directions $\theta_i = i\pi/h$, $i = 0 : (h-1)$. For each direction $\mathbf{n}_i = [\cos\theta_i, \sin\theta_i]$, the directional discrepancy $d(\mathbf{n}_i)$ is evaluated as

$$d_i = d(\mathbf{n}_i) = \frac{1}{4(k-1)} \sum_{\mathbf{p} \in P} (f(\mathbf{p} + t(\mathbf{p})\,\mathbf{n}_i) - f(\mathbf{p}))^2,$$

where P is the set of all pixels in C and $t(\mathbf{p})$ is chosen such that the line $\mathbf{y}(t) = \mathbf{p} + t\,\mathbf{n}_i$ intersects the contour C at $\mathbf{p}$ and $\mathbf{p}' = \mathbf{p} + t(\mathbf{p})\,\mathbf{n}_i$. Even though $\mathbf{p}$ is a pixel location, $\mathbf{p}'$ may not be, in which case $f(\mathbf{p}')$ is linearly interpolated from two adjacent pixel values. From the evaluated sequence $\{d_0, ..., d_{h-1}\}$, we find the minimizer $d_j = \min\{d_0, ..., d_{h-1}\}$ and set the least discrepancy direction $\mathbf{m}(B_k) = \mathbf{n}_j$.

3.3 Oriented Finite Elements

Once the least discrepancy direction is known, the radiance function is approximated by a finite element function whose elements are oriented along the least discrepancy direction. This finite element approximation is a continuous function consisting of bilinear elements (quadratic polynomials). Fig. 3 (e) through (h) describes oriented finite elements for an 8×8 block with $h = 8$ (the angular range $0 \le \theta < \pi$ is discretized into eight different directions). In this case, there are eight different types of oriented finite elements, one for each discretized direction. Only four of them are shown in the figure; the other four are obtained from the ones shown by a 90-degree rotation. The integer values in Fig. 3 (e) mark the locations of the pixel centers on the block boundary. These locations are also the locations for the node values of the finite elements. In Fig. 3 (e) and (h), there are nodes situated halfway between two pixels. For a node of this sort, the node value is taken to be the average of the two adjacent pixels. In general, for an arbitrary θ some nodes of the bilinear elements may not coincide with the pixel locations, and these nodes values are linearly interpolated from the adjacent pixels.

To compare the quality of images generated using oriented finite elements and Painter's adaptive stochastic sampling method [23], Fig. 4 (bottom) examines zoomed views of the same region in Fig. 2 (c) and Fig. 4 (top) (both images are filtered down from their work images using a Gaussian). For the same sampling rate, the DCM already produces a high-quality image while Painter's method suffers from artifacts including heavily jagged edges, missing objects parts, and missing high-frequency details. Fig. 5 shows the sampling patterns of Painter's method and the DCM. Also compare the zoomed views in Fig. 4 with the zoomed sampling patterns in Fig. 5 (the zoomed sampling pattern of the DCM does not include the extra samples needed for the first-order test described in Section 4.3, but the extra sampling is included in the 6% sampling rate reported).

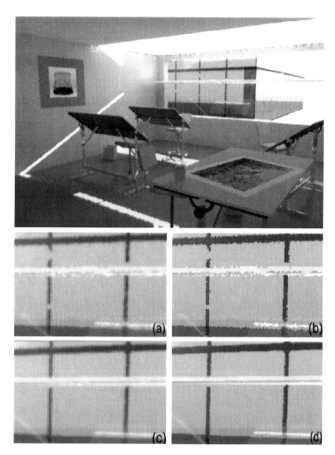

Figure 4: Comparison between the DCM and adaptive stochastic sampling with the office example. The top image, rendered by sampling 6% of the pixels using Painter's adaptive stochastic sampling technique, should be compared with the 6% DCM image in Fig. 2 (c). The bottom image contains four zoomed views of the same region: 6% Painter image in (a) with its work image in (b), and 6% DCM image in (c) with its work image in (d).

Notice that Painter's method very gracefully locates the features, but the number of samples at our disposal is just too small to make this method effective. We have also compared the DCM with adaptive super-sampling [35] and stratified sampling [19]. Painter's method performs much better than the other two because its underlying hierarchical integration sampling technique combines the strengths of adaptive and stratified sampling by stratifying samples with strata that are dynamically adjusted as more samples are taken [16].

3.4 Directional Coherence

Why does the least discrepancy direction work? Simply stated, it works because of image-space coherence. According to Sutherland [29], coherence is the degree to which parts of a scene or its projection exhibit local similarities. Often we think of a discontinuity edge as the break of coherence, since image data change abruptly across the edge. However, discontinuities do not break all forms of coherence. Specifically, image data are typically coherent along the direction of the discontinuity edge even if they change abruptly across the edge [21]. Contour-based image coding (e.g. [21]) and more broadly, second generation image coding [18] takes advantage of this form of coherence. For a block with a simple discontinuity edge, the least discrepancy direction is really the direction

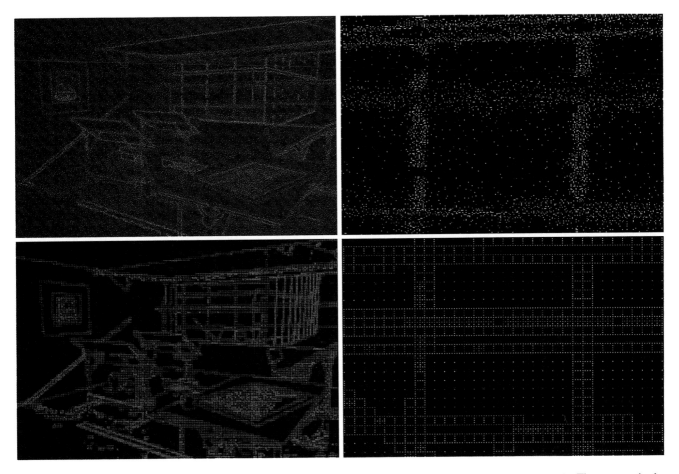

Figure 5: Comparison of the sampling patterns of adaptive stochastic sampling (top row) and the DCM (bottom row). The patterns in the left column are taken from RADIANCE work images described in Section 5. Some of the fine features are shown in zoomed views of the sampling patterns in the right column. These zoomed views correspond to the same region as the zoomed views in Fig. 4.

of maximal coherence as can be inferred from the evaluated boundary pixels. By orienting the finite elements along this direction, we maximize the likelihood of capturing the discontinuity edge along with its characteristics (section 4.3 on block simplicity tests for the treatment of more complex discontinuities such as corners).

4 Coherence Map Construction and Refinements

A DCM consists of a partition of the image plane into square blocks, with some selected blocks having a direction θ ($0 \leq \theta < \pi$) assigned to each of them. These selected blocks are called edge blocks; all other blocks are smooth blocks. The boundary of every edge block is densely evaluated, whereas a smooth block only has its four corners evaluated. To reconstruct an approximate image, we bilinearly interpolate each smooth block and build a finite element approximation on every edge block, with the elements oriented to the direction recorded in the DCM.

The main reason for separating edge and smooth blocks is efficiency. Since it is much more expensive to sample an edge block, we wish to reserve edge blocks for areas with discontinuities. In our block classification procedure, we select edge blocks based on evaluated pixel radiance and object-space data. Thus projections of object boundaries are taken into consideration from the beginning even for small objects. To further reduce the chance of missing blocks with discontinuities, a smooth block is not automatically

subdivided into four smooth quads in the block refinement step. Instead, each quad is reevaluated to see if it contains discontinuities.

The DCM is a divide-and-conquer technique: it aims to partition the image plane into blocks with simple structures (i.e., blocks crossed by at most one discontinuity edge). At any given stage of the progressive radiance evaluation, the oriented finite elements produce good results on edge blocks with simple structures; the results on more complex edge blocks are less certain. Naturally, we wish to identify these complex blocks so that we can focus our sampling efforts on them at the next stage of the radiance evaluation. With this goal in mind, we have designed block simplicity tests for edge blocks. An edge block is a simple edge block if it passes these simplicity tests; otherwise it is a complex edge block.

A big concern with the block simplicity tests is that, in general, it is not possible to guarantee that a block is crossed by at most one edge as long as the block interior is not fully sampled. Nevertheless, with the evaluated block boundary we can identify many offending blocks. Our experiments indicate that with carefully designed simplicity tests, we can identify and subdivide sufficiently many offending blocks for the purpose of generating high-quality images. To further avoid mistreating a block with complex interior discontinuities, we constantly reassess the simplicity of a block as more evaluated pixels become available. This verification is done as part of the lazy boundary evaluation described later.

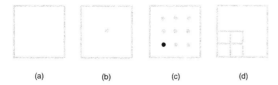

Figure 6: Lazy boundary evaluation on a simple edge block. (a) A simple edge block, with the light grey boundary representing evaluated pixels. (b) The difference between a newly evaluated pixel (marked by the grey dot) and the value predicted by the finite element approximation is within the prescribed tolerance, and no boundary evaluation is invoked. (c) One of the newly evaluated pixels, marked by the black dot, deviates too much from the value predicted by the current finite element approximation. (d) Boundary evaluations are triggered for the surrounding blocks.

4.1 Refinement Steps for the DCM

As mentioned in Section 2, the iterations for the DCM construction and refinements begin after the regular subdivision stage has partitioned the image plane into elementary blocks. Each iteration of the DCM refinement takes five steps. First, the block classification step examines the pool of smooth blocks to select edge blocks. For the first iteration, this pool consists of all elementary blocks. In any later iteration, the pool is formed by collecting the four quads subdivided from the smooth blocks in the previous iteration. The classification also marks as edge blocks the four quads of every complex edge block from the previous iteration. In the second step, the boundary evaluation procedure densely samples the block boundary of every edge block. Then, the simplicity test step analyzes every edge block and labels as complex edge blocks those that fail any block simplicity test. The fourth step builds oriented finite elements, and the fifth step subdivides every block into four quads for the next iteration.

The four quads B_i, $i = 1 : 4$ of a simple edge block B from the previous iteration are computed using a lazy boundary evaluation procedure as shown in Fig. 6. Since B is a simple edge block, we already have a finite element approximation $f(\mathbf{x})$ on B. Our experiments indicate that this finite element approximation is usually of very good quality unless some complex structures in the interior of B have gone undetected in the previous iteration. Thus before going through the normal boundary evaluation with B_i, we evaluate the corner pixels of B_i and compare the resulting pixel values with the pixel values predicted by the existing finite element approximation $f(\mathbf{x})$. If the predicted values are within a prescribed tolerance (1% relative error in our system) from the evaluated pixel values, then the simplicity of B is re-confirmed and we continue to use $f(\mathbf{x})$ on the new blocks B_i with small modifications. More specifically, we skip the normal boundary evaluation procedure and substitute $f(\mathbf{x})$ for the pixel values everywhere on the boundary of B_i except at the corners, where the evaluated pixels are used. With the block boundary so obtained, we construct a finite element approximation $f_i(\mathbf{x})$ on B_i with the least discrepancy direction of B. By incorporating the evaluated pixels into $f_i(\mathbf{x})$, we force the approximate image to converge to the final image as rendered by the baseline system.

4.2 Block Classification

A smooth block can be reclassified as an edge block through the following two steps. First, a block contrast value is computed for each block and this value is tested against the prescribed contrast threshold t_c. The block is classified as an edge block if its block contrast value exceeds the threshold t_c. Second, a visible-line rendering of

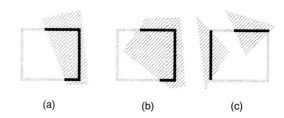

Figure 7: Block simplicity test examples. Case (a) passes both the zero order and first order tests. Case (b) passes the zero order test but not the first order. Case (c) fails both tests. The black and light grey line segments on the block boundary are spans.

the scene is generated, and every block crossed by a visible line is classified as an edge block.

Contrast Thresholding. For an elementary block with corner luminance values $\{g_1, ..., g_4\}$, the block contrast quantifies the ratio between the average luminance $\bar{g}$ and the deviation Δg from the average. Following Mitchell [22], we compute the block contrast as $\frac{\max - \min}{\max + \min}$, where max and min are the maximum and minimum of the corner luminance values $\{g_1, ..., g_4\}$ respectively. The criterion for locating high-frequency details has a significant impact on the effectiveness of the initial edge block selection. The issue here is not the loss of details since the progressive rendering eventually produces the same image as the baseline rendering system. The main concern is whether certain details will appear at earlier stages of the rendering process. In this regard, a criterion based on contrast $\Delta g/\bar{g}$ compares favorably with methods that use deviation Δg alone [19], because the nonlinear human visual sensitivity to the change in light intensity is closely modeled by the contrast $\Delta g/\bar{g}$ rather than just Δg. This logarithmic contrast perception model is the most widely used among other models [15]. In our implementation, we set $t_c = 0.05$.

Computing Visible Lines. The visible lines that we choose include both object boundaries from the scene geometry and their reflections in planar mirrors. These visible lines are efficiently computable through the standard graphics pipeline [36], which supports both polygonal objects and commonly-used curved objects. We use polygon offset to avoid the "stitching" artifact that could result from a naive Z-buffer implementation [36], because stitching turns a solid line into a dotted line and thus allows it to pass through an elementary block undetected. For a curved object the visible-line renderer is instructed to draw the silhouette only [36]. The mirror reflections of visible lines are computed as in [24].

Note that a pure contrast-driven classification can be deceptive for large blocks. To alleviate this problem, we use visible lines to account for object boundaries and at each iteration we reclassify smooth blocks to recover features missed in the previous iteration due to the larger blocks and fewer available samples.

4.3 Block Simplicity Tests

The simplicity tests in our system are designed systematically based on the traditional methodology of proof-by-contradiction. First we assume that the block is crossed by at most one edge. From this assumption, we derive facts about the discontinuities on the block boundary. The derived facts can be verified using the known radiance values on the block boundary. The block fails the tests if any contradiction arises. Fig. 7 provides examples for some of the following tests.

Zero Order Test. For a block crossed by a single edge, we should be able to find a luminance threshold t_b, such that the block can be divided into two simply connected regions (connected and having no holes): one for pixels with luminance above the threshold and

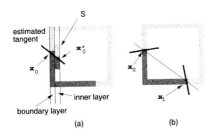

Figure 8: The first order test for block simplicity. (a) The tangent direction for the edge passing through x_0 can be estimated from the transition points x_0 and x'_0 on two adjacent layers. (b) To pass the first order test, the line segment $[x_0\ x_1]$ (the thin black line) and the tangent directions at the two transition points x_0 and x_1 (the two thick black lines) must be nearly parallel.

the other for those below. The zero order test identifies the blocks that cannot be so divided, using the evaluated boundary pixels of the block. In our system, we set $t_b = 0.5(b_1 + d_1)$, where b_1 is the highest luminance on the block boundary and d_1 the lowest.

Thresholding with t_b converts the block boundary into a binary pattern consisting of "1-pixels" that exceed t_c and "0-pixels" that do not. Juxtaposed 1-pixels can be collected together to form a "1-span", and likewise 0-pixels form "0-spans" (Fig. 7). Two spans are separated by a transition point, which is defined as a 1-pixel having at least one 0-pixel neighbor. To simplify this binary pattern, we apply a median filter of length three to eliminate spans of one-pixel long. This simplification is needed because of the Monte Carlo component in the baseline ray tracing system, and the median filtering helps to eliminate the spurious spans caused by Monte Carlo noise. To reduce noise effects, we also apply a length-three Bartlett filter to the luminance values on the block boundary before thresholding. The filtered values are only used for computing the spans, not for constructing the block radiance approximation. With spans of length one removed, the number of transition points on the block boundary must be even. If there are more than two transition points, the block fails the zero order test. Otherwise the block survives the test and moves onto the first order test.

First Order Test. A block with no transition points passes the first order test by default. For a block having two transition points, let the transition points be x_0 and x_1. If the block is crossed by a single edge passing through x_0 and x_1, the tangent vectors of the edge at the two points should be close in direction. The first order test computes the tangent vectors at x_0 and x_1 and measures the difference between the tangent directions against a prescribed tangent threshold t_m. If the measured difference exceeds the threshold, the block fails the test. Let θ_{01} be the direction of the line segment $[x_0\ x_1]$ that connects x_0 and x_1, whose tangent directions are determined by angles θ_0 and θ_1 respectively. The difference of the tangent directions is measured by $m_{01} = \max(|\theta_0 - \theta_{01}|, |\theta_1 - \theta_{01}|)$. Fig. 8 (b) illustrates the geometry. The threshold t_m is set to 0.05π times the L_2 norm $\|x_1 - x_0\|_2$ in our implementation.

A challenging technical problem in the first order test is the efficient computation of tangent vectors at the transition points. We have developed a technique that estimates tangent directions at the cost of a few additional pixel radiance evaluations. To estimate the angle θ_0 at x_0, we evaluate the luminance function at pixels along a short line segment S next to x_0 on the inner layer of pixels, as is shown in Fig. 8 (a). The luminance threshold t_b and a length-three median filter are applied to these additional luminance values to extend the binary pattern from the boundary layer to the line segment S. The evaluation process starts from the pixel next to x_0 in the inner layer and elongates S in both directions, stopping as soon as the transition point x'_0 corresponding to x_0 is found on S. At pixel

resolution, the transition points x'_0 and x_0 determine the tangent angle θ_0.

Binarizing images to extract geometric patterns is not new; researchers have used this technique in the field of video coding [15]. An example is the geometric-structure-based directional filtering proposed by Zeng [39]. Even though the patterns extracted in his work are complex and uncertain, he has successfully used these patterns to improve block-based video coding at low bit rates.

Object Test. We enforce the constraint that no more than two object tags are allowed on the boundary of a block. In addition, the object tags also form object spans similar to the spans in the zero order test, and only two object spans are allowed on the block boundary. A block violating these constraints will not be considered simple. The object tags are returned by the baseline ray tracer as by-products of pixel radiance evaluations.

If a block fails any of the above block simplicity tests, it is labeled as a complex edge block. In the next iteration of block refinement, we devote more sampling to a complex edge block B_c by performing real (i.e. not lazy) boundary evaluations on the four quads subdivided from B_c.

4.4 Discussion

The DCM is useful because it allows us to generate high-quality images from a small percentage of evaluated pixels. Unfortunately, the danger of serious approximation errors also grows with the number of unevaluated pixels. For this reason, it is desirable to have a technique that uses known data (e.g. scene geometry and evaluated pixels) to bound the errors, possibly with the help of some analytical formulation [31, 26, 1]. We have not derived such a technique. Instead, we have built two simple principles into the DCM construction. First, we always incorporate the newly evaluated pixels into the DCM and never overwrite them. As a result, the approximate image is guaranteed to converge to the final image as rendered by the baseline system, and all approximation errors are thus eliminated eventually. The second principle is that we regularly re-examine our previous decisions in partitioning blocks to detect errors: smooth blocks are tested for discontinuities and simple edge blocks are probed for complex structures. These error detections are done using newly evaluated pixels as part of the block classification and lazy boundary evaluation.

In practice, failure to detect discontinuities means the delay of high-quality images. In this regard, the DCM performs better with object boundaries than shadows and highlights, which can go undetected with larger blocks. In fact, small highlights and shadows in the block interior will certainly go undetected until the block is subdivided. Fig. 2 (c) contains errors of this sort (e.g. the cup on the table). These performance problems often have solutions, albeit at additional cost. For example, one way to improve on shadows is to include shadow edges as in [24].

5 Implementation

We have implemented our progressive rendering algorithm using the RADIANCE system developed by Ward [33]. RADIANCE is a physics-based lighting simulation system that has gained considerable reputation because of its successful use in real-world projects [33]. Our progressive rendering system allows the user to examine the approximate image any time during the rendering process. When their Monte Carlo components are challenged by difficult lighting configurations, RADIANCE and other ray tracing systems for global illumination [27] will become less effective. In this sort of situation, our system uses the confidence relocation technique described in Section 6.2 to generate images of high visual quality.

Progressive Rendering with RADIANCE. In the baseline RADIANCE system, a work image is first generated at a super-sample

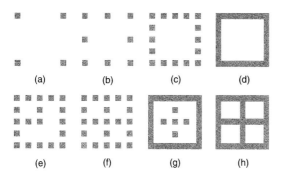

Figure 9: Boundary evaluation procedures for a 8×8 block. The small grey squares stand for evaluated pixels. Other pixels on the block boundary are linearly interpolated. For a simple edge block, we follow the sequence (a), (b), (c), and (d), which evenly distributes evaluated pixels on the block boundary. For a complex edge block, we also need to distribute evaluated pixels in the block interior, and we follow the sequence (a), (b), (c), (e), (f), (g), and (h).

resolution by a hybrid deterministic and Monte Carlo ray tracing program. This work image is then filtered down to the resolution of the output image for anti-aliasing. To generate high-quality images with penumbra from a scene with fine geometric details, as is the case with our examples, the work image is 3×3 times as large as the output image, and every pixel is evaluated through ray tracing.

For pixel radiance evaluation, our progressive rendering system uses exactly the same calculation parameters as the baseline system. Like the baseline system, our progressive system performs the rendering in batch mode. Anytime during the rendering process, the finite element approximation to the radiance function can be assembled "on-demand" in a few seconds, and then re-sampled onto the work image. For the images in this paper, we filtered the work image using the Gauss filter provided with RADIANCE to produce the output image. For the DCM construction, we choose the size of the elementary block to be 8×8 and discretize the angular range $[0, \pi]$ into 8 different directions. All the other DCM-related parameters have been given in the previous sections.

Fig. 9 explains boundary evaluations for 8×8 blocks. The idea is to evenly distribute evaluated pixels in order to allow the construction of oriented finite elements even before every pixel on the block boundary is evaluated. Note that for a complex edge block, we jump from Fig. 9 (c) to (d) because in (c) the distance between evaluated pixels (2) is already smaller than the size of the quads (4) and when this happens we start distributing evaluated pixels on the boundaries of the four quads of a complex edge block.

Generating Better Images by Confidence Relocation. Normally our approximate image progresses towards a final image determined by some given calculation parameters. If this final image suffers from severe artifacts, we must raise the quality standard and progress towards a better final image. This approach is especially relevant to the Monte Carlo components of radiance evaluation. The Monte Carlo computations introduce noise while capturing diffuse interreflections. A common approach to noise reduction is to increase the sampling rates. However, as Rushmeier argues, the sampling rates needed can be impractically high for certain difficult lighting configurations [25].

With the DCM, it is possible to generate images with high visual quality even when the Monte Carlo calculations make it too costly to evaluate every pixel accurately. The basic idea is simple: the Monte Carlo noise is not part of the radiance function by nature, but a manifestation of the limitations of our radiance evaluation techniques. This means that when the pixel values are accurate, they will exhibit the image-space coherence we see in photographs.

image	$L_1(L_2)$ error	time (C)	time (NC)
office 6%	0.008(0.02)	0.9 hrs	8.9 hrs
office final	-	16.5 hrs	38.5 hrs
museum 7%	0.005(0.016)	0.05 hrs	1.2 hrs
museum final	-	1 hrs	5 hrs

Table 1: Progressive rendering statistics. The "time (C)" column lists timings for scenes with cached irradiances, while the "time (NC)" column lists timings for scenes without caching.

In particular, directional coherence will be present and we can use the DCM to reconstruct high-quality images from a small percentage of evaluated pixels. Improvement of pixel accuracy is usually achieved by increasing our confidence in the pixel values through variance reduction. When the available computation is more or less uniformly spread over the entire image plane, so is our confidence in the pixel values. If the resulting image is poor, we can try to improve the accuracy of every pixel, but that usually means a dramatic increase in computational costs. An alternative is to improve the accuracy of pixel values in a progressive system based on the DCM. Since the progressive system can generate high-quality images with a small percentage of evaluated pixels, we usually obtain high-quality images without additional computation. When taking the second approach, we relocate the uniformly spread low confidence to concentrated high confidence in the small percentage of pixels needed by the DCM.

In our implementation, we use hierarchical integration [16] to reduce the variance within each pixel, stopping when a confidence interval test passes [23].

Time and Space Considerations. Compared to the cost of pixel radiance evaluations, the time needed for managing the DCM and oriented finite elements is negligible. More specifically, the time complexity of DCM-related construction is no greater than an inverse discrete cosine transform (DCT), which is used for decoding JPEG images [15]. For a typical image included in this paper, generating an approximate image can be generated on the order of seconds as opposed to the few hours needed for evaluating the pixel radiance. The memory requirements are also modest. In addition to the storage needed by the baseline RADIANCE, we need only store a list of edge blocks and a horizontal strip of the work image. The complete work image is stored on the disk and it is retrieved only when the user demands the system to display the current approximate image.

6 Results

All the high-quality approximate images reported in this paper are obtained after the progressive rendering system finished processing all 4×4 edge blocks. At this point, the approximate images become visually hard to distinguish from the final images for most scenes.

6.1 Progressive Rendering

Fig. 2 shows a series of images progressively rendered from an office scene lit by sunlight transferred through a light shelf. This scene was introduced in [33] to demonstrate how RADIANCE preprocesses "virtual" light sources to optimize light calculations for certain difficult environments. Both the baseline and the progressive systems have included that optimization. As is typical with the other scenes we have tested, 6% evaluated pixels allow us to generate a high-quality image that is hard to distinguish visually from the final image. See Fig. 5 for the locations of the 6% samples. Fig. 10

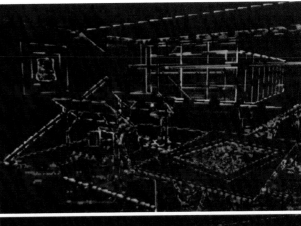

Figure 10: Progressive renderings of a museum scene lit by skylight through the window. Notice the fine shadows cast by the polygonal occluders. The top image is the approximate image after evaluating about 7% of the pixels. The bottom image is the image rendered by the baseline RADIANCE system. The scene model was provided courtesy of Charles Ehrlich.

Figure 11: Error distributions for the office example. The top image shows the errors in the approximate image with 1.6% evaluated pixels. The bottom image is for the approximate image with 6% evaluated pixels. Even though the two distributions are taken from very different stages of the rendering process, the most significant errors are clustered around the image discontinuities for both distributions. This attests to the importance of properly handling discontinuities when generating high-quality images.

shows another example, which is a museum lit by skylight through the window.

To quantify the errors in a high-quality approximate image, we subtract it from the final image F to get an error image E. Then we compute the relative error as either $||E||_1/||F||_1$ or $||E||_2/||F||_2$, where $||.||_1$ and $||.||_2$ is the L_1 and L_2 norms respectively. The resulting L_1 and L_2 errors for the two examples are in Table 1.

Table 1 also compares the computation times for the high-quality approximate images and the final images. All timings are taken on a 180 MHz SGI Indy workstation with 64 Mb of main memory. The time indicated for each final image is the time needed by the baseline RADIANCE system. The time for an approximate image includes not only the time for pixel radiance evaluations but also all the computation related to the DCM.

An important factor that affects the timings is the irradiance caching in RADIANCE [34]. The diffuse interreflections in the rendering equation can be calculated using Monte Carlo ray tracing [16], but to reduce the variance to a tolerable level, hundreds of rays must be spawned for each eye-ray that strikes a surface. To avoid invoking this expensive calculation at every pixel, RADIANCE caches indirect diffuse contributions and interpolates them over each surface in the scene. At an early rendering stage, there is little irradiance cached in the scene to interpolate from, and an eye-ray is more expensive to evaluate. As time goes by, more cached values become available, and the radiance evaluation accelerates.

We tabulate two timings for each example: one measured with the lighting simulation starting without irradiance cached, and the other with the irradiance cached from a previous rendering from a different viewpoint. Note that even when irradiance caching is not a dominant factor, there is no exact correspondence between the time percentage and the percentage of pixels evaluated. In fact, the time percentage can be smaller than the pixel percentage when there is a large amount of irradiance cached in a scene, as is the case with the "museum" example.

Fig. 11 provides error images at different stages of the rendering process. The intensities of both images have been scaled up to make the errors more visible. As a result, the error images mainly show the error distributions.

6.2 Confidence Relocation

Fig. 12 provides an example of generating better images with confidence relocation.[2] Each pixel in the 512×342 image on the left corresponds to 3×3 pixels in the work image, but for the penumbra areas this sampling rate is insufficient. Fig. 12 (a) and (c) show artifacts in the left image with zoomed views of two regions. Fig. 12

---

[2]For information on luminaires, the reader is referred to the scene model at http://radsite.lbl.gov/radiance/pub/models/bath.tar.Z

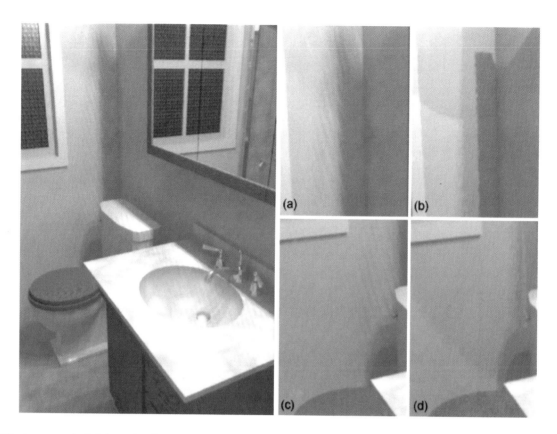

Figure 12: The image on the left is rendered using the baseline RADIANCE system by setting the quality to the highest level available. On the right, (a) and (c) are zoomed views of two regions from the left image. Notice the striping artifacts and missing penumbra boundaries. In (b) and (d), we show zoomed views of the same two regions from an image rendered in less time by our progressive renderer (for the complete image see the Conference Proceedings CD-ROM). The scene model was provided courtesy of Greg W. Larson.

(b) and (d) are zoomed views of the same two regions from an image rendered using confidence relocation. The image generated by confidence relocation is also a 512×342 image, filtered down from a work image 3×3 times as large. But this time, instead of evaluating every pixel of the work image, we only evaluate 6.7% of the pixels and we super-sample these pixels to increase pixel confidence. The computation times for the left image of Fig. 12 and the image with confidence relocation are 5.5 hours and 2.7 hours respectively on our SGI Indy with each computation initiated without irradiance caching. When there is caching, the left image takes 1.4 hours and the image generated with confidence relocation takes about 1/7 of the time. The correctness of the image by confidence relocation has been verified with a benchmark image generated by taking 256 super-samples for each pixel of the final image.

6.3 Discontinuity Varieties

We have tested the DCM on a variety of scenes with very different discontinuities. Fig. 10 is a scene with fine shadows cast by polygonal occluders. For this sort of scene, discontinuity meshing works well. The main advantage of the DCM in this case is the ability to handle large scenes without suffering the storage overhead of meshing.

Fig. 13 is from a scene filled with specular surfaces placed next to each other. Discontinuity meshing cannot cope with this scene well because of the view-dependent specular highlights and curved geometry. Moreover, discontinuity meshing seeks to track down all potential discontinuities prior to radiance evaluation [20], which is extremely difficult to do here due to the closely packed specular sur-

faces. To render the scene, we incorporate the DCM into Rayshade [17], a well-known system for classical ray tracing [35]. We choose to do so partly because RADIANCE does not handle torus primitives – we also wanted to see how easy it is to incorporate the DCM into a typical ray tracing system. Rayshade collects radiance samples for individual pixels of the output image as follows. First, one sample is collected for each output pixel and a contrast value is computed based on the current pixel and its four neighbors. If high contrast is encountered, the current pixel and the four neighbors are anti-aliased by taking 3×3 samples for each pixel (the default setting). To incorporate the DCM into the system, we first create a work image 3×3 times as large as the output image. Then we carry out DCM-related construction as in our RADIANCE implementation.

The top right image in Fig. 13 is rendered after evaluating 10% of the pixels of the work image. The percentage is higher than usual because the complex interactions between the tightly packed specular surfaces lead to high contrast almost everywhere. As shown in Fig. 13 (bottom left), the high contrast also causes much super-sampling in Rayshade. Fig. 13 (bottom row) compares the Rayshade and DCM sampling patterns in the RADIANCE work image using zoomed views of a chosen region (for clarity, the zoomed sampling pattern for the DCM does not include the extra samples needed for the first-order test described in Section 4.3, but the extra sampling is included in the 10% samples reported). On our Indy workstation, the top image of Fig. 13 takes 10 minutes to render with Rayshade, whereas the bottom image takes 1.4 minutes when the DCM is used.

Figure 13: The top left image is a benchmark image rendered by Rayshade. The top right image is rendered using the DCM after a small percentage of pixels have been evaluated. The main purpose of this experiment is to test the DCM's capability in treating discontinuities that cannot be handled by existing discontinuity algorithms. The bottom row provide zoomed views of the sampling patterns for the same region of the work image (left pattern for Rayshade and right for the DCM). The grey dots indicate the locations of the samples. Compared to Rayshade, the DCM performs much less sampling yet can produce an image of similar quality because of the effective treatment of discontinuities. The scene model was provided courtesy of Stuart Warmink.

7 Conclusions

We have presented a progressive refinement algorithm for radiance evaluation, by showing how to handle general radiance discontinuities using a novel technique called the Directional Coherence Map. The DCM subdivides the image plane into blocks with simple discontinuities and captures the discontinuities on each block with the least discrepancy direction and oriented finite elements. By combining object-space data with discontinuity information extracted from evaluated pixel radiance, the DCM achieves both time and storage efficiency. Thus it is possible to treat discontinuities in a complex scene that could barely be loaded into the main memory of our computer. The DCM is also shown capable of effectively treating a variety of discontinuities, including several types that cannot be handled by existing discontinuity algorithms. For a global illumination scene consisting of smooth surfaces, the DCM generates high-quality images much faster than progressive ray tracing systems based on adaptive sampling. When the Monte Carlo components of a lighting calculation system are challenged by very difficult lighting configurations, our algorithm can still produce high-quality images efficiently by relocating the computational resources to the small percentage of pixels needed by the DCM.

Several related research topics remain to be explored. The DCM gains its power from the directional coherence in the image plane. Other forms of coherence in the radiance function should also be investigated. An example is Teller's radiance interpolant, which makes use of the coherence between images from nearby viewpoints [31]. Another area of research is the use of sophisticated color vision models to improve our refinement strategy so that less computation is distributed to areas of little perceptual importance. Bolin's work has shown promising results in this direction [4]. Finally, we expect to see growing interest in image-space discontinuities in the near future. Our experiments not only indicate the importance of properly treating image-space discontinuities, but also demonstrate the power of image-space discontinuity information. In general, we believe techniques for manipulating image data will become more important as the average size of the polygons passing through the graphics pipeline approach the size of individual pixels, and we hope that our work stimulates future research in this increasingly exciting area.

Acknowledgments

I would like to thank Demetri Terzopoulos for his help at several critical moments. Without his help this work would not be possible. Thanks also to Greg W. Larson for his insightful comments on some of the ideas presented and for numerous consultations on RADIANCE, to Bede Liu and Wenjun Zeng for helpful discussions, to John Funge for proofreading part of this paper, and to the anonymous reviewers for their constructive critique.

References

[1] J. Arvo. The Irradiance Jacobian for Partially Occluded Polyhedral Sources. In A. Glassner, editor, *Computer Graphics Proceedings, Annual Conference Series*, pages 75–84, July 1994.

[2] L. D. Bergman, H. Fuchs, E. Grant, and S. Spach. Image Rendering by Adaptive Refinement. In D. C. Evans and R. J. Athay, editors, *Computer Graphics (SIGGRAPH '86 Proceedings)*, volume 20, pages 29–37, August 1986.

[3] J. Bloomenthal. Edge Inference with Applications to Antialiasing. In *Computer Graphics (SIGGRAPH '83 Proceedings)*, volume 17, pages 157–162, July 1983.

[4] M. R. Bolin and G. W. Meyer. A Frequency Based Ray Tracer. In R. Cook, editor, *Computer Graphics Proceedings, Annual Conference Series*, pages 409–418, August 1995.

[5] A. T. Campbell III and D. S. Fussell. Adaptive Mesh Generation for Global Diffuse Illumination. In *Computer Graphics (SIGGRAPH '90 Proceedings)*, volume 24, pages 155–164, August 1990.

[6] S. E. Chen, H. E. Rushmeier, G. Miller, and D. Turner. A Progressive Multi-Pass Method for Global Illumination. In T. W. Sederberg, editor, *Computer Graphics (SIGGRAPH '91 Proceedings)*, volume 25, pages 165–174, July 1991.

[7] N. Chin and S. Feiner. Near Real-Time Shadow Generation Using BSP Trees. In J. Lane, editor, *Computer Graphics (SIGGRAPH '89 Proceedings)*, volume 23, pages 99–106, July 1989.

[8] M. F. Cohen, S. E. Chen, J. R. Wallace, and D. P. Greenberg. A Progressive Refinement Approach to Fast Radiosity Image Generation. In J. Dill, editor, *Computer Graphics (SIGGRAPH '88 Proceedings)*, volume 22, pages 75–84, August 1988.

[9] R. L. Cook, T. Porter, and L. Carpenter. Distributed Ray Tracing. In *Computer Graphics (SIGGRAPH '84 Proceedings)*, volume 18, pages 137–145, July 1984.

[10] F. Crow. Shadow Algorithms for Computer Graphics. In *Computer Graphics (SIGGRAPH '77 Proceedings)*, volume 11, pages 242–248, July 1977.

[11] G. Dretakkis and E. Fiume. A Fast Shadow Algorithm for Area Light Sources Using Backprojection. In A. Glassner, editor, *Computer Graphics Proceedings, Annual Conference Series*, pages 223–230, July 1994.

[12] A. Fujimoto, T. Tanaka, and K. Iwata. ARTS: Accelerated Ray Tracing System. *IEEE Computer Graphics and Applications*, 6(4):16–26, July 1986.

[13] A. Glassner. *Principles of Digital Image Synthesis*, volume 1. Morgan Kaufmann, 1995.

[14] P. Heckbert. Discontinuity Meshing for Radiosity. *Third Eurographics Workshop on Rendering*, pages 203–226, May 1992.

[15] A. Jain. *Fundamentals of Digital Image Processing*. Prentice Hall, 1989.

[16] J. Kajiya. The Rendering Equation. In *Computer Graphics (SIGGRAPH '86 Proceedings)*, volume 20, pages 143–150, August 1986.

[17] C. Kolb. Rayshade User's Guide and Reference Manual. *Rayshade home page at graphics.stanford.edu*, January 1992.

[18] M. Kunt, A. Ikonomopoulos, and M. Kocher. Second-Generation Image Coding Techniques. *Proc. of IEEE*, 73(4):549–574, 1985.

[19] M. E. Lee, R. A. Redner, and S. P. Uselton. Statistically Optimized Sampling for Distributed Ray Tracing. In B. A. Barsky, editor, *Computer Graphics (SIGGRAPH '85 Proceedings)*, volume 19, pages 61–67, July 1985.

[20] D. Lischinski, F. Tampieri, and D. P. Greenberg. Combining Hierarchical Radiosity and Discontinuity Meshing. In *Computer Graphics Proceedings, Annual Conference Series*, pages 199–208, 1993.

[21] S. Mallat and S. Zhong. Characterization of Signals from Multiscale Edges. *IEEE Trans. on Pattern Analysis and Machine Intelligence*, 14(7):710–732, 1992.

[22] D. P. Mitchell. Generating Antialiased Images at Low Sampling Densities. In M. C. Stone, editor, *Computer Graphics (SIGGRAPH '87 Proceedings)*, volume 21, pages 65–72, July 1987.

[23] J. Painter and K. Sloan. Antialiased Ray Tracing by Adaptive Progressive Refinement. In J. Lane, editor, *Computer Graphics (SIGGRAPH '89 Proceedings)*, volume 23, pages 281–288, July 1989.

[24] F. Pighin, D. Lischinski, and D. Salesin. Progressive Previewing of Ray-Traced Images Using Image-Plane Discontinuity Meshing. *Eurographics Workshop on Rendering 1997*, May 1997.

[25] H. Rushmeier and G. Ward. Energy Preserving Non-Linear Filters. In A. Glassner, editor, *Computer Graphics Proceedings, Annual Conference Series*, pages 131–138, July 1994.

[26] P. Schroeder and P. Hanrahan. On the Form Factor between Two Polygons. Technical Report CS-404-93, Princeton University, Computer Science Department, 1993.

[27] P. Shirley. Hybrid Radiosity/Monte Carlo Methods. In *Siggraph 94 Course on Advanced Radiosity*, August 1994.

[28] A. J. Stewart and S. Ghali. Fast Computation of Shadow Boundaries Using Spatial Coherence and Backprojections. In A. Glassner, editor, *Computer Graphics Proceedings, Annual Conference Series*, pages 231–238, July 1994.

[29] I. Sutherland, R. Sproull, and R. Schumacker. A Characterization of Ten Hidden-Surface Algorithms. *ACM Computing Surveys*, 6(1):387–441, March 1974.

[30] S. Teller. Computing the Antipenumbra of an Area Light Source. In *Computer Graphics (SIGGRAPH '92 Proceedings)*, volume 26, pages 139–148, July 1992.

[31] S. Teller, K. Bala, and J. Dorsey. Conservative Radiance Interpolants for Ray Tracing. *Eurographics Workshop on Rendering 1996*, May 1996.

[32] C. Vedel. Computing Illumination from Area Light Sources by Approximate Contour Integration. In *Proceedings of Graphics Interface '93*, Toronto, Canada, May 1993.

[33] G. J. Ward. The RADIANCE Lighting Simulation and Rendering System. In A. Glassner, editor, *Computer Graphics Proceedings, Annual Conference Series*, pages 459–472, July 1994.

[34] G. J. Ward, F. M. Rubinstein, and R. D. Clear. A Ray Tracing Solution for Diffuse Interreflection. In *Computer Graphics (SIGGRAPH '88 Proceedings)*, pages 85–92, August 1988.

[35] T. Whitted. An Improved Illumination Model for Shaded Display. In *Computer Graphics (SIGGRAPH '79 Proceedings)*, volume 13, pages 1–14, August 1979.

[36] M. Woo, J. Neider, and T. Davis. *OpenGL Programming Guide*. Addison Wesley Developers Press, 1996.

[37] G. Wyvill, C. Jay, D. McRobie, and C. McNaughton. Pixel Independent Ray Tracing. In *Computer Graphics: Developments in Virtual Environments (Proc. CG International '95)*, pages 43–55. Springer-Verlag, 1995.

[38] G. Wyvill and P. Sharp. Fast Antialiasing of Ray Traced Images. In *New Advances in Computer Graphics (Proc. CG International '95)*, pages 579–588. Springer-Verlag, 1989.

[39] W. Zeng and B. Liu. Geometric-Structure-Based Error Concealment with Novel Applications in Block-Based Low Bit Rate Coding. *IEEE Trans. Cir. and Sys. for Video Tech.*, to appear, 1998.

Reproducing Color Images Using Custom Inks

Eric J. Stollnitz   Victor Ostromoukhov*   David H. Salesin

University of Washington   *Ecole Polytechnique Fédérale de Lausanne

Abstract

We investigate the general problem of reproducing color images on an offset press using custom inks in any combination and number. While this problem has been explored previously for the case of two inks, there are a number of new mathematical and algorithmic challenges that arise as the number of inks increases. These challenges include more complex gamut mapping strategies, more efficient ink selection strategies, and fast and numerically accurate methods for computing ink separations in situations that may be either over- or under-constrained. In addition, the demands of high-quality color printing require an accurate physical model of the colors that result from overprinting multiple inks using halftoning, including the effects of trapping, dot gain, and the interreflection of light between ink layers. In this paper, we explore these issues related to printing with multiple custom inks, and address them with new algorithms and physical models. Finally, we present some printed examples demonstrating the promise of our methods.

CR Categories: I.3.4 [Computer Graphics]: Graphics Utilities; G.1.6 [Numerical Analysis]: Optimization

Additional Keywords: color reproduction, color printing, gamut mapping, ink selection, Kubelka-Munk model, Neugebauer model, separations

1 Introduction

It is of interest . . . that, regardless of the number of impressions, the inks may be selected solely on the basis of their color gamut. Their colors need not be cyan, magenta, and yellow; nor is it required that they be transparent. The way is therefore opened for entirely new printing processes.

—Hardy and Wurzburg, 1948 [6]

Fifty years ago, the promise of color printing with custom inks appeared imminent. The advantages of such a process are clearly numerous. Freed from the same fixed set of *process color* inks—cyan, magenta, yellow, and black—it should be possible to print more vibrant colors for art reproductions, annual reports, and packaging. Moreover, if the inks are chosen specifically for the particular image being reproduced, it should be possible in many cases to achieve these vivid colors with just a small number of inks—perhaps four—and perhaps at no greater cost than using the four process colors. In addition, it is common today to print boxes and wrappers with four process inks (for images) plus two *spot colors* for corporate logos or large areas of background. By selecting custom inks that complement the required spot colors, we might achieve better quality with six inks or comparable quality with fewer inks.

In recent years, several new color printing processes have been proposed that use a fixed set of six or more standard printing inks [1, 22, 28]. For those willing to use more inks, these new processes do provide more vivid color reproduction. However, Hardy and Wurzburg's fifty-year-old vision of printing with arbitrary custom inks remains elusive. Indeed, there are quite a few difficult problems that stand in the way.

For one, it is very difficult to derive a physical model that accurately predicts how arbitrary inks will interact when printed together, in superposition and in juxtaposition using halftoning. In addition to optical effects, the model must take into account physical effects such as trapping and dot gain.

Furthermore, the gamuts produced by multiple custom inks have irregular, nonconvex shapes. Creating efficient, reliable gamut mapping algorithms for smoothly mapping image colors to the colors that can be achieved with a given set of inks is a nontrivial problem.

Choosing the best set of custom inks to use for a given image is another difficult problem—in this case, a combinatorial challenge, particularly as the number of inks used for printing gets large.

Finally, computing ink separations becomes more difficult for multiple inks. While for two inks there is always a simple analytic solution, for three or more inks the problem can become either over- or under-constrained. The problem becomes over-constrained when the color to be printed cannot be achieved with quantities of ink between 0 and 100%. The problem is under-constrained when there are two or more ways of achieving the same color, using different ink combinations. This situation arises wherever the gamut is doubly covered, a commonplace occurrence with four or more inks.

This paper addresses these challenges in detail with new physical models and algorithms, then demonstrates the potential of our approach with printed examples. Although a great deal more work remains to be done before Hardy and Wurzburg's vision is achieved in its entirety, this paper at least takes some steps toward that goal.

Related work

Power *et al.* [23] showed that for *duotone* printing, in which just two inks are used, choosing the optimal inks for the particular image at hand can result in remarkably good reproductions. Our paper discusses the many issues involved in generalizing their work to three or more custom inks—what we refer to as *n-tone* printing. These issues can be broken down into a number of subproblems.

First, for any given choice of paper and inks, we require a model of the gamut of printable colors. Many existing models have been developed for specific inks and printing processes; unfortunately, these models typically do not apply when printing with custom inks. More general models include the color halftoning model developed by Neugebauer [21], and colorant layering models such as the Beer-Bouguer, Kubelka-Munk, and Clapper-Yule equations (described by Kang [12]). Liu describes a model for process color printing similar to both the Kubelka-Munk layering model and the Neugebauer halftoning model [16]. We model the printing gamuts of custom inks using a similar approach in Section 2, where we combine the Kubelka-Munk and Neugebauer equations while taking into account the effects of dot gain and trapping.

The second subproblem, that of mapping the original image colors into the gamut of available colors, has been addressed previously for monitors and various types of printers. Studies have shown that the least objectionable mappings are those that preserve hue at the expense of luminance and saturation [5, 20]. In accordance with these findings, most existing gamut mapping techniques maintain hue while compressing each color's luminance and saturation in one of two ways: either toward a gray of equal luminance, or toward a fixed gray of medium luminance [10, 14, 27, 29]. In Section 3, we develop a continuous family of gamut mappings filling the gap between these two predominant strategies.

The problem of choosing inks has most often been framed as a search for one fixed palette that reproduces all images well. A number of multicolor printing approaches have been developed to achieve greater fidelity than process inks: the PANTONE Hexachrome system adds an orange and a green to the four process colors; Ostromoukhov [22] adds orange, green, and purple; Boll [1] adds red, green, and blue; and Takaghi *et al.* [28] mention a nine-ink process. Iwata and Marcu [9] touch on the subject of choosing the optimal printing order for a fixed set of inks printed on fabric. However, in none of the previous literature (aside from the work done by Power *et al.* for duotones) are the inks chosen to be optimal for a given image. We discuss criteria and algorithms for choosing optimal inks in Section 4.

The multicolor printing processes mentioned above have corresponding algorithms for computing ink separations. A number of these methods assume the printing gamut is a convex union of tetrahedra [9, 19, 22, 28], but many gamuts violate this assumption. Other separation algorithms, like those for process inks, are tailored for particular inks. Still others use Newton's method [15] or an analytic solution [18, 23] to invert the gamut model, but these approaches do not generalize to more than three inks. In Section 5, we present a robust separation method for arbitrary inks, paying particular attention to the difficulty of obtaining smooth results.

Each of the topics above is treated in more detail in the first author's dissertation [26]. In addition to describing our models and algorithms in the main text of this article, we display our printed results and discuss our experimental procedures in a set of appendices (printed with custom inks and inserted into the proceedings). We conclude in Section 6 with a summary of our work and ways in which it can be extended.

2 Modeling printing gamuts

In order to find the best combination of paper and inks from many possible choices, we need a mathematical model of the gamut of printable colors that results from any particular choice. Power *et al.* use the Neugebauer model of color halftoning in concert with a simple ink layering model to predict duotone gamuts. The accuracy of the gamut model is not crucial for duotone printing, since the user cannot expect a perfect reproduction from only two inks. By contrast, users can be expected to be much more critical when printing with three or more inks, and therefore *n*-tone printing requires a much more accurate gamut model.

We develop a model below that extends the Neugebauer model of color halftoning to account for the fact that an ink does not always adhere to paper and to other inks. This gamut model further requires that we know the colors achieved by overprinting combinations of inks. As we cannot always measure these overprinted colors, we rely on a mathematical model of layered media in addition to the Neugebauer model. We postpone until an appendix a discussion of the experimental procedure we followed to fit the model's parameters to measured data.

2.1 Modeling color halftoning

Most models of color halftone printing used today are based on the equations published by Neugebauer in 1937 [21]. His model assumes that small dots of color are printed in such a way that their edges are sharply defined, their overlapping areas are distributed randomly, and within each overlapping area each ink is either completely present or completely absent. His model also assumes we know the colors of the *printing primaries*: the paper color, the color of each ink printed on paper alone, and the color of each overprinted combination of inks. Under these conditions, the Neugebauer equations state that the overall color of a small area is simply the area-weighted average of the colors of the printing primaries.

Neugebauer's model is easily generalized from its original three-color formulation to incorporate any number of inks. For n inks, there are 2^n printing primaries (since each ink is either present or absent in a primary). The colors of the primaries are typically represented using coordinates in the XYZ color space, though the model applies equally well to reflectance spectra or any linear transformation of XYZ coordinates. With a slight modification of the notation used by Power *et al.* [23], we will refer to the color of paper as g_p, the color of paper covered by the first ink as g_{p1}, the color of paper printed with the first and second inks as g_{p12}, and so on. The fraction of area in which ink i is actually printed is denoted by α_i, and we write these ink amounts collectively as $\boldsymbol{\alpha} = (\alpha_1, \dots, \alpha_n)$.

For a given set of printing primaries, the Neugebauer equations give a printable color c as a function of the ink amounts $\boldsymbol{\alpha}$. For example, three-ink printing yields eight printing primaries, and the Neugebauer model is written as follows:

$$
\begin{aligned}
c(\boldsymbol{\alpha}) = \;& (1-\alpha_1)\,(1-\alpha_2)\,(1-\alpha_3)\,g_p \\
+ \;& (\alpha_1)\,(1-\alpha_2)\,(1-\alpha_3)\,g_{p1} \\
+ \;& (1-\alpha_1)\quad(\alpha_2)\,(1-\alpha_3)\,g_{p2} \\
+ \;& (\alpha_1)\quad\;\;(\alpha_2)\,(1-\alpha_3)\,g_{p12} \\
+ \;& (1-\alpha_1)\,(1-\alpha_2)\quad(\alpha_3)\,g_{p3} \\
+ \;& (\alpha_1)\,(1-\alpha_2)\quad(\alpha_3)\,g_{p13} \\
+ \;& (1-\alpha_1)\quad(\alpha_2)\quad(\alpha_3)\,g_{p23} \\
+ \;& (\alpha_1)\quad\;\;(\alpha_2)\quad(\alpha_3)\,g_{p123}
\end{aligned}
$$

2.2 Adding trapping to the Neugebauer model

Implicit in the Neugebauer model is the assumption that if we intend to cover a fraction α_i of an area with ink i, we can actually achieve that fractional coverage. In reality, because of the physical properties of inks and papers, some of the ink on the printing plate may not stick to the printed page. The portion of ink that does stick is said to be "trapped" by the paper. We will denote by t_{p1} the fraction of ink 1 that sticks to paper, and by t_{pij} the fraction of ink j that sticks to ink i (the *trapping fraction* for ink j on ink i on paper).

With this convention, we can model the color c we get by *trying* to cover a fraction α_1 of the paper with ink 1:

$$
c(\boldsymbol{\alpha}) = (1 - t_{p1}\alpha_1)\,g_p + t_{p1}\alpha_1\,g_{p1} \tag{1}
$$

Now suppose we print a second ink on top of that result. Of the area that was the color of paper g_p, a fraction $t_{p2}\alpha_2$ will get covered by ink 2 and become g_{p2}, while the rest will stay the same. Likewise, in the area that was colored g_{p1}, a fraction $t_{p12}\alpha_2$ will be overprinted with ink 2 and become g_{p12}, while the rest will stay the same. Thus, the result is a weighted average of four colors (as in the Neugebauer model):

$$
\begin{aligned}
c(\boldsymbol{\alpha}) = \;& (1 - t_{p1}\alpha_1)\;(1 - t_{p2}\alpha_2)\,g_p \\
+ \;& (t_{p1}\alpha_1)\;(1 - t_{p12}\alpha_2)\,g_{p1} \\
+ \;& (1 - t_{p1}\alpha_1)\quad(t_{p2}\alpha_2)\,g_{p2} \\
+ \;& (t_{p1}\alpha_1)\quad(t_{p12}\alpha_2)\,g_{p12}
\end{aligned}
\tag{2}
$$

If we add a third ink, the result will be a weighted average of eight colors, and we need seven trapping fractions:

$$
\begin{aligned}
c(\alpha) = \;& (1 - t_{p1}\alpha_1) \; (1 - t_{p2}\alpha_2) \; (1 - t_{p3}\alpha_3)\, g_p \\
+ \;& (t_{p1}\alpha_1) \; (1 - t_{p12}\alpha_2) \; (1 - t_{p13}\alpha_3)\, g_{p1} \\
+ \;& (1 - t_{p1}\alpha_1) \; (t_{p2}\alpha_2) \; (1 - t_{p23}\alpha_3)\, g_{p2} \\
+ \;& (t_{p1}\alpha_1) \; (t_{p12}\alpha_2) \; (1 - t_{p123}\alpha_3)\, g_{p12} \\
+ \;& (1 - t_{p1}\alpha_1) \; (1 - t_{p2}\alpha_2) \; (t_{p3}\alpha_3)\, g_{p3} \\
+ \;& (t_{p1}\alpha_1) \; (1 - t_{p12}\alpha_2) \; (t_{p13}\alpha_3)\, g_{p13} \\
+ \;& (1 - t_{p1}\alpha_1) \; (t_{p2}\alpha_2) \; (t_{p23}\alpha_3)\, g_{p23} \\
+ \;& (t_{p1}\alpha_1) \; (t_{p12}\alpha_2) \; (t_{p123}\alpha_3)\, g_{p123}
\end{aligned}
\tag{3}
$$

In general, for n inks the resulting color will be a weighted average of the 2^n printing primaries, where the weights depend on $2^n - 1$ trapping fractions.

2.3 Adding dot gain to the Neugebauer model

In addition to the effects of trapping, offset printing is subject to *dot gain*. The halftoned dots of an ink appear larger than they should for two reasons: ink spreads out on the paper (*physical dot gain*), and some of the light entering the paper is scattered until it emerges through dots of ink (*optical dot gain*). We can account for both varieties of dot gain using an empirical model that corrects the value of α_i for each ink. When we produce a halftone separation that specifies a coverage $\bar{\alpha}_i$, we find that one minus the actual coverage in the printed result is approximated very closely by a power law:

$$
1 - \alpha_i = (1 - \bar{\alpha}_i)^{\gamma_i} \tag{4}
$$

The parameter γ_i associated with ink i can be determined from experimental data using standard curve-fitting techniques, as discussed in an appendix. Note that if we desire an actual coverage of α_i, we can always solve the equation above for $\bar{\alpha}_i$, the coverage we should specify.

2.4 Modeling the printing primaries

We have so far assumed that we know the colors of the printing primaries. While it is straightforward to measure these colors for a small set of inks (like the process inks) on a small set of papers, it is impractical to do so for all the combinations that could be chosen from large sets of inks and papers. If we want to print on a new paper without measuring all our inks on that paper, we need a model capable of predicting the primaries. There are many levels of complexity we can introduce into a model; we will start with a simple model and progress to more complicated ones.

If we assume that a layer of ink acts as an ideal filter, we need to know only how much light it transmits at each wavelength λ. We will write the transmittance of the ink as T_i, and the reflectance of paper as R_p (for some wavelength λ). The reflectance of ink on paper is given by the amount of light that penetrates the ink (T_i), reflects off the paper (R_p), and emerges through the ink again (T_i):

$$
R_{pi} = T_i^2 R_p \tag{5}
$$

We can measure R_{pi} and R_p using a spectrophotometer, but not T_i because it is a property of the ink layer without paper. However, we can characterize an ink by printing an identical layer of that ink on a variety of papers, measuring R_p and R_{pi} for each paper, then fitting T_i to the model. Unfortunately, a single transmittance spectrum may not be enough information to accurately model an ink on paper, let alone one ink atop another.

One problem with the simple model above is that inks reflect some light in addition to absorbing and transmitting light. If we introduce a reflectance R_i for the ink, we have

$$
R_{pi} = R_i + T_i^2 R_p \tag{6}
$$

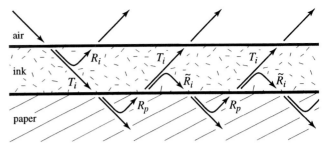

Figure 1 The light reflected by a single layer of ink on paper.

Once again, we can measure R_p and R_{pi} for a single ink on a variety of papers, and fit R_i and T_i to the model.

Equation (6) is subsumed by a more general model, known as the Kubelka-Munk model (described by Judd and Wyszecki [11, pages 420–438] and by Kortüm [13], among others). As Figure 1 illustrates, light can reflect any number of times between the ink and paper before finally exiting the ink layer, making the reflectance of ink on paper an infinite sum of terms:

$$
R_{pi} = R_i + T_i^2 R_p (1 + \tilde{R}_i R_p + \tilde{R}_i^2 R_p^2 + \cdots) = R_i + \frac{T_i^2 R_p}{1 - \tilde{R}_i R_p} \tag{7}
$$

The reflectance of the back side of the ink layer, $\tilde{R}_i$, can differ from the reflectance of its front side because the layer may be inhomogeneous. Now we must fit three reflectance spectra (R_i, $\tilde{R}_i$, and T_i) to measured data in order to characterize an ink. If $\tilde{R}_i$ is identically zero, we are left with equation (6); if R_i is also zero, we are left with equation (5).

Note that we can modify equation (7) to predict the reflectance of one ink on another ink (on paper), assuming the top ink layer behaves the same as it would on paper. If we print on paper p using ink i followed by ink j, we can compute R_{pij} from quantities we have measured or fit to measurements:

$$
R_{pij} = R_j + \frac{T_j^2 R_{pi}}{1 - \tilde{R}_j R_{pi}} \tag{8}
$$

The Kubelka-Munk model can be derived from physical principles, but only under certain assumptions. One assumption is that all the layers have the same index of refraction. However, the index of refraction of a colorant layer is typically between 1.45 and 1.6 [11, page 398], while that of air is very nearly 1. As a result of the difference in indices, some of the incident light will undergo Fresnel reflection at the material interface.

We can correct for Fresnel reflection at the boundary between ink and air using a construction similar to that of the Kubelka-Munk model. Suppose ρ_{ai} is the fraction of diffuse light traveling from air to ink that is reflected by the surface of the ink layer, and ρ_{ia} is the surface reflectance for light going from ink to air. Then, according to Saunderson [25], we find the corrected reflectance R'_{pi} of a layer of ink on paper by modifying the prediction given by equation (5), (6), or (7) as follows:

$$
R'_{pi} = \rho_{ai} + (1 - \rho_{ai})(1 - \rho_{ia}) \frac{R_{pi}}{1 - \rho_{ia} R_{pi}} \tag{9}
$$

Assuming dried ink has an index of refraction of 1.5, ρ_{ai} is approximately 0.1 and ρ_{ia} is about 0.6 for all wavelengths [11, page 417].

Fresnel reflection may also occur at the boundary between ink and paper if the interface is planar. In this case, we adjust our earlier equations using surface reflection coefficients ρ_{ip} (for light going

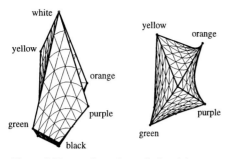

Figure 2 Front and top views of a four-ink gamut.

from ink to paper) and ρ_{pi} (for the opposite direction). We simply replace R_p in equations (5), (6), or (7) with a corrected reflectance R'_p:

$$R'_p = \rho_{ip} + (1 - \rho_{ip})(1 - \rho_{pi})\frac{R_p}{1 - \rho_{pi}R_p} \qquad (10)$$

Uncoated papers consist largely of air, so their indices of refraction are close to 1 and we can use $\rho_{ip} = 0.6$ and $\rho_{pi} = 0.1$. For lack of better knowledge, we use the same numbers for coated papers; however, these papers and modern plastic substrates deserve more study. Note that in the previous two equations R_p and R'_{pi} are measurable quantities, while R_i, $\bar{R}_i$, and T_i are characteristics of the ink that we need to derive from other measurements.

Regardless of the level of complexity we choose for our ink layering model—equation (5), (6), or (7), with or without the corrections in equations (9) and (10)—we often need to convert reflectance spectra into tristimulus XYZ colors for use in the color halftoning model of Section 2.2. Judd and Wyszecki describe this conversion in detail and provide the necessary data for standard illuminants and the XYZ matching functions [11, pages 125–153 and 472–479].

3 Gamut mapping

Suppose we want to reproduce an image using a particular combination of paper and inks. We can use the model presented in the previous section to predict the gamut of all printable colors associated with this choice of paper and inks. In most cases, there will be a number of image colors that are outside the gamut of printable colors. We therefore need to define a gamut mapping function that associates a printable color with each of the original image colors without introducing unnecessary color distortion into the image's appearance.

According to a number of articles that address gamut mapping, it is most important to maintain the hue of a color, while allowing its lightness and saturation to change in order to fit within the printing gamut [5, 10, 14, 20, 27, 29]. In the sections that follow, we devise a hue-preserving gamut mapping strategy that is more general than existing ones, then present its coordinate system and algorithmic details. We conclude our discussion of gamut mapping with some remarks on the special steps we need to take when printing with only one or two inks.

3.1 Strategy of *n*-tone mapping

In general, the gamut of three or more inks occupies a volume in color space. A typical example is shown in Figure 2, illustrating the fact that printing gamuts can take on unusual nonconvex shapes. Because an *n*-tone gamut occupies a volume, we can attempt to preserve hues (though for some choices of inks, not all hues may be printable). Among the hue-preserving gamut mapping algorithms in the literature, there are two predominant strategies for altering luminance and saturation: the first reduces saturation, leaving luminance

fixed [14, 17, 27]; the second simultaneously alters luminance and saturation toward the central gray of the gamut [14, 17].

Because the first approach maps colors into the printing gamut by reducing their radial distances from a central gray axis, we refer to it as a "cylindrical" mapping. Likewise, because the second approach reduces each color's distance from a single central gray point, we refer to it as a "spherical" mapping. Laihanen notes that depending on the image being reproduced, one may be preferable to the other [14]. The cylindrical mapping has the advantage of preserving luminance relationships, but it tends to desaturate brightly colored highlights until they become white. The spherical mapping keeps the highlights more saturated, but reduces their luminance at the same time, resulting in a reordering of brightnesses in the image.

In order to obtain some of the advantages of both the cylindrical mapping and the spherical mapping, we developed a parameterized family of intermediate mappings. While we could simply interpolate between the color given by the cylindrical mapping and the color given by the spherical mapping, there would be no guarantee that the result would lie in the printing gamut (because gamuts are not necessarily convex). Instead, we vary the locus of colors that serve as the centers of projection in the mapping: the cylindrical mapping moves colors toward a fixed line segment along rays orthogonal to a cylinder; the spherical mapping moves colors toward a single point along rays orthogonal to a sphere; our new mapping moves colors toward a line segment whose length is parameterized, along rays orthogonal to an ellipsoid. Figure 3 illustrates the directions in which colors are compressed by each type of mapping. These directions are made explicit in the following section.

3.2 Coordinate system of *n*-tone mapping

The implementation of our *n*-tone gamut mapping makes use of a special-purpose coordinate system that varies according to the parameter k. The coordinate system yields a cylindrical mapping when $k = 0$, a spherical mapping when $k = 1$, and an ellipsoidal mapping for intermediate values. Transforming an XYZ color into this coordinate system takes place in two stages. The first is a linear transform that rewrites the color as a triple (u, v, y), where y represents luminance and u and v hold the chrominance information. This linear transform shears the dark-to-light axis of the printing gamut (while preserving luminance) until it parallels the luminance direction, then applies a uniform scaling and translation that brings the darkest point of the printing gamut to $(0, 0, -1)$ and the lightest to $(0, 0, 1)$. Our linear transform is similar to that of Stone *et al.* [27, Section 5.2], but we have replaced their rotation with a shear in order to preserve luminance relationships throughout the gamut mapping process.

The second stage of the transformation converts (u, v, y) to curvilinear coordinates (r, h, ϕ), where h represents hue and r and ϕ indirectly encode luminance and saturation. These new coordinates are found by inverting the following equations:

$$u = r \cos h \cos \phi$$
$$v = r \sin h \cos \phi$$
$$y = (1 - k^2 + kr) \sin \phi$$

In this coordinate system, lines of constant h and ϕ trace out the normals to the ellipsoid $(u^2 + v^2)/k^2 + y^2 = 1$; these are the lines along which we compress out-of-gamut colors. Note that when $k = 1$, the transformation above gives the standard conversion between spherical and Cartesian coordinates, which is easily inverted. Likewise, when $k = 0$ the equations are only a slight modification of standard cylindrical coordinates, and are also easily inverted. However, for intermediate values of k, we lack an analytic solution and therefore resort to Newton's method to solve a nonlinear equation for ϕ.

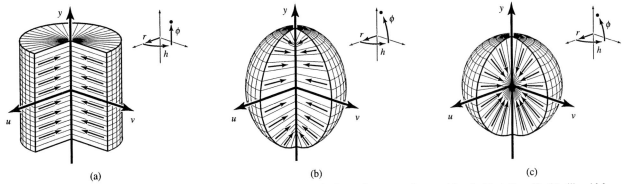

Figure 3 The coordinate systems used by three gamut mapping methods chosen from a continuum: (a) cylindrical ($k = 0$), (b) ellipsoidal ($k = 0.3$), and (c) spherical ($k = 1$). Arrows on the cutaway surfaces indicate the directions in which colors are compressed.

3.3 Steps in n-tone mapping

The first step in our gamut mapping technique is to apply a global mapping to the luminance values of the source image's colors. As noted by Power et al. [23], we can use any monotonically increasing function to compress the image's luminance range into the range of printable luminance values. Experiments in the literature typically rely on clamped or linear mappings [5, 20], but we often use a cubic mapping that has the advantages of both (see Figure 4). This mapping is inspired by the Bézier-curve mapping described by Power et al., but is more easily constructed. We determine a unique cubic function by constraining the minimum and maximum input values to map to the minimum and maximum output values, while choosing for each endpoint a slope between 0 and 1 that yields an increasing function as close as possible to the identity function (Stollnitz [26] provides further details). For most values of k we can skip this first step because subsequent steps will also adjust luminance; it is only when $k = 0$ that we must compress luminance in order for a cylindrical mapping to get all colors into the printing gamut.

The second step is to divide the set of directions that are parameterized by h and ϕ into a two-dimensional array of bins, as indicated by the grid lines in Figure 3. The number of divisions in each direction determines the storage, efficiency, and accuracy of subsequent mapping steps; numbers near 20 are adequate for quick previews, while numbers near 100 are more suitable for high-quality output.

Next, we determine the maximum extent in the r direction of the printing gamut within each (h, ϕ) bin. For each bin, we construct a ray centered within that bin, and intersect it with each of the bilinear surfaces that bound the gamut model described in Section 2.2. We associate with the bin the largest r value encountered in these intersection tests, which we call $\bar{r}_{\text{print}}$.

We also store with each bin a quantity called $\bar{r}_{\text{image}}$, defined as the largest r value of all image colors lying in that bin. If the printing gamut exceeds the image gamut for some bin, we set $\bar{r}_{\text{image}}$ equal to $\bar{r}_{\text{print}}$, so that gamut mapping will not spread similar colors apart.

The final step is to apply a mapping to the r value of each image color, where the mapping varies from one bin to the next. Given an image color, we determine the four bins closest to the (h, ϕ) coordinates of that color, and apply bilinear interpolation to the corresponding values of $\bar{r}_{\text{image}}$ and $\bar{r}_{\text{print}}$. We construct a function that maps zero to zero and the interpolated value of $\bar{r}_{\text{image}}$ to the interpolated value of $\bar{r}_{\text{print}}$. The intermediate values of r can be computed using a clamped, linear, or cubic mapping, as shown in Figure 4. Once all the image colors have been mapped, we can convert them from (r, h, ϕ) coordinates back to XYZ coordinates, and they should all lie within the printing gamut.

3.4 Monotone and duotone mappings

The gamut mapping steps described above (and many other color gamut mapping techniques) rely on assumptions about the shape of the printing gamut that do not always hold. In particular, we assumed that the gamut consists of a volume of colors that includes the line segment connecting the darkest and lightest printable colors. If we are printing with one ink, however, the gamut is a line segment of colors rather than a volume. With two inks, the gamut is a surface rather than a volume. We treat one-ink (monotone) and two-ink (duotone) printing as special cases.

The gamut of colors that can be printed with one ink is given by equation (1); it consists of a line segment parameterized by α_1. According to Stone et al. [27], the most important quality to preserve (aside from the gray axis, which we cannot keep gray) is maximum luminance contrast. Therefore, we first remap the input image's luminance values to lie within the luminance range of the printing gamut. As in the n-tone mapping, we can use any one of the clamped, linear, or cubic mappings illustrated in Figure 4. Once we finish this remapping, we can safely project each image color onto the printing gamut while preserving luminance relationships.

The gamut produced by two inks is a bilinear surface given by equation (2). Once again, because the gamut has lower dimensionality than the space of colors, we must resort to projection within any gamut mapping. The core of the work presented by Power et al. [23] is a method of mapping image colors to a duotone gamut while preserving as much color information as possible. Their algorithm first remaps the input image's luminance values as described above, then remaps a second component (s for "spread") of the image colors that is orthogonal to luminance. This second remapping is a function of luminance, so that the most compression is applied to the darkest and lightest colors, where the printing gamut is the most narrow (and the least compression to the mid-luminance colors, where the gamut

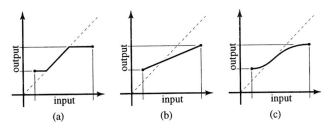

Figure 4 Monotonically increasing mappings: (a) Clamped mapping preserves exact values, except at the endpoints. (b) Linear mapping preserves relationships. (c) Cubic mapping provides a good compromise between the two.

is widest). Finally, each color is projected onto the printing gamut in the direction orthogonal to the first two mappings.

We offer two minor improvements to the method described by Power *et al.* First, we avoid discontinuities in our duotone gamut mapping by applying piecewise-linear (rather than piecewise-constant) interpolation to the bin values approximating the gamut's extent in the *s* direction. Second, we offer a choice of luminance mappings, including the clamped and cubic mappings shown in Figure 4 in addition to the linear mapping used by Power *et al.*

4 Selecting inks

Throughout Sections 2 and 3 we treated the paper and inks as though they were known. Our goal, however, is to find the optimal combination of paper and inks for a given image. This task is difficult because there may be a huge number of possible choices, most of which will result in poor reproductions. Often it is not obvious even to an experienced user whether or not a choice of paper and inks will reproduce an image well; therefore, we are not yet willing to rely on heuristic rules for accepting or rejecting combinations. Instead, we pose the problem of selecting paper and inks as a combinatorial optimization problem and apply a general-purpose algorithm to solve it, just as Power *et al.* [23] did for duotones. We describe below our objective function and optimization algorithm for choosing inks.

4.1 Ink-selection objective function

Our objective function for ink selection is very similar to the one described by Power *et al.* Given an image and a combination of paper and inks, we apply the gamut mapping algorithm discussed in Section 3 to obtain a preview image. Then we compare the preview image pixel-by-pixel to the original image, using the L^2 norm in $L^* a^* b^*$ color space. The value we assign to our objective function is the average over all pixels of the L^2 distance between the preview and original image.

The efficiency of the objective function is an important concern because it gets evaluated often. Fortunately, we don't need to apply our gamut mapping algorithm to each of the tens or hundreds of thousands of distinct colors contained in a typical high-resolution scan. Instead, we can use Heckbert's median-cut algorithm [7] to quantize the image to about 2,000 distinct colors while maintaining its general appearance. Then we need only apply the gamut mapping algorithm to these quantized colors, and weight each color's $L^* a^* b^*$ distance according to the number of pixels of that color in the original image.

4.2 Ink-selection algorithm

Power *et al.* chose a simulated annealing algorithm for their combinatorial optimizer because of its ability to find global minima and relatively good local minima. We prefer to use a genetic algorithm, mainly because it maintains a population of candidate solutions, each of which can be presented to the user as a possibility when the optimizer is finished. Simulated annealing and the genetic algorithm are both stochastic optimization techniques, making use of random changes to intermediate solutions in order to avoid local minima. In fact, Power *et al.* made their simulated annealer slightly closer to a genetic algorithm by using multiple initial conditions to obtain a variety of solutions; likewise, we made our genetic algorithm slightly closer to simulated annealing by assigning a time-varying probability distribution to each of the genetic operators.

Following suggestions made by Davis [3], we include in our implementation a number of variations on the "standard" genetic algorithm. We maintain a population of candidate combinations, each

of which is distinct from the others, and we keep them sorted according to their respective objective function values. At each iteration, we choose a genetic operator according to a time-varying probability distribution, and we choose its operands randomly from the current population. The operators for our application include global mutation, local mutation, and crossover. Global mutation operates on one combination, changing the paper and inks completely randomly; this operator is more likely to be chosen in early iterations. Local mutation also operates on one combination, but changes the paper and inks only to nearby colors; this operator is more likely in later iterations. Crossover takes two combinations and exchanges each of the papers and inks with 50% probability. The likelihood of choosing crossover starts out high, and gradually declines to zero, so as to prevent one solution from dominating the population.

Every time an operator produces a previously untested combination of paper and inks, we evaluate the objective function and compare the result to the current members of the population. If the new combination outperforms the worst member of the population, we replace the old one with the new one. Thus, each iteration maintains or improves the population. We repeat the process for a fixed number of iterations, or until a fixed number of iterations fails to yield a decrease in the objective function. The results are presented to the user as a list of possible paper and ink combinations, sorted from best to worst, from which he or she can choose any one to preview.

5 Computing separations

Once the paper and inks have been selected and a preview has been computed using our gamut mapping algorithm, our only remaining task is to produce separations for each of the inks. More precisely, for each color generated by the gamut mapping algorithm, we need to find the amount of each ink required to reproduce that color. The mathematical model of printing gamuts that we developed in Section 2 gives tristimulus colors as a function of the ink amounts α_i, whereas now we want to find the ink amounts as a function of color. Determining this inverse function is no simple matter, mainly because each tristimulus component of our model is a nonlinear function of the α values. In addition, the inverse is underdetermined when there are more than three inks; there may be many α values that yield the same color. There is another difficulty that arises in practice: some of the colors for which we wish to compute separations may be slightly out of gamut because of imprecisions in the gamut mapping stage, yet we still need to find α values between zero and one that reproduce similar colors.

For more than three inks, we cannot invert the gamut model analytically as Power *et al.* [23] did for two inks, and Mahy and Delabastita [18] did for three. We also cannot treat the printing gamut as a convex union of tetrahedra, as some authors have [9, 19, 22, 28]; many gamuts are actually concave. Instead, we rely on a continuous optimization technique to find the separations that most closely reproduce a desired color while meeting the physical constraints of the printing process. The details of our objective function and optimization algorithm are given below.

5.1 Separation objective function

The goal of the current optimization is to find the ink amounts $\alpha = (\alpha_1, \ldots, \alpha_n)$ for which our gamut model yields the color $c(\alpha)$ closest to a given tristimulus color $\bar{c}$. We formulate the objective function as the sum of four terms:

$$
\begin{aligned}
f(\alpha; \bar{c}, \alpha_{\text{ref}}) = {} & w_1 \left\| c(\alpha) - \bar{c} \right\|^2 \\
& + w_2 \sum_i \max(0, -\alpha_i, \alpha_i - 1)^2 \\
& + w_3 \max\left(0, \sum_i \alpha_i - \alpha_{\text{limit}}\right)^2 \\
& + w_4 \left\| \alpha - \alpha_{\text{ref}} \right\|^2
\end{aligned}
$$

The first term of the objective function is just the square of the distance in XYZ color space between the desired color $\bar{c}$ and the color our gamut model predicts from the α values. For an in-gamut color, the optimizer should find a solution where this term is zero. For an out-of-gamut color, minimizing the first term is akin to projecting onto the nearest point of the gamut, as was done by Stone *et al.* before computing separations [27]. We arbitrarily choose the weight $w_1 = 0.005$, and set the remaining weights by trial and error based on the magnitudes of the terms.

The second and third terms introduce penalties for violating constraints inherent in the printing process. The second term bounds each of the ink amounts between 0 and 1, thereby moving out-of-gamut colors to in-gamut separations. The third term ensures that the total amount of ink does not go over the "ink limit," the point at which ink no longer adheres to the page. The ink limit depends upon the press and the paper; we use $\alpha_{limit} = 3.7$. We typically set $w_2 = w_3 = 1000$ so that ink amounts violating these constraints are strongly penalized.

The final term of the objective function allows us to achieve a unique solution when there are multiple ways to produce the same color. We do so by finding the solution that is closest to a given set of reference values α_{ref}. We use a relatively small weight for this term ($w_4 = 0.025$) so that it does not prevent the color $c(\alpha)$ from matching $\bar{c}$. We can set each component of α_{ref} to 0 or 1 to minimize or maximize the amount of ink used, or choose 0.5 for an intermediate solution.

Unfortunately, we find that these simple choices of reference values often lead to separations containing artificial discontinuities. Because the ink amounts used for adjacent pixels are computed independently, slightly different colors may result in very different separations. While in theory these separations will produce similar colors when printed, in reality even the slightest misregistration reveals the discontinuities. To avoid such artifacts, we try to compute separations that are just as smooth as the input image. One possible solution is to set α_{ref} to the ink amounts of the most similar color among the four adjacent pixels that have already been separated. This approach eliminates many artifacts, but because of the asymmetry inherent in processing pixels from left to right and top to bottom, it may still produce discontinuities in some directions.

We can generate much better separations using a multiresolution algorithm based on image pyramids. The central idea is to compute for each pixel the ink amounts that produce the right color and are as close as possible to the ink amounts of the entire surrounding neighborhood. Of course, the ink amounts that best reproduce a pixel's neighborhood depend in turn on a larger neighborhood, and thus we rely on a recursively defined image pyramid. First, we construct a pyramid of reduced images from the gamut-mapped source image by repeatedly applying a low-pass filter followed by downsampling. We use a separable low-pass filter with coefficients $\frac{1}{16}(1, 4, 6, 4, 1)$; see Burt and Adelson [2] for further details on image pyramids. Next, we compute separations for the lowest-resolution image (with each component of α_{ref} set to 0.5). Then we calculate new separations for each higher resolution image, using as the reference values α_{ref} an enlarged version of the current separations (where enlargement consists of upsampling followed by low-pass filtering). The result is a set of separations at the highest resolution that maintain the smoothness of the original color image. Smoothness comes at the cost of computing separations for the entire image pyramid, but this is only 4/3 the work of computing separations just at the highest level.

5.2 Separation algorithm

There are a plethora of continuous optimization algorithms we could apply to the separation problem. We can choose among them by considering the amount of information they require and their rates of convergence. Because we can efficiently compute the first partial derivatives of all the terms in our objective function, we can use optimization techniques that achieve quadratic convergence rates. These include the conjugate gradient method and "quasi-Newton" methods, among others. We found the BFGS quasi-Newton method to be the most efficient for our problem (even when compared to Newton's method, which uses costly second derivative information as well). Detailed descriptions of these algorithms are given by Press *et al.* [24, pages 420–430].

6 Conclusion

In this paper, we have laid out a general framework for multicolor printing with custom inks, and described algorithms that show promise for solving longstanding problems in color printing. Our gamut model combines previous ink layering and halftoning models with modifications for trapping and dot gain. We introduced a new ellipsoidal gamut mapping that effectively fills a gap between the existing cylindrical and spherical variations of gamut mapping. We described the operators needed to adapt a genetic algorithm to the selection of papers and inks. Finally, we developed a robust multiresolution algorithm that, given any combination of inks, computes separations that are as smooth as the input image.

The appendices present practical results of our experiments in the realm of custom-ink color image reproduction. We outline there the steps required to fit the parameters of our gamut model to measured data, and exhibit a variety of printed images produced with our techniques. While we still see room for improvement in these results, they demonstrate the potential for making color reproductions with custom inks that are more accurate or less costly to produce than with standard process inks.

In general, *n*-tone printing offers the opportunity to match monitor colors better than process color printing because the inks are chosen specifically for the image. Moreover, because we construct a gamut mapping that is customized for the image at hand, we can achieve a much more accurate reproduction than is possible with a gamut mapping designed to bring all monitor colors into the same printing gamut. As a case in point, our gamut mapping will not alter an image whose colors all happen to fall within the printing gamut, while many other algorithms will shift the image colors merely because some colors in the monitor gamut (but not in the image) are not printable.

In the near future, we hope to eliminate some of the remaining artifacts from our results. In particular, we would like to eliminate the extreme desaturation of out-of-gamut hues by introducing a selective hue compression method. By using stochastic screening for our future printing experiments, we will be able to avoid the moiré interference patterns present in traditional halftones when four or more inks are assigned different screen angles. We are also interested in the effects achievable by measuring and printing opaque inks on dark papers.

There are a number of other ways in which this work can be extended. We could model metallic inks by including angular variation in the ink layering model, or capture the behavior of fluorescent inks and papers by treating reflectance and transmittance as functions of both incoming and outgoing wavelength. By substituting a model of the inks and halftoning process of ink-jet printers for our current gamut model, we could suggest custom ink choices and compute separations for these widely available devices (assuming cartridges of custom inks were available).

Our gamut mapping algorithm might be improved by performing the mapping in a perceptually uniform color space like $L^*a^*b^*$ or $L^*u^*v^*$, as recommended by MacDonald [17] and Wolski *et al.* [29].

Montag and Fairchild [20] suggest using different gamut mapping strategies for light colors and dark colors.

We are considering a variety of changes to the way in which the optimizer chooses inks. The user could indicate to the optimizer which colors are most important by painting a weighting function over the original image; these weights would multiply each pixel's $L^*a^*b^*$ distance in the objective function. We could also use the $RLab$ color space [4] or Hunt's color-appearance space [8] instead of $L^*a^*b^*$ to obtain a more accurate estimate of color differences. With more terms in the objective function, we could try to minimize the cost of the materials or their environmental impact (favoring recycled papers and soy inks), maximize the longevity of the reproduction (favoring acid-free papers and fade-resistant inks), or reduce the impact of misregistration artifacts by favoring inks similar in color to the image subject matter. As a more general extension, we might optimize not only the paper and inks, but also the gamut mapping parameters and even the choice of which images to print.

As mentioned earlier, well-chosen heuristics may help to speed up the selection of inks by eliminating poor combinations before any time is spent evaluating them. We hope to accelerate the separation algorithm as well, perhaps by exploiting coherence of image colors in color space, or using a local approximation to our gamut model that is more easily inverted.

Acknowledgments

We are grateful to Safeco Insurance's Graphics & Printing Services for their donation of time and resources. Thanks to Roger Hersch, Pat Lewis, Frédéric Pighin, and Joanna Power for helpful discussions. This work was supported by a grant from the Washington Technology Center and Numinous Technologies, an NSF Presidential Faculty Fellow award (CCR-9553199), an ONR Young Investigator award (N00014-95-1-0728), and industrial gifts from Microsoft and Pixar.

References

[1] Harold Boll. A Color to Colorant Transformation for a Seven Ink Process. In *Device-Independent Color Imaging*, volume 2170 of *Proceedings of the SPIE*, pages 108–118, 1994.

[2] P. J. Burt and E. H. Adelson. The Laplacian Pyramid as a Compact Image Code. *IEEE Transactions on Communications*, 31(4):532–540, April 1983.

[3] Lawrence Davis. *Handbook of Genetic Algorithms*. Van Nostrand Reinhold, New York, 1991.

[4] M. D. Fairchild and R. S. Berns. Image Color-Appearance Specification Through Extension of CIELAB. *Color Research and Application*, 18(3):178–190, June 1993.

[5] R. S. Gentile, E. Walowit, and J. P. Allebach. A Comparison of Techniques for Color Gamut Mismatch Compensation. *Journal of Imaging Technology*, 16(5):176–181, October 1990.

[6] Arthur C. Hardy and F. L. Wurzburg, Jr. Color Correction in Color Printing. *Journal of the Optical Society of America*, 38(4):300–307, April 1948.

[7] Paul Heckbert. Color Image Quantization for Frame Buffer Display. In *Proceedings of SIGGRAPH 82*, pages 297–307, 1982.

[8] R. W. G. Hunt. Revised Colour-Appearance Model for Related and Unrelated Colours. *Color Research and Application*, 16(3):146–165, June 1991.

[9] Kansei Iwata and Gabriel Marcu. Computer Simulation of Printed Colors on Textile Materials. In *Color Hard Copy and Graphic Arts III*, volume 2171 of *Proceedings of the SPIE*, pages 228–238, 1994.

[10] Tony Johnson. A Complete Colour Reproduction Model for Graphic Arts. In *Proceedings of the Technical Association of the Graphic Arts*, pages 1061–1076, 1996.

[11] D. B. Judd and G. Wyszecki. *Color in Business, Science, and Industry*. John Wiley and Sons, New York, 1975.

[12] Henry R. Kang. Comparisons of Color Mixing Theories for Use in Electronic Printing. In *Proceedings of the IS&T/SID Color Imaging Conference: Transforms & Transportability of Color*, pages 78–82, 1993.

[13] Gustav Kortüm. *Reflectance Spectroscopy: Principles, Methods, Applications*, chapter 4, pages 103–169. Springer, New York, 1969.

[14] P. Laihanen. Colour Reproduction Theory Based on the Principles of Colour Science. In *Proceedings of the International Association of Research Institutes for the Graphic Arts Industry*, volume 19, pages 1–36, 1987.

[15] Bruce J. Lindbloom. Accurate Color Reproduction for Computer Graphics Applications. In *Proceedings of SIGGRAPH 89*, pages 117–126, 1989.

[16] Yan Liu. Spectral Reflectance Modification of Neugebauer Equations. In *Proceedings of the Technical Association of the Graphic Arts*, pages 154–172, 1991.

[17] Lindsay W. MacDonald. Gamut Mapping in Perceptual Color Space. In *Proceedings of the IS&T/SID Color Imaging Conference: Transforms & Transportability of Color*, pages 193–196, 1993.

[18] Marc Mahy and Paul Delabastita. Inversion of the Neugebauer Equations. *Color Research and Application*, 21(6):401–411, December 1996.

[19] Gabriel Marcu and Satoshi Abe. Color Designing and Simulation in Non-Conventional Printing Process. In *Applications of Digital Image Processing XVII*, volume 2298 of *Proceedings of the SPIE*, pages 216–223, 1994.

[20] Ethan D. Montag and Mark D. Fairchild. Psychophysical Evaluation of Gamut Mapping Techniques Using Simple Rendered Images and Artificial Gamut Boundaries. *IEEE Transactions on Image Processing*, 6(7):977–989, July 1997.

[21] H. E. J. Neugebauer. Die Theoretischen Grundlagen des Mehrfarbenbuchdrucks (The Theoretical Foundation for Multicolor Printing). *Zeitschrift fuer Wissenschaftliche Photographie*, 36(4):73–89, 1937. Reprinted in *Neugebauer Memorial Seminar on Color Reproduction*, volume 1184 of *Proceedings of the SPIE*, pages 194–202. SPIE, Bellingham, WA, 1990.

[22] Victor Ostromoukhov. Chromaticity Gamut Enhancement by Heptatone Multi-color Printing. In *Device-Independent Color Imaging and Imaging Systems Integration*, volume 1909 of *Proceedings of the SPIE*, pages 139–151, 1993.

[23] Joanna L. Power, Brad S. West, Eric J. Stollnitz, and David H. Salesin. Reproducing Color Images as Duotones. In *Proceedings of SIGGRAPH 96*, pages 237–248, 1996.

[24] William H. Press, Brian P. Flannery, Saul A. Teukolsky, and William T. Fetterling. *Numerical Recipes*. Cambridge University Press, New York, second edition, 1992.

[25] J. L. Saunderson. Calculation of the Color of Pigmented Plastics. *Journal of the Optical Society of America*, 32(12):727–736, December 1942.

[26] Eric J. Stollnitz. Reproducing Color Images with Custom Inks. Ph.D. thesis, University of Washington, 1998.

[27] Maureen C. Stone, William B. Cowan, and John C. Beatty. Color Gamut Mapping and the Printing of Digital Color Images. *ACM Transactions on Graphics*, 7(4):249–292, October 1988.

[28] Atsushi Takaghi, Toru Ozeki, Yoshinori Ogata, and Sachie Minato. Faithful Color Printing for Computer Generated Image Syntheses with Highly Saturated Component Inks. In *Proceedings of the IS&T/SID Color Imaging Conference: Color Science, Systems and Applications*, pages 108–111, 1994.

[29] M. Wolski, J. P. Allebach, and C. A. Bouman. Gamut Mapping: Squeezing the Most out of Your Color System. In *Proceedings of the IS&T/SID Color Imaging Conference: Color Science, Systems and Applications*, pages 89–92, 1994.

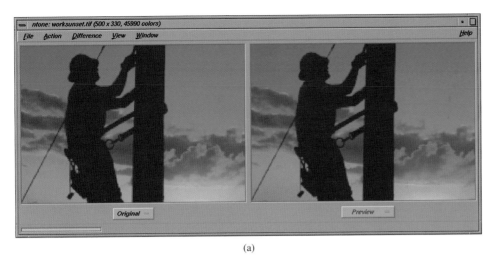

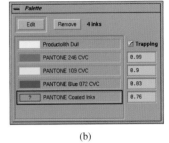

(a)

(b)

Figure 5 The interactive system's image viewer (a) and color palette (b).

Appendices

These appendices were printed with custom inks as an eight-page supplement to the SIGGRAPH proceedings in order to present the results in Examples 1 through 5. In Appendix A we describe the image reproduction system that produced the examples. Next, in Appendix B we discuss techniques for determining the gamut model parameters required by our system, including the trapping, dot gain, and spectral characteristics of papers and inks. Most of these characteristics cannot be measured directly, but we present a data-fitting scheme that allows us to derive them from experimental data. In Appendix C we present the end result of our complete system: color images printed with a variety of custom inks. Finally, in Appendix D we conclude with a discussion of the time required by each stage of our system.

A Implementation features

We developed a system incorporating the gamut model of Section 2 and the gamut mapping, ink selection, and separation algorithms of Sections 3, 4, and 5. The system, which is written in C++, has two modes of operation: batch mode and interactive mode. In batch mode, the system takes the following steps:

1. **Read the input.** The system reads an image and a set of constraints on the paper and inks to be used. The constraints can specify which paper to use, or they can delimit a subset of the available papers from which the system may choose. Likewise, each ink may be fixed by some prior decision, or allowed to vary within a particular subset of all available inks. The input also includes the parameter settings needed to control the remaining steps of the process.

2. **Find the optimal paper and inks.** The system applies the combinatorial optimization techniques of Section 4 to choose the best paper and inks satisfying the given constraints. We can skip this step if the constraints precisely specify all the printing materials.

3. **Perform gamut mapping.** The system maps each of the original image's colors into the printing gamut using the methods of Section 3. The result provides a preview of the image's printed appearance. We can skip this step if most of the image's colors fall within the printing gamut.

4. **Compute color separations.** The separation algorithm of Section 5 generates ink amounts corresponding to each pixel of the gamut-mapped preview image.

5. **Combine the separations.** As a check on the effectiveness of the gamut mapping and the accuracy of the separation algorithm, the system uses the gamut model to combine the ink amounts for each pixel into a "proof" image portraying the precise colors the separations will produce when printed. We can simulate the effect of misregistration in this step by translating each of the separations in different directions before combining them. We can also highlight in the proof any pixels for which the ink amounts exceed the ink limit for a given paper and printing press.

6. **Output the results.** The final step saves the preview image, the color separations, and the proof image. The system also generates a script that composes the separations in a page layout within a desktop publishing application.

The interactive mode of our application performs each of these tasks as well, but provides more flexibility by allowing the user to view intermediate results and alter the parameters of the algorithms at any point in the process. Of particular use is the ability to fine-tune the inks that the combinatorial optimizer selects by trying similar com-

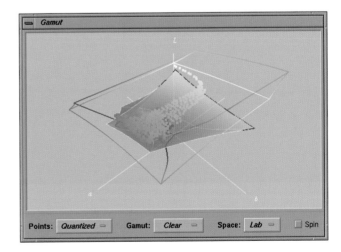

Figure 6 The interactive system's gamut visualization tool. This example displays in $L^*a^*b^*$ color space the printing gamut corresponding to the paper and first three inks in the color palette of Figure 5(b). The cluster of dots shows the location of colors in the original image of Figure 5(a), while the large outlined volume shows the extent of all monitor colors.

Example 1 Process-color reproductions made using Photoshop (a) and using our system (b). The flowers in our process-color print more accurately portray the hues displayed in the original monitor image. Reproductions (c) through (f) use four custom inks chosen from a set of 18 by the genetic algorithm: PANTONE Blue 072, Process Magenta, Process Yellow, and Green. Version (c) was produced by our multiresolution separation algorithm; the image maintains its smoothness when the separations are misregistered in (d). Version (e) demonstrates what goes wrong when we do not use the multiresolution algorithm: discontinuities appear if we attempt to use the least ink possible by separating each pixel independently with the reference ink amounts $\boldsymbol{\alpha}_{\text{ref}}$ set to zero. These discontinuities are amplified by misregistration in (f).

(a) ⬤ ⬤ ⬤ ○   (b) ⬤ ⬤ ○

Example 2 Reproductions of a sunset using process color inks (a) and using three custom inks (b): PANTONE Purple, Blue 072, and Process Yellow. This combination of custom inks was ranked second by the genetic algorithm after evaluating 5,000 possible triples of inks chosen from a set of 18. Though the process color version is better able to reproduce the dark silhouetted areas of the original monitor image, the three-color print more accurately depicts the vibrant purple sky.

binations. The gamut mapping stage quickly provides a preview of the image's printed appearance for the user to compare to the original image. Once the user settles on a choice of inks, he or she can instruct the system to begin the more time-consuming process of computing the appropriate color separations.

The application's user interface includes three major components: the image viewer, the color palette, and the gamut visualization tool. The image viewer, pictured in Figure 5(a), displays two images side-by-side for comparison. The left side always shows the original input image, while the right side can display the preview image resulting from gamut mapping, or any one of the separations. The right side can also show a proof image obtained by recombining the separations, with or without a simulation of the effects of misregistration. The user can pan and zoom the two views simultaneously to compare any region of interest.

The currently selected paper and inks are displayed in the color palette, pictured in Figure 5(b). In the figure, the user has specified a paper and three inks. The question mark in the space reserved for the fourth ink indicates that the user wants the optimizer to choose the best candidates from the specified PANTONE set of inks.

Choosing inks by hand is facilitated by the gamut visualization tool shown in Figure 6. This tool provides a three-dimensional view of color space that can be rotated, translated, and magnified interactively. The visualization displays the printing gamut corresponding to the current choice of paper and inks, as well as the location in color space of the original image colors. By observing how many image colors lie outside the printing gamut, the user gets a sense of how well the current choice of paper and inks will reproduce the image. If the gamut has an obvious shortcoming, the user can choose new inks by selecting colors directly according to their three-dimensional locations within the color space.

B Experimental determination of model parameters

We cannot visualize or model printing gamuts unless we have data characterizing the papers and inks available to us. We conducted an experiment whose goal was to determine R_p for a variety of papers, and the parameters R_i, $\bar{R}_i$, T_i, and γ_i for a number of inks. We also wanted to find how the trapping fractions t_{pi}, t_{pij}, and t_{pijk} depend on paper and inks. Finally, we were curious to see if the corrections for Fresnel reflection in equations (9) and (10) are necessary.

We printed a systematic rectangular grid of varying colors using 18 inks that we refer to as the PANTONE *primaries* (the 14 PANTONE colors used to mix other inks, and the four standard process colors) on 13 papers (five colored uncoated papers, four glossy coated white papers, and four matte coated white papers). The experiment was divided into seven runs, with the ordering and colors of the six inks in the press varying from one run to the next. The grid of 2,745 samples included finely spaced steps of each individual ink, as well as coarsely spaced steps of all possible combinations of three inks. In all, we obtained nearly 250,000 printed color samples. Using a spectrophotometer mounted on a robot arm, we measured absolute spectral reflectances of 153,720 samples from five uncoated colored papers and three coated white papers.

B.1 Characterizing papers

The first task we accomplished with the experimental data was to determine the reflectance of each paper. The measurements included more than 500 reflectance spectra of each unprinted paper from a number of sheets and from varying locations on those sheets. Due to normal variations in the paper colors, the measurements differed by as much as 0.1 in absolute reflectance within each wavelength band. We obtained a single reflectance spectrum for each paper by assigning to R_p the median value of the measured values within each band. Using the median helped to eliminate the occasional outlying value caused by dirty or contaminated samples.

B.2 Characterizing inks

Our next task was to characterize the inks by finding their dot gain, trapping, reflectance, transmittance, and Fresnel reflection parameters. Some of the ink samples were poorly printed, either because of contamination by impurities or because the press did not supply ink consistently across the width of the page. We discarded from our data set all the samples within a given run that incorporated any ink that was printed poorly in that run. These inks were detected algorithmically be examining the range of variation in samples printed with just one ink. For a given ink in a given run, we took the difference between the maximum and minimum measured reflectances (in each wavelength band) for that ink, and labeled the ink as poorly printed if these differences averaged more than 0.1 over all wavelengths. In effect, we discarded inks that varied more on average than the papers did at their worst.

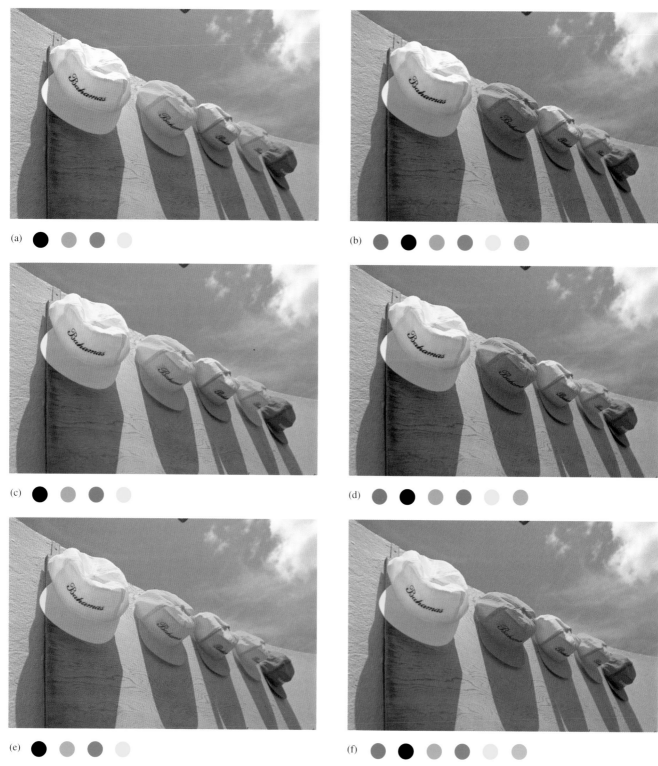

Example 3 An image reproduced using process color inks (a, c, e) and six custom inks (b, d, f). The genetic algorithm selected PANTONE Red 032, Process Black, Process Cyan, Process Magenta, Process Yellow, and Green from a set of 18 inks. Without any appreciable change in the preview, we replaced the first of these inks with Orange 021 in order to improve the results in our next example. The vibrant orange and green hats in the original monitor image are more accurately portrayed with six inks than with the four process colors. The four-color and six-color reproductions include examples of cylindrical, ellipsoidal, and spherical gamut mappings. Differences are most apparent in the highlights on the yellow hat, which turn white under the cylindrical mapping in (a) and (b), and flat yellow under the spherical mapping in (e) and (f). The ellipsoidal mapping in (c) and (d) produces a compromise that appears most like the monitor image, with highlights that are both brighter and whiter than the rest of the yellow hat.

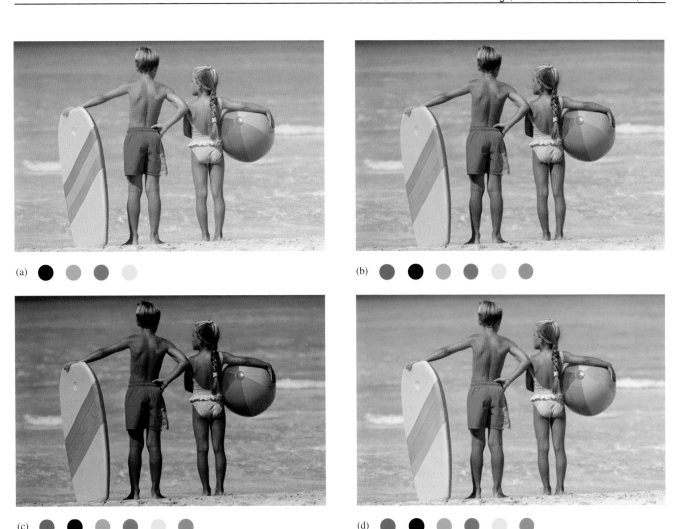

Example 4 A beach scene reproduced using process color inks (a) and using the previous example's six inks (b, c, d). The addition of orange and green inks to the four process colors produces a more saturated orange stripe on the surfboard and more vivid green on the beach ball in version (b). Reproductions (c) and (d) illustrate defects that result when we omit portions of our usual reproduction process. Leaving out the correction for dot gain results in a reproduction that appears too dark in version (c). Omitting the gamut mapping step of our system results in version (d), where the cyan portions of the image stand out with unwanted contrast because these colors are clamped to the gamut's surface.

Among the 18 PANTONE primaries, two inks (Process Yellow and Violet) were not printed well in any of the runs, and therefore our experiment provided no useful data on these inks. We later obtained better samples of Process Yellow along with the other three process colors and two spot colors used in our examples, though these additional samples were only printed on white coated paper.

Dot gain

The property of an ink that is most straightforward to determine is its dot gain. Recall from equation (1) that our gamut model for a single halftoned ink consists of a straight line segment connecting the paper color and the color of the ink printed on paper at 100% coverage. This is true even in the color space of the 36-band spectral measurements made by our spectrophotometer. If we denote by $M(\alpha_i)$ the measured reflectance spectrum of ink i printed with a coverage of α_i, we can rewrite equation (1) in terms of spectral values:

$$M(\alpha_i) = (1 - t_{pi}\,\alpha_i)\,R_p + t_{pi}\,\alpha_i\,R_{pi}$$

Because this equation is linear in α_i, we can rewrite it completely in terms of quantities we can measure:

$$M(\alpha_i) = M(0) + \alpha_i\,(M(1) - M(0))$$

In this form, we can see that the measurement of an ink printed at coverage α_i should lie a fraction α_i along the line segment in color space between the measured color of paper $M(0)$ and the measured color of the full-coverage ink $M(1)$. In practice, the measurements of halftoned samples deviate slightly from a straight line because of variations in paper color or simply because our model's assumptions are faulty. However, we can determine the actual coverage value α_i (as opposed to the intended coverage value $\bar{\alpha}_i$) by projecting the halftoned color $M(\alpha_i)$ orthogonally onto the line segment connecting $M(0)$ and $M(1)$:

$$\alpha_i = \frac{(M(\alpha_i) - M(0)) \cdot (M(1) - M(0))}{\|M(1) - M(0)\|}$$

When we plot the resulting value of α_i versus the corresponding coverage value $\bar{\alpha}_i$ that was specified for a sequence of 32 halftoned samples of a particular ink on a given paper, we get a graph like the one shown in Figure 7. The behavior of the data points can be captured remarkably well by a single parameter γ_i in the power law curve of equation (4) (also shown in the figure). We used a nonlinear curve-fitting procedure provided by the Matlab package to determine γ_i values for each of the 18 inks on one of the coated white papers. The results ranged from 0.43 for PANTONE Process Black

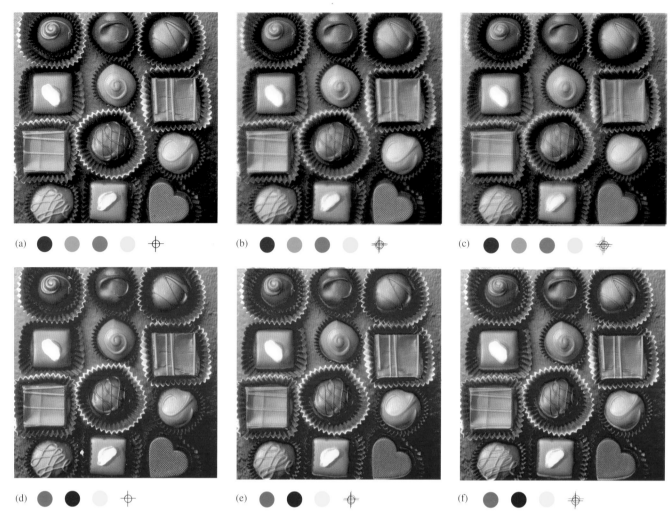

Example 5 Process color reproductions (a, b, c) and three-ink reproductions (d, e, f) of a picture of chocolates. The first column is printed with the separations aligned correctly, while in the middle column each separation is shifted by 0.24 mm in a different direction, and in the third column each is shifted by 0.36 mm. We hypothesized that misregistration artifacts (bands of incorrect hues at the edges of objects) would be less objectionable if we chose inks that closely matched the colors of objects in the image. We chose an image of chocolates because misregistration artifacts are particularly unappealing in pictures of foods, and because the limited range of colors in this image can be closely approximated by the gamut of just three inks (PANTONE 173, Process Black, and 394). The misregistered process color print in (c) exhibits green and orange fringes around the nuts, while the corresponding artifacts in the three-color version (f) are somewhat less noticeable. The three-color version retains more sharpness in the misregistered version, as well. No gamut mapping was used for the reproductions in this example.

to 0.64 for PANTONE Yellow 012 (though there was no obvious pattern to the numbers).

Reflectance, transmittance, trapping, and Fresnel coefficients

It is convenient that we can determine dot gain independently of the other parameters of the gamut model. The remaining properties of inks (reflectance, transmittance, Fresnel coefficients, and trapping fractions) are interrelated in such a way that we cannot easily determine one independently of the others. In order to distinguish between light reflected by an ink and light reflected by the paper after transmission through that ink, we need measurements of the ink printed atop various differently colored backgrounds. Our systematic printed grid offered us samples of each ink printed on many different paper colors, as well as samples of each ink printed atop a number of other inks. We originally used samples of an ink printed individually on all the papers to determine the spectral properties of that ink, but we found that the difference between coated and uncoated papers prevented the model from achieving a good fit to the data. We therefore focused on fitting the spectral parameters of each

ink based on samples printed on just one white paper, but in combination with other inks.

The process of fitting model parameters to data can be posed as a large continuous optimization problem. The objective is to minimize the perceptual difference between colors predicted by the gamut model and the colors we measured—in other words, the average $L^*a^*b^*$ distance between modeled and measured colors. In our case, we want to optimize over the 36-dimensional spectra R_i, $\tilde{R}_i$, and T_i for 16 inks, along with four Fresnel coefficients and a multitude of trapping fractions. Of course, optimizing nearly 2,000 unknowns can be terribly time-consuming, particularly when one evaluation of the objective function involves comparing thousands of spectral reflectances. A more efficient approach is to split the variables according to their dependencies: we treat R_i, $\tilde{R}_i$, and T_i as functions of ink and wavelength, trapping fractions as functions of the paper and inks involved, and the four Fresnel coefficients as unknown constants. With this splitting in mind, we developed a Matlab procedure that iteratively improves the parameters of our gamut model to achieve the best fit to the measured samples. The follow-

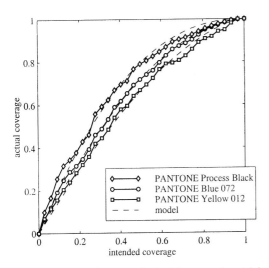

Figure 7 Typical dot gain curves obtained from experimental data.

ing pseudocode outlines the structure of the procedure without the encumbrance of Matlab's technicalities.

function *FitModel*
    initialize all T_i values to 1
    initialize all R_i and $\tilde{R}_i$ values to 0
    initialize all t_{pi}, t_{pij}, and t_{pijk} values to 1
    initialize ρ_{ai}, ρ_{ia}, ρ_{ip}, and ρ_{pi} to 0
    error := $EvaluateError(T_i, R_i, \ldots, \rho_{ip}, \rho_{pi})$
    repeat
        for each ink i and wavelength band λ
            $OptimizeSpectra(T_i(\lambda), R_i(\lambda), \tilde{R}_i(\lambda))$
        for each paper p and ink i
            $OptimizeTrapping(t_{pi})$
        for each paper p, ink i, and ink j
            $OptimizeTrapping(t_{pij})$
        for each paper p, ink i, ink j, and ink k
            $OptimizeTrapping(t_{pijk})$
        $OptimizeFresnel(\rho_{ai}, \rho_{ia}, \rho_{ip}, \rho_{pi})$
        lastError := error
        error := $EvaluateError(T_i, R_i, \ldots, \rho_{ip}, \rho_{pi})$
    until lastError − error < ϵ
end function

The *EvaluateError* function, as its name implies, calculates how well a gamut model with the current ink parameters fits the measured spectral data. We compute this error metric by averaging (over all solid-colored samples in the data set for a given paper) the L^2 norm of the difference in $L^*a^*b^*$ color space between predicted and measured colors. In order to predict the color of a given printed sample, we apply our ink layering model to another measured sample with all but the topmost ink. For example, to predict the color of a sample including inks i, j, and k, we first find a location nearby on the page where a sample M_{ij} has been printed with inks i and j but not k. (We choose a sample that is nearby to reduce the influence on our calculation of the unavoidable variations in paper color and ink density across the page.) We then model the effect of printing ink k atop the sample M_{ij}, and compare the result to the measured sample M_{ijk} with all three inks. The prediction relies on the Kubelka-Munk model of equation (7) and the Fresnel reflection corrections of equations (9) and (10) to determine ideally trapped printing primaries, then applies the modified Neugebauer equations of Section 2.2 to account for imperfect trapping. Note that dot gain does not play a role in the evaluation function since we consider only samples that are printed with 100% coverage.

The *OptimizeSpectra*, *OptimizeTrapping*, and *OptimizeFresnel* functions each use one of Matlab's constrained nonlinear optimization procedures to minimize the *EvaluateError* function over a subset of the ink parameters. We specialized the three optimization functions to efficiently compute just the portion of the objective function that is affected by their particular ink parameters. For example, *OptimizeSpectra* is charged with finding the best reflectance and transmittance parameters for one wavelength band of one ink at a time, assuming the current trapping and Fresnel coefficients are held fixed. Therefore, *OptimizeSpectra* needs to compare predictions to measurements only for samples whose topmost ink is the one in question.

Model variations

As we pointed out at the beginning of this appendix, we are interested not only in obtaining parameter values for our model, but also in determining their relative importance. We therefore used the procedure above to fit twelve variations of the model parameters to the measured data. Table 1 enumerates the variations, some of which constrain R_i and $\tilde{R}_i$ to be zero, while others constrain only $\tilde{R}_i$, and still others permit both to be optimized. Likewise, some of the variations assume perfect trapping while others optimize the trapping fractions; some assume no Fresnel reflection while others optimize the Fresnel coefficients.

One of the conclusions we were able to draw from fitting the model parameters was that the amount of ink trapped by the page depends primarily on the type of paper (coated versus uncoated) and on the number of ink layers already printed. For example, coated papers typically trap between 98 and 100% of the first ink printed and between 88 and 95% of the second ink printed atop the first, regardless of the ink colors. We subsequently treated trapping fractions as functions only of the paper and the number of ink layers, rather than as functions of each particular ink. Half of our model variations constrain the trapping fractions to be 1, while each of the remaining variations yields a similar sequence of decreasing trapping fractions.

Half of the model variations constrain the Fresnel reflection coefficients to be zero. The remaining variations produce quite different results, depending on whether or not we constrain the ink reflectances and back-surface reflectances to be zero. The inks are permitted to reflect light in models G, H, K, and L; in these cases, ρ_{ia} ranges from 0.25 to 0.35, indicating that a significant fraction of the light reflected by the ink pigments is actually trapped within the ink by internal reflection at the interface with air.

In addition to fitting our models to the data obtained for the PANTONE primaries, we also determined ink parameters for two smaller data sets. One of these consisted of the four process colors (cyan, magenta, yellow, and black, denoted CMYK), while the other included two spot colors (PANTONE 173 and PANTONE 394). Because these inks were printed on only one paper and with far fewer overprinted combinations than the primary data set, we were not able to fit all the model parameters for these inks. We relied on the trapping fractions and Fresnel coefficients obtained for the PANTONE

	$\rho = 0$		optimal ρ	
	$t = 1$	optimal t	$t = 1$	optimal t
optimal T; $R = \tilde{R} = 0$	A	B	C	D
optimal T and R; $\tilde{R} = 0$	E	F	G	H
optimal T, R, and $\tilde{R}$	I	J	K	L

Table 1 Variations used in fitting ink models to data. Here ρ stands for all four Fresnel reflection coefficients and t stands for all trapping fractions. Similarly, T, R, and $\tilde{R}$ refer to all wavelengths of transmittance, reflectance, and back surface reflectance of all inks.

primaries, holding these values fixed while we optimized the transmittance and reflectance parameters of the four process colors and the two spot colors. There was not enough data to determine the back-surface reflectance $\tilde{R}_i$, so we could not use model variations I, J, K, or L for any of these inks.

We determined the success of our model-fitting process by examining the average $L^*a^*b^*$ error between predicted and measured colors. Our analysis of this error metric indicated clearly that incorporating trapping fractions less than one into the gamut model improves the accuracy in fitting the larger data set of PANTONE primaries. The CMYK and spot color data sets also show an improved fit when the effect of trapping is included, though the improvement is less significant (perhaps because we could not optimize the trapping fractions for these inks).

We have a harder time drawing conclusions about the other differences between model variations. Using optimized values for ink reflectance R_i in variations E through H brings about a small improvement over variations A through D, while incorporating back-surface reflectance (variations I through L) has little to no beneficial effect. Optimizing over the Fresnel reflection coefficients appears to improve the fit of the models somewhat, but the physical plausibility of the resulting numbers deserves further investigation.

In general, we concluded from our analysis that variations D, G, and H offer the most promising alternatives. Because all the variations result in quite similar error values, we are left with the concern that a significant portion of those errors may be due to the variability inherent in paper colors and press operation. If that is the case and we cannot avoid making somewhat erroneous predictions, the simplicity of model variation A may make it more appealing than any of the others; the determination of ink transmittance alone reduces to a linear least-squares problem. However, after printing many images separated using variations A, D, and H, we found that variation A sometimes reproduced dark areas poorly, while D and H performed much better and could not be distinguished from one another. We chose variation D, the simpler of the two, to produce Examples 1 through 5.

C   Printed examples

The ultimate goal of any color reproduction is the faithful reproduction of physical reality. Unfortunately, it's not easy to obtain a physical image: full-spectrum cameras are rare and expensive. Instead, we often deal with simplified *RGB* images captured by tri-filter cameras and films. In this context, the original full-spectrum image is lost. Consequently, for want of anything better, an *objective* original image is replaced by a *subjective* original image—one that "looks good" on the monitor. We too use this widely accepted criterion and try to match the appearance of images on a calibrated monitor.

We selected a variety of stock photography images with which to test our algorithms. Our goal was to reproduce them as they appeared on our calibrated monitor (a BARCO Reference Calibrator, with stable and known phosphor chromaticities). The images, like most that are commercially available, provided device-dependent *RGB* colors, but without documented reference to any particular device. We therefore converted the colors to device-independent *XYZ* coordinates, treating *RGB* values as though they referred to the red, green, and blue primaries in both Kodak's PhotoCD standard and the HDTV (high-definition television) standard, with a gamma correction of 1.5.

We used the algorithms discussed in Sections 3, 4, and 5 to choose inks, apply gamut mappings, and produce separations for each of the images that appear in Examples 1 through 5. For some of the images, we picked the inks ourselves, while for others we used the genetic algorithm to choose the inks. The genetic algorithm provided

example	resolution	inks	selection time	mapping time	separation time
1(c)	1000×660	4	15 min	6 sec	16 min
2(b)	1000×660	3	5 min	2 sec	7 min
3(d)	1000×660	6	300 min	66 sec	51 min
4(b)	1000×660	6	—	71 sec	75 min
5(d)	660×660	3	—	—	6 min

Table 2 Statistics for printed example images. The genetic algorithm selected inks from the 18 measured in the experiment described in Appendix B. Approximate computation times are given for an SGI O2 workstation with a 174 MHz R10000 processor.

us with a number of good solutions; we chose from these possibilities by considering the subjective appeal of the corresponding preview images. Because we could only print a limited number of inks on a page, we favored inks that helped reproduce other images on the same sheet.

Except where noted otherwise in the example captions, we used the cylindrical gamut mapping strategy (because it preserves luminance relationships) and the multiresolution separation algorithm (because it produces smooth separations). The separations were halftoned at 175 lines per inch using conventional screening and printed by a six-color sheet-fed offset press on 100-pound white Productolith dull coated paper.

D   Timings and complexity

Table 2 presents some statistics for the example images discussed above, and the processing time required by each stage of our algorithm. The time it takes to select optimal inks varies widely depending on the combinatorial complexity of the problem: the time increases exponentially with the number of inks being selected and with the size of the ink set from which they are chosen. We suspect that by adding a few well-chosen heuristics to our general-purpose optimizer, we could eliminate from consideration a large fraction of the bad combinations that we currently spend time evaluating. Our implementation can compute the optimal inks as a preprocessing step, or, in our interactive environment, the user can monitor the progress of the optimizer and interrupt it when it achieves an acceptable solution. Furthermore, because the genetic algorithm maintains a population of possible solutions, we present to the user a number of choices for comparison.

The gamut mapping stage takes only a few seconds, even for six-ink gamuts with fairly complex shapes, making it well suited for use in our interactive application. Users of our system can easily modify their choice of inks or the parameters of the gamut mapping, and quickly see the results of these changes.

The time required to compute separations is roughly proportional to the product of the number of inks and the number of pixels in the original image. Because the separation objective function includes penalties, the continuous optimizer takes more iterations to converge for some colors—particularly those near or outside gamut boundaries—than others. Separations typically take too long to compute in an interactive setting, but fortunately the user can try out many choices of inks (looking at previews) before settling on a combination for which separations are needed. The system can then compute and save the separations as a postprocessing step.

The efficiency of the separator depends on how fast we can evaluate the objective function and its partial derivatives. The major component of these computations is the evaluation of the gamut model and its derivatives. We expect that tuning this part of the code could make the separation algorithm execute at speeds suitable for our interactive application rather than the postprocessing stage.

Realistic modeling and rendering of plant ecosystems

Oliver Deussen[1]   Pat Hanrahan[2]   Bernd Lintermann[3]   Radomír Měch[4]

Matt Pharr[2]   Przemyslaw Prusinkiewicz[4]

[1] Otto-von-Guericke University of Magdeburg
[2] Stanford University
[3] The ZKM Center for Art and Media Karlsruhe
[4] The University of Calgary*

Abstract

Modeling and rendering of natural scenes with thousands of plants poses a number of problems. The terrain must be modeled and plants must be distributed throughout it in a realistic manner, reflecting the interactions of plants with each other and with their environment. Geometric models of individual plants, consistent with their positions within the ecosystem, must be synthesized to populate the scene. The scene, which may consist of billions of primitives, must be rendered efficiently while incorporating the subtleties of lighting in a natural environment.

We have developed a system built around a pipeline of tools that address these tasks. The terrain is designed using an interactive graphical editor. Plant distribution is determined by hand (as one would do when designing a garden), by ecosystem simulation, or by a combination of both techniques. Given parametrized procedural models of individual plants, the geometric complexity of the scene is reduced by *approximate instancing*, in which similar plants, groups of plants, or plant organs are replaced by instances of representative objects before the scene is rendered. The paper includes examples of visually rich scenes synthesized using the system.

CR categories: I.3.7 **[Computer Graphics]**: Three-Dimensional Graphics and Realism, I.6.3 **[Simulation and Modeling]**: Applications, J.3 **[Life and Medical Sciences]**: Biology.

Keywords: realistic image synthesis, modeling of natural phenomena, ecosystem simulation, self-thinning, plant model, vector quantization, approximate instancing.

1 INTRODUCTION

Synthesis of realistic images of terrains covered with vegetation is a challenging and important problem in computer graphics. The challenge stems from the visual complexity and diversity of the modeled scenes. They include natural ecosystems such as forests or grasslands, human-made environments, for instance parks and gardens, and intermediate environments, such as lands recolonized by vegetation after forest fires or logging. Models of these ecosystems have a wide range of existing and potential applications, including computer-assisted landscape and garden design, prediction and visualization of the effects of logging on the landscape, visualization of models of ecosystems for research and educational purposes, and synthesis of scenes for computer animations, drive and flight simulators, games, and computer art.

Beautiful images of forests and meadows were created as early as 1985 by Reeves and Blau [50] and featured in the computer animation *The Adventures of André and Wally B.* [34]. Reeves and Blau organized scene modeling as a sequence of steps: specification of a terrain map that provides the elevation of points in the scene, interactive or procedural placement of vegetation in this terrain, modeling of individual plants (grass and trees), and rendering of the models. This general scheme was recently followed by Chiba *et al.* [8] in their work on forest rendering, and provides the basis for commercial programs devoted to the synthesis of landscapes [2, 49].

The complexity of nature makes it necessary to carefully allot computing resources — CPU time, memory, and disk space — when recreating natural scenes with computer graphics. The size of the database representing a scene during the rendering is a particularly critical item, since the amount of geometric data needed to represent a detailed outdoor scene is more than can be represented on modern computers. Consequently, a survey of previous approaches to the synthesis of natural scenes reflects the quest for a good tradeoff between the realism of the images and the amount of resources needed to generate them.

The scenes synthesized by Reeves and Blau were obtained using (structured) particle systems, with the order of one million particles per tree [50]. To handle large numbers of primitive elements contributing to the scene, the particle models of individual trees were generated procedurally and rendered sequentially, each model discarded as soon as a tree has been rendered. Consequently, the size of memory needed to generate the scene was proportional to the number of particles in a single tree, rather than the total number of particles in the scene. This approach required approximate shading calculations, since the detailed information about the neighborhood trees was not available. Approximate shading also reduced the time needed to render the scenes.

Another approach to controlling the size of scene representation is the reduction of visually unimportant detail. General methods for achieving this reduction have been the subject of intense research (for a recent example and further references see [24]), but the results do not easily apply to highly branching plant structures. Consequently, Weber and Penn [63] introduced a heuristic multiresolution representation specific to trees, which allows for reducing

---
* Department of Computer Science, University of Calgary, Calgary, Alberta, Canada T2N 1N4 (*pwp@cpsc.ucalgary.ca*)

the number of geometric primitives in the models that occupy only a small portion on the screen. A multiresolution representation of botanical scenes was also explored by Marshall *et al.* [35], who integrated polygonal representations of larger objects with tetrahedral approximations of the less relevant parts of a scene.

A different strategy for creating visually complex natural scenes was proposed by Gardner [17]. In this case, the terrain and the trees were modeled using a relatively small number of geometric primitives (quadric surfaces). Their perceived complexity resulted from procedural textures controlling the color and the transparency of tree crowns. In a related approach, trees and other plants were represented as texture-mapped flat polygons (for example, see [49]). This approach produced visible artifacts when the position of the viewpoint was changed. A more accurate image-based representation was introduced by Max [37], who developed an algorithm for interpolating between precomputed views of trees. A multiresolution extension of this method, taking advantage of the hierarchical structure of the modeled trees, was presented in [36]. Shade *et al.* described a hybrid system for walkthroughs that uses a combination of geometry and textured polygons [53].

Kajiya and Kay [26] introduced volumetric textures as an alternative paradigm for overcoming the limitations of texture-mapped polygons. A method for generating terrains with volumetric textures representing grass and trees was proposed by Neyret [40, 41]. Chiba *et al.* [8] removed the deformations of plants caused by curvatures of the underlying terrain by allowing texels to intersect.

The use of volumetric textures limits the memory or disk space needed to represent a scene, because the same texel can be re-applied to multiple areas. The same idea underlies the oldest approach to harnessing visually complex scenes, object instancing [59]. According to the paradigm of instancing, an object that appears several times in a scene (possibly resized or deformed by an affine transformation) is defined only once, and its different occurrences (instances) are specified by affine transformations of the prototype. Since the space needed to represent the transformations is small, the space needed to represent an entire scene depends primarily on the number and complexity of *different* objects, rather than the number of their instances. Plants are particularly appealing objects of instancing, because repetitive occurrences can be found not only at the level of plant species, but also at the level of plant organs and branching structures. This leads to compact hierarchical data structures conducive to fast ray tracing, as discussed by Kay and Kajiya [27], and Snyder and Barr [56]. Hart and DeFanti [20, 21] further extended the paradigm of instancing from hierarchical to recursive (self-similar) structures. All the above papers contain examples of botanical scenes generated using instancing.

The complexity of natural scenes makes them not only difficult to render, but also to specify. Interactive modeling techniques, available in commercial packages such as Alias/Wavefront Studio 8 [1], focus on the direct manipulation of a relatively small number of surfaces. In contrast, a landscape with plants may include many millions of individual surfaces — representing stems, leaves, flowers, and fruits — arranged into complex branching structures, and further organized in an ecosystem. In order to model and render such scenes, we employ the techniques summarized below.

Multilevel modeling and rendering pipeline. Following the approach initiated by Reeves and Blau [50], we decompose the process of image synthesis into stages: modeling of the terrain, specification of plant distribution, modeling of the individual plants, and rendering of the entire scene. Each of these stages operates at a different level of abstraction, and provides a relatively high-level input for the next stage. Thus, the modeler is not concerned with plant distribution when specifying the terrain, and plant distribution is determined (interactively or algorithmically) without considering details of the individual plants. This is reminiscent of the simulations of flocks of birds [51], models of flower heads with phyllotactic patterns [16], and models of organic structures based on morphogenetic processes [14], where simulations were performed using geometrically simpler objects than those used for visualization. Blumberg and Galyean extended this paradigm to *multi-level* direction of autonomous animated agents [5]. In an analogous way, we apply it to multi-level modeling.

Open system architecture. By clearly specifying the formats of inputs and outputs for each stage of the pipeline, we provide a framework for incorporating independently developed modules into our system. This open architecture makes it possible to augment the complexity of the modeled scenes by increasing the range of the available modules, and facilitates experimentation with various approaches and algorithms.

Procedural models. As observed by Smith [55], procedural models are often characterized by a significant *data-base amplification*, which means that they can generate complex geometric structures from small input data sets. We benefit from this phenomenon by employing procedural models in all stages of the modeling pipeline.

Approximate instancing. We use object instancing as the primary paradigm for reducing the size of the geometric representation of the rendered scenes. To increase the degree of instancing, we cluster scene components (plants and their parts) in their parameter spaces, and approximate all objects within a given cluster with instances of a single representative object. This idea was initially investigated by Brownbill [7]; we extend it further by applying vector quantization (*c.f.* [18]) to find the representative objects in multidimensional parameter spaces.

Efficient rendering. We use memory- and time-efficient rendering techniques: decomposition of the scenes into subscenes that are later composited [12], ray tracing with instancing and a support for rendering many polygons [56], and memory-coherent ray tracing [43] with instancing.

By employing these techniques, we have generated scenes with up to 100,000 detailed plant models. This number could be increased even further, since none of the scenes required more than 150MB to store. However, with 100,000 plants, each plant is visible on average only in 10 pixels of a 1K × 1K image. Consequently, we seem to have reached the limits of useful scene complexity, because the level of visible detail is curbed by the size and resolution of the output device.

2 SYSTEM ARCHITECTURE

The considerations presented in the previous section led us to the modular design of our modeling and rendering system EcoSys, shown schematically in Figure 1.

The modeling process begins with the specification of a terrain. For this purpose, we developed an interactive editor TerEdit, which integrates a number of terrain modeling techniques (Section 3). Its output, a *terrain data* file, includes the altitudes of a grid of points superimposed on the terrain, normal vectors indicating the local slope of the terrain, and optional information describing environmental conditions, such as soil humidity.

The next task is to determine plant distribution on a given terrain. We developed two techniques for this purpose: visual editing of plant densities and simulation of plant interactions within an ecosystem

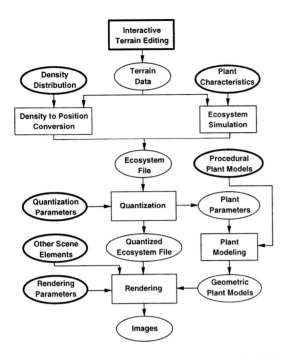

Figure 1: Architecture of the scene synthesis system. Bold frames indicate interactive programs and input files specified by the user.

(Section 4). The editing approach is particularly well suited to model environments designed by people, for example orchards, gardens, or parks. The user specifies the distribution of plant densities using a paint program. To convert this information into positions of individual plants, we developed the program densedis based on a half-toning algorithm: each dot becomes a plant. We can also specify positions of individual plants explicitly; this is particularly important in the synthesis of scenes that include detailed views of individual plants in the foreground.

To define plant distribution in natural environments, such as forests or meadows, we apply an ecosystem simulation model. Its input consists of terrain data, ecological characteristics of plant species (for example, annual or perennial growth and reproduction cycle, preference for wet or dry soil, and shade tolerance) and, optionally, the initial distribution of plants. The growth of plants is simulated accounting for competition for space, sunlight, resources in the soil, aging and death, seed distribution patterns, *etc*. We perform these simulations using the L-system-based plant modeling program cpfg [47], extended with capabilities for simulating interactions between plants and their environments [39]. To allow for simulations involving thousands of plants, we use their simplified geometrical representations, which are subsequently replaced by detailed plant models for visualization purposes.

Specification of a plant distribution may involve a combination of interactive and simulation techniques. For example, a model of an orchard may consist of trees with explicitly specified positions and weeds with positions determined by a simulation. Conversely, the designer of a scene may wish to change its aspects after an ecological simulation for aesthetic reasons. To allow for these operations, both densedis and cpfg can take a given plant distribution as input for further processing.

Plant distribution, whether determined interactively or by ecosystem simulation, is represented in an *ecosystem* file. It contains the information about the type, position and orientation of each plant

(which is needed to assemble the final scene), and parameters of individual plants (which are needed to synthesize their geometric models).

Since we wish to render scenes that may include thousands of plants, each possibly with many thousands of polygons, the creation and storage of a separate geometric plant model for each plant listed in the ecosystem file is not practical. Consequently, we developed a program quantv that clusters plants in their parameter space and determines a representative plant for each cluster (Section 6). The algorithm performs quantization adaptively, thus the result depends on the characteristics of plants in the ecosystem. The quantization process produces two outputs: a *plant parameter* file, needed to create geometric models of the representative plants, and a *quantized ecosystem* file, which specifies positions and orientations of the instances of representative plants throughout the scene.

We employ two modeling programs to create the representative plants: the interactive plant modeler xfrog [10, 32, 33] and the L-system-based simulator cpfg [39, 47]. These programs input parametrized *procedural plant models* and generate specific *geometric plant models* according to the values in the plant parameter file (Section 5). To reduce the amount of geometric data, we extended the concept of instancing and quantization to components of plants. Thus, if a particular plant or group of plants has several parts (such as branches, leaves, or flowers) that are similar in their respective parameter spaces, we replace all occurrences of these parts with instances of a representative part.

Finally, the ecosystem is rendered. The input for rendering consists of the quantized ecosystem file and the representative plant models. Additional information may include geometry of the terrain and human-made objects, such as houses or fences. In spite of the quantization and instancing, the resulting scene descriptions may still be large. We experimented with three renderers to handle this complexity (Section 7). One renderer, called fshade, decomposes the scene into sub-scenes that are rendered individually and composited to form final images. Unfortunately, separating the scene into sub-scenes makes it impossible to properly capture global illumination effects. To alleviate this problem, we use the ray-tracer rayshade [29], which offers support for instancing and time-efficient rendering of scenes with many polygons, as long as the scene description fits in memory. When the scene description exceeds the available memory, we employ the memory-efficient ray-tracer toro [43], extended with a support for instancing.

In the following sections we describe the components of the EcoSys modeling pipeline in more detail. In Section 8, we present examples that illustrate the operation of the system as a whole.

3 TERRAIN SPECIFICATION

We begin the modeling of a scene with the specification of a terrain. The goal of this step is to determine elevation data, local orientations of the terrain, and additional characteristics, such as the water content in the soil, which may affect the type and vigor of plants at different locations.

Terrain data may have several sources. Representations of real terrains are available, for example, from the U.S. Geological Survey [30]. Several techniques have also been developed for creating synthetic terrains. They include: hand-painted height maps [65], methods for generating fractal terrains (reviewed in [38]), and models based on the simulation of soil erosion [28, 38].

In order to provide detailed control over the modeled terrain while taking advantage of the data amplification of fractal methods [55],

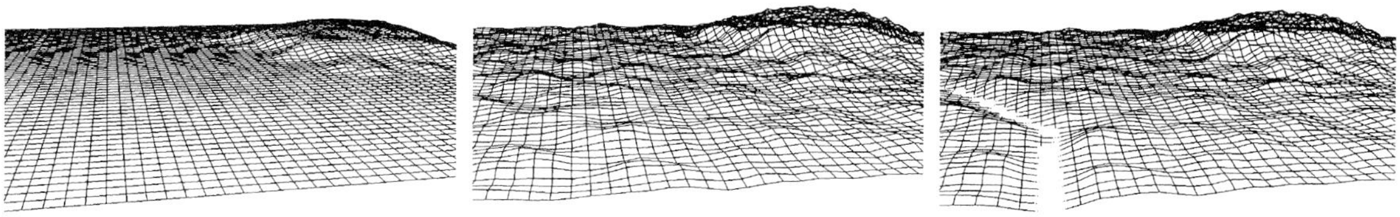

Figure 2: Three stages in creating a terrain: after loading a height map painted by hand (left), with hills added using noise synthesis (middle), and with a stream cut using the stream mask (right).

we designed and implemented an interactive terrain editing system `TerEdit`, which combines various techniques in a procedural manner. Terrain editing consists of *operations*, which modify the terrain geometry and have the spatial scope limited by *masks*. A similar paradigm is used in Adobe Photoshop [9], where *selections* can be used to choose an arbitrary subset of an image to edit.

We assume that masks have values between zero and one, allowing for smooth blending of the effects of operations. Both masks and operations can depend on the horizontal coordinates and the altitude of the points computed so far. Thus, it is possible to have masks that select terrain above some altitude or operations that are functions of the current altitude. The user's editing actions create a pipeline of operations with associated masks; to compute the terrain altitude at a point, the stages of this pipeline are evaluated in order. Undo and redo operations are easily supported by removing and re-adding operations from the pipeline and re-evaluating the terrain.

Examples of editing operations include translation, scaling, non-linear scaling, and algorithmic synthesis of the terrain. The synthesis algorithm is based on noise synthesis [38], which generates realistic terrains by adding multiple scales of Perlin's noise function [42]. The user can adjust a small number of parameters that control the overall roughness of the terrain, the rate of change in roughness across the surface of the terrain, and the frequency of the noise functions used. Noise synthesis allows terrain to be easily evaluated at a single point, without considering the neighboring points; this makes it possible to have operations that act locally. Another advantage of noise synthesis is efficiency of evaluation; updating the wireframe terrain view (based on 256×256 samples of the region of interest) after applying an operation typically takes under a second. On a multiprocessor machine, where terrain evaluation is multi-threaded, the update time is not noticeable.

The editor provides a variety of masks, including ones that select rectangular regions of terrain from a top view, masks that select regions based on their altitude, and masks defined by image files. One of the most useful masks is designed for cutting streams through terrain. The user draws a set of connected line segments over the terrain, and the influence of the mask is based on the minimum distance from a sample point to any of these segments. A spline is applied to smoothly increase the influence of the mask close to the segments. When used with a scaling operation, the terrain inside and near the stream is scaled towards the water level, and nearby terrain is ramped down, while the rest of the terrain is unchanged.

The specification of a terrain using `TerEdit` is illustrated in Figure 2. In the first snapshot, the hill in the far corner was defined by loading in a height map that had been painted by hand. Next, small hills were added to the entire terrain using noise synthesis. The last image shows the final terrain, after the stream mask was used to cut the path of a stream. A total of five operators were applied to make this terrain, and the total time to model it was approximately fifteen minutes.

Once the elevations have been created, additional parameters of the terrain can be computed as input for ecosystem simulations or a direct source of parameters for plant models. Although the user can interactively paint parameters on the terrain, simulation provides a more sound basis for the modeling of natural ecosystems. Consequently, `TerEdit` incorporates a simulator of rain water flow and distribution in the soil, related to both the erosion algorithm by Musgrave *et al.* [38] and the particle system simulation of water on building facades by Dorsey *et al.* [11]. Water is dropped onto the terrain from above; some is absorbed immediately while the rest flows downhill and is absorbed by the soil that it passes through. A sample terrain with the water distribution generated using this approach is shown in Figure 3.

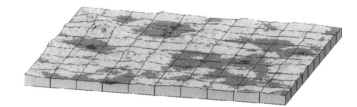

Figure 3: A sample terrain with the water concentration ranging from high (blue) to low (yellow)

4 SPECIFICATION OF PLANT POPULATIONS

The task of populating a terrain with plants can be addressed using methods that offer different tradeoffs between the degree of user control, time needed to specify plant distribution, and biological validity of the results. The underlying techniques can be divided into *space-occupancy* or *individual-based* techniques. This classification is related to paradigms of spatially-explicit modeling in ecology [3, 19], and parallels the distinction between space-based and structure-based models of morphogenesis [44].

The space-occupancy techniques describe the distribution of the *densities* of given plant species over a terrain. In the image synthesis context, this distribution can be be obtained using two approaches:

Explicit specification. The distribution of plant densities is measured in the field (by counting plants that occupy sample plots) or created interactively, for example using a paint program.

Procedural generation. The distributions of plant densities is obtained by simulating interactions between plant populations using an ecological model. The models described in the literature are commonly expressed in terms of *cellular automata* [19] or *reaction-diffusion* processes [23].

The individual-based techniques provide the location and attributes of *individual plants*. Again, we distinguish two approaches:

Explicit specification. Plant positions and attributes represent field data, for example obtained by surveying a real forest [25], or specified interactively by the user.

Procedural generation. Plant positions and attributes are obtained using a *point pattern generation model*, which creates a distribution of points with desired statistical properties [66], or using an *individual-based population model* [13, 58], which is applied to simulate interactions between plants within an ecosystem.

Below we describe two methods for specifying plant distribution that we have developed and implemented as components of EcoSys. The first method combines interactive editing of plant densities with a point pattern generation of the distribution of individual plants. The second method employs individual-based ecological simulations.

4.1 Interactive specification of plant populations

To specify a plant population in a terrain, the user creates a set of gray-level images with a standard paint program. These images define the spatial distributions of plant densities and of plant characteristics such as the age and vigor.

Given an image that specifies the distribution of densities of a plant species, positions of individual plants are generated using a half-toning algorithm. We have used the Floyd-Steinberg algorithm [15] for this purpose. Each black pixel describes the position of a plant in the raster representing the terrain. We also have implemented a relaxation method that iteratively moves each plant position towards the center of mass of its Voronoi polygon [6]. This reduces the variance of distances between neighboring plants, which sometimes produces visually pleasing effects.

Once the position of a plant has been determined, its parameters are obtained by referring to the values of appropriate raster images at the same point. These values may control the plant model directly or provide arguments to user-specified mathematical expressions, which in turn control the models. This provides the user with an additional means for flexibly manipulating the plant population.

Operations on raster images make it possible to capture some interactions between plants. For example, if the radius of a tree crown is known, the image representing the projection of the crown on the ground may be combined with user-specified raster images to decrease the density or vigor of plants growing underneath.

4.2 Simulation of ecosystems

Individual-based models of plant ecosystems operate at various levels of abstraction, depending on the accuracy of the representation of individual plants [58]. Since our goal is to simulate complex scenes with thousands of plants, we follow the approach of Firbank and Watkinson [13], and represent plants coarsely as circles positioned in a continuous landscape. Each circle defines the *ecological neighborhood* of the plant in its center, that is the area within which the plant interacts with it neighbors. Biologically motivated rules govern the outcomes of interactions between the intersecting circles. Global behavior of the ecosystem model is an emergent property of a system of many circles.

We implemented the individual-based ecosystem models using the framework of *open L-systems* [39]. Since L-systems operate on branching structures, we represent each plant as a circle located at the end of an invisible positioning line. All lines are connected into a branching structure that spreads over the terrain.

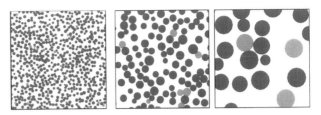

Figure 4: Steps 99, 134, and 164 of a sample simulation of the self-thinning process. Colors represents states of the plants: not dominated (green), dominated (red), and old (yellow). The simulation began with 62,500 plants, placed at random in a square field. Due to the large number of plants, only a part of the field is shown.

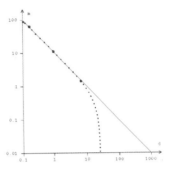

Figure 5: The average area of plants as a function of their density. Small dots represent the results of every tenth simulation step. Large dots correspond to the states of simulation shown in Figure 4.

For example, let us consider a model of plant distribution due to a fundamental phenomenon in plant population dynamics, *self-thinning*. This phenomenon is described by Ricklefs as follows [52, page 339]: "If one plots the logarithm of average plant weight as a function of the logarithm of density, data points fall on a line with a slope of approximately $-\frac{3}{2}$ [called the self-thinning curve]. [...] When seeds are planted at a moderate density, so that the beginning combination of density and average dry weight lies below the self-thinning curve, plants grow without appreciable mortality until the population reaches its self-thinning curve. After that point, the intense crowding associated with further increase in average plant size causes the death of smaller individuals."

Our model of self-thinning is a simplified version of that by Firbank and Watkinson [13]. The simulation starts with an initial set of circles, distributed at random in a square field, and assigned random initial radii from a given interval. If the circles representing two plants intersect, the smaller plant dies and its corresponding circle is removed from the scene. Plants that have reached a limit size are considered old and die as well.

Figure 4 shows three snapshots of the simulation. The corresponding plot shows the average area of the circles as a function of their density (Figure 5). The slope of the self-thinning curve is equal to -1; assuming that mass is proportional to volume, which in turn is proportional to area raised to the power of $-\frac{3}{2}$, the self-thinning curve in the density-mass coordinates would have the slope of $-\frac{3}{2}$. Thus, in spite of its simplicity, our model captures the essential characteristic of plant distribution before and after it has reached the self-thinning curve.

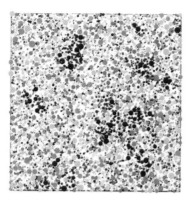

Figure 6: Simulated distribution of eight plant species in a terrain from Figure 3. Colors indicate plant species. Plants with a preference for wet areas are shown in blue.

A slightly more complicated model describes plant distribution in a population of different plant species. Each species is defined by a set of values that determine: (i) the number of new plants added to the field per simulation step, (ii) the maximum size of the plants, (iii) their average growth rate, (iv) the probability of surviving the domination by a plant with a competitive advantage, and (v) a preference for wet or dry areas. An individual plant is characterized by: (i) the species to which it belongs, (ii) its size, and (iii) its vigor. The vigor is a number in the range from 0 to 1, assigned to each plant as a randomized function of water concentration at the plant's location and the plant's preference for wet or dry areas. The competitive ability of a plant is determined as a product of its vigor and its relative size (the ratio between the actual and maximum size). When the circles representing two plants intersect, their competitive abilities are compared. The plant with a smaller competitive ability is dominated by the other plant and may die with the defined probability.

Figure 6 presents the result of a simulation involving a mix of eight plant species growing in a terrain shown in Figure 3. Plants with a preference for wet areas are represented by blue circles. Plants with a preference for dry areas have been assigned other colors. Through the competition between the species, a segregation of plants between the wet and dry areas has emerged.

Similar models can be developed to capture other phenomena that govern the development of plant populations.

5 MODELING OF PLANTS

Interactive editing of plant populations and the simulation of ecosystems determine positions and high-level characteristics of all plants in the modeled scene. On this basis, geometric models of individual plants must now be found.

Recent advances in plant measuring techniques have made it possible to construct a geometric model of a specific plant according to detailed measurements of its structure [54]. Nevertheless, for the purpose of visualizing plants differing by age, vigor, and possibly other parameters, it is preferable to treat geometric models as a product of the underlying procedural models. Construction of such models for computer graphics and biological purposes has been a field of active study, recently reviewed in [45]. Consequently, below we discuss only the issue of model parametrization, that is the incorporation of high-level parameters returned by the population model

into the plant models. We consider two different approaches, which reflect different predictive values of *mechanistic* and *descriptive* models [60].

Mechanistic models operate by simulating the processes that control the development of plants over time. They inherently capture how the resulting structure changes with age [46, 47]. If a mechanistic model incorporates environmental inputs, the dependence of the resulting structure on the corresponding environmental parameters is an emergent feature of the model [39]. The model predicts the effect of various combinations of environmental parameters on the structure, and no explicit parametrization is needed. L-systems [47] and their extensions [39] provide a convenient tool for expressing mechanistic models. Within EcoSys, mechanistic models have been generated using cpfg.

Descriptive models capture plant architecture without simulating the underlying developmental processes. Consequently, they do not have an inherent predictive value. Nevertheless, if a family of geometric models is constructed to capture the key "postures" of a plant at different ages and with different high-level characteristics, we can obtain the in-between geometries by interpolation. This is equivalent to fitting functions that map the set of high-level parameters to the set of lower-level variables present in the model, and can be accomplished by regression [57] (see [48] for an application example). In the special case of plant postures characterized by a single parameter, the interpolation between key postures is analogous to key-framing [62], and can be accomplished using similar techniques. We applied interpolation to parametrize models created using both xfrog and cpfg.

6 APPROXIMATE INSTANCING

Geometric plant models are often large. A detailed polygonal representation of a herbaceous plant may require over 10MB to store; a scene with one thousand plants (a relatively small number in ecosystem simulations) would require 10GB. One approach for reducing such space requirements is to simplify geometric representations of objects that have a small size on the screen. We incorporated a version of this technique into our system by parameterizing the procedural plant models so that they can produce geometries with different polygonizations of surfaces. However, this technique alone was not sufficient to reduce the amount of data to manageable levels.

Instancing was used successfully in the past for compactly representing complex outdoor scenes (*e.g.* [56]). According to the paradigm of instancing [59], geometric objects that are identical up to affine transformations become instances of one object. To achieve a further reduction in the size of geometric descriptions, we extended the paradigm of instancing to objects that resemble each other, but are not exactly the same. Thus, sets of similar plants are represented by instances of a single representative plant. Furthermore, the hierarchical structure of plant scenes, which may be decomposed into groups of plants, individual plants, branches of different order, plant organs such as leaves and flowers, *etc.*, lends itself to instancing at different levels of the hierarchy. We create hierarchies of instances by quantizing model components in their respective parameter spaces, and reusing them.

Automatic generation of instance hierarchies for plant models expressed using a limited class of L-systems was considered by Hart [20, 21]. His approach dealt only with exact instancing. Brownbill [7] considered special cases of approximate instancing of plants, and analyzed tradeoffs between the size of the geometric models and their perceived distortion (departure from the original geometry caused by the reduction of diversity between the components). He achieved reductions of the database size ranging from 5:1 to 50:1 with a negligible visual impact on the generated images (a tree and a field of grass). This result is reminiscent of the observation by Smith [55] that the set of random numbers used in stochastic algorithms for generating fractal mountains and particle-system trees can be reduced to a few representative values without significantly affecting the perceived complexity of the resulting images.

We generalize Brownbill's approach by relating it to clustering. Assuming that the characteristics of each plant are described by a vector of real numbers, we apply a clustering algorithm to the set of these vectors in order to find representative vectors. Thus, we reduce the problem of finding representative plants and instancing them to the problem of finding a set of representative points in the parameter space and mapping each point to its representative. We assume that plants with a similar appearance are described by close points in their parameter space; if this is not the case (for example, because the size of a plant is a nonlinear function of its age), we transform the parameter space to become perceptually more linear. We cluster and map plant parts in the same manner as the entire plants.

This clustering and remapping can be stated also in terms of vector quantization [18]: we store a code book of plants and plant parts and, for each input plant, we store a mapping to an object in the code book rather than the plant geometry itself. In computer graphics, vector quantization has been widely used for color image quantization [22]; more recent applications include reduction of memory needs for texture mapping [4] and representing light fields [31].

We use a multi-dimensional clustering algorithm developed by Wan *et al.* [61], which subdivides the hyperbox containing data points by choosing splitting planes to minimize the variance of the resulting clusters of data. We extended this algorithm to include an "importance weight" with each input vector. The weights make it possible to further optimize the plant quantization process, for example by allocating more representative vectors to the plants that occupy a large area of the screen.

7 RENDERING

Rendering natural scenes raises two important questions: (i) dealing with scene complexity, and (ii) simulating illumination, materials and atmospheric effects. Within `EcoSys`, we addressed these questions using two different strategies.

The first strategy is to to split the scene into sub-scenes of manageable complexity, render each of them independently using ray-casting, and composite the resulting RGBαZ images into the final image [12]. The separation of the scene into sub-scenes is a byproduct of the modeling process: both `densedis` and `cpfg` can output the distribution of a single plant species to form a sub-scene. The ray-casting algorithm is implemented in `fshade`, which creates the scene geometry procedurally by invoking the `xfrog` plant modeler at run time. This reduces file I/O and saves disk space compared to storing all of the geometric information for the scene on disk and reading it in while rendering. For example, the poplar tree shown in Figure 16 is 16 KB as a procedural model (plant template), but 6.7 MB in a standard text geometry format.

A number of operations can be applied to the RGBαZ images before they are combined. Image processing operations, such as saturation and brightness adjustments, are often useful. Atmospheric effects can be introduced in a post process, by modifying colors according to the pixel depth. Shadows are computed using shadow maps [64].

The scene separation makes it possible to render the scene quickly and re-render its individual sub-scenes as needed to improve the image. However, complex lighting effects cannot be easily included, since the renderer doesn't have access to the entire scene description at once.

The second rendering strategy is ray tracing. It lacks the capability to easily re-render parts of scenes that have been changed, but makes it possible to include more complex illumination effects. In both ray-tracers that we have used, `rayshade` [29] and `toro` [43], procedural geometry descriptions are expanded into triangle meshes, complemented with a hierarchy of grids and bounding boxes needed to speed up rendering [56]. `Rayshade` requires the entire scene description (object prototypes with their bounding boxes and a hierarchy of instancing transformations) to be kept in memory, otherwise page swapping significantly decreases the efficiency of rendering. In the case of `toro`, meshes are stored on disk; these are read in parts to a memory cache as needed for rendering computations and removed from memory when a prescribed limit amount of memory has been used. Consequently, the decrease in performance when the memory size has been reached is much slower [43]. We have made the straightforward extension of memory-coherent ray-tracing algorithms to manage instanced geometry: along with non-instanced geometry, the instances in the scene are also managed by the geometry cache.

Because rays can be traced that access the entire scene, more complex lighting effects can be included. For example, we have found that attenuating shadow rays as they pass through translucent leaves of tree crowns greatly improves their realism and visual richness.

8 EXAMPLES

We evaluated our system by applying it to create a number of scenes. In the examples presented below, we used two combinations of the modules: (i) ecosystem simulation and plant modeling using `cpfg` followed by rendering using `rayshade` or `toro`, and (ii) interactive specification of plant distribution using `densedis` in conjunction with plant generation using `xfrog` and rendering using `fshade`.

Figure 7 presents visualizations of two stages of the self-thinning process, based on distributions shown in Figure 4. The plants represent hypothetical varieties of *Lychnis coronaria* [47] with red, blue, and white flowers. Plant size values returned by the ecosystem simulation were quantized to seven representative values for each plant variety. The quantized values were mapped to the age of the modeled plants. The scene obtained after 99 simulation steps had 16,354 plants. The `rayshade` file representing this scene without instancing would be 3.5 GB (estimated); with instancing it was 6.7 MB, resulting in the compression ratio of approximately 500:1. For the scene after 164 steps, the corresponding values were: 441 plants, 125 MB, 5.8 MB, compression 21:1.

The mountain meadow (Figure 8 top) was generated by simulating an ecosystem of eight species of herbaceous plants, as discussed in Section 5. The distribution of plants is qualitatively similar to that shown schematically in Figure 6, but it includes a larger number of smaller plants. The individual plants were modeled with a high level of detail, which made it possible to zoom in on this scene and view individual plants. The complete scene has approximately 102,522 plants, comprising approximately $2 \cdot 10^9$ primitives (polygons and cylinders). The `rayshade` file representing this scene without instancing would be 200 GB (estimated), with the instancing it was 151 MB, resulting in a compression ratio of approximately 1,300:1.

Figure 7: A *Lychnis coronaria* field after 99 and 164 simulation steps

Figure 8: Zooming in on a mountain meadow

The time needed to model this scene on a 150 MHz R5000 Silicon Graphics Indy with 96 MB RAM was divided as follows: simulation of the ecosystem (25 steps): 35 min, quantization (two-dimensional parameter space, each of the 8 plant species quantized to 7 levels): 5 min, generation of the 56 representative plants using cpfg: 9 min. The rendering time using rayshade on a 180 MHz R10000 Silicon Graphics Origin 200 with 256 MB RAM (1024 × 756 pixels, 4 samples per pixel) was approximately 8 hours. (It was longer using toro, but in that case the rendering time did not depend critically on the amount of RAM.)

In the next example, the paradigm of parameterizing, quantizing, and instancing was applied to entire groups of plants: tufts of grass with daisies. The number of daisies was controlled by a parameter (Figure 9). The resulting lawn is shown in Figure 10. For this image, ten different sets of grass tufts were generated, each instanced twenty times on average. The total reduction in geometry due to quantization and instancing (including instancing of grass blades and daisies within the tufts) was by a factor of 130:1. In Figure 11, a model parameter was used to control the size of the heaps of leaves. The heap around the stick and the stick itself were modeled manually.

Interactive creation of complex scenes requires the proper use of techniques to achieve an aesthetically pleasing result. To illustrate the process that we followed, we retrace the steps that resulted in the stream scene shown in Figure 15.

We began with the definition of a hilly terrain crossed by a little stream (Figure 2). To cover it with plants, we first created procedural models of plant species fitting this environment (Figure 12). Next, we extracted images representing the terrain altitudes and the stream position (Figures 13a and 13b) from the original terrain data. This provided visual cues needed while painting plant distributions, for example, to prevent plants from being placed in the stream.

After that, we interactively chose a viewpoint, approximately at human height. With the resulting perspective view of the terrain as a reference, we painted a gray scale image for each plant species to define its distribution. We placed vegetation only in the areas visible from the selected viewpoint to speed up the rendering later on. For example, Figure 13c shows the image that defines the density distribution of stinging nettles. Since the stinging nettles grow on wet ground, we specified high density values along the stream. The density image served as input to densedis, which determined positions of individual plants. The dot diagram produced by densedis (Figure 13d) provided visual feedback that was used to refine the density image step by step until the desired distribution was found.

Figure 9: Grass tufts with varying daisy concentrations

Figure 10: Lawn with daisies

Figure 12: Sample plant models used in the stream scene. Top row: apple, stinging nettle, dandelion; bottom row: grass tuft, reed, yellow flower.

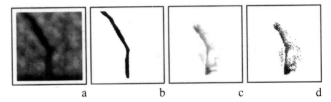

Figure 13: Creating distribution of stinging nettle: the heightmap of the covered area (a), the river image (b), the plant density distribution painted by the user (c), and the resulting plant positions (d).

Once the position of plants was established, we employed additional parameters to control the appearance of the plants. The vigor of stinging nettle plants, which affects the length of their stems and the number of leaves, was controlled using the density image for the nettles. To control the vigor of grass we used the height map: as a result, grass tufts have a slightly less saturated color on top of the hill than in the lower areas. Each tuft was oriented along a weighted sum of the terrain's surface normal vector and the up vector.

At this point, the scene was previewed and further changes in the density image were made until a satisfying result was obtained.

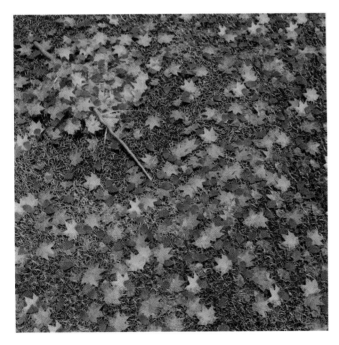

Figure 11: Leaves on grass

Figure 14: OpenGL preview of the stream scene including stinging nettle and yellow flowers

Figure 15: Stream scene

Figure 14 shows the preview of the distribution of stinging nettles and yellow flowers. To prevent intersections between these plants, the painted density image for the yellow flowers was multiplied by the inverted density image for the nettles.

The apple trees were placed by painting black dots on a white image. The final scene (Figure 15) was rendered using fshade. Images representing each species were rendered separately, and the resulting sub-scenes were composited as described in Section 7. The clouds were then added using a real photograph as a texture map. To increase the impression of depth in the scene, color saturation and contrast were decreased with increasing depth in a postprocessing step, and colors were shifted towards blue. Table 1 provides statistics about the instancing and geometric compression for this scene. The creation of this image took two days plus one day for defining the plant models. The actual compute time needed to synthesize this scene on a 195 MHz R10000 8-processor Silicon Graphics Onyx with 768MB RAM (1024 × 756 pixels, 9 samples per pixel) was 75 min.

Figures 16 and 17 present further examples of scenes with interactively created plant distributions. To simulate the effect of shadowing on the distribution of the yellow flowers in Figure 16, we rendered a top view of the spheres that approximate the shape of the apple trees, and multiplied the resulting image (further modified interactively) with the initial density image for the yellow flowers. We followed a similar strategy in creating Figure 17: the most impor-

tant trees were positioned first, then rendered from above to provide visual cues for the further placements. Table 2 contains statistics about the geometry quantization in Figure 17.

plant	obj.	inst.	plant	obj.	inst.
apple	1	4	grass tuft	15	2577
reed	140	140	stinging nettle	10	430
dandelion	10	55	yellow flower	10	2751

Table 1: Number of prototype objects and their instances in the stream scene (Figure 15). Number of polygons without instancing: 16,547,728, with instancing: 992,216. Compression rate: 16.7:1.

plant	obj.	inst.	plant	obj.	inst.
weeping willow	16	16	reed	15	35
birch	43	43	poppy	20	128
distant tree	20	119	cornflower	72	20
St. John's wort	20	226	dandelion	20	75
grass tuft	15	824			

Table 2: Number of prototype objects and their instances in the Dutch scene (Figure 17). Number of polygons without instancing: 40,553,029, with instancing: 6,737,036. Compression rate: 6.0:1

Figure 16: Forest scene

Figure 17: Dutch landscape

9 CONCLUSIONS

We presented the design and experimental implementation of a system for modeling and rendering scenes with many plants. The central issue of managing the complexity of these scenes was addressed with a combination of techniques: the use of different levels of abstraction at different stages of the modeling and rendering pipeline, procedural modeling, approximate instancing, and the employment of space- and time-efficient rendering methods. We tested our system by generating a number of visually complex scenes. Consequently, we are confident that the presented approach is operational and can be found useful in many practical applications.

Our work is but an early step in the development of techniques for creating and visualizing complex scenes with plants, and the presented concepts require further research. A fundamental problem is the evaluation of the impact of quantization and approximate instancing on the generated scenes. The difficulty in studying this problem stems from: (i) the difficulty in generating non-instanced reference images for visual comparison purposes (the scenes are too large), (ii) the lack of a formally defined error metric needed to evaluate the artifacts of approximate instancing in an objective manner, and (iii) the difficulty in generalizing results that were obtained by the analysis of specific scenes. A (partial) solution to this problem would set the stage for the design and analysis of methods that may be more suitable for quantizing plants than the general-purpose variance-based algorithm used in our implementation.

Other research problems exposed by our experience with EcoSys include: (i) improvement of the terrain model through its coupling with the plant population model (in nature vegetation affects terrain, for example by preventing erosion); (ii) design of algorithms for converting plant densities to positions, taking into account statistical properties of plant distributions found in natural ecosystems [66]); (iii) incorporation of morphogenetic plasticity (dependence of the plant shape on its neighbors [58]) into the multi-level modeling framework; this requires transfer of information about plant shapes between the population model and the procedural plant models; (iv) extension of the modeling method presented in this paper to animated scenes (with growing plants and plants moving in the wind); (v) design of methods for conveniently previewing scenes with billions of geometric primitives (for example, to select close views of details); and (vi) application of more faithful local and global illumination models to the rendering of plant scenes (in particular, consideration of the distribution of diffuse light in the canopy).

Acknowledgements

We would like to acknowledge Craig Kolb for his implementation of the variance-based quantization algorithm, which we adapted to the needs of our system, and Christain Jacob for his experimental implementations and discussions pertinent to the individual-based ecosystem modeling. We also thank: Stefania Bertazzon, Jim Hanan, Richard Levy, and Peter Room for discussions and pointers to the relevant literature, the referees for helpful comments on the manuscript, Chris Prusinkiewicz for editorial help, and Darcy Grant for system support in Calgary. This research was sponsored in part by the National Science Foundation grant CCR-9508579-001 to Pat Hanrahan, and by the Natural Sciences and Engineering Research Council of Canada grant OGP0130084 to Przemyslaw Prusinkiewicz.

REFERENCES

[1] Alias/Wavefront; a division of Silicon Graphics Ltd. Studio V8. SGI program, 1996.

[2] AnimaTek, Inc. AnimatTek's World Builder. PC program, 1996.

[3] R. A. Armstrong. A comparison of index-based and pixel-based neighborhood simulations of forest growth. *Ecology*, 74(6):1707–1712, 1993.

[4] A. C. Beers, M. Agrawala, and N. Chaddha. Rendering from compressed textures. In *SIGGRAPH 96 Conference Proceedings*, pages 373–378, August 1996.

[5] B. M. Blumberg and T. A. Galyean. Multi-level direction of autonomous creatures for real-time virtual environments. In *SIGGRAPH 95 Conference Proceedings*, pages 47–54, August 1995.

[6] B.N. Boots. *Spatial tesselations: concepts and applications of Voronoi diagrams*. John Wiley, 1992.

[7] A. Brownbill. Reducing the storage required to render L-system based models. Master's thesis, University of Calgary, October 1996.

[8] N. Chiba, K. Muraoka, A. Doi, and J. Hosokawa. Rendering of forest scenery using 3D textures. *The Journal of Visualization and Computer Animation*, 8:191–199, 1997.

[9] Adobe Corporation. Adobe Photoshop.

[10] O. Deussen and B. Lintermann. A modelling method and user interface for creating plants. In *Proceedings of Graphics Interface 97*, pages 189–197, May 1997.

[11] J. Dorsey, H. Køhling Pedersen, and P. Hanrahan. Flow and changes in appearance. In *SIGGRAPH 96 Conference Proceedings*, pages 411–420, August 1996.

[12] T. Duff. Compositing 3-D rendered images. *Computer Graphics (SIGGRAPH 85 Proceedings)*, 19(3):41–44, 1985.

[13] F. G. Firbank and A. R. Watkinson. A model of interference within plant monocultures. *Journal of Theoretical Biology*, 116:291–311, 1985.

[14] K. W. Fleischer, D. H. Laidlaw, B. L. Currin, and A. H. Barr. Cellular texture generation. In *SIGGRAPH 95 Conference Proceedings*, pages 239–248, August 1995.

[15] R. W. Floyd and L. Steinberg. An adaptive algorithm for spatial gray scale. In *SID 75, Int. Symp. Dig. Tech. Papers*, pages 36–37, 1975.

[16] D. R. Fowler, P. Prusinkiewicz, and J. Battjes. A collision-based model of spiral phyllotaxis. *Computer Graphics (SIGGRAPH 92 Proceedings)*, 26(2):361–368, 1992.

[17] G. Y. Gardner. Simulation of natural scenes using textured quadric surfaces. *Computer Graphics (SIGGRAPH 84 Proceedings)*, 18(3):11–20, 1984.

[18] A. Gersho and R. M. Gray. *Vector quantization and signal compression*. Kluwer Academic Publishers, 1991.

[19] D. G. Green. Modelling plants in landscapes. In M. T. Michalewicz, editor, *Plants to ecosystems. Advances in computational life sciences I*, pages 85–96. CSIRO Publishing, Melbourne, 1997.

[20] J. C. Hart and T. A. DeFanti. Efficient anti-aliased rendering of 3D linear fractals. *Computer Graphics (SIGGRAPH 91 Proceedings)*, 25:91–100, 1991.

[21] J.C. Hart. The object instancing paradigm for linear fractal modeling. In *Proceedings of Graphics Interface 92*, pages 224–231, 1992.

[22] P. Heckbert. Color image quantization for frame buffer display. *Computer Graphics (SIGGRAPH 82 Proceedings)*, 16:297–307, 1982.

[23] S. I. Higgins and D. M. Richardson. A review of models of alien plant spread. *Ecological Modelling*, 87:249–265, 1996.

[24] H. Hoppe. View-dependent refinement of progressive meshes. In *SIGGRAPH 97 Conference Proceedings*, pages 189–198, August 1997.

[25] D. H. House, G. S. Schmidt, S. A. Arvin, and M. Kitagawa-DeLeon. Visualizing a real forest. *IEEE Computer Graphics and Applications*, 18(1):12–15, 1998.

[26] J. T. Kajiya and T. L. Kay. Rendering fur with three dimensional textures. *Computer Graphics (SIGGRAPH 89 Proceedings)*, 23(3):271–289, 1989.

[27] T. L. Kay and J. T. Kajiya. Ray tracing complex scenes. *Computer Graphics (SIGGRAPH 86 Proceedings)*, 20(4):269–278, 1986.

[28] A. D. Kelley, M. C. Malin, and G. M. Nielson. Terrain simulation using a model of stream erosion. *Computer Graphics (SIGGRAPH 88 Proceedings)*, 22(4):263–268, 1988.

[29] C. Kolb. Rayshade. http://graphics.stanford.edu/~cek/rayshade.

[30] M. P. Kumler. An intensive comparison of triangulated irregular networks (TINs) and digital elevation models (DEMs). *Cartographica*, 31(2), 1994.

[31] M. Levoy and P. Hanrahan. Light field rendering. In *SIGGRAPH 96 Conference Proceedings*, pages 31–42, August 1996.

[32] B. Lintermann and O. Deussen. Interactive structural and geometrical modeling of plants. To appear in the *IEEE Computer Graphics and Applications*.

[33] B. Lintermann and O. Deussen. Interactive modelling and animation of natural branching structures. In R. Boulic and G. Hégron, editors, *Computer Animation and Simulation 96*. Springer, 1996.

[34] Lucasfilm Ltd. The Adventures of André and Wally B. Film, 1984.

[35] D. Marshall, D. S. Fussel, and A. T. Campbell. Multiresolution rendering of complex botanical scenes. In *Proceedings of Graphics Interface 97*, pages 97–104, May 1997.

[36] N. Max. Hierarchical rendering of trees from precomputed multi-layer Z-buffers. In X. Pueyo and P. Schröder, editors, *Rendering Techniques 96*, pages 165–174 and 288. Springer Wien, 1996.

[37] N. Max and K. Ohsaki. Rendering trees from precomputed Z-buffer views. In P. M. Hanrahan and W. Purgathofer, editors, *Rendering Techniques 95*, pages 74–81 and 359–360. Springer Wien, 1995.

[38] F. K. Musgrave, C. E. Kolb, and R. S. Mace. The synthesis and rendering of eroded fractal terrains. *Computer Graphics (SIGGRAPH 89 Proceedings)*, 23(3):41–50, 1989.

[39] R. Měch and P. Prusinkiewicz. Visual models of plants interacting with their environment. In *SIGGRAPH 96 Conference Proceedings*, pages 397–410, August 1996.

[40] F. Neyret. A general and multiscale model for volumetric textures. In *Proceedings of Graphics Interface 95*, pages 83–91, 1995.

[41] F. Neyret. Synthesizing verdant landscapes using volumetric textures. In X. Pueyo and P. Schröoder, editors, *Rendering Techniques 96*, pages 215–224 and 291, Wien, 1996. Springer-Verlag.

[42] K. Perlin. An image synthesizer. *Computer Graphics (SIGGRAPH 85 Proceedings)*, 19(3):287–296, 1985.

[43] M. Pharr, C. Kolb, R. Gershbein, and P. Hanrahan. Rendering complex scenes with memory-coherent ray tracing. In *SIGGRAPH 97 Conference Proceedings*, pages 101–108, August 1997.

[44] P. Prusinkiewicz. Visual models of morphogenesis. *Artificial Life*, 1(1/2):61–74, 1994.

[45] P. Prusinkiewicz. Modeling spatial structure and development of plants: a review. *Scientia Horticulturae*, 74(1/2), 1998.

[46] P. Prusinkiewicz, M. Hammel, and E. Mjolsness. Animation of plant development. In *SIGGRAPH 93 Conference Proceedings*, pages 351–360, August 1993.

[47] P. Prusinkiewicz and A. Lindenmayer. *The algorithmic beauty of plants*. Springer-Verlag, New York, 1990. With J. S. Hanan, F. D. Fracchia, D. R. Fowler, M. J. M. de Boer, and L. Mercer.

[48] P. Prusinkiewicz, W. Remphrey, C. Davidson, and M. Hammel. Modeling the architecture of expanding *Fraxinus pennsylvanica* shoots using L-systems. *Canadian Journal of Botany*, 72:701–714, 1994.

[49] Questar Productions, LLC. World Construction Set Version 2. PC program, 1997.

[50] W. T. Reeves and R. Blau. Approximate and probabilistic algorithms for shading and rendering structured particle systems. *Computer Graphics (SIGGRAPH 85 Proceedings)*, 19(3):313–322, 1985.

[51] C. W. Reynolds. Flocks, herds, and schools: A distributed behavioral model. *Computer Graphics (SIGGRAPH 87 Proceedings)*, 21(4):25–34, 1987.

[52] R. E. Ricklefs. *Ecology. Third Edition*. W. H. Freeman, New York, 1990.

[53] J. Shade, D. Lischinski, D. Salesin, T. DeRose, and J. Snyder. Hierarchical image caching for accelerated walkthroughs of complex environments. In *SIGGRAPH 96 Conference Proceedings*, pages 75–82, August 1996.

[54] H. Sinoquet and R. Rivet. Measurement and visualization of the architecture of an adult tree based on a three-dimensional digitising device. *Trees*, 11:265–270, 1997.

[55] A. R. Smith. Plants, fractals, and formal languages. *Computer Graphics (SIGGRAPH 84 Proceedings)*, 18(3):1–10, 1984.

[56] J. M. Snyder and A. H. Barr. Ray tracing complex models containing surface tessellations. *Computer Graphics (SIGGRAPH 87 Proceedings)*, 21(4):119–128, 1987.

[57] R. R. Sokal and F. J. Rohlf. *Biometry. Third Edition*. W. H. Freeman, New York, 1995.

[58] K. A. Sorrensen-Cothern, E. D. Ford, and D. G. Sprugel. A model of competition incorporating plasticity through modular foliage and crown development. *Ecological Monographs*, 63(3):277–304, 1993.

[59] I. E. Sutherland. Sketchpad: A man-machine graphical communication system. Proceedings of the Spring Joint Computer Conference, 1963.

[60] J. H. M. Thornley and I. R. Johnson. *Plant and crop modeling: A mathematical approach to plant and crop physiology*. Oxford University Press, New York, 1990.

[61] S. J. Wan, S. K. M. Wong, and P. Prusinkiewicz. An algorithm for multidimensional data clustering. *ACM Trans. Math. Software*, 14(2):135–162, 1988.

[62] A. Watt and M. Watt. *Advanced animation and rendering techniques: Theory and practice*. Addison-Wesley, Reading, 1992.

[63] J. Weber and J. Penn. Creation and rendering of realistic trees. In *SIGGRAPH 95 Conference Proceedings*, pages 119–128, August 1995.

[64] L. Williams. Casting curved shadows on curved surfaces. *Computer Graphics (SIGGRAPH 78 Proceedings)*, 12(3):270–274, 1978.

[65] L. Williams. Shading in two dimensions. In *Proceedings of Graphics Interface 91*, pages 143–151, June 1991.

[66] H. Wu, K. W. Malafant, L. K. Pendridge, P. J. Sharpe, and J. Walker. Simulation of two-dimensional point patterns: application of a latice framework approach. *Ecological Modelling*, 38:299–308, 1997.

A Multiscale Model of Adaptation and Spatial Vision
for Realistic Image Display

Sumanta N. Pattanaik   James A. Ferwerda   Mark D. Fairchild*   Donald P. Greenberg

Program of Computer Graphics,† Cornell University

Abstract

In this paper we develop a computational model of adaptation and spatial vision for realistic tone reproduction. The model is based on a multiscale representation of pattern, luminance, and color processing in the human visual system. We incorporate the model into a tone reproduction operator that maps the vast ranges of radiances found in real and synthetic scenes into the small fixed ranges available on conventional display devices such as CRT's and printers. The model allows the operator to address the two major problems in realistic tone reproduction: wide absolute range and high dynamic range scenes can be displayed; and the displayed images match our perceptions of the scenes at both threshold and suprathreshold levels to the degree possible given a particular display device. Although in this paper we apply our visual model to the tone reproduction problem, the model is general and can be usefully applied to image quality metrics, image compression methods, and perceptually-based image synthesis algorithms.

CR Categories: I.3.0 [Computer Graphics]: General;

Keywords: realistic imaging, visual perception, tone reproduction, adaptation, spatial vision

1 INTRODUCTION

The range of light we encounter in natural scenes is vast. The *absolute level* of illumination provided by direct sunlight can be 100 million times more intense than starlight. The *dynamic range* of light energy can also be large, on the order of 10,000 to 1 from highlights to shadows, or higher if light sources are visible.

Although physically-based rendering methods and new techniques that utilize the output of digital cameras [Debevec97] now allow us to produce *radiance maps* that accurately represent the wide variations of light energy in scenes, neither of these methods specify how to realistically display these images on conventional

---

*On sabbatical leave from: Munsell Color Science Laboratory, Center for Imaging Science, Rochester Institute of Technology, 54 Lomb Memorial Drive, Rochester, NY 14623-5604, USA. Web address: http://www.cis.rit.edu/people/faculty/fairchild

†580 Rhodes Hall, Cornell University, Ithaca, NY 14853, USA.
E-mail addresses: {sumant,jaf,mdf,dpg}@graphics.cornell.edu
Web address: http://www.graphics.cornell.edu.

electronic and print-based media which have only moderate output levels and typical dynamic ranges of less than 100 to 1.

Recently graphics researchers have started to address this issue by developing *tone reproduction operators* that map scene radiances to display outputs with the goal of producing a visual match between the scene and the display. There are two major problems to be solved in realistic tone reproduction:

- to find an operator that maps the vast ranges of radiances found in scenes into the range that can be produced by a given display device.

- to be certain that this operator produces images that match our perceptions of the scenes.

The critical element that links these two problems is the *visual model* used in the tone reproduction operator. Visual models are used to relate the perceptual responses of a scene observer to the responses of the display observer in order to specify a mapping that produces a visual match between the scene and the display. A central issue is that different tone reproduction operators have made use of different visual models to determine what constitutes a match.

Tumblin and Rushmeier's [1993] operator is based on Stevens' [1961] model of *brightness and contrast perception* illustrated in Figure 1b. The operator attempts to produce images that capture the changes in *suprathreshold brightness and apparent contrast* that occur with changes in the level of illumination. Ward [1994] introduced an operator based on a model of *contrast sensitivity* derived from threshold vs. intensity (TVI) functions similar to those shown in Figure 1a. Its goal is to match the *threshold visibility* of features in the image to features in the scene. Ferwerda [1996] developed an operator based on a model of adaptation that like Ward's matches threshold visibility, but also accounts for the changes in *visual acuity* and *color discriminability* that occur with the changes in the level of illumination.

Both threshold and suprathreshold models of vision capture important aspects of our visual experience, and a realistic tone reproduction operator should produce a mapping that matches both aspects. Unfortunately, threshold models don't scale well to predict suprathreshold appearance, and suprathreshold models don't accurately predict visual thresholds.

Recently much effort has been devoted to developing tone reproduction operators for *high dynamic range* scenes. Chiu [1993], Schlick [1995], and Jobson [1996] introduced spatially-varying operators that compress high dynamic range scenes into the limited range available on display devices, but the ad-hoc visual models they incorporate limits what can be said about the visual fidelity of the mappings. Tumblin [1997] has recently introduced an operator for high dynamic range scenes based on a model of *perceptual constancy*. Although this operator produces attractive images, the model it uses is not quantitative, and therefore the operator can't predict whether an image will be a visual match to a scene. Finally, Ward-Larson [1997] has introduced an operator that extends the work of Ward [1994] and Ferwerda [1996] with a model of *local adaptation*, to produce a threshold-based operator that can handle

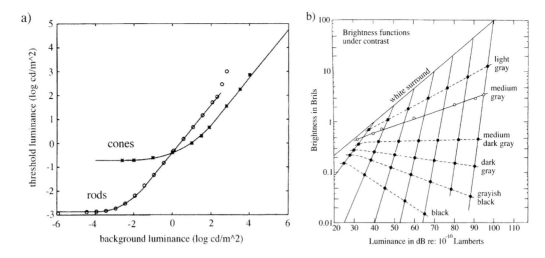

Figure 1: Threshold and suprathreshold models of vision: a) Threshold vs. intensity (TVI) functions for the rod and cone systems. The curves plot the smallest threshold increment ΔL necessary to see a spot against a uniform background with luminance L. b) Stevens' model of suprathreshold brightness and apparent contrast. The curves plot the changes in brightness and apparent contrast of gray targets and a white surround as the level of illumination rises (1 Bril = apparent brightness of a target with a luminance of 1 μLambert). Adapted from [Ferwerda96, Stevens61].

high dynamic range scenes, and also match the changes in threshold visibility, visual acuity and color discriminability that occur with changes in the level of illumination.

Although the innovations introduced in each of these operators represent significant advances toward addressing the two fundamental problems of realistic tone reproduction, overall the problems have been attacked piecemeal. Thus some operators can only handle achromatic scenes, or scenes illuminated at daylight levels. Others can handle wide absolute ranges of illumination in chromatic scenes, but can't handle high dynamic ranges. Still others can handle full ranges of scene radiances, but can't guarantee that the images will match the scenes in any meaningful way. Finally, those that do produce visual matches differ on whether they match threshold measures like visibility and visual acuity, or suprathreshold measures like brightness and apparent contrast. Since the images these operators produce depend upon the visual models they incorporate, a comprehensive solution to the problems of realistic tone reproduction requires a more complete model of visual perception.

In this paper we develop a computational model of adaptation and spatial vision for realistic tone reproduction. The model incorporates a multiscale representation of luminance, pattern, and color processing in human vision that accounts for the changes in threshold visibility, visual acuity, color discriminability, and suprathreshold brightness, colorfulness, and apparent contrast that occur with changes in scene illumination. We incorporate the model into a tone reproduction operator that maps the vast ranges of radiances found in real and synthetic scenes into the small fixed ranges available on conventional display devices such as CRT's and printers. The model allows the operator to address the two major problems in realistic tone reproduction: images of wide absolute range and high dynamic range scenes can be displayed; and the displayed images match our perceptions of the scenes at both threshold and suprathreshold levels to the limits possible on a given display.

2 BACKGROUND

2.1 Adaptation and Visual Thresholds

The range of light we encounter in natural scenes is vast, but the responsive range of the neurons that make up the visual system is

small. Our visual system copes with this vast range of illumination through *adaptation*. Although adaptation allows the visual system to function over a wide range of illumination levels, this does not mean that we see equally well at all levels. At low, *scotopic* levels our eyes are very sensitive and can detect small luminance differences, however visual acuity and the ability to discriminate colors are both poor. In contrast, at high, *photopic* levels, we have sharp color vision, but absolute sensitivity is low and luminance differences have to be large to be detectable. To produce realistic images that capture the visual appearance of scenes we need to understand these adaptation-related changes in vision.

The effects of adaptation on visual sensitivity have been measured in threshold experiments. Figure 1a shows the results of a threshold experiment that measured the changes in visibility that occur with changes in the level of illumination. The curves plot the smallest luminance increment ΔL that can be detected at a particular background luminance L and are known as threshold-vs.-intensity (TVI) functions. The two curves show the TVI functions for the rod and cone systems.

Over a wide range of background luminances, the size of the threshold increment increases in proportion to the background luminance making the functions linear on a log-log scale. This linear relationship $\Delta L = kL$ is known as *Weber's law* and indicates that the visual system has constant contrast sensitivity since the *Weber contrast* $\Delta L/L$ is constant over this range.

Constant contrast sensitivity is a desirable attribute for the visual system to have, since contrast in the retinal image is a function of surface reflectances and is invariant with respect to changes in the level of illumination. This "discounting of the illuminant" through adaptation is a major factor in perceptual constancy which underlies our ability to recognize objects under different illumination conditions [Shapley84]. Weber-like adaptation processes within the different cone systems (known as von Kries adaptation [Wyszecki82]) can also help explain chromatic adaptation and the perceived constancy of surface colors as the chromaticity of the illuminant changes.

2.2 Threshold Models of Spatial Vision

Although the TVI functions shown in Figure 1a give us useful information about the changes in visual sensitivity that occur with

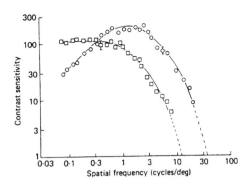

Figure 2: Threshold contrast sensitivity as a function of spatial frequency for a monochromatic luminance grating ($\circ$; $green$; $526nm$) and a isoluminant chromatic grating ($\square$; $red/green$; $602, 526nm$). Adapted from [Mullen85].

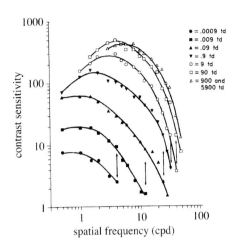

Figure 3: Contrast sensitivity functions for sinusoidal gratings illuminated at different mean luminance levels. Levels are specified in Troland (Td) units of retinal illuminance (Trolands = luminance in cd/m^2 x pupil area). Adapted from [vanNes67].

changes in the level of illumination, it's difficult to understand how to generalize from the results of these studies on the detectability of spots on uniform backgrounds to predicting the visibility of real objects (e.g. tanks, tumors) in complex scenes. In the 1960's vision researchers began to measure visual sensitivity for sinusoidal grating patterns to understand the properties of spatial vision.

The contrast sensitivity functions (CSF's) shown in Figure 2 plot visual sensitivity for detecting sinusoidal gratings as a function of their spatial frequency. Here sensitivity is defined as (1/threshold contrast) using the *Michaelson* definition of contrast: $(L_{max} - L_{min})/(L_{max} + L_{min})$ where L_{max} and L_{min} are the luminances at the peaks and troughs of the gratings [Laming91].

There is substantial evidence that the responses of the rod and cone photoreceptors are organized at an early stage in the visual system into responses in an achromatic channel sensitive to luminance variations and two chromatic channels, one sensitive to variations along a red/green axis and the other sensitive along a yellow/blue axis [Hurvich81]. The two curves in Figure 2 show the CSF's of the achromatic and red/green chromatic channels.

There are several things to notice about the CSF's. The first is that the spatial frequency response of the achromatic channel ($\circ$) has the characteristics of a bandpass filter. Contrast sensitivity is highest for gratings with frequencies around 2 to 4 cycles/degree of visual angle (cpd) and sensitivity drops for both higher and lower spatial frequencies. On the other hand, the spatial frequency response of the red/green chromatic channel ($\square$) has the characteristic of a lowpass filter. Sensitivity is good for low spatial frequencies, but declines at higher frequencies. The contrast sensitivity function of the yellow/blue channel shows a similar pattern of response after correction for chromatic abberation.

The high frequency cutoffs of the CSF's indicate the limits of spatial resolution in the two channels. The achromatic channel has a cutoff at approximately 30 cpd which is in good correspondence with the limits of visual acuity measured in clinical tests. The high frequency cutoff for the chromatic channels is only around 11 cpd. This means that the chromatic channels have much lower spatial resolution than the achromatic channel.

The contrast sensitivity functions have been widely used to model the visual system's response to complex objects. If the image of an object can be described in terms of its sinusoidal Fourier components, then the visibility of that object can be measured by applying the contrast sensitivity function to the components. When the components are above threshold the object will be seen, when they're below threshold it will be invisible.

This approach to predicting the visibility of complex objects has

been widely used, but there is a severe limit on its generality that is often overlooked which will lead to gross errors in the predictions, namely that all the grating patterns used to measure the CSF's have the same mean luminance. While the contrast sensitivity functions show how sensitivity varies with spatial frequency, they do not take into account the changes in sensitivity caused by adaptation. To account for changes in the visibility of real objects in real scenes, we need to understand the interactions of adaptation with threshold spatial vision.

2.3 Adaptation and Threshold Spatial Vision

The results of a classic study on the effects of adaptation on threshold spatial vision are shown in Figure 3. van Nes [1967] measured contrast sensitivity functions for achromatic gratings illuminated at a wide range of different levels. Each curve in the graph represents the CSF measured at a particular luminance level.

There are several things to notice in the graph. The first is that overall, contrast sensitivity improves with the level of illumination. Peak contrast sensitivity changes from a value of 8 (threshold contrast of 12%) at an illumination level of 0.0009 Trolands (Td) to a value of 500 (threshold contrast of 0.2%) at 5900 Td.

The next thing to notice is that the shape of the CSF changes from being lowpass at the lowest illumination levels to being bandpass at higher levels. This reflects the transition from rod vision in the scotopic range to cone vision at photopic levels.

The final thing to notice is that as the level of illumination increases, the high frequency cutoff of the CSF moves to higher and higher spatial frequencies. This corresponds to the improvement in spatial resolution and visual acuity that we experience at higher luminance levels. The cutoff changes from about 4 cpd at 0.0009 Td to about 50 cpd at 5900 Td which corresponds to an improvement in acuity from around 20/150 at the lowest level to almost 20/10 at the highest.

The curves in Figure 3 show the effects of adaptation on spatial contrast sensitivity in the achromatic channel of the visual system. Data from van der Horst [1969] shows a similar pattern of results in the chromatic channels.

These data begin to give us a clearer picture of the interactions between adaptation and threshold spatial vision. From these data we can begin to understand in a unified framework, the changes in

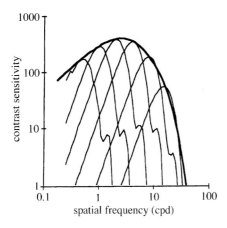

Figure 4: Multiscale bandpass mechanisms underlying the contrast sensitivity functions. Adapted from [Lubin95].

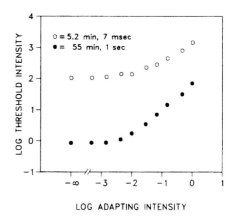

Figure 5: Threshold-vs.-intensity functions for spot patterns with different spatial and temporal parameters. Adapted from [Barlow72].

visibility, acuity, and color discrimination that occur with changes in the level of illumination. However there is one more aspect of these interactions that we need to investigate to have a more complete understanding, and this is the effect of local adaptation.

2.4 Local Adaptation and Multiscale Models of Threshold Spatial Vision

As we look from place to place in a scene our eyes adapt locally to the prevailing conditions of illumination. This local adaptation greatly enhances our ability to see in high dynamic range scenes where some portions of the scene are brightly illuminated and others are in shadow. How does local adaptation work?

Physiological and psychophysical evidence now indicates that the early stages of visual processing can be described as the filtering of the retinal image by visual mechanisms sensitive to patterns of different scale whose response characteristics are bandpass in the spatial frequency domain [Wilson91]. These multiple mechanisms are sensitive to different ranges of spatial frequencies, and the CSF's that are measured in psychophysical experiments are the envelope of these mechanism sensitivities. Figure 4 shows the achromatic CSF described in this way. Losada [1994] has shown that the chromatic CSF's can be described in a similar way.

Now if we look back at van Nes's data (Figure 3) on the changes in spatial contrast sensitivity that occur with changes in the level of illumination, it can be seen that the CSF curves don't simply shift upwards with increasing illumination, but change shape as well. This is a reflection of the fact that these bandpass mechanisms adapt to the average luminance within a region of a scene defined by their spatial scale. In a complex scene, this average is going to be different at different scales so the mechanisms will all be in different states of adaptation.

Thus local adaptation is not only spatially local within different regions of the visual field, but is also local with respect to the scale and spatial frequency filtering characteristics of the bandpass mechanisms involved in early visual processing. Therefore, to correctly account for the changes in visual sensitivity that occur with changes in the level of illumination, we need to describe the effects of local adaptation at different spatial scales.

Peli [1990] has suggested that an appropriate way to characterize the effects of local adaptation is to determine the *band-limited local contrast* at each location in the scene. Band-limited local contrast is calculated by first filtering the retinal image into a set of bandpass images defined by the filter characteristics of the visual mech-

anisms, and then dividing the signals in these images by lowpass images that represent the average local luminance at each location in the image at different spatial scales. This produces a multiscale representation of the image where the signals in each band represent the effective contrasts at each scale, having taken the effects of local adaptation into account. Both Peli and Lubin [1995] have shown that this kind of representation corresponds well with perceived threshold contrasts in complex images.

2.5 Suprathreshold Models of Vision

Threshold models of vision allow us to define the borders between the visible and the invisible. These models have a long and useful history in applied vision research, but because threshold models only define the limits of vision, they don't really tell us much about ordinary "seeing" where the contrasts, sizes of spatial details, and color saturations are typically well above threshold. To characterize how changes in the level of illumination affect the everyday appearances of objects in scenes, suprathreshold models of vision are needed.

Stevens' [1961] model of brightness and apparent contrast shown in Figure 1b summarizes much of what is known about the intensity dependence of surface appearance at suprathreshold levels. Stevens had subjects estimate the apparent brightnesses of gray patches seen against a white surround at different illumination levels. The brightness of the surround increased as a power function (exponent 0.33) of its luminance. The brightnesses of the gray patches either increased, decreased or remained constant depending on their contrast with respect to the surround. Overall, the diverging curves quantify a familiar aspect of our visual experience: as we turn up the light, the world becomes more vivid. Whites become brighter, blacks become deeper and the whole range of apparent contrasts expands. Although Stevens only tested achromatic surfaces, Hunt [1995] has measured a related set of phenomena for chromatic displays, where the vibrancy and *colorfulness* of colored surfaces increases at higher levels of illumination.

While these suprathreshold changes in brightness, colorfulness, and apparent contrast are certainly true to our everyday experience, it is difficult to reconcile these results with the predictions of threshold models and Weber's law which show that adaptation produces a visual system with constant contrast sensitivity, and imply that apparent suprathreshold contrasts should be constant over changes in the level of illumination within the Weber range. Differences in the TVI functions for different kinds of visual stimuli suggest a solution to this conundrum.

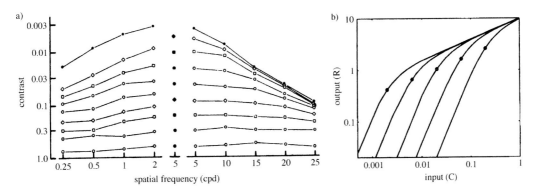

Figure 6: Suprathreshold contrast constancy and non-linear contrast transducers in human vision. Adapted from [Georgeson75, Watson97b].

2.6 Adaptation and Suprathreshold Vision

Figure 5 shows photopic TVI functions measured by Barlow [1972] for incremental spot patterns with different spatial and temporal characteristics. The lower curve shows thresholds measured for a large spot presented in a long exposure. The upper curve shows thresholds for a small, briefly flashed spot. There are two important differences between the curves. First, threshold values for the large/long spot are everywhere lower than thresholds for the small/brief spot. Second, although the slope of the large/long TVI curve follows Weber's law at higher background levels, the short/brief TVI has a lower slope indicating sub-Weber behavior.

The significance of the differences between these two TVI's is that low threshold values, and the constant contrast sensitivity implied by Weber's law, are only obtained under optimal conditions in laboratory experiments, such as those shown in the lower curve in this experiment or those given in the experiments that measured the rod and cone TVI's shown in Figure 1a. The TVI function for the small/brief spot is more like what we should expect under natural conditions where our eyes are continually moving across a complex scene and both the visual stimuli and our state of adaptation will be changing rapidly. Here threshold sensitivity is limited by both incomplete adaptation and quantal fluctuations in the stimulus, making thresholds higher-than-optimal, but also producing a TVI with a sub-Weber slope, where threshold contrast sensitivity continues to improve at higher illumination levels because the magnitude of the visual response to a constant physical contrast increases as the level of illumination rises. The insights provided by this experiment are the key that allow us to unify the predictions of threshold and suprathreshold models in one coherent framework. To complete the picture we've been developing of a model that can explain the interactions of adaptation and spatial vision at threshold and suprathreshold levels, we need to understand the properties of suprathreshold spatial vision.

2.7 Adaptation and Suprathreshold Spatial Vision

A CSF describes how threshold contrast sensitivity varies for sinusoidal gratings of different spatial frequencies. The upper curve in Figure 6a shows an achromatic CSF measured by Georgeson [1975]. This typical curve shows that we are most sensitive to gratings with frequencies around 4-5 *cpd* and that sensitivity falls off at both higher and lower frequencies. This CSF was measured as part of a suprathreshold *contrast matching* experiment. In this experiment subjects matched the apparent contrast of different frequency test gratings to the apparent contrast of a standard grating of 5 *cpd*. In separate trials, the physical contrast of the standard was varied from less than 1% to more than 75%. The lower curves in Figure 6a summarize the results.

At low standard contrasts, the matches followed the form of the threshold CSF. High and low frequency gratings had to have higher physical contrast to have the same apparent contrast as the standard. But at standard contrasts above about 20% the curves flattened out. Gratings matched in apparent contrast when they had the same physical contrast. Georgeson called this phenomenon *contrast constancy*.

The differences in the shapes of the threshold CSF and the suprathreshold contrast matching functions indicates the existence of nonlinear contrast transduction processes in the visual system. Brady [1995] has suggested that these contrast nonlinearities reflect differences in the signal/noise characteristics of the bandpass visual mechanisms which can explain both the curvature of the threshold CSF and the flatness of the suprathreshold contrast matching functions.

Watson and Solomon [1997b] have developed a model of these contrast nonlinearities as part of their work on the closely related phenomenon of visual masking. The transducer functions for a set of hypothetical bandpass mechanisms are shown in Figure 6b. The horizontal axis indicates the input contrast, the vertical axis plots the response. At low input contrast levels, the transducers all have different cutoffs. The differences in these cutoffs imply that the mechanisms all have different sensitivities, since at any particular low level, the input signal will be above the cutoffs for some mechanisms and below for others. This characteristic of the transducer functions accounts for CSF-like responses at low contrast levels. But at higher input contrast levels, the transducer functions converge, which means that given the same input contrast, all the mechanisms will produce the same response. This characteristic accounts for the contrast constancy observed at higher contrast levels. The action of these transducer functions, which mimics the contrast nonlinearity in the visual system, provides a coherent framework for understanding threshold and suprathreshold spatial vision.

2.8 Summary

In the previous sections we have outlined a coherent framework for understanding the changes in vision that occur with changes in the level of illumination in scenes. The framework relates research on adaptation with research on spatial vision to provide a unified view of variations in threshold performance and suprathreshold appearance at different illumination levels. The framework allows us to account for the changes in threshold visibility, visual acuity, and color discrimination, and suprathreshold brightness, colorfulness, and apparent contrast that occur under different illumination conditions. The key features of the framework are:

- Multiscale processing of the retinal image by visual mechanisms in the rod and cone pathways with bandpass spatial frequency response characteristics.

- Adaptation processes operating within these bandpass mechanisms that act as "luminance gain controls" to produce visual signals that are primarily correlated with scene contrasts, but are still luminance dependent and increase in magnitude with increasing luminance. Independent adaptation processes within the bandpass mechanisms in the rod and cone pathways account for "local" adaptation, chromatic adaptation, and changes in sensitivity over the scotopic to photopic range.

- Organization of the bandpass mechanisms in the rod and cone pathways into an achromatic and two chromatic channels with different spatial frequency response characteristics.

- Nonlinear transducers operating on the adapted outputs of the mechanisms in these achromatic and chromatic channels that scale the visual signals to produce CSF-like response at threshold levels, and contrast constancy at suprathreshold levels.

In the following section we will develop a computational model of vision based on this framework and apply it to the problem of realistic tone reproduction. The unique features of the model will allow our tone reproduction operator to address the two major problems in realistic tone reproduction: images of wide absolute range and high dynamic range scenes can be displayed on conventional display devices; and these images should match our perceptions of the scenes at threshold and suprathreshold levels.

3 THE COMPUTATIONAL MODEL

3.1 Overview

We will now draw on the psychophysical framework outlined in the previous section to develop a computational model of adaptation and spatial vision for realistic tone reproduction. Figure 7 provides a flow chart of each major step in this computational model. The model has two main parts: the *Visual model* and the *Display model*. The visual model processes an input image to encode the perceived contrasts for the chromatic and achromatic channels in their band-pass mechanisms. The display model then takes this encoded information and reconstructs an output image. The model must be inverted in order to produce equivalent appearances under the viewing conditions of the display device. This procedure does not "undo" the processes of the model since the thresholding and saturation procedures are accomplished and the gain control parameters differ for the original scene and the display. The reconstruction process creates an output image that reproduces the visual appearance of the input image to the limits possible on a given display device. The specific computational procedures that were used to implement each step of the model are described below. A pictorial representation of the signals at each stage of the model is presented in Figure 8.

3.2 Input Image Preprocessing

Prior to applying the visual model, certain preprocessing steps are required to assure that the image data appropriately correspond to the information accessible to the early stages of the human visual system. First, the image must be spatially sampled such that the band pass signals represent appropriate spatial frequencies. For this implementation, band pass mechanisms with peak spatial frequencies of 16, 8, 4, 2, 1, and 0.5 cpd were required. The spatial sampling necessary to produce these band-pass signals depends upon the Gaussian filters chosen for the image decomposition. With the

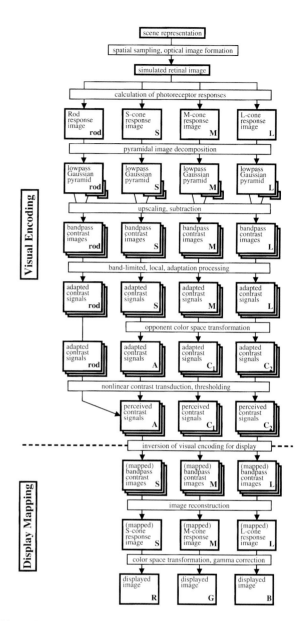

Figure 7: Flow chart of the computational model of adaptation and spatial vision for realistic tone reproduction.

filter described in Section 3.3 it is necessary to sample the image at a rate of 130 pixels/degree.

The next step is to introduce compensations for optical point-spread in the eye and disability glare. Optical point-spread is incorporated via a convolution with a function described by Westheimer [1986] and glare effect is introduced via convolutions with functions described by Spencer [1995].

The image must then be spectrally sampled to represent the visual system's initial photoreceptor responses. This is accomplished by integrating the spectral radiance distribution for each pixel after multiplication by the spectral responsivities of the long-, middle- and short-wavelength sensitive cones (LMS) and the rods. We use the Hunt-Pointer-Estevez [Fairchild98] responsivities for the cones and the CIE scotopic luminous efficiency function, $V'(\lambda)$, [Wyszecki82] for the rods.

In many applications, a spectral radiance image is not available. In such cases, the cone signals can be calculated as a linear transform of the CIE 1931 XYZ tristimulus values as shown in Equation

1.

$$\begin{vmatrix} L \\ M \\ S \end{vmatrix} = \begin{vmatrix} 0.3897 & 0.6890 & -0.0787 \\ -0.2298 & 1.1834 & 0.0464 \\ 0 & 0 & 1 \end{vmatrix} \begin{vmatrix} X \\ Y \\ Z \end{vmatrix} \quad (1)$$

However, it is impossible to obtain the proper rod signals. We derived a linear transform of XYZ tristimulus values as a rough approximation to the rod signal via linear regression of the color matching functions and the $V'(\lambda)$ curve. The resulting transform is given in Equation 2 where R represents the rod response for a pixel.

$$R = -0.702X + 1.039Y + 0.433Z \quad (2)$$

Since it is possible to obtain negative values of R when Equation 2 is applied to some saturated colors, it must be clipped to zero. We chose a simple linear transformation for this approximation since it scales over any range of luminance levels.

Finally the input signals must be calibrated prior to input to the visual transforms. We chose to calibrate the model such that the LMS cone signals and the rod signal are all equal to unity for an equal-radiance spectrum at a luminance of 1.0 cd/m^2.

3.3 Spatial Decomposition

The 4 images representing the calibrated photoreceptor responses are then subjected to spatial processing. The first step is to carry out the spatial decomposition of these images. We carry out this decomposition by the Laplacian pyramid (difference-of-Gaussian pyramid) approach proposed by Burt and Adelson [1983]. This approach guarantees the construction of a non-negative low-pass image in high dynamic range situations, and is perfectly invertible. We first calculate a Gaussian pyramid using a 5 tap filter (with 1D weights: .05 .25 .4 .25 .05) [Burt83]. Each level of the Gaussian pyramid represents a low-pass image limited to spatial frequencies half of those of the next higher level. Our Gaussian pyramid has 7 levels.

Each level of the Gaussian pyramid is then upsampled such that each image is returned to the size of the initial image. Difference-of-Gaussian images are then calculated by taking the image at each level and subtracting the image from the next lower level. This results in 6 levels of band-pass images with peak spatial frequencies at 16, 8, 4, 2, 1, and 0.5 cpd. These images can be thought of as representations of the signals in six band-pass mechanisms in the human visual system. The lowest-level low pass image is retained since it must be used to reconstruct the image for reproduction applications.

3.4 Gain Control

The difference-of-Gaussian images are then converted to adapted contrast signals using a luminance gain control. The gains are set using TVI-like functions that represent the increment thresholds of the rod and cone systems and the growth in response required to allow perceived contrast to increase with luminance level (sub-Weber's law behavior). The gain functions are given for the cones in Equation 3 and the rods in Equation 4.

$$G_{cone}(I) = \frac{1}{0.555(I + 1.0)^{0.85}} \quad (3)$$

$$G_{rod}(I) = \left[\frac{10}{I^2 + 10}\right]\left[\frac{1}{0.908(I + 0.001)^{0.85}}\right] \quad (4)$$

In the above equations, I represents the rod or cone signal that is used to set the level of adaptation and $G(I)$ is the gain-control factor. Equations 3 and 4 were derived to match available psychophysical TVI and brightness matching data. The constraints in

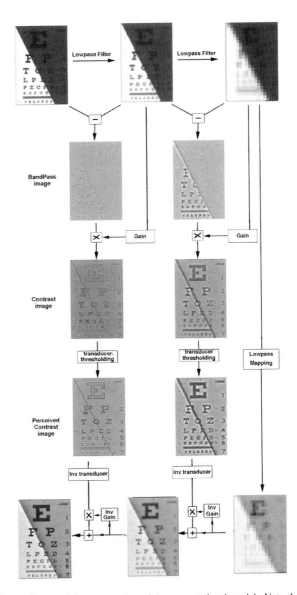

Figure 8: Pictorial representation of the computational model. Note that only 2 out of the 6 spatial mechanisms of one of the channels have been shown for the purpose of illustration. Original image is a Snellen chart with a 30:1 shadow boundary.

their derivation were that both the rod and cone gains were set equal to 1.0 at a 1.0 cd/m^2, the absolute thresholds would be around 1.0 cd/m^2 for cones and 0.001 cd/m^2 for rods, the ultimate slopes of the functions would be 0.85 for sub-Weber's Law behavior, and the rods would saturate, losing 50% of their responsivity at roughly 3 cd/m^2. In our model, each pixel in a given difference-of-Gaussian image is multiplied by the gain derived from the corresponding pixel in the lower-level low-pass image that was used in its derivation. This is illustrated in Equation 5.

$$ACI_n = G\left(LP_{n+1}\right)\left[LP_n - LP_{n+1}\right] \quad (5)$$

ACI_n is the adapted contrast image at level n and LP represents the various low-pass images. The adapted contrast images are analogous to the contrast images that Peli [1990] obtained. However, in our model the magnitude of these images is a function of luminance level as specified by the gain control functions. This is necessary to allow prediction of luminance-dependent appearance effects. The luminance gain controls are applied in the same manner to each of the difference-of-Gaussian images for each of the photoreceptors. Equation 3 is used to calculate the gains for each of the cones and Equation 4 is used for the rods. Note that performing the gain control at this point in the model allows proper prediction of chromatic-adaptation effects.

3.5 Opponent Color Processing

The next stage of the model is to transform the adapted contrast images for the cones into opponent signals. We use the transform of Hunt [1995] that has also been recently adopted in the CIE color appearance model, CIECAM97s [Fairchild98] as given in Equation 6.

$$
\begin{vmatrix} A \\ C_1 \\ C_2 \end{vmatrix} = \begin{vmatrix} 2.0 & 1.0 & 0.05 \\ 1.0 & -1.09 & 0.09 \\ 0.11 & 0.11 & -0.22 \end{vmatrix} \begin{vmatrix} L \\ M \\ S \end{vmatrix} \quad (6)
$$

In the above equation, L, M, S represent the cone signals and A, C_1, C_2 represent luminance, red-green, and yellow-blue opponent signals respectively. This transform is applied without modification to the adapted contrast signals to obtain adapted contrast signals in an opponent color space. This transformation is necessary to model differences in the spatial processing of luminance and chromatic signals. At this stage, the rod images are retained separately since their spatial processing attributes also differ from the cones.

3.6 Adapted Contrast Transducers

The adapted contrast signals are then passed through contrast transducer functions similar to those described by Watson and Solomon [1997]. Different transducer functions are applied to each spatial frequency mechanism in order to model psychophysically derived human spatial contrast sensitivity functions. For example, the transducer for the 16 cpd achromatic mechanism has a higher threshold than the transducer for the 4 cpd achromatic mechanism since we are less sensitive to the higher spatial frequencies. The transducers are also different for the chromatic channels to represent their lower sensitivities and low-pass, rather than band-pass nature. Finally, the rod system has a distinct set of transducers to represent its unique spatial characteristics. At high contrast levels the transducer functions converge to a common square-root form to properly represent perceived contrast constancy and introduce a compressive nonlinearity typically found in color appearance models. The functional form of our transducer functions vary from that proposed by Watson and Solomon [1997] since their function was not analytically invertible and it is necessary to invert our model for image reproduction applications. We chose to use a two-part function consisting of two power functions in order to replicate the two regions of distinct slope in the transducer functions. The contrast transducers used in our model are given by Equations 7 and 8 for the cones and Equation 9 for the rods.

$$
T_{\text{cone,Achromatic}}(c) = \begin{cases} 22.4\,(c/0.536)^{\frac{1}{2}} & \text{if } c \geq 0.536 \\ 22.4\,(c/0.536)^{p} & \text{otherwise.} \end{cases} \quad (7)
$$

$$
T_{\text{cone,Chromatic}}(c) = \begin{cases} 22.4\,(c/0.176)^{\frac{1}{2}} & \text{if } c \geq 0.176 \\ 22.4\,(c/0.176)^{p} & \text{otherwise.} \end{cases} \quad (8)
$$

$$
T_{\text{rod}}(c) = \begin{cases} 22.4\,(c/0.0335)^{\frac{1}{2}} & \text{if } c \geq 0.0335 \\ 22.4\,(c/0.0335)^{p} & \text{otherwise.} \end{cases} \quad (9)
$$

In the above equations, c represents the adapted contrast signals (ACI's) and $T(c)$ represents the output of the transducers. The exponent, p, in Equations 7, 8 and 9 differs for each spatial frequency mechanism as given in the following table.

Peak(cpd)	.5	1.0	2.0	4.0	8.0	16.0
p for A	1.93	1.35	1.15	1.04	1.15	1.40
p for C_1&C_2	1.93	1.93	2.35	2.85	-	-
p for Rod	3.39	3.39	4.50	7.64	-	-

If c is negative, the absolute value of c is taken and then the negative sign is replaced after transformation.

Equations 7 through 9 were derived by specifying the desired thresholds for the various spatial and chromatic mechanisms at 1000 cd/m^2 for the cones and 0.5 cd/m^2 for the rods. The lower parts of the functions were forced to pass through 1.0 for the desired threshold contrast. At sinusoidal contrasts greater than 5% (at these calibration luminance levels) the functions converge to the square-root form that produces contrast constancy. The square root is derived to mimic the compressive nonlinearities typically found in color appearance models. These transducers do produce CSF behavior that changes with luminance as illustrated in Figure 3 since the input adapted contrast signals vary with luminance due to the sub-Weber gain control functions. Transducers for the chromatic cone channels and the rod channel do not exist for spatial frequencies above those represented by the mechanism centered at 4 cpd since these systems cannot resolve contrast at higher spatial frequencies. (Note that the 4 cpd mechanism carries information out to about 16 cpd which is thus the acuity limit of the mechanism.) The contrast transducer functions are calibrated such that psychophysical contrast sensitivity function data are modeled and sinusoidal contrasts above about 5% produce contrast constancy as a function of spatial frequency and sinusoidal contrasts of 100% produce transducer output of approximately 100. It should be recalled that in our model, these levels will be luminance dependent. The contrast transducer functions are also designed such that contrasts that are below threshold have an output level with magnitude less than 1.0.

One of the key functions of the transducers is to set the threshold level such that image content that is imperceptible for a given set of viewing conditions can be removed. To accomplish this, the output of the transducer functions is thresholded such that all absolute values less than 1.0 are set to 0.0. An alternative approach would be to replace all absolute values less than 1.0 with a random number between 0.0 and 1.0. This might better replicate the appearance of visual noise at low contrast levels.

In addition to establishing thresholds, the transducer functions are used to model saturation of the visual neurons that signal contrast. Thus, the transducer functions are limited to maximum values of 50 to simulate the typical physiological dynamic range. [Hunt95] Since the contrast mechanisms are bipolar, this represents a 100:1 dynamic range in each spatial mechanism and therefore even larger perceptual dynamic ranges in fully reconstructed images. This saturation is also not a severe restriction on the image content since the gain control mechanisms already accomplish a high degree of dynamic-range compression.

3.7 Combination of Rod and Cone Signals

Up to this point in the model it is necessary to keep the rod signals separate in order to appropriately integrate their unique adaptation and spatial vision properties. After the contrast transducers, the rod and cone signals can be combined to produce signals that represent the three-dimensional color appearances of the input image. We assume that the rods contribute only to the luminance signal and thus combine the A signal from the cones with the rod signal, denoted A_{rod}, to produce a total achromatic signal, A_{total}, using Equation 10.

$$
A_{total} = A_{cone} + A_{rod}/7 \quad (10)
$$

The differential weighting of the rod and cone signals is a result of the model calibration necessary to establish the rod and cone gain controls and transducer functions. It results in a total achromatic output that is monotonic with luminance.

At this stage in the model we have three channels representing achromatic, red-green, and yellow-blue apparent contrast for 6 band-pass mechanisms. These signals model threshold behavior, in that any contrast signals that could not be perceived have been eliminated at the contrast transducer functions. They also represent suprathreshold appearance since the contrast signals grow with luminance and the chromatic channels will become zero at luminance levels below the cone threshold. At this stage, the model has also accomplished a significant level of dynamic-range compression since the contrast signals range only 2 orders of magnitude (1 to around 100) for luminance differences ranging over 10 orders of magnitude. This compression is accomplished by both the gain control functions and the nonlinear transducers.

3.8 Treatment of the Low Pass Image

The lowest level low-pass image from the upsampled Gaussian pyramid must be retained in order to reconstruct an image from the adapted contrast images that have been passed through the model (each a band-pass image). To this point, we have not discussed the application of the visual model to this low pass image. The best approach to processing the low-pass image depends on the application. For simple images of low dynamic range (*e.g.*, less than 50:1), an appropriate treatment of the low-pass image is to multiply it by a constant gain factor derived from the image mean. This technique will do little to compress the range of high-dynamic range images since the contrast within the low pass image will be preserved. An alternative that produces maximum dynamic-range compression is to multiply each pixel in the low-pass image by a gain factor derived from the pixel itself. (The gain factors are derived using Equations 3 and 4.) Techniques intermediate between these two might produce optimal image reproductions for various applications. The above treatment of the low-pass image is consistent with the full model of visual perception and can be thought of as a treatment of the effects of eye movements on the perception of a scene. In the extreme case of adapting the low pass image to its own values, the treatment mimics the visual response assuming that observer fixated on each and every image location and judged them completely independent of one another. For the other extreme case of adapting the low pass image using the mean signal, the treatment simulates completely random and continuous eye movements uniformly distributed across the scene. Intermediate treatments between these two extremes might more accurately model real world eye movements which are scene dependent and represent some average between fixating each image element of interest and randomly viewing all locations in a scene.

Transducer functions are necessary for the low pass image as well since the rod and cone information is combined after the transducer stage. We have adopted low-pass transducers that are simple power functions based on typical practice in color appearance modeling. [Fairchild98] The scaling of the low-pass transducers is set to preserve equal magnitude of signals for the low-pass and band-pass model output for a sinusoidal grating. The low-pass transducers are given in Equations 11, 12 and 13 for the achromatic and chromatic cone signals and rod signals respectively.

$$T_{LP\_cone,Achromatic}(LP) = 30.5\,(LP)^{\frac{1}{2}} \qquad (11)$$

$$T_{LP\_cone,Chromatic}(LP) = 53.3\,(LP)^{\frac{1}{2}} \qquad (12)$$

$$T_{LP\_rod}(LP) = 122\,(LP)^{\frac{1}{2}} \qquad (13)$$

T represents the output of the low-pass transducers and LP represents the pixel values in the adapted, opponent-transformed, low-pass image.

3.9 Image Reconstruction for Display

The output of the visual model consists of appearance signals in an achromatic and two chromatic channels and six spatial band-pass mechanisms plus a low-pass image. We now take these appearance signals backward through the model to recreate cone signals (and ultimately device signals such as RGB or CMYK) that replicate the full color appearance of the image on a photopic, trichromatic display device such as a CRT display.

The first step of the inversion process is to go through the inverse of the transducer functions given in Equations 7, 8, 11 and 12. The AC_1C_2 signals are then transformed to adapted LMS cone signals using the inverse of the matrix transformation given in Equation 6. At this point we have adapted contrast signals that have been subjected to the appropriate visibility thresholding and saturation by the contrast transducer functions.

The next step is to reverse the gain control process for the viewing conditions of the output display. This begins by determining the gain control factors for the mean luminance of the target display device using Equation 3. The adapted low-pass images are then divided by the display-mean gain control factors to produce images that represent the appropriate LMS cone responses for the display low-pass image. This display low-pass image is then used to begin the process of reconstruction of a full-resolution image from the six adapted contrast signal images.

Gain control factors are calculated for each pixel of the display low-pass image using Equation 3 and these are used to scale the lowest frequency (0.5 cpd peak) adapted contrast signal image back to the display. This image is then added to the low-pass image to produce a new low-pass image that includes the contrast information from the 0.5 cpd image. This image is then used to calculate gain control factors that are applied to the next level (1.0 cpd peak). The resulting image is again added to the new low-pass image to generate yet another low-pass image that incorporates the information from both the 0.5 and 1.0 cpd mechanisms. The process is repeated at each level until all of the spatial frequency mechanisms have been scaled to the display and added to the output image.

At this point in the reconstruction we have an LMS image representing the cone signals that are desired when viewing the output display. These must be converted to signals appropriate for the given display device using typical device-independent color imaging procedures. For a CRT this involves a linear transform from LMS to CIE XYZ (inverse of Equation 1) followed by a second linear transform from CIE XYZ to device RGB. The second transform is defined by the CIE tristimulus values of the display primaries. At this point we have linear RGB signals that must either be transformed through the inverse of the CRT display transfer function (often referred to as gamma correction) or displayed on a system with linearizing video look-up tables. A similar, although more complex, process is required for printing devices.

Finally, it is not uncommon that the desired display colors simply cannot be produced on a given device (i.e., they are out of gamut). This includes the mapping of the desired luminance level and range into that of the display. There are a wide variety of techniques that have been suggested to address this issue the details of which are beyond the scope of this paper. The approach that is taken depends on the particular application. Some of the issues that are encountered with this particular model are discussed in the next section with respect to the rendering on paper and on CRT monitor of the various example images.

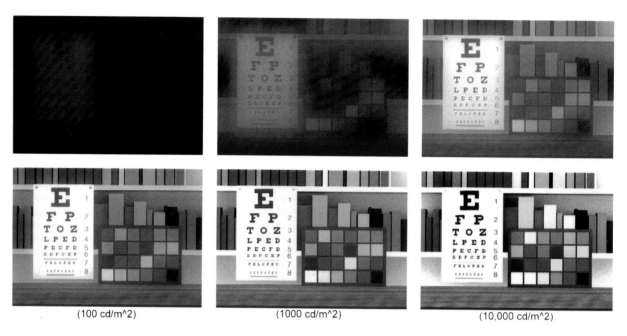

(100 cd/m^2)   (1000 cd/m^2)   (10,000 cd/m^2)

Figure 9: Application of the model to a wide range of illumination levels.

4 APPLYING THE MODEL

4.1 Wide Absolute Range

The series of images in Figure 9 illustrate application of the model to a wide range of luminance levels spanning six orders of magnitude from 0.1 to 10,000 cd/m^2. These images were created using the model as described in section 3 with the low-pass images adapted to the mean luminance of the input images. The size of the original image was about $15° \times 10°$. For image reconstruction as printed images, a mean adapting luminance of 700 cd/m^2 was assumed. This is approximately the luminance of a standard print viewing booth. Thus this series of images should provide faithful reproductions of the visual impression at the various luminance levels when the printed figure is viewed at a mean luminance of 700 cd/m^2. The gamut-mapping selected for this demonstration was a linear scaling that placed the white areas of the 1000 cd/m^2 image at the paper white. While the model can be applied successfully over a wider absolute range, it is impossible to reproduce the results within the limited dynamic range (approximately 50:1) of the printed images unless a variable scaling is used.

Features to note in Figure 9 include: the decrease in luminance contrast and colorfulness as luminance is decreased, the loss of color vision upon the transition from cone to rod vision below 1 cd/m^2, the decrease in spatial acuity with decrease in luminance, and the changes in relative visibility of various colors and patterns. The Purkinje shift (blue to gray and red to black) is also correctly predicted upon changes from photopic to scotopic luminance levels. All of these features illustrate that the model has appropriately encoded aspects of threshold visibility and suprathreshold appearance over a wide range of luminance levels.

4.2 Chromatic Adaptation

Figure 10 shows the unique feature of this model that it can handle changes in chromatic, as well as luminance-level, adaptation. The top row of images illustrate a scene illuminated by a very reddish light source, a nearly-white incandescent light source, and a very

blue light source as they would be rendered by a system incapable of chromatic adaptation. The shift in color balance of the reproduced prints is objectionable since the human visual system largely compensates for these changes in illumination color through its mechanisms of chromatic adaptation. Since our model treats gain control in each of the classes of cone photoreceptors independently, it is capable of predicting changes in chromatic adaptation similar to those that would be predicted by a von Kries model. However, due to the nature of the gain control functions used to obtain increases in contrast and colorfulness with luminance, the degree of chromatic adaptation predicted by the model is less than 100% complete.

The bottom row of images illustrate the output of the visual model when the low-pass images are adapted to the mean signal levels in the image and the reconstructed images are created assuming adaptation to an equal-energy white. All of the computations were completed at a mean luminance of 50 cd/m^2. The gamut-mapping selected for these images was a linear scaling that mapped 100 cd/m^2 in the reconstructed image to the monitor white. 100 cd/m^2 is approximately the maximum luminance of a display monitor. The sizes of the original images were $10° \times 8°$. These images illustrate that the model almost completely accounts for the changes in illumination color. However, as expected the reproduced appearance from the reddish light source retains a slight reddish cast while the reproduction from the bluish light source retains a slight bluish cast. These reproductions match our perceptions of changes in illumination color and replicate the incomplete nature of chromatic adaptation that is widely recognized in the color science literature. [Fairchild98]

4.3 High Dynamic Range

Figure 11 illustrates application of the model to the tone mapping of high-dynamic range images. The original images have areas of detail that are in high illumination levels and other areas that are in low illumination levels. The left most image in Figure 11 is a global illumination rendering. The other two were constructed from successive photographic exposures using the technique of Debevec and

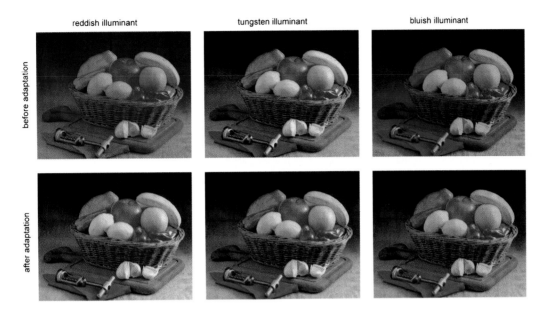

Figure 10: Illustration of chromatic adaptation.

Malik [1997]. To provide the higher degree of compression necessary for high-dynamic-range mapping, the low pass image was adapted to itself. The reproduced images were reconstructed for display at a mean luminance of 50 cd/m^2.

The images on the top row of Figure 11 are linear mappings of the original high-dynamic range images into the limited dynamic range of the output device. The original images had luminance ranges of approximately 10,000:1. The images on the bottom row represent the mapping obtained by application of the visual model. In Figure 11 it is clear that far more detail can be observed in both shadow and highlight regions when the images are mapped using the visual model.

5 CONCLUSIONS AND FUTURE WORK

In this paper we have introduced a new visual model for realistic tone reproduction. The model is based on a multiscale representation of luminance, pattern, and color processing in the human visual system, and provides a coherent framework for understanding the effects of adaptation on spatial vision. The model allows us to account for the changes in threshold visibility, visual acuity, and color discrimination, and suprathreshold brightness, colorfulness and apparent contrast that occur with changes in the level of illumination in scenes.

We have applied the visual model to the problem of realistic tone reproduction and have developed a tone reproduction operator that addresses the two major problems in realistic tone reproduction: images of wide absolute range and high dynamic range scenes can now be displayed on conventional display devices like CRTs and printers; and these images are faithful visual representations that match our perceptions of the scenes at threshold and suprathreshold levels to the limits possible on a given display. This work should have major impact on the field of digital imaging. Scenes that could never be reproduced before can now be imaged with high visual fidelity.

Beyond the clear applications of this work in realistic tone reproduction, the visual model presented in this paper can be usefully applied in a variety of other areas in digital imaging where the characteristics of threshold and suprathreshold vision are important. Potential application areas include: image quality metrics; image coding and compression methods; perceptually-based image synthesis algorithms; image-based rendering; and advanced display system design.

There is still much work to be done in this area. First, this is a static model of vision. Future models should incorporate knowledge about the temporal aspects of visual processing in order to allow both dynamic scenes, and scenes where the level of illumination is dynamically changing to be properly displayed. Second, we hope to integrate our visual model with ongoing work in the color science community on appearance models [Fairchild98] for predicting how images look under different viewing conditions. We should also draw on the testing methods developed by researchers in this community to verify that our images are in fact good visual matches to actual scenes. Finally, a number of researchers [Gilchrist77, Adelson93] in the vision community have shown that threshold and suprathreshold properties of scenes aren't simply a function of the two dimensional patterns of luminances in the retinal image, but also depend upon our perceptions of the spatial arrangement of surfaces and illumination in three dimensions. Future work should address how these 3D issues affect our perceptions of scenes and influence the development of operators for realistic tone reproduction.

ACKNOWLEDGEMENTS

Special thanks to David Hart, Steve Marshner, Hurf Sheldon, Chris Williams, Ben Trumbore, Eric Lafortune and Dan Kartch for their help in preparing this paper.

This work was supported by the NSF Science and Technology Center for Computer Graphics and Scientific Visualization (ASC-8920219) and by NSF grant ASC-9523483 and was performed on workstations generously provided by the Hewlett-Packard Corporation.

References

[Adelson93] Adelson, E.H. (1993) Perceptual organization and judgment of brightness. Science, 262, 2042-2044.

[Barlow72] Barlow, H.B. (1972) Dark and Light Adaptation: Psychophysics. In D. Jameson and L. Hurvich (Eds.), Handbook of Sensory Physiology, V. 7(4), New York: Springer, 2-27.

Figure 11: Tone mapping of high-dynamic range images. The images on the top are linear mappings of the original high-dynamic range images. The images on the bottom are the mapping obtained by application of the visual model.

[Brady95] Brady, N. and Field, D.J. (1995) What's Constant in Contrast Constancy? The Effects of Scaling on the Perceived Contrast of Bandpass Patterns. Vision Res., 35(6), 739-756.

[Burt83] Burt, P.J., and Adelson, E.H. (1983) The Laplacian Pyramid as a Compact Image Code. IEEE Transaction on Communication, 31(4), 532-540.

[Chiu93] Chiu, K., Herf, M., Shirley, P., Swamy, S., Wang, C., and Zimmerman, K. (1993) Spatially Nonuniform Scaling Functions for High Contrast Images. Proceedings Graphics Interface 93, 245-254.

[Debevec97] Debevec, P.E. and Malik, J. (1997) Recovering High Dynamic Range Radiance Maps from Images. Proceedings SIGGRAPH 97, 369-378.

[Fairchild98] Fairchild, M.D. (1998) *Color Appearance Models.* Reading, MA: Addison-Wesley.

[Ferwerda96] Ferwerda, J.A., Pattanaik, S.N., Shirley, P., and Greenberg, D. (1996) A Model of Visual Adaptation for Realistic Image Synthesis. Proceedings SIGGRAPH 96, 249-258.

[Georgeson75] Georgeson, M.A. and Sullivan, G.D. (1975) Contrast Constancy: Deblurring in Human Vision by Spatial Frequency Channels. J. Physiol., 252, 627-656.

[Gilchrist77] Gilchrist, A.L. (1977) Perceived Lightness Depends on Perceived Spatial Arrangement. Science, 195, 185-187.

[Hunt95] Hunt, R.W.G. (1995) *The Reproduction of Color.* 5th edition, Kingston-upon-Thames, England: Fountain Press.

[Hurvich81] Hurvich, L. (1981) *Color Vision.* Sunderland, MA: Sinauer Assoc.

[Jobson96] Jobson, D.J., Rahman, Z., and Woodell, G.A. (1996) Retinex Image Processing: Improved Fidelity to Direct Visual Observation. Proceedings 4th Color Imaging Conference, Society for Imaging Science and Technology, 124-126.

[Laming91] Laming D. (1991) Contrast Sensitivity. In J.J. Kulikowski, V. Walsh, and I.J. Murray (Eds.) *Limits of Vision,* Vol. 5, Vision and Visual Dysfunction. Boca Raton, FL, CRC Press, 35-43.

[Lubin95] Lubin, J. (1995). A Visual Discrimination Model for Imaging System Design and Evaluation. In E. Peli (Ed.) *Vision Models for Target Detection.* Singapore, World Scientific, 245-283.

[Losada94] Losada, M.A., and Mullen, K.T. (1994) The Spatial Tuning of Chromatic Mechanisms Identified by Simultaneous Masking. Vision Res., 34(3), 331-341.

[Mullen85] Mullen, K.T. (1985) The Contrast Sensitivity of Human Color Vision to Red-Green and Blue-Yellow Chromatic Gratings. J. Physiol., 359, 381-400.

[Peli90] Peli, E. (1990) Contrast in Complex Images. J. Opt. Soc. Am. A, 7(10), 2032-2040.

[Schlick95] Schlick, C. (1995) Quantization Techniques for High Dynamic Range Pictures. In G. Sakas, P. Shirley, and S. Mueller, (Eds.), *Photorealistic Rendering Techniques,* Berlin: Springer-Verlag, 7-20.

[Shapley84] Shapley, R. and Enroth-Cugell, C. (1984) Visual Adaptation and Retinal Gain Controls. In N. Osborne and G. Chader (Eds.). *Progress in Retinal Research,* V. 3, Oxford: Pergamon Press., 263-347.

[Spencer95] Spencer, G., Shirley, P., Zimmerman, K., Greenberg, D. P. (1995) Physically-based Glare Effects for Computer Generated Images. Proceedings SIGGRAPH 95, 325-334.

[Stevens61] Stevens, S.S. (1961) To Honor Fechner and Repeal His Law. Science, 133, 13 Jan., 80-86.

[Tumblin93] Tumblin, J., and Rushmeier, H. (1993) Tone Reproduction for Realistic Images, IEEE Computer Graphics and Applications, 13(6), 42-48.

[Tumblin97] Tumblin, J., Hodgkins, J. and Guenter, B. (1997) Display of High Contrast Images Using Models of Visual Adaptation. Visual proceedings SIGGRAPH 97, 154.

[vanNes67] van Nes F.L. and Bouman M.A. (1967) Spatial Modulation Transfer in the Human Eye. J. Opt. Soc. Am., 57, 401-406.

[vanderHorst69] van der Horst, G.J.C. and Bouman, M.A. (1969) Spatiotemporal Chromaticity Discrimination. J. Opt. Soc. Am., 59(11), 1482-1488.

[Ward94] Ward, G. (1994) A Contrast-based Scalefactor for Luminance Display. In P.S. Heckbert (Ed.), Graphics Gems IV, Boston: Academic Press Professional.

[Ward-Larson97] Ward-larson, G., Rushmeier, H., and Piatko, C. (1997) A Visibility Matching Tone Reproduction Operator for High Dynamic Range Scenes. IEEE Transactions on Visualization and Computer Graphics, 3(4), 291-306.

[Watson97] Watson, A.B. and Solomon, J.A. (1997) Model of Visual Contrast Gain Control and Pattern Masking. J. Opt. Soc. Am. A, 14(9), 2379-2391.

[Westheimer86] Westheimer, G. (1986) The Eye as an Optical Instrument. In K. Boff, L. Kaufman, and J. Thomas (Ed.), *Handbook of Perception and Human Performance,* New York: Wiley and Sons.

[Wilson91] Wilson, H.R. (1991). Psychophysical Models of Spatial Vision and Hyperacuity. in D. Regan (Ed.) *Spatial Vision,* Vol. 10, Vision and Visual Dysfunction. Boca Raton, FL, CRC Press, 64-81.

[Wyszecki82] Wyszecki G., and Stiles W.S. (1982) Color Science: Concepts and Methods, Quantitative Data and Formulae (2nd edition). New York: Wiley.

A Perceptually Based Adaptive Sampling Algorithm

Mark R. Bolin[*]   Gary W. Meyer[†]

Department of Computer and Information Science
University of Oregon
Eugene, OR 97403

Abstract

A perceptually based approach for selecting image samples has been developed. An existing image processing vision model has been extended to handle color and has been simplified to run efficiently. The resulting new image quality model was inserted in an image synthesis program by first modifying the rendering algorithm so that it computed a wavelet representation. In addition to allowing image quality to be determined as the image was generated, the wavelet representation made it possible to use statistical information about the spatial frequency distribution of natural images to estimate values where samples were yet to be taken. Tests on the image synthesis algorithm showed that it correctly handled achromatic and chromatic spatial detail and that it was able predict and compensate for masking effects. The program was also shown to produce images of equivalent visual quality while using different rendering techniques.

CR Categories and Subject Descriptors: I.3.3 [Computer Graphics]: *Picture/Image Generation;* I.3.7 [Computer Graphics]: *Three-Dimensional Graphics and Realism;* I.4.0 [Image Processing and Computer Vision]: *General.*

Additional Key Words and Phrases: Adaptive Sampling, Perception, Masking, Vision Models.

1   Introduction

The synthesis of realistic images would be greatly facilitated by employing an algorithm that makes image quality judgements while the picture is being created instead of relying upon the user of the software to make these evaluations once the image is complete. In this way it would be possible to find the artifacts in a picture as it was being rendered and to invest additional effort on those areas. By targeting those parts of the picture where problems are visible, the overall time necessary to compute the picture could be reduced. It would also be possible to have the algorithm stop when the picture quality had reached a predetermined level. This

[*]e-mail: mbolin@cs.uoregon.edu
[†]e-mail: gary@uoregon.edu

would permit the use of radically different rendering algorithms but still have them produce an equivalent visual result.

Image quality evaluation programs have been developed by vision scientists and image processors to determine the differences between two pictures. Given a pair of input images, this software returns a visibility map of the variations between the two image arrays. While these programs are capable of making the visual judgements required by a perceptually based image synthesis algorithm, they are currently too expensive to execute every time a decision is necessary about where to cast a ray into an image or when the overall visual quality of the picture is acceptable. Their efficient evaluation also requires a frequency or a wavelet representation for the images instead of the usual pixel based scheme.

The objective of this paper is to integrate an existing image quality evaluation algorithm into a realistic image synthesis program. This is to be done in such a way that image quality judgements can be made as the image is produced without severely impacting the overall execution time of the rendering program. This will require that the image quality metric be made to run more efficiently without sacrificing its ability to detect visible artifacts. It will also necessitate that the coefficients of a frequency or a wavelet representation are computed by the image synthesis algorithm instead of the individual pixels of the final image. This will have the side benefit of allowing the algorithm to make use of statistical information about the frequency content of natural images when actual data from the scene being rendered is not available.

Including this introduction, the paper is divided into seven major sections. In the second section, previous work on vision based rendering algorithms is reviewed and existing image processing based vision models are described. A simplified version of a vision model is developed in the third section and is integrated into a rendering algorithm in the fourth section. In the fifth section the statistics of natural images are used to make guesses about unknown values as the image is computed. Finally, the results of the algorithm are discussed in the sixth section and some conclusions are drawn in the seventh section.

2   Background

A few attempts have been made to develop image synthesis algorithms that, as the picture is created, detect threshold visual differences and direct the algorithm to work on those parts of the image that are in most need of refinement. There have also been image processing algorithms invented, both inside and outside the field of computer graphics, that can be used to determine the visibility of differences between two images. In this section we review work in each of these areas in preparation for describing how we have combined an image processing and image synthesis algorithm to create a new image rendering technique.

2.1 Vision Based Rendering Algorithms

Mitchell [21] was the first to develop a ray tracing algorithm that considered the perception of noise and attempted to operate near its threshold. He adopted a Poisson disk sampling pattern to concentrate aliasing noise in high frequencies where the artifact is less conspicuous. He also employed an adaptive sampling technique to vary the sampling rate according to frequency content. A contrast calculation was performed in order to obtain a perceptually based measure of the variation in the signal. Differential weighting was applied to the red, green, and blue contrasts to account for color variation in the eye's spatial sensitivity.

Meyer and Liu [20] developed an image synthesis algorithm that took full advantage of the visual system's limited color spatial acuity. To accomplish this they used an opponents color space with chromatic and achromatic color channels. They employed the Painter and Sloan [23] adaptive subdivision algorithm to compute a k-D tree representation for an image. Because lower levels of the tree contained the higher spatial frequency content of the picture, they descended the k-D tree to a lesser depth in order to determine the chromatic channels of the final image.

Bolin and Meyer [2] were the first to use a simple vision model to make decisions about where to cast rays into a scene and how to spawn rays that intersect objects in the environment. The model that they employed consisted of three stages: receptors with logarithmic response to light, opponents processing into achromatic and chromatic channels, and spatial frequency filtering that is stronger for the color channels. They computed a spatial frequency representation from the samples that they took. As higher image frequencies were determined the number of rays spawned was decreased. This allowed them to exploit the phenomena of masking in their algorithm.

Gibson and Hubbold [10] have used a tone reproduction operator to determine display colors during the rendering process. This made it possible to compute color differences in a perceptually uniform color space and control the production of radiosity solutions. They used this technique on the adaptive element refinement, shadow detection, and mesh optimization portions of the radiosity algorithm.

2.2 Image Processing Based Models of the Visual System

The architectures of image processing based models of the visual system share a number of common elements. The first stage of the models is usually a nonlinear intensity transformation. This is done to account for the visual system's difference in detection capability for information in light and dark areas of a scene. The second stage typically involves some spatial frequency processing. Most contemporary models break the spatial frequency spectrum into separate channels. The sensitivity of the individual channels is controlled so that the overall bandpass corresponds to the contrast sensitivity function. The spatial frequency hierarchy makes it possible to determine whether a signal will be masked or facilitated by the presence or absence of background information with a similar frequency composition. Finally the outputs of the separate frequency channels that are above threshold are summed to create a final representation.

Two important examples of image processing based models of the visual system are the Daly Visual Difference Predictor (VDP) [5] and the Sarnoff Visual Discrimination Model (VDM) [17]. The Daly VDP takes a more psychophysically based approach to vision modeling. As such it uses a power law representation for the initial nonlinearity and it transforms the image into

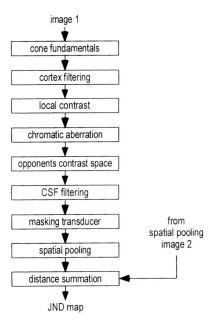

Figure 1: Block diagram of vision model.

the frequency domain in order to perform its filtering operations. The Sarnoff VDM focuses more attention on modeling the physiology of the visual pathway. It therefore operates in the spatial domain and does a careful simulation of such things as the optical point spread function.

In recent work, the Daly VDP and the Sarnoff VDM have been applied to precomputed computer graphic imagery. Rushmeier, et. al [25] used the initial stages of the Daly VDP (and other vision metrics) to compare a simulated and a measured image. Ferwerda, et. al. [7] extended the Daly VDP to include color and modified how it handles masking. The result was a new image processing based model of the visual system that they used to demonstrate how surface texture can mask polygonal tessellation. Li [15,16] has used computer graphic pictures to compare the Daly VDP and the Sarnoff VDM. She found that the two models performed comparably, but that the Sarnoff VDM gave better image difference maps and required less recalibration. The Sarnoff VDM was also determined to have better execution speed than the Daly VDP but required the use of significantly more memory. As a result of this comparison we have decided to use the Sarnoff VDM as the basis for our new vision based rendering algorithm.

3 Simplified Vision Model

The vision model that we have developed bears many similarities to the Sarnoff VDM discussed in the previous section. In creating a new model of visual perception we were motivated by two primary factors. The first and foremost criteria is the speed of the visual model. Modern visual difference predictors have gone to great lengths to accurately model the perceptual sensitivity of the human visual system. However, efficiency is seldom a design criteria in developing these systems. This fact limits the utility of these algorithms in applications where speed is a primary concern. The second factor that motivated our development of a new model is the correct handling of color. The majority of visual difference predictors have been designed only for gray scale images, and the ones that include color have neglected the significant effect of chromatic aberration.

The perceptual model that will be described has been imbedded into a visual difference predictor. This difference predictor receives as input two images specified in CIE XYZ color space. It returns as output a map of the perceptual difference between the two images specified in terms of just noticeable differences (JND's). One JND corresponds to a 75% probability that an observer viewing the two images would be able to detect a difference, and the units correspond to a roughly linear magnitude of subjective visual differences [17].

A block diagram of our visual difference predictor is given in Figure 1. The steps *cone fundamentals* through *spatial pooling* are carried out independently on both input images. The differences between the two images are accumulated in the *distance summation* step.

In the first stage of the vision model entitled *cone fundamentals*, the pixels of the input image are encoded into the responses of the short (S), medium (M) and long (L) receptors found in the retina of the eye. This is accomplished using the transformation from CIE XYZ to SML space specified by Bolin and Meyer [2].

There is now abundant evidence for the existence of channels in the visual pathway that are tuned to a number of specific frequencies and orientations [17]. The visual processing that occurs on a channel is relatively independent of all other channels. In the Sarnoff VDM this *cortex filtering* stage is accomplished by transforming the image into a Laplacian pyramid and applying a set of oriented filters. The net result is a pyramidal image decomposition that is tuned to seven spatial frequencies and four angular directions. This transform is the primary source of expense in the Sarnoff VDM. In order to reduce the cost of this operation we decided to model the spatial frequency and orientation selectivity of the visual system through the use of a simple Haar wavelet transform. A number of other wavelet bases were considered, including Daubechies' family of wavelets [6] and the biorthogonal bases of Cohen, *et. al.* [4]. However, these transforms were discarded due to their expense. The two-dimensional non-standard Haar decomposition can be expressed as:

$$c_{l-1}[\frac{x}{2}, \frac{y}{2}] = (c_l[x, y] + c_l[x+1, y] +$$
$$c_l[x, y+1] + c_l[x+1, y+1])/4$$
$$d^1_{l-1}[\frac{x}{2}, \frac{y}{2}] = (c_l[x, y] - c_l[x+1, y] +$$
$$c_l[x, y+1] - c_l[x+1, y+1])/4$$
$$d^2_{l-1}[\frac{x}{2}, \frac{y}{2}] = (c_l[x, y] + c_l[x+1, y] -$$
$$c_l[x, y+1] - c_l[x+1, y+1])/4$$
$$d^3_{l-1}[\frac{x}{2}, \frac{y}{2}] = (c_l[x, y] - c_l[x+1, y] -$$
$$c_l[x, y+1] + c_l[x+1, y+1])/4 \quad (1)$$

where c_l specifies the lowpass coefficients of the level l Haar

d3	d2	d3
d1	c	d1
d3	d2	d3

Figure 2: Angular tuning of Haar coefficients.

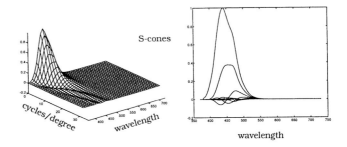

Figure 3: Effect of chromatic aberration on the S-cone photopigment sensitivity. Right diagram takes cross sections through left diagram at intervals of 4 cpd (from Marimont and Wandell [19]).

basis, d^1_l, d^2_l and d^3_l are the detail coefficients of the three two-dimensional level l Haar wavelets, and $c_{levels-1}[x, y]$ corresponds to the response of either the small, medium or long receptors at a pixel location (where $levels$ represents the number of levels in the quad-tree). This decomposition is carried out for each of the S, M and L channels and is stored in a quad-tree representation with the highest frequency details at the bottom and lowest frequency at the top. The detail coefficients of the Haar transform constitute our cortex transform. These detail terms represent variations in the image that are localized in space, frequency and angular direction. The frequency selectivity of the detail terms at a given level of the tree is defined as the frequency in cycles per degree (cpd) to which the wavelet at that level is optimally tuned. The detail coefficients are tuned to three angular directions as illustrated in Figure 2. We acknowledge that the poor filtering and limited orientation tuning of the Haar wavelet is a limitation of this approach. However, the efficiency gains are substantial.

In the next stage labeled *local contrast* the eye's non-linear contrast response to light is modeled. This is accomplished by dividing the detail coefficients of each color channel by the associated lowpass coefficient one level up in the quad-tree. This operation produces a local contrast value which is functionally equivalent to the standard cone contrast calculation of $\frac{\Delta S}{S}$, $\frac{\Delta M}{M}$, and $\frac{\Delta L}{L}$. It additionally avoids the assumption, found in other models [5,7], that the eye can adapt at the resolution of a pixel.

The next step in the visual model incorporates the effect of *chromatic aberration*. Chromatic aberration describes the defocusing of light as a function of wavelength by the optics of the eye. The original chromatic contrast sensitivity experiments performed by Mullen [22] corrected for chromatic aberration. In order to accurately apply the results of her work it is necessary to reintroduce this effect. Chromatic aberration most strongly affects the sensitivity of the short wavelength receptors. The loss of sensitivity in the short wavelength receptors is demonstrated in Figure 3. This illustration shows that the sensitivity drops to less than half its original value at 4 cpd and is virtually non-existent at frequencies higher than 8 cpd. Chromatic aberration is simulated in our model by lowpass filtering the local contrasts of the S cone receptors as a function of spatial frequency. The lowpass filter used was generated by a fit to the data of Marimont and Wandell [19].

The following stage in the model consists of a transformation of the cone contrasts to an *opponents contrast space*. This space consists of a single achromatic (A) and two opponent color channels (C_1 and C_2). There is significant evidence that the signals produced by the cones undergo this type of transformation. The transformation matrix used to convert the cone contrasts is found in [2].

The sixth step of the vision model, labeled *CSF filtering*, in-

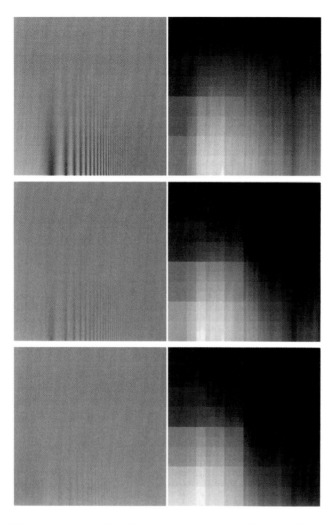

Figure 4: Achromatic and chromatic contrast sensitivity functions and comparison against a uniform gray field.

corporates variations in achromatic and chromatic contrast sensitivity as a function of spatial frequency. The gray scale contrast sensitivity illusion in the top left of Figure 4 demonstrates the sensitivity variation of the achromatic channel. In this demonstration contrast increases logarithmically from top to the bottom of the image and frequency increases logarithmically from left to right. The subjective contour in the shape of an inverted "U" that can be seen along the top of the image is generated by the points at which the contrast of the sinusoidal grating becomes just noticeably different from the gray background. This image demonstrates that achromatic sensitivity reaches its peak at around 4 cpd and drops off significantly at higher and lower spatial frequencies. The equation for the achromatic contrast sensitivity function that is used in our model is presented by Barten [1].

The middle and bottom images on the left side of Figure 4 contain contrast sensitivity illusions for the C_1 and C_2 color channels respectively. In these illustrations it should be observed that the peak sensitivity to chromatic contrast is less than that for achromatic contrast, and that the cutoff for the chromatic sensitivity function occurs at a much lower spatial frequency than in the achromatic illustration. The reader should also see that the shape of the subjective contour is strictly lowpass, with no drop-off at low spatial frequencies. The fact that the cutoff for the C_2 color channel is less than that for the C_1 is the result of axial chromatic aberration which was modeled at an earlier stage of

the algorithm. In our algorithm the chromatic contrast sensitivity function is modeled with a Butterworth filter that has been fit to the chromatic contrast sensitivity data from Mullen [22].

At this stage in the algorithm the square of the contrast for each of the A, C_1 and C_2 channels is multiplied by the square of that channel's contrast sensitivity as a function of spatial frequency. The square of the contrast and contrast sensitivity function is used to model the energy response that occurs for complex cells, as described in the Sarnoff VDM. This transformation has the result of making the model less sensitive to the exact position of an edge, which is a property shared by the human visual system as well [17]. The illustrations on the right side of Figure 4 show the output of our visual difference predictor when comparing the contrast sensitivity illusions on the left side of this figure with a constant gray image. White indicates areas of large visual difference while black denotes regions of low visual difference. In these images we see that the algorithm is able to correctly predict the shape and cutoff of the subjective contour.

The next stage of the model labeled *masking transducer*, incorporates the effect of visual masking. Masking describes the phenomena where strong signals of a given color, frequency and orientation can reduce the visibility of similar signals. This property of the visual system is incorporated through the use of a non-linear, sigmoid transducer described in the Sarnoff VDM

$$T(A) = \frac{2A^{2.25/2}}{A^{2.05/2} + 1}, \qquad (2)$$

where T(A) is the transducer output and A is the weighted contrast output from the previous stage of the model. This transducer is applied independently to the contrasts of each of the A, C_1, and C_2 color channels.

In computer graphic renderings, error primarily is manifested in the form of noise. Therefore, it is worthwhile to give special attention to the issue of noise masking. Noise in the achromatic channel is often the result of aliasing due to undersampling or can result from poor Monte Carlo light source integration. An illustration of the grayscale contrast sensitivity illusion perturbed by the introduction of random noise is given in the upper left of Figure 5. In this image the noise is readily apparent above and to the sides of the subjective contrast sensitivity contour, but is less perceptible in areas where the sinusoidal grating is visible. This result occurs because the strong visual sensitivity to these frequencies masks the presence of a portion of the frequency spectrum of the noise. The image in the upper right of this figure shows the output of our visual difference predictor when comparing the original contrast sensitivity illustration to the contrast sensitivity illustration with noise added. In this image we see that the visual model has correctly predicted that the error is less visible in the lower-center region where masking is strongest.

Noise in the chromatic channels can arise when Monte Carlo integration is performed with multiple colored lights or is used to compute diffuse inter-reflections. Fine grained noise is not masked significantly in the color channels due to the lower frequency cutoff for the chromatic contrast sensitivity function. However, masking can still have a strong affect on the visibility of coarse grained noise. In the middle left and bottom left images in Figure 5 we have overlaid the chromatic contrast sensitivity illusions with coarse grained noise. In these illustrations the noise is very apparent in regions where sensitivity to the chromatic grating is low (top and right of the images), but less visible in regions where the chromatic grating is very perceptible (lower left of the images). The images on the right once again show the output of the visual difference predictor when comparing the images with noise to the original chromatic contrast sensitivity illustrations. In these illustrations we see that the algorithm has correctly predicted that the coarse grained noise is less perceptible in the lower left region of

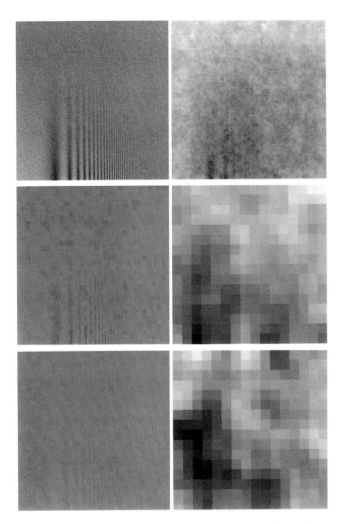

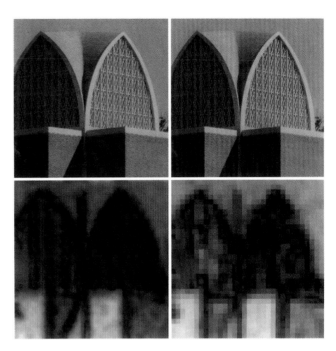

Figure 6: Top - Original chapel (left) and chapel with sinusoidal distortion (right). Bottom - Results of the Sarnoff VDM (left) and simplified vision model (right) visual difference predictions.

Figure 5: Achromatic and chromatic contrast sensitivity functions with noise, and comparison with noiseless contrast sensitivity functions.

the images.

In the next stage of the model labeled *spatial pooling*, the transducer outputs are filtered over a small neighborhood of surrounding nodes at each level of the quad-tree. This is similar to the pooling operation performed in the Sarnoff VDM. It captures the fact that foveal human sensitivity is at a maximum for sine wave gratings containing at least 5 cycles. The pooling filter that is used in our model is:

$$\begin{bmatrix} \frac{1}{16} & \frac{1}{8} & \frac{1}{16} \\ \frac{1}{8} & \frac{1}{4} & \frac{1}{8} \\ \frac{1}{16} & \frac{1}{8} & \frac{1}{16} \end{bmatrix} . \qquad (3)$$

The decision to use a 3x3 filter rather than the 5x5 filter specified in the Sarnoff VDM was made to improve the speed of the algorithm.

In the final *distance summation* stage the differences between the pooling stages of the two input images are computed and used to generate a visual difference map. The local visual difference at each node of the quad-tree is defined to be the sum across all orientations (θ) and color channels (c) of the differences of the pooling stages (P_1 and P_2) of the two images raised to the 2.4

power:

$$LD = \sum_{\theta=1}^{3} \sum_{c=1}^{3} (P_1[\theta, c] - P_2[\theta, c])^{2.4} \qquad (4)$$

The final difference map is generated by accumulating visual differences across levels. This is accomplished by summing local difference down each path in the quad-tree and storing the result in the leaves. The visual difference map that is the output of the algorithm is given by the leaf differences raised to the 1/2.4 power.

Figure 6 shows a comparison between the results of the original Sarnoff VDM and our simplified version for a set of complex images. The inputs are illustrated in the top row of the figure and consist of a chapel image and the chapel image perturbed by a sinusoidal grating. A visual comparison of these two images shows that the sinusoidal distortion is most evident in the dark regions at the base of the chapel. This is due to the eye's non-linear contrast response to light. Within the arches at the top of the chapel, there is no perceptible difference between the two images. This is because the lattice-work in these regions masks the presence of the sinusoidal grating. The visual difference map that is produced by the new algorithm contains a number of blocking artifacts that are caused by the Haar wavelet decomposition. However, the results of both algorithms are similar and correspond well with a subjective comparison of the input images. The Sarnoff VDM processed one channel in a gray-scale image representation and the new model processed three color channels. The new model executed in $1/60^{th}$ of the time of the original model.

4 Adaptive Sampling Algorithm

An adaptive sampling algorithm has been developed that is based on the visual model described in the preceding section. This algorithm receives sample values as input, and specifies the placement of samples at the image plane as output. The goal of

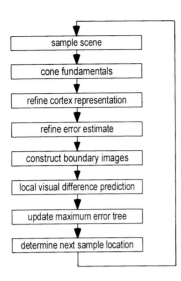

Figure 7: Block diagram of adaptive sampling algorithm.

the adaptive algorithm is to iteratively place each sample at the location that currently contains the largest perceptual error.

The key to developing this perceptually based adaptive sampling algorithm comes from two primary insights. The first is that an estimate of the image and its error can be used to construct two boundary images that may be used as input into a visual difference predictor. The output of this difference prediction can then be used to direct the placement of subsequent samples. The second insight is that a given sample only affects the value and accuracy of a very limited number of terms at each level of a Haar wavelet image representation. This fact makes the algorithm tractable because it implies that only a small number of operations are necessary to refine the image approximation, its error estimate and the visual difference prediction for any given sample.

The algorithm proceeds through a few basic steps. First, as samples are taken of the scene, a Haar wavelet image approximation is generated and refined. Next, a multi-resolution error estimate is developed and similarly refined. This error estimate is expressed in terms of the variance of the detail terms in the Haar representation. The image approximation and error estimate is then used to construct two boundary images which serve as input to the visual difference predictor. The output of the difference predictor is accumulated in a hierarchical tree. The nodes of this tree specify the maximum visual difference present at the current nodes and the children below it. This tree is traversed choosing the branch with the largest visual difference in order to determine the location on the image plane with the greatest perceptual error.

A block diagram of the algorithm is illustrated in Figure 7. As samples are taken their values are first transformed from CIE XYZ to SML space in the step labeled *cone fundamentals*. The Haar image representation and its error estimate are constructed in this space.

In the *refine cortex representation* stage the Haar image approximation is created and refined. This is done through a technique similar to the "splat and pull" method used by Gortler, *et. al.* [11]. The Haar image representation is stored in a quad-tree data structure. The leaves of this structure are defined to contain the intensity of single pixels in the image plane and the interior nodes contain the lower resolution lowpass and detail terms of the Haar representation. As a sample is passed into this stage it is "splatted" at the leaf containing the sample. The intensity at this leaf is simply the average of the samples taken within the pixel it is defined to cover. The lower resolution lowpass and detail terms

are generated by "pulling" the updated leaf intensity up through the tree. During this process, if all children of a node contain at least a single sample, then the lowpass and detail terms are given by Equation 1. If only a single child contains a sample, then the detail terms are left undefined and the lowpass term is set equal to the lowpass of the child containing the sample. If only two or three children contain samples, then a simple scheme is used to fit the lowpass and one or two detail terms, respectively, to the values of the defined children. In this manner the image representation is gradually resolved as samples are taken of the scene. It is also worth noting that this process is very fast since the addition of a sample only requires the updating of a single path up the tree.

At the next step labeled *refine error estimate*, the error of the current Haar approximation is determined. This process is similar in some respects with the algorithm described by Painter and Sloan [23]. The error estimate is expressed in terms of the variance of the lowpass and detail coefficients. For leaf nodes containing at least two samples the variance of the pixel approximation is given by the variance of the samples in the leaf divided by the number of samples in the leaf [3,13]. The error of the lowpass and detail terms in the interior nodes is defined with respect to the error of their children. If the variance is defined for all children of a node, then the variance of the lowpass and detail terms at the node is equal to the sum of the variance of the four children divided by 16. This result comes from the rule

$$V[\sum^i a_i x_i] = \sum^i a_i^2 V[x_i] \qquad (5)$$

(where V denotes variance) and inspection of Equation 1. If the error is not defined for all children of a node and at least 2 samples have been taken, then the variance is given by the variance of the samples taken within the node divided by the number of samples in the node. As in the case of refining the Haar representation, updating the multi-resolution error estimate requires that only a single path in the tree be modified for the addition of each sample.

The next stage in the algorithm labeled *construct boundary images* is concerned with defining the two input images for the visual difference predictor. These input images are described by the magnitude of their detail coefficients which are used to determine the local contrast at an early stage in the vision model. Since the image approximation and error estimate has only changed along a single path in the tree, the detail terms for the boundary images only need to be updated along this path as well. The details for the two boundary images are derived from the details in the current image approximation and the variance of those details. The magnitude of the approximated detail specifies a mean value and the square root of the variance defines the spread of the standard deviation curve. The magnitudes of the details for the boundary images are taken from the 25% and 75% points on this curve. In this manner two boundary images are specified which should contain the true value 50% of the time. The boundary images are organized so that image 1 contains the detail of minimum energy contrast and image 2 contains the detail of maximum energy contrast.

A *local visual difference prediction* is performed at the updated nodes in the next step of the algorithm. The detail terms in the boundary images are passed through the *local contrast* to *spatial pooling* stages of the vision model. The transducer outputs at the current node is stored in the tree for fast re-use in the pooling stages of neighbor nodes.

In the step labeled *update maximum error tree* a value is stored at each updated node in the quad-tree which represents the maximum visual difference contained at the current node and the nodes below it. The local error at a node is defined as in the *distance summation* stage of the vision model (i.e. by the sum of visual distance between the boundary images across each detail and color channel raised to the 2.4 power). The maximum error is defined to be the local error plus the largest maximum error contained in either of the four children. The maximum error of the root node is raised to the 1/2.4 power and represents the largest visual error contained at any location within the image plane. The maximum error in the interior nodes are used to determine which branch of the tree contains the greatest visual difference for the purpose of finding the next location to sample.

In the final stage labeled *determine next sample location* a sample location is selected at the point of maximum visual difference. The location is selected by traversing the quad-tree in a top-down fashion and, at each node, selecting the branch of maximum visual error. This traversal continues until a leaf node is encountered or an interior node is found which contains less than eight samples. If a leaf node is reached, a sample is randomly placed within it. If the traversal stops at an interior node, then a sample location is chosen randomly from a child's quadrant so that the number of samples in each child node is balanced to a tolerance of one sample.

The discussion thus far has assumed that only a single path in the quad-tree is affected by a given sample. However, this is not strictly the case. Due to the local contrast and spatial pooling stages of the vision model the modification of one node in the quad-tree can have an affect on the visual difference at neighboring nodes. One solution to this problem is to update multiple paths up the tree. However, this approach was deemed too expensive. Instead the problem can be effectively solved by adding a small amount of randomness to the traversal of the maximum error tree. As each node in the tree is visited, there is some likelihood a neighboring node will be chosen instead. In this manner, if a particular path is traversed often, there is a chance of selecting neighboring paths. This creates the opportunity to incorporate updated values into the local contrast and spatial pooling calculations for these paths.

The algorithm continues recursively until the maximum error of the root node drops below a specified tolerance. The output image is reconstructed by simply doing an inverse Haar transform of the image representation and converting pixel values from SML to the frame buffer space. This technique can also be used to construct an iterative display of the image during the progression of the algorithm.

5 Selecting Values for Unknown Quantities

A difficulty with adaptive sampling algorithms that are based on the sample variance is knowing when and to what extent to believe the error estimate obtained from the samples. This is especially true for the hierarchical variance estimation scheme described in this paper. If the first two samples obtained from the scene return exactly the same values and therefore have zero variance, can we conclude that the image has been computed exactly and stop? What if the image has been sampled densely and two samples from within a particular pixel of the image plane are the same, can we say that the intensity of the pixel has been computed correctly? A person analyzing these two situations would certainly believe that the scene has not been adequately sampled in the first case, but would probably be willing to stop sampling in the second case. The reason for this difference stems from the statistics of natural images.

A number of authors have analyzed the statistics of images commonly encountered in nature [8,9,24,26]. These authors have found that the frequency spectra of natural images is not random, but tends to be highly correlated and contains a 1/f drop-off in the magnitude of the frequency terms. Therefore, if only two samples have been taken of a scene, we have just begun to compute the low end of the frequency spectra. Based on our experience with images found in the natural world, we know that an average image

contains higher frequency detail, and therefore believe that the scene has not been adequately sampled. Thus, we have some apriori knowledge about the error of an image approximation. If a portion of the frequency spectra has not been computed, then, on average, the approximation of the image will contain an amount of error that is equivalent to the 1/f magnitude of the uncomputed spectra.

We can also draw upon the statistics of natural scenes when we must choose unknown values for the chromatic channels. The frequency content of naturally occurring spectral reflectances is known to be very low [18]. This means that reflectances are more likely to be uniform across the spectrum than they are to be spikey. The result of this is that the average color in the natural world is quite desaturated. This implies that in the absence of other knowledge about the chromatic content of an object, setting the chromatic channels close to zero is as good a choice as one can make.

The statistics of natural images discussed in this section have been employed within our adaptive sampling algorithm. This is accomplished by initializing the two boundary images to a uniform gray for one, and a statistically average image for the other. The visual difference predictor is run on these two input images and the output is used to seed the visual difference at each node in the quad-tree. Initially, the estimated visual difference of the rendering is based on the comparison of the gray and statistically average image. As the algorithm progresses and the image approximation and error estimate is calculated at new nodes in the tree, the visual difference based on the average statistics is traded for the visual difference that is based on the variance and content of the scene samples.

6 Results

In this section we discuss the results of applying our image synthesis algorithm to three dimensional environments. Simple texture mapped disks are considered first followed by a scene with more complicated geometry and lighting. Two shading techniques will be used in these examples, direct and Monte Carlo light source sampling. The direct sampling method uses a simple shading algorithm in which point light sources are directly sampled each time a ray strikes a surface. The Monte Carlo method uses area light sources and blind Monte Carlo integration to evaluate the shading integral. In this approach the incident radiance at a surface point is evaluated by spawning a number of rays at random orientations across the positive hemisphere. We realize that blind integration is not the most efficient means of evaluating the shading integral. However, this technique provides a simple means of demonstrating a situation where noise is present within the illumination calculation.

Figure 8 shows three arrays of texture mapped disks in which the spatial frequency of the texture increases from left to right but the contrast of the texture decreases from bottom to top. In the top disk array the color of the texture varies along the A axis of AC_1C_2 space, in the middle disk array along the C_1 axis, and in the bottom array along the C_2 axis. The three arrays of texture mapped disks are rendered using direct light source sampling. In this case there is no noise generated and the spatial frequency content of the textures is the primary determinant of the sampling rate that is used. All of the disk arrays were rendered to the same visual tolerance. As can be seen in the figure, the sampling density decreases from high frequency to low frequency. Achromatic colors receive far more samples than chromatic colors due to the higher spatial frequency cut off of the achromatic contrast sensitivity function, while colors that vary in C_1 are sampled more often than colors that change in C_2. This difference in sampling between the two color channels is clear evidence of the filtering

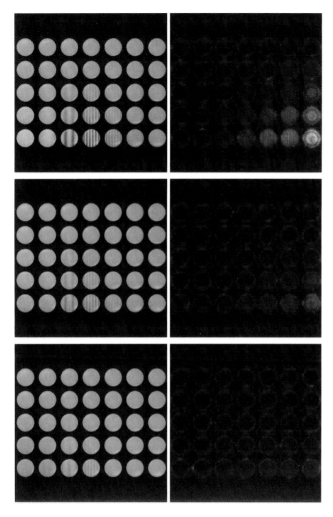

Figure 8: Sampling densities for direct light source sampling.

a given perceptual tolerance, the algorithm holds each type of artifact to a similar level of visual impact.

The approach taken in this algorithm is to compute the perceptual metric for every ray that is cast into the scene. The cost to do this computation is 1 ms on a 100 MHz processor. Evaluation of the algorithm on a number of different test environments shows that it takes fewer samples than either a uniform sampling method or an adaptive approach with an objective error metric (90% less in certain cases). Timing tests reveal that the algorithm is able to provide the perceptual stopping criteria demonstrated in Figure 11 while remaining competitive with either the uniform sampling or standard adaptive sampling techniques. The method is faster than either uniform or standard adaptive sampling on every environment where it was tested, but it was not the overall winner in all cases. Additional work is necessary to exploit the algorithm's excellent spatial sampling rates and determine the optimal number of samples to be taken between evaluations of the perceptual metric.

7 Conclusion

An existing vision model has been incorporated into an image synthesis algorithm to control where samples are taken as a picture is created. The results obtained with the new algorithm on three dimensional scenes track the results obtained using the visual model by itself on two dimensional images. The impact on the execution time of the rendering program has been minimized while the amount of memory required has been increased. The contributions of this work can be summarized as follows:

1. A new image quality model has been developed. This new model is an efficient implementation of an existing algorithm. It executes in a fraction of the time of the original method without a significant sacrifice in accuracy. The model has also been extended for color including the effect of chromatic aberration in the optics of the eye.

2. An image synthesis system has been created that directly computes a wavelet representation for an image. This is a functional (instead of an explicit pixel based) scheme for describing a picture that facilitates the computation of a visual metric. It also permits the use of statistical information regarding the frequency distribution of natural images to estimate values in regions where samples have yet to be taken. In the same manner, guesses regarding unsampled colors were improved by using an opponents color space to store color.

3. A perceptually based approach to image synthesis has been produced. An image quality model was used to decide where to take the next sample in a picture. This can result in a savings in execution time because samples are only

that is done by the visual model due to chromatic aberration in the eye.

In Figure 9 the achromatic disks from Figure 8 are rendered again using Monte Carlo light source sampling. In this case a significant amount of noise is generated and the effect of visual masking becomes important. As can be seen from the figure, the spatial sampling pattern is radically different from the direct light source sampling case in Figure 8. While disks with high frequency textures still receive the most samples, in this case the low frequency disks also get many samples because the noise can be seen on their surfaces. On the other hand, the middle of the spatial frequency range receives relatively few samples because the noise is less visible due to masking. In Figure 10 the environment and the lighting is made more complex but a similar result is obtained. When there is no noise, high achromatic spatial frequency transitions receive the most samples. When noise is present, more samples across the entire image are required, but fewer are necessary for frequencies where the noise is masked.

As a final example, identical scenes were synthesized to the same visual tolerance using two different rendering techniques. As can be seen in Figure 11, the images that resulted are comparable even though the sampling patterns and illumination calculations are very different. In the case where direct sampling of the light sources is performed, aliasing artifacts are the most prevalent defect; while for the scene where Monte Carlo sampling of the light sources was done, noise is the dominant problem. However, for

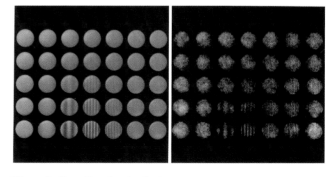

Figure 9: Sampling density for Monte Carlo light source sampling.

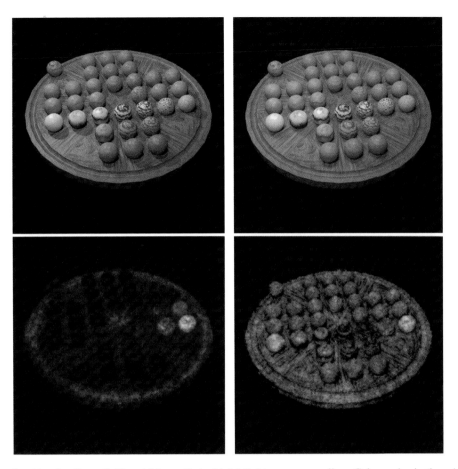

Figure 10: Sampling densities for direct (left) and Monte Carlo (right) light source sampling. Color varies in the middle three rows along the C_2, C_1, and A axes of AC_1C_2 space. Contrast of the middle three balls in the C_2 and A rows is decreased in the top two and bottom two rows respectively.

taken in areas where there are visible artifacts. The image quality model is also used to decide when enough samples have been taken across the entire image. This provides a visual stopping condition and makes it possible to employ different rendering algorithms but still produce equivalent pictures.

This work represents a first attempt to imbed a sophisticated image processing vision model into an image synthesis algorithm. While the results are encouraging it is clear that the approach taken here puts a certain amount of overhead onto every ray that is cast into the scene. An alternative tactic might be to initially sample the image at a low rate and compute the visual difference map from these values. The visual difference map can then be used to select regions of the image which require further sampling. The use of the imbedded version of the vision model might be saved until the image is more fully developed and the masking effects have become completely apparent.

8 Acknowledgements

The authors would like to thank Jae H. Kim for his help in creating Figures 8, 9, 10, and 11 and for his assistance in assembling all of the color figures in this paper. This research was funded by the National Science Foundation under grant number CCR 96-19967.

9 References

[1] Barten, P. G. J., "The Square Root Integral (SQRI): A New Metric to Describe the Effect of Various Display Parameters on Perceived Image Quality," *Human Vision, Visual Processing, and Digital Display*, Proc. SPIE, Vol. 1077, pp. 73-82, 1989.

[2] Bolin, M. R. and Meyer G. W., "A Frequency Based Ray Tracer," *Computer Graphics, Annual Conference Series*, ACM SIG-GRAPH, pp. 409-418, 1995.

[3] Bolin, M. R. and Meyer G. W., "An Error Metric for Monte Carlo Ray Tracing," *Rendering Techniques '97*, J. Dorsey and P. Slusallek, Editors, Springer-Verlag, New York, pp. 57-68, 1997.

[4] Cohen, A., Daubechies, I., and Feauveau, J. C., "Biorthogonal Bases of Compactly Supported Wavelets," *Communications on Pure and Applied Mathematics*, Vol. 45, No. 5, pp. 485-500, 1992.

[5] Daly, S., "The Visible Differences Predictor: An Algorithm for the Assessment of Image Fidelity," *Digital Images and Human Vision*, A. B. Watson, Editor, MIT Press, Cambridge, MA, pp. 179-206, 1993.

[6] Daubechies, I., "Orthonormal Bases of Compactly Supported Wavelets," *Communications on Pure and Applied Mathematics*, Vol. 41, No. 7, pp. 909-996, 1988.

[7] Ferwerda, J. A., Shirley, P., Pattanaik, S. N., and Greenberg, D. P., "A Model of Visual Masking for Computer Graphics," *Computer Graphics, Annual Conference Series*, ACM SIGGRAPH, pp. 143-152, 1997.

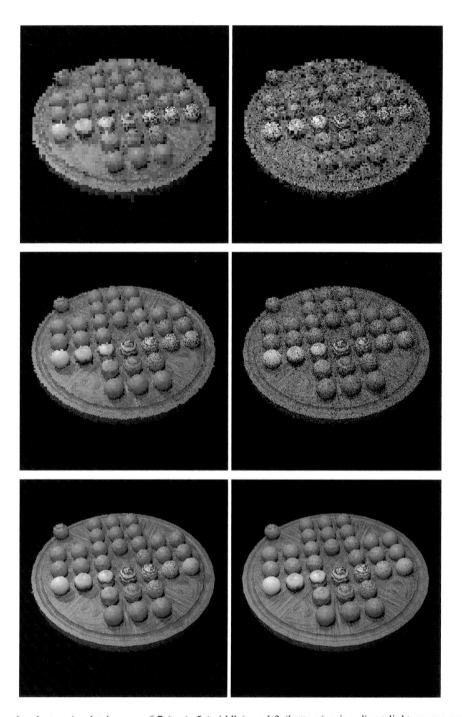

Figure 11: Image rendered at a visual tolerance of 7 (top), 5 (middle), and 3 (bottom) using direct light source sampling (left column) and Monte Carlo light source sampling (right column).

[8] Field, D. J., "Relations Between the Statistics of Natural Images and the Response Properties of Cortical Cells," *J. Opt. Soc. Am. A*, Vol. 4, pp. 2379-2394, 1987.

[9] Field, D. J., "What the Statistics of Natural Images Tell Us About Visual Coding," *Human Vision, Visual Processing, and Digital Display*, Proc. SPIE, Vol. 1077, pp. 269-276, 1989.

[10] Gibson, S. and Hubbold, R. J., "Perceptually-Driven Radiosity," *Computer Graphics Forum*, Vol. 16, pp. 129-140, 1997.

[11] Gortler, S. J., Grzeszczuk, R., Szeliski, R., and Cohen, M. F., "The Lumigraph," *Computer Graphics, Annual Conference Series*, ACM SIGGRAPH, pp. 43-54, 1996.

[12] Kirk, D. and Arvo, J., "Unbiased Sampling Techniques for Image Synthesis," *Computer Graphics, Annual Conference Series*, ACM SIGGRAPH, pp. 153-156, 1991.

[13] Lee, M. E., Redner, R. A., and Uselton, S. P., "Statistically Optimized Sampling for Distributed Ray Tracing," *Computer Graphics, Annual Conference Series*, ACM SIGGRAPH, pp. 61-67, 1985.

[14] Legge, G. E. and Foley, J. M., "Contrast Masking in human vision," *Journal of the Optical Society of America*, Vol. 70, pp. 1458-1470, 1980.

[15] Li, B., "An Analysis and Comparison of Two Visual Discrimination Models," *Master's Thesis, University of Oregon*, June 1997.

[16] Li, B., Meyer, G. W., and Klassen, R. V., "A Comparison of Two Image Quality Models," to appear in *Human Vision and Electronic Imaging III*, B. E. Rogowitz and T. N. Pappas, Editors, Proc. SPIE, Vol. 3299, 1998.

[17] Lubin, J., "A Visual Discrimination Model for Imaging System Design and Evaluation," *Vision Models for Target Detection and Recognition*, Eli Peli, Editor, World Scientific, New Jersey, pp. 245-283, 1995.

[18] Maloney, L. T., "Evaluation of linear models of surface spectral reflectance with small numbers of parameters," *J. Opt. Soc. Am. A*, Vol. 3, pp. 1673-1683. 1986.

[19] Marimont, D. H. and Wandell, B. A., "Matching Color Images: The Impact of Axial Chromatic Aberration," *J. Opt. Soc. Am. A*, Vol. 12, pp. 3113-3122, 1993.

[20] Meyer, G. W. and Liu, A., "Color Spatial Acuity Control of a Screen Subdivision Image Synthesis Algorithm," *Human Vision, Visual Processing, and Digital Display III*, Bernice E. Rogowitz, Editor, Proc. SPIE, Vol. 1666, pp. 387-399, 1992.

[21] Mitchell, D. P., "Generating Antialiased Images at Low Sampling Densities," *Computer Graphics, Annual Conference Series*, ACM SIGGRAPH, pp. 65-72, 1987.

[22] Mullen, K. T., "The Contrast Sensitivity of Human Colour Vision to Red-Green and Blue-Yellow Chromatic Gratings," *J. Physiol. (Lond.)*, Vol. 359, pp. 381-400, 1985.

[23] Painter, J. and Sloan, K. "Antialiased Ray Tracing by Adaptive Progressive Refinement," *Computer Graphics, Annual Conference Series*, ACM SIGGRAPH, pp. 281-288, 1989.

[24] Ruderman, D. L., "Origins of Scaling in Natural Images," *Human Vision, Visual Processing, and Digital Display*, Proc. SPIE, Vol. 2657, pp. 120-131, 1996.

[25] Rushmeier, H., Ward, G., Piatko, C., Sanders, P., and Rust, B., "Comparing Real and Synthetic Images: Some Ideas About Metrics," *Rendering Techniques '95*, P. M. Hanrahan and W. Purgathofer, Editors Springer-Verlag, New York, pp. 82-91, 1995.

[26] Schreiber, W. F., *Fundamentals of Electronic Imaging Systems*, Springer-Verlag: Berlin Heidelberg, 1993.

Efficient Simulation of Light Transport in Scenes with Participating Media using Photon Maps

Henrik Wann Jensen   Per H. Christensen

mental images*

Abstract

This paper presents a new method for computing global illumination in scenes with participating media. The method is based on bidirectional Monte Carlo ray tracing and uses photon maps to increase efficiency and reduce noise. We remove previous restrictions limiting the photon map method to surfaces by introducing a volume photon map containing photons in participating media. We also derive a new radiance estimate for photons in the volume photon map. The method is fast and simple, but also general enough to handle nonhomogeneous media and anisotropic scattering. It can efficiently simulate effects such as multiple volume scattering, color bleeding between volumes and surfaces, and volume caustics (light reflected from or transmitted through specular surfaces and then scattered by a medium). The photon map is decoupled from the geometric representation of the scene, making the method capable of simulating global illumination in scenes containing complex objects. These objects do not need to be tessellated; they can be instanced, or even represented by an implicit function. Since the method is based on a bidirectional simulation, it automatically adapts to illumination and view. Furthermore, because the use of photon maps reduces noise and aliasing, the method is suitable for rendering of animations.

CR Descriptors: I.3.7 [**Computer Graphics**]: Three-Dimensional Graphics and Realism — *color, shading, shadowing, and texture; raytracing*; I.6.8 [**Simulation and Modeling**]: Types of Simulation — *Monte Carlo*.

Additional keywords: participating media, light transport, global illumination, multiple scattering, volume caustics, nonhomogeneous media, anisotropic scattering, rendering, photo-realism, photon tracing, photon map, ray marching.

---
*mental images GmbH & Co. KG, Fasanenstraße 81, D-10623 Berlin, Germany. E-mail: {henrik,per}@mental.com.

1   Introduction

A physically correct simulation of light transport in participating media is necessary to render realistic images of fog, clouds, dusty air, smoke, fire, silty water, etc. Such images are important for applications dealing with the visibility of objects (for example road signs in fog or fire exit signs in smoke-filled rooms), for visualization of underwater scenes, and for high-quality visual special effects. See [30] for a more detailed discussion of the application areas.

The first methods taking participating media into account only considered direct illumination (single scattering) [5, 17, 21]. This approximation is applicable to optically thin media such as the atmosphere (where secondary scattering is less important), but fails to capture important effects in optically thick media such as clouds. Single scattering in water has been simulated in [38] where refracted light from a water surface is approximated using polygonal illumination volumes.

Multiple scattering has been simulated with finite element, point collocation, and Monte Carlo methods.

Finite element methods divide participating media into discrete volume elements and simulate the exchange of light between these volume elements. Point collocation methods choose a set of points in the volume and compute the illumination at these points. Isotropic scattering can be simulated by representing the radiance from each volume element or point by one value [29, 31]. To simulate anisotropic scattering, directional distributions are needed at each volume element or point. Some methods use spherical harmonics [3, 16, 33], while others divide the sphere of directions into a finite number of solid angles [20, 22, 25]. Finite element and point collocation methods are most useful when simulating softly illuminated isotropic media. The simulation of sharp illumination edges requires many volume elements, and directional distributions require complex representations of the illumination. In both cases a huge amount of memory is required.

Monte Carlo methods are more versatile and require less memory. However, pure Monte Carlo path tracing (including bidirectional path tracing) uses significant amounts of computation time to render images without noise, particularly in the presence of participating media [19]. One way to speed up rendering is to use particle tracing combined with a discretization of the scene and the volume for representing the illumination [26]. However, this imposes the same limitations on the algorithm as is the case with finite element methods.

A hybrid method [29] uses a finite element preprocess to increase the efficiency of Monte Carlo rendering. This makes the method less general than pure Monte Carlo techniques and imposes limitations on the supported types of scattering. The finite element preprocess increases memory usage and makes it necessary to discretize the volumes. Even though this is more efficient than pure Monte Carlo rendering, it still uses considerable amounts of computation time to render images without noise.

A detailed overview of previous solution methods and additional references can be found in [27]. None of the existing methods can efficiently simulate effects such as volume caustics where light is focused in a medium. Furthermore, all of the methods except the Monte Carlo path tracing methods are based on a tight coupling of geometry and volumes with the simulation of light transport. This makes them unsuitable for complex scenes.

In this paper we present an extension of the photon map method for global illumination [13, 14] to scenes with participating media. We introduce a *volume photon map* containing photons (particles with energy) within participating media and derive a formula for estimating radiance in a participating medium based on these photons. We also present techniques for using this radiance estimate to efficiently render effects such as multiple volume scattering, color bleeding between surfaces and volumes, and volume caustics. Volume caustics are formed when light reflected from or transmitted through specular surfaces is scattered in a medium. An example of volume caustics is the beams of light in a silty underwater environment [7]. The use of photons makes it easy to simulate homogeneous as well as nonhomogeneous media, and the fact that we include the incoming direction with each photon allows us to directly render media with anisotropic scattering. The photon map is decoupled from the geometry and the volumes, and it is capable of handling any type of representation that can be ray traced. This makes it possible to render for example an implicit function representing a cloud without using any geometry. Another notable aspect of the method is the automatic adaptation to illumination and view: photons are only stored in the illuminated parts of the scene and photon map lookups are only done where required for rendering. The photon map approach provides the same flexibility as pure Monte Carlo path tracing, but is significantly more efficient. It has very little noise and aliasing, making it suitable for rendering animations with participating media.

The remainder of the paper is organized as follows: In section 2, we give an overview of light transport in participating media. The photon map method for surfaces is summarized in section 3, and in section 4 we describe our new extension for handling participating media. In section 5, we present our results, and in section 6 we discuss the method and ideas for future work. Lastly, in section 7 we close with a conclusion.

2   Light transport in participating media

Light transported through a participating medium is affected by emission, in-scattering, absorption, and out-scattering [32]. Taking these four terms into account, the change in (field) radiance L at a point x in direction $\vec{\omega}$ is

$$\frac{\partial L(x, \vec{\omega})}{\partial x} = \alpha(x) L_e(x, \vec{\omega}) + \sigma(x) L_i(x, \vec{\omega}) - \alpha(x) L(x, \vec{\omega}) - \sigma(x) L(x, \vec{\omega}), \quad (1)$$

where L_e is the emitted radiance, L_i is the in-scattered radiance, α is the absorption coefficient, and σ is the scattering coefficient. This equation holds for each wavelength separately, but we will ignore wavelength here. If the scattering and absorption coefficients are constant throughout the medium, we call the medium homogeneous or uniform.

The last two terms of equation (1), for absorption and out-scattering, can be combined to an extinction term $\kappa(x) L(x, \vec{\omega})$, where the extinction coefficient κ is defined as

$$\kappa(x) = \alpha(x) + \sigma(x). \quad (2)$$

The in-scattered radiance L_i depends on radiance L from all directions $\vec{\omega}'$ over the sphere Ω. The in-scattered radiance is

$$L_i(x, \vec{\omega}) = \int_{\Omega} f(x, \vec{\omega}', \vec{\omega}) L(x, \vec{\omega}') d\omega'. \quad (3)$$

While the scattering coefficient σ determines how much of the incident light is scattered at point x, the normalized phase function f determines how much of the scattered light at x is scattered in direction $\vec{\omega}$. The product $\sigma(x) f(x, \vec{\omega}', \vec{\omega})$ expresses the fraction of the differential irradiance from direction $\vec{\omega}'$ to point x that is scattered (as radiance) in direction $\vec{\omega}$. The normalized phase function integrates to 1 over the sphere. If the phase function is constant $(1/4\pi)$, we call the scattering isotropic or diffuse; if not, we call the scattering anisotropic or directional.

Inserting equations (2) and (3) into equation (1) we get the integro-differential equation

$$\begin{aligned}\frac{\partial L(x, \vec{\omega})}{\partial x} &= \alpha(x) L_e(x, \vec{\omega}) \\ &+ \sigma(x) \int_{\Omega} f(x, \vec{\omega}', \vec{\omega}) L(x, \vec{\omega}') d\omega' \\ &- \kappa(x) L(x, \vec{\omega}).\end{aligned}$$

Integrating both sides of the equation along a straight path from x_0 to x (in direction $\vec{\omega}$) gives the following integral equation [32]:

$$\begin{aligned}L(x, \vec{\omega}) &= \int_{x_0}^{x} \tau(x', x) \alpha(x') L_e(x', \vec{\omega}) dx' \\ &+ \int_{x_0}^{x} \tau(x', x) \sigma(x') \int_{\Omega} f(x', \vec{\omega}', \vec{\omega}) L(x', \vec{\omega}') d\omega' dx' \\ &+ \tau(x_0, x) L(x_0, \vec{\omega}), \quad (4)\end{aligned}$$

where $\tau(x', x)$ is the transmittance along the line segment from x' to x,

$$\tau(x', x) = e^{-\int_{x'}^{x} \kappa(\xi) d\xi},$$

and similar for $\tau(x_0, x)$.

Equation (4) can be simplified if the medium is homogeneous or the scattering is isotropic, but not in the general case which we consider here.

3   The photon map method for surfaces

The photon map method was originally developed for global illumination simulation in scenes without participating media [13]. It is a two-pass method where the first pass is the construction of two view-independent photon maps and the second pass is optimized rendering using these photon maps.

The photon maps are generated by emitting photons from the light sources and tracing these through the scene using photon tracing. Every time a photon hits a nonspecular surface it is stored in the photon map(s). The result is a large number of photons distributed on the surfaces within the scene.

The first photon map is a high quality caustics photon map which consists of all photons that have been traced from the light source through a number of specular reflections or transmissions before intersecting a diffuse surface. This path can be expressed as LS^+D using the notation introduced in [12]. The second photon map is a global photon map which is less accurate than the caustics photon map. It contains all photons representing indirect illumination on a nonspecular surface, $L(S|D)^+D$.

A key aspect of the method is the use of a balanced kd-tree [2, 15] to efficiently and compactly handle these photons. This structure makes it possible to represent each photon using only 20 bytes [13].

The rendering pass is a distribution ray tracer optimized in several ways using the two photon maps. The caustics photon map is used to render caustics directly. This is a significant optimization since caustics are nearly impossible to compute using ray tracing from the eye [37]. The global photon map is used to limit the number of reflections traced by the distribution ray tracer and to sample indirect illumination more efficiently.

The photon map can be used to estimate radiance at any given surface position x using the information about the flux $\Delta\Phi_p$ carried by each photon p in direction $\vec{\omega}'_p$. By locating the n photons with the shortest distance to x it is possible to estimate the photon density around x. The estimate of the reflected radiance from a surface is then computed as [13]

$$L_r(x, \vec{\omega}) \approx \sum_{p=1}^{n} f_r(x, \vec{\omega}'_p, \vec{\omega}) \frac{\Delta\Phi_p(x, \vec{\omega}'_p)}{\pi r^2}, \qquad (5)$$

where f_r is the bidirectional reflectance distribution function and r is the distance to the nth nearest photon. This approach can be seen as expanding a sphere centered at x until it contains n photons. Then r is the radius of the sphere and the denominator in the formula is the projected area of this sphere as illustrated in figure 1(a).

The photon map method has the full flexibility of bidirectional Monte Carlo path tracing [18, 34]: all possible light paths can be simulated, including caustics. Tessellating the geometry is not necessary, and the aliasing problems in methods using texture maps [1, 12] or simple geometric primitives [36] to represent the illumination are significantly reduced. Furthermore, since the photon map radiance estimate is inherently a low-pass filter, the high-frequency, grainy noise present in pure Monte Carlo methods disappears. At the same time, the Monte Carlo method's ability to compute precise illumination details is maintained since the photon density is high where the illumination is intense. The photon map radiance estimate is valid as long as the surface is locally flat, and the estimate converges to the correct value as more photons are used.

The Metropolis light transport algorithm [35], a recent improvement over bidirectional path tracing, focuses its computations on the light paths that contribute most to the rendered image. This gives improved performance for scenes containing for example underwater caustics seen through a wavy water surface. The photon map method also handles such scenes efficiently: in the first pass, photons are refracted by the water surface, hit the diffuse pool bottom, and are stored in the caustics photon map; in the second pass, rays from the eye are refracted to the appropriate position on the pool bottom, and photon map lookups return the intensities of the caustics. For soft indirect illumination, the Metropolis algorithm tends to use the same amount of computation time as brute force bidirectional Monte Carlo path tracing.

The illumination in participating media is mostly soft due to the continuous scattering taking place everywhere in the medium. This makes a possible extension of the Metropolis algorithm less attractive for this application.

4 Extending the photon map to participating media

Simulating light transport in participating media requires extension of several aspects of the photon map method. Photons can be scattered and absorbed by the media. To efficiently render the medium, it is necessary to store information about these scattering events. For this purpose several strategies have been considered.

4.1 Algorithmic considerations

One might consider discretizing the media into a finite set of volume elements for which the volume radiance is computed. This strategy would, however, result in unnecessary restrictions and aliasing problems. Another alternative would be to store photons on the surfaces of the media. In this way, the surface radiance estimate in equation (5) could be used to extract information about the radiance leaving or entering a medium. The drawback of this approach is that it would fail to efficiently capture illumination details such as volume caustics inside the medium. Also, it would not work in situations where the viewpoint is within the medium. A better strategy is to store the photons explicitly in the volume. Since the photon map is based on a three-dimensional data structure, this can be done without changing the underlying algorithms. Storing the photons explicitly in the volume has several advantages: the photons can be concentrated where necessary to represent intense illumination, the media do not have to be discretized (it is possible to directly render implicitly defined volumes), and anisotropic scattering can be handled by storing the incoming direction of each photon.

The photons in volumes and on surfaces must be separated when the photon map is queried for information about the incoming flux. This is necessary because the relationship between the density of the photons and the illumination is different on surfaces and in volumes (as described in section 4.3). The separation of the two types of photons could be done by tagging the volume photons and storing them in the global photon map. This would, however, result in more computationally expensive lookups due to the larger size of the kd-tree and the need to separate the photons. Instead we introduce a separate volume photon map for the photons that are scattered in participating media. The volume photon map is used to compute the illumination inside a participating medium, and the global photon map is used — as before — to compute the illumination on surfaces.

The direct illumination of participating media is easy to compute using traditional ray tracing techniques. Therefore we only use the photon map to represent indirect illumination. That is, we only store photons that have been reflected or transmitted by surfaces before interacting with the media, and photons that have been scattered at least once in the media. This is a tradeoff between memory and speed since the photon map is perfectly capable of computing the direct illumination at the expense of using more photons to obtain the desired accuracy.

4.2 Photon tracing

In the first pass, the photon maps are built using photon tracing. A photon traced within a participating medium can either pass unaffected through the medium, or it can interact with it (be scattered or absorbed). If the photon interacts with the medium, and does not come directly from a light source, it is stored in the photon map. The cumulative probability density function, $F(x)$, expressing the probability of a photon interacting with a participating medium at position x is

$$F(x) \;=\; 1 - \tau(x_s, x) \;=\; 1 - e^{-\int_{x_s}^{x} \kappa(\xi)\,d\xi},$$

where x_s is the point at which the photon enters the medium. The transmittance $\tau(x_s, x)$ is computed using ray marching.

If a photon interacts with the medium, Russian roulette decides whether the photon is scattered or absorbed. The probability of a photon being scattered is given by the scattering albedo $\sigma(x)/\kappa(x)$. The new direction of a scattered photon is chosen using importance sampling based on the phase function at x.

4.3 Estimating radiance

The photons stored in a volume photon map can be used to compute an estimate of the in-scattered radiance $L_i(x, \vec{\omega})$. This illumination is determined by the photons closest to x, as is the case with the technique used for surfaces. However, we cannot directly use the radiance estimate for surfaces since it is based on the definition of radiance for surfaces. Instead, we can utilize the relationship between scattered flux Φ and radiance L in a participating medium [32],

$$L(x, \vec{\omega}) \;=\; \frac{d^2\Phi(x, \vec{\omega})}{\sigma(x)\,d\omega\,dV}.$$

By combining this relation with equation (3) we get

$$
\begin{aligned}
L_i(x, \vec{\omega}) \;&=\; \int_\Omega f(x, \vec{\omega}', \vec{\omega})\, L(x, \vec{\omega}')\,d\omega' \\
&=\; \int_\Omega f(x, \vec{\omega}', \vec{\omega})\, \frac{d^2\Phi(x, \vec{\omega}')}{\sigma(x)\,d\omega'\,dV}\,d\omega' \\
&=\; \frac{1}{\sigma(x)} \int_\Omega f(x, \vec{\omega}', \vec{\omega})\, \frac{d^2\Phi(x, \vec{\omega}')}{dV} \\
&\approx\; \frac{1}{\sigma(x)} \sum_{p=1}^{n} f(x, \vec{\omega}_p', \vec{\omega})\, \frac{\Delta\Phi_p(x, \vec{\omega}_p')}{\frac{4}{3}\pi r^3}, \qquad (6)
\end{aligned}
$$

where Φ is the in-scattered flux and dV is the differential volume containing the photons. This differential volume is approximated by $\frac{4}{3}\pi r^3$, corresponding to the smallest sphere containing the n nearest photons (this is effectively a nth nearest neighbor density estimate). Notice the relationship between this formula and formula (5) for estimating radiance on surfaces. The main difference is that the density on a surface is computed using the projected area, whereas the density in a medium is computed using the full volume — as shown in figure 1.

Using formula (6) we can compute a radiance estimate at any given point inside a participating medium. Since we know the incoming direction $\vec{\omega}_p'$ of each photon, we can handle anisotropic phase functions as well as isotropic phase functions.

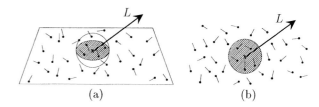

Figure 1: Radiance estimate for (a) surfaces and (b) volumes.

As already mentioned, we split the computation of in-scattered radiance into two parts: direct $L_{i,d}$ and indirect $L_{i,i}$. The direct part $L_{i,d}$ is computed by sampling of the light sources using ray marching. The indirect part $L_{i,i}$ is estimated using the volume radiance estimate from equation (6),

$$L_{i,i}(x, \vec{\omega}) \;\approx\; \frac{1}{\sigma(x)} \sum_{p=1}^{n} f(x, \vec{\omega}_p', \vec{\omega})\, \frac{\Delta\Phi_{p,i}(x, \vec{\omega}_p')}{\frac{4}{3}\pi r^3},$$

where $\Delta\Phi_{p,i}$ is the flux carried by the photons that correspond to the indirect illumination.

Since we store and use all photons that interact with a medium (even photons that are subsequently absorbed), $L_{i,i}$ has to be multiplied by the scattering albedo $\sigma(x)/\kappa(x)$. This leads to the following formula for computing the in-scattered radiance:

$$L_i(x, \vec{\omega}) \;=\; L_{i,d}(x, \vec{\omega}) + \frac{\sigma(x)}{\kappa(x)}\, L_{i,i}(x, \vec{\omega}).$$

4.4 Rendering

In the second pass, the image is rendered using the photon maps. We render the surfaces in the scene using the same approach as described in [13]. To incorporate participating media into this method we need to consider those rays that pass through a medium.

The radiance of a ray traversing a participating medium is computed with an adaptive ray marching algorithm [9] that iteratively computes radiance at points along the ray. In each step, the radiance from the previous point is attenuated and the contribution from emission and in-scattering within the step is added, corresponding to equation (4). The emitted and in-scattered radiance is approximated as being constant within each step. With this approximation, the radiance at points x_k along a ray in direction $\vec{\omega}$ is computed iteratively as

$$
\begin{aligned}
L(x_k, \vec{\omega}) \;=\; & \alpha(x_k)\, L_e(x_k, \vec{\omega})\, \Delta x_k \\
& + \sigma(x_k)\, L_i(x_k, \vec{\omega})\, \Delta x_k \\
& + e^{-\kappa(x_k)\,\Delta x_k}\, L(x_{k-1}, \vec{\omega}),
\end{aligned}
$$

where $\Delta x_k = |x_k - x_{k-1}|$ is the step size and x_0 is the nearest intersection point of the ray with a surface (or the back side of the volume).

The step size is recursively halved if the currently computed radiance differs too much from the radiance in the previous point. This adaptation to illumination makes the ray marcher capable of rendering media efficiently while still capturing small illumination details. The size of each step is also varied using jittering to eliminate the aliasing problems that can occur with a fixed step size.

5 Results

We have implemented the presented method as a part of mental ray, a commercial rendering program that supports parallel ray tracing and has a flexible shader interface [6]. We use a parallelized photon map algorithm as described in [14], where one photon map is shared between all processors. The implementation supports nonhomogeneous media and anisotropic scattering. We use Schlick's two-lobed phase function [4] to approximate Mie scattering [23]. Other phase functions such as the Rayleigh or Henyey-Greenstein phase functions [10] could be used as well. We have not implemented emitting media, but this could easily be added.

The images in figures 2–5 have been rendered on an HP S-class computer with sixteen 180 MHz PA-8000 processors, while the images in figures 6–8 have been rendered on an SGI Origin 2000 computer with sixteen 195 MHz MIPS R10000 processors. Each image is 1024 pixels wide and rendered using up to 16 samples per pixel.

Figure 2 shows a volume caustic created as light is focused by a glass sphere in an isotropic (diffuse) homogeneous medium. The light is emitted from a point light source (a big bright halo around the light source is visible in the upper left corner of the image). The volume photon map contains 100,000 photons, and 500 photons were used in the radiance estimate. Building the volume photon map took 5 seconds, and rendering the image took 41 seconds.

Figure 2: A volume caustic.

Figure 3 illustrates the effect of multiple scattering in a nonhomogeneous, anisotropic medium. The cloud is modeled using an implicitly defined function consisting of 10 blobs combined with turbulent noise [8]. The anisotropic scattering is modeled using an approximation of hazy Mie scattering. In figure 3(a) only single scattering has been simulated (no photons), whereas figure 3(b) demonstrates multiple scattering (using just 10,000 photons in the photon map and 60 photons in the radiance estimate). Despite the low number of photons, the cloud in 3(b) is brighter and looks more realistic. Figure 3(a) took 61 seconds to render. The photon map for image 3(b) was generated in 8 seconds and the image was rendered in 92 seconds.

Our next test case, a variation of the "Cornell box", is

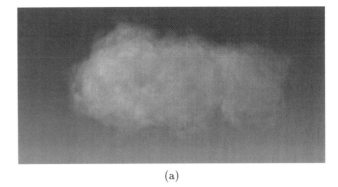

(a)

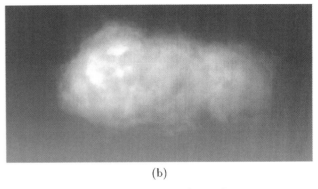

(b)

Figure 3: The cloud is an anisotropic, nonhomogeneous participating medium: (a) direct illumination (single scattering), (b) global illumination (multiple scattering).

shown in figure 4. The box has diffuse reflection on the walls, floor, and ceiling. It contains a glass sphere, a mirror sphere, and a participating medium. To make it easier to see the participating medium, the box has no front or back wall. The geometry is represented using approximately 25,000 triangles, and the scene is illuminated by a square-shaped area light source.

Figure 4(a) shows direct illumination on surfaces and in the volume (an isotropic, homogeneous medium). It took 1 minute 49 seconds to render this image. Because of the area light source, the shadow of the sphere is sharp close to the sphere and gets blurry further away.

Figure 4(b) has full global illumination on the surfaces and in the isotropic, homogeneous participating medium. Notice that the caustic created by the glass sphere becomes visible in the fog, that the halo around the light source gets slightly bigger because of multiple volume scattering, and that the fog gets red and blue tints near the colored walls of the box. The volume caustic under the glass sphere is wider than in figure 2 since the light source is an area light source. The image was computed using a total of 200,000 photons in the photon maps, out of which 65,000 were in the volume photon map. The radiance estimate in the volume used 100 photons. It took 4 seconds to generate the photon maps, and 3 minutes 32 seconds to render the image.

In figure 4(c) the medium has anisotropic scattering. The scattering is mainly forward; it is modeled using Schlick's scattering model with a single lobe of eccentricity $k = 0.8$. As a result of the forward scattering, the halo around the light source changes shape. Also, the volume caustic gets dimmer since most of the light in it gets scattered in a direction perpendicular to the eye. Photon map building took 4 seconds and rendering took 4 minutes 3 seconds.

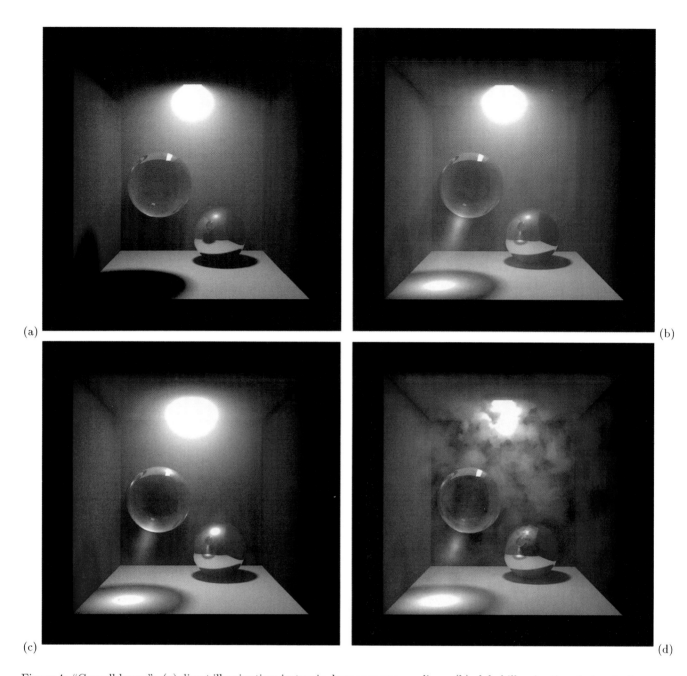

(a)

(b)

(c)

(d)

Figure 4: "Cornell boxes": (a) direct illumination; isotropic, homogeneous medium. (b) global illumination; isotropic, homogeneous medium. (c) global illumination; anisotropic, homogeneous medium. (d) global illumination; isotropic, nonhomogeneous medium.

In figure 4(d) the participating medium is nonhomogeneous. A 3D turbulence function [28] was used to model the spatial variation of scattering and extinction coefficients. Generating the photon maps with 200,000 photons took 6 seconds, and rendering took 7 minutes 54 seconds. The radiance estimate in the volume used 50 photons. The higher rendering time is caused by the evaluation of the turbulence function and the fine illumination details which must be resolved by the ray marcher.

Figure 5 shows scattering of sunlight shining through a stained glass window into a dusty room. Some of the photons that pass through the stained glass window are scattered by the dust in the air (using Schlick's approximation of murky Mie scattering). This is particularly visible near the cognac glass on the table top. An important optimization in this scene is that the bright beam of light shining through the window is rendered as direct illumination. This is a reasonable approximation considering the fact that the window glass is thin. The optimization allows the scattering effects in the dusty air to be represented using just 80,000 photons. The illumination of the surfaces in the room is represented using 220,000 photons. The walls, the floor and the ceiling are all displacement mapped and the geometry is approximated using 2.3 million triangles. The photon maps were generated in 27 seconds and the image was rendered in 5 minutes 27 seconds.

Figure 6: Caustics in a swimming pool seen through a wavy water surface.

Figure 5: Dusty room illuminated by sunlight through a stained glass window.

Figure 6 illustrates a swimming pool with caustics created as light is focused by a wavy water surface. In this scene, the photon maps are used only to simulate the caustics (including volume caustics) resulting from the water in the swimming pool. This is achieved by ignoring all photons which has not intersected the water surface upon the interaction with a diffuse surface. The water surface is displacement mapped and the scene is represented using a total of 2.0 million triangles. Since the water is clear and its extinction coefficient is low, few photons interact with the water before hitting the pool bottom. Therefore only

25,000 photons are stored in the volume photon map. The caustics photon map representing the caustics on the pool bottom and sides contains 475,000 photons. The caustics in the pool are crisp even through the number of photons in the caustics photon map is less than the number of pixels in the image. This is possible since the photons inherently are concentrated where light is focused and intense. The photon maps for this scene were generated in 19 seconds and rendering with a lens simulation to achieve depth-of-field took 1 minute 56 seconds.

Figure 7 shows a simulation of surface and volume caustics in an an underwater scene. The scene is modeled using 1.5 million triangles — these triangles are used primarily for the plants, the pufferfish and the displacement mapped water and sand surfaces. The scene also contains reaction-diffusion textures on the humphead wrasse and glossy reflection on the lowrider crab. The water is modeled as a participating medium to capture the effect of silt particles and plankton, and has highly directional forward scattering. To simulate the caustics and the beams of light in the water, we used 3.0 million photons of which 2.0 million were used in the volume photon map. In order to get sufficiently many photons in the volume photon map, we artificially increased the probability of a photon interacting with the medium (similar to the forced interaction technique used in [26]). This technique can be used to increase the density of photons in the parts of the scene where they contribute most to the overall quality of the illumination representation. The photon maps were generated in 4 minutes 20 seconds and the image was rendered in 24 minutes.

The two images in figure 8 illustrate another simulation of volume caustics in an underwater environment. The two images are from an animation sequence demonstrating gently moving volume caustics. The volume caustics are seen as bright beams of light formed as sunlight is focused due to refraction by the water surface. This particular view of the sun is often seen in pictures of underwater environments;

Figure 7: Underwater scene with volume caustics.

striking examples can be found in [7]. We used 3.0 million photons in the volume photon map for both pictures and a few thousand photons in the caustic photon map to represent the caustics on the fish. For the image in figure 8(a), the photon maps were constructed in 28 seconds and the rendering time was 31 minutes. The image in figure 8(b) required 37 seconds for construction of the photon maps and the rendering time was 32 minutes. The longer rendering time for these images are caused by the fact that the ray marcher must perform a very dense sampling of the medium to adequately capture the crisp beams of light.

The underwater scene in figure 7 was the most memory consuming scene that we rendered (mainly due to the geometry and textures). For the simulation on sixteen processors it reached a maximum resident memory size of 660 MB. By contrast the cloud used 7 MB on one processor of which 4 MB was used for the frame-buffer.

We have tested the method presented here with both Monte Carlo and strictly deterministic quasi-Monte Carlo [24] techniques. In our experience, quasi-Monte Carlo sampling outperforms classical Monte Carlo sampling by distributing the photons more evenly. This leads to an improved photon map radiance estimate with less noise.

We have measured the speedups of the parallel implementation, and for our scenes we achieved speedups between 14.1 and 15.2 on the HP, and speedups between 12.0 and 14.2 on the SGI.

6 Discussion and future work

As our results indicate, the extension of the photon map method to scenes with participating media works very well. The storing of photons in volumes provides a flexible framework and enables this method to simulate complicated media. Our test scenes demonstrate that, in some cases, even a low number of photons in the volume photon map can give very good results. If the lighting situation is more complex, a higher number of photons is required. For the underwater scenes, which contain multiple volume caustics and have large extents, we had to use up to 3.0 million photons in the volume photon map in order to adequately capture the volume caustics. Fortunately, the use of a balanced kd-tree provides an efficient and compact way of handling such a large number of photons.

The radiance estimate for participating media works surprisingly well even with a low number of photons. We compute multiple estimates along each ray traced through a medium, which gives good results using only 50–100 photons per estimate. We found that the combination of ray traced direct illumination and photon map based indirect illumination gives good results. We avoid the costly use of a distribution ray tracer (ie., a final gathering step) to compute the directly visible in-scattered radiance in the participating media. One potential problem with this approach is that the radiance estimate can be incorrect close to the boundary of

(a)

(b)

Figure 8: Underwater sunbeams.

a volume if there are too few photons in the photon map. In this situation, the sphere containing the nearest volume photons extends outside of the medium. The volume is still computed as the full sphere and the estimated density of the photons will therefore be too low. Similarly, false photons might be included in the estimate. Most of these problems can be avoided by looking at the incoming direction of the photons, and in our test scenes we have not experienced any visible artifacts due to this.

The memory usage of the photon map method is very favorable in complex scenes. We were able to render high-quality solutions of complex scenes using less than one photon per triangle. The photon map method does not require any additional links between geometry as in for example hierarchical radiosity [11]. It does not use any more memory than what is required for just the photons. This decoupling from the geometry is the primary reason why it can render very complex scenes. It also makes it possible to handle scene geometry represented using for example instancing or implicitly defined functions.

Although the scenes in the result section have only one light source, it would not be a problem to simulate scenes with many light sources. Each light source then contributes relatively less to the illumination in the scene, and therefore less photons should be emitted from each light source.

Even though our results are very encouraging, we believe there is room for further improvements. In particular one might consider the use of visual importance to guide the photons towards the parts of the scene which contribute most to the image. This could be used to reduce the number of photons required in for example the underwater scene. One way of implementing this could be to use an importance map (along the lines of the photon map) which stores importance-carrying particles emitted from the camera. Visual importance might also help address the difficult problem of automatically determining the number of photons needed in the photon maps to obtain an image of a given quality.

Another interesting possibility would be to implement emitting media such as flames. For complex emitting media the sampling of the direct illumination might be too costly. In this case, one could consider storing the photons corresponding to the direct illumination from the media.

7 Conclusion

We have extended the photon map method to simulate global illumination in scenes with participating media by introducing a volume photon map in which photons representing indirect illumination are stored. Furthermore, we have derived a new technique for estimating radiance based on photons stored in volumes. Since the photon map is detached from the geometry, the method is capable of simulating global illumination in complex scenes. For the same reason, the method can use implicit volumetric representations directly. Even though the method is simple, it provides a general framework for simulating light transport in various types of participating media. It can efficiently handle both homogeneous and nonhomogeneous media with isotropic or anisotropic scattering. The method can simulate global illumination effects such as volume caustics, multiple scattering, and color bleeding between surfaces and volumes.

The results demonstrate that the method can handle complex illumination and geometry, has a low level of noise, and is applicable to animations. While simulation of global illumination in scenes with participating media is still computationally expensive, it is now within reach of high-end animation production.

Acknowledgements

Many thanks to Charlotte "Lowrider" Manning for modeling the scenes in figures 5–8 and for use of the lowrider crab. Steffen Volz animated the fish in figure 8. Modeling and animation was done using Softimage|3D. Hoang-My Christensen and Rolf Herken proofread several drafts of this paper. Eric Lafortune, Alexander Keller, and the SIGGRAPH reviewers provided helpful comments. Finally, we would like to thank our colleagues at mental images for providing a creative environment and for discussions about this paper. The research and development described herein is funded in part by the European Commission in ESPRIT project 22765 (DESIRE II).

References

[1] James R. Arvo. Backward ray tracing. *ACM SIGGRAPH 86 Course Notes — Developments in Ray Tracing*, 12, 1986.

[2] Jon L. Bentley. Multidimensional binary search trees used for associative searching. *Communications of the ACM*, 18(9):509–517, 1975.

[3] N. Bhate and A. Tokuta. Photorealistic volume rendering of media with directional scattering. *Proceedings of the 3rd Eurographics Workshop on Rendering*, pages 227–245, 1992.

[4] Philippe Blasi, Bertrand Le Saëc, and Christophe Schlick. A rendering algorithm for discrete volume density objects. *Computer Graphics Forum (Proceedings of Eurographics '93)*, 12(3):201–210, 1993.

[5] James F. Blinn. Light reflection functions for simulation of clouds and dusty surfaces. *Proceedings of ACM SIGGRAPH 82*, pages 21–29, 1982.

[6] Per H. Christensen. Global illumination for professional 3D animation, visualization, and special effects. *Rendering Techniques '97 (Proceedings of the 8th Eurographics Workshop on Rendering)*, pages 321–326, 1997.

[7] David Doubilet. *Light in the Sea*. National Geographic, 1989.

[8] David S. Ebert. Volumetric modeling with implicit functions (A cloud is born). *Visual Proceedings of ACM SIGGRAPH 97*, page 147, 1997. Technical Sketch.

[9] David S. Ebert, F. Kenton Musgrave, Darwyn Peachey, Ken Perlin, and Steven Worley. *Texturing and Modeling: A Procedural Approach*. AP Professional, 1994.

[10] Andrew S. Glassner. *Principles of Digital Image Synthesis*. Morgan Kaufmann, San Francisco, CA, 1995.

[11] Pat Hanrahan, David Salzman, and Larry Aupperle. A rapid hierarchical radiosity algorithm. *Proceedings of ACM SIGGRAPH 91*, pages 197–206, 1991.

[12] Paul Heckbert. Adaptive radiosity textures for bidirectional ray tracing. *Proceedings of ACM SIGGRAPH 90*, pages 145–154, 1990.

[13] Henrik Wann Jensen. Global illumination using photon maps. *Rendering Techniques '96 (Proceedings of the 7th Eurographics Workshop on Rendering)*, pages 21–30, 1996.

[14] Henrik Wann Jensen. *The Photon Map in Global Illumination*. PhD thesis, Technical University of Denmark, Lyngby, Denmark, 1996.

[15] Henrik Wann Jensen. Rendering caustics on non-Lambertian surfaces. *Proceedings of Graphics Interface '96*, pages 116–121, 1996.

[16] James T. Kajiya and Brian P. von Herzen. Ray tracing volume densities. *Proceedings of ACM SIGGRAPH 84*, pages 165–174, 1984.

[17] R. Victor Klassen. Modeling the effect of the atmosphere on light. *ACM Transactions on Graphics*, 6(3):215–237, 1987.

[18] Eric P. Lafortune and Yves D. Willems. Bi-directional path tracing. *Proceedings of Compugraphics '93*, pages 145–153, 1993.

[19] Eric P. Lafortune and Yves D. Willems. Rendering participating media with bidirectional path tracing. *Rendering Techniques '96 (Proceedings of the 7th Eurographics Workshop on Rendering)*, pages 92–101, 1996.

[20] Eric Languénou, Kadi Bouatouch, and Michelle Chelle. Global illumination in presence of participating media with general properties. *Proceedings of the 5th Eurographics Workshop on Rendering*, pages 69–85, 1994.

[21] Nelson L. Max. Light diffusion through clouds and haze. *Computer Vision, Graphics, and Image Processing*, 33(3):280–292, March 1986.

[22] Nelson L. Max. Efficient light propagation for multiple anisotropic volume scattering. *Proceedings of the 5th Eurographics Workshop on Rendering*, pages 87–104, 1994.

[23] Gustav Mie. Beiträge zur optik trüber medien, speziell kolloidaler metallösungen. *Annalen der Physik*, 25(3):377–445, 1908.

[24] Harald Niederreiter. *Random Number Generation and Quasi-Monte Carlo Methods*, volume 63 of *Regional Conference Series in Applied Mathematics*. Society for Industrial and Applied Mathematics (SIAM), Philadelphia, Pennsylvania, 1992.

[25] Tomoyuki Nishita, Yoshinori Dobashi, and Eihachiro Nakamae. Display of clouds taking into account multiple anisotropic scattering and sky light. *Proceedings of ACM SIGGRAPH 96*, pages 379–386, 1996.

[26] S. N. Pattanaik and S. P. Mudur. Computation of global illumination in a participating medium by Monte Carlo simulation. *Journal on Visualization and Computer Animation*, 4(3):133–152, 1993.

[27] Frederic Pérez, Xavier Pueyo, and François X. Sillion. Global illumination techniques for the simulation of participating media. *Rendering Techniques '97 (Proceedings of the 8th Eurographics Workshop on Rendering)*, pages 309–320, 1997.

[28] Ken Perlin. An image synthesizer. *Proceedings of ACM SIGGRAPH 85*, pages 287–296, 1985.

[29] Holly E. Rushmeier. *Realistic Image Synthesis for Scenes with Radiatively Participating Media*. PhD thesis, Cornell University, Ithaca, New York, 1988.

[30] Holly E. Rushmeier. Rendering participating media: Problems and solutions from application areas. *Proceedings of the 5th Eurographics Workshop on Rendering*, pages 35–56, 1994.

[31] Holly E. Rushmeier and Kenneth E. Torrance. The zonal method for calculating light intensities in the presence of a participating medium. *Proceedings of ACM SIGGRAPH 87*, pages 293–302, 1987.

[32] Robert Siegel and John R. Howell. *Thermal Radiation Heat Transfer, 3rd Edition*. Hemisphere Publishing Corporation, New York, 1992.

[33] Jos Stam. Multiple scattering as a diffusion process. *Rendering Techniques '95 (Proceedings of the 6th Eurographics Workshop on Rendering)*, pages 41–50, 1995.

[34] Eric Veach and Leonidas Guibas. Bidirectional estimators for light transport. *Proceedings of the 5th Eurographics Workshop on Rendering*, pages 147–162, 1994.

[35] Eric Veach and Leonidas J. Guibas. Metropolis light transport. *Proceedings of ACM SIGGRAPH 97*, pages 65–76, 1997.

[36] Bruce Walter, Philip M. Hubbard, Peter Shirley, and Donald P. Greenberg. Global illumination using local linear density estimation. *ACM Transactions on Graphics*, 16(3):217–259, 1997.

[37] Gregory J. Ward. The RADIANCE lighting simulation and rendering system. *Proceedings of ACM SIGGRAPH 94*, pages 459–472, 1994.

[38] Mark Watt. Light-water interaction using backward beam tracing. *Proceedings of ACM SIGGRAPH 90*, pages 377–385, 1990.

Fast Calculation of Soft Shadow Textures Using Convolution

Cyril Soler and François X. Sillion

*i*MAGIS – GRAVIR/IMAG

Abstract

The calculation of detailed shadows remains one of the most diffi-cult challenges in computer graphics, especially in the case of ex-tended (linear or area) light sources. This paper introduces a new tool for the calculation of shadows cast by extended light sources. Exact shadows are computed in some constrained configurations by using a convolution technique, yielding a fast and accurate so-lution. Approximate shadows can be computed for general con-figurations by applying the convolution to a representative "ideal" configuration. We analyze the various sources of approximation in the process and derive a hierarchical, error-driven algorithm for fast shadow calculation in arbitrary configurations using a hierar-chy of object clusters. The convolution is performed on images rendered in an offscreen buffer and produces a *shadow map* used as a texture to modulate the unoccluded illumination. Light sources can have any 3D shape as well as arbitrary emission characteristics, while shadow maps can be applied to groups of objects at once. The method can be employed in a hierarchical radiosity system, or directly as a shadowing technique. We demonstrate results for various scenes, showing that soft shadows can be generated at in-teractive rates for dynamic environments.

Keywords: Soft shadows, Convolution, Shadow map, Error-Driven illumination, Texture.

1 Introduction

The computation of *soft shadows*, i.e. shadows cast by extended light sources, is one of the most difficult challenges in rendering for computer graphics. Soft shadows are a result of the continuous variation of illumination across a receiving surface, when the light source becomes partially occluded by other objects in the scene. Their appearance is mainly controlled by the shape and location of *penumbra* regions, which are the regions on a receiver where the light source is partially visible.

Soft shadows play a key role in the overall realism of computer-generated images, because they provide important visual cues about the 3D arrangement of objects [26]. The location of cast shadows with respect to the blocking objects informs the viewer about the main directions of illumination, and the sharpness of the penum-

*i*MAGIS is a joint research project of CNRS, INRIA, INPG and UJF. Postal address: *i*MAGIS/IMAG, B.P. 53, 38041 Grenoble Cedex 9, France. Email: [Cyril.Soler|Francois.Sillion]@imag.fr.
Web: http://www-imagis.imag.fr/~Cyril.Soler

bra helps understand the distance relationships between the source, blocker and receiver.

Unfortunately, the calculation of soft shadows is also very diffi-cult. It can be restated as an area *visibility determination* problem, since the goal is to identify the regions of partial source visibility, as well as quantifying the relative area of the source that is visible. There are many methods for computing hard shadows (from point light sources), including some texture-based algorithms that can run in real-time on graphics computers. However, the two main avenues for the treatment of extended light sources each have severely lim-iting problems. Analytic techniques such as discontinuity mesh-ing suffer from excessive time and memory costs, and numerical robustness problems, while sampling techniques are prone to an-noying image artifacts unless they are pushed to a stage where they become too expensive.

In this paper, we present a new method for the calculation of soft shadows, which is able to provide pleasant, artifact-free images in a very efficient way. The method is based on the calculation of *shadow maps*, which are textures created from images of the light sources and occluders using a convolution technique. The convo-lution is performed with images of the light source and the set of occluders, rendered in offscreen buffers. The shadow textures are then used to modulate direct light source illumination across the re-ceiving objects. Exact images are obtained for some specific cases (parallel polygons), while for general configurations some approx-imation is necessary. We analyze the error incurred and the various sources of approximation, and show how the overall approximation can be controlled using a spatial hierarchy of object clusters. This is achieved by combining shadow maps of the sub-clusters hierar-chically.

The resulting error-driven algorithm automatically computes soft shadows at interactive rates for extended light sources of arbitrary shape and exitance distribution, while avoiding excessive approxi-mation under a feature-based error metric. The method can be used in any rendering technique, with the only requirement of a hierar-chy of spatial clusters in order to use the hierarchical combination. The algorithm is naturally adaptive and eliminates the difficulties associated with light source sampling. The error-driven hierarchi-cal combination of shadow maps lets us adapt the effort to user-specified approximation tolerances.

Because it uses a single rendered image of the blocker to gen-erate the soft shadows, our technique effectively trades graphics performance for raw computing performance in the form of FFT calculations and image manipulation, which makes it interesting for computers with low or mid-range graphics capabilities.

The remainder of this paper is organized as follows: Section 2 re-views previous approaches to shadow generation and discusses our goals; Section 3 explains the basic convolution method for comput-ing shadow maps, and Section 4 extends the technique to general source and receiver configurations. A number of implementation choices and details are presented in Section 5. Section 6 then dis-cusses the different sources of error and presents our error-driven hierarchical combination method for shadow maps. We present re-sults obtained in a variety of configurations in Section 7, discuss the merits of the approach in Section 8 and conclude in Section 9.

2 Previous work

Woo *et al.* present an excellent survey of the vast literature on shadow algorithms [31], and we will only briefly review here some of the main approaches, especially the few that allow the computation of soft shadows.

Sampling methods

Ray tracing algorithms compute shadows by casting a ray between a point lying on a surface, and a designated light source [29]. This blends very nicely with the rest of the ray tracing technique, but is quite expensive since each ray must in effect sample the scene for potential occluders. Soft shadows are generated in *distributed ray tracing* by casting several rays towards a set of sample points on an extended light source [5].

Another sampling option is to create a depth image from the point of view of the light source [30]. This *shadow buffer* can be used to check whether a given point, visible in the final image, is visible from the source. The severe aliasing issues experienced in a naive approach can be treated using elaborate depth filtering [21]. This approach uses a single point on the light source and therefore can not render penumbrae due to extended light sources.

Using auxiliary data structures

To avoid the cost of brute force sampling, a specific data structure can be created that represents the visibility relationships in the scene. Such structures vary widely in complexity and cost, and essentially allow a time gain because they let us benefit from the *coherence* of visibility in space.

Shadow volumes are constructed relatively easily from a point light source and polygonal occluders [6], and visible points can be quickly tested for inclusion in object space when rendering an image. Complex volumes can be represented and used efficiently through the use of BSP trees [3]. Approximate soft shadows are obtained by combining several shadow volumes, each corresponding to a sample point on the extended source [2].

A better structure for extended light sources records visibility information on the surfaces of the scene, in the form of a *discontinuity mesh* that includes all lines where the illumination function has discontinuities of various orders. Unless an occluder touches a receiver, the illumination function from an extended source is continuous, and exhibits discontinuities only in its derivatives. Techniques for computing discontinuity meshes operate by considering all possible *visual events* and inserting critical lines in an explicit mesh structure [11, 15], which makes them both quite expensive to use and subject to robustness issues. However, they can provide exact visibility [8] and produce images of the highest quality.

Interactive shadow generation

Shadows can be generated while displaying the scene, using one or more extra rendering passes. This is of course especially interesting when hardware acceleration is available to perform the various passes and combine the results. For instance, shadow maps from point or directional light sources can be created by the rendering pipeline and applied using texture mapping operations [23]. Shadow volumes can be combined using the stencil buffers [7].

The only method we are aware of for pre-calculating soft shadows at interactive rates is Heckbert and Herf's [13], where a number of shadow images are created, registered and averaged on the receiver. Each image corresponds to a sample point on the light source, and they are all combined using the accumulation buffer [9]. This method works very well on high-end graphics machine, but essentially produces a superposition of "hard" shadows. The shadows cast by the individual samples are usually noticeable unless a very large number of samples is used.

Shadows and illumination techniques

The radiosity method is often credited with a unique ability to render subtle effects such as soft shadows and illumination details. Radiosity techniques are based on a surface mesh used to compute, store and reconstruct illumination functions. The exchange of energy between mesh elements is evaluated using *form factors* to represent the effect of orientation, geometric attenuation and visibility. Most modern form factor calculation methods actually decouple the estimation of an "unoccluded" form factor based on the radiosity kernel, from that of a *visibility factor* expressing the fraction of the area of the source element that is visible from the receiver [4, 27, 10].

Zatz [32] pushes this idea further by proposing the separate calculation of sampled *shadow masks* to represent the effects of visibility in a separate step. Several authors observed that in the case of ideal diffuse scenes, the entire illumination can be recorded into *radiosity textures*. Such textures can be precomputed off-line, then allowing high-quality rendering with soft shadows at interactive rates [12, 18]. Keller's "instant radiosity" technique [14] computes radiosity textures in a manner similar to Heckbert's, by averaging shadow images from point samples chosen on the surfaces.

In order to simulate the complex shadows due to sunlight and skylight under tree canopies (as shown in the "Sun and Shade" movie [16]), Max used the convolution of a radiance image of the sky with a transparency mask of the canopy [17].

Multiresolution shadows

Experimental evidence suggests that while shadows are important in a 3D rendering, they need not necessarily be exact [28]: this is well known by drawing artists who often sketch an approximate shadow with "appropriate" characteristics to increase realism. This idea was applied to the calculation of multi-resolution visibility factors in the context of hierarchical radiosity and clustering [24]. For a given source/receiver pair, an "appropriate" level in the hierarchical representation of the occluders is selected, and used to create an approximate shadow based on an analogy with semi-transparent volumes. This work effectively produces shadows of variable resolution and cost, but does not provide bounds on the error incurred. Such bounds can be computed in a simplified 2d case [26] but appear very difficult to compute in 3D, mainly because the identification of a cluster to a semi-transparent object is too crude.

Discussion

Our goal is to provide a shadowing algorithm running at interactive rates, in a manner similar to Heckbert's. However, we want to avoid the sampling artifacts produced when averaging hard shadows, without having to resort to very large numbers of samples (more than 100 can be necessary for large sources [20]). On the other hand, we do not want to build expensive data structures to represent visibility, but rather to compute necessary information on the fly. The convolution algorithm explained below can be seen as an extension of Max's method [17], and meets these goals by always providing a smooth image in soft shadow regions.

3 Obtaining soft shadows with convolution

In this section we present the basis of our technique in the form of an algorithm for producing a shadow map across a given receiver, subject to the illumination of an extended light source and to shadows cast by a set of objects. We first explain how the shadow can be expressed as a convolution operation, in the special case of parallel objects, and then propose an extension to the general case.

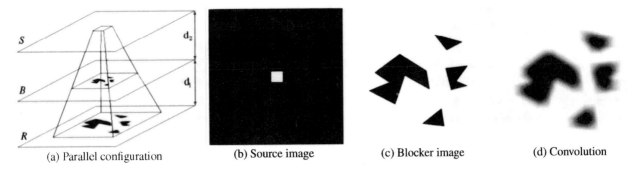

| (a) Parallel configuration | (b) Source image | (c) Blocker image | (d) Convolution |

Figure 1: A simple case of parallel light source (S), occluder (B) and receiver (R). The source image is convolved with the blocker image to obtain the shadow map.

3.1 Convolution formula for a set of parallel objects

Let us first consider the special case where the light source, the receiver and the occluder are all planar, and lie in parallel planes (Figure 1). The irradiance [23] at a point y on the receiver is:

$$H(y) = \frac{E}{\pi} \int_S \frac{\cos(\theta(x,y))\cos(\theta'(x,y))}{d(x,y)^2} v(x,y) dx$$

where E is the exitance [23] of the source, $d(x,y)$ the distance between x and y, θ and θ' the incident angles of the ray $x \longrightarrow y$ on the source and the receiver, and $v(x,y)$ a binary *visibility function* indicating whether x and y are mutually visible.

A common approximation, e.g. in radiosity algorithms, consists of separating the visibility factor in a distinct integral to obtain:

$$H(y) \approx E \underbrace{\int_S \frac{\cos\theta\cos\theta'}{\pi d^2} dx}_{F_S(y)} \underbrace{\int_S v(x,y) dx}_{V(y)} \qquad (1)$$

The first term $F_S(y)$ is the unoccluded *point-to-polygon* form factor from y to the source, and the second term $V(y)$ is the visible area of the source as seen from y. This approximation implicitly assumes a low correlation between the variations of visibility and the radiosity kernel, an assumption that is reasonable in most cases. In this paper we are focusing on the calculation of $V(y)$. The unoccluded form factor can be computed using integration formulae [20] or approximated using the hardware shading model [13].

Computing $V(y)$ is equivalent to projecting the blocker onto the source from y and measuring the remaining unoccluded area of the source. In the present case, because all three components are parallel, the projection of the blocker simply translates on the source as y moves on the receiver. This is precisely why the unoccluded area of the source can be expressed as a convolution between the source and blocker images.

More formally, let us now introduce the following *characteristic* functions of the source and blocker in their respective planes:

$$S(x) = \begin{cases} 1 & \text{if } x \text{ is on the source} \\ 0 & \text{elsewhere} \end{cases}$$

$$P(x) = \begin{cases} 0 & \text{if } x \text{ is on the occluder} \\ 1 & \text{elsewhere} \end{cases}$$

We can use P to express the binary visibility value between two points x and y, by introducing the point of intersection of the xy line and the plane of the blocker. The visibility factor can then be written as

$$V(y) = \int_S P\left(\frac{d_1 x + d_2 y}{d_1 + d_2}\right) dx$$

To show that this expression is a convolution, let us transform $V(y)$ by extending the integration over the entire plane:

$$V(y) = \int_{\mathbb{R}^2} S(x) P\left(\frac{d_1 x + d_2 y}{d_1 + d_2}\right) dx$$

$$= \left(\frac{d_2}{d_1}\right)^2 \int_{\mathbb{R}^2} s_\alpha(-t) p_{1+\alpha}(t+y) dt$$

$$= \frac{1}{\alpha^2} (s_\alpha \star p_{1+\alpha})(y)$$

where

$$\alpha = \frac{d_1}{d_2} \qquad s_\alpha(x) = S(-\frac{1}{\alpha}x) \qquad p_{1+\alpha}(x) = P(\frac{1}{1+\alpha}x) \qquad (2)$$

and $\star$ denotes a convolution operation. Therefore, in this particular geometric configuration, the visibility factor reduces to the convolution of the scaled characteristic functions of the source and blocker.

Note that this particular form of the visibility term implies that it is continuous, therefore implicitly creating soft shadow variations on the receiver. An example of convolution between source and blocker images is presented in Figure 1. For a diffuse surface, we can express the radiosity function B on the receiver by introducing the diffuse reflectance $\rho(y)$ and using Eq. (1):

$$B(y) \approx \frac{\rho(y)E}{\alpha^2} F_S(y)(s_\alpha \star p_{1+\alpha})(y) \qquad (3)$$

Therefore, a possible algorithm for displaying soft shadows is to compute a shadow map using the convolution formula, and use it as a texture to modulate the illumination function $\rho(y)EF_S(y)$ across the receiver.

3.2 Computation of soft shadows in general configurations

We will see in Section 5 that Equation (3) can be used in an efficient algorithm to create illumination textures. But its value is of course severely limited by the assumption that all objects are planar and parallel. In real applications, not only can light sources and receivers be placed at arbitrary orientations, but occluders can also in general occupy a complex volume in 3D.

In a general source/blocker/receiver configuration, it is not possible to derive a convolution formula similar to Eq.(3). Nevertheless, we propose to approximate the resulting shadow effect by using the convolution method for a *virtual geometry* that obeys the preceding requirements, and transform the associated result to fit the actual geometry of the scene. This involves the following operations:

a) choosing a direction $\mathcal{D}$ and a set of three planes containing respectively a virtual source S_v, a virtual blocker B_v and a virtual receiver R_v, all planar and orthogonal to $\mathcal{D}$;

b) computing the illumination function on the virtual receiver using the convolution formula (3);

c) projecting the result back on the actual receiver.

Clearly, depending on the actual geometry of the scene, such an approximation may produce some artifacts. The different sources of error and the way to control them are addressed in Section 6. We now discuss each of these steps in more detail.

3.2.1 Choice of the virtual geometry

The choice of the direction of projection $\mathcal{D}$ is the first issue to be addressed. Obviously, the nature and importance of the approximation will largely depend on this choice. We will discuss this question in more detail in Section 5.1. For now, we observe that it seems natural to have $\mathcal{D}$ be some average of the directions actually involved in the transfer of energy. Therefore we suggest as a possibility to choose $\mathcal{D}$ to be the mean direction of all possible rays between the source and the receiver (Figure 2.(a)).

Once $\mathcal{D}$ has been chosen, it defines the orientation of the three virtual planes. Let us denote by Z an axis parallel to $\mathcal{D}$. Then, we choose altitude values z_s, z_b and z_r for the three virtual planes (Figure 2.(b)). The choice of these values is discussed in Section 5.2.

Each component is now projected onto its virtual plane: The virtual source is obtained from the source by orthographic projection along $\mathcal{D}$. Thus, viewed from the blocker, this virtual source has nearly the same aspect as the original one (See Figure 2.(c)).

The virtual blocker is the projection of the original blocker on the virtual blocker plane. The projection used is a perspective projection, with eye set to the center of the source (See Figure 2.c). Using the same projection onto the virtual receiver plane, we obtain the virtual receiver from the original one. Viewed from the center of the source, the original and virtual blockers (resp. receivers) are thus identical.

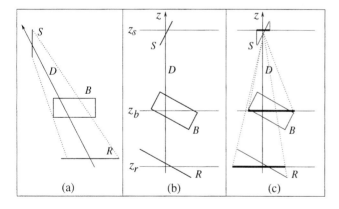

(a)   (b)   (c)

Figure 2: Construction of a virtual source, blocker and receiver for a general shadow configuration. (a) Choosing a preferred direction. (b) Choosing altitudes for the virtual planes. (c) Projecting the original elements to obtain their virtual counterparts.

3.2.2 Back to the actual geometry

Once computed for the virtual receiver, the visibility term $V(y)$ is projected back to the actual receiver where it is multiplied by the direct illumination factor from the source $\rho E F_S(y)$. In practice, the convolution image is set as a shadow texture and modulated by direct illumination values for uniformly sampled points on the receiver.

4 Extensions to the basic principle

In this section we show that our convolution method can be adapted with little modification to even more general lighting conditions. Non-uniform light sources, sources with complex 3D shapes, and complex receiver shapes can all be simulated. Practical examples for each of the three cases are presented in Section 7. In particular, we show that groups of objects can be used to model sources or receivers in a single shadow map calculation.

4.1 Dealing with non-uniform radiosity over light sources

When the source is not uniform, but still planar, we can modify the derivation of Section 3, replacing the uniform exitance term E by a non-uniform exitance $E(x)$:

$$
\begin{aligned}
B(y) &= \frac{\rho}{\pi} \int_S \frac{\cos\theta\cos\theta'}{d^2} E(x)v(x,y)dx \\
&= \frac{\rho}{\pi} \int_S \frac{\cos\theta\cos\theta'}{d^2}dx \int_S E(x)v(x,y)dx
\end{aligned}
$$

Replacing S by $S \times E$ in the derivation of Equation 3, the "visibility" term $V(y)$ turns into:

$$
\begin{aligned}
V(y) &= \int_{\mathbb{R}^2} S(x)E(x)v(x,y)dx \\
&= \frac{1}{\alpha^2}(s'_\alpha \star p_{1+\alpha})
\end{aligned}
$$

Where

$$
s'_\alpha(x) = S(-\frac{1}{\alpha}x)E(-\frac{1}{\alpha}x)
$$

This is another convolution, which can easily be calculated using our method by equipping the source with a texture containing its relative exitance function before rendering it to the offscreen buffer. We essentially include the variations of the source's emission in the visibility integral, with the double advantage that (a) the calculation of the unoccluded illumination is not modified, and (b) the potential correlation between visibility and source emission is properly accounted for.

Note that the same approach could lead to adapt our method for translucent occluders by replacing the binary term $P(x)$ by a more general one varying in the range $[0, 1]$. However, translucent object generally operate in a non linear manner on light propagation (because of refraction and diffusion), which prevents us from deriving a proper convolution based formula.

4.2 Complex light source shapes

Three-dimensional light sources do not require much more computation than a planar light source: All we need is the projection of the source onto its virtual plane. Apart from computing its projection in the offscreen buffer, using a volumetric source requires attention to be paid to the choice of direction $\mathcal{D}$, which will not follow the same criteria as those described for a planar light source.

4.3 Simultaneously shadowing a group of objects

Just as for a polygonal receiver, a shadow map can be assigned to an entire cluster. The shadow map is then shared among objects, while each surface receives its own texture coordinates.

Note that this does not address self shadowing in the cluster, which may be achieved by applying our method using one part of the receiving cluster as a potential occluder for the remaining part.

5 Practical computation of shadow textures

We now describe our implementation, in which we use the convolution operation to create soft shadow textures. We have integrated this algorithm in our research testbed for hierarchical radiosity, but it should be noted that it can be used in other environments as well. We make use of two features of the radiosity system: first, we use the form factor calculation routines to evaluate the unoccluded illumination term. Second, we use the hierarchy of object clusters to select potential occluders between a given pair of source and receiver. Other techniques could be used to compute the illumination, such as Heckbert's combination of hardware point sources [13]. As for the cluster hierarchy, common structures such as hierarchies of bounding volumes are easily constructed and provide the necessary hierarchy.

Let us assume for now that we have selected a light source, a receiver object and a cluster of occluders. Such configurations can be automatically selected by ranking their potential for the creation of soft shadows, as a function of their absolute and relative sizes and distances. For each of the issues discussed below, we suggest a suitable strategy or solution.

5.1 Choice of the direction of projection

As suggested earlier, the direction of projection $\mathcal{D}$ must adequately represent the set of all possible rays between the source and the receiver. If the source and receiver are planar surfaces, we first determine a *useful receiver* by clipping the receiver by the source plane and a *useful source* by clipping the source by the receiver plane. This operation prevents $\mathcal{D}$ from being parallel to the source, which would produce a empty source image, or parallel to the receiver, which would make the computed texture projection fail. We then restrict the set of rays between the useful source and receiver to rays that actually encounter the blocker (that is, the extent of the cluster's bounding box). The direction of projection is chosen as a median value into this set.

The choice of the direction $\mathcal{D}$ does not affect the placement of umbra and penumbra regions, but for some special cases, such as the subdivision of the receiver, we shall see that it can be important not to choose $\mathcal{D}$ for each receiver independently.

5.2 Choice of the virtual planes

The choice of the altitudes of the virtual planes directly affects the size of the resulting penumbra regions in the computed texture. Altitudes for the virtual planes of the receiver, source, and blocker could simply be chosen as the centers of the altitude ranges of the three elements (See Figure 2.(b)), but more accuracy can be achieved on the resulting shadow texture by choosing the altitudes so as to obtain penumbra regions of median sizes in the range of those actually produced.

We will explain in Section 6.2 how to compute the size of the actual and computed penumbra. Using this calculation we can compute an "optimal" virtual blocker altitude which creates the desired median size: denoting by z_s and z_r the virtual source and receiver altitudes, and by z_b^{min} and z_b^{max} the extremal altitudes of blocking objects, the optimal altitude for the virtual blocker is

$$z_b^{opt} = \frac{D_1 z_b^{min} + D_2 z_b^{max}}{D_1 + D_2} \quad \text{where} \quad D_1 = z_s - z_b^{max} \quad \text{and} \quad D_2 = z_s - z_b^{min}$$

5.3 Sampling the virtual source and blocker characteristic functions

In order to perform the convolution, we need two images of the scaled characteristic functions following Equation (3). These images of the virtual source and blocker are obtained by rendering the objects that constitute the real source and blocker, using the projections previously described, in an offscreen buffer of desired size.

Source and blocker frustum are scaled to achieve the required α and $1 + \alpha$ scaling factor with respect to the intrinsic dimensions of the objects, as dictated by Equation (2).

Polygons are rendered in white over a black background, with no z-buffering. Note that a non-uniform source is rendered with a texture modulating its color to follow its relative exitance function. The blocker image is inverted while reading pixel values from the offscreen buffer. In addition, the negative sign in the convolution Equation (2) means that the source image must be reflected across its horizontal and vertical axes. This is achieved by scaling the geometric model of the source with a negative factor when rendering.

Selection of the blocker frustum

The blocker frustum actually used is computed as the intersection of the receiver and blocker frustums viewed from the source (Figure 3). This avoids the computation of large unshadowed areas when the blocker is too small, and the computation of too large a texture when the receiver is too small or when the source is very close to the blocker. The *near* and *far* clipping planes are set so as to capture the blocking polygons in this regions and to avoid projecting irrelevant geometry.

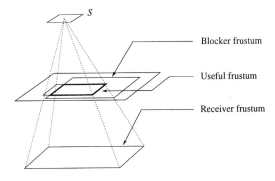

Figure 3: Construction of the blocker projection frustum

Computing the convolution

Once computed, the source and blocker images can be convolved using the following well known property:

$$(f \star g)(y) = \mathcal{F}^{-1}(\mathcal{F}(f) \times \mathcal{F}(g))$$

where $\mathcal{F}(f)$ denotes the Fourier transform of function f. Since we are dealing with 2D images, we perform a two dimensional FFT on each image, multiply them and finally transform the result by a normalized inverse FFT. The result is a sampled version of the visibility function $V(y)$. We use the standard FFT library supplied by SGI on our systems.

5.4 Security zone for proper convolution

When performing the convolution of two images with a Fourier transform, we implicitly assume the images to be periodic. This is obviously true for the source image by construction (because the source is strictly contained in the image), but it is not always the case for the blocker image, because of the clipping operation by the receiver frustum. As a result, the sum of the image space sizes s_1 and s_2 of the windows actually occupied by the source and blocker sampled functions must not exceed the total sampling window size *s*. To ensure this property, we further scale both frustums by a factor of $\frac{s}{s_1+s_2}$, which is the secure scale factor that allows the greatest relative resolution for the effective texture (See Figure 4).

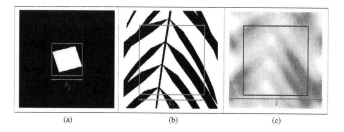

Figure 4: An example convolution between a source image (a) and a blocker image (b), for which the receiver clips the blocker frustum. The red square on the blocker image indicates the interesting area for the given receiver. The source and blocker frustums have been equally scaled until $s_1 + s_2 < s$ (note that enlarging the frustum reduces the effective size s_1 and s_2). In the resulting image (c), pixels outside the blue region are spoiled by FFT wrap-around effects and are not used in the shadow map.

5.5 Resolution issues

The resolution of the shadow map should be chosen carefully. On the one hand, it determines the resolution of all auxiliary images for the convolution operation, and the cost of the convolution itself (See the results in Section 7). On the other hand, it should be appropriate for the size of the receiver in object space and the variations of penumbra across its surface: Whereas a nearly hard shadow due to a small spotlight demands a large texture to be rendered accurately, a very smooth shadow mainly based on penumbra does not require very dense sampling. Such situations can be easily characterized since they simply depend on α. Section 7 shows practical examples of scenes with the texture sizes used.

Due to the different scaling factors, and especially for small values of α, the source sample can actually have a different area (ratio between the numbers of white and black pixels) than that of an ideally sampled image. This area plays an important role in the texture as it determines the maximum value of the convolution. Thus, a wrong area value on the source produces inappropriately normalized shadow maps, with annoying discontinuity artifacts. This problem can be addressed using antialiased rendering for the source, so that the area of the source sample has a more accurate value. Unfortunately, depending on the OpenGL implementation, the value of a pixel in an antialiased polygon is not always exactly the area of the pixel fractions covered by the polygon [17].

Blocker aliasing does not affect the resulting textures in the same way, but antialiasing is also required for the blocker characteristic function to avoid inconsistencies or discontinuities in the penumbra regions, caused by very long and fine blocking objects. The images of the mobile in Figure 12 would be particularly affected without antialiasing.

5.6 Using the shadow texture

As previously stated, the computed convolution image is used as a shadow texture on the receiver, modulated by direct illumination values.

Since we need to represent the variations of the unoccluded illumination across the receiver, we create –for display purposes only– a regular mesh of vertices P_i. Each vertex of this mesh is equipped with a color value computed as $\rho(P_i)EF_S(P_i)$.

When rendering, the receiver is displayed as a textured triangle strip set. For each vertex, texture coordinates are computed by projecting the corresponding receiver point onto the virtual receiver plane. These coordinates can either be pre-computed and stored with the mesh, or directly computed by *OpenGL* by adequately setting the texture projection matrix[17]. However, since texture coordinates are provided only for those vertices, the mesh size must account for both the illumination gradient on the receiver, and the strength of the deformation due to the projection from the virtual receiver. Practically, typical mesh sizes range from 2×2 for small polygons (For example the cubes in Figure 14) to 20×20 for walls.

The unoccluded point to area form factors are computed using the exact point-to-polygon formula[1]. When the receiver is a cluster of objects, each surface receives its own display mesh of adequate size.

6 Error-driven shadow computation

Although, by construction, our method places umbra and penumbra regions in the right place, the different approximations do not lead to exact illumination values. In this section, we first examine the different sources of error and the way to quantify this error. We then review possible refinement techniques to produce more accurate results, and finally present a hierarchical algorithm to compute the shadow texture with a given precision.

6.1 Qualitative discussion of error sources

Virtual blocker

To characterize the error due to the use of the virtual blocker, let us consider the case where the receiver is parallel to the source. Since the light source is not a single point, the umbra of the (planar) virtual blocker will differ from that of the actual blocker in the following two respects:

- When projecting the actual blocker to the virtual one, all the triple-edge discontinuity curves [15] of the discontinuity mesh collapses into Edge-Vertex events. This modification of the discontinuity mesh's internal topology affects the illumination gradient into penumbra regions. This effect is all the more noticeable that the source is large.

- Since all parts of the virtual blocker share the same altitude, all computed penumbra regions will have the same sharpness. This is the most obvious visual effect of using a virtual blocker.

Projection on the receiver

Let us consider the blocker to be planar and parallel to the source, and study the difference between the umbra directly computed on the actual receiver and that projected back from the virtual one.

Although the projection of the shadow texture back onto the actual receiver tends to produce a general shadow region of the right size, it also conserves the size ratio of penumbra and umbra regions. This ratio on an actual receiver strongly depends on the distance between the receiving point and the source. Thus the computed shadow on a large receiver may show umbra where there actually is penumbra, or the reverse.

6.2 Measuring the error

A simple way to estimate the error would be to derive a bound on the difference between the exact and computed shadow functions, depending on the virtual geometry parameters. Although such a method based on standard L_1, L_2 or L_∞ distances would produce conservative bounds on the global error, it would not allow a reliable characterization of the shadow artifacts, because of its inherent non-locality and its lack of coherence towards human perception criteria [22]. We instead consider a form of perceptual error, and study its variation in terms of the virtual geometry parameters.

The most noticeable artifact due to the use of the virtual geometry is the production of penumbra regions of inadequate size. We propose to estimate the ratio between the computed and exact penumbra sizes. The range of variation of this ratio for all points in the configuration will serve as an error measure for the use of the virtual geometry.

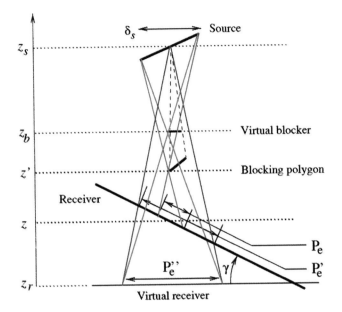

Figure 5: Sizes of computed and exact penumbra regions for a given source/blocker/receiver configuration and virtual planes altitudes z_s, z_b and z_r.

Our error estimate is derived below with a simple reasoning in two dimensions. As shown in Figure 5, the penumbra regions on the virtual receiver (follow red lines), due to a polygon side of the virtual blocker, at a given altitude z_b, have size

$$P_e'' = \alpha \delta_s \quad \text{where} \quad \alpha = \frac{z_b - z_r}{z_s - z_b}$$

After projection (blue lines) onto the actual receiver, at altitude z, the computed penumbra will have approximate size:

$$P_e'(z) = \alpha \delta_s \frac{1}{\cos \gamma} \frac{z_s - z}{z_s - z_r}$$

The penumbra due to the actual blocking polygon at altitude z' can also be approximated by:

$$P_e(z', z) = \delta_s \frac{1}{\cos \gamma} \frac{z' - z}{z_s - z'}$$

Thus, the relative error between the true and computed penumbra will be

$$\Delta_e(z', z) = \frac{P_e'(z)}{P_e(z', z)} = \frac{(z_s - z')(z_s - z)}{z' - z} \times \frac{z_b - z_r}{(z_s - z_r)(z_s - z_b)}$$

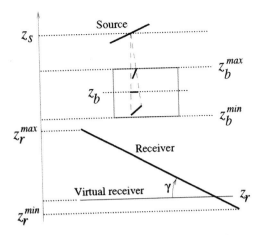

Figure 6: Altitude ranges for the blocker and receiver

Let us assume that the set of blocking objects lies between altitudes z_b^{min} and z_b^{max}, and that the receiver is bounded by z_r^{min} and z_r^{max} (Figure 6). We assume without loss of generality that

$$z_r^{max} < z_b^{min}$$

In this case, the approximation error $\Delta_e(z', z)$ reaches its maximum value for $z = z_r^{max}$ and $z' = z_b^{min}$, and its minimum value for $z = z_r^{min}$ and $z' = z_b^{max}$. The difference between these two extremal values is the maximal error amplitude for the current configuration:

$$E_{max}(Receiver, Blocker) = \Delta_e(z_b^{min}, z_r^{max}) - \Delta_e(z_b^{max}, z_r^{min}) \quad (4)$$

As expected, this error estimate decreases to zero when the blocker and receiver become planar and parallel.

6.3 Reducing the error

Now that we can estimate the amount of approximation incurred, we consider the options available to reduce it. We first list all potential parameters of the problem, and focus on the combination of several shadow maps corresponding to sub-clusters of a given occluder.

6.3.1 Parameters influencing shadow quality

Source subdivision Subdividing the source would help reducing the discontinuity mesh topological error described in Section 6.1, and also improve on the kernel-visibility low correlation assumption. Since these two kinds of error do not significantly affect the visual aspect of the shadow, except for very large light sources, we currently ignore this option.

Image resolution Improving on the shadow texture resolution or on the choice of the direction of projection helps reduce their specific error, but it does not lead to arbitrarily accurate shadow textures, in terms of penumbra accuracy.

Therefore, it is generally more efficient and practical to subdivide either the receiver or the blocker as sketched in Figure 7.

Receiver subdivision Subdividing the receiver into two or more sub-receivers accounts for the different ratios of characteristic sizes of umbra and penumbra for different receiving regions (Figure 7.a).

In this case, a shadow texture is computed separately for each sub-receiver, using the convolution method. This increases the

 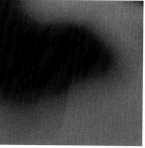 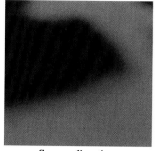 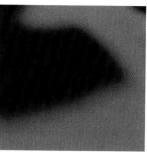

Automatic choice of direction   Source direction   Receiver direction

Figure 8: Artifacts produced along a subdivision boundary on the receiver.

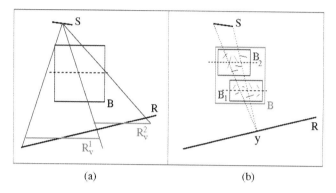

(a)   (b)

Figure 7: (a) A receiver subdivided into two receivers, with their associated virtual receiver. (b) A blocking cluster subdivided into two blocking sub-clusters, with their associated virtual blockers.

computation time, due to the larger number of convolutions to compute, but takes into account different α configurations for the different parts of the subdivided receiver.

Particular attention should be paid to the choice of direction $\mathcal{D}$ for each sub-receiver, as illustrated in Figure 8. As each texture is projected back to its own receiver, boundary artifacts may appear: in this Figure, a receiver patch is subdivided into four receivers (left). The next three images (from left to right) show a shadow detail in the boundary region of two sub-receivers, with three different choices for $\mathcal{D}$:

automatic $\mathcal{D}$ is chosen independently for the four receivers as described in Section 5.1. Note the discontinuity along the boundary, due to non-matching shadow textures.

source $\mathcal{D}$ is the source's normal direction. The four receivers thus have the same direction $\mathcal{D}$, but penumbrae still have different sharpness. The discontinuity is barely noticeable in the penumbra.

receiver $\mathcal{D}$ is the receiver's normal. The four receivers have the same virtual plane, and shadows fit together perfectly.

Thus we see that a proper choice of $\mathcal{D}$ (the same direction for all receivers, in this case) can reduce or eliminate most of the artifacts.

Blocker subdivision When a large set of blocking objects (grouped in a cluster) projects shadows on the receiver, it produces penumbra regions of different sizes. In such a configuration, subdividing the receiver would not suffice. We can expect a more accurate result by considering separately subsets of objects in the cluster (Figure 7.b), computing their associated shadow texture using our convolution method with suitable virtual blockers.

Such a subdivision requires a procedure for combining shadow maps created from the subclusters into a shadow map corresponding to the entire blocking cluster. This issue is addressed in the next section.

6.3.2 Combination of shadow maps from different subclusters

When two blockers are treated separately, all information on their spatial correlation is lost. Thus, exact recombination of the two shadow maps requires the knowledge of the correlation function of the two blockers. The simple experimental case described in Figure 9 illustrates the impossibility of retrieving an exact shadow map value knowing only that of the subclusters.

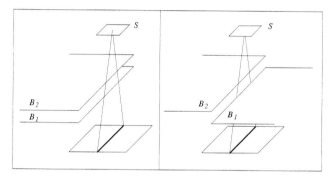

Figure 9: Extremal situations for blocker-to-blocker correlation. For any receiver point y on the bold line, the visibility values $V_1(y)$ and $V_2(y)$ for each separate blocker are exactly $\frac{1}{2}S$. But the actual visibility $V(y)$ is $\frac{1}{2}S$ in the left-hand case, and 0 in the right-hand one. These extremal values are in fact those given by Equation (5).

We propose an approximation method to achieve such a combination for the case of a subdivision into two subclusters. This combination method generalizes readily for more sub-clusters. Let us call $V_1(y)$ and $V_2(y)$ the shadow maps computed for each sub cluster separately, and $V(y)$ the shadow texture associated to the parent cluster. Recalling that the value of the shadow texture is the area of the portion of the source that is visible from a receiver point, we can consider the worst and best correlation cases between blockers 1 and 2 and write:

$$V_2(y) - (S - V_1(y)) \le V(y) \le \min(V_1(y), V_2(y))$$

and thus:

$$\max(0, V_1(y) + V_2(y) - S) \le V(y) \le \min(V_1(y), V_2(y)) \quad (5)$$

(S is the area of the source). Thus, we can use the following median

A test scene.

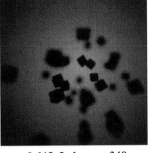

$\varepsilon = 1.0$, 1 cluster, 160 ms.

$\varepsilon = 0.645$, 2 clusters, 340 ms.

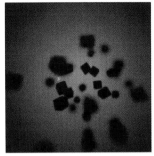

$\varepsilon = 0.452$, 10 clusters, 1055 ms.

Figure 10: Hierarchical combination of shadow maps using a variable number of clusters. In each image, the final shadow map is assembled from as many partial maps as there are selected clusters. Cluster selection is performed using the error estimation described in the text. The reference solution was obtained with ray casting.

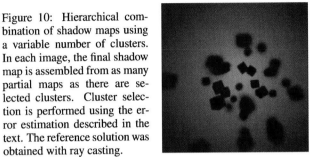

$\varepsilon = 0.387$, 34 clusters, 3.38 s.

$\varepsilon = 0.0$, 210 clusters, 21 s.

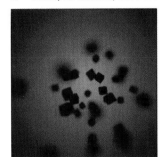

Reference solution.

value for the combined texture, as an approximation of $V(y)$:

$$V_{1,2}(y) = \frac{1}{2}\left(\min(V_1(y),V_2(y)) + \max(0,V_1(y)+V_2(y)-S)\right) \quad (6)$$

The maximum error incurred by this approximation arises in the two configurations depicted in Figure 9 where it reaches the value $\frac{1}{4}S$. It should be noted that such configurations rarely occur, only when two polygons sharing an edge (as viewed from the source) are treated as separate blockers. This is the case in the last image of Figure 10 where the 210 polygons forming the cubes have been used as separate blockers. The visible effect is a slightly faster variation of the penumbra around the shadow of the cubes in comparison to the reference solution.

6.4 Shadow approximation algorithm

We can now organize the preceding elements into a complete hierarchical refinement algorithm, controlled by explicit error estimation.

Refinement criterion

For a given configuration, Equation (4) gives an estimation of the error due to the use of the convolution method. By comparing the error estimates for the two separate cases of blocker and receiver subdivision, we can decide which choice leads to the smallest error on the final texture:

$$
\begin{aligned}
E(R_1,...,R_n,B) &= \max\left(E_{max}(R_1,B),...,E_{max}(R_n,B)\right) \\
E(R,B_1,...,B_p) &= C_{Err} + \max\left(E_{max}(R,B_1),...,E_{max}(R,B_p)\right)
\end{aligned}
$$

C_{Err} is a *combination error* term, that is a bound on the error due to the correlation of sub-cluster shadow maps. It turns out to be negligible in practice. An important property is that for any subcluster b of B, and any sub-receiver r of R, we have

$$E(r,b) \le E(R,B)$$

Equality occurs only when $b = B$ and $r = R$. The refinement algorithm is summarized in Figure 11, where the procedure *ConvolutionTexture(S,B,R)* computes the shadow texture using the given source, blocker and receiver. *CombineTextures* performs the combination of Eq.6 and *PasteTextures* makes a single texture from the texture of the four sub-receivers. When subdividing the cluster of occluders, we save and re-use the Fourier transform of the source image, and adapt the scale of the occluder images to account for the fixed size of the source, thereby saving the cost of one FFT per occluder used. Figure 10 shows the results of the application of this algorithm for different error thresholds. It clearly shows that for a single cluster, all penumbra regions have the same extent, while the range of possible penumbra sizes increases with the number of clusters. The reference solution was computed using ray casting on the true geometry, with 1024 rays per pixel.

```
Texture ComputeTexture(S,B,R)
    if E_max(S,R,B) < ε_max
        return ConvolutionTexture(S,B,R)
    else
        if E(R_1,...,R_n,B) < E(R,B_1,...,B_p)
            T_1 = ComputeTexture(S,B,R_1)
            ...
            T_n = ComputeTexture(S,B,R_n)
            return PasteTexture(T_1,...,T_n)
        else
            T_1 = ComputeTexture(S,B_1,R)
            ...
            T_p = ComputeTexture(S,B_p,R)
            return CombineTextures(T_1,...,T_p)
```

Figure 11: Algorithm for shadow texture computation

Discussion of convergence

Each leaf of the cluster hierarchy contains one or more surfaces, arbitrarily oriented. Thus we cannot refine the blocking clusters into arbitrarily small subclusters. The maximum extent δ_z of atomic objects in the blocking cluster produces the minimum possible error of the computed texture, using criterion (4). The associated texture artifact will be localized in the shadow region produced by the object, and can be imputed to the object model quality.

Conversely, the possibility of refining the receiver is only limited by the allowed computation time for the shadow map.

Our subdivision criterion does not take into account the size and orientation of the source, which means that it does not capture the totality of the error, and that the images do not fully converge to the true images.

7 Results

We present in this section a number of images illustrating the results of our algorithm. As a general rule, shadowed polygons (walls, objects) are entirely illuminated using our convolution method, whereas blockers themselves are illuminated using standard radiosity computation, without any extra visibility treatment. Computation times are given for the shadow texture treatment only, since any illumination method could be used for other objects, including hardware lighting.

7.1 Breakdown of computation time

The scenes used for the following images contain between 212 and 45,000 polygons, mainly concentrated into the blockers. Offscreen rendering times range from less than 1 ms to about 160 ms on SGI Onyx2/iR and $O2$ computers. The cost of one FFT calculation is proportional to $n \log n$, where n is the number of pixels in the images. Therefore this cost is very sensitive to the resolution of the shadow maps. On the Onyx2 we observe the following computation times (in milliseconds, for the calculation of a single representative map such as that the floor). The corresponding images can be seen in Figure 10 (Cubes, 212 polygons), Figure 14 (Pyramid, 4340 polygons) and Figure 12 (Mobile, 45000 polygons).

Text. size	FFT	Cubes	Pyramid	Mobile
128	6	50	60	220
256	25	170	170	340
512	110	610	620	770
1024	500	2510	2540	2730

For comparison, the same operations on the $O2$ take similar amounts of time:

Texture size	FFT	Cubes	Pyramid
512	170	1100	1190
1024	770	5440	4980

In each case we indicate the total time to compute a shadow map, and in the FFT column the time for a single FFT operation. Three FFTs are needed to obtain a shadow map, and other image-based operations take another 140% of the time of a single FFT. We see that the cost of FFTs dominates for textures of 512^2 pixels and higher. Note that these are fairly large texture sizes, used only for large polygons (walls...) in the images. Smaller textures suffice for most objects.

7.2 Hierarchical combination of shadow maps

Figure 12 demonstrates the use of the hierarchical shadow map combination of Section 6.3.2. The scene contains 45,000 polygons, mostly in the complex objects attached to the mobile. The resolution of the three shadow maps is 256×256 for the images shown, although it should be noted that half this size produces almost indistinguishable results. Therefore we indicate computation times for both 128 and 256 resolution.

7.3 Casting shadows on several surfaces at once

Figure 14 shows a cluster of cubes for which a single 128×128 shadow map has been calculated. Each polygon of the cluster is equipped with a coarse display mesh (2×2 to 3×3) containing unoccluded form factor to the source. 512×512 shadow maps are used for the floor and walls. The same occluding cluster containing the plant has been used for all maps. The plant itself is made out of $4,340$ polygons.

7.4 Complex light sources

Figure 13.(a) illustrates the lighting effects that can be simulated when a light source with a complicated shape casts shadows. The "98" shape is three-dimensional text, made of 360 triangles. A 256×256 texture has been computed for each of the three walls using the "hole" cluster as an occluder.

Figure 13.(b) shows how a single convolution can create the effect of several small sources. Note that the stepping effect is normal here, because there really are four distinct small sources in the scene. A single image of the cluster of light sources is used (shown in Figure 13.(c)).

Figure 13.(d) demonstrates shadows cast by elongated light sources: with neon tubes, penumbra regions are smooth in the direction parallel to the tubes, but exhibit a stepping effect in the direction perpendicular, to the axes of the tubes.

8 Discussion

Our results demonstrate the advantage of a convolution method over an explicit sampling method, in that penumbra regions are always continuous. Note that we are still performing a discrete sampling of the source via the offscreen rendering step, but we are able to treat many samples in a single operation (and the samples are antialiased). Our method can be considered to encompass Heckbert's [13] since we can simulate an extended light source with non-uniform exitance distribution, where only a fixed number of sample points have non-zero energy. In our images, we have chosen to use light sources of small or moderate size, so that shadows contained identifiable penumbra/umbra regions. Naturally our method works for light sources of any size, whereas sampling methods would have to use very large numbers of samples.

Even when no subdivision is performed (i.e. with a single occluding cluster grouping all potential occluders), the method produces visually pleasing images without stepping effects. Note that all occluders are always taken into account exactly once with their complete shape, no matter how many clusters are used in the hierarchical subdivision. In this respect, our method provides a better solution to multi-resolution shadow calculation than the simple volume approximation of [22]. As more hierarchical levels are used to recombine shadow maps, better shadows are obtained, and the computation time becomes dominated by the cost of the FFT.

Interestingly, we observe that our method in essence trades graphics performance for raw compute power, since it renders a single image of the source and occluder but requires a number of FFT calculations. This paradigm shift appears consistent with the

1 cluster, 660 ms / 980 ms.   7 clusters, 1.1s / 2.75s.   21 clusters, 2.2s / 7.4s.

Figure 12: Hierarchical combination of shadow maps: results obtained with different error thresholds, requiring more and more shadow textures to be computed. Two timings are given for each image (3 textures in each), for texture resolutions of 128^2 and 256^2 pixels.

  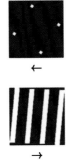 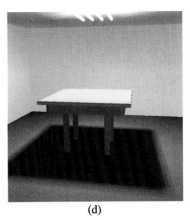

(a)   (b)   (c)   (d)

Figure 13: Shadows cast by complex light sources: (a) 3D source (b) set of small sources (c) light source images (d) elongated sources .

Figure 14: A single 128×128 shadow map was computed for the cluster of cubes, and used to obtain shadows on each individual cube according to its location in space.

evolution of computer technology. We also note that DSP chips are commonly found on multimedia computers, and significantly accelerate FFT calculations. In fact, tests run on DSP-equipped *O2* computers show that the FFT cost for large images is comparable to that of the Onyx2.

Finally, the algorithm is highly parallelisable. Not only can we compute FFTs in parallel, but also the recombination operations for blocker or receiver subdivision.

As for any approximation method, there exist extremal cases where our algorithm does not work properly. One example of this could be obtained using a large blocking polygon that lies in a plane containing the direction $\mathcal{D}$. In such a case, the blocker image is nearly empty and hardly no shadow is produced. Subdividing the source into two regions that see a particular side of the polygon and adding the associated shadow maps together would correct this problem.

Large objects touching the receiver also produce bad configurations unless they can be subdivided because the ideal α values for such objects range from 0 (for parts of the polygons that touch the receiver) to larger values that produce smoother shadows. For a table lying on the floor, for example, although the shadows are produced in the right place, they appear to be too smooth where the table legs touch the floor. In such a configuration, explicit sampling methods would produce better results [13].

9 Conclusions and Future Work

We have presented a new calculation method for soft shadows from extended light sources. The method is based on the expression of visibility functions using convolution operations. It allows the simulation of soft shadows from complex light sources or clusters, having complex shapes and non-uniform exitance distributions. Receivers can be individual surfaces or object clusters, in which case shadows are correctly cast on all objects of the cluster. Occluders can be arbitrary object clusters.

The approximations introduced by the formulation as a convolution have been discussed, and a hierarchical algorithm has been proposed for the combination of shadow maps from sub-clusters. A subdivision criterion was derived to limit the error incurred in the size of the penumbra regions. The algorithm is automatic and can be readily integrated in existing rendering systems.

Future work includes the extension of the convolution approach to other illumination problems. For instance the illumination by the hemispherical sky dome can also be expressed as a convolution. This was first shown by Max in a restricted case where a horizontal plane is used to model skylight [17]. The expression of the illumination kernel, in the absence of occlusion and for parallel source/receiver pairs, is also a convolution.

The current hierarchical combination algorithm will not be able to compute an exact shadow if the clusters contain an object whose "vertical" extent (along the direction of interest) is too large. More elaborate refinement criteria should include provisions to identify such cases and provide alternate methods to compute associated shadow maps, which can then be combined in the same way with those obtained by convolution.

Another important research direction is the re-use of source and occluder images: saving the cost of the associated FFT would significantly accelerate the process for large textures. Image-based rendering methods could perhaps be adapted to derive such images from a set of precomputed images. Such a derivation would have to take place in the Fourier domain to be really effective.

10 Acknowledgments

This work was supported in part by grants from the Région Rhône-Alpes (EMERGENCE) and the European Union (Esprit LTR 24 944: ARCADE). The anonymous reviewers provided a wealth of useful suggestions and comments, which greatly helped improving the paper. Many thanks to Frédo Durand, George Drettakis, and all the iMAGIS team for fruitful discussions and moral support.

References

[1] Daniel R. Baum, Holly E. Rushmeier, and James M. Winget. Improving Radiosity Solutions Through the Use of Analytically Determined Form-Factors. *Computer Graphics*, 23(3):325–334, July 1989. Proceedings SIGGRAPH '89.

[2] Lynne Shapiro Brotman and Norman I. Badler. Generating soft shadows with a depth buffer algorithm. *IEEE Computer Graphics and Applications*, 4(10):5–24, Oct. 1984.

[3] Norman Chin and Steven Feiner. Near real-time shadow generation using bsp trees. *Computer Graphics*, 23(3):99–106, July 1989. Proceedings SIGGRAPH '89.

[4] Michael F. Cohen and Donald P. Greenberg. The hemi-cube : A radiosity solution for complex environments. *Computer Graphics*, 19(3):31–40, July 1985. Proceedings SIGGRAPH '85.

[5] Robert L. Cook, Thomas Porter, and Loren Carpenter. Distributed Ray Tracing. *Computer Graphics*, 18(3):137–145, July 1984. Proceedings SIGGRAPH '84.

[6] Franklin C. Crow. Summed-area tables for texture mapping. *Computer Graphics*, 18:207–212, July 1984. Proceedings SIGGRAPH '84.

[7] Paul J. Diefenbach and Norman I. Badler. Multi-pass pipeline rendering: Realism for dynamic environments. In *1997 Symposium on Interactive 3D Graphics*. ACM SIGGRAPH, 1997.

[8] George Drettakis and Eugene Fiume. A fast shadow algorithm for area light sources using backprojection. In *Proceedings SIGGRAPH '94*, pages 223–230, 1994.

[9] Paul Haeberli and Kurt Akeley. The accumulation buffer: Hardware support for high-quality rendering. *Computer Graphics*, 24(4):309–318, August 1990. Proceedings SIGGRAPH '90.

[10] Pat Hanrahan, David Saltzman, and Larry Aupperle. A rapid hierarchical radiosity algorithm. *Computer Graphics*, 25(4):197–206, August 1991. Proceedings SIGGRAPH '91.

[11] Paul Heckbert. Discontinuity meshing for radiosity. *Third Eurographics Workshop on Rendering*, pages 203–226, May 1992.

[12] Paul S. Heckbert. Adaptive radiosity textures for bidirectional ray tracing. *Computer Graphics*, 24(4):145–154, August 1990. Proceedings SIGGRAPH '90.

[13] Paul S. Heckbert and Michael Herf. Simulating soft shadows with graphics hardware. Technical Report TR CMU-CS-97-104, Carnegie Mellon University, January 1997. See also the technical sketch *"Fast Soft Shadows"* at SIGGRAPH'96.

[14] Alexander Keller. Instant radiosity. In *Proceedings SIGGRAPH '97*, pages 49–56, 1997.

[15] Daniel Lischinski, Filippo Tampieri, and Donald P. Greenberg. Discontinuity Meshing for Accurate Radiosity. *IEEE Computer Graphics and Applications*, 12(6):25–39, November 1992.

[16] Nelson Max. Sun and shade, 1988. SIGGRAPH Video Review, ACM. Issue 36, Segment 8. Available from First Priority, P.O. Box 576, Itasca, IL 60143.

[17] Nelson Max. Unified sun and sky illumination for shadows under trees. *CVGIP: Graphical Models and Image Processing*, 53(3):223–230, May 1991.

[18] Karol Myszkowski and Tosiyasu L. Kunii. Texture mapping as an alternative for meshing during walkthrough animation. In *Photorealistic rendering techniques (Proceedings of the Fifth Eurographics Workshop on Rendering)*, pages 375–388. Springer-Verlag, June 1994.

[19] Jackie Neider, Tom Davis, and Mason Woo. *OpenGL Programming Guide*. Addison-Wesley, Reading MA, 1993.

[20] Pierre Poulin and John Amanatides. Shading and shadowing with linear light sources. In *Eurographics '90*, pages 377–386. North-Holland, September 1990.

[21] William T. Reeves, David H. Salesin, and Robert L. Cook. Rendering antialiased shadows with depth maps. *Computer Graphics*, 21(4):283–291, July 1987. Proceedings SIGGRAPH '87.

[22] Peter Schröder and Pat Hanrahan. On the Form Factor Between Two Polygons. In *Proceedings SIGGRAPH '93*, pages 163–164, 1993.

[23] Mark Segal, Carl Korobkin, Rolf van Widenfelt, Jim Foran, and Paul Haeberli. Fast shadows and lighting effects using texture mapping. *Computer Graphics*, 18(2):249–252, July 1992.

[24] François Sillion and George Drettakis. Feature-Based Control of Visibility Error: A Multiresolution Clustering Algorithm for Global Illumination. In *Proceedings SIGGRAPH '95*, pages 145–152, 1995.

[25] François Sillion and Claude Puech. *Radiosity and Global Illumination*. Morgan Kaufmann publishers, San Francisco, 1994.

[26] Cyril Soler and François Sillion. Accurate Error Bounds for Multi-Resolution Visibility. In *Rendering Techniques '96 (Proceedings of the Seventh Eurographics Workshop on Rendering)*, pages 133–142. Springer-Verlag/Wien, 1996.

[27] John R. Wallace, Kells A. Elmquist, and Eric A. Haines. A ray tracing algorithm for progressive radiosity. *Computer Graphics*, 23(3):315–324, July 1989. Proceedings SIGGRAPH '89 in Boston.

[28] Leonard R. Wanger, James A. Ferwerda, and Donald P. Greenberg. Perceiving spatial relationships in computer-generated images. *IEEE Computer Graphics and Applications*, 12(3):44–58, May 1992.

[29] Turner Whitted. An Improved Illumination Model for Shaded Display. *Communications of the ACM*, 23:343–349, 1980.

[30] Lance Williams. Casting curved shadows on curved surfaces. *Computer Graphics*, 12(3):270–274, August 1978. Proceedings SIGGRAPH '78.

[31] Andrew Woo, Pierre Poulin, and Alain Fournier. A survey of shadow algorithms. *IEEE Computer Graphics and Applications*, 10(6):13–32, Nov. 1990.

[32] Harold R. Zatz. Galerkin radiosity: A higher-order solution method for global illumination. In *Proceedings SIGGRAPH '93*, pages 213–220, August 1993.

Interactive Reflections on Curved Objects

Eyal Ofek   Ari Rappoport

Institute of Computer Science, The Hebrew University

Abstract

Global view-dependent illumination phenomena, in particular reflections, greatly enhance the realism of computer-generated imagery. Current interactive rendering methods do not provide satisfactory support for reflections on curved objects.

In this paper we present a novel method for interactive computation of reflections on curved objects. We transform potentially reflected scene objects according to reflectors, to generate *virtual objects*. These are rendered by the graphics system as ordinary objects, creating a reflection image that is blended with the primary image. Virtual objects are created by tessellating scene objects and computing a virtual vertex for each resulting scene vertex. Virtual vertices are computed using a novel space subdivision, the *reflection subdivision*. For general polygonal mesh reflectors, we present an associated approximate acceleration scheme, the *explosion map*. For specific types of objects (e.g., linear extrusions of planar curves) the reflection subdivision can be reduced to a 2-D one that is utilized more accurately and efficiently.

CR Categories: I.3.3 [Computer Graphics]: Picture/Image Generation; I.3.7 [Computer Graphics]: Three-Dimensional Graphics and Realism.

Keywords: ray tracing, interactive reflections, virtual objects method, reflection subdivision, explosion map.

1 Introduction

Interactive photo-realistic rendering is a major goal of computer graphics. Global view-dependent illumination phenomena greatly enhance image quality. An extremely important type of view-dependent phenomenon is reflection. Reflections on curved object are not supported well by current interactive rendering techniques. In this paper we address the problem of interactive rendering of reflections on curved objects.

Background. Current interactive graphics systems utilize hardware acceleration that directly supports hidden surfaces removal, simple local shading models and texture mapping. While the polygon throughput of these systems is impressive, the range of shading effects they provide hasn't changed much since their introduction. In particular, they lack support for global illumination phenomena in dynamic scenes.

Global illumination phenomena greatly enhance the quality of synthetic imagery. They can be coarsely classified to view-independent and view-dependent phenomena. Among the former, diffuse illumination in static scenes [Sillion89] and shadows [Segal92] can be interactively rendered using current hardware. However, global *view-dependent* phenomena are crucial for providing life-like realism. When only view-independent effects are provided, the visual nature of the result can be dull and lifeless, even when the scene is dynamic.

An extremely important view-dependent illumination phenomenon is reflection. The dominant method for generating reflections is ray tracing [Whitted80, Glassner89]. In spite of extensive work on ray tracing acceleration schemes, [Jansen93] states that the only hope for interactive ray tracing lies in massively parallel computers, and even then satisfactory performance is not guaranteed.

Environment mapping [Blinn76, Greene86, Haeberli93, Voorhies94] generates at interactive rates reflections that are approximately correct when the reflected objects are relatively far from the reflector. However, when this condition is violated the results are of very poor accuracy.

It is well-known that reflections on planar surfaces can be generated by (1) mirroring the viewer along the reflecting plane, (2) creating a reflection image by rendering the scene from the new point of view, and (3) merging the main image with the visible portion of the reflector in the reflection image. Surprisingly, although this method can significantly accelerate ray tracing, it has been accurately documented only recently. The descriptions in [Foley90] (in which the method is called 'reflection mapping') and [McReynolds96] are correct only when the original viewer and all objects lie on the same side of the reflecting plane. A correct description is given in [Hall96]. [Diefenbach97] shows how to use variants of this method for interactive simulation of various general reflectance functions of planar objects. The concept of a reflected virtual world was also used in [Rushmeier86, Wallace87, Sillion89] for supporting specular reflections from planar objects in a radiosity context.

Contribution. In this paper we present a method for interactive rendering of reflections on *curved* objects, based on merging a primary image and a reflection image. The reflection image is generated by creating and rendering *virtual objects* corresponding to reflections of scene objects. Virtual objects are rendered like ordinary polygons, thus taking advantage of the features supported by the graphics system. They are created using a structure called the *reflection subdivision* and an associated approximate acceleration scheme, the *explosion map*.

The method presents a novel approach to the computation of reflections in computer graphics, and is unique in providing approximate reflections on curved objects at interactive rates. Moreover, the rendered scenes can be completely dynamic; no pre-processing is necessary. The method provides higher quality than environment mapping, because it allows reflected objects to be nearby the reflector and it supports equally well reflectors having a large curvature. For scenes in which reflected images of objects occupy more than a

Institute of Computer Science, The Hebrew University, Jerusalem 91904, Israel. http://www.cs.huji.ac.il/~arir,~eyalp   arir,eyalp@cs.huji.ac.il few pixels and in which the depth complexity of the reflection image is not large, the method is much more efficient than ray tracing, because it efficiently exploits the spatial coherency of the reflection image. The price paid for the advantages of the method is that its performance is less efficient than that of environment mapping and the generated images are only polygonal approximations (as in most interactive systems). In addition, its accuracy depends upon the geometric nature of the reflector.

The paper is structured as follows. Section 2 gives an overview of the method. Sections 3, 4 and 5 deal with convex reflectors, discussing respectively the reflection subdivision, the explosion map, and special reflectors. Section 6 deals with non-convex reflectors. Results and an in-depth discussion are given in Sections 7 and 8.

2 Method Overview

In this section we give an overview of the virtual objects method. We present the general idea (2.1), image merging alternatives (2.2), a brief discussion on planar reflectors (2.3), and a high-level outline on non-planar reflectors (2.4).

2.1 General Idea

The virtual objects method is inspired by the following observation. Consider an image containing reflections. Two kinds of entities are visible: reflecting objects, or *reflectors*, and *reflected images* of reflected 3-D objects. When the reflector is a perfect planar one, the geometry of the reflected images is identical to images of the reflected objects from some other viewpoint. In fact, we cannot distinguish between 'real' objects and reflected images of objects. Interior designers utilize this phenomenon when covering walls with mirrors in order to make rooms seem larger. For non-planar reflectors, the appearance of reflected objects is a deformed version of their ordinary appearance. In general, there is no viewpoint from which they appear identical to their reflected images. The nature of the deformation depends upon the geometry of the reflector. Convex reflectors deform reflected objects to seem smaller, and concave reflectors produce reflected images that may seem larger than the reflected object or degenerate into strange chaotic images.

This observation inspires the following algorithm for generation of reflections (Figure 1): for every reflector and every object potentially reflected in it, compute a *3-D virtual object,* that, when rendered using ordinary 3-D rendering methods, will produce an image having a visual appearance similar to the object's reflected image. If depth relationships between the virtual objects are still correct, the rendered images of the virtual objects can be merged together using some hidden surfaces removal algorithm. The result can now be alpha blended with a reflector image containing view-independent lighting to produce the final image. The alpha blending coefficients are determined by the relative reflectivity of the reflector.

SceneRender (Scene S, View E):
(1) Render S without reflections into primary image I.
(2) For every visible reflector $R \in S$
(3)   For every potentially reflected object $O \in S$
(4) $O' \leftarrow$ **VirtualObject** (R, O, E).
(5)   Render O' into a reflection image I'.
(6)   If multiple levels of reflections are desired
             Call the algorithm recursively.
(7)   Alpha blend I' and I, according to
         the reflectivity of R.

Figure 1 The virtual objects method.

When virtual objects can be computed efficiently, the resulting method is very attractive, since reflected images are generated at the object, rather than the pixel, level. Most of this paper deals with step 4, efficient generation of virtual objects. Naturally, only visible reflectors are considered, and the scene can be stored in a data structure that supports culling of scene objects that cannot be reflected.

A comment about shading: for planar reflectors we can reflect the light sources as well as the scene objects and simply use the reflected ones. For non-planar reflectors, it is more accurate to compute shading values for vertices at the world coordinate system, and then use these values for the virtual vertices. On current architectures, this shading is most efficiently computed in software, and the hardware is used for rasterization and texturing.

2.2 Image Merging

The primary and reflection images can be merged in two ways. First, the reflection image can be used as a texture when rendering a reflector. Alternatively, the reflection image can be directly rendered on the screen (using a stencil bit-plane defining the screen image of the reflector.) The view-independent component of the reflector is now rendered, alpha blending it with the reflection image.

Texture mapping and stencil-guided image merging are standard features in interactive graphics systems, even current low-end ones. The choice of method depends on the actual graphics architecture available, especially on its memory organization. For more details, see [Ofek98, McReynolds96, Hall96].

2.3 Planar Reflectors

The method of [McReynolds96, Hall96, Diefenbach97] is a special case of the virtual objects method, when the reflectors are planar and when we consider the objects, rather than the viewpoint, as being mirrored. Note that in this case the method is essentially an image-space version of beam tracing [Heckbert84]. An attractive property of planar reflectors is that the location of a virtual point is a simple affine transformation, *mirroring,* of the real point. Moreover, this transformation does not depend on the viewer location, only on that of the reflector. In Figure 2(a), the location of the virtual image Q' of a scene point Q remains constant for two viewpoints E_1 and E_2. Hence, the same simple affine transformation can be used for all reflected polygons. Full details on how to generate the mirroring transformation are given in the above references.

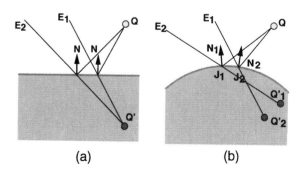

(a)   (b)

Figure 2 For planar reflectors, the virtual location of a point does not depend upon the viewpoint (a). This does not hold for curved reflectors (b).

Note that as presented so far, the method produces correct results only when the viewpoint and the reflected polygon are on the same side of the reflector. Consider a polygon lying on the other side of the reflector. After the mirroring transformation, it can erroneously obscure the reflector from the viewer, because they lie on the same side of it. This problem can be overcome by not mirroring a polygon if all of its vertices lie behind the reflector. The test is done by plugging the vertex coordinates into the reflector plane equation and testing the sign of the result. However, this method does not solve the case when the polygon lies only partially behind the reflector. In many cases such polygons do not cause incorrect results because the virtual front part falls outside of the reflector stencil anyway. For planar reflectors, the problem can be solved very efficiently by defining the reflector plane as a front clipping plane.

2.4 Non-Planar Reflectors

Generation of virtual objects for non-planar reflectors is more difficult than for planar reflectors, because the main property of the planar case does not hold: the location of a virtual point is not a simple affine transformation independent of the viewer position (Figure 2(b)). In general, every reflected point is transformed differently.

Our approach is outlined in Figure 3. The reflected object is tessellated into polygons (step 1). The fineness of the tessellation depends upon the desired accuracy of the resulting reflection image. Tessellations are further discussed in Sections 7 and 8. In steps 2–5, virtual polygons are generated by computing virtual vertices for the tessellation vertices. The collection of all virtual polygons forms the desired virtual object rendered in step 5 of Figure 1. The main step is 4, computing a single virtual vertex; its description occupies much of the rest of the paper.

VirtualObject (Reflector R, Object O, View E):
(1) Tessellate O into polygons.
(2) For each polygon P
(3)   For each vertex Q of P
(4) $Q' \leftarrow$ **VirtualVertex** (R, Q, E).
(5)   Connect the Q's to form a virtual polygon P'.
(6) Connect the P's to form the virtual object O'.

Figure 3 Computing a virtual object O' for a potentially reflected object O on a non-planar reflector R.

Rendered polygons are consistent and possess no holes, because virtual objects are formed by connecting virtual vertices. Visibility relationships between virtual objects are preserved due to the usage of a hidden surfaces removal mechanism (in practice, a z-buffer) for them.

3   The Reflection Subdivision

In this section we start detailing our approach towards computing virtual vertices for curved reflectors. We assume here that the reflector is convex. Concave and other non-convex reflectors are discussed in Section 6. Our approach is based on approximating the reflector by a polygonal mesh. In many cases this is the format in which objects are given anyway; when they are given in a higher-level representation (e.g., a NURBS surface) they are tessellated. For simplicity, we assume that mesh polygons are triangles, but this is not necessary.

Intuition. Given a reflector R and an arbitrary scene point Q, we want to generate the corresponding virtual point Q' (consult Figure 2(b)). If we knew the point of reflection J and normal N on the boundary surface of R, we could easily compute Q' by mirroring Q along the tangent plane to R at J. In some cases, when we know the geometric nature of the reflector (e.g., a sphere), J can be computed

by a direct formula. However, for a general convex polygonal mesh there is no direct formula.

We use an approximation. Every reflector triangle defines two space cells: a *reflected cell* and a *hidden cell*. Suppose that we can find the cell C, defined by triangle T, in which the scene point Q lies. A naive method would mirror Q across the plane containing T. However, this would clearly show the linear approximation of the reflector (imagine a reflecting sharply cut diamond!). Instead, we use the relative location of Q inside C to define a triplet of barycentric coefficients. These coefficients are used to interpolate the three tangent planes at the vertices of T, yielding a new tangent plane that is now used for mirroring Q.

In this section we study the space subdivision defined by the reflector and also explain why we need to compute virtual points for points that are not reflected. The full details of the computation are given in Sections 4 and 5.

The subdivision. Each vertex V_i of the tessellated reflector possesses a normal N_i. Reflector vertices are either *front-facing* or *back-facing*, according to whether their normals point towards or away from the viewer (a normal orthogonal to the line of sight is considered front-facing). Due to the convexity of the reflector, every front-facing vertex is visible by the viewer (when there are no other obscuring objects). Note that back-facing vertices might still be visible (this is a tessellation artifact). When all vertices of a mesh triangle are front-facing (back-facing), we refer to the triangle as being front-facing (back-facing). Otherwise we say that the triangle is a *profile* triangle.

For each front-facing vertex V_i we define two rays: (1) a *reflection ray* R_i, mirroring the ray from V_i to the viewer across the normal N_i, and (2) a *hidden ray* H_i, originating at V_i and extending to infinity in the opposite direction to that of the viewer. Figure 4 shows a 2-D version of the situation. In (a), reflection rays are shown in red and hidden rays in blue.

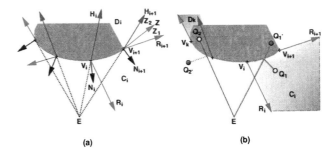

(a)   (b)

Figure 4 (a) The reflection subdivision in 2-D. C_i and D_i are the reflected and hidden cells defined by reflector vertices V_i, V_{i+1}. The ray Z bisects the unreflected region on the right into two parts Z_1, Z_2. (b) Computation of virtual vertices: the point Q_1 in the reflected cell C_i is transformed to Q'_1 inside the hidden cell D_i; the point Q_2 in the hidden cell D_k is transformed to Q'_2 outside the reflector in the reflected cell C_k.

Two reflection rays R_i, R_j corresponding to adjacent front-facing mesh vertices V_i, V_j define a ruled bi-linear parametric surface $s(V_i + tR_i) + (1 - s)(V_j + tR_j)$. Note that in general this surface is not planar, because the two rays are usually not co-planar. The two hidden rays H_i, H_j span an infinite truncated triangle containing the edge V_i, V_j.

Now consider the three vertices V_i, V_j, V_k of a front-facing mesh triangle V_{ijk}. The triangle induces two space regions: (1) A *reflected cell* C_{ijk} bounded by the three ruled surfaces corresponding to the triangle edges and by V_{ijk} itself (figure 10). (2) A *hidden cell* D_{ijk}, which is the infinite part of the truncated pyramid bounded by V_{ijk} and the triangles spanned by the hidden rays. We refer to the union of the reflected (hidden) cells as the reflected (hidden) region.

An important property of the reflected and hidden cells is that they do not intersect each other, since the reflector is convex. Therefore, we can define the *reflection subdivision* as the subdivision of space induced by these cells. Note, however, that these cells do not *cover* space; we call the part of space not covered by reflection or hidden cells the *unreflected region*. In Figure 4(a), the part of the unreflected region lying on the right side of the reflector is the union of Z_1, Z_2 (the reason for subdividing this region and the meaning of the ray Z are explained below). Points in the unreflected region can (in principle) be seen by the viewer, but cannot be reflected by the reflector. A point is potentially reflected by the reflector if and only if it lies in the reflected region. We say 'potentially' because its reflection may be obscured by the reflection of another point.

The unreflected and hidden regions. We compute virtual images for vertices of potentially reflected scene polygons (Figure 3, step 4). These virtual vertices are connected in order to generate virtual polygons, which are then rendered to create the reflection image (Figure 1, step 5). Scene polygons that lie completely in the hidden or unreflected regions can be discarded. However, *mixed polygons*, lying partially in these regions and partially in the reflected region, pose a problem. For such polygons, we would like to render the reflection of the part that lies in the reflected region. However, if we compute only one or two virtual vertices, we would not be able to connect these in order to generate virtual polygons. In some sense, the vertices lying in hidden or unreflected regions are representatives of a polygon area that we want to see reflected.

A naive way to deal with mixed polygons is to intersect them (exactly or approximately) with the region boundaries, thus forcing them to have a uniform classification. However, this is inefficient because the regions depend on the viewpoint. Another way is to subdivide them into smaller polygons, effectively doing an adaptive tessellation of scene objects. Subdivision is stopped when the 'lost' areas are deemed to be small enough.

A more efficient and elegant method is to define a virtual vertex for *every* polygon vertex, even for hidden and unreflected ones (e.g., vertex Q_2 in Figure 4(b)). These *doubly virtual* vertices are not real reflections; their sole purpose is to 'close' virtual polygons so that the graphics system could render them. In general, they lie outside the image of the reflector. Note that this actually is the approach taken in the planar reflector case. Hidden cells are easy to take care of, because there is a one-to-one correspondence between hidden and reflected cells. Moreover, it is possible to define a transformation that maps a reflected cell to exactly cover the corresponding hidden cell, and maps a hidden cell to exactly cover its corresponding reflected cell (see Section 4.2).

The unreflected region is more problematic. We would like to define a transformation for this region such that (1) the part of the region adjacent to a reflected cell will be transformed to be adjacent to its corresponding hidden cell (and vice versa), and (2) there is some continuity of the transformation between the unreflected and the reflected regions. To achieve such a transformation, we define for every contour edge of the reflector an auxiliary *bisecting surface* Z, which extends the edge into the unreflected region. Figure 4(a) shows a 2-D example. In 2-D we have a contour vertex and not a contour edge (it is simply the extreme vertex V_{i+1}), and the bisecting surface is simply a ray Z. Z is orthogonal to the normal N_{i+1} at V_{i+1} and extends V_{i+1} into the unreflected region, thus bisecting the region into two parts Z_1, Z_2. The desired transformation is simply a linear mirroring transformation that mirrors Z_1 into Z_2 and vice versa. In 3-D, the bisecting surface is non-linear, and we do not

define it explicitly; it is defined implicitly by the transformation we use for computing virtual vertices (Section 4.2).

As in the planar case, doubly virtual vertices might cause their virtual polygon to obscure the reflector. The solution in the planar case, a front clipping plane, can be generalized to non-planar reflectors by utilizing a second z-buffer containing the reflector's geometry. Every pixel generated during rendering of the virtual polygons will be tested twice: once against the ordinary z-buffer, in order to produce correct depth relationships between all virtual polygons, and once against the reflector z-buffer, to ensure that pixels in front of the reflectors are discarded.

A second z-buffer is not easy to define efficiently on today's graphics architectures. Alternatives that are currently more practical are: (1) do not do anything, anticipating that the obscuring pixels will fall outside the screen mask of the reflector, (2) approximate the reflector using six clipping planes, an option available on standard architectures, and (3) tessellate the scene so that mixed polygons are very small. Surprisingly, the first approach works well in the vast majority of cases, due to the way objects are usually positioned relative to each other and the way they are viewed. The second option reduces the problem but does not guarantee the resulting quality. The third option also reduces the problem, but requires more computations since there are more virtual vertices to compute. Tessellations are discussed in Sections 7 and 8.

4 The Explosion Map Acceleration Method

In some cases it is very efficient to compute the reflection subdivision and search it to find the cell in which a point lies (Section 5). In the general 3-D case, a faster indexing scheme is preferable.

In this section we describe an approximation method, the *explosion map*, which is a data structure for accelerating the computation of virtual vertices. It is prepared for each reflector separately, and recomputed whenever the viewpoint or the reflector are moved. The map is an image whose pixel values hold IDs of reflector triangles, and which represents a spherical 2-D cross section of the subdivision. To compute a virtual image of a scene point, we compute explosion map coordinates for it, thus yielding the ID of a specific triangle. The virtual image is computed using that triangle.

The explosion map is somewhat similar to a circular environment map [Haeberli93] in that it is an image in which a circle corresponds to the reflection directions (Figure 5(b)). However, it is unlike an environment map in that the latter contains renderings of other scene objects, while the explosion map contains only the reflector (Figure 5(a)). We next detail the computation (4.1) and utilization (4.2) of the map.

4.1 Computing an Explosion Map

An explosion map is a function of the tessellated reflector, the viewpoint, a 3-D sphere, and a desired resolution. The sphere should be centered at a point that is an intuitive 'center' of the reflector (as in environment mapping), and its radius should be large enough so that it bounds the reflector (actually, a sphere is not essential; we need any convex geometric object that approximates the reflector's shape). The map resolution should be large enough so that there are substantially more map pixels than reflector triangles. In practice, a resolution of 200^2 is sufficient when the reflector has been tessellated into several hundred triangles. The depth resolution of the map should have enough bits to hold unique IDs for all reflector vertices plus one more bit (needed to distinguish between ordinary triangles and extension polygons, defined below).

The basic operation in computing the map, **MapCoords**, involves

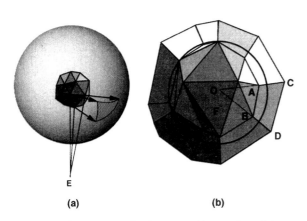

Figure 5 Explosion map: (a) reflection rays and intersection points on a bounding sphere; (b) the resulting map. C and D are extension vertices of A and B.

ExplosionMap (Reflector R, View E, Center C, Distance d, Resolution r):
(1) Let S be a sphere centered at C having radius d.
(2) Let M be an image of size $r \times r$.
(3) For each reflector vertex V_i
        If V_i is front-facing
            Let R_i be the reflection ray of V_i.
            Let I_i be the intersection of R_i with S.
            Let J_i be the normalized direction from C to I_i.
            $T_i \leftarrow$ **MapCoords** (J_i, r).
        Else
(4)   Denote V_i as back-facing.
(5) For each reflector triangle V_{ijk}
        If V_{ijk} is front-facing
            Fill the triangle T_i, T_j, T_k on M,
            using the ID of V_{ijk} as the color.
(6)   Else if V_{ijk} is a profile triangle
(7)   Fix its back-facing normals.
(8)   Compute and fill T_i, T_j, T_k as before.
(9) **ExtendMap** (R, M).

Figure 6 Computing an explosion map.

4.2 Computing Virtual Vertices

The explosion map circle represents a mapping of all possible reflection directions. We use it to directly generate the final virtual vertex Q' corresponding to a potentially reflected scene vertex Q. For each reflector we compute two explosion maps: a *near map* and a *far map*. The near map is computed using a sphere that bounds the object but does not intersect any other object, and the far map is computed using a sphere that bounds all the scene. It is important to understand that although the topologies of the two maps are quite similar (because cells do not intersect each other), their geometries are different; reflection rays, which determine the geometry of map vertices, evolve non-linearly.

In addition to the explosion maps, we store a *hidden map* and an auxiliary z-buffer of the reflector. The hidden map is simply an item buffer of the visible mesh triangles. In other words, it is a discrete map in which a visible mesh triangle is mapped to a 2-D triangle filled by the ID of the mesh triangle. The map resolution can be smaller than that of the frame buffer (say, 200^2).

The basic operation needed is **MapToVirtualVertex**, whose arguments are a map M, a 3-D point Q and a corresponding map point I. Assume that the ID in $M(I)$ is that of an ordinary mesh triangle V (not an extension polygon) having 2-D vertices A, B, C (these are the T_i's computed in step 3 of Figure 6). The output is the virtual point Q'. The operation is implemented in three steps: (1) compute barycentric coordinates s, t of I relative to V by solving the two linear equations in two variables $(1 - (s+t))A + sB + tC = I$; (2) use s, t as weights in a weighted average of the 3-D vertices and normals of V that yields a plane of reflection U; and (3) mirror Q across U to produce Q'. Note that negative barycentric coordinates are perfectly acceptable. The computation can be performed in integers or floating point, to reduce aliasing artifacts resulting from the discrete nature of the map. Extension polygons are handled similarly, using four bilinear coordinates instead of three. This treatment of extension polygons effectively implements the non-linear mirroring transformation of the unreflected region motivated in Section 3.

Computation of virtual vertices for a scene vertex Q is shown in Figure 7. We first determine if Q is hidden (steps 1, 2), by testing it in screen coordinates against the reflector's z-buffer. If it is, Q's virtual image is computed by the hidden map (step 3). Note that an obvious optimization here is to do this only for hidden vertices that belong to mixed polygons, since we don't need virtual images for polygons that are hidden completely.

---

deriving the map coordinates $T = (t_x, t_y)$ corresponding to a normalized direction vector $N = (x, y, z)$ going from the center of the sphere to an arbitrary direction. If the resolution of the map is r^2, N is mapped to $T = (\frac{sx}{(2(z+1))^{1/2}} + s/2, \frac{sy}{(2(z+1))^{1/2}} + s/2)$, where s is a number a little smaller than r. This mapping is similar to that used for generating a circular environment map from a map rendered on the faces of a box [Haeberli93]. The pixels to which directions are mapped all fall inside a circle of radius $s/2$. The circle represents all possible reflection directions.

The map itself is computed as follows (Figure 6). For every front-facing reflector vertex, we compute map coordinates by intersecting its reflection ray with the sphere and calling **MapCoords** with the direction from the sphere's center to the intersection point (step 3). Back-facing vertices are denoted as such (step 4) to facilitate fast identification of profile triangles in step 6. For each front-facing reflector triangle (recall that a triangle is called front-facing if all its vertices are front-facing, and is called profile if only some of its vertices are front-facing), the corresponding triangle defined by the map coordinates is filled on the map, using its unique ID as color (step 5). Polygon fill can be done by the graphics hardware. For profile triangles, the normals of their back-facing vertices are projected in the direction of the viewer such that they are orthogonal to the line from the viewer through the vertex (step 7). The triangles thus become front-facing, and are now filled on the map as done for triangles that were front-facing originally (step 8).

So far, the interior of a map circle of radius $s/2$ has been partially filled, but not completely. This is due to the existence of the unreflected region and the fact that the filled map triangles are linear. As we explained in Section 3, we want the directions into the unreflected region to be filled on the map as well so that we could use it to compute doubly virtual vertices. To ensure that all directions are filled on the map, in **ExtendMap** the map is extended to cover the circle as follows. For each profile triangle V_{ijk} having two back-facing vertices (say V_i, V_j), we define an *extension polygon* E_{ij} in map coordinates and fill it with the ID of V_{ijk}. The vertices of E_{ij} are T_i, T_j, and extensions of each of these vertices in the direction away from the circle's center (in Figure 5(b), the extensions of vertices A, B are C, D). The extensions should be long enough so that the circle is completely covered. In practice, it is enough that the length of the segment from the center to each extended vertex is $0.6s$. Extension polygons effectively comprise an implicit representation of the bisecting surfaces Z explained in Section 3. Other methods for representing the unreflected region on the map are discussed in [Ofek98].

VirtualVertex (Reflector R, Point Q, View E):
(1) Let I be the screen coordinates of Q (using E).
(2) If Q is hidden by a mesh triangle V
(3)   Return **MapToVirtualVertex** (*HiddenMap*, Q, I).
(4) Let c be the direction from the center of R to Q.
(5) $T \leftarrow$ **MapCoords** (c, r).
(6) $Q'_n \leftarrow$ **MapToVirtualVertex** (*NearMap*, Q, T).
    $Q'_f \leftarrow$ **MapToVirtualVertex** (*FarMap*, Q, T).
(7) Let d_n, d_f be the relative distances of Q from
    the near and far spheres.
    Return $\frac{Q'_n/d_n + Q'_f/d_f}{1/d_n + 1/d_f}$.

Figure 7 Computing virtual vertices using the explosion and hidden maps.

When Q is not hidden we use the explosion maps. The normalized direction from the center of the reflector to Q is used to obtain map coordinates, in the same way used for creating the maps (steps 4, 5). Note that the map coordinates T are the same for both maps, but the triangle IDs found at T are different. In general, none of these triangles corresponds to the correct reflection cell in which Q is located, because we approximated the correct ray of reflection of Q by a ray from the center of the reflector (when higher accuracy is desired, we can use an improved approximation or locally search the correct cell [Ofek98].) Each of these triangles defines an auxiliary virtual vertex (step 6), and a weighted average of those is taken to obtain the final virtual vertex (step 7). There may be other ways to choose the weights than the obvious one shown. Figure 13 shows near and far explosion maps, in which polygon IDs are encoded by colors for visualization purposes.

5 Improved Efficiency for Linear Extrusions

For some common reflectors, it is possible to compute virtual vertices more efficiently than the explosion map, by directly utilizing the reflection subdivision to find the cell in which a scene point lies. Among these reflector are linear extrusions of planar curves (e.g., cylinders) and cones. For spheres, there is an efficient method that does not use the reflection subdivision at all. In general, if an implicit equation defining the reflector is available, the reflection point can be computed as in [Hanrahan92] (although this method is slow). Below we detail the case of an extruded reflector. The direct computation for cones and spheres is simple and given in [Ofek98].

Consider a 2-D reflection subdivision, as shown for example in Figure 4. We can optimize the step of identifying the cell in which a point lies by organizing the reflection cells in a hierarchy. Define $C_{i,j}$ to be the region bounded by reflection rays R_i, R_j and the line segment (V_i, V_j). Note that $C_{i,j}$ contains every cell $C_{k,r}, i \leq k < r \leq j$. Classifying a point with respect to a cell $C_{i,j}$ amounts to a few 'line side' tests, implemented by plugging the point into the line's equation and testing the sign of the result. If we find that the point is not contained in $C_{i,j}$, we know that it is outside all contained cells $C_{k,r}$. A binary search can thus be performed on the hierarchy. Note that there are no actual computations involved in generating the hierarchy, since it is implicitly represented by the numbering of the reflector vertices. A similar hierarchy can be defined for the hidden cells as well. Membership in the two (at most) unreflected cells can be tested easily. Consequently, the cell in which a point is located can be found using a small number ($O(\log n)$ where n is the reflector tessellation resolution) of 'line side' tests.

Suppose that the reflector is a linear extrusion of a convex 2-D planar curve. We can reduce the computation of a virtual vertex to 2-D by (1) projecting the viewer and all scene points onto the plane,

(2) performing the 2-D computation, obtaining a line of reflection L_Q for each scene vertex, (3) extruding L_Q to 3-D to form a plane of reflection T, and (4) computing a final virtual vertex by mirroring the original vertex across T. The screen in Figure 17 is a linear extrusion of a convex planar curve.

6 Non-Convex Reflectors

Concave reflectors. The computations we perform for concave reflectors are identical to those for convex ones, but it is interesting to note that concave reflectors produce significantly more complicated visual results. In Figure 8 we see a viewer E in front of a concave reflector and three reflection rays. The reflection of an object located in region A (left) looks like an enlarged, deformed version of the object. The reflection of an object located in region B (middle) looks like an enlarged, deformed, upside-down version of the object. The reflection of objects located in region C (right) is utterly chaotic. This chaotic nature is inherent in the physics of reflections and is not an artifact of computations or approximations.

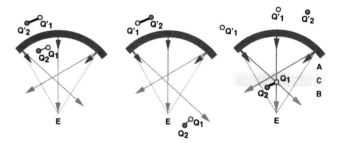

Figure 8 Behavior of reflections on concave reflectors.

Reflections of objects lying in regions A and B can be computed exactly as for convex reflectors, because in these regions the reflection subdivision is well-defined (since the reflection cells are disjoint). Reflections of objects lying in region C or intersecting that region are unpredictable and chaotic anyway, so almost any policy for computing virtual vertices will be satisfactory. In particular, we can simply use the value computed by the explosion map, thereby treating concave reflectors exactly as convex ones.

Figure 11 shows a concave reflector. On the right, we see the reflector, the reflection rays, a reflected planar object, and the computed virtual object, all these from a point of view different from the viewer's. On the left we see the final image from the viewer's point of view. The two explosion maps and the hidden map are shown at the bottom right. Note that reflected objects must be very close to this reflector to cross from region B to regions A or C.

Reflectors of mixed convexity. Reflectors that are neither convex nor concave should be decomposed into convex and concave parts. For many objects this can be done fully automatically [Spanguolo92]. Some polygonal surfaces contain saddles, resulting in a decomposition that is too fine. In such cases it is advised that users decompose the object manually. Note that the actual requirement is not of pure convexity of concavity, but rather that the reflection cells would not self-intersect in areas where reflected objects lie. Devising automatic algorithms that take this into consideration when decomposing the object is an interesting topic for future work. When manual decomposition is used, reflectors cannot dynamically change their shape in an arbitrary way, but the scene can still be dynamic. Figure 9 shows a reflector with a convex part (red) and a concave part (green). Note the seamless transition of the reflection image between the convex and concave parts.

7 Results

We have implemented our algorithms using OpenGL on SGIs running Irix and on PCs running Windows '95 and NT. Figure 12 shows a cylinder reflector modeled as a linear extrusion of a circle. Figure 13 demonstrates the effect of varying reflector tessellation resolution. The bottom part shows the near and far explosion maps. We see that using 128 triangles the reflection image already has an approximately correct geometric form, and that using 2048 rather than 512 triangles barely makes a difference. Figure 14 shows the effect of varying the tessellation of the reflected object (using 512 reflector triangles). A tessellation of 7x7 is sufficient. A lower resolution would suffice for objects farther away from the reflector,

Figure 16 shows a scene with four reflecting spheres, a table, and a window, rendered by our method (top) and by Rayshade, a well-known raytracer (bottom). A checkerboard texture was used in order to emphasize the reflections. The geometric shapes of the reflections in the two images are visually very similar. The texture in the bottom image is sharper because we use the graphics hardware for texture mapping.

On an SGI O_2, the top image required **less than a second**, and the bottom one required **50 seconds**. For Rayshade, we turned off shadows rays, highlights, and anti-aliasing, and we used a single sample per pixel and a manually tuned uniform grid as an acceleration scheme. Image resolution is 512^2.

Figure 15 shows the same scene, from a slightly different viewpoint and using real textures. The shadows are pre-computed textures. Figure 17 shows a reflecting TV modeled as an extrusion of a convex planar curve. Figure 18 shows recursive reflections on a planar mirror. Figure 19 shows a mask composed of several convex and concave pieces. Note the correct reflections of the red and green spheres on both 'cheeks' of the mask and on the nose. Figure 20 shows several reflecting polyhedra and a reflecting sphere. All of these scenes (except Figure 19) are displayed in real-time on an SGI Infinite Reality. We haven't tried the scene of Figure 19 on such a machine; on an SGI O_2, Figure 19 requires about a second with our method, and 1.5 minutes using Rayshade.

8 Discussion

The virtual objects method is the first method capable of accurately approximating reflections on curved objects at interactive rates. In this paper we presented the basic method for a single level of reflection and its implementation for general polygonal meshes and for linear extrusions. Clearly, the method possesses both advantages and disadvantages. We discuss these below, both in isolation and in the context of other methods.

Quality. In general, the quality produced by the method is satisfactory, especially for interactive use. The explosion map gives good results even for planar or nearly planar reflectors. Like any approximation method, ours might produce visible artifacts. The most noticeable ones occur when objects are not tessellated finely enough, in which case their reflections look too much like their real-world images and are not deformed according to the geometry of the reflector. In addition, reflections might be slightly translated inaccurately because we do not compute the exact explosion map cells to which vertices are mapped.

Other visible artifacts can be seen near the boundaries of the reflector, when the transformation used to create doubly virtual vertices is not a good approximation to the correct reflection. In this case the seam between convex and concave regions might be visible. Even in this case, reflections are self-consistent and do not exhibit holes.

When the reflector shape on the explosion map is far from convex, our heuristic for representing the unreflected region (extension polygons) might yield visible artifacts. Obviously, doubly virtual vertices might still hide the reflector when not using a second z-buffer. However, as we noted earlier, this usually does not happen because their screen images tend to fall outside the screen image of the reflector.

An attractive property of the method that has not been mentioned so far is that it supports interactive rendering of *refractions,* by using refraction rays instead of reflection rays. There are some additional differences, detailed in [Ofek98].

Tessellation strategies. As shown in Section 7, some tessellation of reflected objects is usually essential for providing sufficient accuracy. The finer the tessellation, the more accurate the reflections. At the same time, increasing the tessellation has an adverse impact on performance. These considerations are identical to those employed in interactive rendering of curved objects in general. There are two standard approaches: (1) usage of uniform tessellations, pre-computed such that quality is satisfactory, and (2) usage of hierarchical tessellations (levels of detail, etc).

Both approaches can be taken in our case as well. When the distances from a reflector to reflected objects and viewer remain approximately constant, we can pre-compute a uniform tessellation. The tessellation resolution of the reflected object should be chosen such that its virtual polygons cover several dozen pixels. Otherwise, hierarchical tessellations can be used. These can exhibit the same artifacts as when they are used for ordinary objects, e.g. discontinuities during animation. Note that the reflector tessellation resolution can be lower than that used when rendering its view-independent image. Using hierarchical tessellations is a topic for future work.

Performance. In the worst-case, all scene points can indeed be reflected on every convex part and every concave part of every reflector. Denote by r the number of visible reflectors and by $n(n')$ the number of vertices in the original (tessellated) scene. The time complexity of the method is $O(r \times n')$, which is thus worst-case optimal for a given degree of tessellation. For a single reflector, the step of computing the explosion and hidden maps is linear in the size of the reflector and is roughly equivalent to rendering the reflector three times at low resolution. The step of computing a virtual vertex for a scene vertex requires a relatively small *constant* number of operations. Moreover, the operations performed are highly regular, and are probably not too difficult to parallelize or implement in hardware. The cost of rendering virtual polygons is similar to rendering the whole scene. If deforming reflectors are desired, they should be subdivided into convex and concave parts on each frame, which costs time linear in their size. Naturally, as the depth complexity of the reflection image increases, the time complexity of our method diverges from the optimal.

The scenes shown in this paper run interactively (1-30 frames per second) on an SGI O_2 workstation. This performance was achieved *without any optimization;* in particular, no method for culling objects that cannot be reflected has been used. On today's systems, without further optimizations the number of reflected objects cannot be much larger than shown while still guaranteeing interactive performance.

Comparison to other methods. We can compare our method to environment mapping or ray tracing, which are currently the only techniques capable of computing reflections on curved objects. Both visual accuracy and efficiency should be considered.

Environment mapping is relatively accurate only when reflected objects are relatively far from the reflector and when the curvature of the reflector is not large. When the scene is static, time complexity is linear in the size of the reflector, because the map can be pre-computed. This is in general much faster than our method. When the scene is dynamic, the map must be recomputed on each frame for each reflector. This also holds when only the viewer changes, unless the special hardware of [Voorhies94] is used. Complexity is $r \times n$, which is closer to our method but still more efficient. To what degree depends on the amount of tessellation. However, environment mapping simply does not provide realistic accuracy. Seeing reflections of objects that are nearby as if they are very far creates an uneasy feeling and definitely cannot be qualified as realistic.

Ray tracing obviously produces higher quality images than our method and supports a wider range of illumination phenomena. Regarding efficiency, the relevant characteristics of our method are: (1) it operates at the object level rather than the pixel level (we have an object and we want to know where it is reflected, rather than having the point of reflection and seeking an object), (2) it transforms the problem into one that standard graphics systems can handle, (3) it transforms the computation into a local one involving a single reflector-reflected pair, instead of the global ray tracing computation ('find the nearest object'); global visibility relationships are automatically handled by the z-buffer, and (4) it uses both the CPU and the graphics system, dividing (but not necessarily balancing) the load between them. When these properties are significant, our method is more efficient than ray tracing. Ray tracing can be expected to perform better when (1) reflected objects do not cover many pixels, (2) there are many curved reflectors, or (3) the depth complexity of the reflected images is large. It may or may not be faster when there is no graphics hardware. Note that our method scales much better than ray tracing to larger image resolutions, while ray tracing scales better with scene depth complexity.

It is very difficult to predict the point from which ray tracing is more efficient. On the relatively simple scenes shown in this paper, the method is at least an order of magnitude more efficient than Rayshade, a well-known available ray tracer, even when it uses a manually tuned acceleration scheme.

Future work. Both efficiency and quality issues should be further investigated. Efficiency issues include: acceleration using global scene organization techniques, hierarchical tessellations, possible hardware implementation, acceleration using time coherence, and usage of the method to accelerate other illumination methods. Quality issues include refining the initial approximation given by the explosion map, improved methods for filling the unreflected region on the map, using the method for rendering refractions, automatic decomposition of reflectors of mixed convexity, quantifying the degree of error introduced by our approximations, and additional levels of recursive reflections.

Conclusion. We feel that correct reflections from small objects are not very important. Such reflections, reflections on complex mixed convexity objects, and reflections of distant objects can be convincingly emulated using environment mapping. High quality reflections are therefore needed for relatively large objects with relatively uniform convexity (or concavity). A typical scene does not contain too many curved objects like these. As a result, although the time complexity of the method is theoretically quadratic in the number of reflectors, in practice its complexity is linear in the size of the scene (it can be sub-linear if scene databases are used for culling objects). Applicability will increase with increases in processing power and graphics hardware. Even today, there are many applications in which the number of objects in the scene is less important than the rendering quality. In these cases, our method is at least

an order of magnitude faster than ray tracing and provides higher visual quality than environment mapping.

Our experience is that interacting with scenes containing reflections is immensely more enjoyable than with scenes without reflections. Reflections bring dull and lifeless scenes to life.

Acknowledgements. We thank Dani Lischinski for commenting on a draft of this paper and for fruitful discussions. We also thank Amichai Nitsan for his involvement in part of the implementation. Lastly, we warmly thank Leo Krieger for his continuous support.

References

[Blinn76] Blinn, J., Newell, M., Texture and reflection in computer generated images. *Comm. ACM*, 19:542–546, 1976.

[Diefenbach97] Diefenbach, P.J., Badler, N.I., Multi-pass pipeline rendering: realism for dynamic environments. Proceedings, *1997 Symposium on Interactive 3D Graphics*, ACM Press, 1997.

[Foley90] Foley, J.D., Van Dam A., Feiner, S.K., Hughes, J.F., Computer Graphics: Principles and Practice, 2nd ed., Addison-Wesley, 1990.

[Glassner89] Glassner, A. (ed), An Introduction to Ray Tracing. Academic Press, 1989.

[Greene86] Greene, N., Environment mapping and other applications of world projections. *IEEE CG&A*, 6(11), Nov. 1986.

[Haeberli93] Haeberli, P., Segal, M., Texture mapping as a fundamental drawing primitive. Proceedings, *Fourth Eurographics Workshop on Rendering*, Cohen, Puech, Sillion (eds), 1993, pp. 259–266.

[Hall96] Hall, T., Tutorial on planar mirrors in OpenGL, posted to comp.graphics.api.opengl, Aug. 1996.

[Hanrahan92] Hanrahan, P., Mitchell, D., Illumination from curved reflectors. Proceedings, Siggraph '92, ACM Press, pp. 283–291.

[Heckbert84] Heckbert, P.S., Hanrahan, P., Beam tracing polygonal objects. *Computer Graphics*, 18:119–127, 1984 (Siggraph '84).

[Jansen93] Jansen, F.W., Realism in real-time? Proceedings, *Fourth Eurographics Workshop on Rendering*, Cohen, Puech, Sillion (eds), 1993.

[McReynolds96] McReynolds, T., Blythe, D., Programming with OpenGL: Advanced Rendering, course #23, Siggraph '96.

[Ofek98] Ofek, E., Modeling and Rendering 3-D Objects. Ph.D. thesis, Institute of Computer Science, The Hebrew University, 1998.

[Rushmeier86] Rushmeier, H.E., Extending the radiosity method to transmitting and specularly reflecting surfaces. Masters's thesis, Cornell University, 1986.

[Segal92] Segal, M., Korobkin, C., van Widenfelt, R., Foran, J., Haeberli, P., Fast shadows and lighting effects using texture mapping. *Computer Graphics*, 26:249–252, 1992 (Siggraph '92).

[Sillion89] Sillion, F., Puech, C., A general two-pass method integrating specular and diffuse reflection. *Computer Graphics*, 23(3):335–344 (Siggraph '89).

[Spanguolo92] Spanguolo, M., Polyhedral surface decomposition based on curvature analysis. In: *Modern Geometric Computing for Visualization*, T.L. Kunii and Y. Shinagawa (Eds.), Springer-Verlag, 1992.

[Voorhies94] Voorhies, D., Foran, J., Reflection vector shading hardware. Proceedings, Siggraph '94, ACM Press, pp. 163–166.

[Wallace87] Wallace, J.R., Cohen, M.F., Greenberg, D.P, A two-pass solution to the rendering equation: a synthesis of ray tracing and radiosity methods. *Computer Graphics*, 21:311–320, 1987 (Siggraph '87).

[Whitted80] Whitted, T., An improved illumination model for shaded display. *Comm. of the ACM*, 23(6):343–349, 1980.

Fig. 9: Mixed convexity reflector, with seamless reflections.

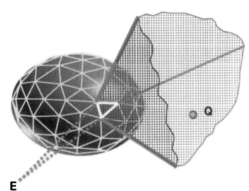

Fig. 10: A 3–D reflected cell.

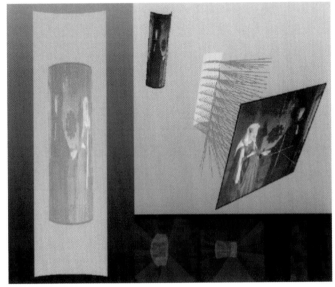

Fig. 11: Virtual object and reflection rays.

Fig. 12: Linear extrusion.

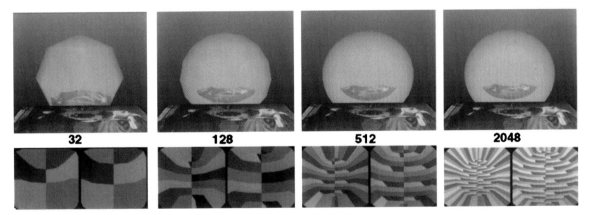

Fig. 13: Varying the tessellation resolution of the reflector.

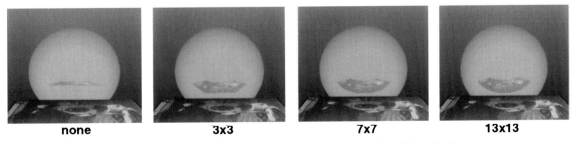

Fig. 14: Varying the tessellation resolution of the reflected object.

Fig. 15: Four reflecting spheres.

Fig. 17: TV.

Fig. 16: Top: our method. Bottom: Rayshade.

Fig. 18: Recursive reflections.

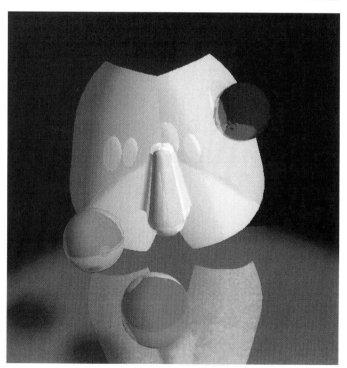

Fig. 19: Reflector containing several convex and concave pieces.

Fig. 20: Polyhedra and sphere.

Non-Distorted Texture Mapping For Sheared Triangulated Meshes

Bruno Lévy[*]   Jean-Laurent Mallet[†]

GOCAD

ENSG, rue du doyen Marcel Roubeault, 54500 Vandoeuvre

Abstract

This article introduces new techniques for non-distorted texture mapping on complex triangulated meshes. Texture coordinates are assigned to the vertices of the triangulation by using an iterative optimization algorithm, honoring a set of constraints minimizing the distortions. As compared to other global optimization techniques, our method allows the user to specify the surface zones where distortions should be minimized in order of preference. The modular approach described in this paper results in a highly flexible method, facilitating a customized mapping construction. For instance, it is easy to align the texture on the surface with a set of user defined isoparametric curves. Moreover, the mapping can be made continuous through cuts, allowing to parametrize in one go complex cut surfaces. It is easy to specify other constraints to be honored by the so-constructed mappings, as soon as they can be expressed by linear (or linearizable) relations. This method has been integrated successfully within a widely used C.A.D. software dedicated to geosciences. In this context, applications of the method comprise numerical computations of physical properties stored in fine grids within texture space, unfolding geological layers and generating grids that are suitable for finite element analysis. The impact of the method could be also important for 3D paint systems.

CR Categories: I.3.3 [Computer Graphics] Picture/Image Generation ; I.3.5 [Computer Graphics]: Three-Dimenstional Graphics and Realism—Color, shading, shadowing and texture; I.4.3 [Image processing]: Enhancement—Geometric Correction, Texture

Keywords: Non Distorted Texture Mapping, Parametrization, Discrete Smooth Interpolation, Optimization

1   INTRODUCTION

Texture mapping is widely used to improve the visual richness of 3D surfaces in computer generated images. Each 3D surface is put in correspondence with a planar image through a function called a *mapping*. Such a *mapping* assigns a pair of coordinates (u, v) referring to a pixel of the planar image to each point of a surface. Thus, for instance, the latitude and longitude can define a trivial mapping of a sphere. This technique was introduced by Catmull in [Cat74], and first applied to bicubic patches using a recursive

*levy@ensg.u-nancy.fr, GOCAD and INRIA Lorraine/CNRS

†mallet@ensg.u-nancy.fr, director of the GOCAD consortium

subdivision algorithm. Unfortunately, these methods often produce highly distorted textures in the resulting images.

First attempts to minimize these distortions were made in [Pea85] and in [BS86] by separating the process into two steps. The texture pattern is first applied to a simple intermediate surface such as a box or a cylinder for which texture mapping is trivial. Then, this intermediate surface is projected on the target object. The choice of the intermediate surface, its orientation together with the projection method dramatically affect the results, and great deal of user interaction is therefore required.

Another idea is to consider that assigning texture coordinates to any surface is equivalent to flattening it. Such a technique is described in [SMSW86]. The idea consists in unfolding a polygonal surface from a user selected seed. A similar idea has been developed in [BVI91]. This latter method means a parametric surface may be unfolded by allowing cuts to appear on the mapped texture when the discrepancy of the geodesic curvature goes beyond a given threshold.

Minimizing the distortions induced by texture mapping can be also realized using optimization techniques. In the method proposed in [ML88], a mapping of any surface is constructed by starting from a grid of points sampled on the surface. The grid is then iteratively optimized by minimizing a global distortion criterion. Krishnamurthy proposes in [KL96] a similar approach for converting a triangulated mesh into a set of B-Spline surfaces. It is also possible to construct a mapping by assigning (u, v) coordinates to the vertices of the mesh. This naturally leads to the use of harmonic maps, as described in [ERDH95]. This method consists in minimizing a *metric dispersion* criterion. Unfortunately, this does not always preserve angles accurately. Another approach is introduced in [Flo97], generalizing the *barycentric mapping* method introduced in [Tut60]. The (u, v) texture coordinates are found to be the solution of a linear system, where each (u, v) point is a convex combination of its neighbors. Floater[Flo97] proposes a way of choosing the coefficients of these convex combinations to mimic the chord length parametrization for curves. These global methods give good results for most surfaces, but suffer from several limitations when applied to complex surfaces. For these kinds of methods, since the criterion to be minimized is hardwired in the optimization algorithm, it is often difficult to take into account user defined information. For instance, as most surfaces are not developable, distortions will still remain, and the user may want to specify the distribution of these distortions.

This article proposes a new global optimization method. As compared to other similar techniques, the method is based on a modular approach enabling the way the mapping is constructed to be customized. For instance, it is possible to tune the perpendicularity and homogeneous spacing of isoparametric curves all over the surface, thus specifying the surface zones where distortions should be minimized in order of preference. It is also possible to make the mapping respect a set of user specified isoparametric curves. Moreover, the mapping can be made continuous through cuts, hence allowing the mapping of a texture on a complex cut surface in one go. The method can be extended easily to honor other kind of linear constraints. All these constraints allow the method to take into account user specified information while beeing much more automatic than other interactive mapping methods [Ped95, LM94, MYV93], where the parametrization is partially or completely defined by the user.

The first section of the paper summarizes the notions involved in texture mapping on triangulated meshes, and shows how a mapping can be constructed using an iterative optimization algorithm. In Section 2, the criteria to be met in constructing a non-distorting mapping are introduced. These criteria are expressed as a set of linear constraints in Section 3, where the algorithm previously introduced is modified in order to honor them. This results in a general algorithm that can be extended easily to take into account user specified information, as shown in Section 4. In this latter section, we show how to respect user specified isoparametric curves, and how to make mappings continuous through cuts. Section 5 presents some applications and results. The paper concludes with some suggestions for future developments.

2 PARAMETRIZING A TRIANGULATION

In this section, the notion of mapping function defined on a triangulated mesh is recalled, and a new method for constructing such mapping functions is described, based on an iterative optimization algorithm. How these mappings can be optimized in order to minimize the distortions is then explained in Section 3.

2.1 Mapping Function Φ and Discrete Mapping φ

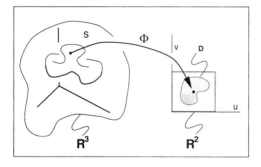

Figure 1: Mapping Φ from a surface $\mathbf{S}$ of $\mathbf{R}^3$ to $\mathcal{D} \subset \mathbf{R}^2$.

As shown in Figure 1, given an open surface $\mathbf{S}$ of $\mathbf{R}^3$, a *mapping* Φ is a one-to-one transform that maps the surface $\mathbf{S}$ to a subset $\mathcal{D}$ of $\mathbf{R}^2$.

$$(x, y, z) \in \mathbf{S} \quad \rightarrow \quad \Phi(x, y, z) = \begin{bmatrix} \Phi^u(x, y, z) \\ \\ \Phi^v(x, y, z) \end{bmatrix}$$

Regarding a mapping, the following definitions can be given:

- $\mathcal{D}$ is called the *parametric (u, v) domain*.

- As Φ is, by definition, a one-to-one function, it has an inverse function $\mathbf{x} = \Phi^{-1}$, called a *parametrization* of the surface:

$$(u, v) \in \mathcal{D} \quad \rightarrow \quad \mathbf{x}(u, v) = \Phi^{-1}(u, v) = \begin{bmatrix} x(u, v) \\ y(u, v) \\ z(u, v) \end{bmatrix}$$

If a surface has a parametrization $\mathbf{x}$ defined, the inverse $\Phi = \mathbf{x}^{-1}$ of this parametrization naturally provides a mapping function. Catmull applied this technique to cubic splines in [Cat74], in which a recursive subdivision scheme is described, making it possible to avoid inverting of the parametrization directly.

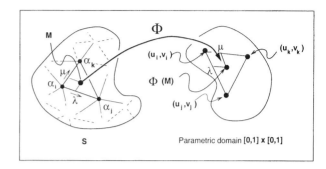

Figure 2: Mapping function Φ interpolated over a triangle.

In what follows, the surface $\mathbf{S}$ is provided with a triangulation $\mathcal{G} = \{\Omega, \mathcal{T}\}$, where Ω is the set of the vertices of the triangulation, and $\mathcal{T}$ the set of the triangles of $\mathcal{G}$, defined as vertex triplets. For the sake of simplicity, Ω will be identified with the interval $[1 \ldots M]$ of integers, where $M = |\Omega|$ denotes the number of vertices of the triangulation. The geometric location at a vertex $\alpha \in \Omega$ is denoted $\mathbf{p}(\alpha)$ in what follows.

For this kind of surface, it is natural to define the value of Φ at the vertices Ω of the triangulation $\mathcal{G}$. This information can be stored as a set of (u_i, v_i) values, where $1 \leq i \leq M$. How to choose these (u_i, v_i) values is explained in Section 4. This defines a discrete function $\varphi : \Omega \to \mathbf{R}^2$ such that $\forall \alpha_i \in \Omega, \varphi(\alpha_i) = \{\varphi^u(\alpha_i), \varphi^v(\alpha_i)\} = (u_i, v_i)$. As shown in Figure 2, a mapping function Φ can be then defined as the linear interpolation of φ over each triangle $\mathbf{T} = (\alpha_i, \alpha_j, \alpha_k)$ of $\mathcal{T}$. For each point $\mathbf{p}$ in $\mathbf{T}$, Φ is given by:

$$\begin{cases} \Phi(\mathbf{p}) &= & (1 - \lambda - \mu) & \cdot & \varphi(\alpha_i) \\ & + & \lambda & \cdot & \varphi(\alpha_j) \\ & + & \mu & \cdot & \varphi(\alpha_k) \end{cases}$$

where:

- λ and μ are the local barycentric coordinates at the point $\mathbf{p}$ in $\mathbf{T}$

- $\varphi(\alpha_i) = (u_i, v_i)$, $\varphi(\alpha_j) = (u_j, v_j)$, $\varphi(\alpha_k) = (u_k, v_k)$

2.2 Discrete Smooth Interpolation

Given a triangulation $\mathcal{G} = \{\Omega, \mathcal{T}\}$, we want to assign (u, v) coordinates to each vertex $\alpha \in \Omega$. Floater has shown in [Flo97] that verifying the following two sufficient conditions constructs a mapping:

1. The image of the border of the surface through φ in the parametric (u, v) domain is a convex polygon.

2. Each internal node is a convex combination of its neighbours.

One must keep in mind that these two conditions are **sufficient** and not necessary to define mappings. We show in Section 4 how the first one can be replaced by a less restrictive condition.

More formally, the second condition can be written as follows (see Equation 1):

$$\forall k \in \Omega, \quad \sum_{\alpha \in N(k)} v^\alpha(k).\varphi(\alpha) = 0 \quad (1)$$

where:

- $N(k)$ denotes the set of nodes directly connected to k, including k.

- the $v^\alpha(k)$ are **given** coefficients such that:

$$\left\{ \begin{array}{lll} v^\alpha(k) & > & 0 \qquad\qquad\quad \forall \alpha \in N(k) - \{k\} \\[2mm] v^k(k) & = & -\displaystyle\sum_{\substack{\alpha \in N(k) \\ \alpha \neq k}} v^\alpha(k) \neq 0 \quad \forall k \in \Omega \end{array} \right. \quad (2)$$

Once boundary nodes have been mapped to a convex polygon in parametric domain space, (u, v) coordinates must be assigned to the internal nodes of the triangulation. Instead of finding φ by directly solving Equation 1 as done in more classical approaches, the method described in this article consists of minimizing a global criterion *in a least square sense*, honoring at the same time a set of linear constraints, as will be shown in the next section. The algorithm is based on the *Discrete Smooth Interpolation* (D.S.I.), that we describe in [Mal89, Mal92]. The reader is referred to these two articles where the notions of *generalized roughness*, *linear constraints*, and the iterative D.S.I. algorithm introduced further on in this document are described in depth. The criterion minimized by the D.S.I. method is called the *roughness R*, and is defined in Equation 3 below:

$$R(\varphi) = \sum_{k \in \Omega} \sum_{\nu \in \{u,v\}} \left\{ \sum_{\alpha \in N(k)} v^\alpha(k).\varphi^\nu(k) \right\}^2 \quad (3)$$

The minimum of this functionnal is reached if $\partial R(\varphi)/\partial\varphi^\nu(\alpha) = 0$ for each $\alpha \in \Omega$ and for each $\nu \in \{u, v\}$, where ν denotes one of the two components of φ. This yields the following equation:

$$\varphi^\nu(\alpha) = -\frac{G^\nu(\alpha|\varphi)}{g^\nu(\alpha)}$$

where:

$$\left| \begin{array}{lll} G^\nu(\alpha|\varphi) & = & \displaystyle\sum_{k \in N(\alpha)} \left\{ v^\alpha(k). \sum_{\substack{\beta \in N(k) \\ \beta \neq \alpha}} v^\beta(k).\varphi^\nu(\beta) \right\} \\[4mm] g^\nu(\alpha) & = & \displaystyle\sum_{\alpha \in N(\alpha)} \{v^\alpha(k)\}^2 \end{array} \right. \quad (4)$$

The following algorithm computes iteratively the assignments of (u, v) coefficients minimizing the roughness given in Equation 3. We have proven in Mallet[Mal89] that it does converge to a unique solution, as soon as at least one node α has its value $\varphi(\alpha)$ fixed, and provided that the chosen $v^\alpha(k)$ coefficients honor Equation 2. Later in this document, we show how this method can be enhanced using D.S.I. constraints.

let I be the set of nodes where φ is unknown
let $\varphi_{[0]}$ be a given initial approximated solution
while (more iterations are needed) {
    for_all($\alpha \in I$) {
        for_all($\nu \in \{u, v\}$) {
            $\varphi^\nu(\alpha) := -\frac{G^\nu(\alpha)}{g^\nu(\alpha)}$
        }
    }
}

Where the $v^\alpha(k)$ coefficients are concerned, several choices are available. One possible choice described by Floater[Flo97] is referred to as the *shape preserving* weighting, and ensures that the location of a vertex in parametric space relative to its neighbors mimics the local geometry around the vertex being considered. The approach described in this article is quite different, as by separating the criteria minimizing the distortions from those which ensure that a valid mapping is constructed, we can obtain a finer control on the way the surface is parametrized. For this reason, the simple harmonic weighting defined as follows is used for the $\{v^\alpha(k)\}$:

$$v^\alpha(k) = \left\{ \begin{array}{ll} 1 & \text{if} \quad \alpha \in N(k) - \{k\} \\ -degree(k) & \text{if} \quad \alpha = k \end{array} \right.$$

where $degree(k)$ denotes the number of neighbors of k. Clearly, one of the previously mentioned more sophisticated weightings such as the *shape preserving* or *gaussian* weightings could have been used instead, since they both satisfy Equation 2, but it is shown in the next section that by using linear constraints, the same effect can be obtained with higher flexibility.

3 NON-DISTORTED MAPPING

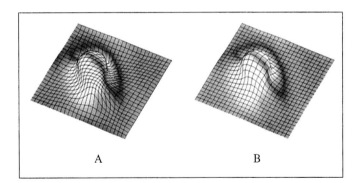

A   B

Figure 3: Isoparametric curves obtained without (A) and with (B) non-distortion constraints.

In this section, we define the criterion to be minimized in order to construct a non-distorted texture mapping. In a nutshell, this criterion preserves the perpendicularity and constant spacing of the isoparametric curves traced on the surface, as shown in Figure 3. In other words, the gradients of u and v should be perpendicular one to another and constant all over the surface (see [Car76]). This requires defining the gradient of a function interpolated over a triangulated mesh from the vertices of the triangulation, definition given below. The way the algorithm presented in the previous section can be modified to take into account this criterion is then explained.

Data in Figure 3 shows the effect of the constraints described in this section as applied while parametrizing a triangulated mesh.

The isoparametric curves obtained when applying the algorithm described in Section 2 are shown in Figure 3-A, whereas the constraints described further on give the result shown in Figure 3-B.

3.1 Gradient of a Discrete Function φ Interpolated over a Triangulation $\mathcal{G}$

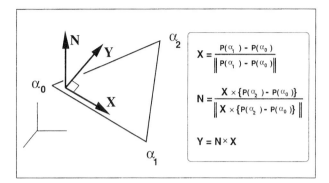

Figure 4: Local orthonormal basis $(\mathbf{X}, \mathbf{Y})$ of a triangle $\mathbf{T} = (\alpha_0, \alpha_1, \alpha_2)$.

As shown in Figure 4, each triangle $\mathbf{T} = (\alpha_0, \alpha_1, \alpha_2)$ of $\mathcal{T}$ can be provided with a local orthonormal basis $(\mathbf{p}(\alpha_0), \mathbf{X}, \mathbf{Y})$. The function $\varphi_T^\nu(X, Y)$ denotes the linear interpolation of φ^ν over the triangle $\mathbf{T}$, where $\nu \in \{u, v\}$ represents one of the two components of φ and where (X, Y) are the local coordinates in the orthonormal basis $(\mathbf{p}(\alpha_0), \mathbf{X}, \mathbf{Y})$ of $\mathbf{T}$.

In this basis, one can check that the gradient of φ_T^ν is constant over $\mathbf{T}$ and is a linear combination of the values of φ_T^ν at the three vertices of the triangle $\mathbf{T}$. The six coefficients $D_X(\alpha_j)$ and $D_Y(\alpha_j)$ given in Equation 5 below are solely dependent on the geometry of the triangle $\mathbf{T}$.

$$
\left|
\begin{aligned}
\frac{\partial \varphi_T^\nu}{\partial X} &= \sum_{j=0}^{2} D_X(\alpha_j).\varphi^\nu(\alpha_j) \\[1ex]
\frac{\partial \varphi_T^\nu}{\partial Y} &= \sum_{j=0}^{2} D_Y(\alpha_j).\varphi^\nu(\alpha_j)
\end{aligned}
\right.
$$

$$
\text{where:} \left\{
\begin{aligned}
D_X(\alpha_0) &= (y_1 - y_2)/d \\
D_X(\alpha_1) &= (y_2 - y_0)/d \\
D_X(\alpha_2) &= (y_0 - y_1)/d \\
D_Y(\alpha_0) &= (x_2 - x_1)/d \\
D_Y(\alpha_1) &= (x_0 - x_2)/d \\
D_Y(\alpha_2) &= (x_1 - x_0)/d \\[1ex]
d &= (x_1 - x_0).(y_2 - y_0) - (x_2 - x_0).(y_1 - y_0) \\[1ex]
x_j &= (\mathbf{p}(\alpha_j) - \mathbf{p}(\alpha_0)).\mathbf{X} \\
y_j &= (\mathbf{p}(\alpha_j) - \mathbf{p}(\alpha_0)).\mathbf{Y}
\end{aligned}
\right. \quad \forall j \in \{0, 1, 2\}
$$

$$(5)$$

Using this definition of the gradient of φ, it is possible to write the equations corresponding to the orthogonality and homogeneous spacing of the isoparametric curves. The orthogonality of the iso-u and iso-v curves in a triangle $\mathbf{T}$ is given by:

$$
\begin{bmatrix} \frac{\partial \varphi_T^u}{\partial X} & \frac{\partial \varphi_T^u}{\partial Y} \end{bmatrix} . \begin{bmatrix} \frac{\partial \varphi_T^v}{\partial X} \\ \frac{\partial \varphi_T^v}{\partial Y} \end{bmatrix} = 0 \qquad (6)
$$

If we consider that φ^u is fixed and that φ^v is to be determined, replacing in Equation 6 the gradient of φ^v with its expression given in Equation 5 yields the following equation, which **linearly** combines the values of φ^v at the three vertices $(\alpha_0, \alpha_1, \alpha2)$ of $\mathbf{T}$. The equation to be used when φ^u is interpolated can be obtained by exchanging u and v in Equation 7.

$$
\sum_{j \in \{0,1,2\}} \left\{ \varphi^v(\alpha_j). \left(\frac{\partial \varphi_T^u}{\partial X}.D_X(\alpha_j) + \frac{\partial \varphi_T^u}{\partial Y}.D_Y(\alpha_j) \right) \right\} = 0
$$

$$(7)$$

The remaining condition on φ concerns the homogeneous spacing of the isoparametric curves. In other words, the gradient must not vary from one triangle to another. This requires that a common basis for two adjacent triangles $\mathbf{T}$ and $\tilde{\mathbf{T}}$ be defined, as shown in Figure 5. The same expressions as introduced in Figure 4 are used. The vector $\mathbf{X}$ is shared by the two bases, and $\tilde{\mathbf{Y}}$ is such that $\mathbf{Y}$ and $\tilde{\mathbf{Y}}$ would become colinear if the pair of triangles $(\mathbf{T}, \tilde{\mathbf{T}})$ was unfolded along their common edge $[\alpha_0, \alpha_1]$.

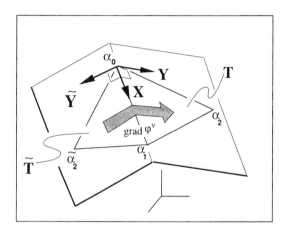

Figure 5: Constant gradient across the common edge of two triangles $\mathbf{T}$ and $\tilde{\mathbf{T}}$.

The homogeneous spacing of the isoparametric curves is verified if, and only if, for each edge of $\mathcal{T}$ the equation below is verified:

$$
\left\{
\begin{aligned}
\frac{\partial \varphi_T^u}{\partial X} &= \frac{\partial \varphi_{\tilde{T}}^u}{\partial X} & ; & & \frac{\partial \varphi_T^u}{\partial Y} &= -\frac{\partial \varphi_{\tilde{T}}^u}{\partial \tilde{Y}} \\[1ex]
\frac{\partial \varphi_T^v}{\partial X} &= \frac{\partial \varphi_{\tilde{T}}^v}{\partial X} & ; & & \frac{\partial \varphi_T^v}{\partial Y} &= -\frac{\partial \varphi_{\tilde{T}}^v}{\partial \tilde{Y}}
\end{aligned}
\right.
$$

$$(8)$$

By replacing in Equation 8 the gradients of φ^u and φ^v by their expressions in $\mathbf{T}$ and $\tilde{\mathbf{T}}$, the following four **linear** equations are obtained (see Equation 9), concerning the two components X and Y of the gradients of φ^u and φ^v. The term δ_W takes into account the fact that $\mathbf{Y}$ and $\tilde{\mathbf{Y}}$ point in an opposite direction.

$$
\begin{aligned}
&\forall \nu \in \{u, v\}, \\
&\forall W \in \{X, Y\},
\end{aligned}
\left|
\begin{aligned}
&\varphi^\nu(\alpha_0). \left\{ D_W(\alpha_0) + \delta_W.\tilde{D}_W(\alpha_0) \right\} + \\
&\varphi^\nu(\alpha_1). \left\{ D_W(\alpha_1) + \delta_W.\tilde{D}_W(\alpha_1) \right\} + \\
&\varphi^\nu(\alpha_2). \left\{ D_W(\alpha_2) \right\} + \\
&\varphi^\nu(\tilde{\alpha}_2). \left\{ \delta_W.\tilde{D}_W(\tilde{\alpha}_2) \right\} = 0
\end{aligned}
\right.
$$

$$
\text{where} \quad \delta_W = \begin{cases} -1 & \text{if} \quad W = X \\ +1 & \text{if} \quad W = Y \end{cases}
$$

$$(9)$$

3.2 Honoring Linear Constraints

We have shown in Section 2 how D.S.I. can be used to construct a mapping of a triangulated mesh. What we want to do now is to take into account the two criteria minimizing the distortions of the mapping, namely the perpendicularity and homogeneity criteria previously introduced. These two criteria can be written as a set of linear equations. As it is not possible to honor these constraints for a non-developable surface, they will be respected *in a least square sense*, thus *minimizing* the distortions. The general form of such a constraint is given in Equation 10 below:

$$\sum_{\alpha \in \Omega} \{ A_{c^\nu}(\alpha).\varphi^\nu(\alpha) \} = b_{c^\nu} \qquad (10)$$

where the values $A_{c^\nu}(\alpha)$ and the scalar b_{c^ν} are constant **given** coefficients defining the constraint c.

Equation 7, corresponding to the perpendicularity of the isoparametric curves in the triangle $\mathbf{T} = (\alpha_0, \alpha_1, \alpha_2)$, yields two constraints $c_{\mathbf{T}}^u$ and $c_{\mathbf{T}}^v$ to be honored when interpolating φ^u and φ^v respectively. The expression of $c_{\mathbf{T}}^v$ is given below in Equation 11. The expression of the twin constraint $c_{\mathbf{T}}^u$ can be obtained by permuting u and v in this equation.

$$\left|
\begin{aligned}
\forall j \in \{0,1,2\}, & \\
A_{c_{\mathbf{T}}^v}(\alpha_j) &= \frac{\partial \varphi_{\mathbf{T}}^u}{\partial X}.D_X(\alpha_j) + \frac{\partial \varphi_{\mathbf{T}}^u}{\partial Y}.D_Y(\alpha_j) \\
\forall \alpha \notin \{\alpha_0, \alpha_1, \alpha_2\}, & \\
A_{c_{\mathbf{T}}^v}(\alpha) &= 0 \\
b_{c_{\mathbf{T}}^v} &= 0
\end{aligned}
\right. \qquad (11)$$

The homogeneity criterion specified by Equation 9 can be expressed by the following four constraints $c_{\mathbf{E}}^{uX}$, $c_{\mathbf{E}}^{uY}$, $c_{\mathbf{E}}^{vX}$ and $c_{\mathbf{E}}^{vY}$ yielded by Equation 12 below, to be taken into account at each edge $\mathbf{E} = (\alpha_0, \alpha_1)$ of the triangulation $\mathcal{G}$. The vertices α_2 and $\tilde{\alpha}_2$ denote the two remaining vertices of the two triangles $\mathbf{T}$ and $\tilde{\mathbf{T}}$ sharing the edge $\mathbf{E}$.

$$\left|
\begin{aligned}
A_{c_{\mathbf{E}}^{\nu W}}(\alpha_0) &= \left\{ D_W(\alpha_0) + \delta_W.\tilde{D}_W(\alpha_0) \right\} \\
A_{c_{\mathbf{E}}^{\nu W}}(\alpha_1) &= \left\{ D_W(\alpha_1) + \delta_W.\tilde{D}_W(\alpha_1) \right\} \\
A_{c_{\mathbf{E}}^{\nu W}}(\alpha_2) &= D_W(\alpha_2) \\
A_{c_{\mathbf{E}}^{\nu W}}(\tilde{\alpha}_2) &= \delta_W.\tilde{D}_W(\tilde{\alpha}_2) \\
A_{c_{\mathbf{E}}^{\nu W}}(\alpha) &= 0 \quad \forall \alpha \notin \{\alpha_0, \alpha_1, \alpha_2, \tilde{\alpha}_2\} \\
b_{c_{\mathbf{E}}^{\nu W}} &= 0
\end{aligned}
\right.$$

where:

$$\nu \in \{u,v\} \;\; ; \;\; W \in \{X,Y\} \;\; ; \;\; \delta_W = \left\{ \begin{aligned} -1 & \quad \text{if} \quad W = X \\ +1 & \quad \text{if} \quad W = Y \end{aligned} \right. \qquad (12)$$

The *roughness* criterion which D.S.I. minimizes can be generalized in order to honor a set $\mathcal{C}$ of linear constraints in a least square sense. In our case, the set $\mathcal{C}$ of constraints is given by Equation 13, where $\mathcal{E}$ denotes the set of the edges of the triangulation $\mathcal{G}(\Omega, \mathcal{T})$.

$$\mathcal{C} = \left(\bigcup_{\mathbf{T} \in \mathcal{T}} \{ c_{\mathbf{T}}^u, c_{\mathbf{T}}^v \} \right) \cup \left(\bigcup_{\mathbf{E} \in \mathcal{E}} \{ c_{\mathbf{E}}^{uX}, c_{\mathbf{E}}^{uY}, c_{\mathbf{E}}^{vX}, c_{\mathbf{E}}^{vY} \} \right) \qquad (13)$$

The *generalized roughness* $R^*(\varphi)$, taking into account the degree of violation of the constraints $\mathcal{C}$, is given by Equation 14 below. In addition to the equation of the roughness given in Section 3 (Equation 3), several terms correspond to the linear constraints, as described further on:

$$R^*(\varphi) = R(\varphi) \;\; + $$
$$\phi.\sum_{c \in \mathcal{C}} \varpi_c. \left\{ \left(\sum_{\nu \in \{u,v\}} \sum_{\alpha \in \Omega} A_c^\nu(\alpha).\varphi^\nu(\alpha) \right) - b_c \right\}^2 \qquad (14)$$

In Equation 14, the term $R(\varphi)$ is the *roughness* (see Equation 3), and the second term represents the degree of violation of the linear constraints. Each constraint c is ponderated by a given $\varpi_c > 0$ coefficient, allowing to tune the relative importance of the constraints. For instance, it is possible to make the mapping respect the perpendicularity rather than the homogeneity. Moreover, since each triangle $\mathbf{T}$ and edge $\mathbf{E}$ has an individual constraint defined, as well as an individual associated ϖ_c coefficient, it is possible to select the surface zones where the distortions are to be minimized in order of preference. The remaining coefficient $\phi \in]0, +\infty[$ is a given parameter called the *fitting factor* and representing the importance of the constraints relative to the roughness.

The functionnal $R^*(\varphi)$ is a quadratic form, whose minimum is reached if $\partial R^*(\varphi)/\partial \varphi^\nu(\alpha) = 0$ for each $\nu \in \{u, v\}$ and for each $\alpha \in \Omega$. This yields the following equation, which solution minimizes $R^*(\varphi)$:

$$\varphi^\nu(\alpha) = -\frac{G^\nu(\alpha|\phi) + (\phi.\varpi).\Gamma^\nu(\alpha|\varphi)}{g^\nu(\alpha) + (\phi.\varpi).\gamma^\nu(\alpha)} \qquad (15)$$

$$\left|
\begin{aligned}
\Gamma^\nu(\alpha|\varphi) &= \sum_{c \in \mathcal{C}} \varpi_c.\Gamma_c^\nu(\alpha|\varphi) \\
\gamma^\nu(\alpha) &= \sum_{c \in \mathcal{C}} \varpi_c.\gamma_c^\nu(\alpha)
\end{aligned}
\right. \qquad (16)$$

with:

$$\left\{
\begin{aligned}
\gamma_c^\nu(\alpha) &= (A_c^\nu(\alpha))^2 \\
\Gamma_c^\nu(\alpha|\varphi) &= A_c^\nu(\alpha). \left\{ \sum_{\beta \neq \alpha} A_c^\nu(\beta).\varphi^\nu(\beta) - b_c \right\}
\end{aligned}
\right. \qquad (17)$$

The orthogonality constraint suggests a modification in the iterative D.S.I. algorithm. The two internal loops iterating on the components of φ and on the nodes of Ω respectively have been inverted. At each iteration, φ^u is interpolated while φ^v is considered to be constant, then the roles of φ^u and φ^v are permuted. The resulting algorithm given below assigns (u, v) coordinates to the vertices of the triangulation while respecting the specified set of constraints.

```
let I be the set of nodes where φ is unknown
let φ[0] be a given initial approximated solution
while (more iterations are needed) {
    for_all( ν ∈ {u, v}) {
        for_all( α ∈ I ) {
```
$$\varphi^\nu(\alpha) := -\frac{G^\nu(\alpha) + \Gamma^\nu(\alpha|\phi)}{g^\nu(\alpha) + \gamma^\nu(\alpha)}$$
```
        }
    }
}
```

4 LOCALLY CONSTRAINING A MAPPING

The constraints defined so far in this paper provide the user with a *global* control on the mapping function. Even if the orthogonality and perpendicularity constraints can be weighted locally to specify the zones where distortions are preferably to be minimized, this may be not sufficient for some applications, where a more precise set of local constraints is required. For instance, it may be necessary to align some details of textures with details of models, which can be achieved by specifying isoparametric curves. Moreover, the model to be texture mapped can present cuts, and the user may want do define a single mapping function for a cut model instead of sewing together several patches. This requirement can be fulfilled by making the mapping continuous through cuts as described further on.

4.1 Specifying an Isoparametric Curve

As shown in Figure 6, we consider that we have a given polygonal curve $L = \{\mathbf{p}_0, \ldots, \mathbf{p}_m\}$ associated with a given value u_0 of the parameter u. We describe here the constraints to be honored for making the isoparametric of the mapping defined by $(u = u_0)$ correspond to the projection of L on the surface $\mathbf{S}$. Each point $\mathbf{p}_i$ of L yields a constraint $c_{\mathbf{p}_i}$ ensuring that the isoparametric curve $u = u_0$ of the mapping φ passes near the projection $\mathbf{p}'_i$ of $\mathbf{p}_i$ on $\mathbf{S}$.

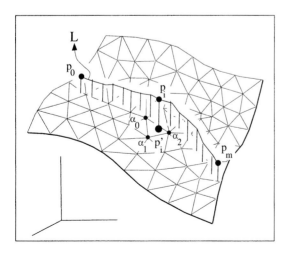

Figure 6: Aligning details of the texture to details of the model by specifying an isoparametric curve.

The triangle $\mathbf{T} = (\alpha_0, \alpha_1, \alpha_2)$ is the triangle of $\mathbf{S}$ that contains $\mathbf{p}'_i$, and $(\lambda_0, \lambda_1, \lambda_2)$ are the barycentric coordinates of $\mathbf{p}'_i$ in $\mathbf{T}$. The linear relation to be honored is given in Equation 18 below.

$$\left|\quad \begin{aligned} &\sum_{j \in \{0,1,2\}} \lambda_j \cdot \varphi^u(\alpha_j) = u_0 \\[2mm] &\text{where:} \begin{cases} \displaystyle\sum_{j \in \{0,1,2\}} \lambda_j \cdot \mathbf{p}(\alpha_j) = \mathbf{p}'_i \\[2mm] \displaystyle\sum_{j \in \{0,1,2\}} \lambda_j = 1 \end{cases} \end{aligned} \right. \qquad (18)$$

Equation 19 below gives the expression of the constraint $c_{\mathbf{p}_i}$ in the form of Equation 10 in Section 2. Such a constraint per point $\mathbf{p}_i$ is added to the set $\mathcal{C}$ to be honored by D.S.I., introduced in the previous section.

$$\begin{cases} A_{c_{\mathbf{p}_i}}(\alpha_j) &= \lambda_j \quad \forall j \in \{0,1,2\} \\[2mm] A_{c_{\mathbf{p}_i}}(\alpha) &= 0 \quad \forall \alpha \notin \{\alpha_0, \alpha_1, \alpha_2\} \\[2mm] b_{c_{\mathbf{p}_i}} &= u_0 \end{cases} \qquad (19)$$

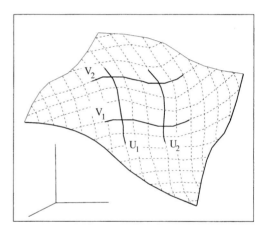

Figure 7: Extrapolating a mapping from four user specified isoparametric curves.

Remark:

As mentioned in Section 2, the two following **sufficient** conditions ensure that a discrete function φ defines a mapping:

1. The image of the border of the surface through φ in the parametric (u, v) domain is a convex polygon.

2. Each internal node is a convex combination of its neighbors.

Introducing the constraints to ensure that the isoparametric curves are orthogonal, with homogeneous spacing means the first condition can be replaced by a less restrictive one. As shown in Figure 7, it is then sufficient to specify four arcs of isoparametric curves $\{u_1, u_2, v_1, v_2\}$ using the constraint previously introduced. Thus, by enabling us to use the algorithm not only as an *interpolator*, but also as an *extrapolator*, it is possible to construct mappings for surfaces having complex shaped borders by leaving φ unspecified on the border.

4.2 Constructing a Mapping for a Cut Surface

Let us now consider that the surface has cuts, and that we want the mapping function Φ to be continuous through these cuts. Instead of using several distinct patches and making the edges of the patches match as described in [Blo85], the surface is considered here as a single patch (as it was before being cut), as suggested in [CEM97]. The set of constraints described below allows us to assign (u, v) coordinates to the vertices of the triangulation in such a way that the two borders of a cut are mapped to the same curve by the interpolated Φ mapping function. In other words, the cuts are sewn in (u, v) domain space.

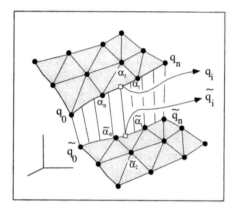

Figure 8: Connecting two borders of a cut in texture space.

As shown in Figure 8, twin set of points $\{\mathbf{q}_i, i = 0 \ldots n\}$ and $\{\tilde{\mathbf{q}}_i, i = 0 \ldots n\}$ are sampled on the twin borders of the cut. We describe now how to make the mapping match at each pair $(\mathbf{q}_i, \tilde{\mathbf{q}}_i)$ of points. More precisely, we want to respect the following conditions:

$$\forall \nu \in \{u, v\} \left| \begin{array}{lll} (1) & \varphi_T^\nu(\mathbf{q}_i) & = & \varphi_{\tilde{T}}^\nu(\tilde{\mathbf{q}}_i) \\ (2) & \mathbf{grad}\varphi_T^\nu & = & \mathbf{grad}\varphi_{\tilde{T}}^\nu \end{array} \right. \quad (20)$$

where T and $\tilde{T}$ denote the triangles containing $\mathbf{q}_i$ and $\tilde{\mathbf{q}}_i$ respectively. The gradient $\mathbf{grad}\varphi_T^\nu$ is computed as described in Section 3 (see Equation 5), using the basis shown in Figure 4.

Using the methods introduced in the previous two sections, it is easy to translate these two conditions into the D.S.I. constraints $c_{\mathbf{q}_i, \tilde{\mathbf{q}}_i}^\nu$ and $c_{\mathbf{q}_i, \tilde{\mathbf{q}}_i}^{\nu W}$, given below in the equations 21 and 22 respectively.

$$\left| \begin{array}{llll} A_{c_{\mathbf{q}_i, \tilde{\mathbf{q}}_i}^\nu}(\alpha_j) & = & \lambda_j & \forall j \in \{0, 1\} \\ A_{c_{\mathbf{q}_i, \tilde{\mathbf{q}}_i}^\nu}(\tilde{\alpha}_j) & = & -\tilde{\lambda}_j & \forall j \in \{0, 1\} \\ A_{c_{\mathbf{q}_i, \tilde{\mathbf{q}}_i}^\nu}(\alpha_j) & = & 0 & \forall \alpha \notin \{\alpha_0, \alpha_1, \tilde{\alpha}_0, \tilde{\alpha}_1\} \\ b_{c_{\mathbf{q}_i, \tilde{\mathbf{q}}_i}^\nu}(\alpha_j) & = & 0 \end{array} \right. \quad (21)$$

where $\lambda_{j, j \in \{0, 1\}}$ and $\tilde{\lambda}_{j, j \in \{0, 1\}}$ denote the barycentric coordinates of $\mathbf{q}_i$ in $[\mathbf{p}(\alpha_0), \mathbf{p}(\alpha_1)]$ and $\tilde{\mathbf{q}}_i$ in $[\mathbf{p}(\tilde{\alpha}_0), \mathbf{p}(\tilde{\alpha}_1)]$ respectively.

The four constraints $c_{\mathbf{q}_i, \tilde{\mathbf{q}}_i}^{uX}$, $c_{\mathbf{q}_i, \tilde{\mathbf{q}}_i}^{uY}$, $c_{\mathbf{q}_i, \tilde{\mathbf{q}}_i}^{vX}$, and $c_{\mathbf{q}_i, \tilde{\mathbf{q}}_i}^{vY}$ yielded by Equation 22 below ensure a constant gradient of the mapping through the cut. In other words, an isoparametric curve points in the same direction in the two corresponding triangles $\mathbf{T}$ and $\tilde{\mathbf{T}}$.

$$\left| \begin{array}{llll} A_{c_{\mathbf{q}_i, \tilde{\mathbf{q}}_i}^{\nu W}}(\alpha_j) & = & D_j & \forall j \in \{0, 1, 2\} \\ A_{c_{\mathbf{q}_i, \tilde{\mathbf{q}}_i}^{\nu W}}(\tilde{\alpha}_j) & = & \delta_W . \tilde{D}_j & \forall j \in \{0, 1, 2\} \\ A_{c_{\mathbf{q}_i, \tilde{\mathbf{q}}_i}^{\nu W}}(\alpha) & = & 0 & \forall \alpha \notin \{\alpha_0, \alpha_1, \alpha_2, \tilde{\alpha}_0, \tilde{\alpha}_1, \tilde{\alpha}_2\} \\ b_{c_{\mathbf{q}_i, \tilde{\mathbf{q}}_i}^{\nu W}}(\alpha) & = & 0 \end{array} \right.$$

where:

$$\nu \in \{u, v\} \;\; ; \;\; W \in \{X, Y\} \;\; ; \;\; \delta_W = \left\{ \begin{array}{lll} -1 & \text{if} & W = X \\ +1 & \text{if} & W = Y \end{array} \right. \quad (22)$$

5 RESULTS AND APPLICATIONS

One can see in Figure 9 the results of the method applied to a triangulated mesh representing a face (see Figure 9-A). The effect of the orthogonality and homogeneity constraints can be brought to the fore by comparing Figure 9-B (no constraint used) and Figure 9-E (orthogonality and homogeneity enforced), where a checker pattern is mapped to the mesh. The isoparametric curves corresponding to this latter image are displayed in Figure 9-D, where one can check that the iso-u curves shown in red are perpendicular to the iso-v shown in blue. In Figure 9-C, the same non-distorting mapping function is used with a fancier texture. For all these pictures, the constraints ensuring the continuity of the mapping through cuts have been specified at the mouth and the eyes of the model. This model has 3000 triangles, and has been parametrized after 100 iterations in approximatively one minute using an R4000 machine.

As with any other texture mapping method, or more precisely as with any parametrization algorithm, our techniques may be applied to problems other than those associated with texture mapping. In the realm of geosciences, several different methods based on our technique have been implemented into a widely used geology oriented C.A.D. software. Among all the possible applications, to name but a few:

- Unfolding surfaces representing the boundaries of geological layers while preserving the volume of the layers;

- Generating grids suitable for finite elements analysis;

- Beautifying triangulated meshes by remeshing in (u, v) domain space.

- Constructing Spline surfaces from triangulated meshes;

- Performing computations such as *geostatistical simulations* in (u, v) domain space.

Not only do these applications require that mappings present non-distorting properties, which is fulfilled by our method, but in addition, these applications will benefit from the ability of our method to take into account additional information expressed in the form of linear constraints.

The method applied to geological data is demonstrated in Figure 10. In Figure 10-A, one can see a mapping of a complex cut surface, corresponding to a boundary of a geological layer presenting faults. In Figure 10-B, the isoparametric curves of the mapping are displayed, and one can see that the mapping is continuous through the cuts of the surface. In Figure 10-(C,D,E), a surface representing a dome of salt is parametrized. For this kind of surfaces which are far from developable, distortions will still remain, and one can choose a compromise between the orthogonality and the homogeneity of the mapping by tuning the weightings ϖ_c of the two constraints. In Figure 10-C, the orthogonality is respected, but the sizes of the squares differ in a great deal, whereas in Figure 10-E the squares have approximatively the same size while the isoparametric curves are far from orthogonal. An average solution is shown in Figure 10-D, where the same weighting has been used for the two constraints. One can see in Figure 10-F a mapped surface with an isoparametric curve specified. As shown in Figure 10-G, the texture has been aligned to this curve.

CONCLUSIONS

We have presented in this paper new techniques for non-distorted mapping. In addition to the other methods based on global minimization of distortions, our method can easily take into account various additional information. It is thus possible to specify the zones where distortions should be minimized in order of preference, to make a set of isoparametric passes through user specified curves, and to sew the cuts of a surface in texture space. Moreover, it is very easy to extend the method by defining new constraints, once these constraints can be expressed as linear (or linearizable) relations.

The method can be easily implemented, since it does only require an efficient representation of triangulated meshes, which is provided by most C.A.D. packages. Thus, the algorithm has been integrated as a basic algorithm into a widely used C.A.D. software dedicated to geology, and several methods other than these associated with texture mapping have been developped based on this algorithm, such as unfolding geological layers and performing computations in texture space.

One of the limitations of the technique is that it can be applied to planar graphs only, i.e. to surfaces topologically equivalent to a disk. A generalization of the method working on arbitrary topology could be realized, by dividing the surface into (topological) disks using a Voronoi based approach, as proposed in [ERDH95]. A method such as the one descrined in [Tur91] could be also used to choose the sites of the Voronoi diagram. A constraint ensuring the continuity of the gradient from one domain to another could be added (see Equation 22), thus blurring the limits of the base triangles that appear when directly applying the method described in [ERDH95]. The interactivity of the tool could also be improved by speeding up the algorithm, using a conjugate gradient method. This latter improvement together with a large set of possible local constraints could have an important impact on 3D paint systems. Future research also comprise the extension of the method to tetrahedralized meshes, enabling to assign (u, v, w) coordinates to the vertices of tetrahedralizations.

AKNOWLEDGEMENTS

This research has been performed in the frame of the G◯CAD project, and the authors want to thank here the sponsors of the consortium, especially *Gaz de France* who supports this work. Thanks also to the reviewers for their interresting comments.

References

[Blo85] J. Bloomenthal. Modeling the Mighty Maple. In *SIGGRAPH 85 Conference Proceedings*, volume 19, pages 305–311. ACM, July 1985.

[BS86] E. Bier and K. Sloan. Two-Part Texture Mapping. *IEEE Computer Graphics and Applications*, pages 40–53, September 1986.

[BVI91] C. Bennis, J.M. Vézien, and G. Iglésias. Piecewise Surface Flattening for Non-Distorted Texture Mapping. In *SIGGRAPH 91 Conference Proceedings*, volume 25, pages 237–246. ACM, July 1991.

[Car76] M.F. Do Carmo. *Differential Geometry of Curves and Surfaces*. Prentice Hall, Englewood Cliffs, Inc., 1976.

[Cat74] E. Catmull. A Subdivision Algorithm for Computer Display of Curved Surfaces. *PhD thesis*, Dept. of Computer Sciences, University of Utah, December 1974.

[CEM97] R. Cognot, T. Aït Ettajer and J.L. Mallet. Modeling Discontinuities on Faulted Geological Surfaces. In *SEG Technical Program*, pages 1711–1718, November 1997.

[ERDH95] M. Eck, T. DeRose, T. Duchamp, H. Hoppes, M. Lounsbery and W. Stuetzle. Multiresolution Analysis of Arbitrary Meshes. In *SIGGRAPH 95 Conference Proceedings*, pages 173–182. ACM, August 1995.

[Flo97] M.S. Floater. Parametrization and Smooth Approximation of Surface Triangulations. *Computer Aided Geometric Design*, 14(3):231–250, April 1997.

[KL96] V. Krishnamurthy and M. Levoy. Fitting Smooth Surfaces to Dense Polygon Meshes. *SIGGRAPH 96 Conference Proceedings*, pages 313–324. ACM, August 1996.

[LM94] P. Litwinowicz and G. Miller. Efficient Techniques for Interactive Texture Placement. In *SIGGRAPH 94 Conference Proceedings*, pages 119–122. ACM, July 1994.

[Mal89] J.L. Mallet. Discrete Smooth Interpolation in Geometric Modeling. *ACM-Transactions on Graphics*, 8(2):121–144, 1989.

[Mal92] J.L. Mallet. Discrete Smooth Interpolation. *Computer Aided Design Journal*, 24(4):263–270, 1992.

[ML88] S.D. Ma and H. Lin. Optimal Texture Mapping. In *EUROGRAPHICS'88*, pages 421–428, September 1988.

[MYV93] J. Maillot, H. Yahia, and A. Verroust. Interactive Texture Mapping. In *SIGGRAPH 93 Conference Proceedings*, volume 27. ACM, 1993.

[Pea85] Peachey, R. Darwyn. Solid Texturing of Complex Surfaces. In *SIGGRAPH 85 Conference Proceedings*, volume 19, pages 287–296. ACM, July 1985.

[Ped95] H.K. Pedersen. Decorating Implicit Surfaces. In *SIGGRAPH 95 Conference Proceedings*, pages 291–300. ACM, 1995.

[SMSW86] Samek, Marcel, C. Slean, and H. Weghorst. Texture Mapping and Distortions in Digital Graphics. *The Visual Computer*, 2(5):313–320, September 1986.

[Tur91] G. Turk. Generating Textures on Arbitrary Surfaces Using Reaction-Diffusion. In *SIGGRAPH 91 Conference Proceedings*, pages 289–298. ACM, 1991.

[Tut60] W.T. Tutte. Convex Representation of Graphs. In *Proc. London Math. Soc.*, volume 10, 1960.

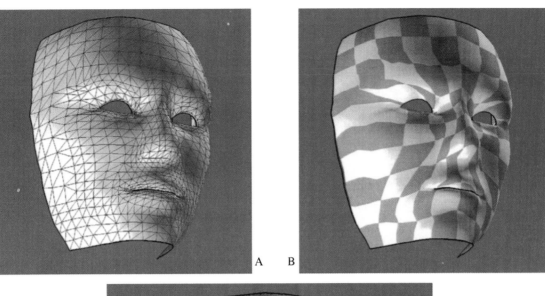

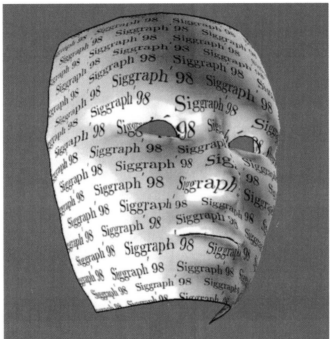

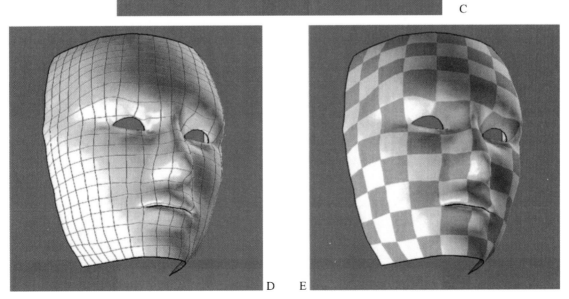

Figure 9: Texture mapping on a face.

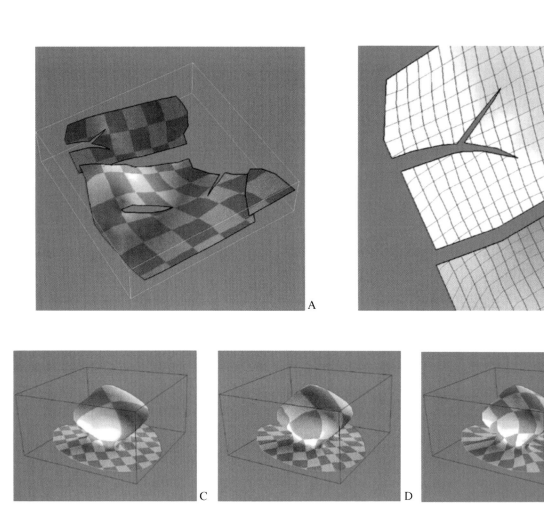

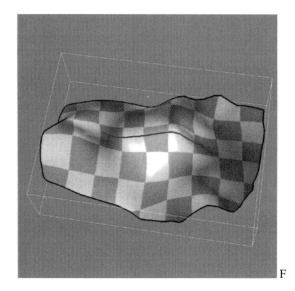

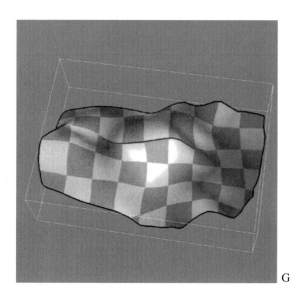

Figure 10: Applications to geology.

Techniques for Handling Video in Virtual Environments

Gianpaolo U. Carraro, John T. Edmark, J. Robert Ensor

Bell Laboratories

Abstract

This paper discusses ways to incorporate video displays into virtual environments. It focuses on the virtual worlds created by a distributed multi-user simulator. Still images or video streams represent spaces within these three-dimensional worlds. The paper introduces techniques to deal with avatar movement into and out of video regions. In one technique—*media melding*—when an object moves from one region to another, the media used to represent that object correspondingly change. In a second technique—*object tracing*—when an object moves from one region to another, its actions in the second region are represented by a *trace object* in the first region. *Pyramidic panels* provide a means of dealing with viewpoint changes so that two-dimensional images and video clips can successfully simulate three-dimensional spaces. The paper concludes by suggesting ways to extend our techniques and by listing possible future studies.

CR Categories and Subject Descriptors: H.5.1 [Information Systems]: Multimedia Information Systems—Artificial Realities; I.3.7 [Computer Graphics]: Three-Dimensional Graphics and Realism—Virtual Reality; I.3.2 [Computer Graphics]: Graphics Systems—Distributed/Network Graphics

Additional Keywords: virtual worlds, virtual environments, camera placement, VRML

1 INTRODUCTION

We have built a sports simulator, called Peloton[1, 5], suitable for athletic training and competition. It creates virtual road courses for walking, running, and bicycle riding. Users participate in simulations by walking or running on treadmills or by pedaling stationary bicycles. An exercise apparatus is attached to each user's local computer and serves as the primary input/output device for the simulation participant. The simulator senses the user's progress along a virtual road course and changes the incline of the treadmill or alters the pedaling resistance of the bicycle to create force feedback corresponding to the

4F-601, 101 Crawfords Corner Road, Holmdel, NJ 07733
paolo@bell-labs.com

changing terrain. Users may exercise alone or they may communicate over the World Wide Web to share Peloton virtual spaces with each other.

The visual component of the simulator's virtual environment is a synthetic, three-dimensional landscape, modeled in the Virtual Reality Modeling Language (VRML)[19]. Parts of these worlds are displayed as three-dimensional graphical objects; other regions are displayed as still images or video streams. We chose this combination of media to create worlds that show the positions of simulation participants on three-dimensional terrains and to enrich these terrains through photo-realistic display elements. The combination also gives us a chance to tailor displays to the computing and communication resources of system users. People with powerful machines but poor network connections can specify that a world be displayed primarily (or exclusively) as locally rendered three-dimensional objects. On the other hand, users with network computers—offering high-end network connections but less processing power—can specify that a world be displayed primarily as streamed video.

Figure 1 is a view from a Peloton virtual world, which models New York City's Central Park. The central portion of this view is a video stream, which is displayed as a texture on a large rectangle—a two-dimensional video "screen." In the surrounding region, graphical elements represent the road and some roadside objects. The bicyclist avatars represent multiple users who are exploring this world concurrently.

As simulation participants move along a virtual roadway, their avatars can move from one region to another. Participants are often spread over different regions of a virtual world, and each participant is likely to see competitors' avatars move to and from image/video regions. In Figure 1, for example, the blue avatar is on a section of road displayed as three-dimensional objects, while the red and green avatars have moved ahead to a road segment displayed as a video region. Also, as Peloton users move around the virtual environment, they see image/video displays as parts of an encompassing, coherent three-dimensional space. To maintain visual continuity with their surrounding regions, these two-dimensional displays must dynamically respond to the moving user viewpoints.

We have developed techniques to deal with the movement of objects into and out of video regions and also with the integration of images into their three-dimensional contexts. Two techniques deal with object movement. In one—*media melding*—when an object moves from one region to another, the media used to represent that object correspondingly change. The red avatar of Figure 1 demonstrates media melding. Upon entering a video region, it became a video object. In the second technique—*object tracing*—when an object moves from one region to another, its actions in the second region are represented by a *trace object* in the first region. The green avatar of Figure 1 is a three-

Figure 1: A Peloton Virtual Environment Representing New York City's Central Park

dimensional trace object representing a cyclist in the video region. A third technique deals with viewing images from multiple viewpoints. *Pyramidic panels* and their associated transforms provide means for dealing with viewpoint changes, so that two-dimensional images and video clips can successfully represent three-dimensional spaces. These three techniques are the main contribution of our work and are the focus of this paper.

2 BACKGROUND

Peloton has basic characteristics in common with other distributed, multi-party simulators. However, Peloton's virtual environments are distinctive because they permit objects to move between video and graphical regions in response to user actions. In addition, image and video displays within Peloton virtual worlds undergo specialized distortions as they respond to changing user viewpoints.

2.1 Simulating Bicycle Rides

A few bicycle simulation programs are commercially available. For example, CompuTrainer[3], the Virtual Reality Bike[16], and UltraCoach VR[18] create shared virtual environments for simulations among people who ride computer-based bicycling devices. Similarly, people can use exercycles to navigate Diamond Park[20], an experimental three-dimensional synthetic environment for social interactions. In addition, Cuesta has posted a VRML based bicycling game, called *Cycling World: The Virtual Tour*[3], on the World Wide Web. However, this game does not involve exercise devices, and it does not create multi-user worlds. Unlike the virtual worlds of these games and simulators, Peloton worlds contain video regions as well as three-dimensional graphical regions.

2.2 Combining Graphics and Images/Videos

Photographs are commonly used as textures and background elements in three-dimensional models. Image based modeling

techniques, *e.g.*, [4] and [12], permit creation of three-dimensional models from two-dimensional photographs, and objects in the resulting virtual worlds can be textured with the images used to generate their structure. In a virtual world by Gossweiler[8], surface textures are selected according to viewpoint location and velocity. However, none of these systems treat the image textures themselves as three-dimensional spaces. Hence they do not accommodate object movement to and from the textures.

Computer-generated graphics and recordings of live action are often combined in special effects for movies. *Who Framed Roger Rabbit*, for example, illustrates a successful combination of these media. Of course, these movies are fixed compositions; their effects cannot vary. On the other hand, Peloton's effects are generated as real-time responses to user actions and viewpoint changes.

Virtual sets, *e.g.*, [7], [10], and [17], are a form of electronic theater in which live actors can move within computer-generated settings. Augmented reality systems, *e.g.*, [6], create another type of composition—they lay computer-generated graphics over video inputs. The Interspace system[14], which supports real-time multimedia, multiparty conferences on the Internet, creates virtual spaces in which avatars have live video streams as "heads." [15] and [21] discuss virtual reality systems, containing video displays, in which graphical objects are assigned priorities, and these priorities help control video transmission streams. The graphical objects in these systems can be manipulated in response to real-time events, *e.g.*, changes of camera position. However, none support movement of objects between their graphical and video elements.

The MPEG-4 proposal[13], currently under development, is expected to permit specification of data displays as compositions of video and graphical objects. Hence, this standard might provide a means of specifying hardware and software infrastructure to support our techniques straightforwardly and efficiently.

2.3 Manipulating Images

A significant body of work, *e.g.*, [2] and [11], involves interpolations among images to create visual continuity during motion or other changes within three-dimensional virtual spaces. Pyramidic panel transforms can be used to generate interpolations, but do not perform this role in Peloton. [9] discusses an approach for creating a static three-dimensional model from a single image. Parts of the original image provide texture for a background, while separate model elements are generated from foreground portions of the image. Pyramidic panel transforms do not produce spatial models from images, nor do they create multiple panels from a single image. Rather, our technique distorts an image in response to viewpoint changes. Other techniques for applying distortions to images, *e.g.*, [22], have been described. Pyramidic panel transforms are more specialized than these general deformation processes. Hence, they are appropriate only for a limited image domain. However, the domain can be broadened somewhat by modifying the transforms according to information about the virtual world that surrounds an image. Furthermore, our techniques avoid complex texture mapping calculations by taking advantage of rendering functions found in most three-dimensional graphics engines.

3 CREATING REGIONS

Each Peloton virtual world is partitioned into regions. To create visual continuity among these subspaces, we calibrate their basic geometric properties. We have given most of our attention to the integration of image/video regions and graphical regions, and, in this section, we describe how we calibrated these region interfaces when we built a model of Central Park. (For the remainder of this paper, we shall use the terms video region and video panel to denote a region displayed as either still images or video clips.)

We gathered data for the Central Park course from a topographical map, measuring road coordinates at regular intervals. We measured the road's width directly at a few locations. We modeled the road from these data only. By using such an elementary description of the real world, we created a somewhat stylized virtual road—it does not change widths, it has no banked turns, and it contains no complex curves between elevation data points. The roadside terrain is modeled as extensions of road elevations. Meanwhile, we recorded our video clips of the road course. We mounted our camera at a known height and orientation on a car, and we then taped the video while driving along the center of the road. The tape provided us with information used to build additional objects in the graphical region. We were able to identify objects, such as trees, by their appearance in the video recording. Using a triangulation process based on the video images, we placed these items at their proper positions in the graphical model.

A static two-dimensional image of an arbitrary space can "fit into" an encompassing three-dimensional world only when it
i)   is placed in a unique position in this world, and
ii)   is viewed from a unique position in this world.
The unique placement position corresponds to the image's original context, while the unique viewing location corresponds to the position from which the image was recorded. Section 5 will discuss pyramidic panel transforms, a set of image deformations that relax the viewing restriction. However, we must still place the images in their unique correct positions within the graphical model.

We used a single video frame as a calibration reference for all video images within the Central Park world. We were able to use this simplified calibration for two reasons. Our graphical road closely approximates the videotaped road segment, and our videotape images are all constrained with respect to the road surface. (The taping constraints include a fixed focal length camera, a camera platform at a fixed height and orientation to the road surface, and a camera path along the center of the road.) While viewing the reference image from its center of projection, we scaled and cropped it to create an alignment of the road's display in the video and graphical regions. The alignment produced by this calibration is the basis for continuity between the video displays and their surroundings. The continuity is enforced by other structures that appear in both the video panel and the adjacent graphical region, *e.g.*, fences, sidewalks, and trees, (as shown in Figure 1).

Visual continuity among regions depends on more than geometric parameters. Lighting, for example, greatly impacts a region's appearance. Even carefully aligned objects may exhibit significant discontinuities when straddling regions with lighting differences. In our Central Park world, we reduced discontinuities between graphical and video regions by using a high level of ambient lighting in the graphical region and by shooting video footage on an overcast day. The resulting video images have several desirable properties, including the lack of strong distinct shadows and shading, and a featureless, uniformly colored sky. Thus, we have avoided the need to render shadows in the corresponding graphical regions, and we can more easily match colors between regions.

Peloton video panels can move. This capability causes time to become a parameter of our calibration process. Our videotape of Central Park provides us with a collection of images, and each video frame corresponds to a position in our graphical model of the park. To maintain alignment with adjacent graphical objects, these images must be displayed at the correct positions. There are two means of controlling this display synchronization. One is to update images according to panel positions; the other is to update panel positions according to images. In the current version of Peloton, the video panel moves along the road at a speed determined by the video frame update rate. Because we traveled at a constant speed when taping our Central Park video, this frame update rate produces a fixed distance between the locations for successive frame displays.

Since we did not individually calibrate the frames of our videotape with the corresponding locations of the Central Park virtual world, most of these images do not align exactly with their surroundings. However, simulation participants report that they still perceive this virtual world as an effective integration of video and graphical regions.

Figure 2: Red Avatar as Merge-in

Figure 3: Red Avatar as Trace Object

Figure 4: Merge-in, Behind-the-scenes

Figure 5: Trace Object, Behind-the-scenes

4 MOVING OBJECTS

One of Peloton's distinguishing characteristics is the movement of objects between its video regions and its graphical regions. The system generates these moves during real-time responses to events. When an object moves into a new region, it is handled by one of two techniques. When being handled by the *media melding* transformation, the medium in which the object is represented is changed to match the medium of the region it has just entered. Alternatively, a moving object can be handled by the *object tracing* transformation. In this approach, when an object leaves a three-dimensional foreground region to enter a video region, it is represented by a trace object in the foreground.

4.1 Media Melding

To undergo media melding, an object must have different media representations. In Peloton, each cyclist avatar has three representations—a three-dimensional graphical object, a still image, and a video clip—that allow the avatar to meld into any region of a Peloton world.

4.1.1 Merge-in

A *merge-in* is a particular type of media melding. It occurs when a graphical object changes to a video element in response to its movement from a graphical region into a video-based one. We call this transform a merge-in because, in a sense, the object "merges into" the two-dimensional video display. In Peloton simulations, this transform typically occurs when a cyclist gains a big lead over the viewing cyclist. For example, Figure 2 illustrates a situation in which the red cyclist has moved into the video region ahead of the viewer—the yellow cyclist—and has become a video element.

Figure 4 is a behind-the-scenes view of this merge-in. On the far left, the semi-transparent avatar represents the red cyclist's "real"

position in the virtual world. In conventional three-dimensional worlds, the video panel would occlude the yellow cyclist's view of the red cyclist's position. However, by performing this merge-in, Peloton allows the leading cyclist to remain visible from the yellow cyclist's point of view. When Peloton's animation module detects that the red avatar has intersected the video panel, the avatar is removed from the module's list of graphical objects and is added to its list of the video elements. The red cyclist's representation then becomes a small video panel, which is placed between the existing video panel and the yellow cyclist's point of view. (In this case, the small video is positioned directly in front of the large video panel.) The relationship between the red cyclist's "real" position and the yellow cyclist's point of view is now used to control scaling and translation of the red cyclist's video panel.

These transforms attempt to create the illusion that the merge-in video panel is moving within the space represented by the existing video panel. However, Peloton's implementation of the technique has significant limitations. Most obviously, the cyclist's video is displayed on a rectangular panel that creates noticeable discontinuities with its surrounding video. Also, objects within the surrounding video cannot occlude the cyclist's video, and the cyclist's actual orientation is not reproduced in the merge-in video panel.

4.1.2 Pop-out

A *pop-out* is the complementary operation to a merge-in. It occurs when a previously merged-in video element changes back to a graphical object in response to its movement from a video-based region into a graphical one. We call this transform a pop-out because the two-dimensional element seems to "pop out" of the video. In Peloton simulations, this transform typically occurs when the viewing cyclist moves closer to a leading cyclist—one who had been riding ahead in a video region. The cyclist returns to its three-dimensional form in order to keep its representation visible in the graphical region.

4.2 Object Tracing

We have developed an alternative to media melding; it's called *object tracing*. Objects may be designated as traceable objects. When a traceable object moves from a three-dimensional region to intersect a video panel, it does not become a video element. Instead, it is replaced in the three-dimensional foreground by a *trace object*. Figure 3 shows the red cyclist's trace object from the yellow cyclist's point of view.

Figure 5 is a behind-the-scenes view of the same situation. As in Figure 4, the semi-transparent red avatar on the left shows the red cyclist's "real" position. When Peloton's animation module detects that the red avatar has intersected the video panel, it creates a trace object to represent the red cyclist from the yellow cyclist's point of view. The trace object is a copy of the red avatar, and it is placed just in front of the existing video panel. As with media melding, the red cyclist's "real" simulation position is used to control scaling and translation of the trace object. Furthermore, the trace object reproduces the cyclist's actual orientation. In this case, the desired illusion is successful—from yellow's viewpoint, one cannot distinguish between the red cyclist's avatar and its trace object.

5 MOVING VIEWPOINTS

As discussed in Section 3, achieving continuity between an image and its surrounding environment requires careful placement and sizing of the image. Even after an image and its surroundings have been calibrated, there exists only one viewpoint from which that image's contents properly correspond to the surrounding environment. We call this unique location the image's *IVP (Ideal Viewing Point)*. Figure 2 contains an image seen from its IVP. From this view, the image aligns well with surrounding objects.

Peloton users rarely view an image from its IVP. As simulation participants move left or right on a road, as they round curves, or as they move closer to or farther from a video panel, they see an image from positions other than its IVP. Figure 7a shows an image seen from a point to the left of its IVP; objects within the image do not align with surrounding objects.

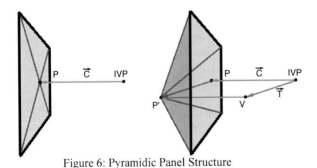

Figure 6: Pyramidic Panel Structure

5.1 Pyramidic Panels

We have developed a structure, called the *pyramidic panel*, for displaying images within a surrounding three-dimensional space. The transforms associated with a pyramidic panel dynamically distort images according to viewer positions. As the viewer

moves away from an image's IVP, the distortions act to limit the discontinuities between the image and its surroundings. The pyramidic panel technique exploits a characteristic common to all Peloton course images—they are views down a road. In these images, the road and its immediate vicinity are treated as a kind of corridor whose floor is formed by the roadbed, whose ceiling is formed by the sky, and whose walls are formed by the roadside objects. This treatment allows single point perspective principles to be used for distorting the Peloton course images according to the movement of the viewer.

Pyramidic panels for images of straight road segments are created as follows:

1) An image of the road, captured and positioned according to the procedure described in Section 3, is clipped so that the left and right road edges pass through the left and right bottom corners of the image, respectively. This clipping ensures that the roadbed maps to the floor of the hypothetical corridor.

2) The location of the vanishing point for this image is determined. Using the virtual world's road model, a vector corresponding to the road's direction is projected from the image's IVP through the image panel. The point of intersection with the panel is the image's vanishing point. (If the road direction is very different from a normal to the image panel, the vanishing point may be out of bounds of the image. In this case, it is adjusted to bring it within the image.) As shown in the left-hand side of Figure 6, the image is then segmented into four triangular faces—one for each of the hypothetical corridor's surfaces. The intersection point of the four faces corresponds to the vanishing point for the corridor.

3) The intersection point of the four faces is then coupled with the viewer's location in the following manner. "Coupling" vector $\bar{C}$ projects from IVP to the image's vanishing point, P, found in step 2. "Translation" vector $\bar{T}$ projects from IVP to the viewer's current location, V. As the viewer moves, the new vanishing point, P', is calculated as $P' = IVP + \bar{T} + \bar{C}$. As shown in the right-hand side of Figure 6, this coupling results in a four sided pyramid. Its fixed base corresponds to the original image panel, and its peak moves in concert with the viewer's location.

Figures 7 through 11 compare the display of an image on a flat panel with the display of the same image on a pyramidic panel. Part a of each figure shows the image texture-mapped onto a flat panel, while part b of the corresponding figure shows the same view of the image texture-mapped onto a pyramidic panel. Part c of each figure is a behind-the-scenes view of the pyramidic panel that is producing the distortion for part b. The yellow movie camera represents the viewpoint for parts a and b. Red lines clarify the pyramidic panel's distortion.

In Figure 7, the viewpoint is to the left of the image's IVP. Part a shows a discontinuity of the road edge between the three-dimensional region and the video panel. Part b shows how the pyramidic panel transforms have eliminated this discontinuity. In Figure 8, the viewpoint is higher than the image's IVP. Part a again shows a discontinuity in the road edge. In addition, the horizon lines do not align between the graphical and video regions. The road seems to be heading down into the ground in

Figure 7a: Flat Panel, Left of IVP

Figure 7b: Pyramidic Panel, Left of IVP

Figure 7c: Behind-the-scenes View

Figure 8a: Flat Panel, Above IVP

Figure 8b: Pyramidic Panel, Above IVP

Figure 8c: Behind-the-scenes View

Figure 9a: Flat Panel, Close Range

Figure 9b: Pyramidic Panel, Close Range

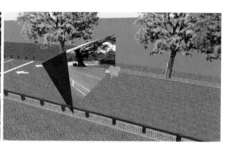
Figure 9c: Behind-the-scenes View

Figure 10a: Flat Panel, Side Corner

Figure 10b: Pyramidic Panel, Side Corner

Figure 10c: Behind-the-scenes View

Figure 11a: Flat Panel, Looking Back

Figure 11b: Pyramidic Panel, Looking Back

Figure 11c: Behind-the-scenes View

the first image, whereas in part b the roadbed appears flush with the surrounding model's ground. In Figure 9, the viewpoint is very close to the image. Part a shows a nearly unintelligible collection of pixels, whereas part b shows a comprehensible view of the road. In Figure 10, the viewpoint is far to the right, close to the panel, and turned to the left. Part a shows a large discontinuity between the road in the graphical region and the road on the panel. Part b shows that the pyramidic panel's image maintains continuity quite well. In Figure 11, the viewpoint has gone through the flat panel and turned around to face backwards. In part a we see only the back of the panel, whereas in part b we see the pyramidic panel surrounding our view onto the model. (In part c, the camera cannot be seen because it is inside the pyramid.)

5.2 Articulated Pyramidic Panels

The basic pyramidic panel technique described above is less effective when applied to an image of a curved road. Such a road contains multiple vanishing points. Choosing a single vanishing point based on one section of the road leads to distortions in other sections of the road. For example, Figure 12 shows a pyramidic panel containing an image of a curved road. The panel is being viewed from a point higher than the image's IVP. The vanishing point was chosen to correspond to the direction of the road in the foreground of the image. Although the technique yields reasonable results for this foreground road section, it breaks down for the more distant sections of the road. Figure 13 shows the same image from the same viewpoint. However, the image is now displayed using an *articulated pyramidic panel (APP)*. An articulated pyramidic panel uses multiple vanishing points to segment the basic pyramidic panel. The APP in Figures 13 contains two vanishing points. Figure 14 shows the same APP from the image's IVP.

A two-vanishing-point APP is created as follows:
1. An image of the road is captured, placed and clipped as in step 1 of the basic pyramid procedure.
2. The road is treated as two straight corridors placed end-to-end, extending back from the panel. Each corridor's direction and length is calculated from the virtual world's model of the road. Using the directions of the two road segments—the two corridors—the corresponding vanishing points, P1 and P2, are determined. Using the first corridor's vanishing point, P1, an initial pyramidic panel is constructed as in step 2 of the basic pyramid procedure. (See Figure 14.)
3. The *coupling ratio*, α, for the first corridor is calculated: $\alpha = l/(l+d)$, where l is the length of the first corridor, and d is the distance between the image's IVP and the base of the pyramidic panel.
4. Each line segment connecting a corner of the panel to the vanishing point is divided into two segments by a point placed according to the coupling ratio. Specifically, the length l' of the line segment from the corner of the panel to this point is given by the following formula: $l' = \alpha l''$, where l'' is the total length of the segment between the corner of the panel and the vanishing point. These four points—Q1 through Q4 in Figure 14—are connected to form the base of a smaller pyramidic panel embedded within the larger one. The intersection point of the four triangles of this embedded

pyramidic panel is then moved to the location of the second vanishing point, P2.

This APP now has five internal points that must be coupled with the viewer's movement. The coupling of the second vanishing point is the same as for the basic pyramidic panels. The coupling, Qi, for the other four points, Q1 through Q4, is computed as follows: $Qi = IVP + \alpha\bar{T} + \bar{C}$. (Recall that IVP, $\bar{T}$, and $\bar{C}$ are defined in Section 5.1.)

Figure 12: Curve Using Single Vanishing Point

Figure 13: Curve Using Multiple Vanishing Points

Figure 14: Articulated Pyramidic Panel Structure

6 FUTURE WORK

The techniques described in this paper have several apparent extensions. Media melding can be enhanced in several ways. The Peloton implementation of merge-ins is based on a "stacking" of video panels. This approach has important shortcomings and often yields crude visual effects. By replacing the stacking approach with a composition of video objects (which might be possible with future MPEG-4 terminals), we could reduce our present occlusion deficiencies as well as achieve more cohesive combinations of video elements. Our current implementation of pop-outs is also restricted; we only allow pop-outs of avatars. By using various image-processing techniques on video frames, a system could automatically detect video elements of interest and determine when they leave a video panel. Image-based modeling techniques could then create and place the pop-out objects in three-dimensional regions. Pyramidic panels could be extended to handle a wider range of image content. For example, non-rectilinear corridors and corridors with changing cross sections could be accommodated by additional pyramidic constructions and manipulations.

Media combinations other than graphics and video are possible and potentially useful. For example audio-only regions could be added to Peloton worlds. An object represented as a video or graphical element could meld into an audio clip, (*i.e.*, presenting the sound of a spinning bicycle wheel or the live speech of a user) when moving into this new region.

A variety of new applications could be developed with the techniques introduced here. For example, education applications could allow students to pick objects from a movie, move them into a region of three-dimensional objects, and study them there by viewing and animating their three-dimensional representations. Similarly, shopping applications could allow shoppers to pick objects from a catalog and see them displayed in a movie. A region can serve as a level of detail specification for groups of objects. For example, a region near the viewer (camera) can be displayed in one medium, while more distant parts of a virtual world can be displayed through other media. These multimedia levels of detail, then, support applications that highlight information for users as they explore virtual worlds.

7 SUMMARY

This paper has described techniques useful for building three-dimensional virtual worlds with subspaces displayed as two-dimensional images or video clips. Two techniques for representing movement of objects between graphical and video regions—media melding and object tracing—were described. Pyramidic panels were introduced as a means of dealing with viewpoint changes so that two-dimensional images and video clips can better simulate three-dimensional spaces. We have used these techniques in creating virtual worlds for a bicycling simulator. Simulator users report that these techniques help create virtual worlds in which still images and video clips successfully represent parts of a single, cohesive three-dimensional space.

References

[1] Carraro, G., Cortes, M., Edmark, J., and Ensor, J., "The Peloton Bicycling Simulator," Proc. VRML '98, Monterey, CA, 16-19 February, 1998.

[2] Chen, S. and Williams, L., "View Interpolation for Image Synthesis," Proc. SIGGRAPH 93, 1-6 August, 1993, Anaheim, CA, pp. 279-288.

[3] Cuesta J., Cycling World. In El Faro Web Site: http://www.elfaro.com/vrml20/cycling/thegame/

[4] Debevec, P., Taylor, C., and Malik, J., "Modeling and Rendering Architecture from Photographs: A hybrid geometry-and image-based approach," Proc. SIGGRAPH 96, 4-9 August, 1996, New Orleans, LA, pp. 11-20.

[5] Ensor, J. and Carraro, G., "Peloton: A Distributed Simulation for the World Wide Web," Proc. 1998 International Conf. On Web-based Modeling and Simulation, San Diego, CA, 12-14 January, 1998.

[6] Feiner, S., Macintyre, B., and Seligmann, D., "Knowledge-Based Augmented Reality," Communications of the ACM, (36, 7), June 1993, pp. 53-62.

[7] 3DK: The Virtual Studio. In GMD Web Site: http://viswiz.gmd.de/DML/vst/vst.html

[8] GPIR. In Rich Gossweiler Web Site: http://reality.sgi.com/rcg/vrml/gpir/playground/playground.html

[9] Horry, Y., Anjyo, K., and Arai, K., "Tour Into the Picture: Using a Spidery Mesh Interface to Make Animation from a Single Image," Proc. SIGGRAPH ,97, 3-8 August, 1997, Los Angeles,CA, pp. 225-232.

[10] Katkere, A., Moessi, S., Kuramura, D., Kelly, P., and Jain, R., "Towards Video-based Immersive Environments," Multimedia Systems, May 1997, pp. 69-85.

[11] Kelly, P., Katkere, A., Kuramura, D., Moezzi, S., Chatterjee, S., and Jain, R., "An Architecture for Multiple Perspective Interactive Video," Proc. Multimedia '95, San Francisco, CA, 1995, pp. 201-212.

[12] McMillan, L. and Bishop, G., "Plenoptic Modeling: An Image-Based Rendering System," Proc. SIGGRAPH 95, 6-11 August, 1995, Los Angeles, CA, pp. 39-46.

[13] MPEG Home Page. In http://drogo.cselt.stet.it/mpeg

[14] Interspace VR Browser. In NTT Software Corp. Web Site: http://www.ntts.com Interspace

[15] Oh, S., Sugano, H., Fujikawa, K., Matsuura, T., Shimojo, S., Arikawa, M., and Miyahara, H., "A Dynamic QoS Adaptation Mechanism for Networked Virtual Reality," Proc. Fifth IFIP International Workshop on Quality of Service, New York, May 1997, pp. 397-400.

[16] Virtual Reality Bike. In Tectrix Web Site: http://www.tectrix.com/ products/VRBike/VR_Bike.html

[17] Thalmann, N., and Thalmann, D., "Animating Virtual Actors in Real Environments," Multimedia Systems, May 1997, pp. 113-125.

[18] UltraCoach VR. In Ultracoach Web Site: http://www.ultracch.com

[19] Virtual Reality Modeling Language (VRML) Version 2.0. In VRML Consortium Web Site: http://www.vrml.org/ Specifications/VRML2.0/

[20] Waters, R. et al., Diamond Park and Spline: Social Virtual Reality with 3D Animation, Spoken Interaction, and Runtime Extendability. Presence. Vol. 6 No. 4 pp.461-481. MIT Press

[21] Yamaashi, K., Kawanata, Y., Tani, M., and Matsumoto, H., "User-Centered Video: Transmitting Video Images Based on the User's Interest," Proc. Chi '95.

[22] Zorin, D. and Barr, A., "Correction of Geometric Perceptual Distortions in Pictures," Proc. SIGGRAPH 95, 6-11 August, 1995, Los Angeles, CA, pp. 257-264.

A Distributed 3D Graphics Library

Blair MacIntyre and Steven Feiner[1]
Department of Computer Science
Columbia University

Abstract

We present Repo-3D, a general-purpose, object-oriented library for developing distributed, interactive 3D graphics applications across a range of heterogeneous workstations. Repo-3D is designed to make it easy for programmers to rapidly build prototypes using a familiar multi-threaded, object-oriented programming paradigm. All data sharing of both graphical and non-graphical data is done via general-purpose remote and replicated objects, presenting the illusion of a single distributed shared memory. Graphical objects are directly distributed, circumventing the "duplicate database" problem and allowing programmers to focus on the application details.

Repo-3D is embedded in Repo, an interpreted, lexically-scoped, distributed programming language, allowing entire applications to be rapidly prototyped. We discuss Repo-3D's design, and introduce the notion of *local variations* to the graphical objects, which allow local changes to be applied to shared graphical structures. Local variations are needed to support transient local changes, such as highlighting, and responsive local editing operations. Finally, we discuss how our approach could be applied using other programming languages, such as Java.

CR Categories and Subject Descriptors: D.1.3 [**Programming Techniques**]: Concurrent Programming—*Distributed Programming*; H.4.1 [**Information Systems Applications**]: Office Automation—*Groupware*; I.3.2 [**Computer Graphics**]: Graphics Systems—*Distributed/network graphics*; I.3.6 [**Computer Graphics**]: Methodology and Techniques—*Graphics data structures and data types*; I.3.7 [**Computer Graphics**]: Three-Dimensional Graphics and Realism—*Virtual reality*.

Additional Keywords and Phrases: object-oriented graphics, distributed shared memory, distributed virtual environments, shared-data object model.

1 INTRODUCTION

Traditionally, *distributed graphics* has referred to the architecture of a single graphical application whose components are distributed over multiple machines [14, 15, 19, 27] (Figure 1a). By taking advantage of the combined power of multiple machines, and the particular features of individual machines, otherwise impractical applications became feasible. However, as machines have grown more powerful and application domains such as Computer

1. {bm,feiner}@cs.columbia.edu, http://www.cs.columbia.edu/graphics

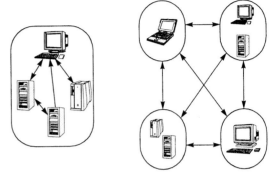

Figure 1: Two meanings of *distributed graphics*: (a) a single logical graphics system with distributed components, and (b) multiple distributed logical graphics systems. We use the second definition here.

Supported Cooperative Work (CSCW) and Distributed Virtual Environments (DVEs) have been making the transition from research labs to commercial products, the term *distributed graphics* is increasingly used to refer to systems for distributing the shared graphical state of multi-display/multi-person, distributed, interactive applications (Figure 1b). This is the definition that we use here.

While many excellent, high-level programming libraries are available for building stand-alone 3D applications (e.g. Inventor [35], Performer [29], Java 3D [33]), there are no similarly powerful and general libraries for building distributed 3D graphics applications. All CSCW and DVE systems with which we are familiar (e.g., [1, 7, 11, 12, 16, 28, 30, 31, 32, 34, 37, 41]) use the following approach: A mechanism is provided for distributing application state (either a custom solution or one based on a general-purpose distributed programming environment, such as ISIS [4] or Obliq [8]), and the state of the graphical display is maintained separately in the local graphics library. Keeping these "dual databases" synchronized is a complex, tedious, and error-prone endeavor. In contrast, some non-distributed libraries, such as Inventor [35], allow programmers to avoid this problem by using the graphical scene description to encode application state. Extending this "single database" model to a distributed 3D graphics library is the goal of our work on Repo-3D.

Repo-3D is an object-oriented, high-level graphics package, derived from Obliq-3D [25]. Its 3D graphics facilities are similar to those of other modern high-level graphics libraries. However, the objects used to create the graphical scenes are directly distributable—from the programmer's viewpoint, the objects reside in one large distributed shared memory (DSM) instead of in a single process. The underlying system replicates any of the fine-grained objects across as many processes as needed, with no additional effort on the part of the programmer. Updates to objects are automatically reflected in all replicas, with any required objects automatically distributed as needed. By integrating the replicated objects into the programming languages we use, distributed applications may be built using Repo-3D with little more difficulty than building applications in a single process.

No matter how simple the construction of a distributed application may be, a number of differences between distributed and monolithic applications must be addressed. These include:

- *Distributed control.* In a monolithic application, a single component can oversee the application and coordinate activities among the separate components by notifying them of changes to the application state. This is not possible in a non-trivial distributed application. Therefore, we must provide mechanisms for different components to be notified of changes to the distributed state.

- *Interactivity.* Updates to distributed state will be slower than updates to local state, and the amount of data that can be distributed is limited by network bandwidth. If we do not want to sacrifice interactive speed, we must be able to perform some operations locally. For example, an object could be dragged locally with the mouse, with only a subset of the changes applied to the replicated state.

- *Local variations.* There are times when a shared graphical scene may need to be modified locally. For example, a programmer may want to highlight the object under one user's mouse pointer without affecting the scene graph viewed by other users.

Repo-3D addresses these problems in two ways. First, a programmer can associate a *notification* object with any replicated object. The notification object's methods will be invoked when the replicated object is updated. This allows reactive programs to be built in a straightforward manner. To deal with the second and third problems, we introduce the notion of *local variations* to graphical objects. That is, we allow the properties of a graphical object to be modified locally, and parts of the scene graph to be locally added, removed, or replaced.

In Section 2 we describe how we arrived at the solution presented here. Section 3 discusses related work, and Section 4 offers a detailed description of the underlying infrastructure that was used. The design of Repo-3D is presented in Section 5, followed by some examples and concluding remarks in Sections 6 and 7.

2 BACKGROUND

Repo-3D was created as part of a project to support rapid prototyping of distributed, interactive 3D graphical applications, with a particular focus on DVEs. Our fundamental belief is that by providing uniform high-level support for distributed programming in the languages and toolkits we use, prototyping and experimenting with distributed interactive applications can be (almost) as simple as multi-threaded programming in a single process. While care must be taken to deal with network delays and bandwidth limitations at some stage of the program design (the languages and toolkits ought to facilitate this), it should be possible to ignore such issues until they become a problem. Our view can be summarized by a quote attributed to Alan Kay, "Simple things should be simple; complex things should be possible."

This is especially true during the exploration and prototyping phase of application programming. If programmers are forced to expend significant effort building the data-distribution components of the application at an early stage, not only will less time be spent exploring different prototypes, but radical changes in direction will become difficult, and thus unlikely. For example, the implementation effort could cause programs to get locked into using a communication scheme that may eventually prove less than ideal, or even detrimental, to the program's final design.

Since we are using object-oriented languages, we also believe that data distribution should be tightly integrated with the language's general-purpose objects. This lets the language's type system and programming constructs reduce or eliminate errors in the use of the data-distribution system. Language-level integration

also allows the system to exhibit a high degree of *network data transparency*, or the ability for the programmer to use remote and local data in a uniform manner. Without pervasive, structured, high-level data-distribution support integrated into our programming languages and libraries, there are applications that will never be built or explored, either because there is too much programming overhead to justify trying simple things ("simple things are not simple"), or because the added complexity of using relatively primitive tools causes the application to become intractable ("complex things are not possible").

Of the tools available for integrating distributed objects into programming languages, client-server data sharing is by far the most common approach, as exemplified by CORBA [26], Modula-3 Network Objects [5], and Java RMI [39]. Unfortunately, interactive graphical applications, such as virtual reality, require that the data used to refresh the display be local to the process doing the rendering or acceptable frame refresh rates will not be achieved. Therefore, pure client-server approaches are inappropriate because at least some of the shared data must be replicated. Furthermore, since the time delay of synchronous remote method calls is unsuitable for rapidly changing graphical applications, shared data should be updated asynchronously. Finally, when data is replicated, local access must still be fast.

The most widely used protocols for replicated data consistency, and thus many of the toolkits (e.g., ISIS [4] and Visual-Obliq [3]), allow data updates to proceed unimpeded, but block threads reading local data until necessary updates arrive. The same reason we need replicated data in the first place—fast local read access to the data—makes these protocols unsuitable for *direct* replication of the graphical data. Of course, these protocols are fine for replicating application state that will then be synchronized with a parallel graphical scene description, but that is what we are explicitly trying to avoid. Fortunately, there are replicated data systems (e.g., Orca [2] or COTERIE [24]) that provide replicated objects that are well suited to interactive applications, and it is upon the second of these systems that Repo-3D is built.

3 RELATED WORK

There has been a significant amount of work that falls under the first, older definition of distributed graphics. A large number of systems, ranging from established commercial products (e.g., IBM Visualization Data Explorer [21]) to research systems (e.g., PARADISE [19] and ATLAS [14]), have been created to distribute interactive graphical applications over a set of machines. However, the goal of these systems is to facilitate sharing of application data between processes, with one process doing the rendering. While some of these systems can be used to display graphics on more than one display, they were not designed to support high-level sharing of graphical scenes.

Most high-level graphics libraries, such as UGA [40], Inventor [35] and Java 3D [33], do not provide any support for distribution. Others, such as Performer [29], provide support for distributing components of the 3D graphics rendering system across multiple processors, but do not support distribution across multiple machines. One notable exception is TBAG [13], a high-level constraint-based, declarative 3D graphics framework. Scenes in TBAG are defined using constrained relationships between time-varying functions. TBAG allows a set of processes to share a single, replicated constraint graph. When any process asserts or retracts a constraint, it is asserted or retracted in all processes. However, this means that all processes share the same scene, and that the system's scalability is limited because all processes have a copy of (and must evaluate) all constraints, whether or not they are interested in them. There is also no support for local variations of the scene in different processes.

Machiraju [22] investigated an approach similar in flavor to ours, but it was not aimed at the same fine-grained level of interactivity and was ultimately limited by the constraints of the implementation platform (CORBA and C++). For example, CORBA objects are heavyweight and do not support replication, so much of their effort was spent developing techniques to support object migration and "fine-grained" object sharing. However, their fine-grained objects are coarser than ours, and, more importantly, they do not support the kind of lightweight, transparent replication we desire. A programmer must explicitly choose whether to replicate, move, or copy an object between processes when the action is to occur (as opposed to at object creation time). Replicated objects are independent new copies that can be modified and used to replace the original—simultaneous editing of objects, or real-time distribution of changes as they are made is not supported.

Of greater significance is the growing interest for this sort of system in the Java and VRML communities. Java, like Modula-3, is much more suitable as an implementation language than C or C++ because of its cross-platform compatibility and support for threads and garbage collection: Without the latter two language features, implementing complex, large-scale distributed applications is extremely difficult. Most of the current effort has been focused on using Java as a mechanism to facilitate multi-user VRML worlds (e.g., Open Communities [38]). Unfortunately, these efforts concentrate on the particulars of implementing shared virtual environments and fall short of providing a general-purpose shared graphics library. For example, the Open Communities work is being done on top of SPLINE [1], which supports only a single top-level world in the local scene database.

Most DVEs [11, 12, 16, 31, 32] provide support for creating shared virtual environments, not general purpose interactive 3D graphics applications. They implement a higher level of abstraction, providing support for rooms, objects, avatars, collision detection, and other things needed in single, shared, immersive virtual environments. These systems provide neither general-purpose programming facilities nor the ability to work with 3D scenes at a level provided by libraries such as Obliq-3D or Inventor. Some use communication schemes that prevent them from scaling beyond a relatively small number of distributed processes, but for most the focus is explicitly on efficient communication. SIMNET [7], and the later NPSNet [41], are perhaps the best known large-scale distributed virtual-environment systems. They use a fixed, well-defined communication protocol designed to support a single, large-scale, shared, military virtual environment.

The techniques for object sharing implemented in recent CSCW toolkits [28, 30, 34, 37] provide some of the features we need, particularly automatic replication of data to ease construction of distributed applications. However, none of these toolkits has integrated the distribution of data into its programming language's object model as tightly as we desire. As a result, they do not provide a high enough level of network data transparency or sufficiently strong consistency guarantees. In groupware applications, inconsistencies tend to arise when multiple users attempt to perform conflicting actions: the results are usually obvious to the users and can be corrected using social protocols. This is not an acceptable solution for a general-purpose, distributed 3D graphics toolkit. Furthermore, none of these CSCW systems provides any support for asynchronous update notification, or is designed to support the kind of large-scale distribution we have in mind.

Finally, while distributed games, such as Quake, have become very popular, they only distribute the minimum amount of application state necessary. They do not use (or provide) an abstract, high-level distributed 3D graphics system.

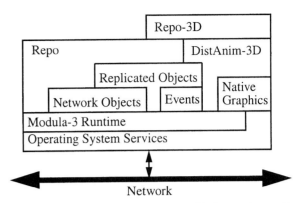

Figure 2: The architecture of Repo-3D. Aside from native graphics libraries (X, Win32, OpenGL, Renderware) the Modula-3 runtime shields most of the application from the OS. The Replicated Object package uses an Event communication package and the Network Object package. DistAnim-3D is implemented on top of a variety of native graphics libraries and Replicated Objects. Repo exposes most of the useful Modula-3 packages, as well as using Network Objects and Replicated Objects to present a distributed shared memory model to the programmer.

4 UNDERLYING INFRASTRUCTURE

Our work was done in the Modula-3 programming language [18]. We decided to use Modula-3 because of the language itself and the availability of a set of packages that provide a solid foundation for our infrastructure. Modula-3 is a descendant of Pascal that corrects many of its deficiencies, and heavily influenced the design of Java. In particular, Modula-3 retains strong type safety, while adding facilities for exception handling, concurrency, object-oriented programming, and automatic garbage collection[2]. One of its most important features for our work is that it gives us uniform access to these facilities across all architectures.

Repo-3D relies on a number of Modula-3 libraries, as illustrated in Figure 2. Distributed data sharing is provided by two packages, the Network Object client-server object package [5], and the Replicated Object shared object package [24] (see Section 4.1). DistAnim-3D is derived from Anim-3D [25], a powerful, non-distributed, general-purpose 3D library originally designed for 3D algorithm animation (see Section 4.2). Finally, Repo itself is a direct descendant of Obliq [8], and uses the Replicated Object package to add replicated data to Obliq (see Section 4.3).

4.1 Distributed Shared Memory

Repo-3D's data sharing mechanism is based on the Shared Data-Object Model of Distributed Shared Memory (DSM) [20]. DSM allows a network of computers to be programmed much like a multiprocessor, since the programmer is presented with the familiar paradigm of a common shared memory. The Shared Data-Object Model of DSM is particularly well suited to our needs since it is a high-level approach that can be implemented efficiently at the application level. In this model, shared data is encapsulated in user-defined objects and can only be accessed through those objects' method calls. The DSM address space is partitioned implicitly by the application programmer, with an object being the smallest unit of sharing. All shared data is fully network transpar-

---

2. The Modula-3 compiler we used is available from Critical Mass, Inc. as part of the Reactor programming environment. The compiler, and thus our system, runs on all the operating systems we have available (plus others): Solaris, IRIX, HP-UX, Linux, and Windows NT and 95.

ent because it is encapsulated within the programming language objects.

Distribution of new objects between the processes is as simple as passing them back and forth as parameters to, or return values from, method calls—the underlying systems take care of the rest.[3] Objects are only distributed to new processes as necessary, and (in our system) are removed by the garbage collector when they are no longer referenced. Furthermore, distributed garbage collection is supported, so objects that are no longer referenced in any process are removed completely.

There are three kinds of distributed object semantics in our DSM:
- *Simple* objects correspond to normal data objects, and have no special distributed semantics. When a simple object is copied between processes, a new copy is created in the destination process that has no implied relationship to the object in the source process.
- *Remote* objects have client-server distribution semantics. When a remote object is copied between processes, all processes except the one in which the object was created end up with a proxy object that forwards method invocations across the network to the original object.
- *Replicated* objects have replicated distribution semantics. When a replicated object is passed between processes, a new replica is created in the destination process. If any replica is changed, the change is reflected in all replicas.

The Network Object package provides support for remote objects. It implements distributed garbage collection, exception propagation back to the calling site, and automatic marshalling and unmarshalling of method arguments and return values of virtually any data type between heterogeneous machine architectures. The package is similar to other remote method invocation (RMI) packages developed later, such as the Java RMI library [39]. All method invocations are forwarded to the original object, where they are executed in the order they are received.

The Replicated Object package supports replicated objects. Each process can call any method of an object it shares, just as it can with a simple or remote object. We will describe the Replicated Object package in more detail, as Repo-3D relies heavily on its design, and the design of a replicated object system is less straightforward than a remote one. The model supported by the Replicated Object package follows two principles:
- All operations on an instance of an object are *atomic* and *serializable*. All operations are performed in the same order on all copies of the object. If two methods are invoked simultaneously, the order of invocation is nondeterministic, just as if two threads attempted to access the same memory location simultaneously in a single process.
- The above principle applies to operations on single objects. Making sequences of operations atomic is up to the programmer.

The implementation of the Replicated Object package is based on the approach used in the Orca distributed programming language [2]. A full replication scheme is used, where a single object is either fully replicated in a process or not present at all. Avoiding partial replication significantly simplifies the implementation and the object model, and satisfies the primary rationale for replication: fast read-access to shared data. To maintain replication consistency an update scheme is used, where *updates* to the object are applied to all copies.

The method of deciding what is and is not an update is what makes the Orca approach particularly interesting and easy to implement. All methods are marked as either *read* or *update* methods by the programmer who creates the object type. Read methods are assumed to not change the state of the object and are therefore applied immediately to the local object without violating consistency. Update methods are assumed to change the state. To distribute updates, arguments to the update method are marshalled into a message and sent to all replicas. To ensure all updates are applied in the same order, the current implementation of the Replicated Object package designates a *sequencer* process for each object. There may be more than one sequencer in the system to avoid overloading one process with all the objects (in this case, each object has its updates managed by exactly one of the sequencers.) The sequencer is responsible for assigning a sequence number to each message before it is sent to all object replicas. The replicas then execute the incoming update messages in sequence. The process that initiated the update does not execute the update until it receives a message back from the sequencer and all updates with earlier sequence numbers have been executed.

There are three very important reasons for choosing this approach. First, it is easy to implement on top of virtually any object-oriented language, using automatically generated object subtypes and method wrappers that communicate with a simple runtime system. We do this in our Modula-3 implementation, and it would be equally applicable to an implementation in C++ or Java. For example, the JSDT [36] data-sharing package in Java uses a similar approach.

Second, the Replicated Object package does not pay attention to (or even care) when the internal data fields of an object change. This allows the programmer great flexibility in deciding exactly what constitutes an update or not, and what constitutes the shared state[4]. For example, objects could have a combination of global and local state, and the methods that change the local state could be classified as *read* methods since they do not modify the global state. Alternatively, *read* methods could do some work locally and then call an *update* method to propagate the results, allowing time-consuming computation to be done once and the result distributed in a clean way. We took advantage of both of these techniques in implementing Repo-3D.

Finally, the immediate distribution of update methods ensures that changes are distributed in a timely fashion, and suggests a straightforward solution to the asynchronous notification problem. The Replicated Object package generates a *Notification Object* type for each Replicated Object type. These new objects have methods corresponding to the *update* methods of their associated Replicated Object. The arguments to these methods are the same as the corresponding Replicated Object methods, plus an extra argument to hold the Replicated Object instance. These notifiers can be used by a programmer to receive notification of changes to a Replicated Object in a structured fashion. To react to updates to a Replicated Object instance, a programmer simply overrides the methods of the corresponding Notification Object with methods that react appropriately to those updates, and associates an instance

---

3. An important detail is how the communication is bootstrapped. In the case of the Network and Replicated Object packages, to pass a first object between processes, one of them exports the object to a special *network object demon* under some known name on some known machine. The second process then retrieves the object.

4. Of course, it falls squarely on the shoulders of the programmer to ensure that the methods provided always leave the object in a consistent state. This is not significantly different than what needs to be done when building a complex object that is simultaneously accessed by multiple threads in a non-distributed system. For example, if a programmer reads an array of numbers from inside the object and then uses an update method to write a computed average back into the object, the internal array may have changed before the average is written, resulting in a classic inconsistency problem. In general, methods that perform computations based on internal state (rather than on the method arguments) are potentially problematic and need to be considered carefully.

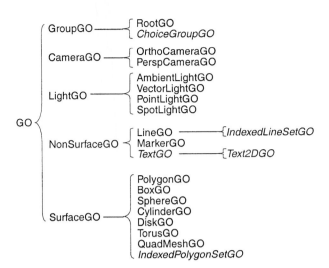

Figure 3: The Repo-3D GO class hierarchy. Most of the classes are also in Obliq-3D; the italicized ones were added to Repo-3D.

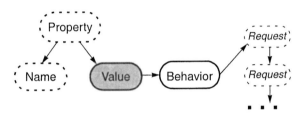

Figure 4: The relationship between properties, names, values, and behaviors. Each oval represents an object and arrows show containment.

of it with the Replicated Object instance. Each time an update method of the Replicated Object is invoked, the corresponding method of the Notifier Object is also invoked. Notification Objects eliminate the need for object polling and enable a "data-driven" flow of control.

4.2 Obliq-3D

Obliq-3D is composed of Anim-3D, a 3D animation package written in Modula-3, and a set of wrappers that expose Anim-3D to the Obliq programming language (see Section 4.3). Anim-3D is based on three simple and powerful concepts: *graphical objects* for building graphical scenes, *properties* for specifying the behavior of the graphical objects, and input event *callbacks* to support interactive behavior. Anim-3D uses the *damage-repair* model: whenever a graphical object or property changes (is damaged), the image is repaired without programmer intervention.

Graphical objects (GOs) represent all the logical entities in the graphical scene: geometry (e.g., lines, polygons, spheres, polygon sets, and text), lights and cameras of various sorts, and groups of other GOs. One special type of group, the RootGO, represents a window into which graphics are rendered. GOs can be grouped together in any valid directed acyclic graph (DAG). The GO class hierarchy is shown in Figure 3.

A *property* is a defined by a *name* and a *value*. The name determines which attribute is affected by the property, such as "Texture Mode" or "Box Corner1". The value specifies how it is affected and is determined by its *behavior*, a time-variant function that takes the current animation time and returns a value. Properties, property values, and behaviors are all objects, and their relationships are shown in Figure 4. When a property is created, its name

and value are fixed. However, values are mutable and their behavior may be changed at any time. There are four kinds of behaviors for each type of properties: *constant* (do not vary over time), *synchronous* (follow a programmed set of *requests*, such as "move from A to B starting at time t=1 and taking 2 seconds"), *asynchronous* (execute an arbitrary time-dependent function to compute the value) and *dependent* (asynchronous properties that depend on other properties). Synchronous properties are linked to *animation handles* and do not start satisfying their requests until the animation handle is signalled. By linking multiple properties to the same handle, a set of property value changes can be synchronized.

Associated with each GO *g* is a partial mapping of property names to values determined by the properties that have been associated with *g*. A property associated with *g* affects not only *g* but all the descendants of *g* that do not override the property. A single property may be associated with any number of GOs. It is perfectly legal to associate a property with a GO that is not affected by it; for example, attaching a "Surface Color" property to a GroupGO does not affect the group node itself, but could potentially affect the surface color of any GO contained in that group. A RootGO sets an initial default value for each named property.

There are three types of input event callbacks in Anim-3D, corresponding to the three kinds of interactive events they handle: *mouse* callbacks (triggered by mouse button events), *motion* callbacks (triggered by mouse motion events) and *keyboard* callbacks (triggered by key press events). Each object has three callback stacks, and the interactive behavior of an object can be redefined by pushing a new callback onto the appropriate stack. Any event that occurs within a root window associated with a RootGO *r* will be delivered to the top handler on *r*'s callback stack. The handler could delegate the event to one of *r*'s children, or it may handle it itself, perhaps changing the graphical scene in some way.

DistAnim-3D is a direct descendant of Anim-3D. In addition to the objects being distributed, it has many additional facilities that are needed for general-purpose 3D graphical applications, such as texture mapping, indexed line and polygon sets, choice groups, projection and transformation callbacks, and picking. Since DistAnim-3D is embedded in Repo instead of Obliq (see Section 4.3), the resulting library is called Repo-3D.

4.3 Obliq and Repo

Obliq [8] is a lexically-scoped, untyped, interpreted language for distributed object-oriented computation. It is implemented in, and tightly integrated with, Modula-3. An Obliq computation may involve multiple threads of control within an address space, multiple address spaces on a machine, heterogeneous machines over a local network, and multiple networks over the Internet. Obliq uses, and supports, the Modula-3 thread, exception, and garbage-collection facilities. Its distributed-computation mechanism is based on Network Objects, allowing transparent support for multiple processes on heterogeneous machines. Objects are local to a site, while computations can roam over the network. Repo [23] is a descendant of Obliq that extends the Obliq object model to include replicated objects. Therefore, Repo objects have state that may be local to a site (as in Obliq) or replicated across multiple sites.

5 DESIGN OF REPO-3D

Repo-3D's design has two logical parts: the *basic design* and *local variations*. The *basic design* encompasses the changes to Obliq-3D to carry it into a distributed context, and additional enhancements that are not particular to distributed graphics (and are therefore not discussed here). *Local variations* are introduced to handle two issues mentioned in Section 1: transient local changes and responsive local editing.

5.1 Basic Repo-3D Design

The Anim-3D scene-graph model is well suited for adaptation to a distributed environment. First, in Anim-3D, properties are attached to nodes, not inserted into the graph, and the property and child lists are unordered (i.e., the order in which properties are assigned to a node, or children are added to a group, does not affect the final result). In libraries that insert properties and nodes in the graph and execute the graph in a well-defined order (such as Inventor), the *siblings* of a node (or subtree) can affect the attributes of that node (or subtree). In Anim-3D, and similar libraries (such as Java 3D), properties are only inherited *down* the graph, so a node's properties are a function of the node itself and its ancestors—its siblings do not affect it. Therefore, subtrees can be added to different scene graphs, perhaps in different processes, with predictable results.

Second, the interface (both compiled Anim-3D and interpreted Obliq-3D) is programmatical and declarative. There is no "graphical scene" file format per se: graphical scenes are created as the side effect of executing programs that explicitly create objects and manipulate them via the object methods. Thus, all graphical objects are stored as the Repo-3D programs that are executed to create them. This is significant, because by using the Replicated Object library described in Section 4.1 to make the graphical objects distributed, the "file format" (i.e., a Repo-3D program) is updated for free.

Converting Anim-3D objects to Replicated Objects involved three choices: what objects to replicate, what methods update the object state, and what the global, replicated state of each object is. Since replicated objects have more overhead (e.g., method execution time, memory usage, and latency when passed between processes), not every category of object in Repo-3D is replicated. We will consider each of the object categories described in Figure 4.2 in turn: graphical objects (GOs), properties (values, names, behaviors, animation handles) and callbacks. For each of these objects, the obvious methods are designated as update methods, and, as discussed in Section 4.1, the global state of each object is implicitly determined by those update methods. Therefore, we will not go into excessive detail about either the methods or the state. Finally, Repo-3D's support for change notification will be discussed.

5.1.1 Graphical Objects

GOs are the most straightforward. There are currently twenty-one different types of GOs, and all but the RootGOs are replicated. Since RootGOs are associated with an onscreen window, they are not replicated—window creation remains an active decision of the local process. Furthermore, if replicated windows are needed, the general-purpose programming facilities of Repo can be used to support this in a relatively straightforward manner, outside the scope of Repo-3D. A GO's state is comprised of the properties attached to the object, its name, and some other non-inherited property attributes.[5] The methods that modify the property list are update methods. Group GOs also contain a set of child nodes, and have update methods that modify that set.

5.1.2 Properties

Properties are more complex. There are far more properties in a graphical scene than there are graphical objects, they change much more rapidly, and each property is constructed from a set of Modula-3 objects. There are currently 101 different properties of

seventeen different types in Repo-3D, and any of them can be attached to any GO. A typical GO would have anywhere from two or three (e.g., a BoxGO would have at least two properties to define its corners) to a dozen or more. And, each of these properties could be complex: in the example in Section 6, a single synchronous property for a long animation could have hundreds of requests enqueued within it.

Consider again the object structure illustrated in Figure 4. A property is defined by a name and a value, with the value being a container for a behavior. Only one of the Modula-3 objects is replicated, the property *value*. Property values serve as the replicated containers for property behaviors. To change a property, a new behavior is assigned to its value. The state of the value is the current behavior.

Animation handles are also replicated. They tie groups of related synchronous properties together, and are the basis for the interaction in the example in Section 6. In Anim-3D, handles have one `animate` method, which starts an animation and blocks until it finishes. Since update methods are executed everywhere, and block access to the object while they are being executed, they should not take an extended period of time. In creating Repo-3D, the `animate` method was changed to call two new methods: an update method that starts the animation, and a non-update method that waits for the animation to finish. We also added methods to pause and resume an animation, to retrieve and change the current relative time of an animation handle, and to stop an animation early. The state of an Animation handle is a boolean value that says if it is active or not, plus the start, end, and current time (if the handle is paused).

Most of the Modula-3 objects that comprise a property are not replicated, for a variety of reasons:

- *Properties* represent a permanent binding between a property value and a name. Since they are immutable, they have no synchronization requirements and can simply be copied between processes.

- *Names* represent simple constant identifiers, and are therefore not replicated either.

- *Behaviors* and *requests* are not replicated. While they can be modified after being created, they are treated as immutable data types for two reasons. First, the vast majority of behaviors, even complex synchronous ones, are not changed once they have been created and initialized. Thus, there is some justification for classifying the method calls that modify them as part of their initialization process. The second reason is practical and much more significant. Once a scene has been created and is being "used" by the application, the bulk of the time-critical changes to it tend to be assignments of new behaviors to the existing property values. For example, an object is moved by assigning a new (often constant) behavior to its `GO_Transform` property value. Therefore, the overall performance of the system depends heavily on the performance of property value behavior changes. By treating behaviors as immutable objects, they can simply be copied between processes without incurring the overhead of the replicated object system.

5.1.3 Input Callbacks

In Repo-3D, input event callbacks are not replicated. As discussed in Section 4.2, input events are delivered to the callback stacks of a RootGO. Callbacks attached to any other object receive input events only if they are delivered to that object by the programmer, perhaps recursively from another input event callback (such as the one attached to the RootGO). Therefore, the interactive behavior of a root window is defined not only by the callbacks attached to its RootGO, but also by the set of callbacks associated with the graph rooted at that RootGO. Since the RootGOs are not replicated, the

---

5. Some attributes of a GO, such as the arrays of Point3D properties that define the vertices of a polygon set, are not attached to the object, but are manipulated through method calls.

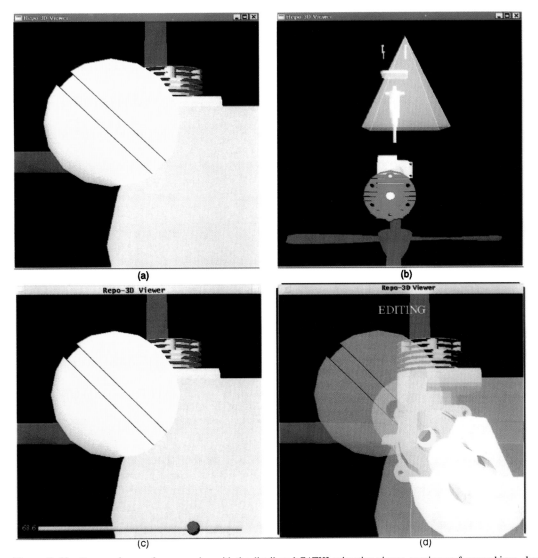

Figure 5: Simultaneous images from a session with the distributed CATHI animation viewer, running on four machines, showing an animation of an engine. (a) Plain animation viewer, running on Windows NT. (b) Overview window, running on Windows 95. (c) Animation viewer with local animation meter, running on IRIX. (d) Animation viewer with local transparency to expose hidden parts, running on Solaris.

callbacks that they delegate event handling to are not replicated either. If a programmer wants to associate callbacks with objects as they travel between processes, Repo's general-purpose programming facilities can be used to accomplish this in a straightforward manner.

5.1.4 Change Notification

The final component of the basic design is support for notification of changes to distributed objects. For example, when an object's position changes or a new child is added to a group, some of the processes containing replicas may wish to react in some way. Fortunately, as discussed in Section 4.1, the Replicated Object package automatically generates Notification Object types for all replicated object types, which provide exactly the required behavior. The Notification Objects for property values allow a programmer to be notified of changes to the behavior of a property,

and the Notification Objects for the various GOs likewise allow notification of updates to them.

5.2 Local Variations

Repo-3D's *local variations* solve a set of problems particular to the distributed context in which Repo-3D lives: maintaining interactivity and supporting local modifications to the shared scene graph.

If the graphical objects and their properties were always strictly replicated, programmers would have to create local variations by copying the objects to be modified, creating a set of Notification Objects on the original objects, the copies of those objects, and all their properties (to be notified when either change), and reflecting the appropriate changes between the instances. Unfortunately, while this process could be automated somewhat, it would still be extremely tedious and error prone. More seriously, the overhead of creating this vast array of objects and links between them would make this approach impractical for short transient changes, such as highlighting an object under the mouse.

To overcome this problem, Repo-3D allows the two major elements of the shared state of the graphical object scene—the properties attached to a GO and the children of a group—to have *local variations* applied to them. (Local variations on property values or animation handles are not supported, although we are considering adding support for the latter.)

Conceptually, local state is the state added to each object (the additions, deletions, and replacements to the properties or children) that is only accessible to the local copies and is not passed to remote processes when the object is copied to create a new replica. The existence of local state is possible because, as discussed in Section 4.1, the *shared state* of a replicated object is implicitly defined by the methods that update it[6]. Therefore, the new methods that manipulate the local variations are added to the GOs as *non-update* methods. Repo-3D combines both the global and local state when creating the graphical scene using the underlying graphics package.

As mentioned above, local variations come in two flavors:

- *Property variations.* There are three methods to set, unset, and get the global property list attached to a GO. We added the following methods to manipulate local variations: add or remove local properties (overriding the value normally used for the object), hide or reveal properties (causing the property value of the parent node to be inherited), and flush the set of local variations (removing them in one step) or atomically apply them to the global state of the object.
- *Child variations.* There are five methods to add, remove, replace, retrieve, and flush the set of children contained in a group node. We added the following ones: add a local node, remove a global node locally, replace a global node with some other node locally, remove each of these local variations, flush the local variations (remove them all in one step), and atomically apply the local variations to the global state.

This set of local operations supports the problems local variations were designed to solve, although some possible enhancements are discussed in Section 7.

6 EXAMPLE: AN ANIMATION EXAMINER

As an example of the ease of prototyping distributed applications with Repo-3D, we created a distributed animation examiner for the CATHI [6] animation generation system. CATHI generates short informational animation clips to explain the operation of technical devices. It generates full-featured animation scripts, including camera and object motion, color and opacity effects, and lighting setup.

It was reasonably straightforward to modify CATHI to generate Repo-3D program files, in addition to the GeomView and Render-Man script files it already generated. The resulting output is a Repo-3D program that creates two scene DAGs: a camera graph and a scene graph. The objects in these DAGs have *synchronous behaviors* specified for their surface and transformation properties. An entire animation is enqueued in the requests of these behaviors, lasting anywhere from a few seconds to a few minutes.

We built a distributed, multi-user examiner over the course of a weekend. The examiner allows multiple users to view the same animation while discussing it (e.g., via electronic chat or on the phone). Figure 5 shows images of the examiner running on four

machines, each with a different view of the scene. The first step was to build a simple "loader" that reads the animation file, creates a window, adds the animation scene and camera to it, and exports the animation on the network, requiring less than a dozen lines of Repo-3D code. A "network" version, that imports the animation from the network instead of reading it from disk, replaced the lines of code to read and export the animation with a single line to import it. Figure 5(a) shows an animation being viewed by one of these clients.

The examiner program is loaded by both these simple clients, and is about 450 lines long. The examiner supports:

- Pausing and continuing the animation, and changing the current animation time using the mouse. Since this is done by operating on the shared animation handle, changes performed by any viewer are seen by all. Because of the consistency guarantees, all users can freely attempt to change the time, and the system will maintain all views consistently.
- A second "overview" window (Figure 5(b)), where a new camera watches the animation scene and camera from a distant view. A local graphical child (representing a portion of the animation camera's frustum) was added to the shared animation camera group to let the attributes of the animation camera be seen in the overview window.
- A local animation meter (bottom of Figure 5(c)), that can be added to any window by pressing a key, and which shows the current time offset into the animation both graphically and numerically. It was added in front of the camera in the animation viewer window, as a local child of a GO in the camera graph, so that it would be fixed to the screen in the animation viewer.
- Local editing (Figure 5(d)), so that users can select objects and make them transparent (to better see what was happening in the animation) or hide them completely (useful on slow machines, to speed up rendering). Assorted local feedback (highlighting the object under the mouse and flashing the selected object) was done with local property changes to the shared GOs in the scene graph.

Given the attention paid to the design of Repo-3D, it was not necessary to be overly concerned with the distributed behavior of the application (we spent no more than an hour or so). Most of that time was spent deciding if a given operation should be global or a local variation. The bulk of programming and debugging time was spent implementing application code. For example, in the overview window, the representation of the camera moves dynamically, based on the bounding values of the animation's scene and camera graphs. In editing mode, the property that flashes the selected node bases its local color on the current global color (allowing a user who is editing while an animation is in progress to see any color changes to the selected node.)

7 CONCLUSIONS AND FUTURE WORK

We have presented the rationale for, and design of, Repo-3D, a general-purpose, object-oriented library for developing distributed, interactive 3D graphics applications across a range of heterogeneous workstations. By presenting the programmer with the illusion of a large shared memory, using the Shared Data-Object model of DSM, Repo-3D makes it easy for programmers to rapidly prototype distributed 3D graphics applications using a familiar object-oriented programming paradigm. Both graphical and general-purpose, non-graphical data can be shared, since Repo-3D is embedded in Repo, a general-purpose, lexically-scoped, distributed programming language.

Repo-3D is designed to directly support the distribution of graphical objects, circumventing the "duplicate database" problem and allowing programmers to concentrate on the application function-

---

6. The local state is not copied when a replicated object is first passed to a new process because the Repo-3D objects have custom *serialization* routines (or Picklers, in Modula-3 parlance). These routines only pass the global state, and initialize the local state on the receiving side to reasonable default values corresponding to the empty local state.

ality of a system, rather than its communication or synchronization components. We have introduced a number of issues that must be considered when building a distributed 3D graphics library, especially concerning efficient and clean support for data distribution and local variations of shared graphical scenes, and discussed how Repo-3D addresses them.

There are a number of ways in which Repo-3D could be improved. The most important is the way the library deals with time. By default, the library assumes all machines are running a time-synchronization protocol, such as NTP, and uses an internal animation time offset[7] (instead of the system-specific time offset) because different OSs (e.g., NT vs. UNIX) start counting time at different dates. Hooks have been provided to allow a programmer to specify their own function to compute the "current" animation time offset within a process. Using this facility, it is possible to build inter-process time synchronization protocols (which we do), but this approach is not entirely satisfactory given our stated goal of relieving the programmer of such tedious chores. Future systems should integrate more advanced solutions, such as adjusting time values as they travel between machines, so that users of computers with unsynchronized clocks can collaborate[8]. This will become more important as mobile computers increase in popularity, as it may not be practical to keep their clocks synchronized.

The specification of local variations in Repo-3D could benefit from adopting the notion of *paths* (as used in Java 3D and Inventor, for example). A path is an array of objects leading from the root of the graph to an object; when an object occurs in multiple places in one or more scene graphs, paths allow these instances to be differentiated. By specifying local variations using paths, nodes in the shared scene graphs could have variations *within* a process as well as *between* processes. One other limitation of Repo-3D, arising from our use of the Replicated Object package, is that there is no way to be notified when local variations are applied to an object. Recall that the methods of an automatically generated Notification Object correspond to the update methods of the corresponding Replicated Object. Since the methods that manipulate the local variations are non-update methods (i.e., they do not modify the replicated state), there are no corresponding methods for them in the Notification Objects. Of course, it would be relatively straightforward to modify the Replicated Object package to support this, but we have not yet found a need for these notifiers.

A more advanced replicated object system would also improve the library. Most importantly, support for different consistency semantics would be extremely useful. If we could specify semantics such as "all updates completely define the state of an object, and only the last update is of interest," the efficiency of the distribution of property values would improve significantly; in this case, updates could be applied (or discarded) when they arrive, without waiting for all previous updates to be applied, and could be applied locally without waiting for the round trip to the sequencer. There are also times when it would be useful to have support for consistency across multiple objects, either using *causal ordering* (as provided by systems such as ISIS and Visual-Obliq)*, or some kind of transaction protocol to allow large groups of changes to be applied either as a unit, or not at all. It is not clear how one would provide these features with a replicated object system such as the one used here.

While a library such as Repo-3D could be built using a variety of underlying platforms, the most likely one for future work is Java. Java shares many of the advantages of Modula-3 (e.g., threads and garbage collection are common across all architectures) and the

packages needed to create a Repo-3D-like toolkit are beginning to appear. While Java does not yet have a replicated object system as powerful as the Replicated Object package, a package such as JSDT [36] (which focuses more on data communication than high-level object semantics) may be a good starting point. Work is also being done on interpreted, distributed programming languages on top of Java (e.g., Ambit [9]). Finally, Java 3D is very similar to Anim-3D, even though its design leans toward efficiency instead of generality when there are trade-offs to be made. For example, the designers chose to forgo Anim-3D's general property inheritance mechanism because it imposes computational overhead. By combining packages such as Java 3D, JSDT, and Ambit, it should be possible to build a distributed graphics library such as Repo-3D in Java.

Acknowledgments

We would like to thank the reviewers for their helpful comments, as well as the many other people who have contributed to this project. Andreas Butz ported CATHI to use Repo-3D and helped with the examples and the video. Clifford Beshers participated in many lively discussions about the gamut of issues dealing with language-level support for 3D graphics. Tobias Höllerer and Steven Dossick took part in many other lively discussions. Xinshi Sha implemented many of the extensions to Obliq-3D that went into Repo-3D. Luca Cardelli and Marc Najork of DEC SRC created Obliq and Obliq-3D, and provided ongoing help and encouragement over the years that Repo and Repo-3D have been evolving.

This research was funded in part by the Office of Naval Research under Contract N00014-97-1-0838 and the National Tele-Immersion Initiative, and by gifts of software from Critical Mass and Microsoft.

References

[1]   D. B. Anderson, J. W. Barrus, J. H. Howard, C. Rich, C. Shen, and R. C. Waters. Building Multi-User Interactive Multimedia Environments at MERL. Technical Report Research Report TR95-17, Mitsubishi Electric Research Laboratory, November 1995.

[2]   H. Bal, M. Kaashoek, and A. Tanenbaum. Orca: A Language for Parallel Programming of Distributed Systems. *IEEE Transactions on Software Engineering*, 18(3):190–205, March 1992.

[3]   K. Bharat and L. Cardelli. Migratory Applications. In *ACM UIST '95*, pages 133-142, November 1995.

[4]   K. P. Birman. The Process Group Approach to Reliable Distributed Computing. *CACM*, 36(12):36–53, Dec 1993.

[5]   A. Birrell, G. Nelson, S. Owicki, and E. Wobber. Network Objects. In *Proc. 14th ACM Symp. on Operating Systems Principles*, 1993.

[6]   A Butz, Animation with CATHI, In *Proceedings of AAAI/IAAI '97*, pages 957–962, 1997.

[7]   J. Calvin, A. Dickens, B. Gaines, P. Metzger, D. Miller, and D. Owen. The SIMNET Virtual World Architecture. In *Proc. IEEE VRAIS '93*, pages 450–455, Sept 1993.

[8]   L. Cardelli. A Language with Distributed Scope. *Computing Systems*, 8(1):27–59, Jan 1995.

[9]   L. Cardelli and A. Gordon. Mobile Ambients. In *Foundations of Software Science and Computational Structures*, Maurice Nivat (Ed.), LNCE 1378, Springer, 140–155. 1998.

[10]   R. Carey and G. Bell. The Annotated VRML 2.0 Reference Manual. Addison-Wesley, Reading, MA, 1997.

[11]   C. Carlsson and O. Hagsand. DIVE—A Multi-User Virtual Reality System. In *Proc. IEEE VRAIS '93*, pages 394–400, Sept 1993.

[12]   C. F. Codella, R. Jalili, L. Koved, and J. B. Lewis. A Toolkit for Developing Multi-User, Distributed Virtual Environments. In *Proc. IEEE VRAIS '93*, pages 401–407, Sept 1993.

---

7. Computed as an offset from January 1, 1997.
8. Implementation details of the combination of Network and Replicated Objects made it difficult for us to adopt a more advanced solution.

[13] C. Elliott, G. Schechter, R. Yeung and S. Abi-Ezzi. TBAG: A High Level Framework for Interactive, Animated 3D Graphics Applications, In *Proc. ACM SIGGRAPH 94*, pages 421–434, August, 1994.

[14] M. Fairen and A. Vinacua, ATLAS, A Platform for Distributed Graphics Applications, In *Proc. VI Eurographics Workshop on Programming Paradigms in Graphics*, pages 91–102, September, 1997.

[15] S. Feiner, B. MacIntyre, M. Haupt, and E. Solomon. Windows on the World: 2D Windows for 3D Augmented Reality. In *Proc. ACM UIST '93*, pages 145–155, 1993.

[16] T. A. Funkhouser. RING: A Client-Server System for Multi-User Virtual Environments. In *Proc. 1995 ACM Symp. on Interactive 3D Graphics*, pages 85–92, March 1995.

[17] G. Grimsdale. dVS—Distributed Virtual Environment System. In *Proc. Computer Graphics '91 Conference*, 1991.

[18] S. P. Harbison. *Modula-3*. Prentice-Hall, 1992.

[19] H.W. Holbrook, S.K. Singhal and D.R. Cheriton, Log-Based Receiver-Reliable Multicast for Distributed Interactive Simulation, *Proc. ACM SIGCOMM '95*, pages 328–341, 1995.

[20] W. Levelt, M. Kaashoek, H. Bal, and A. Tanenbaum. A Comparison of Two Paradigms for Distributed Shared Memory. *Software Practice and Experience*, 22(11):985–1010, Nov 1992.

[21] B. Lucas. A Scientific Visualization Renderer. In *Proc. IEEE Visualization '92*, pp. 227-233, October 1992.

[22] V. Machiraju, A Framework for Migrating Objects in Distributed Graphics Applications, Masters Thesis, University of Utah, Department of Computer Science, Salt Lake City, UT, June, 1997.

[23] B. MacIntyre. Repo: Obliq with Replicated Objects. Programmers Guide and Reference Manual. Columbia University Computer Science Department Research Report CUCS-023-97, 1997.}

[24] B. MacIntyre, and S. Feiner. Language-level Support for Exploratory Programming of Distributed Virtual Environments. In *Proc. ACM UIST '96*, pages 83–94, Seattle, WA, November 6–8, 1996.

[25] M. A. Najork and M. H. Brown. Obliq-3D: A High-level, Fast-turn-around 3D Animation System. *IEEE Transactions on Visualization and Computer Graphics*, 1(2):175–145, June 1995.

[26] R. Ben-Natan. CORBA: A Guide to the Common Object Request Broker Architecture, McGraw Hill, 1995.

[27] D. Phillips, M. Pique, C. Moler, J. Torborg, D. Greenberg. Distributed Graphics: Where to Draw the Lines? Panel Transcript, SIGGRAPH 89, available at:
http://www.siggraph.org:443/publications/panels/siggraphi89/

[28] A. Prakash and H. S. Shim. DistView: Support for Building Efficient Collaborative Applications Using Replicated Objects. In *Proc. ACM CSCW '94*, pages 153–162, October 1994.

[29] J. Rohlf and J. Helman, IRIS Performer: A High Performance Multiprocessing Toolkit for Real-Time {3D} Graphics, In *Proc. ACM SIGGRAPH 94*, pages 381–394, 1994.

[30] M. Roseman and S. Greenberg. Building Real-Time Groupware with GroupKit, a Groupware Toolkit. *ACM Transactions on Computer-Human Interaction*, 3(1):66–106, March 1996.

[31] C. Shaw and M. Green. The MR Toolkit Peers Package and Experiment. In *Proc. IEEE VRAIS '93*, pages 18–22, Sept 1993.

[32] G. Singh, L. Serra, W. Png, A. Wong, and H. Ng. BrickNet: Sharing Object Behaviors on the Net. In *Proc. IEEE VRAIS '95*, pages 19–25, 1995.

[33] H. Sowizral, K. Rushforth, and M. Deering. The Java 3D API Specification, Addison-Wesley, Reading, MA, 1998.

[34] M. Stefik, G. Foster, D. G. Bobrow, K. Kahn, S. Lanning, and L. Suchman. Beyond The Chalkboard: Computer Support for Collaboration and Problem Solving in Meetings. *CACM*, 30(1):32–47, January 1987.

[35] P. S. Strauss and R. Carey, An Object-Oriented 3D Graphics Toolkit, In *Computer Graphics (Proc. ACM SIGGRAPH 92)*, pages 341–349, Aug, 1992.

[36] Sun Microsystems, Inc. The Java Shared Data Toolkit, 1998. Unsupported software, available at:
http://developer.javasoft.com/developer/earlyAccess/jsdt/

[37] I. Tou, S. Berson, G. Estrin, Y. Eterovic, and E. Wu. Prototyping Synchronous Group Applications. *IEEE Computer*, 27(5):48–56, May 1994.

[38] R. Waters and D. Anderson. The Java Open Community Version 0.9 Application Program Interface. Feb, 1997. Available online at:
http://www.merl.com/opencom/opencom-java-api.html

[39] A. Wollrath, R. Riggs, and J. Waldo. A Distributed Object Model for the Java System, In *Proc. USENIX COOTS '96*, pages 219–231, July 1996.

[40] R. Zeleznik, D. Conner, M. Wloka, D. Aliaga, N. Huang, P. Hubbard, B. Knep, H. Kaufman, J. Hughes, and A. van Dam. An Object-oriented Framework for the Integration of Interactive Animation Techniques. In *Computer Graphics (SIGGRAPH '91 Proceedings)*, pages 105–112, July, 1991.

[41] M. J. Zyda, D. R. Pratt, J. G. Monahan, and K. P. Wilson. NPSNET: Constructing a 3D Virtual World. In *Proc. 1992 ACM Symp. on Interactive 3D Graphics*, pages 147–156, Mar. 1992.

Constellation™: A Wide-Range Wireless Motion-Tracking System for Augmented Reality and Virtual Set Applications

Eric Foxlin*, Michael Harrington, and George Pfeifer

InterSense Incorporated

Abstract

We present a new tracking system for augmented reality and virtual set applications, based on an inertial navigation system aided by ultrasonic time-of-flight range measurements to a constellation of wireless transponder beacons. An extended Kalman filter operating on 1-D range measurements allows the inertial sensors to filter out corrupt range measurements and perform optimal smoothing and prediction, while at the same time using the pre-screened range measurements to correct the drift of the inertial system. The use of inside-out ultrasonic tracking allows for tetherless tracking over a building-wide range with no acoustic propagation latency. We have created a simulation to account for error sources in the ultrasonic ranging system. The fully implemented tracking system is tested and found to have accuracy consistent with the simulation results. The simulation also predicts that with some further compensation of transducer misalignment, accuracies better than 2 mm can be achieved.

CR Categories and Subject Descriptors: I.3.6 [Computer Graphics]: Methodology and Techniques - Interaction Techniques I.3.7 [Computer Graphics]: 3-Dimensional Graphics and Realism-Virtual reality; I.3.1 [Computer Graphics]: Hardware Architecture-Input devices.

Additional Keywords: motion tracking, inertial, ultrasonic, kalman filtering, augmented reality, virtual sets, accuracy, latency, sensor fusion

1. INTRODUCTION

There is an ever expanding set of interactive graphics applications which require smooth and fast free-space tracking of some part of the user's body, or some hand-held object. Head-mounted displays (HMDs) for immersive virtual environment simulations have stimulated a tremendous amount of activity since the early 1990s. Many virtual prototyping systems were developed, often using "goggles and gloves" for interaction. While the media has been distracted by the new phenomenon of the world-wide web, virtual environment technology has made great strides, especially in the area of real-time rendering on affordable hardware, and has been silently catapulted out of the laboratory and into real-world applications.

73 Second Ave., Burlington, MA 01803, ericf@isense.com

Recently, there has been considerable interest in wearable Augmented Reality (AR) systems and virtual set generation for television studios. While these seem to present fairly dissimilar tracking problems (tracking a headset v. tracking a camera), they both require a long-range tracking solution with very high accuracy that will work reliably in an uncontrolled environment full of interference sources. The most immediately promising applications for AR seem to be wearable or mobile computers to assist workers in assembly or maintenance of complex machinery from aircraft [18,19] to buildings [6] to human patients [21]. In the case of assembling wire bundles for aircraft, the workpiece may be over 100 feet long, and the AR tracking system must operate over this span with undiminished performance. Likewise, in the virtual studio it is necessary to track a camera which is being carried about freely in a very large space full of metal, electronics and bright dynamic lighting. In addition to long range and difficult operating environments, both applications share the need for tracking accuracy sufficient for visual registration of computer generated and real objects. Tracking is an urgent unsolved problem for these two applications. This paper is an effort to address it.

With such a plethora of different graphics applications that depend on motion-tracking technology for their very existence, a wide range of interesting motion-tracking solutions have been invented and brought to various stages of maturity over the years. Surveys of the myriad magnetic, optical, acoustic, and mechanical tracking systems are available in [2,7,17]. Many HMD applications only require motion over a small region, and these traditional tracking approaches are usable, although there are still difficulties with interference, line-of-sight, jitter, and latency. We have previously described an alternative solution based on inertial sensing technology with automatic drift correction [9] which overcomes the problems with interference, line-of-sight, jitter and latency. In fact, that drift-corrected inertial tracking system is sourceless and operates over an unlimited range. However, it is only able to track 3-DOF orientation. To correct positional drift in a 6-DOF inertial tracking system requires some type of range or bearing measurements to fiducial points in the environment.

In this paper we present a new tracking system concept, a working system based on this concept, test results and a demonstration of the capabilities of this system in a mock virtual set camera-tracking application. The new concept is an extension of our previous work on inertial orientation tracking technology. The inertial tracker provides a self-contained orientation tracking system with unlimited range which does not suffer from the drawbacks associated with source-based or mechanically-linked tracking systems. It also contains triaxial accelerometers which are double integrated to obtain changes in position, relative to a known starting position. The double integration leads to an unacceptable rate of positional drift and must be corrected frequently by some external source.

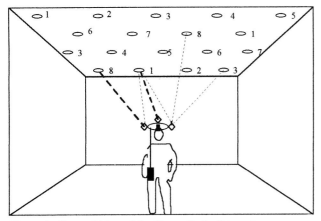

Figure 1: General idea of the Constellation™ system

The CONSTELLATION tracking system is similar in its basic principles of operation to an aided inertial navigation system (INS), except that it operates indoors, has much finer resolution and accuracy, and uses acoustic rather than RF technology for range measurements. Figure 1 illustrates the system, configured for tracking an HMD in a wide-range VR or AR application. The HMD is equipped with an integrated inertial sensing instrument called the InertiaCube™ and, in this example, 3 ultrasonic rangefinder modules (URMs). The rangefinder modules communicate with a constellation of transponder beacons which may be mounted at any known locations in the environment. The beacons are activated one-at-a-time by infrared trigger codes emitted by the rangefinder modules. As each beacon receives its own unique code, it responds by emitting an ultrasonic pulse. The rangefinders count the time-of-flight (TOF) until the pulse arrives, and use the speed of sound to convert the TOF into a distance. These range measurements are fed into an extended Kalman filter (EKF) which makes small adjustments to the position and orientation trajectory which is being update at a high rate by the strapdown INS. At least 6 range measurements, connecting between at least 3 HMD-mounted microphones and at least 3 fixed transponder beacons, are required to completely determine the position and orientation of the HMD. Figure 1 shows an example of 6 suitable ranges, which illustrates that multiple nearly simultaneous measurements from each triggered beacon can be used if available, but are not required. Two degrees of freedom can be resolved by stabilizing with respect to gravity, so only 4 of the myriad potential lines-of-sight need to be open to continue tracking indefinitely, and fewer than 4 can be sufficient to sustain reasonable tracking for a while.

We believe this new tracking system architecture has several compelling advantages:

- It is simple and practical compared to other systems with scaleable-range capabilities

- It is possible to wear the whole tracking system, including all of the sensors and the computational unit. This results in a tracker that is completely untethered.

- It is inertial sensor-based, conferring high update rates and superior smoothness and predictive capability. It can withstand

the loss or corruption of a large portion of its acoustic range measurements without a significant degradation in performance.

- The acoustic ranging system is inside-out compared to other acoustic trackers. Since the sound waves propagate spherically *from* the fixed beacons *to* the moving target, the TOF recorded at the moment of detection represents the instantaneous radius measurement with no latency.

1.1 Previous Work

We are not the first to brave the design of a scaleable-range tracking system. A system called the optical ceiling tracker has been in development for many years at UNC-Chapel Hill [22]. It uses a cluster of head-mounted cameras looking at an array of computer-controlled infrared-emitting diodes (IREDs) mounted in ceiling tiles. Although it is an optical tracker and ours is a hybrid acousto-inertial tracker, both systems are based on an array of fiducial markers on the ceiling and designed to offer the same advantages of high accuracy, potentially limitless range, and relative immunity to occlusion through redundancy. Further, both use extended Kalman filtering algorithms to process single measurements at a time [23]. Another optical constellation-based approach was recently proposed [14] which makes use of quadcells instead of lateral effect photodiode cameras. Quadcells are extremely simple and inexpensive optical direction-sensors which eliminate the need for lenses and the weight and optical distortion they introduce. However, quadcells detect the direction to a light source based on the ratios of the illumination received on each of four photocells, and these ratios may be affected by both diffuse and specular reflection of the LED beacon strobes off of various surfaces.

There are a variety of reasons why we chose to employ acoustic range-finding instead of optical bearing-angle measurement to correct the positional drift in our system:

- It requires no head-mounted cameras, only a few tiny ultrasonic microphones, leading to lower weight, power consumption and cost.

- The orientation is already available from the inertial system. The cumbersome head-mounted camera approach was developed to achieve superior orientation resolution. The simpler acoustic and outside-in optical trackers are sufficient for tracking position even though they are not very precise for orientation.

- The mathematics are simpler. Three range measurements pin down the position. Six bearing angles (normally measured two at a time) are required to solve for position and orientation.

- Microphones are available with very wide fields of view compared to cameras. Thus it is possible to use fewer beacons in the constellation and still be sure there will be several redundant lines of sight available.

In addition to the two aforementioned constellation-type tracking systems, there has been much previous work on inertial and acoustic technologies. At least three authors have exploited the motion derivatives provided by inertial sensors to add prediction capability to HMD tracking systems [1][4][15]. In the navigation arena, the aided inertial navigation approach used in this paper has been well known, and a wide variety of radio-frequency navigational aids have been used, including LORAN, OMEGA, radar, GLONASS, and GPS for maritime and aviation applications, as well as star-trackers for space navigation.

Finally, ultrasonic time-of-flight ranging techniques have been used in numerous commercial products for 3-D motion tracking (Logitech 6-D Mouse, Mattel Power Glove, Lipman VSCOPE, Kantek Ringmouse). In particular, the Lipman VSCOPE and Kantek ring-mouse have wireless infrared-triggered transponders. Also, [20] describes a large-volume extension of the Logitech device in which, based on the current position of the tracked object, the nearest of a number of switchable reference triangles is automatically selected and used.

1.2 Contribution

This paper contributes the following new concepts and results in motion tracking for interactive graphics:

- A novel acousto-inertial hybrid tracking approach and a working system. (Demonstrated on video performing an uninterrupted tracking sequence spanning several rooms.)

- The first TOF motion tracker with latency less than the flight time of the ranging signals. This is possible due to the unique inside-out configuration of the transmit-receive pairs, which in turn is possible because the use of inertial tracking allows for processing of non-simultaneous range measurements.

- An example of the usefulness of single-constraint-at-a-time Kalman filtering for designing robust sensor-fusion based motion-trackers.

- An analysis of the tracker's Geometric Dilution of Precision (GDOP) and simulation results to understand its sensitivity to systematic error sources.

2. SYSTEM DESCRIPTION

2.1 Hardware Overview

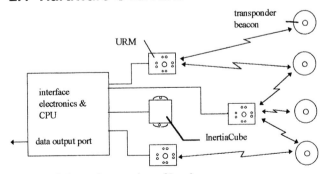

Figure 2:Schematic overview of hardware

Figure 2 illustrates the main hardware components of the tracking system. Just as GPS has a space-based constellation of satellites and a vehicle-born receiver with antennae, this system has a ceiling-based constellation of transponder beacons and a camera- or person-worn tracker unit with ultrasonic rangefinder modules (URMs) and an InertiaCube™ inertial sensing device.

Figure 3 shows a diagram and a photograph of the InertiaCube integrated inertial sensing device manufactured by InterSense for

this and related applications [11]. The InertiaCube senses angular rate about and linear acceleration along each of three orthogonal body axes, as illustrated in Figure 3. A portion of a floppy disk is visible in the photograph to highlight the InertiaCube's compact dimensions: 2.7 X 3.4 X 3 cm.

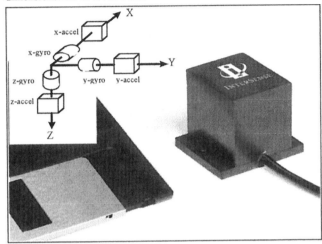

Figure 3: Schematic and photograph of InertiaCube

Each URM consists of a 40 kHz ultrasonic microphone, 4-8 infrared emitting diodes (IREDs) and the necessary electronics, as illustrated in Figure 4. It is not necessary for the IREDs and microphones to be physically mounted together, but it makes logical sense since a blocked line of sight between a beacon and a microphone makes it futile to trigger that beacon.

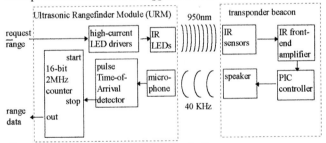

Figure 4: URM and transponder block diagrams

2.2 Software

The tracker system software has two major tasks: acquisition, and tracking. Acquisition occurs whenever the powered-up tracker enters or re-enters a room that has transponder beacons. The purpose of acquisition is for the tracker to determine its initial estimate of position and orientation (a.k.a. pose) so that the tracking algorithm can begin the process of recursively refining and updating the pose estimates. There are currently only eight differently coded beacon types (we are working on increasing this). The acquisition algorithm works as follows:

1. Identify the nearest 4 beacons.

2. Search throughout the entire constellation (which must be pre-known to the tracker) for places that have this combination of beacons in close proximity. Test each such hypothesis to see if a self-consistent trilateration solution can be found using the actual range measurements with the hypothesized beacons .

3. If only one combination of beacons passes the test, use the starting pose determined in this self-consistent trilateration of all three microphones and move on to tracking.

4. If there are multiple 4-tuples in the constellation which are consistent with the initial set of range measurements, try to use range measurements to other beacons to resolve ambiguities.

Note that with only 8 different beacon codes, there are only C(8,4) =70 different combinations, which means that a large constellation would have a lot of repetitions of the same group of four adjacent codes. To overcome this we are increasing the number of beacon codes to 16, which would provide 1820 unique 4-tuples. Even larger constellations would require a different scheme using zone codes and specific beacon codes, because the acquisition time to sequence through more than 16 beacons would be too long.

Once there is a successful acquisition, the state and covariance matrix of the EKF get initialized and tracking begins. Figure 5 illustrates the tracking algorithm. The most important point to note is that the integrated inertial sensors have direct feed-through to the outputs, which insures low latency. The angular rates measured by the gyros are integrated once to obtain orientation, which is output directly. The orientation is also used to transform the accelerations measured by the accelerometers in the constantly changing body-referenced frame into a steady and level navigation frame (hereafter "nav-frame" or N-frame) with its z-axis vertical. The unwanted effect of gravity on this virtual z-accelerometer is first canceled, and then the nav-frame acceleration is double integrated to obtain position, which is output directly. The EKF uses the range measurements to estimate the amount of accumulated error in the orientation, gyro biases, position, and velocity. It applies these error estimates immediately to the appropriate integrator outputs as tiny corrections which prevent the accumulation of error and insure that the EKF is always linearizing about the most accurate possible state. Complementary Kalman filtering is discussed in [3], and the details of our complementary EKF approach are provided in [10].

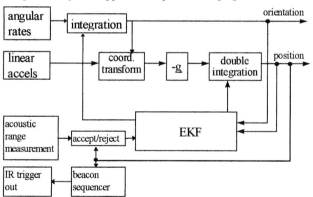

Figure 5: Tracking algorithm flow chart

The selection and utilization of the range measurements is very interesting and deserves some elaboration. First of all, the tracker makes immediate use of individual range measurements as they come in, rather than saving up measurements from 3 beacons, performing a trilateration and feeding the computed position into the Kalman filter as a measurement vector. This technique of processing several scalar measurements instead of one vector measurement is called sequential update Kalman filtering, and it is known to be both faster and numerically more robust because it avoids the matrix inversion in the Kalman gain update step. When measurements containing only partial information about the state

are applied during different update cycles, the process has been called single-constraint-at-a-time (SCAAT) tracking [23]. In non-inertial tracking systems, this allows the tracker to have partial updates at a higher update rate, resulting in lower latency and jitter. In our aided inertial design, the pose output gets essentially complete updates (with a little drift) at a high rate of about 500 Hz, but it is still more convenient to make partial drift correction updates immediately upon receiving each range measurement, because at this time an accurate measurement residual can be formed by differencing the measured range and the predicted range computed using the most recent inertial state update.

Secondly, when the tracker receives a new range measurement, it already knows where it is, and it also knows, based on the diagonal elements of the error covariance matrix, approximately how much uncertainty there is in this self-position estimate. Since it knows the location of the beacon that sent the pulse, it can predict what the range measurement should be. If the range measurement doesn't match within the tolerance computed from the covariance matrix, it can be rejected. This is an extremely useful feature in an acousto-inertial tracker. Acoustic range measurement devices always detect the first arrival: a pulse is sent and a counter is started. Since the direct pulse arrives before its echo, the counter is stopped by the first detected pulse at the receiver. Unfortunately, there is occasionally a random background noise or an echo from a previous sampling period which arrives before the real pulse and stops the counter. In our system, we know when to expect the real pulse and can gate the receiver open only during the window of time when the returned pulse is expected. This can likely prevent over 90% of premature pulse detection problems. Because we use the diagonal elements of the covariance to dynamically adjust the acceptance time window, if the tracker misses some measurements it will widen the window and accept subsequent measurements to bring it back on course, instead of becoming completely lost.

3. Constellation Geometry and Error Sensitivity

The constellation may be set up in many geometrical configurations in order to adapt to different types of surroundings. This invites the questions 1) What geometry will result in the highest tracking performance? , 2) What will the performance be for some particular geometry? and 3) How many transponders are really needed? In this section, we develop a simulation to evaluate the sensitivity of the position and orientation calculations to all the known error sources, both random and systematic.

A standard metric used in GPS and other range-based position location systems to evaluate the effect of geometry on positioning uncertainty is the Geometric Dilution of Precision (GDOP):

$$GDOP \equiv \frac{\sqrt{\sigma_x^2 + \sigma_y^2 + \sigma_z^2}}{\sigma_r} = \frac{\sqrt{tr(P)}}{\sigma_r}, \quad (1)$$

where P is the error covariance of the position solution [16]. This expression is a function of position and it describes, at a given point (x,y,z), how much positional uncertainty there will be if all of the range measurements have the same uncertainty of σ_r. The GDOP is useful for estimating the amplification of random noise in the range measurements, but there are other systematic error sources which may be present:

1. error in the beacon positions

2. temperature error

3. constant time-delay errors in beacons (due to part-to-part variation or electronics drift)

4. constant time-delay errors in URMs (due to part-to-part variation or electronics drift)

5. transducer angle related errors

We have developed a simulation in MATLAB to probe the sensitivity to all these error sources for any desired geometry. The simulation allows the user to enter magnitudes for all of the above systematic error sources, and any desired constellation geometry, then it computes the resulting systematic error and GDOP at a sampling of points within a user-defined test volume.

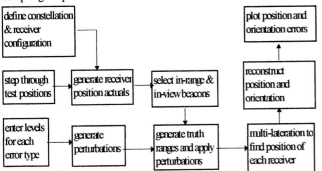

Figure 6: Error sensitivity simulation

Figure 6 shows a block diagram of the simulation. The main flow of the simulation is as follows. First the user is given the opportunity to set up a "trial" constellation for evaluation, and to specify the desired tracking region beneath the constellation. A random horizontal and vertical error are then applied to each beacon in the constellation, uniformly distributed over user-specified intervals. In the main loop of the simulation, the program steps through test positions within the desired tracking volume. At each position it rotates the whole simulated tracker (headset or camera configuration) to a variety of angles, generating the appropriate set of truth positions for all the microphones on the tracker. All beacons which are within range of the tracker are selected using

$$rangelimit = (5m)\sqrt{\cos(\theta_t)\cos(\theta_r)}$$

where $\cos(\theta_t)$ and $\cos(\theta_r)$ approximate the off-axis attenuation patterns of our 40 kHz transmitters and receivers. Having selected an active set of beacons, range measurements are calculated, including all appropriate error perturbations, and fed into a multi-lateration algorithm which solves for the positions of all the receivers. There are numerous trilateration and multilateration algorithms in the literature [16][5][13][12]. Although [16] provides an exact closed form solution that is both general and computationally efficient, we chose to employ the classic iterative least-squares approach [12], because it is a closer simulation of the extended Kalman filter used in the tracker. In fact, in the absence of motion, the EKF converges to the same solution as the recursive least-squares approximation used here [12].

Figures 7 and 8 display some simulation results for a constellation which consists of an infinite square array with 2 foot

(61cm) grid-spacing and 3 meter height. In all cases, the test volume extended from 0-2.5 meters in the z (height) dimension, and 0-1 foot in the x and y dimensions. Due to the symmetries of an infinite square array, any (x,y) point is equivalent to some point inside of this single-quadrant test region. Therefore, the range of errors displayed in these volumetric visualizations represents the whole range of errors that a tracker would experience over any size workspace, as long as it does not approach too closely the edge of the constellation. (We have not simulated edge effects, but would expect higher errors near the edges). The systematic error levels were set for this simulation run to the following values:

error in beacon positions:	+/-2mm horizontal/ +/-4mm vertical, uniform distribution
temperature error:	0.2° C
beacon variations:	+/- 1mm, uniform distribution
URM variations:	+/- 1mm, uniform distribution
transducer angle related errors:	+/-2.5mm range perturbations at 60° off axis

Table 1: Error source inputs for simulation in Fig. 7-8

These error levels were chosen to reflect what we believe to be the actual systematic error levels in the current setup in our laboratory. They result in a combined systematic positional error shown in Figure 7 which ranges from 2.3-4.7 mm from floor level to 2.5 meters height. By contrast, the positional resolution of pure ultrasonic range measurements, shown in Figure 8, is 0.7-1.5 mm in most of the active volume, increasing to 2.5 mm near the floor. These numbers are obtained via Equation 1 from the estimation error covariance returned by the multilateration algorithm which has been fed individual range noise sigmas corresponding to our hardware test results in Section 4.1.

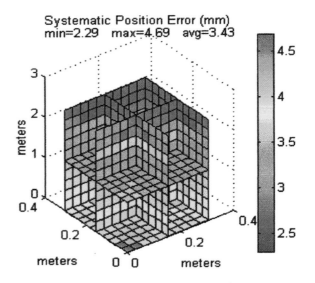

Figure 7: Systematic position errors, assuming error sources listed in Table 1.

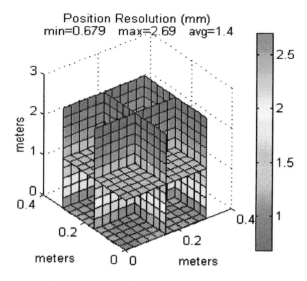

Figure 8: Position resolution

The errors in Figure 7 are largely caused by the transducer misalignment angle errors. We are in the process of developing calibration procedures to better model and compensate for these effects. In Figure 9 we show simulation results predicting approximately 1 mm accuracy when the residual error due to mis-modeled transducer angle effects has been reduced to 1 mm per radian of misalignment, and URM part-to-part variations are measured and compensated out. This excellent accuracy is achieved even in the presence of random beacon placement errors of +/-2 mm horizontal and +/-4 mm vertical, probably because the random errors from the 20-40 beacons participating in the multilateration tend to cancel each other out.

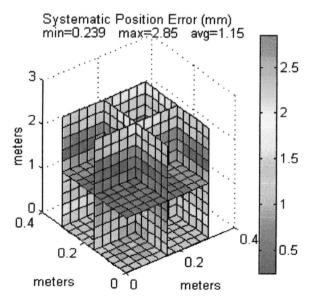

Figure 9: Position errors, assuming improved compensation of systematic error sources

Accuracy of acoustically measured orientation is a function of baseline separation of microphones, so the simulation was run at several different baselines, and the resulting minimum, maximum, and average orientation error throughout a test volume ranging

from 1-2 meters below the beacon constellation are plotted in Figure 10. The plotted error is the root-sum-square combination of yaw, pitch, and roll error, with pitch and roll errors truncated to 0.25 degrees because the inertial sensor is able to correct pitch and roll to this level without any ultrasonic aiding [11]. This data is based on the improved error compensation used in Figure 9. As can be seen from the plot, 15 cm of microphone separation, which can be conveniently arranged on an AR head-mounted display, is sufficient to achieve good orientation accuracy. Wider separations, which can easily be arranged on a camera, lead to even higher accuracy.

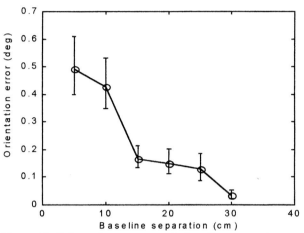

Figure 10: Orientation errors v. mic. baseline separation

4. Test Results

4.1 1-D Ranging Results

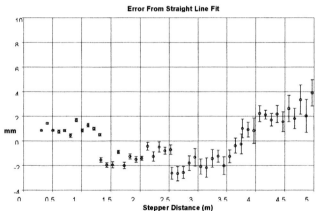

Figure 11: One dimensional ultrasonic ranging results

Figure 11 shows results of testing our ultrasonic ranging hardware prototypes for resolution and linearity. The test was performed using one URM and a transponder mounted on the carriage plate of a leadscrew-driven 4-foot long linear actuator. The rail was moved 4 times to collect approximately 5 meters of data. A single straight line was fit to the entire collective data set, and the residual errors are plotted in Figure 11. The discontinuities in the data were caused by inexact placement of the rail after moving it. Despite these discontinuities, the experiment provides a meaningful assessment of the 1-D ultrasonic ranging performance. The linearity is approximately 0.1% FS, and the range noise of 1mm per meter of range used in the previous section to generate the GDOP appears justified.

4.2 3-DOF Position Tracking Accuracy

To test the accuracy of the 6-DOF tracking system, we set up a 3 by 3 grid (with one corner missing) of transponder beacons on 2 foot centers on a drop ceiling grid. 1.5 meters below the grid we leveled a table with a 1" grid marked on it, and registered this grid to the constellation coordinates using plumb bobs. A 5-DOF digitizer arm (Immersion Corp.) was placed on this table and registered to its grid with a calibration procedure that involves touching four reference points. The tip of the arm was then attached to a camera-tracker head containing an InertiaCube and 3 URMs separated with horizontal and vertical baseline distances of about 28 cm and 25 cm respectively. The camera tracker was manually moved to 30 locations spaced throughout the test volume reachable by the arm. For comparison to the simulation, Figure 12 plots the root-sum-square (RSS) of the 3 position error components at each point. While the average error is the same as the simulation results in Figure 7, the worst case error is 2 mm larger. This is to be expected because the constellation for this test was equipped with only 8 beacons. When the simulation is run with 8 beacons, it also predicts errors of about 1 to 8 mm.

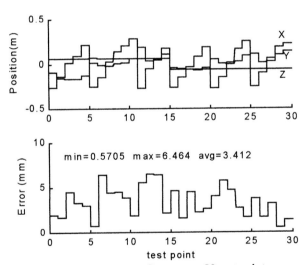

Figure 12: RSS of X,Y, and Z errors at 30 test points

5. Conclusions & Future Work

A new type of motion tracker has been presented which combines inertial orientation and acceleration sensors with ultrasonic ranging devices in a fashion that allows the inertial sensors to filter out corrupt range measurements (ie. echoes and acoustic interference), and perform optimal motion smoothing and prediction, while at the same time using the pre-screened range measurements to correct the drift of the inertial sensors.

Some simulations were performed which indicated that the tracker will be capable of achieving 1-3 mm accuracy levels if used beneath a transponder constellation with 2 ft. spacing that extends 9 ft. beyond the tracking region on each side. Edge effects have not been simulated, but we expect that any dilution of precision near

the edges of a room could be overcome by extending the transponder array part-way down the wall.

The prototype ultrasonic distance measuring hardware was tested in a controlled 1-dimensional measurement set-up in order to characterize the error performance and provide meaningful input data for the simulation. The 3-D position locating accuracy was tested in a benchtop configuration with 8 beacons, and found to conform with the simulation's predictions. Finally, the fully functional 6-DOF tracking system was used to record a videotape to demonstrate qualitatively it's resolution, dynamic performance, and range.

The dynamic performance has not yet been tested quantitatively, but in theory there are expected to be no appreciable sources of latency in this system. The range measurements reflect the instantaneous position when received, and the integration of the rate and acceleration data and incorporation of range measurements by means of Kalman filter updates runs at 400-600 Hz. Thus the effective latency of the system is expected to be about 2.5 ms, even though range measurements are received much less frequently.

The simulation indicates that higher levels of accuracy can be obtained by compensating for part-to-part transducer variations. Ultrasonic transducers have an angular dependence which causes a shift of up to 1 mm at 20° misalignment angle [8], and we find even more at larger angles. We have constructed a computer controlled 2-axis rotation device to characterize this dependency and begun to use the data in the firmware to compensate for the effects.

While the wireless nature of the transponder beacons makes this system easier to set up than other wide-range tracking systems, it is still necessary to accurately measure the beacon locations and download them into the tracking system prior to tracking. This can be time-consuming, and if not done very carefully can become a dominant source of tracking error. In subsequent work, we plan to explore the feasibility of an auto-mapping algorithm that enables a user to install the constellation using the following procedure:

1. A "seed" constellation consisting of 3 rigidly mounted beacons is first hung which establishes the reference frame.

2. The rest of the beacons are hung randomly in any convenient locations. They need not be coplanar.

3. The tracker begins tracking using only the seed beacons. Then it starts trying one additional beacon code at a time until it finds one that responds. The new beacon's position is estimated and entered into the constellation database. As the user walks around the workspace, the tracker finds and auto-installs all the beacons with approximate positions.

4. In a subsequent auto-calibration step, or during normal tracking, there is continuous slow refinement of beacon positions using recursive estimation.

Step 4 has been shown to work in the UNC optical ceiling tracker [23]. It is likely to work here as well if systematic errors other than beacon placement errors have been sufficiently compensated such that the system can track its position to an accuracy substantially better than the placement accuracy of the individual beacons. The simulation results in Figure 9 show that even with random beacon placement errors of +/- 2-4 mm, the tracker is able to find its own position to about 1 mm accuracy. This suggests that auto-calibration in this system may indeed lead to successive refinement of accuracy rather than degradation.

6. Acknowledgments

We are thankful to Wallace VanderVelde for many invaluable insights and lessons on inertial navigation and Kalman filtering, to Gary Bishop, Greg Welch, and David Mizell for enlightening discussions, and to our SIGGRAPH reviewers for many insightful and useful comments and suggestions.

7. References

[1] R. Azuma and G. Bishop. Improving Static and Dynamic Registration in an Optical See-through HMD. In *SIGGRAPH 94 Conference Proceedings*, ACM Annual Conference Series, Orlando, FL, August 1994.

[2] D. K. Bhatnagar, Position Trackers for Head Mounted display Systems: A Survey. *University of North Carolina, Chapel Hill TR93-010*, March 1993.

[3] R. G. Brown and P. Y. C. Hwang. Introduction to Random Signals and Applied Kalman Filtering, 2nd ed. New York: John Wiley & Sons, 1992.

[4] S. Emura and S. Tachi. Compensation of Time Lag Between Actual and Virtual Spaces by Multi-Sensor Integration. In *Proc. IEEE International Conference on Multisensor Fusion and Integration for Intelligent Systems (MFI 94)*, pp. 463--469.

[5] B.T. Fang. Trilateration and Extension to Global Positioning System Navigation. *Journal of Guidance, Control and Dynamics*, 9(6), Nov.-Dec. 1986.

[6] S. K. Feiner, A. C. Webster, T. E. Krueger III, B. MacIntyre, and E. J. Keller. Architectural Anatomy. *Presence*, 4(3): 318-325, Summer 1995.

[7] F. J. Ferrin. Survey of Helmet Tracking Technologies. In *Proc. SPIE*, vol. 1456, pages 86-94, April 1991.

[8] J.F. Figueroa. Ranging Errors Caused by Angular Misalignment Between Ultrasonic Transducer Pairs. *Journal of the Acoustical Society of America*, 87(3), Mar. 1990.

[9] E. Foxlin and N. Durlach. An Inertial Head-Orientation Tracker with Automatic Drift Compensation for use with HMD's. In *Proc. Virtual Reality Software & Technology 94*, G. Singh, S. K. Feiner, and D. Thalmann, Eds. Singapore: World Scientific, pages 159-174, August 1994.

[10] E. Foxlin. A Complementary Separate-Bias Kalman Filter for Inertial Head-Tracking. In *Proc. IEEE VRAIS 96*. IEEE Computer Society Press, March-April 1996.

[11] E. Foxlin, M. Harrington, and Y. Altshuler. Miniature 6-DOF Inertial System for Tracking HMDs. In *Proc. SPIE Helmet and Head-Mounted Displays III*, vol. 3362, Orlando, April, 1998.

[12] W. H. Foy. Position-Location Solutions by Taylor Series Estimation. *IEEE Transactions on Aerospace and Electronic Systems*, 12(2), Mar. 1976.

[13] K.C. Ho and Y.T. Chan. Solution and Performance Analysis of Geolocation by TDOA. *IEEE Transactions on Aerospace and Electronic Systems*, 29(4), Oct. 1993.

[14] D. Kim, S. Richards, T. Caudell. An Optical Tracker for Augmented Reality and Wearable Computers. In *Proc. IEEE VRAIS 97*, p.p. 146-151, IEEE Computer Society Press.

[15] U. H. List. Nonlinear Prediction of Head Movements for Helmet-Mounted Displays. *Air Force Human Resources Laboratory, Technical Paper AFHRL 83-45*

[16] D. Manolakis. Efficient Solution and Performance Analysis of 3-D Position Estimation by Trilateration. *IEEE Trans. on Aerospace and Electronic Systems*, 32(4), Oct. 1996.

[17] K. Meyer, H. L. Applewhite, and F. A. Biocca. A Survey of Position Trackers. *Presence*: 1(2), pp. 173--200, 1992.

[18] J. Nash. Wiring the Jet Set. *Wired Magazine*, Oct. 1997.

[19] J. Seagull and M. Beauer. A Field Usability Evaluation of a Wearable System In *Proc. International Symposium on Wearable Computers*, Oct. 1997

[20] H. Sowizral and D. Barnes. Tracking Position and Orientation in a Large Volume. In *Proc. IEEE VRAIS 93*, p.p. 132-139. IEEE Computer Society Press.

[21] A. State, M. A. Livingston, W. F. Garrett, G. Hirota, M. C. Whitton, E. D. Pisano, and H. Fuchs. Technologies for Augmented Reality Systems: Realizing Ultrasound-Guided Needle Biopsies. In *SIGGRAPH 96 Conference Proceedings*, ACM Annual Conference Series, pages 439-446.

[22] M. Ward, R. Azuma, R. Bennet, S. Gottschalk, H. Fuchs. A Demonstrated Optical Tracker with Scalable Work Area for Head-Mounted Display Systems. In *Proc. 1992 Symposium on Interactive 3D Graphics*, Cambridge, MA, March 1992.

[23] G. Welch and G. Bishop. Single-Constraint-at-a-Time Tracking. In *SIGGRAPH 97 Conference Proceedings*, ACM Annual Conference Series.

mediaBlocks: Physical Containers, Transports, and Controls for Online Media

Brygg Ullmer, Hiroshi Ishii, and Dylan Glas[*]
Tangible Media Group
MIT Media Lab

Abstract

We present a tangible user interface based upon *mediaBlocks:* small, electronically tagged wooden blocks that serve as physical icons ("phicons") for the containment, transport, and manipulation of online media. MediaBlocks interface with media input and output devices such as video cameras and projectors, allowing digital media to be rapidly "copied" from a media source and "pasted" into a media display. MediaBlocks are also compatible with traditional GUIs, providing seamless gateways between tangible and graphical interfaces. Finally, mediaBlocks act as physical "controls" in tangible interfaces for tasks such as sequencing collections of media elements.

CR Categories and Subject Descriptors: H.5.2 [User Interfaces] Input devices and strategies; H.5.1 [Multimedia Information Systems] Artificial, augmented, and virtual realities

Additional Keywords: tangible user interface, tangible bits, phicons, physical constraints, ubiquitous computing

1 INTRODUCTION

Computers have traditionally recorded digital information on both "fixed" and "removable" storage media. While removable media have often been limited in capacity, speed, and accessibility, these factors have been offset by the expanded storage and mobility removable media affords.

However, the rise of widespread online connectivity for both computers and other digital media devices (cameras, projectors, etc.) alters this historical role division. Extended capacity and instant mobility are now better afforded by keeping media online. Does removable media risk obsolescence in the online age?

From a user interface standpoint, the process of online media exchange between digital whiteboards, projectors, computers, and other devices is still far from seamless. Reference and manipulation of online media is at present generally limited to GUI-based interaction with file paths, URLs, and hyperlinks – a process quite at odds with most media interfaces.

We believe that coupling the physicality of removable media with the connectivity and unlimited capacity of online content offers a potential solution to this problem. Moreover, we believe this approach suggests new physical-world interface possibilities that go beyond the pervasive graphical user interface.

In this paper, we introduce a tangible user interface (TUI) based upon *mediaBlocks[*]*: small wooden blocks that serve as physical icons ("phicons") [15] for the containment, transport, and manipulation of online media. MediaBlocks do not actually store media internally. Instead, they are embedded with ID tags that allow them to function as "containers" for online content, or alternately expressed, as a kind of physically embodied URL.

MediaBlocks interface with media input and output devices such as video cameras and projectors, allowing digital media to be rapidly "copied" from a media source and "pasted" into a media display. MediaBlocks are also compatible with traditional GUIs, providing seamless gateways between tangible and graphical interfaces. Finally, mediaBlocks are used as physical "controls" in tangible interfaces for tasks such as sequencing collections of media elements.

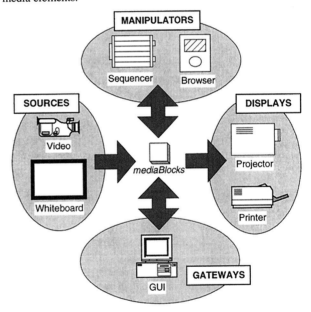

Figure 1: mediaBlocks design space

The mediaBlocks design space is illustrated in Figure 1. MediaBlocks serve as a medium of interchange between media source and display devices; between media devices and GUI-based computers; and between these pre-existing devices and new tangible interfaces for media manipulation. In this fashion, mediaBlocks fill the user interface gap between physical devices, digital media, and online content.

[*]Note: Our mediaBlocks have no relation to the Magnifi Inc. software product of the same name.

2 FUNCTIONALITY OVERVIEW

The following paragraphs describe the basic functionality of our mediaBlocks interfaces. Detailed consideration of interface use and implementation follows later in the paper.

2.1 Physical Containers

MediaBlocks are phicons (physical icons, [15]) embodied as small wooden blocks. MediaBlocks do not actually store digital media internally. Instead, they physically contain ID tags that are dynamically associated with sequences of online media elements. When used in environments where many media devices are linked to online computation, mediaBlocks act as physical "containers" for online media.

As such, mediaBlocks have a variety of interesting properties. Because contents remains online, mediaBlocks have unlimited "capacity" and rapid transfer speed (copying is instantaneous, while playback is a function of network bandwidth). For the same reason, a lost block is easily replaced. MediaBlocks may also contain live streaming media.

2.2 Physical Transports

One role of mediaBlocks is support for simple physical transport and interchange of media between media devices. While inter-application "copy and paste" is core to the modern GUI, comparably lightweight equivalents have not existed for physical media devices. We have realized a physical analog of "copy and paste" by combining mediaBlocks with physical slots mounted upon associated media devices.

We have implemented mediaBlock support for four media devices: a desktop video projector, network printer, video camera, and digital whiteboard. Inserting a block into the slot of a media source begins recording to an online server. Recording stops when the block is removed. This can be understood as "copying" from the media source into the block. Similarly, contents may be "pasted" into a media display by inserting a block into the associated slot. This will display block contents, with removal halting playback.

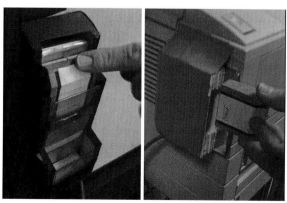

Figure 2: Whiteboard, printer mediaBlock slots

2.3 Physical Gateways

MediaBlock slots have also been implemented for use on general-purpose computers. Slots are mounted on the right margins of computer monitors. When a mediaBlock is inserted into the slot, a GUI window scrolls "out of the block" from the slot's left edge (contiguous with the screen). This window provides GUI access to block contents. (Figure 3)

Figure 3: mediaBlock monitor slot

MediaBlock contents may then be transferred to the desktop or to GUI applications with conventional mouse-based "drag and drop" support. Media may also be copied into blocks in this fashion. In this way, mediaBlocks can be used to seamlessly exchange content between computers and media sources, displays, or other computers.

2.4 Physical Browsers

While the transport function of mediaBlocks allows media to be exchanged between various output devices, it does not address interactive control of media playback, especially for mediaBlocks containing multiple media elements. The *media browser* is a simple tangible interface for navigating sequences of media elements stored in mediaBlocks. (Figure 4)

The browser is composed of a detented browse wheel, video monitor, and mediaBlock slot. Useful both in casual viewing and formal presentation contexts, the browser supports the interactive navigation of mediaBlocks sequences for projector-based display, as well as displaying media on its local screen.

Figure 4: Media browser device

2.5 Physical Sequencers

The media browser provides interactive physical control of mediaBlock display, but does not support modification of media-Block contents. The *media sequencer* is a tangible interface using mediaBlocks both as containers and *controls* for physically sequencing media elements. (Figure 5)

Where earlier sections have introduced mediaBlock slots, the sequencer uses physical *racks*, *stacks*, *chutes*, and *pads* as structures that physically and digitally operate upon mediaBlocks. In particular, the rack is a *physical constraint* used to digitally index and sequence mediaBlock contents as a function of the blocks' physical configuration on the rack.

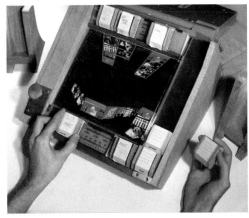

Figure 5: Media sequencer device

2.6 Integrated Functionality

In addition to illustrating the above mediaBlock functions, the accompanying video figure demonstrates the creation of a multimedia presentation integrating all behaviors we have described.

In less than four minutes of uncut footage, we show recording and transport of digital video and whiteboard content; selecting photographs and authoring textual slides for inclusion; assembling these contents into an integrated presentation; rendering the presentation to a network printer; and presenting this content on the browser-controlled video projector. The resulting content is also Web-accessible at each stage of authoring and delivery.

We believe this interface example is significant for several reasons. First, this example shows the creation, manipulation, and use of complex multimedia content with a simplicity and speed that we believe to be highly competitive with other approaches. Simultaneously, it is key to note that the only keyboard, mouse, or other GUI interaction present in the entire sequence is the composition of a textual slide.

In the remainder of the paper, we will continue to develop the interface process, technical operation, and functional roles that we believe represent a powerful new approach for interaction between people, physical objects, and online digital information.

3 RELATED WORK

The mediaBlocks project was most directly influenced by the metaDESK/Tangible Geospace prototype [15, 8] that introduced the phicon concept. Tangible Geospace was based upon an augmented physical desktop and phicons representing geographical landmarks. Manipulation of phicons controlled the position, rotation, and scaling of spatially coincident graphical landscapes.

Tangible Geospace was developed in part to explore physical instantiation of the GUI metaphor. As the GUI system of windows, controls, and icons itself drew from a metaphor of the physical desktop, the physical analogs of lenses, instruments, and phicons (physical icons) seemed a promising first step towards the realization of tangible interfaces.

In practice, Tangible Geospace served to illustrate a number of major differences between graphical and tangible UIs. The fundamental malleability and extent of control over the GUI's

graphical workspace differs substantially from the object persistence and cumulative, potentially inconsistent physical degrees of freedom expressed by TUI elements. In short, the GUI metaphor appeared unable to generalize across the potential design space of tangible user interfaces.

Subsequent research with Triangles and inTouch made a key insight towards resolving this shortcoming [7, 2]. Instead of relying upon pre-existing metaphors of GUI or the physical world (e.g., the metaDESK's optical metaphor [8]), these projects developed new interface metaphors based on the affordances unique to physical/digital artifacts. Both projects served as partial inspiration for mediaBlocks, which continues this design aesthetic.

The whiteboard-based mediaBlock functionality draws upon an earlier whiteboard TUI called the transBOARD [8]. The transBOARD used paper cards called *hypercards* as physical carriers for live and recorded whiteboard sessions. However, the hypercard interaction relied upon barcode wanding, which was found cumbersome in practice.

The ubiquitous computing vision of [16] speaks to moving computation and networking off the desktop and into many devices occupying niche contexts within the physical environment. This insight is core to the mediaBlocks system. Still, the interface prototypes of [16] continued to rely primarily upon GUI-based approaches.

The Bricks work [5] made dynamic association between digital properties and physical handles through the tray device. Also an inspiration for the mediaBlocks work, the Bricks work did not develop physical objects as digital containers or physical manipulation outside of the "Active Desk" context.

Bishop's Marble Answering Machine [3] made compelling demonstration of passive marbles as "containers" for voice messages. Later work by Bishop demonstrated physical objects associated with diverse digital content, and prototyped an early object-GUI gateway.

The Pick-and-Drop work of [11] provides strong support for file exchange between palmtop, desktop, and wall-based GUIs with a pen stylus. However, the technique less directly addresses media exchange between non-GUI devices, or with devices that are not spatially adjacent.

Molenbach's LegoWall prototype (discussed in [6]) used LEGO structures to contain information about ocean-going ships. These objects were combined with display and control objects that, when plugged adjacent to containers, could display shipping schedules, send this data to hardcopy printers, etc.

The AlgoBlock system uses the manipulation of physical blocks to create computer programs [13]. Connections between the blocks create LOGO programs that may be rearranged by the user, esp. in an educational context.

The Digital Manipulatives research of Resnick, Borovoy, Kramer, et al. [12] has developed "societies of objects" including badges, buckets, beads, balls, and stacks. Each is associated with digital semantics responsive to physical manipulations such as shaking, tossing, and stacking objects, or dunking objects in buckets of "digital paint." The manipulatives work makes strong progress towards developing objects with rich digital/physical couplings.

4 SYSTEM OVERVIEW

Figure 6 illustrates our current implementation of the media-Blocks interface. The center column, media devices, lists the physical devices for which we have integrated mediaBlock support. The left column shows devices supporting operation of mediaBlock slots. The right column presents the computers that manage media recording and playback. The media browser and sequencer SGI machines play additional roles as the controllers for these tangible interfaces. However, these details are beyond the scope of our illustration.

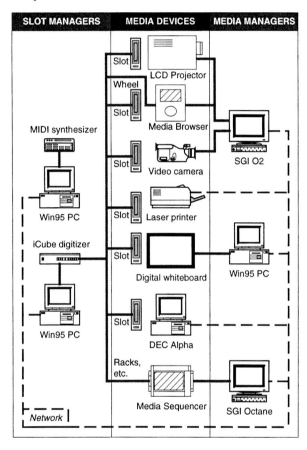

Figure 6: First-generation mediaBlocks system diagram

The mediaBlocks system was implemented with a Tcl- and [incr Tcl]-based tangible interface software/hardware toolkit called 3wish [14]. 3wish includes modules supporting MIDI-based digitizers and synthesizers, Inventor-based 3D graphics, computer vision and magnetic field trackers, etc. 3wish also supports a distributed architecture called *proxy-distributed* or *proxdist computation* [15], which provides strong abstractions for mixed physical/digital systems such as the mediaBlocks interface.

Development of 3wish support for the media sequencer and mediaBlock slots has consumed a large part of the mediaBlocks effort. The mediaBlock idea of objects as physical proxies for online content and computation grew out of early proxdist research, and the influence of 3wish's distributed architecture is visible in the half-dozen computers and tangible interfaces composing Figure 6. However, detailed discussion is beyond the scope of this paper, and is left to [14,15] and future treatments.

5 PHYSICAL CONTAINERS

The paper has emphasized the role of mediaBlocks as "containers" for media, as well as the use of mediaBlock slots for media interchange between various devices. However, a range of removable media devices have realized this basic function. For instance, videotapes and floppy disks are both "physical containers" for electronic media that support media interchange through systems of "physical slots." How do mediaBlocks relate to these well-known technologies?

The comparison will be explored for floppy disks (and other removable media analogs), which share the ability to store digital media of various formats. First, it is clear that mediaBlocks and floppy disks are technically quite different. Floppy disks function by taking information offline, recording media onto the disk's own storage. MediaBlocks instead work by moving information online, referenced by the internal ID of the mediaBlock object.

It is also interesting to note that mediaBlocks transparently support media with widely varying bandwidths. For instance, media-Blocks are equally practical for digital whiteboard and digital video recordings, even though the characteristic bit rates differ by five orders of magnitude (~100KB vs. ~10GB per hour).

From a user interface standpoint, mediaBlocks and floppy disks also have a number of differences. Floppy disk contents are accessed indirectly through graphical or textual interaction on a host computer. In contrast, mediaBlock contents may be accessed through physical manipulation of the mediaBlock object itself. For example, inserting a target mediaBlock into a digital whiteboard's slot initiates recording "into" the block. Similarly, moving a host mediaBlock on our media sequencer's position rack allows sequences of images to be navigated (see section 6.1).

Building from this distinction, mediaBlocks possess a simplicity and "lightweight" mode of operation rarely found with the floppy disk medium. Media recording, playback, and exchange between our example whiteboard, camera, printer, projector, and computer are all as simple as inserting and withdrawing a mediaBlock from the respective slots.

The mediaBlock support for physical media exchange does not force a "sneaker-net" ethic upon users. Instead, mediaBlocks offer the simplicity and directness of physically referencing *which data* and *which device* when physical proximity is a convenient delimiter. Common "reference in absence" tasks such as dispatching jobs to remote printers for later pick-up or delivery may be supported by shortcut controls (e.g., a "print" button on the whiteboard), or by inserting mediaBlocks into TUI or GUI devices providing remote printer access.

Thus, mediaBlocks act not as a *medium of storage*, but rather a *mechanism of physical reference and exchange*. In this sense, the use of mediaBlocks more closely resembles the interactive process of "copy and paste" propagated out into the physical world than the storage medium of floppy disks. Conceptually consistent with the premise of tangible user interface, this is a major distinction that colors the spectrum of mediaBlocks applications.

Also in point of fact, neither floppy disks nor other removable media are native to our projector, printer, or whiteboard, nor do we know of these features in comparable products. The absence of media drives from these well established and commercially competitive products provides market evidence that mediaBlocks serve new or different conceptual roles.

5.1 Implementation

MediaBlocks are constructed as 5x5x2cm wooden blocks embedded with electronic ID tags. First-generation blocks are tagged with resistor IDs. New efforts use Dallas Semiconductor iButton™ devices, which incorporate both digital serial numbers and nonvolatile memory. It is worth noting that the physical form of mediaBlocks is a product of their intended use, not of technical limitations. Both tag technologies are available as surface-mount devices a few millimeters in diameter, rendering block size technically near arbitrary.

Both resistor- and iButton-based mediaBlocks couple to slots, racks, and other TUI elements with a pair of electrical contacts. For resistor-based blocks, ID is determined with a voltage-divider circuit against a reference resistor, sampled by an Infusion Icube MIDI A/D converter. For the iButton implementation, an interface using Microchip's PIC 16F84 microcontroller was implemented, based upon the iRX 2.0 board [10].

MediaBlocks operate in conjunction with a number of different interface devices. The most common of these is the slot. Slots were prototyped in foamcore, with copper tape contacts. Audio feedback for slot entrance, exit, and status events is currently supported by an external MIDI synthesizer.

MediaBlock phicons are separated from their media "contents" by several levels of indirection. These mappings include:

a) physical block → network address

b) network address → mediaBlock data structure

c) data structure element → individual media contents

The individual steps of this mapping process are illustrated in Figure 7. First, insertion of an ID-tagged block (1) is detected electronically by the slot (2). The ID value is registered by a computer hosting the slot's tag reader (3), and transmitted as a block entrance event to the display device's media manager (4). The slot and media managers could be hosted on the same machine. In our implementation, the libraries supporting tag readers and media displays were specific to PC and SGI platforms, respectively, requiring separate computers for (3) and (4).

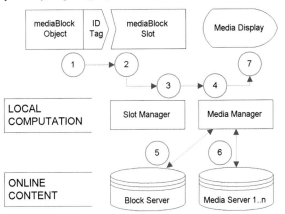

Figure 7: mediaBlock display flow diagram

Once an ID value has been obtained for a mediaBlock, the block server (5) provides a data structure describing the block's digital contents, presented in Table 1. With the resistor ID scheme, a central block server is responsible for mapping block IDs to block data structures for all compatible block devices. However, the resistor-based approach does not scale for distributed operation.

The iButton-based mediaBlocks solve this problem by storing the URL of their hosting block server within internal nonvolatile RAM (4096 bits for our chosen model), allowing truly distributed operation. iButtons also support storage of encrypted data, potentially useful for authenticating mediaBlocks and granting read or write permissions by a given media device.

After retrieving the block data structure, the device media manager retrieves the specified media contents from one or more media servers (6). This content is finally sent to the media display under control of display-specific MIME registries (7), similar to Web browser plug-in registries.

---

mediaList: *List of contained media element addresses*

physidType: *Type of physical ID tag on block*

physidInst: *ID of block tag (usually a number)*

mediaHost: *Media stored on media- or block-server?*

recordBehavior: *New media appends or overwrites old?*

lastObservedLocale: *Last location block observed*

lastObservedTime: *Timestamp of last block sighting*

blockLabel: *Text describing block contents*

blockLabelColor: *Color of paper block label*

Table 1: mediaBlock data structure

Earlier sections have discussed the use of mediaBlocks as a medium of exchange between graphical and tangible interfaces. This works particularly well in conjunction with Microsoft's Internet Explorer 4.0 "Internet shortcuts" feature (and equivalencies provided by other operating systems). "Internet shortcuts" allow distributed online media (e.g., URL-referenced HTTP sources) to be manipulated by the Windows95 desktop and applications indistinguishably from files on local disk drives.

We have explored the synthesis of Internet Shortcuts from media elements dragged out of monitor-slot mediaBlocks with GUI drag and drop. This combination represents a significant step towards truly seamless integration between the online media spaces of graphical and tangible interfaces.

6 PHYSICAL CONTROLS

The previous section discussed the physical containment, transport, and interchange aspects of mediaBlocks. The section also noted that in this capacity, the use of mediaBlocks more closely resembles the software process of "copy and paste" than the storage function of floppy disks.

However, the earlier section did not discuss how users might actively manipulate mediaBlock contents. For example, while both video decks and MS Windows95 CD-ROM drives support "auto-launch" capabilities analogous to mediaBlock slot playback, these systems also provide additional controls for more sophisticated interactions.

Following these examples, we might model interfaces on the physical play/stop buttons and jog/shuttle wheels of VCRs, as we have done with our media browser. We might also use traditional graphical interfaces to manipulate mediaBlock contents, as we have done with the GUI monitor slot.

At the same time, it is interesting to explore new interface possibilities specific to tangible user interfaces. The slot-based "copy and paste" functionality illustrates the first step of such an approach, binding digital semantics to the insertion of mediaBlocks into physical slots.

We have carried this approach forward in our work with the *media sequencer* interface. Here, we introduce *racks, stacks, chutes,* and *pads* as physical constraints that enable mediaBlocks to act as physical *controls* for directly manipulating block contents (Fig. 8).

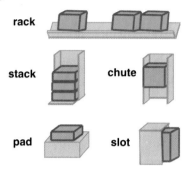

Figure 8: Media sequencer physical constraints,
used in combination with mediaBlocks as physical controls

The mediaBlock *rack* is the primary physical constraint elements used in the media sequencer. The mediaBlocks rack was inspired by the Scrabble™ board game's combination of letter tiles and the tile rack. In Scrabble, the rack allows letter tiles to be rapidly inserted, sequenced, and grouped into meaningful patterns. In the sequencer context, these physical attributes of position, sequence, and adjacency may be digitally recast as indexing, sequencing, and Boolean AND/OR operations, respectively.

6.1 User Interface

The media sequencer prototype is illustrated in Figures 5, 9, and 10. Sequencer operation is dominated by two physical constraint structures: the *position rack* and *sequence rack*.

When a mediaBlock is placed in the position rack, its contents are shown on the sequencer display as a perspective wall [9]. The focus position of the perspective wall is interactively controlled by the relative position of the mediaBlock on the position rack (Figure 10). Moving the block to the rack's left edge moves the perspective wall to focus on the block's first element. Similarly, the right edge of the position rack corresponds to the block's last element.

The combined position rack and perspective wall serve several purposes. First, they support the interactive viewing of mediaBlock contents with imaging of both detail and context [9]. Secondly, they allow the position rack to select an individual media element for copying between mediaBlocks.

Towards this end, a destination mediaBlock can be placed in the sequencer's *target pad*, physically adjacent the position rack (see Figure 9). Pressing the block on the target pad will append the currently selected media element into the destination block. This is confirmed with audio feedback and a haptic "click," as well as an animation of the selected media transferring "into" the target

block. Pressing and holding the block, followed by moving the source mediaBlock to a new location, will copy a range of elements into the target block (analogous to dragging out a selection range with a mouse).

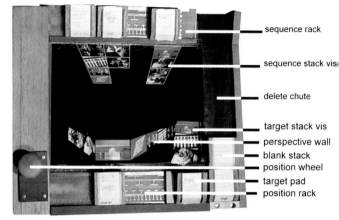

Figure 9: Media sequencer components

We believe this concept of using mediaBlock phicons to physically manipulate their internal contents generalizes to a powerful new interaction technique. Here, we are using mediaBlocks as *physical controls* for directly acting upon their internal state. The nearest equivalent in GUIs might be dragging a graphical folder icon across a scrollbar to index through folder contents. While a somewhat bizarre behavior for the GUI, we believe that use of mediaBlocks as physical controls holds substantial promise in the TUI context.

The *sequence rack* extends the control functionality of mediaBlocks. This rack allows the user to combine the contents of multiple mediaBlocks into a single sequence, which can then be associated with a new mediaBlock carrier on the target pad. When a mediaBlock is placed onto the sequence rack, its contents scroll out of the block into the sequencer display space (Figure 9). Multiple mediaBlocks may be arranged to construct a new sequence.

Figure 10: Media sequencer perspective wall (alternate view)
associated with movement of mediaBlock on position rack;
a compact disk's music is "contained" within this block

Both the sequencer screen and target pad are shared between the position and sequence racks. When a mediaBlock is located on the position rack, the target pad is bound to selections from the perspective wall display. When the position rack is clear, the target pad is associated with recording of the sequence rack's aggregate elements.

The use of mediaBlocks as physical controls services only part of the sequence rack's behavior. Especially when a source media-Block contains many elements, navigating the perspective wall by incremental steps may be more convenient than using the position rack. The *position wheel* supports such incremental navigation. Haptic detents provide the user with physical feedback, where each detent corresponds with movement of one media element.

6.2 Implementation

The media sequencer platform was assembled of wood and acrylic, and embedded with a 1280x1024-pixel 32cm-diagonal flat panel display. Position and sequence rack sensing was performed with a custom contact-grid board. The position wheel was tracked with a shaft encoder. Sensor inputs were digitized with the Infusion Systems Icube device, and acquired through the 3wish extensions to the Tcl language [14] using C++ wrappers over the Rogus MIDI interface suite [4]. The position rack perspective wall and other graphical visualizations were written with 3wish's Open Inventor-based routines, and executed on an SGI Octane workstation.

7 DISCUSSION

While mediaBlocks make progress towards broader vocabularies for tangible interface design, the project also illustrates some of the challenges in designing TUIs. As a case in point, we consider some of the design decisions leading to our sequencer prototype's current form. Some readers have questioned the sequencer's integration of a central graphic display, given our research focus upon tangible interface.

While the sequencer indeed integrates a flat-panel display, we argue that the design is the product of a particular interface task and set of design constraints. Our motivating task was the sequencing of presentation media, especially images and video. Our interface inspirations were the Scrabble tile/rack constraint system, and the brick/tray function of [5]. As our task centered upon manipulation of visual media, a graphic display of some sort was essential.

Our original hope was to integrate this display into a rack's footprint, displaying the graphical contents of transparent media-Blocks in a fashion following the metaDESK's passive lens [15]. However, given that mediaBlocks usually contain multiple media elements, we had difficulty determining an effective method of display within a block's 5x5cm footprint. Thus, we decided upon a visual display external to the mediaBlock/rack system, while maintaining visual contiguity with the associated mediaBlock container.

Here, we explored use of back-projected, front-projected, and integrated displays. While each had advantages, we selected a 32cm-diagonal 1280x1024-pixel integrated flat panel display on the basis of resolution, dot pitch, and compactness of integration. We wished adequate display resolution to support the visually-intensive task. We were also interested in a relatively small, compact device, even at the cost of greater display real estate such as provided by the metaDESK [15].

This was because we wished to make extensive use of physical constraints to support the sequencing task. Simultaneously, we imagined our users making simultaneous use of multiple complementary devices, such as the combination of a general-purpose computer for authoring new content, and the sequencer for assembling and manipulating the presentation. These usage constraints, coupled with the drive for proximity between physical controls and visual displays, drove the system to its current form.

Aspects of the sequencer design remain challenging, including potential inconsistency between the position wheel and rack; linkage between rack-based mediaBlocks and screen-based displays; and the shared screen use by position and sequence racks. Additionally, it is possible that the position rack + media-Block selection mechanism is less efficient than (say) directly selecting contents with one's finger. A second-generation sequencer design is under development to add this direct content-selection ability, increase display real estate, and rationalize the behavior of sequencer racks, while maintaining mediaBlock controls for sorting, sequencing, and transporting media into and out of the sequencer.

We believe mediaBlocks' underlying containment and transport functions are fundamentally sound. MediaBlocks' use as physical controls makes a significant extension to this transport function, and has been demonstrated useful in tasks like the video figure's presentation example. Thus, while less well-established than the transport function, our implementation leaves us optimistic about the interface potential of phicon controls.

8 FUTURE WORK

While part of our research motivation lies in seeking new paradigms for interface outside the well-explored GUI context, it is interesting to explore parallels between graphical and physical interaction techniques. One such instance is the historical emergence of consistent interface behavior across multiple GUI applications, notably articulated in the Apple Human Interface Guidelines [1].

Our design of mediaBlock slots and sequencer constraints has been shaped by an interest in TUI analogs for GUI inter-application behaviors. Our use of mediaBlocks for media transport and interchange develops a physical analog of the GUI "copy-and-paste" functionality. Similarly, the sequencer's racks, chute, and other constraints have parallels to GUI "interaction primitives" (e.g., desktop-based clicking, dragging, etc. of icons), without directly embodying GUI widgetry as with the metaDESK [15].

As much of the TUI appeal lies in a diversity of physical embodiments to address specific interface tasks, it is unclear how far analogies to [1] might extend. Nonetheless, prospects for consistent TUI interface vocabularies and widespread TUI/GUI interoperability are highly attractive.

Finally, mediaBlock's online aspect suggests their ability to "contain" live, streaming content: in other words, the ability to operate as media "conduits." We have demonstrated mediaBlocks containing both streaming media sources such as RealAudio™ and RealVideo™ media, as well as pairs of mediaBlock conduits which together broadcast and receive streaming video.

At the same time, the conduit functionality of mediaBlocks represents a significant conceptual expansion with its own user interface questions. For instance, if a user wishes to both record and broadcast a whiteboard session, or both display and store a live video stream, how are these aggregate behaviors best accommodated? These and other open questions remain. As a result, we leave conduits for further discussion in future work.

9 CONCLUSION

We have presented a system of tangible user interface based upon *mediaBlocks*: small, electronically tagged wooden blocks that serve as physical containers, transports, and controls for online media. MediaBlocks do not store media internally, instead serving as phicons (physical icons) which give physical embodiment to online media.

MediaBlocks provide a mechanism for seamlessly exchanging digital contents between diverse media devices, including media sources, displays, general-purpose computers, and specialized tangible interfaces. Towards these ends, we have demonstrated the ability of mediaBlocks to physically "copy" media from a whiteboard and camera source, and "paste" this content into a printer and projector.

We have also shown the use of mediaBlock slots as physical gateways between tangible and graphical interfaces, allowing media to be swiftly exchanged with traditional GUIs.

Additionally, mediaBlocks are used as physical controls for operating upon their own digital "contents." We have demonstrated this ability in the media sequencer by swiftly composing a presentation integrating video, photographs, whiteboard recordings, and text. While the sequencer supports this task with a graphical display, the entire task is accomplished without a keyboard, pointer, or cursor, except for the GUI-based entry of the textual slide.

Finally, we have discussed analogs between TUI media exchange between diverse physical devices, and GUI support for consistent multi-application operation and communication. Similarly, we have demonstrated new roles and visions for seamless interaction with online content beyond the traditional GUI context.

In conclusion, we believe mediaBlocks are a powerful tangible interface for the seamless exchange and manipulation of online content between diverse media devices and people. More generally, we believe mediaBlocks represent a step towards broader tangible interface use as an interaction technique uniting people, computational media, and the physical environment.

10 ACKNOWLEDGEMENTS

Many people have contributed to this work. John Alex and Paul Grayson helped with software and hardware implementation. John Underkoffler and Paul Yarin assisted video production. Andrew Dahley and Andrew Hsu provided design assistance. Matt Gorbet, Scott Brave, and Victor Su provided additional helpful input. Ben Denckla helped with early Rogus efforts. Paul Grayson, Hannes Vilhjalmsson, Joe Marks, Tara Rosenberger, and others provided feedback on paper drafts. This research was sponsored in part by the MIT Media Lab's Things That Think consortium and a Mitsubishi fellowship.

11 REFERENCES

[1] Apple Computer, Inc. *Apple Human Interface Guidelines: The Apple Desktop Interface.* New York: Addison Wesley, 1987.

[2] Brave, S., and Dahley, A. inTouch: A Medium for Haptic Interpersonal Communication. In *CHI'97 Extended Abstracts,* pp. 363-364.

[3] Crampton Smith, G. The Hand That Rocks the Cradle. *I.D.,* May/June 1995, pp. 60-65.

[4] Denckla, B. Rogus C++ MIDI Suite. `http://theremin.media.mit.edu/rogus/`

[5] Fitzmaurice, G., Ishii, H., and Buxton, W. (1995). Bricks: Laying the Foundations for Graspable User Interfaces. *Proc. of CHI'95,* pp. 442-449.

[6] Fitzmaurice, G. *Graspable User Interfaces.* Ph.D. Thesis, University of Toronto, 1996.

[7] Gorbet, M., Orth, M., and Ishii, H. Triangles: Tangible Interface for Manipulation and Exploration of Digital Information Topography. In *Proc. of CHI'98.*

[8] Ishii, H., and Ullmer, B. Tangible Bits: Towards Seamless Interfaces between People, Bits, and Atoms. In *Proc. of CHI'97,* pp. 234-241.

[9] Mackinlay, J., Robertson, G., & Card, S. The Perspective Wall: Detail and context smoothly integrated. In *Proc. of CHI'91,* pp. 173-179.

[10] Poor, R. The iRX 2.0 ...where Atoms meet Bits. `http://ttt.media.mit.edu/pia/Research/iRX2/`

[11] Rekimoto, J. Pick-and-Drop: A Direct Manipulation Technique for Multiple Computer Environments. In *Proc. of UIST'97,* pp. 31-39.

[12] Resnick, M., Berg, F., et al. Digital Manipulatives: New Toys to Think With. In *Proc. of CHI'98.*

[13] Suzuki, H., Kato, H. AlgoBlock: a Tangible Programming Language, a Tool for Collaborative Learning. In *Proc. of 4th European Logo Conference,* Aug. 1993, Athens Greece, pp. 297-303.

[14] Ullmer, B. 3wish: Distributed [incr Tcl] Extensions for Physical-World Interfaces. In *Proc. of Tcl/Tk'97,* pp. 169-170.

[15] Ullmer, B., and Ishii, H. The metaDESK: Models and Prototypes for Tangible User Interfaces. In *Proc. of UIST'97,* pp. 223-232.

[16] Weiser, M. The Computer for the 21st Century. In *Scientific American,* 265(3), pp. 94-104.

Non-Uniform Recursive Subdivision Surfaces

Thomas W. Sederberg[1]
Jianmin Zheng[2]
Brigham Young University

David Sewell[3]
Sewell Development
Provo, Utah

Malcolm Sabin[4]
Numerical Geometry Ltd.
Cambridge, UK

Abstract

Doo-Sabin and Catmull-Clark subdivision surfaces are based on the notion of repeated knot insertion of uniform tensor product B-spline surfaces. This paper develops rules for non-uniform Doo-Sabin and Catmull-Clark surfaces that generalize non-uniform tensor product B-spline surfaces to arbitrary topologies. This added flexibility allows, among other things, the natural introduction of features such as cusps, creases, and darts, while elsewhere maintaining the same order of continuity as their uniform counterparts.

Categories and Subject Descriptors: I.3.5 [Computer Graphics]: Computational Geometry and Object Modeling–surfaces and object representations.

Additional Key Words and Phrases: B-splines, Doo-Sabin surfaces, Catmull-Clark surfaces.

1   INTRODUCTION

Tensor product non-uniform rational B-spline surfaces have become an industry standard in computer graphics, as well as in CAD/CAM systems. Because surfaces of arbitrary topological genus cannot be represented using a single B-spline surface, there has been considerable interest in the generalization, based on knot insertion, called 'recursive subdivision,' which removes this limitation.

However, despite being based on knot insertion, the recursive subdivision techniques published so far are the analogues of equal interval, *uniform* B-splines rather than of *non-uniform* B-splines.

This paper explores the possibility of achieving the extra flexibility of unequal knot intervals in a recursive subdivision scheme including, for example, the ability to express features such as creases and darts by simply setting some

of the knot intervals to zero. Schemes are presented for achieving non-uniform Doo-Sabin and Catmull-Clark surfaces. We will refer to these collectively as Non-Uniform Recursive Subdivision Surfaces (NURSSes).

Figure 1 (left) shows a Doo-Sabin surface, and Figure 1 (right) shows an example of a non-uniform Doo-Sabin surface in which the knot spacings along certain control edges have been set to zero (as labeled), thereby creating a G^0 discontinuity along the oval edge on the left. Figure 2 shows

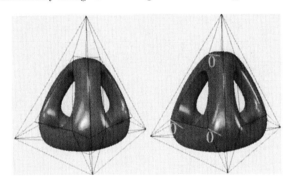

Figure 1: Uniform and non-uniform Doo-Sabin surfaces.

two non-uniform Catmull-Clark surfaces. The one on the left contains a dart formed by setting two pairs of control-edge knot spacings to zero. The one on the right shows shape modification induced by changing the knot spacing along the top edges to 10 and along the center horizontal edges to 0.1. The control net used here has the topology of a B-spline control net, but these shapes cannot be obtained using NURBS or uniform Catmull-Clark surfaces.

1.1   Background

The concept of image space subdivision as a graphics technique had been around for a long time when recursive subdivision appeared as an object definition technique. The first relevant result in parametric space subdivision of sculptured surfaces was the de Casteljau algorithm, which both evaluated a point on a Bézier curve and provided the control points for the parts of the curve meeting there. This was generalized to B-splines in the form of the Oslo algorithm [6] and Boehm subdivision [3] and used as a basis for interrogation methods applying parametric space subdivision.

However, what sparked the imagination of the graphics and modeling communities in 1975 was a much more specific

[1] tom@byu.edu

[2] zheng@cs.byu.edu (On leave from Zhejiang University)

[3] dave@sewelld.com

[4] malcolm@geometry.demon.co.uk

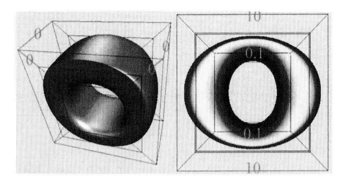

Figure 2: Non-uniform Catmull-Clark surfaces.

subdivision of a quadratic B-spline, proposed by Chaikin as a curve rendering technique [5], and recognized for what it was by Forrest [11] and by Riesenfeld [26]. It later turned out that the concept of a curve being the limit of a polygon under the operation of cutting off the corners had been explored by de Rham in the 1940s and 50s. His results were translated into modern terminology by de Boor [7].

It was quickly appreciated that the curve ideas could give surface techniques just by applying the concept of tensor product, but the important key concept, that subdivision could overcome the rigid rectangular partitioning of the parametric domain — one of the major limitations of tensor products — was reached more or less simultaneously by Catmull and Clark [4] and by Doo and Sabin [8]. Since then there have been five major directions of development:

1. The analysis of what happens near an extraordinary point, started in the Doo-Sabin paper [8], was taken up by Ball and Storry. This led to an optimization of the coefficients for the cubic case [1, 2] which unfortunately missed one of the possible variations, and the task was completed by Sabin [28], in a paper which also identified that a cubic construction could never give full G^2 continuity at the singular points, and that continuity at such points was in fact a much more complicated question than had been assumed. Further analysis was carried out by Reif [25]. The nature of the behavior around the extraordinary points is now well understood.

2. Constructions based on box-splines, rather than on tensor products, were explored by Farin [10] and by Loop [15], and a collection of possible constructions was assembled by Sabin [27].

3. Constructions that interpolate the control points were explored by Dyn, Gregory and Levin [9], and an improved scheme was derived by Zorin, Schröder and Sweldens [31]. Kobbelt [14] proposed an alternative for quadrilateral nets with arbitrary topology. The simpler ones in this category can be viewed as duals of quadratic B-spline constructions.

4. Nasri [17] studied the problems of efficient implementation and practical edge-conditions and extended this to modifications of the basic technique to achieve various interpolation conditions [18, 19, 20]. Halstead, Kass, and DeRose showed that a fairness norm could be computed exactly for Catmull-Clark surfaces [12], enabling the determination of more fair limit surfaces.

5. The idea of using just a small number of subdivision steps, and then using n-sided combinations of patches

to fill in a configuration made more regular in some sense by those steps, was explored by Loop [16], Peters [21, 22, 23] and Prautzsch [24]. Ball and Storry [29] took the opposite line, of using subdivision to define an n-sided patch.

What was not explored until now was that the general topology subdivision schemes were as rigid as the equal interval splines from which they were derived.

1.2 Overview

Section 2 reviews knot-doubling for non-uniform B-spline curves of degree two and three and introduces a simple approach for labeling the knot intervals on the control polygon— an idea that is crucial for the extension to subdivision surfaces. Section 3 then gives the corresponding expression for knot doubling of non-uniform tensor product B-spline surfaces. Section 4 proposes subdivision rules for non-uniform Doo-Sabin and Catmull-Clark surfaces, which reduce to non-uniform B-spline surfaces when the control net is a rectangular grid and when all knot intervals along every given row and column are the same. A continuity analysis is given in section 5, showing that non-uniform Doo-Sabin surfaces are G^1 and non-uniform Catmull-Clark surfaces are generally G^2, but G^1 at certain points. Section 6 makes some observations on NURSSes, and offers a conclusion.

2 CURVE KNOT DOUBLING

For a quadratic periodic B-spline curve, each vertex of the control polygon corresponds to a single quadratic curve segment. It is convenient then to express the knot vector by writing the knot interval d_i of each curve segment next to its corresponding control vertex $\mathbf{P}_i$. If a new knot is inserted at the midpoint of each current knot interval, the resulting control polygon has twice as many control points, and their coordinates $\mathbf{Q}_k$ are:

$$\mathbf{Q}_{2i} = \frac{(d_i + 2d_{i+1})\mathbf{P}_i + d_i\mathbf{P}_{i+1}}{2(d_i + d_{i+1})}$$

$$\mathbf{Q}_{2i+1} = \frac{d_{i+1}\mathbf{P}_i + (2d_i + d_{i+1})\mathbf{P}_{i+1}}{2(d_i + d_{i+1})} \quad (1)$$

as illustrated in Figure 3.

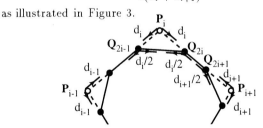

Figure 3: Non-uniform quadratic B-spline curve.

For cubic periodic B-spline curves, each *edge* of the control polygon corresponds to a single cubic curve segment, and so we write the knot intervals adjacent to each edge of the control polygon. The equations for the new control points $\mathbf{Q}_k$ generated upon inserting a knot midway through each knot interval are:

$$\mathbf{Q}_{2i+1} = \frac{(d_i + 2d_{i+1})\mathbf{P}_i + (d_i + 2d_{i-1})\mathbf{P}_{i+1}}{2(d_{i-1} + d_i + d_{i+1})} \quad (2)$$

$$\mathbf{Q}_{2i} = \frac{d_i\mathbf{Q}_{2i-1} + (d_{i-1} + d_i)\mathbf{P}_i + d_{i-1}\mathbf{Q}_{2i+1}}{2(d_{i-1} + d_i)} \quad (3)$$

as shown in Figure 4.

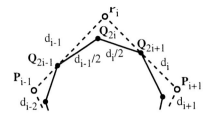

Figure 4: Non-uniform cubic B-spline curve.

3 SURFACE KNOT DOUBLING

The knot-doubling formulae for B-spline curves extend easily to surfaces. Non-uniform B-spline surfaces are defined in terms of a control net that is topologically a rectangular grid, for which all horizontal knot vectors are scales of each other, and all vertical knot vectors are scales of each other.

3.1 Quadratic Case

The formulae for the new control points $\mathbf{F}_A$ can be written in Doo-Sabin form, which is significant because in this form the new control points are seen as being in groups, creating a new face in each old face, and the vertices of each such new face are in 1:1 correspondence with the vertices of the old, whereas under the tensor product form we merely see all the new vertices as forming a new regular array (see Figure 5).

$$\mathbf{F}_A = \frac{\mathbf{V} + \mathbf{A}}{2} + \frac{ac(\mathbf{B} + \mathbf{C} - \mathbf{A} - \mathbf{D})}{4(ad + ac + bc + bd)}, \tag{4}$$

where

$$\mathbf{V} = \frac{bd\mathbf{A} + ad\mathbf{B} + bc\mathbf{C} + ac\mathbf{D}}{bd + ad + bc + ac}. \tag{5}$$

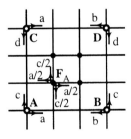

Figure 5: Knot doubling, quadratic B-spline.

3.2 Cubic Case

For non-uniform cubic B-spline surfaces, the refinement rules can be written as follows (see Figure 6). First, each face is replaced with a new vertex F_i. For example,

$$\mathbf{F_1} = [(e_3 + 2e_4)(d_2 + 2d_1)\mathbf{P_0} + (e_3 + 2e_4)(d_2 + 2d_3)\mathbf{P_1}$$

$$+(e_3 + 2e_2)(d_2 + 2d_3)\mathbf{P_5} + (e_3 + 2e_2)(d_2 + 2d_1)\mathbf{P_2}]$$

$$/[4(e_2 + e_3 + e_4)(d_1 + d_2 + d_3)]. \tag{6}$$

Then, each edge is split with an edge vertex E_i, e.g.

$$\mathbf{E_1} = \frac{e_2\mathbf{F_1} + e_3\mathbf{F_4} + (e_2 + e_3)\mathbf{M_1}}{2(e_2 + e_3)}, \tag{7}$$

where

$$\mathbf{M_1} = \frac{(2d_1 + d_2)\mathbf{P_0} + (d_2 + 2d_3)\mathbf{P_1}}{2(d_1 + d_2 + d_3)}. \tag{8}$$

Finally, each original control point is replaced with a vertex point $\mathbf{V}$

$$\mathbf{V} = \frac{\mathbf{P_0}}{4} + \frac{d_3e_2\mathbf{F_1} + d_2e_2\mathbf{F_2} + d_2e_3\mathbf{F_3} + d_3e_3\mathbf{F_4}}{4(d_2 + d_3)(e_2 + e_3)} +$$

$$[d_3(e_2 + e_3)\mathbf{M_1} + e_2(d_2 + d_3)\mathbf{M_2} + d_2(e_2 + e_3)\mathbf{M_3}$$

$$+e_3(d_2 + d_3)\mathbf{M_4}]/[4(d_2 + d_3)(e_2 + e_3)]. \tag{9}$$

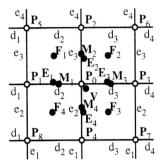

Figure 6: Face, edge and vertex points.

4 NURSS REFINEMENT

In uniform B-spline surfaces, all knot spacings are the same. Doo-Sabin and Catmull-Clark proposed generalizations of uniform B-spline surface schemes that allow for vertices of the control mesh to have valence other than four, and the faces of the control mesh to have other than four sides. Their subdivision rules were designed such that when the control mesh happens to be a rectangular grid, the subdivision rules are equivalent to knot doubling of uniform B-spline surfaces. The subdivision surfaces are then defined as the limit of the control meshes when these subdivision rules are applied an infinite number of times.

We here define generalizations of non-uniform B-spline surfaces. As in the cubic curve case, each edge in the control polyhedron of a non-uniform Catmull-Clark surface is assigned a knot spacing. For a non-uniform Doo-Sabin surface, each vertex is assigned a knot spacing (possibly different) for each edge radiating from it. Our objective is to devise a set of refinement rules for NURSSes such that if all knot intervals are equal, the quadratic NURSS reduces to Doo-Sabin and the cubic NURSS reduces to Catmull-Clark. There are actually two distinct rules to be devised. First, we need to revise the Doo-Sabin and Catmull-Clark rules for the new point coordinates, taking the knot spacings into account. Second, we need rules for determining the new knot spacings.

Note that "NURSS" could just as well stand for "Non-Uniform *Rational* Subdivision Surfaces," because it is a simple matter to first project rational control points to 4-D, then apply our rules, and finally to project back to 3-D.

In this section, bold capital letters stand for points, and non-bold typeface for knot spacings. The indices for knot spacing d_{ij}^k indicate that the spacing pertains to an edge with $\mathbf{P}_i$ as one endpoint. Referring to Figure 8, the notation d_{ij}^0 indicates the knot spacing for edge $\mathbf{P}_i$–$\mathbf{P}_j$. Rotating counter-clockwise about $\mathbf{P}_i$, d_{ij}^1 denotes the knot spacing for the first edge encountered, d_{ij}^2 indicates that of the second edge, etc. For the cubic case, each edge has a single knot spacing, so $d_{ij}^0 = d_{ji}^0$.

4.1 Quadratic Case

In the quadratic case, refinement proceeds in a manner identical to Doo-Sabin subdivision: A polyhedron spawns a refined polyhedron for which new faces (of type F, type E and type V respectively) are created for each face, edge, and vertex of the previous polyhedron. During the subdivision step, each face is replaced by a new face connected across the old edges and across the old vertices by other new faces. In such refinement schemes, the extraordinary points are at the "center" of n-sided faces with $n \neq 4$. After one iteration, every vertex of the new polyhedron will have valence four, and the number of faces with other than four sides will remain constant.

Refer to Figure 7 for labels. The new vertex $\bar{\mathbf{P}}_i$ is computed:

$$\bar{\mathbf{P}}_i = \frac{\mathbf{V} + \mathbf{P}_i}{2} + (d^0_{i+1,i+2} d^0_{i+3,i+2} + d^0_{i-1,i-2} d^0_{i-3,i-2})$$

$$\times \frac{-n\mathbf{P}_i + \sum_{j=1}^{n} \left(1 + 2\cos\left(\frac{2\pi|i-j|}{n}\right)\right)\mathbf{P}_j}{8\sum_{k=1}^{n} d^0_{k-1,k} d^0_{k+1,k}} \quad (10)$$

where

$$\mathbf{V} = \frac{\sum_{k=1}^{n} d^0_{k-1,k} d^0_{k+1,k} \mathbf{P}_k}{\sum_{k=1}^{n} d^0_{k-1,k} d^0_{k+1,k}}.$$

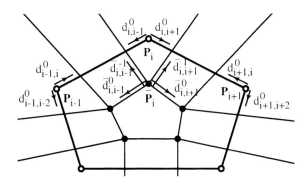

Figure 7: Quadratic refinement rules.

4.1.1 New knot spacings

New knot spacings $\bar{d}^k_{ij}$ can be specified in numerous ways. Here are two straightforward options:

$$\bar{d}^0_{i,i+1} = \bar{d}^{-1}_{i,i-1} = d^0_{i,i+1}/2$$

$$\bar{d}^0_{i,i-1} = \bar{d}^1_{i,i+1} = d^0_{i,i-1}/2$$

or

$$\bar{d}^0_{i,i+1} = d^0_{i,i+1}/2, \quad \bar{d}^{-1}_{i,i-1} = (d^0_{i,i+1} + d^{-1}_{i,i-1})/4$$

$$\bar{d}^0_{i,i-1} = d^0_{i,i-1}/2, \quad \bar{d}^1_{i,i+1} = (d^0_{i,i-1} + d^1_{i,i+1})/4$$

The former allows the refinement matrix to remain constant after a few iterations. The latter seems to produce more satisfactory shapes.

4.2 Cubic Case

Our development parallels that for Catmull-Clark surfaces. As shown in Figure 8, the face point for a face with n sides is computed as

$$\mathbf{F} = \frac{\sum_{i=0}^{n-1} w_i \mathbf{P}_i}{\sum_{i=0}^{n-1} w_i}, \quad (11)$$

where

$$w_i = (d^0_{i+1,i} + d^2_{i+1,i} + d^{-2}_{i+1,i} + d^0_{i-2,i-1} + d^2_{i-2,i-1} + d^{-2}_{i-2,i-1})$$

$$\times (d^0_{i-1,i} + d^2_{i-1,i} + d^{-2}_{i-1,i} + d^0_{i+2,i+1} + d^2_{i+2,i+1} + d^{-2}_{i+2,i+1}) \quad (12)$$

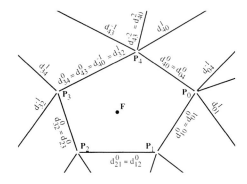

Figure 8: Face point.

The edge point is computed (see Figure 9a):

$$\mathbf{E} = (1 - \alpha_{ij} - \alpha_{ji})\mathbf{M} + \alpha_{ij}\mathbf{F}_{ij} + \alpha_{ji}\mathbf{F}_{ji}, \quad (13)$$

where

$$\alpha_{ij} = \frac{d^1_{ji} + d^{-1}_{ij}}{2(d^1_{ji} + d^{-1}_{ij} + d^{-1}_{ji} + d^1_{ij})} \quad (14)$$

if $d^1_{ji} + d^{-1}_{ij} + d^{-1}_{ji} + d^1_{ij} \neq 0$ and $\alpha_{ij} = 0$ otherwise.

$$\mathbf{M} = \frac{(d^0_{ji} + d^2_{ji} + d^{-2}_{ji})\mathbf{P}_i + (d^0_{ij} + d^2_{ij} + d^{-2}_{ij})\mathbf{P}_j}{d^0_{ji} + d^2_{ji} + d^{-2}_{ji} + d^0_{ij} + d^2_{ij} + d^{-2}_{ij}} \quad (15)$$

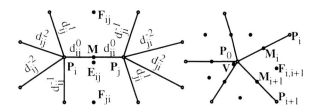

Figure 9: a) Edge point.   b) Vertex point.

The vertex point for a point of valence n is expressed (see Figure 9b):

$$\mathbf{V} = c\mathbf{P}_0 + \frac{3\sum_{i=1}^{n}(m_i\mathbf{M}_i + f_{i,i+1}\mathbf{F}_{i,i+1})}{n\sum_{i=1}^{n}(m_i + f_{i,i+1})}. \quad (16)$$

where $\mathbf{M}_i$ are defined as (15), $\mathbf{F}_{i,i+1}$ as (11), and

$$m_i = (d^1_{0i} + d^{-1}_{0i})(d^2_{0i} + d^{-2}_{0i})/2 \quad (17)$$

$$f_{ij} = d^0_{0i} d^{-1}_{0j} \quad (18)$$

$$c = \frac{n-3}{n} \quad \text{if } \sum_{i=1}^{n}(m_i + f_{i,i+1}) \neq 0 \quad (19)$$

otherwise, $c = 1$.

4.2.1 New knot spacings

Each n-sided face is split into n four sided faces, whose knot spacings are determined as shown in Figure 10.

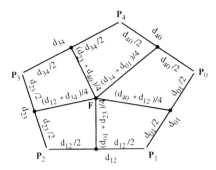

Figure 10: New knot spacings.

5 CONTINUITY ANALYSIS

For each construction, we consider the behavior of the limit surface for all the knot spacings being positive.

5.1 Quadratic case

5.1.1 Limit surface structure

After one iteration, all type V and type E faces are four-sided, with the property that the intervals crossing the original edges are equal as seen from the two sides. Thus each such type V face reduces to a mesh that is equivalent to a uniform biquadratic B-spline, while each type E face reduces to a mesh that is equivalent to a non-uniform biquadratic B-spline. This leaves only the regression in the type F faces to analyze for continuity.

The limit surface for a face consists of patches in the structure as shown in Figure 11a. The face is four-sided in this example.

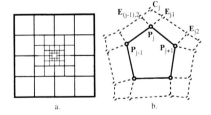

Figure 11: a) Sequence of quadratic polynomial pieces for a four-sided face; b) Configuration surrounding type F face.

5.1.2 Continuity at face-centers

It is convenient to consider four-sided faces alongside the more general n-sided faces. After at most two subdivisions, the configuration surrounding a type F face may be represented as in Figure 11b. In the center lies the face (of type F) $P_1 P_2 \ldots P_n$. Each edge of this face (for example $P_j P_{j+1}$) is adjacent to a four-sided face of type E with vertices $P_j P_{j+1} E_{j2} E_{j1}$. The neighborhood of each vertex P_j is completed by a four-sided face of type V with vertices $P_j E_{j1} C_j E_{(j-1)2}$.

Let the configuration around this type F face be represented by the vector of points

$$M = [P_1, \ldots, P_n, E_{11}, E_{12}, \ldots, E_{n1}, E_{n2}, C_1, \ldots, C_n]^T,$$

and $\bar{M}$ be the corresponding configuration after subdivision. Then $\bar{M} = S_n M$, where S_n is a $4n \times 4n$ matrix called the refinement matrix. Here we only consider the first option for the new knot spacings in which case S_n remains constant through all the subsequent subdivision steps. Thus we can use the eigenstructure of S_n to analyze continuity.

We carried out an algebraic eigenanalysis for orders 3 to 8 based on the discrete Fourier transform technique in an exercise reported in [30]. This leads us to

Theorem 1 *For orders 3 to 8, if all knot spacings $d_{i,j} > 0$, then the refinement matrix S_n is not defective and its eigenvalues are*

$$\lambda_1 = 1 > \lambda_2 = \lambda_3 = \frac{1}{2} > |\lambda_4|, |\lambda_5|, \cdots, |\lambda_{4n}|.$$

By an argument similar to one used in [12] we can conclude that, provided that all the knot spacings are greater than zero, the limit surface generated by the non-uniform Doo-Sabin scheme is G^1 continuous both at all ordinary points and at extraordinary points of valence less than 9.

5.2 Cubic Case

5.2.1 Limit surface structure

After one subdivision, every face is four-sided, and after two more, the pattern of knot intervals over the group of 16 subfaces replacing each original face is as shown in Figure 12a. The h_i are in arithmetic sequence as are the v_i.

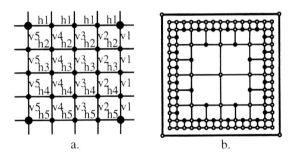

Figure 12: a) Knot intervals after three subdivisions; b) Sequence of cubic polynomial pieces.

When these values are substituted into (11), (13) and (16), the positions of the new vertices in, or on the boundary of, the innermost four sub-faces are exactly the same as if all the horizontal intervals had been equal and all the vertical intervals equal likewise. The innermost four sub-faces therefore converge towards uniform bicubic B-splines, giving a pattern of bicubic pieces as shown in Figure 12b, where the largest square represents the face of a non-uniform Catmull-Clark net with different knot intervals along each edge. The pattern of smaller squares shows schematically the infinite progression of Bézier patches that make up the limit surface. The interior of the limit surface of every such face is therefore G^2. We need only concern ourselves with the continuity at the edges and at the vertices, where there is a regression.

5.2.2 Continuity at vertices

In this section we consider continuity at vertex points of valence ≥ 3 (i.e., exceptional points, as well as vertex points of valence four). Unfortunately, since the refinement matrix changes at each iteration, it is difficult to perform an eigenanalysis to determine if non-uniform Catmull-Clark surfaces are G^1 at vertex points, except for simple numerical cases. One of the few cases that yield a constant refinement matrix is the valence three vertex in Figure 13 (right). In this case, the second and the third eigenvalues are generally *different*.

To find out what is going on in the neighborhood of this point, we performed a numerical study, chosing a cube as a control polyhedron with various knot spacings. Figure 13

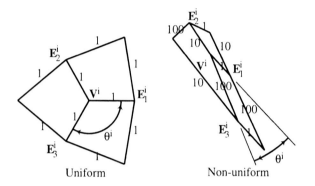

Figure 13: Neighborhood of valence 3 vertex point after 25 iterations.

shows the neighborhood of a vertex point $\mathbf{V}^i$ (that began as a corner of the cube) after 25 iterations. The figure on the left shows the uniform knot spacing; everything is symmetric as expected. The figure on the right came from the same vertex on the same cube, only with knot intervals of value 100 assigned to one set of four parallel edges on the cube; of value 10 assigned to another set of four parallel edges, and of 1 assigned to the remaining four edges, again after $i = 25$ iterations. Notice that the angles are no longer equal. In fact, it turns out that angle $\theta^i = \angle \mathbf{E}_1^i - \mathbf{V}^i - \mathbf{E}_3^i$ tends to zero as $i \to \infty$. However, the three faces become coplanar at a *much* faster rate, as shown in the following table. Here, $\Delta \mathbf{N}^i$ refers to the maximum angle between the planes $\mathbf{E}_1^i - \mathbf{V}^i - \mathbf{E}_2^i$, $\mathbf{E}_1^i - \mathbf{V}^i - \mathbf{E}_3^i$, and $\mathbf{E}_2^i - \mathbf{V}^i - \mathbf{E}_3^i$.

	Uniform		Non-uniform	
i	$\Delta \mathbf{N}^i$ π radians	θ^i π radians	$\Delta \mathbf{N}^i$ π radians	θ^i π radians
0	5×10^{-1}	0.5	5×10^{-1}	0.5
5	5×10^{-3}	0.6665	2×10^{-2}	0.37
25	7×10^{-10}	0.666667	5×10^{-8}	0.15
50	1×10^{-20}	0.666667	9×10^{-15}	0.043
75	2×10^{-30}	0.666667	1×10^{-21}	0.013
100	6×10^{-40}	0.666667	2×10^{-28}	0.004

The normals are becoming parallel at a rate that is roughly 10^7 times faster than the rate at which θ^i is approaching zero. After 100 iterations, the configuration is as close to G^1 as anyone could possibly have need for. The facets are 25 orders of magnitude smaller than they need to be for any practical use (five iterations are plenty for most graphics applications).

We also did a similar study on valence four, using widely varying knot spacings, and again observed a fast convergence of normal vectors, but *no* tendency of any face angles to tend

to zero. Hence, we are confident that valence four points are G^1. Preliminary experiments with $n > 4$ indicate very similar behavior.

5.2.3 Continuity across edges

Across the interior of an edge, the situation may be regarded as a standard non-uniform B-spline with a perturbation due to the original variation between the knot intervals. This perturbation tends to zero with a convergence rate of $O(2^{-i})$. Note that the non-uniform B-spline is C^2 and the surrounding vertices converge to a plane configuration with a rate of $O(4^{-i})$. Therefore, in the limit, the non-uniform Catmull-Clark surface is G^1 across every edge.

6 DISCUSSION

Figure 14 shows the effect that knot spacing can have on a surface. In the grid at the left, all edges are assigned knot spacing of 1, except for the four edges labeled with a 0. Two steps of non-uniform Catmull-Clark subdivision result in the meshes shown (minus a few outer layers of quadrilaterals). This configuration of knot spacings causes the limit surface to interpolate the center point with G^0 continuity.

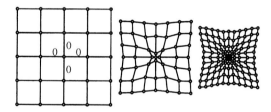

Figure 14: Effect of non-uniform knot spacing.

In the absence of non-uniform subdivision surfaces, Hoppe et. al. proposed a scheme for imposing features such as creases, corners, and darts on an otherwise G^1 subdivision surface that uses special-case "masks" [13]. NURSSes can provide for such features without the need for special masks. For example, Figure 1 shows a crease imposed on a Doo-Sabin surface by setting three knot spacings to zero. Figure 2 (left) shows a dart on a non-uniform Catmull-Clark surface, created by setting four knot intervals to zero.

Figures 16–19 show a variety of shapes that can be attained using NURSSes, but not using uniform subdivision surfaces. The initial control polyhedra are shown in wireframe. Sharp features can be imposed by setting to zero the knot spacing of appropriate edges.

Another use for knot spacing is in shape modification. Figure 2 (right) shows the effect of altering the knot spacing on several control polygon edges of a torus-shaped Catmull-Clark surface. Figure 17 shows a uniform Doo-Sabin surface (on the left) and two non-uniform counterparts, formed by choosing different knot spacings as shown. The sphere in Figure 18 cannot be expressed exactly using uniform subdivision surfaces, rational or otherwise. Figure 19c,e,h are other examples of non-uniform Catmull-Clark surfaces.

In summary,

- this method extends the known general topology methods by permitting unequal knot intervals, thus allowing a single surface description the strengths of both the standard non-uniform tensor products and the uniform recursive subdivision surfaces in one representation.

- Even in the situation where there are no extraordinary points, this theory extends current capability by giving a G^1 surface when the knot intervals are chosen individually for every edge in the control polygon, not constrained to support a tensor product structure.
- This scheme provides a lot of freedom to adjust the shape of the surface. In particular, it can model sharp features by properly setting certain knot spacings to zero.

Future work will design a convenient modeling interface for the interactive purpose and determine how to use knot spacing to best advantage.

ACKNOWLEDGEMENTS

The first two authors received partial financial support for this project through an NSF grant. Kris Klimaszewski made several helpful suggestions, as did the referees.

REFERENCES

[1] A A Ball and D J T Storry. Recursively Generated B-spline Surfaces. *Proc. CAD84*, pages 112–119, 1984. ISBN 0408 01 4407.

[2] A A Ball and D J T Storry. Conditions For Tangent Plane Continuity Over Recursively Generated B-spline Surfaces. *ACM ToG*, 7:83–102, 1988.

[3] W Boehm. Inserting New Knots Into B-spline Curves. *Computer-Aided Design*, 12:199–201, 1980.

[4] E Catmull and J Clark. Recursively Generated B-spline Surfaces On Arbitrary Topological Meshes. *Computer-Aided Design*, 10:350–355, 1978.

[5] G Chaikin. An Algorithm For High-speed Curve Generation. *Computer Graphics and Image Processing*, 3:346–349, 1974.

[6] E Cohen, T Lyche, and R F Riesenfeld. Discrete B-splines And Subdivision Techniques In Computer Aided Design And Computer Graphics. *Computer Graphics and Image Processing*, 14:87–111, 1980.

[7] C de Boor. Cutting Corners Always Works. *Computer Aided Geometric Design*, 4:125–131, 1987.

[8] D Doo and M Sabin. Behaviour Of Recursive Division Surfaces Near Extraordinary Points. *Computer-Aided Design*, 10:356–360, 1978.

[9] N Dyn, D Levin, and J A Gregory. A 4-point Interpolatory Subdivision Scheme For Curve Design. *Computer Aided Geometric Design*, 4:257–268, 1987.

[10] G Farin. Designing C^1 Surfaces Consisting Of Triangular Cubic Patches. *Computer-Aided Design*, 14:253–256, 1982.

[11] A R Forrest. Notes On Chaikin's Algorithm. Technical Report Memo CGP74/1, University of East Anglia, Norwich, UK, 1974.

[12] M Halstead, M Kass, and T DeRose. Efficient, Fair Interpolation Using Catmull-Clark Surfaces. *Computer Graphics (SIGGRAPH 93 Conference Proceedings)*, 27:35–44, 1993.

[13] H Hoppe, T DeRose, T Duchamp, M Halstead, H Jin, J McDonald, J Schweitzer, and W Stuetzle. Piecewise Smooth Surface Reconstruction. *Computer Graphics (SIGGRAPH 94 Conference Proceedings)*, 28:295–302, 1994.

[14] L Kobbelt. Interpolatory Subdivision On Open Quadrilateral Nets With Arbitrary Topology. *Computer Graphics Forum (Eurographics 96)*, 1996.

[15] C Loop. *Smooth Subdivision Surfaces Based On Triangles*. Master's thesis, University of Utah, Dept. of Mathematics, 1987.

[16] C Loop. Smooth Spline Surfaces Over Irregular Meshes. *Computer Graphics (SIGGRAPH 94 Conference Proceedings)*, 28:303–310, 1994.

[17] A Nasri. *Polyhedral Subdivision Methods For Free-form Surfaces*. PhD thesis, University of East Anglia, 1984.

[18] A Nasri. Polyhedral Subdivision Methods For Free-form Surfaces. *ACM ToG*, 6:29–73, 1987.

[19] A Nasri. Surface Interpolation On Irregular Network With Normal Conditions. *Computer Aided Geometric Design*, 8:89–96, 1991.

[20] A Nasri. Curve Interpolation In Recursively Generated B-spline Surfaces Over Arbitrary Topology. *Computer Aided Geometric Design*, 14:13–30, 1997.

[21] J Peters. Joining Smooth Patches Around A Vertex To Form A C^k Surface. *Computer Aided Geometric Design*, 9:387–411, 1992.

[22] J Peters. Smooth Free-form Surfaces Over Irregular Meshes Generalizing Quadratic Splines. *Computer Aided Geometric Design*, 10:347–361, 1993.

[23] J Peters. C^1 Surface Splines. *SIAM J Num Anal*, 32:645–666, 1995.

[24] H Prautzsch. Freeform Splines. *Computer Aided Geometric Design*, 14:201–206, 1997.

[25] U. Reif. A Unified Approach To Subdivision Algorithms Near Extraordinary Vertices. *Computer Aided Geometric Design*, 12:153–174, 1995.

[26] R F Riesenfeld. On Chaikin's Algorithm. *Computer Graphics and Image Processing*, 4:304–310, 1975.

[27] M A Sabin. Recursive Division. In J Gregory, editor, *The Mathematics of Surfaces*, pages 269–282. Clarendon Press, Oxford, 1986. ISBN 0 19 853609 7.

[28] M A Sabin. Cubic Recursive Division With Bounded Curvature. In P J Laurent, A le Mehaute, and L L Schumaker, editors, *Curves and Surfaces*, pages 411–414. Academic Press, 1991. ISBN 0 12 438660 1.

[29] D J T Storry and A A Ball. Design Of An N-sided Surface Patch From Hermite Boundary Data. *Computer Aided Geometric Design*, 6:111–120, 1989.

[30] J Zheng, T Sederberg, and M A Sabin. Eigenanalysis Of Non-Uniform Doo-Sabin Surfaces. Technical report, Brigham Young University, Department of Computer Science (appears as an appendix in the electronic version of this paper), November 1997.

[31] D Zorin, P Schröder, and W Sweldens. Interpolating Subdivision For Meshes With Arbitrary Topology. *Computer Graphics (SIGGRAPH 96 Conference Proceedings)*, 30:189–192, 1996.

Non-Uniform Recursive Subdivision Surfaces

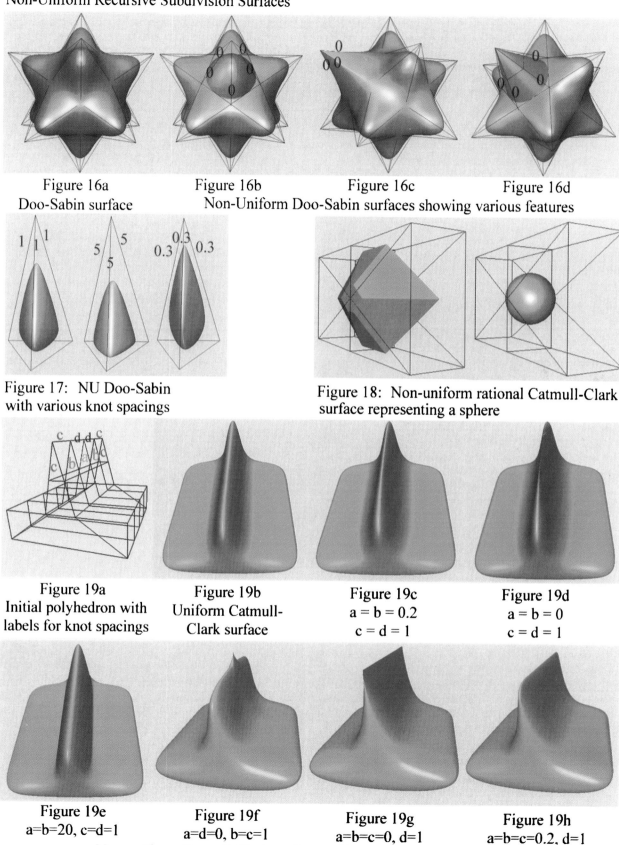

Figure 16a
Doo-Sabin surface

Figure 16b

Figure 16c

Figure 16d

Non-Uniform Doo-Sabin surfaces showing various features

Figure 17: NU Doo-Sabin
with various knot spacings

Figure 18: Non-uniform rational Catmull-Clark
surface representing a sphere

Figure 19a
Initial polyhedron with
labels for knot spacings

Figure 19b
Uniform Catmull-
Clark surface

Figure 19c
$a = b = 0.2$
$c = d = 1$

Figure 19d
$a = b = 0$
$c = d = 1$

Figure 19e
$a=b=20, c=d=1$

Figure 19f
$a=d=0, b=c=1$

Figure 19g
$a=b=c=0, d=1$

Figure 19h
$a=b=c=0.2, d=1$

Non-uniform Catmull-Clark surfaces with various knot spacings

Exact Evaluation Of Catmull-Clark Subdivision Surfaces At Arbitrary Parameter Values

Jos Stam*

Alias | wavefront, Inc.

Abstract

In this paper we disprove the belief widespread within the computer graphics community that Catmull-Clark subdivision surfaces cannot be evaluated directly without explicitly subdividing. We show that the surface and all its derivatives can be evaluated in terms of a set of *eigenbasis* functions which depend only on the subdivision scheme and we derive analytical expressions for these basis functions. In particular, on the regular part of the control mesh where Catmull-Clark surfaces are bi-cubic B-splines, the eigenbasis is equal to the power basis. Also, our technique is both easy to implement and efficient. We have used our implementation to compute high quality curvature plots of subdivision surfaces. The cost of our evaluation scheme is comparable to that of a bi-cubic spline. Therefore, our method allows many algorithms developed for parametric surfaces to be applied to Catmull-Clark subdivision surfaces. This makes subdivision surfaces an even more attractive tool for free-form surface modeling.

CR Categories: I.3.5 [Computer Graphics]: Computational Geometry and Object Modeling—Curve, Surface, Solid, and Object Representations J.6 [Computer Applications]: Computer-Aided Engineering—Computer Aided Design (CAD)

Keywords: subdivision surfaces, eigenanalysis, linear algebra, parametrizations, surface evaluation, Catmull-Clark surfaces

1 Introduction

Subdivision surfaces have emerged recently as a powerful and useful technique in modeling free-form surfaces. However, although in theory subdivision surfaces admit local parametrizations, there is a strong belief within the computer graphics community that these parametrizations cannot be evaluated exactly for arbitrary parameter values. In this paper we disprove this belief and provide a non-iterative technique that efficiently evaluates Catmull-Clark subdivision surfaces and their derivatives up to any order. The cost of our technique is comparable to the evaluation of a bi-cubic surface spline. The rapid and precise evaluation of surface parametrizations is crucial for many standard operations on surfaces such as picking, rendering and texture mapping. Our evaluation technique

allows a large body of useful techniques from parametric surfaces to be transfered to subdivision surfaces, making them even more attractive as a free-form surface modeling tool.

Our evaluation is based on techniques first developed to prove smoothness theorems for subdivision schemes [3, 5, 1, 4, 7, 6]. These proofs are constructed by transforming the subdivision into its eigenspace[1]. In its eigenspace, the subdivision is equivalent to a simple scaling of each of its eigenvectors by their eigenvalue. These techniques allow us to compute limit points and limit normals at the vertices of the mesh, for example. Most of the proofs, however, consider only a subset of the entire eigenspace and do not address the problem of evaluating the surface everywhere. We, on the other hand, use the entire eigenspace to derive an efficiently evaluated analytical form of the subdivision surface everywhere, even in the neighborhood of extraordinary vertices. In this way, we have extended a theoretical tool into a very practical one.

In this paper we present an evaluation scheme for Catmull-Clark subdivision surfaces [2]. However, our methodology is not limited to these surfaces. Whenever subdivision on the regular part of the mesh coincides with a known parametric representation [7], our approach should be applicable. We have decided to present the technique for the special case of Catmull-Clark subdivision surfaces in order to show a particular example fully worked out. In fact, we have implemented a similar technique for Loop's triangular subdivision scheme [5]. The details of that scheme are given in a paper on the CDROM Proceedings [8]. We believe that Catmull-Clark surfaces have many properties which make them attractive as a free-form surface design tool. For example, after one subdivision step each face of the initial mesh is a quadrilateral, and on the regular part of the mesh the surface is equivalent to a piecewise uniform B-spline. Also, algorithms have been written to fair these surfaces [4].

In order to define a parametrization, we introduce a new set of *eigenbasis functions*. These functions were first introduced by Warren in a theoretical setting for curves [9] and used in a more general setting by Zorin [10]. In this paper, we show that the eigenbasis of the Catmull-Clark subdivision scheme can be computed analytically. Also, for the first time we show that in the regular case the eigenbasis is equal to the power basis and that the eigenvectors then correspond to the "change of basis matrix" from the power basis to the bi-cubic B-spline basis. The eigenbasis introduced in this paper can thus be thought of as a generalization of the power basis at extraordinary vertices. Since our eigenbasis functions are analytical, the evaluation of Catmull-Clark subdivision surfaces can be expressed analytically. As shown in the results section of this paper, we have implemented our evaluation scheme and used it in many practical applications. In particular, we show for the first time high resolution curvature plots of Catmull-Clark surfaces precisely computed around the irregular parts of the mesh.

The paper is organized as follows. Section 2 is a brief review of the Catmull-Clark subdivision scheme. In Section 3 we cast this subdivision scheme into a mathematical setting suitable for analysis. In Section 4 we compute the eigenstructure, to derive our eval-

*Alias | wavefront, 1218 Third Ave, 8th Floor, Seattle, WA 98101, U.S.A. jstam@aw.sgi.com

[1]To be defined precisely below.

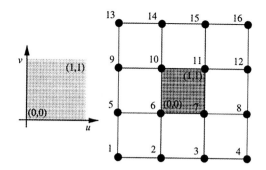

Figure 1: A bi-cubic B-spline is defined by 16 control vertices. The numbers on the right show the ordering of the corresponding B-spline basis functions in the vector $\mathbf{b}(u, v)$.

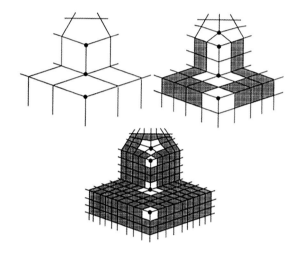

Figure 2: Initial mesh and two levels of subdivision. The shaded faces correspond to regular bi-cubic B-spline patches. The dots are extraordinary vertices.

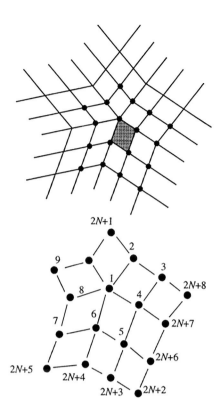

Figure 3: Surface patch near an extraordinary vertex with its control vertices. The ordering of the control vertices is shown on the bottom. Vertex 1 is the extraordinary vertex of valence $N = 5$.

uation. Section 5 is a discussion of implementation issues. In Section 6 we exhibit results created using our technique and compare it to straightforward subdivision. Finally in Section 7 we conclude, mentioning promising directions for future research.

1.1 Notations

In order to make the derivations below as clear and compact as possible we adopt the following notational conventions. All vectors are assumed to be columns and are denoted by boldface lower case roman characters, e.g., $\mathbf{v}$. The components of the vector are denoted by the corresponding italicized character: the i-th component of a vector is thus denoted v_i. The component of a vector should not be confused with an indexed vector such as $\mathbf{v}_k$. Matrices are denoted by uppercase boldface characters, e.g., $\mathbf{M}$. The transpose of a vector $\mathbf{v}$ (resp. matrix $\mathbf{M}$) is denoted by $\mathbf{v}^T$ (resp. $\mathbf{M}^T$). The transpose of a vector is simply the same vector written row-wise. Therefore the dot product between two vectors $\mathbf{u}$ and $\mathbf{v}$ is written "$\mathbf{u}^T\mathbf{v}$". The vector or matrix having only zero elements is denoted by $\mathbf{0}$. The size of this vector (matrix) should be obvious from the context.

2 Catmull-Clark Subdivision Surfaces

The Catmull-Clark subdivision scheme was designed to generalize uniform B-spline knot insertion to meshes of arbitrary topology [2]. An arbitrary mesh such as the one shown on the upper left

hand side of Figure 2 is used to define a smooth surface. The surface is defined as the limit of a sequence of subdivision steps. At each step the vertices of the mesh are updated and new vertices are introduced. Figure 2 illustrates this process. On each vertex of the initial mesh, the *valence* is the number of edges that meet at the vertex. A vertex having a valence not equal to four is called an *extraordinary vertex*. The mesh on the upper left hand side of Figure 2 has two extraordinary vertices of valence three and one of valence five. Away from extraordinary vertices, the Catmull-Clark subdivision is equivalent to midpoint uniform B-spline knot insertion. Therefore, the 16 vertices surrounding a face that contains no extraordinary vertices are the control vertices of a uniform bi-cubic B-spline patch (shown schematically Figure 1). The faces which correspond to a regular patch are shaded in Figure 2. The figure shows how the portion of the surface comprised of regular patches grows with each subdivision step. In principle, the surface can thus be evaluated whenever the holes surrounding the extraordinary vertices are sufficiently small. Unfortunately, this iterative approach is too expensive near extraordinary vertices and does not provide exact higher derivatives.

Because the control vertex structure near an extraordinary vertex is not a simple rectangular grid, all faces that contain extraordinary vertices cannot be evaluated as uniform B-splines. We assume that the initial mesh has been subdivided at least twice, isolating the extraordinary vertices so that each face is a quadrilateral and contains at most one extraordinary vertex. In the rest of the paper, we need to demonstrate only how to evaluate a patch corresponding to a face with just one extraordinary vertex, such as the region near vertex 1 in Figure 3. Let us denote the valence of that extraordinary vertex by N. Our task is then to find a surface patch $\mathbf{s}(u, v)$ defined over the unit square $\Omega = [0, 1] \times [0, 1]$ that can be evaluated directly in terms of the $K = 2N + 8$ vertices that influence the shape of

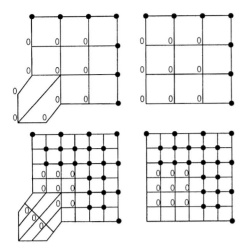

Figure 4: The effect of the seven outer control vertices does not depend on the valence of the extraordinary vertex. When the $2N+1$ control vertices in the center are set to zero the same limit surface is obtained.

the patch corresponding to the face. We assume in the following that the surface point corresponding to the extraordinary vertex is $\mathbf{s}(0,0)$ and that the orientation of Ω is chosen such that $\mathbf{s}_u \times \mathbf{s}_v$ points outside of the surface.

A simple argument shows that the influence on the limit surface of the seven "outer control vertices" numbered $2N+2$ through $2N+8$ in Figure 3 can be accounted for directly. Indeed, consider the situation depicted in Figure 4 where we show a mesh containing a vertex of valence 5 and a regular mesh side by side. Let us assume that all the control vertices are set to zero except for the seven control vertices highlighted in Figure 4. If we repeat the Catmull-Clark subdivision rules for both meshes we actually obtain the same limit surface, since the exceptional control vertex at the center of the patch remains equal to zero after each subdivision step. Therefore, the effect of the seven outer control vertices is simply each control vertex multiplied by its corresponding bi-cubic B-spline tensor product basis function. In the derivation of our evaluation technique we do not need to make use of this fact. However, it explains the simplifications which occur at the end of the derivation.

3 Mathematical Setting

In this section we cast the informal description of the previous section into a rigorous mathematical setting. We denote by

$$\mathbf{C}_0^T = (\mathbf{c}_{0,1}, \cdots, \mathbf{c}_{0,K}),$$

the initial control vertices defining the surface patch shown in Figure 3. The ordering of these vertices is defined on the bottom of Figure 3. This peculiar ordering is chosen so that later computations become more tractable. Note that the vertices do not result in the 16 control vertices of a uniform bi-cubic B-spline patch, except when $N = 4$.

Through subdivision we can generate a new set of $M = K + 9$ vertices shown as circles super-imposed on the initial vertices in Figure 5. Subsets of these new vertices are the control vertices of three uniform B-spline patches. Therefore, three-quarters of our surface patch is parametrized, and could be evaluated as simple bi-cubic B-splines (see top left of Figure 6). We denote this new set of vertices by

$$\mathbf{C}_1^T = (\mathbf{c}_{1,1}, \cdots, \mathbf{c}_{1,K}) \text{ and } \bar{\mathbf{C}}_1^T = \left(\mathbf{C}_1^T, \mathbf{c}_{1,K+1}, \cdots, \mathbf{c}_{1,M} \right).$$

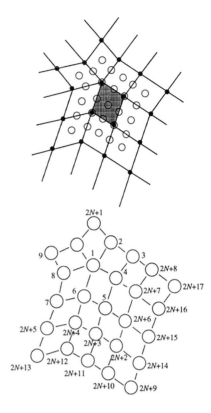

Figure 5: Addition of new vertices by applying the Catmull-Clark subdivision rule to the vertices in Figure 3.

With these matrices, the subdivision step is a multiplication by an $K \times K$ (extended) subdivision matrix $\mathbf{A}$:

$$\mathbf{C}_1 = \mathbf{A}\mathbf{C}_0. \tag{1}$$

Due to the peculiar ordering that we have chosen for the vertices, the extended subdivision matrix has the following block structure:

$$\mathbf{A} = \begin{pmatrix} \mathbf{S} & \mathbf{0} \\ \mathbf{S}_{11} & \mathbf{S}_{12} \end{pmatrix}, \tag{2}$$

where $\mathbf{S}$ is the $2N+1 \times 2N+1$ subdivision matrix usually found in the literature [4]. The remaining two matrices correspond to the regular midpoint knot insertion rules for B-splines. Their exact definition can be found in Appendix A. The additional points needed to evaluate the three B-spline patches are defined using a bigger matrix $\bar{\mathbf{A}}$ of size $M \times K$:

$$\bar{\mathbf{C}}_1 = \bar{\mathbf{A}}\mathbf{C}_0,$$

where

$$\bar{\mathbf{A}} = \begin{pmatrix} \mathbf{S} & \mathbf{0} \\ \mathbf{S}_{11} & \mathbf{S}_{12} \\ \mathbf{S}_{21} & \mathbf{S}_{22} \end{pmatrix}. \tag{3}$$

The matrices $\mathbf{S}_{21}$ and $\mathbf{S}_{22}$ are defined in Appendix A. The subdivision step of Equation 1 can be repeated to create an infinite sequence of control vertices:

$$\begin{aligned} \mathbf{C}_n &= \mathbf{A}\mathbf{C}_{n-1} = \mathbf{A}^n \mathbf{C}_0 \text{ and} \\ \bar{\mathbf{C}}_n &= \bar{\mathbf{A}}\mathbf{C}_{n-1} = \bar{\mathbf{A}}\mathbf{A}^{n-1}\mathbf{C}_0, \quad n \geq 1. \end{aligned}$$

As noted above, for each level $n \geq 1$, a subset of the vertices of $\bar{\mathbf{C}}_n$ becomes the control vertices of three B-spline patches. These

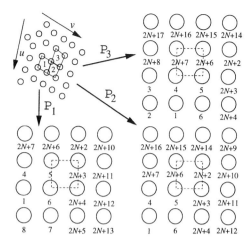

Figure 6: Indices of the control vertices of the three bi-cubic B-spline patches obtained from $\bar{\mathbf{C}}_n$.

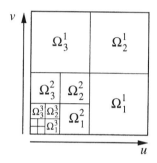

Figure 7: Partition of the unit square into an infinite family of tiles.

control vertices can be defined by selecting 16 control vertices from $\bar{\mathbf{C}}_n$ and storing them in 16×3 matrices:

$$\mathbf{B}_{k,n} = \mathbf{P}_k \bar{\mathbf{C}}_n,$$

where $\mathbf{P}_k$ is a $16 \times M$ "picking" matrix and $k = 1, 2, 3$. Let $\mathbf{b}(u, v)$ be the vector containing the 16 cubic B-spline basis functions (see Appendix B). If the control vertices are ordered as shown on the left of Figure 1, then the surface patch corresponding to each matrix of control vertices is defined as

$$\mathbf{s}_{k,n}(u, v) = \mathbf{B}_{k,n}^T \mathbf{b}(u, v) = \bar{\mathbf{C}}_n^T \mathbf{P}_k^T \mathbf{b}(u, v), \tag{4}$$

where $(u, v) \in \Omega$, $n \geq 1$ and $k = 1, 2, 3$. Using the ordering convention for the B-spline control vertices of Figure 1, the definition of the picking matrices is shown in Figure 6. Each row of $\mathbf{P}_k$ is filled with zeros except for a one in the column corresponding to the index shown in Figure 6 (see Appendix B for more details). The infinite sequence of uniform B-spline patches defined by Equation 4 form our surface $\mathbf{s}(u, v)$, when "stitched together". More formally, let us partition the unit square Ω into an infinite set of tiles $\{\Omega_k^n\}$, $n \geq 1$, $k = 1, 2, 3$, as shown in Figure 7. Each tile with index n is four times smaller than the tiles with index $n - 1$. More precisely:

$$
\begin{aligned}
\Omega_1^n &= \left[\frac{1}{2^n}, \frac{1}{2^{n-1}}\right] \times \left[0, \frac{1}{2^n}\right], \\
\Omega_2^n &= \left[\frac{1}{2^n}, \frac{1}{2^{n-1}}\right] \times \left[\frac{1}{2^n}, \frac{1}{2^{n-1}}\right], \\
\Omega_3^n &= \left[0, \frac{1}{2^n}\right] \times \left[\frac{1}{2^n}, \frac{1}{2^{n-1}}\right].
\end{aligned}
\tag{5}
$$

A parametrization for $\mathbf{s}(u, v)$ is constructed by defining its restriction to each tile Ω_k^n to be equal to the B-spline patch defined by the control vertices $\mathbf{B}_{k,n}$:

$$\mathbf{s}(u, v)\big|_{\Omega_k^n} = \mathbf{s}_{k,n}(\mathbf{t}_{k,n}(u, v)). \tag{6}$$

The transformation $\mathbf{t}_{k,n}$ maps the tile Ω_k^n onto the unit square Ω:

$$
\begin{aligned}
\mathbf{t}_{1,n}(u, v) &= (2^n u - 1, 2^n v), & \tag{7} \\
\mathbf{t}_{2,n}(u, v) &= (2^n u - 1, 2^n v - 1) \quad \text{and} & \tag{8} \\
\mathbf{t}_{3,n}(u, v) &= (2^n u, 2^n v - 1). & \tag{9}
\end{aligned}
$$

Equation 6 gives an actual parametrization for the surface. However, it is very costly to evaluate, since it involves $n - 1$ multiplications of the $K \times K$ matrix $\mathbf{A}$. The evaluation can be simplified considerably by computing the eigenstructure of $\mathbf{A}$. This is the key idea behind our new evaluation technique and is the topic of the next section.

4 Eigenstructure, Eigenbases and Evaluation

The eigenstructure of the subdivision matrix $\mathbf{A}$ is defined as the set of its eigenvalues and eigenvectors. In our case the matrix $\mathbf{A}$ is non-defective for any valence. Consequently, there always exists K linearly independent eigenvectors [4]. Therefore we denote this eigenstructure by $(\mathbf{\Lambda}, \mathbf{V})$, where $\mathbf{\Lambda}$ is the diagonal matrix containing the eigenvalues of $\mathbf{A}$, and $\mathbf{V}$ is an invertible matrix whose columns are the corresponding eigenvectors. The computation of the eigenstructure is then equivalent to the solution of the following matrix equation:

$$\mathbf{A}\mathbf{V} = \mathbf{V}\mathbf{\Lambda}, \tag{10}$$

where the i-th diagonal element of $\mathbf{\Lambda}$ is an eigenvalue with a corresponding eigenvector equal to the i-th column of the matrix $\mathbf{V}$ ($i = 1, \cdots, K$). There are many numerical algorithms which can compute solutions for such equations. Unfortunately for our purposes, these numerical routines do not always return the correct eigenstructure. For example, in some cases the solver returns complex eigenvalues. For this reason, we must explicitly compute the eigenstructure. Since the subdivision matrix has a definite block structure, our computation can be done in several steps. In Appendix A we analytically compute the eigenstructure $(\mathbf{\Sigma}, \mathbf{U}_0)$ (resp. $(\mathbf{\Delta}, \mathbf{W}_1)$) of the diagonal block $\mathbf{S}$ (resp. $\mathbf{S}_{12}$) of the subdivision matrix defined in Equation 2. The eigenvalues of the subdivision matrix are the union of the eigenvalues of its diagonal blocks:

$$\mathbf{\Lambda} = \begin{pmatrix} \mathbf{\Sigma} & 0 \\ 0 & \mathbf{\Delta} \end{pmatrix}.$$

Using the eigenvectors of $\mathbf{S}$ and $\mathbf{S}_{12}$, it can be proven that the eigenvectors for the subdivision matrix must have the following form:

$$\mathbf{V} = \begin{pmatrix} \mathbf{U}_0 & 0 \\ \mathbf{U}_1 & \mathbf{W}_1 \end{pmatrix}.$$

The matrix $\mathbf{U}_1$ is unknown and is determined from Equation 10. If we replace the matrices $\mathbf{\Lambda}$, $\mathbf{V}$ and $\mathbf{A}$ by their block representations, we obtain the following matrix equation:

$$\mathbf{S}_{11}\mathbf{U}_0 + \mathbf{S}_{12}\mathbf{U}_1 = \mathbf{U}_1\mathbf{\Sigma}. \tag{11}$$

Since $\mathbf{U}_0$ is known, $\mathbf{U}_1$ is computed by solving the $2N + 1$ linear systems of Equation 11. In principle, this equation could be solved symbolically. In practice, however, because of the small sizes of the linear systems (7×7) we can compute the solution up to machine accuracy (see the next section for details). The inverse of our eigenvector matrix is equal to

$$\mathbf{V}^{-1} = \begin{pmatrix} \mathbf{U}_0^{-1} & \mathbf{0} \\ -\mathbf{W}_1^{-1}\mathbf{U}_1\mathbf{U}_0^{-1} & \mathbf{W}_1^{-1} \end{pmatrix}, \qquad (12)$$

where both $\mathbf{U}_0$ and $\mathbf{W}_1$ can be inverted exactly (see Appendix A). This fact allows us to rewrite Equation 10:

$$\mathbf{A} = \mathbf{V}\boldsymbol{\Lambda}\mathbf{V}^{-1}.$$

This decomposition is the crucial result that we use in constructing a fast evaluation scheme of the surface patch. Indeed, the subdivided control vertices at level n are now equal to

$$\bar{\mathbf{C}}_n = \bar{\mathbf{A}}\mathbf{A}^{n-1}\mathbf{C}_0 = \bar{\mathbf{A}}\mathbf{V}\boldsymbol{\Lambda}^{n-1}\mathbf{V}^{-1}\mathbf{C}_0 = \bar{\mathbf{A}}\mathbf{V}\boldsymbol{\Lambda}^{n-1}\hat{\mathbf{C}}_0,$$

where $\hat{\mathbf{C}}_0 = \mathbf{V}^{-1}\mathbf{C}_0$ is the projection of the K control vertices into the eigenspace of the subdivision matrix. Using this new expression for the control vertices at the n-th level of subdivision, Equation 4 can be rewritten in the following form:

$$\mathbf{s}_{k,n}(u,v) = \hat{\mathbf{C}}_0^T \boldsymbol{\Lambda}^{n-1} \left(\mathbf{P}_k\bar{\mathbf{A}}\mathbf{V}\right)^T \mathbf{b}(u,v).$$

We observe that the right most terms in this equation are independent of the control vertices and the power n. Therefore, we can precompute this expression and define the following three vectors:

$$\mathbf{x}(u,v,k) = \left(\mathbf{P}_k\bar{\mathbf{A}}\mathbf{V}\right)^T \mathbf{b}(u,v) \quad k = 1, 2, 3. \qquad (13)$$

The components of these three vectors correspond to a set of K bi-cubic splines. In Appendix B we show how to compute these splines. Notice that the splines $x_i(u,v,k)$ depend only on the valence of the extraordinary vertex. Consequently, we can rewrite the equation for each patch more compactly as:

$$\mathbf{s}_{k,n}(u,v) = \hat{\mathbf{C}}_0^T \boldsymbol{\Lambda}^{n-1}\mathbf{x}(u,v,k) \quad k = 1, 2, 3. \qquad (14)$$

To make the expression for the evaluation of the surface patch more concrete, let $\mathbf{p}_i^T$ denote the rows of $\hat{\mathbf{C}}_0$. Then the surface patch can be evaluated as:

$$\mathbf{s}(u,v)\Big|_{\Omega_k^n} = \sum_{i=1}^{K}(\lambda_i)^{n-1}\,x_i(\mathbf{t}_{k,n}(u,v),k)\mathbf{p}_i. \qquad (15)$$

Therefore, in order to evaluate the surface patch, we must first compute the new vertices $\mathbf{p}_i$ (only once for a given mesh). Next, for each evaluation we determine n and then scale the contribution from each of the splines by the relevant eigenvalue to the power $n-1$. Since all but the first of the eigenvalues are smaller than one, their contribution decreases as n increases. Thus, for large n, i.e., for surface-points near the extraordinary vertex, only a few terms make a significant contribution. In fact for $(u,v) = (0,0)$ the surface point is $\mathbf{p}_1$, which agrees with the definition of a limit point in [4].

Alternatively, the bi-cubic spline functions $\mathbf{x}(u,v,k)$ can be used to define a set of *eigenbasis functions* for the subdivision. For a given eigenvector λ_i we define the function φ_i by its restrictions on the domains Ω_k^n as follows:

$$\varphi_i(u,v)\Big|_{\Omega_k^n} = (\lambda_i)^{n-1}x_i(\mathbf{t}_{k,n}(u,v),k),$$

with $i = 1, \cdots, K$. By the above definition these functions satisfy the following scaling relation:

$$\varphi_i(u/2, v/2) = \lambda_i\varphi_i(u,v).$$

The importance of these functions was first noted by Warren in the context of subdivision curves [9]. More recently, Zorin has defined and used eigenbasis functions to prove smoothness conditions for very general classes of subdivision schemes [10]. However, explicit analytical expressions for particular eigenbases have never appeared before. On the other hand, we can compute these bases analytically. Figures 8 and 9 show the complete sets of eigenbasis functions for valences 3 and 5. In the figures we have normalized each function such that its range is bounded within -1 and 1. In particular, the first eigenbasis corresponding to an eigenvalue of one is always a constant function for any valence. A closer look at Figures 8 and 9 reveals that they share seven identical functions. In fact as shown in Appendix B, the last seven eigenbasis functions for any valence are always equal to

$$\left\{\frac{1}{36}u^3v^3, \frac{1}{6}u^3, \frac{1}{6}u^3v, \frac{1}{2}u^3v^2, \frac{1}{6}v^3, \frac{1}{6}uv^3, \frac{1}{2}u^2v^3\right\}.$$

Furthermore, by transforming these functions back from the eigenspace using $\mathbf{W}_1^{-1}$ we obtain the seven tensor B-spline basis functions

$$b_4(u,v), b_8(u,v), b_{12}(u,v), \cdots, b_{16}(u,v),$$

i.e., the basis functions corresponding to the "outer layer" of control vertices of Figure 3. This should not come as a surprise since as we noted above, the influence of the outer layer does not depend on the valence of the extraordinary vertex (see Figure 4).

In the regular bi-cubic B-spline case ($N = 4$), the remaining eigenbasis can be chosen to be equal to the power basis

$$\{1, u, v, u^2, uv, v^2, u^2v, uv^2, u^2v^2\}.$$

The scaling property of the power basis is obvious. For example, the basis function u^2v corresponds to the eigenvalue $1/8$:

$$(u/2)^2(v/2) = (1/2)^2(1/2)u^2v = \frac{1}{8}u^2v.$$

This relationship between the Catmull-Clark subdivision and the power basis in the regular case has not been noted before. Note also that the eigenvectors in this case correspond to the "change of basis matrix" from the bi-cubic B-spline basis to the power basis. The eigenbasis functions at extraordinary vertices can thus be interpreted as a generalization of the power basis. However, the eigenbases are in general not polynomials. In the case of the Catmull-Clark subdivision they are piece-wise bi-cubic polynomials. The evaluation of the surface patch given by Equation 15 can now be rewritten exactly as:

$$\mathbf{s}(u,v) = \sum_{i=1}^{K}\varphi_i(u,v)\mathbf{p}_i. \qquad (16)$$

This is the key result of our paper, since this equation gives a parametrization for the surface corresponding to any face of the control mesh, no matter what the valence is. There is no need to subdivide. Equation 16 also allows us to compute derivatives of the surface up to any order. Only the corresponding derivatives of the basis functions appearing in Equation 16 are required. For example, the partial derivative of the i-th eigenbasis with respect to u is:

$$\frac{\partial}{\partial u}\varphi_i(u,v)\Big|_{\Omega_k^n} = 2^n(\lambda_i)^{n-1}\frac{\partial}{\partial u}x_i(\mathbf{t}_{k,n}(u,v),k),$$

where the factor 2^n is equal to the derivative of the affine transformation $\mathbf{t}_{k,n}$. Generally a factor 2^{pn} will be present when the order of differentiation is p.

5 Implementation

Although the derivation of our evaluation technique is mathematically involved, its implementation is straightforward. The tedious task of computing the eigenstructure of the subdivision matrix only has to be performed once and is provided in Appendix A. In practice, we have precomputed these eigenstructures up to some maximum valence, say `NMAX=500`, and have stored them in a file. Any program using our evaluation technique can read in these precomputed eigenstructures. In our implementation the eigenstructure for each valence `N` is stored internally as

```
typedef
  struct {
    double L[K];         /* eigenvalues */
    double iV[K][K];     /* inv of the eigenvectors */
    double x[K][3][16];  /* coeffs of the splines */
  } EIGENSTRUCT;
EIGENSTRUCT eigen[NMAX];,
```

where `K=2*N+8`. At the end of this section we describe how we computed these eigenstructures. We emphasize that this step only has to be performed once and that its computational cost is irrelevant to the efficiency of our evaluation scheme.

Given that the eigenstructures have been precomputed and read in from a file, we evaluate a surface patch around an extraordinary vertex in two steps. First, we project the control vertices surrounding the patch into the eigenspace of the subdivision matrix. Let the control vertices be ordered as shown in Figure 3 and stored in an array `C[K]`. The projected vertices `Cp[K]` are then easily computed by using the precomputed inverse of the eigenvectors:

```
ProjectPoints(point *Cp,point *C,int N){
  for ( i=0 ; i<2*N+8 ; i++ ){
    Cp[i] = (0,0,0);
    for ( j=0 ; j<2*N+8 ; j++ ){
      Cp[i] += eigen[N].iV[i][j] * C[j];
    }
  }
}
```

This routine is called only whenever one of the patches is evaluated for the first time or after an update of the mesh. This step is, therefore, called at most once per surface patch. The second step of our evaluation, on the other hand, is called whenever the surface has to be evaluated at a particular parameter value `(u,v)`. The second step is a straightforward implementation of the sum appearing in Equation 15. The following routine computes the surface patch at any parameter value.

```
EvalSurf ( point P, double u, double v,
    point *Cp, int N ) {
/* determine in which domain Ω_k^n the parameter lies */
n = floor(min(-log2(u),-log2(v)));
pow2 = pow(2,n-1);
u *= pow2; v *= pow2;
if ( v < 0.5 ) {
  k=0; u=2*u-1; v=2*v;
}
else if ( u < 0.5 ) {
  k=2; u=2*u; v=2*v-1;
}
else {
  k=1; u=2*u-1; v=2*v-1;
}
/* Now evaluate the surface */
P = (0,0,0);
for ( i=0 ; i<2*N+8 ; i++ ) {
```

```
    P += pow(eigen[N].L[i],n-1) *
      EvalSpline(eigen[N].x[i][k],u,v)*Cp[i];
  }
}
```

The function `EvalSpline` computes the bi-cubic polynomial whose coefficients are given by its first argument at the parameter value `(u,v)`. When either one of the parameter values `u` or `v` is zero, we set it to a sufficiently small value near the precision of the machine, to avoid an overflow that would be caused by the `log2` function. Because `EvalSpline` evaluates a bi-cubic polynomial, the cost of `EvalSurf` is comparable to that of a bi-cubic surface spline. The extra cost due to the logarithm and the elevation to an integer power is minimal, because these operations are efficiently implemented on most current hardware. Since the projection step is only called when the mesh is updated, the cost of our evaluation depends predominantly on `EvalSurf`.

The computation of the p-th derivative is entirely analogous. Instead of using the routine `EvalSpline` we employ a routine that returns the p-th derivative of the bi-cubic polynomial. In addition, the final result is scaled by a factor `pow(2,n*p)`. The evaluation of derivatives is essential in applications that require precise surface normals and curvature. For example, Newton iteration schemes used in ray surface computations require higher derivatives of the surface at arbitrary parameter values.

We now describe how we compute the eigenstructure of the subdivision matrix. This step only has to performed once for a given set of valences. The efficiency of this step is not crucial. Accuracy is what matters here. As shown in the appendix, the eigenstructure of the two matrices S and S_{12} can be computed analytically. The corresponding eigenstructure of the extended subdivision matrix A requires the solution of the $2N+1$ linear systems of Equation 11. We did not solve these analytically because these systems are only of size 7×7. Consequently, these systems can be solved up to machine accuracy using standard linear solvers. We used the `dgesv` routine from LINPACK to perform the task. The inverse of the eigenvectors is computed by carrying out the matrix products appearing in Equation 12. Using the eigenvectors, we also precompute the coefficients of the bi-cubic splines $x(u,v,k)$ as explained in Appendix B. For each valence N we stored the results in the data structure `eigen[NMAX]` and saved them in a file to be read in at the start of any application which uses the routines `ProjectPoints` and `EvalSurf` described above.

6 Results

In Figure 10 we depict several Catmull-Clark subdivision surfaces. The extraordinary vertex whose valence N is given in the figure is located in the center of each surface. The position information within the blue patches surrounding the extraordinary vertex are computed using our new evaluation technique. The remaining patches are evaluated as bi-cubic B-splines. Next to each surface we also depict the curvature of the surface. We map the value of the Gaussian curvature onto a hue angle. Red corresponds to a flat surface, while green indicates high curvature. We have purposely made the curvature plot discontinuous in order to emphasize the iso-contour lines. Both the shaded surface and the curvature plot illustrate the accuracy of our method. Notice especially how the curvature varies smoothly across the boundary between the patches evaluated using our technique and the regular bi-cubic B-spline patches. The curvature plots also indicate that for $N \neq 4$ the Gaussian curvature takes on arbitrarily large values near the extraordinary vertex. The curvature at the extraordinary vertex is in fact infinite, which explains the diverging energy functionals in [4].

Figure 11 depicts more complex surfaces. The patches in blue are evaluated using our technique.

7 Conclusion and Future Work

In this paper we have presented a technique to evaluate Catmull-Clark subdivision surfaces. This is an important contribution since the lack of such an evaluation scheme has been sited as the chief argument against the use of subdivision scheme in free-form surface modelers. Our evaluation scheme permits many algorithms and analysis techniques developed for parametric surfaces to be extended to Catmull-Clark surfaces. The cost of our algorithm is comparable to the evaluation of a bi-cubic spline. The implementation of our evaluation is straightforward and we have used it to plot the curvature near extraordinary vertices. We believe that the same methodology can be applied to many other subdivision schemes sharing the features of Catmull-Clark subdivision: regular parametrization away from extraordinary vertices. We have worked out the details for Loop's triangular scheme, and the derivation can be found in the accompanying paper on the CDROM proceedings [8]. Catmull-Clark surfaces and Loop surfaces share the property that their extended subdivision matrices are non-defective. In general, this is *not* the case. For example, the extended subdivision matrix of Doo-Sabin surfaces cannot generally be diagonalized. In this case, however, we can use the Jordan normal form of the extended subdivision matrix and employ Zorin's general scaling relations [10].

Acknowledgments

I wish to thank the following individuals for their help: Eugene Lee for assisting me in fine tuning the math, Michael Lounsbery and Gary Herron for many helpful discussions, Darrek Rosen for creating the models, Pamela Jackson for proofreading the paper, Gregg Silagyi for his help during the submission, and Milan Novacek for his support during all stages of this work.

A Subdivision Matrices and Their Eigenstructures

The matrix S corresponds to the extraordinary rules around the extraordinary vertex. With our choice of ordering of the control vertices the matrix is:

$$\mathbf{S} = \left(\begin{array}{c|cccccccccc} a_N & b_N & c_N & b_N & c_N & b_N & \cdots & b_N & c_N & b_N & c_N \\ \hline d & d & e & e & 0 & 0 & \cdots & 0 & 0 & e & e \\ f & f & f & f & 0 & 0 & \cdots & 0 & 0 & 0 & 0 \\ d & e & e & d & e & e & \cdots & 0 & 0 & 0 & 0 \\ f & 0 & 0 & f & f & f & \cdots & 0 & 0 & 0 & 0 \\ \vdots & & & \vdots & & & \ddots & & \vdots & & \\ d & e & 0 & 0 & 0 & 0 & \cdots & e & e & d & e \\ f & f & 0 & 0 & 0 & 0 & \cdots & 0 & 0 & f & f \end{array}\right)$$

where

$$a_N = 1 - \frac{7}{4N}, b_N = \frac{3}{2N^2}, c_N = \frac{1}{4N^2}, d = \frac{3}{8}, e = \frac{1}{16}, f = \frac{1}{4}.$$

Since the lower right $2N \times 2N$ block of S has a cyclical structure, we can use the discrete Fourier transform to compute the eigenstructure of S. This was first used in the context of subdivision surfaces by Doo and Sabin [3]. The discrete Fourier transform can be written compactly by introducing the following $2N \times 2N$ "Fourier matrix";

$$\mathbf{F} = \left(\begin{array}{cccccccc} 1 & 0 & 1 & 0 & \cdots & 1 & 0 \\ 0 & 1 & 0 & 1 & \cdots & 0 & 1 \\ 1 & 0 & \omega^{-1} & 0 & \cdots & \omega^{-(N-1)} & 0 \\ 0 & 1 & 0 & \omega^{-1} & \cdots & 0 & \omega^{-(N-1)} \\ & \vdots & & & \ddots & \vdots & \\ 1 & 0 & \omega^{-(N-1)} & 0 & \cdots & \omega^{-(N-1)^2} & 0 \\ 0 & 1 & 0 & \omega^{-(N-1)} & \cdots & 0 & \omega^{-(N-1)^2} \end{array}\right),$$

where $\omega = \exp(i2\pi/N)$. Using these notations we can write down the "Fourier transform" of the matrix S compactly as:

$$\hat{\mathbf{S}} = \left(\begin{array}{c|c|c|c} \hat{S}_0 & 0 & 0 & 0 \\ \hline 0 & \hat{S}_1 & 0 & 0 \\ \hline \vdots & 0 & \ddots & 0 \\ \hline 0 & 0 & 0 & \hat{S}_{N-1} \end{array}\right) = \mathbf{T}\,\mathbf{S}\,\mathbf{T}^{-1},$$

where

$$\mathbf{T} = \left(\begin{array}{cc} 1 & 0 \\ 0 & \frac{1}{N}\mathbf{F} \end{array}\right), \quad \mathbf{T}^{-1} = \left(\begin{array}{cc} 1 & 0 \\ 0 & \mathbf{F}^* \end{array}\right),$$

$$\hat{S}_0 = \left(\begin{array}{ccc} a_N & Nb_N & Nc_N \\ d & 2f & 2e \\ f & 2f & f \end{array}\right) \text{ and}$$

$$\hat{S}_l = \left(\begin{array}{cc} e\left(\omega^{-l} + \omega^l\right) + d & e\left(1 + \omega^{-l}\right) \\ f\left(1 + \omega^l\right) & f \end{array}\right),$$

$l = 1, \cdots, N-1$. The eigenstructure of the Fourier transform $\hat{S}$ is computed from the eigenstructures of its diagonal blocks. The first block $\hat{S}_0$ has eigenvalues

$$\mu_1 = 1, \quad \mu_2, \mu_3 = \frac{1}{8N}\left(-7 + 3N \mp \sqrt{49 - 30N + 5N^2}\right)$$

and eigenvectors

$$\hat{K}_0 = \left(\begin{array}{ccc} 1 & 16\mu_2^2 - 12\mu_2 + 1 & 16\mu_3^2 - 12\mu_3 + 1 \\ 1 & 6\mu_2 - 1 & 6\mu_3 - 1 \\ 1 & 4\mu_2 + 1 & 4\mu_3 + 1 \end{array}\right).$$

Similarly, the two eigenvalues of each block $\hat{S}_l$ $(l = 1, \cdots, N-1)$ are equal to:

$$\lambda_l^{\mp} = \frac{1}{16}\left(5 + \cos\left(\frac{2\pi l}{N}\right) \mp \cos\left(\frac{\pi l}{N}\right)\sqrt{18 + 2\cos\left(\frac{2\pi l}{N}\right)}\right),$$

where we have used some trigonometric relations to simplify the resulting expressions. The corresponding eigenvectors of each block are

$$\hat{K}_l = \left(\begin{array}{cc} 4\lambda_l^- - 1 & 4\lambda_l^+ - 1 \\ 1 + \omega^l & 1 + \omega^l \end{array}\right).$$

We have to single out the special case when N is even and $l = N/2$. In this case the corresponding block is

$$\hat{K}_{N/2} = \left(\begin{array}{cc} 1 & 0 \\ 0 & 1 \end{array}\right).$$

The eigenvalues of the matrix $\hat{S}$ are the union of the eigenvalues of its blocks and the eigenvectors are

$$\hat{\mathbf{K}} = \left(\begin{array}{c|c|c|c} \hat{K}_0 & 0 & 0 & 0 \\ \hline 0 & \hat{K}_1 & 0 & 0 \\ \hline \vdots & 0 & \ddots & 0 \\ \hline 0 & 0 & 0 & \hat{K}_{N-1} \end{array}\right).$$

Since the subdivision matrix $\mathbf{S}$ and its Fourier transform $\hat{\mathbf{S}}$ are similar, they have the same eigenvalues. The eigenvectors are computed by inverse Fourier transforming these eigenvectors:

$$\mathbf{K} = \mathbf{T}^{-1}\,\hat{\mathbf{K}}.$$

Consequently, we have computed the eigenvalues and eigenvectors of $\mathbf{S}$. However, in this form the eigenvectors are complex valued and most of the eigenvalues are actually of multiplicity two, since $\lambda_l^- = \lambda_{N-l}^+$ and $\lambda_l^+ = \lambda_{N-l}^-$. We relabel these eigenvalues as follows:

$$\mu_4 = \lambda_1^-, \mu_5 = \lambda_1^+, \mu_6 = \lambda_2^-, \mu_7 = \lambda_2^+, \cdots$$

Since we have rearranged the eigenvalues, we have to rearrange the eigenvectors. At the same time we make these eigenvectors real. Let $\mathbf{k}_1, \cdots, \mathbf{k}_{2N+1}$ be the columns of $\mathbf{K}$, then we can construct the columns of a matrix $\mathbf{U}_0$ as follows:

$$\begin{aligned}
\mathbf{u}_1 &= \mathbf{k}_1, \quad \mathbf{u}_2 = \mathbf{k}_2, \quad \mathbf{u}_3 = \mathbf{k}_3, \\
\mathbf{u}_{2l+2} &= \frac{1}{2}\left(\mathbf{k}_{l+3} + \mathbf{k}_{2N-l+2}\right) \quad \text{and} \\
\mathbf{u}_{2l+3} &= \frac{1}{2i}\left(\mathbf{k}_{l+3} - \mathbf{k}_{2N-l+2}\right).
\end{aligned}$$

More precisely $\mathbf{u}_1, \mathbf{u}_2, \mathbf{u}_3, \mathbf{u}_{2l+2}$ and $\mathbf{u}_{2l+3}$ are equal to

$$\begin{pmatrix} 1 \\ 1 \\ 1 \\ \vdots \\ 1 \\ 1 \end{pmatrix}, \begin{pmatrix} 16\mu_2^2 - 12\mu_2 + 1 \\ 6\mu_2 - 1 \\ 4\mu_2 + 1 \\ \vdots \\ 6\mu_2 - 1 \\ 4\mu_2 + 1 \end{pmatrix}, \begin{pmatrix} 16\mu_3^2 - 12\mu_3 + 1 \\ 6\mu_3 - 1 \\ 4\mu_3 + 1 \\ \vdots \\ 6\mu_3 - 1 \\ 4\mu_3 + 1 \end{pmatrix},$$

$$\begin{pmatrix} 0 \\ 4\mu_{l+3} - 1 \\ 1 + C_l \\ (4\mu_{l+3} - 1)C_l \\ C_l + C_{2l} \\ \vdots \\ (4\mu_{l+3} - 1)C_{(N-1)l} \\ C_{(N-1)l} + 1 \end{pmatrix} \quad \text{and} \quad \begin{pmatrix} 0 \\ 0 \\ S_l \\ (4\mu_{l+3} - 1)S_l \\ S_l + S_{2l} \\ \vdots \\ (4\mu_{l+3} - 1)S_{(N-1)l} \\ S_{(N-1)l} \end{pmatrix},$$

respectively, where $l = 1, \cdots, N_2$, $N_2 = N - 1$ when N is odd and $N_2 = N - 2$ when N is even, and

$$C_k = \cos\left(\frac{2\pi k}{N}\right) \quad \text{and} \quad S_k = \sin\left(\frac{2\pi k}{N}\right).$$

When N is even the last two eigenvectors are

$$\begin{aligned}
\mathbf{u}_{2N}^T &= (0, 1, 0, -1, 0, 1, 0, \cdots, -1, 0) \quad \text{and} \\
\mathbf{u}_{2N+1}^T &= (0, 0, 1, 0, -1, 0, 1, \cdots, 0, -1).
\end{aligned}$$

Finally, the diagonal matrix of eigenvalues is

$$\mathbf{\Sigma} = \mathrm{diag}\left(1, \mu_2, \mu_3, \mu_4, \mu_4, \cdots, \mu_{N+2}, \mu_{N+2}\right).$$

The inverse of the eigenvectors $\mathbf{U}_0$ can be computed likewise by first computing the inverses of each block $\hat{\mathbf{K}}_l$ in the Fourier domain and then setting

$$\mathbf{K}^{-1} = \hat{\mathbf{K}}^{-1}\,\mathbf{T}.$$

With the same reshuffling as above we can then compute $\mathbf{U}_0^{-1}$. The resulting expressions are, however, rather ugly and are not reproduced in this paper.

The remaining blocks of the subdivision matrix $\mathbf{A}$ directly follow from the usual B-spline knot-insertion rules.

$$\mathbf{S}_{12} = \begin{pmatrix} c & b & c & 0 & b & c & 0 \\ 0 & e & e & 0 & 0 & 0 & 0 \\ 0 & c & b & c & 0 & 0 & 0 \\ 0 & 0 & e & e & 0 & 0 & 0 \\ 0 & 0 & 0 & 0 & e & e & 0 \\ 0 & 0 & 0 & 0 & c & b & c \\ 0 & 0 & 0 & 0 & 0 & e & e \end{pmatrix}, \ \mathbf{S}_{11} = \begin{pmatrix} c & 0 & 0 & b & a & b & 0 & 0 & \mathbf{0} \\ e & 0 & 0 & e & d & d & 0 & 0 & \mathbf{0} \\ b & 0 & 0 & c & b & a & b & c & \mathbf{0} \\ e & 0 & 0 & 0 & 0 & d & d & e & \mathbf{0} \\ e & 0 & 0 & d & d & e & 0 & 0 & \mathbf{0} \\ b & c & b & a & b & c & 0 & 0 & \mathbf{0} \\ e & e & d & d & 0 & 0 & 0 & 0 & \mathbf{0} \end{pmatrix},$$

where

$$a = \frac{9}{16}, \quad b = \frac{3}{32} \quad \text{and} \quad c = \frac{1}{64}.$$

For the case $N = 3$, there is no control vertex $\mathbf{c}_8$ ($\mathbf{c}_8 = \mathbf{c}_2$) and the second column of the matrix $\mathbf{S}_{11}$ is equal to $(0, 0, c, e, 0, c, e)^T$.

The eigenstructure of the matrix $\mathbf{S}_{12}$ can be computed manually, since this matrix has a simple form. Its eigenvalues are:

$$\mathbf{\Delta} = \mathrm{diag}\left(\frac{1}{64}, \frac{1}{8}, \frac{1}{16}, \frac{1}{32}, \frac{1}{8}, \frac{1}{16}, \frac{1}{32}\right),$$

with corresponding eigenvectors:

$$\mathbf{W}_1 = \begin{pmatrix} 1 & 1 & 2 & 11 & 1 & 2 & 11 \\ 0 & 1 & 1 & 2 & 0 & 0 & 0 \\ 0 & 1 & 0 & -1 & 0 & 0 & 0 \\ 0 & 1 & -1 & 2 & 0 & 0 & 0 \\ 0 & 0 & 0 & 0 & 1 & 1 & 2 \\ 0 & 0 & 0 & 0 & 1 & 0 & -1 \\ 0 & 0 & 0 & 0 & 1 & -1 & 2 \end{pmatrix}.$$

The inverse $\mathbf{W}_1^{-1}$ of this matrix is easily computed manually.

The other two matrices appearing in $\hat{\mathbf{A}}$ are:

$$\mathbf{S}_{21} = \begin{pmatrix} 0 & 0 & 0 & 0 & f & 0 & 0 & \mathbf{0} \\ 0 & 0 & 0 & 0 & d & e & 0 & \mathbf{0} \\ 0 & 0 & 0 & 0 & f & f & 0 & \mathbf{0} \\ 0 & 0 & 0 & 0 & e & d & e & \mathbf{0} \\ 0 & 0 & 0 & 0 & 0 & f & f & \mathbf{0} \\ 0 & 0 & 0 & e & d & 0 & 0 & \mathbf{0} \\ 0 & 0 & f & f & 0 & 0 & 0 & \mathbf{0} \\ 0 & 0 & e & d & e & 0 & 0 & \mathbf{0} \\ 0 & 0 & f & f & 0 & 0 & 0 & \mathbf{0} \end{pmatrix}, \mathbf{S}_{22} = \begin{pmatrix} f & f & 0 & 0 & f & 0 & 0 \\ e & d & e & 0 & e & 0 & 0 \\ 0 & f & f & 0 & 0 & 0 & 0 \\ 0 & e & d & e & 0 & 0 & 0 \\ 0 & 0 & f & f & 0 & 0 & 0 \\ e & e & 0 & 0 & d & e & 0 \\ 0 & 0 & 0 & 0 & f & f & 0 \\ 0 & 0 & 0 & 0 & e & d & e \\ 0 & 0 & 0 & 0 & 0 & f & f \end{pmatrix}.$$

B   Eigenbasis Functions

In this appendix we compute the bi-cubic spline pieces $\mathbf{x}(u, v, k)$ of the eigenbasis defined in Equation 13. The vector $\mathbf{b}(u, v)$ contains the 16 tensor B-spline basis functions ($i = 1, \cdots, 16$):

$$b_i(u, v) = N_{(i-1)\%4}(u)N_{(i-1)/4}(v),$$

where "%" and "/" stand for the remainder and the division respectively. The functions $N_i(t)$ are the uniform B-spline basis functions:

$$\begin{aligned}
6N_0(t) &= 1 - 3t + 3t^2 - t^3, \\
6N_1(t) &= 4 - 6t^2 + 3t^3, \\
6N_2(t) &= 1 + 3t + 3t^2 - 3t^3 \quad \text{and} \\
6N_3(t) &= t^3.
\end{aligned}$$

The projection matrices $\mathbf{P}_1, \mathbf{P}_2$ and $\mathbf{P}_3$ are defined by introducing the following three permutation vectors (see Figure 6):

$$\mathbf{q}^1 = (8, 7, 2N + 5, 2N + 13, 1, 6, 2N + 4, 2N + 12,$$

$$4, 5, 2N + 3, 2N + 11, 2N + 7, 2N + 6, 2N + 2,$$
$$2N + 10),$$

$$\mathbf{q}^2 = (1, 6, 2N + 4, 2N + 12, 4, 5, 2N + 3, 2N + 11,$$
$$2N + 7, 2N + 6, 2N + 2, 2N + 10, 2N + 16,$$
$$2N + 15, 2N + 14, 2N + 9),$$

$$\mathbf{q}^3 = (2, 1, 6, 2N + 4, 3, 4, 5, 2N + 3, 2N + 8, 2N + 7,$$
$$2N + 6, 2N + 2, 2N + 17, 2N + 16, 2N + 15,$$
$$2N + 14).$$

Since for the case $N = 3$ the vertices $\mathbf{c}_2$ and $\mathbf{c}_8$ are the same vertex, $q_1^1 = 2$ instead of 8 for $N = 3$. Using these permutation vectors we can compute each bi-cubic spline as follows:

$$x_i(u, v, k) = \sum_{j=1}^{16} V_{q_j^k, i} \, b_j(u, v),$$

where $i = 1, \cdots, K$ and $\mathbf{V}$ are the eigenvectors of the subdivision matrix.

References

[1] A. A. Ball and J. T. Storry. Conditions For Tangent Plane Continuity Over Recursively Defined B-spline Surfaces. *ACM Transactions on Graphics*, 7(2):83–102, April 1988.

[2] E. Catmull and J. Clark. Recursively Generated B-Spline Surfaces On Arbitrary Topological Meshes. *Computer Aided Design*, 10(6):350–355, 1978.

[3] D. Doo and M. A. Sabin. Behaviour Of Recursive Subdivision Surfaces Near Extraordinary Points. *Computer Aided Design*, 10(6):356–360, 1978.

[4] M. Halstead, M. Kass, and T. DeRose. Efficient, Fair Interpolation Using Catmull-Clark Surfaces. In *Proceedings of SIGGRAPH '93*, pages 35–44. Addison-Wesley Publishing Company, August 1993.

[5] C. T. Loop. *Smooth Subdivision Surfaces Based on Triangles*. M.S. Thesis, Department of Mathematics, University of Utah, August 1987.

[6] J. Peters and U. Reif. Analysis Of Generalized B-Splines Subdivision Algorithms. To appear in SIAM Journal of Numerical Analysis.

[7] U. Reif. A Unified Approach To Subdivision Algorithms Near Extraordinary Vertices. *Computer Aided Geometric Design*, 12:153–174, 1995.

[8] J. Stam. Evaluation Of Loop Subdivision Surfaces. SIGGRAPH'98 CDROM Proceedings, 1998.

[9] J. Warren. Subdivision Methods For Geometric Design. Unpublished manuscript. Preprint available on the web at http://www.cs.rice.edu/~jwarren/papers/book.ps.gz.

[10] D. N. Zorin. *Subdivision and Multiresolution Surface Representations*. PhD thesis, Caltech, Pasadena, California, 1997.

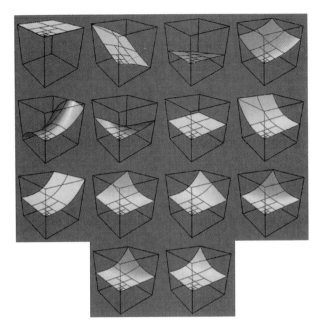

Figure 8: The complete set of 14 eigenbasis functions for extraordinary vertices of valence $N = 3$.

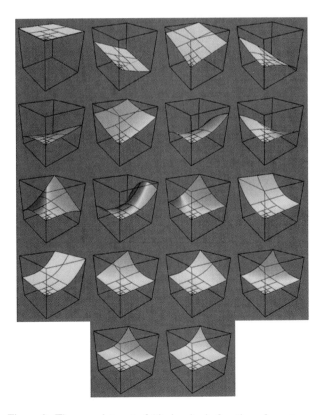

Figure 9: The complete set of 18 eigenbasis functions for extraordinary vertices of valence $N = 5$.

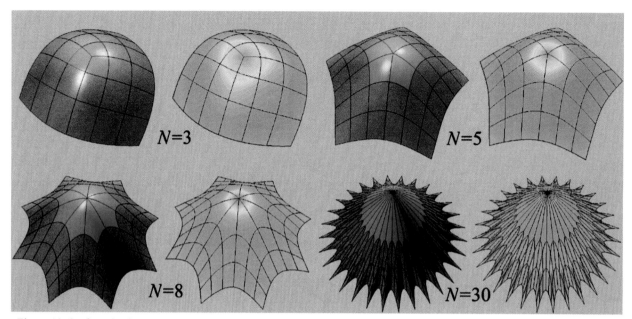

Figure 10: Surfaces having an extraordinary vertex in the center. For each surface we depict the patches evaluated using our technique in blue. Next to them is a curvature plot. Derivative information for curvature is also computed near the center vertex using our technique.

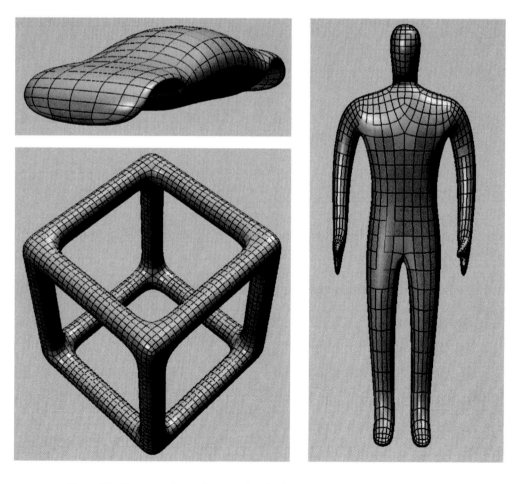

Figure 11: More complex surfaces rendered using our evaluation technique (in blue).

Wires: A Geometric Deformation Technique

Karan Singh

Eugene Fiume*

Alias|wavefront

Abstract

Finding effective interactive deformation techniques for complex geometric objects continues to be a challenging problem in modeling and animation. We present an approach that is inspired by armatures used by sculptors, in which *wire* curves give definition to an object and shape its deformable features. We also introduce *domain curves* that define the domain of deformation about an object. A wire together with a collection of domain curves provide a new basis for an implicit modeling primitive. Wires directly reflect object geometry, and as such they provide a coarse geometric representation of an object that can be created through sketching. Furthermore, the aggregate deformation from several wires is easy to define. We show that a single wire is an appealing direct manipulation deformation technique; we demonstrate that the combination of wires and domain curves provide a new way to outline the shape of an implicit volume in space; and we describe techniques for the aggregation of deformations resulting from multiple wires, domain curves and their interaction with each other and other deformation techniques. The power of our approach is illustrated using applications of animating figures with flexible articulations, modeling wrinkled surfaces and stitching geometry together.

Keywords: deformations, implicit models, interactive graphics, animation.

1 Introduction

The modeling and animation of deformable objects is an active area of research [1, 2, 7, 8, 10, 12, 13, 15]. Free-form deformations (FFDs) [13] and their variants [6, 7, 9, 10], for example, are popular and provide a high level of geometric control over the deformation. These approaches involve the definition and deformation of a lattice of control points. An object embedded within the lattice is then deformed by defining a mapping from the lattice to the object. The user thus deals with a level of detail dictated by the density of the control lattice. While very useful for coarse-scale deformations of an object, the technique can be difficult to use for finer-scale deformations, where a very dense and customized control lattice shape [7, 10] is usually required. Arbitrarily shaped lattices can be cumbersome to construct and it is often easier to deform the underlying geometry directly than to manipulate a dense control lattice.

*Alias|wavefront, 210 King St. E., Toronto, Canada M5A 1J7. ksingh@aw.sgi.com, elf@aw.sgi.com

Axial deformations provide a more compact representation in which a one-dimensional primitive, such as a line segment or curve, is used to define an implicit global deformation [12]. Our approach, called *wire* deformations, is related to axial deformations, although we have a different motivation and formulation. Our main point of departure is our desire to bring geometric and deformation modeling closer together by using a collection of wires as both a coarse-scale representation of the object surface, and a directly manipulated deformation primitive that highlights and tracks the salient deformable features of the object. As can be seen in Figure 1, projections of the wire curves provide a sketch-like representation of the object, which is how many artists prefer doing design.

Wire deformations may be likened to a constructive sculpting approach in which the wires of an armature provide definition to the object and control its deformable features. As in sculpture, the wire curves themselves give a coarse approximation to the shape of the object being modeled. A wire deformation is independent of the complexity of the underlying object model while easily allowing finer-scale deformations to be performed as either object or deformation complexity increases. In fact, an animator can interact with a deformable model, namely the wires, without ever having to deal directly with the object representation itself. Wires can control varying geometric representations of the same object and can be reused on different objects with similar deformable features.

There are two stages in the wire deformation process. In the first, which is typically computed once, an object is bound to a set of wires. In the second, any manipulation of a wire effects a deformation of the object. Implicit function based techniques are used to implement wire deformations. The deformation algorithm is conceptually simple and efficient. Through several examples, we shall illustrate the expressiveness of wires for feature based object design and animation, including facial animation.

Section 2 presents the wire deformation algorithm. Section 3 introduces the use of domain curves to refine the regions affected by a wire. Section 4 describes the techniques used to provide user control over aggregate wire (or other) deformations. Section 5 demonstrates the power of wires for the modeling and animation of wrinkled surfaces, flexible articulated structures and stitched surfaces. Section 6 concludes with discussion of our results.

2 Wire Definition and Algorithm

A *wire* is a curve whose manipulation deforms the surface of an associated object near the curve. We define a wire as a tuple $\langle W, R, s, r, f \rangle$, where W and R are free-form parametric curves, s is a scalar that controls radial scaling around the curve, and r is a scalar value defining a radius of influence around the curve; the scalar function $f : \mathbb{R}^+ \to [0, 1]$ is often referred to in implicit function related literature as a *density function* [15]. Normally, f is at least C^1 and monotonically decreasing with $f(0) = 1, f(x) = 0$ for $x \geq 1$ and $f'(0) = 0, f'(1) = 0$. [1]

---

[1] Wire deformations on a surface preserve continuity up to the degree of continuity of the function f. As an example, we use a C^1 function $f(x) = (x^2 - 1)^2, x \in [0, 1]$, in our implementation.

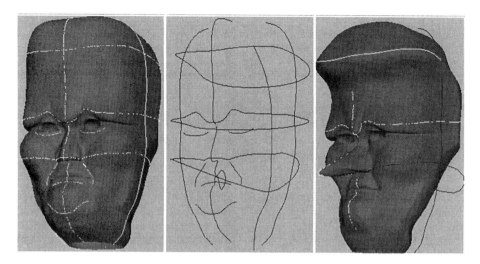

Figure 1: Wires: A geometric deformation technique.

The parameters f and r can be used to define a volume about a curve bounded by an offset surface at a distance r from the curve [4]. Together with a scale factor s, and given r and f, a wire is defined by specifying a curve W and a congruent copy of the curve, R. We refer to W as the *wire curve* and R as the *reference curve* for a wire. When an object is bound to the wire, the domain of influence of the wire is demarkated by the offset surface of radius r defined around the reference curve R. The influence for points of the object within this offset volume are calculated using the density function f. Subsequent manipulation of W results in a change between W and R, which is used along with s to define the deformation. The actual deformation applied to a point is modulated by its influence calculated when the object was bound to the wire.

Let $C(u)$ be a space curve, parametrized without loss of generality by $u \in [0, 1]$. For any point $P \in \mathbb{R}^3$, let $p_C \in [0, 1]$ be the parameter value that minimizes the Euclidean distance between point P and curve $C(u)$. If there is more than one minimum, we arbitrarily define p_C to be the parameter with the smallest value.[2] For any point P and curve C, we define the function $F(P, C)$ as

$$F(P, C) = f\left(\frac{||P - C(p_C)||}{r} \right).$$

From the properties of f it is clear that $F(P, C)$ varies from zero for $||P - C(p_C)|| \geq r$ (points on and outside the offset volume defined by C and r), to $F(P, C) = 1$ when $||P - C(p_C)|| = 0$ (P lies on C). $F(P, C)$ defines the influence that a curve C has on a point P. This is the usual function definition for implicitly defined offset shapes [4], and it will be used below in defining the semantics of the deformation.

As with any deformation, a wire deformation is a pointwise function mapping $\mathbb{R}^3$ onto $\mathbb{R}^3$. For each object O, let $\mathbf{P}_O$ be the point-based representation to which the wire deformations will be applied. Typically $\mathbf{P}_O$ contains all points necessary to construct or approximate an object's surface. $\mathbf{P}_O$ could thus be a set of control vertices for freeform surfaces, a set of vertices in a polymesh, or an unstructured set of points in space.

When an object O is bound to a wire $\langle W, R, s, r, f \rangle$, the parameters p_R and $F(P, R)$ are computed for every point $P \in \mathbf{P}_O$. Only points on the object within the offset volume of radius r from the curve R will be deformed (i.e., points P with $F(P, R) > 0$). Figure 3(a) shows how one wire with a larger r affects a larger region of the object, the other deformation parameters being identical.

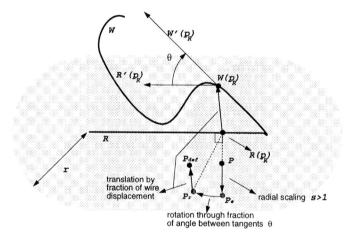

Figure 2: Deformation of a point P to P_{def} by a wire W.

The deformation at a point P is related to the deviation of the closest point on the reference curve $R(p_R)$ from a corresponding point on the wire curve W. We use a direct correspondence between curves R and W based on parameter value, but correspondences such as an arc-length parametrization can instead be used. The computation thus far defines the region of the object to be deformed.

When W is manipulated, the object is deformed for every point P of the undeformed object for which $F(P, R) > 0$ (see Figure 2):

1. Uniformly scale P about point $R(p_R)$ resulting in point P_s. Specifically, $P_s = P + (P - R(p_R)) \cdot (1 + (s-1) \cdot F(P, R))$.
2. Let $C'(u)$ be the tangent vector to curve C at u, and let θ be the angle between $W'(p_R)$ and $R'(p_R)$. Rotate P_s by the modulated angle $\theta \cdot F(P, R)$, around the axis $W'(p_R) \times R'(p_R)$, about point $R(p_R)$. This provides a screw-like deformation, resulting in point P_r (see Figure 2). Rotational transformations such as a twist along the wire can be easily specified as in Section 3, and composed with the rotation specified here.
3. Finally add the translation $(W(p_R) - R(p_R)) \cdot F(P, R)$ to the result of the rotation P_r. The resulting deformed point P_{def} is thus $P_{def} = P_r + (W(p_R) - R(p_R)) \cdot F(P, R)$.

---

[2]In most cases, this is an effective choice, but it can be overly simple in geometrically delicate situations, which we discuss in Section 6.

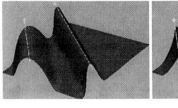 

(a) Varying r (b) Varying s

Figure 3: Varying r and s on wires.

Observe the following properties of our formulation.

- Objects are not deformed upon initial creation of wire and reference curves: R, being a copy of W, coincides with it, so no rotation or translation is applied. For a default scale parameter of $s = 1$, no deformation is applied to the object.

- Points on the object outside the offset volume of radius r from the reference curve (points P with $F(P, R) = 0$) are not deformed regardless of the value of s. This is because $F(P, R)$ attenuates each step of the deformation.

- Points on the object that are on the reference curve, when the object is bound to the wire, track the wire curve precisely. For a point P on the undeformed object that coincides with a point on the reference curve, $R(p_R)$ is identical to P and thus $F(P, R) = f(0) = 1$. The scale and rotation have no effect as they are applied about point $R(p_R)$ itself. P thus moves to $P + (W(p_R) - R(p_R))$ or the point $W(p_R)$ on W.

- The deformation of points on the object between those on the reference curve and those outside its realm of influence is smooth and intuitive. The factor $F(P, R)$ controls the attenuation of the deformation, varying from precise tracking for points on the reference curve to no deformation at or beyond the offset volume boundary. The properties of the function f dictate the behavior of $F(P, R)$ and the smoothness properties of the deformation.

- For $s = 1$, the cross-section of the deformed object surface in a plane perpendicular to the wire curve at a point closely resembles the profile of f (see Figure 3(a)). Manipulating f provides intuitive control over the shape of the deformed object surface and directly controls the degree of continuity preserved by the deformed surface. Figure 3(b) also shows how reducing s on one wire and increasing it on the other provides sucking or bulging control over the deformation.

Axial deformations [12] also use the notion of a reference curve R and closest point computation p_R for a point P. The axial deformation technique relates two Frenet frames attached at $W(p_R)$ on the deformed curve and $R(p_R)$ on the reference curve. The deformation imparted to point P is a portion of the transformation from the reference curve's Frenet frame to the Frenet frame on the deformed curve. The proportion is based on an interpolation of the closest distance of P to the reference curve $\|P - R(p_R)\|$ between two cut-off radii R_{in} and R_{out}.

While axial deformations and the deformation of a single wire share some similarities, a wire has several differences. First, the separation of the scale, rotation and translational components of the wire deformation provides a user with more selective control over the resulting deformation than the integrated transformation of a Frenet frame. Second, Frenet frames are harder to control and have orientation problems when the curvature of a curve vanishes. Third, simple non-linear transformations can be incorporated seamlessly into the deformation algorithm at the appropriate point. For example, as seen in Figure 4, an interpolated twist around the wire can be implemented by rotating the point around the axis along the

reference-curve $R'(p_R)$ by a specified angle as part of the rotational step of the deformation algorithm. Fourth, using an implicit function to control the spatial influence of the wire on the deformed objects makes the technique accessible to more general implicit surface animation techniques. The extensions in Section 3 will show how implicit functions can be overlaid by a user to determine what parts of the deformed objects are affected and by how much.

Figure 5 shows the effect of the various deformation parameters. A cylindrical object with an associated wire is depicted in Figure 5(a). Figure 5(b) shows the deformation to the surface as a result of moving a control point on the wire curve. A more global deformation to the entire object as result of a large increase to r is illustrated in Figure 5(c). Another control point is moved in Figure 5(d). When r is large, the entire object tracks the wire. Figure 5(e) depicts the effect of reducing the scale factor s on the configuration in Figure 5(d). Figure 5(f) further illustrates how the three stages of deformation can be tuned individually by attenuating the rotational aspect and inducing a shear on the configuration in Figure 5(d).

3 Controlling Wire Parameters

Our technique was designed with usability and direct manipulation in mind. We are thus interested in ways of giving finer user control over the deformation parameters. Allowing a specified portion such as a subset of control vertices on an object to be deformed affords some degree of control. However, continuity properties may be compromised in parts of the object surface defined by control vertices that are selectively deformed. This is shown in Figures 6(a,b). Usually one would expect a smoother dropoff based on the region selected, such as that shown in Figure 6(c).

3.1 Locators

One solution involves using *locators* along a wire curve to specify the values of parameters along the wire. An animator can position locators along curves as needed to control locally not only the radius of influence r but any attribute related to wire deformation. We calculate the attribute being localized at a parameter value p as an interpolation between the attribute values specified at the two locators that bracket p. Two wire locators are used to model the cone-spherical shape of an Adam's apple in Figure 7(a) by varying r. Local control over the amplitude of deformation causes the transformation from an "I" in Figure 7(b) to an "i" in Figure 7(c). Locators can also be used to incorporate non-linear transformations such as a twist (see Figure 4), where they are used to control the twist angle along the wire.

As mentioned in Section 2, the implicit function F can be combined with other functions. In particular, we can get directional control by modulating F with an implicit function for an angular dropoff around an axis perpendicular to the wire. Both the directional axis and dropoff angle can be interpolated by locators.

3.2 Domain Curves

Locators provide radially symmetric local control along and around a wire curve. Anisotropic directional control is provided by domain curves as illustrated in Figure 6(c). *Domain curves* along with an associated wire's reference curve define an implicit primitive function over a finite volume. This provides incremental, direct control over what parts of the object are deformed (using domain curves) and by how much they are deformed (using wire curves). We shall deal here with a single domain curve for a given wire. The use of multiple domain curves will be discussed in Section 4.

As illustrated in Figure 6(c), a domain curve demarkates a region of the object surface to be deformed, and along with the reference

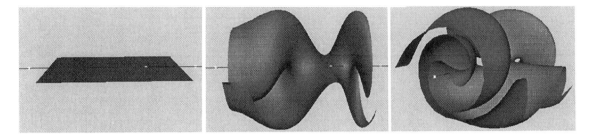

Figure 4: Interpolated twist around a wire.

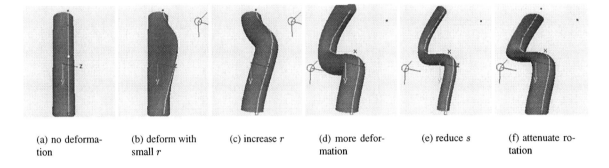

(a) no deformation

(b) deform with small r

(c) increase r

(d) more deformation

(e) reduce s

(f) attenuate rotation

Figure 5: More variations of r and s on wires.

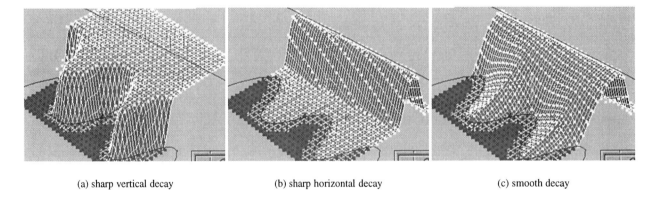

(a) sharp vertical decay

(b) sharp horizontal decay

(c) smooth decay

Figure 6: Region of influence of a wire.

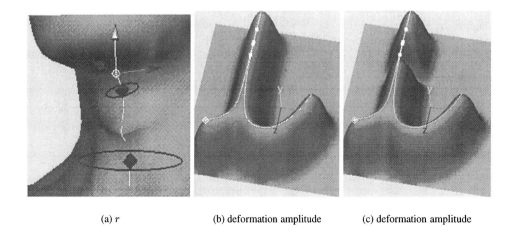

(a) r

(b) deformation amplitude

(c) deformation amplitude

Figure 7: Varying deformation parameters along a wire.

curve it acts as an anchor for the deformation. More generally, we defined the domain curve to be a free-form curve rather than a closed curve on the object surface. Such a domain curve does not unambiguously determine which control points on the object surface will be deformed. Most animators, however, have a very good idea of how a given domain curve will affect the region of the object to be deformed, based on the spatial relationship between the reference curve, domain curve and the object surface. In our implementation we use distance and angle computations between points on the object surface, the domain curve and reference curve to determine if and by how much the point will be influenced.

In Figure 6(c), we chose the domain curve to have a *one-sided* influence region affected by the wire. The other side is affected by the conventional dropoff radius r. Our formulation of one-sided domain curves is as follows.

We first determine if the domain curve D will be used to define the function f at a point P. Let $cosangle = (D(p_D) - R(p_R)) \cdot (P - R(p_R))$. The domain curve will define the function if $cosangle > 0$. This heuristic attempts to select points P that are thought to lie on the same side of R as D (even though the concept of *side* is not well-defined mathematically). As can be seen in the Figure 8, this notion of same side tends to be captured by an acute angle subtended at $R(p_R)$, for the triangle with vertices at P, $D(p_D)$ and $R(p_R)$. With this edge condition,

$$F(P, R) = f\left(\frac{\|P - R(p_R)\|}{\|R(p_R) - D(p_D)\|}\right).$$

For points considered to be outside the domain defined by the domain curve, the conventional dropoff radius calculation can be applied. This formulation is likely to lead to a discontinuity in the neighbourhood of points where $cosangle = 0$. The discontinuity may be removed by specifying a $\delta \in (0, 1)$, so that for $cosangle \in [0, \delta]$,

$$F(P, R) = f\left(\frac{\|P - R(p_R)\|}{Interp(cosangle)}\right),$$

where the function $Interp$ gives a smoothly interpolated value from r to $\|R(p_R) - D(p_D)\|$ as $cosangle$ varies from 0 to δ.

Figure 9 uses a domain curve under the eye to limit the influence of the wire to the figure's cheek. Domain curves can easily be used to control other spatially variable parameters.

4 Multiple wires

Recall that our approach is driven by the interaction of multiple wires that together provide an overall definition of the object's shape (cf. Figure 1). We appeal to a sculptor's armature metaphor to give the expected behavior of a deformation in regions where more than one wire has an effect. In an armature, an overall shape deformation can be seen as a smoothed union of the deformations caused by each wire. This behavior is evident in the **X** pulled out of a plane by two wires in Figure 10(a). The results are distinct from the traditional superposition of the deformations due to each wire as in Figure 10(b). This behavior is analogous to that discussed in [4] distinguishing implicit function based convolution and distance surfaces. We further require that subdividing a wire curve into two curves does not affect the deformation applied to the object (such as an unwanted bulge where the two curves abut).

The problem of unwanted aggregate blobs is circumvented in [7, 10] by making deformations due to multiple deformers incremental. While Coquillart's technique for FFDs can be readily applied to wires[7], it would defeat our main purpose of getting interesting aggregate behavior from many interacting wires.

Our solution is as follows. Let the ith wire curve deforming an object be $\langle W_i, R_i, s_i, r_i, f_i \rangle$. Let us suppose the deformation of a point P on an object induced by wire i results in P_{def_i} (as defined in Section 2). Let $\Delta P_i = P_{def_i} - P$. The deformed point P_{def} as influenced by all wires is defined as the following blend:

$$P_{def} = P + \frac{\sum_{i=1}^{n} \Delta P_i \cdot \|\Delta P_i\|^m}{\sum_{i=1}^{n} \|\Delta P_i\|^m}.$$

The resulting behavior varies with m from a simple average of the ΔP_i when $m = 0$, converging to $\max\{\Delta P_i\}$ for large m (see Figure 11). When m is negative, it is technically possible to have a singular denominator. But if we reformulate this expression as

$$P_{def} = P + \frac{\sum_{i=1}^{n} \Delta P_i \cdot \prod_{j \neq i} \|\Delta P_j\|^{|m|}}{\sum_{i=1}^{n} \prod_{j \neq i} \|\Delta P_j\|^{|m|}},$$

we note that the singularity is removable. In practice, it is preferable to use the original formulation even for negative m and simply omit those ΔP's that are zero. Observe that as m gets increasingly negative, the displacement approaches $\min\{\Delta P_i\}$. Indeed, each wire i could have its own exponent m_i, giving finer control over its contribution to the result in regions of interaction.

It is easy to verify that the above formulation has several desirable properties for typical values of $m \geq 1$:

1. In a region where only one wire is relevant, the result is precisely the deformation of that wire.

2. When several wires produce the same deformation, the result is the deformation induced by any one of those wires.

3. In general, the result is an algebraic combination of the individual wire deformations, with a bias (controlled by m) toward the deformations of larger magnitude.

Figure 10: Multiple wires on multiple surfaces with differing deformations. Left, (a): integrated deformation that avoids blobby superposition. Right, (b): the traditional additive deformation.

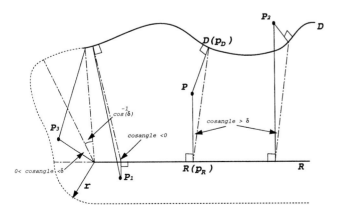

Figure 8: Implicit function defined using a domain curve.

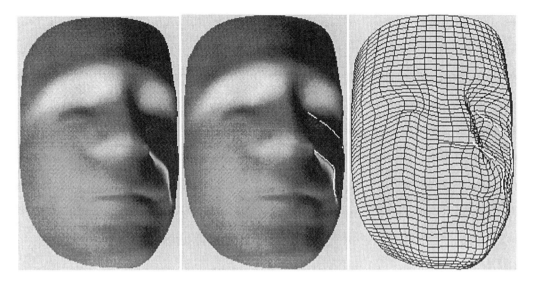

Figure 9: Using domain curves to animate a facial crease.

Many augmentations of our formulation are possible. For example, we can blend the above deformation with an aggregation of wire deformations given by $P_{def} = P + \sum_{i=1}^{n} \Delta P_i$. We can also attach different exponents to each domain curve, allowing us to introduce domain curves that refine an implicit volume in an additive or subtractive fashion controlled by the sign of each exponent.

Another useful variation is to introduce a local influence of a wire at a point on an object's surface relative to other wires. In the formulation above, only wires that directly deform a point are of consequence. In Figure 12(b), the central straight wire lifts a large portion of the surface when it is translated upward. Because the outer curve did not move, it did not influence the surface. In Figure 12(c), however, it acts as an anchor, exercising a local influence on the surface that is independent of the deformation it imparts (in this case none), but depends on the proximity of points in space to the curve. We use $F(P, R_i)$ as a measure of proximity or local influence for the wire. The formulation used for this behavior is

$$P_{def} = P + \frac{\sum_{i=1}^{n} \Delta P_i \cdot F(P, R_i)^k}{\sum_{i=1}^{n} F(P, R_i)^k}.$$

The factor k has a similar effect that m had earlier. A parameter *localize* combines this deformation with the others defined earlier.

A similar effect can be seen in Figure 13, where wires simulate the behavior of an FFD lattice. A wire curve is generated along each lattice line. Large dropoff radii ensure that planarity is preserved on the deformed cube when the right face of the lattice is translated outward, as can be seen in Figures 13(b,c). The difference in behavior with and without the localized influence computation is evident from the more global deformation in Figure 13(c) over 13(b). The formulations we have described are equally applicable to other deformation techniques and can be used to combine the results of different deformation approaches.

5 Applications

We shall illustrate the versatility of wires with three examples that exercise different aspects of wire deformations. We show how wires may be used to control wrinkle formation and propagation on a surface. Such *surface oriented* deformations are localized to increase surface detail. We apply wires to stitching and tearing geometry, which again is a surface oriented deformation. Lastly, we describe a *volume oriented* deformation, in which a flexible skeletal curve is

generated from a traditional joint hierarchy and is used to bind articulated geometry as a wire. Figures 5(b) and (c) distinguish between surface and volume oriented deformations.

5.1 Wrinkles

Wrinkles and creases can greatly enhance the realism of animated deformable objects. Cloth animation has become an important area of computer animation, especially related to human figure animation [11]. We show here how wires are effective in animating the crease lines along which wrinkles propogate. Wrinkle creases are either drawn as curves on the object surface by the animator or automatically generated in a set of predefined patterns.

Typical properties such as wrinkle thickness, intensity and stiffness of the material are easily captured by the various wire deformation parameters. The extent of wrinkle propagation can also be controlled. Figure 14(a) shows two wire curves as magnified wrinkles. Figure 14(b) shows the wrinkles propagating along the object surface. While one wrinkle is pulled along, remaining anchored, the other travels along the surface. The travelling wrinkle in Figure 14(b) is a result of pulling the reference curve R along the object surface with the wire curve W.

Figure 15 shows wrinkles that are procedurally generated by specifying parameters such as the number of crease lines, thickness, intensity, stiffness, and resistance to propagation. The approach is geometric and fast; it allows the animator to intuitively control over many salient visual features of wrinkle formation and propagation. Figure 16 illustrates this with a curtain animated using wires. A dynamic simulation of the wire curves results in a bead-curtain like animation. The wires then deform the object surface.

5.2 Stitching Object Surfaces

A wire-based geometry stitcher is a two step process. The first is the creation of wire curves along two edges of the geometry to be stitched. The wire curves are then blended pairwise to common seams. The object surfaces track the common seam, resulting in a stitch. We reparametrize the matching edges to a common domain before defining the stitch. Figure 17 depicts the stitching of one edge onto the other. Figure 18 demonstrates the levels of control available as various parameters are changed. These parameters give control not only over the stitch but also over the tearing of the stitch through the use and animation of locators along the seam (see Figure 18(f)). Figure 19 shows the results of a four-way stitch.

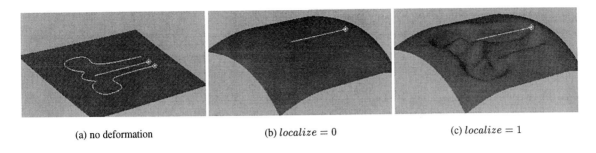

(a) no deformation   (b) $localize = 0$ (c) $localize = 1$

Figure 12: Localized influence of wires.

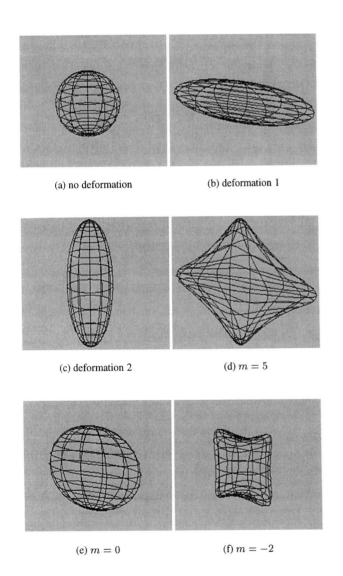

(a) no deformation   (b) deformation 1

(c) deformation 2   (d) $m = 5$

(e) $m = 0$ (f) $m = -2$

Figure 11: Integration of two squash-stretch deformations using wires and different values of m.

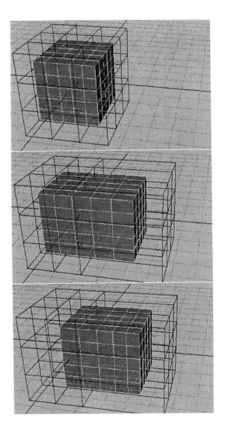

Figure 13: Wires simulating a free-form deformation lattice. Above, (a): no deformation. Middle, (b): deformed with $localize = 1$. Below, (c): deformed with $localize = 0$.

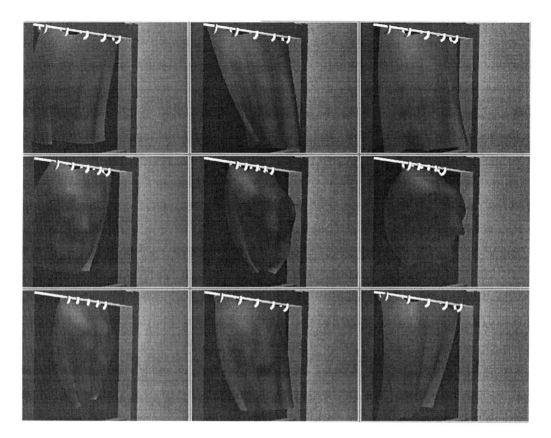

Figure 16: Curtain animation.

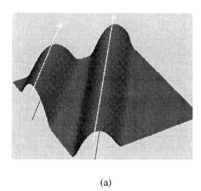

(a)

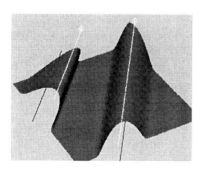

(b)

Figure 14: Wrinkle propagation using reference curves.

There are two shortcomings of the above approach. The first is that since each object is deformed independently, high orders of surface continuity across the stitch cannot be guaranteed. The control afforded by wire parameters r, s and f in particular, alleviates this to an extent. Second, seams are currently stitched pair-wise, thus imposing a stitching order, which can be restrictive.

5.3 Kinematics for flexible skeletons

Inverse kinematics on joint chains driving attached object geometry is popular for articulated-figure animation. Most IK solvers, especially efficient single chain solvers, have a problem with segments that scale non-uniformly during animation. This is essential if, for example, we wish to model a character with partially elastic bones. We replace a joint chain with a curve passing through it, so the control polygon of the curve acts like an articulated rigid body. We also introduce a rubberband like behavior by transforming the control points of the curve proportionally along the joint chain based on the motion of the end effector. The result is a semi-elastic skeletal curve. The curve then deforms the object geometry associated with the joint hierarchy as a wire. We use a large dropoff radius r so we can assume that every point on the geometry will track the curve equally and precisely (see Figure 5(b)). This in itself takes care of smoothing the regions around joints that often require special techniques to solve. Further, the arc-length of the wire curve is used to modulate the wire scale factor s, providing visually realistic volume preservation of the geometry on elastic deformations. Figure 20 shows the deformation to an arm as the kinematic solution is varied from perfectly rigid to perfectly elastic.

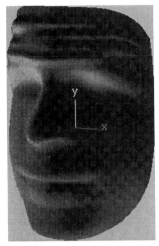

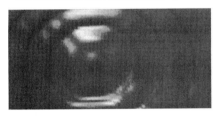

Figure 15: Procedural wrinkles. Top, (a): Tangential. Middle, (b): Radial. Bottom, (c): Ripple.

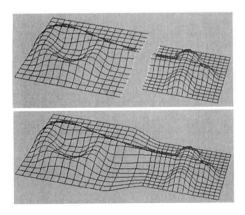

Figure 17: Simple stitch on two surfaces.

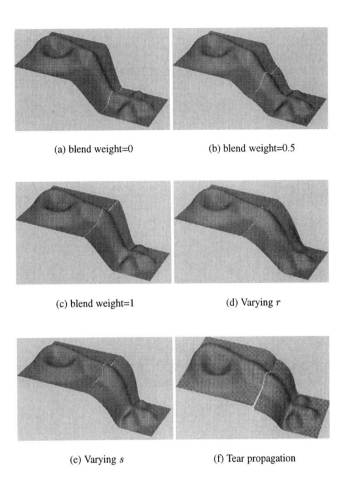

(a) blend weight=0   (b) blend weight=0.5

(c) blend weight=1   (d) Varying r

(e) Varying s (f) Tear propagation

Figure 18: Control over stitch parameters.

6 Discussion

This paper has presented an effective geometric deformation technique, employing space curves and implicit functions that cleanly aggregate to deform an object. Our system has been completely implemented as a module in Alias|wavefront's *Maya* production modeling, animation and rendering graphics product. The slowest part of the algorithm is the closest-point on curve [14] calculation p_R for points P of the object geometry. Fortunately, this can be precomputed for each point P and must be recalculated only if the reference curve R is changed. In such cases, many values can be preprocessed, reducing the online wire deformation algorithm to a few vector operations per control vertex of the object geometry. Multiple wire interactions are accumulated incrementally in one pass.

Wire deformations work very well alone or in combination with existing techniques. FFDs, for example, are well suited for volume-oriented deformations. Arbitrarily shaped lattices can be cumbersome to construct for finer surface-oriented deformations. FFD lattices also usually have far more control points than wire curves for deformations of similar complexity. Wire curves can help by providing higher level control for lattice points to make complex FFD lattices more tractable (see Figure 21). Conversely, wires can emulate FFD lattices (see Figure 13).

Wires allow one to localize the complexity of a deformation on an object, and they provide a caricature of the object being modeled. The coupling of deformation and geometry is a significant advantage of wires. The technique also makes it easy to work in a

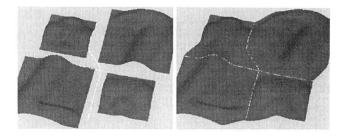

Figure 19: Four-Way stitch. Above, (a): the individual patches. Below, (b): the stitched patches.

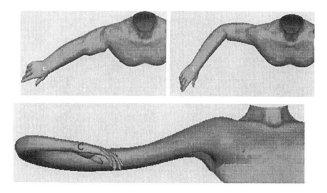

Figure 20: Inverse Kinematics for highly flexible skeletons.

multi-scale fashion. At the highest level a user may simply create a few wire curves, associate them with an object and move them around to verify that the object's surface properly tracks the motion of the curves. The region of the surface to be influenced can then be refined by adding domain curves and locators to the wires; finer-scale deformations can be added with more wires.

A point of comparison to our approach is "curve on surface" manipulation techniques that are found in some CAGD systems. There, least-squares techniques are used to isolate the control vertices relevant to a curve placed on or near a surface so that motion of the curve displaces the control points, which in turn changes the surface. Wires in most ways are a superior interaction technique because they are easier for a user to control, they are efficiently computed, and they apply to more general object representations. For surface patches with a low density of control points, changing a surface by deforming control points may not be as precise as a least squares solution, and it can suffer from aliasing artifacts.

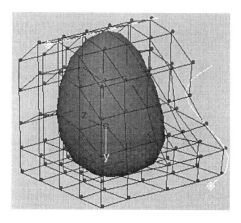

Figure 21: Deformation of a lattice by a wire.

In our implementation, some of our geometric algorithms could be made more efficient. Both finding the closest-point on curve and finding the region of influence of domain curves are good candidates for reworking. In our formulation in Section 2, we noted that there may be several closest points on a curve to a point in space. In cases of wire curves with of high curvature, the policy of picking the closest point with the smallest parameter value can cause singularities in the deformation. Such cases can be handled heuristically by breaking a wire curve into multiple wire curves in regions of high curvature.[3] While subdivision is rarely necessary, it is worth improving our policy to see if extreme cases can be handled automatically.

Acknowledgements

We thank Tom Sederberg and Kris Klimaszewski for their editorial help in the final stages of the paper, as well as the anonymous reviewers. Jeff Bell, Lincoln Holme and the animator geeks of Alias|wavefront were invaluable for their technical and creative help with this project. Finally, our congratulations and gratitude to the wonderful technical staff at Alias|wavefront who made *Maya* a reality. It is a remarkable accomplishment.

References

[1] A. Barr. Superquadrics and angle-preserving transformations. *IEEE Computer Graphics and Applications*, 1:1–20, 1981.

[2] T. Beier and S. Neely. Feature based image metamorphosis. *Computer Graphics*, 26(2):35–42, 1992.

[3] J. Bloomenthal and B. Wyvill. Interactive techniques for implicit modeling. *Computer Graphics*, 24(4):109–116, 1990.

[4] J. Bloomenthal and K. Shoemake. Convolution surfaces. *Computer Graphics*, 25(4):251–256, 1991.

[5] J. Chadwick, D. Haumann and R. Parent. Layered construction for deformable animated characters. *Computer Graphics*, 23(3):234–243, 1989.

[6] Y.K. Chang and A.P. Rockwood. A generalized de Casteljau approach to 3D free-form deformation. *Computer Graphics*, 28(4):257–260, 1994.

[7] S. Coquillart. Extended free-form deformations: A sculpting tool for 3D geometric modeling. *Computer Graphics*, 24(4):187–196, 1990.

[8] M.-P. Gascuel. An implicit formulation for precise contact modeling between flexible solids. *Proc. of SIGGRAPH*, pages 313–320, 1993.

[9] W. Hsu, J. Hughes and H. Kaufman. Direct manipulation of free-form deformations. *Computer Graphics*, 26(2):177–184, 1992.

[10] R. MacCracken and K. Joy. Free-form deformations with lattices of arbitrary topology. *Computer Graphics*, 181–189, 1996.

[11] N. Magnenat-Thalmann and Y. Yang. Techniques for cloth animation. *SIGGRAPH Course Notes C20*, 151–163, 1991.

[12] F. Lazarus, S. Coquillart, and P. Jancene. Axial deformations: an intuitive deformation technique. *Computer-Aided Design*, 26(8):607-613, August 1994.

[13] T. Sederberg and S. Parry. Free-form deformation of solid geometric models. *Computer Graphics*, 20:151–160, 1986.

[14] P. Schneider. Solving the Nearest-Point-on-Curve Problem. *Graphics Gems*, Academic Press, vol.1:607–612, 1990.

[15] G. Wyvill, C. McPheeters and B. Wyvill. Animating soft objects. *Visual Computer*, 2:235–242, 1986.

---

[3]Recall from Section 4 that our formulation ensures that abutting wires do not introduce seaming or bulging artifacts.

A New Voronoi-Based Surface Reconstruction Algorithm

Nina Amenta*
UT - Austin

Marshall Bern
Xerox PARC

Manolis Kamvysselis[†]
M.I.T.

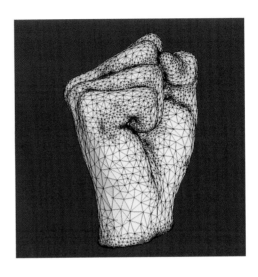

Abstract

We describe our experience with a new algorithm for the reconstruction of surfaces from unorganized sample points in $\mathbb{R}^3$. The algorithm is the first for this problem with provable guarantees. Given a "good sample" from a smooth surface, the output is guaranteed to be topologically correct and convergent to the original surface as the sampling density increases. The definition of a good sample is itself interesting: the required sampling density varies locally, rigorously capturing the intuitive notion that featureless areas can be reconstructed from fewer samples. The output mesh interpolates, rather than approximates, the input points.

Our algorithm is based on the three-dimensional Voronoi diagram. Given a good program for this fundamental subroutine, the algorithm is quite easy to implement.

Keywords: Medial axis, Sampling, Delaunay triangulation, Computational Geometry

1 Introduction

The process of turning a set of sample points in $\mathbb{R}^3$ into a computer graphics model generally involves several steps: the reconstruction of an initial piecewise-linear model, cleanup, simplification, and perhaps fitting with curved surface patches.

We focus on the first step, and in particular on an abstract problem defined by Hoppe, DeRose, Duchamp, McDonald, and Stuetzle [14]. In this formulation, the input is a set of points in $\mathbb{R}^3$, without any additional structure or organization, and the desired output is a polygonal mesh, possibly with boundary. In practice, sample sets for surface reconstruction come from a variety of sources: medical imagery, laser range scanners, contact probe digitizers, radar and seismic surveys, and mathematical models such as implicit surfaces. While the most effective reconstruction scheme for any one of these applications should take advantage of the special properties of the data, an understanding of the abstract problem should contribute to all of them.

The problem formulation above is incomplete, since presumably we should require some relationship between the input and the output. In this and a companion paper [2], we describe a simple, combinatorial algorithm for which we can prove such a relationship. A

---

*Much of this work was done while the author was employed by Xerox PARC, partially supported by NSF grant CCR-9404113.

[†]Much of this work was done while the author was an intern at Xerox PARC.

Figure 1. The fist mesh was reconstructed from the vertices alone. Notice that the sampling density varies. Our algorithm requires dense sampling only near small features; given such an input, the output mesh is provably correct.

nontrivial part of this work is the fitting of precise definitions to the intuitive notions of a "good sample" and a "correct reconstruction". Although the actual definition of a good sample is rather technical, involving the medial axis of the original surface, Figure 1 gives the general idea: dense in detailed areas and (possibly) sparse in featureless ones.

The algorithm is based on the three-dimensional Voronoi diagram and Delaunay triangulation; it produces a set of triangles that we call the *crust* of the sample points. All vertices of crust triangles are sample points; in fact, all crust triangles appear in the Delaunay triangulation of the sample points.

The companion paper [2] presents our theoretical results. In that paper, we prove that given a good sample from a smooth surface, the output of our reconstruction algorithm is topologically equivalent to the surface, and that as the sampling density increases, the output converges to the surface, both pointwise and in surface normal.

Theoretical guarantees, however, do not imply that an algorithm is useful in practice. Surfaces are not everywhere smooth, samples do not everywhere meet the sampling density conditions, and sample points contain noise. Even on good inputs, an algorithm may fail to be robust, and the constants on the running time might be prohibitively large. In this paper, we report on our implementation of the algorithm, its efficiency and the quality of the output.

Overall, we were pleased. The program gave intuitively reasonable outputs on inputs for which the theoretical results do not apply. The implementation, using a freely available exact-arithmetic Voronoi diagram code, was quite easy, and reasonably efficient: it can handle 10,000 points in a matter of minutes. The main difficulty, both in theory and in practice, is the reconstruction of sharp edges.

2 Related work

The idea of using Voronoi diagrams and Delaunay triangulations in surface reconstruction is not new. The well–known *α-shape* of Edelsbrunner et al. [9, 10] is a parameterized construction that associates a polyhedral shape with an unorganized set of points. A simplex (edge, triangle, or tetrahedron) is included in the α-shape if it has some circumsphere with interior empty of sample points, of radius at most α (a circumsphere of a simplex has the vertices of the simplex on its boundary). The *spectrum* of α-shapes, that is, the α-shapes for all possible values of α, gives an idea of the overall shape and natural dimensionality of the point set. Edelsbrunner and Mücke experimented with using α-shapes for surface reconstruction [10], and Bajaj, Bernardini, and Xu [4] have recently used α-shapes as a first step in the entire reconstruction pipeline.

An early Delaunay-based algorithm, similar in spirit to our own, is the "Delaunay sculpting" heuristic of Boissonnat [6], which progressively eliminates tetrahedra from the Delaunay triangulation based on their circumspheres. In two dimensions, there are a number of recent theoretical results on various Delaunay-based approaches to reconstructing smooth curves. Attali [3], Bernardini and Bajaj [5], Figueiredo and Miranda Gomes [11] and ourselves [1] have all given guarantees for different algorithms.

A fundamentally different approach to reconstruction is to use the input points to define a signed distance function on $\mathbb{R}^3$, and then polygonalize its zero-set to create the output mesh. Such *zero-set* algorithms produce approximating, rather than interpolating, meshes. This approach was taken by Hoppe et al. [14, 13] and more recently by Curless and Levoy [8]. Hoppe et al. determine an approximate tangent plane at each sample point using least squares on k nearest neighbors, and then take the signed distance to the nearest point's tangent plane as the distance function on $\mathbb{R}^3$. The distance function is then interpolated and polygonalized by the marching cubes algorithm. The algorithm of Curless and Levoy is tuned for laser range data, from which they derive error and tangent plane information. They combine the samples into a continuous volumetric function, computed and stored on a voxel grid. A subsequent hole-filling step also uses problem-specific information. Their implementation is especially fast and robust, capable of handling very large data sets.

Functionally our crust algorithm differs from both the α-shape and the zero-set algorithms. It overcomes the main drawback of α-shapes as applied to surface reconstruction, which is that the parameter α must be chosen experimentally, and in many cases there is no ideal value of α due to variations in the sampling density. The crust algorithm requires no such parameter; it in effect automatically computes the parameter locally. Allowing the sampling density to vary locally enables detailed reconstructions from much smaller input sets.

Like the α-shape, the crust can be considered an intrinsic construction on the point set. But unlike the α-shape, the crust is naturally two-dimensional. This property makes the crust more suitable for surface reconstruction, although less suitable for determining the natural dimensionality of a point set.

The crust algorithm is simpler and more direct than the zero-set approach. Zero-set algorithms, which produce approximating rather than interpolating surfaces, inherently do some low-pass filtering of the data. This is desirable in the presence of noise, but causes some loss of information. We believe that some of our ideas, particularly the sampling criterion and the normal estimation method, can be applied to zero-set algorithms as well, and might be useful in proving some zero-set algorithm correct.

With its explicit sampling criterion, our algorithm should be most useful in applications in which the sampling density is easy to control. Two examples are digitizing an object with a hand-held contact probe, where the operator can "eyeball" the required density, and polygonalizing an implicit surface using sample points [12], where the distribution can be controlled analytically.

3 Sampling Criterion

Our theoretical results assume a *smooth surface*, by which we mean a twice-differentiable manifold embedded in $\mathbb{R}^d$. Notice that this allows all orientable manifolds, including those with multiple connected components.

3.1 Geometry

We start by reviewing some standard geometric constructions. Given a discrete set S of sample points in $\mathbb{R}^d$, the *Voronoi cell* of a sample point is that part of $\mathbb{R}^d$ closer to it than to any other sample. The *Voronoi diagram* is the decomposition of $\mathbb{R}^d$ induced by the Voronoi cells. Each Voronoi cell is a convex polytope, and its vertices are the *Voronoi vertices*; when S is nondegenerate, each Voronoi vertex is equidistant from exactly $d + 1$ points of S. These $d + 1$ points are the vertices of the *Delaunay simplex*, dual to the Voronoi vertex. A Delaunay simplex, and hence each of its faces, has a circumsphere empty of other points of S. The set of Delaunay simplices form the *Delaunay triangulation* of S. Computing the Delaunay triangulation essentially computes the Voronoi diagram as well. See Figure 5 for two-dimensional examples.

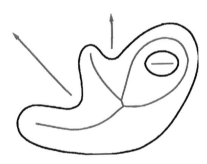

Figure 2. The red curves are the medial axis of the black curves. Notice that components of the medial axis lie on either side of the black curves.

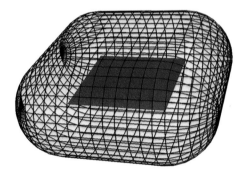

Figure 3. In three dimensions, the medial axis of a surface is generally a two-dimensional surface. Here, the square is the medial axis of the rounded transparent surface. A nonconvex surface would have components of the medial axis on the outside as well, as in the 2D example of Figure 2.

The *medial axis* of a $(d - 1)$-dimensional surface in $\mathbb{R}^d$ is (the closure of) the set of points with more than one closest point on the surface. An example in $\mathbb{R}^2$ is shown in Figure 2, and in $\mathbb{R}^3$ in Figure 3. This definition of the medial axis includes components on the exterior of a closed surface. The medial axis is the extension to continuous surfaces of the Voronoi diagram, in the sense that the to continuous surfaces of the Voronoi diagram, since the Voronoi diagram of S can be defined as the set of points with more than one closest point in S.

In two dimensions, the Voronoi vertices of a dense set of sample points on a curve approximate the medial axis of the curve. Somewhat surprisingly—a number of authors have been misled—this nice property does not extend to three dimensions.

3.2 Definition

We can now describe our sampling criterion. A good sample is one in which the sampling density is (at least) inversely proportional to the distance to the medial axis. Specifically, a sample S is an *r-sample* from a surface F when the Euclidean distance from any point $p \in F$ to the nearest sample point is at most r times the distance from p to the nearest point of the medial axis of F.

The constant of proportionality r is generally less than one. In the companion paper [2], we prove our theorems for rather small values of r such as $r \leq .06$, but the bounds are not tight. So very dense sampling to really apply the theoretical results.

We observe that in practice $r = .5$ generally suffices. Figure 4 shows a reconstruction from a dense sample, and from a sample thinned to roughly $r = .5$. We did not compute the medial axis, which can be quite a chore. Instead, we used the distance to the nearest "pole" (see Section 4.2) as a reasonable, and easily computed, estimate of the distance to the medial axis.

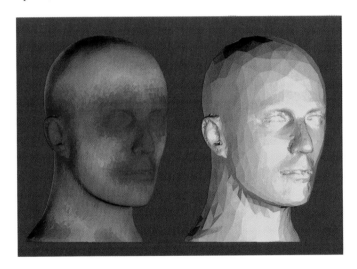

Figure 4. The sampling spacing required to correctly reconstruct a surface is proportional to the distance to the medial axis. On the left is a surface reconstructed from a dense sample. The color represents estimated distance to medial axis—red means close. On the right, we use the estimated distance to thin the data to a .5-sample (meaning that the distance to the nearest sample for any point on the surface is at most half the distance to the medial axis), and then reconstruct. There were about 12K samples on the left and about 3K on the right.

Notice that our sampling criterion places no constraints on the distribution of points, so long as they are sufficiently dense. It inherently takes into account both the curvature of the surface—the medial axis is close to the surface where the curvature is high—and also the proximity of other parts of the surface. For instance, although the middle of a thin plate has low curvature, it must be sampled densely to resolve the two sides as separate surfaces. In this situation an r-sample differs from the distribution of vertices typically produced by mesh simplification algorithms, which only need to consider curvature.

At sharp edges and corners, the medial axis actually touches the surface. Accordingly, our criterion requires infinitely dense sam-

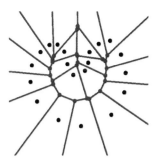

Figure 5. The two-dimensional algorithm. On the left, the Voronoi diagram of a point set S sampled from a curve. Just as S approximates the curve, the Voronoi vertices V approximate the medial axis of the curve. On the right, the the Delaunay triangulation of $S \cup V$, with the crust edges in black. Theorem 1 states that when S is an r-sample, for sufficintly small r, the crust edges connect only adjacent vertices.

pling to guarantee reconstruction. Sharp edges are indeed a problem in practice as well, although the reconstruction errors are not noticable when the sampling is very dense. We discuss a heuristic approach to resolving sharp edges in Section 6, and propose a stronger theoretical approach in Section 7.

4 The crust algorithm

4.1 Two Dimensions

We begin with a two-dimensional version of the algorithm [1]. In this case, the crust will be a graph on the set of sample points S. We define the crust as follows: an edge e belongs to the crust if e has a circumcircle empty not only of all other sample points but also of all Voronoi vertices of S. The crust obeys the following theorem [1].

Theorem 1. *The crust of an r-sample from a smooth curve F, for $r \leq .25$, connects only adjacent sample points on F.*

The medial axis provides the intuition behind this theorem. An important lemma is that for any sample S, an edge between two nonadjacent sample points cannot be circumscribed by a circle that misses both the medial axis and all other samples. When S is an r-sample for sufficinetly small r, the Voronoi vertices approximate the medial axis, and any circumcircle of an edge between nonadjacent samples contains either another sample or a Voronoi vertex. An edge between two adjacent samples, on the other hand, is circumscribed by a small circle, far away from the medial axis and hence from all Voronoi vertices.

The definition of the two-dimensional crust leads to the following simple algorithm, illustrated in Figure 5. First compute the Voronoi diagram of S, and let V be the set of Voronoi vertices. Then compute the Delaunay triangulation of $S \cup V$. The crust consists of the Delaunay edges between points of S, since those are the edges with circumcircles empty of points in $S \cup V$. Notice that the crust is also a subset of the Delaunay triangulation of the input points; adding the Voronoi vertices filters out the unwanted edges from the Delaunay triangulation. We call this technique *Voronoi filtering*.

4.2 Three Dimensions

This simple Voronoi filtering algorithm runs into a snag in three dimensions. The nice property that all the Voronoi vertices of a sufficiently dense sample lie near the medial axis is no longer true.

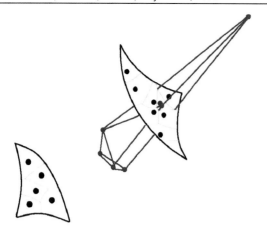

Figure 6. In three dimensions, we can use only a subset of the Voronoi vertices, since not all Voronoi vertices contribute to the approximation of the medial axis. Here, one sample on a curved surface is colored blue, and the edges of its three-dimensional Voronoi cell are drawn in red. One red Voronoi vertex lies near the surface, equidistant from the four samples near the center. The others lie near the medial axis, near the center of curvature on one side and halfway to an opposite patch of the surface on the other.

On the other hand, many of the three-dimensional Voronoi vertices *do* lie near the medial axis. Consider the Voronoi cell V_s of a sample s, as in Figure 6. The sample s is surrounded on F by other samples, and V_s is bounded by bisecting planes separating s from its neighbors, each plane nearly perpendicular to F. So the Voronoi cell V_s is long, thin and roughly perpendicular to F at s. V_s extends perpendicularly out to the medial axis. Near the medial axis, other samples on F become closer than s, and V_s is cut off. This guarantees that some vertices of V_s lie near the medial axis. We give a precise and quantitative version of this rough argument in [2].

This leads to the following algorithm. Instead of using all of the Voronoi vertices in the Voronoi filtering step, for each sample s we use only the two vertices of V_s farthest from s, one on either side of the surface F. We call these the *poles* of s, and denote them p^+ and p^-. It is easy to find one pole, say p^+: the farthest vertex of V_s from s. The observation that V_s is long and thin implies that the other pole p^- must lie roughly in the opposite direction. Thus in the basic algorithm below, we simply choose p^- to be farthest vertex from s such that sp^- and sp^+ have negative dot-product. Here is the basic algorithm:

1. *Compute the Voronoi diagram of the sample points S*

2. *For each sample point s do:*

    (a) *If s does not lie on the convex hull, let p^+ be the farthest Voronoi vertex of V_s from s. Let n^+ be the vector $sp+$.*

    (b) *If s lies on the convex hull, let n^+ be the average of the outer normals of the adjacent triangles.*

    (c) *Let p^- be the Voronoi vertex of V_s with negative projection on n^+ that is farthest from s.*

3. *Let P be the set of all poles p^+ and p^-. Compute the Delaunay triangulation of $S \cup P$.*

4. *Keep only those triangles for which all three vertices are sample points in S.*

Notice that one does not need an estimate of r to use the crust algorithm; the basic algorithm requires no tunable parameters at all. The output of this algorithm, the *three-dimensional crust*, is a set of triangles that resembles the input surface geometrically. More precisely, we prove the following theorem [2].

Theorem 2. *Let S be an r-sample from a smooth surface F, for $r \leq .06$. Then 1) the crust of S contains a set of triangles forming a mesh topologically equivalent to F, and 2) every point on the crust lies within distance $5r \cdot d(p)$ of some point p on F, where $d(p)$ is the distance from p to the medial axis.*

The crust, however, is not necessarily a manifold; for example, it often contains all four triangles of a very flat "sliver" tetrahedron. It is, however, a visually acceptable model.

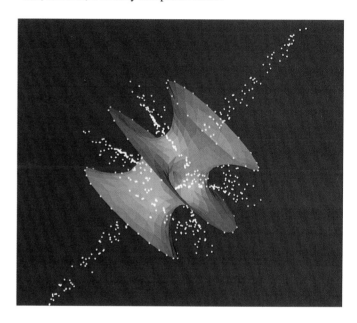

Figure 7. The crust of a set of sample points and the poles (white points) used in its reconstruction. Each sample selects the two vertices of its Voronoi cell that are farthest away, one on either side of the surface, as poles. The poles lie near the medial axis of the surface, sketching planes separating opposite sheets of surface that degenerate to one-dimensional curves where the cross-section of the surface is circular.

4.3 Normal Estimation and Filtering

Additional filtering is required to produce a guaranteed piecewise-linear manifold homeomorphic to F, and to ensure that the output converges in surface normal as the sampling density increases.

In fact, whatever the sampling density, the algorithm above may output some very thin crust triangles nearly perpendicular to the surface. We have an important lemma [2], however, which states that the vectors $n^+ = sp^+$ and $n^- = sp^-$ from a sample point to its poles are guaranteed to be nearly orthogonal to the surface at s. The angular error is linear in r. The intuition (put nicely by Ken Clarkson) is that the surface normal is easy to estimate from a point far away, such as a pole p, since the surface must be nearly normal to the largest empty ball centered at p.

We can use these vectors in an additional *normal filtering* step, throwing out any triangles whose normals differ too much from n^+ or n^-. When normal filtering is used, the normals of the output triangles approach the surface normals as the sampling density increases. We prove in [2] that the remaining set of triangles still contains a subset forming a piecewise-linear surface homeomorphic to F.

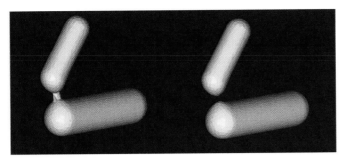

Figure 8. The crust of points distributed on an implicit surface (left). The additional normal filtering step is needed to separate the two connected components (right), which are undersampled at their closest point. Triangles are deleted if their normals differ too much from the direction vectors from the triangle vertices to their poles. These vectors are provably close to the surface normals.

Normal filtering can be useful in practice as well, as shown in Figure 8. In the usual case in which r is unknown the allowable difference in angle must be selected experimentally. Normal filtering can be dangerous, however, at boundaries and sharp edges. The directions of n^+ and n^- are not nearly normal to all nearby tangent planes, and desirable triangles might be deleted.

We note that n^+ and n^-, our Voronoi-based estimates of normal direction, could be useful in the zero-set reconstruction methods, which depend on accurate estimation of the tangent planes. For the algorithm of Hoppe et al. [14], a Voronoi-based estimate could replace the estimate based on the k-nearest neighbors. The Voronoi-based estimate has the advantage that it is not sensitive to the distribution; whereas, for instance, on medical image data, all k nearest neighbors might lie in the same slice, and so would the estimated tangent plane. In the algorithm of Curless and Levoy [8], the Voronoi-based estimate could be checked against the bounds on normal direction derived from the laser-range scanner.

4.4 Manifold Extraction

After the normal filtering step, all the remaining triangles are roughly parallel to the surface. We can define a sharp edge as one which is adjacent to triangles only on one side of a plane through the edge and roughly perpendicular to the surface. Notice that an edge of degree one counts as a sharp edge. If the surface F is indeed a smooth manifold without boundary, we are guaranteed that the normal-filtered crust contains a piecewise-linear manifold homeomorphic to F. Any triangle adjacent to a sharp edge cannot belong to this piecewise-linear manifold, and can be safely deleted. We continue recursively until no such triangle remains. A piecewise-linear manifold can then be obtained by a *manifold extraction* step which takes the outside surface of the remaining triangles on each connected component. This simple approach, however, cannot be applied when F is not a smooth manifold without boundary. In that case we do not know how to prove that we can extract a manifold homeomorphic to F.

4.5 Complexity

The asymptotic complexity of the crust algorithm is $O(n^2)$ where $n = |S|$, since that is the worst-case time required to compute a three-dimensional Delaunay triangulation. Notice that the number of sample points plus poles is at most $3n$. As has been frequently observed, the worst-case complexity for the three-dimensional Delaunay triangulation almost never arises in practice. All other steps are linear time.

5 Implementation

5.1 Numerical Issues

Robustness has traditionally been a concern when implementing combinatorial algorithms like this one. Our straightforward implementation, however, is very robust. This success is due in large part to the rapidly improving state of the art in Delaunay triangulation programs. We used Clarkson's *Hull* program. *Hull* uses exact integer arithmetic, and hence is thoroughly robust, produces exact output, and requires no arithmetic tolerancing parameters. The performance cost for the exact arithmetic is fairly modest, due to a clever adaptive precision scheme. We chose *Hull* so that we could be sure that numerical problems that arose were our own and did not originate in the triangulation. Finding the exact Delaunay triangulation is not essential to our algorithm.

Hull outputs a list of Delaunay tetrahedra, but not the coordinates of their circumcenters (the dual Voronoi vertices) which always contain some roundoff error. Fortunately, the exact positions of the poles are not important, as the numerical error is tiny relative to the distance between the poles and the surface. We computed the location of each Voronoi vertex by solving a 4×4 linear system with a solver from *LAPACK*. The solver also returns the condition number of the coefficient matrix, which we used to reject unreliable Voronoi vertices. Rejected Voronoi vertices were almost always circumcenters of "slivers" (nearly planar tetrahedra) lying flat on the surface; for a good sample such vertices cannot be poles. It is possible that this method also rejects some valid poles induced by very flat tetrahedra spanning two patches of surface. We have not, however, observed any problems in practice. Presumably there is always another Voronoi vertex nearby that makes an equally good pole.

5.2 Efficiency

Running times for the reconstruction of some large data sets are given in the table below; the reconstructions are shown in Figure 9. We used an SGI Onyx with 512M of memory.

Model	Time (min)	Num. Pts.
Femur	2	939
Golf club	12	16864
Foot	15	20021
Bunny	23	35947

The running time is dominated by the time required to compute the Delaunay triangulations. *Hull* uses an incremental algorithm [7], so the running time is sensitive to the input order of the vertices. The triangulation algorithm builds a search structure concurrently with the triangulation itself; the process is analogous to sorting by incrementally building a binary search tree. When points are added in random order, the search structure is balanced (with extremely high probability) and the expected running time is optimal. In practice, random insertions are slow on large inputs, since both the search structure and the Delaunay triangulation begin paging. We obtained better performance by first inserting a random subset of a few thousand points to provide a balanced initial search structure, and then inserting the remaining points based on a crude spatial subdivision to improve locality.

Most likely much greater improvements in efficiency can be achieved by switching to a three-dimensional Delaunay triangulation program that, first, does not use exact arithmetic, and second, uses an algorithm with more locality of reference.

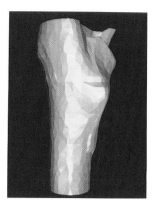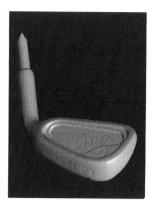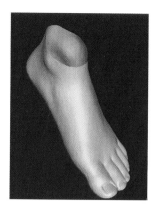

Figure 9. Femur, golf club, foot and bunny reconstructions. Notice the subtle "3" on the bottom of the club (apparently a 3-iron), showing the sensitivity of the algorithm. The foot, like all our reconstructions, is hollow. The bunny was reconstructed from the roughly 36K vertices of the densest of the Stanford bunny models in 23 minutes.

6 Heuristic Modifications

As we have noted, our algorithm does not do well at sharp edges, either in theory or in practice. The reason is that the Voronoi cell of a sample s on a sharp edge is not long and thin, so that the assumptions under which we choose the poles is not correct. For example, the Voronoi cell of a sample s on a right-angled edge is roughly fan-shaped. The vector n^+ directed towards the first pole of s might be perpendicular to one tangent plane at s, but parallel to the other. The second pole would then be chosen very near the surface, punching a hole in the output mesh.

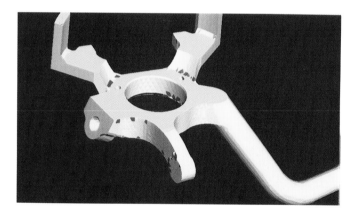

Figure 10. We resolve the sharp edges on this model of a mechanical part by using the two farthest Voronoi vertices as poles, regardless of direction. The basic algorithm forces the poles to lie in opposite directions, but is only guaranteed to work properly on a smooth surface. The red triangles do not appear in the reconstruction when using the basic algorithm.

We experimented with other methods for choosing the second pole. We found that choosing as p^- the Voronoi vertex with the greatest negative projection in the direction n^+ gave somewhat better results. This modification should retain the theoretical guarantees of the original algorithm. The best reconstructions, however, were produced by a different heuristic: choosing the farthest and the second farthest Voronoi vertices, regardless of direction, as the two poles (see Figure 10). This heuristic is strongly biased against choosing poles near the surface, avoiding gaps near sharp edges but sometimes allowing excess triangles filling in sharp corners. We believe that pathological cases could be constructed in which this fill causes a topologically incorrect reconstruction irrespective of the sampling density.

Boundaries pose similar problems in theory, but the reconstructions produced by the crust algorithm on surfaces with boundaries are usually acceptable. Figure 7 and the foot in Figure 9 are examples of perfectly reconstructed boundaries. When the boundary forms a hole in an otherwise flat surface, with no other parts of the surface nearby, the crust algorithm fills in the hole.

Undersampling also causes holes in the output mesh. For example, consider a sample in the middle of a a flat plate. Although its second pole lies in the correct direction, if there are too few sample points on the opposite side of the plate, the pole may fall near the surface on the opposite side and cause a hole. We experimented with heuristics to compensate for this undersampling effect, and for similar reconstruction errors in undersampled cylindrical regions. We found that moving all poles closer to their samples by some constant fraction allowed thin plates and cylinders to be reconstructed from fewer samples, while sometimes introducing new holes on other parts of the model. We were sometimes able to get a perfect reconstruction by taking the union of a crust made with this modification and one without.

7 Research Directions

We have identified a number of future research directions.

7.1 Noise

Small perturbations of the input points do not cause problems for the crust algorithm, nor do a few outliers. But when the noise level is roughly the same as the sampling density, the algorithm fails, both in theory and in practice. We believe, however, that there is a Voronoi-based algorithm, perhaps combining aspects of crusts and α-shapes, that reconstructs noisy data into a "thickened surface" containing all the input points, some of them possibly in the interior. See Melkemi [15] for some suggestive experimental work in $\mathbb{R}^2$.

7.2 Sharp Edges and Boundaries

We would like to modify the crust algorithm to handle surfaces with sharp edges and to provide theoretical guarantees for the reconstruction of both sharp edges and boundaries. Interpolating reconstruction algorithms like ours have an advantage here, since approximating reconstruction algorithms smooth out sharp edges. One important goal is to develop reliable techniques for identifying samples that lie on sharp edges or boundaries. As noted, the Voronoi cells of such samples are not long and thin. This intuition could be made precise, and perhaps combined with more traditional filtering techniques.

7.3 Using Surface Normals

A variation on the problem is the reconstruction of surfaces from unorganized points that are equipped with normal directions. This problem arises in two-dimensional image processing when connecting edge pixels into edges. In three dimensions, laser range data comes with some normal information, and we have exact normals for points distributed on implicit surfaces. It should be possible to show that with this additional information, reconstruction is possible from much sparser samples. In particular, when normals are available, dense sampling should not be needed to resolve the two sides of a thin plate, suggesting that a different sampling criterion than distance to medial axis is required.

7.4 Compression

One intriguing potential application (pointed out by Frank Bossen) of interpolating, rather than approximating reconstruction, is that it can be used as a lossless mesh compression technique. A model created by interpolating reconstruction can be represented entirely by its vertices, and no connectivity information at all must be stored. A model which differs only slightly from the reconstruction of its vertices can be represented by the vertices and a short list of differences. These differences might be encoded efficiently using some geometrically defined measure of "likelihood" on Delaunay triangles. The vertices themselves could then be ordered so as to optimize properties such as compressibility or progressive reconstruction by an incremental algorithm. With the current best geometry compression method [16], most of the bits are already used to encode the vertex positions, rather than connectivity, but the connectivity is encoded in the ordering of the vertices. Allowing arbitrary vertex orderings could improve compression; we are experimenting with an octree encoding.

Our current crust algorithm is not incremental, and our implementation is too slow for real-time decompression, so this application motivates work in both directions.

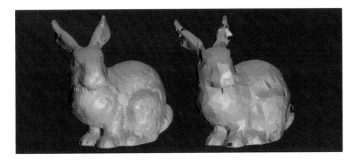

Figure 11. Reconstructions from subsets of the samples resemble the final reconstructions. The crust of the first 5 % of the points in an octree encoding of the bunny samples is still quite recognizable (right); the crust of 20 % of the points is on the left. Rough reconstructions like these could be shown during progressive transmission.

Acknowledgments

We thank David Eppstein (UC–Irvine) for his collaboration in the early stages of this research, and Frank Bossen (EPF–Lausanne) and Ken Clarkson (Lucent) for interesting suggestions. We thank Ping Fu (Raindrop Geomagic) for the fist and the mechanical part, Hughes Hoppe (Microsoft) for the head, the golf club and the foot, Chandrajit Bajaj (UT–Austin) for the femur, Paul Heckbert (CMU) for the hot dogs, and the Stanford Data Repository for the bunny. We thank Ken Clarkson and Lucent Bell Labs for *Hull*, and The Geometry Center at the University of Minnesota for *Geomview*, which we used for viewing and rendering the models.

References

[1] Nina Amenta, Marshall Bern and David Eppstein. The Crust and the β-Skeleton: Combinatorial Curve Reconstruction. To appear in *Graphical Models and Image Processing*.

[2] Nina Amenta and Marshall Bern. Surface reconstruction by Voronoi filtering. To appear in *14th ACM Symposium on Computation Geometry*, June 1998.

[3] D. Attali. r-Regular Shape Reconstruction from Unorganized Points. In *13th ACM Symposium on Computational Geometry*, pages 248–253, June 1997.

[4] C. Bajaj, F. Bernardini, and G. Xu. Automatic Reconstruction of Surfaces and Scalar Fields from 3D Scans. *SIGGRAPH '95 Proceedings*, pages 109–118, July 1995.

[5] F. Bernardini and C. Bajaj. Sampling and reconstructing manifolds using α-shapes, In *9th Canadian Conference on Computational Geometry*, pages 193–198, August 1997.

[6] J-D. Boissonnat. Geometric structures for three-dimensional shape reconstruction, *ACM Transactions on Graphics* 3: 266–286, 1984.

[7] K. Clarkson, K. Mehlhorn and R. Seidel. Four results on randomized incremental constructions. *Computational Geometry: Theory and Applications*, pages 185–121, 1993.

[8] B. Curless and M. Levoy. A volumetric method for building complex models from range images. In *SIGGRAPH '96 Proceedings*, pages 303–312, July 1996.

[9] H. Edelsbrunner, D.G. Kirkpatrick, and R. Seidel. On the shape of a set of points in the plane, *IEEE Transactions on Information Theory* 29:551-559, (1983).

[10] H. Edelsbrunner and E. P. Mücke. Three-dimensional Alpha Shapes. *ACM Transactions on Graphics* 13:43–72, 1994.

[11] L. H. de Figueiredo and J. de Miranda Gomes. Computational morphology of curves. *Visual Computer* 11:105–112, 1995.

[12] A. Witkin and P. Heckbert. Using particles to sample and control implicit surfaces, In *SIGGRAPH '94 Proceedings*, pages 269–277, July 1994.

[13] H. Hoppe. Surface Reconstruction from Unorganized Points. Ph.D. Thesis, Computer Science and Engineering, University of Washington, 1994.

[14] H. Hoppe, T. DeRose, T. Duchamp, J. McDonald, and W. Stuetzle. Surface Reconstruction from Unorganized Points. In *SIGGRAPH '92 Proceedings*, pages 71–78, July 1992.

[15] M. Melkemi, $\mathcal{A}$-shapes and their derivatives, In *13th ACM Symposium on Computational Geometry*, pages 367–369, June 1997

[16] G. Taubin and J. Rossignac. Geometric compression through topological surgery. *Research Report RC20340*, IBM, 1996.

Computer-Generated Floral Ornament

Michael T. Wong   *Douglas E. Zongker*   *David H. Salesin*

University of Washington

Abstract

This paper describes some of the principles of traditional floral ornamental design, and explores ways in which these designs can be created algorithmically. It introduces the idea of "adaptive clip art," which encapsulates the rules for creating a specific ornamental pattern. Adaptive clip art can be used to generate patterns that are tailored to fit a particularly shaped region of the plane. If the region is resized or reshaped, the ornament can be automatically regenerated to fill this new area in an appropriate way. Our ornamental patterns are created in two steps: first, the geometry of the pattern is generated as a set of two-dimensional curves and filled boundaries; second, this geometry is rendered in any number of styles. We demonstrate our approach with a variety of floral ornamental designs.

CR Categories: I.3.3 [Computer Graphics]: Picture/Image Generation; I.3.4 [Computer Graphics]: Graphics Utilities—Picture description languages.

Additional Keywords: adaptive clip art, conventionalization, pattern generation, plant development, ornamentation, texture generation

1   Introduction

> *If I were asked to say what is at once the most important production of Art and the thing most to be longed for, I should answer, A beautiful House; and if I were further asked to name the production next in importance and the thing next to be longed for, I should answer, A beautiful Book. To enjoy good houses and good books in self-respect and decent comfort, seems to me to be the pleasurable end towards which all societies of human beings ought now to struggle.*
>
> — William Morris, 1892 [23]

Ornament is among the oldest forms of human expression, already well developed by the Neolithic Age [6]. Nearly all the commissioned writing of the Middle Ages was decorated with ornament, and the illuminated manuscripts of the 13th century rank among the most beautiful books ever produced.

Even the earliest printed books were often illuminated by hand, but by about 1530 such carefully crafted illumination had all but disappeared [23]. Today, documents are produced with greater ease and in greater number than ever, thanks to ubiquitous desktop publishing tools—yet, beyond the use of static "clip art" elements, these tools provide precious little support for ornamenting the page. Similarly, in architecture, ornament has historically played a critical and famous role. However, most modern buildings, despite the help of sophisticated CAD tools, are largely devoid of these beautiful decorations.

Though technological advances have virtually ignored the creation of ornament, they have at the same time provided new opportunities for its use. The dynamic nature of Web documents encourages ornament to be generated on the fly to accommodate different browser configurations and fonts. New printing processes make it feasible to print on fabric or wallpaper in small runs, raising the possibility of their custom design and production.

This paper therefore provides an early exploration into how aesthetically pleasing ornaments might be generated algorithmically. The method we describe attempts to capture the "essence" of an ornamental pattern, encoding it as a set of rules, which we call *adaptive clip art*. This encoding allows the ornament to be defined in a manner that is independent of a specific areal boundary. The adaptive clip art so described can be used to generate ornaments that are automatically tailored to any particular re-

Figure 1 Design element categories. (a) Geometric forms (after Alhambra tile) [29, plate 29]. Natural forms (b) plants (Gothic vine) [10, fig. 82], (c) animal/human forms (border detail, Germany 1518) [4, plate 30], (d) physiographic forms (17th century Japanese wave motif) [9], (e) artificial objects (Renaissance torches) [21, plate 80].

gion of interest; moreover, if the region is changed, the ornament can be regenerated to fill the new area in an appropriate way.

The automatic creation of aesthetically pleasing ornament is a monumental challenge, which we by no means claim to solve here. Nevertheless, we hope that this paper will offer some interesting new directions, with the hope that further advances may someday help in the creation of beautiful ornaments for our houses and books—and online chat rooms and web pages!

1.1 Problem statement

The problem space of all possible ornamental design is simply enormous. In order to approach the problem at all, we need to limit our domain. We therefore make the following taxonomy (adapted from Meyer [21]).

First, the *elements* of ornamental design can be broken down into three broad categories:

1. *geometrical elements*, such as lines, polygons, ovals, and the like (Figure 1a);
2. *natural forms*, which can be further classified as
    1. plants (Figure 1b),
    2. animal/human forms (Figure 1c),
    3. physiographic features (Figure 1d); and
3. *artificial objects*, such as shields, ribbons, or torches (Figure 1e).

Second, for our purposes we will similarly divide the *applications* of ornament into four main contexts:

A. to *bands*, which have finite thickness in one dimension and are infinitely repeating in the other (Figure 2a);
B. to *half-open borders*, which are tightly constrained along one or more edges, but open in other directions (Figure 2b);
C. to *panels*, which are arbitrary bounded regions of the plane (Figure 2c); and
D. to the *open plane*, in which the ornament typically becomes a repeating pattern (Figure 2d).

In this paper, we restrict the problem space to the case of producing floral growth within panels (case 2.1-C in the classification above). In particular, we will look at the challenging issues of structuring floral ornament according to various principles of ornamental design, such as balance, analogy, and intention—as described in Section 2. We will not, however, focus here on designs involving strict symmetries. As we shall see, the resulting design space is still quite large; however, it is at least constrained enough that we can explore a series of related approaches within the confines of a single research paper. Moreover, we expect that many of the approaches suggested here will be useful, in some form, for other cases in the taxonomy.

In the rest of this paper, we describe a number of principles of floral ornamental design, and we discuss ways in which such designs can be created algorithmically.

Figure 2 Applications of ornament: (a) bands (16th century Germany) [31, plate 34] (b) half-open borders [24, opening page of chapter 7], (c) panels (oak leaf vine from the cathedral of Toledo) [10, fig. 104], (d) open plane [35, fig. 270].

1.2 Related work

The area of ornamental design synthesis has received relatively little attention in the computer graphics community, to our knowledge.

At SIGGRAPH '75 (the 2nd annual SIGGRAPH conference), Alexander described a Fortran program for generating the 17 symmetry patterns in the plane [1]. Grünbaum and Shephard used a more sophisticated computer program to generate periodic tilings and patterns in their landmark text on the subject [14]. However, in both of these cases, the ornamental designs produced are purely geometric and purely on the open plane.

Glassner examined the synthesis of frieze patterns, which can be used for generating textures for band ornaments [11].

Siromoney and Siromoney examined the synthesis of kolam patterns: a form of ephemeral ornament practiced in India where grains of rice are used to trace out designs forming intricate lattices [32]. Their goal, however, was to show how graph grammars could be used to generate instances of such geometric patterns, rather than to create ornament to fill a specified region.

Arvo and Kirk introduced the modeling of plant growth with environmentally sensitive automata [2], Greene examined the growth of plant-like branching structures in voxel space [13], and Prusinkiewicz *et al.* examined the generation of ornamental topiary plant forms with open L-systems [26]. The synthetic structures described in these papers were adaptive to space, but not designed to grow according to conventions of 2D ornamentation.

Smith introduced the graphics community to the modeling of plant growth with a class of parallel rewriting grammars he termed "graftals" [33]. The grammars were used to generate a branching structure, which could then be given visual character through a post-processing step. We use a similar two-step procedure to create first the structure and then the rendering of our ornaments.

In their paper on graphical style sheets, Beach and Stone introduced the idea of procedurally generating a simple repeating border pattern that is warped to follow the path of a spline [3]. This idea was subsequently elaborated by Hsu and Lee, in their papers on "skeletal strokes," to the warping of predefined vector clip art along a path [15, 16]. Skeletal strokes—whose commercial implementation, MetaCreations Expression, we have used to render many of the illustrations in this paper—may be thought of as a rudimentary form of adaptive clip art along curvilinear paths. The work described in this paper builds on their approach by creating a higher-level mechanism for the automatic arrangement of skeletal strokes within arbitrary regions of the plane.

1.3 Overview

The rest of this paper is organized as follows. Section 2 surveys the key principles of floral ornamental design. Section 3 discusses how these principles can be encapsulated algorithmically. Section 4 discusses the framework of our ornamental growth engine. Section 5 presents some of our results, and Section 6 suggests areas for future research. Finally, Appendix A shows in detail some simple examples of using our system.

2 Principles of ornamental design

For our purposes, we will define *ornament* as the aesthetic enrichment of the surfaces of man-made objects in ways not directly contributing to their functional utility. In order to provide a sense of the richness and depth of the problems involved in creating ornament, we will briefly describe some of the principles that underlay its design. The system we have implemented so far addresses only a fraction of these principles.

Let's first look at some of the methods ornamentalists use in conveying a perception of order. We will then explore the particulars of *floral* ornamental design.

2.1 Order in ornament

If there is any one underlying principle of ornament, it is the conveyance of a sense of order or design [12]. Ornamentalists use three principal techniques in conveying a perception of order: repetition, balance, and conformation to geometric constraints [10, 12, 36].

2.1.1 Repetition

Perhaps the most fundamental ordering principle is *repetition*. The repetition of even the simplest mark can form the basis of an ornament. When forms are repeated, they may be repeated exactly through translation and rotation (Figure 3a). Or they may be reflected about some axis, yielding *bilateral symmetry* (Figure 3c) or *glide reflection* (Figure 3b). In many patterns containing rotational symmetries, the point of radiation is positioned off-center from the design elements it controls, leading to a *bilaterally symmetric radiation* (Figure 3d).

A more subtle form of repetition is the use of *analogy*, in which similar, rhythmic controlling lines are used to place and constrain different floral or figurative elements (Figure 3e). In addition, the recurrence of almost any ratio, or *proportion*, in a design can impart a pleasing unity of form. *Color* is another powerful attribute of patterns, orthogonal to shape, that can be used to unify a design through repetition.

While designs based on rigid repetition may appeal to a clean, austere aesthetic, other patterns use *variation* within a class of forms to add organic dynamism to their composition (Figure 3h). This variation may be achieved through *alternation* of color or form (Figure 3f), or through *scaled repetition* (Figure 3g).

2.1.2 Balance

The principle of *balance* requires that asymmetrical visual masses be made of equal weight. Figure 4a shows this principle applied to several compositions. We can also speak of balance in the implicit motion of lines. Crane [8] describes this phenomenon as each new

Figure 3 Repetition: (a) simple translation [4, plate 142], (b) glide reflection [10, plate 14], (c) reflection [36, cover illustration], (d) radiation (late Gothic "pine" ornament) [10], (e) analogous (rhythmic lines in the frieze of the Parthenon) [8], (f) alternation [34, plate 78], (g) scaled [9], (h) organic variation [34, plate 27].

line posing a question that requires an answering line (Figure 4b). We can see both these principles at work in Figure 4c.

The principle of balanced masses, combined with the primal motivation for ornamentation, *horror vacui*, yields the principle of *uniform density*: ornament should uniformly fill its allotted space. In some ornaments, elements of similar mass are distributed non-uniformly in space. In this case, their unequal distribution can be balanced with different elements of a smaller scale. This type of ordering leads to a balance within and among levels of hierarchies of visual mass (Figure 4d).

2.1.3 Conformation to geometric constraints

Since ornament must live within the boundaries of the objects it seeks to enrich, the design process must generally begin with a consideration of geometric constraints.

First and foremost, a careful *fitting to boundaries* is a hallmark of ornament from many cultures. Often, the period of a meandering vine, for instance, has to be adjusted not only to fit properly between the

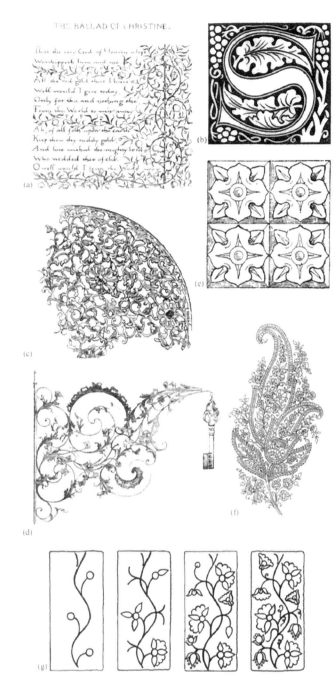

Figure 4 Balance: (a) in composition [8], (b) question and answer within lines [8], (c) combined [36, fig. 126], (d) hierarchical [5, title page].

top and bottom edges of the panel, but also to provide appropriate positions for secondary shoots to invade other portions of the ornamented region (Figure 5a). In addition, the shapes of the design elements themselves are sometimes deformed to better fill space (Figure 5b).

In many vining motifs, elements are made to grow together tangentially. This principle of *tangential junction* lends a powerful sense of *teleological*, or ends-driven, design to the composition. For obvious reasons of structural integrity, tangential junction is also important for ornament that is "cut through" or must otherwise hang together, such as the open-work bronze basket in Figure 5c, and the sign support in Figure 5d.

A further principle ordering the layout of motifs is placement at signal geometric points such as points of maximum concavity or convexity, as in the rosettes of Figure 5e. When filling a region that has distinct corners, a design element is almost always dedicated to the task of filling each corner. When accomplishing this task with a growth motif, the growth is often coordinated by the skeleton of the region to be filled, as demonstrated by the paisley in Figure 5f.

The design of ornament frequently proceeds through the subdivision of an area followed by the filling of the divisions. Figure 5g shows the sequence of steps taken by a 19th-century textile designer from India in laying out a woodblock print. Since the act of filling may also be viewed as one of subdivision, the process may be recursively repeated, leading to a many-tiered *hierarchical composition* in the final design.

2.2 Floral ornament

For our purposes, we will define *floral ornament* as any ornamental design process involving plant-like growth models, such as branching structures; or plant-like elements, such as vines, leaves, or flowers.

In this section we will first examine the peculiar qualities of *growth* that distinguishes it as a progenitor of ornamental design. We will then discuss how plant-like structures can be transformed into ornamental elements through the process of *conventionalization*.

Figure 5 Conformation to geometric constraints: (a) fitting meander period (drawn after [22, p. 35]), (b) deformation of design elements [24], (c) tangential junction (drawn after [19, p. 107]), (d) tangential junction (drawn after [12, fig. 66]), (e) signal geometric points [36, fig. 99], (f) following skeleton of a region [25], (g) hierarchical subdivision [6, fig. 213].

2.2.1 Growth

To begin with, it is worth noting that most of the ornamental principles discussed so far are already principles of growth. As Owen Jones observed in the *Grammar of Ornament* [17], "whenever any style of ornament commands universal admiration, it will always be found to be in concordance with the laws which regulate the distribution of form in nature."

Growth is a particularly good source for continuous patterns that fill space and that can logically transport a design into new regions. In Figure 6, design elements are transported by linear trunks and sinuous meanders. Space is filled by smaller spiral branches and half-

Figure 6   Growth transporting a design [10, plate 77].

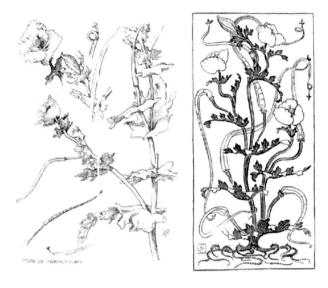

Figure 7   Natural vs. conventional representation [8].

spiral leaves. In addition, the non-rigid repetition of forms derived from natural growth can be used to breathe life into a design.

Another issue of growth as represented in ornament is that it tends to be more highly structured, or ordered, in this context. This ordering property can be described as *intention*. Intention can be defined as the aesthetic perception of teleological growth or placement of form, discernible from multiscale features of a design: its high-level layout; its sinuous sub-motifs and their serial and hierarchical compositions; and, at the lowest level, the continuous change in curvature along a line, a line's modulation in width, and the angles of crossings of lines. In other words, intention is not just the process of growth in the absence of external influences, but rather a way of expressing growth even under such influences. Examples include growth toward pre-placed flowers, or the cooperative formation of symmetric structures, sometimes even from non-analogous locations in an overall branch structure.

2.2.2   Conventionalization

While in common usage the term "convention" has a pejorative ring, implying lack of invention, in ornamental design it can have just the opposite meaning. *Conventionalization* in ornament is the development of abstractions of natural form, a highly creative process. When artists develop a conventionalization they perform a sort of inventive prefiltering of phenomenal reality followed by a creative resynthesis of form. The focus is to extract essential features of form from the vagaries of environmental influence.

In Figure 7 we see a side-by-side comparison of a study drawn from nature and a conventional representation based on that study. Note how the subtle wave of the leaf margins of the poppy get amplified and regularized in its conventionalization. Note also how the form of the seed pods has been stylized to fill space.

3   Approach

We will represent a given adaptive clip art pattern as a set of *elements*, which describe the geometric primitives that comprise the ornament, together with a set of *growth rules*, which describe how the elements are structured in relation to one another and to the boundaries of the panel. The growth rules are invoked by a controlling framework to produce the ornamental pattern, customized for any planar region.

L-systems would appear to be the natural choice for expressing our growth rules, as they have been used to model many plant-like structures. In the rest of this section, therefore, we will take a closer look at the use of L-systems for ornament and discuss the reasons we ultimately chose not to use them. We will then discuss the approach

we took in encoding our adaptive clip art in more detail.

3.1   Using L-systems for ornament

L-systems were developed by biologists seeking to model the development of plants, and they have been extended by the computer graphics community [27, 28, 33] to create realistic plant images and animations. Traditional L-systems do not receive information about the environment. More recently, *open L-systems* have been introduced to allow information from the model's environment to also affect growth [20, 26]. Open L-systems are therefore a reasonable choice for encoding growth rules for ornament. As we discuss below, however, the generation of ornament differs from the growth of real plants in several significant ways that we felt limited the applicability of open L-systems in this context.

First, while floral ornaments may involve leaves, flowers, vines, and so forth, in their conventionalization these elements are often connected and arranged in ways that no plant would ever produce. Biological models are therefore not directly applicable. Indeed, we felt it would be easier, in most cases, to model the *appearance* of an ornament rather than some underlying *process* to produce it. Also, by modeling the appearance of the output directly, we felt we could have tighter control over it.

Second, the environmental feedback loop for real plant growth is indirect: the environment at a given point in space produces chemical changes in the plant that act to alter its further growth. Open L-systems model this loop by alternating "rule application" phases with "environment query" phases—productions leave symbols in the L-string to indicate where queries should be answered by the environment process. These answers can only affect productions in future iterations of the simulation. Thus, a rule for growth that incorporates environment queries must be split into a *set* of productions. We felt that in our case it would be easier to design rules in the form of *procedures*, which could both query the environment and directly act on the results of those queries in placing graphical elements of the ornament.

Finally, L-systems apply all productions to a string in parallel: each element in the string is simultaneously replaced with the result of a rule acting on the element. Rather than trying to define the semantics of parallel rule application when each rule is a procedure, we have chosen to apply our rules serially. A successful iteration of our system, then, consists of the selection of a single element, followed by the incremental growth of that element according to a certain growth rule associated with it. This process also provides an opportunity to integrate some form of global planning into both the selection of the element and the rule being applied.

3.2 Adaptive clip art

Adaptive clip art consists of two parts: *elements* and *growth rules*.

Elements correspond to the 2D geometric primitives that appear in the ornament (e.g., flowers, leaves, and stems); they are the objects upon which the growth rules operate. To provide simplicity without sacrificing the ability to draw detail, each element is defined as a collection of one or more *proxies*. A proxy is a relatively simple geometric shape that represents the element (or a part of the element) for the purposes of locating empty spaces and testing for intersections. When producing final output, a more complicated rendering procedure can be invoked. The use of proxies, therefore, keeps the details of rendering an element separate from the mechanics of positioning it in the design.

Our *growth rules* are specified as procedures. When a rule is invoked on a parent element, the code associated with that rule (the *rule body*) is executed. This code can perform environmental queries and create child elements, among other things. A support library is provided for common environmental queries and for conveniently manipulating geometrical primitives such as proxy shapes.

Finally, our framework for elaborating adaptive clip art uses a limited form of planning in selecting the element for growth on each new iteration. As described in more detail in the next section, the framework attempts first to grow the ornament into large open space, then shifts to filling in corners of the desired region.

4 Implementation

The current implementation consists of approximately 600 lines of Perl (the *preprocessor*) and 3,600 lines of C++ (the *framework*). The preprocessor reads a *rule file* which encodes an ornamental pattern. The preprocessor output is a C++ source file and a corresponding header file, which are compiled with the framework code to produce an executable. This executable can take a region specification and produce the ornamental pattern to fill that particular region. The output generated is a PostScript file. A default rendering is provided for every element, which simply draws each proxy of the element in outline form. The user can attach arbitrary C++ code to each element type within the rule file to generate custom PostScript output if desired. Alternatively, the PostScript output can be converted to paths and rendered with skeletal strokes [15, 16] to produce a wide variety of effects.

We will take a top-down approach to describing the implementation in the next three sections, first describing the way in which elements and rules are selected for growth, then covering the details of how they are specified.

4.1 Rule invocation

The main job of the framework is to decide which elements to "grow" with the rules in order to fill the given space. Let R represent the region to be filled with a pattern. Our heuristic is simple: it finds the largest circle C (modulo some approximation error) that does not intersect the boundary R or any element of the design, and tries invoking rules on the elements within a distance δ of that circle. Elements are tried in order of their distance from the circle. When a rule succeeds (or when all possibilities are exhausted), the iteration ends and a new circle C is selected.

To find the desired circle, we keep a (relatively) low-resolution buffer into which we render the proxies of already placed elements, along with the boundary of the region R. We start small test circles at various points within the region and increase the radius of each circle until it intersects an element or the boundary. If the inflation procedure for a given circle is stopped because the circle hits a boundary, the circle is discarded, since the circle is not adjacent to the existing ornament. If inflation is stopped by hitting an element, the circle is kept. The largest kept circle is chosen as C. The center and radius of C are made available within rule bodies so that rules may direct their growth based on the circle's location.

To determine at which points to center the test circles, we perform a medial axis transformation (MAT) [30] using the Manhattan distance metric. A circle is centered on each pixel whose transform value is at least as great as those of its neighbors. We use these skele-

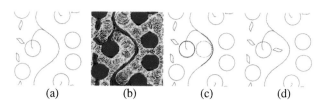

Figure 8 One iteration of the main loop. (a) Elements already in place at the start of the iteration. (b) The render buffer, with points covered by elements and/or the region boundary (in red). Eligible empty-region circles are superimposed in yellow, ineligible circles (on the exclude list) in green. (c) The selected empty circle C (dashed blue lines) and the nearby elements that are candidates for growth (thick purple lines). (d) The ornament after a rule has placed a new leaf.

ton points as centers of the candidate circles to avoid having to perform the circle inflation, which is relatively slow, starting at every uncovered point in the region. The MAT is updated incrementally after each new element is placed.

It is possible that all the rules on all the elements near a given circle C may fail to place new elements. In this case, C would continue to be the largest empty circle available and would immediately be tried again. To prevent the algorithm from falling into an infinite loop, we keep a list of points called the *exclude list*. No circle that intersects a point on the exclude list can be selected as C. If all the elements near a given circle fail to produce new elements, then the center of the circle is placed on the exclude list. A point can be removed from the exclude list in one of two ways. Whenever a rule is successful in placing elements for a circle C, all points within ϵ of that circle's center are removed from the list. The idea is that we want to prevent a failed circle from being eligible until some change has occurred in its vicinity; then it can be tried again. The other way is for a rule body to explicitly clear the list (useful, for instance, if some state change within the rule code allows previously unavailable possibilities for placing elements).

The overall algorithm can be summarized with the following pseudocode. The *FindEmptyCircle* procedure locates the largest empty circle in the region, subject to the two restrictions above. The effects of one iteration of the main loop are illustrated in Figure 8.

```
initialize element tree with seed points
render boundary elements into buffer
compute initial MAT
initialize empty exclude list
repeat
    C ← FindEmptyCircle()
    find elements within δ of C
    try elements in order of distance from C
        try rules in order specified in rule file
            if rule succeeds, break
    if some rule succeeded
        update element tree
        render new elements into buffer
        incrementally update MAT
        remove points on exclude list within ε of C
    else
        add center of empty circle to exclude list
```

4.2 Elements and rules

Each design element has a *type*. The set of available types is declared in the rule file. Each element type is associated with one or more proxies, and zero or more user fields. Available proxies include circles (`circle`), arcs (`arc`), cubic Bézier segments (`bezier`), line segments (`linesegment`), etc. Each element contains a few standard fields (such as the number of children the element has), any user fields given in the element declaration, and proxy objects of the types specified in the declaration. The fields of each proxy are dependent on its type: a `circle` proxy, for instance, has `center` and `radius` fields.

Each rule file must declare the element type `seed`, with a single `point` proxy. Seed elements are placed by the framework in user-selected locations at the beginning of the run to start the ornament.

After the element declaration section of the file is the rule section. Each rule specifies what element type the rule acts on (the *parent*) and what types of children the rule produces. The set of children created by the rule consists of the static children declared in the rule preamble, plus any dynamic children created within the rule. The only difference between static and dynamic children is how they are initialized and how they are referenced within the rule body.

The body of the rule looks very much like a block of C++ code. Anything that is legal within a C++ function is legal within a rule body. Additionally, special dollar-sign tokens provide convenient access to the fields of the parent and child elements. The preprocessor translates these tokens into C++ expressions referring into the data structures of the elements.

Each rule returns a flag to indicate success or failure. On success, the children created by the rule are permanently added to the ornament and a new iteration begins. On failure, the children elements are discarded, and the framework proceeds to try other element/rule combinations as discussed in Section 4.1.

Two detailed examples of patterns implemented with this system are given in Appendix A.

5 Results

Our first set of results shows four different ornamental patterns, each elaborated over two regions.

The first pattern (Figure 9) is based on a pattern taken from a Chinese vase [18, plate 47]. The pattern has two types of stylized flowers laid down in a grid pattern and connected by curving stems. The remaining space is filled with small hook-shaped curves, which themselves are adorned with smaller teardrop shapes. In addition to exhibiting constraints to geometric bounds, this example was chosen to demonstrate "intentional" growth: the large vine appears to deliver its flowers to predefined locations on the grid.

The second pattern (Figure 10) demonstrates the principle of hierarchical growth. The pattern starts from the seed points by growing the vines. It then adds the red flowers and the yellow and blue shapes, connecting them to the main vine structure with shorter subsidiary vines. Next, leaves are added, either attached to a vine or floating on their own, and finally the small double-quote-shaped structure is used to fill in small gaps. This ordering of rule phases is imposed on the system by adding "state" preconditions to each rule, so that any rule that is invoked when the program is not in the right state automatically fails.

The third pattern (Figure 11) is a somewhat less successful attempt, motivated by a William Morris willow-leaf wallpaper. There is only one rule, which grows through the empty circle by adding a curved stem with alternating leaves while preventing the leaves from overlapping too much. This pattern illustrates a shortcoming in our approach, which is that it is difficult to do significant global planning of a design. In our current system, rule invocation is controlled by the empty-space-finding algorithm, so growth always proceeds from the nearest element. For many patterns, it would be better to fill a given space with growth from a more distant element that curves so as to naturally pass through that space. Our "willow" pattern, while covering the region well, is jumbled in comparison to the more elegant original.

The fourth pattern (Figure 12) uses a motif based on an equal-angle spiral, a shape that can be seen in diverse natural forms, from the spiral of a nautilus shell to the curve of a vine tendril [7]. This same pattern is also used, with a different rendering style, to generate the border on the first page of this paper. Each spiral is composed of multiple curved segments, making heavy use of dynamic child creation, since spirals of different lengths require different numbers of segments in order to appear smooth. Each spiral curve is given an orientation opposite to that of its parent. Note how the pattern generates a rhythmic repeat with a period that is related to the changing width of the space; the pattern also simplifies as it wanders into narrower spaces. Although the rules that generate this pattern are not explicitly hierarchical, the appearance of hierarchical structuring is nonetheless formed by placing new elements in, and scaling them to, the largest empty circle adjacent to the growing ornament. The resulting ornament reveals large-scale structures placed in relation to the outline of the boundary space, with finer-scale details placed

in relation to both the boundary space and the evolving ornament.

Figure 13 shows each of these four patterns again, elaborated over differently-shaped panels.

Figure 17 shows the breadth of rendering possibilities provided by the skeletal strokes technique [16]. The same spiral design is rendered with four different strokes, producing a variety of effects. Although the underlying spiral growth motif is more subtly felt in the more abstract renderings, its ordering properties structure the distribution and scaled repetition of design elements, creating an organic feel to the compositions.

6 Conclusion

In this paper, we have described a mechanism for encapsulating growth principles for ornamental design into "adaptive clip art" patterns.

Although we have so far implemented only a rudimentary testbed for these ideas, we envision, ultimately, a powerful interactive authoring system for designing these patterns. The artistic tool so derived—unlike most previous work in computer-generated artistic rendering—might be more than just a digital form of an existing artistic medium: it could essentially provide a new medium of artistic expression, one that yields "living," dynamic patterns that adapt to their environments. As we gain more experience with the novel parameter space of this new medium we hope to encapsulate our knowledge in high-level, interactive tools that novices and artists alike will be able to use for creating new instances of these patterns.

In addition to creating better high-level design tools, there are a huge number of other important areas for future research:

Ornaments over manifolds. We would like to extend our work to creating ornaments over arbitrary manifolds. Such techniques would allow the ornamentation of 3D objects (vases, mugs, T-shirts, etc.) without the distortion that results from simply mapping a planar ornament onto the surface.

Incorporating global planning strategies. Our strategy of growth towards the largest empty region is a simple, relatively local one. A more sophisticated approach might be developed to look at the design more globally and better incorporate ornamental design principles such as balance and symmetry.

Putting an artist "in the loop." In applications such as web page ornamentation, the adaptive clip art must be generated purely automatically, on the fly. However, in other applications, such as wallpaper design, there is no reason not to put an artist in front of the computer to help guide the growth of the pattern and improve its appearance artistically, since both the cost of manufacturing the resulting artwork and the longevity of the finished piece are both relatively high. It would be interesting to explore semi-automatic algorithmic design processes and user interfaces for use in these situations.

Acknowledgements

We would like to thank Przemyslaw Prusinkiewicz, Ned Greene, and Victor Ostromoukhov for many helpful discussions. This work was supported by an NSF Presidential Faculty Fellow award (CCR-9553199), an ONR Young Investigator award (N00014-95-1-0728), an NSF Graduate Research Fellowship, and industrial gifts from Microsoft and Pixar.

References

[1] Howard Alexander. The computer/plotter and the 17 ornamental design types. In *Proceedings of SIGGRAPH '75*, pages 160–167. 1975.

[2] J. Arvo and D. Kirk. Modeling plants with environment-sensitive automata. In *Ausgraph 88 proceedings*, pages 27–33. 1988.

[3] Richard Beach and Maureen Stone. Graphical style—towards high quality illustrations. In *Proceedings of SIGGRAPH '83*, pages 127–135. 1983.

[4] Albert Fidelis Butsch. *Handbook of Renaissance Ornament: 1290 Designs from Decorated Books*. Dover Publications, Inc., New York, 1969.

[5] William Caxton. *History of Reynard the Foxe*. Kelmscott, Hammersmith, England, 1892.

[6] Archibald H. Christie. *Traditional Methods of Pattern Designing*. The Clarendon Press, Oxford, 1929.

[7] Theodore A. Cook. *The Curves of Life*. Constable and Company, London, 1914.

Figure 9   Red Chinese vase pattern.

Figure 10   Flowers and leaves pattern.

[8] Walter Crane. *Line and Form*. G. Bell & Sons, London, 1902.

[9] Joseph D'Addetta. *Traditional Japanese Design Motifs*. Dover Publications, Inc., New York, 1984.

[10] Lewis F. Day. *Nature in Ornament*. B.T. Batsford, London, 1898.

[11] Andrew Glassner. Frieze groups. *IEEE Computer Graphics and Applications*, 16(3):78–83, May 1996.

[12] E.H. Gombrich. *The Sense of Order*. Phaidon Press Limited, London, 1994.

[13] N. Greene. Voxel space automata: Modeling with stocastic growth processes in voxel space. In *Proceedings of SIGGRAPH '89*, pages 175–184. 1989.

[14] Branko Grünbaum and G. C. Shephard. *Tilings and Patterns*. W.H. Freeman, New York, 1987.

[15] Siu Chi Hsu, I. H. H. Lee, and N. E. Wiseman. Skeletal strokes. In *Proceedings of UIST '93*, pages 197–206. 1993.

[16] Siu Chi Hsu and Irene H. H. Lee. Drawing and animation using skeletal strokes. In *Proceedings of SIGGRAPH '94*, pages 109–118. 1994.

[17] Owen Jones. *Grammar of Ornament*. Day and son, London, 1856.

[18] Owen Jones. *The Grammar of Chinese Ornament*. Portland House, New York, 1987.

[19] Sherman E. Lee. *The Genius of Japanese Design*. Kodansha International, Tokyo, 1981.

[20] Radomír Měch and Przemyslaw Prusinkiewicz. Visual models of plants interacting with their environment. In *Proceedings of SIGGRAPH '96*, pages 397–410. 1996.

[21] Franz S. Meyer. *Handbook of Ornament*. Dover Publications, New York, 1957.

[22] William Morris. *A Book of verse*. Kelmscott, Hammersmith, England, 1870.

[23] William Morris. *Ideal Book: Essays and Lectures on the Arts of the Book*. University of California Press, Berkeley, 1982.

[24] William Morris and A.J. Wyatt. *The Tale of Beowulf*. Kelmscott Press, Hammersmith, England, 1895.

[25] K. Prakash. *Paisleys and Other Textile Designs from India*. Dover, New York, 1994.

[26] Przemyslaw Prusinkiewicz, Mark James, and Radomír Měch. Synthetic topiary. In *Proceedings of SIGGRAPH '94*, pages 351–358. 1994.

[27] Przemyslaw Prusinkiewicz and Aristid Lindenmayer. *The Algorithmic Beauty of Plants*. Springer-Verlag, New York, 1990.

Figure 11   Willow leaf pattern.

[28] Przemyslaw Prusinkiewicz, Aristid Lindenmayer, and James Hanan. Developmental models of herbaceous plants for computer imagery purposes. In *Proceedings of SIGGRAPH '88*, pages 141–150. 1988.

[29] Auguste Racinet. *Polychromatic Ornament*. Firmin Didot freres, fils & cie, Paris, 1873.

[30] A. Rosenfeld and A. C. Kak. *Digital Picture Processing*. Academic Press, New York, 1976.

[31] Henry Shaw. *The Encylopedia of Ornament*. J. Grant, Edinburgh, 1898.

[32] Gift Siromoney and Rani Siromoney. Rosenfeld's cycle grammars and kolam. In *Graph-Grammars and Their Application to Computer Science*, pages 564–579. Springer-Verlag, Berlin, 1986.

[33] Alvy Ray Smith. Plants, fractals, and formal languages. In *Proceedings of SIGGRAPH '84*, pages 1–10. 1984.

[34] M.P. Verneuil. *Floral Patterns*. Dover, New York, 1981.

[35] Otto von Falke. *Decorative Silks*. W. Helburn, Inc., New York, 1922.

[36] James Ward. *The Principles of Ornament*. Scribner, New York, 1896.

Figure 12   Bamboo spirals pattern.

A   Examples

Our first example pattern is a simple cluster of circular dots (Figure 14). The first dot is centered on the seed point, and subsequent dots are placed adjacent to the existing ornament. Dots may be at most 3 units in radius. Table 1 explains the dollar-sign tokens used within the rules in this appendix.

```
%element
seed point       // the seed element is required
%endelement

%element
dot circle
int order;       // number each dot in order of placement
%endelement

%source                  // declare a global variable
int dot_count = 0;       // to count the dots placed
%endsource
```

Figure 13 All four patterns, elaborated over different shapes. The line width variation in the outer spiral arch has been reversed from that of Figure 12 to give a filigreed effect.

```
%rule
seed --> dot
{
    // place a maximum-sized dot on the initial seed
    $0.set( $, 3.0 );
    $$0.order = dot_count++;

    // prevent the seed from being used again
    $$.sterile = 1;

    return SUCCESS;
}
%endrule

%rule
dot --> dot
{
    // ignore tiny empty spaces.
    if ( $goal.radius < 0.5 ) return FAILURE;

    // determine the radius of the new dot.
    double r = min( 3.0, $goal.radius );

    // place the new dot adjacent to the parent dot.
    $0.set( $.center.offset( $goal.center - $.center,
                             $.radius + r ), r );
    $$0.order = dot_count++;

    return SUCCESS;
}
%endrule
```

token	meaning
$$	the parent element
$	proxy 0 of the parent
$(k)	proxy k of the parent
$$j	the j'th declared child element
$j	proxy 0 of the j'th declared child
$j(k)	proxy k of the j'th child
$$var	dynamic child element in *var*
$var	proxy 0 of a dynamic child
$var(k)	proxy k of a dynamic child
$goal	the empty circle C

Table 1 Explanation of dollar-sign tokens used in rule bodies.

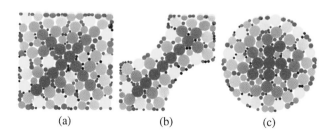

Figure 14 A simple example applied to three different regions. Parts (a) and (b) were seeded near the lower left corner, while part (c) was seeded at the center.

The $0.set call is the critical line. It places the new child dot by taking the center of the parent dot ($.center), and offsetting it by the sum of the parent and child radii ($.radius + r) in the direction from the center of the parent dot to the center of the goal circle C.

Figure 14 shows this pattern applied to three different regions. For this example, we have colored the dots, using the order field, to indicate the order in which they were placed, from oldest (red) to newest (purple). This example illustrates how the empty-circle heuristic first extends the ornament along the skeleton of the region, then fills in smaller and smaller regions successively.

A more complex example involves an arrangement of flowers, leaves, and stems. This rule file has the following declaration section:

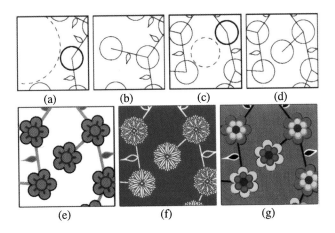

Figure 15 Two applications of the second example rule. Part (a) shows the parent flower (bold), and the empty goal circle (dashed). The center of the goal circle lies more than 8 units away, so the rule produces (b) a flower, a stem, and a leaf. When the rule is applied in the situation of part (c), where the goal circle is smaller, only the flower and stem are produced (d). Parts (e)–(g) show the elements of part (d) in a variety of rendering styles.

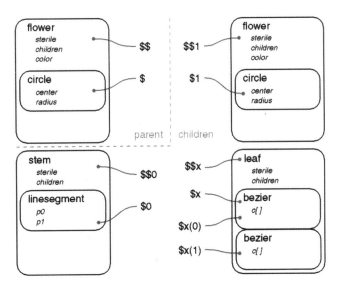

Figure 16 Data structures and dollar-sign tokens for the rule in the second example.

```
%element
seed point              // the required seed element type
%endelement

%element
flower circle           // flower: a circle proxy
int color;              // this element type has a user field
%endelement

%element
stem linesegment        // stem: a line segment proxy
%endelement

%element
leaf bezier bezier      // leaf: two Bezier segment proxies
%endelement
```

Here three element types are declared, in addition to the required seed type: flower, which is proxied by a single circle; stem, which is proxied by a line segment; and leaf, proxied by two Bézier segments. The flower element contains an integer user field called color.

This pattern also has only two rules. One rule places a flower on top of the initial seed point, and so is invoked only once. We will omit the code for of this rule. The other rule is more interesting: it places a new flower connected to an existing flower with a new stem segment, and adds a leaf to the stem only if the stem is long enough. Thus, the number of children produced is variable (two or three). The effects of this rule are pictured in Figure 15.

Here is the preamble to the rule, which creates a set of elements whose relationships are depicted in Figure 16:

```
%rule
flower --> stem flower
* x leaf
```

The last line of the preamble tells the preprocessor that the variable x within the rule body will point to an element of type leaf. This declaration is necessary so that when the preprocessor sees a dollar-sign construction involving the variable x, it knows the type of x and can insert appropriate typecasts.

Here is the remainder of the rule:

```
{
    Direction to_goal = $goal.center - $.center;
    double distance;

    // determine how far away to place the child flower.
    // ~ on the difference between two points gives
    // the distance between them.
    distance = ~($goal.center - $.center);
    if ( distance > 10.0 )
        distance = 10.0;

    // place the flower centered "distance" units away
    // in the direction of the goal, with a radius of 3.
    $1.set( $.center.offset( to_goal, distance ), 3.0 );

    // if the new flower intersects any
    // already-placed element, cancel this rule.
    if ( intersection( $$1 ) )
        return FAILURE;

    // the stem extends from the center of the parent
    // flower to the center of the child flower.
    $0.set( $.center, $1.center );

    // if the new flower was placed far enough away
    // add a leaf as well.
    if ( distance > 8.0 )
    {
        leaf *x = new leaf;

        // the base of the leaf is the stem midpoint.
        Point leaf_base = ( $1.center - $.center ) / 2;

        // place the leaf at a right angle to the stem,
        // and make it 3 units long.
        Direction leaf_dir = to_goal + M_PI/2;
        Point leaf_tip = leaf_base.offset(leaf_dir, 3.0);

        // a leaf is proxied by two Bezier segments.
        // each is placed giving position and tangent
        // direction and magnitude.
        $x(0).set( leaf_base, leaf_dir+M_PI/4, 0.6,
                   leaf_tip, leaf_dir, 0.4 );
        $x(1).set( leaf_base, leaf_dir-M_PI/4, 0.6,
                   leaf_tip, leaf_dir, 0.4 );

        // add the newly created leaf to the
        // child set of this rule.
        new_child( $$x );
    }

    // commit the set of children to the design.
    return SUCCESS;
}
%endrule
```

Figure 17 Results of applying different skeletal strokes to a single design.

Texture Mapping for Cel Animation

Wagner Toledo Corrêa[1]   Robert J. Jensen[1]   Craig E. Thayer[2]   Adam Finkelstein[1]

[1]Princeton University
[2]Walt Disney Feature Animation

(a) Flat colors

(b) Complex texture

Figure 1: A frame of cel animation with the foreground character painted by (a) the conventional method, and (b) our system.

Abstract

We present a method for applying complex textures to hand-drawn characters in cel animation. The method correlates features in a simple, textured, 3-D model with features on a hand-drawn figure, and then distorts the model to conform to the hand-drawn artwork. The process uses two new algorithms: a silhouette detection scheme and a depth-preserving warp. The silhouette detection algorithm is simple and efficient, and it produces continuous, smooth, visible contours on a 3-D model. The warp distorts the model in only two dimensions to match the artwork from a given camera perspective, yet preserves 3-D effects such as self-occlusion and foreshortening. The entire process allows animators to combine complex textures with hand-drawn artwork, leveraging the strengths of 3-D computer graphics while retaining the expressiveness of traditional hand-drawn cel animation.

CR Categories: I.3.3 and I.3.7 [Computer Graphics].

Keywords: Cel animation, texture mapping, silhouette detection, warp, metamorphosis, morph, non-photorealistic rendering.

1   INTRODUCTION

In traditional cel animation, moving characters are illustrated with flat, constant colors, whereas background scenery is painted in subtle and exquisite detail (Figure 1a). This disparity in rendering quality may be desirable to distinguish the animated characters from the background; however, there are many figures for which complex textures would be advantageous. Unfortunately, there are two factors that prohibit animators from painting moving characters with detailed textures. First, moving characters are drawn differently from frame to frame, requiring any complex shading to be replicated for every frame, adapting to the movements of the characters—an extremely daunting task. Second, even if an animator were to re-draw a detailed texture for every frame, temporal inconsistencies tend to lead to disturbing artifacts wherein the texture appears to "boil" or "swim" on the surface of the animated figure. This paper presents a method for applying complex textures to hand-drawn characters (Figure 1b). Our method requires relatively little effort per frame, and avoids boiling or swimming artifacts.

In recent years, the graphics community has made great progress in 3-D animation, leading up to full-length feature animations created entirely with 3-D computer graphics. There are advantages to animating in 3-D rather than 2-D: realism, complex lighting and shading effects, ease of camera motion, reuse of figures from scene to scene, automatic in-betweening, and so forth. Furthermore, it is easy to apply complex textures to animated figures in 3-D. Thus, one might consider using 3-D computer graphics to create *all* animated figures, or at least the characters that have interesting textures. However, it turns out that there are several reasons why hand-drawn 2-D animation will not be replaced with computer-generated 3-D figures. For traditional animators, it is much easier to work in 2-D rather than in 3-D. Hand-drawn animation enjoys an *economy of line* [14], where just a few gestures with a pen can suggest life and emotion that is difficult to achieve by moving 3-D models. Finally, there exists an entire art form (and industry) built around hand-drawn animation, whose techniques have been refined for more than 80 years [27]. While the industry is increasingly using computer-generated elements in animated films, the vast majority of characters are hand-drawn in 2-D, especially when the figure should convey a sense of life and emotion.

In this project, we begin with hand-drawn characters created by a traditional animator. Next, a computer graphics animator creates a crude 3-D model that mimics the basic poses and shapes of the hand-drawn art, but ignores the subtlety and expressiveness of the character. The 3-D model includes both a texture and the approximate camera position shown in the artwork. Our algorithm distorts the model within the viewing frustum of the camera, in such a way that the model conforms to the hand-drawn art, and then renders the model with its texture. Finally, the rendered model replaces the flat colors that would be used in the ink-and-paint stage of traditional cel animation. This process combines the advantages of 2-D and 3-D animation. The critical aspects of the animation (gestures, emotion, timing, anticipation) are created in 2-D with the power and expressiveness of hand-drawn art; on the other hand, effects that give shape to the texture occur in 3-D, yielding plausible motion for the texture. The hand-drawn line art and the texture are merged for the final animation.

To implement the process outlined above, this paper offers two new algorithms: a silhouette detection scheme and a depth-preserving warp. The silhouette detector (which is based on the frame buffer) is efficient, simple to implement, and can be used for any application where visible silhouette detection is necessary. The warp has two main advantages over previous warps that make it appropriate for our problem: it works with curved features, and it provides 3-D effects such as wrapping, foreshortening, and self-occlusion. It also has other potential applications: texture acquisition, and manipulation of 3-D objects using hand-drawn gestures. (These applications are described in Section 9.)

The remainder of this paper is organized as follows. Section 2 surveys previous work related to this project. Section 3 presents an overview of our process. In Sections 4, 5, and 6, we describe in detail how we correlate features on the model with features on the art, how our system warps the model to conform to the art, and how to control the warp. In Section 7, we present some resulting animations. Section 8 discusses some limitations of our technique, while Section 9 describes several applications for this technology other than its use in traditional cel animation. Finally, Section 10 outlines some possible areas for future work.

2 RELATED WORK

A variety of previous efforts have addressed the use of computer graphics for animation, though to our knowledge nobody has successfully solved the specific problem described here. Researchers have largely automated the image processing and compositing aspects of cel animation [6, 18, 25, 28], wherein the conventional ink-and-paint stage could be replaced with the textures resulting from our system. Wood *et al.* [35] demonstrate the use of 3-D computer graphics in the design of static background scenery; in contrast, this paper addresses animated foreground characters. Sabiston [20] investigates the use of hand-drawn artwork for driving 3-D animation, which, although not the main focus of our work, is similar to the application we describe in Section 9.2. Finally, animators at Disney actually applied a computer graphics texture to color a hand-drawn magic carpet in the film *Aladdin* [30], but their process involved meticulously rotoscoping a 3-D model to match each frame of artwork—an arduous task that would have benefitted from a system such as the one we describe.

The heart of our method is a new warp. Critical for visual effects such as metamorphosis (or *morphing*), image warps have been extensively studied. Beier and Neely's warp [2] distorts images in 2-D based on features marked with line segments; it was the inspiration for the warp that we describe, which works with curved feature markers and provides 3-D effects such as occlusion and foreshortening. Litwinowicz and Williams [13] describe a warp (based on a thin-plate smoothness functional) that behaves more smoothly than that of Beier and Neely in the neighborhood of feature markers; perhaps a hybrid approach could combine these smoothness properties into the warp that we describe. Lee *et al.* [10] have described a user-interface based on *snakes* [9] that is useful for feature specification, as well as a new warp based on free-form deformations [24]. Warps have been applied in other domains as well, such as the work of Sederberg *et al.* [23] on 2-D curves, Witkin and Popović [33] on motion curves for 3-D animation, and Lerios *et al.* [11] on volumes.

This paper also presents a scheme for silhouette detection based on rendering the 3-D model into a frame buffer. In general, silhouette detection is closely-related to hidden surface removal, for which there are a host of methods [7]. Markosian *et al.* [14] present some improvements and simplifications of traditional algorithms, and are able to trade off accuracy for speed. Most algorithms dealing with polyhedral input traverse the mesh tagging edges of the model as silhouettes. In our work, we are only interested in *visible* silhouettes (since they correspond to features that appear in the drawing). Furthermore, we want our algorithm to produce smooth, continuous silhouette curves on the actual model. As described in Section 4, our method generates this kind of output, and solves the problem of bifurcation along the silhouette edge by rendering the 3-D model colored with texture coordinates into a frame buffer. Saito and Takahashi [21] employed a similar technique for highlighting edges in technical illustrations, and Wallach *et al.* [29] used this idea for finding frame-to-frame coherence in 3-D animations.

This project shares much in spirit with the recent progress of the computer graphics community toward non-photorealistic rendering (NPR), although the actual NPR aspects of our work (the shape of the animated figure and often its texture) are created by an artist. For the researchers who have investigated animation and video in simulated media (oil paint for Meier [15] and Litwinowicz [12]; pen and ink for Markosian *et al.* [14] and Winkenbach *et al.* [32]; and watercolor for Curtis *et al.* [4]) a challenge has been to maintain temporal coherence in the individual strokes of the artwork to avoid "boiling." In our project, this challenge is circumvented because we use a single texture throughout the animation.

3 THE PROCESS

In this section we present our system from the user's point of view. The details of the algorithms mentioned here are explained in later sections.

For each shot in the animation, we follow these steps (Figure 2):

(a) A person scans in the cleaned-up hand-drawn artwork.

(b) A person creates a simple 3-D model that approximates roughly the shape of the hand-drawn character.

(c) The computer finds border and silhouette edges in the model.

(d) A person traces over edges of the line art that correspond to border and silhouette features of the 3-D model.

(e) The computer warps the 3-D model to match the shape of the line art, and then renders the model.

(f) The computer composites the rendered model with the hand-drawn line art and background scenery.

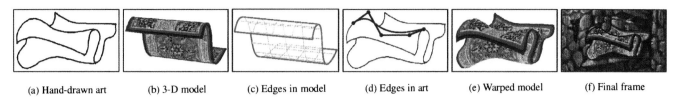

(a) Hand-drawn art   (b) 3-D model   (c) Edges in model   (d) Edges in art   (e) Warped model   (f) Final frame

Figure 2: The process of creating one texture mapped frame.

Our method fits into the existing production pipeline for cel animation [6, 18]. Steps (a) and (f) are stages in the current digital production process, with the ink-and-paint stage between them. We are offering, as an alternative to the constant colors of the ink-and-paint stage, a process that applies complex textures to the drawings.

The problem of applying textures to hand-drawn artwork poses a challenge: the line art must be interpreted as some kind of shape. Given a set of black lines on white paper, the computer must acquire at least a primitive model for the 3-D forms conveyed by the art. This information is necessary if we are to provide 3-D effects for the texture such as self-occlusion and foreshortening. (See, for example, the difference in occlusion between Figures 2b and 2e or the foreshortening shown in Figure 7.) Note that with the constant colors of the traditional ink-and-paint stage, these 3-D effects are unnecessary. The viewer does not expect the constant orange color of the front of the carpet in Figure 1a to appear to recede as it crosses over a silhouette; however the texture of the carpet in Figure 1b must recede. Thus, some form of 3-D information must be available to the algorithm. Since interpreting hand-drawn line art as a 3-D figure is tantamount to the computer vision problem (which has not as yet been solved), we resort to human intervention for steps (b) and (d) above. These phases of our process can be labor-intensive, and we believe that partial automation of these tasks through heuristic methods is a critical area for future work.

In step (b) above, we create a simple 3-D model that corresponds to the animated figure. As seen from a set of specific camera perspectives, the model should have the approximate form of the hand-drawn figure. By "approximate form" we mean that the model projected into screen space should have a similar set of features in a similar arrangement as the features of the line art. For example, the artwork and 3-D model and in Figures 2a and 2b both have four border edges and an upper and lower silhouette edge. Note that in this example the warp succeeds even though the order of the upper silhouette edge and the backmost edge of the carpet is reversed between the hand-drawn artwork and the 3-D model. For the animations shown in this paper, our models were represented by tensor product B-spline patches [5]. However, before performing the warp described in Section 5, we convert our models to polygon meshes. Thus, the method should be applicable to any model that can be converted to polygons, provided that the model has a global parameterization, which is generally necessary for texture mapping.

4   SPECIFYING MARKERS

In this section we show how we specify *marker curves*—curves that identify features on the 3-D model and on the 2-D artwork. We call feature curves on the model *model markers* and feature curves on the drawing *drawing markers*. These curves will be used by the warp described in Section 5 to deform the 3-D model so that it matches the drawing.

Section 4.1 explains how we automatically find model markers by detecting visible border edges and silhouette edges on the model. Section 4.2 explains how these edges are converted to form smooth curves on the model. Section 4.3 shows how to guarantee that these

edges can be safely used later as the input to the warp. Section 4.4 shows how to specify the edges on the 2-D drawing that correspond to the edges found on the 3-D model.

4.1   Silhouette Detection

In this section we describe a scheme for finding visible silhouette and border edges in a 3-D model represented by a polygon mesh. These features are likely to correspond to features in the hand-drawn line art; such correspondences are the primary input to the warp we describe in Section 5. We also allow the user to specify model markers by drawing them directly on the 3-D model, but it would be cumbersome to have to specify *all* model marker curves this way. Thus, we automatically construct model markers for all visible border and silhouette edges, and allow the user to pick the useful marker curves (often, all of them).

To get started, we need to define some terminology, consistent with that of Markosian *et al.* [14]. A *border edge* is an edge adjacent to just one polygon of the mesh. A *silhouette edge* is an edge shared by a front-facing polygon and a back-facing polygon (relative to the camera).

Standard silhouette detection algorithms will identify the subset of edges in the mesh that are silhouette edges. Treated as a group, these edges tend to form chains. Unfortunately, in regions of the mesh where many of the faces are viewed nearly edge-on, the chains of silhouette edges can bifurcate and possibly re-merge in a nasty tangle. For our warp, we are interested in finding a smooth, continuous curve that traces the silhouette on the model, rather than identifying the exact, discrete set of silhouette edges in the mesh. Furthermore, we are only interested in *visible* silhouettes because they tend to correspond to features that appear in the drawing. Finally, we want to distinguish border edges from other silhouette edges.

To detect the border and silhouette edges of a 3-D model, we proceed as follows. Using Gouraud shading (*without* lighting effects or antialiasing) we render the 3-D model over a black background as a polygon mesh whose vertices are colored $(R, G, B) = (u, v, \text{ID})$, where u and v are the parametric coordinates of each vertex, and ID identifies the texture (Figure 3b). Let us call the resulting image the *uv-image*. The method accommodates models with multiple texture maps, but so far in our animations all of our models have only used a single texture, whose ID is 1. The ID 0 is reserved for the background.

When a pixel on the *uv*-image corresponds to a point on the surface of the model, we say that the pixel is *covered by* the model. Also, a *pixel corner* is one of the four corners of a pixel, while a *pixel boundary* is the line segment joining two pixel corners shared by two adjacent pixels. For example, in Figure 4, p_1 and p_2 are pixels, c_1 and c_2 are pixel corners, and e is a pixel boundary.

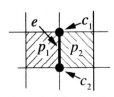

Figure 4: A few pixels.

Borders and silhouettes generate color discontinuities in the resulting image (Figure 3c). To find these discontinuities, we construct a directed graph $G = (V, E)$, where V are the vertices

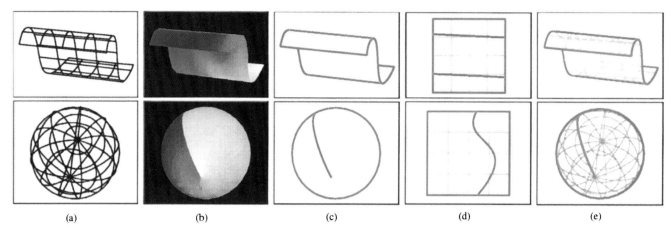

Figure 3: Detecting border and silhouette edges on a 3-D model. (a) Wireframe 3-D model. (b) 3-D model shaded with vertices colored (u, v, ID). (c) Discontinuities in color. (d) Model marker curves in parameter space. (e) Marker curves on model.

of the graph, and E are directed edges in the graph. V consists of the pixel corners in the uv-image, and E is constructed by the following classification process:

```
CLASSIFY(G)
1   for every boundary between two neighboring pixels
2       p₁ ← pixel closer to the camera
3       p₂ ← pixel farther from the camera
4       if p₁.color ≉ p₂.color
5           e ← ADD_EDGE(G, p₁, p₂)
6           if p₁ is an extremum
7               e.type ← corresponding kind of border edge
8           else
9               e.type ← silhouette edge
```

In steps 2 and 3, we determine which of the two pixels of a boundary is closer to the camera, using one of three methods. First, if exactly one of the pixels is covered by the model, then it is the closer pixel (because the other pixel corresponds to background). Second, we can read from the depth buffer the z-values of the two pixels and compare them. Third, if the depth value is unavailable (as on some machines for which z-buffering is implemented in hardware) then we can read the u and v parameters of the part of the model that covered those pixels, evaluate the model at those parametric locations, and compare their distances from the camera.

In step 5, we add to G a directed edge e between the two corners shared by p_1 and p_2 in such a way that p_1 is on the left of e, and p_2 is on the right. If the parametric space is periodic then the border edges should be ignored. For example, in Figure 3, the carpet has two silhouette edges (upper and lower) and four border edges (at $u = 0$, $u = 1$, $v = 0$, and $v = 1$); the ball only has silhouette edges because the interior line in Figure 3c is ignored. In the actual implementation, we generate for each edge a confidence value for each of the possible kinds of edge. If, for example, the u parameter at p_1 was found to be very near 0, and u at p_2 was large, then we could say with high confidence that the edge between these pixels represents a border at $u = 0$. Finally, we choose the highest confidence value to represent the type of the edge.

After the classification process is finished, finding the edges on the model is equivalent to finding the connected components of G, which can be done efficiently using depth-first search [3, 26]. We traverse the graph, finding paths of edges that have the same edge type and the same color (within a tolerance). The running time of depth-first search is $\Theta(|V|+|E|)$ [3]. In our case, both $|V|$ and $|E|$ are linear in the number of pixels. Furthermore, the classification

process is linear in the number of pixels because it makes a single pass over the entire image, adding a number of edges to the graph that is bounded by a constant multiple of the number of pixels. Thus, the silhouette detection scheme described here is linear in the number of pixels in the image. The image resolution dictates the accuracy of the resulting silhouette curves. We have found that a resolution of 512×512 is sufficient for the simple models we have used in our animations.

Having found the connected components of G, we have a set of lists of pixel boundaries that correspond to border edges and silhouette edges on the model. In the next section we will describe how to fit smooth curves to this data. These curves are the model marker curves (Figure 3e) used by the warp in Section 5.

The benefits of this silhouette detector are that it is simple to implement, it leverages existing support for hidden surface removal and texture mapping, it works for any object with a well-defined parameter space, and produces smooth, visible silhouette curves.

4.2 Curve Fitting

To represent each marker curve, we use a chord-length parameterized endpoint-interpolating uniform cubic B-spline [5, 19]. These curves have several desirable properties: they are smooth; they can be linked "head to tail" (without a break between them); the rate of change of the curve with respect to the parameter is uniform; and they are well understood. We obtain each curve by fitting it to a set of data. These data are either chains of pixels (as in the previous section) or the result of user input (as in Section 4.4).

To fit the curves, we typically have many more data points than degrees of freedom: a chain of hundreds of pixels generated by the silhouette detector (or generated by tracing on the drawing) may be smoothly approximated by a spline with only a few control points. To calculate the control points, we solve an overdetermined linear system using least squares data fitting techniques that minimize the root-mean-square error between the data and the resulting curve [1, 17, 19, 22]. Our fitting procedure attempts to use as few control points as possible, given a maximum error threshold.

4.3 Ghostbusting

The marker curves created in this section drive the warp described in Section 5. Beier and Neely [2] observe that image warps tend to fail if feature lines cross, producing what they call *ghosts*. Near the intersection between two feature lines, both features exert a strong influence on the warp. If crossed feature lines do not "agree" about the warp, then there tend to be sharp discontinuities in the resulting warp leading to unpleasant artifacts. Thus, conventional wisdom regarding image warps warns: "do *not* cross the streams."

For the warp of Section 5, there are some configurations of crossed feature markers that are dangerous and others that are benign. Our warp distorts a 3-D model, so feature markers that cross *on the model* lead to sharp discontinuities in the warp.

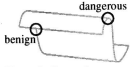

Figure 5: Crossed streams.

On the other hand, feature markers that cross in image space (but are distant on the model) do not cause any ill artifacts. An example of each kind of crossing is shown in Figure 5. Our application automatically detects dangerous crossings, and splits model marker curves where they cross. Since the silhouette detector described in this section builds feature markers based on finding discontinuities in parameter space, it is easy to use this information to distinguish dangerous crossings from benign crossings. At dangerous crossings we split marker curves so that they meet only at their endpoints. For example, after splitting, three curves in Figure 5 meet at the point labeled "dangerous." Furthermore, our application trims the feature curves a small distance away from the crossing point, so the resulting curves do not touch. The splitting procedure ensures that the resulting marker curves "agree" about the warp at their intersection. The trimming step, though not strictly necessary, causes the warp to behave even more smoothly in the neighborhood.

4.4 Specifying Markers on the Drawing

We have described the creation of model marker curves based on features in the 3-D model. Next the user picks model marker curves, and specifies corresponding drawing marker curves. To specify these curves, the user traces over features in the hand-drawn art— a time-consuming and tedious task. To reduce user-intervention, we use contour tracing techniques similar to those presented by Gleicher [8] and Mortensen and Barrett [16] in which the cursor automatically snaps onto nearby artwork. For each drawing marker, tracing results in a list of pixels that we subsequently approximate with a smooth curve, as described in Section 4.2.

We now have a collection of model and drawing markers. These curves identify features on the model that correspond to features on the hand-drawn artwork. In the following section, we describe a warp that uses this information to guide the distortion of the 3-D model so that it matches the hand-drawn artwork.

5 THE WARP

This section describes our method for warping a given 3-D model to match hand-drawn line art. The inputs to the warp are the model, camera parameters, and a set of pairs of (model and drawing) marker curves. The warp is applied to points on the model *after* they have been transformed into the screen space for the given camera but before the model has been rendered. The warp, which maps a point in screen space to a different point in screen space, has the following important properties:

- Each warped model marker lies on its associated drawing marker as seen from the camera.

- The surface warped between two markers varies smoothly, avoiding puckering or buckling.

- The warp preserves approximate area in image space, so that foreshortening effects are still apparent.

- The warp leaves depth information (relative to the camera) unchanged.

5.1 The Warp for One Pair of Markers

To begin, let us assume we only have a single pair of marker curves in screen space: a model marker curve $M(t)$ (generated by the silhouette detector in Section 4.1) and a drawing marker curve $D(t)$ (traced on the drawing by the user as described in Section 4.4). In the next section we will describe how this works with multiple pairs of marker curves.

For a given point p in the screen-space projection of the model, we want to find the corresponding point q on the drawing. For a particular value of t, we define two coordinate systems: one on the model marker curve and one on the drawing marker curve (Figure 6). The model coordinate system has origin at $M(t)$, and abscissa direction $\hat{x}_m(t)$ given by the tangent of M at t. Likewise, the drawing coordinate system has origin at $D(t)$, and abscissa direction $\hat{x}_d(t)$ given by the tangent of D at t. For now, the ordinate directions $\hat{y}_m(t)$ and $\hat{y}_d(t)$ are oriented to be perpendicular to the respective abscissa. However, in Section 6.4 we will modify the ordinate direction to get a smoother warp.

We find the x and y coordinates of p in relation to the model coordinate system in the usual way:

$$
\begin{aligned}
x(t) &= (p - M(t)) \cdot \hat{x}_m(t) \\
y(t) &= (p - M(t)) \cdot \hat{y}_m(t)
\end{aligned}
$$

Next we define a tentative drawing point $q(t)$ corresponding to $p(t)$:

$$q(t) = D(t) + x(t)\,\hat{x}_d(t) + y(t)\,\hat{y}_d(t) \qquad (1)$$

This is the location to which we warp $p(t)$, taking into account *only* the coordinate systems at parameter t. Of course, we have a continuum of coordinate systems for all parameters t, and in general they do not agree about the location of $q(t)$. Thus, we take q to be a weighted average of $q(t)$ for all t, using a weighting function $c(t)$:

$$q = \frac{\displaystyle\int_0^1 c(t)\,q(t)\,dt}{\displaystyle\int_0^1 c(t)\,dt} \qquad (2)$$

We want the contribution $c(t)$ to fall off with the growth of the distance $d(t)$ between the 3-D points that project to p and $M(t)$. Intuitively, we want nearby portions of the marker curves to have more influence than regions of the markers that are far away. We compute $d(t)$ in one of two ways. We either approximate the

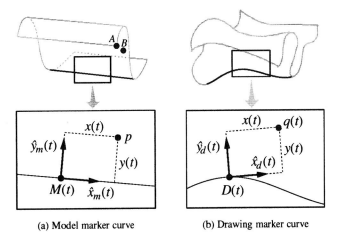

(a) Model marker curve   (b) Drawing marker curve

Figure 6: Coordinate systems for the warp.

distance along the surface of the model, or we compute world-space distance on an undeformed reference mesh. This is an important difference between our warp and traditional warps: traditional warps would use the 2-D distance between the origins of the coordinate systems. Although our warp happens in 2-D space, it takes into account 3-D information. Thus, the marker curves at point A in Figure 6a have little influence on the warp of point B, even though they are very near each other in the image plane. Thus, we choose the contribution to be:

$$c(t) = \frac{1}{\epsilon + d(t)^f} \qquad (3)$$

where ϵ is a small constant to avoid singularities when the distance is very near zero, and f is a constant that controls how fast the contribution falls off with distance. We discuss the nature of these parameters in greater detail in Section 6.1.

5.2 The Warp for Multiple Pairs of Markers

The warp in equation (2) only considers a single pair of marker curves. Here we generalize the warp to handle multiple pairs of curves. We assign a user-specified weight w_i to each pair i of curves, $i = 1, 2, \ldots, m$, balancing the relative contribution of each pair to the overall warp. Finally, we compute the drawing point q as a weighted average using $q_i(t)$ and $c_i(t)$ from equations (1) and (3), for each marker pair i:

$$q = \frac{\sum_{i=1}^{m} \left(w_i \int_0^1 c_i(t)\, q_i(t)\, dt \right)}{\sum_{i=1}^{m} \left(w_i \int_0^1 c_i(t)\, dt \right)} \qquad (4)$$

The main features of our warp are: it uses curved features; it is visually smooth; it is scale, translation, and screen-space rotation independent; and, most importantly, it maps model markers to drawing markers while preserving 3-D effects.

5.3 Computing the Warp

In practice, we evaluate the integrals in equation (4) numerically, by uniformly sampling the marker curves. This can be computed quickly for all vertices in the model by caching the coordinate systems at sample locations.

Our warp uses *forward mapping* [34]: for each point in the source texture, it finds where the point is mapped in the destination. The motivation in this case is that we get self-occlusion and hidden-surface removal for free using normal z-buffered rendering. Also, this permits us to compute the warp at low resolution for the interactive parts of the process, and later perform the final rendering at high-resolution. Litwinowicz and Williams [13] also use forward mapping, whereas Beier and Neely [2] use *inverse mapping*: for each point in the destination, they find the location at which to sample the input image. We sample the map by calculating the warp only at vertices in the 3-D model; thus, we can render the warped model using conventional texture mapping simply by modifying the coordinates of vertices in the mesh and then rendering the usual way.

6 CONTROLLING THE WARP

Many factors influence the behavior of the warp described in Section 5. In this section we describe some of these influences in better detail.

6.1 Contribution Parameters

The factors ϵ and f of equation (3) can be modified to achieve different effects. By varying ϵ, we can get different levels of smoothness and precision. If ϵ is large, the warp is smoother. If ϵ is small, the warp is more precise. By varying f, we control how fast the contribution falls off with distance. If f is large, distant points will have almost no influence. (The factors ϵ and f are similar to the factors a and b of the warp of Beier and Neely [2].) The figures in this paper use $\epsilon = 10^{-4}$ and f between 2 and 3.

6.2 Modeling and Viewing Parameters

Our warp is based on the projection of the 3-D model into screen space. By varying the modeling and viewing parameters we produce different projections of the model, and obtain different results. Figure 7 shows the results of the warp for two different camera views. In both cases, the hand-drawn art and the 3-D model are the same. Notice that without the texture the drawing would be ambiguous. We do not know whether the drawing is smaller at the top or recedes into the distance. The foreshortening effect helps resolve this ambiguity. Thus, use of a texture in a figure may provide the viewer with information about spatial arrangement that is not available in conventional flat-colored figures. Since it only takes a few seconds to rotate the model and re-render the frame, it is easy to interactively switch between the two views like those of Figure 7 to choose one that has the desired effect.

6.3 Extra Markers

So far we have only mentioned model marker curves detected automatically. In the actual implementation, the user can specify extra markers on the model and the corresponding ones on the drawing, to match features that were not detected automatically. For example, Figure 8 shows how extra markers can be used to tell the carpet how to fold over a set of stairs. Also, one could add *marker points*— control points that add to the formula like marker curves, but have a single coordinate system that is embedded in the

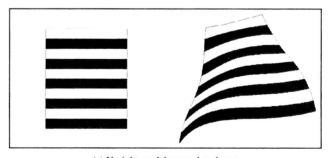

(a) Upright model warped to the art

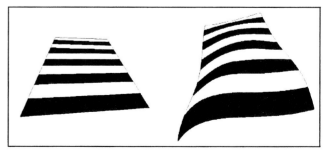

(b) Tilted model warped to the art

Figure 7: Influence of modeling and viewing parameters.

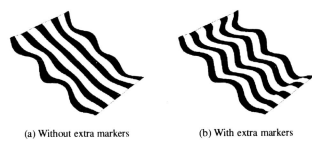

(a) Without extra markers   (b) With extra markers

Figure 8: Effect of defining extra markers on the warp.

plane—although we have not yet found it necessary to use marker points for any of our animations.

6.4 Ordinate Direction Adjustment

In Section 5 we described a warp that uses coordinate systems whose ordinate and abscissa directions are perpendicular to each other. This approach leads to puckering when there is a great disparity between the orientation of nearby drawing coordinate systems (Figure 9a). Instead, we adjust the ordinate direction of the drawing coordinate systems so that they conform better to the actual artwork. The algorithm produces drawing coordinate systems whose axes are linearly independent, but not necessarily orthogonal. The result is a smoother and more intuitive warp (Figure 9b).

To understand how our method works, let us suppose we have a drawing coordinate system with axes $(\hat{x}_d, \hat{y}_d)$, and a corresponding model coordinate system with axes $(\hat{x}_m, \hat{y}_m)$ as shown in Figures 10a and 10b. Also, let us assume that we have a single drawing marker curve D and a corresponding model marker curve M. For a given value of t, we want to find the ordinate direction $\hat{y}_d'$ taking into account the drawing coordinate system with origin at $D(t)$ and axes $(\hat{x}_d(t), \hat{y}_d(t))$, as well as the corresponding model coordinate system with origin at $M(t)$ and axes $(\hat{x}_m(t), \hat{y}_m(t))$. We find the rotation that maps $\hat{y}_m(t)$ to $\hat{y}_m$, and apply this same

rotation to $\hat{y}_d(t)$ to obtain $\hat{y}_d'(t)$, which is where the coordinate system at $D(t)$ "thinks" that $\hat{y}_d$ should be. Using an approach similar to the one we used for the warp, we find $\hat{y}_d'$ as a weighted combination of $\hat{y}_d'(t)$, using a weighting function $c'(t)$:

$$\hat{y}_d' = \frac{\int_0^1 c'(t)\,\hat{y}_d'(t)\,dt}{\int_0^1 c'(t)\,dt} \tag{5}$$

We want the contribution $c'(t)$ to have two properties. First, it should fall off with the distance $d'(t)$ between the model coordinate systems, computed as in Section 5. Second, it should be larger when the corresponding coordinate systems in parameter space (Figure 10c) are perpendicular to each other. Intuitively, the bottom edge of the carpet in Figure 9 should have a strong influence over the ordinate direction along the right edge of the carpet, because they are perpendicular in parameter space. This leads to "isoparameter lines" in the drawing space that follow the shape of the lower boundary curve. The contribution is then:

$$c'(t) = \frac{1 - \hat{y}_p \cdot \hat{y}_p(t)}{\epsilon' + d'(t)^{f'}}$$

where $\hat{y}_p$ and $\hat{y}_p(t)$ are the vectors in parameter space that correspond to $\hat{y}_m$ and $\hat{y}_m(t)$, respectively. The parameters ϵ' and f', and the distance function $d'(t)$ have the same roles as in equation (3). As with the warp in Section 5, we compute the final ordinate direction by promoting equation (5) to include all marker curves, but here we do not use weights w_i. When all coordinate systems are parallel to each other in parameter space, the result of this algorithm is undefined. In this special case, we simply use the original orthogonal $\hat{y}_d$.

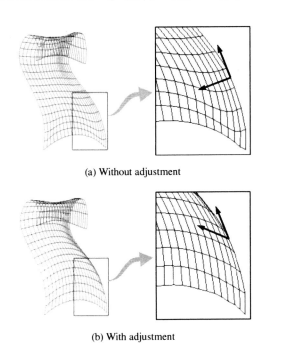

(a) Without adjustment

(b) With adjustment

Figure 9: Effect of ordinate direction adjustment on the warp.

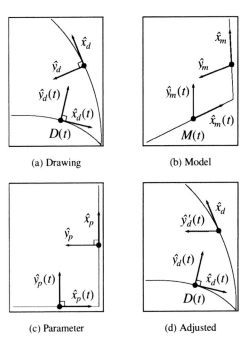

(a) Drawing   (b) Model

(c) Parameter   (d) Adjusted

Figure 10: Coordinate systems for ordinate direction adjustment.

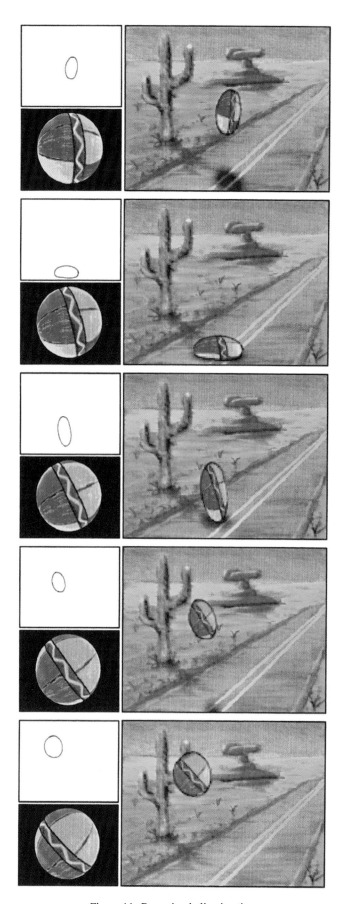

Figure 11: Bouncing ball animation.

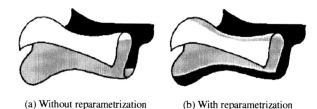

(a) Without reparametrization   (b) With reparametrization

Figure 12: Effect of reparameterizing the texture.

6.5 Reparameterizing the Texture

As we mentioned in Section 4, the marker curves are approximately chord length parameterized. This leads to an interpretation of which part of the overall texture should be visible that is often, but not always, correct. We provide a mechanism for pulling occluded texture back over a silhouette horizon, or pushing visible texture over the horizon so it becomes occluded. For example, for the carpet in Figure 12, the lower silhouette curve corresponds to two different regions in parameter space. We simply move the texture on the underformed model, essentially reparameterizing the texture on the surface. We can perform such reparameterization easily by warping the texture in parameter space prior to rendering, guided by feature curves such as the borders of the texture and the desired silhouette positions. However, we have not yet found it necessary to use this feature for any of our animations.

7 RESULTS

In this section we describe several animations we created with our application.

Figure 11 shows an animation of a ball bouncing along a desert highway. For each row, the upper left picture shows the hand-drawn artwork, the lower left picture shows the 3-D model with the texture applied to it, and the right picture shows the final frame from the movie: hand-drawn art composited with the warped model and the background. In these frames the ball exhibits "squash and stretch", a fundamental principle of traditional cel animation [27]. The 3-D model for this case is a simple sphere with a hand-painted beach-ball texture applied to it. The sphere rotates with respect to the camera, so that it appears to be rolling. To guide the warp for this simple model, we used exactly one pair of marker curves per frame.

In Figure 14 we show the line art, model, and final frames for an animated carpet on a staircase. In these frames, the carpet "stands up" to look around. For this animation we used about 5 or 6 marker curves per frame. Section 6.3 describes a method for specifying extra marker curves that would cause the carpet to follow the contours of the steps more closely, but we did not use that feature in this animation. The frames demonstrate 3-D effects such as self-occlusion and foreshortening—as well as temporal coherence in a complex texture—that would be very difficult to produce with traditional cel animation. Also note that even though the character is computer-rendered using a highly-symmetric, repeating texture, it blends aesthetically with the background art due to the hand-drawn shape.

Finally, Figure 15 shows a hand-drawn animation of a fish. The 3-D model of the fish contains only the body of the fish (with a simple checkerboard texture). Not shown are the three fins of the fish (which are planar quadrilaterals) and the two eyes of the fish (which are simple spheres). These were modeled, rendered, and composited as separate layers—in the style of traditional, multi-layer animation [27]—although they all share the same hand-drawn art. The model is rigid throughout the animation, only rotating back and forth with respect to the camera. Nonetheless, in the final frames of the animation the fish appears to bend and flex as it swims. The fins and tail are semi-transparent (using a hand-painted matte embedded in the texture of the model) and thus it is possible to see the reeds of the background through transparent parts of the fish.

To create the hand-drawn artwork for the fish, it took several hours to draw 23 frames. Building the 3-D model was easier (approximately an hour) because the motion is simple rotation. The computer found the model markers in just a few seconds per frame. Drawing markers were specified by hand, requiring about two minutes per frame. Finally, rendering and compositing required tens of seconds per frame. For the ball and carpet animation (which have simpler art and simpler models) these steps required less time.

8   LIMITATIONS

There are several classes of line art for which our process does not work well. First, cel animation has developed a "vocabulary" for conveying texture by modifying the edges of characters. For example, tufts of fur on a character may be suggested or by drawing a few sharp wiggles rather than a smooth edge (Figure 13a). A character illustrated with *both* "hinted" texture (in its line art) and the kind of textured-fill described in this paper would probably suffer visually from this mixed metaphor; moreover, the texture near the sharp wiggles would be likely to stretch and pucker unpleasantly in order to conform to the wiggles of the line art. Our process also does not work well with figures for which it is difficult to generate the 3-D model—most notably, clothing. Cloth is typically drawn showing creases and folds, which would be difficult to replicate well in a 3-D model (Figure 13b). Other drawings use a few lines to suggest greater geometric complexity. The interior folds in the knotted carpet would have to be modeled explicitly if we expect the texture to look right. Figure 13c shows an example of how some drawings do not correspond to any reasonable 3-D geometry. Here the nose is drawn in profile, the eyebrows float off the surface, and the hair is a crude representation. There are other limitations inherent in using quadrilateral patches to represent complex shapes. The body, legs, and tail of the cat Figure 13d could not reasonably be represented with a single patch.

Figure 13: Line art that would be difficult to texture.

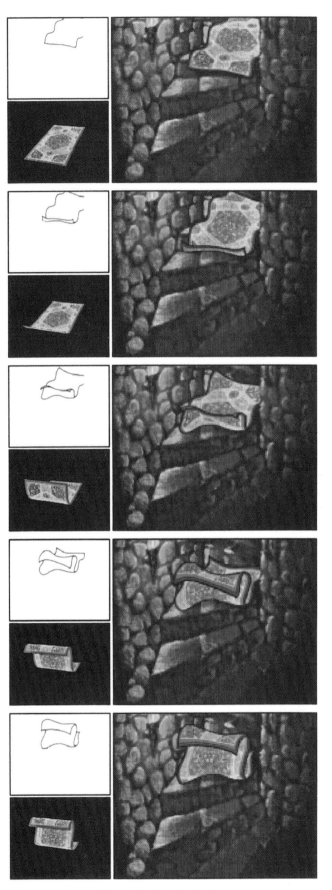

Figure 14: Carpet animation.

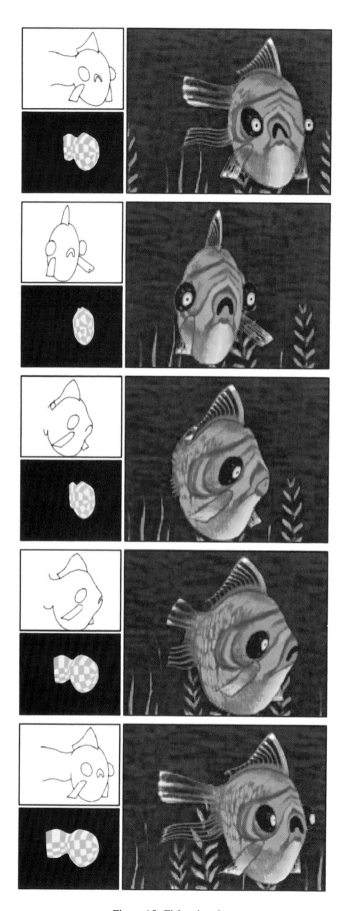

To solve these problems we either need to use multiple patches and solve continuity issues, or switch to a more general surface representation. Subdivision surfaces could be used in the warp if we devised a method of representing surface curves and some concept of orthogonality in parameter space.

9   OTHER APPLICATIONS

In this section we briefly talk about some other applications that might benefit from this technology.

9.1   Shading Effects

Once we have this correspondence between a 3-D model and the artwork, it is easy to incorporate many traditional computer graphics effects such as highlights, shadows, transparency, environment mapping, and so forth. Since this draws us further away from the look and feel of traditional animation, we have not investigated these effects in our work (except for the use of transparency in the fins of the fish in Figure 15).

9.2   3-D Shape Control for Animation

While it is not the focus of this work, we are currently developing a variation of this method as a new form of control in 3-D animation. It would fit into the 3-D animation pipeline just before rendering. An animator could add detail or deformations to the 3-D geometry by *drawing* on the image plane (Figure 16). This is better than distorting the final image because it affects the *actual* geometry, correctly modifying occlusion and shading. Note that after the warp, the model should only be viewed from the original camera position, as the figure may appear distorted when viewed from other directions.

 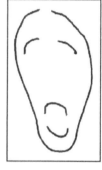 

(a) Original 3-D model   (b) Hand-drawn art   (c) Warped 3-D model

(d) Perplexed face   (e) Goofy face

Figure 15: Fish animation.

Figure 16: Controlling a 3-D model by drawing.

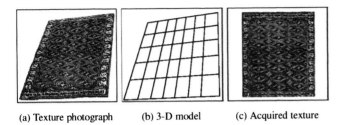

(a) Texture photograph   (b) 3-D model   (c) Acquired texture

Figure 17: Texture acquisition.

9.3 Texture Acquisition

Sometimes we find pictures of objects with textures that we would like to apply to other objects. Often these textures are not available in a perfect orthogonal view as it is necessary for texture mapping. Our technique can be used in reverse to acquire the texture. For example, shown in Figure 17 is a photograph of a carpet on the floor. Since the camera was not directly over the carpet, it appears in perspective; furthermore, since the carpet is not rigid the edges are not completely straight. Thus, the image of the carpet is not the kind of rectangle one would like to use for texture mapping. We build a 3-D model of the carpet (a rectangle), position and orient the model in space so its projection on screen space is similar to the picture, associate markers on the picture and on the model, and apply the inverse of our warp to extract the texture form the picture and apply it to the model. Of course, if parts of the figure were occluded in the original photograph this could lead to holes in the final texture map.

10 FUTURE WORK

This project suggests a number of areas for future work, several of which are described below.

Computer Vision.   We would like to reduce the amount of effort required to construct and position the 3-D model. One strategy is to investigate the applicability of computer vision algorithms to reconstruct the 3-D geometry from the 2-D drawings. Perhaps the animator could draw hints in the artwork using Williams's scheme [31] for conveying depth information through line-drawings. Computer vision techniques would also be useful for discerning camera position, inferring model deformations, and applying kinematics constraints. The computer could orient and deform the 3-D model based on the 2-D drawings. Finally, perhaps the computer could also guess the correspondence between a curve in the drawing and a curve in the 3-D model using simple heuristics based on location, orientation and shape.

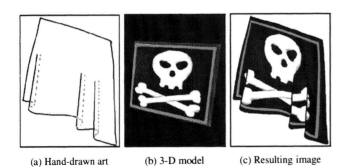

(a) Hand-drawn art   (b) 3-D model   (c) Resulting image

Figure 18: Applying texture to hand-drawn cloth.

Frame-to-Frame Coherence.   In an animation sequence, two consecutive frames are likely to be similar. We would like to minimize user intervention by exploiting frame-to-frame coherence, reusing information such as association between drawing and approximating 3-D model, detection and association of feature curves, and model and camera adjustment.

Cloth.   As mentioned in Section 8 there are some kinds of figures for which our process does not yet work. Perhaps the most challenging (and probably the most rewarding) class of figures would be those with complex surface textures such as cloth and hair. One of the difficulties with cloth is understanding and how it folds, based on the line art. Given the right set of marker curves, our warp can produce the right kind of behavior. For example, in Figure 18 we show how adding extra marker curves by hand (shown as dashed blue) can disambiguate the line art.

Acknowledgements

We thank Kiran Joshi for posing this problem, as well as Brent Burley, Aliza Corson, Mauro Maressa and Paul Yanover at Disney for their help and advice on this project. We also thank Cassidy Curtis for his guidance, and Tim Milliron for the 3-D examples. Finally, we are grateful to Ronen Barzel, John Hughes, Dan Wallach, and the anonymous reviewers for many improvements to the paper. This work was supported in part by CNPq (Conselho Nacional de Desenvolvimento Científico e Tecnológico), Brazil.

References

[1] Kendall E. Atkinson. *An Introduction to Numerical Analysis.* John Wiley & Sons, New York, 1988.

[2] Thaddeus Beier and Shawn Neely. Feature-Based Image Metamorphosis. In Edwin E. Catmull, editor, *SIGGRAPH 92 Conference Proceedings*, Annual Conference Series, pages 35–42. ACM SIGGRAPH, Addison Wesley, July 1992.

[3] Thomas H. Cormen, Charles E. Leiserson, and Ronald L. Rivest. *Introduction to Algorithms.* MIT Press, Cambridge, Mass., 1990.

[4] Cassidy J. Curtis, Sean E. Anderson, Joshua E. Seims, Kurt W. Fleischer, and David H. Salesin. Computer-Generated Watercolor. In Turner Whitted, editor, *SIGGRAPH 97 Conference Proceedings*, Annual Conference Series, pages 421–430. ACM SIGGRAPH, Addison Wesley, August 1997.

[5] Gerald Farin. *Curves and Surfaces for Computer Aided Geometric Design: a Practical Guide.* Academic Press, 1997.

[6] Jean-Daniel Fekete, Érick Bizouarn, Éric Cournarie, Thierry Galas, and Frédéric Taillefer. TicTacToon: A Paperless System for Professional 2-D Animation. In Robert Cook, editor, *SIGGRAPH 95 Conference Proceedings*, Annual Conference Series, pages 79–90. ACM SIGGRAPH, Addison Wesley, August 1995.

[7] James D. Foley, Andries van Dam, Steven K. Feiner, and John F. Hughes. *Computer Graphics, Principles and Practice.* Addison-Wesley, Reading, Massachusetts, second edition, 1990.

[8] Michael Gleicher. Image Snapping. In Robert Cook, editor, *SIGGRAPH 95 Conference Proceedings*, Annual Conference Series, pages 183–190. ACM SIGGRAPH, Addison Wesley, August 1995.

[9] Michael Kass, Andrew Witkin, and Demetri Terzopoulos. Snakes: Active Contour Models. *International Journal of Computer Vision*, pages 321–331, 1988.

[10] Seung-Yong Lee, Kyung-Yong Chwa, Sung Yong Shin, and George Wolberg. Image Metamorphosis Using Snakes and Free-Form Deformations. In Robert Cook, editor, *SIGGRAPH 95 Conference Proceedings*, Annual Conference Series, pages 439–448. ACM SIGGRAPH, Addison Wesley, August 1995.

[11] Apostolos Lerios, Chase D. Garfinkle, and Marc Levoy. Feature-Based Volume Metamorphosis. In Robert Cook, editor, *SIGGRAPH 95 Conference Proceedings*, Annual Conference Series, pages 449–456. ACM SIGGRAPH, Addison Wesley, August 1995.

[12] Peter Litwinowicz. Processing Images and Video for an Impressionist Effect. In Turner Whitted, editor, *SIGGRAPH 97 Conference Proceedings*, Annual Conference Series, pages 407–414. ACM SIGGRAPH, Addison Wesley, August 1997.

[13] Peter Litwinowicz and Lance Williams. Animating Images with Drawings. In Andrew Glassner, editor, *SIGGRAPH 94 Conference Proceedings*, Annual Conference Series, pages 409–412. ACM SIGGRAPH, Addison Wesley, July 1994.

[14] Lee Markosian, Michael A. Kowalski, Samuel J. Trychin, Lubomir D. Bourdev, Daniel Goldstein, and John F. Hughes. Real-time Nonphotorealistic Rendering. In Turner Whitted, editor, *SIGGRAPH 97 Conference Proceedings*, Annual Conference Series, pages 415–420. ACM SIGGRAPH, Addison Wesley, August 1997.

[15] Barbara J. Meier. Painterly Rendering for Animation. In Holly Rushmeier, editor, *SIGGRAPH 96 Conference Proceedings*, Annual Conference Series, pages 477–484. ACM SIGGRAPH, Addison Wesley, August 1996.

[16] Eric N. Mortensen and William A. Barrett. Intelligent Scissors for Image Composition. In Robert Cook, editor, *SIGGRAPH 95 Conference Proceedings*, Annual Conference Series, pages 191–198. ACM SIGGRAPH, Addison Wesley, August 1995.

[17] Michael Plass and Maureen Stone. Curve Fitting with Piecewise Parametric Cubics. In Peter Tanner, editor, *SIGGRAPH 83 Conference Proceedings*, Annual Conference Series, pages 229–239. ACM SIGGRAPH, July 1983.

[18] Barbara Robertson. Disney Lets CAPS out of the Bag. *Computer Graphics World*, pages 58–64, July 1994.

[19] D. F. Rogers and J. A. Adams. *Mathematical Elements for Computer Graphics*. McGraw-Hill, New York, second edition, 1990.

[20] Walter Roberts Sabiston. Extracting 3D Motion from Hand-Drawn Animated Figures. M.Sc. Thesis, Massachusetts Institute of Technology, 1991.

[21] Takafumi Saito and Tokiichiro Takahashi. Comprehensible Rendering of 3-D Shapes. In Forest Baskett, editor, *SIGGRAPH 90 Conference Proceedings*, Annual Conference Series, pages 197–206. ACM SIGGRAPH, Addison Wesley, August 1990.

[22] Philip J. Schneider. An Algorithm for Automatically Fitting Digitized Curves. In Andrew S. Glassner, editor, *Graphics Gems*, number I, pages 612–626. Academic Press, 1990.

[23] Thomas W. Sederberg, Peisheng Gao, Guojin Wang, and Hong Mu. 2D Shape Blending: An Intrinsic Solution to the Vertex Path Problem. In James T. Kajiya, editor, *SIGGRAPH 93 Conference Proceedings*, Annual Conference Series, pages 15–18. ACM SIGGRAPH, Addison Wesley, August 1993.

[24] Thomas W. Sederberg and Scott R. Parry. Free-Form Deformation of Solid Geometric Models. In David C. Evans and Russell J. Athay, editors, *SIGGRAPH 86 Conference Proceedings*, Annual Conference Series, pages 151–160. ACM SIGGRAPH, August 1986.

[25] Michael A. Shantzis. A Model for Efficient and Flexible Image Computing. In Andrew Glassner, editor, *SIGGRAPH 94 Conference Proceedings*, Annual Conference Series, pages 147–154. ACM SIGGRAPH, Addison Wesley, July 1994.

[26] Robert E. Tarjan and Jan van Leeuwen. Worst-Case Analysis of Set Union Algorithms. *Journal of the ACM*, 31(2):245–281, April 1984.

[27] Frank Thomas and Ollie Johnston. *Disney Animation: The Illusion of Life*. Walt Disney Productions, New York, 1981.

[28] B. A. Wallace. Merging and Transformation of Raster Images for Cartoon Animation. In Henry Fuchs, editor, *SIGGRAPH 81 Conference Proceedings*, Annual Conference Series, pages 253–262. ACM SIGGRAPH, August 1981.

[29] Dan S. Wallach, Sharma Kunapalli, and Michael F. Cohen. Accelerated MPEG Compression of Dynamic Polygonal Scenes. In Andrew Glassner, editor, *SIGGRAPH 94 Conference Proceedings*, Annual Conference Series, pages 193–197. ACM SIGGRAPH, Addison Wesley, July 1994.

[30] Walt Disney Home Video. Aladdin and the King of Thieves. Distributed by Buena Vista Home Video, Dept. CS, Burbank, CA, 91521. Originally released in 1992 as a motion picture.

[31] Lance R. Williams. Topological Reconstruction of a Smooth Manifold-Solid from its Occluding Contour. Technical Report 94-04, University of Massachusetts, Amherst, MA, 1994.

[32] Georges Winkenbach and David H. Salesin. Computer-Generated Pen-and-Ink Illustration. In Andrew Glassner, editor, *SIGGRAPH 94 Conference Proceedings*, Annual Conference Series, pages 91–100. ACM SIGGRAPH, Addison Wesley, July 1994.

[33] Andrew Witkin and Zoran Popović. Motion Warping. In Robert Cook, editor, *SIGGRAPH 95 Conference Proceedings*, Annual Conference Series, pages 105–108. ACM SIGGRAPH, Addison Wesley, August 1995.

[34] George Wolberg. *Digital Image Warping*. IEEE Computer Society Press, Washington, 1990.

[35] Daniel N. Wood, Adam Finkelstein, John F. Hughes, Craig E. Thayer, and David H. Salesin. Multiperspective Panoramas for Cel Animation. In Turner Whitted, editor, *SIGGRAPH 97 Conference Proceedings*, Annual Conference Series, pages 243–250. ACM SIGGRAPH, Addison Wesley, August 1997.

A Non-Photorealistic Lighting Model For Automatic Technical Illustration

Amy Gooch   Bruce Gooch   Peter Shirley   Elaine Cohen

Department of Computer Science
University of Utah
http://www.cs.utah.edu/

Abstract

Phong-shaded 3D imagery does not provide geometric information of the same richness as human-drawn technical illustrations. A non-photorealistic lighting model is presented that attempts to narrow this gap. The model is based on practice in traditional technical illustration, where the lighting model uses both luminance and changes in hue to indicate surface orientation, reserving extreme lights and darks for edge lines and highlights. The lighting model allows shading to occur only in mid-tones so that edge lines and highlights remain visually prominent. In addition, we show how this lighting model is modified when portraying models of metal objects. These illustration methods give a clearer picture of shape, structure, and material composition than traditional computer graphics methods.

CR Categories: I.3.0 [Computer Graphics]: General; I.3.6 [Computer Graphics]: Methodology and Techniques.

Keywords: illustration, non-photorealistic rendering, silhouettes, lighting models, tone, color, shading

1 Introduction

The advent of photography and computers has not replaced artists, illustrators, or draftsmen, despite rising salaries and the decreasing cost of photographic and computer rendering technology. Almost all manuals that involve 3D objects, e.g., a car owner's manual, have illustrations rather than photographs. This lack of photography is present even in applications where aesthetics are a side-issue, and communication of geometry is the key. Examining technical manuals, illustrated textbooks, and encyclopedias reveals illustration conventions that are quite different from current computer graphics methods. These conventions fall under the umbrella term *technical illustrations*. In this paper we attempt to automate some of these conventions. In particular, we adopt a shading algorithm based on cool-to-warm *tones* such as shown in the non-technical image in Figure 1. We adopt this style of shading to ensure that black silhouettes and edge lines are clearly visible which is often not the case when they are drawn in conjunction with traditional computer graphics shading. The fundamental idea in this paper is that when silhouettes and other edge lines are explicitly drawn, then very low

Figure 1: *The non-photorealistic cool (blue) to warm (tan) transition on the skin of the garlic in this non-technical setting is an example of the technique automated in this paper for technical illustrations. Colored pencil drawing by Susan Ashurst.*

dynamic range shading is needed for the interior. As artists have discovered, adding a somewhat artificial hue shift to shading helps imply shape without requiring a large dynamic range. This hue shift can interfere with precise albedo perception, but this is not a major concern in technical illustration where the communication of shape and form are valued above realism. In Section 2 we review previous computer graphics work, and conclude that little has been done to produce shaded technical drawings. In Section 3 we review the common technical illustration practices. In Section 4 we describe how we have automated some of these practices. We discuss future work and summarize in Section 5.

2 Related Work

Computer graphics algorithms that imitate non-photographic techniques such as painting or pen-and-ink are referred to as *non-photorealistic rendering* (NPR). The various NPR methods differ greatly in style and visual appearance, but are all closely related to conventional artistic techniques (e.g., [6, 8, 10, 13, 14, 16, 20, 26]). An underlying assumption in NPR is that artistic techniques developed by human artists have intrinsic merit based on the evolutionary nature of art. We follow this assumption in the case of technical illustration.

NPR techniques used in computer graphics vary greatly in their level of abstraction. Those that produce a loss of detail, such as semi-randomized watercolor or pen-and-ink, produce a very high level of abstraction, which would be inappropriate for most technical illustrations. Photorealistic rendering techniques provide little abstraction, so photorealistic images tend to be more confusing than less detailed human-drawn technical illustrations. Technical illustrations occupy the middle ground of abstraction, where the important three-dimensional properties of objects are accented while extraneous detail is diminished or eliminated. Images at any level of abstraction can be aesthetically pleasing, but this is a side-effect rather than a primary goal for technical illustration. A rationale for using abstraction to eliminate detail from an image is that, unlike the case of 3D scene perception, the image viewer is not able to use motion, accommodation, or parallax cues to help deal with visual complexity. Using abstraction to simplify images helps the user overcome the loss of these spatial cues in a 2D image.

In computer graphics, there has been little work related to technical illustration. Saito and Takahashi [19] use a variety of techniques to show geometric properties of objects, but their images do not follow many of the technical illustration conventions. Seligmann and Feiner present a system that automatically generates explanation-based drawings [21]. Their system focuses primarily on what to draw, with secondary attention to visual style. Our work deals primarily with visual style rather than layout issues, and thus there is little overlap with Seligmann and Feiner's system, although the two methods would combine naturally. The work closest to our own was presented by Dooley and Cohen [7] who employ a user-defined hierarchy of components, such as line width, transparency, and line end/boundary conditions to generate an image. Our goal is a simpler and more automatic system, that imitates methods for line and color use found in technical illustrations. Williams also developed similar techniques to those described here for non-technical applications, including some warm-to-cool tones to approximate global illumination, and drawing conventions for specular objects [25].

3 Illustration Techniques

Based on the illustrations in several books, e.g. [15, 18], we conclude that illustrators use fairly algorithmic principles. Although there are a wide variety of styles and techniques found in technical illustration, there are some common themes. This is particularly true when we examine color illustrations done with air-brush and pen. We have observed the following characteristics in many illustrations:

- edge lines, the set containing surface boundaries, silhouettes, and discontinuities, are drawn with black curves.

- matte objects are shaded with intensities far from black or white with warmth or coolness of color indicative of surface normal; a single light source provides white highlights.

- shadowing is not shown.

- metal objects are shaded as if very anisotropic.

We view these characteristics as resulting from a hierarchy of priorities. The edge lines and highlights are black and white, and provide a great deal of shape information themselves. Several studies in the field of perception have concluded that subjects can recognize 3D objects at least as well, if not better, when the edge lines (contours) are drawn versus shaded or textured images [1, 3, 5, 22]. However, when shading is added in addition to edge lines, more information is provided only if the shading uses colors that are visually distinct from both black and white. This means the dynamic range available for shading is extremely limited. In most technical illustrations, shape information is valued above precise reflectance information, so hue changes are used to indicate surface orientation rather than reflectance. This theme will be investigated in detail in the next section.

A simple low dynamic-range shading model is consistent with several of the principles from Tufte's recent book [23]. He has a case-study of improving a computer graphics animation by lowering the contrast of the shading and adding black lines to indicate

direction. He states that this is an example of the strategy of *the smallest effective difference*:

> *Make all visual distinctions as subtle as possible, but still clear and effective.*

Tufte feels that this principle is so important that he devotes an entire chapter to it. The principle provides a possible explanation of why cross-hatching is common in black and white drawings and rare in colored drawings: colored shading provides a more subtle, but adequately effective, difference to communicate surface orientation.

4 Automatic Lighting Model

All of the characteristics from Section 3 can be automated in a straightforward manner. Edge lines are drawn in black, and highlights are drawn using the traditional exponential term from the Phong lighting model [17]. In Section 4.1, we consider matte objects and present reasons why traditional shading techniques are insufficient for technical illustration. We then describe a low dynamic range artistic tone algorithm in Section 4.2. Next we provide an alogrithm to approximate the anisotropic appearance of metal objects, described in Section 4.3. We provide approximations to these algorithms using traditional Phong shading in Section 4.4.

4.1 Traditional Shading of Matte Objects

In addition to drawing edge lines and highlights, we need to shade the surfaces of objects. Traditional diffuse shading sets luminance proportional to the cosine of the angle between light direction and surface normal:

$$I = k_d k_a + k_d \max\left(0, \hat{\mathbf{l}} \cdot \hat{\mathbf{n}}\right) \qquad (1)$$

where I is the RGB color to be displayed for a given point on the surface, k_d is the RGB diffuse reflectance at the point, k_a is the RGB ambient illumination, $\hat{\mathbf{l}}$ is the unit vector in the direction of the light source, and $\hat{\mathbf{n}}$ is the unit surface normal vector at the point. This model is shown for $k_d = 1$ and $k_a = 0$ in Figure 3. This unsatisfactory image hides shape and material information in the dark regions. Additional information about the object can be provided by both highlights and edge lines. These are shown alone in Figure 4 with no shading. We cannot effectively add edge lines and highlights to Figure 3 because the highlights would be lost in the light regions and the edge lines would be lost in the dark regions.

To add edge lines to the shading in Equation 1, we can use either of two standard heuristics. First we could raise k_a until it is large enough that the dim shading is visually distinct from the black edge lines, but this would result in loss of fine details. Alternatively, we could add a second light source, which would add conflicting highlights and shading. To make the highlights visible on top of the shading, we can lower k_d until it is visually distinct from white. An image with hand-tuned k_a and k_d is shown in Figure 5. This is the best achromatic image using one light source and traditional shading. This image is poor at communicating shape information, such as details in the claw nearest the bottom of the image. This part of the image is colored the constant shade $k_d k_a$ regardless of surface orientation.

4.2 Tone-based Shading of Matte Objects

In a colored medium such as air-brush and pen, artists often use both hue and luminance (greyscale intensity) shifts. Adding blacks and whites to a given color results in what artists call *shades* in the case of black, and *tints* in the case of white. When color scales are

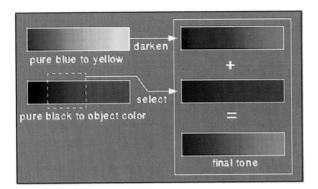

Figure 2: *How the tone is created for a pure red object by summing a blue-to-yellow and a dark-red-to-red tone.*

created by adding grey to a certain color they are called *tones* [2]. Such tones vary in hue but do not typically vary much in luminance. When the complement of a color is used to create a color scale, they are also called tones. Tones are considered a crucial concept to illustrators, and are especially useful when the illustrator is restricted to a small luminance range [12]. Another quality of color used by artists is the *temperature* of the color. The temperature of a color is defined as being warm (red, orange, and yellow), cool (blue, violet, and green), or temperate (red-violets and yellow-greens). The depth cue comes from the perception that cool colors recede while warm colors advance. In addition, object colors change temperature in sunlit scenes because cool skylight and warm sunlight vary in relative contribution across the surface, so there may be ecological reasons to expect humans to be sensitive to color temperature variation. Not only is the temperature of a hue dependent upon the hue itself, but this advancing and receding relationship is effected by proximity [4]. We will use these techniques and their psychophysical relationship as the basis for our model.

We can generalize the classic computer graphics shading model to experiment with tones by using the cosine term $(\hat{\mathbf{l}} \cdot \hat{\mathbf{n}})$ of Equation 1 to blend between two RGB colors, k_{cool} and k_{warm}:

$$I = \left(\frac{1 + \hat{\mathbf{l}} \cdot \hat{\mathbf{n}}}{2}\right) k_{cool} + \left(1 - \frac{1 + \hat{\mathbf{l}} \cdot \hat{\mathbf{n}}}{2}\right) k_{warm} \quad (2)$$

Note that the quantity $\hat{\mathbf{l}} \cdot \hat{\mathbf{n}}$ varies over the interval $[-1, 1]$. To ensure the image shows this full variation, the light vector $\hat{\mathbf{l}}$ should be perpendicular to the gaze direction. Because the human vision system assumes illumination comes from above [9], we chose to position the light up and to the right and to keep this position constant.

An image that uses a color scale with little luminance variation is shown in Figure 6. This image shows that a sense of depth can be communicated at least partially by a hue shift. However, the lack of a strong cool to warm hue shift and the lack of a luminance shift makes the shape information subtle. We speculate that the unnatural colors are also problematic.

In order to automate this hue shift technique and to add some luminance variation to our use of tones, we can examine two extreme possibilities for color scale generation: blue to yellow tones and scaled object-color shades. Our final model is a linear combination of these techniques. Blue and yellow tones are chosen to insure a cool to warm color transition regardless of the diffuse color of the object.

The blue-to-yellow tones range from a fully saturated blue: $k_{blue} = (0, 0, b), b \in [0, 1]$ in RGB space to a fully saturated yellow: $k_{yellow} = (y, y, 0), y \in [0, 1]$. This produces a very sculpted but unnatural image, and is independent of the object's diffuse reflectance k_d. The extreme tone related to k_d is a variation of dif-

fuse shading where k_{cool} is pure black and $k_{warm} = k_d$. This would look much like traditional diffuse shading, but the entire object would vary in luminance, including where $\hat{\mathbf{l}} \cdot \hat{\mathbf{n}} < 0$. What we would really like is a compromise between these strategies. These transitions will result in a combination of tone scaled object-color and a cool-to-warm undertone, an effect which artists achieve by combining pigments. We can simulate undertones by a linear blend between the blue/yellow and black/object-color tones:

$$\begin{aligned} k_{cool} &= k_{blue} + \alpha k_d \\ k_{warm} &= k_{yellow} + \beta k_d \end{aligned} \quad (3)$$

Plugging these values into Equation 2 leaves us with four free parameters: b, y, α, and β. The values for b and y will determine the strength of the overall temperature shift, and the values of α and β will determine the prominence of the object color and the strength of the luminance shift. Because we want to stay away from shading which will visually interfere with black and white, we should supply intermediate values for these constants. An example of a resulting tone for a pure red object is shown in Figure 2.

Substituting the values for k_{cool} and k_{warm} from Equation 3 into the tone Equation 2 results in shading with values within the middle luminance range as desired. Figure 7 is shown with $b = 0.4$, $y = 0.4$, $\alpha = 0.2$, and $\beta = 0.6$. To show that the exact values are not crucial to appropriate appearance, the same model is shown in Figure 8 with $b = 0.55$, $y = 0.3$, $\alpha = 0.25$, and $\beta = 0.5$. Unlike Figure 5, subtleties of shape in the claws are visible in Figures 7 and 8.

The model is appropriate for a range of object colors. Both traditional shading and the new tone-based shading are applied to a set of spheres in Figure 9. Note that with the new shading method objects retain their "color name" so colors can still be used to differentiate objects like countries on a political map, but the intensities used do not interfere with the clear perception of black edge lines and white highlights.

4.3 Shading of Metal Objects

Illustrators use a different technique to communicate whether or not an object is made of metal. In practice illustrators represent a metallic surface by alternating dark and light bands. This technique is the artistic representation of real effects that can be seen on milled metal parts, such as those found on cars or appliances. Milling creates what is known as "anisotropic reflection." Lines are streaked in the direction of the axis of minimum curvature, parallel to the milling axis. Interestingly, this visual convention is used even for smooth metal objects [15, 18]. This convention emphasizes that realism is not the primary goal of technical illustration.

To simulate a milled object, we map a set of twenty stripes of varying intensity along the parametric axis of maximum curvature. The stripes are random intensities between 0.0 and 0.5 with the stripe closest to the light source direction overwritten with white. Between the stripe centers the colors are linearly interpolated. An object is shown Phong-shaded, metal-shaded (with and without edge lines), and metal-shaded with a cool-warm hue shift in Figure 10. The metal-shaded object is more obviously metal than the Phong-shaded image. The cool-warm hue metal-shaded object is not quite as convincing as the achromatic image, but it is more visually consistent with the cool-warm matte shaded model of Section 4.2, so it is useful when both metal and matte objects are shown together. We note that our banding algorithm is very similar to the technique Williams applied to a clear drinking glass using image processing [25].

4.4 Approximation to new model

Our model cannot be implemented directly in high-level graphics packages that use Phong shading. However, we can use the Phong lighting model as a basis for approximating our model. This is in the spirit of the non-linear approximation to global illumination used by Walter et al. [24]. In most graphics systems (e.g. OpenGL) we can use negative colors for the lights. We can approximate Equation 2 by two lights in directions $\hat{l}$ and $-\hat{l}$ with intensities $(k_{warm} - k_{cool})/2$ and $(k_{cool} - k_{warm})/2$ respectively, and an ambient term of $(k_{cool} + k_{warm})/2$. This assumes the object color is set to white. We turn off the Phong highlight because the negative blue light causes jarring artifacts. Highlights could be added on systems with accumulation buffers [11].

This approximation is shown compared to traditional Phong shading and the exact model in Figure 11. Like Walter et al., we need different light colors for each object. We could avoid these artifacts by using accumulation techniques which are available in many graphics libraries.

Edge lines for highly complex objects can be generated interactively using Markosian et al.'s technique [14]. This only works for polygonal objects, so higher-order geometric models must be tessellated to apply that technique. On high-end systems, image-processing techniques [19] could be made interactive. For metals on a conventional API, we cannot just use a light source. However, either environment maps or texture maps can be used to produce alternating light and dark stripes.

5 Future Work and Conclusion

The shading algorithm presented here is exploratory, and we expect many improvements are possible. The most interesting open ended question in automatic technical illustrations is how illustration rules may change or evolve when illustrating a scene instead of single objects, as well as the practical issues involved in viewing and interacting with 3D technical illustrations. It may also be possible to automate other application-specific illustration forms, such as medical illustration.

The model we have presented is tailored to imitate colored technical drawings. Once the global parameters of the model are set, the technique is automatic and can be used in place of traditional illumination models. The model can be approximated by interactive graphics techniques, and should be useful in any application where communicating shape and function is paramount.

Acknowledgments

Thanks to Bill Martin, David Johnson, Brian Smits and the members of the University of Utah Computer Graphics groups for help in the initial stages of the paper, to Richard Coffey for helping to get the paper in its final form, to Bill Thompson for getting us to reexamine our interpretation of why some illustration rules might apply, to Susan Ashurst for the sharing her wealth of artistic knowledge, to Dan Kersten for valuable pointers into the perception literature, and to Jason Herschaft for the dinosaur claw model. This work was originally inspired by the talk by Jane Hurd in the SIGGRAPH 97 panel on medical visualization. This work was supported in part by DARPA (F33615-96-C-5621) and the NSF Science and Technology Center for Computer Graphics and Scientific Visualization (ASC-89-20219). All opinions, findings, conclusions or recommendations expressed in this document are those of the author and do not necessarily reflect the views of the sponsoring agencies.

References

[1] Irving Biederman and Ginny Ju. Surface versus Edge-Based Determinants of Visual Recognition. *Cognitive Psychology*, 20:38–64, 1988.

[2] Faber Birren. *Color Perception in Art*. Van Nostrand Reinhold Company, 1976.

[3] Wendy L. Braje, Bosco S. Tjan, and Gordon E. Legge. Human Efficiency for Recognizing and Detecting Low-pass Filtered Objects. *Vision Research*, 35(21):2955–2966, 1995.

[4] Tom Browning. *Timeless Techniques for Better Oil Paintings*. North Light Books, 1994.

[5] Chris Christou, Jan J. Koenderink, and Andrea J. van Doorn. Surface Gradients, Contours and the Perception of Surface Attitude in Images of Complex Scenes. *Perception*, 25:701–713, 1996.

[6] Cassidy J. Curtis, Sean E. Anderson, Kurt W. Fleischer, and David H. Salesin. Computer-Generated Watercolor. In *SIGGRAPH 97 Conference Proceedings*, August 1997.

[7] Debra Dooley and Michael F. Cohen. Automatic Illustration of 3D Geometric Models: Surfaces. *IEEE Computer Graphics and Applications*, 13(2):307–314, 1990.

[8] Gershon Elber and Elaine Cohen. Hidden Curve Removal for Free-Form Surfaces. In *SIGGRAPH 90 Conference Proceedings*, August 1990.

[9] E. Bruce Goldstein. *Sensation and Perception*. Wadsworth Publishing Co., Belmont, California, 1980.

[10] Paul Haeberli. Paint By Numbers: Abstract Image Representation. In *SIGGRAPH 90 Conference Proceedings*, August 1990.

[11] Paul Haeberli. The Accumulation Buffer: Hardware Support for High-Quality Rendering. *SIGGRAPH 90 Conference Proceedings*, 24(3), August 1990.

[12] Patricia Lambert. *Controlling Color: A Practical Introduction for Designers and Artists*, volume 1. Everbest Printing Company Ltd., 1991.

[13] Peter Litwinowicz. Processing Images and Video for an Impressionistic Effect. In *SIGGRAPH 97 Conference Proceedings*, August 1997.

[14] L. Markosian, M. Kowalski, S. Trychin, and J. Hughes. Real-Time Non-Photorealistic Rendering. In *SIGGRAPH 97 Conference Proceedings*, August 1997.

[15] Judy Martin. *Technical Illustration: Materials, Methods, and Techniques*, volume 1. Macdonald and Co Publishers, 1989.

[16] Barbara J. Meier. Painterly Rendering for Animation. In *SIGGRAPH 96 Conference Proceedings*, August 1996.

[17] Bui-Tuong Phong. Illumination for Computer Generated Images. *Communications of the ACM*, 18(6):311–317, June 1975.

[18] Tom Ruppel, editor. *The Way Science Works*, volume 1. MacMillan, 1995.

[19] Takafumi Saito and Tokiichiro Takahashi. Comprehensible Rendering of 3D Shapes. In *SIGGRAPH 90 Conference Proceedings*, August 1990.

[20] Mike Salisbury, Michael T. Wong, John F. Hughes, and David H. Salesin. Orientable Textures for Image-Based Pen-and-Ink Illustration. In *SIGGRAPH 97 Conference Proceedings*, August 1997.

[21] Doree Duncan Seligmann and Steven Feiner. Automated Generation of Intent-Based 3D Illustrations. In *SIGGRAPH 91 Conference Proceedings*, July 1991.

[22] Bosco S. Tjan, Wendy L. Braje, Gordon E. Legge, and Daniel Kersten. Human Efficiency for Recognizing 3-D Objects in Luminance Noise. *Vision Research*, 35(21):3053–3069, 1995.

[23] Edward Tufte. *Visual Explanations*. Graphics Press, 1997.

[24] Bruce Walter, Gun Alppay, Eric P. F. Lafortune, Sebastian Fernandez, and Donald P. Greenberg. Fitting Virtual Lights for Non-Diffuse Walkthroughs. In *SIGGRAPH 97 Conference Proceedings*, pages 45–48, August 1997.

[25] Lance Williams. Shading in Two Dimensions. *Graphics Interface '91*, pages 143–151, 1991.

[26] Georges Winkenbach and David H. Salesin. Computer Generated Pen-and-Ink Illustration. In *SIGGRAPH 94 Conference Proceedings*, August 1994.

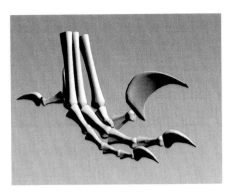

Figure 3: Diffuse shaded image using Equation 1 with $k_d = 1$ and $k_a = 0$. Black shaded regions hide details, especially in the small claws; edge lines could not be seen if added. Highlights and fine details are lost in the white shaded regions.

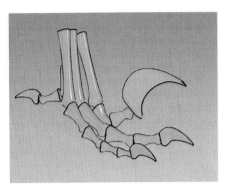

Figure 6: Approximately constant luminance tone rendering. Edge lines and highlights are clearly noticeable. Unlike Figures 3 and 5 some details in shaded regions, like the small claws, are visible. The lack of luminance shift makes these changes subtle.

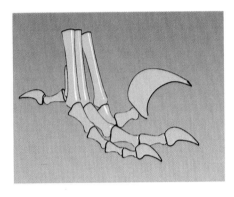

Figure 4: Image with only highlights and edges. The edge lines provide divisions between object pieces and the highlights convey the direction of the light. Some shape information is lost, especially in the regions of high curvature of the object pieces. However, these highlights and edges could not be added to Figure 3 because the highlights would be invisible in the light regions and the silhouettes would be invisible in the dark regions.

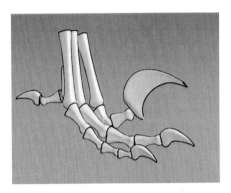

Figure 7: Luminance/hue tone rendering. This image combines the luminance shift of Figure 3 and the hue shift of Figure 6. Edge lines, highlights, fine details in the dark shaded regions such as the small claws, as well as details in the high luminance regions are all visible. In addition, shape details are apparent unlike Figure 4 where the object appears flat. In this figure, the variables of Equation 2 and Equation 3 are: $b = 0.4$, $y = 0.4$, $\alpha = 0.2$, $\beta = 0.6$.

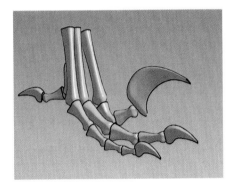

Figure 5: Phong shaded image with edge lines and $k_d = 0.5$ and $k_a = 0.1$. Like Figure 3, details are lost in the dark grey regions, especially in the small claws, where they are colored the constant shade of $k_d k_a$ regardless of surface orientation. However, edge lines and highlights provide shape information that was gained in Figure 4, but couldn't be added to Figure 3.

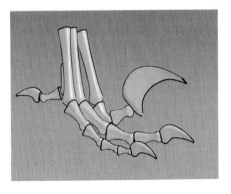

Figure 8: Luminance/hue tone rendering, similar to Figure 7 except $b = 0.55$, $y = 0.3$, $\alpha = 0.25$, $\beta = 0.5$. The different values of b and y determine the strength of the overall temperature shift, where as α and β determine the prominence of the object color, and the strength of the luminance shift.

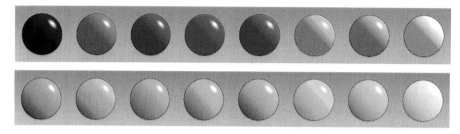

Figure 9: Top: Colored Phong-shaded spheres with edge lines and highlights. Bottom: Colored spheres shaded with hue and luminance shift, including edge lines and highlights. Note: In the first Phong shaded sphere (violet), the edge lines disappear, but are visible in the corresponding hue and luminance shaded violet sphere. In the last Phong shaded sphere (white), the highlight vanishes, but is noticed in the corresponding hue and luminance shaded white sphere below it. The spheres in the second row also retain their "color name".

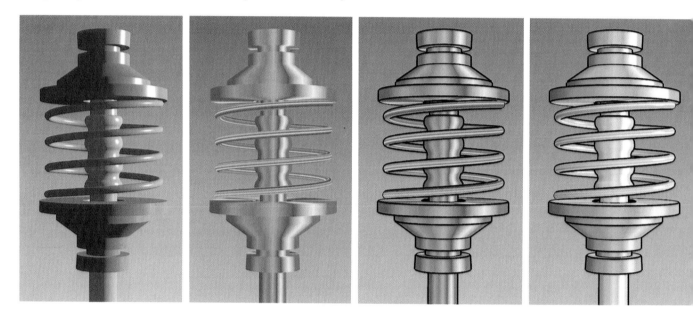

Figure 10: Left to Right: a) Phong shaded object. b) New metal-shaded object without edge lines. c) New metal-shaded object with edge lines. d) New metal-shaded object with a cool-to-warm shift.

Figure 11: Left to Right: a) Phong model for colored object. b) New shading model with highlights, cool-to-warm hue shift, and without edge lines. c) New model using edge lines, highlights, and cool-to-warm hue shift. d) Approximation using conventional Phong shading, two colored lights, and edge lines.

Painterly Rendering with Curved Brush Strokes of Multiple Sizes

Aaron Hertzmann
Media Research Laboratory
Department of Computer Science
New York University

ABSTRACT

We present a new method for creating an image with a hand-painted appearance from a photograph, and a new approach to designing styles of illustration. We "paint" an image with a series of spline brush strokes. Brush strokes are chosen to match colors in a source image. A painting is built up in a series of layers, starting with a rough sketch drawn with a large brush. The sketch is painted over with progressively smaller brushes, but only in areas where the sketch differs from the blurred source image. Thus, visual emphasis in the painting corresponds roughly to the spatial energy present in the source image. We demonstrate a technique for painting with long, curved brush strokes, aligned to normals of image gradients. Thus we begin to explore the expressive quality of complex brush strokes.

Rather than process images with a single manner of painting, we present a framework for describing a wide range of visual styles. A style is described as an intuitive set of parameters to the painting algorithm that a designer can adjust to vary the style of painting. We show examples of images rendered with different styles, and discuss long-term goals for expressive rendering styles as a general-purpose design tool for artists and animators.

CR Categories and Subject Descriptors: I.3.3 [Computer Graphics]: Picture/Image Generation — Display algorithms

Additional Keywords: Non-photorealistic rendering

1. INTRODUCTION

Art and illustration have historically been the sole domain of artists — skilled and creative individuals willing to devote considerable time and resources to the creation of images. Computer technology now allows the quick and easy creation of highly realistic images of natural and imaginary scenes. This technology automates the tedious details of photorealistic rendering, although the process is still driven by the human user, who selects the scene and rendering parameters. The technology for producing non-photorealistic works such as paintings and drawings is less advanced — the user must either "paint" the entire image interactively with a paint program, or else must process an image or 3D model through a narrowly-defined set of non-photorealistic filters. Ideally, a human user

email: *hertzman@mrl.nyu.edu*; URL: *http://www.mrl.nyu.edu/~hertzman*

should be able to choose from a wide range of visual styles, while leaving the mechanical details of image creation to a computer. It is now possible to envision animating a feature-length movie in a watercolor or oil painting style, a feat that would be prohibitively labor-intensive with traditional media. Non-photorealistic rendering can also be used to inexpensively create attractive and concise images for graphic design and illustration.

Most current computer painterly rendering algorithms use very simple brush strokes that are all of equal size and shape. Thus, the resulting images tend to appear mechanical in comparison to hand-made work. In this paper, we present techniques for painting an image with multiple brush sizes, and for painting with long, curved brush strokes. We find the resulting images to be more visually pleasing and "natural" than those produced with previous algorithms.

Artists have long exploited the richness of natural media in a variety of unique styles. Naturally, we would like our computer algorithms to be capable of similar variety. Here we do not attempt to imbue "creativity" into the algorithms, but prefer a more cooperative relationship. Rather, the user selects a composition and a rendering style, and the computer produces an image from these choices. In this paper we show how to create rendering styles suitable for use by a human designer.

1.1 Related work

Two principal challenges face the production of satisfying non-photorealistic images. The first of these, physical simulation, attempts to closely mimic the physical appearance of real-world artistic media. Impressive systems have been demonstrated for watercolor [5] and a variety of other media [7], in which the user places brush strokes interactively or semi-interactively. Wet media such as watercolor and oil paint are the most challenging media to simulate, because of the complex and rich set of effects produced by fluid flow and transparency. In this paper, we are not concerned with a convincing physical simulation; Haeberli [8] and others have shown that striking compositions can be produced even with very simple painting models. A related area of research is multiresolution painting [2,15], a set of techniques for interactive painting at all scales.

This paper extends the complementary line of research: automatic painting and drawing without human intervention. Cohen [4,13] casts the problem in terms of artificial intelligence; his system, named Aaron, follows a set of randomized rules to create original compositions in a specific style. Aaron even has a robotic painting device. Unlike Cohen's work, we assume that the composition is provided to the system in the form of an input image to be painted. Hence, we can focus on creating a painterly style, and need not deal with the problem of creativity in designing a composition. Winkenbach and Salesin [20,21] describe a system for automatically creating pen-and-ink illustrations from 3D models, and Salisbury et al. [16] describe a technique for producing pen-and-ink illustrations from images. Curtis et al. [5] produce watercolor paintings by a semi-automatic algorithm. However, their algorithm does not necessarily produce visible brush strokes, and thus lacks a painterly quality. A common method for processing an image for a painterly effect [1,7,11,14,17,22] is to place a jittered grid of short brush strokes over an image. These brush strokes may be aligned to the normals of image gradients, and all have the same size and shape. (Litwinowicz [11] uses clipped strokes; Treavett and Chen [17] use statistical analysis of the source image to guide stroke size, orientation and placement.) [14] and [17] do vary brush stroke size with respect to local detail levels. They appear to paint each image in a single pass, and thus lack the ability to refine the painting with multiple passes. [14] and [22] allow rendering parameters to be encapsulated and saved as "styles."

1.2 Overview

In the next section, we present a method for painting with different brush sizes to express various levels of detail in an image, and a technique for painting long, curved brush strokes to express continuous color regions in an image. In Section 3, we show how to abstract the rendering process to provide many painting styles. Finally, we discuss some future directions for non-photorealistic rendering.

2. PAINTING TECHNIQUES

2.1 Varying the brush size

Often, an artist will begin a painting as a rough sketch, and go back over the painting with a smaller brush to add detail. While much of the motivation for this technique does not apply to computer algorithms,[1] it also yields desirable visual effects. In Figure 1, note the different character of painting used to depict the blouse, sand, children, boat and sky. Each has been painted with different brush sizes as well as different stroke styles. This variation in stroke quality helps to draw the most attention to the woman and figures, and very little to the ground; in other words, the artist has used fine strokes to draw our attention to fine detail. (Other compositional devices such as shape, contrast and color are also used. These are not addressed in this paper.) To use strokes of the same size for each region would "flatten" the painting; here the artist has chosen to emphasize the figure over the background. In our image processing algorithm, we use fine brush strokes only where necessary to refine the painting, and leave the rest of the painting alone. Our algorithm is similar to a pyramid algorithm [3], in that we start with a coarse approximation to the source image, and add progressive refinements with smaller and smaller brushes.[2]

Our painting algorithm (Figure 2) takes as input a source image and a list of brush sizes. The brush sizes are expressed in radii $R_1 \ldots R_n$. The algorithm then proceeds by painting a series of *layers*, one for each radius, from largest to smallest. The initial canvas is a constant color image.

---

[1] One motivation is to establish the composition before committing fine details, so that the artist may experiment and adjust the composition.
[2] In fact, our original painting algorithm was based on the Laplacian pyramid: difference images (L_i) guided brush stroke placement. However, the difference images assume a perfect reconstruction of the lower levels of the pyramid, and our reconstruction is deliberately imperfect. Thus, refinements at later levels of the pyramid caused unwanted artifacts. Our present algorithm avoids this problem by creating the difference images after every step of the painting.

Figure 1: Detail of At The Seashore, Young Woman having her Hair Combed by her Maid, *Edgar Degas, 1876-7. Note that the small brush strokes are only used in regions of fine detail (such as the children in the background), and draw attention to these regions.*

For each layer R_i, we first create a *reference image* by blurring the source image. Blurring is performed by convolution with a Gaussian kernel of standard deviation $f_\sigma R_i$, where f_σ is some constant factor.[3] The reference image represents the image we want to approximate by painting with the current brush size. The idea is to use each brush to capture only details which are at least as large as the brush size. We use a *layer* subroutine to paint a layer with brush R_i, based on the reference image. This procedure locates areas of the image that differ from the reference image and covers them with new brush strokes. Areas that match the source image color to within a threshold (T) are left unchanged. The threshold parameter can be increased to produce rougher paintings, or decreased to produce paintings that closely match the source image.

This entire procedure is repeated for each brush stroke size. A pseudocode summary of the painting algorithm follows.

```
function paint(sourceImage, R₁ ... Rₙ)
{
    canvas := a new constant color image

    // paint the canvas
    for each brush radius Rᵢ,
         from largest to smallest do
    {
        // apply Gaussian blur
        referenceImage = sourceImage * G(fσ Ri)
        // paint a layer
        paintLayer(canvas, referenceImage, Rᵢ)
    }

    return canvas
}
```

---

[3] Non-linear diffusion [19] may be used instead of a Gaussian blur to produce slightly better results near edges. (Figure 5(a)).

Each layer is painted using a simple loop over the image canvas. The approach is adapted from the algorithm described in [11], which placed strokes on a jittered grid. That approach may miss sharp details such as lines and points that pass between grid points. Instead, we search each grid point's neighborhood to find the nearby point with the greatest error, and paint at this location. All strokes for the layer are planned at once before rendering. Then the strokes are rendered in random order to prevent an undesirable appearance of regularity in the brush strokes.

```
procedure paintLayer(canvas,referenceImage, R)
{
    S := a new set of strokes, initially empty

    // create a pointwise difference image
    D := difference(canvas,referenceImage)

    grid := f_g R

    for x=0 to imageWidth stepsize grid do
        for y=0 to imageHeight stepsize grid do
        {
            // sum the error near (x,y)
            M := the region (x-grid/2..x+grid/2,
                             y-grid/2..y+grid/2)
            areaError := Σ_{i,j∈M} D_{i,j} / grid²
            if (areaError > T) then
            {
                // find the largest error point
                (x_1,y_1) := arg max_{i,j∈M} D_{i,j}
                s :=makeStroke(R,x_1,y_1,referenceImage)
                add s to S
            }
        }

    paint all strokes in S on the canvas,
        in random order
}
```

The following formula for color difference is used to create the difference image:[4] $|(r_1,g_1,b_1) - (r_2,g_2,b_2)| = ((r_1 - r_2)^2 + (g_1 - g_2)^2 + (b_1 - b_2)^2)^{1/2}$. In order to cover the canvas with paint, the canvas is initially painted a special "color" C such that the difference between C and any color is MAXINT.

In practice, we avoid the overhead of storing and randomizing a large list of brush strokes by using a Z-buffer. Each stroke is rendered with a random Z value as soon as it is created. The Z-buffer is cleared before each layer.

"makeStroke()" in the above code listing is a generic procedure that places a stroke on the canvas beginning at (x_1,y_1), given a reference image and a brush radius. f_g is a constant grid size factor. Following [9], Figure 3(a) shows an image illustrated using a "makeStroke()" procedure which simply places a circle of the given radius at (x,y), using the color of the source image at location (x,y). Following [11], Figure 3(b) shows an image illustrated with short brush strokes, aligned to the normals of image gradients.[5] Note the regular stroke appearance. In the next section, we will present an algorithm for placing long, curved brush strokes, closer to what one would find in a typical painting.

Our technique focuses attention on areas of the image containing the most detail (high-frequency information) by placing many small brush strokes in these regions. Areas with little detail are painted only with very large brush strokes. Thus, strokes are appropriate to the level of detail in the source image.

This choice of emphasis assumes that detail areas contain the most "important" visual information. Other choices of emphasis are also possible — for example, emphasizing foreground elements or human figures — but these would require semantic interpretation of the input images, which is known to be an extremely difficult problem in computer vision. The choice of emphasis could also be provided by a human user [16], or as output from a 3D renderer.

2.2 Creating curved brush strokes

Individual brush strokes in a painting can convey shape, texture, overlap, and a variety of other image features. There is often something quite beautiful about a long, curved brush stroke that succinctly expresses a gesture, the curve of an object or the play of light on a surface. To our knowledge, all previous automatic painting systems use a series of small brush strokes, identical aside from color and orientation, or else apply pigment simultaneously to large regions of an image. In contrast, we present a method for painting long, continuous curves. In particular, we focus on painting solid strokes of constant thickness to approximate the coloration of the reference image; exploiting the full expressivity of brush strokes is far beyond the scope of this paper. We model brush strokes as anti-aliased cubic B-splines, each with a given color and thickness. Each stroke is rendered by dragging a circular brush mask along the sweep of the spline.

In our system, we limit brush strokes to constant color, and use image gradients to guide stroke placement. Other authors have also used this concept [11,8,18] for placing strokes. The idea is that the strokes will represent contours of the image with roughly constant color. Our method is to place control points for the curve by following the normal of the gradient. When the color of the stroke deviates from the color under a control point of the curve by more than a specified threshold, the stroke ends at that control point. One can think of this as placing splines to roughly match the isocontours of the reference image.

A more detailed explanation of the algorithm follows. The spline placement algorithm begins at a given point in the image (x_0,y_0), with a given a brush radius R. The stroke is represented as a list of control points, a color, and a brush radius. The control point (x_0,y_0) is added to the spline, and the color of the reference image at (x_0,y_0) is used as the color of the spline.

We then need to compute the next point along the curve. The gradient (θ_0) for this point is computed from the Sobel-filtered luminance[6] of the reference image. The next point (x_1,y_1) is placed in the direction $(\theta_0 + \pi/2)$ at a distance R from (x_0,y_0) (Figure 4(a)). We use the brush radius R as the distance between control points because R represents the level of detail we will capture with this brush size. This means that very large brushes create broad sketches of the image, to be later refined with smaller brushes.

---

[4] We have also experimented with more perceptually correct metrics, such as distance in CIE LUV [6] space. Surprisingly, we found that these often gave worse results.
[5] Note that no stroke clipping is used. Instead, small scale refinements of later layers automatically "fix" the edges of earlier layers.

[6] The luminance of a pixel is computed with $L(r,g,b) = 0.30*r + 0.59*g + 0.11*b$ [6].

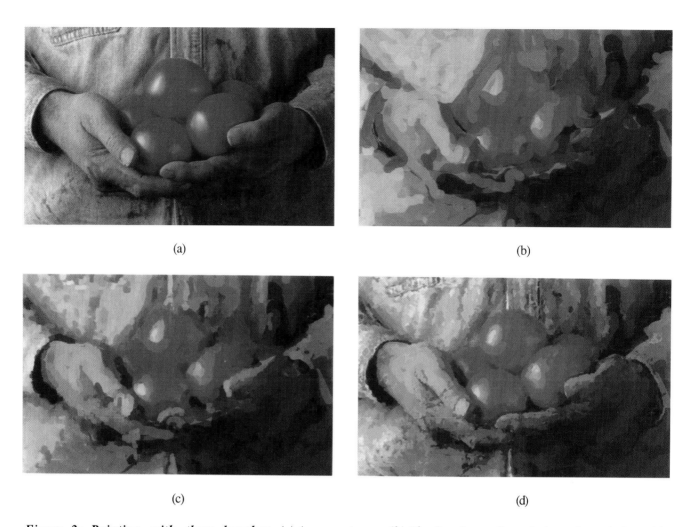

(a)

(b)

(c)

(d)

Figure 2: Painting with three brushes. *(a) A source image. (b) The first layer of a painting, after painting with a circular brush of radius 8. (c) The image after painting with a brush of radius 4. (d) The final image, after painting with a brush of size 2. Note that brush strokes from earlier layers are still visible in the painting.*

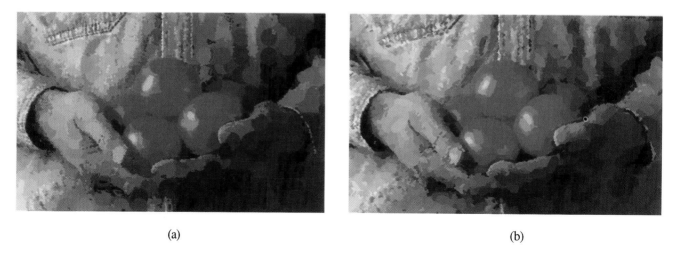

(a)

(b)

Figure 3: Applying the multiscale algorithm to other types of brush strokes. *Each of these paintings was created with brush strokes of radius 8, 4, and 2. (a) Brush strokes are circles, following [9]. (b) Brush strokes are short, anti-aliased lines placed normal to image gradients, following [11]. The line length is 4 times the brush radius.*

The remaining control points are computed by repeating this process of moving along the image normal to the image gradients and placing control points. The stroke is terminated when (a) the predetermined maximum stroke length is reached, or (b) the color of the stroke differs from the color under the last control point more than it differs from the current painting at that point. The maximum stroke length prevents an infinite loop from occurring. For a point (x_i, y_i), we compute a gradient direction θ_i at that point. Note, however, that there are actually two normal directions, and so two candidates for the next direction: $\theta_i + \pi/2$, and $\theta_i - \pi/2$. We choose the next direction so as to minimize the stroke curvature: we pick the direction D_i so that the angle between D_i and D_{i-1} is less than or equal to $\pi/2$. (Figure 4(b)).

We can also exaggerate or reduce the brush stroke curvature by applying an infinite impulse response filter to the stroke directions. The filter is controlled by a single predetermined filter constant, f_c. Given the previous stroke direction $D'_{i-1} = (dx'_{i-1}, dy'_{i-1})$, and a current stroke direction $D_i = (dx_i, dy_i)$, the filtered stroke direction is $D'_i = f_c D_i + (1-f_c) D'_{i-1} = (f_c dx_i + (1-f_c) dx'_{i-1}, f_c dy_i + (1-f_c) dy'_{i-1})$.

A pseudocode summary of the entire stroke placement procedure follows.

```
function makeSplineStroke(x₀,y₀,R,refImage)
{
    strokeColor = refImage.color(x₀,y₀)
    K = a new stroke with radius R
            and color strokeColor
    add point (x₀,y₀) to K
    (x,y) := (x₀,y₀)
    (lastDx,lastDy) := (0,0)

    for i=1 to maxStrokeLength do
    {
        if (i > minStrokeLength and
          |refImage.color(x,y)-canvas.color(x,y)|<
          |refImage.color(x,y)-strokeColor|) then
            return K

        // detect vanishing gradient
        if (refImage.gradientMag(x,y) == 0) then
         return K

        // get unit vector of gradient
        (gx,gy) := refImage.gradientDirection(x,y)
        // compute a normal direction
        (dx,dy) := (-gy, gx)

        // if necessary, reverse direction
        if (lastDx * dx + lastDy * dy < 0) then
         (dx,dy) := (-dx, -dy)

        // filter the stroke direction
        (dx,dy) :=fc*(dx,dy)+(1-fc)*(lastDx,lastDy)
        (dx,dy) := (dx,dy)/(dx² + dy²)^(1/2)
        (x,y) := (x+R*dx, y+R*dy)
        (lastDx,lastDy) := (dx,dy)

        add the point (x,y) to K
    }
    return K
}
```

The minimum stroke length prevents the speckled appearance of very short strokes. To render a curved stroke, the spline is first computed by subdivision. An anti-aliased, circular mask is then drawn along the path of the curve.

We have shown how to draw a long, curved brush stroke, to represent continuous color regions in an image. This method works best in combination with the layering method of Section 2.1; see Figure 2(b) for an example of curved brush strokes without layering. In the future, we would like to enhance this

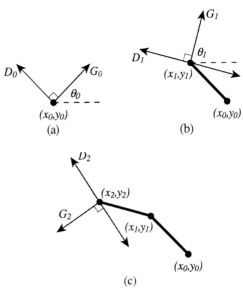

Figure 4: Painting a brush stroke. *(a) A brush stroke begins at a control point (x_0, y_0) and continues in direction D_0, normal to the gradient G_0. (b) From the second point (x_1, y_1), there are two normal directions to choose from: $\theta_1 + \pi/2$, and $\theta_1 - \pi/2$. We choose D_1, in order to reduce the stroke curvature. (c) This procedure is repeated to draw the rest of the stroke. The stroke will be rendered as a cubic B-spline, with the (x_i, y_i) as control points. The distance between control points is equal to the brush radius.*

technique to depict other features, such as contours and texture, and to use a richer stroke model, including pressure, bristles, wetness, and tapering.

3. RENDERING STYLES

There is no one "right" algorithm for non-photorealistic rendering, just as there is no "right" approach to painting. We believe that the graphic designer or artist using a rendering system should be allowed to vary the computer's "artistic approach," rather than being forced to employ a single style of painting for every picture. In order to quantify the notion of painterly styles, we propose the use of *style parameters* to control the rendering process. These parameters should provide an intuitive way to vary visual qualities of the painting. Some possible style parameters include stroke curvature and how closely the painting should approximate the original. To be useful to a designer, style parameters should exhibit, as much as possible, the following four properties:

- **Intuitiveness** — Each style parameter should correspond to a visual quality of the painting. These qualities should be intuitive to an artist without any technical computer knowledge.
- **Consistency** — Styles should produce the same "visual character" for different images. For example, we should be able to choose a style based on a single frame of a video sequence, and then render the rest of the sequence in the same style.
- **Robustness** — Each parameter should produce reasonable results over a predetermined range, without "breaking" for some values. A default value should be available, so that extra parameters provide the user with

more options without adding any extra burden. Increasing a parameter should always monotonically increase or decrease some quality of the painting, rather than cause it to fluctuate.

- **Independence** — Style parameters should be independent of one another. Changing line thicknesses, for example, should not affect the saturation of an image.

A group of style parameters describes a space of *styles*; a set of specific values can be encapsulated in a style. Styles may be designed to imitate the styles of famous artists, or may represent other approaches to painting. Styles can be collected into libraries, for later use by designers. Although there may conceivably be hundreds of rendering parameters, the designer need only adjust the parameters appropriate to an application. Some commercial painterly rendering products [14,22] provide the ability to vary rendering parameters and to save sets of parameters as distinct styles.

3.1　Some style parameters

In the experiments that follow, we have used the following style parameters.

- **Approximation threshold** (T) — How closely the painting must approximate the source image. Higher values of this threshold produce "rougher" paintings. (See Section 2.1)
- **Brush sizes** — Rather than requiring the user to provide a list of brush sizes ($R_1 \dots R_n$), we have found it more useful to use three parameters to specify brush sizes: Smallest brush radius (R_1), Number of Brushes (n), and Size Ratio (R_{i+1}/R_i). We have found that a limited range of brush sizes often works best. (See Section 2.1)
- **Curvature Filter** (f_c) — Used to limit or exaggerate stroke curvature. (See Section 2.2)
- **Blur Factor** (f_σ) — Controls the size of the blurring kernel. A small blur factor allows more noise in the image, and thus produces a more "impressionistic" image. (See Section 2.1)
- **Minimum and maximum stroke lengths** (minLength, maxLength) — Used to restrict the possible stroke lengths. Very short strokes would be used in a "pointillist" image; long strokes would be used in a more "expressionistic" image. (See Section 2.2)
- **Opacity** (α) — Specifies the paint opacity, between 0 and 1. Lower opacity produces a wash-like effect.
- **Grid size** (f_g) — Controls the spacing of brush strokes. The grid size times the brush radius ($f_g R_i$) produces the step size in the "paintLayer()" procedure. (See Section 2.1)
- **Color Jitter** — Factors to randomly add jitter to hue (j_h), saturation (j_s), value (j_v), red (j_r), green (j_g) or blue (j_b) color components. 0 means no random jitter; larger values increase the factor.

The threshold (T) is defined in units of distance in color space. Brush sizes are defined in units of distance; we specify sizes in pixel units, although resolution-independent measures (such as inches or millimeters) would work equally well. Brush length is measured in the number of control points. The remaining parameters are dimensionless.

3.2　Experiments

In this section, we demonstrate four painting styles: "Impressionist," "Expressionist," "Colorist Wash," and "Pointillist." Figure 6 shows the application of the first three

of these styles to two different images. The distinct character of each style demonstrates the consistency of the painting algorithm. (Figures 3(f) and 5 are also rendered in the "Impressionist" style.)

Figure 7 shows a continuous transition between the "Pointillist" style and the "Colorist Wash" style. By interpolating style parameter values, we can "interpolate" the visual character of rendering styles. This demonstrates the robustness of the parameters.

The styles are defined as follows.

- **"Impressionist"** — A normal painting style, with no curvature filter, and no random color. $T = 100$, $R = (8,4,2)$, $f_c = 1$, $f_s = .5$, a=1, $f_g = 1$, minLength=4, maxLength=16
- **"Expressionist"** — Elongated brush strokes. Jitter is added to color value. $T = 50$, $R = (8,4,2)$, $f_c = .25$, $f_s = .5$, a=.7, $f_g = 1$, minLength=10, maxLength=16, $j_v = .5$
- **"Colorist Wash"** — Loose, semi-transparent brush strokes. Random jitter is added to R, G, and B color components. $T = 200$, $R = (8,4,2)$, $f_c = 1$, $f_s = .5$, a=.5, $f_g = 1$, minLength=4, maxLength=16, $j_r = j_g = j_b = .3$
- **"Pointillist"** — Densely-placed circles with random hue and saturation. $T = 100$, $R = (4,2)$, $f_c = 1$, $f_s = .5$, a=1, $f_g = .5$, minLength=0, maxLength=0, $j_v = 1$, $j_h = .3$. (This is similar to the Pointillist style provided by [22].)

4.　DISCUSSION AND FUTURE WORK

We have presented a new algorithm for producing paintings from images. Brush stroke sizes are selected to convey the level of detail present in the source image using a multiscale algorithm. Long, curved brush strokes are created by moving in a direction normal to image gradients. The painting may be made sketchier or more precise by changing a threshold parameter. Stroke curvature may be limited or exaggerated by filtering stroke direction. These and other parameters describe a space of rendering styles that can be created and modified by artists and graphic designers.

Painting is a complex and rich pursuit, involving many approaches and many ways to interpret a scene. Our goal in developing painting algorithms is similar to a goal pursued by artists: to develop expressive visual languages. Future work in this area should extend the strategies available to non-photorealistic rendering algorithms, both image-based and model-based. We should be able to draw inspiration from various artistic approaches, as well as from computer vision, cognitive science, and artificial intelligence.

Brush strokes may convey many physical properties such as color, texture, lighting, 3D shape, gesture, and overlap, as well as semantic elements such as emphasis, mood, and emotion. One long-term goal is to develop an approach to painting that will convey the "important" features of an image with carefully chosen brush strokes.

A relaxation-based approach [8,18] may also be useful for computer painting. Although relaxation algorithms are usually more compute-intensive than are direct algorithms, they do allow many visual constraints to be embedded into a single energy function, some of which may be difficult to achieve by a direct method.

Another interesting line of work is real-time processing of video [11] and models [12] with different styles. New techniques will be required to maintain temporal coherence for complex brush strokes with various size and shape attributes, while maintaining or changing rendering styles. One can envision a real-time interactive system in which the rendering style varies with the mood or the action.

(a)

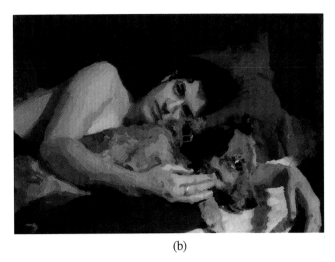

(b)

Figure 5: Two "impressionist" paintings.

Acknowledgements

Many thanks to Ken Perlin for useful discussions and support throughout the course of this work. Thanks to Rich Radke, Jon Meyer, and Henning Biermann for discussions. The source images for Figures 5(b) and 7 were provided by Jon Meyer. The source image for Figure 6(b) was used by kind permission of CND, Inc. The author is supported by NSF grant DGE-9454173.

5.   REFERENCES

[1]   ADOBE SYSTEMS. Adobe Photoshop 4.0

[2]   DEBORAH F. BERMAN, JASON T. BARTELL, DAVID H. SALESIN. Multiresolution Painting and Compositing. *SIGGRAPH 94 Conference Proceedings*, pp. 85-90. July 1994.

[3]   PETER J. BURT AND EDWARD H. ADELSON. The Laplacian Pyramid as a Compact Image Code. *IEEE Transactions on Communications.* 31:532-540, April 1983.

[4]   HAROLD COHEN. The Further Exploits of Aaron, Painter. *Stanford Humanities Review.* Vol. 4, No. 2. pp. 141-158. 1995

[5]   CASSIDY J. CURTIS, SEAN E. ANDERSON, JOSHUA E. SEIMS, KURT W. FLEISCHER, DAVID H. SALESIN. Computer-Generated Watercolor. *SIGGRAPH 97 Conference Proceedings,* pp. 421-430. August 1997.

[6]   JAMES FOLEY, ANDRIES VAN DAM, STEPHEN FEINER, JOHN HUGHES. *Computer Graphics: Principles and Practice*, Addison-Wesley, 1995.

[7]   FRACTAL DESIGN CORPORATION. Fractal Design Painter.

[8]   PAUL HAEBERLI. Paint by numbers: Abstract image representations. *Computer Graphics (SIGGRAPH 90 Conference Proceedings)*, 24(4):207-214, August 1990

[9]   PAUL HAEBERLI. The Impressionist. http://www.sgi.com/graphica/impression

[10]   JOHN LANSDOWN AND SIMON SCHOFIELD. Expressive rendering: A review of nonphotorealistic techniques. *IEEE Computer Graphics and Applications*, 15(3):29-37, May 1995.

[11]   PETER LITWINOWICZ. Processing Images and Video for An Impressionist Effect. *SIGGRAPH 97 Conference Proceedings*, pp. 407-414. August 1997.

[12]   LEE MARKOSIAN, MICHAEL A. KOWALSKI, SAMUEL J. TRYCHIN, LUBOMIR D. BOURDEV, DANIEL GOLDSTEIN, JOHN F. HUGHES. Real-Time Nonphotorealistic Rendering. *SIGGRAPH 97 Conference Proceedings*, pp. 415-420. August 1997.

[13]   PAMELA MCCORDUCK. AARON's CODE: Meta-Art, Artificial Intelligence, and the Work of Harold Cohen. New York: W. H. Freeman & Co. 225 pages. 1991.

[14]   MICROSOFT CORPORATION. Microsoft Image Composer 1.5

[15]   KEN PERLIN AND LUIZ VELHO. LivePaint: Painting with Procedural Multiscale Textures, *SIGGRAPH 95 Conference Proceedings*, pp. 153-160. 1995.

[16]   MICHAEL P. SALISBURY, MICHAEL T. WONG, JOHN F. HUGHES, DAVID H. SALESIN. Orientable Textures for Image-Based Pen-and-Ink Illustration. *SIGGRAPH 97 Conference Proceedings*, pp. 401-406. August 1997.

[17]   S. M. F. TREAVETT AND M. CHEN. Statistical Techniques for the Automated Synthesis of Non-Photorealistic Images. *Proc. 15th Eurographics UK Conference*, March 1997.

[18]   GREG TURK AND DAVID BANKS. Image-Guided Streamline Placement. *SIGGRAPH 96 Conference Proceedings*, pp. 453-460. August 1996.

[19]   JOACHIM WEICKERT, BART M. TER HAAR ROMNEY, MAX A. VIERGEVER. Efficient and reliable schemes for nonlinear diffusion filtering. *IEEE Transactions on Image Processing.* March 1998.

[20]   GEORGES WINKENBACH AND DAVID H. SALESIN. Computer-Generated Pen-and-Ink Illustration. *SIGGRAPH 94 Conference Proceedings*, pp. 91-100. July 1994.

[21]   GEORGES WINKENBACH AND DAVID H. SALESIN. Rendering Parametric Surfaces in Pen and Ink. *SIGGRAPH 96 Conference Proceedings*, pp. 469-476. August 1996.

[22]   XAOS TOOLS. Paint Alchemy 2.0

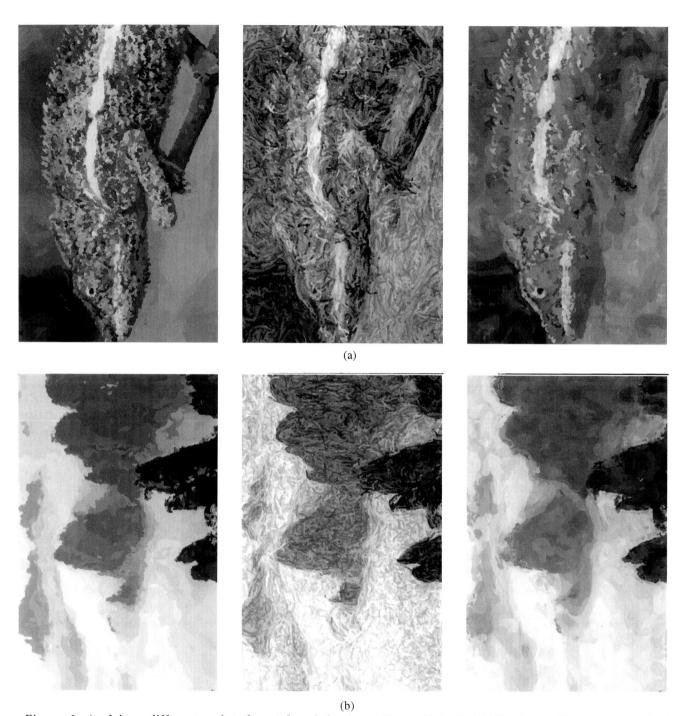

(a)

(b)

Figure 6: Applying different painterly styles. *Left column: "Impressionist." Middle column: "Expressionist." Right column: "Colorist Wash." Note that the styles have a consistent visual appearance when applied to different images.*

(a)   (b)   (c)

Figure 7: Interpolating rendering styles. *Images (a) and (c) are rendered in the "Colorist Wash" and "Pointillist" styles, respectively. The average of their parameters was used to produce the style for (b). (The number of layers (n) was rounded up to 3.)*

SIGGRAPH 98 Committee

SIGGRAPH 98 Conference Chair
Walt Bransford
Thrillistic

SIGGRAPH Conference Chief Staff
Executive
Dino Schweitzer
Capstone Management Group, Inc.

Accounting / Conference Management /
Copy Coordination / Marketing and Media
/ Registration
Smith, Bucklin & Associates, Inc.

Art Gallery: Touchware
Joan Truckenbrod
School of the Art Institute of Chicago

Audio/Visual Support
AVW Audio Visual, Inc.

Community Outreach
Chris Stapleton
Universal Studios
Adele Newton
Newton Associates

Computer Animation Festival
Ines Hardtke
National Film Board of Canada

Conference Administration
Capstone Management Group, Inc.

25th Conference Celebration
Carl Machover
Machover Associates Corporation

Courses
Harry Smith
University of North Carolina

Creative Applications Laboratory
Garry Paxinos
Metro Link Incorporated

Digital Pavilions / Online Technologies
Omar Ahmad
Netscape Communications Corporation

Educators Program
Scott Grissom
University of Illinois at Springfield

Enhanced Realities
Janet McAndless
Sony Pictures Imageworks

Exhibition Management
Hall-Erickson, Inc.

Graphic Design / Editing / Web Site
Q LTD

Interactive Dance Club
Ryan Ulyate
Organized Noise

International Services
Linda Hersom
James Scidmore
Scidmore, Hersom, & Others, Inc.

Networking
CJ Murzyn
University of Illinois at Chicago

Organizational Development
Raoul Buron
Center for Creative Leadership

Panels
Celia Pearce
momentum media group

Papers
Michael Cohen
Microsoft Research

Publications
Stephen N. Spencer
The Ohio State University

Service Contractor
Freeman Decorating Company

SIGGRAPH TV
David Tubbs
Evans & Sutherland Computer
Corporation

sigKIDS
Chris Stapleton
Universal Studios

Sketches
Rick Parent
The Ohio State University

Student Volunteers
Joe Lohmar
Digital Domain

Travel Agent
Flying Colors

SIGGRAPH 96 Conference Chair
John Fujii
Hewlett-Packard Company

SIGGRAPH 97 Conference Chair
G. Scott Owen
Georgia State University

SIGGRAPH 99 Conference Chair
Warren Waggenspack
Louisiana State University

SIGGRAPH 2000 Conference Chair
Jackie White
California State University Los Angeles

SIGGRAPH Chair
Steve Cunningham
California State University Stanislaus

Conference Advisory Group

SIGGRAPH 96 Conference Chair
John Fujii
Hewlett-Packard Company

SIGGRAPH 97 Conference Chair
G. Scott Owen
Georgia State University

SIGGRAPH 98 Conference Chair
Walt Bransford
Thrillistic, LLC

SIGGRAPH 99 Conference Chair
Warren Waggenspack
Louisiana State University

SIGGRAPH 2000 Conference Chair
Jackie White
California State University Los Angeles

SIGGRAPH Conference
Chief Staff Executive (Ex officio)
Dino Schweitzer
Capstone Management Group, Inc.

SIGGRAPH Organization Chair
Steve Cunningham
California State University Stanislaus

SIGGRAPH Executive Committee

Chair
Steve Cunningham
California State University, Stanislaus

Vice Chair
Alain Chesnais
Alias|Wavefront

Director for Communications
John C. Hart
Washington State University

Director for Education
Marc J. Barr
Middle Tennessee State University

Director for Professional Chapters
Scott Lang
Academy for the Advancement of
Science & Technology

Director for Publications
Stephen N. Spencer
The Ohio State University

Directors-at-Large
Chuck Hansen
University of Utah

Theresa-Marie Rhyne
Lockheed Martin Technical Services/
US EPA Scientific Visualization Center

Treasurer
Nan Schaller
Rochester Institute of Technology

Past Chair
Mary C. Whitton
University of North Carolina at Chapel
Hill

SIGGRAPH 97 Conference Chair
G. Scott Owen
Georgia State University

SIGGRAPH Conference
Chief Staff Executive (ex officio)
Dino Schweitzer
Capstone Management Group, Inc.

Papers Committee

Chair
Michael F. Cohen
Microsoft Research

Committee

Kurt Akeley
Silicon Graphics, Inc.

David Baraff
Carnegie Mellon University

Ronen Barzel
Pixar Animation Studios

Gary Bishop
University of North Carolina

Kellogg S. Booth
University of British Columbia

Rob Cook
Numinous Technologies

Frank Crow
Interval Research

Julie Dorsey
Massachusetts Institute of Technology

Irfan Essa
Georgia Institute of Technology

Steve Feiner
Columbia University

Thomas Funkhouser
Princeton University

Hugues Hoppe
Microsoft Research

John Hughes
Brown University

Chris Johnson
University of Utah

David Kirk
NVidia

Greg Ward Larson
Silicon Graphics, Inc.

Marc Levoy
Stanford University

Jitendra Malik
University of California, Berkeley

Joe Marks
Mitsubishi Electric Research Lab

Demitri Metaxas
University of Pennsylvania

Alyn Rockwood
Arizona State University

David Salesin
University of Washington

Tom Sederberg
Brigham Young University

Hans-Peter Seidel
Universität Erlangen

François Sillion
iMAGIS, France

Alvy Ray Smith
Microsoft Research

John Snyder
Microsoft Research

Demetri Terzopoulos
University of Toronto / Intel Corporation

Jane Wilhelms
University of California, Santa Cruz

Panels Committee

Chair
Celia Pearce
Momentum Media

Administrative Assistant
Tom Burkhart

Committee

John Snoddy
GameWorks

Clark Dodsworth

David Zeltzer
Sarnoff Corporation

Sara Diamond
Banff Centre for the Arts

Barbara Mones-Hattal
Industrial Light + Magic

Turner Whitted
Microsoft

Pauline T'so
Rhythm and Hues

Jeff Jortner
Sandia Laboratories

Courses Committee

Chair
Harry F. Smith
University of North Carolina

Administrative Assistant
Emma Kay Thornton
University of North Carolina

Committee

Barb Helfer
The Ohio State University

Alyce Kaprow
The New Studio

Anselmo Lastra
University of North Carolina

Steve May
The Ohio State University

Nan Schaller
Rochester Institute of Technology

Arnulfo Zepeda
Microsoft Corporation

Courses Reviewers

Andy Adler
Peter Anderson
Steve Anderson
Tony Apodaca
David Backer
Mike Bailey
David Banks
Kathy Barshatzky
Daniel Bergeron
Jack Bresenham
Wayne Carlson
Peter Carswell
Shih-Fu Chang
Claudia Cumbie-Jones
Andy Daniel
David Ebert
David Ellsworth
Nick England
Ken Flurchick
Donald Gambino
Andrew Glassner
David Gorgen
William Grosky
Mary Beth Haggerty
Rob Haimes
Chuck Hansen
Lou Harrison
John Hart
Barb Helfer
Gentaro Hirota
Leo Hourvitz
Donald House
Gil Irizarry
Stephen Jacobs
Lauretta Jones
Alyce Kaprow
James Kent
Scott King
Andrew Kitchen
Steve Kurtz
Anselmo Lastra
Mark Lee
Wm Leler
Mark Levoy
Matthew Lewis
Ming Lin
Zicheng Liu
Mark Livingston
Kevin Luster
William Mark
Mark Mine
Bonnie Mitchell
Steve Molnar
Carl Mueller
Steve Mullins
Ulrich Neumann
Marc Olano
Randy Pausch
Paul Rademacher
Saty Raghavachary
David Reed
Theresa-Marie Rhyne
Kevin Rodgers
Nan Schaller

Ferdi Scheepers
Marla Schweppe
Scott Senften
Andrei State
Don Stredney
Wolfgang Stürzlinger
Edward Swan
Rasmus Tamstorf
Russell Taylor
Paul Tymann
Lawson Wade
Hans Weber
Pat Wenner
Turner Whitted
Mary Whitton
Arnulfo Zepeda

Paper Reviewers

Gregory Abowd
Maneesh Agrawala
John Airey
Kiyoharu Aizawa
Daniel G. Aliaga
John Amanatides
Nina Amenta
P. Anandan
John Anderson
Ken Anjyo
Remi Arnaud
Jim Arvo
Ian Ashdown
Peter Astheimer
Matt Ayers
Ronald Azuma
Norman Badler
Wyeth Bair
Chandrajit Bajaj
Mike Bajura
Harlyn Baker
Kavita Bala
David C. Banks
Gill Barequet
Woodrow Barfield
Tony Barkans
Al Barr
William Barrett
Brian Barsky
Richard Bartels
Joseph Bates
Dan Baum
Ben Bederson
Andrew Beers
Thad Beier
Walter Bender
Jim Bergen
Michael J. Black
Andrew Blake
Jim Blinn
Jules Bloomenthal
Bruce Blumberg
Aaron Bobick
Bobby Bodenheimer
Silviu Borac
Jan Borgerson
James Boritz
Paul Borrel
Rachael Brady
David Breen
Normand Briere
John Bronskill
Armin Bruderlin
Steve Bryson
Richard Bukowski
Andreas Butz
William Buxton
Brian Cabral
Sharon Calahan
Tom Calvert
Swen Campagna
Marie-Paule Cani-Gascuel

Rikk Carey
Loren Carpenter
Gianpaolo U. Carraro
Ed Catmull
Tom Caudell
Bernard Chazelle
Cindy Chen
Eric Chen
Vernon Chi
Norishige Chiba
Eng Wee Chionh
Insook Choi
Peter Chou
Mike M. Chow
Lilian Chu
Paolo Cignoni
Robert Clear
Jeff Close
Elaine Cohen
Jonathan Cohen
Michael Cohen
Danny Cohen-Or
D'nardo Colucci
Perry R. Cook
Satyan Coorg
Sabine Coquillart
Mike Cosman
Michelle Covell
William Cowan
Michael Cox
Alan Craig
Roger Crawfis
Jim Cremer
Carolina Cruz-Neira
Davor Cubranic
Tim Cullip
Brian Curless
Bena Currin
Cassidy Curtis
Niels da Vitoria Lobo
Morten Daehlen
Kristin Dana
Trevor Darrell
Katja Daubert
Larry S. Davis
David Dean
Jeremy De Bonet
Paul Debevec
D. DeCarlo
Michael Deering
Leila DeFloriani
Tony Derose
Rod Deyo
Sven Dickinson
Paul Diefenbach
Suzana Djurcilov
David Dobkin
Steve Dollins
Bruce Rondall Donald
Judith S. Donath
Walt Donovan
Julie Dorsey

George Drettakis
Mark Duchaineau
Tom Duff
Aude Dufresne
Fredo Durand
Charles R. Dyer
David Ebert
Herbert Edelsbrunner
John T. Edmark
Gershon Elber
Matt Eldridge
Steve Ellis
Jihad El-Sana
Nick England
J. Robert Ensor
Carl Erikson
Mark D. Fairchild
Gerald Farin
Olivier Faugeras
Sidney Fels
James A. Ferwerda
Adam Finkelstein
Russ Fish
Eugene Fiume
Kurt Fleischer
Michael Fong
Michael Forkheim
David Forsey
David A. Forsyth
Nick Foster
Farhad Fouladi
Alain Fournier
William Freeman
Henry Fuchs
John Funge
Thomas Funkhouser
Jean Gallier
Michael Garland
Jean-Dominique Gascuel
Simon Gibson
Andrew Glassner
Mike Gleicher
Martin Goebel
Martin Goebel
Jeff Goldsmith
Steven Gortler
Phil Gossett
Ed Granger
Sebastian Grassia
Ned Greene
Guenther Greiner
Cindy Grimm
Larry Gritz
Markus Gross
Brian Guenter
Andre Gueziec
Mukul Gupta
Paul Haeberli
Tom Hahn
James Hahn
Eric Haines
Roy Hall

Mike Halle
Pat Hanrahan
Diane Hansford
Andy Hanson
John Hart
David Haumann
Barbara Hayes-Roth
Christopher Healey
Paul Heckbert
Wolfgang Heidrich
Alan Heirich
Sheila Hemami
Travis Heppe
Roger Hersch
Lambertus Hesselink
Jerry Higgins
Shaun Ho
Larry F. Hodges
Jessica Hodgins
Murray Hodgson
Tobias Hoellerer
Kenny Hoff
Dave Holliday
Robert Holt
Michael Hopcroft
Youichi Horry
Jim Hourihan
Donald H. House
Alex Hsu
Philip Hubbard
David Huffman
Zahid Hussain
Katsushi Ikeuchi
Kori Inkpen
Victoria Interrante
Hiroshi Ishii
Thomas W. Jensen
Dan Jobson
Stephen Johnson
Michael Jones
Ken Joy
Zafer Kadi
Jim Kajiya
Ioannis A. Kakadiaris
Michael Kass
Henry Kaufman
Arie E. Kaufman
Alexander Keller
John Kender
Jim Kent
Scott Kim
Kwansik Kim
David Kirkpatrick
R. Victor Klassen
Reinhard Klein
Brian Knep
Gunter Knittel
Leif Kobbelt
Visa Koivunen
E. Kokkevis
Klaus Kremer
David Kriegman

Paul Kruszewski
Subodh Kumar
Andrew Kunz
Alexandra Kuswik
Kiriakos Kutulakos
Phil Lacroute
David Laidlaw
James Landay
Anselmo Lastra
Jean-Claude Latombe
Asish Law
Mark Leather
Yuencheng Lee
Seungyong Lee
Justin Legakis
Jed Lengyel
David Levin
Hongbo Li
Ming Lin
Erik Lindholm
Peter Lindstrom
Dani Lischinski
James Little
Zicheng Liu
Mark Livingston
Yarden Livnat
N. Lobo
Suresh Lodha
Gerald Lohse
Jack Loomis
Charles Loop
Bill Lorensen
David Lowe
Mark Lucente
David Luebke
Tom Lyche
Kwan-Liu Ma
Carl Machover
Blair MacIntyre
Christine L. MacKenzie
Bruce Madsen
Nadia Magnenat-Thalmann
Mark Manca
Steve Mann
Dinesh Manocha
Martti Mantyla
Bill Mark
Lee Markosian
Paul Martin
Kenji Mase
Nelson Max
David McAllister
Michael McAllister
Michael McCool
Tim McInerney
Leonard McMillan
G. Medioni
Barbara Meier
Christopher Migdal
Victor Milenkovic
Gavin Miller
Tim Miller

Mark Mine
Brian Mirtich
Neelkanth Mishra
Don Mitchell
Joe Mitchell
David Mizell
Steve Molnar
Michael Monks
John Montrym
Henry Moreton
Dave Morgan
Bryan Morse
Mike Moshell
Amitabha Mukerjee
Michael Nagy
Marc Najork
Shree Nayar
Shawn Neely
Ulrich Neumann
Fabrice Neyret
Tom Ngo
Wayne Niblack
Jeffry Nimeroff
Alan Norton
Ryutarou Ohbuchi
Drew Olbrich
Kirk Olynyk
Joseph O'Rourke
Eben Ostby
Victor Ostromoukhov
Dinesh K. Pai
James S. Painter
Alex Pang
Matt Papakipos
Richard Parent
Tony Parisi
Frederic Parke
Steven Parker
Kannan Parthasarathy
Velerios Pascucci
Alexander Pasko
Sumant Pattanaik
Randy Pausch
Darwyn Peachey
Hans Køhling Pedersen
Mark Peercy
Catherine Pelachaud
Shmuel Peleg
Joseph Penn
Sandy Pentland
Ken Perlin
B. Peroche
Bernard Peroche
Hanspeter Pfister
Matt Pharr
Cary Phillips
Frederic Pighin
John Platt
Jean Ponce
Jovan Popovic
Zoran Popović
Hanna-Oskar Porr

Tom Porter
Frits H. Post
Helmut Pottmann
Pierre Poulin
Joanna Power
Apurva Prakash
Gill A. Pratt
Hartmut Prautzsch
John Princen
Dennis Proffitt
Przemyslaw Prusinkiewicz
Kari Pulli
Hong Qin
Sudeep Rangaswamy
Ari Rappaport
Matt Regan
Jun Rekimoto
Sandy Ressler
Craig Reynolds
Bill Ribarsky
George Robertson
Charles Rose
Lawrence J. Rosenblum
Dan Rosenthal
Jarek Rossignac
Holly Rushmeier
Paolo Sabella
Malcolm Sabin
Georgios Sakas
Tim Salcudean
Mike Salisbury
Nick Sapidis
Dietmar Saupe
Harpreet Sawhney
Gernot Schaufler
Andreas Schilling
Christophe Schlick
Bengt-Olaf Schneider
Robert Schneider
Chris Schoeneman
Will Schroeder
Peter Schroeder
Robert Schumacker
Stan Sclaroff
Roberto Scopigno
Mark Segal
Steve Seitz
Doree Seligmann
Carlo Sequin
Jonathan Shade
Mubarak Shah
Rob Shakespeare
Michael Shantz
Michael Shantzis
Linda Shapiro
Chris Shaw
Qin Shen
S. Shin
Peter Shirley
Ken Shoemake
Harry Shum
Kwanak-ku Sillim-dong
Michael Siminovitch
Karl Sims
Mukesh P. Singh
Phil Skolmoski

Mel Slater
Peter-Pike Sloan
Kenneth Sloan
Philipp Slusallek
Brian Smits
Scott Snibbe
Cyril Soler
Bob Sproull
Pierre St. Hilaire
Jos Stam
Marc Stamminger
John Stasko
Andrei State
Anthony Steed
Eckehard Steinbach
Eric Stollnitz
Maureen Stone
Wolfgang Straßer
Paul Strauss
Timothy Strotman
Wolfgang Stürzlinger
Wim Sweldens
Richard Szeliski
Tapio Takala
Steven Tanimoto
Gabriel Taubin
Seth Teller
Patrick Teo
Daniel Thalmann
Craig Thayer
Carlo Tomasi
Ken Torrance
Nicolas Tsingos
Xiaoyuan Tu
Mihran Tuceryan
Jack Tumblin
Greg Turk
Ken Turkowski
Sam Uselton
Michiel van de Panne
Kees van Overveld
Mark VandeWettering
Amitabh Varshney
Eric Veach
Luiz Velho / Gomes
Vivek Verma
Anne Verroust
Lev Virine
Doug Voorhies
James Waldrop
Bruce Walter
Jack Walther
Wenping Wang
Colin Ware
Joe Warren
Keith Waters
Richard C. Waters
Greg Welch
Will Welch
Pierre Wellner
Stephen Westin
Lee Westover
Turner Whitted
Lance Williams
John Willinsky
Andrew Willmott

Georges Winkenbach
Stephanie Winner
Andrew Witkin
George Wolberg
George Wolberg
Hans Wolters
Michael Wong
Daniel Wood
Adam Woodbury
Brian Wyvill
Yaser Yacoob
Hussein Yahia
Harold Zatz
Robert Zeleznik
David Zeltzer
Hansong Zhangh
Jianmin Zheng
Michelle Zhou
Ben Zhu
Andrew Zisserman
Douglas Zongker
Denis Zorin
Michael Zyda

Exhibitors

3D Construction Company
3D Pipeline Corporation
The 3D Shop
3Dlabs, Inc.
3Name3D
4DVISION LLC
5D Ltd.

A K Peters, Ltd.
Academic Press, Inc.
AccelGraphics, Inc.
Accom Inc.
Acuris Inc.
Adaptive Optics Associates, Inc.
Addison-Wesley
Adobe Systems Inc.
Advanced Imaging
Advanced Media Production
Advanced Rendering Technology Ltd.
Advanced Visual Systems Inc.
Advanstar Digital Media Group
aii/Digital Cinema Systems
AJA Video
Alias / Wavefront
Alien Skin Software, LLC
American Cinematographer Magazine
Ampex Corporation
ANDATACO
Animation Magazine
Animation Science
Anthro Corporation
AP PROFESSIONAL
Appian Graphics
Apple Computer, Inc.
The Art Institutes International
Artbeats
Ascension Technology Corporation
ASK LCD, Inc.
ATI Technologies, Inc.
auto.des.sys, Inc.
AutoMedia Ltd.
Avid Technology Inc.

B & H Photo Video-Pro Audio
Balboa Capital
Blue Sky | VIFX
The Bulldog Group

CADCrafts
Caligari Corporation
Cambridge Animation Systems
Cambridge University Press
CBS News Archives
CELCO
CGSD Corporation
Charles River Media
Chroma Graphics, Inc.
Chromatek Inc.
Chyron Corporation
Cinebase Software
Ciprico Inc.
CIRAD

Communications Specialties Inc.
Compaq Computer Corporation
Computer Graphics World
Concept Action Multimedia
Coryphaeus Software
Cyberware
Cygnet Storage Solutions

Dataram Corporation
Dell Computer Corporation
Desktop Engineering Magazine
Desktop Images
Diamond Multimedia
Diaquest Inc.
Digimation, Inc.
Digital Domain
Digital Equipment Corporation
Digital Processing Systems
Digital Semiconductor
Digits 'n Art Software, Inc.
DISC, Inc.
Discreet Logic
DreamWorks
Dynamic Pictures, Inc.

Electric Image, Inc.
ELSA Inc.
Elsevier Science
ENCAD, Inc.
Ensemble Designs
Equilibrium
EUROGRAPHICS
Evans & Sutherland Computer
Corporation
Eyeon Software Inc.

Folsom Research, Inc.
Fujitsu Microelectronics, Inc.
Full Sail Real World Education

General Reality Company
GW Hannaway & Associates

Harlequin, Inc.
Hash Inc.
Hewlett-Packard Company
HPCwire

I.D. Magazine
IBM
IEEE Computer Society
IMAGICA Corporation of America
Imagina - INA
Immersion Corporation
Industrial Light + Magic
Integrated Computing Engines, Inc. (ICE)
Intel Corporation
Interactive Effects /Amazon
Intergraph Corporation
InterSense
Islip Media
ITU Research, Inc.

Jasc Software, Inc.
John Wiley & Sons, Inc.
Journey Education Marketing

Kaydara Inc.
Kinetix
Kingston Technology Company
Knowledge Industry Publications

LambSoft, Inc.
Leadtek Research, Inc.
LEGASYS International, Inc.
Leitch
Lightwave Communications, Inc.
LightWork Design
Linker Systems, Inc.
Live Picture,Inc.
Logitech

MacAcademy/Windows Academy
Mainframe Entertainment, Inc.
Management Graphics, Inc.
Markee
Matrox Video Products Group
MAXSTRAT Corporation
MBNA America
Media 100, Inc.
Media PEGS
MegaDrive Systems, Inc.
Mercury Computer Systems, Inc.
MetaCreations Corporation
Microboards Technology, Inc.
Microsoft Corporation
Miller Freeman Inc.
Minicomputer Exchange
Minolta Corporation
Miranda Technologies
MMS Multi Media Systems GmbH
Morgan Kaufmann Publishers
Motion Analysis Corporation
The Motion Factory
MultiGen, Inc.
Multimedia Content Association of Japan
(MMCA)
MuSE Technologies, Inc. (MTI)

n-Vision, Inc.
NAD Centre
National Display Systems
NeTPower
New Media Magazine
NewTek, Incorporated
Nichimen Graphics, Inc.
Nikkei Computer Graphics
Northern Digital Inc.
nStor Corporation
Numerical Algorithms Group, Inc.
NVision, Inc.

Odyssey Productions
Omnicomp Graphics Corporation

Exhibitors

Ontario Film Development Corporation
Onyx Computing, Inc.
Orphan Technologies
Oxberry LLC

Pacific Data Images
Panasonic Broadcast & Digital Systems
Company
PC Video Conversion
Peak Performance Technologies, Inc.
Phobos Corporation
Photron USA
Pixar
Platform Computing Corporation
Polhemus
Post Digital Software
Post Magazine/Testa Communications
Proxima Corporation
Puffin Designs, Inc.
Pyramid Systems, Inc.

Quantel, Inc.
Quantum 3D
Quantum Corporation
Questar Productions, LLC
QuVIS

Real 3D
REALiZ
REM INFOGRAFICA, S.A.
The Republic Group
Research Systems
RGB Spectrum
Rhythm & Hues Studios
Roland Digital Group

Safework, Inc.
Savannah College of Art and Design
Scientific Placement, Inc.
Screen Actors Guild
SensAble Technologies, Inc.
Sharp Electronics Corporation
Side Effects Software
Sigma Electronics
Silicon Gear Corporation
Silicon Graphics, Inc.
Society of Motion Pictures and TV
Engineers (SMPTE)
Softimage Inc.
Sony
Sound Ideas
Springer-Verlag New York, Inc.
Sprint
Square USA, Inc.
SRS Bit 3 Operations
Storage Concepts
Strata, Inc.
Stratasys, Inc.
Sun Microsystems Inc.
Superscape
Sven Technologies
Symmetric

Synapix, Inc.
SYS-CON Publications

TechImage Ltd.
Tektronix, Inc.
Texas Memory Systems, Inc.
TGS, Inc.
TNT Technologies
Toon Boom Technologies, Inc.
Transoft Technology Corporation
Tri-Star Computer
Trimension Systems Ltd.
Trinity Animation
TV One Multimedia Solutions

University of Advancing Computer
Technology
Unlimited Potential, Inc.
Upside Magazine

Vancouver Film School
Variety's On Production
Vicon Motion Systems
Video Systems Magazine/Intertec
Publishing
Videomedia, Inc.
Viewpoint DataLabs International, Inc.
ViewSonic Corporation
Visible Productions
Vision International
Voxar

Wacom Technology Corporation
The Walt Disney Company
WCB/McGraw-Hill
Westwood Computer & Networking
Winsted Corporation
Workstation Users Alliance

SIGGRAPH Professional Chapters

California

Los Angeles ACM SIGGRAPH
Aliza Corson
PO Box 9399
Marina del Rey, CA 90295
los_angeles_chapter@siggraph.org
http://www.siggraph.org/chapters/los_angeles/

San Diego ACM SIGGRAPH
Nancy Collier
4822 Santa Monica Ave, Suite 179
San Diego, CA 92107
san_diego_chapter@siggraph.org
http://www.siggraph.org/chapters/san_diego/

San Francisco ACM SIGGRAPH
Rob Rothfarb
P.O. Box 1495
El Cerrito, CA 94530-4495
san_francisco_chapter@siggraph.org
http://www.siggraph.org/chapters/sf/

Silicon Valley ACM SIGGRAPH
Alesh Jancarik
PO Box 804
Mountain View, CA 94042-1205
silicon_valley_chapter@siggraph.org
http://www.siggraph.org/chapters/siliconv/

Colorado

Denver/Boulder ACM SIGGRAPH
Mike McCarthy
PO Box 61402
Cherry Creek Station
Denver, CO 80206-8402
denver-boulder_chapter@siggraph.org

Florida

Ft. Lauderdale ACM SIGGRAPH
Garry M. Paxinos
Metro Link Inc
4711 N. Powerline Road
Fort Lauderdale, FL 33309
fort_lauderdale_chapter@siggraph.org
http://www.siggraph.org/chapters/ftlsig/

Orlando ACM SIGGRAPH
Lynn R. Finch
PO Box 2208
Winter Park, FL 32790-2208
orlando_chapter@siggraph.org
http://www.siggraph.org/chapters/orlando/

Tampa Bay ACM SIGGRAPH
Blake Barr (acting chair)
tampa_bay_chapter@siggraph.org
http://www.flsig.org/tampa/

Georgia

Atlanta ACM SIGGRAPH
Mark Feldman
PO Box 769182
Roswell, GA 30076-9182
atlanta_chapter@siggraph.org
http://www.acm.org/chapters/atlanta/

Massachusetts

Boston ACM SIGGRAPH
Olin Lathrop
PO Box 194
Bedford, MA 01730
boston_chapter@siggraph.org
http://www.siggraph.org/chapters/boston/

Minnesota

Minneapolis/St. Paul ACM SIGGRAPH
Stan Bissinger
School of Communication Arts
5401 Elliot Ave. S.
Minneapolis, MN 55417
minneapolis-stpaul_chapter@siggraph.org
http://www.pixel8.com/siggraph/

New Jersey

Princeton ACM SIGGRAPH
Douglas Dixon
P.O. Box 1324
Princeton, NJ 08542
princeton _chapter@siggraph.org

New Mexico

Rio Grande ACM SIGGRAPH
Gwen Sylvan
P.O. Box 8352
Albuquerque, NM 87108-8352
rio_grande_chapter@siggraph.org

New York

New York City ACM SIGGRAPH
Valerie Castleman
60 Gramercy Park, #9A
New York, NY 10010
new_york_city_chapter@siggraph.org

North Carolina

NC Research Triangle ACM SIGGRAPH
Randy Brown
SAS Campus Drive RA 459
Cary, NC 27513
research_triangle_chapter@siggraph.org

Pennsylvania

Pittsburgh
David Egts, acting chair
Concurrent Technologies Corporation
(CTC)
1450 Scalp Ave.,
Johnstown, PA 15904-3374
pittsburgh_chapter@siggraph.org
http://www.vr.ctc.com/siggraph/

Texas

Dallas Area ACM SIGGRAPH
Aaron Hightower
Paradigm Simulation Inc.
14900 Landmark Suite 400
Dallas, TX 75240
dallas_area_chapter@siggraph.org
http://acm.org/~aaronh/das.html

Houston ACM SIGGRAPH
Christine Rosso Paige, Acting Chair
The Art Institute of Houston
1900 Yorktown
Houston, TX 77056
houston_chapter@siggraph.org
http://www.cogniseis.com/HAS/

Washington

Seattle ACM SIGGRAPH
Steve Hollasch
Microsoft
One Microsoft Way
Redmond, WA 98052-6399
seattle_chapter@siggraph.org
http://www.siggraph.org/chapters/seattle/

Tri-Cities Washington ACM SIGGRAPH
Donald R. Jones
Pacific Northwest Lab
MS K1-96
PO Box 999
Richland, WA 99352
tri-cities_chapter@siggraph.org

Brazil

Sao Paulo ACM SIGGRAPH
Sergio Martinelli
Digital Group
Rua Bairi 294
SP-05059
Sao Paulo,
Brazil
sao_paulo_chapter@siggraph.org

SIGGRAPH Professional Chapters

Bulgaria

Sofia ACM SIGGRAPH
Gospodin Jelev
Dept of Prog & Computer Appl
Technical Univ. of Sofia
1756 Sofia,
Bulgaria
sofia_chapter@siggraph.org

Canada

Vancouver B.C. ACM SIGGRAPH
Graeme Gish, chair
Vancouver Film School
420 Homer Street,
Vancouver, B.C.
V6B 2V5
Canada
vancouver_bc_chapter@siggraph.org
http://fas.sfu.ca/cs/research/groups/
    GMRL/ACM-SIGGRAPH

France

Paris ACM SIGGRAPH
Thierry Frey
c/o SUPINFOCOM - Terita 3000
2, rue Henri Matisse
59300 Aulnoye-lez-Valenciennes,
France
paris_chapter@siggraph.org
http://www.siggraph.org/chapters/paris/

Israel

Central Israel ACM SIGGRAPH
Daniel Cohen-Or
Dept of Computer Science
Tel Aviv University
Ramat Aviv,
Israel
central_israel_chapter@siggraph.org
http://www.cs.technion.ac.il/~sudar/icgf.html

Japan

Tokyo ACM SIGGRAPH
Masa Inakage
c/o Yukiko Ozaki
Image Systems Engineering Division
IMAGICA Corporation
2-14-1,Higashi-Gotanda,Shinagawa-ku
Tokyo,141
Japan
tokyo_chapter@siggraph.org
http://www.siggraph.org/chapters/tokyo/

Mexico

Mexico City ACM SIGGRAPH
Eduardo Llaguno Velasco
Calzada de las Aguilas #1124-E-202
Col. San Clemente
Mexico City 01740 D.F.
Mexico
mexico_city_chapter@siggraph.org
http://www.spin.com.mx/sigmex/sighome.htm

Singapore

Singapore ACM SIGGRAPH
Yong Tsui Lee
Nanyang Technological University
Nanyang Avenue
Singapore 639798
Republic of Singapore
singapore_chapter@siggraph.org

In-Formation Chapters

Arkansas

Northwest Arkansas
Preston Smith, Acting Chair
P.O. Box 852
Siloam Springs, AR 72761
northwest_arkansas_chapter@siggraph.org

Illinois

Chicago
Patricia Hamarstrom, Acting Chair
Illinois Institute of Art at Chicago
350 North Orleans
Chicago, IL 60654
chicago_chapter@siggraph.org

Louisiana

New Orleans ACM SIGGRAPH
Irving Blatt
4700 Wichers Drive
Marrero, LA 70072
new_orleans_chapter@siggraph.org

Belgium

Brussels ACM SIGGRAPH
Jean-Yves Roger
Project Officer
European Commission
Directorate General III - Industry
Rue de la loi/Wetstraat 200
B-1049 Bruxelles/Brussel
Belgium
brussels_chapter@siggraph.org

Canada

Toronto ACM SIGGRAPH
Adele Newton, Acting Chair
Newton Associates
6338 Snowflake Lane
Mississauga, Ontario
L5N 6G9
Canada
toronto_chapter@siggraph.org

Italy

Milano
Maria Grazia Mattei, Acting Chair
MGM Digital Communication s.r.l.
via Vivaio 23
20122 Milano Italia
+39 2 798760 (Voice)
+39 2 798701 (Fax)
milano_chapter@siggraph.org

Netherlands

Rotterdam ACM SIGGRAPH
Richard E. Ouwerkerk
Department of Arts and Architecture
Hogeschool Rotterdam & Omstreken
Scheepmakersstraat 7
PO Box 1272
3000 BG Rotterdam
The Netherlands
rotterdam_chapter@siggraph.org

United Kingdom

London ACM SIGGRAPH
Len Breen
c/o Department of Design
Brunel University
Runnymede Campus
Englefied Green
Surrey TW20 0JZ
United Kingdom
london_chapter@siggraph.org

Index

Cover Image Credits

Front Cover

"Dancer with Long Skirt"
Copyright © 1998, David Baraff and Andrew Witkin.

The dancer's swirling skirt and flowing blouse are animated automatically using a new, fast algorithm for simulating cloth dynamics. Alias|Wavefront provided the character animation of the dancer's body, based on motion-capture data provided by Paraform. The simulated clothing follows the dancer's motion, influenced by gravity, air-drag, and the dynamics of the cloth itself. Despite the high spatial resolution of the cloth model, the cloth's motion from this sequence is simulated in less than 30 seconds per frame on a standard desktop workstation.

Reference: "Large Steps in Cloth Simulation," *David Baraff and Andrew Witkin, pp. 43–54.*

Frontispiece

3D reconstructions of the face of an actress talking and making expressions.

Reference: "Making Faces," *Brian Guenter, Cindy Grimm, Daniel Wood, Henrique Malvar, Frédéric Pighin, pp. 55–66.*

Back Cover

Left column, top to bottom:

A swing dance motion adapted to a smaller female character. Left: original motion. Center: only female motion adapted. Right: both characters shown adapted.

Reference: "Retargetting Motion to New Characters," *Michael Gleicher, pp. 33–42.*

"Siamese Pachyderm"
Paul Rademacher

This is a multiple-center-of-projection image of an elephant. It was acquired by sweeping a thin camera around a 92KB polygon model. As the camera was swept, it captured a single-pixel-wide image from each point on its semi-circular path. These thin images were then concatenated to form the full picture shown. This image, along with its corresponding depth map and camera information, can be used to create a regular 3D view of the elephant from any new location. The model was provided by REM Infografica, and was rendered in 3D Studio Max.

Reference: "Multiple-Center-of-Projection Images," *Paul Rademacher and Gary Bishop, pp. 199–206.*

"Foggy Cornell Box"
Copyright © 1998, Per H. Christensen and Henrik Wann Jensen, mental images.

This image shows a variation of the classic "Cornell box." The box has diffuse reflection on the walls, floor, and ceiling. It contains a glass sphere, a mirror sphere, a homogeneous participating medium with anisotropic scattering (mainly in the forward direction), and a square-shaped area light source. The image has been rendered using the photon map method for simulating light transport in scenes with participating media. It illustrates global illumination effects on the surfaces and in the medium: there is a volume caustic created by the focusing of light through the glass sphere, there is color bleeding from the red and blue walls to the fog nearby, and there is multiple volume scattering.

Reference: "Efficient Simulation of Light Transport in Scenes With Participating Media Using Photon Maps," *Henrik Wann Jensen and Per H. Christensen, pp.311–320.*

"Tomatoes"
Copyright © 1998 Aaron Hertzmann,
NYU Media Research Laboratory

This image demonstrates a progressive refinement approach to painting. A loose sketch of the original photograph is created with large, curved brush strokes that follow image contours. The painting is then repeatedly refined with smaller brushes, but only in regions of the painting that do not already look like the corresponding region in the photograph. The final painting contains brush strokes with different shapes and sizes appropriate to the source image.

Reference: "Painterly Rendering with Curved Brush Strokes of Multiple Sizes," *Aaron Hertzmann, pp. 453–460.*

Right column, top to bottom:

"Daisy Dream"
Oliver Deussen

A natural looking meadow is created by combining grass tufts as shown in this image. In our paper we describe how parametrizing plant models and approximate instancing can be used to dramatically reduce geometric complexity for the generation of complex outdoor scenes. This tuft was created by using our interactive plant modeller and instancing was performed so that each model was used approximately ten times. The number of daisies that are present was controlled via a parameter to the model. For achieving a natural appearence, five different species were used.

Reference: "Realistic Modeling and Rendering of Plant Ecosystems," *Oliver Deussen, Patrick Hanrahan, Matt Pharr, Bernd Lintermann, Radomír Měch, Przemyslaw Prusinkiewicz, pp. 275–286.*

Phong-shaded 3D imagery does not provide geometric information of the same richness as human-drawn technical illustrations. Illustrations give a clearer picture of shape, structure, and material composition than traditional computer graphics methods. Although there are a wide variety of styles and techniques found in technical illustration, there are some common themes. This is particularly true when we examine color illustrations done with airbrush and pen. We have observed the following characteristics in many illustrations: edge lines, the set containing surface boundaries, silhouettes, and discontinuities, are drawn with black curves; matte objects are shaded with intensities far from black or white with warmth or coolness of color indicative of surface normal; a single light source provides white highlights; shadowing is not shown; metal objects are shaded as if very anisotropic.

We view these characteristics as resulting from a hierarchy of priorities. The edge lines and highlights are black and white, and provide a great deal of shape information themselves. Several studies in the field of perception have concluded that subjects can recognize 3D objects at least as well, if not better, when the edge lines (contours) are drawn versus shaded or textured images.

Illustrators use a different technique to communicate whether or not an object is made of metal. In practice illustrators represent a metallic surface by alternating dark and light bands. To simulate a milled object, we map a set of twenty stripes of varying intensity along the parametric axis of maximum curvature. The stripes are random intensities between 0.0 and 0.5 with the stripe closest to the light source direction overwritten with white. Between the stripe centers the colors are linearly interpolated.

Reference: "A Non-Photorealistic Lighting Model For Automatic Technical Illustration," *Amy Gooch, Bruce Gooch, Pete Shirley, and Elaine Cohen, pp. 447–452.*

"Bouncing Beach Ball Sequence"
Robert Jensen, Wagner T. Correa, Adam Finkelstein, and Craig Thayer

These images demonstrate a method of applying complex texture maps to traditional cel animation.
The ball was animated in 2D by hand, matched to an approximate 3D version, and then rendered with a beach ball texture over a background image.

Reference: "Texture Mapping for Cel Animation," *Wagner Toledo Corrêa, Robert J. Jensen, Craig E. Thayer, Elaine Cohen, pp. 435–446.*